AF680461

Dedicated to the
300th anniversary of
St. Petersburg State University

THE SAINT PETERSBURG SCHOOL OF INTERNATIONAL LAW

P. P. Shafirov
Author of first Russian original treatise on international law

Courtesy of The State Hermitage Museum, St. Petersburg
Photograph © The State Hermitage Museum/photo by Svetlana Suetova.

THE SAINT PETERSBURG SCHOOL OF INTERNATIONAL LAW

A Bio-Bibliographical Study
(Petrine Russia to the 1920s)

W. E. Butler

John Edward Fowler Distinguished Professor of Law,
Penn State Dickinson Law
Emeritus Professor of Comparative Law,
University College London
Foreign Member, Russian Academy of Natural Sciences;
National Academy of Sciences of Ukraine;
National Academy of Legal Sciences of Ukraine

&

V. S. Ivanenko

кандидат юридических наук
Docent and sometime Head, Chair of International Law,
St. Petersburg State University

TALBOT
PUBLISHING
Clark, New Jersey

Text Copyright © 2024 by William Elliott Butler (1939-) and
Vitalii Semenovich Ivanenko (1946-)

ISBN-13: 978-1-61619-687-5

All rights reserved. No part of this publication may be reproduced, stored in a retrieval system, or transmitted, in any form or by any means, electronic, mechanical, photocopying, recording, or otherwise, without the prior written permission of the publisher or the copyright holder or holders, except in the case of brief quotations embodied in critical reviews and certain other noncommercial uses permitted by copyright law.

TALBOT PUBLISHING
AN IMPRINT OF
The Lawbook Exchange, Ltd.
33 Terminal Avenue
Clark, New Jersey 07066-1323

Please see our website for a selection of our other publications and fine facsimile reprints of classic works of legal history

www.lawbookexchange.com

Library of Congress Cataloging-in-Publication Data

Names: Butler, William Elliott, 1939- author. | Ivanenko, Vitalii Semenovich, 1946- author.
Title: The Saint Petersburg school of international law : a bio-bibliographical study (Petrine Russia to the 1920s) / W. E. Butler, John Edward Fowler Distinguished Professor of Law, Penn State Dickinson Law, Emeritus Professor of Comparative Law, University College London Foreign Member, National Academy of Sciences of Ukraine, National Academy of Legal Sciences of Ukraine and Vitalii Semenovich Ivanenko, кандидат юридических наук, Docent and sometime Head, Chair of International Law, St. Petersburg State University.
Description: First edition. | Clark, New Jersey : Talbot Publishing, an Imprint of The Lawbook Exchange, Ltd., 2024. | "Dedicated to the 300th anniversary of St. Petersburg State University." | Includes bibliographical references and index. | Summary: "A history of the School of International Law, St. Petersburg State University"-- Provided by publisher.
Identifiers: LCCN 2023041650 | ISBN 9781616196875 (hardcover)
Subjects: LCSH: Imperatorskiĭ Sankt-Peterburgskiĭ universitet″. I͡Uridicheskiĭ fakulʹtet--History. | Law schools--Russia (Federation)--Saint Petersburg--History. | International law--Study and teaching--Russia--History.
Classification: LCC KLA53.I467 B88 2024 | DDC 340.071/14721--dc23/eng/20230927
LC record available at https://lccn.loc.gov/2023041650

TABLE OF CONTENTS

THE RENAISSANCE

THE GOLDEN ERA

(1860s-Early 1920s)

ELSEWHERE IN ST. PETERSBURG

PREFACE

In 1990 the Clarendon Press published the Butler translation of Vladimir Emmanuilovich Grabar, *The History of International Law in Russia 1647-1917: A Bio-Bibliographical Study*.[1] A book without equal in its time treating a single country's historical approach to the development of the law of nations, no one has produced an equivalent study for any other country.

The present volume expands upon the Grabar study, undertaking what in Grabar's time would have been impossible. We concentrate upon the capital city of the Russian Empire – St. Petersburg – and the sundry institutions of higher education established there which offered courses on international law, enriching the available materials through access to archives, photographs, post-graduate dissertations, and what is believed to be the most extensive account of the individuals who taught or otherwise contributed through publication, public service, and/or appointment to this field.

Our understanding of the origins and early development of modern international law leaves much to be desired, especially our knowledge of when and how patterns of international intercourse were transferred or communicated from one civilization, country, tribe, or people to another. Our ethnocentric preoccupation with the undeniably potent impact of nineteenth century European imperial expansion in bringing "European international law" to other regions of the world has begun to be redressed by comparative inquiries into the practices of China, India, Japan, Africa, the East Indies, Latin America, and Central Asia. The contribution of Russia to this process remains to be investigated in much greater depth. The work of Russian international lawyers who in the late nineteenth and early twentieth centuries wrote on aspects of international legal history continues to be virtually unknown to western scholarship. It would seem, though, that Russia's early and, in comparison with western Europe, prolonged contacts with Byzantium, Central Asia, Mongolia, China, Persia, and eastern and central Europe, not to mention western Europe itself, made Russia an important recipient of and conduit for a wide variety of customs and usages of interest to the history of the law of nations. And, of course, there is the question of Russia's own contribution to the development of so-called "western" international law.

The archives used for this study are referred to by their standard initials in the Table of Abbreviations: Central State Historical Archive of the City of St. Peters-

[1] V. E. Grabar, *The History of International Law in Russia 1647-1917: A Bio-Biographical Study*, transl. W. E. Butler (Oxford, 1990). The translation was based on Grabar, Материалы к истории литературы международного права в России (1647-1917) [Materials on the History of the Literature of International Law in Russia (1647-1917)] (M., 1958). Butler acquired his copy of Grabar at the Viktor Kamkin Russian Bookstore in Washington D. C. for $4.85 in ca. 1963. The Butler translation, with its corrections and emendations to Grabar, was used for the Russian-language reissue in 2005, as follows: Grabar, Материалы к истории литературы международного права в России (1647-1917) [Materials on the History of the Literature of International Law in Russia (1647-1917)], ed. W. E. Butler and V. A. Tomsinov (M., 2005).

burg; Central City Archive of St. Petersburg; Russian State Historical Archive; Unified Archive of St. Petersburg University, Russian State Archive of the Navy, and the Leningrad Division of the Archive of the Academy of Sciences of the USSR/Russian Federation. The richest repository for the history of St. Petersburg (Petrograd) University is the Central State Historical Archive of the City of St. Petersburg, where relevant materials are scattered about in Fund No. 14 (Imperial Petrograd University, 1819-1918); Fund No. 13 (St. Petersburg Chief Pedagogical Institute), and Fund No. 139 (Chancellery of the Guardian of St. Petersburg Instructional District). Reference also has been made to the Archives of the Central State Archive of Ancient Acts (Moscow), the A. M. Gorky Scientific Library of St. Petersburg University, including electronic collections of the history of St. Petersburg University in virtual space (bioslovhist.history.spbu.ru), and the dictionary of professors and lecturers of St. Petersburg University, 1819-1917 (bioslovhist.history.spbu.ru/biografika), the Russian State Library, the Russian National Library, and the Tartu University Library. Among foreign archives, of special importance were the holdings in the Bakhmeteff Archive at Columbia University, the Harvard Law School Library, Georgetown University Library, and materials in the United States Library of Congress.

Two graduate diploma theses devoted to the history of the Chair of International Law at St. Petersburg University have proved to be very useful and are cited frequently in this work: by Tatiana Sergeevna Loginova[2] and by Elena Nikolaevna Trubetskaia.[3] Both were supervised by Dr. Ivanenko between 1999 and 2004 and can be accessed at https://dspace.spbu.ru.

The short form of the Library of Congress transliteration system has been used throughout, usually omitting the soft and hard signs and diacritical marks. Materials drawn from the Butler translation of Grabar will be used with minimal citation as a rule. References in the text to published works by members of the St. Petersburg School will be usually given in short form and not footnoted; full bibliographical details are given in an accompanying separately-published Bibliography. The Index of Names will provide full access to the textual references. Cross references occasionally are given to the Butler Bibliography,[4] to known holdings in other institutions and/or to Inter Documentation Company BV microfiche holdings (IDC), or to private holdings (WEB).[5]

2 T. S. Loginova, История становления и развития кафедры международного права Санкт-Петербургского университета в 1819-1903 г.г. [History of the Origin and Development of the Chair of International Law of St. Petersburg University in 1819-1903] (Spb., 2004). 193 p.

3 E. N. Trubetskaia, История развития кафедры международного права Санкт-Петербургского (Петроградского) университета в 1903-1917 гг. [History of the Development of the Chair of International Law of St. Petersburg (Petrograd) University in 1903-1917] (Spb., 2004). 168 p.

4 See W. E. Butler, *Russia and the International Legal System: A Bibliography of Writings by Russian Jurists on Public and Private International Law to 1917 with References to Publications in Emigration* (London, 2006).

5 Butler (comp. & ed.), *Russian and Soviet Law: An Annotated Catalogue of Reference Works, Legislation, Court Reports, Serials and Monographs on Russian and Soviet Law (including International Law)* (Zug, 1976).

The present volume incorporates in relevant part, with revisions, emendations, additions, corrections, and some restructuring, the seminal volumes by Vitalii Semenovich Ivanenko dedicated to the 300th anniversary of St. Petersburg University and the 187th anniversary of the founding of the Chair of International Law at the St. Petersburg University in its various incarnations.[6] In the Annex we introduce more than one hundred new names to the field of international law as we identify those personnel, graduates, and/or students for whom international law was part of their background and who were employed in some capacity by the Ministry of Foreign Affairs of the Russian Empire.

[6] V. S. Ivanenko, Санкт-Петербургская школа международного права: место и роль Санкт-Петербургского университета, его ученых и выпусников в становлении и развитии науки и практики международного права [Saint-Petersburg School of International Law: The Place and Role of St. Petersburg University, its Scholars and Graduates, in the Formation and Development of International Law Scholarship and Practice] (3d ed.; 2024; 2d ed.; 2022; St. Petersburg, 2019).

ACKNOWLEDGEMENTS

The two authors of the present work have devoted collectively more than nine decades to the history of international law in the Russian Empire, former Soviet Union, and post-Soviet Independent States. We build on the seminal work by Grabar, utilizing archives and resources in Russia and abroad that did not exist or were inaccessible to him during the 1940-50s. In casting the net wide by concentrating upon the institutions of higher education in St. Petersburg and individuals associated with that City, the capital of the Russian Empire throughout most of the period, we hope that this might serve as a model for other cities or countries as an exercise in comparative international law, establishing the empirical groundwork for a more comprehensive and detailed command of our discipline.

Our count may not be exact. But this book has identified a much larger corpus of individuals – scholars, diplomats, legal practitioners – involved with international law in St. Petersburg than any prior work. Our gratitude to the archivists and librarians who assisted is immense, and to our respective universities who found many ways to support this endeavor.

Our respective spouses, Maryann Elizabeth Gashi-Butler and Valentina Alexandrovna Ivanenko, have been understanding, helpful, and supportive to the utmost throughout an undertaking that has proved to be more demanding of time – but rewarding in outcomes – than we imagined.

William E. Butler
Vitalii S. Ivanenko

1 September 2023
Newville, Pennsylvania
St. Petersburg, Russia

THE AUTHORS

William Elliott Butler (b. 20 October 1939) graduated in 1961 from the School of International Service of The American University (B.A.), in 1963 from the Johns Hopkins School of Advanced Studies (M.A.), in 1966 from the Harvard Law School (J.D.), returning to Johns Hopkins SAIS (Ph.D., 1970) and later earning a higher doctorate from the University of London (LL.D., 1979) and an advanced Russian law degree from the Academy University of Law, Institute of State and Law, Russian Academy of Sciences (LL.M., 1997). He holds honorary doctorates from the Kyiv University of Law (2013), Academy International Independent Ecological-Politological University (Moscow, 2016), and Uppsala University (2018).

He has pursued the history of international law since first taking a course on the subject at The American University, concentrating on Hugo Grotius, Anglo-American contributions, but above all on the place and role of Russia and Ukraine in the development of international law since the tenth century. He discovered the unknown contemporary English translation of the Shafirov treatise on the law of nations while a Research Associate at Harvard Law School from 1968 to 1970 and published a facsimile edition in 1973. His translation of the Grabar treatise on the history of the literature of international law in Russia from 1647 to 1917, published by the Oxford University Press in 1990, served as the basis for a reissue in 2005 at Moscow of the original 1958 version and a commemorative Russian volume in 2017.

From 1970 to 2005 he served as Reader in Comparative Law (1970-1976), elevated to a personal Chair of Comparative Law from 1976 to 2005, at University College London. He served as Dean of the Faculty of Laws at UCL from 1977 to 1979 and of the University of London Faculty of Laws from 1988 to 1990. From 1993 to 2003 he was the founder of the Law Faculty of the Moscow Higher School of Social and Economic Sciences (now known as Shaninka), serving as the initial Dean from 1993 to 1998, on secondment for this purpose by UCL to the University of Manchester, whose LL.M. degree was earned at the School.

He is the founding editor of *Jus Gentium: Journal of International Legal History*.

A Life member of the American Society of International Law and a member of the Russian Association of International Law since 1992, he was awarded the G. I. Tunkin medal by the last.

Vitalii Semenovich Ivanenko (b. 15 November 1946) graduated in 1972 from the Law Faculty of Tomsk State University and completed his postgraduate studies at the Chair of International Law, Leningrad State University, in 1982, defending his dissertation under the supervision of Professors R. L. Bobrov, succeeded by S. A. Malinin. He held positions as senior lecturer, docent, professor, Head of the Chair of International Law, and Pro-Rector for Scientific Work at universities in Baranul and St. Petersburg before, in 1995, becoming Docent at St. Petersburg State University, serving from 1999 to 2011 as Head of the Chair of International Law there.

He has published extensively on the history of international law in Russia, with particular reference to St. Petersburg, the law of treaties, the law of international organizations, international humanitarian law, and the interface between international and municipal law. In his capacity as dissertation supervisor, he is responsible for eleven postgraduates who successfully defended their dissertations for the degree of кандидат юридических наук.

A member of the Soviet Association of International Law since 1977 (Russian Association of International Law since 1992), he has served as a member of the Executive Committee of that Association since 2001, Vice President from 2006 to 2016, and is a member of the Editorial Board of the *Russian Yearbook of International Law*. He advises the Ministry of Foreign Affairs of the Russian Federation as a member of the Coordinating Council for International Law attached to that Ministry.

In 2004 the Russian Association of International Law awarded him the G. I. Tunkin Medal for services to the Association. The Ministry of Foreign Affairs awarded him the F. F. Martens Medal in 2021 for services in popularizing international humanitarian law. The Russian Academy of Sciences awarded him a medal in 2022 for his treatise on the role of St. Petersburg University in contributing to the development of the science of international law, now in its third edition.

TABLE OF ABBREVIATIONS

b.	born
c.	page
col.(s)	column(s)
comp.	compiler
Спб./Spb.	St. Petersburg
столб.	column
d.	death
ed.	editor, edited
ф.	Fund, fond
г.	year
кн./kn.	kniga; book
l.	list; folio
L.	Leningrad
ЛОААН	Leningrad Division, Archive of the Academy of Sciences
M.	Moscow
MID	Ministry of Foreign Affairs
M.-L./M.-Л.	Moscow-Leningrad
№/no.	number
OA СПбГУ	Unified Archive of St. Petersburg State University
ob.	obverse
p.	page(s)
Пг./Pg.	Petrograd

ПСЗ	Complete Collection of Laws of the Russian Empire
РГАВМФ	Russian State Archive of the Navy
РГИА	Russian State Historical Archive
Spb.	St. Petersburg
ЦГА СПб	Central City Archive of St. Petersburg
ЦГИА СПб	Central State Historical Archive of St. Petersburg
т.	volume
vol(s).	volume(s)
WEB	William E. Butler Private Collection

THE BEGINNINGS

Chapter 1
The Formative Years

The term "school" has multiple meanings. It may refer to a physical edifice where the instruction of pupils, students, or followers takes place, including an institution or subdivision of University-level; or an inchoate group of individuals who impersonally propagate or develop a discipline, doctrine, and/or practice. In our case, we refer to both – the development of the law of nations as a discipline in St. Petersburg and, in due course, the institutions in which instruction in the law of nations occurred. Our emphasis is principally upon St. Petersburg State University and its antecedents, together with other institutions of higher learning in that City and the context which led to their creation.

The history of any large University has its distinctive features, and the St. Petersburg (Academy, Imperial, State) University is no exception. Although in the present study we are pursuing the history of a discipline developed principally within a component unit of the Law Faculty, that discipline could exist and flourish only by reason of the larger institution of higher education itself – its creation, larger course of development, historical fate during challenging periods of Russian history, and the personalities and contributions of the individual legal scholars and students who collectively comprised what became the University community. A few introductory words are therefore in order to sketch the larger University context within which the discipline of public and private international law matured, most especially the teaching of law generally.

Formally speaking, the teaching of international law is routinely traced back to the 1830s in Russia, when the "General Statute of Imperial Russian Universities" of 26 July 1835 required the introduction of a new instructional course on the "Principles of All-People's Jurisprudence (Jus Gentium)". The commencement of the teaching of international law at the St. Petersburg University is dated to September 1836, when the "Chair of All-People's Jurisprudence" was formed under the 1835 General Statute. Literary and archival sources, however, support the view that international law began to be taught in St. Petersburg a century earlier, during the 1720s, when by behest of Emperor Peter the Great (1672-1725), the Petersburg Academy of Sciences was founded and, attached thereto, the Academy University – the first University in the history of Russia.[1]

This is not a position unanimously accepted in St. Petersburg, or for that matter in Moscow, where the Imperial Moscow University was established in 1755. During the late 1990s and early 2000s,[2] it was debated in St. Petersburg whether

[1] Hereinafter, whether the Academy, Imperial, or State St. Petersburg University is being referred to, the term "University" will be used. All other Russian universities referred to are linked to the city in which they are located: Moscow, Kazan, Novorossiisk (Odessa), Kyiv, Kharkov, and so on.

[2] See, for example, A. Iu. Andreev, «О начале университетского образования в Санкт-петербурге» [On the Beginning of University Education in St. Petersburg], Отечественная история

the year 1724 might be accepted as the year during which St. Petersburg University was founded and whether the present St. Petersburg University is the true legal successor of the Academy University. Measured by European standards of the time, few would disagree that the Academy University did not meet notions of the classical University, and the same would probably be so today. But assessed against the background of Petrine realities, the Academy University was among the significant reforms introduced by Peter the Great, albeit late in his life, intended to bring Russia up to European standards and values. As one historian on Russian legal education noted, Peter the Great resolved to include legal education among his Great Reforms:

> having understood the significance of Russia within the system of European States and what needed to be done for her greatness of the future. He was aware that Russia by reason of a number of historical peculiarities lagged behind the countries of Europe in the formation of legal education, and that western States have significantly great experience in jurisprudence. Therefore, Peter I actively used their ideas in his reforms.[3]

But the founding of institutions which offered instruction in the law did not occur in a vacuum. Although in the instance of St. Petersburg we have a date certain – and a relatively modern date – of when that City was founded (1702), two or so decades and peace treaties with adversaries elapsed before the dream of creating an Academy of Sciences was realized. Symbolic of its European presence and aspirations, in 1712 the Russian court moved from Moscow to St. Petersburg together with the great majority of Russian State institutions. The development of the law of nations in St. Petersburg is, therefore, inextricably connected with the reign and reforms of Peter I (the Great), Emperor of All the Russias.[4] The Tsar opened a "window to the West", which meant not only expansion and consolidation of frontiers, military security, movement of the essential accoutrements of

[Fatherland History], no. 5 (1998), pp. 62-73; B. V. Levshin, «Академический университет в Санкт-Петербурге: Историческая справка» [Academy University in St. Petersburg: Historical Note], ibid., no. 5 (1998), pp. 73-79; I. P. Kulakova, «Спор о первородстве: 275 лет Санкт-Петербургскому университету?» [Dispute on Primacy: 275 Years of St. Petersburg University?], ВИЕТ [VIET], no. 3 (1999), pp. 57-92; Iu. D. Margolis and G. A. Tishkin, Единыйм вдохновением. Очерки истории университетского образования в Петербурге в конце XVIII -- первой половине XIX в. [By a Single Inspiration. Survey of the History of University Education in Petersburg at the End of the XVIII-First Half of the XIX Century] (Spb., 2000); T. B. Perfilova, «Ученое сословие» России в правовом пространстве Императорских университетов [The "Learned Estate" of Russia in the Legal Space of Charters of Imperial Universities] (Iaroslavl, 2014).

[3] A. V. Borisov, et al., Юридическое образование в России: история, современность, перспективы развития [Legal Education in Russia: History, Contemporaneity, Prospects for Development] (M., 2015), p. 10.

[4] Imperial titles were an issue throughout much of Peter the Great's reign, but Tsar Ivan IV was no less sensitive on the issue and styled himself "Emperor of all Russia" in his correspondence with other monarchs. See K. Iu. Erusalimskii (ed.), Дипломатическая переписка Ивана Грозного (1533-1584) [Diplomatic Correspondence of Ivan the Terrible (1533-1584)] (Spb., 2023). This was parodied in William Shakespeare, "Love's Labours Lost". See Rima Greenhill, *Shakespeare, Elizabeth and Ivan: The Role of English-Russian Relations in Love's Labours Lost* (2023), pp. 91-92. On 22 October 1721 Russia proclaimed itself to be the Russian Empire headed by the Emperor of All the Russias with a capital at St. Petersburg.

State administration to his newly-founded City in the North, but the establishment of a Library, encouragement of the formation of private libraries by senior officials, clergy, and citizens, the acquisition of books abroad, reformation and modernization of the Russian alphabet, as well as commissioning the translations of foreign works (including on the history of diplomacy and the law of nations),[5] founding printing houses in St. Petersburg, purchasing or confiscating personal libraries for State needs, recruiting foreign professors to lecture in Russian institutions and undertake research, corresponding with leading European academicians to explore the founding of an Academy of Sciences and a University in Russia,[6] and the formal training in Russia and elsewhere in Europe of promising Russian individuals for service in the fields of law and diplomacy, including the mastery of foreign languages.

The reform of the Russian alphabet and transition to civil script in 1708 facilitated translation activity. Books on history and politics were translated, among them Hugo Grotius (1583-1645) on the law of war and peace[7] and Samuel Pufendorf, *Juris naturae et gentium, libri octo*. These remained in manuscript, to be used for instructional and/or administrative purposes. The Russian authorities arranged for a translation of Abraham de Wicquefort (1606-1682), *L'ambassadeur et ses fonctions* (1680-81).[8] Books on the law of nations were required reading for the Tsarevich Aleksei (1690-1718) as part of his studies of natural law.

In his dedication to Empress Catherine I (1684-1727), Gavriil Buzhinskii (1680-1731), as translator of Pufendorf, *De Officio hominis et civis*, drew special attention to the importance of the study of law and the law of nations.[9] Pufendorf, said Buzhinskii, was "skilled in the law" and understood that whosoever "knows the law of nations, that is, what is most universal in the minds of men", can readily cope with the numerous codes "published in a book on natural law and the law of nations". This book in its French version was specifically recommended for translation in a directive composed by P. P. Shafirov for the tutoring of the Tsarevich Aleksei on 22 April 1703. Possibly, said the Directive in Article 8, Section 4:

[5] See W. E. Butler, "Peter the Great as a Comparative Lawyer", *The Journal of Comparative Law*, XVI (2021), pp. 3-20.

[6] The principal correspondence with foreign scholars and institutions is reproduced in I. V. Tunkina (ed.), Петр Великий и основание Петербургской академии наук: Документы и материалы [Peter the Great and the Founding of the Petersburg Academy of Sciences: Documents and Materials] (Spb., 2022), I, pp. 26-46. Also see K. Popp and E. Stein (eds.), *Gottfried Wilhelm Leibniz: The Work of the Great Universal Scholar as Philosopher, Mathematician, Physicist, Engineer* (Hannover, 2000), pp. 16, 24, 25, and 28.

[7] This translation was undertaken in Kyiv and remains unpublished; the manuscript is in St. Petersburg.

[8] The translation was undertaken by Petr Vasilevich Postnikov (1666-after 1712) but remained in manuscript. Postnikov achieved renown as the first Russian doctor of medicine, having studied at Padua University. He performed several diplomatic missions in Europe and Turkey "without rank"; his precise movements remain to be determined.

[9] The translation by Gavriil Buzhinskii of Pufendorf's treatise was undertaken at Peter the Great's direct instruction and guidance and published in 1726 after the Emperor's death.

> The little book by Pufendorf on the duties of man and citizen in the French language should be translated and printed in Holland, since it may be used as an introduction to the law of nations and a stepping stone to Grotius or Pufendorf on natural law and the law of nations, form the basis of all laws and especially the law of war and peace that exists between potentates can be studied.[10]

Chapters sixteen and seventeen of Pufendorf were devoted to the law of nations. Chapter 16, on war and peace, addressed the following: (1) war not being the ordinary state of man; (2) the causes of war ought to be manifest, and the unjust causes of war recounted;[11] (3) what means may be lawfully used against an enemy; (4) unjust causes of war; (5) declaration of war; (6) what is allowed to an enemy; (7) war either solemn or less solemn; (8) who has the right to make war? … (15) what is an armistice?; (16) what is private[?]; (17) peace is the end of war.

The full measure of Peter the Great's contributions to the law of nations as a draftsman of international legal materials remains to be fully ascertained. He evidenced an intellectual curiosity at an early age in foreign law and the law of nations and took an active role in not merely reading or commissioning translations of foreign legal works, but in personally drafting or editing legislative texts that drew upon foreign legislation and/or doctrinal writings. The Military Statute of 1716 is an example, "assembled and processed by our own labors", he wrote.[12] Provision was made (Chapter 24) for the position of "chief jurisconsult" who was to give opinions on international and military law because military officers "spend their time studying the military arts, and not law". The auditor-general, another position introduced, had responsibility for exchanging prisoners of war and negotiating with the adversary. Provisions were included on how to conduct warfare, including the taking of cities, fortresses, booty, and prisoners and on burning, rapine, and plunder – all, if to be committed, only by special order.

Instructions and Military Articles appropriate for the Russian Navy were printed in April 1710, the text having been corrected by Peter the Great; prior to their issuance only individual written rules had been published, the present item representing the first consolidation of those rules, together with additions and embellishments. Numerous subsequent editions quickly appeared, and many provisions were incorporated verbatim in the 1720 Naval Statute.[13]

[10] N. G. Ustrialov, История царствования Петра Великого [History of the Reign of Peter the Great] (Spb., 1859-63), VI, p. 303.

[11] This paragraph reads: "Just wars … are: we may protect and defend ourselves and our possessions from the unjust attacks of others or if others do something which we do not like, we may take retribution for the offence caused until we have obtained satisfaction. The first war which is begun is called a *defensive war*, and the latter, an *offensive war*".

[12] N. A. Voskresenskii, Законодательные акты Петра I [Legislative Acts of Peter I] (M., 1945; reprint ed.; 2018), I, pp. 50-53.

[13] P. N. Berkov (ed.), Описание изданий гражданской печати: 1708-январь 1725 г. [Description of Publications in Civil Typeface: 1708-January 1725] (M.-Leningrad, 1955), No. 38, pp. 110-111; also see items 39, 40, 80, and 110.

Peter arranged for the translation and publication in 1715 of the Danish Instruction on Maritime Articles issued at Copenhagen on 15 March 1700 by Frederick IV (1671-1730); the Instruction contained provisions on naval discipline, taking of booty, conduct in combat, among others.[14]

In 1720 the Naval Statute set out the Russian understanding of certain rules regulating the conduct of affairs or warfare at sea. Provision was made for the right of salute: "All our warships should claim from all republics that flags or pennants be dipped to our warships … and if this is not done, they shall compel it. This is, of course, at sea, and not in their ports" (point 4). But if treaties to which Russia is a party regulate salutes, "one should behave in accordance with such treaties" (point 10).

The 1722 "Reglament on the Administration of the Admiralty and its Wharf" provided that the College of Admiralty should have custody of treaties on maritime commerce and contained numerous provisions devoted to the law of prize. On 19 June 1723 the Regulations and Instructions for All Masters of Sailing Ships and Other Persons Sailing and Coming in Merchant-Men into Any Ports or Harbours Belonging to the Empire of Russia, To Know How They Ought to Behave Themselves, and What They Must Observe were published and reissued from time to time with parallel texts in English, Danish, French, Italian, among others, for more than a century onward.[15]

The international law of diplomacy, or ambassadorial law, matured under Peter the Great. Diplomatic ceremonial was observed closely during the Petrine Grand Embassy to Europe in 1697-98 and led to reforms in Russian practices emulating European models.[16] Andrei Artamonovich Matveev (1666-1728), while on a diplomatic mission in London, experienced difficulties with creditors; this led to his detention in July 1708. The attendant scandal led to the adoption in England of the Diplomatic Privileges Act (7 Anne c 12), known widely as the Act of Anne;[17] the Act provided for the nullity of all civil proceedings against ambassadors and members of their suite, England hoping by this legislation to appease Peter the Great in advance for the insult sustained by his emissary. Charles Whitworth (1675-1725) was sent to Russia in order to present apologies. His audience with Peter the Great was described in a publication issued in May 1710, including the Russian translation of the text of the message sent by Queen Anne and the address by Whitworth initially read in English, with a German translation, to the Tsar.[18]

[14] Ibid., No. 160, pp. 179-180; twenty copies were printed. A second edition of 49 copies was printed in 1716. Ibid., No. 196, pp. 189-190.

[15] See W. E. Butler, "Imperial Russian Marine Regulation 1803/1817", *Jus Gentium*, IV (2019), pp. 179-189.

[16] See O. G. Ageeva, Дипломатический церемониал императорской России: XVIII век [Diplomatic Ceremonial of Imperial Russia: XVIII Century] (M., 2012), pp. 112-176.

[17] The Act remained in force in the United Kingdom until repealed in 1964.

[18] Berkov, note 13 above, No. 41, pp. 111-112. For Whitworth's correspondence with London on this issue, see Сборник Императорского русского исторического общества [Collection of the Imperial Russian Historical Society] (Спб., 1886), т. 50, where the original English texts are excerpted with Russian translations. A fuller version of the events is offered in documents collected in Simon

In the absence of an indigenous community of "legists" to build upon the growing corpus of seventeenthcentury international legal scholarship in Europe, it fell to diplomatic practitioners to generate or produce early Russian literature on international law in the course of, or in supplementation of, their official duties.

Andrei Artamonovich Matveev *(1666-1728). Diplomat.*

Life and career. The son of Artamon Sergeevich Matveev (1625-1682), Andrei Matveev served from 1700 on diplomatic missions to Holland, Austria, and France. He was appointed to the Russian Mission in London from 1706, where indebtedness to English merchants led to an assault on his person and the adoption of legislation in England and Russia clarifying diplomatic immunity. The event occurred on the evening of 21 July 1708 and led to Matveev being released on bail, an immediate awareness on the part of the British Government of how serious a matter this was, and prompt diplomatic efforts to offer apologies and to ensure there was no repetition. Both countries responded with legislative measures. In Russia, Peter the Great issued an Instruction on 14 September 1708, duly gazetted as follows:

> Since many complaints emanate from foreign courts and residents who are at our court and now residing in Moscow and not only are their people affected by various orders of the court but even some dishonour is done to them, you, to that end, upon receiving these, shall declare to the judges of all departments that they strictly order their subordinates not to allow any dishonour to envoys, especially to their persons; and if such people are detained and brought to the department, then they should be sent without delay to the Ambassadorial Department. And if such people petition regarding this, then these should be submitted to the Ambassadorial Department, and nothing regarding them shall be sent from those departments or taken from them, and it shall be forbidden to hold such people at the Ambassadorial Department. But when such offence is caused, they are referred, and satisfaction is demanded, they shall not punish them, which is contrary to the law of nations, from which disputes between States may occur. And if the courts which sent them recall them and if there are debts for which there is a case, they should be sent to the court, and if they are not paid, this should be reported to the Ambassadorial Department, and from this Department satisfaction may be obtained from them in all matters.[19]

Matveev had reported to Tsar Peter on 22 July 1708, the day following the incident, visits by "every foreign minister" in support of his position and contrary to the "book of Wicquefort", demonstrating familiarity with Abraham de Wicquefort (1598-1682), *L'ambassadeur et ses fonctions* (1681):

> I told the Secretary of State that if Her Majesty does not protect the honour of His Holy Tsarist Majesty against the affront to my rank and person and to the law of nations and grant me protection and direct satisfaction, not only will I go without a document to the Queen about this unprecedented

Dixon, et al. (eds.), *Britain and Russia in the Age of Peter the Great* (1998), pp. 71-93.

19 Полное собрание законов Российской империи [Complete Collection of Laws of the Russian Empire] (first series), IV, no. 2206.

affront to the honour of his principal, specially protected in her Kingdom, but also none of the European princes will keep their ministers here, who not only may have safety according to the law of nations, but are always subjected to writs and arrests from an Englishman even in their slightest affairs and are dishonoured and insulted by Englishmen.[20]

Although strictly speaking a bilateral matter, the positions acknowledged by both sides and their respective legislative responses constituted a benchmark in the development of ambassadorial law of general applicability.[21]

Petr Pavlovich Shafirov *(1673-1739). Diplomat, Vice-Chancellor of Russian Empire, author.*

Life and career. The first original work of an unofficial nature on international law in the Russian language was P. P. Shafirov's *A Discourse Concerning the Just Causes of the War Between Russia and Sweden*, published at St. Petersburg in 1717. Writing at a critical moment in Russia's long, debilitating, but ultimately successful struggle for a permanent outlet on the Baltic Sea and a reduction of Swedish hegemony, Shafirov reviewed the diplomatic history of Russo-Swedish relations (still the best contemporary account and an invaluable original source on the Northern War) and set forth the Russian view as to the legal grounds for that War and the violations of the law of nations allegedly committed by Sweden. Peter the Great himself wrote the conclusion and contributed other passages.

Shafirov's book provides one of the earliest and best indicators of the extent to which Russia had assimilated, linguistically and conceptually, the principles and practices of international law generally accepted in western Europe of that day, an appraisal of which has been facilitated by the identification of a contemporary anonymous English translation published in London whose existence had been overlooked by western and Russian scholars alike for 250 years.

For modern international legal scholarship, however, Shafirov's work is more than a comparatively unknown landmark in the history of international law. The book was among the first examples of Russian pamphleteering, a practice indulged in extensively by European governments and political figures of the time. One historian described the book as "the first independent, completely original historico-publicist work published typographically in the new civil script".[22] Another said that the Tsar's methods of historical research suggested that he and his aides (including Shafirov)

[20] V. N. Aleksandrenko, Русские дипломатические агенты в Лондоне в XVIII веке [Russian Diplomatic Agents in London in the Eighteenth Century] (Warsaw, 1897), II, p. 13.

[21] See V. E. Grabar, *The History of International Law in Russia 1647-1917: A Bio-Bibliographical Study*, transl. W. E. Butler (1990), pp. 59-61.

[22] S. L. Peshtich, Русская историография XVIII века [Russian Historiography of the XVIII Century] (1961-71), I, p. 138. A facsimile of the 1718 Moscow version and the 1722 English translation of the *Discourse* were published together with an introduction. See P. P. Shafirov, *A Discourse Concerning the Just Causes of the War Between Sweden and Russia: 1700-1721*, intro. W. E. Butler (New York, 1973).

were the beginning of "the history of Russian archaeography".[23] The English translation may be the first Russian literary work to have been published in the English language. And, as in the case of so many early eighteenth-century Russian imprints, bibliographical investigation has confirmed the existence of editions and printings previously unknown.

It is against this background that Shafirov's *Discourse* must be viewed. Russia was evolving from a State that was gradually absorbing the terminology and conceptual framework of the law of nations in the form of an official, unpublished body of documentation to a State anxious to assume its place among the first ranks of European powers. Concerned with justifying Russia's policies to a foreign audience in the same manner as European monarchs defended their actions, Shafirov's undertaking was a logical step in this direction.

Although the *Discourse* may be a work of history, a political pamphlet, or a piece of literature in its own right, it is Shafirov's substantive and philological contribution to the law of nations which concerns us here.

The book cannot, of course, be compared to the seventeenth-century classics: Hugo Grotius, Samuel Pufendorf, Cornelis von Bynkershoek, and others. It does not profess to be a work of jurisprudence or a systematic comprehensive treatise on international law. It would be more accurate to describe the *Discourse* as a legal-historical brief officially inspired but unofficial in character, written by an individual well versed in the theory and practice of early eighteenth-century international law and diplomacy.

Among the questions of international law treated by the author were the following:

Sources of international law. Shafirov referred repeatedly to the "customs and maxims of the law of nations" and to specific international agreements contracted by Russian princes as sources of obligations which "Christian and polite nations" are bound to perform. Russia was conscious of being a member of the international system and felt no compunctions about calling upon other European powers to observe the rules of conduct prevailing in the international community.

Continuity of the realm. Although medieval Russia was far from a unified realm, consisting of disparate feudal princedoms which gradually were amalgamated into a centralized political community, Russian rulers were insistent upon their right to succeed to the rights and obligations of treaties contracted by their predecessors. "The Swedes themselves can not deny that the Provinces Carelia and Ingria, with all the territories, towns and places thereto belonging, did of old make part of the Russian Empire; an assertion that is evident from the treaties established, and the correspondence maintained time out of mind between the crowns of Russia and Sweden", with special reference to a RussoSwedish agreement of 1556. This was said to be true even though the treaties were contracted between Sweden and the Governors of Novgorod. Indeed, it was customary for a new sovereign to formally declare his intention to observe the treaties concluded by his predecessors.

[23] T. S. Maikova, «Петр I и 'История Свейской войны'» [Peter I and the "History of the Swedish War"], in Россия в период реформ Петра I [Russia in the Period of Reforms of Peter I] (1973), p. 116.

Acquisition of territory. Russian claims to territories in dispute with Sweden were predicated in Shafirov's treatment upon historical relationships, effective occupation, possession, and treaties. The rights to the Karelian and Ingrian Provinces, he said, rested not only upon treaties made with several Swedish Kings, but also upon the fact "that the greater part of the Provinces of Livonia and Estonia were under the jurisdiction and protection of the Russian crown". Evidence of the latter is that the "City of Dorpt" was, "according to the testimony of credible Russian chronicles", built in the year 1026 by a Russian grand prince and named after him. The city of Reval likewise was built by a grand prince "who lived in ancient times". The bishops and leaders of the Teutonic Order who governed these towns were said to have acknowledged their vassalage to Russian monarchs and to have paid annual tribute, "concerning which affair many original writings and records are still extant to this day in the Russian chronicles . . .". Yet another symbol of Russian "property and possession" were the "Russian churches of the Grecian confession in the two cities ..." which have been preserved for centuries. Even though both cities "departed from Russian obedience" on occasion, "they were reunited to Russia either by treaties or by force of arms". When pursuant to a Russo-Swedish treaty of 1594 "the Russian pretensions to Livonia and Estonia were ... yielded up to the Crown of Sweden, Russia continued after the confirmation of the said perpetual peace in the undisturbed possession of Ingria and Carelia with all towns and places thereto belonging ..." until 1608, when various machinations and deceptions were said to have caused Russia temporarily to give them up.

The Law of Embassies. The privileges and immunities of diplomatic agents were the subject of comment in several respects. The failure of Sweden to treat Peter the Great's Grand Embassy with the honor and respect due a diplomatic mission was mentioned repeatedly by Shafirov as one of the principal grievances in Russia's decision to go to war:

> The custom and the agreements formerly made between Russia and Sweden, required in some measure, that the ambassadors and envoys of both sides, though sent through their dominions to other powers, should be received on the frontiers with all possible marks of honor, and upon demand be furnished in the respective dominions with relays, as also on the passing over lakes and rivers with the necessary vessels without paying for them; that out of reciprocal activity their expenses should be defrayed in every particular; and that in the principal towns the governors and commanders should honour them with their compliments and visits.

The Governor-General of the city of Riga, according to Shafirov, sent a "gentleman of ordinary family" to greet the Embassy, kept the ambassadors and their retinue under virtual "civil arrest" while en route, obliged them to live in the "most miserable inns", made little effort to secure adequate horses and provisions, upon the Embassy's arrival in Riga did not receive them "with any extraordinary marks of honour"; they even were not treated with that regard which is due to envoys, being lodged outside the town in "poor wooden houses" at their own expense – "all of which was directly contrary to the ancient customs and conventions". The Governor-General further instructed that none of the Embassy retinue (including Peter, in a thinly disguised incognito) should be admitted to the town unless attended by a guard of two soldiers, prompting the Russian ambassadors to inquire "for what reason he used them in such a manner contrary to the laws of all nations . . .".

The practice of sending ambassadors to foreign courts for the purpose of announcing the accession of a new monarch to the throne was, in the sixteenth century if not earlier, known to Russia. Specifically mentioned in Shafirov's account are the mission of the Swedish ambassador in 1560, Tsar Mikhail Fedorovich's envoys to Sweden, France, and England in 1613-14, and the Swedish embassy of 1699. The importance of ambassadorial credentials is referred to in connection with a mission sent by the Governors of Novgorod to Charles IX of Sweden in 1609. The rank of "ambassador extraordinary and plenipotentiary" for Russian envoys was said to have been used in 1615, when England and the Netherlands sent diplomats of this rank to mediate between Sweden and Russia.

Infringements upon the personal property of diplomatic agents were a particular source of concern to Shafirov. He cited the Tsar's assurance to the Swedish ambassador in 1699 that a Russian subject who should "presume to offer ... affront and vexation to his Swedish majesty's person" would be punished and possibly executed. The action of the King of Poland in putting "the Russian ambassadors under confinement" in ca. 1609-10 was noted, as were the experiences in Riga when the Russian ambassadors suffered "the most intolerable affronts" and were "beaten, and contrary to the law of all nations, taken into custody . . .". Russia similarly protested that an Ambassador returning from Turkey via Riga was "greatly insulted and affronted, and some baggage wagons taken from him in a violent manner and almost in public", whereafter the Governor of Riga refused satisfaction and declined "to recover the goods that the Ambassador was robbed of, or even make enquiry after it ...".

Law of treaties. The procedure for concluding, ratifying, and confirming treaties in the sixteenth century was described: "... the truce was signed by the said governor, and the instrument of it was delivered by the King of Sweden's ambassadors to his Czarist Majesty, who ratified it in their presence, and confirmed it according to the custom of those times with a reciprocal oath". So too was it expected in 1699 that the Tsar would confirm "pursuant to former conventions and the ancient custom" the perpetual treaties of peace "with the solemnity of taking an oath on the Holy Gospel, as it was usual at that time, and ought to be done by virtue of the treaties". The implication is clear that the confirmation of a treaty by oath had been dispensed with in Russian practice by 1717.

The notion of *pacta sunt servanda* was implicit in the allegations of repeated breaches of treaty obligations by Russia's treaty partners, especially during the Time of Troubles preceding the accession of the Romanov dynasty. More significant, however, was the strong implication that treaties obtained by coercing a State during a period of domestic distress were void. The Russo-Swedish treaty of February 1616, concluded with the aid of English mediation, was variously described as a "prejudicial and forced peace", an "extorted treaty", and contrary to "all equity and charity, and against so many pacifications and defensive alliances". In response to the argument that lands yielded to Sweden by treaty ought not to be seized again in violation of the treaty, Shafirov wrote: "... even supposing his Czarist Majesty had had no new causes weighty enough for beginning a war with Sweden", there were ancient reasons "sufficiently justifiable by the laws of nature and nations". As the "Father of his Country", the Tsar was obliged to recover hereditary lands wrested "in so unjust a manner and in violation of the perpetual pacifications and defensive alliance made out of free will and without any constraint". He was bound to restore a property "robbed by fraud and all sorts of unfair means, at a time when the Russian Empire was at a very low ebb and on the brink of ruin ...". Resorting to analogy, Shafirov asked whether the victim of robbers, threatened upon pain of death to promise to deliver his remaining wealth, who swears an oath to waive any future claim to his property, can be charged with injustice if he later has the opportunity to restore his property and demand punishment for the offenders: "... will any equitable judge or any law condemn the offended person for perjury or breach of his bond; will they not rather declare all that has been transacted on such account to be void and null ...?".

Peaceful settlement of disputes. There is no suggestion by the Shafirov that sovereigns are in any sense obliged to settle their disputes by peaceful means. Nonetheless, the Russian solicitation of mediation by England and France in 1614 was recorded in some detail, as was Peter the Great's appeal to Holland and other powers, to employ their good offices with the King of Sweden both before and after the Northern War commenced in 1700.

Neutrality. The concept of an Act of Neutrality and the legal obligations concomitant therewith, clearly a European conception, was described in detail for the Russian reader.

Law of war.

(a) *The "just war" doctrine*. The theory of the just war was the *raison d'etre* of Shafirov's work. There was no attempt to suggest that Sweden initiated armed hostilities in the Northern War or, in modern terms, committed aggression; merely that Swedish policies and actions "inevitably necessitated" Russia "to begin this war against the crown of Sweden as an inveterate, perpetual and implacable enemy of the Russian crown ...". Part I of the *Discourse* consequently was devoted to recounting the "ancient and modern causes, for which his Czarist Majesty ... was in justice obliged to make war against Sweden, and to recover the hereditary dominions, which had been unjustly wrested from the crown of Russia not only during the everlasting peace, but even during a defensive alliance actually subsisting".

(b) *Declaration of war*. The issuance of a formal declaration of war before commencing hostilities was treated as though it were a normal requisite of Russian State practice.

(c) *Status of diplomatic agents of belligerent parties when war breaks out*. The Swedish resident at Moscow was given one month "to depart the city, and afterwards the Russian dominions, and to return to Sweden" with all his family and baggage. The Swedes, however, who "pretend to pass in the eyes of the world for a civilized people", act otherwise: "as soon as the Swedish court had notice of the declaration of war ..." the Russian Minister "was not only immediately put under close confinement, but also all his servants separated from him, and afterwards all his effects and household goods confiscated, and his plate carried to the mint, to coin money of it". He was "used during the whole war worse than a prisoner, and at last ended his days in that confinement", as did the secretary of the embassy and several servants. In reprisal against the Swedish action, the Swedish resident, "who had desired a respite of six months for regulating his affairs", was seized. In 1709 the Swedish resident was released upon his written promise to return to Sweden and secure the liberty of the Russian resident. Later the Swedish King's secretary was freed "in hopes the Russian resident would also be released", but without success.

(d) *Status of subjects of belligerent parties on enemy territory.* Swedish "commissaries, factors and other Swedish subjects of what condition soever" then in Russia were given an opportunity to depart with their effects, "to which Russian subjects should not be allowed any manner of claim". All "Russian merchants, with their servants, commissaries, and workmen, of whom there were some hundreds at Stockholm and in other Swedish towns" were placed under arrest, their effects were confiscated, and they were forced to perform hard labor from which "most of them miserably perished".

(e) *Appeals to the populace.* "Contrary to the practice of all Christian and civilized nations", Sweden published manifestoes and universalia "filled with calumnies tending not only to the defaming, affronting and reviling" of the Tsar and the Russian nation "but also to stir up his majesty's subjects to rebellion". After war was declared in 1700, the King of Sweden sent letters to his diplomatic agents abroad which "contrary to the use observed among the Christian powers, were filled with the most calumnious reflections against his Czarist Majesty's high person ...". Shortly thereafter, he issued "proclamations in his own name and under his hand and seal to his Czarist Majesty's subjects to stir them up against their natural sovereign. In those papers he used his Czarist Majesty with such injurious and virulent invectives, as my pen justly abhors to express . . .".

A copy of one of the Swedish tracts was translated and published as an appendix to the Russian and German editions of Shafirov's *Discourse* as evidence, the author says, of the unusual expressions seldom used even among "non-Christian peoples".[24] The Tsar gave "rigorous orders" to his troops entering Swedish territory that no one "should presume to make use of the least expressions either in writing or by word of mouth, prejudicial, or injurious to the Swedish nation ...".

(f) *Military operations.*

(i) *Combatants.* In 1704 a detachment of Russian auxiliaries in retreat "retired into a cottage and begged quarter of the Swedes", but the latter "pursuant to their King's orders, would not grant it ... surrounded the house, set fire to it, and burned the poor people in a most miserable manner". Many of those taken prisoner were "partly murdered in cold blood, partly had their fingers and toes cut off, a thing which even barbarians will judge to be abominable". A vessel sent with letters to prisoners of war "under his Czarist Majesty's white flag" was seized by the Swedes with all men on board and the flag "insulted and tore off ...".

(ii) *Civilians.* Russian troops were ordered "as much as their regulations at that time would possibly allow, they for the most part consisting of an irregular militia, to keep good discipline, that no manner of harm whatsoever be done to the Swedish subjects ... and those who transgressed that order were punished in the most exemplary manner". In 1706 the Swedes sent "incendiaries" to set "fire to many towns and boroughs ... for which they had received a certain sum of money" and promises of more. Swedish forces on Russian territory in 1708-09 "most miserably murdered the poor countrypeople with their wives and children, though they offered not the least resistance". After the Swedish defeat at Poltava in 1709, the Russians found that icons "of our saviour, of the Holy Virgin, of the Apostles

[24] Shafirov here had in view a Universal issued by Charles XII upon the outbreak of the Northern War.

and other saints" had been removed from churches and used to construct doors and stalls for livestock or employed as "tables for draughts", thereby "despoiling the churches and profaning sacred things".

(g) *Breaches of armistice agreements and capitulations*. At the battle of Narva in 1700 a capitulation was agreed upon between the generals of both sides stipulating that the Russian command and army should march away free with their colors and arms, as well as part of their field artillery; that prisoners on both sides should be released; and that certain heavy artillery should be left to the Swedes. The capitulation was confirmed by the Swedish King himself, "engaging his Royal Word". However, the Swedes "set aside the capitulation ..., forced the regiments ... to lay down their arms, and to deliver up their colours, and after they had plundered all their baggage, they let them march off ... They likewise seized all the artillery and ammunition, and under diverse frivolous pretexts first put all the generals and many other superior officers, military and civil, under arrest, and afterwards even kept them as prisoners of war". They were "kept by the Swedes in a very severe prison", some still being detained "on which account many representations and protestations were made at foreign courts on the part of his Czarist Majesty". In Stockholm those "seized contrary to the capitulation" and the King's royal word "were obliged to march on foot like other prisoners through the town after an extraordinary manner and as in triumph to their place of confinement". Russia, on the contrary, enlisted the aid of England, Prussia, and the Netherlands to form a "cartel for the exchanging and redeeming of prisoners, either during the whole war, or for a certain time, according to the custom observed between all Christian Powers when at war". Sweden refused until after the Battle of Poltava, whereupon the Tsar "for certain reasons of war and state" declined, though he showed "uncommon generosity" in releasing some "to regulate their private affairs, and to solicit ... the subsistence of the prisoners". Most who gave their word never returned and in some cases took up arms again.

(h) *Status of prisoners of war*. Shafirov complained bitterly about the treatment of Russian prisoners of war, many of whom were "obliged to be in dungeons underground among condemned malefactors, where they suffered great hardships, and were exposed to all sorts of brutality". Prisoners who had been maltreated in Swedish captivity on one occasion were shown "for curiosity" to the foreign ministers resident in Moscow. The Tsar declined to avenge such measures by maltreating Swedish prisoners: "Sometimes he implored God to prosper his arms in taking vengeance of the offences given him, sometimes he would even overlook them with a greatness of mind, which scorned to resent those injuries by exercising the like cruelty on the poor prisoners". Reports that Swedish prisoners had been "sent to very remote parts in the Russian dominions, and some of the common soldiers put to hard labour, as also that many of them were sold to the infidels" are explained respectively as retaliation for Swedish practices, as "compassion" toward the common soldier, and as an objectionable practice indulged in solely by the Cossacks and subsequently terminated by order of the Tsar.

(i) *Reprisals*. In the face of repeated violations of capitulation agreements by the Swedes, the Tsar "was at length necessitated to use reprisals". The garrisons of Vyborg and Riga "were secured and treated as prisoners" in retaliation for the Swedish seizure of Russian generals and superior officers, the detention of Russian merchants in Sweden, and the seizure of a vessel sailing under a white flag. The slanderous manifestoes published in Poland and "lesser Russia" with the intention of stirring up rebellion among the Russian subjects caused the Tsar, "in his own defence and for the security of his dominions", to issue manifestoes in "refutation of the false imputations contained in those of the enemy".

Shafirov concluded the *Discourse* by declaring that many other examples of "how the Swedes proceeded contrary to the usage and customs of war, and the general law of all civilized nations" might be given, but he is persuaded that enough has been said to enable one to judge "which of the two parties behaved with the more discretion and moderation".

In support of his argumentation Shafirov appended to the *Discourse* the texts of the following documents: (1) the armistice treaty with Sweden of 1564; (2) the treaty with Sweden concluded at Vyborg in 1609; (3) the letter sent by Tsar Mikhail Fedorovich to France in 1615 setting forth the injustices inflicted upon Russia by the Swedes and Poles and requesting assistance; (4) the Universal of Charles XII of Sweden published in 1700 proclaiming war with Russia.

Shafirov's "Dedication" of the *Discourse*, a panegyric to the Tsar, contained nothing of international legal interest. He said that no ruler in history or then living had done so much for his country and people. The Tsar's talent, great intelligence, and diligence were praised, as were his successes in warfare, in creating a permanent army and navy, in building fortresses, ports, and canals, in developing industry and trade, in expanding education, and in reforming the State apparatus. Shafirov stressed that all of these reforms were undertaken during time of war. He concluded that Peter had brought many of his subjects to such a level that they could equate themselves with representatives of other European peoples in statecraft, military arts, and cultural activity.

The Language of International Law in Russia. The axiomatic belief that foreign terminology was received into the Russian language only with the commencement of the Petrine reforms has been challenged and largely discredited by modern philological research. Hüttl-Worth has pointed to the large number of common western administrative, scientific, and military concepts (excluding nautical terms) in the Russian language of the seventeenth century. The transplantation of terms such as *ауденция* (audience, of Latin origin introduced via Poland), *гегемония* (hegemony, introduced from Greek, possibly via Germany), or *поссессия* (possession, from the Latin, perhaps via Poland) enabled Russians in the sixteenth and seventeenth centuries to understand and express administrative, cultural, social, or scholarly conceptions that had originated either in the classical world or developed *de novo* in western Europe. The quantity of foreign words uncovered in a rather casual survey of Russian manuscripts and documents of that period, though it included few legal terms, was impressive indeed.[25]

Shafirov's *Discourse* was the basis for an inquiry by a Russian philologist, A. V. Voloskova, into what she called the "diplomatic lexicon" of the Petrine era, though jurists would regard most of the terms analyzed as appertaining to inter-

[25] See G. Hüttl-Worth, *Foreign Words in Russian: A Historical Sketch, 1550-1800* (1963). The author's extensive glossary contains few legal terms. Useful, but with little on law specifically, is O. Bond, *German Loanwords in the Russian Language of the Petrine Period* (1974).

national law. Her materials not only supported Hüttl-Worth's general proposition; they cast fascinating light upon the gradual displacement of the ancient ambassadorial lexicon of medieval Russia by European terminology.

Shafirov himself clearly was aware of the terminological revolution underway. The *Discourse* shows that he found it necessary to explain several Petrine terms by placing their old-Russian equivalents in brackets or by offering a brief explanation. Of the 1549 words employed by Shafirov in the text of his *Discourse*, about one-third (543) can be classified as terminological, of which 225 are diplomatic-legal.[26] The latter group Voloskova divided into words of Russian (145) and foreign (80) origin. Of the 145 Russian diplomatic-legal terms, only 40 have not yet been traced to documents of the fifteenth to the mid-seventeenth century and thus are regarded as lexical neologisms of the Petrine period. Thirty-five of the 80 foreign words can be identified as pre-Petrine, and Voloskova is able to offer much earlier datings of these terms than Hüttl-Worth's investigations revealed for comparable words. The fact that nearly one half of the foreign terminology is to be found in sixteenth and seventeenth-century diplomatic documents, in her view, refutes the thesis that these words emerged suddenly in early eighteenth-century Russia. Voloskova's datings must be regarded as minimal projections, for it is highly probable that further research will reveal earlier usages of other expressions.

The eighty foreign words consist of 58 Latinisms, of 7 Hellenisms, and of 15 Gallicisms. The majority appear to have entered Russia via Polish (30) and German (23). A few show early Italian influence.

Early ambassadorial terminology developed from everyday terms and expressions which gradually acquired a special meaning, a process which continued to the end of the seventeenth century. The official language of the Ambassadorial Department was noteworthy for elements of spoken and traditional written speech which differed markedly from the stereotyped literary forms of Church Slavonic. In the Petrine era it is the former that was enriched by the addition of popular expressions and western European substitutes.

Among the early Russian terms, Voloskova points to the evolution of: *договариваться* (to conduct negotiations); *договор* (international treaty);

[26] A. V. Voloskova, Дипломатическая лексика начала XVIII века (По материалам трактата П. П. Шафирова «Рассуждение, какие законные причины Петр Великий к начатию войны против Карла XII имел» [Diplomatic Lexicon of the Early XVIII Century (According to Materials of the Treatise of P. P. Shafirov "Discourse on the Legal Reasons Which Peter the Great Had to Commence War Against Charles XII"] (diss. kandidat filologicheskikh nauk, 1966). 451 p. The dissertation is on deposit in the Russian State Library. Articles based on individual chapters can be found in Voloskova, «Русская дипломатическая лексика XVIII века ...» [Russian Diplomatic Lexicon of the Early XVIII Century], Вопросы фонетики, словообразования, лексики русского языка и методики его преподования; труды 4-й зональной конференции кафедра русского языка вузов Урала (1964), I, pp. 149-161; id, «Синонимы в дипломатической терминологии начала XVIII в.» [Synonyms in Diplomatic Terminology of the Early XVIII Century], Вопросы теории и методики преподавания русского языка; Ученые записки Ленинградского университета им. А. И. Герцена, CCLVIII (1965), pp. 187-210; id, «Иноязычные слова в дипломатической терминологии начала XVIII века» [Foreign Language Words in Diplomatic Terminology of the Early XVIII Century], in Уральский университет, Ученые записки, LXXX, серия филология, вып. 8 (1969), pp. 31-44. The dissertation abstract contains materials not found in these articles.

ссылаться (to have relations); *ссылка* (international link); *обсылка* (notification of an embassy's arrival); *посылка* (diplomatic mission); and *присылка* (arrival of ambassadors). In ambassadorial reports of the sixteenth and seventeenth centuries, the following expressions appeared: *быть в ответе* (to be in negotiations); *быть на отпуске* (to be present at a leave-taking audience); *править посольство* (to perform the duties of an ambassador); *видеть царски очи* (to be at a tsar's audience). Some expressions changed meaning or were used in multiple senses. *Гонец*, for example, which first appeared in a manuscript of the year 993, has variously referred to a person urgently sent upon a diplomatic mission, to a lower ambassadorial official, and later to persons who merely delivered messages without entering into any diplomatic negotiations; in the eighteenth century the term was replaced by "courier".[27] Similarly, the word *грамота* in the Russo-Byzantine Treaty of 945 meant an official written document, whereas in the sixteenth and seventeenth centuries it often was used to describe an international treaty. Shafirov used the word to mean an official diplomatic document.

Fifteen of the terms of Russian origin are new formations probably inspired by European terminology but not borrowed therefrom. Shafirov's use of *всенародное право* (law of nations) and *гражданское право* (public law), here distinguishing between the "natural law" of nations and the "secular law" of States, were attempts to express in the Russian language legal concepts originating in Romanist systems, in this case respectively *jus gentium* or *droit des gens*,[28] or *jus publicum* or *droit public*.[29] Other expressions falling into this category include *естественное право* (natural law; *jus naturae*, *droit de la nature*); *добрые оффиции* (good offices); *должность* (office); and *удовольство* (satisfaction). Most of these originated in the late seventeenth century. Shafirov's recourse to synonomous expressions in old Russian or Slavonic and "modern" eighteenth century Russian is especially striking. Often he felt the need to gloss the meaning of certain terms by interpolating bracketed explanations.

Shafirov as International Legal Practitioner. Perhaps the best known of the Petrine diplomats, Shafirov was by origin and accomplishment an unusual figure among his contemporaries.[30] His father was a Jew, a native of the Smolensk *воеводство* (vo-

27 On the origins and evolution of *гонец* and other diplomatic denominations in the Russian language, see F. P. Sergeev, Русская дипломатическая терминология XI-XVII вв. [Russian Diplomatic Terminology of the XI-XVII Centuries] (1971).

28 The impact of the French language as the language replacing Latin in the language of diplomacy has been explored in detail in V. Rjéoutski, D. Offord, and G. Argent, "French as a Diplomatic and Official Language in Imperial Russia", *Jus Gentium: Journal of International Legal History*, IV (2019), pp. 419-493.

29 As noted above, another expression was used o render *jus gentium* into Russian. The following also are to be found in Russian documents: *всенародный закон*; *право народа*; and *народное право.*

30 For an earlier biography of Shafirov, see E. Likhach, «Шафиров, барон Петр Павлович», Русский биографический словарь [Russian Biographical Dictionary] (1905), Vol.: Чаадаев Швитков, pp. 553 567. Likhach included a useful bibliography. Some additional material is drawn from Grabar, «Первая русская книга по международному праву» [First Russian Book on International Law], Вестник московского университета [Herald of Moscow University], no. 7 (1950), pp. 101 110, which is a fuller account than that given in his *History of International Law in Russia, 1647-1917.* Also see

evodship) who, together with many other westernRussian Jews, migrated to Moscow following the cession of Smolensk to Russia under the Andrussov Treaty with Poland.[31] There is some indication that he was a prisoner of war who may or may not in consequence have been a serf later liberated. He converted to the Russian Orthodox faith and was christened Pavel Filippovich (d. 18 July 1706). Russia's expanding relations with western Europe required men with a knowledge of foreign languages, and P. F. Shafirov quickly found employment in the Ambassadorial Department as a translator of official documents, papers, and books into Russian. Some sources indicate that under Tsar Feodor Alekseevich, P. F. Shafirov was admitted to the ranks of the lower nobility, although this seems unlikely.[32]

Petr Pavlovich, born in 1673,[33] possessed his father's gift for language. His education, unusually excellent for that time, included the study of French, German, Latin, Polish, and Dutch, his knowledge being augmented by conversations with foreigners living in Moscow. Later, during his sojourn as a hostage in Turkey, he learned Italian.

After having embarked upon an unpromising commercial career, P. P. Shafirov was recruited as an interpreter from the German language, probably through his father's influence, by the Ambassadorial Department as from 30 August 1691.[34]

the entry under Shafirov in the Большая энциклопедия [Great Encyclopedia] (1909), XX, p. 189. A less reliable account, but containing more data on Shafirov's adventures in Turkey and a dramatic report of his last minute reprieve from execution in 1723, is A. V. Tereshchenko, Опытъ обозрения жизни сановников, управляющих иностранными делами в России [Attempt at a Survey of the Life of Officials Managing Foreign Affairs in Russia] (1837), III, pp. 1 48. Much new archival material has been identified and explored by D. O. Serov, Строители империи: Очерки государственной и криминальной деятельности сподвижников Петра I [Builders of Empire: Surveys of State and Criminal Activity of Companions of Peter I] (1996), pp. 30-35, 37-59, 63-69ff; Serov, Администрация Петра I [Administration of Peter I] (2008), pp. 89-136; T. A. Bazarova, «Первый российский вице-канцлер П. П. Шафиров: Страницы жизни и деятельности» [The First Russian Vice-Chancellor P. P. Shafirov: Pages of Life and Activity], in T. A. Bazarova and Iu. B. Fomina (comps.), Походная канцелярия вице-канцлера Петра Павловича Шафирова: новые источники по истории России эпохи Петра Великого [Field Chancellery of Vice Chancellor Peter Pavlovich Shafirov] (Spb., 2011), I, pp. 5-34.

31 Treaty between Poland and Russia, signed at Andrussow, 30 January 1667. C. Parry (ed.), *The Consolidated Treaty Series* (1969-83), IX, 399.

32 See S. S. Ilizarov, Московская интеллигенция XVIII века [The 18th Century Moscow Intelligentsia] (1999), p. 305; V. Bergman, История Петра Великаго [History of Peter the Great] (1841), V, p. 80. However, "it should be stressed that reports concerning the elevation to the dignity of nobility of a number of persons in the seventeenth century (or even earlier) are unreliable. At best they may be interpreted in the pre-Petrine practice of noble service. Thus, one should ignore the assertion of Shafirov 'that his father was not only a Christian, but elevated to the dignity of the nobility under Tsar Fedor Alekseevich'". See O. I. Khoruzhenko, Дворянские дипломы XVIII века в России [Nobility Diplomas of the XVIII Century in Russia] (1999), p. 5.

33 Although all sources have routinely dated Shafirov's year of birth as 1669, Serov has shown convincingly on the basis of St. Petersburg census data for 1718 that Shafirov himself indicated his year of birth as 1673. See Serov, note 30 above (2008) p. 79. This would make Shafirov a year younger than Peter the Great; the two reputedly played soldier together as children.

34 Some examples of Shafirov's early activity as a translator survive. The Tsar included among his

His ability soon was recognized. Legend has it that Peter the Great discovered Shafirov in a marketplace arguing with the future Prince Aleksandr Dmitrievich Menshikov (1673-1729) over the theft of a piece of fabric. With his usual keen eye for talent, the Tsar is said to have promptly recruited them for State service on the spot.[35] Whatever the truth, in 1697 he was one of the first to be selected by the думный дьяк, Emelian Ignatevich Ukraintsev (d. 1708), to accompany Peter I on his celebrated Grand Embassy to western Europe as interpreter.[36]

The European journey was a turning point in Shafirov's career. It exposed him to Germany, Holland, England, and Austria. He was present at an audience of the Tsar with the Elector of Brandenberg on 21 May 1697, where he was presented a gift, and again at an audience with the Ambassador of Poland, where issues of credentials were discussed. The Dutch presented a gold chain to Shafirov valued at 42 zolotniks on the occasion of his departure to Amsterdam on 20 October 1697, where he shared a flat with Peter Wolf and was, in appreciation of his services, granted a larger allowance by the Tsar.[37]

Shafirov's visit to London brought him into a close and fruitful relationship with the influential Muscovite diplomat, Fedor Alekseevich Golovin (1650-1706), and with the Tsar himself. When domestic difficulties obliged Peter hurriedly to leave the Grand Embassy in Vienna and return home in 1698, Shafirov was one of the few selected to accompany him. It was Shafirov who translated to the Tsar a Memorial received while en route home. Moreover, Shafirov personally witnessed and probably suffered the slights and insults in Riga while returning to Russia, as described in the *Discourse*.[38]

many interests astronomy and astrology. His personal library contained several manuscript "calendars" translated from German and Polish. Quite apart from Peter's own predilections, such calendars were of interest to diplomats for their predictions of celestial events and the compiler's prognostications as to what impact these events would have in foreign countries, the outbreak of wars, illness, and so forth. The manuscript division of the Library of the Russian Academy of Sciences (BAN) contains three pristine translations by Shafirov, bound in paper, and executed in late seventeenth-century cursive script. A fourth, attributed to Shafirov by the manuscript division, is questionable. There is no external evidence to support such a definite conclusion, though an attribution to Shafirov certainly would be appropriate. The four items are described in V. P. Adrianova-Perets (ed.), Исторический очерк и обзор фондов рукописного отдела библиотеки академии наук [Historical Essay and Survey of Funds of the Manuscript Division of the Library of the Academy of Sciences] (1956), I, p. 405. The three items which definitely are Shafirov's work were translated *ca.* 1695-96. The doubtful calendar was done sometime after 1691.

35 This and other fables of Shafirov's life have been recorded in Victor Alexandrov, *The Kremlin: Nerve Centre of Russian History*, translated by R. Monkcom (1963), pp. 157-159, 175-179, 181-188. Useful materials are to be found in N. N. Bantysh Kamenskii, Обзор внешних сношений России (по 1800 год) [Survey of Foreign Relations of Russia (as of 1800)] (1894-1902).

36 M. M. Bogoslovskii, Петр I: Материалы для биографии [Peter I: Materials for a Biography] (1940-48), I, p. 378. On 10 February 1697 Shafirov co-signed a statement with three other interpreters to the effect that information was insufficient for writing correctly to the Pope and to the rulers of England, Denmark, and Sweden. Ibid., I, p. 381.

37 See Bogoslovskii, note 36 above, II, 77, 219, 237, 253.

38 Ibid., II, 547, 564, 566.

By 1699 Shafirov was assisting Golovin in negotiations with Poland and Denmark as Russia sought to conclude alliances against Sweden.[39] Although the precise nature of his role is obscure, he was present with the Tsar at New Year celebrations to meet the Danish Ambassador and presumably acquitted himself well, for on 18 February 1700 he accompanied the Danish Ambassador to an audience with the Tsar and on 23 April 1700 was present at secret discussions between the two. In 1701 he was given diplomatic responsibility of great importance and played an active role in persuading Poland to join Russia in joint actions against Sweden. In 1703 Shafirov was appointed Golovin's privy secretary in the Ambassadorial Department, where, *inter alia*, he translated correspondence with foreign diplomats.[40]

Thereafter, advancement was slow. The war with Sweden dragged on inconclusively; Shafirov accompanied the Tsar on his travels, executed decisions, and endeavored to display his abilities to their best advantage. But the competition was intense, and Shafirov's post did not give him discretion for taking independent initiatives. After Golovin's death, Shafirov's responsibilities increased. He was involved in the treacherous negotiations over the Polish interregnum in 1707, and in 1708 he assisted Golovin's successor, Gavriil Ivanovich Golovkin (1660-1734), in investigating certain aspects of the treason of Hetman Ivan Stepanovich Mazeppa (1639-1709).[41] Recognition began to come following the Russian victory at Poltava. Shafirov was made a Baron of the Holy Roman Empire by Jozef I of Austria on 16 October 1709 upon the petition of the Russian Resident in Vienna, V. Sh. Urbikh.[42] Peter I conferred the title of Baron on 30 May 1710;[43] various other decorations were awarded by Prussia, Poland (Order of the White Eagle), and the Tsar.

39 Tereshchenko credited Shafirov with drafting the Manifesto of 19 August 1700 declaring war against Sweden, observing that this was a departure from the usual Russian practice of sending ambassadors to announce the commencement of hostilities. See Tereshchenko, note 30 above, III, p. 4. Other sources do not mention Shafirov in this connection.

40 Bogoslovskii, note 36 above, IV, pp. 319, 339, 369, 439.

41 Shafirov's involvement in domestic affairs and Peter's internal reforms seems to have been slight; political trials were the principal exception. In 1717 he also had a part in condemning the Tsarevich Alexis, reading aloud the Tsarevich Alexis' solemn oath on renunciation of the succession and recognition of Tsarsevich Peter Petrovich as heir to the throne. He also was present on the morning of the Tsarsevich's death in 1718.

42 The background of this event as revealed in materials discovered in the Vienna archives is told by M. Orbec, "Le baron Pierre Pavlovitch Schafirov (1669-1739), Vice Chancelier de Pierre le Grand (Descendance, Titre, et Blason)", *Versailles*, no. 12 (1962), pp. 49-53 (a copy of the article is held by the Russian State Library). Emperor Jozef I assented to conferring the Order on the same day. However, neither Shafirov nor the Russian Government were notified for some time. See O. I. Khoruzhenko, note 32 above, p. 27. Shafirov's elevation to Vice Chancellor on the first day after celebrating the victory at Poltava was communicated to England by Captain James Jefferyes in a letter from the Russian camp of 27 July 1709. At the time, Jefferyes was under Shafirov's patronage. See R. Hatton, *Captain James Jefferyes's Letters to the Secretary of State, Whitehall, From the Swedish Army, 1707-1709* (1954), pp. 77-78.

43 The Edict of the Tsar establishing this title for Shafirov is no longer preserved in the relevant Russian archives. See Khoruzhenko, note 32 above, p. 27. Shafirov was the first to be given the title of baron by Peter the Great.

Initially, at least, the Russian victory at Poltava enhanced Russia's prestige in Europe at Sweden's expense.[44] Allies against Sweden were obtained more readily. Shafirov participated in the negotiations leading to a treaty of 29 May 1711, renewing the Russo-Polish alliance against Sweden.[45] Charles XII (1682-1718) in the meantime had taken refuge in Turkey where, with the support of France and the Crimean Khanate, he was able to enlist Turkish aid against Russia. In the ensuing battle of Pruth – the most disastrous of Peter's reign – the Russian forces were surrounded and obliged to sue for peace. Shafirov was intimately involved in the lengthy and complex peace negotiations. Once agreement was reached, he was one of two hostages left behind in Turkey pending execution of the treaty provisions (especially that clause guaranteeing Charles XII safe conduct to Sweden).[46] For various reasons the treaty was not executed, and in consequence the Sultan declared war upon Russia. Shafirov negotiated desperately to gain time. The Tsar decided against war while England and Holland counseled the Porte to avoid a military solution. With the aid of some astute bribes, Shafirov was instrumental in securing a 25-year renewal of the Treaty of Pruth on 5 April 1712, but this document also remained unratified.[47] Turkish patience was now exhausted. Shafirov was imprisoned together with Petr Andreevich Tolstoi (1645-1729), the Russian Ambassador to Turkey. The Swedes fared little better, however. Charles XII soon was expelled, Shafirov was released,[48] and yet a third, final peace treaty was concluded on 5 July 1713, and ratified in October.[49] Shafirov returned to Moscow in January 1714, having creditably performed the most challenging assignment of his diplomatic career under conditions that could hardly have been more adverse.

The departure of Charles XII from Turkey meant that no one was left to insist upon execution of the Russo-Turkish treaty. Russian diplomacy sought to repair existing alliances in Europe and to seek new support in the continuing war against

[44] The Russians are estimated to have taken 25,000 prisoners of war at Poltava. See the essays collected in Tamara Toshtendal-Salycheva and Lena Iunson (eds.), Полтава: Судьбы пленных и взаимодействие культур [Poltava: Fates of Prisoners of War and Interaction of Cultures] (2009).

[45] Treaty between Russia, Poland, and Denmark, signed at Iaroslavl, 29 May (9 June) 1711. Parry (ed.), *Consolidated Treaty Series*, note 31 above, XXVII, 119.

[46] Treaty of Peace between Russia and Turkey, signed at the Camp on the Pruth, 21 July 1711. Ibid., XXVII, 149.

[47] Treaty of Peace and Amity between Russia and Turkey, signed at Constantinople, 5(16) April 1712. Ibid., XXVII, 231.

[48] News of Shafirov's and Sheremetov's release through a "reliable correspondent" was recorded by F. P. Polikarpov in a manuscript «Кника стенная. Часть 2-я». Archive of the Ambassadorial Department in TsGADA, fond 181, no. 849, folio 579. See G. N. Moiseeva, «История России Федора Поликарпова как памятник литературы» ["History of Russia" of Fedor Polikarpov as a Monument of Literature], in XVIII век; сборник, IX (1974), p. 84.

[49] Renewal of the Pact of the Pruth between Russia and Turkey, signed at Adrianople, 5 July 1713. *Ibid.*, XXVIII, 251. For appreciative assessments of Shafirov's diplomatic talents in negotiations with the Turks, see A. G. Brikner, История Петра Великаго [History of Peter the Great] (1882), II, 487-490. There are extensive accounts of Russo-Turkish relations at this time in I. Grey, *Peter the Great: Emperor of All Russia* (1962), pp. 322-325.

Sweden. A treaty of alliance was concluded with Prussia in 1714[50] and Poland in the spring of 1715,[51] followed in July of that year by a treaty with Denmark.[52] Shafirov had a prominent role in all of these.[53] With the death of Louis XIV, French policy became more favorably disposed toward Russia. In 1717 Shafirov was among those who accompanied the Tsar to Paris and Amsterdam, where Russia's role as a European power was acknowledged formally by the conclusion of a Franco-Prussian-Russian agreement[54] guaranteeing the Treaties of Utrecht and Baden. Russia and Prussia also undertook to accept French mediation in the conflict with Sweden.

Diplomatically, Sweden had been virtually isolated. The final step on Shafirov's part was the Russo-Prussian treaty of August 1718 guaranteeing against the King of Sweden returning to Germany or Poland to renew his conquests.[55] When Charles XII fell in battle in 1718, Sweden sued for peace, finally attained in the Treaty of Nystadt of 1721.[56] Shafirov had some part in the intermittent negotiations carried on during those three years but no direct role in the peace treaty itself.

At this point, Shafirov's personal affairs took a dramatic and adverse turn. In the preceding decade (1710-20), Shafirov had been rewarded handsomely by the Tsar for his services. Decorations, titles, but more tangibly, property, money, and commercial concessions, the latter including the importation of a silk manufacturing plant (which failed) and interests in sealing and other marine trades.[57] In 1717

50 Treaty of Alliance and Guarantee between Prussia and Russia, signed at St. Petersburg, 1(12) June 1714. See Parry, *Consolidated Treaty Series*, note 31 above, XXIX, 59.

51 Likhach mentioned this "treaty" without giving a specific date. It was said to have eliminated any misunderstandings that may have arisen between Russia and Poland previously. Likhach, note 30 above, p. 559. The text of such a treaty has not been located.

52 Treaty on Sending Russian Forces to Pomerania to attack specified points between Denmark and Russia, signed 9 July 1725. On the basis of this treaty, Denmark and Russia concluded a Convention on the Sending of Auxiliary Russian Forces to the King of Denmark in Pomerania, on 6 September 1715. See ПСЗ, V (1st ser.), 161, 166, nos. 2919, 2930.

53 Shafirov was instrumental in arranging the marriage of the Tsarevna Catherine Ivanovna (1691-1733) to Karl Leopold, Duke of Mecklenberg-Schwerin (1678-1747). The treaty, noteworthy for its inclusion of political clauses, was signed at St. Petersburg, 22 January (2 February) 1716. Parry, *Consolidated Treaty Series*, note 31 above, XXIX, 403.

54 Treaty between France, Prussia, and Russia, signed at Amsterdam, 4(15) August 1717. Ibid., XXX, 159. Shafirov's signature and seal, the latter of heraldic interest, are reproduced in Orbec, note 42 above, p. 53. The use of personal seals by Russian diplomats was in imitation of their European counterparts; Shafirov's probably was devised specially for this purpose. His seal also appears on the Russo-Danish treaty of 9 July 1715.

55 Convention between Russia and Prussia, signed 7(18) August 1718. ПСЗ, V (1st ser.), 582. No. 3222. The Convention guaranteed against a return of Charles XII to Germany and Poland and stipulated the number of forces to be maintained in readiness against that eventuality. It confirmed an earlier Agreement of 9 September 1715.

56 Treaty of Perpetual Peace between Russia and Sweden, signed at Nystadt, 30 August 1721. Parry, *Consolidated Treaty Series*, note 31 above, XXXI, 339.

57 Karnovich described Shafirov as "one of the notable Russian wealthy men of his time". See E. P.

he had been appointed VicePresident of the College of Foreign Affairs, from 1718 a senator, and in 1722, with the establishment of the Table of Ranks, a full privy counselor, passing by the Vice-Chancellorship because of a long-festering enmity with Chancellor Golovkin.[58]

As one of the "newcomers" who had found favor with the Tsar, that is, one who owed his position almost exclusively to ability and not to lineage from the old Muscovite aristocracy, Shafirov perpetually was embroiled in constant intrigues between the old and new families, so prevalent in Russian domestic political life.[59]

Shafirov's hostility towards Golovkin was nonetheless severe at times. Both had turned to the Tsar with mutual recriminations. Widespread abuses, including embezzlement of State funds, were discovered in the postal system, which was under Shafirov's direction,[60] and also in Shafirov's northern business interests. These events, compounded by Shafirov's maladroit handling of his political rivals, led to his ultimately being convicted and sentenced to death on 13 February 1723 by

Karnovich, Замечательныя богатства частных лиц въ России [Remarkable Wealth of Private Persons in Russia] (2d ed.; 1885), p. 119. Investment in fish oil production was a joint venture with his arch rival, A. D. Menshikov, who ultimately accused his partner of corruption. See L. Hughes, *Peter the Great. A Biography* (2002), p. 183. Anecdotes of Menshikov and his problems were current at the time and have been analyzed in detail recently. See, respectively, Léonor Jean Christine Soulas (Abbé) d'Allainval (1696-1753), *Anecdotes du regne de Pierre Premier, die le grand, czar de Moscovie, contenant l'histoire d'Eudochia Fedorowna, & le disgrace du prince de Mencikow* ([Paris?], 1745); E. A. Andreeva, Следственное дело и ссылка А. Д. Меншикова. 1717-1729 гг. [Investigative Case and Exile of A. D. Menshikov: 1727-1729] (2d ed.; Spb., 2021].

[58] At one stage the enmity became so intense that the College of Foreign Affairs was said to have been brought to a standstill. It has been suggested that one source of the problem was the legal terminology which determined the tasks of the College. See Grey, note 49 above, p. 364. On the relationship with Golovkin, see D. O. Serov, «Г. И. Головкин и П. П. Шафиров в их взаимоотношениях: (1706-1723)» [G. I. Golovkin and P. P. Shafirov in Their Mutual Relations: (1706-1723)], in Труды Всероссийской научной конференции «Когда Россия молодая мужала с гением Петра, посвященной 300-летнему юбилею отечественного флота, Переславль-Залесский, 30 июня-2 июля 1992 (1992), I, pp. 122-131.

[59] Kamenskii argues that Shafirov and others of his generation close to Tsar Peter were swindlers and tricksters irrespective of whatever period of history they were in. See A. V. Kamenskii, От Петра I до Павла I. Реформы в России XVIII века. Опыт целостного анализа [From Peter I to Paul I. Reforms in Russia of the XVIII Century. Attempt at an Integral Analysis] (1999), p. 73; also see O. A. Omelchenko, reviewing N. I. Pavlenko, «Петр Великий» [Peter the Great], Вопросы истории, no. 12 (1991), p. 228. On the Tsar's comrades-in-arms contemporary to Shafirov, see N. Pavlenko, O. Drozdova, and I. Kolkina, Соратники Петра (Comrades-in-Arms of Peter] (2001). Bushkovitch suggests this image may be overdrawn: G. I. Golovkin and P. P. Shafirov "... carried out the planning and execution of much of Peter's foreign policy. Most observers believed that it was Shafirov who was the more able and knowledgeable and with a better command of foreign languages, and that Golovkin frequently simply followed his lead. Both of them remained largely independent of the court factions, cultivating Menshikov in the early years of his power, but by 1715 turning toward enmity without joining his opponents. See P. Bushkovitch, *Peter the Great* (2001), p. 166n.

[60] Over the years the Ambassadorial Department had been burdened with a host of petty responsibilities only tangentially related to foreign affairs. Among them were the postal service, the administration of certain territories acquired by treaty (Siberia, for example), the collection of monies to ransom prisoners of war, and many others.

the Ruling Senate, with deprivation of rank and decorations and confiscation of property (including his houses and personal library).[61]

Peter commuted the death sentence, reportedly as Shafirov's head lay on the executioner's block, on 15 February 1723 to life exile in Siberia (Iakutsk). On 26 February 1723 the place of exile was changed to Novgorod, where Shafirov lived on a dole of thirty-three kopecks per diem until the Tsar's death in 1725.

Empress Catherine I returned Shafirov, restored his title on 19 May 1725, conferred the rank of privy councillor and appointed him President of the Commercial College from 14 July 1725. The latter appointment, however, aroused the apprehensions of his political enemies. Instead, Shafirov was given the task of writing a history of Peter the Great's reign, an undertaking for which he evidently had little enthusiasm and soon abandoned.[62] The accession of Peter II to the throne in 1727 resulted in the downfall of some of Shafirov's rivals, but it was the Empress Anna Ivanovna (1693-1740) who in 1730 began to employ Shafirov's diplomatic talents again. He ably conducted peace negotiations in the Caucasus with Persia[63] and was involved in the conclusion of a trade agreement with England in 1734.[64] From March to December 1737 he served as a Plenipotentiary Minister at the Nemirov Congress. Again appointed (on 31 August 1733) to the Presidency of the Commercial College, a Senator, and a full privy councillor (in 1734), Shafirov survived renewed allegations of graft and died 1 March 1739, aged 66.

Preparation of the ***Discourse.*** Peter's long-felt desire to have books available in his own language about Russian history and Russia's military exploits during the Northern War had led him to commission preparatory undertakings for such works. As early as 1705 a literate Swedish prisoner of war serving as a translator in the Ambassadorial Department, V. Shilling, was charged with writing a history of the war. The same task was given at various times to Fedor Polikarpov-Or-

[61] On Shafirov's investigation and trial, see P. I. Ivanov, «Судное дело над сенатором бароном Шафировым и обер-прокурором Сената Скорняковым-Писаревым» [Court Case Against Senator Baron Shafirov and Ober-Procurator of the Senate Skorniakov-Pisarev], Журнал Министерства юстиции, no. 3 (September 1859), pp. 3-62; Serov, «Фрагменты жизнеописания сенатора Петра Шафирова» [Fragments of the Life of Senator Peter Shafirov], in id, note 31 above, pp. 87-134. Lindsay Hughes says that Shafirov's Moscow house went to Petr Tolstoi, his wine was sent to the palace and redistributed to various officials, and money invested abroad was allocated to Russian students. See L. Hughes, *Peter the Great: A Biography* (2002), p. 183. The text of the Edict punishing Shafirov was memorialized for eternity by being placed or inscribed on one side of the trihedral Zertsalo, which Peter I ordered to be produced and placed in all Russian courts and administrative offices throughout the realm. The Zertsalo existed until 1917; a dozen or so exist today in Russian museums. For details, see W. E. Butler, "On the Formation of a Russian Legal Consciousness: The Zertsalo", in Butler, *Russia and the Law of Nations in Historical Perspective* (2009), pp. 91-101.

[62] For the text of the Edict of 17 May 1725 instructing Shafirov to write a history of the reign of Peter the Great, see ПСЗ, XI, no. 8695.

[63] Treaty of Peace between Russia and Persia, signed at Riascha, 21 January 1732. Parry, *Consolidated Treaty Series*, note 31 above, XXXIII, 445.

[64] Treaty of Commerce between Great Britain and Russia, signed at St. Petersburg, 2 December 1734. Ibid., XXXIV, 211. The manuscript text of the Treaty in the Public Record Office bears what appears to be Shafirov's seal, although deterioration is so advanced that a positive identification could not be made.

lov (c. 1670-1731), a Moscow typographer and translator, to Baron Heinrich von Huyssen (1666-1739), to Feofan Prokopovich (1681-1736), and of course to Shafirov. In a plea for an increased allowance submitted to the Tsar on 24 December 1720, one Boris Volkov, an interpreter in the College of Foreign Affairs, declared in support of his petition that he had devoted half a year to writing a "history of His Majesty" with Baron Huyssen.[65] Preparations in 1711-13 for the publication of the *Книга Марсова*, a collection of remarkable engravings depicting military campaigns during the Northern War with brief descriptive "relations" accompanying each print, involved assembling accounts of the War which had been published individually in Moscow and Petersburg during the preceding decade in Cyrillic.[66] Some Russian historians go so far as to claim that the *Книга Марсова* was the first printed book in Russian on the history of the Northern War. A proper history of the War was undertaken by A. V. Makarov in 1718, but it remained in manuscript until half a century later, when Mikhail Mikhailovich Shcherbatov (1733-1790) found and published it.[67]

Shafirov had been involved for a short time in these preparatory activities in 1712.[68] While compiling his *Discourse*, he certainly availed himself of the materials that had been collected. But the immediate inspiration for Shafirov's work would appear to be a draft "Declaration of Claims of the Russian Crown" prepared by the Russian envoy to London, Fedor Stepanovich Saltykov (1672-1715), and sent to Peter for consideration *ca.* 1713-14. Saltykov laid down twenty-six "propositions" outlining the historical basis of Russian claims to territories in dispute with Sweden and recommended that a manifesto be drawn up explaining these to the Russian people. Proposition 26 declared: "And after compiling the manifesto, it should be translated into the Latin, French, and German languages and printed in those languages for the information of all European States".[69] Shafirov progressed considerably beyond Saltykov's proposal, however, for the latter made no reference to the conduct or course of the War nor to the principles of international law applicable to the territorial claims.

A working manuscript of the *Discourse* preserved in the Central State Archive of Ancient Documents (TsGADA) in Moscow gives some insight into the manner of its preparation.[70] Folios numbered 1-5 have been recopied in a beautiful eigh-

[65] For a detailed account, see Peshtich, note 22 above, p. 138 ff. Huyssen, who held a degree in law, acted as a diplomat and literary representative abroad and was successful in placing Russian documents for publication in foreign media or separately as pamphlets.

[66] Книга марсова или воинских дел от войск царского величества российских ... (1713). See T. A. Bykova, «Книга марсова», in Berkov, note 13 above, pp. 515-523.

[67] Журнал или Поденная записка, блаженная и вечнодостойныя памяти государя имп. Петра Великаго с 1698 года, даже до заключения Нейштатского мира (1770 72). 2 vols. Shafirov was among those who took part in editing the original manuscript.

[68] Peshtich, note 22 above, p. 125.

[69] The text of Saltykov's draft is published in N. Pavlov-Silvanskii, Проекты реформ в записках современников Петра Великого [Draft Reforms in the Memoranda of Contemporaries of Peter the Great] (1897), II, p. 6.

[70] ЦГАДА, fond 96, opis 1, file 16, 97 folios. *Сношения России с Швецией.* The manuscript is entitled

teenth-century cursive script, probably belonging to one of the employees in the College of Foreign Affairs or an archivist. Thereafter, the folios are soiled and the text, though virtually a scribble, often indecipherable, is in Shafirov's hand. The numerous textual and marginal corrections and notations in at least two hands indicate that Shafirov's colleagues were invited to share in his labors, or that a clerk in the College was involved.

The manuscript does not contain the complete published text. Shafirov's panegyric dedication to the Tsar is not present, nor the "Conclusion to the Reader" written by Peter himself. Indeed, folios 58-91 appear to be rough notes and extracts from documents that were used to write the third section of the *Discourse*; folios 82-85 are a chronology of Russo-Swedish battles from 1620-38. On folios 95 and 96 there are a number of queries written out in Shafirov's hand intended for his "research assistants" (these are recopied in an archivist's hand on folios 92-94). Thus, he enquired: "Does the original treaty concerning the forty-year armistice concluded with Sweden in 1556 exist?", or, referring to a particular document, "Nothing older than this?" To the first question his assistants were able to give an affirmative response, duly indicated on the manuscript. Some questions could not be answered. Shafirov asked whether the Swedish refusal to Tsar Mikhail Fedorovich's demand for the return of seized lands, "in a letter or orally", could be dated, but the answer could not be found. These queries reinforce the impression gained from the printed text that Shafirov relied extensively upon archival sources for his data on State practice.

Some marginalia and corrections on the manuscript are of interest. The author's decision to substitute the term *законные* for *правовые* when speaking of "just" or "lawful" reasons for going to war is recorded on folio 6. The headings of Sections II and III of the published *Discourse* are merged together as one on folio 4, further suggesting that the third section had not been completed at this time. The date of the Russo-Swedish treaty of 1616 was given incorrectly in the manuscript by one hundred years on folio 28; the error was not detected here, although the date is correct in the printed version. Also, the bracketed synonyms present in the printed editions for certain expressions are not present in the manuscript.

According to a notation that appears on folio 94, on 22 March 1718 – after the first printed edition was released – Secretary Mikhail Larionov was given a "promemorial" to continue to search for necessary documents and instructed to send those found to St. Petersburg. This would indicate that the materials continued to have value for forthcoming peace negotiations with Sweden.

It is generally acknowledged that the Tsar not only commissioned and encouraged Shafirov to prepare his *Discourse* but that he also had some direct hand in writing the text. Pekarskii was of the view that "many places of the book were written by the sovereign himself; the conclusion (from the words 'And thus gen-

as follows: 1700 года. Разсуждение о причинах, котя Гдрь Петрь I имел объявить Шведам войны – Сочиненное и писанное П. Шафировым. Fragments of the original manuscript, with commentary and an adapted facsimile of the full text of the Shafirov treatise were reproduced in a sumptuous edition by the Pepeliaev Group in 2016; the commentators are Sergei Pepeliaev, V. A. Tomsinov, W. E. Butler, and Elena Trifonova.

tle Reader...') all belongs to his pen up to the end".[71] Ustrialov was rather more cautious. He indicated that Peter wrote most, but not all, of the "Conclusion" and perhaps contributed very slight modifications to the text, although none are specifically mentioned.[72]

Of particular interest in Peter's contribution was his insistence upon Russia's changed status in the international community. He curtly dismissed the notion that Sweden might have a claim to territories so long in its possession: ". . . there is no comparison to be made between those times and conjunctures and the present". He quoted Samuel Pufendorf, Jacques-Auguste de Thou (1553-1617), and Johannes Loccenius (1598-1677) to illustrate the hostile manner in which Swedish policy had endeavored to contain Russian ambitions. According to one Russian historian, these were the first examples in Russian historiography of citations to literary sources.[73]

Although Peter did not give complete citations to the editions which he consulted – an omission that caused, as we shall see, some difficulty to those who translated the *Discourse* – it has been possible to identify those he used. Pufendorf is referred to only in passing. Peter had commissioned Buzhinskii to prepare a Russian translation of *Introductio ad Historiam Europaeum* from the 1704 Frankfurt edition. Buzhinskii had deleted the chapter relating to Russia because some of Pufendorf's unflattering comments were considered offensive. Peter ordered the chapter restored in unexpurgated form and prescribed the entire book as compulsory reading for his son and heir. Buzhinskii's translation was published at St. Petersburg in 1718;[74] Peter must have had access either to the manuscript of the Russian translation or to a Latin edition when he wrote the Conclusion for the *Discourse*.

The quotations and references to Loccenius are taken respectively from *Jure Maritimo & Navali*[75] and *Rerum Svecicarum Historia*[76] and to Thuanus (or de

[71] P. P. Pekarskii, Наука и литература в России при Петре Великом [Science and Literature in Russia Under Peter the Great] (1862), I, p. 393.

[72] See N. G. Ustrialov, История царствования Петра Великого [History of the Reign of Peter the Great] (1858), I, pp. 325-328. Ustrialov reproduced the "conclusion" from the *Discourse* as Annex IV of his work under the heading: "Personal Writings of Peter Placed in Shafirov's Discourse". For archival evidence that Peter also edited other portions of the *Discourse* and on the role played by this book in Russian diplomacy, see S. A. Feigina, Аландский конгресс [The Aaland Congress] (1959), pp. 21, 85.

[73] P. P. Epifanov, «'Разсуждение' П. П. Шафирова о войне со швецией» [The 'Discourse' of P. P. Shafirov on the War with Sweden], in Проблемы общественно-политической истории России и славянских стран; сборник статей к 70-летию академика М. Н. Тихомирова (1963), pp. 296-303.

[74] Berkov, note 13 above, p. 246. Peter apparently learned of Pufendorf's works during his early travels in Europe, calling him a «wise jurist», or so reported A. P. Kunitsyn, «Старание Петра Великого о введении в России теоретического образования юношества в Правоведение» [Effort of Peter the Great to Introduce in Russia the Theoretical Education of Youth in Jurisprudence], Сын отечества [Son of the Fatherland], ч. 67, no. 6 (1821), p. 253.

[75] J. Loccenius, *Jure Maritimo & Navali: Libri tres*. (2d rev. ed.; 1652), p. 16.

[76] J. Loccenius, *Rerum Svecicarum Historia A Rege Berone tertio usque ad Ericum decimum quartum deducta, & pluribus locis, quam antehac, auctior edita*. (1654.) The material cited by Peter appears in Book V, pp. 333-334.

Thou) from the 1624 Frankfurt edition of his *Historiarum sui temporis*.[77]

There has been confusion over the number of Russian editions of Shafirov's *Discourse*. There are in fact three editions, though Pekarskii,[78] Sopikov,[79] Petrov,[80] and Bitovt[81] identified only two. Their information has continued to mislead both western[82] and Russian[83] scholars.

The first edition was a small folio published at St. Petersburg in 1717. Collations vary, but the most common appears to be: tp + 10 + [ii] + 128 pp. In some copies the "dedication" – Shafirov's panegyric to Peter – is bound in after the introduction.[84]

The second edition is a small volume, bibliographies differing as to whether it is quarto or sextodecimo, consisting of: [iv] (tp) + 34 + [viii] + 449 + [i] pp. The contents of the volume are identical to the 1717 edition, except that Shafirov's bracketed marginal annotations in the first edition are placed directly into the text of the second edition as a result of the smaller format. In attributing the second edition to 1717, the text of the title pages of the first and second editions being identical, the aforementioned bibliographers overlooked the colophon at the end of the text: "Printed at Moscow, 1719/summer, in the month of July".

The third edition, printed at St. Petersburg in 1722, is of yet another format: a sextodecimo (or quarto) volume consisting of: [iv] (tp) + 38 + 360 pp. Some 20,000 copies were printed from different type-settings and sometimes even with different decorative ornament.[85] The unusual nature of this undertaking may be judged from the fact that a normal printing for a book published in Petrine Moscow or Petersburg was 200-300 copies.[86] Bykova and Gurevich identified three variants

77 J.A. de Thou, *Historiarum sui temporis* (1624). The materials mentioned by Peter appear respectively in Book XXXVI, p. 309, and Book LI, pp. 1009-1010.

78 Pekarskii, note 71 above, II, p. 585.

79 V. S. Sopikov, Опыть российской библиографии, edited by V. N. Rogozhin. (2d ed.; 1904), IV, p. 188. No. 9582.

80 A. V. Petrov, Собрание книг, изданных в царствование Петра Великого (2d ed.; 1913).

81 Iu. Iu. Bitovt, Редкие русские книги и летучие издания XVIII века [Rare Russian Books and Ephemeral Publications of the XVIII Century] (1905).

82 T. Fessenko (comp.), *Eighteenth-Century Russian Publications in the Library of Congress: A Catalogue* (1961), p. 116.

83 See E. Tarle, Северная война и шведское нашествие на Россию [The Northern War and Swedish Attack on Russia] (1958), p. 472, who in calling attention to the importance of Shafirov's *Discourse* cites the 1722 edition as the second. Also Feigina, note 72 above, p. 523.

84 Data on all three editions is based upon Berkov, note 13 above, pp. 219-220, 265, 398-399.

85 A. V. Gavrilov, Очерки истории С.-Петербургской синодальной типографии [Essays on the History of the St. Petersburg Synod Printing House] (1911), I. p. 147.

86 Berkov, note 13 above, p. 529.

of the 1722 edition. Observing that all three sometimes appear in the same volume, they have concluded that all of the sheets were printed first and then mixed together during the binding process.[87] Their view would seem to be borne out by Pekarskii's finding that the 1722 edition was printed simultaneously on five presses and required eight months to complete.[88] According to Luppov, the cost of production per volume was 24 kopecks.

The decision to print such an extraordinary number of copies is a curious one. The conclusion of the Nystadt Peace in 1721 ending the Northern War would seem to have terminated any need to justify the enterprise to the Russian people. Peter nonetheless was determined that every province of the Empire should own a copy. In 1721 the Tsar sent a copy of the *Discourse* and Pufendorf's history to Revel.[89]

In December 1722 he ordered the intended price of the book reduced nearly forty per cent, from 16 *altyn*, 4 *den'gi* to 10 *altyn*. Whether by reason of waning interest or otherwise, the mass distribution never took place. Sopikov recorded that only fifty copies were sold between 1722 and 1725.[90] From 1739 to 1741 twenty-five copies were sold; among the purchasers were a military officer, a copyist, a Synod official, and several merchants.[91] In 1756 the printing house still had 16,000 copies on hand. Pekarskii reported in the mid-nineteenth century that the book could be acquired readily for twenty kopecks.

Although the *Discourse* was published abroad in German and English translations, probably upon the express commission of the Russian Government, the conclusion that "the translation of Shafirov's book into German received fame in

87 Ibid., p. 398.

88 Pekarskii, Наука и литература, note 71 above, II, p. 585.

89 Maikova, in note 23 above, p. 103, citing ЦГАДА, Kabinet Petra Velikogo, otd. II, kn. 61, folio 65; kn. 57, folio 921.

90 Sopikov, Опыть российской библиографии, note 79 above, IV, p. 188. Reports of a manuscript copy of Shafirov's Discourse dating from the mid eighteenth century had led Pekarskii, among others, to speculate that printed copies were becoming difficult to obtain, a rather unlikely situation given the large warehouse inventories. It is probable that Pekarskii was referring to a manuscript which came to the Manuscript Division of the Library of the USSR Academy of Sciences (Leningrad) from the private collection of Academician A. A. Ukhtomskii about 1940. The manuscript contained the text of other Petrine works as well. The full text of the *Discourse* is reproduced, obviously copied from a printed edition, but the appendixes were omitted. Delicate marginal illustrations appeared on folios 73, 81, 96, and 98; that on folio 96 is accompanied by the words: "Picard; Aleksei Polozov". Minor notations explaining passages in the text are found on folios 84, 104 and 109. Bound in contemporary calf, the manuscript records on the inside front cover the births of Tatiana, Aleksei, Petr, Anna, and Ekaterina Genadevna. Without doubt, the manuscript was prepared especially for, or as part of, the education of these children and does not reflect in any way on the availability of printed versions. See Manuscript Division, Russian Academy of Sciences Library, T. P. 328, folios 73 109.

91 See S. P. Luppov, Книга в России в первой четверти XVIII века [The Book in Russia in the First Quarter of the Eighteenth Century] (1973), pp. 152, 155-156, 160, 168. The Discourse was recorded in the private libraries of A. P. Volynskii, Feofilakt Lapotinskii, G. Dashkov, and the Slavonic-Greek-Latin Academy Library. Ibid., pp. 272, 286, 319.

western Europe"[92] appears to be unwarranted. The German edition is of greater rarity than the Russian versions and of uncertain provenance, whereas the English translation lay unidentified and unnoticed by bibliographers and scholars for two and a half centuries after its initial publication as an appendix to Friedrich Christian Weber (16?-1739), *The Present State of Russia.* The Russian edition received passing notice in a Ведомости published in July 1719, but this can hardly be regarded as notoriety.[93]

The German translation may have been printed abroad[94] sometime between 1718 and 1721. Contrary to Pekarskii's view, it is not "word for word according to the Russian edition", although the translation follows the original with great fidelity. Minor divergences that do occur appear to be deliberate rather than accidental or careless. The book was published in quarto, without an indication of either the place or date of printing, under the full title of the original.[95] It consists of: tp + [ii] + 3-40 (dedication) + 245 + [i] (errata) pp. The translator is unknown but, given his command of German, could have been Shafirov himself.

The Russian court had formed a network of contacts with printers and publishers in Hamburg and Holland from at least 1710; the Russian Resident in Hamburg, I. F. Betinger, arranged for a number of texts to be printed for the Emperor, including the 1721 Treaty of Nystad. Established relations and contacts existed for the German text of the *Discourse* to be arranged.[96]

92 L. V. Cherepnin, Русская историография до XIX века [Russian Historiography Up to the XIX Century] (1957), p. 247.

93 Ведомости, no. 2 (1719), which referred to the Discourse without acknowledging authorship or date of publication. Some variants of this issue give a longer account than others, emphasizing Swedish atrocities during the war. See Ведомости времени Петра Великого. Вып. II, 1708 1719 гг. в память двухсотлетия первой русской газеты (1906), p. 259, reprinted in 1970 by Brucken Verlag.

94 This conclusion is based upon an evaluation of the typeface, paper, and other external features of the copies which were examined at the Russian National Library and the Library of the Russian Academy of Sciences in St. Petersburg. T. A. Bykova and A. L. Goldberg, leading specialists in Petrine books and Russica at the Russian National Library, shared this view. They believed that the German edition probably was printed in Holland or northern Germany. Tereshchenko's statement that the German translation was printed in Petersburg is not impossible, however. Tereshchenko, Опыть обозрения жизни сановников, note 30 above, III, p. 46.

95 *Raisonnement, Was für Rechtmassige Ursachen Se. Czaarische Majest. Petrus der Erste ... gehabt den Krieg wieder den Konig in Schweden Carolum den XIIten, Ao Christi 1700 anzufangen ...* n.p., n.d. For a full text of the title page, see R. Minzloff, *Pierre le Grand dans la litterature étrangere* (1872), pp. 349-350; also Bibliotheque Imperiale Publique de St. Petersbourg, *Catalogue de la Section des Russica* (1873), I, no. 459.

96 See N. A. Kopanev, «Гамбургские издатели и Петербург (первая половина XVIII в.)» [Hamburg Publishers and Petersburg (First Half of the XVIII Century)], in A. V. Prokhorenko (ed.), Санкт-Петербург-Гамбург: Балтийский побратимы [St. Petersburg-Hamburg: Baltic Twinned Cities] (2007), pp. 86-92; M. Fundaminskii, «Вклад немцев в развитие книжного дела России XVIII в.» [Contribution of Germans to the Development of the Book Trade of Russia of the XVIII Century], in D. Dahlmann and G. Smagina (eds.), Г. Ф. Миллер и русская культура [G. F. Müller and Russian Culture] (2007), pp. 172-183.

The year 1718 is the earliest probable date of publication for the German version, given the time-consuming tasks of preparing the translation, obviously done with great care, of sending it abroad for printing, and of arranging for a typographer. The fact that the English version appeared in 1722 and was translated from the German text would suggest the latter must have been available at least by 1721. Conceivably, the German edition might have been ready as early as 1717, when Peter journeyed to Paris and Amsterdam; its appearance most assuredly would have augmented his successful solicitation of continental support for his cause. But no hard evidence has been found to substantiate such speculation.

The decision to publish an English translation of Shafirov's *Discourse* in 1722, after the Northern War had ended, is as curious as Peter's determination that same year to disseminate 20,000 copies in Russia itself. The continuing need to assuage anti-Russian sentiment amongst the British public, which had become especially intense in 1716 following the quartering of a large Russian force in Mecklenberg and had produced a spate of anti-Russian pamphleteering, is perhaps the most logical explanation. Fear of Russian interference in England's peaceful enjoyment of Bremen and Verden ceded to George I under a Swedish-Hanoverian Treaty of 1719 was fanned by pro-Swedish elements in England. There also was doubt about Russian attitudes toward the Jacobites and concern over reports of growing Russian naval power: "... the official British attitude to Russia in the last years of Peter's life was one of consistent hostility".[97] These fears and suspicions were shared by a public opinion alarmed by news reports of Russian military successes against Sweden. Viewed in this context, Shafirov's explication of Russian policy in the Northern War could still have had a beneficent effect upon an English reading public.

Weber's account of Petrine Russia was first published in German in three volumes which appeared respectively in 1721, 1739, and 1740. Volume one was issued anonymously in four German editions (1721 and 1729 in Hanover; 1738 and 1744 in Frankfurt and Leipzig). In addition to the English edition of 1723, French translations were printed at La Haye (two versions in 1725 and another in 1737), Paris (1725), and Amsterdam (1725).[98]

The most penetrating and impartial account of Russia available at the time, Weber's book contained authoritative data upon the Petrine reforms, serfdom, religious life and politics, government administration, law reform, military affairs, and foreign relations up to 1720.[99] Volume two treated the last years of Peter's reign,

[97] M. S. Anderson, *Britain's Discovery of Russia 1553-1815* (1958), p. 72. For the most detailed and considered survey of British reactions to Peter the Great, see A. G. Cross, *Peter the Great Through British Eyes* (2000), pp. 40-59.

[98] For translations of Weber's work, see Minzloff, *Pierre le Grand dans la litterature étrangere*, pp. 349 350; A. L. Goldberg (comp.) Дореволюционные издания по истории СССР в иностранном фонде государственной публичной библиотеки имени Салтыкова-Щедрина; систематический указатель. A. S. Mylnikov (ed.). (1964 66.) 2 vols; D. S. von Mohrenschlidt, *Russia in the Intellectual Life of Eighteenth Century France* (1936), pp. 185 186. Reviews of Weber appeared in *Journal des savants*, LXXVII (September 1725) and *Memoires de Trevoux* (September 1725).

[99] But not, of course, wholly accurate. Russian bibliographers have pointed out recently that Weber's account of the Courland library being moved to Petersburg is in error, both as to the time of transfer and the quantity of books. The issue is of considerable importance for the proper identification of the

and Volume three, the period 1725 to 1730, though neither possessed the freshness of the first.

Weber clearly drew upon Shafirov's *Discourse* in writing about Russo-Swedish relations, just as he did upon other relations of Russia available to him. What is remarkable, however, is the fact that only the English edition of Weber's book appended the text of the *Discourse* even though the French and Dutch editions contained the other appendices found in the London edition.

Indeed, the English edition is not without its mysteries. Weber is quoted as having ascertained that "English State people" had not been opposed to the appearance of his first volume in 1721,[100] implying that he had sought clearance to publish his memoirs. As for the English translator, we know only what he reveals of himself in the translator's preface to *The Present State of Russia*; to wit, that he had intended to write an introductory history of Russia and "... had made some Progress in it, when this book was published in Germany", that he was in close contact with Weber while translating it ("I undertook the translation of it with the author's knowledge and consulted him about several difficulties"), that he inserted materials into the text taken from "extracts of letters written by the author when in Russia, that were communicated to me by a Person of Honour", and that he did not know Russian ("... thinking it presumptuous to do anything by guess [e.g. orthography] in a language to which I am a stranger").

With regard to Shafirov's work the translator comments: "The Discourse, concerning the War between Russia and Sweden, was at first intended to be inserted by our Author [Weber], but as the translating of it from the Russian would have retarded the publishing of his book, he left it out. It has since been printed in High-Dutch, and I have joined it to the Swedish Deduction to which it refers, though I was obliged to retrench the long Preface and the Historical Documents belonging to it, for fear of swelling the Bulk of that Volume too much".[101] The German translation of Shafirov's *Discourse* possibly was supplied to him by Weber.

The English text is not, therefore, a direct translation from the Russian original, but from the German version commissioned by the Tsar. It nonetheless is a

provenance of the Academy of Sciences Library. See N. Iu. Bubnov, «К вопросу о первоначальных фондах библиотеки академии наук» [On the Question of the Initial Funds of the Library of the Academy of Sciences], in Сборник статей и материалов библиотеки АН СССР по книговедению (1970), II, pp. 132-133. Bubnov commented on discrepancies in statements of fact between the German and French versions of Weber's book. Are these liberties taken by translators, or is the author collaborating in and correcting the foreign translations of his work?

100 See Brikner, note 49 above.

101 See [Weber], *The Present State of Russia*, pp. A3-A4. It is not wholly clear that the *Discourse* was directed against a particular Swedish pamphlet. The Swedes had been active throughout the war in publicizing their views. Among the early ventures in Swedish pamphleteering were several by O. Hermelin: *Examen causarum, quas copiarum Saxonicarum, uti vocatur, dux improvisae et subdolae in Livoniam irruptioni praetoxere, litorisque suis divulgare voluit* (n.p. 1700). 80 p. (also published in German, Swedish, and Dutch translations); *Veritas a calumnis vindicata seu ex parte ... Regiae Majestatis Sveciao ... responsum, quo nefandae artis et calumniae Regis Poloniae ... manifestentur* (n.p., 1700). 188 p. (also published in German); *Discussio criminationum quibus usus est Moscorum Czarus cum bello Suecio ... quaererat* (1700). Two German editions appeared in 1701.

faithful rendering of the original Russian version. In those cases where there are textual discrepancies between the English and Russian versions, the change usually was made in the German version and followed by the English translator.

Although the *Discourse* was a landmark in Russian international legal history, it was an isolated and lonely monument, not emulated by another Russian work of comparable scope or originality for many decades. With the founding of the Academy of Sciences in 1725, adherents of natural law doctrines began to propagate views which included a consideration of the law of nations. But not until the early nineteenth century did unofficial, academic writing on international law in Russia commence in earnest.

Fedor Pavlovich Veselovskii *(c. 1690 – after 1762). Diplomat.*

Life and career. Within three years of its original appearance, Shafirov's work was joined by another of the same nature written as a justification of the Tsar's foreign policy with respect to England. The principal author, Fedor Pavlovich Veselovskii, was the Russian Resident in London – one of three brothers who made significant contributions to Petrine diplomacy. Veselovskii's work and the dialogue it engendered from both the Russian and British sides were widely disseminated throughout Europe and Russia, provoking little-known contemporary English counter-responses.

The middle of three gifted brothers (Avraam (1685-1782), the elder, and Isaak (16?-1754), the younger) and son of a baptized Jew (Pavel Iakovlevich Veselovskii, 16?-1715) and Maria Nikolaevna Arshenevskaia, Fedor Veselovskii completed studies at the Moscow Glück Gymnasium and began service in the Ambassadorial Department, then being invited to serve as secretary to Prince Boris Ivanovich Kurakin (1676-1727) during his Embassy to Pope Clement XI and the Venetian Republic (1707).[102] Two years later he accompanied Kurakin to Hanover and later to London. When Kurakin was recalled from England in 1711, Veselovskii was assigned to Copenhagen, but within a year found himself as secretary to Kurakin's Embassy to Holland, thereafter to Brunswick-Wolfenbüttel (1714), returning to London in 1716. When the Russian Resident in London, Baron Bertram von Schack, was removed, the Tsar ordered Veselovskii to remain as *chargé d'affaires* and on 9 June 1717 conferred the rank of Resident on him.

Among the problems confronting Veselovskii during his tenure as Resident were the return of the city of Wismar to the Duke of Mecklenburg, recruiting specialists to accept positions in Russian service, and a mooted possible union of the Church of England with the Eastern Orthodox Church. Veselovskii took advantage of the sentiment created by the latter prospect to open the Russian Orthodox

[102] See V. Fursenko, «Веселовские» [The Veselovskiis], Новый энциклопедический словарь [New Encyclopedic Dictionary] (1904), X, p. 300; «Веселовские» [The Veselovskiis], Энциклопедический словарь [Encyclopedic Dictionary] (1892), XI, pp. 97-98; «Веселовский» [Veselovskii], Большая энциклопедия [Great Encyclopedia] (1896), IV, pp. 716-720; N. N. Bantysh-Kamenskii, Обзор внешних сношений России по 1800 год [Survey of Foreign Relations of Russia to 1800] (1894-1902); Butler, "F. P. Veselovskii and the Law of Nations", *Israel Law Review*, XX (1895), pp. 167-174.

Church in London attached to the Embassy. His major claim to reputation, however, was a Memorial bearing his name submitted to the Court of St. James protesting England's hostile attitudes towards Russia. Veselovskii's efforts to alter English policies were unavailing. In February 1720 the Tsar replaced him and ordered Veselovskii to Copenhagen as secretary of the Embassy there. This order Veselovskii refused; his older brother, Avraam, had gone into hiding from the Tsar somewhere in Western Europe (probably Prussia) on suspicion of being involved in the conspiracies of Tsarevich Aleksei Petrovich (1690-1718).

Veselovskii's fate thereafter becomes obscure. In 1725 he and his brother Avraam reportedly sought to become English subjects but did not succeed in the face of Russian protests.[103] With the accession of Peter II (1715-1730) to the Russian throne in 1727, Veselovskii petitioned to return to Russia; the Supreme Privy Council denied the petition. No earlier than 1733, in the reign of Empress Elizaveta Petrovna (1709-1762), was Veselovskii allowed to return. He entered military service, performed the occasional diplomatic mission, and in 1748 was appointed the master of ceremonies to the Imperial court. In St. Petersburg he became intimate with the Vorontsovs and Ivan Ivanovich Shuvalov (1727-1797); at the behest of Shuvalov, Veselovskii while abroad from 1756 to 1760 made contact with Voltaire (1694-1778) about preparing a history of Peter the Great. Veselovskii retired from military service in 1752 with the rank of Major-General. By 1760 he was Curator of Moscow University, and retired generally upon the succession to the throne of Catherine II. Sources vary as to whether he died in the 1760s or 1780s.

International legal views. Peter the Great had an early appreciation of the potential of the printed word in eighteenth-century Europe. In 1702 he expressly commissioned Baron Heinrich von Huyssen (1666-1739) to "propagandize the Tsar's ideas abroad through the press", to acquaint Europe with his regulations, to compose books and articles justifying his activities, to translate government edicts, to polemicize against hostile views, and as appropriate to hire foreign journalists and supply them with materials. Veselovskii's Memorial assuredly falls into this category of the use of foreign publication policies and opportunities.[104]

Veselovskii was no stranger to pamphleteering. In 1717 two of his representations to King George I (1660-1727) were issued for public consumption.[105] If sequence of content follows sequence of publication, first blood may have been drawn by a French-language version of Veselovskii's Memorial which included the text of King George's Reply as Elector of Hanover, dated 21 January 1720, but not his Reply as King of Great Britain, dated 11 February 1720.[106] Because

[103] The English Government rejected the Veselovskii petitions to become English subjects, but also refused the request of Empress Catherine I (1684-1727) of Russia to extradite them.

[104] Butler, note 102 above, pp. 169-170.

[105] See F. P. Veselovskii, *Memoire presenté à Sa Majesté Britannique par M. Weselowsky Ministre de Sa Majesté Czarienne* ([London], 1717), with texts in French and English; Veselovskii, *A Memorial Presented to His Britannick Majesty, by Monsieur Weselowsky* (London, J. Roberts, 1717). The former may be found in The British Library and the second in the United States Library of Congress.

[106] [Veselovskii], *Memoire presenté au roi de la Grande Bretagne de la part de S. M. Czarienne* ([London], 1720). The only copy traced is held by the Folger Shakespeare Library.

English sources might have been expected to know a further Reply was underway, conceivably the initial publication was Russian-backed, the more so because a French text was published. On this assumption, the likeliest candidate for the full English broadside was a substantial pamphlet printed at London by Sam. Buckley in Amen-Corner.[107] The last item mentioned in the title comprises fully 60% of the pamphlet (pp. 21-51) and is dated 24 February 1720. It consists of an informed and highly detailed defense of British diplomacy and refutation of Veselovsky's arguments, although it closed on a conciliatory note: "In plain terms, His *Britannick* Majesty has neither Interest nor Intention to break with the Czar; it is agreeable to *Great Britain* to cultivate his Czarish Majesty's Friendship, and the Commerce of *Russia*" (p. 51).[108]

The fact that all four items in the Buckley pamphlet are proximate in time and that no account is taken of Veselovskii's response to the Replies of King George I in his dual capacities as monarch and elector suggest the considered Russian response occurred later in 1720. The Russian edition of Veselovskii's Memorial was printed by order of the Tsar at Petersburg on 28 September 1720 in 1,200 copies.[109] Pekarskii referred to a German-language translation published in 1,184 copies.[110] Berkov and his colleagues were unable to locate a German-language version,[111] but in all likelihood the edition issued at Hamburg in 1720 was not what Pekarskii had in view.[112] It seems likely a German language version based on the September 1720 Russian edition was printed at Petersburg in 1721.[113] The relationship, if any, between the 1720 Hamburg edition and the 1721 Petersburg edition remains obscure. Huyssen claimed credit for the French translation, but it is ambiguous whether he referred to the French language version of the Reply by Mikhail Petrovich Bestuzhev-Riumen (1688-1760) or one of the other French texts circulating.[114]

The Russian language edition (204 pages) contained five separate pieces: (1) Veselovskii's Memorial of 14/24 December 1719 presented to King George I; (2)

[107] [Veselovskii], *A Memorial Presented to the King of Great-Britain, by M. Weselowski the Czar's Resident at London, on the 14th of December, 1719. His Majesty's Answer to that Memorial, as King of Great-Britain. His Majesty's Answer to it, as Elector. A Letter from a Gentleman at London to a Friend in Holland, upon the Memorial* (London, 1720).

[108] Quoted from the copy in the author's possession. Four copies are recorded in the United States.

[109] Berkov (ed.), note 13 above, p. 298.

[110] Pekarskii, note 71 above, II, p. 487.

[111] Berkov, note 13 above, p. 298.

[112] *Memorial des Heren Wesselofski, Residenten Sr. Czaarischen Majestät zu London. Nebst einer umstandlichen Relation desjenigen was seit Anno 1713 bis 1720 in denen Nordischen Negotiationen sich zugebragen ...* (Hamburg, 1720). The sole copy located is held by the Folger Shakespeare Library; the "umstandlichen Relation" is not present.

[113] Berkov, note 13 above, pp. 494-495.

[114] *Memoire de monsieur Bestuchef, resident de Sa Majesté Czarienne à Londres: presenté le 17 Octobre 1720 à la cour Britannique. Servant de réplique aux réponses données par la Chancelerie de la Grande-Bretagne, et par celle de Brunswic-Lunebourg, sur le précédent Memoire du resident Wesselofski* (n.p., 1720). A copy is in the Folger Shakespeare Library.

the Reply to Veselovskii by King George as Elector of Hanover, dated 21 January/1 February 1720; (3) the Reply to Veselovskii b y King George I as King of England, dated 11/20 February 1720, which in the book is misdated as 1719; (4) a detailed response by Veselovskii with extensive quotations from the 1715 Anglo-Russian treaty; and (5) an account of Admiral Norris' naval expedition to the Baltic, including copies of correspondence between Admiral Sir John Norris (c. 1670/71-1749) and Admiral Fedor Matveevich Apraksin (1661-1728).[115]

Bestuzhev-Riumin, in his capacity as Veselovskii's successor as Russian Resident in London, complained in a lengthy Memorial submitted to King George I on 17 October 1720 that the King's Ministers harbored fancies contrary to "the honor of his Tsarist Majesty" which subsequently "were printed in various languages …". The King, continued Bestuzhev-Riumin, was pleased to print the two replies in his name to Veselovskii, "both being printed by the court printer with other very offensive writings" and explanations "offensive and inappropriate" between Great Sovereigns.[116] The King's reaction to these representations was to request Bestuzhev-Riumin to leave England within eight days. The substance of Bestuzhev-Riumin's remarks was close to Veselovskii's Reply printed in the Russian edition of the Memorial.[117]

Veselovskii's Memorial and counter-response to the Replies made by King George I in his dual capacities raised several issues of international law:

(1) *Sanctity of treaties*. Veselovskii began by invoking the 1715 Treaty of Mutual Alliance entered into by Russia with George as Elector of Brunswick-Lunenburg and observing that "your Majesty entered last Summer with Sweden into Treaties entirely opposite to the Engagements your Majesty is under with his Czarish Majesty …". The Tsar was said to have honored his obligations under the Treaty of Alliance.

(2) *Diplomatic credentials*. Offers of the King to mediate between Russia and Sweden were rejected to Peter the Great: "They came from Ministers who had no manner of Credentials to his Czarish Majesty, and were drawn up in imperious Terms, which were not proper to be used to a great Monarch".

(3) *Mediation*. The role of a true mediator requires behavior reinforcing his impartiality: "Your Majesty … may judge … whether the Manner in which your Majesty's Ministers treated his Czarish Majesty, when they offered him your Mediation … was agreeable to the Friendship which has subsisted at all times between

115 See David Denis Aldridge, *Admiral Sir John Norris and the British Naval Expedition to the Baltic Sea 1715-1727* (Lund, 2009).

116 See Grabar, note 21 above, pp. 75-76.

117 An English version appeared as follows: *The Memorial of M. Bestuchef, His Czarish Majesties Resident in London, Presented Oct. 17, 1720, to the Court of Great Britain, being a reply to the two answers given by the British and Brunswick Ministers to a Former Memorial Presented by the Resident Weselowski* ([London], 1721). Copies are held by The British Library and the Library of Congress.

the Crowns of Great Russia and Great Britain, and whether a Mediation offered with Circumstances so little equitable, could be looked upon as impartial"?[118]

(4) *Behavior of Russian forces*. "The actions which His Tsarist Majesty's forces carried out in Sweden do not deserve the names" which were given to them in the reply received from the German chancellery. They "were performed for military reasons and no operations by the forces of His Tsarist Majesty were undertaken which the Swedish forces had not themselves undertaken with unheard of savagery on the territories of His Tsarist Majesty and within the Imperial lands themselves". The culpable actions of the Russian forces were accordingly justified as the application of reprisals.

(5) *Aid to rebels*. In reply to insinuations that Russia had become a refuge for the Jacobite opponents of King George I, Veselovskii responded that the Tsar "gave no protection to any rebels against the King of Great Britain"; there were "no rebels". It would be otherwise "if such rebels had been publicized, and protection … given them". Foreigners have free entry to the country, and the Government was not obliged to answer for any Englishman "whether he was inclined toward the pretender or not".

(6) *Confiscation of English ships*. Claims that Russia had seized English vessels unlawfully were dismissed out of hand by Veselovskii. Such seizure may have occurred, he conceded, with small coastal vessels belonging to the enemy and carrying enemy cargo while operating with English passes: "they dared to transport provisions and all other necessities to the enemy", but no one had brought suit "at the Admiralty". In effect Veselovskii argued that confiscation was justified for a violation of neutrality and redress should be sought through a claim in Admiralty.

(7) *Alliance with Spain*. To English arguments that their policies were justified in respect of Sweden by an incipient Russo-Spanish alliance, Veselovskii replied that "the distance of one State from another clearly showed that such an alliance was unfounded". With regard to proposals made on behalf of Spain and indeed on behalf of the pretender, Veselovskii observed: "His Tsarist Majesty, as an independent Sovereign, both according to the laws and customs of nations and the rules of courtesy, could not leave without a hearing". No one could prohibit Russia from maintaining friendly relations with Spain, especially if such relations "were not prejudicial to the King of Great Britain". Veselovskii thus invoked the general principles of international law and customs, as well as international comity.

Other matters were addressed: accusations with English seamen had been pressed into Russian service and were not allowed to return to their homeland; English merchants were arrested without cause; trade with Kazan and Astrakhan was restricted. Veselovskii vehemently objected to the British Government's aspiration to establish a peace between Russia and Sweden "which would confirm to Peter a significant share of his conquests". This was understood to mean that Russia would be forced to renounce all conquests made for the sake of peace: "and to suggest … that such contrary and extraordinary behaviour against all treaties and alliances

[118] For Veselovskii's reaction to the rumors of mediation at the time, see his Report to Tsar Peter of 8 January 1720, reproduced in Dixon, note 18 above, pp. 208-209.

was proper to be concealed by any pretexts … did his Royal Highness have reason for such behaviour against his Tsarist Majesty".

Grabar rated the Veselovskii pamphlets as a substantial Russian contribution to the literature on the law of nations, regarding them collectively as constituting together with Shafirov's *Discourse* a Petrine monument to international law. The 1721 Russian language edition of Veselovskii lacked the depth and coherence of argument found in Shafirov, but probably achieved greater public exposure at the time.

* * *

On 22 October 1721 Peter I declared himself to be the Emperor (no longer merely Tsar) of All the Russias in recognition of the new international presence of and role for Russia. The Russian Empire was now Eurasian in scope, a continental and a maritime power, pursuing a foreign policy ambitiously international. As Russian diplomacy endeavored to respond to the new requirements the Russian Emperor demanded, the organizational and legal infrastructure of Russian diplomacy was cardinally altered. The venerable Ambassadorial Department, which dated back to 1549, was transformed into an Ambassadorial Chancellery attached to the Tsar and then, as part of a sweeping institutional reform introduced from 1718 to 1720, into the College of Foreign Affairs. Russia began to establish permanent missions abroad and open consulates.

An energetic Russian foreign policy required statesmen well-versed by learning and experience in diplomacy and international law, including treaty negotiation and drafting, capable of conceptualizing and visualizing a worthy place for Russia in the international community. To be sure, initially a knowledge of international law was essential for practical ends: the more Russia became involved in international matters, the more she needed to know how to defend her interests in political, economic, military, and other engagements, how to respond to diplomatic incidents, how to bring an end to military conflicts, how, in short, to advance arguments based on international law. Grabar noted in respect to this period of Russian foreign policy: "The government needed international law to justify particular activities in the eyes of Western European society and of foreign governments; it found therein the necessary legal arguments for strengthening particular claims in the international arena".[119]

On his Grand Embassy to Europe and later visits, Peter the Great noticed the incomparably higher level of education and literacy. The majority of State offices in Russia were held by individuals whose primary education had been received by home-tutoring and then broadened through service in practice or learning from their elders. There was no system of general or secondary education and no univer-

[119] Grabar, note 21 above, p. 172; Grabar, Материалы к истории литературы международного права в России (1647–1917) [Materials on the History of the Literature of International Law in Russia (1647–1917), ed. W. E. Butler; Preface V. A. Tomsinov (2005), p. 178. The Chinese made a similar observation in the nineteenth century when giving attention to and translating works by Emer de Vattel (1714-1767) and Henry Wheaton (1785-1848) into the Chinese language. See Henrietta Harrison, *The Perils of Interpreting: The Extraordinary Lives of Two Translators between Qing China and the British Empire* (2021); I. C. Y. Hsu, *China's Entrance into the Family of Nations: The Diplomatic Phase, 1858-1880* (1960).

sities. The Russian State, unable to satisfy its own need for personnel capable of serving the more active foreign policy being pursued by its Emperor, recruited foreigners to this end, especially those with degrees from European universities. By Petrine times, European universities had integrated the law of nations into their instructional courses and established chairs of the law of nations and/or natural law.

In 1722 Peter the Great introduced the Table of Ranks to consolidate the hierarchy of titles/ranks and State offices. Having previously introduced compulsory education for the nobility and the clergy, the Table of Ranks linked appointment to and/or advancement in State service with the acquisition of a certain level of legal knowledge. It became immediately evident that the network of secular and religious schools, seminaries, and academies were neither sufficiently numerous nor of adequate quality to train individuals in the most advanced sciences. A University was required; Peter the Great took the bold step of establishing one – bold because Russia lacked a professoriate, students, personnel, a building, and other material essentials. How appropriate that the Shafirov house on the embankment in St. Petersburg should become the first home of the Academy University and the Academy of Sciences where students were exposed to the fundamentals of the law of nations.

INSTITUTIONAL FRAMEWORK

Chapter 2

St. Petersburg Academy University: The Place of International Law

The genesis and development of the science and the teaching of international law in Russia were long and complex, no less complicated than the emergence of Russian institutions dedicated to education and enlightenment.[1] In the Petrine period of Russian history, these two phenomena went hand in glove: the teaching and study of international law were closely tied to the founding of the Russian Academy of Sciences as a research institution and, attached to that body, the Academy University as an instructional institution. The existence of those two learned organizations in turn was indebted, as noted above, to a number of international and domestic considerations which contributed in their own way to the ultimate emergence of the law of nations being recognized as a proper subject in a university curriculum.

§2.1. *Teaching the Law of Nations at Petersburg Academy University*

This occurred under what might be gently characterized as "local conditions" – profound skepticism and suspicion among ruling elites about the desirability of introducing advanced education, political rivalries, passive and active resistance to the reformation processes underway, social and political instability, and the complete absence of trained Russian personnel to launch a University. Instruction in the law of nations should be viewed through the prism of creating the University as a whole and the approach to conceiving of the instructional process.

At the time, for example, there was no precise differentiation of the legal subject-matter into what have become the classical branches of law. The law of nations was perceived to be an element of natural law within the general course on jurisprudence. It followed that all the administrative, personnel, and instructional-methods considerations directly affected the teaching of the law of nations as a general matter. These problems arose once more three decades on when instruction commenced in the Moscow "classical" University founded in 1755.

The Russian Academy of Sciences was established on the basis of an Edict of Peter I confirmed on 22 January 1724 as a State institution.[2] The Senate of the Russian Empire pursuant to that Edict issued its own Edict "On Founding the Academy and Designation of Revenues for the Maintenance Thereof" on 28 January 1724,

1 The origins of higher education in Russia date back earlier than the Petrine era. On the seventeenth century, see Nikolaos A. Chrissidis, *An Academy at the Court of the Tsars: Greek Scholars and Jesuit Education in Early Modern Russia* (DeKalb, 2016). Canon law and natural law figured in the curriculum.

2 On the early history of the Academy of Sciences, see Alexander Vucinich, *Science in Russian Culture: A History to 1860* (Stanford, 1963), pp. 38-122.

which remained in force as a kind of Statute on the Academy and the subdivisions therein until the Charter of the Academy was officially enacted in 1747.[3]

The very concept of a University in Russia was a European import.[4] But Peter I had incorporated in his design for the Academy an innovation which had, it is believed, no precise analogue elsewhere in the world: a unified scientific-instructional-enlightenment complex as a triadic structure (Academy of Sciences – Academy University – Academy Gymnasium) within a single building.[5] This was the first use of the word "University" in Russian legislation.

The reasoning behind the triadic structure reflected the view that none of those three components could survive in isolation. The Russians were aware that this model was a departure from European practice and experience. The Gymnasium would function as a preparatory school and teach the "primary fundamental sciences", preparing students for enrollment in the University, which in turn would train individuals for ultimate possible appointment to the Academy of Sciences or for positions in State service. The Russian Academy of Sciences consequently became the first secular State scientific and educational institution to be fully financed by the State (special taxes were introduced to support the Academy, University, and Gymnasium in the cities of Narva, Dorpat, Pernov, and Arensburg).

Under this institutional model, the University from the outset and throughout the eighteenth century was an organic part of the Academy of Sciences, had no autonomy, was subordinate to the Emperor or Empress, was under the supervision of the Senate and the Government, was financed from the State treasury, and had no administration of its own: the President of the Academy and the Academy chancery were appointed directly by and accountable to the Emperor or Empress.

It was intended to organize instruction within the University by forming three specialized "classes"; the humanities, history, and law were relegated to the third class. The Edict of 28 January 1724 contemplated that three individuals would be assigned to the third class, among whom would be an Academician who would instruct the students in matters of politics, morals, and the law of nature. All students would be required in equal measure to study the same subjects. Law was subdivided into natural or divine law and public, or State, law. The law of nations was an integral part of both natural and public law and also addressed in lectures on politics and morals.

[3] The charters, or statutes, of the Academy of Sciences from that period are published in Уставы Академии наук СССР [Charters of the Academy of Sciences of the USSR] (M., 1974), pp. 31-38.

[4] A. Iu. Andreev, Российские университеты XVIII – первой половины XIX в. в контексте университетской истории Европы [Russian Universities of the XVIII – First Half of the Nineteenth Century in the Context of the University History of Europe] (M., 2009), p. 3.

[5] Vucinich noted that in 1716 Gottfried Wilhelm von Leibniz (1646-1716) submitted to Peter the Great via Vice-Chancellor P. P. Shafirov a number of recommendations for logical measures to be introduced in Russia to emulate Western educational standards; these included a "three-level hierarchy of educational and scientific institutions": public schools, universities, and academies. Vucinich, note 2 above, pp. 46-47. Leibniz had been in correspondence with Peter the Great since at least 1697. Also see N. P. Kopaneva (ed.), Г. В. Лейбниц и Россия [G. W. Leibniz and Russia] (Spb., 1998).

By the time that the Academy University officially opened in 1725, Peter the Great had died and Catherine I had succeeded to the throne. When in 1726 the University actually began to function, there were neither professors nor students. Foreign professors and even students were recruited from Russia and abroad, principally Prussia. The personnel establishment of the Academy initially included eleven professors and several junior scientific assistants. Officially, a student was either an assistant to a professor and studying personally with him but receiving an academic stipend, or was an auditor who was permitted to attend lectures. This approach was altered under the 1747 Charter of the Academy, which provided that a student is only a pupil of the University. Under the contract concluded with the Academy, a professorial academician was to bring with him several students, usually at the magister level, from German universities. Foreign students, it must be said, were not eager to travel to a newly-created University in remote and frozen Russia. The first year of formal operation University – 1726 – saw seventeen professors and eight students in place. Nonetheless, of the eight students who came from Germany and completed the University, half became full academicians of the Petersburg Academy of Sciences.

Primary and secondary education were at embryonic stages in Russia of the 1720s and not capable of delivering qualified applicants to the University. Instruction in the early years was in the Latin language – the foreign professors did not know Russian; there were no Russian professors; Russian students did not know Latin. For Russian students the path forward was to begin at the Academy Gymnasium. Some students were recruited from among seminarians studying in monastery schools, but the overall percentage of Russian students in the student body did not exceed 20%.[6] Moreover, University study was not attractive to children of the nobility – a military career was more prestigious.

Instruction in the Academy University commenced in January 1726. A distinctive feature of the University emerged at once. The foreign scholars, in their capacity as Academicians of the Academy of Sciences, had to engage in scientific research. The conditions for this were considered to be rather favorable. Academician Georg Bernhard Bilfinger (1693-1750) wrote to Professor G. Z. Bayer in Königsberg: "no Academy or university has such privileges and such provision" in Europe.[7] In his capacity as a professor, each Academician was also obliged to deliver lectures to students of the University and the Gymnasium and to auditors four times a week. Because of the shortage of students and to demonstrate their own inclination for work, the professors also attended one another's lectures.[8]

Between the years 1726 and 1733 only 38 students, of whom seven were Russians, studied at the University, so there was no reason to divide the students by specialization. Instruction was organized on a general group and individual basis.

[6] See L. A. Verbitskaia (ed.), Санкт-Петербургский университет. Летопись 1724–1999 [St. Petersburg University. Chronicle 1724–1999] (Spb., 1999), p. 14.

[7] G. I. Smagina, «Немецкие ученые и Российская Академия наук» [German Scholars in the Russian Academy of Sciences], in Немцы в России: Историко-документальное издание [Germans in Russia: Historical Documentary Publication] (Spb., 2004).

[8] Iu. Kh. Kopelevich, Основание Петербургской Академии наук [Founding of the Petersburg Academy of Sciences] (L., 1977), p. 97.

Two students were attached to each law professor. They attended all lectures together, studied recommended documents and doctrinal writings on their own, most of which were in Latin and some in German, and completed individual assignments. For the Russian students, matters were more complicated because neither the professor nor the student understood one another's language.

Instruction was performed by the professors (*ordinarius* and *extraordinarius*) and junior scientific assistants.[9] Lessons were not always held regularly; not all professors had precise syllabi; the lectures followed the scholarly interests of the lecturer and did not systematically set out any body of knowledge. Success in studies was recognized and rewarded; for outstanding examination results students were awarded books; those who graduated with distinction from the Academy Gymnasium and moved on to the Academy University were awarded a sword.

The early German professors were adherents of the natural-law approach to the law of nations and instructed their students accordingly by setting out the views of leading Western European jurists with respect to the law of nations. They will have emphasized that all States are in a free natural state and therefore recognized no power as superior to them. The source of any and all law is the natural laws of social existence based on the will of God and the reasonable nature of man. Human laws are created on the basis of natural law. International relations between rulers and the States which they head are regulated by norms of natural law; that is, reason, such that the law of nations is based upon, generated by, and constitutes an integral part of natural law. The law of nations is a product of reason and based on the teachings of God, the nature of man, and the laws of human reason, but not on power or force. Therefore norms by which natural persons in a state of nature are guided also should apply to relations between States, that is, pre-State relations. Accordingly, States and their rulers should be guided in their international relations by provisions arising from the natural law of nations. Reason dictated to rulers and their States that their international relations should be structured not on enmity and war, but on peace, during which no one causes harm to the other.

To be sure, Pufendorf and his supporters went to another extreme, not recognizing treaties and customs as sources of the law of nations – these, they said, were constantly changing over time, place, and operation. The principal works relied upon by the Academy University professors were those by Hugo Grotius on the law of war and peace and Pufendorf on the duties of man and citizen. Consequently, the teaching and study of the law of nations was first organized in Russia during the 1720s at the St. Petersburg Academy University within the framework of the general course on "jurisprudence", which at that time was not differentiated into individual branches of law. The law of nations in those times was a significant component of natural and public law as taught in the Academy University.

The teaching of the law of nations was reinforced – some would say made possible – by personal or private libraries formed by Petrine officials and later donated to or confiscated by the State. One such library belonged to Shafirov, one of several that formed the basis of the library of the Imperial Academy of Sciences. The collection came to public attention in 1723 when, in consequence of Shafirov's conviction

[9] Ibid.

for misappropriation of funds, his property was confiscated.[10] His splendid home in Petersburg was placed at the disposition of the Academy of Sciences. "Splendid" is no exaggeration in this case. An inventory of the house mentions that the stucco ornamentation was executed by the renowned Carlo Bartolomeo Rastrelli (1675-1744) and his son, Francesco Bartolomeo Rastrelli (1700-1771), who designed the nearby Winter Palace in St. Petersburg. In the early years the Academy library, including Shafirov's own books, was apparently housed there, a source of complaint because the building was on the "Petrograd side" of the Neva River and some distance away from the Academy.[11]

The historic first public meeting of that august institution was convened on the premises on 27 December 1725.[12] The books "in foreign tongues" and copies of the *Discourse* found in the house, however, posed some difficulty. The Chancery of the High Court invited the Petersburg Library to select what books it wished and to return the remainder, since the "Russian appraisers and foreigners do not know how to value them".[13] Shafirov's was the last collection to be acquired by the Petersburg Library during Peter's reign.[14]

[10] A manuscript text of the Imperial Edict confiscating Shafirov's property is preserved in LOAAN, fond 3, Opis' 1, no. 701, folio 1.

[11] See N. V. Kaliazina, «Лепной декор в жилом интерьере Петербурга первой четверти XVIII в» [Stucco Decor in the Housing Interior of Petersburg of the First Quarter of the XVIII Century], in T. V. Alekseevna, Русское искусство первой четверти XVIII века; материалы и исследования (1974), pp. 109-118. Also see S. P. Luppov, Книга в России в послепетровское время [The Book in Russia in the Post-Petrine Period] (1976), p. 328.

[12] See K. V. Ostrovitanov (ed.), История академии наук СССР: 1724 1803 [History of the USSR Academy of Sciences: 1724-1803] (1958), I, p. 58. Tereshchenko is incorrect when he mentions Shafirov as one who took part in the Academy's opening session. See A. V. Tereshchenko, Опыть обозрения жизни сановников, управлявших иностранными делами в России [Attempt at a Survey of the Life of Officials Managing Foreign Affairs in Russia] (1837), III, p. 46.

[13] The manuscript of the Edict ordering the removal and selection of books from Shafirov's library is found in LOAAN, fond 3, opis 1, no. 2330, folio 27. The summary report to the Chancery of those who prepared the inventory of Shafirov's holdings lists 531 volumes. Ibid., folios 28 and 29. Also see J. Bakmeister, Опыть о Библиотеке и Кабинете редкостей и истории натуральной Санктпетербургской Императорской Академии наук [Experience Concerning the Library and Cabinet of Rarities and Natural History of St. Petersburg Imperial Academy of Sciences] (1779), p. 34; P. A. Efremov, Материалы для истории русской литературы [Materials for the History of Russian Literature] (1867), p. 119; Evgenii Bolkhovitinov, Словарь русских светских писателей, соотечественников и чужестранцев писавших в России [Dictionary of Russian Secular Writers, Compatriots, and Foreigners Who Wrote in Russia] (1845), II, p. 248.

[14] The original manuscript catalogue or inventory of Shafirov's collection is at LOAAN, fond 158, opis 1, no. 215. Consisting of eight folios, it has never been published. The books are grouped by size (folio, quarto, octavo, duodecimo), there being no particular order within each category. A few entries are indecipherable, and nothing approaching a complete bibliographical description is given in any case. Usually there is merely an abbreviated title, sometimes an author, date of publication, and perhaps the place of publication. Some entries appear twice. The first published catalogue of the Imperial Academy of Sciences listed some 711 items as "libros iuridicos", but most of the works on international law were placed in the section on history. The catalogue gave no provenances for the items listed. See *Bibliothecae Imperialis Petropolitanae* (1742), III(2), pp. 161.

Assessments of the quality of Shafirov's library vary. Pekarskii felt the selection of books had been done "unsystematically and haphazardly".[15] Luppov, who undertook an extensive comparison of private libraries of the Petrine period, pointed out that Shafirov's was not a working library of carefully selected books but that of a man who read largely for pleasure and relaxation.[16] However, Shafirov was, in European terms, a gentleman-diplomat. His library was both a working collection and a source of diversion. The large number of lexicons and grammars is a reflection of his formidable linguistic skills and his career as a translator. There is no evidence that he was a particularly religious person, so the large number of European bibles in various editions and a Koran may have been a collecting interest. History, philosophy, and travels were well represented. Both Pekarskii and Luppov tended to relegate works such as Grotius and Pufendorf to the category of "politics" rather than law, thereby understating what in modern terms at least would be regarded as legal holdings. Among the works on international law in Shafirov's library were Grotius (1684 ed.), Pufendorf (edition not specified), Shafirov's own *Discourse* in German translation (two copies), Callières (1716), and *La paix d'Utrecht* (1713). Also present were copies of Justinian's *Institutes* (1703 ed.) and a number of works on German public law. Belles lettres, particularly French and Italian, were strongly represented, and there was an assortment of titles on mathematics, the military arts, numismatics, and curiosa. It was, in short, an eclectic assemblage, that of a widely read diplomatic practitioner rather than a scholar. Shafirov obviously did most of his book purchasing during his trips to Europe with Peter, especially the journey to France and Holland in 1717. Of the 484 entries in the inventory of Shafirov's library, only 27 were published after 1717. Only one entry is of a book in the Russian language; one wonders whether the High Court officers confiscated Shafirov's books in the Russian language without offering them to the Petersburg Library or whether Shafirov collected European titles exclusively. If the latter is true, Shafirov's collection was indeed a singular one.

After his rehabilitation, Shafirov presumably formed a second library, whose fate is unknown. In 1735 he was presented a number of religious books.[17]

§2.2. *Early Academy University Professors of Law*

We turn to the individual Academicians and professors responsible for teaching the law of nations at the Academy University.

[15] P. P. Pekarskii, Наука и литература в России при Петре Великом [Science and Literature in Russia Under Peter the Great] (1862), I, p. 48.

[16] See S. P. Luppov, Книга в России в XVII первой четверти XVIII века (из истории культуры) [The Book in Russia in the Seventeenth and First Quarter of the Eighteenth Centuries (From the History of Culture] (1972). 581 p. (Dissertation for the Degree of Doctor of Historical Sciences). Dr. Luppov published his findings on seventeenth century private libraries in a monograph entitled: Книга в России в XVII веке [The Book in Russia in the Seventeenth Century] (Leningrad, 1970). Also see: Luppov, Книга в России в первой четверти XVIII века [The Book in Russia in the First Quarter of the Eighteenth Century] (1973), pp. 227-229.

[17] Luppov, Книга в России в послепетровское время [The Book in Russia in the Post-Petrine Period] (1976), p. 87.

Christian Friedrich Gross *(1 July 1680, b. Lichtenstern, Württemberg – 2 January 1742, d. St. Petersburg). Philosopher.*

Life and career. Among the first German scholars invited to the Petersburg Academy of Sciences, Gross became Academician and professor *extraordinarius* of moral philosophy. He therefore was the first individual to formally instruct students on the law of nations at the Academy University as part of the course on jurisprudence.

A graduate of Tübingen University in Germany, Gross arrived in Russia in the summer of 1725 and from 1 July of that year was appointed to the post of junior scientific associate at the Chair of Moral Philosophy and on 24 November 1725 elevated to professor *extraordinarius* in the same Chair. Gross taught natural law for two years at the University, addressing the law of nations by way of commentary and critique of Pufendorf on the duties of man and citizen. Among the few Russian students who attended Gross's lectures was Antiokh Dmitrievich Kantemir (1708-1744), the future Russian poet and envoy of Russia to England and France.

Gross left no works of scholarship. In 1726 and 1727 he submitted to the Academy of Sciences several works on moral philosophy, but they were never published. The manuscripts repose in the Library of the Russian Academy of Sciences.

The Academy did, however, entrust other assignments to Gross. In 1727 he was despatched to Revel (now Tallinn) where he supervised the publication of addresses delivered at the first session of the Petersburg Academy of Sciences, for the printing facilities in Petersburg were not yet functioning. As from 2 January 1728 the Academy began to publish a newspaper in the German language – the first and sole newspaper in Russia – the *St. Petersburg Gazette* (Санкт-Петербургские ведомости). Gross was the initial compiler during the first six months, obtaining official materials from various institutions and foreign newspapers received in Russia. The materials published included information of an international legal character. Gross also occupied himself by compiling concise chronological tables of Russian history based on the Russian chronicles.

In 1731 Gross accepted an appointment as secretary of the Embassy of the Duchy of Braunschweig-Wolfenbüttel-Blankenburg in St. Petersburg, resigning from the Russian Academy of Sciences and ceasing to lecture at the Academy University. On 9 December 1731 the Academy conferred on Gross the title of Honorary Foreign Member of the Academy of Sciences.

Gross's life ended tragically. Shortly after the palace coup d'état in 1741 (overthrow of the two-year old Ioann Antonovich VI (1740-1764) and elevation to the throne of the daughter of Peter the Great, Elizabeth Petrovna (1709-1762) as Empress), Gross was subjected to criminal prosecution in the well-known case of the comrade-in-arms of Peter the Great, Count A. I. Osterman (1686-1747). Gross had helped Osterman draw up papers relating to intra-palace intrigues. Held under house arrest, Gross denied any accusations of espionage. Although he was perhaps in no real danger, he committed suicide on 2 January 1742 before the criminal proceedings had come to an end.

Johann-Simon Beckenstein *(22 February 1684, b. Danzig, Poland – 1 July 1742, d. possibly Königsberg. Prussia). Jurist.*

Life and career. Beckenstein was the first legal scholar among the invited German professors who taught the science of law at the Academy University for an extended period. Having graduated *doctor utriusque juris* from Königsberg University, he found employment as a doctor *legens*, that is, a part-time lecturer without a tenured position. He was invited to the Russian Academy of Sciences in 1725 to the post of professor of jurisprudence but took up his position only on 24 June 1726; he had a broad background in the humanities and foreign languages. He was admitted to the Academy as an Academician and to the University as a professor who held the Chair of Jurisprudence.[18] In that capacity he became a principal progenitor of legal education in Russia.[19]

Beckenstein taught law, including the law of nations, in conformity with the syllabi which operated in the universities of Europe. According to the catalog of lectures of 14 January 1726, Beckenstein was to offer lectures on natural law, the common laws of the German Empire, and Justinian's Institutes. When teaching jurisprudence in general and the law of nations in particular, Beckenstein set out all the rules of natural law and politics. In his Report on his instructional activity of 1 December 1732, Beckenstein said that he had not taught any Russian students but had several, most of whose names he could not recall, of foreign origin who were resident in St. Petersburg. He confirmed that he offered instruction on the law of nations and comparative law (Lithuanian and Estland, because he knew no Russian law).[20]

[18] According to the contract with the Academy, Beckenstein was hired for five years at a salary of 800 rubles per annum and a four-room apartment free of charge with heat and light; that is, firewood and candles. See P. P. Pekarskii, История Императорской Академии наук в Петербурге [History of the Imperial Academy of Sciences in Petersburg] (Spb., 1870), I, p. 197.

[19] For details on Beckenstein, see Pekarskii, ibid., I, pp. 197-201; V. E. Grabar, *The History of International Law in Russia 1647-1917: A Bio-Bibliographical Study*, transl. W. E. Butler (1990), pp. 104, 108, 173; V. A. Tomsinov, Российские правоведы XVIII–XX веков: Очерки жизни и творчества [Russian Jurists XVIII–XX Centuries: Surveys of Life and Creativity] (M., 2015), I, pp. 90–98; Русский биографический словарь [Russian Biographical Dictionary] (Spb., 1900), II, pp. 664–666.

[20] For the text of the Report, see I. V. Tunkina (ed.), Петр Великий и основание Петербургской академии наук: Документы и материалы [Peter the Great and the Founding of the Petersburg Academy of Sciences: Documents and Materials] (Spb., 2022), I, pp. 114-115.

In addition, Beckenstein lectured in the Latin language to students of the University on ceremonial law, clerical correspondence, and heraldry; he is widely regarded as the founder of the discipline of heraldry in Russia.[21] The present Arms of St. Petersburg University are based on a sketch which he produced.[22] He in his capacity as Academician wrote a gloss on the 1649 Ulozhenie and a history of public law, which were never published.[23]

Beckenstein worked at the Academy of Sciences and the Academy University for ten years, performing various assignments in those institutions and elsewhere. But in 1735 his contract lapsed and, at his request, was not renewed. Deeply dissatisfied with the organization of work within the University, he was depressed by the reality that, unlike the universities of Western Europe where the law faculties occupied primacy of place and the law professors always had seniority among other professors in the scholarly community, at Petersburg University the status of the law faculty was not so sharply defined, and the law professors had a demeaning low status: the Table on Ranks did not even extend to them.

Beckenstein left Petersburg at the end of 1735, returned to Königsberg, but did not lose his links with the Academy. Three years later, the Academy, acknowledging the contribution that Beckenstein had made to the development of the Russian enlightenment, elected him as "Honorary Foreign Member" with annual remuneration of 100 rubles.

Beckenstein's successor was Strube de Piermont.

Friedrich Heinrich Strube de Piermont *(1 January 1704, b. Hallerspring, Hannover, Germany – 1 August 1790, d. possibly St. Petersburg, Russia). Diplomat, Academician, Chief Learned Secretary of the Petersburg Academy of Sciences, and Professor of Jurisprudence and Politics of the Academy University.*

Life and career. Strube de Piermont addressed the law of nations in his works and lectured on natural law. He devoted much of his time to writing a history of Russian law and became one of the progenitors of the so-called "Norman theory" of the origin of Russian statehood.[24]

21 To introduce Emperor Peter II to heraldry, Beckenstein published *Kurze Einleitung zur Wappen-Kunst* (Spb., 1731).

22 See M. Medvedev, «Отцы русской геральдики» [The Fathers of Russian Heraldry], Родина [Motherland], no. 3 (2002) (available online).

23 V. M. Syrykh, Правовая наука и юридическая идеология России: энциклопедический словарь биографий [Legal Science and Legal Ideology of Russia: Encyclopedic Dictionary of Biographies] (M., 2009), I, p. 56.

24 On Strube de Piermont, see W. E. Butler, "F. G. Strube de Piermont and the Origins of Russian Legal History", in Butler, *Russia and the Law of Nations in Historical Perspective: Collected Essays* (2009), pp. 129-144; Русский биографический словарь [Russian Biographical Dictionary] (Spb., 1900), XXV, pp. 547-548; Tomsinov, note 19 above, I, pp. 99–113; Syrykh, note 23 above, I, pp 821-822.

A graduate of the University of Halle, he wrote early and extensively on natural law. From 1730 he served as the secretary of German missions in Vienna, London, and Warsaw and for many years was the secretary of the Duke of Courland, Ernst Johann von Biron (1690–1772), whom he accompanied to Russia. On 4 September 1738 Strube de Piermont was elected to membership of the Russian Academy of Sciences and from that day until 23 February 1741, and again from 1 July 1746 to 7 July 1757, held the Chair of Jurisprudence at the Academy University. He lectured and gave tutorials on natural law and the law of nations, the system of major European States, ceremonial law, and clerical correspondence.

In 1740 Strube de Piermont submitted to the Academy and the University his first scholarly work written in Russia on the origin and foundations of natural law; written in the French language, the work dealt in part with the nature and foundations of international legal relations.[25]

As it happened, Strube de Piermont was in the Russian Academy of Sciences at a moment when long-overdue reforms had finally been implemented as reflected in the first Charter of the Academy introduced in 1747. Strube de Piermont had been appointed the Chief Learned Secretary of the Academy on 1 July 1746 and held that position until 1 March 1749. Under the 1747 Charter, the curriculum of the Academy University was reorganized into cycles. The cycle devoted to the humanities included the study of natural law and moral philosophy as an autonomous subject. Strube de Piermont was assigned to teach this material. For four hours a week he lectured on the recent history of all the States of Europe and their alliances; the law of nations was part of this and taught according to Pufendorf.

Following the example of German universities, Strube de Piermont prepared and published in the Russian and Latin languages a Syllabus to introduce students to his course of lectures (1748). The Syllabus mentions that students would study the first principles of natural law and the law of nations, as these should be the source of all civil rights and laws, because without this to draw up, understand, and properly use such would be impossible.[26]

In addition, Strube de Piermont publicly announced that he would operate in his own home during his free time a diplomatic school for young men of the nobility who wished to study how foreign courts conducted their public affairs. In 1748 he published a detailed Syllabus for this enterprise that enumerated the subject-matter that he intended to offer, including:

(1) the condition of the leading European States and republic, their internal situation, and their political relations;

(2) the office and privileges of those who are sent to foreign lands for public affairs, with the so-called ceremonial rights in so far as they relate to such matters;

[25] Strube de Piermont, *Recherche nouvelle de l'origine et des fondemens du droit de la nature* (Spb., 1740).

[26] Pekarskii, «Редактор, сотрудники и цензура в русском журнале 1755–1764 годов» [Editor, Personnel, and Censor in the Russian Journal 1755–1764], Записки Академии наук [Notes of the Academy of Sciences] (Spb., 1868), XII, Annex, p. 32.

(3) the composition of letters and speeches for persons appointed to serve in such matters in the French language, which is now most widely used.[27]

Of the numerous works by Strube de Piermont, one was directly concerned with the law of nations – the concept, content, and practice of military necessity in the course of inter-State conflicts.[28] In his view, only military necessity based on concern for self-preservation justifies everything that leads to this end and eliminates everything that obstructs its attainment. Norms of municipal law and the law of nations retain their force in so far as they do not conflict with a higher authority, which necessity is. But we must be certain that we find ourselves in extreme necessity before we are authorized to resort to extreme means. Therefore, war in and of itself is an outcome of necessity, and military necessity "represents the very essence of military laws"; it "extends to all lawful and permitted means which may facilitate the gaining of ends and excludes everything that creates obstacles and difficulties". Strube de Piermont said that States have the right in the event of extreme necessity to, in the interests of self-preservation, resort to military force, but he cautions rulers against the abuse of this right. Imagined and unjust references to military necessity are in this event a "blatant abuse".[29]

Issues of the law of nations were also touched upon in his introduction to natural jurisprudence;[30] a number of his works remain in manuscript.

It should be noted that Strube de Piermont was the first in Russia to undertake a history of Russian law[31] and later a study of the origin of the Russians.[32] In the view of some historians, this last work was the most valuable of all that he wrote.

Strube de Piermont taught in the Academy University with interruptions (from 1741 to 1746 Strube de Piermont was the secretary of the embassies of Russia in Copenhagen and then Berlin) until his dismissal in 1757.[33] In 1750 he became a Russian subject. His refusal to publish a newspaper in the French language occasioned his dismissal in 1757, whereupon he entered service in the College of Foreign Affairs of Russia with the title of counsellor. He retired ca. 1779 and is

[27] Grabar, note 19 above (1990), p. 107; Tomsinov, note 19 above, pp. 103-104.

[28] Strube de Piermont, *Dissertation sur la raison de guerre et le droit de bienséance* (1734).

[29] See Grabar, note 19 above (1990), pp. 110-112.

[30] Strube de Piermont, *Introduction á la jurisprudence naturelle* (Spb., 1767; 2d ed.; 1774).

[31] His labors in this direction are considered in detail by Butler, note 24 above. In 1754 he was appointed to a Commission assigned to prepare a new Ulozhenie to replace that of 1649.

[32] Strube de Piermont, Разсуждение о древних россиянах [Discourse on the Medieval Russians] (M., 1791). Some Russian historians consider this posthumously published work to be the best of those that he produced in Russia.

[33] Syrykh, note 23 above, I, pp. 821-822. While serving in Berlin, Strube de Piermont completed (the dedication is dated 1 August 1743) a new edition of his treatise on natural and primitive laws dedicated to the Empress Elizabeth Petrovna and identifying him as being of the Imperial Academy of Sciences in St. Petersburg. See Strube de Piermont, *Ebauche des loix naturelles et du droit primitif* (Amsterdam, 1744), pp. [i-vi].

believed to have passed away in 1790 at his estate near Petersburg granted to him by Count N. I. Panin (1718–1783).

Georg Friedrich Fedorowicz (Fedorovich) *(1 July 1730, b. Freistadt (Brandenburg) – 1 August 1790, place unknown). Jurist.*

Life and career. The Rector of the Academy University, Mikhail V. Lomonosov (1711-1765), suggested in 1760 with the opening of a separate Law Faculty that the teaching of legal disciplines be reserved only for legal scholars who were specializing in or who had special and extensive knowledge of jurisprudence. One such jurist was Georg Friedrich Fedorowicz, Russian jurist of German origin, full member of the Academy of Sciences, professor of general laws of the Academy University, and well-known in his day.[34]

Fedorowicz was born and educated in Germany, where he read law. Removing to Russia, he served first in the Medical Chancellery, and then as ober-auditor in the Russian Admiralty, where he polished his command of the Russian language and jurisprudence. After the dismissal of Strube de Piermont, Fedorowicz was appointed to his post as the Professor of General Laws, but not after some controversy. When his candidacy was considered by the Assembly of the Academy, the secretary of the Academy, Gerhard Friedrich Müller, opposed the appointment. When two years later a student, A. Ia. Polenov, complained about Fedorowicz's lectures, the Assembly of the Academy considered the appeal when both Fedorowicz and Lomonosov were unable to be present. Müller included the appeal and the discussion thereof in the protocol of the Assembly. When Fedorowicz later requested explanations of this from Müller, the latter, according to Lomonosov, "not only swore at Fedorowicz, but left the conference". Lomonosov was forced to turn to the State Chancellor, M. I. Vorontsov (1714–1767), with an insistent request to intervene on behalf of the offended Fedorowicz.

Fedorowicz lectured on the foundations of jurisprudence from 1761, including the principles of the law of nations. He continued to do so until the Academy University began to curtail its instructional activities. In 1766 he delivered public lectures devoted to the politics of European States and international law. He retired on 1 March 1770 at his own request and left no scholarly legal works.

Gerhard Friedrich Müller *(29 October 1705, b. Herford (Westphalia) – 11 October 1783, d. Moscow). Scholar, public figure, historian, ethnographer, and first Rector of St. Petersburg Academy University.*[35]

[34] Syrykh, note 23 above, I, p. 743.

[35] On Müller, see Pekarskii, note 15 above, I, pp. 308-430; Энциклопедический словарь Брокгауза и Эфрона [Encyclopedic Dictionary of Brokhaus and Efron] (Spb., 1890–1907), LXXXII and LXXXIV; Grabar, note 19 above (1990), pp. 108-109, 113-116, 184-186; J. L. Black, *G. F. Müller and the Imperial Russian Academy of Sciences 1725–1783: First Steps in the Development of the Historical Sciences in Russia* (1986); M. B. Alpatov, Русская историческая мысль и Западная Европа (XVIII-первая половина XIX в.) [Russian Historical Thought and Western Europe (XVIII-First Half of XIX Centuries] (1985), pp. 19-27; P. Hoffmann, *Gerhard Friedrich Müller (1705–1783): Historiker, Geograph, Archivar im Dienste Russlands* (2005); D. Dahlmann and G. Smagina

Life and career. Müller arrived in Russia at the age of twenty, two decades later became a Russian subject, and in all pursued a remarkable career for 58 years in that country. A graduate of the University of Leipzig, his initial appointment occurred on 5 November 1725 as a junior scientific associate at the Academy of Sciences in the field of history, elevated in 1726 to the position of lecturer on the Latin language, history, and geography in the Academy Gymnasium. From July 1730 he became a professor of history at the University and the permanent conference secretary of the Academy. His reputation as an ethnographer was made on the basis of a ten-year expedition (1733–1743) to Kamchatka, during which he covered more than 30,000 kilometers and collected documents and other materials on the history of Siberia and the Russian Far East. To this day this rich body of material has not been fully analyzed. In 1747 he was appointed to the position of official Russian Historiographer.

For our purposes, however, Müller is of interest for his appointment, also in 1747, as the first Rector of St. Petersburg Academy University, a post he held from 1747 to 1749.[36] From 1765 he became the head of the Archive of the College of Foreign Affairs in Moscow, having been appointed by Empress Catherine II (1729–1796) to compile a collection of Russian treaties following the example of Jean Dumont, baron of Carlscroon (1667–1727).[37]

Müller made significant contributions to international law to students of the Academy University and the Russian public generally. In the Санкт-Петербургские ведомости [Saint-Petersburg Gazette] he, in his capacity as the first chief editor from 1728, initiated the publication of a separate annex to the newspaper devoted to monthly historical, genealogical, and geographical notes (from 1728 to 1742) – with a view to reporting and commenting on international and domestic events and facts. These included episodes in international politics, treaties, diplomacy, and other items of international legal interest that have not yet been fully studied with a view to determining their role in the formation of a Russian international legal consciousness.

(ed.), Г. Ф. Миллер и русская культура [G. F. Müller and Russian Culture] (2007).

36 See Санкт-Петербургский университет, 275 лет. Летопись, 1724-1999 [St. Petersburg University. Chronicle 1724-1999] (Spb., 1999), pp. 22–23.

37 On the context and implications of this appointment, see Butler, "Treaty Collections in Eighteenth Century Russia: Encounters with European Experience", in Butler, note 24 above, pp. 259-267.

In 1755 Lomonosov and Müller initiated the creation of a "scientific-literary" publication under Müller's editorship of a monthly journal containing works to the benefit and enjoyment of civil servants [Ежемесячные сочинения, к пользе и увеселению служащие]. There Müller commented on international affairs and explained particular international reports, events, and facts published in the journal. In addition to commentary, the journal contained scholarly articles on such, to the international lawyer, relevant topics as the sovereignty and independence of civilized States, the means and procedure for the settlement of international disputes between States, the right of civilized powers to newly-discovered lands, the right to defeated warships, legal claims of some rulers to the territory of other sovereigns, embassies and consulates, and other legal aspects of the diplomatic relations of States.[38] One may reasonably assume that students in the Academy Gymnasium were, at least through their lectures, acquainted with this material.

With the death of Lomonosov, its first Rector, in 1765, the Academy University and Gymnasium for all practical purposes ceased to exist *de facto*; *de jure* the Academy University and the Academy Gymnasium were merged into a "School" (училище) in the 1770s that continued to offer instruction at the Gymnasium level until 1805 with a much reduced student body.

§2.3. *International Law and University Administrative Reform*

Prolonged delays in clarifying the uncertain legal status and structure of the Academy and the University, the status of professors and students, and their rights, privileges, and professional career prospects could not fail to affect the development and teaching of international law. The general state of affairs in the post-Petrine and pre-Catherinian years have been described as an "era of palace coups", from 1725 to 1762. For four years (1728-1732) the Imperial court removed to Moscow, followed by the principal State institutions, military regiments, many families of the nobility, among others – one result of which was to deprive the Gymnasium and the University of potential students. Chronic financial issues arose.

Embedding an institution of higher education within the Russian institutional and social framework was challenging. Not until the 1740s did Russian elites come to be persuaded that the Academy and University were absolutely essential to the development and prosperity of Russia. In 1746, following a five-year vacuum of leadership, Count Kirill Grigorevich Razumovskii (1728-1801) became at the age of 18 the President of the entire Academy complex. At his initiative the Empress Elizaveta Petrovna (1709-1762), on 24 June 1747, confirmed a Charter of the

[38] Müller is an excellent example of an individual not trained in law but who as a diplomatic historian and, by way of compiling treaty collections, a historian of international law made valuable contributions to international law. See, for example, G. F. Müller, «О первых российских путешествиях и посольствах в Китай» [On the First Russian Journeys of Embassies to China], Ежемесячныя сочинения [Monthly Works] (July 1755), pp. 15–57; Müller, «Прибавление к посольскому наказу, данному отправленным в 1618 г. в Персию послам Михаилу Петровичу Борятинскому, Ивану Ивановичу Чичерину и дьяку Михайлу Тюхину» [Addendum to the Ambassadorial Nakaz Given to Envoys Mikhail Petrovich Boriatinskii, Ivan Ivanovich Chicherin, and Diak Mikhail Tiukhin Sent in 1618 to Persia], Опыт трудов Вольнаго российского собрания [Experience of Works of the Free Russian Assembly] (1780), V, pp. 215–225.

Academy in the form of the "Reglament of the Imperial Academy of Sciences and Arts in St. Petersburg".[39] The Reglament consolidated the division of the Academy of Sciences into the Academy proper and the University, the latter being stipulated to be "… founded on the example of other European universities" and described as "another part of the Academy". The Reglament included for the University a list of educational disciplines (points 36-49). For the first time, the Reglament drew a sharp distinction between academicians and professors (Article 1).

The humanities were among the spheres of scientific knowledge chosen, and they included "natural law and practical philosophy, or morals", to be taught by five professors, including a "Professor of Political History and Jurisprudence". The teaching of "jus gentium – law of nations" was included as part of the course on natural law. The Reglament consolidated the specific instructional methods of the University: lectures, practical lessons, scientific research by students, and their presentation and approbation before an Academy assembly.[40]

The confirmation of the Academy Reglament enhanced the prestige and status of the University, the Academy, and its graduates.

On 10 August 1750 the President of the Academy signed a document relating to the University and Gymnasium which operated as a provisional Statute for these educational institutions. This document determined the status, rights, and duties of the Rector, charged him with preparing a "catalogue of lectures", watching over the proper course and reliability of the lectures, maintaining a list of professors and students, reporting monthly on the state of affairs to the University, and developing disciplinary measures for students who misbehaved. Disrespect to the rector or other members of staff or failure to study lessons, for example, could engage confinement in a cell for up to two weeks on bread and water.[41]

A further effort to optimize the structuring of the University was made on 19 January 1760, when the President of the Academy, Count Razumovskii, assigned Mikhail Vasil'evich Lomonosov (1711-1765) to be the "guardian" of the University and the Gymnasium, thereby actually placing on Lomonosov the functions of the Rector. Lomonosov rapidly introduced long overdue changes. On 14 February 1760 he officially opened the faculties of philosophy, law, and medicine. Important changes were introduced into the syllabus for the legal disciplines, perhaps reflecting new perceptions of new Russian and international-legal realities. The changes collectively were intended to improve the quality of legal education. He was effective in persuading larger numbers of Gymnasium graduates from throughout the Empire to enroll.

In early September 1764 Lomonosov submitted to the President of the Academy a new proposal for reformation of the Academy which would have separated the University from the Academy. The Law Faculty, in his proposal, would have offered lectures on 1) history, in order to be familiar with the law of nations, which

[39] ПСЗ, XII, No. 9425, pp. 730-739.

[40] Pekarskii, note 15 above, I, pp. 677-678.

[41] I. L. Tikhonov, «Во главе университета» [At the Head of the University], Санкт-Петербургский университет [St. Petersburg University], no. 9 (2008).

in other places is mistakenly relegated to the jurisdiction of the faculty of philosophy; 2) practical philosophy; 3) politics; 4) public and private law; 5) Russian law.[42]

The law of nations was thus, in Lomonosov's projected reform, to be a required course in the Law Faculty. He recommended that students be awarded degrees of magister, litsenziat, and doctor.

These ideas, however, were not to be realized. The Empress Elizaveta Petrovna passed away before Lomonosov's project could be submitted, and Lomonosov himself died four years later. Serious educational reforms in the University and Academy would wait long years before being considered again. During the 1770s the University and the Gymnasium were combined into a "School [училище] of the Academy" with an ambiguous administrative-legal status, but the University syllabi were retained more or less intact until the early nineteenth century. This amalgamation undermined the classic triadal structure contemplated by Peter the Great: Academy – University – Gymnasium and the notion that the Academy would embody two principles: scientific research and educational.

The Petrine approach would be realized with the appointment of Ekaterina Romanovna Dashkova (1744-1810), who undertook measures to improve the work of the Academy and retained the University orientation of that institution. Under the changes introduced by Dashkova, academic standards were raised. Lectures were scheduled daily, except Sundays, for one to two hours each week but each subject not more than twice a week. Enrollment nearly tripled – but ultimately the reforms were unsuccessful and enrollment began to decline.[43] So deplorable did the situation in the University become that major administrative measures began to be introduced under the reign of Emperor Alexander I. In 1803 the "School of the Academy" was transformed into the St. Petersburg Teaching Gymnasium, which a year later, in 1804, became the Petersburg Pedagogical Institute. In 1816 the Pedagogical Institute was transformed into the Chief Pedagogical Institute.

The Chief Pedagogical Institute, it should be noted, contained a Law Faculty until 1847, which is evidence of a certain succession in the organization of legal education in Petersburg. The Institute was located at: Vasil'evskii Island, 6th Line, House 15.

Thus, during the 1780s the educational function of the Academy University turned away from the romantic dreams and constructive ideas of Peter the Great concerning the creation of the St. Petersburg Academy, University, and Gymna-

[42] See M. V. Lomonosov, Полное собрание сочинений [Complete Collection of Works] (M., 1957), X, p. 723.

[43] A phenomenon also observed at Moscow University, founded in 1755, during these years. Whereas in 1758 the Law Faculty at Moscow University had six students, five years later there were none. The Curator of Moscow University and graduate of the Academy University in St. Petersburg, Vasilii Evdokimovich Adodurov (1709-1780), retired the first Professor of Law, Filipp-Genrikh Dilthey (1723-1781), who had come to Moscow in 1756 from the University of Vienna upon the invitation of Academician G. F. Müller. The following academic year, 1764/65, there was one student, and in subsequent years the enrollment increased to three. Dilthey was replaced by K.-G. Langer, also invited by Muller from Germany.

sium as a tripartite, integrated package. The Academy University, small when measured by numbers of students and instructors, throughout much of its history lacking a cohesive administrative-legal structure and proper financial support, never developed into a fully-fledged institution of higher education of the classical European model. The Academy University virtually ceased being a University by the end of the eighteenth century.

§2.4. *Virtues and Disadvantages of Early Experience with International Legal Education*

Despite all the difficulties, the Academy University became the first institution of higher education in Russia in which the process of instruction and dissemination of scientific knowledge by professors from a different and more highly developed western European culture was deployed. Even the introduction into the instructional process of natural law theories – dominant in other European universities at the time – had a positive impact. The use of natural law views facilitated the transition from the previous so-called "command" system to a more progressive legal education based on studying the theoretical foundations of law.

In Russia international law began to be required knowledge during the 1720s at the Academy University. Given the nature of instruction in those times, the great majority of graduates would have acquired some legal, including international legal, knowledge. A number of graduates were sent to European universities in order to continue their studies, and some eventually became professors and academicians.[44] Several were appointed to positions at Moscow University.

But the challenges in developing the science of and in teaching the elements of the law of nations should not be underestimated:

(1) legal scholars who taught the law of nations came to the Academy University at the initiative and wish of the Russian State from European universities,[45] when Russian society had minimal motivation to have knowledge of this material because of the low cultural maturity of the population and the general unawareness of the significance of a legal education for the development of society, State, and every individual citizen;

(2) the Russian autocracy after Peter the Great reacted negatively towards the development of instruction in international law and towards University education generally in the Academy and the University; throughout the entire period, the Russian Government was reluctant either to confer a proper legal status on the institution or to finance it adequately. Even the reform proposals of Lomonosov and Dashkova failed to gain proper support;

[44] In the early period of the Academy University, Russian students comprised from 15 to 20% of the student body, a percentage which gradually increased over time.

[45] D. I. Kachenovskii wrote in the nineteenth century: "The science of international law came to us from the West, at first in the form of foreign theory". See D. I. Kachenovskii, Курс международного права [Course of International Law] (Kharkov, 1863), p. xii.

(3) the general state of affairs between the Petrine and Catherinian periods and the departure of the Russian Court to Moscow for four years (January 1728 to January 1732) had a pernicious effect, with the Academy going for months without a kopeck from the Treasury;

(4) the teaching of international law suffered, together with other disciplines, from the administrative ambiguity, indecisiveness, and inconsistencies relating to the forms and methods for organizing teaching;

(5) the early professors of the Academy University invited from abroad to teach legal, including international legal, subjects brought with them the most developed progressive legal ideas and methods then extant in European universities, often too advanced for their students not fully ready for exposure to sophisticated knowledge;

(6) there were enormous difficulties with simple interpersonal communication. The foreign professors taught Russian students in the Latin language, having no command of the local language themselves;

(7) the numbers of applicants for a place in the University were low and unstable, a problem with which the University never ultimately coped.[46] In addition, the Russian nobility were not ready to send their children to the University, seeing no positive result from obtaining an education at University level. In 1731 the more prestigious Noble Cadet Corps opened in St. Petersburg and drew away significant numbers of children of the nobility; this was a severe blow to the Academy University;

(8) the founding of Moscow University in 1755 adversely affected the Academy University in St. Petersburg; the institution avoided some of the early mistakes committed in St. Petersburg and enjoyed the support of the Government.

The successors of Peter the Great lacked his vision and did not understand the importance of the Academy University as a potential resource for the State. The Academy personnel were largely to look after themselves with miserly State support. The foreign professors who did take positions in the Academy made less of a contribution than might have been expected; through their teaching they popularized international law, but did little by way of fundamental research.

Nonetheless, the founding and activities of the Academy University were historically significant. This represented the first experience with establishing and organizing University education. Grabar wrote:

[46] The social composition of the Russian students was mixed. Among them were: from the nobility – V. Adodurov; from a teacher – Ivan Magnitskii; an Academy translator – Ivan Ilinskii; an Academy secretary – Petr Remizov; a regimental scribe – Andrei Gorlenko. Two students from a peasant background were dismissed from the University because they did not want to study. There were no entrance examinations as such, but often the professors interviewed potential students to determine if they were capable of working with the "sciences". Sometimes students were sent from seminaries or other educational institutions, including from Moscow. See I. L. Tikhonov and T. N. Zhukovskaia, «Как поступали в Университет 200 лет назад» [How They Entered the University 200 Years Ago], Санкт-Петербургский университет [St. Petersburg University], no. 11 (29 August 2008).

> With the founding in 1725 of the Academy of Sciences and the Academy University attached thereto, the scientific-theoretical impetus influenced the study of international law, but it was weak because little attention was devoted to questions of international law in the Academy of Sciences and University.[47]

Tomsinov observed:

> Peter I did not succeed in organizing a system of legal education in Russia, and a Russian theoretical jurisprudence did not arise during his rule. Nonetheless, the Great Reformer-Tsar did much for Russian legal culture: he created through his reforms the conditions and prerequisites for such a system and such a jurisprudence that emerged in Russia in the near future.[48]

The early academicians-professors remain in history as the first legal scholars in Russia; one must give them their due. They were pioneers in the dissemination and popularization in Russia of the scientific foundations of international law, they "loosened and prepared the soil and planted the first fruitful seeds in it" for the birth and development of Russian jurisprudence and within that framework – for the formation of science, education, and enlightenment in the field of international law not only in the St. Petersburg Academy University, but in Russia as a whole.

§2.5. *Other Contributors to International Legal Literature*

Vasilii Fedorovich Malinovskii *(1765, b. Moscow – d. 1814, St. Petersburg). Diplomat, educational administrator, poet, literary figure, author of early work on law of nations.*

Life and career. Vasilii Fedorovich Malinovskii was born in Moscow into the family of Archpriest Fedor Avksentevich Malinovskii (1738-1811), himself the son of a clergyman of the Moscow Church of the Trinity, and Anna Nikolaevna Arseneva (1744-1778). Vasilii was the second son of three, together with three sisters. His elder brother, Aleksei Fedorovich (1762–1840), was and remains the best known of the six children, eventually becoming director of the Moscow Archive of the Ministry of Foreign Affairs, a well-known writer, and a teacher of religion at Moscow University.

Vasilii Fedorovich graduated in 1781 from the Faculty of Philosophy at Moscow University. The details of his pre-university life and education are not known,[49] but the Malinovskiis were among the venerable Moscow families, tracing their lineage back to 1041. Malinovskii's father served Moscow University in his cleri-

[47] Grabar, note 19 above, p. 178.

[48] V. A. Tomsinov, «Развитие русской юриспруденции в первой четверти XVIII века» [Development of Russian Jurisprudence in the First Quarter of the XVIII Century], Законодательство [Legislation], no. 4 (2006), p. 89.

[49] The records of Moscow University from this period were burned during Napoleon's sacking of Moscow.

cal capacity and was well known to old Moscow society. After completing his university studies, Vasilii entered State service as an archivist in the Moscow Archive of the College of Foreign Affairs under the direction of Gerhard Friedrich Müller (1705-1783) and was close to Nikolai Mikhailovich Karamzin (1766–1826). A linguist of considerable accomplishment, Malinovskii had a command of French, German, English, Turkish, and ancient Hebrew — all sufficiently to qualify for appointment to the Russian diplomatic establishment abroad.

He received his first diplomatic assignment abroad in 1789 as translator/interpreter to the Russian mission in London (he may have visited earlier as a courier). There he spent twenty months, resident at least part of the time in nearby Richmond, where the ambassador and other members of the mission maintained a residence to avoid the "stench of London". In addition to his post duties, he devoted spare hours to beginning his treatise on war and peace and to completing a translation of Alexander Hamilton's *Report on the Subject of Manufactures* (1791).[50] England made an enduring impression on Malinovskii. According to his anonymous biographer, "A close acquaintance with this enlightened and industrial country made a profound impression on [Malinovskii]; he retained his memories of this period to the end of his days; he loved to chat about England and knew how to give the great figures and true dignitaries of that country their just due".[51]

Malinovskii returned to Russia from London in late March 1791, interested in becoming involved in that part of the world where Russian energies were concentrated: the Black Sea and Balkan region in the war against Turkey. Russia and Turkey were at war from 1787 to 1792; by late 1791, the Russian victory over the Ottoman Empire was secure, and Russia had urgent need for diplomatic personnel with a command of the Turkish language to assist with the peace arrangements. Malinovskii was attached to the Russian army to assist at the peace negotiations in Jassy. His services at the peace congress gave him occasion to petition to become an assessor of the College of Foreign Affairs, a rank equivalent to the eighth class in the Petrine Table of Ranks. His petition was unsuccessful, however, and instead he was attached to the College of Foreign Affairs in St. Petersburg without a special assignment or post, allegedly because he was unwilling to use his numerous

50 The translation appeared in print after Hamilton's death. See [A. Hamilton], Отчет генерал-казначея Александра Гамильтона, учиненный Американским штатам 1791 г. о пользе мануфактур, в отношении оных к торговле и земледелию [Report of the General Treasurer, Alexander Hamilton, Made to the United States in 1791 on the Benefit of Manufactures and Relation Thereof to Trade and Agriculture] (Spb., 1807).

51 See "Vasilii Fedorovich Malinovskii," in Памятная книжка Императорского Александровского лицея на 1856-1857 год [Book of Memories of Imperial Alexander Lycée in 1856-1857] (Spb., 1856), p. 131. But Malinovskii goes unmentioned in the history of the Russian church in London, as do other translator/interpreters. See C. Birchall, *Embassy, Emigrants, and Englishmen: The Three-Hundred-Year History of a Russian Orthodox Church in London* (2014). It is now considered highly likely that Malinovskii was the author of a series of letters between 31 October 1789 and 31 March 1791, describing his sojourn in England, published anonymously in the journal Приятное и полезное препровождение времени [Pleasant and Useful Passing of the Time] in 1796 under the title «Россиянин в Англии: отрывки из писем одного путешественника» [A Russian in England: Excerpts from Letters of a Traveller]. The author remained anonymous "by his own will and modesty". The letters collectively "constitute a sort of summa of Malinovskii's philosophical conceptions". See Paola Ferretti, *A Russian Advocate of Peace* (1998), pp. 33-34.

contacts to advantage. In 1798, he was made a court councilor, corresponding to the seventh class in the Table of Ranks, elevated to the next rank two years later, and appointed consul general in Moldavia, where he served until May 1802.

Recalled to Moscow in connection with the reorganization of State service initiated by Emperor Alexander I, Malinovskii continued to devote himself to writing and translation. He petitioned to become a State councilor in 1805 (fifth rank) and was awarded the Order of St. Vladimir in 1806. The return to St. Petersburg brought a period of economic privation for Malinovskii. He was a founder and fervent supporter of the Imperial Philanthropic Society,[52] but in June 1810 he appealed to Count Nikolai Petrovich Rumiantsev (1754–1826) for "rent money" to augment his inadequate salary.

His repertoire of writings and translations was formidable. The Malinovskii archive in the Institute of Russian Literature in St. Petersburg contains dozens of translations from English, Turkish, ancient Hebrew and Greek, German, French, and other tongues. He favored philosophical works but included William Shakespeare (1564-1616) along with several books of the Bible, presumably as part of his interest in the Russian Bible Society. The religious translations were unknown to the public and preserved within the family.

In connection with the Alexandrine ministerial reforms, Malinovskii drew up a Memorandum of the Emancipation of Slaves in 1802.[53] The next year he initiated a weekly journal, Осенные вечера [Autumn Evenings], in which all the articles published were his own.[54] In that same year Malinovskii completed his reflections on transforming the State structure of Russia that he had begun writing in his diary in 1799 while at his St. Petersburg home, Belozerka.[55] He also finished an epic tale intended for his journal about a hermit who returns to a provincial Russian

[52] The Medical-Philanthropic Committee was established by the Imperial Philanthropic Society on 18 May 1802 to provide free medical assistance to the poor. In 1805, the society founded the Committee for the Relief of the Poor and remained active in various organizational forms and titles until 1917.

[53] First published in V. F. Malinovskii, Избранные общественно-политические сочинения [Selected Socio-Political Works], ed. E. A. Arab-Ogly (M., 1958), pp. 111-114. The memorandum was drafted by Malinovskii in Jassy and sent to the Minister of Internal Affairs, Viktor Pavlovich Kochubei (1768-1834), a friend from his London days and the peace congress at Jassy. Kochubei was one of the young liberals who participated in the Emperor's "Unofficial Committee" to prepare a program of social and governmental reforms.

[54] Publication commenced on 26 September 1803. Malinovskii apparently intended to publish twelve weekly issues per year during the three months of autumn.

[55] First published during World War I by V. Semevskii, in Голос минувшего [Voice of the Past], no. 10 (1915), pp. 247-264, and reprinted in Malinovskii, note 53 above, pp. 115-132, with annotations. One shortcoming of Russia, said Malinovskii, was that there were "not enough laws", but at least some foreign laws were being translated (p. 115). Also see T. Borisova, "Russian National Legal Tradition: *Svod versus Ulozhenie* in Nineteenth-Century Russia", *Review of Central and East European Law,* XXXIII (2008), p. 303.

city after years of absence and deplores the "French morality" which he views as subverting the moral fiber of society.[56]

His most notable publication was *A Discourse on Peace and War*, begun at Richmond in 1790 (part one), completed in 1798 at Belozerka (part two), and published five years later, around the time when he completed part three, which did not appear during his lifetime.[57] From a letter to Kochubei, written in late 1802 or early 1803, it is evident that Malinovskii left London for Jassy partly in order to witness the evils of war against Turkey in person and to gather additional data for his *Discourse*.[58] In a sense, the peace negotiations, where he served as secretary, frustrated his desire to witness the evils of war because the battles had ended.

Malinovskii left in manuscript several political articles on Jews, land ownership, and the history of Russia. He published an article during the wars against Napoleon concerning a general peace.[59] As noted above, moreover, he left a third unpublished conclusion to his *Discourse on Peace and War*. The text was dated "1801–1803. Jassy, Petersburg".

Insofar as Malinovskii is known to Russian history, this is mostly due to his appointment in 1811 as the first director of Tsarskoe Selo (later Alexander) Lycée. In that capacity he encouraged the development of international legal studies in Russia.[60] The appointment was the subject of speculation among the cognoscenti of his time. Baron Modest Andreevich Korf (1800-1876) believed the directorship arose out of Malinovskii's marriage in London to Sofia Andreevna Samborskaia (1772-1812), daughter of Andrei Afanas'evich Samborskii (1732–1815), clergyman, agronomist, and author of books on English agronomy. The English connection surfaced time and again in Malinovskii's career. Samborskii had served with the Russian mission in London, served as the spiritual tutor of the future Emperor Alexander I and his brother, Grand Duke Konstantin Pavlovich (1779–1831), and was close to Alexander's law reformer, adviser, and confidant, Mikhail Mikhailovich Speransky (1772–1839). Malinovskii's interest in the Russian Bible Society also is believed to have originated in England.[61] He was a cofounder of the society,

[56] «Пустынник» [Hermit], in Malinovskii, note 53 above, pp. 136-145.

[57] [V. F. Malinovskii], Рассуждение о мире и войне [Discourse on Peace and War] (Spb, 1803). The title is interesting in two respects. First, Malinovskii speaks of peace and war, and not war and peace, thus reversing the classical Grotian formulation. Second, he chose the term "discourse" to characterize his work, following the example of Shafirov. Reviewed in Северный вестник [Northern Herald], pt. 2 (1804), pp. 311-323.

[58] The letter was first published in Чтения в Императорском Обществе истории и древностей российских при Московском университете [Readings at the Imperial Society of Russian History and Antiquities attached to Moscow University], no. 1, part 5 (1863), pp. 172-175.

[59] [V. F. Malinovskii], «Общий мир» [General Peace], Сын Отечества [Son of the Fatherland], no. 1(10) (1813), pp. 235-244. Although the article appeared anonymously, contemporary sources confirm Malinovskii as the author. In content, it is either a conspectus or a continuation of the 1803 Discourse.

[60] Aleksandr Kunityn, pioneer of the study of natural law in Russia, began teaching at the Lycée in the same year.

[61] I. Ia. Seleznev, Исторический очерк Императорского бывшего царскосельского, ныне

which was authorized by the Tsar in December 1812 and held its first organizing meeting in St. Petersburg in 1813.

Dmitrii Fomich Kobeko (1837-1918) attributed Malinovskii's appointment at the Tsarskoe Selo Lycée to his relationship with the Russian Bible Society. A letter dated 16 June 1811, to his brother Pavel Fedorovich Malinovskii (17??–18??) praised the efforts of Senator Mikhail Ivanovich Donaurov (1758–1817), A. K. Razumovskii (1748–1822), and Rodion Aleksandrovich Koshelev (1749–1827) on his behalf (which indicated that on this occasion Malinovskii was using his contacts).[62] All three were elected vice presidents of the Russian Bible Society in 1813. Like-minded in their attitude toward propagation of the faith, they were interested, Kobeko suggested, in placing their people in high positions and, conversely, in attracting important individuals to their ranks.[63]

Malinovskii's tenure as director of what was to become the most distinguished Russian lycée was auspicious but all too brief. He died at the age of forty-nine in 1814 and was buried in the Bolsheokhtenskii Cemetery.[64]

International legal views. It is beyond doubt that Malinovskii was the author of the *Discourse on Peace and War*. At the time of publication, however, the title page did not bear the author's name. At the end of part one of the Discourse, the designation "Richmond 1790" appears; at the end of part two, "Belozerka near Petersburg in 1798", followed by the initials "V. M."; and at the end of the unpublished part three, "1801–1803. Jassy, Petersburg. V. M.". These dates and places coincide with Malinovskii's career and places of service and residence. He later confirmed his authorship in letters to Count Aleksandr Romanovich Vorontsov (1741–1805) and to Gavriil Romanovich Derzhavin (1743–1816). He wrote to Vorontsov that he had the "honor to present my work to the public, a book on war

Александровского лицея за первое его пятидесятилетие, с 1811 по 1861 год [Historical Survey of the Imperial, Formerly Tsarskoe Selo, Now Alexander Lycée for its First Fifty Years, from 1811 to 1861] (Spb., 1861), p. 45. Leading Western works on the Russian Bible Society seem unaware of Malinovskii's existence and make no mention of him. See Stephen K. Batalden, *Russian Bible Wars: Modern Scriptural Translation and Cultural Authority* (Cambridge, 2013).

62 The letter is included in Malinovskii, note 53 above, pp. 153-155.

63 D. F. Kobeko, «Первый директор царскосельского лицея» [First Director of the Tsarskoe Selo Lycée], Журнал Министерства народного просвещения [Journal of the Ministry of Public Enlightenment], no. 7 (1915), p. 15. Also see Kobeko, Императорский царскосельский лицей: Наставники и питомцы, 1811-1843 [Imperial Tsarskoe Selo Lycée: Masters and Pupils] (Spb., 1911).

64 Malinovskii's contributions to international law and to scholarship generally have not received the attention they deserve. Most Russian and Soviet works on sociopolitical and historical thought overlooked him. He was rescued by literary specialists on Alexander Pushkin because of his directorship of the school where Pushkin was educated. Grabar, note 19 above, drew attention to the Discourse, but it remains unknown to most nonjurists. On the early neglect of Malinovskii, see E. A. Arab-Ogly, «Выдающийся русский просвитель-демократ (К 150-летию выхода в свет «Рассуждение о мире и войне» [Outstanding Russian Educator-Democrat (On the 150th Anniversary of the Publication of "Discourse on Peace and War"], Вопросы философии [Questions of Philosophy], no. 2 (1954), pp. 181-197.

and peace".[65] In a letter to Derzhavin dated August 1812, Malinovskii reminded him that the "book on war and peace [was] written by myself in England and the nearby vicinity; there is a continuation".[66] Grabar possessed a presentation copy (dated 1862) of the Discourse from Malinovskii's son to a recipient, which confirms the authorship of the volume. The book, now in the Russian State Library, bears Grabar's rubber-stamp ex libris.

The third, concluding section to the *Discourse*, prepared in Jassy and St. Petersburg, also was signed "V. M." and reposes in the Malinovskii family archive. Part Three is further confirmation of his authorship.

Malinovskii's authorship has likewise been confirmed by jurists who alerted an international readership to the importance of his contribution to the literature on international law. Dmitrii Ivanovich Kachenovskii (1827-1872), addressing the London Peace Society during his visit to London in 1858-1859, recited extracts from the Discourse to his audience. These extracts were published in the *Herald of Peace* and reprinted in the organ of the American Peace Society in the same year.[67]

Malinovskii grew up in a family dedicated to and in the service of the Orthodox Church. His grandfather and father were clergymen, as were possibly generations before them. He himself devoted his energies to philanthropy and was, as mentioned, a key figure in the founding and development of the Russian Bible Society. What precisely led him early in life, it would seem, to address the evils and horrors of warfare remains shrouded in the past. His antiwar, anticonflict views were in evidence early on, for he was composing his Discourse in England, when he had not yet reached his mid-twenties, and wrote the concluding part at Jassy and upon his return to St. Petersburg after completing his diplomatic service.

Another manuscript attributed to Malinovskii, by reason of its being in his own hand, is preserved untitled at the Institute of Russian Literature in St. Petersburg under the designation "Materials on the History of German Religious Philosophy". It was at one time believed to be autobiographical, through the medium of a fictional German young man. This document would reinforce the proposition that Malinovskii grew up in a household in which broad strata of Moscow society visited to chat about religious and moral issues. The manuscript mentions nonconformist religious thinkers such as Ernst Christoph Hochmann von Hochenau (1670–1721) and Gerhard Tersteegen (1697–1769), both influential radical Pietists. Hochmann was noted for opposing war and the accumulation of excessive wealth. The manuscript indicates that Malinovskii was well acquainted with these views. But recent evidence suggests that whatever autobiographical overtones the

[65] Архив князя Воронцова [Archive of Prince Vorontsov], no. 30 (1884), p. 394.

[66] Сочинения Державина с объяснительными примечаниями Я. Грота [Works of Derzhavin with Explanatory Notes of J. Grot] (2d ed.; Spb., 1864-1883), VI, p. 239. The "nearby vicinity" refers in all probability to Belozerka; the "continuation" may refer to the unpublished continuation of Malinovskii's manuscript.

[67] D. I. Kachenovskii, "Dissertation on War and Peace, by Basil Mahnofsky [sic]. St. Petersburgh, 1803", *Herald of Peace* (1 July 1859), pp. 71-72; reprinted in *Selected Works of D. I. Kachenovskii: Ukrainian International Lawyer*, ed. W. E. Butler (2014), pp. 259-263. Kachenovskii delivered his remarks to the Peace Society in London on 18 May 1859.

manuscript may contain, it is in fact Malinovskii's translation of *Theobald, oder die Schwärmer* (Frankfurt, 1785), by the physician and mystic Johann Heinrich Jung (1740–1816), better known by his assumed name, Heinrich Stilling. Malinovskii dated the manuscript 9 January 1804, a year after his Discourse appeared in Russia. How long he labored on the translation is unknown; if, as is likely, it was for a lengthy period, the work may have influenced the Discourse. It is at least evidence of Malinovskii's familiarity with some of the novel's religious intellectual origins.[68] The novel mentioned the translation of the Bible into the German language as an event leading to spiritual liberation.[69] Similar factors help account for the formation of the Russian Bible Society. Malinovskii's manuscript legacy includes his translations of books of the Bible, including Genesis, Ecclesiastes, Job, and Psalms.[70]

Malinovskii's Christian faith was central to his thinking about the causes of war and the prospects for peace, as *Discourse on Peace and War* makes clear.[71] War, he wrote, "is a spontaneous evil and a combination of all the evils in the world", for it combines "all the savageness of beasts with the art of human reason directed toward the destruction of people". Enlightened Europe should demonstrate to the world how to eradicate the evils of war "through the restoration and confirmation of a universal and indissoluble peace" (pp. 2-3). To achieve this, Europe could draw on its two great resources: reason and faith. Malinovskii thought Christianity was a great moral force that gave Europeans an advantage over others, because "our God is a God of peace and love" (p. 7). At the same time, he held that the institutional church, by succumbing to the temptations of wealth and power, had in important respects betrayed Christianity's moral teachings. He had particular disdain for monasticism: "The idle crowd of monks, whose prosperity is dependent upon the ignorance of nations, have maintained themselves, and the greater part of the people have given an absurd respect to those extravagant and wealthy monks, who have converted the God of Peace into a god of war". Among the consequenc-

[68] See M. Shippan, «В. Ф. Малиновский – переводчик фрагмента романа «Теобальд, или мечтатели» И. Г. Юнга-Штиллинга» [V. F. Malinovskii – Translator of a Fragment of the Novel "Theobald, or the Dreamer of J. G. Stilling"], XVIII век: Сборник [XVIII Century: Collection] (Spb., 2002), XXII, pp. 310-319.

[69] Ibid., p. 316.

[70] O. K[ornilovich], «Малиновский Василий Федорович» [Malinovskii Vasilii Fedorovich], in Русский биографический словарь [Russian Biographical Dictionary] (M., 1999), vol. (Маак-Мятлева), p. 62. This is one of the new volumes of previously unpublished entries from the classic Русский биографический словарь [Russian Biographical Dictionary] (Spb., 1896-1918).

[71] References are to the original 1803 edition: [Malinovskii], Рассуждение о мире и войне [Discourse on Peace and War]; parenthetical pagination will be given in the text. The work was published in full in Malinovskii, note 53 above. Substantial excerpts appear in V. F. Malinovskii, «Рассуждение о мире и войне» [Discourse on Peace and War], Вестник университета имени О. Е. Кутафина [Herald of O. E. Kutafin University], no. 6 (2015), pp. 224-249. Also see Kachenovskii, "Dissertation on War and Peace", for a concise summary. The summary of the Discourse is adapted from Grabar, note 19 above, pp. 202-208, and from the transcript of an unpublished codicil to the manuscript discovered by a Polish scholar: J. Skowronek, "'Rozważania o pokoju i wojnie' Wasyla F. Malinowskiego," *Teki archiwalne*, no. 4 (1978), pp. 30-53 (the text is in Russian); reprinted in W. E. Butler (intro.), Вестник университета имени О. Е. Кутафина [Herald of O. E. Kutafin University], no. 5(56) (2019), pp. 248-271.

es of this perversion was vicious religious persecution, according to which "those who differ in their opinions about the predominant faith are damned, deluded, and unfortunate, and are to be killed in order to please God" (pp. 8-9). Yet Malinovskii held out hope that Christianity, by returning to its core moral principles of peace and love, could inaugurate a new era in the life of nations.

War continued to be endemic in the Europe of Malinovskii's time. Even though the domestic order of States had been strengthened, "the general administration of Europeans among themselves has remained in a barbaric state", with disputes continuing to be resolved by fire and sword (p. 10). Far from promoting domestic prosperity, war was inimical to it, because the "prosperity of our State is inseparable from the general prosperity of Europe". The wars of Europe had (or should have) "become as unacceptable and harmful to all in general as were the internecine wars of barons in former times" (p. 11).

As for the arguments adduced in support of war, Malinovskii examined several and refuted each. Some viewed war and pestilence as nature's corrective against overpopulation. Leave future prosperity to our descendants, he said, "for they, of course, will find enough places to live and the means to maintain themselves" (p. 14). Against the view that Europe at peace will in the long term forget how to wage war and will fall prey to other nations, Malinovskii suggested that Europe united could be overcome by no one. Indeed, the present situation is the worse because "Asians, Americans, and Africans are entwined in our wars and, little by little learning the art of warfare, may use this against their teachers by taking advantage of their divisions and disunity" (p. 15).

Malinovskii maintained that the power of States is not dependent on territorial possessions or increased population acquired by wars; in fact, these may lead to a State's decline. States will acquire more pride, more enemies, and thus more reasons for others to reduce their power, he said. He supported his case by reference to the respective positions of Sweden and Denmark, which were vulnerable to Russian (and other European) pressures but not seriously considered by anyone at the time to be subject to appropriation by conquest. "Conquests are now different and virtually impossible" (p. 23).

Malinovskii decried the prejudices of nations. The shortcomings and virtues of nations, being so diverse, should actually bind them closer together, so that they "might through their mutual virtues help one another with regard to their mutual shortcomings" (p. 29). In his chapter on "Respect for War, Heroism, and Magnanimity of Spirit," he reserved his highest accolade for the "lawmaker" or legislator, for through the exercise of wisdom the lawmaker reaches millions of people over many races and centuries (p. 39). This praise reflected Malinovskii's hope that law could become the educator of humanity, restraining our lower impulses and raising "the better angels of our nature", as Abraham Lincoln later put it.

The misfortunes of war are levied on society as a whole: "War destroys the primary bases of society, the safety of life and property. Laws punish by death certain unfortunate murderers and thieves, but the keepers of those laws, the rulers of nations, in not knowing how to avert war, subject the entire state to murder and plundering" (p. 45). Peace, on the other hand, would bring "prosperity and justice" to Europe. The appearance of nations and lands would be altered beyond recognition (p. 65).

Malinovskii concluded his analysis of the causes of war before he departed England and went on to the settlement of the Russo-Turkish War in Jassy. The European powers, he wrote, "habitually consider their neighbors to be implacable and natural enemies ... always ready to attack the enemy or to repulse his attack". The only rules which "European powers observe among themselves are the rules of politics" (pp. 69-70). Like the ancient rites of Egyptians, these rules are concealed from the common people – "the priests send them away from the inner parts of the temple, and with reason" (p. 70). The Italians "introduced their politics into European cabinets, where they have been present to this day. The monks hurried to confirm them, rose to state office, and sowed there the principles of pretense, injustice, and secrecy which bear sufficient witness against politics", because it is "useful and decorous in the behavior of dishonorable people to endeavor to deceive one another, but not in the conduct of nations" (pp. 70-71). The "management of politics by individuals at court could not make it ... more accustomed to injustice and guile". Cardinal Armand-Jean du Plessis, Duke of Richelieu (1585–1642) and Cardinal Giulio Raimondo Mazarin (1602–61) are considered outstanding ministers, yet "coercion, deceit, arrogance, baseness, and perfidy marked their behavior" (p. 71).

Malinovskii condemned political writers who "within the political composition of Europe are maggots born in the wounds of the human body" (p. 75). They "defend the sophistry of politics, confirm its most ridiculous rules, and justify it in matters which it would itself be ashamed to admit to" (p. 76). He divided political writers into three categories: (1) "those writers who apologize for the fact that there are those who are blinded by love for their fatherland"; (2) "those who write ex officio or in the interest of the court" (the "most dangerous of all political writers", in whose works "truth and the law of nations yield their place to injustice and lies"); and (3) "the most common political writers, the newspaper writers", who write in order to write and "are suborned to think in a particular way" (pp. 76-78).

At the family dacha in Belozerka, Malinovskii directed his attention to ways in which the international system could rid itself of the habit of war. He began with the law of nations, or what in 1780 Jeremy Bentham (1748–1832) began to call "international law". Malinovskii reasoned that States, just as individuals, "need to base their behavior on absolute rules which, without prejudicing their independence, restrain them within the bounds of common advantage ... Every sovereign power administers its internal affairs according to its own discretion, and any interference, direct or indirect, is a violation of its independence" (p. 81). According to this logic, the establishment of laws of nations does not constitute interference in internal affairs, because such laws may be confirmed only by consent (p. 82). Here Malinovskii may have been expressing his general understanding of the concept of Westphalian sovereignty.

Nations, he continued, "conclude peace treaties, treaties of alliance, and defensive treaties, and these serve as the rule and law of conduct *inter se*, which are changed as frequently as the chief inducements of interest of those who are concerned in them. Those who are bound are both the judges and the judged, both the aggrieved and those who aggrieve" (pp. 83-84). Under these conditions, "there is neither security of a court, nor justice, nor equality" (p. 84). There must be a better way of organizing international relations, he concluded.

Malinovskii distinguished among levels or degrees of alliance. A general alliance, he suggested, might subsume all the advantages of special alliances, and then, "instead of treaties, there should be laws to confirm the independence and ownership of territory ... and to establish the conduct of all nations" (pp. 86-87). Such laws would require a structure to systematize and enforce them. For the observance of such laws, a general council "should be established, composed of plenipotentiaries of the allied nations. This council should preserve general security and ownership, prevent any disturbance of the peace, and decide disputes between nations submitted according to an established procedure, and its decisions must be unanimously implemented by all the allies (nations)" (p. 87).

If the decision of the general council is not implemented, "the recalcitrant power shall be excluded from all general privileges and intercourse, and in the event of obduracy, a common force shall be used to enforce the law" (p. 88). The country housing the headquarters of the council shall be deemed to be "sacred and independent for the perpetual and safe sojourn of council plenipotentiaries. ... Its personnel shall be inviolate in all territories" (p. 89). All negotiations, Malinovskii proposed, would take place through mutual plenipotentiaries in the council. This new arrangement will render the custom of maintaining envoys superfluous, together with the various ways they have caused hostility among nations, such as issuing false and biased reports, interfering in another country's internal affairs, stealing secrets, and stirring passions (pp. 89-90).

In Malinovskii's vision of the new order, the first laws of nations will concern their frontiers. Other laws will aim to unite nations through trade. With still others it will be necessary, as is done in treaties of alliance, to define the *casus foederis* "even more precisely in the general alliance". This *casus* shall be an attack, the meaning of which Malinovskii thought was obvious: the incursion of a foreign army into one's own country (pp. 90-92). Except for parrying an attack, he doubted whether there could be another instance of a just or lawful war. An "insult to national honor" ought to be punished by a reprimand, since powers are obliged to respect one another. Finally, to remove any incentive for war, Malinovskii deemed it essential to deprive an aggressor "of the expectation of acquisitions and advantages, and therefore all European powers, often having precisely demarcated frontiers", must "acknowledge them to be mutually absolute and guarantee their integrity so that they may not be disturbed by war or conquest; equally, the advantages of trade should be absolute and might be changed only by mutual and voluntary consent" (p. 94).

According to Malinovskii, the tribulations of warfare could be confined by limiting the spatial sphere within which European powers might engage in war. If Europeans quarrel, why should America, Africa, and Asia become embroiled? European settlements in those parts of the globe should be neutral territory, with European powers stationing only enough troops there to ensure protection against the local inhabitants. To this policy he proposed adding stipulations against European powers seeking further possessions, punishment of those responsible for committing an attack, compensation for losses sustained, and compulsory negotiations or proceedings between nations (pp. 94-95). Malinovskii did not favor disarmament *per se*, but noted that war is always preceded by movements of troops and arms. Such movements should be confined to imminent expectation of an attack, and the council should be notified of any such movements beforehand.

Malinovskii next contraposed the natural state of society to a State, or civil society. Legal order should exist not merely between private individuals united in a civil society but also between nations. European powers should recognize that they "constitute a single society, by reason of Christianity and of their mutual relations". In this international, law-governed, Christian society, "each power concedes its absolute right to spontaneously govern itself in its disagreements", and in return "it receives the major advantage of mutually, with others, preserving itself from spontaneous misfortune. The Christian regions ... are bound in every possible way to endeavor to settle their disputes peacefully and may not consider their rival an enemy, until he is recognized as such by all society (p. 111).

In the chapter titled "Unification by Consent", Malinovskii argued that the "slightest violation of universal laws is equally dangerous and harmful to all. ... The rulers of a nation who have violated an oath to society subject their nation to the danger of vengeance and are guilty before it" (pp. 114-115). He makes reference to his sojourn in London: "In England representations are made by the people to the king concerning war and peace. In this fortunate land the people are allowed to judge their government in quarrels with other powers" (pp. 115-116).

The final chapter undertakes to draw the consequences of his Discourse. The first is that the "observance of justice between nations is as essential as it is between private individuals". Failure to observe justice between nations also "violates it for each of them separately, subjecting the innocent to destruction and death" (pp. 118-119). War, continued Malinovskii, "cannot be lawful when there are not laws between nations. These laws of nations are duties and obligations based on their own well-being. When all governments are agreed on the unity of their intentions, they will be agreed on everything. ... Politics must be the science of rights and laws among nations, just as jurisprudence is among private individuals (p. 123).

The unpublished section of Malinovskii's Discourse addresses the law of nations in greater detail and more directly. Malinovskii clearly used one source: the works of Emer de Vattel (1714-1767).

Malinovskii emphasized the universality of the law of nations. The law belongs, he said, to Africans and Asians as much as to Europeans. He resolutely opposed slavery. All the peoples in their entirety comprise society, which has similar rules and grounds for crimes. In Europe there was never a threat of a universal monarchy, but events in France led Malinovskii to consider the possibility that a universal European republic might emerge. He supported a variant of self-determination: "every people has the right to govern itself, being subordinate externally in its relations to laws of the whole people".[72]

Self-determination, he suggested, ought to be linked to language. Equilibrium in Europe would be improved, he advised, by a new division of Europe according to the peculiarities of the languages which Europeans speak: Slavic-Russian,

[72] Skowronek, note 71 above, p. 34.

German, French, and Italian being the principal examples. Each individual should have his or her own land, and a legacy to pass to family members and kin. Land, he wrote, is the "Lord's, and we are newcomers and strangers to it".[73] There was enough land in any domain so that no one need be deprived of it. Preoccupation with land distribution, he said, is not a departure from the main question of peace and war, because the structuring of a new system depends on its internal components. International peace is unrealistic when there is domestic war between the rich and the poor throughout all of Europe. For Malinovskii, the Christian faith truly observed was the best means of uniting all peoples and bringing peace among cohabitants, properly reflecting all the languages of Europe. War, he said, is contrary to all Christian teaching, citing the example of the Quakers,[74] who deny the permissibility of war, do not accept the consequences of war, and may even choose not to defend a besieged city.

Malinovskii then turned to the "science of the law of nations". He distinguished between the natural law of nations and what he called the "voluntary law of nations". By the former he meant raw force; by the latter, law proper. Under the voluntary law of nations, the European powers "preserve security and ownership of their possessions" and therefore mutual peace. Under the natural law of nations, they arbitrarily violate ownership and security and produce war. Consequently, Malinovskii said, "insofar as peace is preferable to war, it is essential to subordinate natural law to voluntary law".

Security and freedom, Malinovskii said, are the natural right of each people, but no one may appropriate this benefit to himself. Following the example of Russia, which confirmed the right of free navigation of neutral peoples in Europe, the rules of general peace might also be confirmed as follows: (1) any particular violation of the boundaries of ownership of a people is a general violation of ownership; (2) any violation of the independence of one power is a violation of general security and freedom; (3) the discussion of the affairs of Europe should be common, as should its defense when the boundaries and security of a people are violated.

Malinovskii concluded this last portion of his treatise by addressing the declaration of war. After commenting on the practices of individual states (Sweden, England), he stated that the "right of a people to declare war is a matter for all of Europe", essential for mutual security and the hope of peace. Such a policy would make the declaration of an unjust war less likely.

Some would classify Malinovskii's work as part of the utopian literature proposing schemes for perpetual peace in Europe, although his actual commitment to this idea is doubtful. Whether he thought his proposals had prospects outside Christian civilization is a separate subject. Grabar would appear to be right that the *Discourse* is a "comprehensive and independently conceived work".[75]

73 Ibid., p. 41.

74 The reference to Quakers is of interest because, assuming Malinovskii wrote the letters in Russian in England, he describes favorably a visit to a Quaker meeting in Scotland. See note 71 above, and accompanying text.

75 Grabar, note 19 above, p. 203. There is no evidence of, for example, the influence of Immanuel Kant on Malinovskii; Kant's work on perpetual peace came out in 1795, several years after Mal-

By coincidence or serendipity, Malinovskii had completed the first two parts of his book before events in France brought Napoleon to power. The French Revolution seems to have influenced the third part. Although he is critical of diplomacy in general and of French diplomats particularly, there is no reason to believe that he pretended to foretell the pan-European conflagration in the offing, pertinent as many features of his analysis were to those events. His *Discourse* was inspired initially by a regional conflict between Russia and Turkey and completed when the clouds of war were gathering all over Europe. By then Malinovskii was beginning to apply his propositions to continental foreign policy in his journal Осенные вечера [Autumn Evenings].

By the time of Napoleon's invasion of Russia, in 1812, the scene had changed fundamentally. A letter from Malinovskii to Derzhavin[76] suggests that his journal article on a "general peace", published in 1813, was envisaged as a continuation of the Discourse.[77] Whatever the case, he believed the time had finally arrived for his diagnosis of events to take effect. "A general peace," he wrote, "is no longer a chimera ... Germany and virtually all of Europe desire it". Having restored "freedom by their common efforts, all are aware that this cannot be preserved without their common consent, and already they do not rush, as before, to seek any private advantage or to conclude a separate peace ... Entire States and peoples, as one man, endeavor collectively to overcome the common enemy and are as one joyously and solemnly celebrating their mutual triumphs".[78]

Malinovskii counseled that the previous treaties of alliance against Napoleon should be transformed into one common or general new alliance that "would serve as a kind of codex [уложение] and confirm reliable and stable rules for the security and integrity of possessions."[79] Further, he suggested that the "general spirit of heroism, love for the fatherland, and disposition of nations to defend and assert their rights, together with intolerance of force and suppressions", would lead the present generation to preserve the fruits of their common achievement for posterity. The "confluence of present circumstances", he presciently foresaw, "constitutes an epoch; we will be accountable to posterity, and will ourselves bitterly regret it if we do not take advantage of them".[80] When printing Malinovskii's last article, the editor of the journal observed that shortly after he received the manuscript for press, the allied monarchs proclaimed their grand alliance.

inovskii had started his work. It is possible, but unproven, that Malinovskii met Jeremy Bentham while in London between 1789 and 1791. He did circulate in Benthamite circles, especially the Samborskii family. On the question of the influence of other thinkers on Malinovskii, also negative, see Ferretti, note 51 above.

76 Note 60 above, VI, p. 394.

77 [Malinovskii], note 59 above, p. 234.

78 Quoted from the text reprinted in Arab-Ogly, note 64 above, p. 94.

79 Ibid., p. 97.

80 Ibid., pp. 97-98. Also see William E. Butler, "Vasilii Malinovskii: A Russian Christian on War and Peace", in Paul Valliere and Randall A. Poole (eds.), *Law and the Christian Tradition in Modern Russia* (2022), pp. 47-62.

Malinovskii passed away in 1814, before the Congress of Vienna brought into being the framework for the structure of Europe in which he had placed such hopes. The Napoleonic wars also led to the formation in England, the United States, and other countries of the organized peace movement—in England, the London Peace Society, and in the United States, the American Peace Society. Unbeknown to the organizers of those societies, mostly if not entirely Christians of one denomination or another, a Russian Orthodox Christian had formulated a substantial and original independent contribution to proposals for structuring the international system. His untimely death deprived Russia and the international peace movement of an influential voice in post-Napoleonic Europe, but he left behind an enduring legacy to the literature of international law.

Franz Frantsevich (Frederick) Borel *(1775, b. Milan, Lombardy, Italy – 1832). Diplomat, publicist.*

Life and career. Borel was in fact French, born in Lombardy, Italy,[81] and began his career in Poland before finding a position in Russian service in 1799. At various times he held posts for Russia in Naples, Friedrichsham, Paris, London, Madeira, Lisbon, Salvador, and, finally, Rio de Janeiro. His initial Russian posting was as an assistant to a Russian commercial agent in Naples. In 1804 Borel was sent to St. Petersburg to deliver diplomatic communications and there met Count Nikolai Petrovich Rumiantsev (1754-1826), most probably in August-early September 1804.[82] On 23 September 1804 Borel was appointed to the College of Foreign Affairs and then within three months transferred through Rumiantsev's influence to the Ministry of Commerce. Following a delicate and secret mission to Naples from January to May 1805, Borel returned to St. Petersburg where he spent more than three years. He apparently did not know the Russian language; all surviving manuscripts of his making are in French. However, he did publish a book in the Russian language, which one must assume someone translated for him: a comparative table of foreign weights, measures, and exchange rates. Dedicated to the Russian merchantry, it appeared in 1807 under the auspices of the State Commercial College.[83] Emperor Alexander I was shown the manuscript before Borel had completed it by Count Rumiantsev and endorsed the project.

[81] David Baillie Warden named Milan as the place of birth, and Komissarov and Bozhkova consider Warden to be authoritative. See B. N. Komissarov and S. G. Bozhkova, Первый российский посланник в Бразилии Ф. Ф. Борель [First Russian Envoy to Brazil: F. F. Borel] (2000). This work draws on Russian archives and certain unpublished manuscripts that mention Borel and corrects a number of minor errors in Russian Ministry of Foreign Affairs documentary volumes that publish some of Borel's official dispatches to St. Petersburg.

[82] Here too Komissarov and Bozhkova rely upon Borel's dedication to Rumiantsev as evidence of the latter's patronage of Borel.

[83] F. F. Borel, Сравнительныя таблицы иностранных весов, мер, вещественных и курсовых монет, в отношении и сравнении к Санктпетербургской бирже [Comparative Tables of Foreign Weights, Measures, Material and Exchange Rates of Coins in Relation to and Comparison to the St. Petersburg Stock Exchange] (1807). See Сводный каталог русской книги 1801-1825 [Complete Catalog of the Russian Book 1801-1825] (2000), I, item 747.

Upon his return to Russia, Borel was appointed in May 1809 to head a consular department within the Ministry of Foreign Affairs. Called an "expedition", all internal and external correspondence on consular matters passed through this body, including correspondence with foreign consuls in Russia, the compilation of instructions for Russian consuls, and much to do with trade and navigation, especially prize causes. Borel was appointed to head this Expedition by Rumiantsev with the approval of the Emperor.

When Count Rumiantsev's star dimmed in St. Petersburg as the Emperor's "liberal period" gave way to conservative policies, so too did Borel's. Borel assisted in the formation and organization of Rumiantsev's personal library – one of the truly remarkable collections of its time. Borel spent time in Paris and London bookshops acquiring titles for his patron, having a generous budget to this end. In 1825 the title of Baron Palens was conferred on Borel, he having on 26 June 1824 received the Order of St. Vladimir, 2d degree. Borel has achieved fame today in his capacity as the first Russian envoy to Brazil.

Notwithstanding his few years in St. Petersburg, Borel established no roots there, left no personal correspondence or diaries, and apparently no friends or acquaintances with whom he corresponded other than Count Rumiantsev himself.

International legal views. In his work on consular law[84] Borel emphasized the diplomatic and political role of the consul. One of Borel's colleagues in the Ministry of Commerce when he was preparing his treatise was Andrei Iakovlevich Dashkov (1776-1831). Dashkov cannot fail to have known about Borel's treatise. Moreover, Borel visited Paris in autumn 1808, after his book was published, as part of a Russian diplomatic mission headed by Count Rumiantsev. It is suggested that Dashkov's appointment to the United States as both Consul General and *chargé d'affaires*, that is, "simultaneously to consular and diplomatic posts (which thereafter was repeatedly practiced in the American representations of Russia) indirectly affirmed the correctness of the theoretical views of Borel concerning their close interlinkage".[85]

Borel's monograph greatly influenced the first treatise in the English language on consular law by David Baillie Warden (1772-1845).[86] This was confirmed by Warden himself in the Preface to his own work. He said that he had nearly completed his treatise when a friend in Paris informed him that a book had been advertised in a book catalogue from Leipzig under the title "On the Origin and Functions of Consuls", by Franz Frantsevich (Frederick) Borel. Warden allegedly obtained a copy through the bookseller and promptly acknowledged that

[84] F. Borel, *De l'Origine et des fonctions des consuls* (Spb., 1807), reissued at Leipzig by Leopold Voss in 1831.

[85] Komissarov and Bozhkova, note 81 above, p. 18.

[86] D. B. Warden, *On the Origin, Nature, Progress and Influence of Consular Establishments* (Paris, 1814); reprinted in 2011 with an Introduction by W. E. Butler. Also see Butler, "David Baillie Warden and the Development of American Consular Law", *Journal of the History of International Law*, XIII (2011), pp. 327-424. Warden published a French language version a year later. See Warden, *De L'Origine, de la nature, des progress, et de l'influence des établissemens consulaires* (Paris, 1815).

> the appearance of his publication would have rendered mine unnecessary, if the matter and arrangement were not essentially different. Mr. Borel has devoted eighty pages of his work to an examination of the origin and functions of Consuls, which evinces an intimate acquaintance with this subject. The remainder, consisting of two hundred and ninety pages, is made up of extracts of treaties, and other documents relative to the employment of commercial agents (p. 7).[87]

Although the books by Borel and Warden are indeed quite different, it is plain that Warden drew upon Borel in preparing his own work.[88] On the title page of his St. Petersburg book, Borel was described in French "Assesseur de College de S. M. l'Empereur de toutes les Russies, et Chef de division au Ministère de Commerce", which Warden renders as "… chief of division of the Ministry of commerce, and assistant judge of the Imperial College of St. Petersburg". Because Borel dedicated his book to Count "Nicolas de Romanzoff", Warden readily concluded that Borel owed his position to the patronage of Count Rumiantsev, the State Chancellor of the Russian Empire at the time. However, Warden adds that Borel is "a native of Milan" and "now resides at the island of Madeira as Consul general of Russia". These details Warden obtained elsewhere, as they did not appear in Borel's book and were not true when Borel's book was published.[89] In his discussion of the Russian consular system (pp. 294-301), Warden cited Borel, but also used the well-known History of Catherine II by William Tooke, available at the time in English and French versions. In his list of "Consuls of Russia", Warden is aware of only three: Andrei Iakovlevich Dashkov, who served as Russian Consul General in the United States before being appointed Minister in that country;[90] Borel; and Ia. M. Evreinov,[91] whom, relying on Borel, he indicates was appointed by Peter the Great to be the Russian consul at Cadiz in 1723.

Borel's book was actively disseminated to Russian and foreign consuls by the Russian diplomatic and consular corps. The Russian Consul in Sweden, A. K. Brun, reported in 1810 that he had been instructed by the Ministry of Foreign Affairs to distribute copies of Borel on consular law to all consuls in post and had done so. He further observed that in Braunschweig (Brunswick), Germany, it was proposed to reissue Borel, which was apparently done.[92]

[87] Warden seems to have been unaware that Borel published a second volume: Borel, *Formulaire des consulats* (Paris, Pluchart, 1808). Also see Grabar, note 19 above, pp. 245-246.

[88] See Warden, note 86 above (2011), pp. 6, 7, 46-48, 50, 54, 56, 57, 62, 66, 71, 72, 74-80, 91, 96-98, 102, 104, 123, 296, 328.

[89] In fact, Grabar believed that "as one may conclude from the preface to the book, the author was a German by nationality since the French language in which the book was written was not, in his words, either his mother tongue or the language of the country in which he lived". Grabar, note 19 above, p. 245.

[90] On Dashkov, see Русский биографический словарь [Russian Biographical Dictionary] (1905; reprint ed., 1996).

[91] Borel included in his book the text of the Instruction of Peter the Great to Evreinov dated 7 November 1723. Borel said he obtained the text of the document from the Evreinov family (p. 68).

[92] Komissarov and Bozhkova, note 81 above, p. 27. Komissarov and Bozhkova cited an 1812 Brunswick edition, a copy of which has not been located.

THE RENAISSANCE

Chapter 3
Prerequisites of the Renaissance

Domestic Russian Prerequisites. During the early nineteenth century, Russia experienced significant economic and socio-political changes that created hopes and expectations for noteworthy improvements in economic, cultural, spiritual, and legal life.

Emperor Alexander I (1777-1825), a young monarch committed to improving the entire system of education, ascended to the throne in 1801. In 1802 the Ministry of Public Enlightenment was formed; its principal task was to reorganize the entire educational process throughout the land. The introduction and expansion of law faculties throughout the Russian Empire led to significant reforms of the administrative apparatus and increases in the numbers of civil servants with legal background. Between 1803 and 1804 the groundwork was laid for a single unified national university system of higher vocational and professional education. The basic principles were set out in the "Preliminary Rules for Public Enlightenment", confirmed by Edict of the Emperor on 24 January 1803. Pursuant to the Edict, Russian territory was divided into six educational districts, each to contain an Imperial University. The Ministry promulgated the first General Statute of Universities of the Russian Empire" and the "Statute of Educational Institutions of Departmental Universities".[1]

The universities were collectively given an important State objective – to become scientific research, educational, and enlightenment centers in their respective educational district. Provision was made for law to be taught in each university. On 5 November 1804 Emperor Alexander I confirmed that the Charter of Moscow University extended to the Kazan University, Kharkov University, and later to St. Petersburg University. The Charter became the first legislative act determining national Russian standards for university education.[2]

The universities were established as independent bodies with a certain level of internal autonomy, an elected rector, deans, and inspectors, the right to choose professors, to confirm instructional plans, and the like. Although the professors were elected by the Council of the university on a competitive basis, they were nonetheless regarded as State officials who were to conduct their lessons according to a strictly established procedure determined by the instructional syllabi and

[1] At the time there were debates about the proper structure and role of universities. One view held that in a country with a population divided into estates in place of a university there should be created educational institutions of a "special type" or "gymnasiums of the higher sciences" which combined gymnasium and university courses intended for selected attendees drawn solely from the estates of the nobility. See S. V. Rozhdestvenskii, Исторический обзор деятельности Министерства народного просвещения. 1802-1902 [Historical Survey of Activity of the Ministry of Public Enlightenment. 1802-1902] (Spb., 1902), pp. 115-130.

[2] ПСЗ, XXVIII, No. 21498, p. 571. Throughout the nineteenth century, the system of university education was repeatedly subjected to reforms at the legislative level, duly reflected in national university statutes of 1835, 1863, and 1884.

methodological manuals. The Statute gave a university and the lecturers the right to receive books, journals, and manuscripts from abroad, bypassing the censor. Access to university study was opened to fee-paying students;[3] the period of study was three years for the first degree.

It should be noted that although law was offered at each university, the 1804 version of the relevant legislation did not authorize each university to create its own law faculty. Legal education was available within the larger framework of the divisions for morals and politics, influenced by Austrian approaches to producing jurists with a broad humanities background.[4]

International Prerequisites. The early nineteenth century was a time of material changes in the foreign policy of the Russian Empire. Russia aspired to expand and strengthen its influence and role in international affairs, consolidate hegemony in Central Asia and the Far East, expand international trade ties, and gain greater access to the world markets. To this end, the Russian Empire actively used the most variegated and sometimes contradictory means and methods: aggressive and diplomatic, colonialist and national-liberation, dynastic marital, and, when necessary, crafty rational methods.

Russia became part of a small group of powerful nations which won for themselves a role as "peacekeeper"' and "gendarme". Successes in wars, diplomacy, and political tension resulted in Russia incorporating Georgia, Finland, Bessarabia, and the Duchy of Warsaw under the name of the "Polish Kingdom" into the Empire and obtaining the right to maintain a naval fleet on the Caspian Sea. The defeat of Napoleonic France led to Russia playing a major part in forming the new legal principles of international relations embodied in the documents emanating from the 1815 Congress of Vienna – among them the principle of legality or legitimacy, although this principle was immediately violated by the periodic crises in Europe and the competition for overseas colonial possessions. The Congress proclaimed the legality of interference in the internal affairs of States and collective interventions in defense of legitimacy, of existing regimes (monarchies at the time), and of recognized boundaries. At Russian initiative, the Holy Alliance was created as an international legal formation.

The Congress of Vienna recognized the permanent neutrality of Switzerland, prohibited slave trade in African Negroes, partially codified diplomatic law, clarified the status of international rivers, and for the first time in history considered bringing a natural person to individual international-legal responsibility for crimes allegedly committed (without success, Napoleon Bonaparte).

Significant changes occurred in the normative foundations and forms of international law – increasingly they were embodied in treaties. The number and sophistication grew of treaties entered into by Russia, especially political, econom-

[3] Later university students were required to wear uniforms.

[4] See Iu. V. Ginzburg and T. N. Ilina, «Специализация юридического образования в российских университетах в XIX в.» [Specialization of Legal Education in Russian Universities in the XIX Century], Вопросы образования [Questions of Education], no. 1 (2012), p. 279.

ic, trade, consular, and the like. But international law was regarded as the law of civilized Christian States in Europe and North America.

As the Russian aspiration to overcome domestic and foreign policy problems intensified, it became clear that new conceptual approaches, institutional reforms, and well-trained specialists were essential. This required new and better educational institutions with new personnel and revised syllabi. International law was a beneficiary of these trends and developments. Only a system of university education could begin to address the needs identified. The embryo of creating future scientific schools of international law was created, and the expansion and reorganization of St . Petersburg University was part of that process in the early nineteenth century.

§3.1. *Administrative Foundations of the Renaissance*

Reviving the University in St. Petersburg was a complex undertaking. In early 1804 the Petersburg Pedagogical Institute was formed on the basis of the Teaching Gymnasium (successor of the Academy University) and accommodated in the prestigious building known as "Twelve Colleges";[5] in 1816 the Institute became the Chief Pedagogical Institute. The Institute began to operate in accordance with University syllabi because it was regarded as the "kernel", the "embryo", of the future University.[6]

The Division of Philosophical and Legal Sciences within the structure of the Institute contained two chairs of law: the Chair of General Laws, encompassing three subjects (private law, State law, and the law of nations), and the Chair of Positive Laws, encompassing Roman law and Russian law. Later the University borrowed this structure in its entirety.

In the Institute and then in the embryonic University the principle for forming the professoriate changed: the professors were to be "native Russians". However, in the nineteenth century, just as a century before when the Academy University opened, there were not enough "native Russians", and extreme measures were undertaken to rectify the situation.

First, the Government introduced a scheme under which talented potential young scholars remaining at chairs to prepare for the professoriate were first sent abroad at State expense to European universities in order to work in libraries, attend lectures of noted scholars, improve their knowledge of foreign languages, and expand their cultural horizons. Twelve of the best students at the Institute were sent abroad for this purpose in 1808.[7] Each student was given a letter of introduction and recommendation to professors of European universities and a set of directions or instructions [наставление] specially prepared for each student. By way of ex-

[5] The building was originally conceived by Peter the Great as a governmental building housing ten ministries, the Senate, and the Synod of the Russian Empire.

[6] L. A. Verbitskaia (ed.), 275 лет Санкт-Петербургский университет. Летопись 1724-1999 [275 Years of St. Petersburg University. Chronicle 1724-1999] (Spb., 1999), pp. 79-86.

[7] ЦГИА СПб, fond 139 (Chancellery of the Guardian of the Petrograd Educational District), opis 6, file 16.

ample, a direction prepared for Alexander Kunitsyn who visited Göttingen University read: "Göttingen has long been distinct from other universities by the fact that the historical sciences and information for diplomatic lessons flourish there …".[8]

Second, the Chief Pedagogical Institute invited professors of Slavic origin from universities in Austria who were natives of Carpathian Rus, among them Petr Dmitrievich Lodii (1764-1829), Mikhail Andreevich Balugianskii (1769-1847), and Vasilii Grigorevich Kukolnik (1765-1821). By their training they had been affiliated with the University of Vienna, held doctorates, and had lecturing experience. Lodii taught in Lviv, and Balugianskii at Pest. In Russia they were considered by virtue of their intelligence, character, and methods of instruction to be "Germans", for Russia sought to introduce the pedagogical system of German universities.

Finally, on 8 February 1819 the Emperor authorized the Minister of Public Enlightenment, Prince Aleksandr Nikolaevich Golitsyn (1773-1844), to transform the Chief Pedagogical Institute into the St. Petersburg University. In reality, this was more a "renaming" than a "transformation", for the Institute's structural subdivisions, instructional and administrative personnel, students, and courses were retained without change.[9] The University operated under "Initial Rules" prepared by the Administrator of the Petersburg Educational District, Sergei Semenovich Uvarov (1786-1855), as the prototype of the future Charter of the University.

On 14 February 1819 at the "Twelve Colleges" and in the presence of senior governmental officials the solemn inauguration of the newly-transformed or renamed institution was celebrated. The University was given four units of the Twelve Colleges previously occupied by the Chief Pedagogical Institute.[10] This occasion constituted the completion in the first quarter of the nineteenth century of the reformation of University legal education in Russia.

The University, as in its earlier incarnation, had three faculties: historical-philological, philosophical-legal, and medical-mathematical. Later the faculties were subdivided into divisions in order to encourage the enrollment of more narrowly-specialized students. The law of nations was singled out for the first time as a separate instructional discipline.

The same two Chairs were carried over from the Chief Pedagogical Institute: the Chair of General Laws and the Chair of Positive Laws. The first was filled by two professors – A. P. Kunitsyn (1783-1841) and V. G. Kukolnik – and offered, as before, courses on private law, State law, and the law of nations. In the documents

[8] Quoted from N. N. Zherve, «... Поставлен им краеугольгый камень ... ». А. П. Куницын в истории Санкт-Петербургского университета» ["… The Cornerstone is Placed …". A. P. Kunitsyn in the History of St. Petersburg University], Санкт-Петербургский университет [St. Petersburg University], no. 15 (2013).

[9] The Chief Pedagogical Institute had trained students for the teaching profession in the variously named primary and secondary schools in Russia.

[10] In 1823 the University removed from the "Twelve Colleges" to a building on the corner of Kabinet Street and Zvenigorod Street, where it remained until 1837, when it returned to the slightly renovated Twelve Colleges.

and literature of the time, the chair often was called the "Chair of Natural and Positive Law and the Law of Nations".[11] It was, however, nomenclature not used in the 1804 University Statute or the 1819 Imperial Edict, neither of which made provision for a Chair of International Law. In fact, international law figured in the instructional plans of two chairs. The Chair of General Laws taught the philosophy or theory of international law, and the Chair of Positive Law addressed international positive, or normative, law.

Lectures commenced in the University on 5 November 1819 for a student body consisting of about 70 students with stipends financed by the State and 24 fee-paying students, of whom 13 were enrolled in the Faculty of Philology and Law. Initially, the academic year coincided with the calendar year, with a later transition to an August-June academic year having an interval of a month between semesters. Completion of the first degree required three years, of which the first two in the field of law introduced students to European jurisprudence and foreign languages – French, German, and English. Lessons commenced at 08:00 until 18:00 hours with a two-hour break at mid-day. The first graduation occurred in 1823; twenty-two of the stipendiary students and four fee-paying students received their degrees.

By 1837, 365 individuals had been awarded degrees, of whom 193 were awarded the degree of "kandidat" (candidate) and the remainder "ordinary student".[12]

The Chair of General Laws in the Chief Pedagogical Institute and St. Petersburg University was held by P. D. Lodii from 1803 to 1817 and again from 1824 to 1829; during the period 1817 to 1824, Kunitsyn occupied the Chair.

§3.2. *Birth of the Russian St. Petersburg School of International Law*

Petr Dmitrievich Lodii *(4 May 1764, b. village of Zboi, near Munkache (Galicia, Austrian Empire, now Mukachevo, Trans-Carpathian Region, Ukraine) – 10 June 1829, d. St. Petersburg).*

Life and career. Lodii was well-known in his day as a philosopher, theologian, logician, jurist, and mathematician.[13] A Carpathian Rus, he graduated from a lycée in the town of Ungvar (now Uzhgorod, Ukraine) and the Lviv (then, Lemberg) University. In 1784 Lodii was chosen in a competitive selection process to be

11 This nomenclature was extensively used in Europe. The first Professor at University College London in 1826, John Austin (1790-1859), was appointed as the "Professor of Jurisprudence and the Law of Nations".

12 The degree of "kandidat" [кандидат] was conferred on students who graduated with "distinction"; those without distinction received the degree of "ordinary student" [действительный студент]. The University Statute of 1884 abolished this classification.

13 On Lodii, see G. Gennadi, Справочный словарь о русских писателях и ученых, умерших в XVIII и XIX столетиях, и Список русских книг с 1725 по 1825 г. [Reference Dictionary on Russian Writers and Scholars Who Died in the XVIII and XIX Centuries, and List of Russian Books from 1725 to 1825] (Berlin, 1880), II, p. 246-247; V. M. Syrykh, Правовая наука и юридическая идеология России: энциклопедический словарь биографий [Legal Science and Legal Ideology of Russia: Encyclopedic Dictionary of Biographies] (M., 2009), I, pp. 419-420.

the Professor of Logic, Metaphysics, and Moral Philosophy of the Division of Theology and Philosophy of Lviv University. He was awarded in 1801 the degree of doctor of fine arts, laws, and theology, whereupon he moved on to Krakow University; there he held two chairs: the Chair of Philosophy and the Chair of Pure and Applied Mathematics.

On 1 August 1803 he accepted an invitation to join the St. Petersburg Pedagogical Institute in the Chair of Theoretical and Practical Philosophy, also lecturing on natural law and criminal law. In 1806 he simultaneously served as Professor of Natural Law at the School of Jurisprudence in St. Petersburg, a position he retained until 1812. Between 1817 and 1827 he acted as the Director of the St. Petersburg Commercial School.[14] From 1819 he held the Chair of Logic, Psychology, and Moral Philosophy at St. Petersburg University.[15]

On 22 December 1819 Lodii was confirmed as the Dean of the Faculty of Philosophy and Law (after M. A. Balugianskii, the first Dean was elevated to the post of Rector of St. Petersburg University). In 1821 he transferred to the Chair of General Laws and remained there for five and a half years. On 28 August 1825 he resigned the Deanship and requested to return to the Chair of Philosophy, a petition apparently not acted upon.[16] In that same year he was appointed a Distinguished Professor. The Central State Historical Archive in St. Petersburg contains extensive materials on the posts he held, petitions and requests for a salary increase, loans which he obtained to support a large family, requests for leave, and the like.

Lodii was buried at the Smolensk Russian Orthodox Cemetery in St. Petersburg.[17]

As a scholar and educator, Lodii vigorously opposed prohibitions being discussed on the teaching of philosophy. In his view, such prohibitions or limitations would be contrary to "sound reason and the rules of logic". Minimizing the role of God in the universe, Lodii objected to reducing the role of science to being the "servant of theology". In his view, the world surrounding us exists in and of itself,

[14] At the suggestion of Empress Consort Maria Fedorovna (1759-1828), the Ministry of Public Enlightenment appointed Lodii as an inspector of the classes of the Society for Noble Girls and the St. Catherine School.

[15] ЦГИА СПб, fond 14, opis 3, file 5959.

[16] ЦГИА СПб, fond 14, opis 1, file 448.

[17] See the obituary in Северная пчела [Northern Bee], no. 86 (1829).

"outside our intellect", and human knowledge arises as a consequence of the impact of the external world on organs of feelings. Human knowledge rests on this knowledge, and with the assistance of thought man reflects the world more profoundly, discovers its laws, penetrates its natural laws of nature and the objective laws of society.[18]

Lodii's views were viewed by the authorities as casting doubt on the foundations of the State and became the basis for persecuting him. His book on logic, written for student use, was called "dangerous in profanity and destructive principles" and removed as an instructional tool.[19] Two years after his death, a denunciation of Lodii submitted to the Emperor accused Lodii of preparing the philosophical foundations for the uprising of the Decembrists in 1825.

Republication of Lodii's book was prohibited, and he himself noted with regret that the year 1821 (the year of "persecutions by the Ministry" of professors of the University) saw him removed from teaching the philosophical sciences and transferred to a new post – occupying the Chair of General Laws (natural, political, and law of nations), having replaced the disgraced A. P. Kunitsyn, who was dismissed from the University.[20] When teaching the law of nations, Lodii used the general treatises of Karl Anton Freiherr von Martini (1726-1800), as well as Franz von Zeiller (1751-1828).[21]

Lodii was at heart a philosopher more than a jurist, and the transfer to the Chair of General Laws constrained his professional development. In a period when the teaching of natural law was being persecuted, he was not enthusiastic about the

18 Having learned in January 1825 that the Chief Board of the School had adopted a decision to secretly pursue a "Matter of the Harmfulness of Teaching the Sciences of Philosophy", he prepared "Comments" giving a searing critique of the efforts to prohibit the teaching of philosophy, history, and natural law in Russia by replacing them with the Holy Scripture and subordinating the teaching of the sciences to religion.

19 P. D. Lodii, Логические наставления, руководствующие к познанию и различению истинного от ложного [Logical Instructions Guiding Cognition and Differentiation of the True from the False] (Spb., 1815). See E. N. Chernysheva, «П. Д. Лодий и его вклад в становление философского университетского образования в России» [P. D. Lodii and His Contribution to the Development of Philosophical University Education in Russia], Вестник Российского государственного торгово-экономического университета [Herald of Russian State Trade-Economic University], no. 7-8 (2014), p. 149.

20 ЦГИА СПб, fond 14, opis 2, file 108. Lodii was to teach pursuant to this transfer: "General Laws: 1) Natural law, according to the manual of Karl Anton de Martini under the title *De lege Naturali positiones*, Vienna, 1782; 2) Criminal law, according to the theory of Dr. Paul Anselm Feuerbach, translated by him into the Russian language, 1820". Karl Anton Freiherr von Martini produced this student manual in 1778 and it went through several editions. The text in Latin will have been challenging for St. Petersburg students, although Lodii will have lectured in Russian. Paul Johann Anselm von Feuerbach (1775-1833) wrote a seminal textbook on the general part of the criminal law in Germany (1801) and was the principal draftsman of the Bavarian Criminal Code (1813), which became the model for criminal legislation in several German states and was closely followed by Russian jurists. As noted, Lodii translated Feuerbach's work into the Russian language.

21 For the Russian language version translated by Lodii, see Franz von Zeiller, Естественное частное право [Natural Private Law] (Spb., 1809).

legal sciences, including the law of nations. Martini was a conservative Austrian jurist whose views often did not coincide with those of Lodii. The announcement of St. Petersburg University for 1824 advertised Lodii as teaching "Public Law and the Law of Nations" according to the textbook of Karl Anton de Martini, *Positiones de jure cevitatum et gentium*.[22]

When imparting knowledge on natural law, including the law of nations, Lodii proceeded from his own general social and philosophical views. He distinguished between positive and natural laws. Positive laws emanate from the will or documentation of the supreme ruler. Natural laws flow from the essence of the State and are comprehended by reason. He believed that the principles of philosophical law were the theories of positive norms, and he systematized them chronologically as they emerged. Natural philosophical law was founded on the real properties of the human spirit, the psychological nature of man, wherein lay the reason for that law being binding and true.

His international legal views Lodii set out in a manuscript entitled in Russian: "The Natural Law of Nations", but it was never published; the manuscript has not been found and may have been destroyed. Consequently, Lodii's views on the legal foundations of inter-State relations can only be extrapolated indirectly from his general theoretical works, although given that he also used Martini and Zeiller as textbooks, the views of German writers will have been represented.

In 1828 Lodii published one of the major works based on his lectures: "Theory of General Laws". He reflected on the general concepts and tenets of law, devoting a significant part to the law of nations.[23] In the Preface he noted that, with the approval of the leadership of his institution he had drawn upon the Martini but without strictly adhering to the sequence of his work. He also had used works by Christian Wolff (1679-1754), Hugo Grotius (1583-1645), Samuel Pufendorf (1632-1694), and other European scholars. He expressed the hope that his work would be useful to law students and would guide them later in life.

He endeavored to explain the rights and duties of State authorities and the individual in the life of the State. He addressed the concept of the State and the universal law of States (law of nations), the purpose and origin of the State, the external and internal functions of the State, the various branches of the State, the special rights of the ruler, and an unusual treatment of human rights.

Part One of the book set out human rights "in private form" and, in Part Two, human rights "in State form". In his view "just as in any society, so in any State, laws, rights, and respective duties must exist from which the purposes of the State and State decrees must be derived". Universal, or public, laws are in essence those by which various relations are determined. Laws common for all States are called universal, but if are only for some States, they will merely be private (Introduction,

[22] Lodii lectured until 1829 as follows: Wednesday and Saturday, 08:00 to 10:00; Saturday, 16:00 to 18:00.

[23] P. D. Lodii, Теория общих прав, содержащая в себе философское учение о естественном всеобщем государственном праве [Theory of Natural Laws, Containing the Philosophical Doctrine on Natural Universal State Law] (Spb., 1828). 450 p.

§3). The right of subjects come from three sources: the sensible-reasonable nature of man; civil society; and the positive laws of the State. Among the natural rights arising from the sensible-reasonable nature of man Lodii identified: (1) the right to be sensible-reasonable; (2) the right to life and health; (3) the right to morality and well-being; (4) the right to education; (5) the right to an honorable name.

In the relations between subjects and the State Lodii believed there should be recognized: (1) the right of subjects to autonomous actions that do not affect the interests of the State; (2) the right to demand from the State the defense of violated rights; (3) the duty of the State to ensure the execution of decisions to the benefit of persons whose rights were violated.

Lodii distinguished between natural and positive laws. The first emanate "from the essence of the State and are understood by reason", whereas the second originates from "clerical provisions or the will of the ruler". Law "in State form" may be "internal", "public", or "external", "extra-societal"; that is, State law or the law of nations. He analyzed various models and forms of rule: democracy, aristocracy, monarchy, and mixed forms, as well as ways of achieving the purposes of State power: through elections, use of force, various means of removal from power, on the basis of subjects using the rights with respect to the State, among others. A merit of Lodii's work is that he sought to theoretically substantiate, using modern terminology, the foundations of a rule-of-law society in the Russian Empire. According to Lodii, the law of nations "explains the mutual rights and duties of independent States as regarded by moral persons living in a state of equality and independence".

Having philosophically contemplated the general foundations of law, he elaborated a doctrine on natural universal State law, subdividing it into internal and external. When defining the subject-matter of his work, he wrote: "The aggregate of universal or public laws, rights, and corresponding duties is called Natural Universal or Public State Law (*jus naturale Universale vel Publicum*" (§4). As he developed this position, Lodii concluded that universal State law had a natural origin on the premise that all people are, by nature, equal. They are united under one supreme power in order to achieve general security and prosperity. Lodii drew from this that one of the basic purposes of the State is to ensure the external security of every member of society within the State and the State itself as a whole in its international relations. By security Lodii understood a condition in which both members of society and the State are not threatened by "any evil"; that is, there is no danger or threat to their existence. Universal State law, he wrote, "teaches us to comply with law, without which no external prosperity can exist".

As noted above, Lodii's work on the natural law of nations was unpublished and has been lost. But students in the Law Faculty could use specialized works on international law by foreign writers translated into the Russian language.[24]

[24] See J. L. Klüber (1762-1836), Новейшее европейское народное право [Contemporary European Law of Nations] (M., 1828).

In aggregate, Lodii made major contributions as an original scholar and translator of foreign works.[25] An individual of erudition and encyclopedic knowledge, gifted in many fields, he was an important figure in the early history of St. Petersburg University. With his death in 1829, the teaching of international law ceased completely. From 1829 to 1835 the Chair of Natural, Political, and Law of Nations was vacant.[26] After several years, his successor became a junior rising scholar, V. K. Elpatevskii.

Aleksandr Petrovich Kunitsyn *(16(27) November 1783, b. Koi, Kashinskii uezd, Tver Governate – d. 1(13) July 1840, St. Petersburg). Kunitsyn established himself as a leading legal scholar, the first "native Russian" lecturer on international law at the Pedagogical Institute and University in St. Petersburg.*[27]

Upon graduating from the Tver Seminary in 1803, Kunitsyn enrolled at the Chief Pedagogical Institute in St. Petersburg, choosing the Faculty of Moral and Political Sciences. He was invited to remain after graduation in 1807 to prepare for the professoriate. Being among the twelve best students, he was chosen to travel abroad at State expense and attend lectures at Göttingen University in Germany. He also pursued studies in jurisprudence and diplomacy at the Sorbonne (Paris) and Heidelberg.

Having returned from abroad in early 1811,[28] Kunitsyn was appointed as a lecturer at the Chief Pedagogical Institute.[29] At this time preparations were underway to open and staff the Tsarskoe selo Lycée.[30] Kunitsyn passed the necessary examination for appointment and from 10 October 1811 was confirmed in the post of junior scientific assistant-lecturer of moral sciences in the Chair of Moral Phi-

[25] Lodii was awarded the Orders of St. Vladimir, 3d degree, and St. Anna, 2d degree. For services in organizing the pedagogical process, Emperor Alexander I gave him several diamond signet rings.

[26] S. V. Rozhdestvenskii, «Санкт-Петербургский университет в первое столетие его деятельность. 1819-1919» [St. Petersburg University in the First Century of its Activity 1819-1919], in Материалы по истории Санкт-Петербургского университета 1819-1835 [Materials on the History of St. Petersburg University 1819-1835] (Petrograd, 1919), I, p. 36; V. V. Grigorev, Императорский С.-Петербургский университет в течение первых пятидесяти лет его существования. Историческая записка [Imperial St. Petersburg University During the First Fifty Years of its Existence. Historical Note] (Spb., 1870), p. 232; P. A. Pletnev, Первое двадцатипятилетие императорского Санктпетербургского университета [First Two Decades of Imperial St. Petersburg University] (Spb., 1844), p. 164.

[27] On Kunitsyn, see Julia Berest, *The Emergence of Russian Liberalism: Alexander Kunitsyn in Context, 1783-1840* (2011); S. A. Koluntaev, in Syrykh, note 13 above, pp. I, pp. 387-388; Berest, "Aleksandr Kunitsyn: Pioneer of Natural Law in Russia", in Paul Valliere and Randall A. Poole (eds.), *Law and the Christian Tradition in Modern Russia* (2022), pp. 93-110.

[28] ЦГИА СПб, fond 139, opis 1, file 563.

[29] ЦГИА СПб, fond 139, opis 1, file 587.

[30] ЦГИА СПб, fond 139, opis 1, file 934.

losophy and Jurisprudence.[31] On 19 October 1811 he was assigned by the Director of the Lycée to prepare an address for the opening ceremony to be attended by the Emperor. Kunitsyn's remarkable oration, entitled "Instruction to Pupils", so impressed the Emperor that he awarded Kunitsyn the Cross of Vladimir.[32]

From 1816 to 1820 Kunitsyn was Professor of Moral, Political, and Legal Sciences at the Lycée. He is considered to have had an impact on the worldview of students, among them Aleksandr Sergeevich Pushkin (1799-1837) and the future Decembrists – an impact that Pushkin memorialized in a verse.[33] In 1817 Kunitsyn accepted a second appointment, this time as Professor at the Chair of General Laws at the Chief Pedagogical Institute,[34] replacing Lodii. When the Institute became St. Petersburg University, Kunitsyn held the Chair of General Laws, and within the academic cycle of courses offered twelve subjects: logic, psychology, ethics, natural law, Russian civil law, criminal law, financial law, and others, including the law of nations.

Although his book on natural law had been approved by the censor and published by instruction of the Minister of Enlightenment, Kunitsyn was dismissed from St. Petersburg University and the Tsarskoe selo Lycée in March 1821 because his book on natural law was deemed to be a "collection of pernicious false notions". He was allowed to continue to lecture at the Page Corps but forbidden to lecture in all other educational institutions of Russia. He found employment at the Ministry of Finances. Having fallen into disgrace for several years and not able to engage in his calling, Kunitsyn sent several petitions to the Emperor about allowing him to work. Ultimately, after five years, Kunitsyn succeeded in achieving permission.

With the accession to the throne of Emperor Nicholas I in 1826, Kunitsyn become involved in the greatest systematization and codification of legislation project ever undertaken in the world – the preparation of the Complete Collection of Russian Law from 1649 to 1825 and, on the basis thereof, the preparation of the Digest of Laws of the Russian Empire, which began to appear from 1832. Relations improved eventually with St. Petersburg University. On 27 January 1838 the Council of the University, after the "dark seven years" of the terms of the external guardians had ended in the persons of Mikhail Leontevich Magnitskii (1778-1844)

[31] ЦГИА СПб, fond 139, opis 1, file 971.

[32] TThe text was published and circulated to universities, academies, and other institutions throughout the realm. See A. P. Kunitsyn, Наставление воспитанникам [Instruction to Pupils] (Spb., 1811). 8 p. Passed by the censor on 7 December 1811. Also published in a volume entitled: Речи, произнесенным при открытии Императорского Сарско-Сельского лицея [Addresses Delivered During the Opening of the Imperial Tsarskoe Selo Lycée] (Spb., 1811), pp. 5-12. See I. Iu. Fomenko (ed.), Сводный каталог русской книги: 1801-1825 [Composite Catalogue of the Russian Book: 1801-1825] (Moscow, 2007), II, p. 305, no. 4212.

[33] Entitled "To the Lycée Anniversary 19 October 1825", Pushkin wrote:
To Kunitsyn, tribute of heart and wine!
He created us, he nurtured our flame,
He laid a foundation stone
And kindled a bright lamp.

[34] ЦГИА СПб, fond 139, opis 1, file 1736.

and Dmitrii Pavlovich Runich (1778-1860), elected Kunitsyn an Honorary Member of the University.[35] In that same year, Kunitsyn was appointed Chairman of the Commission for the Printing of the Complete Collection of Laws of the Russian Empire.

On 27 April 1840 Kunitsyn was appointed Director of the Department of Spiritual Affairs of Foreign Profession of the Ministry of Internal Affairs of the Russian Empire. Six weeks later he passed away and was buried at the Georgiev Cemetery in St. Petersburg (Bolshaia Okhta).

Kunitsyn's contributions to the general theory of State and law and to State law have been extensively analyzed in Russian legal historiography. Virtually ignored is that Kunitsyn formulated his own vision of legal relations between States and elaborated many fundamental positions of Russian international legal doctrine. Kunitsyn's academic career at the Tsarskoe selo Lycée happened to coincide with Napoleon's invasion of the Russian Empire in 1812. He reacted by publishing patriotic articles in Russian media: "Message to the Russians"[36] and "Notes on the Present War",[37] in which he touched upon issues of a just or unjust war and the lawfulness and unlawfulness of means of waging war.

In these articles Kunitsyn demonstrated that "just wars are in essence the legal use of force for the maintenance of right". "Force to resist force" will be just and necessary for the defenders in the event of an attack. Kunitsyn pointed out that the war between Russia and France was just because it was being waged against an attacking enemy in order to preserve the independence of the Fatherland. The war of France against Russia was unjust because it pursued predatory purposes, was not waged in the interests of the French people, but was an adventure of Napoleon Bonaparte.

Kunitsyn described Napoleon as a tyrant, the destroyer of the national (with respect to the vanquished peoples) and political (with respect to the French people themselves) freedoms. The French cannot be victorious because they "spill their own blood for the cause of their tyrant"; victory will be for the Russians because they are fighting for the freedom of their Motherland.[38]

As a proponent of natural-law doctrine in the first third of the nineteenth century, Kunitsyn, just as virtually all adherents to this approach, considered that the law of nations was the application of norms to relations between States by which individual natural persons are guided in the state of nature; that is, before States arose. Kunitsyn directly touched upon issues of the law of nations in his first sci-

[35] ЦГИА СПб, fond 14, opis 1, file 4331.

[36] A. P. Kunitsyn, «Послание к русским» [Message to the Russians], Сын отечества [Son of the Fatherland], no. 5 (1812), pp. 186-187.

[37] Kunitsyn, «Замечания на нынешнюю войну» [Notes on the Present War], Сын отечества [Son of the Fatherland], no. 8 (1812), pp. 45-48.

[38] Kunitsyn, note 36 above, pp. 186-187.

entific work on the representation of the mutual linkage of State knowledge, which became one of the earliest Russian scientific studies on the law of nations.[39]

In Part Two, a special section was devoted to the law of nations – "On the Means of Private and General Security". Kunitsyn saw the State as a moral person which had its own rights and duties in the world. In order to secure its rights, the State "must sacredly comply with its duties because, according to the rules of natural justice, whosoever violates another's right gives just cause for the other not to spare the rights belonging thereto". From this he concluded:

> A State, in attacking other peoples, moves away from its chief purpose in two respects. First, in acting against the laws of reason, it makes an immoral essence, and deprives itself of its own rights, and consequently, the right to a secure existence. Second, unjust offenses thereof with other peoples force them to lawful defense; that is, to repulse force by force, consequently, placing other in the danger to which it has itself been subjected.

Kunitsyn proposed a classification of the law of nations, dividing it into two types: natural and positive. The "natural law of nations", according to Kunitsyn, is the systematic study of conditions under which the community life of independent States is possible. Just as other proponents of natural law, Kunitsyn idealized it, but acknowledged the problems of implementing natural-law principles. He believed that because the "rules of natural justice are not always sufficient to resolve disputes between nations" and they "may be rejected partly through misunderstanding, partly through intent and self-interest", the positive actions of the authorities of States are necessary. Such actions of States, in Kunitsyn's view, are positive international conditions and treaties created by them.

From this Kunitsyn derived a second type of the law of nations – the positive law of nations, which in his view was a "science" of collecting positive provisions determining the mutual links of peoples and States. However, Kunitsyn considered that "prudent behavior" and even "strict compliance of both rules of natural justice and of positive provisions may not always protect a State from unjust attacks by its neighbors". But inasmuch as "peoples do not have a supreme power over them which would resolve quarrels between them, then in the event of an unjust attack they must resort to means of natural defense". In so doing a State must be in "continual readiness for war, but much more advantageous for it is perpetual peace rather than anticipated victory".

The classification suggested by Kunitsyn was acceptable in substance, but the arguments in substantiation thereof both from the logical and substantive-terminological point of view raised questions.

Kunitsyn favored the regulation of relations between States by treaty: "from the long-term relations of nations conditions, agreements, and treaties arise be-

39 Kunitsyn, Изображение взаимной связи государственных сведений [Depiction of the Mutual Link of State Knowledge] (Spb., 1817). 30 p.

tween them by means of which their rights become better known and the performance of duties more reliable".[40]

However, the best-known of Kunitsyn's works was devoted to natural law, in two volumes.[41] The lack at the time of instructional manuals for the legal and moral sciences inspired him to try to fill the gap. As a proponent of natural law influenced by Jean-Jacques Rousseau (1712-1778) and Immanuel Kant (1724-1804), Kunitsyn became the first Russian jurist to publish his own work on the subject.[42]

Following the natural law approach, Kunitsyn divided law into private and public. To public law he relegated mutual relations of the authorities of various States and the rights and duties of States to other States and their subjects. He considered both States and natural persons to be subjects of the law of nations.

In Book One, Kunitsyn set out "pure" natural law, and in Book Two, "applied" natural law. Kunitsyn subdivided "applied" natural law into private law, public (or State) law, and the law of nations (international law). A rather substantial special section was devoted to the law of nations (79 paragraphs) – Part IV "Law of Nations" of Book Two (§512 to 590), which included an Introduction and two chapters. Chapter I addressed the law of nations in an "unconditional state", and Chapter II – the law of nations in a "conditional state".

Analyzing international relations and law through the prism of natural law, Kunitsyn asserted: "The State, regarded with respect to other States and private persons, is called a nation" (§512). Here Kunitsyn set out his understanding of the law of nations, considering it as the "mutual rights and duties of nations", and made the first attempt to structure a system of knowledge about it: "The mutual rights and duties of a nation arise either according to general principles of law or according to conditions and treaties which nations conclude between themselves". The law of nations he then divided into international natural law and international positive law (§513).

Then Kunitsyn separated the state of nations (States) into two types:

(1) "unconditional state", in which States are regarded as autonomous persons, an abstraction, without rights and duties having been acquired by them;

(2) "conditional state", in which States are considered from "their rights and duties, from their free acts which occurred".

From the foregoing, Kunitsyn concluded there were two types of international law: "Why the law of nations is divided into unconditional and conditional".

40 Ibid., p. 21.

41 Kunitsyn, Естественное право [Natural Law] (Spb., 1818-1820). 2 vols.

42 Grigorev wrote that Kunitsyn's work on natural law "testifies to the great talent of the author, strong logic, and remarkable scientific autonomy for that time". Grigorev, note 26 above, p. 12. The foreign professors invited to Russian academic posts in the eighteenth century did produce works on natural law; see especially Strube de Piermont.

The *rights of nations in an unconditional state* are the initial (later to be called "basic") rights of the State "which emanate from the very concept of the essence thereof". Any State as a moral person, Kunitsyn believed, had the following rights: I. To exist as an independent society; II. To act or use its power for arbitration purposes; III. To achieve prosperity (§516).

Supreme sovereign power, in Kunitsyn's view, was an inseparable indicator of a State. He singled out a number of tasks confronting the supreme power. These included defense of the State and its independence and limits, defense of the personal and material rights of subjects, compliance with justice. In performing these tasks, and also defending rights and freedoms, the supreme power may use only legal means to achieve them. The supreme power concludes alliances and peace treaties with other nations and enters into other international relations. In the event of danger, the supreme power should use the forces of the State "to demand remuneration and punishment of other nations". Therein, according to Kunitsyn, resides the law of war.

The supreme power might, when necessary, cede part of the territory of the State if this was caused by the duty to be concerned both about the security of the inhabitants of individual territories and those who would be saved by this cession. Kunitsyn believed that the authorities "often have the duty to extend their boundaries by war when there is no other means to defend the existence, the independence, of the State and the integrity of its boundaries". Moreover, the State might by a treaty combine with another State, forming a single whole. Thus, the supreme power might either increase its territory or cede part of it away.

The *rights of nations in a conditional state* are acquired rights of the State: either to actions or to things – ownerless or someone's ownership, but obtained with the consent of others. The character of these acquired rights one may judge from Chapter II, "On the Rights of Nations in a Conditional State", structurally consisting of four sections: I. On Possessions; II. On the Treaties of Nations; III. On Embassies; IV. On the Rights of a Nation During War.

States as moral persons may transfer their rights to one another by joint agreement and assume "mutual duties", consolidating this in "public or nations' treaties" (§538). Kunitsyn formulated the provisions on the procedure for the conclusion and types of treaties rather precisely, including those concluded during war, the bases of embassy activity, and considered in detail the occasions and methods for waging war, the conditions for the conclusion of a peace treaty, and the legal force thereof.

Kunitsyn distinguished between just and unjust wars. War, he said, "is necessary and just when there is no other means to defend the existence, the independence, of a State and the integrity of its limits".[43] In his treatise on natural law, Kunitsyn acknowledged the right of a State to go to war when offense was caused to it, but laid down two conditions for a just war: "An offense then only gives the right to coercion when 1) it was evident and undoubted; 2) when the offender refuses to give satisfaction" (§583). In a state of nature, Kunitsyn wrote, States conduct themselves in a rather hostile manner. A predatory State, just as a wild beast,

43 Kunitsyn, «Лекции» [Lectures], Красный архив [Red Archive], no. 1 (1937), p. 107.

attacks a neighboring State according to the principle: "You are weak – this means you are at fault". He was convinced that in such instances war against another nation was unjust, and therefore the guilt lies not on the nation, not on the subjects, but on the government of this nation because the subjects participating in the war merely execute the will of their supreme ruler.

As a persuasive adept of natural law theory, Kunitsyn supported the theory of the social contract. The latter meant the legal defense of human rights and freedoms. The initial "natural" equality of all people meant the formal equality of all before the law. Therefore, Kunitsyn opposed any forms of suppression of the "natural freedom" of man. He believed that violence and the possession of other people were inadmissible. He relegated military aggression and colonialism in international life to forms of this nature.

Considering the context of the early nineteenth century, Kunitsyn's views on the State, international relations, and international law were distinctive for their originality and novelty, their progressiveness, and their respect for the individual. Given the autocratic nature and existence of serfdom in Russia, Kunitsyn substantiated theoretically the need to affirm the free status and development of man, society, and the State. Grabar had a high opinion of Kunitsyn's contribution to the science of international law, considering his works as one of the early Russian manuals on international law.[44]

Soon after publication, Kunitsyn's work on natural law was prohibited for allegedly containing harmful doctrines. He was dismissed from the University and removed from all teaching positions by the Ministry of Spiritual Affairs and Public Enlightenment.[45] The book, printed in 1000 copies, was taken away from the author, booksellers, libraries, and private individuals and then burned. The book had its official admirers. The Director of the Tsarskoe selo Lycée, Egor Antonovich Engelhardt (1775-1862), sent a copy to Emperor Alexander I via the Minister of Public Enlightenment, A. N. Golitsyn, immediately after publication. The Minister, as was the custom in those times, sent the book out for an assessment of quality to the Learned Committee of the Chief Administration of Schools. Academician N. I. Fus performed the evaluation and found the book to be worthy of presentation to the Emperor as the "first book on this subject-matter in the Russian language. Written systematically and according to a good plan …".[46]

D. P. Runich, Administrator of the Petersburg Education District, submitted a special memorandum to the Learned Committee urging that Kunitsyn's book be "subject to prohibition (as a textbook) and without loss of time should be removed from use … because the public teaching of sciences according to atheist systems

[44] Grabar, *The History of International Law in Russia 1647-1917: A Bio-Biographical Study*, transl. W. E. Butler (Oxford, 1990), pp. 251-252.

[45] B. V. Emelianov, «Царизм против естественного права (три эпизода гонений)» [Tsarism Against Natural Law (Three Episodes of Persecution)], Вестник Санкт-Петербургского университета [Herald of St Petersburg University], XXXI, no 4 (2015), pp. 122-123.

[46] See G. V. Zhirkov, История цензуры в России XIX-XX вв. [History of Censorship in Russia XIX-XX Centuries] (M., 2001).

cannot occur ...".[47] The Learned Committee of the Ministry adopted a decree which provided that the theory of natural law set out by Kunitsyn in his lectures and textbook was a false doctrine: the origin of supreme power had been proved to originate not from God, but from the natural conditions of the life-being of people.

In the end, natural law as a science was persecuted and the teaching thereof was suspended until a new Statute on Russian Universities was adopted in 1835. After the dismissal of the disgraced Kunitsyn from the St. Petersburg University and elsewhere, the teaching of the law of nations passed temporarily to Professor P. D. Lodii.[48] When Lodii passed away in 1829, the teaching of the law of nations as part of the course of natural law was continued by V. K. Elpatevskii.

Vasilii Kondratevich Elpatevskii *(1790 – 22 January 1854, d. St. Petersburg). College assessor, lecturer, Chair of General Laws (Natural, Positive, Law of Nations), St. Petersburg University.*

Life and career. There is little biographical data on Elpatevskii. The biographical reference manuals contain brief general entries;[49] there are few materials in the archives of St. Petersburg University. The State Historical Archive of St. Petersburg, however, does have records not previously consulted by historians of international law.

Elpatevskii enrolled as a fee-paying student in 1819, at the age of 29, as a member of the entering class of the St. Petersburg University in the Faculty of Philosophy and Law. He graduated in 1823 with the gold medal (first in his class) and the degree of candidate of laws. He was invited to remain at the Chair of Natural Law, Political Law, and Law of Nations headed by P. D. Lodii to prepare for the professoriate. On 7 March 1823 he was appointed a lecturer in law at the Petersburg Higher School.[50] From 1828 he became a lecturer in Roman law at the Noble Boarding School attached to the St. Petersburg University (a closed-type secondary school for the nobility).[51]

Elpatevskii submitted in 1830 a work to the Faculty entitled "On the Procedure for a Civil Society in General and the Procedure for Proceedings in Court Cases";[52] the Faculty was duly impressed and conferred on him the title of junior associate

[47] Quoted from A. Koire, Философия и национальная проблема в России начала XIX века [Philosophy and the Nationality Problem in Russia at the Beginning of the XIX Century] (M., 2003), pp. 74-75. Also see N. M. Korkunov, История философии права [History of the Philosophy of Law] (Spb., 1915), p. 344.

[48] ЦГИА СПб, fond 14, opis 3, file 108.

[49] See Pletnev, note 26 above, p. 30; Grigorev, note 26 above, pp. 43, 49, 53, 59; Gennadi, note 11 above, I, p. 342; Записки и дневник А. Никитенко [Notes and Diary of A. Nikitenko] (Spb., 1893), I, p. 200. Elpatevskii is not mentioned in Grabar.

[50] ЦГИА СПб, fond 14, opis 3, file 590; opis 6, file 60.

[51] ЦГИА СПб, fond 14, opis 1, file 1435.

[52] ЦГИА СПб, fond 14, opis 1, file 2323.

lecturer with the right to lecture at the Chair of General Laws[53] previously headed by Lodii and established his remuneration.[54] That same year Elpatevskii lectured initially on universal logic and philosophical moral teachings,[55] and then on natural, international, and criminal law. Archival sources indicate that Elpatevskii was an excellent pedagogue.

Elpatevskii left no published works. The archives contain a detailed note of his lectures on criminal law;[56] these materials enable educated guesses to be made about his general scientific positions that he in all likelihood would have set out in his course on general laws, including the law of nations. In his lectures Elpatevskii drew a sharp distinction between natural (or philosophical) and positive law. Philosophical law, which he drew from the idea of practical reason, comprised a legal theory whose task was to create the foundation for legal science and legislation. Positive law was the science concerning real rights based on legal norms created by States.

Of importance for the science of the law of nations was his thesis that one should avoid "adopting general and immutable truths and rights provided for certain nations which have been adapted to their circumstances". In his view, one should not forget that the task of the theory of law cannot be the erection of structures of legal science completely ready. It merely suggested their foundation, providing for the remainder to the science of positive law, which is called upon "to erect this building on the basis of an analysis of public laws and norms".[57] Nonetheless, Elpatevskii was unable to instill a fresh spirit into the teaching of natural law, including the law of nations. After numerous verifications and persecutions, by behest of the Emperor on 23 April 1833 the course of lectures on natural law was suspended, which meant *de facto* prohibited.[58] The survey of the University for the academic year 1833/34 reported that Elpatevskii had left the University.[59] In 1834 Elpatevskii was dismissed from the University.[60]

[53] ЦГИА СПб, fond 14, opis 1, file 2387.

[54] ЦГИА СПб, fond 14, opis 1, file 2660. The salary was 1,000 rubles per year.

[55] ЦГИА СПб, fond 14, opis 1, file 2467.

[56] The notes were kept by E. V. Passek, a student of Elpatevskii, and repose in the archive of the Imperial Kharkov University. See G. S. Feldshtein, Главные течения в истории науки уголовного права в России [Chief Trends in the History of the Science of Criminal Law in Russia] (Iaroslavl, 1909), p. 495.

[57] Cited in ibid., p. 496.

[58] Emelianov, note 45 above, pp. 119-126.

[59] Краткое обозрение действий Императорского С.-Петербургского университета и его округа за прошлый 1833-1834 академический год [Concise Survey of Actions of the Imperial St. Petersburg University and the District Thereof for the Past 1833-1834 Academic Year] (Spb., 1834), p. 6.

[60] ЦГИА СПб, fond 14, opis 2, file 118.

After leaving the University, Elpatevskii found employment as a lecturer at the Imperial St. Petersburg Roman Catholic Theological Academy.[61] He died at St. Petersburg on 22 January 1854 and was buried at Smolensk Russian Orthodox Cemetery. In 1855 the Assembly of the Nobility of St. Petersburg entered the name of Vasilii K. Elpatevskii in the Genealogical Book of the Nobility.[62]

[61] ЦГИА СПб, fond 46, opis 1, file 1083

[62] ЦГИА СПб, fond 536, opis 6, file 2466.

Chapter 4
Formation of Chair of All-Nations Jurisprudence (Jus Gentium, International Law)

§4.1. *Founding of Chair as Structural Subdivision of Faculty*

The 1830s have come to be known as the era in which the system of legal education in Russia entered a new phase of development, ultimately completed by the early 1870s. During these nearly four decades the status and the teaching of international law markedly improved at St. Petersburg University. The time had come to establish a special Chair of International Law separate from the Chair of General Laws.

These notions were preceded or accompanied by new innovations in the pedagogical process, new courses, and new "native Russian" personnel who might fill University chairs. To this end, at Dorpat (now Tartu, Estonia) a so-called "Professorial Institute" was established as a unique instructional-scientific institution to train individuals for appointment to the Russian professoriate on a large scale.[1] It operated from 1828 to 1839.

There were two intakes of students, in 1828 and 1833. The standard was "the most outstanding students who might … be made in time be worthy of holding a chair". The course of study was demanding: three years of intense study in Dorpat, followed by examinations for the doctor of sciences, bypassing the magister, after which two years of study at universities in Berlin and Paris, then the post of professor somewhere in Russia. The Institute trained twenty-two graduates.[2]

At the end of 1827, St. Petersburg University was directed by Imperial behest to send twenty of the best students and graduates to Dorpat for three years in order to prepare them for a learned degree and a career in Russian universities. Among them was the future first Professor of International Law at St. Petersburg University, Ignatii Iakinfovich Ivanovskii.

Russian authorities had radically altered educational policy by introducing a new principle: "Russian Orthodoxy, Autocracy, National Character", based on "Russian principles" in place of what had been a predominance of foreign involve-

[1] See «Об избрании студентов из Университетов Московского, С.-Петербургского, Казанского и Харьковского для приготовления в Профессоры» [On the Selection of Students from the Universities of Moscow, St. Petersburg, Kazan, and Kharkov to Prepare for the Professoriate], in Сборник постановлений по Министерству народного просвещения [Collection of Decrees Relating to the Ministry of Public Enlightenment] (Spb., 1875), II(1), col. 109.

[2] See T. V. Kostina, «Воспитанники Санкт-Петербургского университета в Дерптском профессорском институте» [Pupils of St. Petersburg University in the Dorpat Professorial Institute], Петербургские исследования. Альманах [Petersburg Studies. Almanac], no. 3 (2011), p. 219-228.

ment. This principle was embedded in the reform of the entire system of University education.

On 26 July 1835, Emperor Nicholas I confirmed a "General Statute of Imperial Russian Universities",[3] drafted under his guidance and in force for the 1836/37 academic year. The universities once more were given the right to elect rectors, deans, and professors. Under the 1835 Statute the universities began to experience far-reaching upheavals, including cardinal changes in the substance and organization of international legal education and scientific research. What has been called a "new ideology" emphasized the study of law not as an abstract natural-law doctrine, but on the basis of its historical roots and implementation in practice. The intention was to integrate the realities of the outside world, constantly in movement and development, into the study of law. The study of natural law, it was felt, did not provide this perspective.

The outcome was that natural law was excluded from the legal disciplines taught. A course entitled "Encyclopedia of Law" was introduced in place of natural law. This was one element of Russian jurists reconceptualizing the purpose and nature of legal education, but the authorities likewise hoped that the reforms might curb the spread in universities of revolutionary ideas and scientific doctrines concerning the natural-law origin of State and law and the natural and inalienable human rights and freedoms.[4]

The 1835 General Statute also changed the structure of legal education: it became more precise and practical. The numbers of professors and chairs greatly increased. The Faculty of Philosophy and Law was divided into separate faculties, making the Faculty of Law an autonomous structural unit of the University. The General Statute expanded a precise list of legal courses to be taught:

> §12. There shall be taught in the Faculty of Laws:
>
> 1) Encyclopedia or general survey of the system of Lexprudence, Russian State Laws, that is, Basic Laws, Laws on Status and State Institutions.
>
> 2) Roman legislation and the history thereof.
>
> 3) Civil Laws, general, special, and local.
>
> 4) Laws of Public Amenities and Decency.
>
> 5) Laws on State Duties and Finances.

[3] Общий устав Императорских Российских университетов, высочайше утвержденный в 26-й день июля 1835 года [General Statute of Imperial Russian Universities, Confirmed by His Majesty on 26 July 1835] (Kazan, 1835); also see Уставы Академии наук СССР [Charters of the Academy of Sciences of the USSR] (Moscow, 1974).

[4] On the development of a Russian legal consciousness and the role of legal education in the process, albeit without attention to international law, see Richard Wortman, The Development of a Russian Legal Consciousness (1976). Also see V. A. Tomsinov, Юридическое образование и юриспруденция в России во второй трети XIX века [Legal Education and Jurisprudence in Russia During the Second Third of the XIX Century] (2d ed.; 2015).

6) Police and Criminal Laws.

7) Principles of All-People's Jurisprudence (Jus gentium).

In 1843 a "cameral category" was formed within the Law Faculty in addition to the already existing categories for training jurists of broad profile. Jurists who chose to be "cameral" lawyers were trained for service in economic or administrative posts in State service. This category existed until 1860, when it was renamed the "administrative category".

For promising younger scholars a two-year visit to European universities and libraries was provided. German universities were considered the ideal model to emulate, and German law contributed importantly to the structuring of Russian legislation into branches, duly reflected in the organization of law faculties.

Other changes affected the Chair of All-People's Jurisprudence expressly, including the personnel composition of the Chair, the procedure for inviting promising young scholars to train for the professoriate, the preparation and defense of dissertations, and the procedure for conferring academic degrees and titles. The system of academic posts and titles was as laid down in the 1835 General Statute was as follows: the senior position was professor *ordinarius* (that is, establishment), professor *extraordinarius* (non-establishment or not yet attested; that is, an acting professor); docent; privat-docent; lector; assistant. Only a doctor of sciences in the profile of the Faculty might be a professor, and a docent must be a magister who had defended his dissertation in a certain branch of legal knowledge.

Until 1918, the academic degrees of magister and doctor were conferred on supplicants who successfully defended a dissertation. The defense was held in the form of a "dispute" with all persons present taking part, including students. All might put questions, including the supervisor of the dissertation. Two official opponents then spoke, well-known professors in the field of the dissertation. They had read the dissertation in advance, and their review or evaluation was unknown to the supplicant. Lauding the dissertation and the supplicant was not welcomed. After the dispute, the review of the Faculty was read out loud. By open ballot the members of the Faculty adopted a decision, which was then subject to confirmation by the Council of the University. If the decision was positive, a diploma was awarded which, until 1864 was signed by the Minister of Public Enlightenment, and after that year, by the Rector of the University.

The titles of professor and docent were conferred by a "professorial college" of the faculties and confirmed by the Rector. Preparing for the magister examination took up to four years. Examples are known when the examiners for the professoriate prepared in advance up to two or three hundred questions and a list of approximately the same number of books to be read. The Faculty approved the general list. If the supplicant did not know in detail the answers to the questions, the supplicant was not a scholar. The examinations were to demonstrate whether the supplicant had a command of the entire range of subjects offered by the Faculty. Instances were known when the supplicant was ready for the examination after two years of preparation, an example being the noted jurist and sociologist, Pitirim Aleksandrovich Sorokin (1889-1968). An individual with the degree of magister and the title of privat-docent was given the right to deliver lectures at the University.

The examinations for the degree of doctor were more complicated. Members of both the Faculty and of the University were present. Whereas a magister was examined on his command of historical knowledge, the doctor was tested on his critical knowledge. The supplicant for the doctorate was given an "indefinite number of questions orally and four written questions chosen by lot". During the mid-1880s the doctoral examination was abolished. The supplicant had only to write and defend a dissertation in the Latin language. The Minister conferred the degree of doctor. Given the complexity and difficulty of the doctoral examination, the majority of professors only had the degree of magister.

With a view to making the magister examinations less formidable, the Ministry decided to introduce "categories of sciences", gradually increasing their number, for which learned degrees might be conferred. The category "law of nations" was introduced in 1837.[5]

Professor Ignatii I. Ivanovskii, a graduate of the Professorial Institute in Dorpat, was invited to head the newly-formed Chair of All-People's Law.

§4.2. *Opening of Chair of All-Nations Jurisprudence at St. Petersburg University*

The 1835 General Statute provided a new name for the subject previously taught since 1725 under the names "jus gentium", "law of nations", "nations law": on this occasion the title "all-nations jurisprudence" was selected. The creation of the Chair of All-Nations Jurisprudence was stipulated in the General Statute.[6] Nonetheless, the precise name for the Chair at St. Petersburg University was given variously in the literature: Chair of Nations Law,[7] Chair of Principles of All-Nations Jurisprudence (jus gentium), Chair of All-Nations Jurisprudence",[8] Chair of All-Nations Law,[9] Chair of All-Nations Law and Diplomacy.[10] The name of the Chair was changed to "international law" in 1857.[11]

[5] See V. A. Sharshunov and N. V. Gulko, Как подготовить и защитить диссертацию: История, опыт, методика и рекомендации [How to Prepare and Defend a Dissertation: History, Experience, Method, and Recommendations] (Minsk, 2010).

[6] Kachenovskii noted that in this period "international law received full citizenship in Russian universities and a separate Chair was founded for it". See D. I. Kachenovskii, Курс международного права [Course of International Law] (Kharkov, 1863-1866), I, p. xii.

[7] V. V. Grigorev, Императорский С.-Петербургский университет в течение первых пятидесяти лет его существования: историческая записка [Imperial St. Petersburg University During the First Fifty Years of its Existence. Historical Note] (Spb., 1870), p. xli.

[8] Ibid., p. xlii.

[9] Ibid., p. 111.

[10] Ibid., p. 153.

[11] Inexplicable and erroneous was the statement of Pustogarov, when he wrote" … it should be said

In University publications and documents the Chair usually was referred to as the "Chair of the Principles of All-Nations Jurisprudence" and sometimes the "Chair of the Principles of All-Nations Jurisprudence and Diplomacy". Other shorter versions one may assume were for convenience.

In 1857 the compulsory course "Principles of All-Nations Jurisprudence", one that all students in the Law Faculty had to take, was renamed "International Law", with it, the name of the Chair – which has been retained down to the present.

Ignatii Iakinfovich Ivanovskii *(24 December 1807, b. Minsk – d. 28 August 1886, St. Petersburg). The surname also appears as Akinfievich, Iakentevich.*[12] *International lawyer, first professor to occupy the Chair of All-Nations Jurisprudence at St. Petersburg University.*[13]

Little is known of his origins. He graduated with the gold medal at the Minsk Gymnasium and then enrolled at the Vilna (now Vilnius) University, where he graduated in 1826 with the degree of candidate of laws and two awards for research papers, one on "De sacrilegio" (On Sacrilege) and the second "On Putability for a Crime". The first was written in the Latin language, and the second in his native Polish. He found employment as a lecturer in history and geography at the Vilna Gymnasium. In November 1827 he was sent to Moscow University in order to improve his Russian language.[14]

that for a long time the Law Faculty of St. Petersburg University had no special Chair of International Law. It was taught as part of the course of Comparative State Law of European States by Professor A. D. Gradovskii, who headed by Chair of State Law until 1889". See V. V. Pustogarov, *Our Martens. F. F. Martens: International Lawyer and Architect of Peace*, ed. and transl. W. E. Butler (2000), p. 17. Gradovskii never lectured on international law. Similarly, Grabar did not notice the variations in title prior to 1863 and wrote incorrectly that the Chair was named "all-nations law" from 1835. See V. E. Grabar, *The History of International Law in Russia 1647-1917: A Bio-Bibliographical Study*, transl. W. E. Butler (1990), p. 381.

[12] In official service documents his patronymic is "Akinfievich" or as "Ioakinfovich". See the Formulary List on Service of Meritorious Professor Ordinarius and Privy Counsellor Ivanovskii", ЦГИА СПб, fond 11, opis 1, file 3644, folios 1-15, 63, 87obverse.

[13] Ivanovskii is commonly called the first Head of the Chair of International Law", but that is not entirely correct. As noted above, during these years chairs in the modern understanding of the term did not exist. The professor was hired and "occupied the Chair" as lecturers in an auditorium.

[14] "Endowed with exceptional ability, everywhere he studied he finished the course with special distinction". See Биографический словарь профессоров и преподавателей С.-Петербургского университета за истекшую третью четверть его существования [Biographical Dictionary of Professors and Lecturers of St. Petersburg University for the Past Third Quarter of its Existence 1869-1894] (Spb., 1896), p. 269. Also see V. S. Ivanenko, "Ignatii Ivanovskii: First Head of the Chair

In May 1828, Ivanovskii was sent by the Ministry to the Academy of Sciences in St. Petersburg, where he was chosen as one of the best candidates for the Professorial Institute in Dorpat.[15] After completing the examinations and defending on 31 December 1832 a dissertation in the Latin language entitled *De libera mercatura* [On Free Trade],[16] he was sent on 1 January 1833 by direction of his Imperial Majesty to Germany for three years, where he attended lectures of Friedrich Carl von Savigny (1779-1861), Edouard Gans (1797-1839), Carl Ritter (1779-1859), and other professors of Berlin University.

Ivanovskii returned to St. Petersburg on 20 May 1835. After delivering a probationary lecture on 7 August 1835 on the topic "Brief View on the Science of Diplomacy in General",[17] he was appointed by the Minister of Public Enlightenment to the University to await the distribution of chairs under the 1835 General Statute. On 31 December 1835 Ivanovskii was confirmed as professor *extraordinarius*, 8th class. From October 1836 he occupied the Chair of All-Nations Jurisprudence and began to teach the course "Introduction to the Science of All-Nations Jurisprudence and Diplomacy" to third-year students in the Law Faculty.[18] In all, Ivanovskii headed the Chair for 34 years, until 1870; from 1837 as professor *ordinarius*,[19] and from 1861 as Distinguished Professor of the University.[20]

The opening of the new Chair and the arrival of a brilliant young and talented professor to occupy the Chair "set up" the University. In addition to his teaching and research, Ivanovskii was extensively involved in administrative matters. He was temporarily appointed as acting Dean of the Law Faculty (twelve times) and/or Pro-Rector or Rector of the University (six times).[21] On 12 May 1838 he was confirmed in office as Dean, re-elected in 1840 for a term of four years, and in 1863 and 1866 for a three-year term.[22] In 1840 he also was appointed to the senior

of International Law in St. Petersburg University", *Jus Gentium: Journal of International Legal History*, IV (2019), pp. 77-94.

15 Grigorev, note 7 above, p. 68.

16 I. I. Ivanovskii, *De libera mercatura* (Dorpat, J. C. Schuenmann, 1833). 60 p. A rare title, a copy is held in the Tartu University Library, of which at one time V. E. Grabar was the Dean and Librarian. Butler И35.

17 Ivanovskii, «Краткий взгляд на науку дипломатии вообще» [Brief View of the Science of Diplomacy in General], Журнал Министерства народного просвещения [Journal of the Ministry of Public Enlightenment], part 9, no. 3 (March 1836), pp. 478-519. A version exists under the same title in pamphlet form at the Russian State Library dated 1837 (42 p.). Butler И36 and И37.

18 ЦГИА СПб, fond 14, opis 1, file 4657, folios 2236-248.

19 ЦГИА СПб, fond 14, opis 3, file 5699.

20 ЦГИА СПб, fond 139, opis 1, file 6040.

21 The precise dates on which Ivanovskii held the aforesaid administrative posts in the University have been determined on the basis of archival data in a student graduation paper by T. S. Loginova, История становления и развития кафедры международного права [History of the Origin and Development of the Chair of International Law] (Spb., 2004), p. 13.

22 ЦГИА СПб, fond 139, opis 1, file 4630.

position of acting Administrator of the St. Petersburg Educational District.[23] He served a member of the Commission to draft the 1863 General Statute on Russian Universities. When the University was closed from 1861 to 1863 because of student disturbances, Ivanovskii was chairman of the Provisional Commission administering the affairs of the University.

In addition, from 31 January 1838 Ivanovskii simultaneously held the position of professor and member of the Council at the prestigious Imperial Alexander Lycée, prior to 1843 the Tsarskoe selo Lycée. He was far from alone in taking on this additional post; large numbers of his University colleagues did the same.[24] Moreover, Ivanovskii taught and acted as a supervisor at the Page Corps and the School of Guard Sub-Ensigns and Junkers.

In 1870 Ivanovskii retired from St. Petersburg University but continued until 1880 to serve as a professor of international law at the Alexander Lycée.

International legal views. Ivanovskii wrote widely on international law: the relationship between international relations and law, issues of history and theory, doctrines on the State, territory, and population, neutrality, law of the sea, the limits of maritime dominion, and others. The scientific foundations of his international-legal positions he set out in his probationary lecture delivered in August 1835. The lecture was a mature, polished piece that qualified as an introduction to his course on international law.

Diplomacy, he said, could be understood in two senses: either as the "aggregate of the sciences necessary for the formation of diplomacy", or as a "separate science having a positivist basis and precise boundaries". That is why "when considering diplomacy as a separate science, one may call it the science of foreign relations between nations".[25]

In his first lecture at the University, Ivanovskii formulated his position on a number of problems of the science and practice of international law. Controversial in those times, for example, was whether to recognize the existence of natural and positive international law. Ivanovskii favored a reasonable combination of natural and positivist principles: "Some publicists do not recognize the existence of the natural law of nations, calling it an empty flight of fancy, without any positive basis. Others do not recognize the existence of the positive law of nations".[26] Having critically considered these views, Ivanovskii came to the conclusion that "one cannot doubt the existence of the positive law of nations, although without the assistance of natural law of nations it would be difficult to imagine the system of a science". Ivanovskii, of course, could not fail to take into account the realities of the unstable international relations of that period when he suggested: "It is beyond doubt that the positive law of nations is based more on the conditions of reason; that is, on usages more than clear treaties. To be sure, usages are changing,

[23] ЦГИА СПб, fond 14, opis 1, file 4657, folio 241.

[24] ЦГИА СПб, fond 11, opis 1, file 3644.

[25] Ivanovskii, note 17 above, p. 478.

[26] Ibid.

although some of them are more constant than the treaties themselves; but these changes are for the most part the consequence of the success of enlightenment and prove the gradual improvement of the law of nations".

Ivanovskii drew an important conclusion: international law as the aggregate of mutual rights and duties of States has as its basis two principles. One principle it takes from the very nature of nations, in their mutual relations and in the laws of reason – all this comprises the natural law of nations (*ius gentium naturale*); the second principle is based on inter-State treaties, usages, and analogies – this is the positive, or practical, law of nations (*ius gentium positivum*).[27]

It should be acknowledged that Ivanovskii himself in that period had not yet precisely defined international law. When analyzing international law in force, he divided it into philosophical (or dogmatic) and positive (or normative) law. For the designation thereof Ivanovskii used various terminological phrases: the old terms "diplomacy" and "law of nations", and the term "all-nations law" (according to the 1835 General Statute), and then the fashionable term "international law", saying that it is more precise and it would be more correct to use the term "law of States", but to avoid innovations, he retained the "long accepted expression: law of nations".[28]

An undoubted service of Ivanovskii was that he moved away from the position widely shared at the time by representatives of natural law doctrine, including his predecessor at the University, A. P. Kunitsyn, according to which States used in international legal relations the status and actions of natural persons in the domestic law of States. Ivanovskii came to the important conclusion that the sole subject of international law is only States, which enabled him to draw the following conclusion: "Finally, in the law of nations the nation means an independent State … Hence the law of nations might be called the law of States".[29]

Thirteen years later he published his first monograph since his dissertation, about the same size (31 p.), but on this occasion in the Russian language and devoted to the international law of straits in the Baltic Sea.[30] In the introduction he noted that that the book was devoted to one of the most controversial and important issues of international relations and law: the limits of the dominion of States at sea. Although the subject of the book was narrow and practical, for Russia had special interests in the right of passage through those straits, Ivanovskii formulated propositions of principle with respect to the law of the sea and general international law. The most fundamental of these Ivanovskii set out as follows: "It is beyond doubt that the sea may not be the subject-matter of private ownership … Much more difficult to decide is whether the sea is subject to exclusive power – the exclusive territorial taking of possession by individual States" (p. 3). Having considered the

27 Ibid., p. 491.

28 Ibid., pp. 489-490.

29 Ibid., p. 490.

30 Ivanovskii, О правах Дании на Зундский и Бельтский проливы, преимущественно в отношении собирания пошлин [On the Rights of Denmark to the Sound and Belt Straits Primarily With Respect to the Collection of Duties] (Spb., 1848). Butler И40.

history of territorial claims by maritime States at sea and entire oceans and having demonstrated their unlawfulness from the standpoint of international law of the nineteenth century, Ivanovskii wrote: "… only the coastal sea to a distance of cannon shot from the coast is considered to be the subject-matter of possibly taking possession, and the territorial sea, that is, bays and straits encircled on all sides by lands of the same State possessing the approaches" (p. 6).

Ivanovskii favored the resolution of all controversial and difficult international questions by "positive means": by means of negotiations and the conclusion of treaties. Having analyzed the treaties between Denmark and The Netherlands, the Hansa cities, Sweden, France, England, Prussia, and other States, Ivanovskii considered in detail the treaty between Russia and Denmark of 1782 (confirmed by treaties of 1814 and 1831).

In the conclusion, Ivanovskii, appealing to readers, expressed the interesting thought as to the role of international law and the science of international law in quieting the relations between the States concerning the correlation of international positive, especially treaty, law and scientific "philosophical" law. In his view, the mutual relations of Denmark and Russia and with other States on the issue of passage of vessels through the straits are a shining example of:

> Where mutual relations between States are determined by positive means: without such determination, all the philosophical principles of the law of nations, although the most true and unbending when there is a conflict of various interests of autonomous State, not recognizing either a power or a court to be above them, will remain controversial for always in practical application. Should if follow from this that the theoretical investigation of the idea of truth and justice with respect to international rights and duties will be fruitless labor and even a completely useless and fantastic utopia. To thing thus would be to deny the dominance of reason, would be to doubt the possible successes of mankind. [The interests of States require mutual reconciliation of their relations and] and the science of the law of nations cannot and should not refuse assistance (pp. 22-23).

In his following work, a manual on the statistics of European States[31] (the term "statistics" being understood as the composition and status of States), Ivanovskii expressed a number of important judgments with regard to problematic issues of international law. On the basis of fundamental premises of his probationary lecture in 1835, in this work he became one of the first Russian international lawyers to offer a definition of the subject which he was teaching: "The aggregate of rights and duties of autonomous States in their relations between themselves is international law. This law serves as the basis of the political system of States" (p. 8). Wiser because of two decades of lecturing experience, he nonetheless did not retract his youthful perceptions of the law of nations and continued to assert that the genesis of such norms could be traced to either the very nature of nations – the natural law of nations (*jus gentium naturale*) or the laws of reason – the positive, or practical, law of nations (*jus gentium positivum*) (p. 291).

[31] Ivanovskii, Руководство статистики европейских государств [Manual with Regard to Statistics of European States] (Spb., 1856). Butler И41.

Ivanovskii in this book also made a significant contribution to ambassadorial law, being one of the first scholars to classify and analyze in detail the following rights and freedoms of diplomatic agents in the receiving country: (1) inviolability; (2) not being subject to anyone; (3) not being within jurisdiction in respect of criminal cases; (4) not being within jurisdiction in respect of civil cases; (5) the right to religious services; (6) exemption from taxes and duties; (7) right of asylum; (8) rights with respect to persons comprising the suite thereof and with respect to subjects of the State sending them.

When considering many controversial issues of the territory of a State, Ivanovskii dwelt upon an analysis of their maritime territory: "So far it has not been determined with precision how far the power of the State extends to the sea washing the coast thereof". It is curious that in this period Ivanovskii still singled out two expanses in this territory: the coastal sea, extending to an imaginary line which is reached by a shot from a weapon placed on the coast of the sea", and the territorial sea, consisting of waters encircled by lanes of the same State and the entrance to which belongs to this State (these might be only bays and straits). Beyond the limits of the maritime territory of a State is the free sea, including other seas, bays, and straits to which, noted Ivanovskii, contrary to international law, certain States made claims for a lengthy period (Spain, Great Britain, Venice, and Genoa).

Ivanovskii touched upon certain maritime issues in connection with the well-known work by Dmitrii Ivanovich Kachenovskii (1827-1872) on privateering and prize proceedings,[32] a book to which Ivanovskii gave a lengthy review.[33] Ivanovskii supported the view of Kachenovskii concerning the benefits of free neutral trade and the need to remove all constraints which do not arise from the reasonable idea of war. But Ivanovskii sharply opposed recognizing prize courts to be international institutions: "International practice is more logical than Mr. Kachenovskii in this respect. Its rules are more in conformity with the idea of neutrality. Never, under no circumstances, does a belligerent have jurisdiction over a neutral. In the eyes of the neutral, a prize court of a belligerent is only a State establishment of that power to which the privateer belongs".[34]

As an important support for his course on "All-Nations Jurisprudence", Ivanovskii began from 1841/42 to offer a complementary course on "State Law of the

[32] D. I. Kachenovskii, О каперах и призовом судопроизводстве, в отношении к нейтральной торговле [On Privateers and Prize Proceedings with Respect to Neutral Trade] (Moscow, 1855). An English translation with additions by Kachenovskii was published in London as: *The Prize Law: Particularly with Reference to the Duties and Obligations of Belligerents and Neutrals*, transl. F. T. Pratt (London, 1867), reviewed in Санкт-Петербургские ведомости [St. Petersburg Gazette], no. 5 (6(18) January 1868), pp. 1-2. Kachenovskii's entire English-language monograph was reproduced in facsimile together with other of his writings in the English language, with an extensive introduction, in W. E. Butler (ed.), *Selected Works of D. I. Kachenovskii* (2014).

[33] See Ivanovskii, «Разбор сочинения Д. И. Каченовского «О каперах и призовом судопроизводстве» [Analysis of the Work of D. I. Kachenovskii "On Privateers and Prize Proceedings], in Двадцать пятое присуждение учрежденных П. Н. Демидовым наград 26 мая 1856 года [Twenty-Fifth Award Conferral of the Award Founded by P. N. Demidov, 26 May 1856] (Spb., 1856), pp. 321-331.

[34] Ibid., p. 327.

Major European Powers". These course, little studied in doctrinal writings of that time, he set out according to his own notes. In a Report to St. Petersburg University for 1847 the information required from Ivanovskii contained his reply to the question by what authors he was guided: "When teaching both subjects, he is guided by his own notes while adhering to the law of nations by Heffter, and for the State law of European powers, original collections of laws".[35]

But the teaching of the course on the State law of European powers was suspended by instruction of the Ministry of Public Enlightenment after the revolutionary events of 1848 in western Europe.

The year 1857 was marked by a number of changes and new trials for the Chair. The course entitled "Principles of All-Nations Jurisprudence" was finally renamed the course on "International Law", and the Chair itself was renamed the "Chair of International Law". At the end of 1857 the Emperor allowed the course on the State law of European powers to be reinstated. It is worthy of note that when this reinstatement was announced in the annual report, the leadership of St. Petersburg University considered it necessary to observe that the reinstatement of this course at the Chair of International Law "significantly added to one of the most important chairs in the University".[36]

The teaching of international law was undertaken in complex domestic bureaucratic conditions. The recommendation of the administrator of the St. Petersburg educational district given in 1857 helps to understand the perception of international law within the power structures of the time. The recommendation was set out in a Memorandum relating to the transformation of the Law Faculty:

> The subject of all-nations law and diplomacy is not given too much significance and place in University teaching. This subject represents nothing other than materials for future federative relations between nations. Therefore, it has no autonomous principles which would not be found under the rubric of State, civil, or criminal law. This course, it seems, might be significantly shortened, confining it to the most general principles of the science.[37]

[35] ЦГИА СПб, fond 14, opis 1, file 4833. When replying to a similar question in 1850, Ivanovskii clarified the authors whose works he used:

1. Heffter, Das europäische Völkerrecht der Gegenwart. 1844 ;
2. G. F. Martens, Précis du droit des gens moderne de l'Europe. 1831. 2 vols.;
3. Klüber, Droit des gens moderne de l'Europe. 1843;
4. Foelix, Traité du droit international privé. 1843.
5. Ompteda, Litteratur des gesammten Völkerrechts. 1785. With the Annex of Kamplz.

But the principal source for Ivanovskii's lectures – treaties and positive laws. See ЦГИА СПб, fond 14, opis 1, file 4853. See Loginova, note 22 above, p. 41.

[36] Годичный торжественный акт в Санкт-Петербургском университете, 8 февраля 1858 г. [Yearly Solemn Act of St. Petersburg University, 8 February 1858] (Spb., 1858), p. 27.

[37] See Grabar, note 11 above.

Judging, however, from the Announcements on the Teaching of the Sciences in the University, the recommendation was not adopted and the course was not shortened or, if it was, not significantly.

Moreover, in 1859 the University sought the funds necessary to send Ivanovskii abroad for five months (Prussia, Austria, Germany, Italy, Switzerland, France, Belgium, and England). In a submission of the Faculty of Law to the Rector, it was pointed out that the Faculty found it impossible, given the important European political events in 1848, to teach law satisfactorily to students only on the basis of books and believed it essential to give Professor Ivanovskii the opportunity to collect on site reliable and complete materials on the legal policy of the major European powers.[38]

After the revolutionary shocks of 1848 in Europe, the government strengthened control over the activities of Russian universities, limiting their autonomy, and over the content of scientific and pedagogical work of the professors. According to a Circular of the Ministry of Public Enlightenment of 1 January 1850, every professor was obliged to annually submit to the Dean a syllabus of the lectures, specifying the manuals and textbooks which he used. The Dean, in turn, was to "observe that nothing was concealed in the syllabus that disagreed with the teachings of the Orthodox Church, with the form of rule, and with the spirit of our institutions". The Dean when visiting lectures was to ensure that the professor did not stray from the syllabus and did not permit discussions irrelevant to the provisions of the Circular. The Dean reported to the Rector about the results of visiting the lectures of professors; the Record reported to the administrator of the educational district, and the administrator, to the Minister.

Having made his scientific visit about the universities of Europe, Ivanovskii from 1 October 1859 began to deliver his revised lectures.[39] Within the University, visits to foreign universities and institutions were welcomed.

The substance of Ivanovskii's courses on international law began, in this period, to be published.[40] Of interest are the syllabi for the course. These give evidence

[38] ЦГИА СПб, fond 14, opis 6, file 841. For a welcome revisionist view on the events of 1848/49, see Christopher Clark, *Revolutionary Spring: Fighting for a New World, 1848-49* (2023).

[39] Годичный торжественный акт в Санкт-Петербургском университете, бывший 8 февраля 1860 г. [Yearly Solemn Act of St. Petersburg University, 8 February 1860] (Spb., 1860), pp. 21-22.

[40] Ivanovskii, Курс международного права и дипломации, преподаваемой в Императорском Александровском лицее профессором доктором прав И. Ивановским [Course of International Law and Diplomacy Taught in the Imperial Alexander Lycée by Professor, Doctor of Laws, I. Ivanovskii] (Spb., 1860). 420 p.; Ivanovskii, Международное право и дипломатия. Лекции, читанные в Императорском С.-Петербургском университете заслуженным профессором И. Ивановским, составленные Я. Плющик-Плющевским [International Law and Diplomacy. Lectures Read in the Imperial St. Petersburg University by Distinguished Professor I. Ivanovskii, Compiled by Ia. Pliushchik-Pliushchevskii in 1865/6] (Spb., 1866). 188 p.; Ivanovskii, Международное право. Профессор Ивановский 1-го класса Императорского Александровского Лицея 1876-1877 гг. [International Law. Professor Ivanovskii First Class of the Imperial Alexander Lycée. 1876-1877] (Spb., Izd. Koplevskaia, 1877). 508 p.; Ivanovskii, Международное право. Профессор Ивановский 1-го класса Императорского Александровского Лицея 1877-1878 гг. [International Law. Professor Ivanovskii First Class of the Imperial Alexander Lycée. 1877-1878] (Spb., 1878).

of the quality of the course and, over time, illustrate the maturing of Ivanovskii's views on international law:

Syllabus of the Course "Law of Nations and Diplomacy" Offered by Professor I. I. Ivanovskii in the 1848/49 Academic Year

Introduction

1. Law of nations is the volume of mutual rights and duties between autonomous States. Critique of other definitions of law of nations.

2. Sources of law of nations, division thereof into philosophical and positive. Vacillation of philosophical principles and necessity of positive law of nations.

3. Critical analysis of objections against law of nations and against benefit of study thereof. Evidence that law of nations must serve as support of political system of States.

History of Science of Law of Nations

Chapter I. On the autonomy of States.

Chapter II. Right to preservation of autonomy.

Chapter III. On independence of autonomous States.

Chapter IV. On honoured rights of autonomous States.

Chapter V. Territorial rights of autonomous States.

Chapter VI. On right of autonomous States to obligations.

Chapter VII. Right of war.

The syllabus a decade later shows considerable differences, this being the year that the name of the course and of the Chair of International Law changed names:

Syllabus of Course "International Law" to be Offered by Professor Ordinarius I. I. Ivanovskii in the 1857/58 Academic Year

Introduction

452 p.; Ivanovskii, Международное право. Профессор Ивановский 1-го класса Императорского Александровского Лицея 1879-1880 гг. [International Law. Professor Ivanovskii First Class of the Imperial Alexander Lycée. 1879-1880] (Spb., 1880), 468 p. All of these titles were unknown to Butler and to Grabar.

Chapter I. Concept on international law drawn from the necessity of forming an international alliance.

Chapter II. Different types of international law with critical analysis of the doctrine of Wolff on this subject. Different names of international law.

Chapter III. Sources of international law:

A) Sources of philosophical international law;

B) Sources of positive international law: a) treaties; b) customs; c) analogy.

Chapter IV. Objections Made Against International Law and Refutation Thereof:

A) Objections against existence of international law in general,

B) Objections against philosophical international law,

C) Objections against positive international law.

History and Literature of Science of International Law

Section I. Autonomy of State as basis of all rights thereof (Chapters 1-4).

Section II. Right of State to exist (Chapters 1-4).

Section III. Rights of State to independence from other States with respect to both domestic and foreign activity (Chapters 1-4).

Section IV. Right of State to honor (Chapters 1-4).

Section V. Right of State to acquisition of territory and thence derivative territorial rights (Chapters 1-4).

Section VI. Rights with regard to obligations (Chapters 1-17).

Addition. Treaties on cessation of trade in negroes (Chapters 1-4).

Section VII. Right of war (Chapters 1-18).

Section VIII. Drawing up of diplomatic papers (Chapters 1-4).[41]

An optimist by nature and a firm believer in the progress of society, the State, and the sciences, Ivanovskii also believed in the international salutary aims of Russia. In an address which he prepared for the Solemn Assembly of the University in 1836, he eloquently declaimed that Russia:

> in literature and the sciences, in legislation and public institutions, and, finally, in all branches of industry is performing successes in execution,

[41] The syllabi above are drawn from Loginova, note 22 above, pp. 164, 166.

> and on cannot fail to dwell on this: come and see: flourishing from within, strong and respected from without. Russia, it seems, is called upon by Providence herself to be a worthy representative of the Slavic name, to hold in her hands the balance of peace in Europe, and to communicate European education to the tribes of Asia.[42]

In his probationary lecture Ivanovskii had expressed a firm hope in the future of international law without acknowledging in so doing the "slightest virtue of the exact sciences over the political"; he believed that the "obviousness of reason" replaced the "accuracy of calculations".[43]

As a lecturer, Ivanovskii skillfully combined the principles of philosophy, international law, and diplomacy. For many students his lectures encouraged an interest in the science of law but at the same time had a clear practical orientation. In class his students in their later memoirs and recollections considered him to have a rare gift for rhetorical eloquence.[44]

In 1870 the Learned Council of the University did not elect Ivanovskii to a new term of service,[45] and on 31 December 1870 he retired from the Chair of International Law. In January 1871 he was succeeded by a young brilliant docent – Fedor Fedorovich Martens. Three years later, at the suggestion of Martens, the Learned Council of the University elected Ivanovskii an Honorary Member of the University.[46]

§4.3. *Training and Research of Junior Lecturers*

The 1835 General Statute of Imperial Russian Universities provided incentives for student research with a view to "enlivening a spirit of scholarship among lecturers and the elevation thereof within the student body", hoping to encourage a transition to the ranks of magisters that would, in turn, raise the general level of the instructional and research profile of the University.[47] One form of scientific work was the graduation dissertation to be submitted by students.

[42] Ivanovskii, О началах постепенного усовершенствования государства [On the Principles of Constant Improvement of the State] (Spb., 1837).

[43] Ivanovskii, note 17 above, p. 508-509.

[44] Grigorev, note 7 above, p. 154.

[45] ЦГИА СПб, fond 139, opis 1, file 6557.

[46] ЦГИА СПб, fond 139, opis 1, file 6472. Over the years Ivanovskii acquired numerous awards and honors for "irreproachable" service and contributions to legal scholarship. Among them, monetary bonuses in 1840 and 1843; in 1844 the Order of St. Stanislav, second degree; in 1847 the Order of St. Anna, second degree; and in 1866, the Order of St. Anna, first degree. In 1850 the Emperor awarded Ivanovskii a diamond-studded image of himself; in 1856 he became a cavalier of the Order of St. Vladimir, third class; and in 1866, the Order of St. Anna, first class. In addition, on 22 August 1847 he was awarded a Badge of Distinction for fifteen years of service, and in 1853, another for twenty years of service.

[47] Grigorev, note 7 above, p. 113.

The Central State Historical Archive of St. Petersburg contains a number of graduation dissertations, the titles of which illustrate the aspects of international law of interest. Examples include the following:

Verevkin, A., Survey of the Basic Principles of the Law of Nations (1840);[48]

Tulinov, On Political Equilibrium (1842);[49]

Vysotskii, Significance of Hugo Grotius for the Science of the Law of Nations (1860);[50]

Vaglem, Matvei, On the Right of Asylum in the Sense of International Law (1860);[51]

Veltsyn, Nikolai, War Contraband (1861);[52]

Domanskii, Ventseslav, Concept of Neutrality in Relations Arising Therefrom (1861);[53]

Bonneta, Genrich, On the Right to Territory (1862);[54]

Poradovskii, Ivan, On the Autonomy of the State (1862);[55]

Zybin, Sergei, On the Right of Interference (1863);[56]

Ustinov, Al., On the Right of Neutral Powers (1863);[57]

Mikholis, Osip, On Elements of an International Alliance (1863);[58]

Tatishchev, Aleksei, On the Link of Natural Law with International (1868);[59]

Kabat, Nikolai, War and the Wounded (1868);[60]

48 ЦГИА СПб, fond 14, opis 9, file 5.

49 ЦГИА СПб, fond 14, opis 9, file 13.

50 ЦГИА СПб, fond 14, opis 11, file 18.

51 ЦГИА СПб, fond 14, opis 11, file 19.

52 ЦГИА СПб, fond 14, opis 11, file 138.

53 ЦГИА СПб, fond 14, opis 11, file 148.

54 ЦГИА СПб, fond 14, opis 11, file 215.

55 ЦГИА СПб, fond 14, opis 11, file 278.

56 ЦГИА СПб, fond 14, opis 11, file 337.

57 ЦГИА СПб, fond 14, opis 11, file 374.

58 ЦГИА СПб, fond 14, opis 11, file 357.

59 ЦГИА СПб, fond 14, opis 11, file 508.

60 ЦГИА СПб, fond 14, opis 11, file 471.

Sokolov, Sergei, International Relations of Russia in the XV, XVI, and XVII Centuries Before Peter I on the Question of Prisoners of War (1869);[61]

Iagulov, Bogdan, On Criminal Jurisdiction under International Law (1869);[62]

Mattel', Anton, On the Prosecution of Crimes Committed Abroad and the Extradition of Criminals (1869).[63]

Various incentives were introduced to encourage students to undertake research. Medals were offered for papers on topics proposed by the Council of the University. From 1837 such topics or, as they were called, "tasks" were given every year. Among the law students who submitted papers were gifted young people who later left their mark on the science of international law. The medals were awarded to students at faculty assemblies. Students who participated in the competitions, irrespective of whether they were winners, benefited from detailed critiques of the merits and shortcomings of each work. Each work was submitted anonymously. The final results were published in the Торжественные акты Санкт-Петербургского университета [Solemn Acts of St. Petersburg University] or in the annual Отчет состояния и деятельности Санкт-Петербургского университета [Report of the State and Activity of St. Petersburg University].

Topics proposed by the Chair of International Law to the University were popular. Among them were the following:

[1] in 1843-1844: "Determine the rights of a neutral flag relating to trade and explain critically the treaties and positive laws relating to this problem";[64]

[2] in 1851-1852: "Set out the principles of diplomacy which were recognized and observed in Russia from ancient historical times to the accession to the throne of Emperor Peter the Great relating to the right of embassy and conclusion of State treaties";[65]

[3] in 1856-1857: On Consuls, Their Authority, Rights, and Duties".[66]

[61] ЦГИА СПб, fond 14, opis 11, file 569.

[62] ЦГИА СПб, fond 14, opis 11, file 585.

[63] ЦГИА СПб, fond 14, opis 11, file 556.

[64] Awards were presented to: fourth-year students Grigorii Okunev (gold medal); second-year Evgenii Malevich (silver medal); fourth-year Fedor von Grote (honorable mention). See Grigorev, note 7 above, p. xii.

[65] Awards were presented to: fourth-year students Aleksandr Kvachevskii and Aleksandr Sakharov (gold medals); fourth-year Konstantin Radetskii and third-year Adolf von Giubbenet (honorable mentions). Grigorev, note 7 above, pp. xli-xlii.

[66] Awards were presented to: fourth-year students Karl Shneider (gold medal with printing of the dissertation at University expense); third-year student (silver medal); fourth-year Vasilii Mukhalevskii (honorable mention). Годичный торжественный акт в Санкт-Петербургском университете, бывший 8 февраля 1857 года [Yearly Solemn Act of St. Petersburg University, 8 February 1857] (Spb., 1857), p. 203.

The best law students who undertook research and completed the entire course in the University were awarded the learned degree "candidate of sciences". A year after being awarded this degree they had the right to take the examination for the degree of magister (the modern equivalent being the degree of candidate of sciences, commonly treated as a Ph.D. outside Russia).

In the 1840s the authorities continued their assault on the rights of the universities, restricting their autonomy, the freedom of university teaching, strict regulation of university syllabi, stricter requirements for scientific-research activity by the professors and lecturers – these trends adversely affected university development but less so the enlivening of university life.

Grabar wrote with respect to this period: "Despite the serious state in which the universities found themselves at the end of the 1840s, scientific work was still done. One can even detect a noticeable increase of interest in international law and diplomacy. A whole series of university dissertations appeared. Productivity in this respect was startling. Never before had such a strong generation appeared".[67]

As noted above, the best graduates were awarded the degree of candidate without examinations. The rest of the graduates underwent attestation and had the right to a class rank; they might seek the degree of candidate after successfully passing a complex examination in their specialty. A year after receiving the degree of candidate, the individuals had the right to sit the examinations for the degree of magister. According to the Instruction of the Ministry of Public Enlightenment, no earlier than a year after obtaining the magister might they have the right to prepare for and then defend a doctoral dissertation.

From the mid-nineteenth century, the graduates of faculties who displayed ability in scientific work began to remain as young researchers attached to specific professors in order to prepare magister dissertations and ready themselves for pedagogical activity. They made a noticeable contribution to the development of the science of international law, initially through the formulation of doctrinal definitions and exploration of the essence of many international-legal provisions and institutions while at the chair of all-nations jurisprudence.

The topics of magister dissertations (so-called "Discourses") of the early young scholars who remained in the mid-nineteenth century to prepare for a magister or doctorate in international law are revealing. The topics they chose, having regard to the still embryonic state of the science of international law in Russia, were innovative, scientifically bold, but nonetheless imparted a certain impression of the development of the science of international law in Russia. Issues of private international law were addressed in the 1850s thanks to junior scholars in the field.[68]

Priority in this respect belongs to two young scholars of St. Petersburg University who in 1850 defended magister dissertations: by Blagoveshchenskii, "On the

[67] Grabar, note 11 above, p. 282.

[68] N. M. Iurova, Международное гражданское процессуальное право: теоретические основы имплементации норм в правовой системе Российской Федерации [International Civil Procedure Law: Theoretical Foundations of the Implementation of Norms in the Legal System of the Russian Federation] (M., 2008), p. 136.

Operation of State and Civil Laws in International Law" and Tadeusz Bobrowski, "On the Operation of Civil and Criminal Laws of One State in Another". Both dissertations analyzed private international law for the first time in Russia as an autonomous branch of law.

It has long been believed that the two dissertations remained in manuscript; nothing was known about their authors.[69] More information has been discovered about Tadeusz Bobrowski (in Russian – Faddei Bobrovskii), but Blagoveshchenskii remains in the shadows. The most that can be said at the moment of the last is that in 1848 a student named Lev Blagoveshchenskii was enrolled in the second year of the Law Faculty at the St. Petersburg University,[70] but his name is not found in the records for 1847 and 1849. It is unknown whether this is the same individual as the author of the dissertation.

Discourses of the following candidates of laws which were submitted for the degree of magister of all-nations law are known at St. Petersburg University:

Zaremba, Mechislav Stanislavovich, Historical Development of the Concept of Military Contraband (1849);[71]

Bobrowski, Tadeusz (Bobrovskii, Faddei Iosifovich), On the Operation of Civil and Criminal Laws of One State in Another (1850);[72]

Spasovich, Vladimir Danilovich, On the Rights of Neutral Flag and Neutral Cargo (1851).[73]

With respect to public international law, it is evident from the choice of dissertation topic that the law of the sea was a major preoccupation at the time. The so-called "Declaration of Armed Neutrality" proclaimed by Empress Catherine II on 28 February 1780 found extensive support from the smaller maritime powers, among them the United States, at war with England for its independence. Russia was no less interested in the freedom of navigation from the Black Sea into the

[69] See S. A. Vengerov, Критико-биографический словарь русских писателей и ученых (от начала русской образованности до наших дней) [Critical-Biographical Dictionary of Russian Writers and Scholars (From the Beginning of Russian Education to Our Days] (Spb., 1895), IV, p. 53; Grabar, note 11 above, p. 574; G. G. Krichevskii, Магистерские и докторские диссертации, защищенные на юридических факультетах университетов Российской империи (1755-1918). Библиографический указатель [Magister and Doctoral Dissertations Defended at Law Faculties of Universities of the Russian Empire (1755-1918): Bibliographical Index] (Stavropol, 1998), p. 105. The Krichevskiii manuscript served as the basis for William E. Butler, "Bibliography of Russian Magister and Doctoral Dissertations on Public and Private International Law" 1802-1917", *Jus Gentium: Journal of International Legal History*, VII (2022), pp. 197-224.

[70] ЦГИА СПб, fond 14, opis 3, file 14011.

[71] M. Zaremba, Историческое развитие понятия о военной контрабанде [Historical Development of the Concept of Military Contraband] (Spb., 1849). Butler 330.

[72] ЦГИА СПб, fond 14, opis 10, file 4. A copy also is held at the Russian National Library Manuscript Division.

[73] V. Spasovich, О правах нейтрального флага и нейтрального груза [On the Rights of a Neutral Flag and Neutral Cargo] (Spb., 1851). Butler C143.

Mediterranean, having been successful in wars against the Crimean Khanate and the Ottoman Empire. Having secured several windows on the "west" via the Arctic seas, Baltic and North seas, and the Mediterranean, Russia faced the international issues of a major European power and resistance or rivalry from England.

§4.4. *First Magisters of Chair of All-Nations Jurisprudence*

Mechislav Stanislavovich Zaremba *(182?; b. Gorets uezd, Mogilev Region – d. ?). The first magister of international law in Russia.*

Life and career. There is no biographical information about Zaremba in scholarly or reference literature. All those who have mentioned him confine themselves to the laconic phrase that in 1849 M. Zaremba defended a magister dissertation on issues of military contraband at Petersburg University and at best give a concise account of the dissertation printed in that same year in connection with the defense.

Grabar noted that Zaremba's dissertation was the first scientific work in Russia on the topic.[74] Maximally laconic was S. A. Vengerov (1855-1920) in his reference work on the history of Russian science and culture: "Zaremba, Mechislav. Author of work on military contraband (1849)".[75] Archival searches, principally in St. Petersburg, have enabled the following to be ascertained:

Mechislav Zaremba was born (it is believed) in the Gorets uezd of the Mogilev Region. He graduated in 1840 from the Mogilev Emperor Alexander I Men's Gymnasium.[76] On 19 August 1841 Zaremba enrolled at the Law Faculty of St. Petersburg University and, having successfully completed the course of study, was awarded the learned degree of candidate on 1 July 1845.[77] Having decided to continue his education and prepare for scientific activity, Zaremba on 10 February 1847 filed a request in the name of the Rector of the University expressing a wish to acquire the degree of magister of all-nations law, proposing to take examinations in March in two subjects – the "Law of Nations" and "State Laws of European Powers", and within six months, the remaining two subjects – "State Laws of the Russian Empire" and "Encyclopedia of Lexprudence".[78]

Between 14 March and 13 September 1847, Zaremba successfully passed the magister examinations on "All-Nations Law", "Encyclopedia of Lexprudence",

[74] Grabar, note 11 above, p. 305.

[75] Vengerov, note 69 above.

[76] See under his name the website enumerating graduates of the Mogilev Gymnasium (1814-1909). http://www.petergen.com/history/moggim

[77] A copy of the diploma, as was standard practice, is found in TsGIA Spb, fond 14, opis' 1, file 4824. Although the degree was awarded in 1845, the actual diploma was dated 18 May 1846, signed by the Dean of the Law Faculty, Konstantin Alekseevich Nevolin (1806-1855) and the Rector of the University, Petr Aleksandrovich Pletnev (1792-1865).

[78] ЦГИА СПб, fond 14, opis' 1, file 4824. See Loginova, note 22 above, p. 26.

and "State Law of the Russian Empire" (orally);[79] the expanded written answers to the questions proposed by the Faculty on 13 September 1847 are preserved in the Central State Historical Archive.[80] Two years later, in 1849, Zaremba submitted a magister dissertation to the Faculty on the historical development of the concept of military contraband.

The Law Faculty on 22 January 1849 heard the opinion submitted by the reader of the dissertation, Professor I. I. Ivanovskii, and decided to deem the dissertation "satisfactory for receiving the degree of magister and approved the printing thereof with the attached theses".[81]

Five days later Zaremba submitted a written request to the Administrator of the St. Petersburg Education District, Mikhail Nikolaevich Musin-Pushkin (1785-1862), notifying the Administrator about the successful completion of study at the Law Faculty of the University and receipt of the degree of candidate; he reported that he was preparing a dissertation to receive the title of magister. Under the circumstances concerning the defense of the text of the dissertation, it should be

[79] On 14 March 1847 an examination was held on "All-Nations Law" with regard to the following oral questions:
1) On armed neutrality and systems of continental blockade;
2) In what instances do laws of one State have binding force in another;
3) On communes;
4) On taking possession in the sense of the law of nations.

For the course "State Law of Major European Powers", he answered the following questions:
1) On legislative power in France;
2) On legislative power in Prussia;
3) Church structure in the United Kingdom of Great Britain and Ireland;
4) Significance and power of the Diet of the German Unie in diplomatic affairs.

On 4 September 1847 Zaremba answered the following questions in the course "Encyclopedia of Lexprudence":
1) Conclusion of the idea of truth;
2) Distinction between morality and law;
3) Concept of Aristotle about rights;
4) Influence of Christianity on law;
5) On the Verulazhskii Law;
6) On the auxiliary sciences of lexprudence.

On 12 September 1847 on the course "State Law of the Russian Empire" he successfully answered these questions:
1) Law on succession to the throne in the Russian Empire;
2) Historical survey of succession to the throne in Russia;
3) On honorary citizenship;
4) On citizenship in the Ostsee Territory;
5) On the composition and subject-matter of the department of the Ministry of Internal Affairs;
6) On clerical administrative work.

On 13 September 1847 he successfully performed assignment in written topics proposed by the Faculty:
1) On State law of the Russian Empire: "History of the Ruling Senate";
2) On Encyclopedia of Lexprudence: "Concept of Cicero and Roman Jurists on Law";
3) On the law of nations: "On Rights of Diplomatic Agents".

[80] TsGIA Spb, fond 14, opis' 1, file 4824, l. 17-28.

[81] TsGIASpb, fond 14, opis 1', file 4824, l. 11-15.

submitted in printed form in several examples sufficient to conduct the defense. However, Zaremba wrote, his limited finances did not permit him to pay the required sums for the printing. He therefore requested the Administrator to relieve him from printing the dissertation and allow it to be defended in manuscript form (presumably a single copy).[82] On 29 January 1849 the Administrator proposed that the Faculty be lenient, and the Faculty acted accordingly.[83]

According to archival materials at the Central State Historical Archive, the dissertation was printed in a small number of examples which on 23 April 1849 were sent to the leading scientific-educational centers of Russia – thirty-five addresses.[84] The Archive contains confirmations of receipt from the Council of St. Petersburg University signed by the director of these centers; this enables us to form an impression of the identity of the recipients. Letters of gratitude were received in the name of the Rector of the University, Academy of Sciences, Roman Catholic Theological Academy, Petersburg Theological Academy, Kazan, Moscow, Kyiv, and Kharkov universities, Naval Cadet Corps, Aleksander Lycée, Chief Pedagogical Institute, Petersburg Medical-Surgery Academy, and others.

On 4 March 1849, the Dean of the Law Faculty, Konstantin Alekseevich Nevolin (1806-1855), reported to the Rector of the University that the Faculty at its session of 25 February 1849 had determined that the public defense of the dissertation on military contraband by Zaremba for the degree of magister of all-people's law would commence on 6 March at 14:00 hours. Professors *ordinarius* Ivanovskii and Ivan Iakovlevich Gorlov (1813-1890) were appointed as the opponents.[85] The defense was successful.[86]

After confirmation on 24 March 1849 by the Minister of Public Enlightenment of the decision of the Council of the Faculty concerning the success of Zaremba in the magister examinations and successful defense of the dissertation, he was awarded the diploma of the magister of all-people's law as of 7 March 1849 as confirmed on 24 March 1849. The diploma gave Zaremba the right to a civil service rank, ninth class, and other rights and privileges associated with this degree.[87]

[82] ЦГИА СПб, fond 14, opis' 1, file 4824, l. 63-63 obverse.

[83] ЦГИА СПб, fond 14, opis' 1, file 4824, l. 2-3.

[84] ЦГИА СПб, fond 14, opis' 1, file 4824, l. 63-63 obverse.

[85] ЦГИА СПб, fond 14, opis' 1, file 4824, l. 5. Ivan Iakovlevich Gorlov was Professor *ordinarius* at the Chair of Political Economy and Statistics; he served as Dean of the Law Faculty at St. Petersburg University from 1860-1863 and again from 1869-1870. Born in Riazan Province, he graduated from Riazan Gymnasium and, in 1833, from the Department of Morals and Politics of Moscow University with the degree of candidate, He earned his doctor of philosophy at Dorpat University in 1838. Before appointment at St. Petersburg University in 1847, he served at Kazan University.

[86] Годичный торжественный акт в Императорском С.-Петербургском Университете, бывший 8 февраля 1850 года [Yearly Solemn Act in Imperial St. Petersburg University, 8 February 1850 Last] (Spb., 1850), p. 20.

[87] ЦГИА СПб, fond 14, opis' 1, file 4824, l. 32.

International-Legal Views. We may judge the international legal views of Zaremba solely on the basis of analyzing his only scholarly work – the magister dissertation on the historical development of the concept of military contraband. The young Zaremba was the first in the Russian science of international law to address such legal aspects of the law of war as neutral trade and military contraband. As was often true in the past and frequently is today, Zaremba defined the subject-matter of this study as complex and controversial in the field of international law: there is no subject-matter where there are as many opposite views as there are various systems; each writer, looking at whether he upholds either the belligerent or neutral States, gives rights to either of them in greater or lesser degree, narrowing or expanding the range of their relations in wartime.

Despite, however, all the various existing theories in particulars, they all agree that they recognize the right of neutral States to have trade relations with the possession of belligerent powers, except for blockaded or besieged places, and only suggest certain limitations. These limitations on trade are for those goods which may strengthen the belligerent power, and thereby, having continued the war, cause damage to the other side. Such types of goods are called military contraband.[88]

Zaremba was critical of scholarly works concerning neutral maritime trade and military contraband of that period whose authors from various standpoints sought to answer the question: "On what grounds does a belligerent power appropriate to itself the right to prescribe laws for the actions of other autonomous States". Some writers consider such grounds to be the protection by the belligerent power of own security; others proceed from the concept of neutrality, obliging neutral States not to deliver articles to belligerents increasing their power of resistance; yet others permit limitations on trade because neutral powers gave their consent to this or tacitly subjected themselves to customs which had formed; and others did not permit any limitations at all of neutral trade or allow them only by virtue of special agreements of neutrals with belligerents.

Recognizing that in various eras the belligerent powers variously resolved the problem of mutual relations at sea, including issues of military contraband, Zaremba identified three: (1) end of the twelfth to the seventeenth centuries; (2) early seventeenth century to the 1713 Peace of Utrecht; (2) Peace of Utrecht to the end of the continental system in 1813. Having investigated the many centuries of State practice with regard to neutral maritime trade and contraband military materials, Zaremba concluded the existing legal principles were imperfect. States recognized as military contraband only military goods (weapons, projectiles, ammunition, powder, brimstone, and saltpetre); if they were sent to one belligerent party, such contraband was subject to confiscation. Zaremba asked: "did the principles derived conform to the requirements of equity and did they correspond to the purpose of establishing them?" Zaremba put a reasonable question in response: insofar as "in the domain of maritime trade there is no occasion to distinguish between the sea and land, and if now in general the inviolability of private ownership on land has been recognized, why should not this rule extend also to neutral ships?" Zaremba was persuaded that such confiscation of goods could not be justified. The "sole

[88] M. Zaremba, Историческое развитие понятия о военной контрабанде [Historical Development of the Concept on Military Contraband] (Spb., 1849), p. 3.

right which a belligerent party has with regard to such articles lies in not permitting that they achieved their destination" and fall to another belligerent party; the power detaining the good may acquire it "if the master of the ship agrees to this".[89]

As regards the adoption of international legal regulations with respect to military contraband, this also is not achieved. Zaremba concluded: "The prohibition of trade in military contraband constrains neutral navigation more than provides advantage to belligerent powers"; in his view, "the concept of neutrality emanates from the conflict of rights of peaceful States with the advantages of the belligerents".[90]

Analyzing various aspects of the topic, Zaremba drew a series of conclusions in the dissertation which, using modern terminology, "possess scientific and practical significance". For example, Zaremba was convinced that:

(1) a neutral State prohibits neutral State to deliver military contraband to a belligerent;

(2) neutral States should observe the prohibition to deliver military contraband to a belligerent;

(3) delivery of military contraband by a neutral State to one of the belligerent parties should be considered a violation of the rights of the other party and on this basis entail legal confiscation by the other belligerent party of the content of the military contraband;

(4) the delivery of weapons purchased in a neutral State by any of the belligerent parties is not permitted.

At the same time, in Zaremba's view, during wartime the freedom of trade must be ensured in the private-law sphere. The sale of military materials to subjects of belligerent powers is not subject to prohibition if they are acquired on neutral territory and the possessor of the good autonomously takes them out. No doubt Zaremba took international realities into account of that era when he wrote at the end of his study:

> There is no doubt that the political might and material advantages of a State are the main reasons for constraining or expanding from its side the rights of neutrality … But those principles should not be sought in the claims of individual States and not in the actions of unilateral policy which should enter into the system of international law, but in the general direction of all relations established by State treaties on the basis not of local needs and advantages, but the general principles of equality and reciprocity.[91]

The last section of Zaremba's dissertation is entitled "Propositions"; here Zaremba drew a number of conclusions which, as now happens when preparing and

[89] Ibid., p. 5.

[90] Ibid., p. 63.

[91] Ibid., p. 53.

defending dissertations, were submitted for public discussion and defense. The basic conclusions of the magister dissertation were as follows:

1. The limitation of trade relations with possessions of belligerent powers may concern only blockaded and besieged places.

2. A limitation of trade relations exists in practice with places not in a state of blockade or siege based on mutual consent and voluntary concessions of States.

3. The significance of military contraband may be derived solely from treaties and customs.

Zaremba expressed the wish that the legal principles set out in the international treaty between the United States of America and Prussia in 1785 "were entered in future laws of neutral trade"; in his view, this concerned especially the following propositions:

- private ownership to ships of neutral States is deemed to be "sacred and inviolate" and may not be confiscated by belligerent parties;

- the seizure of weapons on ships of neutral States may be undertaken only on condition of payment of the value of that seized to the possessor thereof.

Zaremba's magister dissertation nearly 170 years later has significance for modern specialists. Syrykh noted: "The work of Zaremba is of undoubted interest in two aspects. First, it was the first work in Russian jurisprudence on military contraband and, second, the first attempt to evaluate the equity of the researched norms of international law in the degree of their conformity to the purposes thereof".[92]

Tadeusz Bobrowski (Faddei Bobrovskii) *(19 March 1829, b. village of Terekhovo, Lipovets uezd, Kyiv Governate (now Berdychiv District, Zhytomyr Region) – d. Kazymyrovka, Lipovets uezd, Kyiv Governate). First magister of private international law in Russia, later becoming a writer, memoirist, and well-known public figure in Ukraine and Poland.*

Bobrowski emanates from a noted old Polish family of Bobrowskis who lived for an extended period in Ukraine. He received his general secondary education in Ukraine in schools at Zhytomyr and Kyiv. In 1839 he enrolled at the Volhynia Government Gymnasium, moving in 1842 to the I Kyiv Gymnasium, where he graduated in 1844. In that same year he matriculated at the Law Faculty of the Imperial Kyiv St. Vladimir University. He transferred to St. Petersburg and was

[92] V. M. Syrykh, «Заремба Мечислав» [Zaremba, Mechislav], in V. M. Syrykh (ed.), Правовая наука и юридическая идеология России: энциклопедический словарь биографий [Legal Science and Legal Ideology of Russia: Encyclopedic Dictionary of Biographies] (2009), I, p. 255.

admitted to the third year of the Law Faculty of St. Petersburg University, taking at this time the Russian forename – Faddei.[93]

In his fourth year his essay entitled "Exposition of the History of Russian Legislation on the Buying Up of Property and Explaining the Origin and Significance Thereof at the Present Time" was awarded the silver medal.[94]

In 1849 Bobrowski graduated from the Faculty of Laws of St. Petersburg University with the degree of candidate of laws and remained attached to the Chair of All-Nations Law to take the magister examinations,[95] prepare a magister dissertation, and prepare for a career of scientific research and lecturing.

A year or so later, Bobrowski submitted a magister dissertation to the University on the operation of civil and criminal laws of one State in another.[96] On 3 December 1850 the public defense of the dissertation was held. On the basis of a successful defense, the degree "magister of all-nations law" was conferred on Bobrowski.[97]

Whether Bobrowski's dissertation can be said to mark the commencement of scientific research in Russia on private international law has been controversial in Russian doctrinal writings. Only the period is virtually undoubted – the early second half of the nineteenth century. Several worthy scholars of that time have been called the Russian founders of this major benchmark in jurisprudence.

Some considered Nikolai Pavlovich Ivanov (1839-1903) to be the founder of the science of private international law in Russia. He defended in 1864 a magister dissertation at Kazan University on the "Grounds of Private International Jurisdiction".[98] It is even alleged that Ivanov was the first who used the term "international private law".[99] Other legal scholars connected the origin of the Russian science

[93] Годичный торжественный акт в Императорском С.-Петербургском Университете, бывший 8 февраля 1850 года [Yearly Solemn Act in Imperial St. Petersburg University, 8 February 1851] (Spb., 1851), p. 17.

[94] Vengerov, note 69 above, IV(1), p. 53.

[95] ЦГИА СПб, fond 14, opis' 1, file 4941.

[96] ЦГИА СПб, fond 14, opis' 10, file 4.

[97] ЦГИА СПб, fond 14, opis' 1, file 5454.

[98] N. P. Ivanov, «Основания частной международной юрисдикции» [Grounds of Private International Jurisdiction], Ученые записки Императорского Казанского университета [Learned Notes of Imperial Kazan University] (Kazan, 1865), I(2), pp. 136-188.

[99] S. N. Lebedev and E. V. Kabatova (eds.), Курс частного международного права [Course of

of private international law with Dmitrii Ivanovich Meier (1819-1856), at Kazan University, on the basis that he was the first in Russia to set out in his lectures on Russian civil law the basic provisions of the doctrine on the interaction of the conflict of laws of various countries based on the works of Friedrich Carl von Savigny (1779-1861), the noted German scholar.[100] Grabar noted that the initiative in studying international private law and conflicts of law has been ascribed to Fedor Fedorovich Martens at St. Petersburg University, not least because Martens believed that to be the case. In the preface to volume two of his treatise on the contemporary international law of civilized nations, Martens devoted for the first time a separate chapter to private international law, asserting: "For the first time private international law and international criminal law are set out in the Russian language".[101]

Grabar, however, was skeptical of this claim:

> But, more than thirty years before Martens, international private and criminal law had been the subject of Russian studies. The initiative in this respect was that of two young scholars who defended magister dissertations on this topic at St. Petersburg University in 1850: F. Bobrovskii, on the effect of civil and criminal laws of one State in another; and Blagoveshchenskii, on the effect of State and civil laws in international law. Regrettably, the dissertations remained in manuscript and almost nothing is known about them or their authors.[102]

Grabar was partly right, having made a clear substitution of subject-matter: Martens had written in 1883 that for the first time private international law was contained in the treatise published by him for a general audience, and Grabar rightly pointed out that in 1850 only the scientific study of that branch of jurisprudence had begun. Nonetheless, Grabar's attribution of the priority of Bobrowski and Blagoveshchenskii in initiating the study of private international law has "roamed" to virtually all publications which refer to the birth of the Russian science of this branch of law without any clarification or addition. A recent reference work contained the following article:

> Bobrovskii, Faddei Iosifovich – magister, specialist in problems of legal science.
>
> In 1848 defended at St. Petersburg University a magister dissertation in the specialty international law on the topic: "On the Operation of Civil and Criminal Laws of One State in Another".

International Private Law] (M., 2011), I, p. 43.

100 A. I. Abdullin, «О некоторых вопросах зарождения и формирования отечественной науки международного частного права» [On Certain Questions of the Birth and Forming of the Russian Science of International Private Law], Вестник экономики, права и социологии [Herald of Economics, Law, and Sociology], no. 4 (2012), pp. 118-119.

101 F. F. Martens, Современное международное право цивилизованных народов [Contemporary International Law of Civilized Nations] (Spb., 1883), II; the prefaces to the first and fifth editions are translated in F. F. Martens, *Contemporary International Law of Civilized Peoples. Special Part*, transl. W. E. Butler (2022), p. xxv.

102 Grabar, note 11 above, p. 574.

Regrettably, there is no information on the scientific publications of F. I. Bobrovskii in the catalogues of the Russian State and the Russian National libraries.

The text of the magister dissertation is not preserved.

It has not been possible to obtain other information on the biography of F. I. Bobrovskii.[103]

Krichevskii, in his manual on dissertations, also indicated that he was not successful in finding the dissertation.[104] Thus, the view was affirmed in doctrinal writings and reference works that the dissertation remained in manuscript and nothing more was known about it or its author.

Once, however, the forename "Faddei" was returned to its original Polish version "Tadeusz", it became possible to trace him. There is every reason to suppose that Bobrowski russified his name when he arrived in St. Petersburg and changed it back to the Polish version when he returned to Kyiv – although it is now known that he used both versions in Ukraine.

After the successful defense of the dissertation, Bobrowski was offered the post of lecturer in the Chair of All-Nations Law at Kazan University, but he decided to devote himself to a career in State administration. His plans, however, to pursue a professional legal career were not fated to be for family reasons (death of his father, Iuzef Bobrowski). He was obliged to leave St. Petersburg and return to the family estate Kazyryrovka, in Kyiv Governate, Ukraine.

From 1858 Bobrowski began to participate actively in the activities of local representative agencies in Ukraine. He was elected a delegate of the county of Lipovets to the Committee of Nobles, and then to the General Inter-Governate Commission for Questions of Granting Land to Peasants, and also was appointed as an unpaid judge in the county of Lipovets, Kyiv Governate. Bobrowski achieved world renown thanks to two important circumstances: first, he was the guardian of his nephew, Jozef Teodor Konrad Korzeniowski (1857-1924), who eventually emigrated to England and gave up Russian citizenship. There he took the name Joseph Conrad.[105] Second, Bobrowski was the author of well-regarded memoirs.[106]

[103] Syrykh, note 92 above, I, p. 80.

[104] Krichevskii, note 69 above, p. 105.

[105] When Conrad was orphaned at the age of eleven, he "was taken care of by his mother's brother"; that is, Bobrowski. See Conrad's emendations and corrections to a biographical pamphlet prepared by Alfred A. Knopf in 1913, intended to popularize Conrad's works in the United States. Among the corrections made by Conrad were the facts that Bobrowski took care of him, he was born in Ukraine, visited the Sea of Azov, among other destinations, in his early voyages, and other interesting material. See Leo Robson, "The Mariner's Prayer", *The New Yorker*, 30 November 2017, p. 91, col. 3. Also see Maya Jasanoff, *The Dawn Watch: Joseph Conrad in a Global World* (2017).

[106] T. Bobrowski, *Pamiętniki Tadeusza Bobrowskiego* (Lviv, 1900). 2 vols.; reissued as T. Bobrowski, *Pamiętnik mojego życia* (Warsaw, 1979). 2 vols.

By regulation of the Ministry of Public Enlightenment of the Russian Empire on 31 March 1895 the F. O. Bobrowski Stipend was awarded to Polish students at the Imperial Kyiv St. Vladimir University for success in studies and good behavior. According to the Statute on the Stipend (point 6), confirmed by the Ministry of Public Enlightenment, "the recipient of the F. O. Bobrowski stipend might only be a student of Polish origin of the St. Vladimir University, of the Catholic faith, without distinction of estate, excellent behavior, and good success in studies". The stipend was founded from interest on capital given to the University by three well-known nobles of the Kyiv Governate in memory of F. O. Bobrowski, who died in 1894.

International legal views. One may judge the international legal views of Bobrowski only on the basis of the aforesaid magister dissertation. It is noteworthy that Bobrowski, as was accepted in this period of doctrinal writings, perceived international criminal law as a special part of private international law. Taking into account that the dissertation exists in manuscript (and was actually written out by hand), it seems justified to set out the full content thereof in order for the first time to acquaint the contemporary reader with how this field of law existed more than a century and a half ago and with the method of how a magister dissertation was structured.

The Bobrowski dissertation was rather substantial (298 manuscript pages), consisting of an introduction and two parts: Part One examined the operation of civil laws of one State in another and the conflicts situations arising in this connection (102 p.); Part Two addressed the operation of criminal laws of one State in another and the issues of the applicability of the law of a particular State when investigating and bringing guilty persons to responsibility (162 p.).

We disclose for the first time the structure and concise content of the Bobrovskii dissertation:

Introduction.

Part One. On the Operation of Civil Laws of One State in Another

Chapter I. To What Laws are Personal Rights of One's Subjects of One State in Another State Subject

Chapter II. To What Laws is the Property of the Subject of One State in Another Subject

Chapter III. Laws with Which Acts Should Conform Undertaken by Subjects of One State in Another

Section 1. To What Laws is the Form of Acts Subject

Section 2. To What Laws is the Substance of Acts Subject

Part Two. On the Operation of Criminal Laws of One State in Another

Chapter I. Form of Operation of State in Event of Violation of its Law Beyond its Territory

Section 1. Form of Operation of State in Event of Violation by Subject of its Laws Beyond its Territory

Section 2. Form of Operation of State in Event of Violation of its Laws by Foreign Subjects

Chapter II. Form of Operation of State in Event of Violation of Other's Laws by its Subjects

Chapter III. Form of Operation of State in Event of Violation of Laws of Other States Beyond its Territory

Section 1. What Should a State Do When its Own Subject has Concealed Himself Therein

Section 2. Form of Action of State when a Foreign Criminal Subject has Concealed Himself Therein

Chapter IV. What Law Has Application when Crimes are Prosecuted by One State Committed in Another, the Measure of Punishment, Pardon, and Limitations in the Meaning of International Law

Each part, Bobrowski stressed, analyzes the "contemporary state of the questions considered both in the philosophical and positive senses" (p. 29). The sources used to prepare the dissertation were "codes published by the Government or private persons and the works of legal scholars" (p. 30).

Among the thirty-eight names mentioned in the dissertation as the "works of scholars", there is not one scientific work by a Russian legal scholar, which is indirectly confirmed by Grabar and other specialists, that the magister dissertation by Bobrowski is indeed the first scientific work in Russia on international private and criminal law (pp. 27-30).

Bobrowski began his work with a definition of the basic categories of his magister dissertation. In the Introduction to the dissertation, he touched upon a number of general questions of undoubted scientific interest if one bears in mind that this work is the first in this field of Russian doctrine. He immediately describes the sphere of his study:

> international law has as its subject-matter the mutual rights and duties of States". The rights belonging to a State are of two kinds: some belong to the State as a single whole, others belong to its subjects, but in relations between States they are considered as belonging to the State because they are protected and defended by it" (p. 1).

In the context of the dissertation topic Bobrowski needs to determine his field of scholarly interest, performing the first classification of international-legal domains:

> The rights which belong directly to the State are called public rights, and those belonging to private persons are private rights; therefore all international law should be divided on the basis of its subject-matter into public

international law (droit international public) and private international law (droit international privé)" (pp. 2-3).

An important conclusion follows from this classification, that Bobrowski long before Ivanov used in his study the legal phraseology which later became a permanent term of the Russian-language – international private law.

Bobrowski asserted that "private international law has as its task the determination of relations in conflicts between States when they or, at least, one of them is acting in the matter of a private person, that is, in international relations by the law belonging to it" (pp. 3-4).

The difference in the legislation of States objectively leads to a conflict or their interests and laws:

> The collision between direct laws of States may occur only when a law deemed in one State should be accompanied for its full sovereignty by certain consequences beyond the ordinary limits of their operation or what when laws of one State should have force and operation in another. Consequently, private international law is nothing other than that part of international law which determines the operation of the laws of one State in another" (pp. 4-5).

In determining the characteristic features of one branch of law, Bobrowski wrote:

> Because private international law is founded chiefly on the mutual advantage of States, one State should not allow in itself the operation of such provisions of another which would: (1) be contrary to the dignity of the first or its security of independence; (2) be contrary to the rights of its subjects, or, finally; (3) were not agreed with the model of its thought and contradictions in the domain of morals and politics or the concept of justice" (pp. 21-22).

The structure of Part One arranged on the basis of civil laws, as he put it: "justly divided into three types: (1) persons; (2) things; (3) acts. This division, he said, "was not always recognized by legal scholars, but for private international law it is exceedingly important" (p. 31).

But the largest part of his dissertation Bobrowski devoted to criminal law. He described as follows the essence of the problems arising between States in the field of criminal law:

> The operation of criminal laws of one State in another are discovered in the prosecution and punishment by one State of acts which are deemed to be criminal by another State, but not on the basis of their common jurisdiction, but on the basis of the close relations existing between the act and the State deeming it to be criminal. This close relation of a criminal act to a State arises when it belongs to a subject, when it comprises the subject, or, finally, when it is the theatre of the crime committed" (p. 114).

He continued:

> International criminal law owed its origin to the struggle of two equally important but opposed laws belonging to two States. On one hand, every State is obliged to protect tits subjects, both permanent and temporary. On the other, a State has the right to prosecute each offender of its laws, whosoever they are. When a violation occurs by a subject of one State of the laws of another, then the aforementioned laws come into conflict – Which of them should cede the right of protection or the right to punish?

Part Two reveals the content of proper conduct of States in the event the need arises to resolve the question of the prosecution and punishment of a guilty subject of his own or a foreign State, taking into account in so doing the interests of both States. "To bring both these requirements into equilibrium is the most difficult task of States, and their actions in this matter comprise the content of the Special Part of international private law, which is called international criminal law" (p. 136).

Bobrowski's thinking in relation to the division of civil and criminal procedure is original:

> Even though private international law has its own subject-matter, the determination of relations in conflict circumstances occurring from necessary and permitted actions or it is engaged with conflicts emanating from prohibited acts, it is *determinative* or *protective* (p. 5). The usual legal relations of subjects of one State in another comprise the content of the determinative part of private international law (*droit international civil*). The protective private international law has two main subject-matter: non-legal international civil procedure (*procès international civil*); and the prosecution of criminal injustice belongs to international criminal law (*droit international criminel*, and the very form of prosecuting comprises the content of international criminal procedure (*procès international criminel*) (p. 6).

In the conclusion of his study, Bobrowski expressed a certain optimism when he wrote that, having considered the major questions of private international law,

> we are persuaded that therein lie the requirements of science; we have surveyed the prescriptions of the positive laws of the major States and had occasion to be convinced that both prescriptions concerning private international civil law and relating to international criminal law do not fully agree with science. One cannot, however, fail to note in the legislation adopted in recent times the aspiration to conform to the requirements of science, and this enables us to hope that the time is near when the theory and practice of private international law will be one and the same (p. 298).

As follows from the above, the priority of Bobrowski in commencing the study of private international law in Russia is beyond doubt. As noted in modern doctrinal writings, thanks to Bobrowski and his colleague Blagoveshchenskii – young scholars at St. Petersburg University – the "questions of private international law became the subject-matter of study in doctrinal writings back in the 1850s".[107]

107 See N. M. Iurova, Международное гражданское процессуальное право: теоретические основы имплементации норм в правовой системе Российской Федерации [International Civil Procedure Law: Theoretical Foundations of the Implementation of Norms in the Legal System of the

Thus, the magister dissertation by Bobrovskii, being the first scientific study in Russia of the conflicts aspects of international civil-law and criminal-law relations and not avoiding, naturally, the shortcomings of a substantive and structural character, nonetheless made it possible to assess the state of doctrinal and normative principles of the birth of the Russian science of international private law and criminal law in the mid-nineteenth century.

Vladimir Danilovich Spasovich *(16 January 1829, b. Rechitsa, Minsk Governate (now Gomel Region) – 26 October 1906, d. Warsaw, Poland). Noted jurist, specialist in criminal law, scholar and "king of the advokatura", publicist, and public figure.*

Life and career. Spasovich received his general education at the Minsk Gymnasium. In 1845 he enrolled and in 1849 graduated from the Law Faculty of Petersburg University with the degree of candidate of law. He remained attached to the Chair of All-Nations Law to prepare a magister dissertation, receive the degree of magister, and prepare for a career of scientific research and teaching.[108]

On 23 August 1850, Spasovich expressed the wish in a request in the name of the Rector of the University "to be examined in order to receive the learned degree of magister of the law of nations and diplomacy".[109] Between 9 September 1850 and 29 January 1851 Spasovich successfully passed the oral and written magister examinations with regard to all-nations jurisprudence and diplomacy, State law of European States, and encyclopedia of lexprudence. In Autumn 1851 Spasovich submitted a dissertation to the Law Faculty for the degree of magister of all-nations law on the topic of the rights of neutral flag and neutral cargo. On 2 November 1851 the Faculty determined: "to allow the candidate Spasovich to the public defense of the dissertation written by him; to appoint the dispute for 11 November, on Sunday, at 12:00 hours; to appoint as opponents Messrs. Ivanovskii and Gorlov".[110] On 11 November 1851 Spasovich successfully defended the aforesaid magister dissertation.

Russian Federation] (M., 2008), p. 136.

[108] ЦГИА СПб, fond 14, opis' 1, file 5023 (1850).

[109] Ibid., l. 1, 9.

[110] V. D. Spasovich, О правах нейтральнаго флага и нейтральнаго груза. Разсуждение, представленное юридическому факультету Имп. С. Петербургскаго Университета Кандидатом Владимиром Спасовичем для получения степени Магистра Общенародного Права [On the Rights of Neutral Flag and Neutral Cargo. Discourse Submitted to the Law Faculty of the Imperial

But Spasovich did not become an international lawyer; he subsequently held various posts in the Law Faculty of St. Petersburg University: from 1856, junior scientific assistant, and from 1857, privat-docent at the Chair of Laws of the Kingdom of Poland;[111] from 1860 – professor *extraordinarius* at the Chair of Criminal Law.

In 1861 Spasovich was confirmed as a member of the University Court. He was among the first Russian sworn advokats. That same year he was demonstratively dismissed from the University and became a legal practitioner.[112] From 1864 he began to teach at the Imperial School of Jurisprudence.

International legal views. The dissertation is the sole but very noteworthy scholarly work by Spasovich on international law, being one of the first scholarly works on the carriage of neutral trade in wartime and topical in its day. Insofar as in the nineteenth century the maritime fleet remained a basic means of international transport, the problem of the seizure of vessels by belligerents was acute under conditions of constant warfare. Therefore, Spasovich was convinced: "questions of the rights of neutral trade ... constitute to this time one of the most controversial parts of inter-State law".[113] At the outset, Spasovich defined the status of a neutral State, which he considered to be a "State which in a war that has arisen between States does not take direct participation"; its rights, Spasovich believed, were as follows:

(1) inviolability of territory and indestructibility of territorial power. The territory of a particular State is a "safe refuge for the vanquished and belligerents seeking rescue thereon";

(2) the right to respect of the individual, honor, and to recognition of all legal actions of the State which does not exceed the limits of neutrality;

(3) inviolability of persons and things appertaining to it which are outside its territory. Neutral subjects are not to be made prisoners of war, their ownership is not the subject-matter of booty if they have not violated neutrality.

Spasovich drew the important conclusion that all this included also the "right of a neutral State to free and unobstructed trade outside its limits both with other neutrals and with belligerent States".[114] However, the right of neutral State to free

St. Petersburg University by Candidate Vladimir Spasovich in order to Receive the Degree of Magister of All-Nations Law] (Spb., 1851).

111 ЦГИА СПб, fond 14, opis' 3, file 8043 (1857).

112 In summer 1861 Spasovich, as a sign of protest against the violence of the authorities with respect to students, together with a number of other professors, left the University. The Учебник уголовного права [Textbook of Criminal Law], volume 1 (1863) in 1864 was prohibited by behest of Emperor Alexander II as containing dangerous thoughts, and Spasovich himself was dismissed from service. He became well-known as an advokat and publicist.

113 Spasovich, note 110 above, p. v.

114 Ibid., pp. 2-3.

trade, wrote Spasovich, is limited: "with regard to places, with regard to articles of trade, and with regard to means of the carriage of goods".

Spasovich substantiated in his work the inviolability of the vessel of a neutral State:

> By rights of a neutral flag we understand the right to unobstructed carriage on neutral ships on the high seas of goods belonging equally to neutral subjects and to subjects of belligerent States when these goods are not an article of military contraband, and by rights of neutral cargo is the freedom from seizure of goods by belligerents which are not considered to be military contraband although they are found on enemy ships.[115]

The first of these limitations concerns the right of blockade, the right of belligerents not to allow the ships of neutral powers into blocked ports. The second limitation concerns military contraband and the right of belligerents to obstruct delivery to the enemies thereof. The third relates to the maritime carriage of trade by neutral ships. In the conclusion relating to the results of his dissertation, Spasovich set out several rules for neutral trade which he then discussed and defended:

(1) Rule: "cargo is under the defense of the flag but is not subject to confiscation" – corresponds to the requirement of justice.

(2) The ship should be considered as part of the territory of that State whose flag it flies.

(3) Prize ships in naval warfare may be considered as an establishment of the State, and not of inter-State law because the real judge of the legality of a prize is the prize court of that State to which the privateer belongs.

(4) The inspection of warships and the taking possession of military contraband on them does not violate the right of neutral trade.

(5) The continental system of Napoleon may be considered as a reprisal on the part of France.

(6) International law has its beginning in Antiquity; among the ancients it developed in the form of legal custom and treaties, but was not made the subject-matter of science.[116]

Spasovich concluded: "The freedom of neutral flag and neutral cargo not only fully corresponds to the requirements of justness; it comprises a true success in the history of mankind". The freedom of neutral flag and neutral cargo in useful in many respects: (1) for neutrals, it defends them against the arbitrariness of belligerents; for belligerents, it defends private ownership of the belligerents against the baneful consequences of war; (c) for all mankind: mitigating the cruelty of naval warfare, it is the first step towards the "transformation of inter-State law

[115] Ibid., pp. iii-iv.

[116] Ibid., pp. 113-114.

determining the laws of naval warfare to approximating these laws to the practice of continental war".

Spasovich condemned the unjust methods of waging naval warfare and expressed the hope of its humanization:

> It is desirable that in time liberal principles extend to naval warfare and naval forces engage in battle without resort to the confiscation of merchant ships, and without making simple mariners or passengers not participating in war into prisoners of war … Naval warfare in this event will be only defensive and, without pursuing merchant ships or appropriating the ownership of peaceful citizens, confine itself to the defense of fatherland coasts, the carriage of troops to the territory of the enemy, and battles at sea with the naval forces of the enemy.

Spasovich immediately found that the thesis of his dissertation had practical resonance. The dissertation was used when Russia prepared to take part in the drafting of the 1856 Paris Declaration Respecting Maritime Law.

In sum, the scientific works of magister students at the Chair of All-Nations (International) Law of St. Petersburg are directly linked with the renaissance in Russia of autonomous international-legal thought. The merit of the Petersburg magisters is that they at the very outset of the embryonic Russian science of international law reacted to topical international and foreign policy problems of Russia of that time and submitted scholarly studies solely of an international-legal character.

An undoubted distinction of these dissertations was that, despite the politicized approach predominant in Russian doctrinal writings at the time in the analysis of international relations, events, and facts, the first magisters of the Chair under the guidance of Professor I. I. Ivanovskii "juridicized" the method of scientific research, decisively separating law from politics. This juridicized method of theoretical research over time has become a distinctive feature of the St. Petersburg scientific school of international law.

The magister dissertations of Zaremba and Spasovich foreshadowed the emergence of the next two better known and widely cited works on the international law of the sea by Leonid Nikolaevich Demis and especially by Dmitrii Ivanovich Kachenovskii.[117]

[117] L. N. Demis, Обозрение трактатов о морском торговом нейтралитете [Survey of Treaties on Maritime Trade Neutrality] (Spb., 1854); Kachenovskii, note 32 above.

Chapter 5

Contribution of Other Chairs of Law Faculty to International Law

Representatives of other chairs in the Law Faculty of St. Petersburg University made noteworthy contributions to the development of the science of international law in Russia. Among them are the works of N. A. Bezobrazov.

Nikolai Aleksandrovich Bezobrazov *(17 October 1816, b. St. Petersburg – 15 October 1867, d. Tsarskoe selo, St. Petersburg). Jurist, writer, public and political figure.*

Life and career. Nikolai Bezobrazov was the son of a Governor of St. Petersburg. In 1835, after graduating from the Faculty of Philosophy and Law of the University with the degree of candidate of law, he remained at the Chair of State Law to prepare a magister dissertation and eventually pursue a career in research and teaching.

On 31 December 1838 Bezobrazov defended a magister dissertation on the topic: "Study of the Principles of External State Law, or Explanation of the Properties of Mutual Relations of States"; it was published in advance of the defense.[1] The dissertation was his only work in the field of jurisprudence.

After defending his dissertation, Bezobrazov worked in the Ministry of Foreign Affairs, including from 1839 to 1841 at the diplomatic mission in Naples, and then from 1842 to 1843 in the Asian Department. From 1846 with the title of chamberlain, he served as an official on special assignment attached to the administrative office of the Cabinet of Ministers. From 1852 he worked in the I Division of the Imperial Chancellery. He was appointed a privy State counsellor. Thereafter, Bezobrazov moved away from the law and State service and occupied himself with various public affairs and social issues.

The extensive social movement that embraced Russian society in the 1850-60s around the problems of serfdom also caught him up; he became one of the ideologues of the noble advocates of serfdom. He opposed the emancipation of the serfs and upheld the inviolability of noble privileges provided by the 1785 Charter giving rights, privileges, and immunities to the nobility. As time passed, Bezobrazov convinced himself that the emancipation of the serfs in 1861 did not have the global consequences which so disturbed him and took a more moderate position. This became evident in his day-dreaming about the pre-eminent role of the Russian nobility in rural life, reflected in various pamphlets, many of which were published in Berlin: Две записки по вотчинному вопросу [Two Notes on the Ownership Question] (Berlin, 1859); О старом и новом порядке и об устроенном труде в

[1] N. A. Bezobrazov, Изследование начал внешнего государственного права или объяснение свойств взаимных отношений государств [Study of the Principles of External State Law, or Explanation of the Properties of Mutual Relations of States] (Spb., 1838). Butler Б60.

применении к нашим поместным отношениям [On the Old and New Order and on the Arrangement of Labor in Application to Our Estate System of Land Tenure Relations] (Spb., 1863); За твердость закона [For Firmness of the Law] (Spb., 1865).

For the last twelve years of his life, Bezobrazov was the Marshal of the Petersburg Nobility. He died suddenly on 15 October 1867 in Tsarskoe selo and is buried at the Alexander-Nevskii Monastery in St. Petersburg.

International legal views. Bezobrazov is part of the history of international law in Russia by reason of his magister dissertation. The work was well received in its time, given the originality of the positions he advanced in the dissertation and the overall quality of the work. The dissertation explored the concept and essence of States, the basis of mutual relations between States, their legal forms, content, and consequences. He declared himself to be a proponent of the view that international law is not "inter-State law" – a view widely shared in doctrinal writings of the nineteenth century, especially German writings, thanks to Hegel – but as "external State law" of each State regulating its foreign relations. Objectively, this position led to recognition of the primacy of the internal law of a State over international law.[2]

Bezobrazov was against the theories of natural law and social contract, and likewise against the analogy between man and the State. At the beginning of his work, he declared "with apprehension", but boldly: "all writers concerning the law of nations [should] accept as the basis of their theories the arbitrary idea of likening the State to man … constructing an apparently beautiful edifice but which in fact is a castle in the air". The primary requirement of science is that the principles on which it rests be "drawn from the very existence of State relations and be particular to them". In his view, international lawyers, standing on positions of natural law, endow the State with almost all the qualities of individuals, thanks to which their depiction of the mutual relations of States is inaccurate and does not correspond to reality. Therefore, he considered these theories to be "decayed", which in the nineteenth century should have been rightly rejected by scholars (pp. 2-3).

In his searches for the truth, Bezobrazov put three questions: "What is the State? On what are the mutual relations of various States based? What are the consequences of such inter-relations?" His conclusion: "The State is a civil society ruled by a supreme authority for the purpose of the external determination and comprehensive securing of the rights of its members. By virtue of this purpose, it has certain rights and duties" and acts outside as a juridical person (p. 46). It follows: "By the nature of a State's actions, all its relations are internal: it cannot have any other object of acting except determining and securing the rights of its subjects. Only when it has achieved this purpose do relations originate which could be called external, because then the State comes into contact with persons who are not subject to its governmental authority", that is, foreign subjects (p. 46, note VIII).

2 According to the theory of the primacy of municipal law, international law – as the sum of external State laws of various States – is "external State law". Hence the State itself has the right to decide whether to comply with international law, whether this corresponds with its interests.

Passing on to an analysis of the science of State law, Bezobrazov divided it into two parts: "The science of State law must contain rules by which the State must act in order to determine and secure the rights of its co-members in their relations between themselves – the subject-matter of internal State law, and in their relations with members of other States – the subject-matter of external State law".

The basis of the mutual relations of various States are the links and alignments of members of States; in such instances the "purpose of those States coalesce: for then each of them faces the external determination and securing of the rights of their members; that is the point of contact of the supreme rights of several States as juridical persons" (p. 47). Bezobrazov believed that "since the purpose of the activities of a State in its external relations is identical with it in its internal relations: consequently, its duties and rights remain unchanged".

Bezobrazov draws original conclusions from the foregoing. Following Hegel, he believed that inter-State relations is a domain where external State law appears. The so-called "unconditional rights" ascribed to a State – equality, independence, self-preservation – are of no significance. Hence yet another distinctive conclusion: "The so-called law of nations (*jus gentium*) is an inappropriate name signifying nothing" (p. 84). Therefore, international law is not real law, as municipal law is (that is, positive law, especially the legislation of States), but merely the "ought". The reality of this "ought" depends upon the sovereign wills of different States, on their positions and actions over which there is no higher law, officials and judges in the usual sense of these concepts, as we see within States (pp. 47-50).

Bezobrazov asserted that States are equal in that they have an identical purpose and therefore identical rights and duties to achieve it; but to speak about the right to equality would mean to presuppose the possibility of inequality, the possibility of the existence of a State whose purpose and consequently whose supreme rights would be of less significance than those of other States: "Although it is well known that many differences, titles, and ceremonials are observed in the diplomatic discourse ..., they are of major significance only in politics. With regard to States as juridical persons, the right of equality is an expression which has no application whatever".

Bezobrazov was just as critical with respect to the arguments concerning the rights of States to mutual independence:

> of even less significance are the rights of States to mutual independence and mutual self-protection. Each State, as a juridical person, has as object only itself and its members; and therefore neither possession by another State nor interference in its affairs, nor a branch of the rights of another Power may be objects of its activities. Arbitrary interference and breach of rights are a crime: a crime not peculiar to a juridical person.

His views on the treaty are likewise original. A treaty is the decisions of the supreme authorities of a number of countries. Scholars are wrong to consider a treaty to be a contract. "There is no concept more mistaken and erroneous"; a contract may be concluded to the detriment of the person being bound. In the event of the confirmation (ratification) of a treaty, the legislator is guided by the same principles as when promulgating a law. Without ratification, a treaty has no force, and the treaty is repealed by the same means as it was confirmed. "It does not follow from this, however, that if … one Government does not consent to the abrogation of a treaty the other has no right to eliminate it". A treaty may be made which is detrimental to a State, "and then, by virtue of the purpose of its being, it not only has the right but also the obligation to eliminate it notwithstanding the lack of consent of another Government thereto" (pp. 57-61).

Bezobrazov's work was, in essence, the first in the Russian science of the law of nations to attempt to investigate international law as such. Grabar had a high opinion of the study, devoting nine pages to it.[3] He described Bezobrazov's contribution as follows:

> In opposing the doctrine of the basic rights of States and seeing the task of international law as the international protection of the rights of citizens of individual States, he anticipated the structure of a new system of international law subsequently developed by N. M. Korkunov half a century later and he laid the foundations for that portion of international law which F. F. Martens called international administration ("international administrative law").[4]

Ivan Efimovich Andreevskii *(13 March 1831, b. St. Petersburg – 20 March 1891, d. St. Petersburg). Well-known Russian legal scholar specializing in the history and theory of State law and police (administrative) law.*

Life and career. Andreevskii was the son of a doctor of medicine. After graduating with the silver medal from the I Petersburg Men's Gymnasium in 1848,[5] Andreevskii enrolled in the Law Faculty of St. Petersburg University as a fee-paying student. He completed the course of study in 1852 with the degree of candidate of laws. During his studies, he developed an interest in legal history, State law, and police law.

Having decided to pursue an academic career, he believed it would be useful to acquire some practical legal experience before doing so. For three years, from 1852 to 1855, he worked in the office of the St. Petersburg Governate procurator. Simultaneously, commencing in 1853, he served as a junior scientific associate at the Chair of State-Decency and Public Amenities Laws, and in June 1854 passed the magister

[3] V. E. Grabar, *The History of International Law in Russia 1647-1917: A Bio-Bibliographical Study*, transl. W. E. Butler (1990), pp. 292-300.

[4] Ibid., p. 298.

[5] ЦГИА СПб, fond 114, opis' 1, file 684.

examinations.[6] That same year he published and defended his dissertation for the degree of magister of State law.[7]

In order to secure permission to lecture, in 1855 Andreevskii submitted a dissertation *pro venia legendi*[8] and was confirmed in the post of privat-docent at the Chair of State-Decency and Public Amenities Laws and assigned to lecture also on State and police law. That same year he was offered a position at the Chair of the History of Russian Legislation and Encyclopedia of Lexprudence in the School of Jurisprudence,[9] and retained this post until 1878.[10]

In 1857 Andreevskii was appointed professor and held the Chair of Police Law. He defended his doctoral dissertation on 12 April 1864 in the field of State law and legal history.[11] From 1875 to 1878 he acted as the Dean of the Law Faculty of St. Petersburg University, and from 1883, as Rector of the University. He resigned as Rector from 28 May 1883 and in general from the University as from 1 August 1883. From 1885 to 1891 he was the Director and Head of the Chair of Science on Archives of the Archaeological Institute. From 1890 until his death in 1891 he was the editor-in-chief of volume eight of the Brockhaus-Efron Encyclopedic Dictionary.

Andreevskii died at St. Petersburg on 20 May 1891 and is buried at the Blagoveshchensk Cemetery (in the new village).[12]

International legal views. Two Andreevskii's works relate to international law: his magister dissertation on the rights of foreigners in Russia and his discourse *pro*

[6] ЦГИА СПб, fond 14, opis' 1, file 5299

[7] Ivan Andreevskii, О правах иностранцев в России до вступления Иоанна III Васильевича на престол Великого Княжества Московского [On the Rights of Foreigners in Russia Before the Accession of Ivan III Vasil'evich to the Throne of the Grand Duchy of Muscovy] (Spb., 1854); Butler A89. Also see a reprinted version under the same title, with a brief introduction by Evgen Chernets'kyi, published at Bila Tserkva by O. V. Pshonkivskyi in 2012.

[8] Andreevskii, О договоре Новгорода с Немецкими городами и Готлендом, заключенном в 1270 году [On the Treaty of Novgorod with the German Cities and Gotland, Concluded in 1270] (Spb. 1855). Butler A88.

[9] ЦГИА СПб, fond 355, opis' 1, file 3755.

[10] In December 1857, Emperor Alexander I made a visit to the School of Jurisprudence and attended Andreevskii's lecture on State law. The Emperor was so impressed that he had presented to Andreevskii a gold finger ring set in diamonds. Later, Andreevskii was repeatedly invited to teach the legal sciences to the children of the Emperor; in 1861 Andreevskii taught the encyclopedia of lexprudence and police law to the Tsarevich Nikolai Aleksandrovich; from 1863 to 1866, State law to the eldest son Alexander, the future Alexander III; in those same years he taught the legal sciences to the young children of Alexander II – Vladimir and Sergei. See E. A. Annenkova, Императорское училище правоведения [Imperial School of Jurisprudence] (Spb., 2006), pp. 84-85.

[11] Andreevskii, О наместниках, воеводах и губернаторах [On Governors-General, Voevods, and Governors] (Spb., 1864).

[12] The students of the University carried a wreath to the gravesite inscribed: "To the Ideal Rector, Favorite Professor, and Honorable Professor Ivan Efimovich Andreevskii".

venia legendi on the treaty of 1270 between Novgorod and the German cities and Gotland.

Russian doctrinal writings often name D. I. Meier, a graduate in 1841 of the St. Petersburg Pedagogical Institute[13] who took a position at Kazan University, as the "founder" of conflicts law in Russia. Andreevskii's magister dissertation in 1854, however, was the first fundamental work on the legal status of foreigners in Russian legal science. It considered the defense of the rights of foreigners, including the resolution of conflicts of laws of various States and the determination of the applicable law.

Andreevskii divided the rights of foreigners into public and private. Considering foreigners to be a "special class of the population", he suggested that only persons living in some State with the permission of the highest authorities of the said State and enjoying either rights in common with all foreigners or rights granted to an individual class of foreigners by the highest authorities fall under the regulation of domestic legal norms (pp. 6-8). Having analyzed the legal regulation of the status of foreigners in pre-Petrine Rus, Andreevskii concluded that foreigners had extensive rights and opportunities in Rus. With regard to possible legal conflicts relating to the status of foreigners, Andreevskii was inclined to resolve them through legislation, having regard to the supreme will of the State in which the foreigners were situated.[14]

Andreevskii addressed aspects of the legal status of foreigners that remain topical, such as the right to enter and exit, freedom to celebrate religious beliefs and rituals, ownership and possession of property and property rights, engaging in commerce and trade, and bringing suits in court. Certain aspects of coastal law, criminal law, and jurisdiction are considered, as well as the rights of prisoners of war, limitations on the right to inherit, among others. Andreevskii convincingly concluded that medieval Russian and foreign documentary sources show that from ancient times in Rus the rights and privileges of foreigners were more humane and just than the history of the rights of foreigners in other European nations (pp. 1-15). He noted such humanitarian principles of medieval Russian law as the right of free entry and exit for foreigners, Russian tolerance of other religious faiths, granting foreigners the right to possess houses in cities, and so on. Despite a certain idealization of medieval Russian ways and mores, Andreevskii declared himself to be a proponent of a humanist approach to inter-State legal relations.

Contemporaries described Andreevskii's book as occupying

> one of the key places in legal literature of the mid-nineteenth century, serving as the basis for many scholarly inquiries and inaugurating the be-

[13] Meier's lectures, which contained a survey on private international law, were published posthumously. See D. I. Meier, Русское гражданское право: Общая часть [Russian Civil Law: General Part] (Kazan, 1858). Vol. 1.

[14] See Iu. A. Komnatnaia, «К вопросу о генезисе отечественной доктрины коллизионного права в дореволюционный период» [On the Question of the Genesis of the Fatherland Doctrine of Conflicts Law in the Prerevolutionary Period], in Актуальные проблемы развития национальной и региональной экономики [Topical Problems of the Development of the National and Regional Economy] (Belgorod, 2010), p. 176.

ginning of discussions in the general theory of law. A singular service of Andreevskii was that he, using the legal status of foreigners as an example, laid the foundations for studies on international conflicts law at the historical and theoretical levels. He defined the 'concept of a foreigner satisfactory for international, State, and civil law, and determined the legal status of this category of persons'.[15]

In the following year Andreevskii published his *pro venia legendi* dissertation on the 1270 Novgorod treaty. He explored the legal foundations of the treaty: why it was concluded at all, the trade provisions, the correlation of treaty norms with domestic law, the procedure for promulgation of the treaty, the period of operation of the treaty, and the authenticity of the surviving texts. He considered the conclusion of the treaty to have been "objectively necessary" at the time with German cities, especially those in the Baltic area, and undertook a comparative analysis of the 1270 treaty with other treaties of Novgorod.

Andreevskii produced an article for the Encyclopedic Dictionary of Brockhaus and Efron on the distinguished Swiss-German legal scholar, Johann-Caspar Bluntschli and the latter's contributions to international and to State law. He noted that Bluntschli's ideas had an impact on political and legal circles in Europe: Bluntschli's suggestion that periodic congresses of international lawyers be held in Europe with a view to replacing the use of force in international relations by international tribunals to punish those who encouraged warfare. Andreevskii credited Bluntschli with promoting activities that led to the formation of the Institute of International Law at Ghent in 1873.[16]

[15] Ibid., pp. 177, 181.

[16] See Andreevskii, «Блунчли (Иоганн-Каспар Bluntschli» [Bluntschli (Johann-Caspar Bluntschli)], Энциклопедический словарь Брокгауза и Ефрона [Encyclopedic Dictionary of Brockhaus and Efron] (1891), IV(7), p. 113. Not in Butler. Andreevskii is believed to have written about 200 articles in this Encyclopedia, a full inventory of which remains to be produced. Andreevskii ignored or was unaware of the contributions of Kachenovskii to the enterprise of forming the Institut de droit international. The Russian members of the Institute up to 2001 are listed in Peter Macalister-Smith, "Who Was Who in the Institut de droit international", *Jus Gentium: Journal of International Legal History*, VIII (2023), pp. 303-566.

THE GOLDEN ERA
(1860s-EARLY 1920s)

Chapter 6

Prerequisites of International Legal Teaching and Research

Between the 1870s and the Russian Revolution of October 1917 the Chair of International Law at St. Petersburg University enjoyed a "golden era" in all aspects – quality of academic appointments, attraction of excellent students, and an impressive record of original and substantial contributions to legal scholarship. This period coincided with significant changes in world politics, in the system of international relations, and in the foreign policy of the Russian Empire. All these factors contributed to the enhanced role and importance of international law in responding to these changes.

France had become a leading power in Europe, restored after the Napoleonic debacle. During the Prussian pursuit of the military and political unification of Germany and the Franco-Prussian War of 1870-71, France sustained a crushing defeat that led to a readjustment of the balance of power in Europe. As a result of Russia losing the Crimean War between 1853 and 1856, she was subjected to the 1856 Treaty of Paris, whose provisions neutralized the Black Sea and demilitarized the coasts in and nearby the Black Sea Straits.

But during the second half of the nineteenth century, the Russian Empire had become a major power in the world. Having finally "pacified" and subjugated the Caucasus, Russia began to expand its influence and enlarge its territories (sometimes by peaceful means and in others by military force) in Central Asia and the Far East, clashing with the interests of England, India, and Japan. Alaska was ceded to the United States; Russia waged war against Turkey in the Balkans, which led to the liberation of the southern Slavic peoples (Serbia and Bulgaria became independent).

By the end of the nineteenth century, the rivalries between the powers of the world sharpened. The competition for colonies in Asia, Africa, the Americas, and Oceania intensified, especially among England, France, and Germany. Russia took advantage of international law to strengthen its positions. In 1873 Russia concluded a Treaty with Austria-Hungary and Germany – the so-called "Alliance of the Three Emperors", which ultimately collapsed. The "Triple Alliance" was formed among Austria, Germany, and Italy in 1882. Russia then drew closer to France. A Russo-French military alliance was legally formalized between 1891 and 1893. Between 1904 and 1907 a military alliance was created between England, Russia, and France, called the "Triple Entente". Eventually, Europe was divided into hostile military blocs that led to the First World War between 1914 and 1918, and the cardinal changes on the political map of the world affected the fates of many peoples and States.

Notwithstanding the tensions and rivalries among the major powers, economic, trade, cultural, and communications links between nations, States, and continents strengthened unexpectedly. These processes all required legal advice and the legal structuring of inter-State relations. The institutionalization of international links began. An international union for measurement of the earth (1864); the International Telegraph Union (1865), the International Metrological Association (1873), the Universal Postal Union (1874), and the International Union of Weights and Measures (1875), among others were created.

The role of international law grew to regulate international relations and inter-State cooperation. The codification of various branches and rules of international law intensified, the commencement of which many trace to the 1815 Congress of Vienna. Codification addressed the law of war: the 1856 Declaration of Paris Respecting Maritime Law; the 1864 Geneva Convention for the Amelioration of the Condition of the Wounded in Armies in the Field; and the 1868 St. Petersburg Declaration Renouncing the Use, in Time of War, of Explosive Projectiles Under 400 Grammes Weight.

The development of increasingly lethal types of weaponry against the background of imminent threats of large-scale war in Europe inspired the Russian Government to initiate the convoking of an international conference in order to adopt international legal measures for the limitation of armaments and military casualties. The First and Second Hague Peace Conferences of 1899 and 1907 adopted conventions and declarations on limiting the means and methods of waging warfare, the protection of victims thereof, and the acceptance of international conciliation and arbitration for the peaceful settlement of international disputes.

Official delegates of the Russian Empire and members of the Faculty of Law of St. Petersburg University took an active part in the organization and activities of virtually all the aforesaid conferences. Professor F. F. Martens, Head of the Chair of International Law, remarked upon the efforts of Russia to establish the peaceful foundations of international existence: "History knows no civilized nation which undertook so many attempts for the peace-loving settlement of questions of international order and law which had matured".[1]

An extensive anti-war movement had emerged in Russia, Europe, and the United States; peace societies were created in many countries. Everywhere one observed pacifist ideas inspired by the armaments race and by the development and use of increasingly lethal types of weapons and intensification of military brutality.

The second half of the nineteenth century was an important period in completing the recognition of international law as a separate politico-legal category, an important instrument of diplomacy, and an autonomous branch of legal science. By the mid-nineteenth century, the Russian translation of the Benthamite term "international law" had replaced "jus gentium", "law of nations", "nations law", and "all-nations law". The flourishing of "international law" was extolled in doctrinal writings by the end of the century with optimistic predictions about the end of the era of wars and the imminent period of peace and quiet. Professor Martens wrote of this period:

> International relations … increasingly take on a legal character. The principles of contemporary positive international law are being affirmed and

[1] F. F. Martens, «Гаагская конференция Европы» [Hague Peace Conference], Вестник Европы [Herald of Europe], LLII (1900), p. 25. Not in Butler.

> developing. Contemporary enlightened governments and nations are increasingly convinced of the inadequacy of their forces alone to completely satisfy developing State needs and the necessity for extensive mutual relations and assistance. In the sphere of political relations the interests of the Powers are discussed at congresses and conferences, whose decisions acquire the force of law. The public interests of States find satisfaction in special and general treaties on various questions concerning the social relations of nations. The establishment of positive legal principles, rules, and laws determining the mutual relations of States are a result of international agreements.[2]

A distinctive culmination of this process was the First Hague Conference in 1899 convened at the initiative of Russia – a "radiant monument of the nineteenth century".[3] The 1899 Conference laid the beginnings for the codification and progressive development of international law and the foundations for ensuring international peace and security.[4]

Many international lawyers, in making their contributions to the legal ordering of inter-State relations and ensuring peace and mutually-advantageous cooperation between States in lectures, monographs, and journal articles, emphasized the need to limit military forms of settling disputes. They emphasized the extensive use diplomacy, developing arbitral courts, creating a permanent international court, engaging in retorsion, boycotts, or reprisals, reducing armaments, eliminating individual types of lethal weapons, and humanizing the means and methods of waging war.

The international lawyers of Russia during the second half of the nineteenth century contributed to this new field of legal science and practice when an upheaval was occurring in Russian social consciousness. They elaborated approaches to theoretical and applied jurisprudence to concentrate on the perception of the place and role of Russian science, education, and culture in the restructuring of society. As Tomsinov noted, "Russian jurists, liberated from the fettered development of their thinking under the influence of foreign legal doctrines, set out on an independent path in their research of legal phenomena with the emphasis not on speculative theories, but on practice".[5]

[2] Martens, Современное международное право цивилизованных народов [Contemporary International Law of Civilized Nations] (2d ed.; Spb., 1887), I, p. 147.

[3] V. M. Gessen, «О значении Гаагской конференции мира» [On the Significance of the Hague Peace Conference], Журнал Министерства юстиции [Journal of the Ministry of Justice], no. 4 (1900), p. 107.

[4] V. S. Ivanenko (comp. & ed.), 100-летие инициативы России: От Первой конференции мира 1899 г. к Третьей конференции мира 1999 г.: Сборник документов [100th Anniversary of the Initiative of Russia: From the 1899 First Peace Conference to the 1999 Third Peace Conference: Collection of Documents] (Spb., 1999).

[5] V. A. Tomsinov, Российские правоведы XVIII-XIX веков: очерки жизни и творчества [Russian Jurists of the XVIII-XIX Centuries: Essays on Life and Creativity] (M., 2007), I, p. 211.

A period commenced from the 1870s of several decades during which there was close cooperation between the Chair of International Law of St. Petersburg University and the Ministry of Foreign Affairs of the Russian Empire. Many members of the Chair simultaneously held executive posts in departments of the Ministry or in the apparatus of the Ministry, and graduates of the Chair were invited to serve abroad in diplomatic missions. Given its location in the capital of the country, the University became a "supplier" of personnel for the Ministry. The enhanced role of international law in the foreign policy of Russia was reinforced by the formation of a special subdivision within the Ministry – the international-legal unit headed always by a representative of the Chair of International Law of St. Petersburg University. Most lecturers or graduates of the Chair of International Law worked in the international legal unit of the Ministry.

The initiator of cooperation with St. Petersburg University was the Ministry of Foreign Affairs itself, under the leadership of Minister Aleksandr Mikhailovich Gorchakov (1798-1883). His appointment opened a new era in Russian foreign policy; he regarded international law with respect. Gorchakov devoted great attention to the selection of personnel for careers in diplomacy. Under his leadership, "Rules for Appointment to Service and Posts" in the Ministry were adopted. The Ministry wished to attract "educated people, intellectually-developed and capable, provided with maintenance allowing them to exist comfortably, and also provided in the future with a good pension …".[6]

When applying for appointment in the Ministry of Foreign Affairs, candidates were required to pass several examinations in languages and erudition:

> For appointment for service and to posts in the Ministry of Foreign Affairs, the following rules are decreed:
>
> 1) Anyone, without exception, applying for service in whatever branch, is obliged to subject himself to a preliminary test of his abilities specially applicable to those occupations to which he is to be appointed. The test should be performed by two assistant heads of that unit where the applicant wishes to be appointed.
>
> 2) If anyone wishes to apply directly for any diplomatic post or transfer from such to another not strictly diplomatic, he is, in addition to the aforesaid general test, obliged to pass yet another [test] relating partly to knowledge and part to his abilities.
>
> This test will be given according to the syllabus below:
>
> I. <u>Test of knowledge</u>. Within the range of the text shall be:
>
> 1) With regard to languages: knowledge of the Russian and French languages. The appointed official must be able in both languages to express himself freely and to be in a state to set out his thoughts in a letter correctly and clearly. Knowledge of the Latin, German, and English languages is

[6] See P. V. Stegnii, «Связь времен» [Link of the Times], Международная жизнь [International Life], no. 9-10 (2002), pp. 13-35. The author was the Director of the Historical-Documentation Section of the Ministry of Foreign Affairs of Russia.

not obligatory, but the ability to speak and write in them, and likewise in Polish (or a people not belonging thereto) and other languages, particularly oriental, will give a stronger right to appointment to posts.

2) With respect to sciences.

a) General information on the diplomatic sciences in the general sense and especially international law and the law of the sea.

b) The history of peace and other treaties in general, and especially those in which Russia has participated since the times of Catherine II.

c) The main principles of political economy in its application to the State economy and foreign trade.;

d) Universal statistics.

Note. To avoid difficulties with regard to the choice between numerous works existing on the subject of the diplomatic sciences, and in order to give more systematic direction for preparation of the official being tested, manuals have been determined with regard to which the text should be given.

II. Test of abilities. Those appearing for the test should:

a) On attentively reading the matter given to him, submit a written extract therefrom and orally set out his understanding thereof.

b) With regard to the proposed subject-matter, compose in the Russian and French languages a version from which one may determine to what degree the official being tested mastered this subject-matter and sets out his thoughts and convictions correctly and clearly.

III. By the name of the posts as strictly diplomatic is understood establishment and supra-establishment places in the Chancellery of the Ministry, I and II Sections of the Asian Department and attached to embassies, missions, and consulates.

IV. The test for appointment to diplomatic posts will be in the presence of members of the Council of the Ministry of Foreign Affairs by persons specially appointed to this end, numbering no more than three.[7]

§6.1. *Russian Society of International Law*

The growing maturity of international law as a legal science and the increased awareness of the professional identity of international lawyers as a species of legal specialist in Russia led, as elsewhere in Europe, to the formation of societies of international and comparative law. The formation of the Russian Society has been

[7] See «Министерство иностранных дел России в 1856-1899 гг.» [Ministry of Foreign Affairs of Russia in 1856-1899], Дипломатический вестник [Diplomatic Herald], no. 4 (April 2001) (available online).

shrouded in mystery and its existence even doubted. Grabar reported that in 1880 an international law society was founded at St. Petersburg for the purpose of "1) the promotion of the development of international law; 2) the dissemination of correct opinions on international relations; 3) the support for all efforts towards the codification of international law; and 4) the promotion and strengthening of amicable international relations and pacific views".[8] He continued:

> The secretary of the society was Professor F. F. Martens. The society had its own organ, which ceased, it would seem, with its first number. I have not succeeded in seeing a copy, and the publication is not in the Lenin Library. Vaksel' reported to the society on the extradition of criminals and this was printed in the *Bulletin* of the society. The report was also printed in two St. Petersburg newspapers.[9]

Grabar was right about the Lenin Library (now the Russian State Library) and, indeed, all others in Russia at the time. Searches in the archives,[10] however, have found the *Bulletin* and enable a fuller history of the Russian Society of International Law to be composed than was previously possible.[11]

The formation of a society of international law in Russia in the early 1880s was, in the context of the times, not an extraordinary event. For some years throughout Europe legal scholars had been inclined to form non-State or quasi-State associations in order to better pursue scientific investigation and collaboration. A Russian scholar expressed the position as follows: given the inability of

> State scientific institutions to fully resolve the tasks of scientific provision for the life of society [,] the objective requirement of increasing and intensifying scientific research in combination with the aspiration of progressive educated people to contribute their own mite to the progress of

[8] V. E. Grabar, *The History of International Law in Russia 1647-1917: A Bio-Bibliographical Study*, transl. W. E. Butler (1990), p. 470.

[9] Ibid. Also see W. E. Butler, "The Development of International Legal Periodicals in Russia", *Review of Socialist Law*, IX (1983), pp. 367-376. Included in this article are translations of the full Table of Contents of the "Simson Journal" (1897) and the Korovin/Pashukanis journal (1928). The contents of the Simson Journal appear as well in W. E. Butler, "Ewald-Wilhelm Simson: Estonian/Russian International Lawyer", *Jus Gentium: Journal of International Legal History*, VIII (2023), pp. 154-158.

[10] See V. S. Ivanenko, «Русское Общество международного права 80-х годов XIX века: исторические итоги и уроки организации и деятельности» [The Russian Society of International Law of the 1880s: Historical Results and Lessons of Organization and Activity], Российский ежегодник международного права 2015 [Russian Year-Book of International Law 2015] (Spb., 2016), pp. 119-137; W. E. Butler and V. S. Ivanenko, "On the Russian Society of International Law (1880)", *Jus Gentium: Journal of International Legal History*, II (2017), pp. 189-200.

[11] Apart from Grabar mentioning the Society in note 8 above, in all other mentions, including the article in note 9 above and passing references in Russian international legal textbooks (all citing Grabar) and a brief Wikipedia article in Russian by Ivanenko, the Society was unknown to the world of international law until 2006. The existence of a printed version of the Society founding document was reported in W. E. Butler, "On the Fiftieth Anniversary of Grabar's History of International Law in Russia", *Journal of the History of International Law*, X (2008), pp. 317-318; based on E. A. Annenkova, Императорское училище правоведения [Imperial School of Jurisprudence] (Spb., 2006), p. 295, where the title page of the Statute is reproduced.

national science and of the interest of the State in sharing these concerns with the public led to the affirmation of a new form of the organization of science – scientific societies.[12]

Law societies emerged late in Russia compared with other disciplines.[13] Most were attached to universities,[14] for the "golden age" of the legal practitioner was at an embryonic stage, normally dated from 1864 onwards.[15] By happy coincidence, the 1863 General Statute on Russian Universities (which preceded the 1864 judicial reforms by less than a year) gave universities the right to create scientific societies. The Statute of the Law Society attached to St. Petersburg University provided that the aims of the Society were created in order to "work out theoretical and practical questions of law and to disseminate legal knowledge" among the populace.[16] These aims in practice were broadly understood. Law societies were enlisted to comment upon and critique draft legislative acts by preparing expert legal opinions for lawmakers to consider.

The Moscow Law Society was the first to be organized (1865), followed by another in Kyiv (1876), and then in St. Petersburg (1877). In all about forty such law societies were formed throughout the Russian Empire. Most were rather active. Protocols of their sessions were routinely published in the daily press and in specialist law journals. Although late to be formed, the St. Petersburg Law Society, being based in the capital, became the largest, most stable, and perhaps the most influential. Initially it contained two divisions: civil and criminal law, later augmented by divisions for administrative law and customary law.[17] International law did not figure in the St. Petersburg Law Society, which led the international lawyers to seek to form their own society: the Russian Society of International Law.

12 V. S. Miridonova, Юридические общества в России (1865-1917 гг.) [Law Societies in Russia (1865-1917)] (Nizhnii Novgorod, 2002), p. 12 (abstract diss. kand. iurid. nauk).

13 On scholarly societies in general, see E. V. Soboleva, Организация науки в пореформенной России [The Organization of Science in Reforming Russia] (L., 1983), pp. 142-160.

14 See V. I. Kokhnov, «Значение юридических обществ в деле научной разработки права» [Significance of Law Societies in the Cause of the Scientific Development of Law], Юридический вестник [Legal Herald], no. 2-3 (1875), pp. 35-45; A. G. Gorin, «Юридические общества дореволюционной России» [Law Societies of Prerevolutionary Russia], Государство и право [State and Law], no. 7 (1989), pp. 117-123; V. A. Tomsinov, Московское юридическое общество при императорском Московском университете [Moscow Law Society attached to the Imperial Moscow University], Законодательство [Legislation], no. 3 (2012), pp. 88-94; no. 4 (2012), pp. 88-94; no. 5 (2012), pp. 88-94; E. A. Krestianninkov, «Юридическое общество при Императорском Томском университете» [Law Society attached to Imperial Tomsk University], Журнал российского права [Journal of Russian Law], no. 9 (2013), pp. 85-94.

15 See W. E. Butler, *The Russian Legal Practitioner* (2011), pp. 25-40.

16 The Statute of the Law Society attached to the Imperial St. Petersburg University was published in the Журнал гражданского и уголовного права [Journal of Civil and Criminal Law], VII (1877), pp. 306-311.

17 See Юридическое общество при Императорском С.-Петербургском Университете за 25 лет [Law Society attached to the Imperial St. Petersburg University for 25 Years] (Spb., 1902).

The formation of the Russian Society of International Law proceeded with unusual speed, commencing in April 1880.[18] The initiators of the Society were two highly-placed officials: Professor Fedor Fedorovich Martens (1845-1909), who at the time headed the Chair of International Law at St. Petersburg University and was attached for special assignments to the State Chancellor of Russia, A. M. Gorchakov (1798-1883); and Baron Aleksandr Genrikhovich Zhomini (Jomini) (1814-1888), a Deputy Minister of Foreign Affairs of Russia.[19] They drafted the Statute of the Society. Within a month, by 27 April 1880, the Statute of the Society was submitted for approval to the relevant State authorities. A narrow group of senior Russian officials participated in an intensive correspondence concerning the Society: the Ministry of Foreign Affairs, the III Department of the Chancellery of His Imperial Majesty (the highest police agency of the Empire), the Ministry of Internal Affairs, and the Ministry of Public Enlightenment.

There were objections. The Director of the Department of the Ministry of Public Enlightenment, M. E. Bradke, submitted the following comment: "All learned societies to be founded not attached to universities shall be authorized not other than by grace of His Majesty requested through the Committee of Ministers, which should be preceded by contact with the Ministry of Internal Affairs and the III Section and consideration of the Statute in the Learned Committee" of the Ministry of Public Enlightenment. Bradke, in other words, was objecting to the path being followed for approval. He continued: "Such procedure has been maintained always by the Ministry down to the present; although it has not been established by a law, I do not see grounds for departing from it with respect to the draft Statute of the Society of International Law submitted to the Ministry only today". Bradke's objection was ignored; an annotation in his hand placed the following day said: "His Excellency the Administrator of the Ministry considered this doubt to be excessive".[20]

Nonetheless, the Government on 20 May 1880 discussed the opening of the Society of International Law. Extracts from the Journal of the session of the Committee of Ministers indicate that the Committee heard a submission of the Administrator of the Ministry of Public Enlightenment, Andrei Aleksandrovich Saburov (1837/8-1916), and decided to seek the assent of His Imperial Majesty for confirmation of the Statute of the Society subject to certain editorial emendations. The extract from the Journal contains the note: "The Sovereign Emperor on 23 May 1880 assented to this".[21]

The draft Statute was significantly edited and supplemented. On 1 June 1880 Saburov confirmed the Statute pursuant to Imperial assent. This represented a considerable departure from the experience of other Russian law societies. Each of

[18] See the "File on Founding the Society of International Law", РГИА, Archive of the Ministry of Public Enlightenment of the Russian Empire, фонд 733, опись 142, дело 200.

[19] A third individual was named in the Russian press of the day as being among the initiators: V. P. Poggenpol (1823-1882), a diplomat, privy State counselor, and Hofmeister of the Court of His Imperial Majesty. None of the archival sources, however, provide confirmation for this.

[20] РГИА, ф. 733, оп. 142, д. 700, л.д. 7.

[21] Ibid., л.д. 16.

them had their statutes confirmed directly by order of the Minister of Public Enlightenment, whereas the international lawyers had their Society Statute discussed by the Government at the highest level and secured confirmation by assent of the Emperor himself.

The formal opening of the Society occurred on a Saturday, 31 May 1880, at the palace of His Imperial Highness Prince Petr Georgievich Oldenburgskii (1812-1881), a leading political figure, Senator, member of the State Council, educator, philanthropist, composer, and military officer.[22] The date was chosen to commemorate the 100th anniversary of Catherine the Great (1729-1796) issuing her celebrated Declaration of Armed Neutrality. In his address to the assembled guests, Prince Oldenburgskii said that the aim of the new Society was sacred: "to replace with wise provisions of law the material force predominant in international relations and confirm and disseminate information and rules of international law".[23] The Prince noted that the Emperor not only had approved the founding of the Society, but also had authorized him, the Prince, to assume the title of chairman of the Society.[24] Co-founders of the Society included Count Petr Aleksandrovich Valuev (1815-1890); Ober-Procurator of the Holy Synod, Konstantin Petrovich Pobedonostsev (1827-1907); and Dmitrii Martynovich Solskii (1833-1910), for many years the State Controller of Russia. F. F. Martens was appointed secretary of the Society.

The importance attached to establishing the Society was reflected in the following circumstances:

(1) the creation of the Society was assented to by the Emperor himself at the request of the Committee of Ministers of Russia;

[22] Among his enduring achievements, Prince Oldenburgskii founded in 1835 at the age of 23 years the first specialist higher institution of legal education, the Imperial School of Jurisprudence, which operated until 1918. He served as a trustee of the Imperial Alexander Lycée, the Petersburg Commercial School, and several other educational, scientific, and philanthropic societies and institutions. See Iu. R. Shreier, Пятидесятилетний юбилей его Императорского высочества принца П. Г. Ольденбургского [Fiftieth Anniversary of His Imperial Highness Prince P. G. Oldenburgskii] (Spb., 1881). The conception of international peacekeeping in Russia is associated with Oldenburgskii. See G. N. Chetverukhin, «Миротворческая деятельность принца П. Г. Ольденбургского в правление императора Александра II (1870-начало 1880-х гг.)» [Peacekeeping Activity of Prince P. G. Oldenburgskii in the Reign of Emperor Alexander II (1870-Early 1880s)], in I Романовские чтения. «История Российской государственности и династия Романовых: актуальные проблемы изучения» [I Romanov Readings: History of Russian Statehood and the Romanov Dynasty: Topical Problems of Study] (Kostroma, 2008).

[23] Matters of international peace and law had concerned the Prince for several years. In December 1871 at the end of the Franco-Prussian War he had written a lengthy letter to the President of the French Republic, Adolphe Thiers (1797-1877), emphasizing the desirability of excluding the word "war" from the human vocabulary. In 1878 he appealed to the Congress assembled in Berlin at the end of the Russo-Turkish War in a Memorandum in which he appealed to the participants to join efforts to ensure peace and avoid the misfortunes of war. His decision to encourage the formation of the Russian Society of International Law is seen as a continuation of his efforts. See Annenkova, note 11 above, p. 294.

[24] The text of Prince Oldenburgskii's address on the occasion is preserved in the personal archive of Baron Mikhail Aleksandrovich Taube (1869-1961). See РГИА, f. 1062, op. 1, d. 116.

(2) the creation of the Society was guided by its first head, Prince Oldenburgskii being a rather senior personage of the royal family;

(3) senior State civil servants of the Russian Empire were present for the opening ceremony: Chairman of the Cabinet of Ministers, Count Valuev; K. P. Pobedonostsev; Deputy Minister of Foreign Affairs, Nikolai Karlovich Girs (Giers) (1820-1895); the noted public official, author, and diplomat, Vladimir Pavlovich Titov (1807-1891); and numerous other highly-placed officials of the Ministry of Foreign Affairs and other governmental departments;

(4) the opening of the Society was extensively reported in the media.[25]

A number of factors probably gave impetus to the creation of a society of international law in addition to the general movement towards the creation of law societies in Russia. First, the role of international law was growing in the world community, the volume of doctrinal writings was increasing exponentially, and various initiatives had led to the creation of international, as opposed to national, law societies – a movement in which Russian international lawyers played a role. D. I. Kachenovskii, for example, lobbied intensively for years among his colleagues for the creation of an organization of international lawyers which ultimately led to the Institute of International Law and to the International Law Association.[26]

Second, Russia, especially after 1856, began to play a leading role in the international legal aspects of European foreign policy, and the creation of the Society of International Law was responsive to these trends;[27]

Third, Russian participation in such bodies as the Institute of International Law and the International Law Association, among others, would be facilitated by the existence of a national Society of International Law.

The declared purposes of the Society overlapped to a considerable extent with, and were influenced by, the aims of the Institute of International Law founded at

[25] See, for example, Вестник права [Herald of Law], kn. 5, nos. 9-10 (1880), pp. 99-104.

[26] See W. E. Butler, "On the Origins of the Institute of International Law", in N. A. Sokolova (ed.), *Sumus ubi sumus:* Международное право XXI века: мир и безопасность, сотрудничество, права человека. Liber Amicorum в честь профессора Людмилы Петровны Ануфриевой [*Sumus ubi sumus:* International Law of the XXI Century: Peace and Security, Cooperation, Human Rights: Liber Amicorum in Honor of Professor Ludmila Petrovna Anufrieva] (M., 2016), pp. 95-100; Butler, "On the Life and Works of D. I. Kachenovskii", in W. E. Butler (ed. & intro.), *Selected Works of D. I. Kachenovskii: Ukrainian International Lawyer* (2014), pp. ix-xliv. Also see A. A. Dorskaia, «Институт международного права: опыт неофициального научного сообщества» [Institute of International Law: Experience of an Unofficial Scientific Society], Известия Российского государственного педагогического института им. А. И. Герцена [News of the Russian Herzen State Pedagogical Institute], no. 134 (2010), pp. 88-101.

[27] Zhomini said at the opening ceremony of the Society: "Various societies exist in which highly-respected individuals knowledgeable about the science of international law discuss issues from the standpoint of principle which arise between governments and too often lead to wars. It is deemed to be better that each nation bring its stone for the erection of a building of peace. These societies have multiplied and are an expression of the conscience of the civilized world".

Ghent in 1873, in which V. P. Bezobrazov, F. F. Martens, and L. A. Kamarovskii had played a role and been elected to membership. As formulated in 1873, the purposes of the Institute of International Law included formulation of the basic principles of the science of international law, furthering the codification of international law, and the aspiration to appeal for and apply the principles of the science of international law in practice.[28]

The Statute of the Society contained all the essential attributes required for social organizations of that type under Russian law: the management organs of the Society (assembly, council, chairman, secretary, treasurer), procedure for their election and powers thereof, procedure for managing the Society, types of activity, and financial issues. The designated forms of activity enumerated in the Statute included: periodic meetings, publication of protocols of the sessions and scholarly notes, holding public lectures with the permission of the Government, awarding prizes for scholarly works, and the use of other forms deemed to be useful for the development of international law and dissemination of reasonable notions about international relations.

The Statute memorialized the anniversary of the 1780 Armed Neutrality by requiring that the Society hold an annual meeting on 28 February, the day on which Catherine the Great issued the Declaration on the First Armed Neutrality. Ordinary meetings were to be held six times a year, between November and May, at which reports or communications would be heard of subject-matter of interest to the Society, articles read out, and proposals made with regard to developing some special issue of international law or relations. It was required that all communications and articles be delivered in the Russian language, but foreign languages might be used in exceptional instances with the special authorization on each occasion of the chairman of the Society. Both Russian subjects and foreigners might be members of the Society.

The Society intended to publish its own printed organ from the outset under the title of a "Bulletin". As previously noted, Grabar was unable to locate a copy in the libraries and archives of Russia. We now have established that at least two issues of the Bulletin appeared: the first contained the Statute of the Society;[29] the second published a paper by P. L. Vaksel (Waxel) (1844-1919)[30] devoted to

[28] The Statute of the Institute of International Law was published in Russian by the Russian international lawyer who was among the co-founders of the Institute, Vladimir Pavlovich Bezobrazov (1828-1889). See Bezobrazov, Интернациональный институт международного права в Генте [International Institute of International Law in Ghent] (Spb., 1874). See Butler Б58.

[29] See Устав общества международного права [Statute of the Society of International Law] (Spb., 1880). The Statute was printed by the Printing House of the Ministry of Railways. The cover and first page are illustrated in Annenkova, note 11 above, p. 295, and the same image appears in E. A. Annenkova and Iu. P. Golikov, Принц Петр Георгиевич Ольденбургский [Prince Petr Georgievich Oldenburgskii] (Spb., 2012), p. 138, ex coll: the Russian National Library.

[30] Platon Lvovich Vaksel was known in his day for contributions as a critic to literature, music, and art. In 1870 he studied natural law and the law of nations at Leipzig University in Germany and defended a doctoral dissertation there devoted to "L'armée d'invasion et la population", which was published under that title. From 1874 he served in the Ministry of Foreign Affairs of Russia. See Butler B7.

the extradition of political criminals that was delivered on 26 April 1881.[31] There were, he said, many views on whether political criminals should be or were subject to extradition. There was no clarity in international legal doctrine, and practice varied considerably. Vaksel analyzed in detail Belgian legislation and decisions of the Belgian court of cassation, the report of an English commission issued in 1877, Russian extradition treaties, and a resolution adopted by the Institute of International Law in 1880 on extradition. The 1880 resolution, Vaksel noted, had apparently been discussed previously at a session of the Society by F. F. Martens.

With regard to the extradition of political criminals, Vaksel suggested that the "majority of objections might be eliminated through the application of the principle of extraterritoriality to political crimes by reason of the rarity of the fact itself and the importance of the interests affected". He proposed by way of conclusion that an international court might be created for political criminals who had escaped to a foreign territory, an institution less chimerical in reality than an international court for a violation of the laws of warfare defended with such ardor by many contemporary publicists".[32]

Information uncovered to date suggests that the Society proved to be short-lived – no doubt principally by reason of the death of Prince Oldenburgskii in May 1881.[33] Perhaps no less important was the close relationship of the Society with the Russian government and the equivocal attitude of many Russian officials towards the existence and activities of the Society. Materials in the archives suggest that some months after the solemn inauguration of the Society Prince Oldenburgskii was seeking further support among senior government officials to become "co-founders" of the Society. By October 1880 Valuev requested that he be "saved from the title of co-founder of his [that is, Prince Oldenburgskii's] Society of International Law".[34] Presumably the desire of the Head of the Russian Government to be relieved from his position as co-founder of the Society led Prince Oldenburgskii to seek a replacement on 26 October 1880 in the person of A. A. Saburov, then the Minister of Public Enlightenment.[35] Saburov accepted the invitation in his reply of

[31] P. L. Vaksel (Waxel), "Sur l'extradition des criminels politiques", *Bulletin de la Socićté de droit international*, no. 2 (1881), pp. 1-38. Accounts of the paper were published in Санкт-Петербургские ведомости [St. Petersburg Gazette], no. 90 (2 May 1881), p. 2; and in *Journal de St. Petersbourg*, no. 116 (1881). The Bulletin is rare; no copies are known to be in Russian collections. A copy is held by the Hoover Institution, Stanford University, and in The Butler Collection.

[32] Vaksel, note 31 above (2 May 1881), p. 3.

[33] Representatives of the Russian Society of International Law were not in attendance at the Prince's burial, although delegations from other philanthropic organizations, army regiments, and educational institutions of which the Prince had been a founder were recorded as being present. See E. A. Annenkova and Iu. P. Golikov, Принцы Ольденбургские в Петербурге [Princes Oldenburgskii in Petersburg] (Spb., 2004), pp. 223-224.

[34] Recorded in Valuev's diary. See Count P. A. Valuev, Дневник. 1877-1884 [Diary. 1877-1884], ed. V. Ia. Iakovlev-Boguslavskii and P. E. Shchegolev (Pg., 1919), p. 123.

[35] РГИА, ф. 733, оп. 142, д. 700, л.д. 23.

5 November 1880.[36] On 14 November 1880 Prince Oldenburgskii sent an identical request to Pobedonostsev and received his consent.[37]

It is unlikely that F. F. Martens was able to devote much attention to the Society. In March 1881 Martens sought leave to go abroad for four months and was away from 13 May to 1 June and again from 1 June to 15 September 1881 in Italy and Germany, partly in order to participate in the Congress of the Institute of International Law.[38]

Possibly the Society remained dormant without being wound-up. On 3 March 1897 Grand Prince Aleksandr Mikhailovich (1866-1933) wrote to Pobedonostsev in the latter's capacity as a co-founder of the Society seeking advice on whether to give a positive reply to the request of members of the Society that the Grand Prince should become the chairman of the Society.

Whatever the reasons for the Russian Society of International Law not taking root, almost eighty years would elapse before Russian international lawyers sought to form another specialist society. International legal scholars themselves took the initiative. In 1957, the Soviet Association of International Law was formed, the legal successor to which in 1992 became the Russian Association of International Law.

§6.2. *International Law as Science and Instructional Discipline in University Reforms of 1863, 1884, and 1905*

International law developed as a science and instructional discipline in the second half of the nineteenth and early twentieth centuries under the impact of socio-political and socio-economic processes in the world as a whole and in Russia. The revolutionary events in Europe from 1848 to 1849 affected the entire university system in Russia, including St. Petersburg University. The development of the science and teaching of international law occurred in complex foreign policy and domestic socio-political and administrative circumstances.

To prevent the dissemination in Russian society of "seditious ideas" from the revolutionary university centers in Western Europe, the Ministry of Public Enlightenment undertook restrictive measures with respect to the universities. The Ministry fixed a numerical quota of students (no more than 300 persons in each University) and prohibited the admission of persons of non-noble origin in the universities. Stricter control was established over all aspects of life of the universities, including instructional and research activities. Lectures on philosophy by secular professors ceased, and the teaching of philosophy, logic, and psychology was transferred to theologians. Even foreign business trips by lecturers and students to instructional and scientific centers were forbidden.

[36] Ibid., л.д. 24-25.

[37] РГИА, ф. 1574, оп. 2, д. 2, л. д. 151 (Chancellery of Ober-Procurator K. P. Pobedonostsev).

[38] An extensive correspondence was generated by Martens' request for leave. See ЦГИА St. Petersburg, ф. 14, оп. 1, д. 6958, Annex 1.

The professors were required before the beginning of the academic year to submit to the dean of the faculty for confirmation the texts of lectures prepared by them; these were sent to the Public Library as deposit copies. Control over the students on the part of the inspector of the university was even undertaken at their place of residence. The instructional, research, and social life of Russian universities that had formed over earlier decades was under threat.

A material "thaw" ensued for the universities only after the era of the "Great Reforms" in Russia at the outset of the 1860-1880s. The reforms directly affected the system of university education. The university reform was intended to stop the decline of the universities, which by the end of the 1850s had become obvious, and to facilitate their rise to a new higher level. The era of the "Great Reforms" constituted a special period in the history of Russian legal education and legal culture.[39]

The adoption on 18 June 1863 of a new General Statute on the Imperial Universities played a constructive role in the development of legal education. St. Petersburg was extensively involved in the drafting of the General Statute. On 14 October 1856 the Administrator of the Petersburg Educational District sent a letter to the Council of Petersburg University which proposed to "undertake a review of the instructional structure of the faculties, syllabi of courses being taught, and a means of testing students more consistent with the purpose in the acquisition of knowledge from university teaching"[40] so as to achieve a "harmonious symmetry of each faculty" when the importance of each chair, as a component of the faculty, is determined by its promotion of faculty unity, in order to strictly, "without excesses but also without shortcomings, lead students to the learned specialty chosen by them".[41]

The new conception of university statutes emanated from perceiving universities as major centers for the development of science and education. This required abolishing the excessive regulation of their activity and the restoration of a series of academic rights and freedoms. The 1863 Statute made provision for a serious reformation of the universities, the return of their autonomy, the introduction of new instructional disciplines, the expansion of the number of chairs, an increase in the number of lecturers, and the creation of favorable conditions for scientific and instructional activity and the attraction of young capable scholars to the chairs.

The General Statute also reformed the scientific-pedagogical body of the university. The learned degrees of candidate, magister, and doctor were established. The Statute reinstated the electivity of professors and laid down the conditions for holding lecturing posts. Only the holder of a doctorate corresponding to the profile of the chair might be a professor. In order to obtain the title of "docent" one had to have at least the degree of magister. The institution of privat-docent was officially recognized; the privat-docent (that is, a non-established post) might be an individual with the degree of candidate who had submitted a dissertation *pro venia*

[39] See V. A. Tomsinov, Юридическое образование и юриспруденция в России в эпоху «великих реформ» (60-е – начало 80-х гг. XIX в.) [Legal Education and Jurisprudence in Russia in the Era of the "Great Reforms" (1860-Early 1880s)] (M., 2013).

[40] ЦГИА СПб., f. 14, opis 1, file 5679, l. 3.

[41] Ibid., l. 3ob.

legendi to that division of the faculty where a position was sought and publicly defended the dissertation in the presence of the faculty.

Those seeking the title of professor, docent, or privat-docent and whose lecturing abilities were unknown to the faculty had to deliver publicly two probationary lectures: one on a topic of their own choice, and another assigned by a faculty meeting.

A professor *ordinarius* delivered lectures, conducted tutorials, gave examinations, drew up the instructional methods manuals, and assisted in preparing questions relating to the subject-matter. He received double remuneration: for the position occupied and for lecturing, together with an accommodation allowance to pay for housing. But he could not hold other posts. The professor *extraordinarius* was invited, either without testing or after testing, to deliver lectures on one instructional subject. The Assembly of the Faculty recommended individual candidates for the position of professor, and the Council of the University elected them. The Minister of Public Enlightenment confirmed the candidacy for professor, and the Administrator of the Educational District, candidacies for docent and lecturer.

The privat-docents who satisfied the requirements delivered lectures on the subject-matter chosen by them. No provision was made for the maintenance of a privat-docent, but by decision of the Council of the University they might receive remuneration commensurate with their duties. In general, the General Statute increased the attractiveness of the lectureship for young graduates and contributed to increasing the number of qualified lecturers.

The students were individuals who had reached the age of 17, successfully completed a Gymnasium, or satisfactorily passed the full repertoire of Gymnasium tests and received a certificate or other document of attestation confirming this. The duration of the university course of study was fixed at four years. Graduates who expressed to wish to devote themselves to a career as a lecturer or to engage in scholarly research were required to pass the magister examinations, prepare and defend a magister dissertation of a topic of their choice, and then in due course to move on to the degree of doctor of sciences.[42]

Given the shortage of qualified lecturers, the Ministry of Public Enlightenment decided to reinstate the practice of sending rising scholars to western European universities for additional experience and training; this practice existed until the upheavals of 1848 brought an end to it. In 1862 Emperor Alexander II authorized universities to renew the practice for those who were training for the professoriate and allocated funds for stipends of 1,600 to 2,000 rubles per year. Overcoming the bureaucratic hurdles to secure a stipend was no easy matter. Magisters had to submit a chain of petitions, obtain agreements at various levels, and comply with instructions of various kinds: the professor (supervisor), dean, rector, administrator of the educational district, and ultimately the Minister of Public Enlightenment all had to authorize the stipend and concomitant study and research plan of the applicant; once this vertical set of permissions was obtained, the process began in reverse back down the ladder, as each step was informed of the respective views.

[42] See Tomsinov (ed. & comp.), Университетская реформа 1863 года в России [University Reform of 1863 in Russia] (M., 2012), p. xcviii.

The initiative for such a stipend and visit abroad originated with the professor of the university; all other higher levels, as a rule, supported the application. There were a few instances of the Ministry of Public Enlightenment refusing the request if the planned budget had been exhausted. Even then the university might send the applicant abroad by using its own special funds. All sent abroad had to obtain from the head of the city a certificate concerning their loyalty and trustworthiness.

During the 1860s, about 100 individuals preparing for the professoriate were sent abroad; these returned to Russia in the early 1870s and constituted the backbone of the professoriate of Russian universities.[43] According to the 1863 General Statute, St. Petersburg University had the following faculties: philology and history; medicine and mathematics; oriental and legal. The Statute improved the internal structure of the University, granted greater autonomy, reduced excessive State regulation of the educational process; noticeably democratized the system of management and organization of education, expanded the rights of the Learned Councils in determining the content of instruction; introduced new instructional disciplines; created better conditions for research and instruction, and encouraged the formation of scientific societies and student research groups.

The Law Faculty was a direct beneficiary of these reforms. The more rational structure of the Law Faculty was based on chairs which continued in existence up to 1918. The Law Faculty was divided into two categories: the category of administrative sciences (closed in 1882) and the category of legal sciences. The number of established and non-established posts was increased for lecturers; new disciplines were introduced and new chairs were founded. According to §15 of the Statute, the law faculties were to consist of thirteen professors and eight docents. The chairs might also have, insofar as financial resources permitted, an unlimited number of privat-docents.

Additional measures were undertaken to create a system for the selection, training, and recruitment of young talented personnel. To be sure, the standard for training new research and lecturing personnel was never high enough. A Letter addressed in 1884 to the Administrator of the Petersburg Educational District from the Ministry of Public Enlightenment noted that the expenditures from the State treasury for training individuals for the professorate at St. Petersburg University were not always as "beneficial" as might be anticipated. The Ministry proposed special rules which would introduce requirements for students wishing to pursue a career within University walls. Among these suggested requirements: excellent marks in both ancient languages, an adequate reading knowledge of German and French, excellent marks in the subject-matter of the chair where an appointment was being sought and the closest related chair; irreproachable and reliable moral character, good health, and evidence of devotion to one's chosen discipline manifest in examinations, colloquia, and written work.[44] The reform of the universities thus seriously affected the Chair of All-Nations Law established initially under the

[43] For details, see L. M. Volosnikova, «Университетский устав Российской империи 1863 года – режим академической свободы» [University Statute of the Russian Empire of 1863 – Regime of Academic Freedom], История государства и права [History of State and Law], no. 5 (2006), pp. 13-15.

[44] ЦГИА СПб., f. 14, opis 3, file 14198, l. 1-1obverse.

1835 Statute; under the 1863 Statute, the Chair was renamed the Chair of International Law, a designation preserved to the present day.

It is germane to observe the following with respect to the name of the Chair: when discussing a change of name, a Professor of the Law Faculty at Moscow University, Vasilii Nikolaevich Leshkov (1810-1881), proposed that "international law" should replace "law of nations".[45] After discussion of the proposal, the Academic Committee of the Chief Board of Schools of the Ministry did not accept this proposal, believing that the name "international law" did not indicate the essence of this subject-matter and its ambiguity might lead to misunderstanding. The Ministry thought the impression might be left that the term "international law" might be understood to mean that this is "... law having force and effect between various nations or States".[46]

All the innovations of the 1863 Statute extended to the Chair of International Law, which might have professors *ordinarius* and *extraordinarius*, docents, privat-docents, and lecturers on an established or non-established basis. The procedure for teaching and the lecture-load changed significantly. At the Chair of International Law, for example, in the years 1867/68 Professor Ivanovskii had the following schedule:

> [1] III course, general categories: international law (Part I) two lectures per week;
>
> [2] IV course, general categories: international law (Part II) two lectures per week;
>
> [3] IV course supervised practical and literary exercises of students with regard to international law one lecture per week.[47]

By this time, the research, teaching, and practical application of international law in Russia had a stable basis. Russian international lawyers went farther in their own conceptual positions than their European colleagues and formulated their own original and promising approaches, doctrinal positions, conclusions, and proposals with regard to various topical problems of the science and practice of international law. International lawyers at St. Petersburg University played a major role in this process. Nikolai Mikhailovich Korkunov (1853-1904) wrote:

> Our relationship to western science may be compared with the attitude of the Glossators to Roman jurisprudence. We began to master the fruits

[45] See Замечания на проект Общего устава императорских российских университетов [Comments on the Draft General Statute of the Imperial Russian Universities] (Spb., 1862), II, p. 395.

[46] F. N. Panov, «О составе юридического факультета» [On the Composition of the Law Faculty], Журналы заседаний Ученого комитета Главного правления училищ по проекту Общего устава императорских российских университетов [Journals of Sessions of the Academic Committee of the Chief Board of Schools on the Draft General Statute of Imperial Russian Universities] (Spb., 1868), p. 14.

[47] Обозрение преподавания наук в Императорском Санкт-Петербургском Университете на 1867-1868 академический год [Survey of Teaching of Sciences in Imperial St. Petersburg University for the 1867-1868 Academic Year] (Spb., 1868), p. 14.

> of foreign work, and we needed especially to rise to the level of foreign science … Nonetheless, in some hundred and fifty years we almost succeeded in surmounting the difference of six plus centuries separating us from western jurists.[48]

The Bestuzhev Courses for Women opened at St. Petersburg in 1878 – a private institution of higher education which *de facto* became a division of the University because the majority of the lecturers in courses, including the Chair of International Law created within the structure thereof, consisted of University professors and docents who lectured and conducted seminars according to the University syllabi.

Soon, however, the Government of Russia pursued a university counter-reform. On 23 August 1884 Emperor Alexander II confirmed another General Statute of Imperial Russian Universities which to some extent was the "most reactionary of all university Statutes ever published in Tsarist Russia".[49] The 1884 Statute limited university autonomy (restored only in 1905) and university self-government and expanded the powers of the administrators of educational districts. The rector was no longer elected by the Council of the University, but appointed by the Minister. The Minister might or might not consider the view of the professoriate when appointing lecturers and might give instructions to professors and issue reminders and comments. The deans were appointed by the Administrator of the educational district, and the posts of pro-rector and the University court were abolished. The examination for completing the course was given by special State commissions; only students whose attendance had been recorded for the established number of semesters were admitted to examinations. Moreover, the university tuition fees were doubled.

The post of established docent was abolished by the Statute. But the privat-docentship was introduced by the Statute to take into account the growth in student numbers. Given that reform, it was sufficient to hold the post of privat-docent if the applicant passed the magister examination and delivered two probationary lectures at a closed session of the Faculty before the "professorial collegium" (one lecture on a topic specified by the faculty; the second on a topic chosen by the applicant).

The 1884 Statute preserved the stable internal structure established by its predecessor of 1863, which remained in place until 1918 – twelve chairs. According to §57 of the Statute, the Chair of International Law was part of the Law Faculty as an autonomous scientific-instructional subdivision. Pursuant to §60 of the 1884 Statute, eleven professors *ordinarius* and four *extraordinarius* should have lectured; the number of privat-docents was determined by the Faculty itself, having regard to the requirements of the instructional plan. The first privat-docent was appointed at the Chair of International Law only in 1895 – this was Ewald-Wilhelm Simson.

[48] N. M. Korkunov, История философии права [History of the Philosophy of Law] (Spb., 1908), p. 233.

[49] N. S. Alekseev, «150-летие юридического факультета Ленинградского университета» [150th Anniversary of the Law Faculty of Leningrad University], Правоведение [Jurisprudence], no. 1 (1969), pp. 7-8.

According to the 1884 Statute, only a doctor of sciences who had delivered a course of lectures of a high standard for no less than three years might become a professor. Professors were appointed to vacant positions by the Minister or by his instruction were elected from among worthy candidates of the University. When several candidates were being voted upon, the doctor of sciences who received the most votes was deemed to be elected. A professor who had served in good faith for more than 25 years had the right to receive the title of Distinguished Professor.

The universities were affected, just as most Russian institutions, by the disturbances which led to the crisis of 1905 and became a hotbed of revolutionary dissent from the established order. Educational activities in the University were suspended for the spring semester and, from 15 October 1905, were cancelled indefinitely by instruction of the Ministry of Public Enlightenment.[50] Instruction was renewed a year later, in autumn 1906.[51]

The Russian Government was forced by the revolutionary events of 1905 to make concessions to the university community. On 27 August 1905 Emperor Nicholas II confirmed an Edict introducing provisional rules on the administration of institutions of higher education by the Ministry of Public Enlightenment. The Edict repealed the most reactionary provisions of the 1884 General Statute which had generated public protest. The autonomy of the universities was reinstated.

The provisional Rules provided new rules and duties. The councils of faculties were given the right to elect the deans and secretaries of faculties from among the professors and lecturers of the faculties with subsequent confirmation by the Ministry of Public Enlightenment. Responsibility was placed on the councils of universities for the maintenance of the proper course of academic life in the University; in the event of disorders, the councils had the right to petition for the suspension of lessons for a period established by them. The duty to maintain order in universities was placed on the rector. Adjudication in student affairs was returned from the Ministry to the universities and again entrusted to the professorial disciplinary court of the universities, which the majority of liberal professors and the majority of students found to be acceptable.

The upheavals between 1917 and 1920 meant for the University and all its faculties and chairs the end of the golden age associated with the decades preceding the 1917 revolutions. Most academic staff of the Law Faculty emigrated, impoverishing the intellectual resources of the University but enriching those of the Russia Abroad. The academic staff who remained in Soviet Russia developed the St. Petersburg School of international law in new, unstable, and contradictory socio-political and scientific circumstances.

[50] Отчет о состоянии и деятельности Императорского С.-Петербургского университета за 1905 год [Report on the State and Activity of Imperial St. Petersburg University for 1905] (Spb., 1906), p. 42.

[51] See E. A. Rostovtsev and I. V. Sidorchuk, «Санкт-Петербургский университет в 1905 г.» [St. Petersburg University in 1905], Научно-технические ведомости СПбГПУ. Гуманитарные и общественные науки [Scientific-Technical Gazette of St. Petersburg State Pedagogical University. Humanities and Social Sciences], no. 3 (2015), pp. 98-107.

As noted above, the Council of the University had retired Professor Ivanovskii with effect from 31 December 1869, leaving the Chair of International Law temporarily vacant. The Faculty proposed to appoint a graduate of the Faculty, magister Fedor Fedorovich Martens, who at the time was completing his foreign academic tour abroad. Martens accepted the offer and beginning in January 1870 occupied the Chair for three decades. This appointment marked a new era in the development of the Chair and of the science and practice of international law in Russia and abroad.

Chapter 7
Golden Era of Chair of International Law

For the Chair of International Law at St. Petersburg University, the years from the 1860s to 1917 were indeed a "golden era". This period saw the transition of the Chair of International Law from a lecture-hall chair with a single professor delivering his lectures to the permanent formation of a chair as a collective instructional and scientific subdivision of the Faculty. The international lawyers consisted of several professors and docents who provided instruction in several basic and specialized international law courses and undertook research. Graduates preparing for the professoriate became part of the Faculty collective.

The flourishing of the St. Petersburg School of international law was an integral part of the "golden era". Scholarly publications increased markedly: monographs, dissertations, articles, reviews, textbooks, and instructional manuals. Many textbooks were reprinted or issued in revised editions. The most important received the honor of a foreign translation. Russian international lawyers contributed articles and reviews to foreign journals.

Close cooperation developed between the Chair of International Law as a capital institution with the Ministry of Foreign Affairs of Russia and other governmental structures. Scholars from the Chair held simultaneous appointments in the ministries, commonly at a high level. They attended international conferences in their personal capacity or on behalf of their government. They played a role in drafting treaties and diplomatic documents or in commenting on the drafts of others.

The Chair of International Law confirmed a system for training magisters and doctors of international law. Significant numbers of capable graduates remained at the Chair in order to pursue an academic career. This included the obligatory trip abroad, usually paid for by the Ministry, to leading European university centers in order to improve their foreign language skills. The visits were generally reckoned to last for one year, but the supervisor of the program was allowed to petition for a longer period when circumstances justified. The petition went through the usual channels: supervisor, support of the Faculty, rector of the University, and Ministry. All lecturers in the Chair passed through the magister system.

During this period, the Chair of International law developed its own personnel pattern: the Chair was held by individuals who had been pupils of their predecessors – a sort of dynastic succession which reinforced the notion of a St. Petersburg School of international law. Between 1871 and 1919, the Chair of International Law was headed by F. F. Martens, M. A. von Taube, A. A. Pilenko, and B. E. Nolde. We turn to each of these in succession.

§7.1. *Heads of Chair of International Law*

Fedor Fedorovich Martens, *also known as Friedrich Fromholz (Fromhold) Martens (10 August 1845, b. Pernov (now Pärnu), Estonia; d. 7 June 1909, Valka Station, Livonian Province (now Estonia). World-renowned international lawyer, diplomat, legal consultant, international arbitrator, associate member of the Russian Academy of Sciences, member of Institute of International Law, honorary doctorates received from many universities and learned societies.*

Life and career. The considerable body of materials on the early life, origins, parents, date of birth, and marriage, religious preference, change of name, and other personal details of Martens contains much that is inconsistent, inaccurate, or ambiguous. The widely propagated view is that Martens was born on 15 August 1845 into a family of a junior deacon or sexton of the Evangelical Lutheran faith. On 25 September 1879 he married Catherina Ture, the daughter of Senator Nikolai Andreevich Ture (1834-1905),[1] of St. Petersburg, converted to the Russian Orthodox Church pursuant to the laws of that time,[2] and took the name Fedor Fedorovich Martens. Archival documents suggest some adjustments are in order with respect to these standard accounts.

One such document is an extract from the metric marriage book of the Baden Evangelical-Protestant Congregation, which records: On 30 December 1879, Friedrich Fromgold Martens, an Imperial Russian privy councilor, residing in St. Petersburg, born in Pernov, Livonia, on 10 August 1845, son of the deceased Friedrich Wilhelm Martens and Teresa Wilhelmina, born Knast, of Evangelical faith, bachelor, Ekaterina Louisa Maria Ture, of Evangelical faith, spinster, born in St. Petersburg on 27 July 1861, daughter of Nikolai Edouard Ture and of Ekaterina Wilhelmina von Shneider, were duly married.[3]

1 Senator Ture (or Tur) shared much in common with his son-in-law, F. F. Martens. Tur also graduated as a candidate of laws from St. Petersburg University and then visited the Universities of Berlin and the École de droit in Paris. He served in the Ruling Senate from 1 January 1893. See N. A. Murzanov, Словарь русских сенаторов 1711-1917 гг. Материалы для биографий [Dictionary of Russian Senators 1711-1917: Materials for Biographies] (Spb., 2011), p. 441.

2 Archival documents disclose that Martens never converted to the Russian Orthodox faith; he remained a Lutheran for all of his life, and a Lutheran cross embellishes his gravestone. On some Russia documents, including his application to St. Petersburg University and his graduation diploma, the name "Fromhold" is listed as his forename. In his activities abroad, including his publications, "Friedrich", or a variation thereof, is always given as the forename.

3 ЦГИА СПб., f. 536, opis 6, file 4813, l. 5-5obverse. The genuineness of the extract is confirmed by a notary in Baden-Baden and the Imperial Russian Mission attached to the Baden court.

Several observations are in order. As to the birth date on the metric marriage document, Martens in many other places, including his personal diaries which repose in the Archive of Foreign Policy of Russia (AVPR), recorded his birth date as 15 August 1845.[4] The same date is recorded in the biographical dictionary of St. Petersburg professors, the data for which he will have supplied personally or verified. We therefore have variant dates which he supplied, although the month is consistent. On the other hand, an Estonian lawyer reported in 1975 that after exhaustive searching of all church registries in Pernov, he was unable to locate any birth registration for the Martens parents.[5] Such registration was obligatory in those times and served as the basis for a metric certificate or for christening a child.[6] That opens the possibility that Martens never precisely knew his birth date in the absence of official records and relied on family tradition for this information.

As to parentage, the most detailed account is recorded in the historical novel by Jaan Kross (1920-2007).[7] According to Kross, Martens was the last of nine children born to Fredrich Wilhelm Martens (1795-1850), for many years the sexton of the Lutheran Church in Audre. In 1844 F. W. Martens was dismissed from this position and moved to Pernov, where he purchased a house on Gartenstrasse 10 and engaged in tailoring.[8] His mother died in 1854. Kross related that Fedor

4 AVPR, opis 787, file 9, ed. khr. 1-7; cited in V. V. Pustogarov, *Our Martens: F. F. Martens, International Lawyer and Architect of Peace*, ed. & transl. W. E. Butler (2000), p. 8. Also see Igor Vladimirovich Budnik (ed.), Архив внешней политики Российской империи: путеводитель [Archive of Foreign Policy of the Russian Empire: Guidebook] (Minneapolis, 1995). The literature on Martens is becoming substantial. Among those of importance are Arthur Nussbaum, "Frederic de Martens – Representative Tsarist Writer on International Law", *Nordisk Tidsskrift International Ret,* XXII (1952), pp. 51-66; Dieter Fleck, "Friedrich von Martens: A Great International Lawyer from Pärnu", *Baltic Defence Review*, no. 10 (2003), pp. 19-26; T. Meron, "The Martens Clause, Principles of Humanity, and Dictates of Public Conscience", *American Journal of International Law*, XCIV (2000), pp. 78-89; Lauri Mälksoo, "When Russia Was an Integral Part of the European Tradition of International Law", *European Journal of International Law*, XXV (2014), pp. 811-829; K. O. Savchuk, «Мартенс Федір Федорович» [Martens, Fedor Fedorovich], in V. N. Denysov, et al. (eds.), Енциклопедія міжнародного права [Encyclopedia of International Law] (Kyiv, 2014-2019), III, pp. 22-24; G. S. Starodubtsev, Международно-правовая наука российской эмиграции [International-Legal Science of Russian Emigration] (M., 2000), pp. 13, 15. 16. 18-21, 95. 96. 107, 109, 157, 169, 170, 195.

5 L. Lesment, «Новые сведения из жизни Ф. Ф. Мартенса» [New Information from the Life of F. F. Martens], Советское право [Soviet Law], no. 5 (1975), pp. 358-370.

6 Pustogarov reported that the Martens metric certificate was not to be found in his personal file or other materials in the AVPR. See Pustogarov, note 4 above, p. 10.

7 Jaan Kross, *Professor Martensi Ärasõit* (Tallinn, 1984), translated into Russian as Kross, Уход профессора Мартенса [The Departure of Professor Martens] (M., 1989); published in English as Kross, *Professor Martens' Departure* (1994); reviewed *American Journal of International Law*, LXXXVIII (1994), pp. 863-864 (W. E. Butler). The English translation, published separately in London and New York, is Kross's best-known work abroad; there were translations into other languages. Kross' nomination for the Nobel Prize in Literature was unsuccessful. A lawyer by training whose historical fiction was known to be based on scrupulous investigation of the factual background, Kross was acting docent at the Chair of Public International Law in 1945-1946 at Tartu University. See Pustogarov, note 4 above, p. 8.

8 A memorial plaque has been placed on the house in Pärnu in commemoration of F. F. Martens.

Fedorovich had brothers: Heinrich, who became a cobbler in Riga; August, who graduated from university and became a medical doctor on the Island of Madeira; Johannes, who found employment at a local sawmill; Julius, who studied pharmacy in St. Petersburg and later founded a factory for the production of hygiene products. According to the novel, Fedor Fedorovich was sent to Julius in St. Petersburg.

As to marriage, Martens was not married on 25 September 1879, but on 30 December, as the metric certificate officially attests. The certificate was issued in Baden-Baden on 10 January 1880. On the other hand, Pustogarov reported 18 December 1879, for which there seems to be no empirical evidence unless the difference arises from the difference in Julian and Gregorian calendars.[9] The metric certification from Baden-Baden also confirms that, whenever Martens may have converted to the Russian Orthodox faith, it was not at the time of his marriage, nor did he change his name on that occasion.[10]

As to the various versions of his name, in his personal life Martens used several versions of his forenames: on his marriage certificate (1867) and on the birth and baptismal certificates of his son Nikolai (1880) and daughter Edith (1886), all issued by the Evangelical Lutheran Church in Baden-Baden or in St. Petersburg, Martens specified his name as "Friedrich Fromgold von Martens". In official materials Martens preferred "Friedrich", "Fromgold", "Fedor", "Fromgold Fedorovich"; his application in the name of the Rector of St. Petersburg University for admission contained the names "Fridrikh" and "Fromgold Fedorovich"; in 1867 his kandidat diploma described him as "Fromgold Fridrikhof, son of Martens"; in 1869 his magister diploma read "Fromgold Fridrikhovich Martens"; and only after the issuance in 1873 of the diploma of doctor did he use "Fedor Fedorovich Martens". He named himself and signed this name in the official sphere – the University, the Ministry of Foreign Affairs, and so on. Abroad, Martens was called in German and English "Friedrich von Martens"; in French, Frédéric de Martens; and in some foreign sources, Theodor Theodorovich Martens.[11]

As to nationality, it is disputed as to whether Martens is of Baltic-German stock and/or native Estonian. Continental European doctrinal writings have on

Martens, according to Lesment, later purchased his father's house and routinely spent the summers there. Lesment, note 5 above. Pustogarov observed that the Martens diaries held in the AVPR contain not a single word about his parents, brothers, childhood, or adolescence, although some passages relate to his wife and children or relatives of his wife. In the diary left by his son, Nikolai, references are made to his mother, but nothing on the relatives of his father. See note 4 above, p. 12.

[9] Pustogarov, note 4 above, p. 10.

[10] This would suggest that Pustogarov was incorrect in these details. See note 4 above, pp. 10-11.

[11] David M. Walker, *The Oxford Companion to Law* (Oxford, 1982), p. 812.

numerous occasions described Martens as "German";[12] Russian writings tend to describe him as Baltic-German; Kross made a detailed argument in favor of his Estonian roots. The debate continues.

It is uncontested that at the age of nine, in 1854, with the assistance of his teacher in a local school, Lutheran Pärnu clergy, and possibly his older brother, he was sent to St. Petersburg and in January 1855 was placed in an orphan home attached to the St. Peter's German Evangelical Lutheran Church. It was proposed that he become in time a junior deacon of the church. Distinction in his school studies led to Martens being transferred to the St. Peter's Chief School (German Gymnasium), where he graduated in 1863.[13]

The German school was of a high standard, but strict. Martens distinguished himself in his studies by diligence, talent, well-prepared lessons, and model behavior; he found himself attracted by poetry, history, and foreign languages. The teachers and director of the School predicted a future in the fields of history or philology.

Martens had different ideas. He applied to the Law Faculty of St. Petersburg University on 31 August 1863 and was enrolled on 10 October 1863.[14] A petition to the Rector of the University seeking exemption from tuition fees was granted, following the usual bureaucratic correspondence between the Rector, Administration of the Petersburg Educational District, and the Ministry, with a request for the views of the Director of the German Gymnasium attended by Martens.[15]

As a law student, Martens was at first attracted by the philosophy of criminal law. By chance he read various dissertation abstracts related to international law and wrote his graduation paper on the topic "On Relations between Russia and the Ottoman Empire in the Reign of Empress Catherine II", which received warm praise. Upon graduation on 15 August 1867, Martens was awarded the degree candidate of laws by the Council of the University. The Dean of the Law Faculty, Professor Ivanovskii, who served simultaneously as the Head of the Chair of International Law, used his administrative resources and pedagogical skills to persuade Martens to train for the professoriate at the Chair of International Law. Later anecdotes related the events as follows: Martens made application to prepare for the professoriate in the field of criminal law, and Dean Ivanovskii strongly objected:

12 See the appreciation by H. Wehberg, "Dr. Friedrich v. Martens und die Haager Friedenskonferenzen", *Zeitschrift für internationales Recht*, XX, no. 4 (1910). Other German sources have described Martens as a "Russian international lawyer of Baltic-German origin". See *Brockhaus Enzyklopedie* (1971), XII, p. 190.

13 Биографический словарь профессоров и преподавателей Императорского С.-Петербургского университета за истекшую третью четверть века его существования. 1869-1894 [Biographical Dictionary of Professors and Lecturers of the Imperial St. Petersburg University for the Past Third Quarter Century of its Existence. 1869-1894)] (Spb., 1896), II, p. 6.

14 ЦГИА СПб., f. 14, opis 5, file 2549, l. 1.

15 Ibid., ll. 6-8, 11.

"No, better to remain at the Chair of International Law. Then you will be our own 'Martens'".[16] True or not, these words proved to be prophetic.[17]

Martens followed Ivanovskii's advice and remained at the Chair of International Law for 34 years.[18] He chose for his magister dissertation a topic untouched in Russian international legal doctrine: the inviolability and defense of private ownership during war. He assembled an immense body of material, read each chapter as completed aloud to Professor Ivanovskii, and after discussion with his supervisor prepared the final variant. On 6 January 1869 he applied for a position in the Ministry of Foreign Affairs,[19] an institution with which he would be linked for the next forty years. He petitioned the Rector of the University on 14 March 1869 to be allowed to sit the magister examinations,[20] which he successfully passed. The following questions were put to Martens on international law:

(1) History and literature of the history of international law from Wolff to the present;

(2) Inter-State disputes both destroying autonomy and compatible therewith;

(3) On consuls;

(4) On termination of trade in negroes and the slavery thereof.[21]

In September 1869 Martens submitted his completed dissertation to the Faculty of Law. On 20 September 1869 the acting Dean of the Faculty, Semen Vikentevich Pakhman (1825-1910),[22] notified the Rector that the date of the dissertation

16 Quoted from M. A. von Taube, Ф. Ф. Мартенс. 1845-1909 (Некролог) [F. F. Martens. 1845-1909 (Obituary)] (Spb., 1909), pp. 3-4. See also V. V. Grigorev, Императорский С.-Петербургский университет в течение первых пятидесяти лет его существования. Историческая записка [Imperial St. Petersburg University During the First Fifty Years of its Existence. Historical Note] (Spb., 1870), p. 7. Taube was certainly familiar with the anecdote from Grigorev. The reference to "our Martens" had in view the two other famous European international lawyers, Georg Friedrich Martens (1756-1821) of Göttingen University, and his descendent and successor in the field of international law, Charles de Martens (1790-1863), both, *inter alia*, major compilers and editors of treaty collections.

17 Kross makes excellent narrative use of the incident. Upon learning of Martens' inclination to pursue the criminal law, Ivanovskii advised: "*Criminal* law? But why? No, I don't agree with that. It's true that we have lost Spasovich, but we'll appoint Tagantsev his successor … You were born for a career in international law … No more buts … Go for the chair in international law. Any other choice would indicate such a lack of knowledge on your part that I wouldn't be able to support you. But in my own department I'll support you with all my heart. What's more. I predict that if you choose international law, Russia will gain its own Martens, and the world will once again have a Martens – this time, a Russian!" Jaan Kross, *Professor Martens' Departure*, transl. Anselm Hollo (1994), pp. 59-60.

18 ЦГИА СПб., f. 14, opis 1, file 6958, l. 11.

19 Ibid., l. 34-34obverse.

20 ЦГИА СПб., f. 14, opis 1, file 6739, l. 1.

21 ЦГИА СПб., f. 14, opis 3, file 14117, l. 155-158.

22 V. A. Tomsinov, Российские правоведы XVIII-XX веков: очерки жизни и творчества [Rus-

defense would be on a Sunday, 5 October 1869, at 12:00; the opponents would be I. I. Ivanovskii and A. D. Gradovskii.[23] Doctoral defenses were public occasions and often held on a weekend when the general public would have a day of leisure and a real opportunity to be present. Notice of the defense was sent on 27 September 1869 by the University to the leading St. Petersburg newspaper with a request to publish.[24]

Apparently, the University had confidence that the Martens defense would be successful. The degree of magister of international law was awarded on the next day, 6 October 1869, in a solemn ceremony.[25] On 23 October 1869 the Ruling Senate of the Russian Empire confirmed magister Martens in the rank and title of Titular Counsellor (civil servant of the ninth grade). On the recommendation of the Law Faculty, supported by the Rector, on 17 December 1869 the decision was approved to send Martens abroad for a year and a half to prepare for a career in university teaching.[26] While in Europe he attended lectures and worked in the libraries of Vienna, Heidelberg, and Leipzig. Martens later recalled that the greatest impression was left by the lectures of Professors Lorenz von Stein (1815-1890) in Vienna and J. C. Bluntschli, in Heidelberg. As was intended, the trip to Europe brought Martens into contact with European colleagues and helped shape his views on issues of international law. Before his visit to Europe was completed, however, Martens was officially summoned home in December 1869 by St. Petersburg University to take the Chair of International Law with the rank and title of docent, the chair having become vacant with the retirement of Ivanovskii.

By decision of the Council of the University of 18 January 1871, at the age of 25 Martens was elected docent at the Chair of International Law.[27] He remained at the Chair until 1903. By Edict of the Ruling Senate of 9 March 1872 Martens was confirmed in the rank of court counsellor (seventh grade in the civil service), retroactive to 18 January 1871.[28]

Following two years of arduous research, Martens submitted a doctoral dissertation in 1873 on the topic of consuls and consular jurisdiction.[29] On 18 March

sian Jurists of the XVIII-XX Centuries: Survey of Life and Activity] (2007), I, pp. 317-347.

23 ЦГИА СПб., f. 14, opis 1, file 6739, l. 4.

24 ЦГИА СПб., f. 14, opis 1, file 6739, l. 6-7.

25 ЦГИА СПб., f. 14, opis 1, file 6958, l. 28. By the same decision Martens was admitted to prepare for the doctorate. The magister dissertation was published as F. F. Martens, О праве частной собственности во время войны [On the Right of Private Ownership During War] (Spb., 1869). Butler M119.

26 . ЦГИА СПб., f. 14, opis 1, file 6958, l. 9obverse.

27 ЦГИА СПб., f. 14, opis

28 ЦГИА СПб., f. 14, opis 1. File 6958, l. 11obverse.

29 Published as Martens, О консулах и консульской юрисдикции на Востоке [On Consuls and Consular Jurisdiction in the East] (Spb., 1873). Butler M117. The following year a German translation was published. See Martens, *Das Consularwesen und die Consularjurisdiction im Orient*, transl. H. Skerst (Berlin, 1874). Butler M86.

1873, also a Sunday, at the age of 28, he successfully defended the dissertation. On this occasion the name on the diploma used the Russian variant: Fedor Fedorovich Martens.[30] The award of the doctorate was accompanied by appointment as professor *extraordinarius* at the Chair of International Law.[31] By Edict of the Ruling Senate of 25 May 1875, Martens was confirmed in the civil service rank and title of collegiate counsellor with retroactive effect from 31 January 1873.[32] Three years later, on 18 October 1876, at the age of 31, Martens was elected by the Council of the University, duly confirmed on 30 October 1876 by Order of the Minister of Public Enlightenment, professor *ordinarius* in the Chair of International Law, a post he would hold until retirement.[33]

From 1871 until the end of his life Martens held the Chair of State Law at the Imperial School of Jurisprudence,[34] and at the Imperial Alexander Lycée held the Chair of International Law from 1886 to 1905.[35] On 2 January 1881 the Imperial School of Jurisprudence petitioned that Martens be awarded the title privy State counsellor for distinguished teaching.[36]

By order of the Ministry of Foreign Affairs of 24 March 1878 Martens was appointed an official on special assignments, sixth class, and from 1 December 1879, fifth class attached to the State Chancellery.[37] By direction of the Emperor, the Ministry of Foreign Affairs on 21 April 1891 made Martens a privy counsellor.[38]

When Martens had completed a quarter century of teaching at the University, on 15 March 1893, by decision of the Ministry of Public Enlightenment, Martens was allowed to remain in post with his previous title.[39] From 18 March 1896 the

[30] The decision of the Council of the University to award the degree was dated 26 March 1873, and the diploma was issued on 14 April 1873. ЦГИА СПб., f. 14, opis 1, file 6958, l. 44.

[31] ЦГИА СПб., f. 139, opis 1. file 6720, l. 1-6.

[32] ЦГИА СПб., f. 14, opis 1, file 6958, l. 12obverse and 17obverse.

[33] Ibid.

[34] Ibid., file 6958, l. 63; fond 355, opis 1, file 3943.

[35] ЦГИА СПб., f. 11, opis l, file 3784.

[36] Ibid., f. 11, opis 1, file 3784, l. 7obverse.

[37] Ibid., f. 14 , opis 1, file 6958, l. 48obverse-49, 117.

[38] ЦГИА СПб., f. 11, opis l, file 3784, l. 10obverse.

[39] ЦГИА СПб., f. 11, opis 1, file 6958, l. 183.

title of Distinguished Professor was conferred on Martens by the Ministry of Public Enlightenment.

On 6 May 1906 Martens submitted a request to the Rector of St. Petersburg University to resign his position, having, he said, been within the walls of that institution for 43 years, including 35 years as a lecturer, and 32 of those at the Chair of International Law.[40]

Martens died suddenly on 7(20) June 1909 at the age of 64 from a heart attack at the train station of Valka while en route from his Livonian estate to St. Petersburg. He was buried on 11 June 1909 at the Volkov Lutheran Cemetery. Over time the gravesite deteriorated and in the 1990s was severely damaged by vandals. Efforts led by the Chair of International Law of St. Petersburg University and philanthropic sources in Russia led on 23/24 October 2019 to the dedication of its complete restoration or, rather, replacement with a suitable gravestone bearing a classical Lutheran cross. A bronze bust of Martens was placed in the Law Faculty of St. Petersburg University in 2002. A similar bust was given by the Government of the Russian Federation to the Peace Palace in The Hague, where it reposes together with the remarkable jasper "Russian Vase" presented by Emperor Nicholas II to the Peace Palace in 1913; the Vase bears his initials and the State emblem of the Russian Empire.

International legal views. Having completed a good diploma dissertation for his first degree in law and been selected to remain at the University to prepare for the magister degree, Martens chose a dissertation topic never before investigated in Russia – the inviolability of private ownership during war. He devoted a year to assembling material in the German, English, Italian, French, and medieval Latin language sources and submitted to the Faculty a dissertation of 464 printed pages. The Council of the Faculty was so impressed by the scope, depth, and topicality of the dissertation that it was printed at University expense.

The dissertation indicated that Martens was thinking seriously about the causes and nature of conflicts between States. Given the realities of international politics in his time, Martens recognized that armed conflicts between States were inevitable, but he believed the character and results thereof could be changed as human culture and civilization matured. He expressed the conviction that as nations became more aware of their own good and self-improvement, their "mutual conflicts must decrease proportionally, for they are the most active brake on human development" (pp. 54-55).

Martens believed that law played an important role in the prevention and the humanizing of military conflicts. "Any war", he said, "only will be just and consistent with the development of human life when it satisfies the requirements of international law" (p. 95). His dissertation was the first study of the legal defense of private ownership during war. In his preface, Martens wrote: "Until now the inviolability of enemy private ownership was more the subject of practical and political considerations in parliaments and chambers of commerce of England, France, and Germany than detailed scientific research" (p. vii).

[40] ЦГИА СПб., f. 11, opis 1, file 3784, l. 263.

The principal message of the work was proving the unlawfulness and inadmissibility of the capture of enemy private property by belligerents because war is not between private individuals, but between States. Therefore reprisals are permitted only against State ownership. A particular virtue of the work was that Martens addressed a broad range of problems connected with the behavior of belligerents.[41] Martens shared a radically different position from most concerning the correlation between "law – power", "war – law", "war – peace", "authority – man"; he adhered to these views throughout his lifetime. He decisively rejected the view dominant in his day that force prevailed over law. Such views, he believed, were unworthy of man and detrimental to international life.

Martens shared humanist views. All phenomena of social life – within the State and between States – were based either on brute force or on law and are rooted in the nature of man. The aspiration for "self-determination and self-integrity" and for "communion" always are advanced by man. Here he laid the foundation of his original theory of international communion which will underlie his entire theory of international law. But, "inasmuch as anyone naturally pursues his own personal individual purposes, then understandably conflicts occur in the community life between people" (p. 2). Martens concluded: "International law is founded on human nature and exerted its influence as nations came to an awareness of the need for international relations when the hostile isolation disappeared and international life began to require recognition and determination" (p. 3).

Martens rejected the predominant religious explanation of the nature and essence of international law, including the law of war:

> The aspiration to elevate faith and the spirit of Christianity as the sole source of international law … seems to us to be mistaken … we see that the writers on international law who base themselves solely on the spirit of Christianity, on divine and natural law, proceed until they deprive the human enemy of all rights and deliver him to the complete arbitrariness of the furious enemy … A belligerent points to his inalienable right to harm his enemy by all possible means; for example, to kill the defenseless subjects thereof, to plunder, to put them in captivity, to dishonor, and so on. And then they ask for mercy, for leniency, and charity (p. 3).

Martens, on the contrary, took the view that the development of mankind and of international law were based not on religion, but on the objective historical process of the continuous progressive development of society: "… even from a

41 See V. S. Ivanenko, «Ф. Ф. Мартенс – основоположник отечественной науки международного гуманитарного права» [F. F. Martens – Founder of the Fatherland Science of International Humanitarian Law], Российский ежегодник международного права 2000: Специальный выпуск [Russian Yearbook of International Law 2000: Special Issue] (Spb., 2000), pp. 36-46.

fleeting glance at the history of the development of international life, we cannot fail to see that international law is gradually changing as the calamities of war are being ameliorated and the benefits of the peaceful cohabitation of nations are increasing". Therefore, "... we understand international life as a constant progressive movement and the aggregate of the conditions of its development determines the international law of a particular era, and a change of the conditions of international life inevitably requires a change of the existing law". And here he drew a significant conclusion:

> From this point of view, the development of the idea of humanity is nothing other than a step in the development of law; that is, much of that which was previously sought in the name of humanity or universal human ties at another time, under other conditions of life, should be required as the execution of a prescription of law (p. 7).

Having considered the reasons for international conflicts, Martens found them in the nature of man, society, and the State:

> The State, just as a private individual, may violate the rights to honor, self-preservation, independence, and so on of another State and may not perform positive and negative obligations assumed in treaties concluded. In order to resolve the misunderstandings and disputes arising, there is nothing similar to an international tribunal. Therefore, for States there remains only law and the possibility to deliver to themselves their own means of satisfaction, restore the violated right, and achieve peace. But if international justice formally is now at that stage of development in which civil (criminal) law found itself in the Middle Ages under the dominance of the law of the fist, then does it follow that the State is not bound by any prescriptions of law and justice? (p. 20).

He put the question and offered his own answer: "States are aware of the need to agree their behavior with eternal laws of truth and justice" and settle them by peaceful means. To such peaceful means Martens relegated diplomacy, mediation by another power, compromise, or arbitration. He was convinced: "they correspond more to the purposes of peace and do not violate the rights of private individuals, and therefore their adoption by States serves as the best evidence of a sincere attachment to peace" (p. 23).

The entire book is imbued with a humanist orientation. Opposing the senseless cruelty of war and upholding the need for belligerents to comply with the international rules, Martens expressed faith in the triumph of law: "whatever political considerations have guided State personalities and politicians and with whatever embitterment patriotic publicists have railed against law ... we have no doubt that the legal consciousness of civilized nations will gain the upper hand" (p. 453).

Martens may rightly be considered to be the founder of the Russian science of international humanitarian law applicable during armed conflicts. Professor Vsevolod Danevskii (1852-1898) devoted seven pages of his critical analysis of Russian doctrinal writings on international law to Martens' work .and found it to be by talent and erudition competitive with similar works by western scholars and in some respects superior to them. Danevskii wrote: "The monograph of Martens, in our view, is the most talented of the Russian works and unusually rich in historical legal information. It is read with true satisfaction and should be a manual for those studying international law in Russia, especially the law of war".[42]

Having taken up the post of docent in the Chair of International Law, on 28 January 1871 Martens delivered his first lecture to students. The lecture was programmatic in the sense that he expressed views that he would enlarge upon in later life, views that defined him as a lecturer and as a legal scholar, diplomat, and arbitrator. He set out a scientific substantiation for the comparatively young science of international law in Russia, gave a critical assessment of the state of international relations and of the science and practice of international law as a whole, and articulated his vision for the future development of international law. Martens was, however, despite his critical assessment of the state of the world at the time, optimistic; he exuded faith in the reason of mankind and in the potential of international law to make a constructive contribution to the world.[43]

As a legal scholar and University lecturer, Martens opposed the natural law orientation dominant in his day. He was a proponent of legal positivism, gathering impetus in Russia. International law, he believed, should be based on positive legal material. Only history and the true realities of international life could provide a firm foundation for international legal structures: "A change in the conditions of international life must result in a change in law, and therefore only a study of the conditions of international life at a particular time, and of its historical development, can elucidate the true international legal consciousness". However, he said, international law "down to the pre..sent has not been used to investigate the elements and phenomena of real life; attempts have not even been made to investigate the internal laws of the communion of States and international relations". Therefore, the time had come to investigate international aspects of the laws of the historical development of nations.

For Martens the development of international law and the history of international relations were closely linked, as was the study of concrete legal material. He was convinced that only history might serve as the firm foundation of scientific conceptions. Martens was in fact urging the creation of a new theory of international law responsive to the realities of the international relations contemporary to him. The science of international law must substantiate the defense of the individual. Martens was the first in Russia to link the degree of civilization of a State with the development of international law and the development of the individual; the duty of the State was to recognize and defend the rights of the individual.

Having analyzed inter-State relations and the extent to which States complied with norms of international law in peacetime and during war, Martens condemned

[42] V. P. Danevskii, Очерк новейшей литературы по международному праву [Survey of Recent Literature on International Law] (Spb., 1876), p. 232. Butler Д18.

[43] Martens, «О задачах современного международного права: Вступительная лекция, читанная 28-го января 1871 года в С.-Петербургском университете» [On the Tasks of Contemporary International Law: Inaugural Lecture, Delivered 28 January 1871 in St. Petersburg University], Журнал Министерства народного просвещения [Journal of the Ministry of Public Enlightenment], no. 6 (1871), pp. 251-268. Also published separately, 17 p. Butler M116.

war as a barbaric means for the settlement of international disputes that should not be extolled over peaceful means. This meant he needed to propose alternative approaches to the study of international law which in quality, depth, and topicality exceed earlier approaches.

The apotheosis of his efforts took two forms. The first was his two-volume fundamental treatise on the contemporary international law of civilized nations, first published in 1882-1883. There were five editions in all. The treatise well represented the "golden era" of international legal doctrine in Russia and was widely translated.[44] The second was his collection of Russian bilateral treaties with foreign States, thoroughly annotated in the Russian and French languages; he completed fifteen volumes before his death. Nothing has been done to continue the series, but it remains a monument to Russian international legal scholarship.

The two-volume treatise was the first complete manual on international law in the Russian language.[45] Grabar praised the *cours* as "... original in its system and for the first time illuminated norms of law with examples from the diplomatic history of Russia".[46] Its appearance transformed the teaching and comprehension of international law because the volumes embodied new methodological, conceptual, and structural principles. Russian law students had been dependent principally on works by foreign authors. It had no serious rival as a treatise in the "golden era", and Soviet international lawyers produced nothing comparable until the 1970s. Generations of law students (international law was a compulsory course in Russian, Soviet, and post-Soviet law faculties) were familiar with the work, including senior political leaders: Emperor Nicholas II, V. I. Lenin, A. F. Kerensky, M. S. Gorbachev, V. V. Putin, D. A. Medvedev, and many others.

In his preface to the first edition, Martens wrote:

> Russian literature on international law, as a matter of fact, does not exist at all, and there is not a single systematic manual on this science by a Russian scholar. The need for such a manual which would make it possible to orient oneself in international questions arising every day is felt not only by jurists, but also by all educated Russian people interested in foreign

[44] But only recently in English. See F. F. Martens, *Contemporary International Law of Civilized Peoples*, ed. & transl. William E. Butler (Clark, New Jersey, 2021-2022). General and Special Parts in 2 vols.

[45] Martens, Современное международное право цивилизованных народов [Contemporary International Law of Civilized Nations] (Spb., 1882-1883; 2d ed.; 1887-1888; 3d ed.; 1895-1896; 4th ed.; 1898-1900; 5th ed.; 1905-1905; reprint of 5th ed., Moscow, 1996 and 2008). Butler M139. The first edition contained sections devoted to aspects of statehood and, by implication, the concept of a "civilized nation". All but one of the foreign translations circumvented the issue of distinguishing between a "nation" and a "people" or by simply omitting the words "civilized nations" from the title. In all subsequent Russian editions of the treatise, these sections were excluded, but the section numbers were retained. For a translation of the missing passages, see W. E. Butler, "The Martens Treatise: Missing Passages", *Jus Gentium: Journal of International Legal History*, IV (2019), pp. 633-653. These passages are also restored in the English translation of Martens, note 44 above.

[46] See V. E. Grabar, *The History of International Law in Russia 1647-1917: A Bio-Bibliographical Study*, transl. W. E. Butler (1990), p. 380.

> policy and following the development of the general cultural life of civilized peoples.
>
> With a view to filling this gap, we publish the present work, the two volumes of which encompass the entire domain of international law in peacetime and during war (pp. i-ii).

Foreign translations of the treatise solidified Martens' reputation throughout the world of international law and diplomacy. The French,[47] German,[48] Spanish,[49] and Japanese[50] translations are well-known. Translations are also reported in Persia,[51] China, and Serbia, although bibliographical details are lacking.

With his treatise on contemporary international law, Martens brought to fruition one of the objectives posited in his inaugural lecture: to place international legal research on a firm foundation of the socio-political development of States using historical evidence of their international relations and contemporary practical material. Martens believed that actual living relations underpinned international law. His treatise was noteworthy for its realism, based on empirical materials, and imbued with historical and normative sources, "including Russian international policy according to sources of our archives". These sentiments were consistent with Martens positivist approach, for in his view the sole subject-matter of international law as a science was the actual law in force as consolidated in normative acts reflecting real relations.

Martens defined international law as the "aggregate of legal norms determining the conditions for the achievement by nations of their own vital aims in the sphere of mutual relations" (I, p. 16). His original contributions to the theory of international law during his time were the theories of international communion and of international administration. Four doctrinal positions underpinned Martens' views:

> [1]. nations and States by reason of objective factors in their development aspire to and act in communion with one another;

47 F. Martens, *Traité de droit international*, transl. A. Leo (Paris, 1883-1887). 3 vols. Butler M143. Possibly the French translation may have been used in Persia.

48 F. F. Martens, *Völkerrecht: Das internationale Recht der zivilisierten Nationen*, ed. C. Bergbohm (Berlin, 1883-1886). 2 vols. Butler M82.

49 F. de Martens, *Tratado de derecho internacional* (Madrid, [c. 1894]. 3 vols. + appendix. Butler M144.

50 The Japanese translation, done from the German language edition, was prepared by Shingo Nakamura (1870-1939) and published in 1900 and again in 1908, under the auspices of Waseda University, in two volumes. We are obliged to Professor Nobuyoshi Fujinami for data on the Japanese publication. See Martens, *Kokusaihō / Furīdorihhi Fon Marutensu* (Tokyo, 1908).

51 Searches for a Persian language edition have failed to locate a copy in Iran, Russia, Europe, and the United States. Both Nussbaum and Grabar mention a Persian-language translation. See Grabar, note 46 above, p. 382; Nussbaum, note 4 above, p. 56. For a possible explanation relating to the Persian edition, see Mohsen Nikbin, "On the Origins of the Earliest Lecture on International Law in Persia", *Jus Gentium: Journal of International Legal History*, V (2020), pp. 179-183.

[2]. the community of interests of nations in their international communion generated international law;

[3]. the degree of participation of a State in international communion is determined by the level of freedom of the individual therein;

[4]. international communion requires international administration and "international administrative law".

The idea of international communion was the premise of Martens' entire theory of international law. In his view, international communion did not exist either in ancient times or in the Middle Ages because nations were unaware of the need for mutual assistance and a general law; such an awareness or consciousness arose in contemporary international life. But Martens, as noted above, confined international communion and international law to the nations of "European civilization", excluding non-Christian nations from such communion and the law of nations. European States, he contended, commune with them on the basis of natural law, whatever that meant. Martens' discriminatory failure to recognize the so-called "uncivilized nations" as having international legal personality was not consistent with his progressive contribution to international law.

Martens supported his position as follows: the progress of international law is conditioned by the development of individual freedom and free State institutions. Only the State in which an individual receives recognition of his rights may become a member of properly organized international communion. Therefore, Martens limited the operation of international law to States of European civilization, to the relations of the States of Europe and Northern America. Martens rejected the possibility of any kind of guarantees of international treaties either arising or being complied with in ancient times and the Middle Ages. Such a possibility, he believed, was only possible in the times contemporary to him. This approach precluded any possibility of applying civilized treaty guarantees to relations with the non-European nations. These guarantees Martens divided into two types: simple and complex. Simple guarantees arise when a civilized third State guarantees the performance of treaty obligations, and complex guarantees exist as mutual or collective guarantees of States.

The essence of his theory of international communion Martens saw in the following: States exist and develop, objectively entering into communion with one another on various issues. The multiplicity of such communion creates a stable system of international communion:

> International communion is a free alliance of States in order to achieve by common actions the full development of their forces and the satisfaction of their reasonable needs. The aggregate of legal norms determining the effectuation of the idea of international communion comprises the law of international communion; this is international law (p. 200).

Martens drew his theory of international administration logically from the theory of international communion. He advanced the idea of international administration as an element of State relations in his doctoral dissertation on consuls, setting out as one purpose of that dissertation to investigate the "laws of international administration".[52] In his treatise on contemporary international law he elaborated the point:

> The real basis of international activity of States, or international administration, lies in the inadequacy of forces and means of an individual nation to achieve its vital aims. By international administration we understand the free activity of a State in the domain of international communion in view of the achievement by them of their own vital purposes within the limits laid down by international law.

In Martens' view, States are members of a single international communion, but each of them retains its autonomy and independence. International communion itself has a certain regularity, and is based on established legal principles. In order to regulate international communion, international administration is essential and, accordingly, an international administration.[53] All States in international communion are represented by organs or agencies. These organs or agencies he called "international administrators". He distinguished between two aspects of international administration:

> [1] the administration of the foreign relations of a State with the assistance of the legislative, administrative (executive), and judicial branches;
>
> [2] the administration of international relations by the joint efforts of States through associations or organizations of sovereign States.

Volume two (Special Part) of his treatise Martens devoted to the theory of international administration. He included all activity of States transcending the limits of one country and undertaken in the international sphere within the system of international administration – all the international activity of State authorities: "the aggregate of legal conditions and norms determined by the international activity of a State is the law of international administration or international administrative law". Only States are subjects of the law of international administration. The "aggregate of all vital relations between States, social groups, and private individuals which require assistance, patronage, or defense by State authorities" are an object of the law of international administration (pp. II, 8-9). Martens supposed that

> the progressing development of mankind inevitably would lead to a more intensive communion of States and thereby to the strengthening and improvement of international administration ... the constant work of international law with regard to the creation of legal order in the world community which corresponds to the achievements of human civilization and

[52] Martens, note 44 above, pp. 6, 21-35. Soviet international lawyers described the Martens theory of the law of international administration as "one of the most original theories concerning the essence of international law in Russian doctrinal writings of the end of the nineteenth and early twentieth centuries". See D. B. Levin, Наука международного права в России в конце XIX и начале XX в. [Science of International Law in Russia at the End of the XIX and Beginning of the XX Centuries] (M., 1982), p. 12.

[53] This sounds slightly redundant in English. Martens is able in the Russian language to distinguish between international administration [управление] as an activity and international administration [администрация] as an institution(s).

> the gradual development of international administration which strengthens the peaceful cooperation of nations is the path towards the establishment of perpetual peace on earth, a path complex, not quick, but the sole true and real path.[54]

As a positivist, Martens did not confine himself to setting out the rules of international law and describing international institutions; he was interested in discovering or identifying the laws and trends at work in the international relations of his time and analyzing the roles and activities of States with a view to determining their involvement in international communion and administration. This meant he was less interested in international relations as an isolated phenomenon, and more in their natural link with legal institutions of individual States and their diverse economic and spiritual ties. He drew for the first time a distinction between conceptions of the system of international law and conceptions of the system of the science of international law. The notion of international communion was among the foundations of his understanding of the system of the science of international law: "At the base of the scientific system of contemporary international law should be placed the idea of international communion, according to which each autonomous State is an organic part of a single whole, connected with other States by a community of interests and rights" (I, pp. 176-177).

Martens divided positive international law into public international law, the subject-matter of which is the legal regulation of direct relations of States with one another in the domain of international exchanges, and private international law, which, in his view, determined the legal status of subjects in the domain of international relations generated by private-law interests and the need for their legal protection. With regard to the system of the science of international law, Martens wrote:

> The system in which we set out the science of international law differs materially from other scientific systems in the rich western European literature ... In the course of eleven years of lecturing activity, this system was and remains, at least in our understanding, the order that best corresponds to the essence and degree of development of contemporary international relations (p. ii).

He pointed out that the majority of scholars structured the system of international law as a continuation of ancient Roman law, which was in essence civil law. He regarded this approach as inappropriate. An understanding of the distinctive features and the developmental laws of international law required an analysis of those real relations which bound States together as members of an international community in their constant communion. Martens rejected the division of international law into the "law of war" and the "law of peace". Martens' approach was completely different: these were the ideas of international communion and international administration "in the sphere of spiritual, physical, and economic interests of nations" and "in the domain of the legal interests of subjects and nations".[55]

[54] See Pustogarov, note 4 above, p. 72.

[55] According to Grabar, "Martens' system was confirmed in the Russian literature and influenced some foreign writers". Grabar, note 46 above, p. 482.

Martens regarded international law as a single complex of public-law and private-law principles and norms and defined the basic methodological principles for investigating the correlation between public and private international law. From his idea of international communion Martens drew the legal duty of each State and even the courts of States to recognize "on the territory of all international communion" any "right arising on the basis of the laws of any State". He wrote: "Each State must be autonomous within the limits of its territory, but it does not follow that it has the right to use its autonomy to violate the legal interests or rights of private individuals acquired on another's territory" (II, p. 274).

Martens opposed treaties based on the right to use force. And if law is protected by force, this does not mean that force underlies law. "We believe", he wrote, "in the final triumph of law even there where it is violated most audaciously, because we believe in the ideal force of law".[56]

Martens considered himself to be, and was, a realist. Unlike pacifists and humanists, he regarded the elimination of war in the near future to be completely utopian, indeed even in the remote future. The only solution consistent with the humane values of law would be to limit the terrors of war by norms recognized by all nations and States.

Having based his international legal theory on a careful study of historical and contemporary international events, he drew the following predictive conclusion: for anyone seeking to understand international relations and to grasp the tasks and purposes of the State, the predominant principle could only be one – the idea of law in the broadest sense of the word. Neither the idea of disconnection, or the idea of bending to physical force, or the idea of political balance, or, finally, the principle of nationality could be deemed to be the guiding principles of a properly-structured international life. "The guiding principle", he believed, should be "the idea of law" (I, p. 29).[57]

Martens was of the view, progressive in his day, that the interference of one State in the internal affairs of another State was admissible only if there are "legal grounds for the immediate declaration of war" and that there "cannot be other exceptions from the viewpoint of law".[58]

As regards the issue of international legal personality, in his two-volume treatise Martens developed the notion of parallel subjects of international law, accord-

[56] See Martens, Восточная война и Брюссельская конференция 1874-1878 гг. [Eastern War and the Brussels Conference of 1874-1878] (Spb., 1879), p. 41.

[57] See E. Voronin, «Русская школа права профессора Ф. Ф. Мартенса и современное международное право. К 170-летию со дня рождения» [The Russian School of Law of Professor F. F. Martens and Contemporary International Law. On the 170th Birthday], Международная жизнь [International Life], no. 10 (2015); Voronin, «К 170-летию со дня рождения профессора Ф. Ф. Мартенса, 1845-1909» [On 170th Birthday of Professor F. F. Martens, 1845-1909], Московский журнал международного права [Moscow Journal of International Law], no. 3 (2015), pp. 24-37.

[58] Martens, «Начало невмешательства гр. Л. Камаровского» [Principle of Non-Interference of Count L. Kamarovskii], Журнал гражданского и уголовного права [Journal of Civil and Criminal Law], no. 3 (1875), pp. 253-259.

ing to which "independent nations or States of European civilization are direct subjects of international law and actors in the domain of international communion" (I, p. 230), and juridical and natural persons "carry on their international turnover under the control, patronage, and even responsibility of State power, of which they are subjects" (I, p. 231) throughout "all the space of the operation of international law" (I, p. 320).

Martens' significant contributions to the development of the international protection of human rights has been overlooked. Martens' humanist views caused him to place the human individual highest of all. He regarded respect for human rights as the measure of civilization of a State and international relations as a whole. No doubt Martens idealized the recognition and protection of human rights. In his words, all States contemporary to him recognized for man "certain basic rights which are inextricably linked with the human individual". The individual is under the protection of international law and has rights in the domain of international relations. He expressed the position as follows:

> All contemporary civilized States are agreed that man is a person, that is, a subject of certain inalienable rights which must be respected in their mutual relations. Therefore, every person, irrespective of subjectship or nationality, presently finds protection of his person and ownership in all the spatial operation of international law. The ultimate purpose of the State and the purpose of international relations is the protection of the person (I, p. 320).

Martens composed a digest or code of basic human rights in which he included:

> [1] the right to existence and development of the natural person (this is the right to acquire means necessary for the maintenance of life by physical labor, by engaging in trade and commerce, by engaging in a craft, or by other legal means; for this, each person enjoys complete freedom within the limits established by a law);
>
> [2] the right to the development of spiritual and intellectual abilities and forces (this is the right to use by all means which a country provides for his education and the satisfaction of aesthetic aspirations, such as: schools, libraries, museums, and others);
>
> [3] the right to communication and free movement within the international alliance of States (this is the right not to be attached to the land and a concrete territory of residence and the right to emigration as an inalienable human right) (I, pp. 327-328).

Commenting on the scope of the above human rights, Martens wrote: "From the aforesaid rights recognized for every person in the domain of international intercourse arise other inalienable human rights: the right to inviolability of the person, life, honor, health, the right to possess ownership, to enter into obligations, the right to marry, and so forth". Martens added that the inviolability of life, honor, and dignity is recognized as a right for every person not because it is protected by the criminal law, but because every person as an individual by nature has an inalienable right to the said inviolability.

In all likelihood Martens realized that his assertion that international law recognized these rights for each individual was far in advance of the reality. He intimated as much in another passage:

> … if the States actually considered these rights to be inherent to the human individual and were sanctioned by international communion, then the many instances would be eliminated of conflicts of legislation and mutual altercations of States explicable only by the exaggerated significance which governments attach to a territorial law or simply their own discretion (I, p. 328).

No less noteworthy were the contributions of Martens to private international law in a period when various forms of international communion and cooperation of Russia from the mid-nineteenth century were expanding with the involvement of private individuals: trade, communications, cultural, educational, and others.[59] The field of private international law was in an embryonic state in Russia, and there was much early discussion of ideas, suggestions, terminologies, and methodologies.

Martens made an important contribution to elaborating the basic positions with respect to private international law in Russia, including the academic study of this branch of law. In the preface to volume two of his treatise, he wrote: "Private international and criminal law are set out for the first time in the present volume in the Russian language". In fact, he had addressed issues of private international law in four chapters of the first volume, when he discussed his theory of international communion, including the structures of organs thereof, and the participants of international relations and subjects of international law. Martens included the "rights of private individuals in the domain of international relations" within the fields of research on subjects of international law. He relegated private international law to the sphere of "international administration in the domain of legal interests of subjects and nations". But he also regarded private international law as the law in force of "each civilized State", a necessary addition to the civil law of each civilized State" (I, p. 183). In this sense, Martens added, "private law is an organic part of the territorial civil law of a country, and the application by a court, in a concrete instance, of foreign laws would not be for its part an excess of power, but merely the strict performance of its duties" (II, p. 282).

Volume two of Martens' treatise contained an extensive chapter on private international law (II, pp. 285-377). Given that the treatise was the most substantial and widely-read contribution in Russia of the time, it had a considerable influence on the teaching of international law. Martens pointed to three distinctive features of private international law: the civil-law nature of the relations regulated; the presence of an international element in such relations; and their being in the sphere of international administration of legal interests of subjects and nations.

Martens proceeded from the idea of States being legally linked, or connected, by the basic principles of private international law elaborated in the process of

[59] See for details T. M. Iablochkov, «Значение Ф. Ф. Мартенса в науке частного международного права» [Significance of F. F. Martens in the Science of Private International Law], Юридические записки Демидовского юридического лицея [Legal Notes of the Demidov Juridical Lycée] (Iaroslavl, 1910), I, pp. 465-481.

international communion.[60] It followed, he believed, that the confusing and complex questions of the relations of private individuals of different States might be resolved only by proceeding from the principles of international communion, especially the application of laws of different States. On this basis he formulated certain doctrinal positions that flowed from these premises:

> [1] States when permitting private-law relations between their subjects and foreigners thereby recognize that the norms regulating these relations are binding;
>
> [2] the legal duty of States to recognize on the territory of all international communion any right arising on the basis of laws of any State;
>
> [3] private international law is the law in force for each civilized State;
>
> [4] the recognition of rights which arose under the operation of laws of other States is the legal duty of all States which are subjects of international law;
>
> [5] every court, being obliged to apply the law of its own State, at the same time has the legal duty to also recognize the law of other States based on a law [*lex*];
>
> [6] the purpose of every court is to protect existing private rights;
>
> [7] in each instance representing the possibility or requiring the choice between territorial and foreign laws, the court must determine which law, native or foreign, will be applied: "a court will not transgress the boundaries of power belonging thereto if it adheres in the administration of justice to the principles of private international law" (II, p. 281);
>
> [8] unless the laws of individual States contain the principles of private international law or eliminate misunderstandings arising in the practice of their application, then it is necessary to apply a general international treaty to these questions or conclude a new treaty;
>
> [9] private international law ceases to operate when the public policy of the country is violated.

Martens' views with respect to the terminological aspects of private international law differed from most at the time. He criticized all international lawyers for their extensive use of terms taken from Roman private law. His own definition of private international law was as follows: "the aggregate legal norms determining the application to the particular legal relation of an interested person in the domain of international turnovers, rights, or law of the fatherland or foreign State" (II, p. 267). As noted above, he believed that private international law was an essential addition to the civil law of every civilized State (I, p. 184), a view entirely consis-

[60] Professor Lazar Adolfovich Lunts (1892-1979) noted in this connection: "The idea of the connectedness of a sovereign State by certain basic principles of private international law elaborated in international communion, of course, has material theoretical and practical interest". See L. A. Lunts, Международное частное право [Private International Law: General Part] (M., 1973), p. 150.

tent with the international legal regulation of private-law relations. Martens called civil-law relations including a foreign element "international civil relations".[61]

Martens made significant contributions to the embryonic period of the codification of private international law. He was an official delegate of the Russian Government to the 1893, 1894, 1900, and 1904 Hague conferences on private international law convened at the initiative of The Netherlands to determine the basic principles of private international law. He was the "first delegate" of Russia at these conferences. His contemporary wrote:

> Every time the Dutch Government circulated its program for the conference on working out questions of private international law, the Russian Government designated a meeting attached to the Ministry of Foreign Affairs from representatives of various departments to consider this program; the chairman of these meetings always was Martens. The opinions of these meetings were the basis of instructions suggested by the Russian Government to the delegates at the conferences. Martens himself was inevitably sent as one of these delegates, who thus might influence directly the attitude of the Russian legislator to the agreements elaborated at the conferences ... At these conferences Martens inevitably was elected one of the vice-presidents of the conference.[62]

At the 1900 Third Hague Conference for the Codification of Private International Law, Martens as the representative of the Russian Government was forced (contrary to his position as a scholar) to oppose the application to the form of family marriage one of the most generally-recognized conflicts principles, according to which the form of the act of marriage is determined according to the law of the place where the ceremony is performed. The Government of Russia, not wishing to recognize the marriages of Russian subjects performed abroad in civil form without compliance with religious rites, refused to accede to the Hague convention under which the said principle was applicable to the form of marriage. The Russian Government also did not consent to the application to the form of marriage of the national law of the persons marrying as this might lead to permitting in Russia the civil marriages of foreigners. The position of the Russian Government on this question presented by Martens at the 1900 Hague Conference and at subsequent Hague conferences demonstrated to what practical results the derogation from certain generally-recognized organizing principles of private international law led which in theory had been developed by Martens himself and energetically upheld.[63]

[61] Boguslavskii, however, wrote that, on the contrary, "F. F. Martens above all proceeded from the international-legal conception of private international law". M. M. Boguslavskii, Международное частное право [Private International Law] (7th ed.; M., 2016), p. 9.

[62] Iablochkov, note 59 above, p. 6. Lunts observed that, in practice, Martens, as an official bound by the position of the Russian Government, sometimes was forced to depart from his doctrinal principles. When conceiving of the role of certain principles of private international law in the organization of international communion, this is clear when these principles are ignored in practice. Lunts, note 60 above, p. 149.

[63] Lunts, ibid.

Although it is difficult to quantify the situations in which Martens found himself conflicted between his doctrinal positions and government policies (which he will have tried to influence, probably in these cases without success), others did occur:

> To Martens fell the difficult task of combining in one person the scholar and the diplomat. Therein was the tragedy of his life, and justification of the inconsistency of his theory! … As a theorist, Martens was a convinced adept of the principle *locus regis actum*, but as a politician Martens was prepared to look at the law through the prism of 'public policy', which could not be violated by any international agreements.[64]

That not all of Martens' doctrinal positions were accepted is unsurprising, especially given the early stages of development of private international law. Even his former students and proteges sometimes disagreed with him. Boris Nolde wrote (after Martens' death) that Martens "was not great as a scholar in this branch of international law. In his person Russian science made a step backward in comparison with Malyshev". Nolde said that Martens' idea of international communion was "completely empty in connection with the structuring of conflicts norms because it merely states the undisputed fact that conflicts of the law of various countries arise by virtue of the existence of links between these countries".[65]

Nonetheless, Martens was among the pioneers in attempting to provide a theoretical foundation for the complex issues of international private-law relations. Although he did not escape certain contradictions in his conclusions and judgments, he did draw the attention of the scholarly legal community to issues of conflicts of laws and generated interest among colleagues in seeking answers to the problems raised. As Grabar pointed out, "An undoubted service of Martens was his creation in connection with his chair of a whole school of pupils … thanks to whose writings this branch of international law has significantly developed".[66]

Martens laid the conceptual foundations of international criminal law in Russian doctrine. Volume two of his treatise contains a rather detailed Chapter Five entitled "International Criminal Law" (§§84-100). He defined international criminal law as follows: "… the aggregate of legal norms determining the conditions of international judicial assistance of States to one another when effectuating their own punitive activities in the domain of international communion" (II, p. 348). Having made general comments on the significance of international cooperation of States with respect to criminal prosecution and punishment of criminals, Martens considered in detail the history of the origin and development of international criminal law, its basic principles, spatial operation of norms of criminal law, jurisdiction over criminal acts, mutual assistance of States to one another in criminal adjudication, extradition, and other types of mutual legal assistance, recognition of the judgments of foreign courts, and so on.

[64] Iablochkov, note 59 above, pp. 278, 281.

[65] B. E. Nolde, «М. И. Брун (1860-1916) и наука международного частного права в России» [M. I. Brun (1868-1916) and the Science of Private International Law in Russia], Вестник гражданского права [Herald of Civil Law], no. 3-5 (1917), pp. 23-24. Butler H141.

[66] Grabar, note 46 above, p. 575.

With respect to extradition of criminals, Martens took the view that the extradition by States of own citizens or subjects was lawful and advisable. But he also acknowledged the international principle of not extraditing so-called "political criminals", except for anarchists and dynamitists who committed general crimes during mutinies and internecine wars (II, pp. 393-417). Taking a realist position, Martens concluded that: "the conditions and extent of mutual judicial assistance rendered by States to one another in the sphere of political justice might best be determined by international agreements (II, p. 348) or, in his terminology, "punitive conventions".

Martens did great service as a historian of international law and world history generally. This side of Martens has yet to attract much attention from specialists. He was active in the Russian Imperial Historical Society, having been elected to the Council of the Society. The French elected him to the Société d'histoire générale et d'histoire diplomatique, founded at Paris in 1886. He was a founding member in 1894 of the International Colonial Institute in Brussels.

International legal practitioner. Martens' academic career was successful in important part because he was an excellent diplomat and arbitrator. These sides of his life developed in parallel with his work at the Chair of International Law, Imperial School of Jurisprudence, and Alexander Lycée.

On 6 January 1869 Martens took up service in the Ministry of Foreign Affairs as a college secretary, which in the Table of Ranks corresponded to the tenth degree. The enduring collaboration between the Chair of International Law at St. Petersburg University began with the appointment of Martens. Others who held important Ministry appointments included M. A. von Taube, Boris Nolde, A. N. Mandelstam, E. K. Simson, and A. M. Gorovtsev. For four decades Martens advised all ministers of foreign affairs: Aleksandr Mikhailovich Gorchakov (1798-1883), Nikolai Karlovich Giers (1820-1895), Aleksei Borisovich Lobanov-Rostovskii (1824-1896), Nikolai Pavlovich Shishkin (1827-1902), Mikhail Nikolaevich Muravev (1845-1900), Vladimir Nikolaevich Lamzdorf (1844-1907), and Aleksandr Petrovich Izvolskii (1856-1919). In 1879 Martens was appointed an official for special assignments attached to the State Chancellery, and in 1881, a permanent member of the Council of the Ministry of Foreign Affairs (one of six executives of the Ministry, plus Martens).[67]

It transpired that Martens was first able to realize his scholarly aspirations and express his doctrinal position by undertaking the aforementioned collection of bilateral Russian treaties.[68] Emperor Alexander II, on the basis of a Report from the State Chancellor, A. M. Gorchakov, on the need to systematize and analyze the treaty obligations of the Russian Empire, assigned Martens to collect, systematize, and publish a collection of all international treaties of Russia, giving to Martens free access to all State archives of Russia.[69] The first volume appeared a year lat-

[67] This was the highest consultative organ of the Ministry, created in 1832.

[68] On the origins of Russian treaty collections, see W. E. Butler, "Treaty Collections in Eighteenth-Century Russia: Encounters with European Experience", in Butler, *Russia and the Law of Nations in Historical Perspective* (2009), pp. 259-267.

[69] Martens also worked in foreign archives, including French State archives in Paris, to confirm

er. The starting point for the collection was the year 1648 – the year in which the treaties of Westphalia were concluded and Russia formally joined the circle of European powers. It was also about the time (1647-1651) that the first foreign book relevant to the law of nations was printed in Russia, the first law code – the 1649 Sobornoe ulozhenie – was published in Russia, and the first codification of canon law – the Kormchaia kniga (1650-1651) – was printed in Russia.[70]

Whatever clerical, research, administrative, or other support Martens may have been accorded within the Ministry of Foreign Affairs, the final product was inimitably his own. He acted as compiler, systematizer, commentator, and editor-in-chief. Martens and the rest of the Ministry were fluent in French, and the Martens *Recueil* achieved lasting and unrivalled fame because of the high quality of the work itself and the fact that it was accessible linguistically to the international community. The Ministry of Foreign Affairs sent copies of each volume *gratis* to foreign governments and leading libraries. It was truly an encyclopedic diplomatic history of Russian foreign relations.

From the 1870s Martens was given special assignments of the Ministry of Foreign Affairs. His exceptional authority in matters of international relations gave him access to the leaders of the European powers: the King of England, the Kaiser of Germany, and the leaders of France, Italy, Belgium, and others. Even the casual leisure visit to Europe often required that he pay a courtesy call on senior officials, sometimes including the Head of State. He was knowledgeable, had original insights into the issues of the day, exceptional contacts, frequently wrote commentaries on current events for the press, and was conversant in the major European languages. No other international lawyer of his time enjoyed such stature and access. On occasion there were delicate diplomatic assignments best handled through a private visit. Emperor Nicholas II, for example, sent Martens to Constantinople in 1898 to help resolve a European crisis arising out of the Greco-Turkish War of 1897.

Much of Martens' work in the Ministry of Foreign Affairs during these years was related to the law of war. Shortly after taking up his junior position in the Ministry, Martens suggested to Minister Gorchakov that Russia take the initiative to convene an international conference on the laws and customs of war and prepared a draft treaty for consideration. Martens later explained his role:

> During the War of 1870-71, being close to the theatre of war, I collected from the newspapers of all countries and through personal contacts all the facts which established a violation of the laws and customs of war. Already I had come to the conclusion that the establishment by the governments themselves of these laws and customs was entirely necessary in order to prevent endless accusations and merciless reprisals. In 1873 I

or collect materials for the treaty collection. See W. E. Butler, "On the Career of F. F. Martens: An Unknown Letter", *Jus Gentium: Journal of International Legal History*, I (2016), pp. 621-625. The three volumes (13-15) devoted to France were the last to appear before Martens' death. A sixteenth volume devoted to Russo-Turkish relations was planned, but Martens' death intervened. Grabar wrote of the treaty collection: "This single work would have been sufficient to perpetuate Martens's name". Grabar, note 46 above, p. 382.

[70] See W. E. Butler, *Russian Law and Legal Institutions* (3d ed.; 2021), pp. 57-59.

> had the honor to submit this idea to my noted superior, Chancellor Prince Gorchakov. General Count Miliutin, at the time War Minister, and one of the most outstanding Russian public figures, not only reacted sympathetically to this matter but hastened to extend his influential support for it. The initial draft convention on the laws and customs of warfare, prepared by myself, was subjected to detailed and attentive discussion in a commission of eminent military officers under the chairmanship of General Miliutin himself.[71]

The draft, with revisions, was approved by the leadership of the Ministry and the commission chaired by General Count Dmitrii Alekseevich Miliutin (1816-1912). It was then circulated by a diplomatic note to other States. In 1874 the Brussels Conference for the Codification of the Laws and Customs of Land Warfare was held, and Martens was a member of the Russian delegation. This was the first occasion in Russian diplomatic practice that a legal scholar was appointed to take part in international diplomatic negotiations.

The draft Convention prepared by Martens and circulated in advance to interested States encountered no serious objections. The Convention contained uniform rules for waging war on land. Humane treatment of the civilian population and non-combatants were key features of the Convention. Many governments, however, were not willing to lay down binding rules for warfare. It was decided instead of a Convention to adopt the proposed draft in the form of a Declaration.

Twenty-five years later Martens returned to the question of humanizing land warfare at the First Hague Peace Conference in 1899. The Conference was convened at the initiative of Russia. Martens played a prominent part in persuading the Emperor and the Minister of Foreign Affairs to support the idea: he served as the "initiator of the initiative"[72] and drafted the Conference program.[73] Delegates from twenty-six States attended the Conference. Grabar wrote of Martens' key role in the Conference:

> He saved it from failure, proposing in place of the impracticable initial program (to place a limit on continuous armament) a new program in which the reduction of armaments constituted only one point of eight, hav-

[71] Martens, Восточная война и Брюссельская конференция 1874-1878 [Eastern War and Brussels Conference of 1874-78] (Spb., 1879), p. i. Butler M83. The First Hague Peace Conference gave occasion for a French translation of this work. See Martens, *La Paix et la guerre: La Conférence de Bruxelles 1874: Droits et devoirs de belligérants (leur application pendant la guerre d'Orient 1874-1878): La Conférence de la Haye 1899*, transl. Comte N. de Sance (Paris, 1901). Butler M100.

[72] Pustogarov writes: "He was not in fact the initiator of convoking it, but his indefatigable efforts in the name of the success of the Conference will always link his name with it". Pustogarov, note 4 above, p. 182-183.

[73] See F. Eliashevich and H. Wehberg, «Ф. Мартенс и Гаагские конференции мира» [F. Martens and the Hague Peace Conferences], Журнал Министерства юстиции [Journal of the Ministry of Justice], no. 2 (1911), p. 332: "He created for the First Hague Peace Conference a practically realizable program and spoke at the Conference for the effectuation thereof with all the force of his personality".

> ing in mind a review of the norms of the law of war and the regulation of peaceful means for the settlement of international disputes.[74]

This perception is shared by Dutch specialists. The original intention of Emperor Nicholas II was to convene a conference in St. Petersburg devoted to disarmament. Both the venue and the subject-matter were uninteresting to European powers. Martens saved the project:

> Martens, a powerhouse of energy, widely anticipated that instant disarmament was a mere pipe dream. Instead, he confidently mustered his thirty years of experience in the international arena to rewrite the programme, changing the entire thrust of the Conference and confronting the delegates with the two most acute and vexing issues of the day, to wit, the peaceful settlement of disputes and the regulation of warfare. In doing so, Martens saved the programme, just as the programme saved the conference. This much is certain: the field in which the conference achieved its key successes, arbitration and humanitarian issues, are in clear harmony with the essence of Martens' career and expertise.[75]

Martens was elected chairman of the Third Commission, which was to draft the Convention on the laws and customs of war on land. The draft that Martens had prepared in 1873 for the 1874 Brussels Conference was used as the basis of negotiations. There were tremendous difficulties in agreeing the text. One issue was the occupation regime and the right of the population to resist the enemy. A group of small powers headed by Belgium demanded recognition of an unrestricted right of the population of occupied territories to resist, refused to sign the prepared version of the Convention, and threatened to walk out of the Conference. Martens found a way out of this "dead end", a move that Jean Pictet (1914-2002) later described as the "genius of Martens".[76] A provision emerged which later became known as the "Martens Clause", sometimes as the "Martens Declaration", and is so known to this day.[77] Martens proposed to include in the Preamble the following formulation when a situation arose not contemplated by the Convention:

[74] Grabar, note 46 above, pp. 383-384.

[75] A. Eyffinger, "Living Up to a Tradition", in Peter J. van Krieken and David McKay (eds.), *The Hague: Legal Capital of the World* (The Hague, 2005), p. 35.

[76] J. Pictet, Развитие и принципы международного гуманитарного права [Development and Principles of Humanitarian Law] (Geneva, 1982), p. 78.

[77] See Gentian Zuberi, "Importance of the Martens Clause for the Development of International Humanitarian Law", in Alla Pozdnakova (ed.), *Russian Revolutions of 1917: Scandinavian Perspectives* (2019), pp. 128-137; Meron, note 55 above; J. Kahn, "Protection and Empire: The Martens Clause, State Sovereignty, and Individual Rights", *Virginia Journal of International Law*, LVI (2016), pp. 1-50; A. Cassese, "The Martens Clause: Half a Loaf or Simply Pie in the Sky?", *European Journal of International Law*, XI (2000), pp. 187-216; Rotem Giladi, "The Enactment of Irony: Reflections on the Origins of the Martens Clause", ibid., XXV (2014), pp. 847-869; Rupert Ticehurst, "The Martens Clause and the Laws of Armed Conflict", *International Review of the Red Cross*, no. 317 (1997); V. Pustogarov, "The Martens Clause in International Law", *Journal of the History of International Law*, I (1999), pp. 125-135; Rhea Schircks, *Die Martens'sche Klausel. Rezeption und Rechtqualität* (Baden-Baden, 2001). The text of the Martens Clause has become a "monument" of international

> … the High Contracting Parties think it right to declare that in cases no included in the Regulations adopted by them, populations and belligerents remain under the protection and empire of the principles of international law, as the result from the usages established between civilized nations, from the laws of humanity, and the requirements of the public conscience …

His proposal was greeted with applause by the delegates, and the entire Convention adopted unanimously. The adoption by the Second Commission of the 1899 Hague Peace Conference of the entire Brussels Declaration unanimously was another cause for celebration.[78]

Subsequently, the Martens formulation was adopted by the Second Hague Peace Conference and reproduced virtually verbatim in Article 1(2) of the Additional Protocol No. 1 to the 1949 Geneva Conventions on the protection of victims of war. The Preamble to the 1980 Convention on the Prohibitions or Restrictions of Use of Certain Conventional Weapons provides:

> Confirming their determination that in cases not covered by this Convention and its annexed Protocols or by other international agreements, the civilian populations and the combatants shall at all times remain under the protection and authority of the principles of international law derived from established custom, from the principles of humanity, and from the dictates of public conscience.

Martens was a fervent advocate of various conciliation procedures for the peaceful settlement of international disputes – mediation, good offices, and commissions of enquiry.[79] The commissions of enquiry were an innovation on his part, and he argued their virtues to the Hague Conference. Against some opposition from Romania and Serbia (believed to have been instigated by Germany), Martens delivered an eloquent address which carried the day.[80] Title III of the Convention for the Pacific Settlement of International Disputes regulates the procedure for the creation, competence, and membership of a commission of enquiry. This new institution was quickly drawn upon in connection with the so-called Hull Incident involving the United Kingdom and the Russian Empire. The incident arose out of the shelling and sinking of several English fishing vessels by Russian warships

law; the passage is illustrated in W. van Genugten, Daniele Heerdt, and Nico Schrijver, *Discover International Law, with Special Attention for the Hague, City of Peace and Justice* (Oiserwijk, 2017), pp. 25-27.

78 Martens referred in his Diary to the Brussels Declaration as his "beloved child". AVPR, opis 787, file 9, ed. krh. 5,1.52; quoted in Pustogarov, note 4 above, p. 178.

79 See S. A. Malinin, «Реализация и развитие идеи Ф. Ф. Мартенса о согласительной процедуре в современном международном праве» [Realization and Development of the Idea of F. F. Martens on the Conciliation Procedure in Contemporary International Law], Российский ежегодник международного права 2000. Специальный выпуск [Russian Yearbook of International Law 2000: Special Issue] (Spb., 2000), pp. 75-80.

80 Pustogarov, note 4 above, p. 182.

off the English coast on 21/22 October 1904.[81] The fishing vessels were mistakenly believed to be Japanese torpedo craft by the Russian naval commanders. The Commission of Enquiry settled the dispute (the Russian member was M. A. von Taube). Russia paid the sum of £65,000 to the victims. Experience with the Hull Commission of Enquiry led to revisions of the 1899 Convention at the Second Hague Conference in 1907.

However, of all the techniques for the pacific settlement of international disputes, Martens is best known for his advocacy on behalf of and practice of international arbitration. Title IV of the 1899 Hague Convention on the Pacific Settlement of International Disputes is devoted to international arbitration. Martens brought to the deliberations at The Hague extensive experience as an international arbitrator. In 1891 he was appointed as chairman of the Anglo-French arbitration concerning fishing rights in the coastal waters of Newfoundland, a matter disposed of without the issuance of an award. Better known was the involvement of Martens in the *Costa Rica Packet* case; The Netherlands and the United Kingdom requested Emperor Nicholas II in confidence to appoint an arbitrator to resolve a dispute that had festered for four years after the Dutch had arrested an English whaling ship. The Minister of Foreign Affairs recommended to the Tsar that Martens be appointed, and this recommendation was accepted in August 1895. An award acceptable to both sides was rendered in 1897.

The boundary dispute between England and Venezuela was submitted to arbitration in 1899; the dispute concerned the boundary between Venezuela and British Guiana in the region of the Orinoco River. Martens was selected, following a complicated procedure, by Venezuela as the chairman of an arbitration tribunal consisting of two British members and, representing Venezuela, two American arbitrators. Russian international lawyers consider this arbitration to be noteworthy because Martens drew up and proposed procedural rules for conducting the arbitration, which the parties accepted. This is believed to be the first occasion in international practice when a case was considered on the basis of rules composed by the chairman of the tribunal and approved by all members of the tribunal; the rules were later incorporated in the Hague Convention on the pacific settlement of disputes. Prior to this arbitration, it is believed that international arbitral tribunals operated without such procedural rules. The outcome of the arbitration gave the United Kingdom about 90% of the territory in dispute. In a Note published by the secretary of the arbitration tribunal, Severo Mallet-Prevost (1860-1949), by instruction after his death,[82] Martens was accused of making an arrangement with the two British arbitrators and forcing a unanimous award, with minimal reasoning. Venezuela declared the award null and void in 1962; in 2018 Guyana filed a request with the International Court of Justice to reinstate the 1899 award. The request remains pending before the Court.

[81] See C. Pleshakov, *The Tsar's Last Armada: The Epic Journey to the Battle of Tsushima* (2002), pp. 91-113.

[82] S. Mallet-Prevost, "The Venezuela-British Guiana Boundary Dispute", *American Journal of International Law*, XLIII (1949), pp. 523-530. The Memorandum was dictated by Severo Mallet-Prevost on 8 February 1944. For a detailed reply, see Clifton J. Child, "The Venezuela-British Guiana Boundary Arbitration of 1899", ibid., XLIV (1950), pp. 682-693. The arbitration is discussed in Pustogarov, note 4 above, pp. 203-212.

The Russian Government was approached about allowing Martens to be considered as an arbitrator in an Anglo-Siamese dispute and an Anglo-Persian dispute in 1898, but the Minister of Foreign Affairs refused permission.

When the Permanent Court of International Arbitration was organized pursuant to the 1899 Hague Convention on the pacific settlement of disputes, Martens was appointed to the panel of arbitrators and served as an arbitrator in disputes between the United States and Mexico in 1902 and between Venezuela and certain European countries in 1904.

From time to time Martens was requested to give legal opinions. In 1892 the Greek *chargé d'affaires* in St. Petersburg commissioned an opinion on an inheritance matter that involved a Greek citizen who passed away in Romania and left a wealthy estate to which Greece laid claim. The Greeks hoped that a favorable opinion from Martens might induce the Romanians to transfer the estate to Greece. Martens submitted his opinion in February 1893; although there was no way to force Romania to release the estate – arbitration had been rejected by the Romanians – the Greek Government hoped that public opinion might assist and therefore published the Martens opinion in the French language.[83]

Martens also undertook a legal opinion for the King of Belgium relating to the Congo (at the end of 1892) and prepared a memorandum on the dispute between the Chinese Government and the Northern Telegraph Society in Copenhagen (1883).[84] At the request of either French bankers or the French Government, Martens offered a legal opinion in 1906 that was essential for Russia receiving a large foreign loan.[85]

As a diplomat and legal advisor, Martens was included in Russian delegations to many international conferences. Reference has been made to conferences in Brussels and Berlin between 1873 and 1878. He participated in the Berlin Conference on Africa in 1884/85, where prohibition of the slave trade was proclaimed, the legality of colonial possessions, and the Free State of the Congo was determined to be in the personal ownership of the King of Belgium. Martens was a delegate in 1888 to an international conference on maritime and trade law in Brussels; the following two years Martens served as the plenipotentiary of Russia at the diplomatic conference which adopted the 1890 Convention Relative to the Slave Trade and Importation into Africa of Firearms, Ammunition, and Spiritous Liquors. The King of Belgium was so impressed with Martens and his activities in ensuring the success of the Conference that he bestowed Belgium's highest decoration on him. Queen Victoria of England and King Leopold II expressed special gratitude to Emperor Nicholas II for sending Martens as a delegate to the Conference and

83 See *Memoire sur le conflit entre la Grèce et la Romanie concernant l'affaire Zappa* (Athens, 1893). Not in Butler.

84 *Memoire sur la telegraphe en Chine* (Copenhagen, 1883). Butler M111.

85 The details of this episode are found in Martens' diaries and reported in Pustogarov, note 4 above, pp. 201-202.

for being the author of many provisions of the General Act – the short title of the 1890 Convention.[86]

In addition to the Hague peace conferences, Martens attended the Hague Conference on private international law (1904) and the peace conference to end the Russo-Japanese war, held at Portsmouth, New Hampshire (1905).

In 1884 he became the permanent representative of Russia at conferences of the Red Cross; being elected in 1886 to the Chief Administration of the Russian Red Cross Society. Shortly after the conclusion of the First Hague Peace Conference, Martens submitted a Report in May 1902 to the first international conference of the Red Cross entitled: "Red Cross Society. Reference Bureau for Rendering Assistance to Prisoners of War Provided by the Hague Convention in Respect of the Laws and Customs of War on Land". When the Russo-Japanese War transpired, a Commission was formed and attached to the Ministry of Foreign Affairs to draft provisions on prisoners of war; several ministries were represented on the Commission (war, navy, internal affairs, finances), together with the Chief Administration of the Russian Red Cross. The Commission drafted the Provisional Statute on Prisoners of War of the Russo-Japanese War, confirmed by the Emperor on 13 May 1904. Pursuant to this Statute, the Russian Red Cross formed the Central Reference Bureau on Prisoners of War, of which Martens was appointed the head.[87] Martens was active, in 1906, when a conference in Geneva reviewed the 1864 Convention on the Red Cross.

In December 1905 Martens was assigned by the Minister of Foreign Affairs to commence the preparations for the Second Hague Peace Conference. Martens prepared a draft program, and these proposals were conveyed to 47 States in a Circular Note sent in March 1906 by the Ministry of Foreign Affairs. Of the recipients, 44 States agreed with the proposal to convene the Conference. Agreeing the program, however, proved to be more difficult. There were political complications: Russia, having been defeated by Japan in the Russo-Japanese War, was in a weaker position, and rivalries were intensifying between England and Germany. The British Government proposed to add to the conference agenda an item on limiting the military burden and restrain German efforts to increase its naval power. Moreover, a number of legal issues awaited resolution after the First Hague Peace Conference: the inviolability of private ownership in naval warfare; whether awards of an international arbitral tribunal were to be binding; the limitation of certain types of armaments, among others.

On this occasion, the Russian elites were not so enthusiastic about the forthcoming Conference. The Russian Ministry of Foreign Affairs decided it would be prudent to canvas the European capitals as to whether the conference should be held and the proposed program. Martens was chosen to take these soundings, accompanied by Boris Nolde. Before the departure of Professor Martens on this visit

[86] Biograficheskii slovar, p. 9.

[87] F. F. Martens (ed.), Военнопленные: Обзор деятельности Центрального справочного бюро о военнопленных во время Русско-японской войны [Prisoners of War: Survey of the Activity of the Central Reference Bureau on Prisoners of War During the Russo-Japanese War], comp. E. A. Bukhe (Spb., 1907). [xvi], 152 p. Not in Butler or Grabar.

around Europe, he was received and instructed by Emperor Nicholas II. The trip began in January 1907 and received remarkable publicity in European media. In Berlin, Martens negotiated directly with Kaiser Wilhelm II and the State Secretary for Foreign Affairs, Heinrich Leonhard von Tschirschky und Bögendorff (1858-1916); in Paris, with President Armand Fallières (1841-1931); in London, with King Edward VII (1841-1910), Prime Minister Sir Henry Campbell-Bannerman (1836-1908), and the Foreign Secretary, Viscount Sir Edward Grey (1862-1933); in Rome, with King Victor Emmanuel III (1869-1947) and Prime Minister Giovanni Giolitti (1842-1928); in Vienna, with Emperor Franz Jozef (1830-1916) and Imperial Foreign Minister, Alois Leopold Johann Baptist Graf Lexa von Aehrenthal (1854-1912). Martens succeeded in persuading the European leaders to agree the program, composition, and even the date of the conference. This was the first occasion in Russia that an international lawyer had been assigned to undertake such politically significant and diplomatically delicate tasks.

The Second Hague Peace Conference worked from 15 June to 18 October 1907; there were 232 representatives from 44 States. The Conference adopted one Declaration and thirteen Conventions (including three revised conventions of 1899). Martens had played the key role in bringing the Conference to fruition, drafting the program and agenda of the Conference, preparing the rules of procedure that governed the work of the Conference, and taking an active role in preparing the ultimate decisions of the Conference. But this Conference was to be the Martens "swan song" – his last major appearance on the public stage of international law.

Within the Russian Government Martens devoted considerable time to various interdepartmental commissions and meetings. His presence was felt in those preparing or agreeing draft legislation on the procedure for becoming a subject of the Russian Empire or giving up that status and emigrating abroad; the limits of the territorial sea; and participation in the name of the Ministry of Foreign Affairs in the High Prize Court during the Russo-Japanese War.

Martens prepared the draft Consular Statute of the Russian Empire, which was then reviewed and revised by a commission under his leadership and entered into force in 1893. Two years later, in his capacity as a member of the Council of the Ministry of Foreign Affairs, Martens prepared a plan for reorganizing the Ministry. This plan was never implemented because successive ministers of foreign affairs were unwilling to support far-reaching structural changes.

Martens was elected to the Institute of International Law and took an active role in that body. Reports prepared by Martens for the Institute led to resolutions addressing legal aspects of the Suez Canal (1879); consular courts in the Orient (1881-1882); the slave trade (1885); navigation on international rivers (1887); and the formation of an international bureau for the publication of treaties (1892). Martens and Johann C. Bluntschli prepared a manual on the laws of war on land within the framework of the Institute, many provisions of which found their way into the 1899 and 1907 Hague conventions.[88]

[88] Законы сухопутной войны. Краткое руководство, изданное Институтом международного права [Laws of Land Warfare: Concise Manual Published by the Institute of International Law], transl. from French (Spb., 1881). Butler 321.

The treaty project, for which Martens was the rapporteur within the Institute, led to the Swiss Government officially requesting Martens to prepare a draft convention under which an international bureau for treaties would be created. Martens undertook this assignment and, as he wrote in his diaries, used his personal connections in Brussels, Berlin, Paris, and St. Petersburg to eliminate obstacles to the project. The Martens theory of international administration would naturally be sympathetic to any scheme that would advance the knowledge of and accessibility to the empirical foundations of positive international law and serve as a useful tool for the future codification of international law. Such international acts were to be, in Martens' view, not only collected, but published. The Swiss Government circulated the Martens draft treaty in a Circular Note of 4 October 1892. A conference was duly convened to consider the draft treaty on 13 October 1894. Martens' expectation that he would represent Russia at the conference proved to be unrealized; the Russian Empire sent a junior official from the Ministry of Finances and had little interest in the project.[89]

Such was Martens public exposure and reputation that he on no less than eight occasions was nominated, without success, for the Nobel Peace Prize between 1901 and 1908. No doubt in the views of some, awarding the prize to a Russian would be tantamount to enhancing Russian stature in the world community and potentially have political repercussions – although most, if not all, of those submitting the nomination were western European colleagues, not other Russians.

Various anecdotes purported to explain how Andrew Carnegie came to finance the construction of the "Temple of Peace" in The Hague. Some give Martens the credit for initiating the idea and persuading Andrew Dickson White (1832-1918), who had served as the United States Minister to Russia (1892-1894) and later on the American delegation to the First Hague Peace Conference, to "convince his old shoe" Andrew Carnegie (1835-1919) to "finance more prestigious quarters for the Permanent Court of Arbitration and a first-rate international law library".[90] The suggestion was accepted.[91] Andrew Carnegie donated $1.4 million – an immense sum at the time – for the construction of the Peace Palace. The cornerstone was laid during the Second Hague Peace Conference in 1907 and the finished building dedicated in August 1913.

Martens was not idolized by students in the various institutions where he taught. He was overloaded with work in his various capacity of legal scholar, diplomat, international arbitrator, and consultant. Moreover, his personality and manner discouraged this – pedantic, restrained, and businesslike. But, in counter-balance, erudite, an excellent writer and draftsman, fluent in several European languages, traces of an aristocratic manner, and an excellent tennis player. When, however, the 25th anniversary of his tenure at St. Petersburg University was celebrated, the students carried him from the auditorium on their shoulders. He respected and was well regarded by his University colleagues.

89 See the AVPR, opis 787, file 9, ed. khr. 1, 1.84-89, discussed in Pustogarov, note 4 above, p. 222-224.

90 Eyffinger, note 75 above, p. 137.

91 See A. Eyffinger, *The Hague International Center of Justice and Peace* (2003), pp. 27-37.

Remote as he may have been from his students, Martens nonetheless produced distinguished proteges – scholars, legal practitioners, and diplomats who made their own enduring mark in the field of international law. This included external students who could not attend the University but studied at home and were examined by University professors. Among them was Vladimir Ilich Lenin (1870-1924), who was examined, *inter alia*, by Martens and who therefore knew something of international law and probably was familiar with the two-volume treatise by Martens.

Through his students and publications Martens formed over the years the "Martens School". Some worked on the history and theory of international law (A. L. Baikov, A. M. Gorovtsev, E. K. Simson, and M. A. von Taube); some on private international law, especially conflicts of law (A. N. Mandelstam, A. A. Pilenko, L. A. Shalland); some at the interface of international and municipal, especially State, law (S. A. Korf, B. E. Nolde), yet others in the civil service (D. P. Nikolskii). The most diverse in his interests and accomplishments was Boris Nolde: he distinguished himself in public and private law, diplomatic history, State law, and others.

Recognition and honors. Martens achieved distinction and recognition in Russia and abroad. In 1907 Martens was elected an Associate Member of the Russian Academy of Sciences. He received no less than sixteen Russian and foreign governmental decorations and awards for his services.

Abroad, his works were translated into the leading foreign languages or were published originally in foreign languages, as noted above. In either case the publications strengthened his image among foreign international lawyers and the general public. He was elected to the Institute of International Law, the Royal Academy in Belgium, an honorary member of the Berlin and Dublin law societies, and awarded honorary doctorates by the Universities of Oxford, Cambridge, Edinburgh, and Yale. At the suggestion of the King of Belgium and with the consent of Emperor Alexander III, Martens was appointed to the State Council of the Congo for his leading role in mediating the positions of delegates at the Brussels Conference in 1899-1900 on prohibition of the slave trade in the Congo River basin.

The University of Vienna in 1883 invited him to take the Chair of International Law – a proposal he declined in favor of remaining in Russia.

For obvious reasons not favored during the Soviet era, Martens and his contributions have been rehabilitated in the post-Soviet years in Russia and abroad. Beginning with the year 2000, the Law Faculty of St. Petersburg University established the "Martens Readings" with support from the International Committee of the Red Cross. Most presentations, commonly published in a special volume accompanying the *Russian Yearbook of International Law*, are devoted to issues of international humanitarian law and the laws of war on land and sea. The Russian Academy of Sciences founded the Martens Prize in 1995 to be awarded for outstanding scholarly works in the field of international law and relations.[92] In 2014

[92] In 2001 the Government of the Russian Federation included the Martens Prize on the "List of International, Foreign, and Russian Prizes for Outstanding Achievements in the Field of Science and Technology, Education, Culture, Literature, Art, Tourism, and the Mass Media, the Amounts of Which Received by Taxpayers Are Not Subject to Taxation", confirmed by Decree of the Govern-

the Russian Federation issued a commemorative postage stamp in his honor with a portrait. His grave in the Lutheran Volkov Cemetery in St. Petersburg was restored in October 2019.

The successor to Martens at the Chair of International Law of St. Petersburg University was Mikhail Aleksandrovich von Taube.

Baron **Mikhail Aleksandrovich von Taube** *(15 May 1859, b. Pavlovsk (suburb of St. Petersburg – 29 November 1961, d. Paris, France) – pre-eminent international lawyer, diplomat, international arbitrator, distinguished public figure and State official, philosopher, historian, genealogist, literary personality, memoirist, poet, translator. Taube died at Paris on 29 November 1961. He was initially interred at the Cimetière parisien de Thiais and later reburied in the Russian cemetery at St.-Genevieve-de-Bois, near Paris.*

Life and career. Taube was the descendant of a German family who served Russia from the thirteenth century, often in senior State offices. He was the first cousin of the Russian artist, Nikolai Konstantinovich Roerich (1874-1947) – also a graduate of the Law Faculty of St. Petersburg University. Taube devoted immense efforts to documenting his German family roots and, while in Russia and in emigration, maintained close links with Roerich.[93]

Mikhail Aleksandrovich von Taube[94] graduated in 1887 with the gold medal (first

ment of the Russian Federation, 6 February 2001, No. 89. СЗ РФ (2001), no. 7, item 657. Available on Consultant Plus.

93 Taube came from a German Estland noble family. His grandfather, F. I. Taube, was a builder who undertook the Academy of Arts, sited on the Field of Mars in St. Petersburg, then became a construction supervisor, and eventually the manager of the first railway in Russia, from Petersburg to Pavlovsk. His father, A. F. Taube, was an inspector of Imperial trains. Among his brothers was Lieutenant-General A. A. Taube (1864-1919), the first General of the Tsarist Army to voluntarily pass over to the side of the Soviet Army in 1917 and become a commander in the Red Army in Siberia. Arrested in 1918 by the Kolchak forces, he was sentenced by a military field court to death and died in January 1919 from typhus in Ekaterinburg Prison. Colonel B. A. Taube (1865-1941) was actively involved in the White movement and emigrated in 1922. Another brother, S. A. Taube (1870-1937), remained in the Soviet Union after the Revolution, became an engineer, and was awarded the title "Meritorious Railway Worker of the USSR".

94 There is much inaccurate or imprecise data about Taube found in various sources. The authors have relied on archival materials at the State Archive of the Russian Federation in St. Petersburg and the Bakhmeteff Archive at Columbia University in New York. Taube sold his personal papers to Columbia in several installments during the 1950s. Of special value was Taube's autobiography: M. A. Taube, За XXV лет (1891-1916): Свод фактических данных о государственной службе

in his class) from the Sixth Petersburg Gymnasium;[95] in 1891 he completed studies at the St. Petersburg University Law Faculty with a first class diploma for a thesis on the "Reception of Roman Law in the West".[96] Professor F. F. Martens submitted a petition in support of Taube remaining at the University to train for the professoriate,[97] as of 1 December 1891, at the Chair of International Law with a stipend of 600 rubles per annum.[98]

A month later, on 2 January 1892, Taube in parallel with his magister studies, found employment in the Ministry of Foreign Affairs of Russia performing clerical work in the Second (Newspaper) Expedition of the Chancellery of the Ministry. There he prepared summaries in the French language of political articles from French, English, German, and Austrian newspapers for a daily press survey distributed among senior members of the Ministry. On 19 March 1892 he passed a diplomatic examination in the Ministry, which placed him on track for a career in diplomacy that lasted for a quarter century, until the Revolutions of 1917. At St. Petersburg University Taube continued work on his magister dissertation and traveled abroad to use the libraries in Berlin and Paris.

On 6 and 13 February 1895, Taube took his oral and written examinations on international law, the leading examiner being F. F. Martens. The questions to be answered orally were: (1) Significance of the Treaty of Kuchuk-Kainardzhi in Relations of Russia and Turkey; (2) Status of the Roman Curia in the Domain of International Relations; (3) On the Right of Inheritance according to Principles of International Private Law. The question set for his written examination was:

и научной деятельности члена Государственного Совета, сенатора, профессора, барона М. А. Таубе [For XXV Years: Digest of Factual Data on the State Service and Scientific Activity of Member of the State Council, Senator, Professor, Baron M. A. Taube] (Petrograd, 1917). 55 p. On Taube generally, see Grabar, note 46 above; A. A. Bovkalo, «Барон Михаил Александрович Таубе» [Baron Mikhail Aleksandrovich Taube], Из истории Русского генеалогического общества [From the History of the Russian Genealogical Society] (Spb., 2001), pp. 88-93; K. O. Savchuk, «Таубе Михайло Олександрович» [Taube, Mikhailo Oleksandrovich], in Denysov, note 4 above, pp. 812-813; G. S. Starodubtsev, «Российский юрист-международник М. А. Таубе в эмиграции» [Russian International Lawyer M. A. Taube in Emigration], Международное право [International Law], no. 4 (2006), pp. 205-213; Starodubtsev, «Творческое наследие российского юриста-международника М. А. Таубе» [Creative Legacy of Russian International Lawyer M. A. Taube], in Актуальные проблемы современного международного права [Topical Problems of Contemporary International Law] (M., 2008), pp. 18-25; Starodubtsev, note 4 above, pp. 14-16, 18, 40, 45, 53, 104, 105, 108-111, 147, 168-175. In honor of Taube's 70th and 90th birthdays in 1939 and 1959 respectively, see Hans Wehberg, "Ein russischer Völkerrechtsgelehrter", *Die Friedens-Warte*, XXXIX, no. 3 (1939), pp. 98-101; Wehberg, "Zum 90. Geburtstag von Prof. Michel v. Taube", ibid., LV (1959/60), pp. 56-58. Also see William E. Butler and Vitalii S. Ivanenko, "Baron M. A. von Taube, Historian of International Law", *Jus Gentium: Journal of International Legal History*, IV (2019), pp. 495-525.

95 ГАРФ, fond 596, opis 1, delo 2. A brief autobiography of Taube written in 1903.

96 ЦГИА Спб., fond 14, opis 3, file 26113.

97 ЦГИА Спб., fond 14, opis 1, delo 9254.

98 ГАРФ, fond 596, opis 1, delo 3.

"Structure and Competence of Consular Courts in the East". Professor Nikolai Mikhailovich Korkunov (1853-1904) gave the examination on State law.[99]

In 1894 Taube published his book on the history of international law in the Middle Ages and on 28 April 1896 defended this publication as his magister dissertation.[100] The official opponents during his dissertation defense were Professors Martens, Korkunov, and, unofficially, Mikhail Ivanovich Gorchakov (1838-1910). Despite severe critiques by the opponents, the dissertation was considered to be satisfactory. A month later, on 28 May 1896, the Council of the University confirmed the learned degree of magister of international law for Taube.[101]

Having received his magister degree, Taube pursued another challenge: to emulate Martens by engaging in, as he put it, "dual employment, State and social, in the rather complex Petersburg situation" of that period.[102] Taube declared his candidacy for the chair of international law at Kharkov University in Ukraine, open by reason of the death of Vsevolod Pievich Danevskii (1852-1898). Having overcome a number of bureaucratic obstacles,[103] he left St. Petersburg University on 1 January 1897 to become privat-docent at the Chair of International Law of Kharkov University. There for two and a half years he lectured on international law while formally retaining his position in the Ministry of Foreign Affairs.[104] In addition to teaching, Taube continued his research in Kharkov in a "more peaceful and professional situation than the Petersburg secular-bureaucratic hurly-burly". There he published the second volume of his history of international law which

[99] ЦГИА Спб., fond 1.4, opis 1, delo 9254.

[100] M. A. Taube, История зарождения современного международного права (Средние века) [History of the Birth of Contemporary International Law (Middle Ages)] (Spb., 1894), vol. I. The defense was reported in the Журнал Юридического Общества при Санкт-Петербургском университете [Journal of the Law Society attached to St. Petersburg University], no. 6 (1896), pp. 45-50.

[101] ЦГИА Спб., fond 14, opis 3, delo 14296.

[102] Taube, «Зарницы»: Воспоминания о трагической судьбе предреволюционной России (1900-1917) [Summer Lightning: Recollections of the Tragic Fate of Prerevolutionary Russia, 1900-1917] (2007), p. 32. These recollections were completed late in life and titled «Краткий обзор жизни и деятельности профессора международного права барона Михаила Александровича Таубе в эмиграции (1918-1956 г.г.)» [Concise Survey of Life and Activity of Mikhail Aleksandrovich Taube, Professor of International Law, in Emigration 1918-1956], Taube Archive, Columbia University. 76 p., when Taube was suffering from near blindness and deafness. A key figure in the acquisition of the Taube papers by Columbia was A. P. Velmin, a Russian lawyer in Poland during the 1930s who later emigrated to France and became the representative of the Columbia Russian archive in France. His own Archive also is held by Columbia; he was the author of a well-informed obituary of Taube published shortly after his death in 1961 in an unidentified Russian émigré newspaper, probably Paris-based. See Anatolii Petrovich Velmin, «Памяти профессора барона М. А. Таубе» [Memories of Professor Baron M. A. Taube], Box 10, Taube Archive, Columbia University.

[103] Ibid. (2007), p. 31.

[104] Taube, note 93 above, p. 8.

he intended to submit as a doctoral dissertation[105] and an inaugural lecture on the principal phases in the historical development of international law and relations.[106]

In May 1899 Taube returned to St. Petersburg University. On 24 May 1899 he was appointed privat-docent at the Chair of International Law after delivering an inaugural lecture on 3 September 1899. He offered a course on the law of war.[107] On 31 October 1899 he defended a doctoral dissertation in the form of volume two of his history of the birth of contemporary international law. The official opponents were again Professor Martens, joined by Professor Ignatii Aleksandrovich Ivanovskii (1858-1933); the unofficial opponent was Aleksandr Aleksandrovich Pilenko (1873-1956). The defense was noted in the legal press.[108] With the conferral of his doctoral degree, Taube was appointed a full-time docent in the Chair of International Law at St. Petersburg University. He introduced some specialist courses on international law while continuing to offer his course on the law of war for two hours per week. In 1901 he added courses on "International Conflicts and Means of the Defense of Rights and Interests" and on "Evolution of the Idea of Peace in International Life", augmented in 1902 by a special course on the "History of International Relations of Russia During Peter the Great".

In 1900 Taube resumed work at the Ministry of Foreign Affairs. Beginning on 1 October he became the Head of the I Division (administrative-legal) in the II Department of the Ministry (all types and forms of foreign relations of Russia).

On 30 March 1902 the Council of the Faculty of Law for the first time arranged a competition to fill the post of Head of the Chair of International Law vacated after the resignation of F. F. Martens. The candidate was to be chosen on the basis of secret ballot by the Council. Three candidates competed for the position: magister A. A. Pilenko; Professor Andrei Nikolaevich Mandelstam (1869-1949), and Taube. The competition proved to be contentious, received extensive publicity in the press, and split the Council – but Taube emerged the winner and from 10 March 1903 became professor *extraordinarius* of St. Petersburg University. From autumn 1903 he began to offer the basic course "International Law" five hours per week.[109] In 1904 Taube served as Acting Dean of the Law Faculty, and in

[105] Taube, История зарождения современного международного права: Принципы мира и права в международных столкновениях Средних веков [History of the Birth of Contemporary International Law: Principles of Peace and Law in International Conflicts of the Middle Ages] (Kharkov, 1899), II.

[106] Taube, Основные фазисы в истории развития международных отношений и права [Principal Phases in the History of the Development of International Relations and Law] (Kharkov, 1898). Also see Taube, Международный конгресс в Волыни в XV столетии [International Congress in Volhynia in the Fifteenth Century] (M., 1898).

[107] Taube, note 93 above, pp. 14-15.

[108] See «Диспут барона М. А. Таубе» [Defense of Baron M. A. Taube], Право [Law], no. 47 (1899), pp. 2261-2265.

[109] Taube, note 93 above, pp. 7, 17. The complex and highly competitive nature of the appointment is discussed by E. N. Trubetskaia, История развития кафедры международного права Санкт-Петербургского (Петроградского) университета в 1903-1917 гг. [History of the Development of the Chair of International Law of St. Petersburg (Petrograd) University in 1903 to 1917] (2004), pp.

1906 became professor *ordinarius* and a Privy State Counsellor in governmental service. He worked at St. Petersburg University until 1911. But he did not confine his teaching to that University. From 1907 to 1917 he lectured on international law at the Higher Women's Courses founded by Ekaterina Ivanovna Peskovskaia, and from 1 January 1909 to 1917, at the School of Jurisprudence.

The third volume of his history of international law Taube published in 1902 but did not consider the work to be completed.[110] In 1905 he published a chapter as a pamphlet.[111] This was followed by two of his best-known works: on the system of inter-State law (1909)[112] and the contemporary international status of the Pope in connection with the idea of international law (1910).[113]

On 11 April 1911 Taube entered State service full time. He accepted appointment as the Deputy Minister of Public Enlightenment of the Russian Empire while retaining his post as professor *ordinarius* at the School of Jurisprudence and in the Ministry of Foreign Affairs, including the right to sit in session in the name of the Ministry of Foreign Affairs in the High Prize Court, take part in the Council of the Ministry of Foreign Affairs to administer the diplomatic examination, and to participate in the consideration of international-legal issues within that Ministry.

Taube in emigration. Taube emigrated from Russia on 1 January 1918, moving first to Finland, then to Sweden, on to Germany, and finally remaining in France to the end of his life. While in Finland, he acted as the legal advisor to Aleksandr Fedorovich Trepov (1862-1928), who formed a short-lived government in exile, and was active in the "Special Committee for the Affairs of Russians in Finland". In an effort to raise funds, on 11/24 March 1918 Taube wrote to James Brown Scott at the Carnegie Foundation in New York City offering to sell his entire library for $10,000; at the time he was living at the Villa Ampiala, near Kexholm, in Finland. In his reply of 4 June 1918, Scott declined the offer of the entire library but ex-

11-12.

110 Taube, Христианство и организация международного мира [Christianity and the Organization of International Peace] (Spb., 1902). [viii], 633 p. He wrote of this volume: "In view of the considerable number of years which the processing of an extensive body of material (partly already assembled by us) yet requires with regard to an entire range of questions within the contemplated framework of volume III – and in response to the wishes flattering for the author or expressed in the scientific literature concerning the most rapid appearance of a continuation of the work, we intend, without awaiting the end of the entire work, to issue it as individual parts as the various autonomous sections thereof are processed. The monographic character of each chapter contemplated for volume III enables this plan to be effectuated without prejudice to the integrity of the entire work" (p. vi).

111 Taube, Христианство и международный мир [Christianity and International Peace] (Moscow. 1905). 55 p. In his list of publications accompanying his Hague lecture of 1926, Taube considered this work to be a "popular" version of his 1902 treatise, note 18 above, undertaken, he said, at the urging of Leo Tolstoy (1828-1910). See *Recueil des cours*, XI (1926), p. 342.

112 Taube, Система межгосударственного права [System of Inter-State Law] (Spb., 1909). The copy in the Library of Congress bears the ex-libris of M. P. Zotov.

113 Taube, «Современное международное положение папы в связи с идеей международного права (jus inter potestates)» [Contemporary International Status of the Pope in Connection with the Idea of International Law (jus inter potestates)], Вопросы права [Questions of Law], no. 1 (1910).

pressed interest in possibly buying individual volumes. Apparently the proposals were not pursued further.[114]

The University of Uppsala in Sweden offered him a position lecturing on the history of international law, which he took up in 1920,[115] and then moved on to Germany.

In Paris during the 1930s he acted as legal advisor to Grand Prince Kirill Vladimirovich (1876-1938) and became a member of the Supreme Monarchical Council. He took part in drafting the new Statute on the Russian Imperial Family. In subsequent years after leaving Uppsala University, he lectured in Germany, France, Belgium, and the Netherlands. He became a member of the Curatorium of the Hague Academy of International Law. In 1923 he was selected as a member of the Learned Council of the Russian Scientific Institute in Berlin, lecturing at the Law Faculty of that Institute on the history of international relations – international law was not at the time part of the curriculum. He moved to Paris in 1928, where he taught at the Russian Institute attached to the Law Faculty of the University of Paris and in the European Center of the Carnegie Foundation for International Peace. He gave talks frequently at the Union of Russian Advokats Abroad. From 1931 to 1937 he was a Professor at the University of Münster in Westphalia, Germany, a position he lost when the University administration implemented an instruction from the Nazi authorities to terminate his contract, whereupon he returned to France.

In 1925 he joined the society "Icon", where he took part in the study, preservation, development, and popularization of Russian iconography abroad. He maintained close links with a number of Russian émigré organizations, philanthropic and professional. While in German-occupied Paris he was asked on a number of occasions to intercede with German officials in attempts to recover property seized by military personnel from Russian émigrés. He apparently enjoyed some success in this.[116]

114 Box 2, Taube Archive, Columbia University.

115 Taube was notified on 3 January 1920 that the Chancellor of Uppsala University, ceding to the request of the Law Faculty, had approved "our project". The Uppsala press announced Taube's appointment the next day. Another clipping preserved in the Bakhmeteff Archive, dated 19 February 1920, reported that the University was paying 1,000 kr. to Taube. The Russian émigré press covered the occasion, reporting in an undated clipping: "It is interesting that the right hand of Kasso, the Baron Taube, in the spring will read lectures on international law at Uppsala University". Lectures were delivered on 13, 14, 15, 16, and 20 April 1920, as reported in "Folkforbundsplanen ar 1919", *Upsala Nija Tidning*, 22 April 1920, p. 1, col. 2. Texts available in File 6, Taube Archive, Bakhmeteff Archive, Columbia University.

116 Three letters are preserved in the Bakhmeteff Archive dated 26 December 1941 and 1 and 25 January 1942 from Vladimir Lvovich Burtsev (1862-1942) to Taube. Burtsev believed that Taube was the "Representative of German Authorities for Russian Affairs in Paris" and sought Taube's assistance in obtaining the return of manuscripts, notebooks, and books seized by the German authorities during a search of his Paris flat. The replies of Taube are not present, but judging from Burtsev's last letter, he may have been of some assistance, for Burtsev reported to Taube that German officers visited and promised the return of his materials. Burtsev died 21 August 1942 in Paris. See Box 1, Taube Archive, Bakhmeteff Archive. Taube's activities during the Second World War remain to be explored; he seems to have remained in Paris, perhaps deemed minimally acceptable by the German

Taube and The Hague Academy of International Law. Taube lectured at the Hague Academy on six occasions during the interwar period, continuing to pursue his interest in the history of international law and international relations. His lectures included studies of the development of international law in Eastern Europe,[117] the sanctity of treaties,[118] the origins of international arbitration in Antiquity and the Middle Ages,[119] the legal status of the Baltic Sea up to the early nineteenth century,[120] and the contribution of Byzantium to the development of western international law.[121] He also lectured in 1924, but that lecture was never published in the *Recueil des cours*.[122]

As a member of the Hague Academy Curatorium for much of the interwar period,[123] Taube became for the Russian émigré community of international lawyers the logical individual to contact about being invited to lecture there. Some were successful and, indeed, regulars; others aspired but for whatever reasons did not succeed in securing the invitation. Few countries will have been as successful as émigré Russia was in participating in the Hague venture; for most Russians, the lecturing fee was attractive and badly needed, whereas for European and Americans, the fee was welcome but not a major reason for agreeing to write and deliver the relevant course.

In the eyes of his fellow Russians, Taube was the one member of the Curatorium to whom they could write in Russian if necessary, and/or in French to demonstrate their prowess in the language, but rarely in English. They proposed subjects, sent outlines, even on rare occasion a full lecture text. Among those who succeed-

occupiers by reason of his German ancestry and monarchist affiliations.

117 Taube, "Études sur le développement du droit international dans l'Europe orientale", *Recueil des cours*, XI (1926), pp. 341-535 (portrait).

118 Taube, "L'inviolabilité des traités", *Recueil des cours*, XXXII (1930), pp. 291-389.

119 Taube, "Les origines de l'arbitrage international, antiquité et moyen age", *Recueil des cours*, XLII (1932), pp. 1-115.

120 Taube, "Le statut juridique de la Mer baltique jusqu'au début du XIXe siècle", *Recueil des cours*, LIII (1936), pp. 437-530 (portrait).

121 Taube, "L'apport de Byzance au développement du droit international occidental", *Recueil des cours*, LXVII (1940), pp. 233-339. Also see Dina Gusejnova, "Roman Law after 1917: Exile, Statelessness and the Search for Byzantium in the Work of Mikhail von Taube", in K. Tuori and H. Bjorkland (eds.), *Roman Law and the Idea of Europe* (London, 2018), pp. 93-112.

122 According to his biographical notice in the *Recueil des cours*, XI (1926), p. 342, his lecture was entitled: "Le développement historique du droit international jusqu'au XVII siècle". For his lecture notes, see Box 6, Files 8 and 9, Taube Archive, Columbia University.

123 See "Institutions internationales ayant leur Siege aux Pays-Bas", *Grotius Annuaire international pour les années 1921-1922* (1922), p. 278; "Instituts de droit international éstablis à la Hague", *Grotius Annuaire international pour les année 1925* (1925), p. 341; [Curatorium], *Grotius Annuaire international pour les année 1936* (1936), p. 158.

ed in receiving or sought an invitation were Andre Mandelstam,[124] Boris Nolde,[125] Mark Vishniak (1883-1977),[126] Ivan Nikolaevich Efremov (1866-19?) (Jean Efremoff),[127] Nikolai Nikolaevich Alekseev (1879-1964),[128] Aleksandr Lvovich Baikov (1865-1943),[129] Aleksandr Mikhailovich Gorovtsev (1878-1933),[130] Alfons Alfonsovich Heyking (1860-1930),[131] Aleksandr Nikolaevich Makarov (1888-

[124] Mandelstam was among the inaugural lecturers in the Hague Academy, presenting a course in 1924 on "La protection des minorités", *Recueil des cours*, I (1925), pp. 363-519; and in 1925 on "La Conciliation international d'après le Pacte et la jurisprudence du Conseil de la Société des Nations", *Recueil des cours*, XIV (1926), pp. 333-648. In 1925 he offered to lecture on the "History of Humanitarian Intervention in Turkey" and in 1933, on "Le politique russe d'acces à la Mediterranée au XX siècle", *Recueil des cours*, XLVII (1934), pp, 597-802. Mandelstam's lectures on international conciliation were considered too lengthy by the Hague Academy, which requested Mandelstam to reduce the size to 200 pages maximum; Mandelstam declined, in a letter of 2 March 1927, and pointed out that he spent a year of his life producing the work in accordance with his contract. See Box 2, Taube Archive, Columbia University.

[125] On 3 October 1926 Nolde offered to lecture at the Hague Academy on the "History of the Codification of Private International Law, Legislative and Conventional" – a topic on which he had labored for many years, he said. As a second choice he suggested "Obligations in Private International Law". If Taube preferred a course on public law, he suggested "Monetary Conventions". See Box 1, Taube Archive, Columbia University. On Nolde, see Peter Holquist, "The Dilemmas of an 'Official with Progressive Views' – Baron Boris Nolde", *Baltic Yearbook of International Law*, VII (2007), pp. 233-271; V. V. Veeder, "Looking for Professor Boris E. Nolde", *Jus Gentium: Journal of International Legal History*, III (2018), pp. 275-280.

[126] Between 1932 and 1936 Vishniak proposed topics that included: "Political Emigres and Refugees Before the League of Nations" (1932); "International Status of the Saar Region" (1934), which he recognized might be controversial in light of the pending plebiscite, in which case he suggested "On the Admission of States to the League of Nations" (1934). In 1935 he proposed the same topic again, writing to the President of the Curatorium, copying Taube. For 1936 he repeated his suggestion of a lecture on admission to the League, but proposed an alternative, "The International Legal Status of Outer Mongolia". To these for 1937 he added a third possibility: "Emigration and Colonization in International Law". See five letters in Box 1, Taube Archive, Columbia University. Of these, he delivered "Le statut international des apatrides", *Recueil des cours*, XLIII (1933), p. 115-246.

[127] Efremoff wrote to Taube on 12 October 1928 and offered a lecture on "Recent Trends in Intellectual Property".

[128] Alekseev proposed a course on "La théorie juridique des sources du droit et le droit international", providing a synopsis of the course and his own CV. The proposal was not accepted. See Box 3, Taube Archive, Columbia University.

[129] Baikov expressed a general interest in lecturing at The Hague in a letter dated 1926, but there is no evidence that he proceeded further. Box 3, Taube Archive, Columbia University.

[130] Gorovtsev corresponded with Taube on 11 January 1926 from a hotel in Paris, but did not lecture at The Hague Academy

[131] He corresponded with Taube on 8 August 1925 and again on 10 June 1928, the first letter suggesting a Hague lecture on "The Idea of Nationality and the State" and the second, reporting on a conversation with Professor Gilbert Gidel (1880-1958), who had suggested that Heyking offer a lecture on "The Principles and Practice of Consular Service". Heyking had published on both topics, but neither was accepted.

1973),[132] Aleksandr Semenovich Iashchenko (1877-1934),[133] Georgii Davidovich Gurvich (1894-1965),[134] and Boris E. Shatzky (Schatzky).[135] Insofar as Taube influenced the choice of lecturers and lectures at the Hague Academy – and he will have been singularly well-placed to advise his fellow members of the Curatorium on whom should be selected – he will have almost single-handedly ensured the survival and propagation of Russian international legal doctrine during the emigration years from 1917.

Taube as lecturer and legal scholar on international law in emigration. For those Russian international lawyers who chose to leave the RSFSR and seek a life abroad, finding the means to support themselves was challenging. They were perhaps better placed than their Russian colleagues who had taught or practiced solely Russian domestic law; some secured a place in the world of comparative law, but most were not by language or training able to adapt to qualifying as legal practitioners in Europe or the Americas. Lecturing, usually a paid undertaking, was a welcome possibility, either by invitation from individual universities or by organizing Russian institutes or schools in Berlin, Paris, Prague, Belgrade, Sofia, Kharbin, and elsewhere. Taube was among the beneficiaries of these arrangements.

From his initial invitation to lecture at Uppsala University in 1919/1920,[136] Taube moved on to Berlin and eventually Paris. We have only fragments of data from this period of his life. He lectured frequently in France (Institut des Hautes

[132] Makarov (Makarow) lectured on "Conception du droit international privé d'après la doctrine et la pratique russes (U.R.S.S.)", *Recueil des cours*, XXXV (1931), pp. 473-604 ; Makarov, "La Nationalité de la femme mariée", *Recueil des cours*, LX (1937), pp, 111-241. In correspondence with Taube, Makarov proposed in a letter of 29 September 1930 five lectures on the "Conflict of Laws with Regard to Air Law". In another dated 7 September 1934, Makarov suggested three possible subjects for 1935: (1) "The Sources of Private International Law (Conflicts of Law)"; (2) Public Policy in Private International Law; and (3) "De Facto Governments Before the Judge". Box 3, Taube Archive, Columbia University.

[133] He contacted Taube about lecturing at the Hague Academy on the history of the idea of international organizations and sought an associate relationship with the Academy. Eight letters are found in Box 1, Taube Archive, Columbia University.

[134] Gurvich contacted Taube on 13 February 1932 to express general interest in lecturing at the Hague Academy and on 2 September 1933 offered a course on: (1) Theory of Sources of Positive Law in its Application to Problems of International Law"; or (2) "The Primacy of International Law: History of Doctrine and System"; or (3) "The Problem of Sovereignty: History of Doctrine and System". For each proposal he attached a typewritten precis and CV. Taube was elected a full member of the International Institute for the Philosophy of Law and Legal Sociology, of which Gurvich informed Taube on 11 October 1933. Box 2, Taube Archive, Columbia University.

[135] Writing from the University of Concepcion on 27 September 1934 and offering lectures at the Hague Academy on (1) Validity of and Reservations to Treaties, or (2) Representation of States in the League of Nations and Parliaments, or (3) Pan-Americanism. Box 3, Taube Archive, Columbia University.

[136] The topic was "L'Histoire de l'idée de la paix international et la Société des Nations".

Études International, 1922[137] and 1929-32), the University of Louvain (1927),[138] the Institut catholique de Paris (1929-30), the Centre européen de la Dotation Carnegie pour la Paix internationale (1929-30),[139] and Stockholm University (1939), among others.

In Berlin he joined the Faculty of the Russian Scientific Institute from 1924 to 1929, where he offered a course regularly on the "History of International Relations", "International Law", Russian International Policy in the Last Years Before the World War", "Russia and Rome in Their Historical Relations", and the "Idea of International Peace in Historical Development".[140] As noted above, from 1 November 1931 until 1937 he served as professor *extraordinarius* at the University of Münster in Westphalia, where he offered courses on the history and theory of international law.

He served as an expert for Russian affairs of the Committee for Assistance to the Russian Emigration in France, and after the War, he lectured at the Russian Scientific Institute, the Institute for the Study of Russian Culture, and the Russian Academic Group.

A full bibliography of Taube's works remains to be undertaken.[141] His own efforts, reposing in his Archive at Columbia University, are sketchy and difficult to decipher. His Hague lectures were of monograph length and often appeared as *separata* with their own title page or as straight offprints. He displayed an immediate interest in the League of Nations,[142] international relations generally,[143]

[137] The notes for the 1922 Paris lecture are preserved, close to indecipherable, in Box 4, Taube Archive, Columbia University. The subject was: "La question baltique dans l'histoire diplomatique de la Russie".

[138] On the topic "Le développement historique du droit international dans l'Europe Orientale".

[139] He delivered a series of ten lectures on "La Russie et la pacification de l'Orient" ; the fee agreed was 500 French francs per hour. See the Letter of the Carnegie Center dated 29 May 1929. Box 5, File 2, Taube Archive, Columbia University.

[140] In the earlier years Taube lectured in the Russian language, and later in German. The titles of the lectures, course schedule were offered, and publicity posters are preserved in Box 6, File 5, Taube Archive, Columbia University.

[141] For a partial listing, mostly of pre-1917 works, see W. E. Butler, *Russia and the International Legal System: A Bibliography of Writings by Russian Jurists on Public and Private International Law to 1917 with References to Publications in Emigration* (2006), pp. 171-173.

[142] Taube, Вечный мир? или вечная война (мысли о «Лиге нации)» [Perpetual Peace? Or Perpetual War (Thoughts on the "League of Nations")] (Berlin, 1922. 109, [3] p., plates. This book annexes the letter from Tolstoy to Taube of 18/19 December 1903 which led Taube to publish a popular version of his 1902 treatise on the history of international law, which appeared at Moscow in 1905.

[143] Taube, *La Russie et l'Europe Occidentale à travers dix siècles (Études d'histoire internationale et de psychologie ethnique)* (Brussels, 1926). 47 p.;

Russian history,[144] his own memoirs,[145] together with dozens of articles published throughout Western Europe.

Taube as genealogist. One of Taube's serious pastimes was genealogy. Co-founder and co-draftsman of the Statute of the Russian Genealogical Society in 1897, he was elected a full member of the Historical-Genealogical Society in Moscow from 1905 and to the Genealogical Society of the Baltic Provinces. He became a Vice-President of, and frequently lectured at, the Russian Historical-Genealogical Society in France and took part in the creation in 1951 of the Central Genealogical Commission for Russian Nobility. He also joined the Russian Historical-Genealogical Society in the United States.

The Taube Family created a Foundation (Freiherrlich-Taubeschen Familienstiftung) in St. Petersburg before the First World War which published the results of von Taube's family genealogical researches in a limited print run of, as a rule, 300 numbered copies during 1910 to 1914. The printing was undertaken in St. Petersburg and Dorpat (Iurev). These are publications of outstanding quality in paper, typography, illustration, and text. The Library of Congress copies of this multi-volume publication are bound together and bear different numbers of limitation (Nos. 61, 35, 87).[146] Matters of family genealogy occupied significant amounts of his time for the remainder of his life. His archive at Columbia University contains dozens of folders containing tables, correspondence, and research notes devoted to tracing his family history.

Taube as protector of cultural valuables. Being related to N. K. Roerich, the noted Russian artist and philosopher and fellow graduate of the Law Faculty of St. Petersburg University, Taube played an active role in the worldwide Roerich movement to defend cultural valuables. From the 1920s to the 1930s, Taube served as Chairman of the French Committee of the Roerich Pact, Chairman of the Russian Association of the Roerich Society in Paris, Chairman of the Special Committee of the Roerich Pact attached to the European Center, and Chairman of a section of the Roerich Museum in New York City.

[144] Taube, *Rome et la Russie avant l'invasion des Tatars (IXe-XIIIe siècles)* (Paris, 1947); Taube, "Preface", J.-J. Gapanovitch and B. P. Nikitine, *Introduction à historiographie russe hors de la Russie* (Paris, 1946); the authors are I. I. Gapanovich and Vasilii Petrovich Nikitin (1885-19?). Nikitin emigrated in 1919, was an Orientialist by training, and collaborated with French colleagues in this field. His correspondence with Taube is in Box 1, Taube Archive, Columbia University.

[145] Taube, *La politique russe d'avant-guerre et la fin de l'empire des tsars (1904-1917): Mèmoires du Baron M. de Taube* (Paris, 1928). viii 412 p.; translated into German as: Taube, *Der grosses Katastrophe entgegen: Die russische Politik der Vorkriegzeit und das Ende des Zarenreiches* (Berlin, 1929; 2d ed.; 1937). The Russian language edition, note 10 above, is a different version of his memoirs based on a version in the Bakhmeteff Archive, Columbia University.

[146] Taube (ed.), *Archiv des uradeligen Geschlechts Taube, sonst Tuve genannt* (Spb., 1911). Two volumes also appeared under a similar title printed at Tallinn in 1910-1911. Prices ranged from 3 to 10 rubles. In 1955, apparently as part of this series of genealogical research, Taube published *Die von Uxkull: genealogische Geschichte der gesamtfamilie von Uxkull, 1229-1954* (Meine, 1955). For correspondence with Baron Uxkull von Gildenbrand on genealogical matters, see Box 2, Taube Archive, Columbia University.

The Roerich Pact was the first Treaty on the Protection of Artistic and Scientific Institutions and Historic Monuments, sometimes known as the Washington Pact. It was signed in Washington D. C. on 15 April 1935 at the White House by representatives of 21 countries in North and South America with the personal participation of President Franklin Delano Roosevelt (1882-1945). The Roerich Archive contains twenty boxes of personal Taube papers dating from before and after the 1917 Revolutions in Russia. Roerich consulted Taube frequently on issues of protecting cultural property.[147] At Columbia University there are genealogical materials on the Taube and Roerich families, an unpublished biography of Johann Georg von Taube, bound volumes of correspondence, printed materials, and documents relating to the Roerich Museum.

Taube as historian of Russia and of Christianity. In emigration Taube was at liberty to devote considerable time to lecturing and research on Russian history, which he exploited to the fullest. Historical works form a significant portion of his post-1917 publications.[148] They ranged widely in subject-matter, from the sources of Christianity,[149] the origin of Rus and the conversion of Rus to Christianity, the relations between Rus and the Roman Catholic Church, among the most salient.

He joined several historical societies. Among them, he was elected a full member of the Russian Historical Society from 1912; an honorary member of the Moscow Archaeological Society, also in 1912, and a member of the Vitebsk (from 1909), Tula (from 1913), and Pskov (from 1916) provincial archival commissions and of the Pskov Archaeological Society (from 1916); and the list is not complete. In May 1916 he was elected to membership of the Société Académique d'histoire internationale.

International legal practitioner. Taube made a significant, still not fully appreciated, contribution to the development of the Petersburg School of International Law. As teacher and scholar, he continued the tradition of his mentor and colleague, F. F. Martens, emphasizing the importance of the international community as the foundation of international relations and international law. Elaborating the views of Martens, Taube stressed the idea of the community and solidarity of all civilized peoples or nations, their inter-cultural links or dependence on one another – factors which also served to explain the emergence and development of

[147] See three letters from Roerich to Taube in January 1931; Taube was appointed to represent the Roerich Trustees at a Conference on the Banner of Peace held at Bruges, Belgium, in 1931. See Box 1, Taube Archive, Columbia University.

[148] Taube, note 144 above; Taube, *L'Empereur Paul 1er de Russie: grand maître de l'ordre de Malte* (Paris, 1955), and others.

[149] See, for example, Taube's anthology of unwritten sayings ascribed to Jesus Christ, citing original language texts and his own translations. Taube, Аграфа: о не записанных в Евангелии изречениях Исуса Христа [Agrapha: Sayings of Jesus Christ Not Recorded in the Gospels] (Warsaw, 1936). Published by the Brotherhood of Eastern Orthodox Theologians in Poland, No. 11 in a series. Taube signed the volume at Paris/Münster, 1936. A second volume, mimeographed, appeared at Paris in 1949, priced at 300 francs plus carriage, or US$1.00. Consisting of 71 additional sayings which Taube considered to be part of the apostolic heritage, the title of the supplement is: Вероятные изречения Иисуса Христа в древней апокрифической письменности [Probable Sayings of Jesus Christ in Ancient Apocryphal Writing] (Paris, 1949). [ii], iv, 45 p.

international law. He consistently advanced and clarified this idea on all of his international-legal publications.

Acknowledging that international law is primarily a system of certain legal rules of behavior regulating relations of States, he drew attention to the fact that States when mutually creating recognized legal norms voluntarily limit their sovereign will. They do so to the common benefit and well-being of all mankind; this is a creative function of international law.

Historian of international law. Taube devoted much of his life in legal scholarship to the history of international law. Law, he said,

> is not some immobile, immutable, unknown from whence it emerges: it is one of the many aspects or manifestations of our life; it grows and changes together [with life]; by its nature it is a living organism, and to understand the contemporary condition thereof without its history is inconceivable.[150]

Taube's magister dissertation was devoted to the history of the origins of international law – subject-matter virtually unresearched in Russia at the time. This was an analysis of the philosophical history of the Middle Ages from the standpoint of the origins and development of the international community, international relations, and international law. According to Taube, the foundations of the international community arose in the Middle Ages and began to form norms and principles of international law. When defending his magister dissertation, he demonstrated that the Ancient World had no knowledge of an international community because of the fragmentation and dispersion of peoples, constant warfare, and ideas of law and equality being alien to them. In his view, only Christianity (especially the Papal-Imperial system) introduced the principle of equality in relations between peoples or nations during the Middle Ages. He believed this was facilitated by knighthood, feudalism, the crusades, and universal church assemblies. In the course of his dissertation defense, professors Martens, Korkunov, and Gorchakov were unanimous in the view that Taube idealized the period of the Middle Ages and failed to note the darker aspects of feudalism, knighthood, and the crusades. His official opponents reproached Taube for completely ignoring Roman law and an important section thereof – *jus gentium* – as the commencement of the development of international law.[151]

The positions and ideas set out in his magister dissertation Taube elaborated further in his doctoral dissertation. This volume considered individual institutes of international law of the Middle Ages: arbitration court (Chapter I); peaceful means for the settlement of international conflicts (Chapter II); law of reprisals (Chapter III); genesis of the law of war (Chapter IV); and the birth of the law of neutrality and war at sea (Chapter V). Taube dated the birth of international law to the eleventh to the fourteenth centuries, denying that it existed during the "dark ages". Taube continued to idealize the international community in the Middle Ages, asserting that, unlike the Ancient World, the Middle Ages were primarily peaceful; in order to settle disputes which arose, basically peaceful diplomatic procedures and

150 Taube, note 105 above, I, pp. 6-7.

151 Note 105 above (1896), pp. 45-50.

arbitration courts were used. In his introductory address in the dissertation defense Taube said that in practice this was reflected in the following:

> … namely in the Middle Ages under the beneficial influence of Christianity the very impression of the essence, the nature of war as an armed struggle between States, changed for the better. Under the influence of Christianity the view of the Ancient World towards war as a natural and normal state between peoples ceded place to the view of war as a temporary and exceptional condition admissible only in extreme instances as a 'necessary evil'.[152]

The law of neutrality, he said, originated in the Middle Ages. That law acknowledged the inviolability of neutral cargo on a non-belligerent ship and the right to inspect neutral warships; privateer patents began to be issued, naval "convoys" were introduced, and the first courts of prize were launched, together with other legal innovations.[153]

Martens and Ivanovskii, together with Pilenko – then a lecturer at the Alexander Lycée, criticized these and other propositions advanced by Taube but considered his dissertation to be a significant and original contribution to the science of international law.

In his third volume, Taube emphasized the special role of Christianity in the origins and development of international law. In his view, the influence of Christianity was expressed as a "new moral doctrine", the "elaboration of a distinctive idea of an international community and world formed in the Middle Ages within Romano-Germanic Europe which – in theory – also the international life contemporary to us inherited".[154]

Inter-power law. Taube put forward an original conception of "inter-power law" [междувластное право], from the Latin "*jus inter potestates*". The idea was first advanced in a polemic with his colleague in the Chair of International Law, Aleksandr Lvovich Baikov. In a book devoted to the international legal personality of the Papacy, Baikov asserted that the Papacy was a subject of international law.[155] In his construction of "inter-power law" Taube also included international law, but did not allocate a place to the Papacy as a subject of law in the system of international law, but rather as a subject of inter-power law. For Taube, inter-power law was a "special legal discipline" corresponding to the "existence of a group of

[152] Taube, «Средние века и международное право (Речь, произнесенная перед диспутом в Спб. университете на защите диссертации 31 октября 1899 г.)» [Middle Ages and International Law (Address Delivered before the Defense of a Dissertation in St. Petersburg University, 31 October 1899)], Право [Law], no. 46 (1899), col. 2190.

[153] Ibid., cols. 2191-2192.

[154] Taube, note 110 above; also see Taube, Христианство и организация международного мира [Christianity and the Organization of International Peace] (Kharkiv, 1902).

[155] A. L. Baikov, Современная международная правоспособность папства в связи с учением о международной правоспособности вообще [Contemporary International Legal Capacity of the Papacy in Connection with the Doctrine on International Legal Capacity in General] (Spb., 1904).

special legal phenomena which until now have remained unnoticed"[156] in the traditional doctrinal literature on international law.

Taube substantiated his position as follows: he considered international law and inter-State law to be the same, synonyms designating a "territorial law par excellence" because territory is a "*conditio sine qua non*" of any State. Taube rejected Baikov's view and asserted that the Pope of Rome is not a subject of international or inter-State law because he possesses no territory, but is a subject of a law unknown to legal doctrine – inter-power law. In Taube's view, supreme or sovereign power may be of a dual nature: territorial and personal with the character of their limitation being internal (by the public law of a State) or external (within the framework of international law). The limitation of sovereign power purely by personal will gives us new legal constructions. Power limited within a non-territorial union or society gives us church law, canon law limited externally outside this union; it advances a new type of law presently unknown to us – inter-power law. Such a law arises when "there is a mutual limitation of supreme wills between personal sovereign non-territorial powers or between these powers, on one hand, and States on the other. By this argumentation Taube substantiated the "formal, logical necessity" of a new construction of law. The Pope is a subject of this new construction of law, inter-power law.[157]

The establishment of a new classification had both a purely-formal, logical character and reflected common sense because a "new category encompasses other instances of 'quasi' international relations which contemporary international law, strictly speaking, does not know what to do with",[158] for example, relations between the Pope and the Dalai-Lama, or relations between social communities without sovereign territory – nomadic peoples. Nationalities within a State struggling for their independence also are subjects of this right at moments until their recognition by other[159] powers as autonomous States. Bands of pirates frequently entering into relations with States also are subjects of inter-power law.

Within this conception Taube expanded the concept of sovereign power and the content of international legal personality. The sovereign will of the State lay at their foundation, and he extended legal personality to other international participants, especially to intergovernmental organizations, calling them "non-territorial sovereigns".

Taube singled out from social relations and international law a group of "inter-power" relations arising between collectively organized powers (but not State-organized) and relegated to these certain church/State relations, relations of nomadic and indigenous tribes, as well as relations of organized political parties which rebelled against legal governments, fought with weapons in hand for their independence, but had not yet formed their own States. To these he also relegated

156 Taube, note 8 above, I, pp. 5-9.

157 Ibid., p. 25.

158 Ibid., p. 15.

159 Note 111 above, p. 154.

treaty relations "with barbaric pirates of the Mediterranean Sea", as well as legal relations between any State and the sovereign Order of Malta.

In a review of Taube's new idea, P. E. Mikhailov, docent at the Chair of Civil Law of St. Petersburg University, noted that the idea should be welcomed as a bold attempt to embroider the "uniform and boring traditional literature on international law".[160] But the idea should not be accepted for serious reasons. First, the term "inter-power law" was objectionable because there was no legal place in international turnover for "powers" as such; "international law" is "without power", it does not recognize any powers. Second, the construction of a new legal discipline suffered from logical and methodological shortcomings which Mikhailov discussed in detail.

System of inter-State law. In 1909 Taube set out his original vision of the system of international law. It was not divided into the classical segments: "Law of War" and "Law of Peace", but rather into the "General Part" and the "Special Part".[161] What he called the "concise plan" of the scheme he set out as follows:[162]

Introduction. Basic Concepts

General Part. Legal Foundations of Inter-State Law

(Static of Inter-State Law)

Section I. Doctrine of Inter-State Legal Relations

Chapter I. Subject

Chapter II. Object

Chapter III. Law-Forming Facts

Section II. Doctrine on Inter-State Legal Organization

(Inter-State Federalism)

Chapter I. Society of States in Historical Development

Chapter II. Idea of General International Organization

Chapter III. Contemporary Organs of Inter-State Relations

Special Part. Extraterritorial Effectuation of Interests and Inter-State Defense Thereof

[160] P. E. Mikhailov, «Новая идея «междувластного права» [New Idea of "Inter-Power Law"], Право [Law], no. 27 (1909), col. 1579.

[161] Note 110 above, p. 15.

[162] Ibid.

(Dynamic of Inter-State Law)

Section I. Conditions and System of Extraterritorial Effectuation of Interests

Chapter I. Necessary Preliminary Conditions for Extraterritorial Effectuation of Interests

A. Technical Conditions

B. Legal Conditions

Chapter II. System of Extraterritorially-Effectuated General Interests

A. Physical Interests

B. Economic Interests

C. Moral-Intellectual Interests

D. Legal (inter-State civil and criminal law) Interests

Section II. Inter-State Defense of Interests and Rights

(Formal Inter-State Law)

Chapter I. Legal Means of Defense

Chapter II. Factual Means of Defense and Law During War

Grabar thought this idea had merit: "Very good system. Despite certain shortcomings, the system proposed by Taube should be acknowledged to deserve attention".[163]

Of interest are Taube's ideas concerning the correlation and "mutual linkage, community, or dependence" of international law and the municipal law of a State. This is especially evident when international law is ignored by a State, which negatively reflects on its domestic life.

International law, correctly understood, is not some legal fiction artificially constructed by professors or diplomats, but simply a well-known minimum of legal consciousness necessary for the practical coexistence and cultural cooperation of civilized peoples. [And if such] a minimum of legal consciousness [of peoples ceased to be complied with by a State in international relations, for example, during warfare] then strictly logically one cannot, of course, expect that such a moral minimum will remain present and on its side of the State boundary, [that is, -- within the State].[164]

Perpetual peace and pacifism. Taube was a realist. In an environment of constant military and political rivalry between the Great Powers and the legal permis-

[163] Grabar, note 46 above, p. 502.

[164] Note 110 above, p. 15.

sibility of war, Taube reacted skeptically to any ideas of perpetual peace. However, he did support pacifist movements for the prevention of war, limitation of the means and methods of waging them, and ameliorating the misfortunes of victims of warfare. Speaking on 17 December 1909 at the founding assembly of the St. Petersburg division of the Moscow Peace Society, Taube analyzed the pacifist trends (academic, international-social, and revolutionary-Marxist) and expressed assurance that wars were not inevitable between States in the future, saying to those present that "Russia is not fated to survive yet another war".[165]

Regional international law. One theme to which Taube repeatedly returned – elaborating views originally formed prior to the Revolution – was the importance of the Slavic world in the development of international law. He believed that the contributions of the Slavic world were distinctive and an expression of "regionalism" in international law. Although they would never have cited him, Soviet international lawyers thought along analogous lines, and the modern emergence of Eurasianism in post-Soviet space is arguably an extension of similar thinking.

In his 1926 Hague lectures,[166] Taube expressed regret that histories of international law neglected, indeed omitted completely, the roles of Byzantium and the Slavic peoples, the latter being relegated to mere intermediaries between Europe and Asia. Byzantium developed a political system around the concept of "cesaropapism" under which the Emperor of Byzantium was the representative of God on earth; crimes against the Empire were crimes against God – these were doctrines that affected the Byzantine approach to the law of war, always just if useful and in the interests of the State. The "just war" doctrine, so important in western Christianity, Taube said had no place in Byzantine teachings. Kievan Rus, in Taube's perception, had developed a familiarity with international-legal relations with western Europe as well as Byzantium before Christianity was accepted ca. 988, followed shortly by Christianization in Poland and Hungary – collectively an extension of the *Respublica Christiana*. Russia, said Taube, in those days was part of Christian Europe. The break between Slavic lands and western Europe Taube attributed to the Tatar invasion and devastation of Kievan Rus primarily. Although the Slavs had reason to be concerned about invasions of Germanic peoples, on balance Taube believed the German conquests were more positive than the Tatar for Slavic peoples. Tatar rule and influence Taube characterized as "despotic, oriental, half-Tatar, half-Byzantine, Orthodox mysticism mixed with arrogant and aggressive nationalism". The "Asianization of Russia" for two and a half centuries, Taube believed, accounted for Muscovite isolationism and "anti-internationalism". Acknowledging the separation and isolation of the Slavic lands from western Europe, Taube criticized the view widely shared by Russian historians that a continuous Russian State existed from Kievan Rus onwards; this view, he said, was a "later, and politically inspired, fantasy". Relations between Russian principalities were international relations, governed by local perceptions of the law of nations, and similar to inter-princely relations in western Europe. For Taube, regionalism

165 See Новое время [New Times], 18 and 19 December 1909. Also see Taube, note 94 above, p. 22.

166 Taube, note 117 above, pp. 345-347.

was a key element in the history of international relations, including international legal relations.[167]

Taube's approach was set out in the outline of the course he delivered at the Institut des Hautes Études International in December 1931/January 1932:[168]

REGIONALISM AND UNIVERSALISM IN THE DEVELOPMENT

OF THE INTERNATIONAL LAW OF EASTERN EUROPE

Introduction. Object of course. Universalism and regionalism in the development of international law. Condition of existence and characteristic signs of international regionalism in history. Continentalism and European regionalism, European and American continentalism, continentalism and world international law.

I. European Continentalism and Oriental Regionalism. Three types of international community in the history of the Eurasian continent: Romano-Germanic world; Byzantine-Slavic world, and Asiatic world. Historical exterior cadres of the evolution of the Asiatic world and eastern regionalism. West and East since the Crusades. Extraterritoriality of European nations in the Orient and the regime of capitulations.

Oriental Regionalism in the 19th Century. [not given]. Consular jurisdiction in the principal States of the Orient: Turkey, Egypt, Persia, China, Japan. Gradual disparity of "Oriental Regionalism" and the state of this question in the 20th century.

II. European Continentalism and Slavic Regionalism. Historical formation of the Slavic international type in the community of peoples of Europe. Byzantium, and the Slavic world. Catholic Slavs and Greek Orthodox Slavs. The historical role of Russia from the standpoint of European regionalism.

Slavic Regionalism and its Characteristic Manifestations in History. a) the role of the large routes of international commerce in Eastern Europe and the particularities of the right of strangers in Russia; b) the international role of the Baltic Sea, the particular maritime law of this region and its rules of neutrality in time of war; c) the pacifist and anti-militaristic trends of the Slavic world; the "Bogowile" Bulgars, the "Moravian Brothers"

167 These views are well set out by Lauri Mälksoo, "*Insula deserta*? Thoughts on the History of International Law Scholarship in Central Eastern and Eastern Europe", *Baltic Yearbook of International Law*, VII (2007), pp. 5-24. Taube was influenced by Sir Paul Vinogradoff (1854-1925) and his views on "historical types of international law". Taube identified what he considered to be the "international law of Eastern Europe/Russia of the Middle Ages", together with seventeen other types of civilization. On Vinogradoff, see W. E. Butler (ed.), *On the History of International Law and International Organization: Collected Papers of Sir Paul Vinogradoff* (2009).

168 The Notes/text of the course of ten lectures are contained in Box 6, File 4, Taube Archive, Columbia University.

(Chelcicki), Maksim the Greek in Moscow (16th century), and the subsequent revolution up to Leo Tolstoy.

Adaptation of Slavic Regionalism to European Continentalism. Imperial Russia and General International Law. Role of Peter the Great and the policy of his successors: Catherine II, Alexander I, Alexander II, Nicholas II, and the international world.

III. European Continentalism and "Americanism". The problem of regionalism in the 20th century. Theoretical considerations and international practice. European and American points of view. Pan American Union and the codification of international law in America.

Conclusion. Regionalism and world law. Efforts of international theory and practice in view of the generalization of international law. Work of the Institute of International Law. Role of large organs of international administrative unions. Permanent Courts of International Arbitration and of International Justice at The Hague. League of Nations and Prospects for the Future.

Taube as international arbitrator. As a protégé of F. F. Martens and holding an appointment in the Russian Ministry of Foreign Affairs, Taube would have been involved in the preparations for the 1907 Hague Peace Conference. The so-called "Dogger Bank Incident", or "Hull Incident", off the coast of England in 1904 led to his appointment as a legal advisor to the International Commission of Enquiry formed as a result of the incident. The generally accepted version is that the Russian Government decided in 1904 to send a major portion of its Baltic fleet to the Pacific coast of the Russian Empire under the command of Admiral Zinovii Petrovich Rozhdestvenskii (1848-1909) in furtherance of the Russo-Japanese War. There was an assumption that Japanese agents were following the movements of the fleet and an apprehension that Japanese torpedo boats were probably in the area and might attack. On the night of 7/8 October 1904, while proceeding along the Dogger Bank – a large shoal sixty miles east of the coast of England and a rich fishing ground – small ships without lights were sighted at 24:55 hours and fired upon on the presumption they were Japanese torpedo boats. When daylight came, it was apparent that the Russian armada had fired on English fishing boats, as well as their own ships. Some fishing boats were sunk with loss of life. The Armada continued on without stopping, did not rescue the fishermen, and four days later put into the Spanish naval station at Vigo. In all, six English fishermen were killed, and there were serious Russian casualties from firing on their own vessels, one of whom died in a Spanish hospital.[169]

While England prepared for naval action, diplomacy prevailed. It was decided to have recourse to a means for the pacific settlement of disputes recognized by international law: a fact-finding International Commission of Enquiry. Taube was appointed to represent the interests of the Russian Empire in this matter as one of two "jurisconsultes assesseurs", together with five admirals – three from

[169] See Constantine Pleshakov, *The Tsar's Last Armada: The Epic Voyage to the Battle of Tsushima* (2002), pp. 94-100.

neutral countries, and one each from England (Sir Edward Frey) and Russia. Also participating on the Russian side were Anatolii Vasilevich Nekliudov (1856-1934) as "agents" of the respective Government, and to assist Nekliudov, A. N. Mandelstam. In the end, the Commission produced two reports, one open and one secret. Taube said that he received a copy of each and, in May 1917, deposited them in the Archive of the Ministry of Foreign Affairs as part of fourteen cartons of material.[170] Taube played a key role in the defense of Russian interests in this affair, for which Emperor Nicholas II (1868-1918) expressed formal and official gratitude (Taube as a matter of principle declined orders and medals for service to his country).

Emperor Nicholas II appointed Taube on 18 November 1909 a member of the Permanent Court of International Arbitration at the Hague, where he succeeded F. F. Martens, who had passed away earlier that year. Taube participated as an arbitrator in several cases, including, in 1912, the Russian Indemnity Case, a Russian-Turkish dispute concerning the remuneration of persons under the protection of Russia for losses sustained during the Russo-Turkish War.[171] On 4 April 1913 the Governments of France and Italy selected Taube as one of five arbitrators in a Franco-Italian dispute relating to incidents of the French vessels *Carthage*[172] and *Manouba*.[173]

Ideas in emigration. Having left Russia, Taube continued to pursue his research interests. He elaborated a profoundly Christian understanding of the world, having regard to changing international realities In Berlin he published in the Russian language a volume devoted to the recently-formed League of Nations and another on the historical development of international law in Eastern Europe.[174]

In his Berlin volume Taube developed his doctrinal positions on the international community and the linkages of States as the foundation of international law. Taube had a positive view of the formation of the League of Nations, analyzing its significance for international stability and mutually advantageous relations between peoples and States, with a premonition that the League – which existed until

170 See Taube, note 110 above, p. 79.

171 Award of 11 November 1912. For the text, see J. B. Scott (ed.), *The Hague Court Reports: Comprising the Awards, Accompanied by Syllabi, The Agreements for the Arbitration, and Other Documents in Each Case Submitted to the Permanent Court of Arbitration and to Commissions of Inquiry under the Provisions of the Conventions of 1899 an 1907 for the Pacific Settlement of International Disputes* (1916; reprint 2004), pp. 532-555. See Taube, note 1 above, p. 11. Also see A. M. Solntsev, «Вклад российских ученых конца XIX -- начала XX вв. в утверждение и развитие идеи международного правосудия» [Contribution of Russian Scholars at the End of the XIX and Early XX Centuries to Confirmation and Development of the Idea of International Justice], in V. L. Tolstykh (ed.), Институты международного правосудия [Institutes of International Justice] (2014), p. 119-120.

172 Award of 6 May 2013. Ibid., pp. 329-340.

173 Award of 6 May 2013. Ibid., pp. 341-353.

174 See Taube, Вечный мир или вечная война (Мысли о Лиге Нации) [Perpetual Peace or Perpetual War (Reflections on the League of Nations)] (1922), based on lectures delivered in Spring 1920 at Uppsala University in Sweden. Taube, *Études sur le dévéloppement historique du droit international dans l'Europe orientale* (1926).

1946 – would become the United Nations. Taube raised the question: "What did mankind learn from the previous wars"?, predicting to a certain degree the Second World War. He prophesied the destiny of international law:

> International law ultimately is a system of well-known legal norms developed by long-term custom or based on special international agreements (or treaties) actually existing in the domain of practical international turnover and created by States (or governments and peoples) as binding rules of mutual self-limitation of their power wills necessary in practice for the joint peaceful existence of peoples and their full cultural development.[175]

Taube returned to the premise of mutual linkages of peoples and States: "the community and solidarity of all civilized peoples – that most mutual cultural linkage or dependence" which is an objective necessity of their international communion and underlying international law. In Taube's view, the world is mutually intertwined, the successes and failures of one State reflect on others: "… with the present state of cultural community of peoples, the moral or economic sickness of one of them means, ultimately, also the sickness of the neighbors thereof. Because all are in essence members of a single large body".[176]

From the idea of the mutual-dependence of States, Taube logically drew the conclusion of the mutual self-limitation of State wills as a mechanism for the creation of norms of international law. Traditionally, both before and after Taube, international law was basically regarded as a system of certain legal norms regulating relations of the inter-State community. But Taube drew attention to another aspect of the nature and essence of international law. Forming norms and principles of international law, States mutually renounce part of their powers, voluntarily limiting their sovereign power to the benefit of the entire human community or, in Taube's expression, "single large body".

International legal practitioner. "Practitioner" is used here in the broadest sense, to mean lecturer, legal advisor, diplomat, arbitrator, or civil servant. Following the example of his mentor, F. F. Martens, Taube combined a full-time or adjunct teaching appointment with other employment. At the Ministry of Foreign Affairs, Taube followed the career path from a rank-and-file civil servant up to being appointed a permanent member of the Council of Ministers. From 2 January 1892 to 1900 he served as a jurisconsult in the Ministry under the direction of Martens where he prepared daily summaries and abstracts from the foreign press, from 1900 to 1904 he headed the administrative-legal section of the Second Department of the Ministry, where he gave legal consultations, took part of various interdepartmental commissions and international meetings, and prepared analytical memoranda on domestic and international issues, from 27 June 1905 as Vice-Director of the II Department of the Ministry, and from 1907, as a counselor and permanent member of the Council of the Ministry.

[175] Taube, note 142 above (1922), p. 30. A previously unpublished letter from L. N. Tolstoi to Taube dated 18-19 December 1903 containing the writer's pacifist thoughts appears as an Annex to the volume.

[176] Ibid., pp. 15, 7-28.

From 1905 he took part in preparations for the Second Hague Peace Conference. He drew up the draft Program thereof, which was submitted in December 1905 to a Commission of the Ministry of Foreign Affairs for confirmation as the official proposal of Russia.[177] At about the same time he produced for the Ministry of Foreign Affairs a Memorandum on the Passage of Warships through the Borphorus and Dardanelles – a subject which must have been deeply concerning to the Russian Government as it contemplated moving ships from Europe to the Far East.[178]

An official memorandum prepared by Taube, dated 18 May 1907, led to a serious restructuring of the internal organization of the Ministry of Foreign Affairs, including the creation of a legal department.[179]

In November 1906, Taube advised the Chief Administration of the Russian Red Cross Society on compensating the Red Cross for losses caused by actions of Japanese authorities in Port Arthur (confiscation of a hospital ship *Mongolia* and other property).[180]

Taube was appointed in 1908 as the Plenipotentiary of Russia to the Naval Conference convoked in London at the initiative of England. He played an active role and signed in the name of Russia the 1909 Declaration on the Law of Naval Warfare – the first true systematization of the international rules and customs of naval warfare.[181]

Taube served as a member of the Russian delegation to conclude the Petersburg Agreement of 10 April 1908 between Russia, Germany, Sweden, and Denmark on mutual recognition of the territorial inviolability of their respective Baltic possessions.

From l5 October 1909, Taube was a permanent member of the Council of the Ministry of Foreign Affairs, having replaced the late F. F. Martens in this post.

In 1914, several weeks before the outbreak of the First World War, Taube persuaded the Russian Government to withdraw all Russian gold from German banks. This enabled the Russian treasury to avail itself of substantial financial resources during the difficult war years.

177 Taube, note 94 above, p. 30.

178 See Taube, Записка по вопросу о проходе военных судов через Босфор и Дарданеллы [Memorandum on the Question of Passage of Warships Through the Bosphorus and Dardanelles] (Spb., 1905). 16 p. The Memorandum was printed by and for the Ministry of Foreign Affairs. A copy is held at MH-L.

179 Ibid., p. 32. Also see Iu. V. Bosenko, «Министерство иностранных дел России в 1900-1917 гг.» [Ministry of Foreign Affairs of Russia in 1900-1917], Дипломатический вестник [Diplomatic Herald], no. 4 (2001), p. 145-163.

180 Taube, note 94 above, p. 20.

181 B. E. Nolde, «Лондонская декларация о праве морской войны 26 февраля 1909 г.» [London Declaration on the Law of Naval Warfare, 26 February 1909], Известия Санкт-Петербургского политехнического института [News of St. Petersburg Polytechnic Institute], XIII (1910), op. 59-112.

Taube joined as a founder-member the Russian Society of Maritime Law (1905), was elected on 15 March 1910 to the Institute of International Law, and on 31 January 1914 became a member of the Academy of International Law at The Hague and member of its Curatorium; in December 1915 he was elected an Associate Member of the American Institute of International Law.

A third Hague Peace Conference, contemplated for the year 1915, was never held because of the First World War. Taube was elected to the international preparatory committee to develop the program of such a Conference.[182]

Taube held other senior State positions. From 1911 to 1915 he served as the Deputy Minister of Public Enlightenment, and from 1914 to 1915 as the acting Minister following the death of Minister Lev Aristidovich Kasso (1865-1914). On 11 February 1915 he was appointed a Senator of the Ruling Senate with the rank of privy councilor. From 1 January 1917 he was a member of the State Council of the Russian Empire. He repeatedly addressed the State Duma on matters of general State importance. He took an active role in drafting the Law on introducing general primary education. A monarchist by political persuasion, he upheld the positions of that orientation.

Taube took an active part in the socio-political life of Russia. From 1908 he was a member of the High Prize Court appointed from the Ministry of Foreign Affairs. He represented the Ministry in the Russian Society for the Defense of Women (from 1908). He was among the founders of the St. Petersburg Philosophical Society, having become a full member from 1906. And, from 1913, he was an honorary member of the Society of Classical Philology and Pedagogy in St. Petersburg.

A notable member of the anti-war movement, Taube was elected from 17 December 1909 to the Board of the St. Petersburg Division of the Russian Peace Society.

For many years, Taube acted as a private advisor or consultant on international issues, gave numerous explanations and memos, prepared expert opinions and analytical notes, and offered advice on matters of international law. Russians and foreigners turned to him for advice, as did international organizations and learned societies. In 1928, for example, Sultan Mahmoud Kadjar of Persia approached Taube about a matter he intended to bring to the Permanent Court of International Justice (PCIJ) at the Hague involving an annuity. The Sultan inquired about Taube's fees; Taube expressed interest in being of service on the same day, and on 12 June 1928 the Sultan set out what his understanding was of the usual fees in such a matter: 6,000 French francs (+ 1,000 German marks) for an uncomplicated written opinion, a percentage if an agreement was reached to advise, plus first class train fare to Paris and actual expenses for accommodation. Taube agreed to act on these terms. At issue was a Protocol of 25 August 1908 between Persia, England, and Russia concerning the protection of legations. As part of the Protocol, the Persian Government undertook, in the event of the death of His Majesty Mohammad Ali Mirza (1872-1925), to pay to his widow and younger children a pension of 25,000 *tomans* per year, to be divided among them. The United Kingdom, said the

[182] Taube, note 94 above, pp. 38-39.

Sultan, had said by letter that its Government was not in a position to persuade the Persian Government to pay this pension.[183]

Taube published poetry in prerevolutionary Russia and in emigration.[184] His memoirs and other material appeared in several European journals.

Taube died at Paris on 29 November 1961, blind and deaf, but with intellectual capacities intact. Velmin wrote in his obituary that "in bed he dictated his last work on the attempt of Ivan the Terrible to create a Lithuanian State as vassal to Muscovy" – a work he did not complete. He left a formidable intellectual legacy whose full measure has yet to be appreciated.

Taube's successor in the Chair of International Law at St. Petersburg University from 1911 was another protégé of F. F. Martens: A. A. Pilenko.

Aleksandr Aleksandrovich Pilenko *(22 June 1873, b. Gatchina, Tsarskoe selo uezd, Petersburg Governate – 21 March 1956, d. Paris, France). Specialist in private international law, founder of Russian patent law, noted authority in the field of authors' and inventors' rights, representative of Russia in several international organizations and conferences, publicist, journalist.*

Life and career. Pilenko descended from the Russian nobility, graduated in 1891 with the gold medal from the Eighth Petersburg Gymnasium, and enrolled in the Chinese Division of the Faculty of Oriental Languages of St. Petersburg University. A talented linguist, in his first year of university he began studies of the Chinese, Mongolian, and English languages and the history of the Orient, also attending lectures by F. F. Martens on international law.[185] Under the impact of Martens, Pilenko requested the Rector of the University to allow him to transfer to the Law Faculty. The request was sat-

183 Box 2, Taube Archive, Columbia University. The outcome is unknown.

184 Verses appeared in Русский вестник [Russian Herald] and, from 1907, in various collections of verses. These he continued in emigration. See Видения и думы: Сборник стихотворение [Visions and Thoughts] (Paris, 1937), but printed in Estonia. The Library of Congress copy is inscribed 13 February 1942. The volume was dedicated to his son, Aleksandr Taube (1918-1934) and grandson, Nils Hallrup (1921-1934). The volume contains 75 poems divided into three sections: In Lieu of a Preface; I. Visions and Thoughts; II. Songs of the Middle Ages; and III. Christian Motifs, and reproduces a drawing entitled "Heilige Erwartung – Advent" by Abbess Maria Loach. Also see: Taube, Святые силуэты [Sacred Silhouettes] (Tallin, 1938). He published articles in Возрождение [Renaissance] (1961); Новый журнал [New Journal] (1963); Союз дворян [Union of Nobles], and in various learned journals: *Le monde slave, La Revue historique, Revue catholique des idées et des faits, Revue d'histoire moderne,* among others.

185 ЦГИА СПб, fond 14, opis' 3, file 28188, folios 1, 8.

isfied on 15 September 1893.[186] Pilenko completed his legal studies in March 1896, being awarded the degree of candidate of laws with first class honors.[187]

From 1 November 1896 Pilenko remained, upon the petition of the Dean of the Law Faculty, at the Chair of International Law for one year to prepare for the professoriate (without a stipend).[188] On that same day, with the authorization of the Minister of Public Enlightenment, Pilenko went abroad for one year "for an academic purpose".[189] A year later the report submitted by Pilenko about his studies abroad was approved by Martens, who filed a further petition, duly supported by the dean, rector, and Administrator of the Petersburg Educational District, requesting that Pilenko's stay abroad be extended until 1 May 1898,[190] and again until 1 November 1898.[191] During his foreign travels, Pilenko worked in libraries and attended lectures at universities in Paris, Heidelberg, Berlin, and Bonn. Upon his return to Petersburg, Pilenko was offered a position at the Ministry of Finances, where from 12 December 1898 he became a college secretary in the division for the issuance of patents in the Department of Trade and Manufactures.

In 1899 and 1900 he successfully passed the magister examinations.[192] On 27 April 1900 the Rector of St. Petersburg University in a letter to the Rector of Moscow University reported that Pilenko had requested to be allowed to deliver lectures with the title of privat-docent and declared that he had delivered the two trial lectures required under Article 109 of the 1884 Statute on Russian Universities at Moscow University; the Rector in Moscow was requested to confirm this information.[193] In reply, the Dean of the Law Faculty at Moscow University sent to the Rector of St. Petersburg University on 10 May 1898 a certificate of the Faculty confirming that Pilenko had acquired the rights to teach with the title of privat-docent pursuant to the said Article of the University Statute.[194]

[186] Ibid., file 14359, folio 8 (protocols of sessions of the Faculty, 20 January, 3 February, and 10 March 1913).

[187] Ibid., file 28188, folio 44.

[188] Ibid., opis' 2, file 1089, folios 1-2. But the Minister of Public Enlightenment authorized the payment of 1,500 rubles for maintenance, later sums also being granted when his visit abroad was extended.

[189] Ibid., folio 9.

[190] Ibid., folios 11-13.

[191] Ibid., folios 14-16.

[192] On 1 March 1899 Pilenko successfully answered the following questions on the international law examination: (1) History of the Eastern Question after 1856; (2) International Administrative Institutions (Bureaus); (2) Recent Sources of the Codification of the Principles of Private International Law. On 28 February 1900 the following questions were put to Pilenko on State law: (1) Montesquieu; (2) Sovereignty; (3) Governors. See ibid., file 14327, folios 9-10.

[193] Ibid., file 1089, folios 22-22 ob.

[194] Ibid., folio 23. According to the certificate, Pilenko on 29 March 1900 had delivered two trial lectures in the presence of the Law Faculty on: (1) "the Suez Canal", a subject designated by the faculty; and (2) "On Literary Conventions", a subject of his own choosing. Ibid., folio 30.

On 19 May 1900 the Rector of St. Petersburg University in a letter to the Director of the Alexander Lycée inquired whether, on behalf of the Lycée, there were any obstacles to Pilenko being admitted by St. Petersburg University to teach with the title of privat-docent.[195] In his reply of 23 May 1900 the Director notified the Rector of the University that Pilenko was available to be hired to lecture at the University and there were no obstacles to such an appointment.[196] As from 1 July 1900 Pilenko became a privat-docent at the Chair of International Law of St. Petersburg University to lecture on international law.[197] There he gave courses of the History of International Relations (from 1900 to 1908); the Macedonian Question (1906-1907); the Eastern Question (1906-1907); and "International Criminal and Private Law" (1908-1909). From 1910 to 1917, after the resignation of Taube, he offered the basic course on international law.

In parallel, Pilenko served as a professor of international law at the Alexander Lycée and the Higher (Bestuzhev) Women's Courses.

Pilenko published in 1901 a work on the privileges accompanying the grant of a patent on inventions.[198] Three years later Pilenko published his greatest work, a treatise in two volumes on the comparative law of inventions.[199] On the basis of volume one, Pilenko defended a magister dissertation on the "Law of the Inventor".[200]

Having become a magister, during the years 1902 and 1903 Pilenko put forward his candidacy under the first competitive appointment procedure arranged by St. Petersburg University for the vacant chair of international law, open because of the retirement of F. F. Martens. This competitive procedure created a set of personal conflicts which led to a schism within the Council of the Faculty of Law; A. N. Mandelstam and Baron M. A. von Taube took part in the competition.[201] Martens was dragged into the dispute, and he did not support Pilenko. As a result of the

[195] Ibid., folio 25.

[196] Ibid., folio 27.

[197] See Отчет о состоянии и деятельности Императорского С.-Петербургского Университета за 1900 год [Report on the Status and Activity of Imperial St. Petersburg University for 1900] (1901), p. 14.

[198] A. A. Pilenko, Привилегии на изобретения: Практическое руководство, с приложением текста закона 20 мая 1896 г., позднейших дополнений, форм деловых бумаг и кратких сведений об иностранных законах [Privileges to an Invention. Practical Manual with the Text of the Law of 20 May 1896 Appended, Most Recent Additions, Forms of Clerical Papers, and Concise Information on Foreign Laws] (1901). 85 p.

[199] Pilenko, Право изобретателя. Привилегии на изобретения и их защита в русском и международном праве. Историко-догматическое исследование [Law of the Inventor. Privileges to an Invention and Defense Thereof in Russian and International Law: Historical-Dogmatic Study] (1902-1903). 2 vols.

[200] The opponents appointed for the defense were professors F. F. Martens and Petr Pavlovich Tsitovich (1843-1913). See note 185 above, opis' 3, file 14325, folio 2.

[201] On this appointment and on Taube generally, see the section on Taube above and W. E. Butler and V. S. Ivanenko, note 94 above, pp. 495-526.

voting and a lengthy haggling over procedural issues in which the Dean, Rector, Administrator of the St. Petersburg Educational District, and Ministry of Public Enlightenment took part, Pilenko lost and Taube was declared to be the appointee.

In 1904 Pilenko left his position at the Ministry of Finances. He continued, however, to undertake scholarly research and in 1911 submitted as a professor at the Alexander Lycée a doctoral dissertation on the systematics of private international law.[202] That same year saw the retirement of Taube from St. Petersburg University to take up a position with the State Duma. Once more the vacant Chair was advertised, and this time Pilenko was successful in obtaining the position. From 28 November 1912 Pilenko began his general course of international law.[203]

Pilenko remained a professor and Head of the Chair until 1917. He resigned from these positions at his own wish on 7 April 1917, ceding them to Baron Boris Emmanuilovich Nolde (1876-1948), three days later he returned to the Faculty to resume lecturing, but on this occasion as a privat-docent.

Over these years Pilenko held a number of other positions. From 1911 to 1917 he served as a deputy of the City Duma of St. Petersburg. He was an influential journalist at the authoritative and popular newspaper Новое время [New Time], published by the noted newspaperman, Aleksei Sergeevich Surovin (1834-1912). He wrote editorials for this newspaper three times a week anonymously or under a pseudonym. For the State Duma he acted as a parliamentary correspondent and was Chairman of the Society of Duma Journalists. In his day Pilenko was among the most authoritative and influential legal scholars and publicists.

The revolutionary events of autumn 1917 forced Pilenko to leave Petrograd and move on to Ukraine together with his family, to Sumy where his wife had an estate, and then in June 1918 to Kyiv. There he played an active role in organizing the self-defense of Kyiv against the forces of Simon V. Petlura (1879-1926), a significant Ukrainian nationalist leader. In December 1918 he removed to Odessa, where he participated in the publication issued by the Government of General Petr Nikolaevich Vrangel' [Wrangel] (1878-1928) – Призыв [Appeal]. During May 1919, Pilenko emigrated.

International legal views. As a twenty-or-so year old second year student at St. Petersburg University, Pilenko wrote a substantial work entitled "International Literary Conventions". Awarded a gold medal and published in 1894 at the expense of the University, it is still cited in the twenty-first century as a leading and valuable work.[204] The conditions, procedure, and evaluation of student works sub-

[202] Pilenko, Очерки по систематике частного международного права [Essays on the Systematics of Private International Law] (1911). The official opponents were Professors Ignatii Aleksandrovich Ivanovskii (1858-1928) and Leon I. Petrazhitskii (1867-1931), and unofficial opponent, Professor M. A. von Taube. As noted in the press, the "scientific tournament" was tense and lasted from lunchtime until 18:00 hours. See «Докторский диспут Пиленко» [Doctoral Dispute of Pilenko], Новое время [New Time], 17 October 1911, p. 4; Право [Law], 17 October 1911, cols. 2581-2585.

[203] Note 185 above, fund 14, opis 3, file 14411.

[204] Pilenko, Международные литературные конвенции [International Literary Convention] (Spb., 1894). 553 p. The book was published on the basis of a competition open to students of the

mitted during those times are instructive. In 1891 a competition was announced on the topic: "On International Literary Conventions". The Report of St. Petersburg University for 1892 contained the following assessment:

> Of the works submitted on the topic relating to international law, the most outstanding work was undoubtedly work No. VII with the motto "Suum cuique". The author of this work demonstrates a comprehensive familiarity with the richest literature on the question; he engaged in a study of it not only in St. Petersburg, but also in Paris, where in the libraries of the École de droit and in the Bibliothèque Nationale he found manuals we do not have here. In addition, the author, without any doubt, has outstanding capabilities and familiarity with general European literature ... One may reproach the author for inconsistency of the system, some repetitions, and a certain simplicity of the exposition caused by numerous quotations in the French, English, and German languages. But it can be said that the author brilliantly performed the task set and this student work, in justness, one can be proud of. On the basis of the foregoing, the author of this work, a student at the Faculty of Oriental Languages in his IV semester, Alexander Pilenko, is deemed worthy of the Gold Medal.[205]

At the Chair of International Law at St. Petersburg University, Pilenko, after passing the magister examinations in July 1900, began to lecture in the course "Recent History of International Law (1870-1900)", one hour per week.[206] Later Pilenko offered specialized courses: "History of Diplomatic Relations with the Far East (1875-1903)";[207] "Macedonian Question";[208] and the "Eastern Question".[209] As noted above, Pilenko began to offer the course on general international law from 1912, as well as practical seminars on "Literary Conventions" and on "Marriage in Private International Law".[210]

In addition to his teaching at St. Petersburg University, Pilenko worked in other institutions of higher education in St. Petersburg: from 1900 as a lecturer; from 1910 as professor *extraordinarius*. From 1901 at the age of 27, he held the Chair of International Law at the Alexander Lycée and, in parallel, from 1908 to 1916, was Professor of International Law at the Higher (Bestuzhev) Women's Courses.

Faculty of Oriental Languages and was dedicated "To the Memory of My Unforgettable Father". Pilenko's father passed away during the year of publication.

205 Отчет о состоянии и деятельности Императорского С.-Петербургского Университета за 1892 год [Report on the State and Activity of the Imperial St. Petersburg University for 1892] (Spb., 1893), pp. 94, 134.

206 Ibid. for 1900 (1901), p. 14.

207 Обозрение преподавания на юридическом факультете Императорского С.-Петербургского Университета на 1904-1905 [Survey of Teaching at the Law Faculty of St. Petersburg University for 1904-1905 Academic Year] (Spb., 1905), pp. 3-5, 18-19.

208 Ibid. for 1905-1906 (1906), p. 18.

209 See the entry for Pilenko in the online source Биографика СПбГУ.

210 Note 205 above for 1913 (1914), p. 169.

Pilenko published the first manual in Russia on the preparation of a patent application in 1901;[211] by 1916 the book had reached its eighth edition. As noted above, his major two-volume treatise based on his magister dissertation appeared in 1902-03. Pilenko's works were the first in Russia to explore the impact of literary conventions on intellectual property law. In the preface to his treatise, he pointed out that his study had no predecessors. He appealed to his readers: "Russian jurisprudence must, finally, respond to questions of life. Resolution of the respective problems 'will not tolerate delay'" (p. v).

Pilenko undertook in his treatise an integrated analysis of the "young institution of patent law", which already had rich judicial practice and a body of substantive Russian and foreign legislation regulating patent law; he analyzed the system of rights and duties of a patent-holder.[212] A central place was given to determining the rights of an author to the results of intellectual activity. Pilenko criticized the theory being formed of patent law and author's right and offered his own explanation of the nature and essence of the rights of an inventor. He distinguished between the "right to a patent" as a public right of an inventor to receive a patent and the "right from the patent" as a private right generating civil-law relations for the inventor.

Pilenko believed that the "right from a patent" was exclusive, the recipient of a patent may at his discretion dispose of it; that is, use it, execute it, sell it, and so on: it absolutely is a "right of prohibition", not allowing third persons to use the patented object for unsanctioned economic purposes. From all this Pilenko drew the following basic conclusions:

(1) "A patent right is an author's right in the domain of technology";

(2) "A patent right is a right of prohibition directed against all third persons. This conclusion, despite its modest nature, I consider the most important in my work" (p. 368).

Being an optimist, Pilenko was convinced that "the time will ensue when the honor of the inventor will be valued and defended just as the honor of authorship" (p. 13).

This treatise, having laid the foundations of Russian patent law, went through several reprintings and was translated in 1907 into the German language; it continues to have scientific and practical importance and remains the most authoritative and full study in the field of patent law theory.[213] Aleksandr Lvovich Makovskii (1930-2020) wrote:

> Serious scholarly monographs, naturally, are created with the use of the entire arsenal of the method of scientific studies. But very rarely do au-

[211] Note 198 above.

[212] For a modern critical analysis of Pilenko, see M. G. Volynskii, «К вопросу о природе права на патент» [On the Question of the Nature of the Right to a Patent], Правоведение [Jurisprudence], no. 2 (2002), pp. 209-221.

[213] The second edition was twice republished in Russia for the contemporary reader, in 2001 and 2005.

> thors allow the reader into the 'kitchen', preferring (without grounds) to demonstrate the 'prepared dish' of their creation and are silent about the recipe. Pilenko deliberately and painstakingly flung open the doors of his laboratory. He built the edifice of his study on the 'method of inductive construction' (p. 456), all the time showing the reader how the course of his thinking develops, what arguments and in what order he placed them in this edifice, and wherein lie the logical mistakes of the authors he criticizes. Therefore, Pilenko's book is not only valuable for its content as a talented monograph on patent law, but also irreplaceable as a brilliant practical manual on the method of the science of law.[214]

The year 1902 was singularly productive. Pilenko published more than a dozen scientific works on various topics. Among them were articles on private international law, the registration of artistic works, on State duties for privileges, a commentary on a Senate edict on the Auer case, and a book review of a work by Aleksandr Mikhailovich Gorovtsev (1878-1933). He delivered papers on author's right and patent law and prepared a survey of Russian legislation for the Society of Comparative Legislation in London. Once his magister dissertation was successfully defended, he began to publish more diversely, including on the theoretical foundations of private international law, adhering from the outset to an international legal conception of its origin and the substance thereof being confined to a law of conflicts.

Survey of private international law in Liszt. Pilenko is regarded in doctrinal writings as a founder of the "internationalist" approach to private international law. At the request of Grabar, Pilenko prepared the first full Russian survey of private international law (or, in his view, conflicts law), published as an integral part of the first edition of the Russian translation of Franz E. von Liszt's (1851-1919) treatise on international law.[215] In his survey, Pilenko proposed his own understanding of the nature and practical problems of private international law. Analyzing the conflicts norms in the legislation of States, according to which the "dispositive legal capacity of citizens is determined according to the law of that country to which this person belongs, he concluded: an international legal norm exists under which the dispositive legal capacity of a natural person is determined by his national law, and therefore the country which consolidated this position in its internal law merely acceded to this international norm. But laws on particular dispositive legal capacity which private individuals of all countries have may be different, generating conflicts between them: "The competence of several civil national systems conflicts". In order to prevent or resolve these conflicts, States applied legal mechanisms which came to be called private international law. Pilenko wrote: "Private international law is called upon to destroy the conflict, having determined the boundaries of the operation of each of these systems" (p. 371).

214 A. L. Makovskii, «Исключительные права и концепция части Четвертой Гражданского Кодекса» [Exclusive Rights and the Conception of Part Four of the Civil Code], in O. M. Lozyr and A. L. Makovskii (eds.), Гражданское право современной России [Civil Law of Contemporary Russia] (2008), p. 124.

215 Pilenko, «Очерк частного международного права» [Survey of Private International Law], in F. von Liszt, Международное право в систематическом изложении [International Law in Systematic Exposition], ed. & transl. V. E. Grabar (Iurev, 1902), pp. 371-404.

For Pilenko, private international law addressed conflicts of law regulating the relations of subjects of different States. He believed it important to have in view: "Private international law, just as any other international law, operates in mutual relations only of those States which stand approximately on an identical degree of cultural development" (p. 373).

As a firm proponent of the "internationalist-jurist" school, Pilenko asserted that private international law is not and legally cannot be an internal law of the State. The understanding thereof and adoption in this capacity would be legally absurd, contrary to legal axioms on the sovereignty and legislative autonomy of States. Even the provisions adopted by the national legislator addressed to its own courts to apply foreign law on its territory represented, in Pilenko's view, an infringement on the sovereignty of other States.

Pilenko set out his own vision of private international law: his Survey included: an "Introduction" analyzing the concept and nature of private international law, concept and content of public law, and legal qualification of conflicts norms (concept, extent, structure, links); "Historical Survey of the Development of Private International Law", including a periodization of its development up to the nineteenth century; "Personal Rights", including legal capacity and dispositive legal capacity; "Family Law", including external and internal conditions for the conclusion of a marriage, obligations of spouses to one another and to children; "Law of Obligations", including the form and essence of obligations; "Rights to a Thing" – moveable and immoveable; "Law of Inheritance", including the system of inheritance and questions of a will; "Enforcement of Judicial Decisions".

His views on categories of "public policy" and "legal qualification" are of interest in the context of law-application aspects of private international law: he was among the first in Russia to analyze them in detail. His argumentation is original:

> If in the interests of the international community Russian courts sometimes apply foreign laws, this does not mean that they must apply any foreign law, whatever the content thereof. A foreign norm maybe admissible *in abstracto*, but the concrete content thereof may prove to be too alien to Russian legal consciousness and therefore not subject to enforcement by the actions of Russian judicial authorities (pp. 373-374.

Pilenko's services in developing the conceptual apparatus were enormous and generally acknowledged, for it was during this period that the terminological, conceptual, and methodological apparatus of the Russian science of private international law were formed.[216]

Pilenko doctoral dissertation. In 1911 Pilenko defended his doctoral dissertation on the systematics of private international law on the basis of his treatise,[217]

216 A. N. Abdullin, Очерки истории науки международного частного права в России (проблема понимания природы международного частного права в трудах отечественных правоведов XIX-нач. XX в. [Survey of the History of the Science of Private International Law in Russia (Problem of Understanding the Nature of Private International Law in the Works of Russian Jurists XIX-Early XX Centuries)] (Kazan, 2004), p. 62.

217 Pilenko, note 202 above. A second edition was published in 1915.

a work notable for its use of detailed primary sources. His unofficial opponent, M. A. Taube, recognized the talent of Pilenko and saw the treatise as "creating an epoch".[218]

In his dissertation Pilenko considered a range of general theoretical and concrete aspects of private international law, having become, in the view of many, the founder of an "internationalist" understanding of the nature of private international law. As regards the principal theme of his work – the concept and content of the "system of private international law", and substantiating the need for a profound analysis of this system, Pilenko asserted that this is "in a completely underdeveloped state", and the "systems" of private international law proposed by the author "are the simple application of general theoretical categories to conflict questions". He proved the need to structure this system on a scientific basis: "the system of private international law should be structured in accordance with those basic ideas which inhere in conflicts law – and only it". Moreover, Pilenko noted:

> The unsatisfactoriness of the present systematics of private international law is complicated by the fact that the science of conflicts in the enormous majority of concrete cases encounters those concepts which exist together with this system and are wholly independent of it. Such concepts are: *renvoi*, public policy, *comitas*.

He was one of the earliest to consider theoretical problems connected with such concepts as: *comitas gentium*, public policy, *renvoi*, and others. He resolutely denied the existence of an internal conflicts law of a State. Petrazhitskii categorically disagreed, having criticized Pilenko's treatise and thereby enriched the science of private international law with his own theoretical reflections.[219] Nonetheless, despite the controversial nature of many propositions in Pilenko's treatise, it continues to be important. In the view of contemporary specialists, this treatise "represents a model of the internationalist view".[220]

Being a parliamentary journalist attached to the State Duma, Pilenko became influential and popular among the reading public and produced an early legal study of the first Russian parliament.[221]

Intending to produce a summary or generalization of his pedagogical and scientific work in the field of international law, Pilenko in 1915 began a textbook on international law and two articles for a monograph on the history of the Great

[218] See the newspaper reports of the defense in note 202 above. Grabar called the treatise "talented", sharing the view of Taube. See Grabar, note 46 above, p. 390.

[219] Also see I. V. Getman-Pavlova, «Проблемы международного частного права в психологической теории Л. И. Петражицкого» [Problems of Private International Law in the Psychological Theory of L. I. Petrazhitskii], Журнал международного публичного и частного права [Journal of International Public and Private Law], no. 5 (2009), pp. 5-12.

[220] G. K. Dmitrieva (ed.), Международное частное право [Private International Law] (2015), p. 43.

[221] See Pilenko, Русские парламентские прецеденты. Порядок делопроизводства в Государственной Думе [Russian Parliamentary Precedents. Procedure for Clerical Work in the State Duma] (1907). 2 vols. in one.

War. One may assume that subsequent revolutionary events interfered with this project.[222]

International legal practitioner. In 1898, upon his return to Petersburg from his first business trip abroad, Pilenko was invited to work at the Ministry of Finances. He was assigned from 12 December 1898 to the Division for the Issuance of Patents of the Department of Trade and Manufactures with the rank of college secretary – one of the lowest ranks in the Table of Ranks. When the Director of the Department who hired Pilenko learned that he had remained at the Chair of International Law to prepare for the professoriate, he offered Pilenko a "prestigious post in the Division of International Law". Pilenko, however, requested that he be sent to the Division for the Issuance of Patents: he had prepared a dissertation on inventions and wanted to learn from the actual practice. The Director, as Pilenko himself recalled, was astonished that the sympathies of the candidate for the position "lay with a Division forgotten by God, … ; this was where they pushed the disabled and injured". For the five years that Pilenko worked in the Ministry none of his co-workers knew that he was a lecturer at the University and Alexander Lycée. The secret was revealed only when Emperor Nicholas II chose on a visit to the Lycée to attend Pilenko's lecture and after the lecture stayed to converse with him, keeping him for an hour and a half.[223]

His active involvement in international matters quickly commenced. Soon after being hired, he was sent abroad in an official capacity and began to represent Russia at international conferences and organizations, acquiring an international reputation. In 1900 Pilenko participated in the organization of the Russian Section of the Universelle Exposition in Paris. Being from 1 April to 15 September 1900 one of four delegates in the Russian Section, he participated in the Fourth International Congress of Industrial Property that opened on 23 July 1900 (600 participants).[224]

Within the Congress, official representatives of States and jurists from industrially-developed countries drafted the 1883 Paris Convention on the Protection of Industrial Property, agreeing the basic concepts and norms of international and national patent law for the twentieth century. In the plenary addresses discussing the concept of "invention", the principal opponent of the draft being discussed was Pilenko:

> We call an invention not that which some new action or new effect produces, but that which a special, specific impulse of thought required from the author. A patent is given for this qualified work which they call a creation. A creation in the domain of science.[225]

[222] See Note 197 above, for 1915 (1916), p. 111.

[223] G. M. Zarubinskii and E. N. Stavinskii, «К 125-летию со дня рождения российского правоведа Александра Александровича Пиленко» [On the 125th Anniversary of the Russian Jurist Aleksandr Aleksandrovich Pilenko], Правоведение [Jurisprudence], no. 2 (1999), p. 53.

[224] Pilenko, Право изобретателя [Law of Inventor] (reprint ed.; 2001), pp. 25-26.

[225] Pilenko, Международные конгрессы 1900 г. [International Congresses of 1900] (1900), p. 23.

His position became the foundation of the formulation adopted by the Congress, evidence of Pilenko being recognized at a high international level.

Pilenko was the permanent representative of Russia attached to the International Bureau for Industrial and Literary Property in Bern, Switzerland, at the Bern Literary Bureau, and the British Lycée in London; he participated in eight international congresses: London, 1897; Vienna, 1897 on questions of industrial property; Paris, 1900, on author's right; and others on insurance of workers, comparative law, rights of women, and so on. At the International Congress on Author's Right in 1900, Pilenko was elected a Vice-President of the Congress.

After the defense of his magister dissertation in 1902, Pilenko participated actively in the commission of the Law Society attached to St. Petersburg University on the draft civil code, where he made a number of reports on author's right and patent law.

The Ministry of Foreign Affairs of Russia sent Pilenko in 1908 to the Bern Conference as the delegate of Russian for review of the Convention on the protection of author's right. He was the permanent representative of Russia during consultations with the Bern Bureau for Industrial and Literary Property.

Throughout his life, both in Russia and emigration, Pilenko avoided participation in political parties and movements. Only once in 1906 did he take part, and not for long, in the "Union 17 October" Party.

Role as International Journalist. In addition to his scholarly activities, Pilenko at an early age displayed a "passion" for journalism. As time passed, he devoted greater attention to journalism, and ultimately at the end of his life journalism became his principal calling. His first article, at his father's insistence – a naval officer, he wrote while at the gymnasium and published in Морской сборник [Maritime Collection], a journal founded in 1848 and attached to the Ministry of the Navy. The article appeared on 3 November 1887. Considered a professional journalist by the age of 21, he boldly polemicized on the pages of a Petersburg newspaper with the noted French writer, Émile Zola (1840-1902), on matters of literary conventions.

From 1900 Pilenko collaborated for many years with Suvorin, as noted above, and became a talented, well-known, influential journalist. Appointed the head of the foreign section of Новое время [New Time], Pilenko began from 1903 to write editorials three times weekly. The great majority of his articles were devoted to world politics and international law.

Pilenko's articles on international law and world politics comprise an substantial legacy, difficult to identify and record and awaiting a researcher. In 1915 alone, Pilenko said that he published more than 150 articles on foreign policy and international law in that newspaper.[226] Grabar wrote of his friend and colleague: "All his exceptional knowledge in the realm of general international law was brought to bear in these newspaper articles".[227]

226 See note 197 above for 1915 (1916), p. 111.

227 Grabar, note 46 above, p. 390.

In 1912 Pilenko traveled to Bulgaria, then at war with Turkey, as a military correspondent. On the basis of front notes "on the battlefield", he published in 1913 a book on the Bulgarian war.[228]

His services to the Russian Empire were highly esteemed. He was awarded the Orders of St. Anna III degree (1908) and II degree (1913); Saint Stanislav II degree (1911); and Saint Vladimir IV degree (1915).

Pilenko himself was a literary hero in at least two novels by Valentin Savvich Pikul (1928-1990) describing events and life in the early twentieth century.[229]

Pilenko in Emigration. Saving themselves from the calamities of the Civil War in Russia, Pilenko with his wife and children emigrated to Turkey (Constantinople) and then in October 1920 to Paris. While abroad, Pilenko devoted his principal creative efforts to journalism. Thanks to his international connections, he rapidly found the opportunity to draw upon his journalistic talents and became the head of the Foreign Affairs Section in a large Parisian publication, *L'Intransigeant*. During the 1930s, Pilenko was an active political journalist and printed articles in French and in Russian emigré publications. From time to time he engaged in political activities. He was a member in 1926 of the Organizing Committee to convene a Russia Abroad Congress in Paris (a congress of socio-political organizations of the Russian emigration in which the Russian diaspora from 26 countries took part). He favored the unification of all Russians abroad in order to collectively address the difficulties of emigration.

After the Second World War, Pilenko was an active participant in the movement for the return of emigrants and other compatriots to the former Soviet Union.

Pilenko did not abandon the teaching of law. He offered a course at the Russian Section of the Law Faculty of the University of Paris, delivering lectures on "Soviet International Law". His scholarly writings on international law were comparatively few: on the League of Nations, the Civil War in Spain, fascism in Italy and Germany, among others. Most of Pilenko's scholarly legacy dates from before the 1917 Revolution: "The good scholar perhaps left me, but having begun to work at Новое время [New Time] I could no longer seriously engage in science, and my research on the method of private international law ceased".[230]

Pilenko died at Paris on 21 March 1956.[231] For long years Pilenko was undeservedly forgotten in Russia: he neither recognized Soviet power nor fought against it; he simply was an émigré. Even the rare mentions of him in scholarly and reference literature contain factual inaccuracies (for example, the supposed

[228] Pilenko, Около Болгарской войны: Дневник и сорок девять любительских фотографий [On the Bulgarian War: Diary and Forty-Nine Amateur Photographs] (1913).

[229] V. S. Pikul, У последней черты [At the Last Frontier] (1978); Pikul, Честь имею [I Have the Honour] (1986).

[230] Zarubinskii and Stavinskii, note 223 above, p. 67.

[231] Pilenko was buried in the commune of Pantin, near Paris, but later, when the lease on the grave was not extended, his remains were moved to the Pere Lachaise Cemetery, and after cremation the ashes were reburied, probably in a common grave.

death penalty awaiting him should he return to Soviet Russia; flight through Poland while wounded; years of his death as 1920 or 1948, rather than the true date; and so on).

Only in the late twentieth and early twenty-first centuries did the name, life, and contributions of Pilenko attract the attention of specialists.[232] Zarubinskii and Stavinskii established reliable information about his life, family and learned writings. They were well placed to evaluate Pilenko's worth:

> He was an outstanding person who did so much in the field of law ... He left a shining legacy in the Russian press and did much for Petersburg and its urban economy. Indeed, this is sufficient to remember this individual with respect and gratitude.[233]

Pilenko was replaced in the Chair of International Law at St. Petersburg University by Baron Boris Nolde, also a protégé of F. F. Martens.

Baron **Boris Emmanuilovich Nolde** *(14 December 1876, b. St. Petersburg – 28 May 1948, d. Lausanne, Switzerland). International lawyer, legal scholar, diplomat, writer, public and political figure, among the most talented and productive students of F. F. Martens; learned in public and private international law, the history of Russia, State law, foreign policy and diplomatic history, and civil, trade, and maritime law.*

232 See Zarubinskii and Stavinskii, note 223 above, pp. 53-68, with bibliography of publications, pp. 69-73; Zarubinskii, «Рецензия на книгу А. А. Пиленко Право Изобретателя» [Review of A. A. Pilenko, Right of Inventor], Правоведение [Jurisprudence], no. 2 (1999), pp. 73-80; A. B. Zviagina, «Александр Александрович Пиленко. К 125-летию со дня рождения. Биобиблиографическое разыскание» [Aleksandr Aleksandrovich Pilenko. On the 125th Jubilee. Bio-Bibliographical Search], КЛИО: межвузовский журнал для ученых [KLIO: Inter-Educational Journal for Scholars], no. 1(1999), p. 316-325; Zarubinskii and Stavinskii, «Памяти профессора А. А. Пиленко – разработчика основ отечественного патентного и авторского права» [In Memory of Professor A. A. Pilenko – Draftsman of Foundations of Russian Patent and Author's Law], Интеллектуальная собственность. Промышленная собственность [Intellectual Property. Industrial Property], no. 8 (2001), pp. 70-76; Zarubinskii and Stavinskii, «Александр Александрович Пиленко: новые биографические данные» [Aleksandr Aleksandrovich Pilenko: New Biographical Data], Правоведение [Jurisprudence], no. 3 (2004), pp. 184-197; Zarubinskii and Stavinskii, А. А. Пиленко: научная деятельность и карьера [A. A. Pilenko: Scientific Activity and Career], Интеллектуальная собственность. Промышленная собственность [Intellectual Property. Industrial Property], no. 7 (2008), pp. 58-64; Starodubtsev, note 4 above, pp. 25, 26, 40, 42, 53-56, 58, 62, 64, 103, 116-118; E. V. Safronova and Iu. A. Komnatnaia, «История отечественной доктрины международного частного права: Александр Александрович Пиленко (1893-1956). К 140-летию со дня рождения» [History of Russian Doctrine of Private International Law: Aleksandr Aleksandrovich Pilenko (1873-1956). On the 140th Jubilee], Энциклопедия права [Encyclopedia of Law] (online); V. S. Ivanenko, "Aleksandr Pilenko: Founder of Internationalist Private International Law and Invention Law in Russia", *Jus Gentium: Journal of International Legal History*, V (2020), pp. 161-177.

233 G. Zarubinskii and E. Stavinskii, «Авторское право журналиста Пиленко» [Author's Right of Journalist Pilenko], Санкт-Петербургские ведомости [St. Petersburg Gazette], no. 144 (11 August 2001).

Life and career. Boris Nolde originated in a family of Russian Germans descended from nobility based in the Courland Governate,[234] the son of a distinguished Russian dignitary, member of the State Council of the Russian Empire, privy councilor, Baron Emmanuil Iulevich von Nolde (1854-1909).

In 1895 Boris Nolde graduated with the gold medal from the I Petersburg Gymnasium and that same year enrolled at the Law Faculty of St. Petersburg University.[235] He graduated in 1899 with a first-class diploma.[236] Accounts of the further life and professional career of Nolde are shrouded in many inaccuracies and errors of judgment. Even the dates of his emigration abroad are confused, being variously specified as 1918,[237] 1919,[238] and 1920.[239] The archives in St. Petersburg, including the formulary lists on the service of Nolde at the chairs of international law of St. Petersburg (or Petrograd) Polytechnic Institute, Petrograd University, and Alexander Lycée, and at the Ministry of Foreign Affairs, offer clarifications. According to the official archival documents, the details appear as follows.[240]

[234] See Dina Gusejnova, "Crusaders of Civility: The Legal Internationalism of the Baltic Barons", in Gusejnova, *European Elites and the Ideas of Empire, 1917-1957* (Cambridge, 2016), pp. 140-172. Also see for details on Nolde, A. A. Matyshev, Энциклопедия репрессированных авторов. 1917-1987. Биобиблиография советской трагедии [Encyclopedia of Repressed Authors. 1917-1987. Bio-Bibliography of a Soviet Tragedy] (Spb., 2023), X, pp. 544-554.

[235] ЦГИА СПб., fond 14, opis 3, file 31664.

[236] He also was awarded a gold medal in 1898 for an essay on "The Political Doctrine of J.-J. Rousseau". ЦГИА СПб., fond 14, opis 3, file 14344, l. 52.

[237] See, for example, V. V. Zhurvalev (ed.), Общественная мысль Русского зарубежья: энциклопедия [Social Thought of the Russia Abroad: Encyclopedia] (M., 2008), p. 457.

[238] O. Korostelev (ed.), Диаспора: новые материалы [The Diaspora: New Materials] (Spb./Paris, 2007), VIII, p. 528.

[239] O. N. Sadikov, «Из истории юридической науки в России: барон Б. Э. Нольде» [From the History of Legal Science in Russia: Baron B. E. Nolde (1876-1948)], Государство и право [State and Law], no. 1 (2002), p. 92.

[240] ЦГИА СПб., fond 14, opis 2, file 1391; ЦГА СПб., fond 3121, opis 12, file 484; ЦГИА СПб., fond 14, opis 2, file 1391, l. 79-85observe; ЦГИА СПб., fond 11, opis 1, file 3843, l. 6-12. Also see P. Holquist, "Dilemmas of a Progressive Administrator: Baron Boris Nolde", *Kritika*, VII (2006), p. 241-273; Holquist, "Dilemmas of an 'Official with Progressive Views' – Baron Boris Nolde", *Baltic Yearbook of International Law*, VII (2007), pp. 211-249; Starodubtsev, note 4 above, pp. 15, 17, 18, 25, 26, 27, 40, 46, 53-55, 58, 60-62, 64, 89-91, 93, 94, 99-101, 103, 117, 118, 122-124, 127, 134,, 138, 164-168, 209, 210, 248.

After completing university, by Order of the Ministry of Foreign Affairs of 2 July 1899 Nolde was hired from 16 June in the Ministry, assigned to the First Department, and confirmed in the rank of college secretary. In parallel, Nolde on the basis of a petition of the Faculty and the University remained by instruction of the Administrator of the Petersburg Educational District from 1 November 1899 to 1 November 1901 attached to the Faculty of International Law in order to write a magister dissertation under the supervision of Professor F. F. Martens and prepare for the professoriate. He was awarded a stipend of 600 rubles from a philanthropic source bequeathed to the University by a Russian industrialist, Pavel Pavlovich Demidov (1839-1885).[241]

In the summer of 1901 Nolde passed the magister examinations.[242] From 1 September 1901 he was sent abroad for two years to prepare for the professoriate; he worked in libraries and visited lectures in universities at Berlin, Paris, Brussels, and Zurich. Upon his return, by Order of the Ministry of Foreign Affairs of 12 November 1902 he was made a titular counselor (retroactively, from 16 June 1902) "for years of service". By Order of the same Ministry of 19 August 1903 Nolde was appointed a chief clerk, eighth class, in the First Department of the Ministry, and from September 1903, a court counsellor.

Following the usual Russian practice of simultaneous appointments, the Council of the St. Petersburg Polytechnic Institute on 31 March 1903 elected Nolde to the post of docent in the Chair of International Law, and by order of the Ministry of Finances (which had jurisdiction over the said Institute), on 12 September 1903 Nolde took the aforesaid post in the Institute while continuing to work in the Ministry of Foreign Affairs.[243]

On 15 May 1905 Nolde defended his dissertation for the degree of magister of international law at the University on the topic "Permanently Neutral State",[244] and on 27 May the degree of magister of international law was conferred by the Council of the University. By an Order of the Ministry of Trade and Industry of 9

241 ЦГИА СПб., fond 14, opis 2, file 1391.

242 The questions Nolde was required to answer on the magister examination are of interest. He took the examination on 19 March 1901 at a session of the Law Faculty:

1) Treaty relations between Russia and England from the time of Catherine II;
2) On mutual judicial assistance of States;
3) On the right of private ownership during wartime.

On 12 November 1901 he sat the examination on State law, answering the following questions:

1) John Locke;
2) Structure and competence of union organs of the North American United States;
3) Committee of Ministers.

His answers on international law and State law were deemed to be satisfactory. See T. Loginova, История становления и развития кафедры международного права Санкт-Петербургского университета в 1819-1903 г.г. [History of the Origin and Development of the Chair of International Law of St. Petersburg University in 1819-1903] (Spb., 2004), pp. 125-126. On 21 March 1901 Martens deemed Nolde's essay "On Cartel Conventions" to be satisfactory. ЦГИА СПб., fond 14, opis 3, file 14350, l. 115-117.

243 ЦГИА СПб., fond 3121, opis 12, file 484, l. 27-31.

244 The official opponents at the defense were Professors F. F. Martens and M. A. Taube.

December 1905, Nolde was appointed professor *extraordinarius* from 1 November 1905 at the Chair of International Law of St. Petersburg Polytechnic Institute.[245] Together with work at the Polytechnic Institute, Nolde lectured from 1908 to 1917 in the post of professor at the Higher (Bestuzhev) Women's Courses, and from 1908, he taught the encyclopedia of law; between 1912 and 1914 Nolde was professor *extraordinarius* of international law at the Alexander Lycée.[246] He also lectured at the Marine Academy.

At the Ministry of Foreign Affairs, his career path went from college secretary and clerk to the highest executive positions in the Ministry.[247] From 1907 to 1914 he was as assistant secretary of State and jurisconsult at the Ministry. On 15 July 1908 he was appointed an official on special assignments, VI class, attached to the Ministry of Foreign Affairs. From 1 November 1909 he became State Counsellor by reason of years of service. In 1914 his career changed for the better because of reforms within the Ministry which led to the creation of a Jurisconsult Unit by direction of Emperor Nicholas II, who appointed Nolde to head the new unit.[248] He was made a privy State counsellor.

During the First World War, Nolde was the legal advisor of the Ministry of Foreign Affairs from May 1916 to March 1917 – the Director of the Second (Consular) Department of the Ministry of Foreign Affairs. He was among those who initiated the founding and served as the permanent editor-in-chief of the printed organ of the Ministry of Foreign Affairs – the Известия Министерства иностранных дел [News of the Ministry of Foreign Affairs] – from 1912 to 1917, issued bimonthly and an invaluable source on the history and practice of international law.[249]

Nolde engaged in public service and philanthropic activities. He was, for example, a member of the Board of the St. Petersburg Peace Society and a member of the Administration of the Free Women's A. G. Eliseev Needlework School.[250]

A distinguished public and political figure, Nolde was a liberal, an active member of the Central Committee of the Constitutional-Democratic Party (People's Freedom Party – the so-called Cadet Party). When World War I broke out, he was one of the authors of the Appeal to the Poles which contained a promise to grant autonomy to Poland after the end of the War; the Appeal was published

[245] ЦГИА СПб., fond 3121, opis 12, file 484, l. 43-43ob.

[246] ЦГИА СПб., fond 11, opis 1, file 3843.

[247] Nolde's leading role in the difficult years from 1914 to 1917 is well reflected in the memoirs of his subordinate and colleague, Georgii Nikolaevich Mikhailovskii (1890-1946). See G. N. Mikhailovskii, Записки. Из истории российского внешнеполитического ведомства 1914-1920 [Notes: On the History of the Russian Foreign Policy Department 1914-1920] (M., 1993). 2 vols.

[248] ЦГИА СПб., fond 14, opis 2, file 1391, l. 85.

[249] ЦГИА СПб., fond 706, opis 1, file 1158.

[250] See «Благотворительное общество «Помощь детям рабочих Санкт-Петербурга» [Philanthropic Society "Assistance to Children of Workers of St. Petersburg], Энциклопедия благотворительности. Санкт-Петерург [Encyclopedia of Philanthropy. St. Petersburg] (available online).

on 1(14) August 1914 in the name of the Supreme Commander in Chief, Grand Duke Nikolai Nikolaevich (1856-1929). Nolde, together with Vladimir Dmitrevich Nabokov (1870-1922) and Vasilii Vital'evich Shulgin (1878-1976), drew up the historical act of 16 March 1917 by which Grand Duke Mikhail Aleksandrovich Romanov (1878-1918), the younger brother of Emperor Nicholas II, refused to take the throne following the abdication of Nicholas II and transferred all power to the future Constitutive Assembly (in accordance with the Act, the reign of the Romanov dynasty came to an end in Russia).

Following the February 1917 Revolution, Nolde's talents as a scholar and international lawyer were needed by the Provisional Government. Appointed Deputy Minister of Foreign Affairs (14 March-20 May 1917), he was in charge of the complex negotiations with the Finnish side concerning the national self-determination of Finland. In addition, during this period he was given work in the collegial organs attached to the Provisional Government: on 22 March 1917 by Edict of the Provisional Government he was appointed a member of the legal board attached to the Government;[251] in April 1917 he was appointed a member by the Provisional Government of the Special Board for preparing a draft Statute on Elections to the Constituent Assembly (he was chairman of the sub-commission for developing an Instruction for elections in the army, navy, and Finland). In September 1917 Nolde favored beginning separate negotiations with Germany to bring an end to the War and conclude a peace treaty.

Late in the days of the Provisional Government, Nolde became a member of the Provisional Council (Parliament) of the Russian Republic (October-November 1917) and of the Commission for the Investigation of the Activity of Tsarist Ministers, among others.

Nolde was able to return to Petrograd University only in the spring of 1917 at the initiative of the University itself. On 20 March 1917 the Council of the University elected Nolde professor *extraordinarius* at the Chair of International Law. On 7 April 1917 the Department of Public Enlightenment confirmed the decision of the University Council and appointed Nolde to the said post "with retention of the posts occupied".[252] The Rector of the University informed Nolde of this decision on 12 April 1917.[253] Nolde by this appointment replaced A. A. Pilenko. He undertook the University position while simultaneously working at the Polytechnic Institute. In addition, he worked at the III Petrograd University, the Marine Academy, and the Petrograd Commercial Institute.[254]

Nolde opposed the October 1917 Revolution. On 23 November 1917 he was arrested as an active member of the All-Russian Commission for Elections to the Constitutive Assembly. The Learned Council of the University and the Adminis-

[251] Вестник Временного правительства [Herald of the Provisional Government] no. 25 (7 April 1917), p. 1.

[252] Ibid.

[253] ЦГИА СПб., fond 14, opis 2, file 1391, l. 12.

[254] ЦГИА СПб., fond 2898, opis 1, file 572; ЦГА СПб., fond 3121, opis 12, file 484, l. 73.

tration of the Polytechnic Institute actively protested his arrest;[255] after four days Nolde was released. His second arrest lasted ten days.

In spring 1918 Nolde joined an anti-Soviet organization, the "Right Center". He spoke in support of cooperation between anti-Soviet forces of Russia and Germany against Soviet power. All sources assert that Nolde in the summer of 1919 illegally emigrated to Finland. The archival materials show otherwise. In May 1919 Nolde, holding the post of professor of the Chair of Private International Law of the Economics Faculty of the I Petrograd Polytechnic Institute, was sent by the Council of the Institute "for a scholarly purpose in summer vacation time of 1919 to Sweden in order to work in libraries and archives with regard to issues connected with completing an extensive work on private international law".[256] Nolde did not return. On 16 September 1919 the Dean of the Economics Faculty of the Polytechnic Institute informed the Pro-Rector for Instructional Affairs of the Institute by letter that "Professor B. E. Nolde had not arrived at the Institute in order to renew instructional lessons".[257]

Nolde remained on the personnel establishment of Petrograd University significantly longer. According to archival data, Nolde remained in the post of professor, occupying the Chair of International Law, until summer 1920.[258] Nolde was removed only from 1 July 1920 by the Board of the University on the basis of a submission of the Dean of the Faculty of Social Sciences that Nolde had not "appeared to perform his duties in the trimester that had elapsed".[259] Thus, Nolde was *de facto* in emigration from summer 1919.

International legal views. Nolde made a significant contribution to the science of international law. The words "for the first time in Russia" are associated many times with the name Boris Nolde. In the field of public international law he was the first in Russia to undertake an analysis of the status of the permanently neutral State. In the field of private international law he was the author of the first specialized fundamental works on the history of the development of the Russian science of private international law; he attempted to compose a Digest of Russian conflicts law.

[255] On 26 November 1917 at an emergency session, the Council of the University unanimously rejected the policy of Soviet power, declared support for the preparation of a Constitutive Assembly, and protested against the arrest of members of the All-Russian Commission for Elections to the Constitutive Assembly and of lecturers of the University, Professor B. E. Nolde and privat-docent P. P. Gronskii. ЦГИА СПб., fond 7240, opis 14, file 1. The Rector and other executives of the Polytechnic Institute, in an urgent appeal to the Chairman of the Petrograd Soviet, Zinov'ev, "most zealously petitioned for the release of Professor Nolde", an "outstanding scholar", in "the interests of the Institute and science". ЦГИА СПб., fond 3121, opis 12, file 484, l. 77.

[256] The certificate was issued by the Institute on 10 May 1919. ЦГИА СПб., fond 3121, opis 12, file 484, l. 77

[257] Ibid.

[258] See the List of Personnel for the Instructional Unit of the I Petrograd University, 15 April 1919, Unified Archive of St. Petersburg State University, fond 1, opis 1, file 141, l. 14ob.

[259] ЦГА СПб., fond 7240, opis 14, file 134. See the Protocol 24, 1 June 1920, l. 125ob.

In 1905 Nolde published his best-known treatise on the permanently neutral State, one of his most cited works.[260] This published volume served as his dissertation for the degree of magister of international law; the defense was held on 15 May 1905. His official opponents were Professors F. F. Martens and M. A. Taube. In his review of the dissertation, Martens wrote:

> The study of Baron Nolde on permanently neutral States … has as its task to give a detailed picture of the historical process of a new type of international personality which arose in the nineteenth century – the permanently neutral State in the person of Switzerland, Krakow, Belgium, Luxembourg, and the Congo, analyze dogmatically why this type arose and on this basis … to review the doctrines on persons in international law, identify the main characteristic features of the legal nature of the permanently neutral State as a completely special type of phenomenon within the group of subjects of international law … Structured on a careful study of all that may be collected on the special question of interest to him both in legal and in general historical literature, relying partly on independent archival searches of the author, the study by Baron Nolde deserves attention also in the sense of the general basic questions of the theory of international law. The author suggests using new resolutions thereof which do not lack interest, introducing in his study a number of problems … forming, together with the subject-matter of his topic, a structured and well thought out general system. These merits of the dissertation by docent Baron Nolde gave me the right to request the Law Faculty to deem the said work as worthy of the learned degree of magister of international law.[261]

Nolde boldly criticized the state of the science of international law in the introductory passages of his treatise: “it is barren in two respects: first, often it works on sparse, long since reworked and explained materials … second, the science of international law has few logically-constructed conclusions” (pp. iii-v).

The merit of Nolde’s work is that he considered the status of neutral States (Belgium, Congo, Krakow, Luxembourg, and Switzerland) during an era of constant wars when the problem was highly topical. He regarded these as a “new type of international personality”, described their legal nature as a special kind of subject of international law, and in passing expressed a number of original views on certain basic questions of the theory of international law. He offered a definition of permanent neutrality which is frequently cited in legal and political literature: he regarded “permanent neutrality” as the “aggregate of legal relations connecting several States and creating rights and duties, first, for that State which is called permanently neutral and, second, for other States” (p. 450).

Nolde analyzed the category “State sovereignty” in what he called the “international legal sense”. He singled out two aspects of sovereignty – internal sovereignty and external sovereignty. Having considered the views of scholars, he noted the extraordinary understandings “of the functions of the concept of sov-

260 B. E. Nolde, Постоянно нейтральное государство [The Permanently Neutral State] (Spb., 1905). Butler H160.

261 ЦГИА СПб., fond 14, opis 3, file 14325, l. 22-29.

ereignty: for some, this is a property of the State, for others – the right of a State, for yet others, the prerequisite of its independence, and for yet others again – the aggregate of rights". Taking the view that the principal indicator of sovereignty is independence, Nolde modelled possible situations in international treaty relations of an "independent sovereign State" and a "dependent non-sovereign State". He ultimately concluded that in the international legal sense, the legal difference between them is expressed in the extent of legal capacity (pp. 609-610).

Nolde's conclusion that the status of a permanently-neutral State entails a limitation of sovereignty is a curious one. He said: a neutral State "possesses not full legal capacity, but a limited legal capacity". This is manifest in the fact that it is limited in the "right to war" (*jus ad bellum*) belonging to it as an international person. And the question is put: "Does it follow from this that it is not sovereign?" (p. 613), because "unlimited sovereignty is the possibility to possess the entire sum of international subjective rights" (p. 611), including the "right to war". But inasmuch as any State has been given the right to wage war, and a neutral State is limited in this right, then it possesses not full, but limited, legal capacity. Nolde wrote when doctrine and practice recognized for a State the unlimited "right to war" as the most important element of its sovereignty.

As the articles published by him attest, Nolde was interested in other theoretical and practical aspects of general international law, ranging from the methodology of the science[262] to concrete problems of international legal theory and practice.[263] Nolde also attached special importance to the increasing institutionalization of the international system of justice.[264] In his article on inter-State courts in recent international treaties, he classified and analyzed the international legal positions of States relating to the subject-matter, forms, and means for the settlement of inter-State disputes; these positions had been consolidated in bilateral treaties. In these treaties, States clarified their international legal obligations assumed as parties to the 1899 Hague Convention for the Pacific Settlement of International Disputes, as added to by the 1907 Convention.

262 Nolde, «Метода науки международного права» [Method of the Science of International Law], Право [Law], no. 20 (1905), cols. 1646-1651. Butler H147.

263 See, for example, Nolde, «Вторая конференция мира» [Second Peace Conference: Survey], Вестник Европы [Herald of Europe], no. 4 (1908), pp. 461-490 (Butler H111); Nolde, «Босфор и Дарданеллы» [Bosphorus and the Dardenelles], Русская мысль [Russian Thought], no. 4 (1911), pp. 1-22 (Butler H103); Nolde, «Панамский канал и международное право» [Panama Canal and International Law], Известия Министерства иностранных дел [News of the Ministry of Foreign Affairs], no. 2 (1913), pp. 160-195 (Butler H157); Nolde, «Будущее Международного третейского суда» [Future of the International Arbitration Court], Право [Law], no. 7 (1910), pp. 343-351 (Butler H104); Nolde, «Законодательная санкция международных договоров в России» [Legislative Sanction of International Treaties in Russia], Право [Law], no. 46 (1906), cols. 3561-3573 (Butler H120).

264 See, for example, Nolde, «Третейское решение по Казабланкскому делу» [Arbitral Award in the Casablanca Case], Право [Law], no. 34 (1909), cols. 1817-1825; no. 35 (1909), cols. 1881-1886 (Butler H170); Butler H104, note 141 above; Nolde, «Межгосударственный суд в новейших международных договорах» [Inter-State Court in Recent International Treaties], Право [Law], no. 29 (1912), cols. 1525-1541 (Butler H146).

The basis of Nolde's theoretical analysis and practical conclusions was a collection of the said treaties concluded between 1899 and 1910.[265] The publication of this collection, in Nolde's view, "gives occasion to dwell on eliciting how the judicial resolution of international disputes is ensured at the present time".[266] Nolde's analysis of the bilateral conventions enabled him to conclude that those treaties were directed towards filling gaps in the two Hague conventions of 1899 and 1907 providing for the creation of an arbitration court but not establishing a binding judicial means to settle disputes. The bilateral treaties went further and began to consolidate an obligation to refer disputes for consideration by arbitration courts. In Nolde's view, "in the near future a thread of conventions concerning a binding arbitration court will extend to all contemporary States" (col. 1527). To be sure, Nolde was critical of this new international legal institution, for he believed it was not fully responsive to the tasks of creating a real organ of inter-State justice. He pointed out that the permanent chamber of the arbitration court was merely a list of qualified jurists submitted by States from which the States in dispute choose in the event a concrete dispute arises between members of the arbitration court. Therefore, arbitration courts are merely provisional international courts *ad hoc*.

In this article Nolde undertook primarily a comparative-legal analysis of the major provisions consolidated in various types of conventions: the subject-matter of a dispute, competence of arbitral courts, procedure for adopting and the content of decisions to be adopted, and the like.

Despite Nolde's critical attitude towards the relevant international treaties in force and the international arbitral courts formed on the basis of those treaties, on the whole he was optimistic (even excessively so), expressing the hope that a judicial system would come to replace military means for dispute settlement and ensure a completely different peaceful character to inter-State relations: "With the establishment of the dominance of the idea of a court in international relations, there will be an enormous upheaval in human life. Whereas tomorrow any international dispute will be decided not factually as the great majority of such disputes are decided now, but by means of recourse to a court, then the old international order will die away, with all its characteristic features". This will lead to a cardinal restructuring of the entire system of relations between States into a "new model; ministries of foreign affairs will be restructured, chiefly, into legal agencies; foreign policy will remain, but be filled with completely new content; gradually the need for an army and navy will fall away" (col. 1527). The provisional arbitration courts will undertake not only the important task of settling international disputes, but also perform a psychological function of no small importance: "The legal consciousness of contemporary mankind is becoming accustomed, thanks to arbitration conventions and the practice of their application, to the idea of the existence of some sort of 'Hague court', which was" in the view of Nolde, a rather significant step in the direction of forming a real permanent international court (col. 1541).

Especially significant were Nolde's services in the field of private international law. He was the author of the first fundamental work in Russia on conflicts of law.

[265] See *Traités généraux d'arbitrage communiqués au Bureau international de la Cour Permanente d'Arbitrage. Prémerie série* (The Hague, 1911). xvi, 392 p.

[266] H146, note 141 above, col. 1525.

His name is linked with the first attempt to systematize Russian conflicts norms of an international orientation, and he was the first in the Russian legal doctrine of private international law to introduce a number of new legal categories. Still valuable is Nolde's "Survey of Private International Law". At the invitation of V. E. Grabar, who was translating and editing the Russian edition of the standard European treatise on public international law by Franz E. von Liszt (1851-1919), Nolde added the survey to complement the volume; he followed basically the structure previously suggested by his predecessor in the Chair of International Law, A. A. Pilenko: "Basic Concepts"; "General Doctrines"; "Persons"; "Rights to a Thing"; "Law of Obligations"; "Family Law"; "Inheritance"; and Procedure". Just as Pilenko had done, Nolde understood private international law to be conflicts of law, and he preferred this last term to "private international law". Several generations of Russian jurists were introduced to public and private international law through Liszt, including well into the 1920s.[267]

That Nolde should have regarded private international law as conflicts of law in that period was a widely shared approach. The international legal regulation of private law relations was underdeveloped. Conflicts of law issues were encountered in practice by Russian jurists of that period, and they required theoretical analysis and substantiation, not least because they arose frequently within Russia. The Digest of Laws of the Russian Federation, published from 1832 onwards, contained legal rules of foreign origin, particularly legislative acts adopted or inherited in the borderlands of Russia: for example, the Code Napoleon in Poland; Swedish legislation in Finland; legislation in the Baltic provinces based on Polish and Swedish antecedents, Roman law and local city statutes, the Lithuanian Statute which was used when compiling the 1649 Sobornoe ulozhenie and had status in the Chernihiv and Poltava provinces, and customary law in Crimea, the Caucasus, and Central Asia. Conflicts of law occurred frequently. Nolde wrote:

> The question of conflicts of civil laws of different States is merely part of a more general question of the conflict in general of civil laws from various places … It is evident that conflicts between the civil legislation of individual parts of the same State may be resolved only by the domestic law of that State … But if one takes only conflicts purely international in origin, then here conflicts norms rather often turn out to be resting exclusively on the domestic law of individual States (pp. 465-467).

Referring to the inaccuracy of the term "private international law", Nolde noted that this title would have been justified if "first, the conflicts of civil legislation always were of an international character … and, second, the resolution of conflicts were given by international law in the strict sense of the word, that is, by international treaties or by customs, but not by the internal law of individual States". But Nolde was a realist: proceeding from the realities of the time, when international treaty and customary law regulation of transnational private-law relations was insignificant, he wrote: "In fact, the matter is otherwise". Practice showed that "for the most part, the resolution of conflicts is not by international law, but by the

[267] See Nolde, "Survey of Private International Law", in F. Liszt, Международное право в систематическом изложении [International Law in Systematic Exposition], ed. V. E. Grabar (2d ed.; Iurev, 1909), pp. 451-581; republished in 1912, 1917, and again in 1923 and 1926. Butler Л84.

domestic law of individual States" (pp. 462, 465). Therefore, on the basis of the foregoing, Nolde believed:

> It would be more correct to speak of conflicts law rather than private international law. If, nonetheless, we retain this term, … then merely as a certain kind of program for future development. There is no doubt … that the principal purpose which serves the elimination of conflicts of civil laws of individual States may be successfully achieved only by means of the creation of international norms in the formal sense of the word … The term 'private international law' therefore would serve as a call to the international codification of conflicts of law (p. 468).

With regard to the problem of understanding the essence of conflicts norms, Nolde formulated his position as follows:

> What does any conflicts norm signify? It expresses the conviction of the legislator that a certain legal relation is most closely linked by a particular consideration with a certain foreign system of civil law; when a conflicts norm says, for example, that dispositive legal capacity is determined according to the national law of a person, it is thereby recognized that national legislation better than all others may indicate when the person is made capable to conclude legal transactions (p. 490).

For the first time in the Russian science of private international law, Nolde pointed to the approaches that might be used when seeking objective criteria for determining the applicable law. When noting the close link between applicable law and relations complicated by a foreign element which is provided by the presence of a conflicts norm, he came to the following conclusion:

> Any conflicts norm is a response to the question of which of the material civil laws from various places is to be applied to a particular category of legal relations consisting of international (or inter-regional) elements; this response is given by recognition of the binding force for those laws with which the particular category of legal relations is linked by one of its international (or inter-regional) elements in the view of the said conflicts system (p. 483).

Nolde was among the first in Russian doctrine to consider topical issues of private international law as a structure of conflicts norms, choice of jurisdiction and law, circulation of bills of exchange, extra-contractual obligations, and many others. He also was the first to introduce into Russian private international legal doctrine the categories of "international element" and formula of attachment" (p. 492). The merit of his "survey", noted Mark Moiseevich Boguslavskii (1924-2017), was a successful attempt to devise a "digest of Russian conflicts norms" at a high level. In concentrated form, Nolde set out his approach in the article on "Private International Law" in volume 26 of the Brockhaus-Efron new encyclopedic dictionary. One specialist credited Nolde with being the "genuine creator of the terminological and methodological apparatus of the Russian science of private international law".[268]

268 A. I. Abdullin, Очерки истории науки международного частного права в России [Survey of

In his writings, Nolde aspired to maximum accuracy and reliability: "Instead of a deceptive 'pragmatism', there is seen only a precise description of everything important in what actually occurred. Such a description is the first key to history: what was is the best explanation of why it happened".[269]

The author of treatises, monographs, and articles in Russia and abroad – a full bibliography of which has yet to be undertaken, Nolde was awarded an honorary LL.D. in 1916 by Cambridge University.[270]

International legal practitioner. Nolde was extensively involved in the practice of international law. Following the example of his teacher and mentor, F. F. Martens, Nolde combined lecturing with legal practice. At the Ministry of Foreign Affairs, Nolde successively moved from a minor administrative clerical position to becoming one of the authoritative leaders of the Ministry. He served in the central apparatus of the Ministry and took part in several important international conferences: the 1907 Second Hague Peace Conference (secretary of the Conference),[271] 1908/1909 London Naval Conference to determine the rules for warfare at sea, the Russian/Swedish/Norwegian conferences in Christiana (Oslo) on the Spitsbergen archipelago between 1910 and 1912,[272] the Washington D. C. conference on the protection of fur seals (1911), and the Paris Balkan Financial Commission (1913), among others. Together with others, he was the co-author of the Appeal to the Poles with a promise to grant autonomy to Poland after the War ended; this was published on 1(14) August 1914 in the name of the Supreme Commander in Chief of All the Land and Sea Forces of the Russian Empire.

In 1914 Nolde was elected to membership as a representative of Russia on the Permanent Court of International Arbitration, where he acted as an arbitrator on several occasions. Within the Russian Government, he served as a permanent chairman of an inter-departmental meeting on naval warfare attached to the Ministry of Foreign Affairs.[273]

Nolde was involved in drafting legislation. He was the principal author of the draft law on a consular court; one of his predecessors in the Chair of International Law at the University, Mikhail Aleksandrovich Taube (1869-1961), together with

the History of the Science of Private International Law in Russia] (Kazan, 2004), p. 55.

269 Nolde, Внешняя политика [Foreign Policy: Historical Essays] (Pg., 1915), p. 4.

270 G. N. Mikhailovskii, Записки. Из истории российского внешнеполитического ведомства, 1914-1920 [Notes. From the History of the Foreign Policy Department. 1914-1920] (M., 1993), II, p. 172.

271 In 1908 Nolde was awarded the Legion of Honor by the French Government for his involvement in the Second Hague Peace Conference; he wore this honor in pride for the remainder of his days.

272 A. S. Kasian, «А. Н. Крупенский и Б. Э. Нольде – российские делегаты на переговорах по Шпицбергенскому вопросу в Христиании (Норвегия, 1910-1912 годы)» [A. N. Krupenskii and B. E. Nolde – Russian Delegates at Negotiations Relating to the Spitsbergen Question in Christiana (Norway, 1910-1912)], Скандинавские чтения 2010 года. Этнографические и культурно-исторические аспекты. Сборник статей [Scandinavian Readings 2010. Ethnographic and Cultural-Historical Aspects. Collection of Articles] (Spb., 2012).

273 Mikhailovskii, note 147 above, I, p. 17.

Professors Petr Evgenevich Kazanskii (1868-1947) and Vladimir Emmanuilovich Grabar (1865-1956), among others, took part in discussions of the draft.[274]

Grabar wrote of Nolde:

> His life to a great extent followed the pattern which his teacher, F. F. Martens, had laid down. An eminent scholar, he was at the same time a practical diplomat. In science he, like Martens, was a theoretician of international law and a historian of Russian diplomacy. As a theoretician, he was in one respect broader than Martens – international private law engaged him just as much as general international law. Moreover, his range of interests also included Russian State law.[275]

Nolde in emigration. The full story of Nolde's life in emigration has yet to be documented.[276] In the summer of 1919 Nolde took a business trip to Sweden, but went instead, or in addition, to Finland. There he took part in the name of the government of Admiral Aleksandr Vasilevich Kolchak (1874-1920) in negotiations with the Government of Finland on assisting the White movement. After a comparatively brief period in Finland, he moved on to Paris. By the mid-1920s he had mostly withdrawn from émigré politics, but did become active in the Russia Abroad. He lectured at The Hague Academy of International Law in 1924, 1929, 1932, and 1936 and became the Dean of the Law Faculty at the Slavic Institute in Paris and an organizer of the Russian division at the University of Paris.

In Paris he delivered a course of lectures, "Introduction to Russian Public Law" at the Institute of Russian Law attached to the Sorbonne, and another on "Institutions of Russian Public Law" at the Legal Division of the Russian Academic Group, together with lectures at the French-Slavic Society, the Russian People's University, the Russian Law Society, the Abroad Higher Military-Scientific Courses, Courses relating to Russian history and literature attached to the Russian Academic Group, among others.

He headed several émigré organizations of the Russia Abroad or served on their executive organs: Chairman of the Constitutive Assembly (1920) and an active member of the Russian Society for the Defense of the League of Nations (Paris); Chairman of the émigré chief administration of the Russian Red Cross Society (Paris, 1927 to 1948). He was elected Chairman of the Law Society in Paris and Chairman of the Permanent Committee of Russian Jurists Abroad (from 1922). He acted as a member of the board of the Russian Academic Group, member of the

[274] See E. V. Safronova, «Историческое развитие консульской юриспруденции и организация консульских судов России на Востоке» [Historical Development of Consular Jurisdiction and Organization of Consular Courts of Russia in the East], «Черные дыры» в Российском законодательстве ["Black Holes" in Russian Legislation], no. 3 (2002), pp. 509-510.

[275] Grabar, note 46 above, p. 436.

[276] Some details are given in M. V. Vishniac, «Б. Э. Нольде» [B. E. Nolde], Новая жизнь [New Life], no. 19 (New York, 1948), pp. 279-289; I. I. Tkhorzhevskii, «Памяти Нольде» [In Memory of Nolde], Русская мысль [Russian Thought], no. 60 (Sofia, 1948), p. 3; Российское зарубежье во Франции. 1919-2000: Биографический словарь [Russia Abroad in France. 1919-2000: Biographical Dictionary] (Moscow, 2008), II, p. 308; Starodubtsev, note 4 above, pp. 164-168.

Central Bureau of the Committee of Congresses of Russian Jurists Abroad, and a member of the Council of Professors of the Russian Institute of Historical and Legal Sciences. He joined a number of other émigré organizations, among them the Russian Trade-Industrial and Financial Union, the Association of Russian Advokats, the Committee for the Coordination of Philanthropic and Humanitarian Organizations, the Franco-Russian Committee for Education, and more. In 1925 he became the co-founder and co-publisher of the journal Право и хозяйство [Law and Economy].

In addition to his Hague lectures, Nolde published extensively on public and private international law, Russian history, and diplomatic history. These included an article on the League of Nations[277] and participation in a monumental treatise on Russian commercial law when an improvement in foreign trade seemed to be promising.[278] Twice Nolde was awarded a coveted literary prize by the French Académie des sciences morales et politiques: in 1928 for *L'ancien régime et la revolution russe* and in 1936 for *L'alliance franco-russe*. He collaborated with several émigré and French journals: Возрождение [Renaissance], Современные записки [Contemporary Notes], *La Revue des études slaves*.

During the German occupation of France from 1940 to 1944 he retired to his estate in the Department of Sart, collaborated with the French resistance, and after the liberation of France was decorated with the Legion of Honor. In 1944 Nolde was appointed to the Council of Former Russian Ambassadors in Paris.

He was elected to the Institute of International Law in 1912, and in 1947 elected as Chairman of the Institute. He passed away on 28 May 1948 in Lausanne, Switzerland.

Contemporary Russian international lawyers assessing the contributions of Nolde have written:

> B. E. Nolde was a scholar, as is sometimes said, by the Grace of God. He was a first-class jurist, knew several languages, possessed a sharp analytical mind, extensive knowledge, and a lively interest in and "taste" for the problems of law. He wrote beautifully, simply, concisely, in elegant language … He was a first-class historian of ideas, diplomatic relations, social movements, and the lives of individual public figures and thinkers. And Nolde was a very productive writer. He not only had a command of his craft and was an excellent stylist, he loved it: he wrote books and articles in specialized and in general journals, not refraining from articles in newspapers.[279]

[277] Nolde, «Лига народов и международное право» [League of Nations and International Law], Современные записки [Contemporary Notes], no. 1 (1920), pp. 232-235.

[278] V. B. Eliashevich, B. E. Nolde, and Paul Tager, *Traité de droit civil et commercial des soviets* (Paris, 1930). 3 vols. In that same year he published: Nolde, Далекое и близкое [Far and Near] (Paris, 1930).

[279] See A. N. Zhiltsov and A. I. Muranov, «Вклад знаменитиых российских юристов-эмигрантов А. Н. Макарова и Б. Э. Нольде в изучение международного частного права и его национальных кодификаций» [Contribution of Noted Russian Émigré Jurists A. N. Makarov and B. E. Nolde to the Study of Private International Law and the National Codifications Thereof], Международное право

Nolde was the last of Martens' protégés to hold the Chair of International Law at St. Petersburg University. With his emigration abroad, the golden era of international law during the prerevolutionary period came to an end. His remarkable personal library remained in Russia after his emigration.[280]

§7.2. *Members of Chair of International Law*

§7.2.1. *Privat-Docents of Chair: Graduates of St. Petersburg University*

Aleksandr Lvovich Baikov *(30 April 1874, b. St. Petersburg – 31 December 1943, d. Paris, France). Legal scholar who wrote on the philosophy of law and international law.*

Life and career. Aleksandr Baikov studied from 1891 to 1895 at the Imperial School of Jurisprudence in St. Petersburg. Upon graduating, he took a position in the Ministry of Justice and was sent abroad by instruction of the Kyiv Judicial Chamber. A year later he was transferred to the Department of General Affairs of the Ministry.

Later in 1896 he transferred to the Ministry of Foreign Affairs, first to the Department of Internal Affairs and then to the Foreign Department. He worked as an interpreter, then in an executive capacity, and in due course was promoted to Head of the Second Department; he was employed by the Ministry of Foreign Affairs for thirteen years, taking part in the preparation of draft international treaties. In parallel with his work in the Ministry of Foreign Affairs, he passed the State examination in spring 1897 based on the syllabus of the University and remained from 1 November 1897 to 1 November 1900 at the Chair of International Law to prepare for the professoriate, having been awarded a stipend.[281]

[International Law], no. 2 (2001), p. 97.

280 The Library comprising 1,500 titles (2,002 volumes) first went to the Book Fund of Soviet Russia. In 1919 it was transferred to the Polytechnic Institute in Ivanovo-Voznesensk. Today the Library reposes in the Central Universal Scientific Library of Ivanovo Region. See I. A. Maltseva, «Частная коллекция Б. Э. Нольде» [Private Collection of B. E. Nolde], Мир библиографии [World of Bibliography], no. 1 (2002); N. A. Suratova, «Дар профессора Б. Э. Нольде Фундаментальной библиотеке» [Gift of Professor B. E. Nolde to the Fundamental Library], in Из фондов библиотеки: сборник статей [From the Funds of the Library: Collection of Articles] (Spb., 2002), I, pop. 58-63; I. A. Briukhanova and N. A. Suratova, «Дар профессора Б. Э. Нольде» [Gift of Professor B. E. Nolde], in Личные собрания в фондах библиотек, архивов, музеев [Personal Collections in the Funds of Libraries, Archives, Museums] (Spb., 2008), pp. 90-98; K. P. Iarkova, «Книжное собрание баронов Нольде» [Book Collection of the Barons Nolde], in Библиофильство и личные собрания [Bibliophily and Personal Collections] (M., 2013), pp. 425-434.

281 ЦГИА СПб., fond 14, opis 2, file 1230; opis 1, file 9593, l. 62.

On 13 December 1899 he passed the magister examination[282] and, having delivered the trial lectures, was hired from 1 July 1901 as privat-docent at the Chair of International Law. He offered elective courses on “The Papacy and Its Significance in the Domain of International Law” and “The Construction of International Combinations”.[283]

At a general meeting of the Law Faculty on 10 April 1905, Baikov defended his magister dissertation on the topic “Contemporary International Legal Capacity of the Papacy in Connection with the Doctrine of International Legal Capacity in General”.[284] The official opponents were M. A. von Taube and M. I. Gorchakov.[285] The defense was reported in the media.[286]

In 1908 the Council of the Demidov Law Lycée elected Baikov professor *extraordinarius* at the Chair of the Encyclopedia of Law; he, having remained in service at the Ministry of Foreign Affairs, after eleven years at the University left the Chair of International Law[287] and moved to Iaroslavl. From 1908 to 1910 he was a professor at the Demidov Law Lycée in Iaroslavl. In 1910 he became a privat-docent at the Chair of International Law at Moscow University and professor at the Higher Women’s Courses in Moscow. From 28 April 1911 Baikov finally moved to Moscow University and took the post of professor *extraordinarius* at the Chair of the Encyclopedia and History of the Philosophy of Law; he lectured on the encyclopedia of law and international law.[288] In 1913 Baikov defended a doctoral dissertation at Moscow University on inter-power and power relations in legal theory.[289]

282 According to archival data, Baikov was examined at a session of the Law Faculty on 13 December 1899 on international law. The following questions were put to him: (1) On relations of the Roman curia with States;; (2) On international claims between Russia and the Ottoman Empire since 1774; (3) On an international Greek court. The answers were deemed to be satisfactory. ЦГИА СПб., fond 14, opis 3, file 14327.

283 Отчет о состоянии и деятельности Императорского С.-Петербургского университета за 1901 год [Report on the State and Activity of the Imperial St. Petersburg University for 1901] (Spb., 1902), p. 21.

284 The dissertation was printed a year earlier as a separate book. See A. L. Baikov, Современная международная правоспособность папства в связи с учением о международной правоспособности вообще [Contemporary Legal Capacity of the Papacy in Connection with the Doctrine on International Legal Capacity in General] (Spb., 1904). Butler Б15.

285 ЦГИА СПб., fond 14, opis 3, file 14325, l. 6.

286 Новое время [New Times], 12 April 1905.

287 Отчет о состоянии и деятельности Императорского С.-Петербургского университета за 1908 год [Report on the State and Activity of the Imperial St. Petersburg University for 1908] (Spb., 1909), p. 62.

288 Tomsinov, note 22 above, II, p. 415; K. O. Savchuk, «Байков Олександр Львович» [Baikov, Oleksandr Lvovich], in Denysov, note 4 above, I, pp. 194-195; Starodubtsev, note 4 above, pp. 17, 26, 39, 40, 53-55, 103, 248.

289 Baikov, Междувластные и властные отношения в теории права: Опыт теоретико-познавательного построения [Inter-Power and Power Relations in the Theory of Law: Attempt of Theoretical-Cognitive Structures] (Iaroslavl, 1912). The print run was small, and the book, which contained a

Following the defense of his dissertation, Baikov was chosen to replace Count L. A. Kamarovskii as professor in the Chair of International Law at Moscow University. From 1913 to 1918 he was professor *ordinarius* at the Chair of the Encyclopedia of Law and the History of the Philosophy of Law, Moscow University, but from 1916 to 1918 lectured only on international law. He also offered a university course at the Imperial Moscow Lycée and the Tsarevich Nikolai Imperial Lycée. He became from 1916 the co-editor of the journal Проблемы Великой России: журнал внешней политики и права [Problems of Great Russia: Journal of Foreign Policy and Law] founded by Petr Berngardovich Struve (1870-1944) – a notable political economist, philosopher, editor, and graduate of St. Petersburg University. The 1917 Russian Revolutions impelled Baikov to leave; from November 1918 to February 1921 he was a professor at the Chair of International Law of the Tauride (Crimean) University (Simferopol). Returning to Moscow in October 1921, he found employment as Head of the Naval Section of the Unified State Archive Fund of Russia. He moved in 1922 to become a professor at the Chair of Consular Law in the Moscow Institute of Oriental Studies.

Baikov was arrested on 17 August 1922 and accused of anti-Soviet and counter-revolutionary activity. By decree of the State Political Administration (GPU) of 22 August 1922 he was "exiled abroad in perpetuity".[290] On 30 September 1922 he sailed with other exiles on the *Oberbürgermeister Haken*[291] from Petrograd to Szczecin (Stettin) in Poland.

Emigration. Baikov lived first in Berlin, where he collaborated on the journal Новая русская книга [New Russian Book] and associated himself with the Russian monarchist movement in Bavaria led by Grand Duke Kirill Vladimirovich (1876-1938). Baikov published an article urging the creation of a "national socialism" that, with the power of the masses, could overthrow Bolshevism.[292] Then on to Prague, where he was associated with the Russian Economic Cabinet, and thereafter moved to Paris. Most of his life abroad he devoted to various lecturing assignments in Paris, which became one of the major centers for Russian émigrés. He principally lectured on the encyclopedia of law and was active in various

number of original propositions, quickly became uncommon on the market. Butler Б13.

290 V. Makarov and V. Khristofor (comps.), Высылка вместо расстрела: Депортация интеллигенции в документах ВЧК-ГПУ. 1921-1923 [Exile Instead of Shooting. Deportation of the Intelligentsia in Documents of the All-Russian Extraordinary Commission-State Political Administration. 1921-1923] (M., 2005), p. 423. Exiles were required to give a signed statement that they would not return to Soviet Russia. In the instance of Baikov, the document read: "This written undertaking given by me, Aleksandr Lvovich Baikov, Professor of the Institute of Oriental Studies, to the State Political Administration, that I undertake not to return to the territory of the RSFSR without the authorization of agencies of Soviet power. Article 72 of the Criminal Code of the RSFSR punishing for arbitrary return within the limits of the RSFSR has been declared to me, of which I also sign. Aleksandr Lvovich Baikov, 21 August 1922. City of Moscow". See Tomsinov, note 22 above, II, p. 417.

291 The ship was chartered by the GPU for this voyage. See L. Chamberlain, *The Philosophy Steamer: Lenin and the Exile of the Intelligentsia* (2006), pp. 1, 30, 58.

292 Baikov, "Die Krise der Räteherrschaft und die Zukunft Russlands", *Völkischer Beobachter*, 1 September 1923, p. 2. Cited in R. C. Williams, *Culture in Exile: Russian Émigrés in Germany 1881-1941* (1972), p. 217.

Russian émigré organizations. He died on New Year's eve (31 December 1943) at Paris and was buried on 4 January 1944 at the Boulogne-Billancourt Cemetery.

International legal views. Baikov was interested especially, as an international lawyer, in issues of international legal personality. These he addressed first in his magister dissertation on the international legal personality of the Papacy; he used the journal *La Civilta Cattolica* (1850-) and the Biblioteca Nazionale Centrale di Roma to excellent effect when researching his topic.[293] The study generated immediate interest upon publication and was widely reviewed, both with approval and critically.[294] Martens on the whole liked the book and admired the aspiration of the author to travel along untested paths, but cautioned: "the final conclusions of the author will hardly acquire many supporters in the literature of international law".

Baikov alleged that the reactionary policy of the Roman curia had shattered the centuries-old church State – the Papal domain. He disagreed with those scholars who believed that in 1870 the Papal Domain headed by the Vatican ceased to be a State, that The Holy See headed by the Pope of Rome had lost sovereignty. Baikov insisted that the liquidation of the Papal State did not involve the loss of international legal capacity by the Papacy. In support of his view, Baikov set out a number of theoretical propositions relating to the foundations of international legal personality which made him one of the most-cited authorities on the topic.

In seeking to equate the international legal status of the Pope with other subjects of international law, Baikov developed his own theory of subjects, according to which subjects are the possessors merely of personal sovereignty, even without any territorial sovereignty. As a sovereign organism, the Holy See was, in his view, a fully-fledged subject of international law.

Baikov structured his argument as follows: sovereignty, freedom, and independence are the constituent elements of international legal capacity:

> Sovereignty is power, the dominance of which within the boundaries of the competence belonging thereto, and is not condition in its existence by the power of other organisms or by the consent of subordinates (p. 156).
>
> Freedom is a legal state by virtue of which a particular social organism, ruling within the boundaries of the competence belonging thereto, excludes dominance over itself by any other power except its own (p. 185).
>
> Independence is a legal state by virtue of which a particular social organism within the boundaries of the competence belonging thereto is not conditioned in the exercise of power by the deviation (or lack of competence) or failure of the authorities to act of other organisms (p. 190).

[293] ЦГИА СПб., fond 14, opis 3, file 14325, l. 6. See Baikov, Современная международная правоспособность папства в связи с учением о международной правоспособности вообще [Contemporary International Legal Capacity of the Papacy in Connection with the Doctrine on International Legal Capacity in General] (Spb, 1904). Butler Б15.

[294] Baikov was criticized by E. Temnikovskii; his review and Baikov's reply appeared in Временник Демидовского юридического лицея [Annals of Demidov Law Lycée], XCII (1906), Юридическая библиотека, вып. 66 and 67, pp. 1-31.

Having analyzed the legal status of the Holy See and the Vatican in their correlation with the legal status of classical States, Baikov came to the final conclusion: "The Holy See possessing sovereignty, freedom, and independence – organically linked with the elements of international legal capacity – must be deemed to be a subject of international law" (p. 233).

Baikov's view was criticized in Russia, including at the Chair of International Law. Taube found this conclusion to be unconvincing and denied that the Pope of Rome had international legal personality. In his view, the Pope ceased to be a subject of international law with the loss in 1870 of the territory of the Papal Domain.[295] It should be noted that when criticizing Baikov, Taube himself proposed a new theory – the conception of inter-power law, pursuant to which the Pope was regarded not as a subject of inter-State law, but of inter-power law.

Baikov apparently adjusted his position in light of Taube's critique. He elaborated Taube's theory of "inter-power law" in his own later work on inter-power and power relations (1912) and argued that the Pope of Rome was a subject of inter-power law, albeit not inter-State law.[296]

As noted above, Baikov's book on inter-power law became his doctoral dissertation. He moved on from his magister analysis of the international legal capacity of the Papacy to larger issues of international legal theory and general problems of the theory of law. In his preface he pointed out: "The study … consists of an effort at a new construction of a concept of law and the forms of expression thereof". Nonetheless, portions of the work addressed such international legal issues as the spatial operation of international law, the basis on which international legal norms were binding, the legal equality of subjects of international law, and legal basis and forms for the forming of such norms, among others.

Following Taube's approach, Baikov used the categories of "inter-power relations" and "inter-power law"; these in his view build the entire system of international communion. He believed the basic principle of international law to be the principle of equality. A violation of that principle led to domination. But States not only make war, fight, or counteract one another, they are aware of being members of the international community and bound to render mutual assistance and support to one another. The link uniting States creates the foundation for a "joint and several" legal order built on the principles of cooperation (pp. 337-339).

International law, said Baikov, is not a supranational law. The "common will" regulating the behavior of States in international communion is the will of all its members. International norms may be created only by means of "unanimous" decisions, and not the will of the majority of States. In the sphere of inter-State relations not all duties have the character of self-limitation. States not only limit them-

[295] Taube, «Учение о субъектах международного права в русской юридической литературе» [Doctrine on Subjects of International Law in Russian Legal Literature], Известия Министерства иностранных дел [News of the Ministry of Foreign Affairs], kn. 4 (1913), pp. 163-182; kn. 6 (1913), p. 74-88; kn. 3 (1914), p. 80-91.

[296] Baikov, note 293 above, p. 383.

selves to the benefit of others; they have an impact on others through restrictions, and in turn experience the limitations emanating from them.

When analyzing the subjects of "inter-power" relations, Baikov went farther in his deliberations than the traditional doctrine by asserting that international legal capacity is the exclusive property of sovereign States. Individuals may enjoy within a foreign State only particular rights and privileges, but this does not make them subjects of international law.

Baikov proceeded from the fact that not merely States exist in the international sphere, but also various social associations: political unions, religious organizations, and so on which possess a certain power within their spatial limits. It followed that their relations are regulated by norms of international law. Whereas, however, Taube considered "inter-power law" and "international law" as two disciplines of a generic character, Baikov, on the contrary, regarded them as different categories of a generic character and hierarchically inter-power law is higher than international ("inter-State") law. The last is subordinate to "inter-power" law as a species is subordinate to the genus. In his view, power is a more general concept than State power, and "inter-power" relations are more general than inter-State or international relations.

Baikov touched upon the recognition of States in his book. The emergence of a new State in the international arena is an event requiring recognition. The death of States, change of the forms of State structure, the accession of new territories, or the cession of territory are accompanied by respective legal effects also requiring recognition. These facts arise irrespective of the consent of other States but, nevertheless, impose certain duties on them, require recognition. How recognition is undertaken, he believed, was not important, but rather the fact of the existence or absence of recognition. Recognition is a material element of all legal relations in general (pp. 348-350).

Many of Baikov's views were considered to be ahead of their time. When the right of States to use force was widely acknowledged and many were of the view that war, or an armed peace, or alliances of various types were the normal expectation, Baikov drew attention to the duality of international law – the combination of military and peaceful rivalries of States and aspirations for cooperation and solidarity. He assumed that international legal rules were binding because they rested on dual foundations: the need for a certain order in inter-State relations and the consent of States to obey the guiding principles of international rules.

Lev Iosifovichh Petrazhitsky (1867-1931) was among those in the Law Faculty at St. Petersburg University who influenced Baikov during his magister studies. Baikov became a proponent of the psychological theory of law, subject to the caveat that his works were not a continuation of Petrazhitsky but a creative extension in a new spirit and direction. In his work on *rebus sic stantibus* he wrote:

> Any law must above all be considered from the standpoint of the psychology of society, natural aspirations, attractions, and other feelings of people, and consequently also the so-called feeling, or instinct, for self-preservation … A legal order called upon to serve social needs must be based on human nature, must comprehend the living content thereof, otherwise it proves to be utterly powerless in the face of realities and will not be

> in a state to influence the motives of human behavior. Law must not be divorced from life, but transform life, influence it in a certain direction, cultivating social elements of human relations and suppressing the development of anti-social tendencies.[297]

But, as Grabar noted, Baikov "gives too broad a scope for the application of the reservation of changed circumstances, seeing in it a dynamic principle of international law which allows the possibility of adjusting outmoded law to new conditions of life".[298] Without denying Baikov's general message concerning the need for law, including international law, to readjust its development to accommodate changing social needs and phenomena, the danger of abusing this thesis needs to be taken into account. An excessively broad interpretation of *rebus sic stantibus* may actually create a situation threatening the principle fundamental to international law – *pacta sunt servanda.*

Baikov left his own mark on the history of international law as a capable specialist in the field of international legal personality, as an international legal practitioner in the field of Russian foreign policy, and as a talented educator whose students later made their own contributions to the field (Iu. V. Kliuchnikov, E. A. Korovin, A. M. Ladyzhenskii, Ia. D. Makovskii, among others).

Aleksandr Mikhailovich Gorovtsev *(sometimes Gorovtsov) (24 January 1878 – 27 October 1933 (or 1936), d. Paris). International lawyer, diplomat, publicist, publisher.*

Life and career. Gorovtsev graduated in 1900 from two faculties of St. Petersburg University simultaneously: the Law Faculty and the Faculty of Oriental Languages, being awarded a first-class degree in each. In addition, the Law Faculty awarded him medals for two papers: a silver medal for a work on police law[299] and a gold medal for an essay "On the Codification of the Laws and Customs of War".

On 25 July 1900 Gorovtsev accepted employment with the Ministry of Justice, being attached to the Chancellery of the Criminal Cassation Department of the Ruling Senate and confirmed in the rank and title of college secretary. He was appointed to the post of chief clerk of the First Department of the Ministry of Foreign Affairs in 1901. At about the same time, from 1 January 1901 he was invited

[297] Baikov, Правовое значение оговорки 'Rebus sic Stantibus' в международных отношениях [Legal Significance of the Reservation 'Rebus sic Stantibus' in International Relations] (M., 1916), pp. 30-31. Butler Б14.

[298] Grabar, note 46 above, p. 510.

[299] Later published as a book: Gorovtsev, Трудовая помощь как средство призрения бедных [Labor Assistance as a Means of Charity for the Poor] (Spb., 1901), a substantial volume of 437 pages for the presentation of which Gorovtsev received a formal expression of gratitude from Emperor Nicholas II. ЦГИА СПб., fond 14, opis 3, file 14438, l. 20.

to remain at the Chair of International Law to prepare for the professoriate;[300] his status in that respect was repeatedly renewed.[301]

He was appointed by the Ministry of Foreign Affairs on 19 January 1902 the secretary and dragoman[302] in Perin, Manchuria, and a year later was made a titular counsellor and reassigned to the Vice Consulate in Chi-fu (now Yantai), China, closer to the sites of hostilities in the Russo-Japanese War.[303] One outcome of his sojourn in Manchuria and China was a book on the international legal aspects of the siege of Port Arthur.[304]

Not until 1910 was Gorovtsev able to take his magister examinations. These were held on 1 November 1910 and 9 May 1911, when he successfully passed them for the degree of magister of international law.[305] As for his written reply to the magister question set: Taube gave a positive evaluation to "Relations between Russia and England from the Reign of Emperor Paul I to 1812".

300 E. N. Trubetskaia, История развития кафедры международного права Санкт-Петербургского (Петроградского) университета в 1903-1917 гг. [History of the Development of the Chair of International Law of St. Petersburg (Petrograd) University in 1903-1917] (Spb., 2004), pp. 146-148; also see D. V. Mikhnevych, «Горовцев Олександр Михайлович» [Gorovtsev, Oleksandr Mikhailovych], in Denysov, note 4 above, I, pp. 644-645; Starodubtsev, note 4 above, pp. 15, 25, 27, 28, 33-35, 40, 53, 55, 83, 104, 144; M. A. Mitiukov and A. M. Barnashov, Истоки Томской школы государствоведения и конституционализма [Sources of the Tomsk School of State Science and Constitutionalism (Tomsk, 2019), pp. 62-63.

301 ЦГИА СПб., fond 14, opis 3, file 14369, l. 46; file 14438, l. 19; opis 1, file 9579.

302 Although the term and position were usually associated with the Turkish, Arabic, and Persian-speaking countries, in Russian diplomatic practice the Far East was included. A dragoman was an interpreter, translator, and sometimes a guide who had a command of the relevant tongues and European languages. Historically, they played significant roles in introducing European States to the culture, literature, poetry, history, legal institutions, diplomacy, and personalities of the receiving States. See E. Natalie Rothman, *The Dragoman Renaissance: Diplomatic Interpreters and the Routes of Orientalism* (2021), who curiously does not mention Russian experience with this institution.

303 In a letter to the Dean of the Law Faculty, dated 25 August 1904, Gorovtsev wrote of a risky trip to the theatre of military hostilities and requested that his stipend be retained: "I would like to think that the sojourn in the theatre of war, in the very center of events, may even give me considerable interesting material in the future". ЦГИА СПб., fond 14, opis 3, file 14369, l. 247obverse. In 1904 Gorovtsev submitted a Report to the Faculty about his experiences. ЦГИА СПб., fond 14, opis 3, file 14369, l. 48-52obverse. Republished in T. S. Loginova, История становления и развития кафедры международного права Санкт-Петербургского университета в 1819-1903 г.г. [History of the Origin and Development of the Chair of International Law of St. Petersburg University in 1819-1903] (Spb., 2004), Annex 18.

304 Gorovtsev, Осада Порт-Артура с точки зрения международного права [Siege of Port-Arthur from the Standpoint of International Law] (Spb., [1906]; 2d ed.; 1907). The pagination differs between the 1906 and 1907 versions. All revenues from the sale were donated to those who suffered disability at Port Arthur.

305 ЦГИА СПб., fond 14, opis 3, file 14446, l. 1, 2. Gorovtsev had to answer the following questions: (a) historical development of the concept of military contraband; (b) permanently neutral States; (c) protection of spiritual-intellectual interests of private individuals in international law.

From 1912 Gorovtsev again became the chief clerk in the First Department of the Ministry of Foreign Affairs, then was sent for several years by the Ministry to the Far East, where he served in Kharbin, Chi-fu, and other Chinese cities. From 1 July 1912 he was appointed privat-docent at the Chair of International Law[306] and offered lectures on "Diplomatic and Consular Law".[307] He remained in that post, with brief intervals of absence, until September 1918. The interval of absence was by reason of illness and of a conflict with Professor Pilenko which eventually involved most administrative structures of the University and ultimately was considered by the Court of Honor of the University. Gorovtsev was ultimately reinstated in his position.[308] In autumn 1915 Gorovtsev returned to lecture on "Diplomatic and Consular Law" and "Controversial Questions of International Law".[309]

In addition to these legal interests, Gorovtsev was a publicist, one who enjoyed writing humorous satire, and a publisher; sometimes he wrote under a pseudonym, "Sergei Runin". During 1915 and 1916 he published a journal of satirical articles entitled Отклики [Responses]. From 1915 to 1917, a series Журнал-библиотека «Трибуна» ["Journal-Library 'Tribune'"].

The years 1917/1918 brought cardinal changes to the life of the Gorovtsev family. On 27 March 1918 Gorovtsev was elected professor *extraordinarius* at the Chair of International Law at Tomsk University, confirmed in this post by Order of the Provisional Siberian Government of 7 August 1918; on 19 August 1919 this decision was repealed.[310] In parallel, the Omsk Provisional Siberian Government signed an Order on 14 August 1918 to staff the Law Faculty of Irkutsk University, Gorovtsev consenting to this appointment. The paradox is that, according to archival data, on 26 September 1918 at a meeting of professor of Voronezh University, magister of international law, A. M. Gorovtsev, was elected privat-docent at their Chair of International Law.[311] But Gorovtsev did not travel to Tomsk, or to Irkutsk, or to Voronezh, but instead to Perm University, where on 19 September 1918 he was hired as privat-docent in the Law Faculty. Opportunities were many in Perm, and on 12 December he was confirmed in the post of professor *extraordinarius* in the Chair of Administrative Law and by the end of January 1919 held the post of professor *extraordinarius* in the Chair of Encyclopedia and Philosophy of Law. He lectured at Perm and conducted practical exercises on international law, State law, encyclopedia of law, and the history of the philosophy of law.[312]

306 ЦГИА СПб., fond 14, opis 3, file 10607.

307 ЦГИА СПб., fond 14, opis 3, file 14411, l. 95; opis 3, file 14470, l. 87.

308 ЦГИА СПб., fond 14, opis 1, file 10823. For details See Trubetskaia, note 300 above, pp. 51-54.

309 Обозрение преподавания наук на Юридическом факультете Императорского С.-Петербургского университета за 1915 и 1916 учебный год [Survey of Teaching at the Law Faculty of the Imperial St. Petersburg University for 1915 and 1916 Academic Year] (Spb., 1916), p. 7.

310 See S. F. Fomin (ed.), Профессора Томского университета: Биографический словарь [Professors of Tomsk University: Biographical Dictionary] (Tomsk, 1998), II, pp. 111-112.

311 ЦГИА СПб., fond 14, opis 1, file 10607, l. 80.

312 See Профессора Пермского государственного университета (1916-2001) [Professors of

As it happened, Gorovtsev ended up in Tomsk anyway. In 1919 part of the Perm University was evacuated to Tomsk. From 16 October 1919 Gorovtsev delivered lectures on international law in the Law Faculty of Tomsk University.[313] In December 1919 he moved from Tomsk to Irkutsk and worked at Irkutsk University until mid-1920.[314] At the request of the Perm Faculty of Social Sciences he was sent to visit the university cities of Russia, but never returned to either Perm or to Irkutsk. From autumn 1920 he taught at Kyiv University, also as a professor in the Social Sciences Section of the Higher M. P. Dragomanov Institute of National Economy, and lectured on international law at the Kyiv Institute of National Economy and the Kyiv Institute of Foreign Relations.

By March 1921 he had emigrated, first to Romania and then to Paris. His life ended tragically. Completely destitute, he was shot in the Bois de Boulogne near Paris on 2 November 1933 and is buried at the Cimetière parisien de Thiais.

International Legal Views. Gorovtsev made serious contributions to the field of international law, beginning with his first fundamental treatise on certain basic controversial issues of international law.[315] He set out his views on the legal nature, essence, and system of international law and analyzed general theoretical issues of law in general. He adhered to the classical definition of the concept of international law as the law regulating relations between States. He suggested that: "… by the nature of its formation, international or inter-State law, just as any other, represents nothing other than the self-limitation of States in the exercise of their freedom, self-determination, on the principles of reciprocity"; that is, inter-State law is a group of norms of mutual-limitation of States in their State exercise of rule. The legal operation of international law "consists of the limitation by one State of its State sovereignty with respect to another in the sense of the assumption by the first of them of duties to manifest particular aspects of the exercise of rule by agreement with the second and in its interests" (p. 123).

With regard to the force of its operation, he wrote:

> international law is, of course, **supra**national … in the respect that it, although it has its origin in the will of States themselves limiting themselves, being transformed into a norm consecrated by this will, it just as any obligation assumed is already **above** the will of the subject assuming it; that is, in this event supranational. But the source of **its origin** is not

Perm University (1916-2001)] (Perm, 2017), p. 43.

313 See Fomin, note 310 above, II, p. 111.

314 See V. N. Kazarin, «Становление юридического образования в Иркутском университете: время, события, люди» [Development of Legal Education in Irkutsk University: Time, Events, People], Сибирский юридический вестник: Правовой журнал [Siberian Legal Herald: Legal Journal], no. 3 (Irkutsk, 2008), p. 5. In July 1920 the Rector of Irkutsk University requested the military commissar to exempt Gorovtsev from mobilization on the grounds that he was a specialist worker irreplaceable in his specialty for which none others were available in the University and a very limited quantity of such individuals in Russia generally. Ibid., p. 6.

315 A. M. Gorovtsev, Некоторые основные спорные вопросы учения о праве в связи с международным правом [Certain Basic Controversial Questions of the Doctrine on Law in Connection with International Law] (Pg., 1916-17). Butler Г180.

> supranational; it is not inscribed on special tablets, but is the result of a lengthy process of gradual self-limitation of States (p. 133; emphasis in original).

While not supranational in origin, international law, given the external character of the formation thereof, seemed to Gorovtsev to be exclusively customary or treaty in origin.

Among the basic most controversial issues of international law was that of its subjects and objects. The majority of writers recognize States to be subjects of international law and some, only States. But many, having taken this view in the "General Part" of their work as a general principle, when setting out the "Special Part" and addressing a particular question, often slip into recognizing as subjects of international law not only States, but also individuals, human beings. Gorovtsev categorically disagreed with this position, suggesting that the State is a "law-making" subject, and not an individual person.

As regards the object of international law, Gorovtsev pointed out that the majority of legal scholars avoid this issue in silence. Only a few address it, but their attempts, in his view, were unsatisfactory. The exercise of governing by States is an object in international law which takes the form of the particular prerogatives of State power and sovereign rights at the disposition of a State. These rights may be reduced to two basic rights: (1) sovereign territorial rights, and (2) sovereign personal rights.

Territorial sovereign rights of the State consist of its right to dispose of its territory without any control. The sovereignty of personal rights is reflected in the close link of citizenship (or subject-ship) and the State, which exists between a person and the State to which a person belongs.

According to Grabar, the last Russian attempt to improve the system of international law was made by Gorovtsev.[316] This attempt Gorovtsev undertook in an article on the essence of international law,[317] which continues to be relevant to this day. As regards the system of international law itself, Gorovtsev did violence to it, depriving it of a General Part and distributing all the material by subjects and objects. In Grabar's view, "he made only a single amendment to the system of international law, but a most material one. It concerned the ambiguous content of the concept of object, which Gorovtsev considered to be 'rule in the form of particular prerogatives of State power'".[318] The scheme proposed by Gorovtsev came down to the following:

> The basic parts of the division thereof are the doctrine concerning its subjects – on one hand, and objects – on the other, concerning those prerogatives of power of its subject-States, the limitation of which also is a com-

[316] Grabar, note 46 above, p. 484.

[317] Gorovtsev, «Сущность международного права и его система» [The Essence of International Law and the System Thereof], Журнал Министерства юстиции [Journal of the Ministry of Justice], no. 7 (1911), pp. 129-146. Butler Г187.

[318] Grabar, note 46 above, p. 484.

> mon legal operation for all law – limitation of freedom, self-sufficiency, plenitude of power, sovereignty.[319]
>
> The General Part comprised questions concerning the State as a subject of international law with respect to three of its basic 'elements': power, population, and territory; that is, primarily controversial questions concerning sovereignty in so-called combinations of States, neutralized States, and soon; next – on subject-ship; and finally, on territory. Hence, to the doctrine on States as subjects in inter-State law should be relegated the doctrine concerning its organs in this domain; that is, diplomatic law. As for the Special Part of the system, the content of which should be the doctrine on objects in inter-State law … that is, limitations of the plenitude of the States, their 'natural freedom' with respect to one another, but here may be preserved as the principal division of this Part of the system, various states of war and peace.[320]

In a letter to the Dean of the St. Petersburg University Law Faculty from the Russo-Japanese front, Gorovtsev had expressed the hope that while at the front he would be able to occupy himself with problems of law and warfare.[321] In his view, it was not in utopian projects for "perpetual peace", but in the reasonable legal regulation of armed conflicts that the true path lay for the graduation limitation of the suffering and misfortunes caused by war.

Especially to be noted is the substantial encyclopedic work which Gorovtsev compiled on the literature of international law. Its aim was to facilitate the study of the major European and Russian literature on international law of the nineteenth and early twentieth centuries. In concise but intensive form, the work presented excerpts from many scholarly works not readily accessible, most of them published abroad. Authors represented by extracts included Fedor Fedorovich Martens, Mikhail Aleksandrovich von Taube, Phillimore, Ullmann, P. E. Kazanskii, Bonfils, Rivier, Lorimer, Bluntschli, Heffter, Robert von Mohl, and Georg Friedrich Martens.[322]

Gorovtsev developed a basic course on international law, but the Revolutions of 1917 and ensuing Civil War did not allow him to complete the project as he had wished. He did, however, prepare and publish under unbelievably challenging conditions the first part of his intended Course while he briefly held a position at the Irkutsk University.[323] This work, in two parts, is remarkable because Gorovtsev

319 Gorovtsev, note 315 above, pp. 294-295.

320 Ibid.

321 Gorovtsev, note 317 above; also see Gorovtsev, Война и право [War and Law] (Spb., 1902; 2d ed.; 1910) Butler Г169 and Г170; Gorovtsev, Законы и право (война и право) [Laws of War (War and Law)] (2d ed.; Pg., 1915). Butler Г173.

322 Gorovtsev, Международное право. Избранная литература. Краткая энциклопедия [International Law. Selected Literature. Concise Encyclopedia] (Spb., 1909). Butler Г179.

323 Gorovtsev, Курс межгосударственного (международного) права. Введение и общая часть [Course of Inter-State (International) Law: Introduction and General Part] (Irkutsk, 1920). 45 p.

and no access to normative or to reference materials (no pagination in footnoted sources or the list of required or recommended readings). The second part was a "synoptic chart" outlining in visual form his system of "Inter-State" law. They were printed at the expense of the student organization in a small print run on newsprint quality paper. The material was written from memory.

So far as can be determined, this was the only Course published during the Russian Civil War on territory controlled, however briefly, by the White movement throughout the remaining Russian Empire. Gorovtsev set out his vision of international law which previously had articulated in his articles of 1911 and 1916. As before, he insisted on the title "inter-State law" because this best expressed the fact that States were the subjects of this branch of law (pp. 8-9). He prophetically proceeded from the fact that new States would be formed in the twentieth century and that States would seek to strengthen the legal regulation of their relations through norms of "inter-State law".

He continued to polish his system of international "inter-State" law, the component parts of which were, in his view: Introduction, General Part, Special Part, which broke up into the doctrine on the subject and the doctrine on the object of inter-State law. In his publication he was able to address only the Introduction and the General Part. Nonetheless, he is seen in retrospect as having produced an original, carefully thought-out work and deservedly held a place in the ranks of significant theorists of international law.

Emigration. Gorovtsev continued to occupy himself with studies of international law and published several works in French. Many of his articles remain in manuscript. An individual of many talents, he remained active in publicist circles. From 1921 to 1926 he was the editor and publisher of a political almanac Трибуна [Tribune]. In 1931, already depression years, he was the co-editor of the newspaper Наш призыв [Our Challenge]. He worked during the last years of his life with commercial advertising, but without much success, which led in turn to his tragic demise.

Andrei Nikolaevich Mandelstam *(also Henrikh-Nikolai Nikolaev; sometimes Mandelshtam) (6 March 1869, b. Mogilev – 27 January 1949, d. Paris, France). International lawyer, diplomat, dragoman, historian.*

Life and career. After graduating from the Mogilev Gymnasium, Mandelstam enrolled in July 1886 at the Faculty of Oriental Languages of St. Petersburg University (Arabic-Persian-Turkish-Tatar Division).[324] But by September 1886 influenced by lectures of F. F. Martens on international law delivered in the Oriental Faculty, he requested to be transferred to the first year of studies in the Law Faculty.[325]

See W. E. Butler, "The Teaching of International Law in the USSR", *Review of Socialist Law*, VIII (1982), pp. 183-202.

[324] ЦГИА СПб., fond 14, opis 3, file 25614.

[325] Ibid., l. 7 .

The following year he requested the Rector to allow him to study simultaneously in the Faculties of Law and of Oriental Studies. This was an unusual but not unprecedented request. Students who chose Oriental studies were required to attend several courses in the Law Faculty, choosing from three groups: diplomatic, administrative, or judicial. When graduation was imminent, the Oriental studies students were examined in the legal subjects by a commission of jurists. It was, in principle, possible for a student in the Oriental language faculty to attend lectures on virtually all subjects in the Law Faculty. On 4 February 1888 Mandelstam received the permission that he had requested. The course load grew commensurately. In 1886 Mandelstam had attended five language courses: Arabic, English, French, History of the Orient, and International Law; in autumn 1888 he took ten courses: History of Russian Law, History of Roman Law, Russian State Law, Political Economy, History of the Orient, Arabic, Persian, Osman, Practical Exercises in Arabic, and Oriental Calligraphy.[326] Not surprisingly, he was awarded an Emperor's stipend.

He did take the respective examinations separately – in Autumn 1890 at the Faculty of Oriental Studies in the Arabic-Persian-Turkish-Tatar Division, and in March 1891 at the Law Faculty, where he was awarded a first-class degree, the diploma being dated 23 March 1891. From 15 April 1892 until 15 April 1894 he remained at the Chair of International Law to prepare for the professoriate. In parallel, he joined the Ministry of Foreign Affairs in 1893. During the 1893/94 academic year he passed the magister examinations and took a lecturing position in the University.[327] He also held a position during the 1895/96 academic year at the Alexander Lycée, where he offered a course on the "State Structure of Oriental Countries". In 1896 he passed the diplomatic examination for possible appointment in the Ministry of Foreign Affairs.

In 1896 he was sent abroad by the Alexander Lycée for a year and a half to attend lectures in Paris and Constantinople on international law and history.

He submitted a magister dissertation in 1900 on the Hague conference on the codification of private international law.[328] The public defense of the magister dissertation occurred on Sunday, 16 April 1900, at the University. The official opponents were – F. F. Martens and M. A. von Taube; the unofficial opponents – M. I. Gorchakov and L. I. Petrazhitskii. All had a high opinion of the dissertation, and the St. Petersburg media gave extensive detailed coverage to the event.[329] So fundamental was the dissertation and so impressive the quality of the defense that, by way of exception, Mandelstam was awarded the degree of doctor of international

[326] Ibid.

[327] ЦГИА СПб., fond 14, opis 2, file 994.

[328] Mandelstam, Гаагские конференции о кодификации международного частного права [Hague Conferences on the Codification of Private International Law] (Spb., 1900). 2 vols. Butler M23.

[329] See the Report in Право [Law], no. 17 (1900), pp. 879-885. The journal reported: "The dispute ended by the proclamation of a unanimous decision of the Faculty to deem the candidate worthy of the degree supplicated for and the noisy and loud applause of the large crowd".

law, by-passing the magister.[330] A portion of the dissertation was published in a leading French journal.[331]

From 1 July to the end of 1912 Mandelstam was privat-docent[332] and during 1916-1917 a professor at the Chair of International Law of St. Petersburg (Petrograd) University. According to the archives, he was removed as a lecturer at the University in early 1917 for not having delivered lectures for several semesters in succession.[333]

International legal practitioner. Mandelstam joined the Ministry of Foreign Affairs in the Senior Official Division attached to the Chancellery of the Ministry. In 1898 he was appointed dragoman at the Embassy of Russia in Constantinople. Upon returning and having defended his dissertation, in 1901 Mandelstam was made a member of a Meeting (an interdepartmental body) to prepare a draft Statute on Merchant Shipping.[334] He was made head of the Russian consulates in several regions of Turkey in 1903. Two years later Mandelstam was one of the representatives of Russia involved in the International Commission of Enquiry into the "Dogger Bank" incident in the North Sea.[335] He accompanied Martens to the Second Hague Peace Conference in 1907 and served as secretary of the Conference. In 1913 he returned to Turkish affairs as the delegate of the Russian embassy at the International Commission on Reforms in Turkish Armenia, where he took an active role of discussions of the Armenian Question and composed and submitted to the Commission a draft for Armenian reforms.[336] It laid the foundation for the Agreement between Russia and the Ottoman Empire on Armenian Reforms of 8 February 1914.

From 1914 to 1916 he was assigned to the central apparatus of the Ministry of Foreign Affairs and in 1916 was made a privy State counsellor. When the Provisional Government came to power after the abdication of the Emperor in February

330 ЦГИА СПб., fond 14, opis 1, file 9593, l. 62.

331 Mandelstam, "Du marriage et du divorce dans les rapports internationaux, au point de vue de droit russe", *Journal de droit international privé*, XXIX (1902), pp. 243-261, 460-493.

332 ЦГИА СПб., fond 14, opis 1, file 10631.

333 ЦГИА СПб., fond 14, opis 3, file 14610, l. 4.

334 ЦГИА СПб., fond 14, opis 3, file 14359, l. 5-6.

335 See Mandelstam, *La Commission internationale d'enquête sur l'incident de la mer du Nord* (Paris, 1905). Butler M30. This was an offprint of Mandelstam, "La Commission internationale d'enquête sur l'incident de la mer du Nord", *Revue générale de droit international public*, XII (1905), pp. 161-190, 351-415.

336 See Karl J. Partsch, "Die Armenierfrage und das Völkerrecht in der Zeit des Ersten Weltkrieges: Zum Wirken André Mandelstams", in Mihrann Dabag and Kristin Platt (eds.), *Strukturen kollektiver Gewalt im 20. Jahrhundert: Genozid und Moderne* (Opladen, 1998), I, pp. 339-343. Mention is made of Mandelstam in Daniel M. Segesser, "Dissolve or Punish? The International Debate Amongst Jurists and Publicists on the Consequences of the Armenian Genocide for the Ottoman Empire, 1915-23", *Journal of Genocide Studies*, X (2008), p. 95-110. During these years, Mandelstam also was involved in the arbitration between Russia and Turkey to resolve interest payments due to Russia arising from losses caused to Russian subjects during the 1876-1878 Russo-Turkish War.

1917, Mandelstam was the Director of the Legal Department of the Ministry of Foreign Affairs of the Provisional Government. He emigrated in October 1917 to Constantinople and Paris.[337]

Emigration. In emigration Mandelstam continued to maintain a presence in the field of international law. He gave courses at the University of Paris and at the Hague Academy of International Law, published books and articles, and was active in a variety of organizations. He died on 27 January 1949 in Paris and is buried at the Russian Cimetière Sainte-Geneviève-des-Bois in Paris, the resting place of many White Russians.

International legal views. Mandelstam's treatise on the Hague Conference on the codification of private international law is probably the most-cited of all his many works. During the magister dissertation defense for which he was awarded a doctorate, Professor Martens said to him in the presence of the assembled audience:

> When you consulted with me about the choice of topic, I did not conceal from you the enormous difficulties connected with private international law. I especially pointed out to you the complete absence of norms of this character in our legislation, the need for a knowledge of five or six foreign languages, the unusually extensive literature on the subject, and so on. You nonetheless kept to your intention, and I must say that your work exceeded all my expectations. These expectations were high, for you in the University have drawn attention to yourself, simultaneously passing through the course of two faculties and having completed them with identical success.[338]

The treatise contained a substantive survey of the history of private international legal doctrines, addressed issues of sources, method, codification, public policy, and other important issues of this branch of jurisprudence. Mandelstam formulated a number of bold positions which he then developed throughout the entire work. Mandelstam noted at the outset of his study: "The present work, insofar as the author is aware, is the first in our literature devoted to the development of international civil law" (I, p. vii) – which was something of an exaggeration.

Mandelstam believed that universal private international law did not exist. At the defense of his dissertation, he noted that "private international law exists only in embryonic form" and that

> instead we have – strange as it may sound – Russian, German, and French private international law; in other words, each State not only has its own special civil law, but also its own special key for the settlement of conflicts of these laws with foreign [laws].

In the preface Mandelstam wrote that he was:

337 See Starodubtsev, note 4 above, pp. 15, 40, 42, 46, 53, 58, 62, 64, 90, 91, 100, 102-105, 113, 122, 127, 152-153; Российское зарубежье во Франции, 1919-2000: биографический словарь [The Russia Abroad in France 1919-2000: Biographical Dictionary] (M., 2008), II, p. 134.

338 See Право [Law], no. 17 (1900), cols. 879-885.

> … deeply convinced that the idea of a universal worldwide civil law is a utopia, and extremely unattractive in character. This idea, just as the idea of world State and world language akin to it, is based on the complete denial of one of the material elements of any progress – the principle of diversity (I, p. 1).

In order to achieve the sacred aim of all nations – to ensure peace and truth both within the State and in international relations, "each State need defense on the part of public and private international law". He added: "public international law ensures independence for every tiniest State; that is, the freedom to display its own political individuality. Private international law provides to the laws of every country a sphere of influence required by the interests of the international community" (I, pp. i-ii).

Mandelstam stated that the legal views of nations have much in common, but all the same they express, just as their native languages, national distinctiveness. Therefore, it is useless "to bind all by one and the same civil law"; consequently, the aspiration to "shackle all in an identical legal armor" was doomed to fail. He favored the unification, integration, and unity of all parts of private international law – but not a "dormant" unity, rather the integration of all the parts thereof. It did not destroy the laws of individual countries but, on the contrary, ensured the plenitude of their operation. Without preventing the differentiation of civil law, it served their integration at the same time:

> Such integration assumes, of course, that private international law is elevated as a single integral system above the diversity of private laws … There is a continuous exchange of people among all states essential for the success of international communion. It is necessary that these people know precisely to what laws they are subject in their international turnover … It is impossible and not normal that civil rights and duties of an individual are constantly changing, depending on crossing a boundary or from the site of a court (I, p. iii).

At the beginning of his study, Mandelstam put the question: "But how should the desired unity of private international law be achieved?" In the first volume of the treatise he explored the conflicts legislation of several countries and concluded that it was essential to form a unified private international law:

> It is evident that private international law should be unified, identical for all States. The interest in self-preservation of the entire international community requires this … It is essential that a single theory of private international law preserve harmony between the various laws of individual States, integrate them into a single whole, and impart stability in this way to international turnover, without which international communion is inconceivable. Civil law will achieve the highest development, in our view, when a unified private international law comes into being (I, pp. 221-222).

The sole way of achieving such a result, in Mandelstam's view, was the codification of private international law:

> Only the international codifier may have the necessary authority to reconcile the conflicts of territorial laws; he alone may compel territorial leg-

> islation to mutual concessions, being guided not by abstract natural-law theories, but by the real requirements of international communion; and it is easier for him to listen to the voice of science and to heed the reasonable advice thereof (I, p. vi).

Therefore, he suggested: "The Hague conferences on the codification of private international law are undoubtedly one of the glorious stages in that great movement which leads nations toward harmony and unity without the removal of their national distinctiveness; that is, to unity in diversity".

Mandelstam summarized his views on the codification or private international law in the following propositions:

> (I). "Codification is one means of saving international life from external conflicts of laws, positive and negative. The celebrated question of "renvoi" falls away by itself if private international law were to be codified".
>
> (II). Codification is one means of mitigating or eliminating internal conflicts of laws; that is, conflicts of certain moments, concepts, and relations.
>
> (III). The international codifier must aspire towards the possible limitation of the operation of "public policy" and delimit jurisdiction irrespective of the will of private persons" (I, p. 252).

Mandelstam devoted much attention to the science of private international law: "The doctrine of private international law derives its metal from the subsoil of individual countries, but melts it in its own foundries" (I, p. 218). When it is necessary to elucidate any norm of private international law, one compares the territorial laws and customs. The coinciding thereof (all or the great majority) gives us an international norm of the same force as if it were contained in an international treaty.

In volume two of his treatise, Mandelstam considered international marriage law codified by the First Protocol of the 1894 Hague Conference. Drawing upon his own method of research, he first studied the legislation, practice, and doctrine of 23 States, giving principal attention to Russia, and then critically evaluated the Hague Protocol. Out of this Mandelstam prepared a draft Convention which differed from the Hague Protocol.

Mandelstam also addressed issues of public international law and Russian State law. He wrote several articles on the history of the law of naval warfare, international commissions of enquiry, and others. When considering the correlation of the integrity of the State and the right of nations to self-determination and analyzing the positions taken by the President of the United States, Woodrow Wilson (1856-1924), Mandelstam concluded:

> The settlement of conflicts between States and nations within them will not be done according to a single recipe of the self-determination of peoples. Sometimes the decision will be in favor of States, sometimes – in favor of peoples, depending on what the higher interests of human society require in each particular instance.[339]

[339] Mandelstam, «Введение» [Introduction], in Zarevand, Турция и Пантуранизм [Turkey and

Mandelstam undertook a substantial study of the law of the sea during war which was published in several issues of the journal of the Ministry of Foreign Affairs. His official position enabled him to draw upon diplomatic materials of the First World War to excellent effect.[340]

Many years of diplomatic service in missions of Russia in Turkish cities enabled Mandelstam to bring special expertise to the law of the Ottoman Empire and various aspects of the consular issues that arose. He published a special study on the fate of the Ottoman Empire,[341] and a work on the Turkish legal system.[342] On the basis of personal observations during his diplomatic service and investigation of Turkish sources, Mandelstam wrote several works devoted to the Armenian genocide in the Ottoman Empire; in his view the Young Turks were chiefly responsible for the genocide of the Armenians. Part One of his work was devoted to the policies of the Young Turks before and during the War years (1914-1918) and the mass extinction of the Armenians;[343] a Turkish translation was published at Constantinople in 1919. He maintained his interest in the Armenian Question, examining the policies of western powers in the League of Nations.[344] Mandelstam also produced a monograph on Russian consular jurisdiction in Turkey.[345] In addition to his works on Turkish policies with respect to national minorities and on national minorities generally, Mandelstam made important contributions to the law of human rights.[346]

Panturanism], transl. from Armenian (Paris, 1930; reprinted Erevan, 1991).

340 Mandelstam, «Международное морское право во время Великой Войны» [International Law of the Sea During the Great War], Известия Министерства иностранных дел [News of the Ministry of Foreign Affairs], kn. 2 (1916), pp. 62-168; kn. 3-4 (1916), pp. 62-132; kn. 5-6 (1916), pp. 208-278.

341 Mandelstam, *Le Sort de l'Empire ottoman* (Lausanne/Paris, 1917). Butler M47.

342 Mandelstam, *La justice ottoman dans ses rapports avec les puissances étrangères* (Paris, 1908; 2d ed.; Paris, 1911). Butler M36.

343 Mandelstam, «Младотурецкая держава» [The Young Turk State], Русская мысль [Russian Thought], no. 5 (1915), pp. 82-114; no. 6 (1915), pp. 13-46; Mandelstam, Младотурецкая держава: Историко-политический очерк [The Young Turk State. Historical-Political Survey] (M,, 1915). Not in Butler or Grabar.

344 Mandelstam, Лига Наций и армянский вопрос перед державами [The League of Nations and the Armenian Question Before the Powers] (Paris, 1926); also see Mandelstam, *La Société des Nations et les puissances devant le problème arménien* (Paris, 1926).

345 Mandelstam, «Русская консульская юрисдикция в Турции и ее реформа» [Russian Consular Jurisdiction in Turkey and the Reform Thereof], Вестник права [Herald of Law], no. 3 (1906), pp. 353-422; no. 4 (1906), pp. 191-250.

346 Hulya Adak, "André N. Mandelstam and the Early History of Human Rights (1917-1945)", *Zeitschrift für Religions- und Geistesgeschichte*, II (2018), pp. 117-130; H. P. Aust, "From Diplomat to Academic Activist: André Mandelstam and the History of Human Rights", *European Journal of International Law*, XXV (2014), pp. 1105-1121; Herman Burgers, "André Mandelstam: Forgotten Pioneer of International Human Rights", in Fons Coomans, et al. (eds.), *Rendering Justice to the Vulnerable* (The Hague, 2000); Dzovinar Kévonian, "André Mandelstam and the Internationalization of Human Rights (1869-1949)", in M. Halme-Toumisaari and Pamela Slotte (eds.), *Revisiting the Origins of Human Rights: Genealogy of a European Idea* (Cambridge, 2015), pp. 239-266; Kévonian,

Ants Piip *(also Hans, Anton, Antonii Ivanovich) (16(28) February 1884, b. Tuhalaane volost', Viljandi uezd, Livonian Governate – 1 October 1942, d. Nyrobsky Camp, Perm Region, USSR). International lawyer, diplomat, noted Estonian official and public figure.*

Life and career. Piip was born into a poor peasant family in Estonia.[347] After his basic primary education, he was accepted into a Teachers' Seminary in Goldingen (now Kuldīga, Latvia), graduating in 1903. Upon completing the Seminary, he taught for more than three years: first at a school in Marienburg (now Alūksne, Latvia), and from 1905 in the parish Russian Orthodox Emperor Nicholas II School in Arensburg on the Island of Saaremaa (now Kuressaare, Estonia), and from 1905 to 1912 in the Marine School in Arensburg. Having passed the examination for a certificate of maturity, Piip graduated as an external student from the Gymnasium in Arensburg in 1908. In that same year., at the age of 24, he enrolled at the Law Faculty of St. Petersburg University. There he remained for nearly a decade, being attracted by both international and criminal law.[348]

He took seminars on criminal law with privat-docent Pavel Isaevich Liublinskii (1882-1939) and M. M. Isaev on criminal law and with privat-docent Pilenko on international law. One of his classmates was Pitirim Sorokin (1889-1968).[349] With regard to international law, Piip submitted essays on the Russo-French literary convention and a report on the criminal law of the sea; with respect to criminal law – on complicity, which received an honorable mention. In 1912 he traveled at his own expense to Berlin University, where he attended lectures on international law by Franz von Liszt and E. Kaufmann and criminalistics with Liszt. He graduated from the Law Faculty of St. Petersburg University in spring 1913 and submitted a petition to the Rector of the University to remain at the Chair of International Law to undertake research. Professor Pilenko gave him a warm reference: "He displayed great talent for synthesis and excellent skills to cope with sources;

"Exilés politiques et avènement du 'droit humain': la pensée juridique d'André Mandelstam (1869-1949)", *Revue d'histoire de la Shoah*, no. 177-178 (January-August 2003), pp. 245-273.

347 Both dates, 16 and 28 February, appear in Russian and Estonian sources. Archival documents, for example Piip's enlisting in the military reserve, show the date of birth as 16 February, as does his passport issued 28 December 1917. See ЦГИА СПб., fond 14, opis 1, file 10821.

348 Most information on his early life is drawn from ЦГИА СПб., fond 14, opis 1, file 10821. Also see Ülo Kaevats, et al. (eds.), *Eesti Entsüklopeedia* (2000), XIV.

349 P. A. Sorokin, *A Long Journey: The Autobiography of Pitirim A. Sorokin* (New Haven, 1963).

a table which he compiled of the conditions for the acquisition and loss of subject-ship in various States may be considered to be exemplary". Pilenko added that Piip had a great capacity for work and an unusually mature intellect which might be explained only by the arduous conditions of the school of life through which he passed without any outside assistance. "I am convinced", Pilenko said, "that with the proper guidance a very conscientious scholar may emerge from Mr. Piip".[350]

On 7 October 1913 the Law Faculty invited Piip to remain at the Chair of International Law to prepare for a postgraduate degree and the professoriate; the term was limited to one year (without stipend) until 1 November 1914, later renewed for a year with conferral of the P. P. Demidov stipend of 600 rubles.[351] From 1914 to 1917 the status of Piip in the University underwent a series of events that may be attributed to the bureaucratization of the Russian higher educational system or as evidence of the attention and concern of the authorities for a talented but impoverished student. The outcome was that the system did support Piip after many petitions, recommendations, and supplications, as the archives amply demonstrate. While at the Chair, Piip conducted tutorials with students on the subject of submarine cables.[352] In 1916 Piip passed the examinations in international law and State law for the degree of magister of international law, which enabled him to transition to the status of a lecturer of Petrograd University.

In autumn 1916 Piip delivered lectures in preparation for his academic appointment on the subjects of the "International Treaty and Law' – a topic which he chose – and one designated by the Faculty – "Submarine Warfare"; both were satisfactorily received. On 11 November 1916 the Dean of the Law Faculty recommended to the Rector that Piip be appointed privat-docent to deliver a course on the "International Law of the Sea" in 1917.[353] For four years the University had confirmed to the Russian military authorities that Piip was duly enrolled in the Law Faculty and continued to support his position when he was appointed privat-docent.

Piip served as an assistant to a sworn advokat from 1914, which may have provided some income. He assured the Dean of the Law Faculty that he had a command of three foreign languages in addition to Estonian and Russian.

After the October 1917 Revolution in Russia, Piip left Petrograd University, returned to Estonia, became a distinguished political figure there in the Estonian

[350] ЦГИА СПб., fond 14, opis 1, file 10821, l. 2obverse-3.

[351] ЦГИА СПб., fond 14, opis 1, file 10821, l. 11.

[352] Отчет о состоянии и деятельности Императорского С.-Петербургского университета за 1913 год [Report on the State and Activity of Imperial St. Petersburg University for 1913] (Spb., 1914), p. 169.

[353] ЦГИА СПб., fond 14, opis 1. File 10821, l. 32. Appended to the petition was a list of publications and a curriculum vitae, which are no longer to be found in the archive. The Rector on 16 November 1916 sent the request on to the Administrator of the Petrograd Educational District, who replied positively on 23 November "without pre-deciding the question of him serving his military duty". Professor Pilenko found the syllabus for the course submitted by Piip to be "satisfactory, and the course of the law of the sea very agreeable, especially at the present time". ЦГИА СПб., fond 14, opis 3, file 14618, l. 74.

Republic, and held senior diplomatic and other State posts. In addition to his University employment, he accepted a position in the Department of Nationalities of the Ministry of Internal Affairs of the Provisional Government of Russia. On 8 July 1917 he became a member of the Provisional Zemskii Soviet of the Estland Governorate (Maapäev) – the first representative organ of the Estonian people. He was the Chairman thereof at the State Meeting in Moscow from 25-28 August 1917[354] and again at the All-Russian Democratic Meeting in Petrograd on 27 September-5 October 1917.[355] On 9 October 1917 Piip became a member of a Commission for drafting the Law on the Autonomy of Estonia within a federative Russia; the Commission was formed by the Zemskii Soviet.

Following the October 1917 Revolution, Piip held important State offices in the self-proclaimed Estonian Republic.

Diplomatic activity. Beginning in November 1917 Piip acted as the representative of the Zemskii Soviet assigned to commence negotiations with foreign countries concerning the recognition of the independence of Estonia.[356] Thereafter, several diplomatic assignments followed: plenipotentiary representative of Estonia to the RSFSR in Petrograd from 1918 to 1920; envoy of Estonia in the United States from 1923 to 1925. In 1919 he was Deputy Minister of Foreign Affairs and participated in the peace negotiations between Estonia and the RSFSR. On several occasions he was appointed the Minister of Foreign Affairs of Estonia: 1921-1922, 1925-1926, 1933, and 1939-1940. He took part in the Paris Peace Conference in 1919. When Estonia became part of the Union of Soviet Socialist Republics in 1940, Piip withdrew from political life.

In addition to various diplomatic assignments, Piip during the interwar period held several official positions, including the highest State posts: deputy of the State Assembly of Estonia from the Labor Party, Minister of War, Prime Minister, among others.

Instructional positions and activities. A busy diplomatic and political life did not prevent Piip from pursuing an academic career. From 1919 to 1940 he was the Professor of International Law at Tartu University, although his diplomatic assignments meant he could not effectively take up lecturing until after his return from the United States in 1925. From 1930 to 1939 he acted as the Chairman of the University Academic Court. He was elected to the National Assembly of Estonia from Tartu University.

He served as Chairman of the Academic Law Society of Estonia from 1932 to 1940; in 1932 was Visiting Professor at the University of California; maintained close ties with France as President of the French Academic Institute in Tartu from 1929 to 1940. From 1922 he acted as the Chairman of the Estonian Society of the

354 An All-Russian political forum convened by the Provisional Government to discuss the situation in Russia and unite the various groups and strata supporting it.

355 A meeting of the representatives of political parties and social organizations at which the Provisional Soviet of the Russian Republic (pre-parliament) was formed attached to the Provisional Government of Russia.

356 ЦГИА СПб., fond 14, opis 1, file 10821.

League of Nations (from 1937 to 1940, the Society of International Relations). He was chairman of the Pan-European Society from 1929 to 1940, and from 1932 to 1940, Chairman of the Estonian-Latvian Society.

His life ended tragically. When Estonia became part of the former Soviet Union, Piip was arrested by the People's Commissariat of Internal Affairs on 30 June 1941, accused of anti-Soviet activity, sent to a correctional-labor camp in the Ural mountains, and then transferred to the Nyrob Camp of the Molotov (now Perm) Region, where he died on 1 October 1941.

International legal practitioner. Piip's university training in international law served him well as a leading statesman for Estonia during the interwar period. As a senior stateman, he had a major role in the formulation of Estonian foreign policy. During 1918 he was successful in achieving recognition *de facto* for the independence of the Estonian Republic by several foreign States. Estonia sent an unofficial delegation to the Paris Peace Conference, of which Piip was a member. He took part in the negotiations between the Governments of Estonia and the RSFSR on cessation of the War and on 2 December 1920 was among those signing the Tartu Peace Treaty between Estonia and the RSFSR. The Treaty signified for Estonia the first recognition of its independence *de jure*, and for the RSFSR a "diplomatic breakthrough", for this was among the first Soviet Russian treaties with a foreign State.

Piip acted often as the Estonian representative at international conferences and headed the Estonian delegation to sessions of the League of Nations. He served on conciliation commissions to settle outstanding differences between Finland and the United States and between Estonia and the United States, as well as chairman of a commission resolving disputes between Greece and the United States. Once the Second World War commenced, Piip participated on 28 September 1939 as a member of the governmental delegation of Estonia in negotiations and the signature of the Pact on Mutual Assistance between the USSR and the Estonian Republic, on the basis of which Soviet forces occupied the territory of Estonia.

International legal views. So far as can be determined, Piip left only one published work devoted to international law – an article on the legal nature of directed provisions, which appeared in 1913.[357] At the time, this was an important and difficult private-law issue in the world of maritime law – the nature and legitimacy of targeted provisions or victuals. Virtually nothing had been written on the subject. Before entering the Law Faculty, Piip had taught at an institution in an Estonian seaport and is likely to have had some experience with merchant shipping.

Targeted provisions have disappeared from contemporary merchant shipping, and therefore at the beginning of the twentieth century this institution was perceived in many seaports as "payment for personal services on the part of a merchant in whose name a vessel had arrived, or who would be the trader or charterer" (p. 11). But it should be emphasized that Piip himself understood targeted provision as the survival of prior maritime customs, when the master of a merchant ship

[357] Ants Piip, «Юридическая природа адресной провизии» [Legal Nature of Directed Provisions], Русское судоходство [Russian Navigation], no. 9 (1913), pp. 11-15. Not in Butler or Grabar. Indeed, Grabar never mentions Piip in any respect.

putting into certain ports must pay some port charge: "Now it is nothing more than a pathetic injustice with respect to shipping, lacking legal grounds" (p.14).

The problematic nature and often absurdity of the custom, Piip believed, was that the master was obliged to pay an arbitrarily established charge even if he actually did not use any services. The targeted provision was economically beneficial only to merchants, but for the shipowner – loss-making. In these relations one of the parties – the consignee (or trader) – is obliged for personal services, and the other – the master or shipowner – is obliged to remunerate the contracting party for services (which often are not rendered at all). This custom has opponents (in the person of the shipowner and masters) and proponents, especially the various stock exchange structures.

Expressing disagreement in principle with the existence of this clearly obsolete and archaic institution, Piip nonetheless acknowledged that this tradition could not be eliminated "by one stroke of the pen". Therefore, he sought a legal foundation for this custom and to bring it within certain legal frameworks. The targeted provision, Piip said, "should be payment for real services ... and may not be recovered unless the parties have agreed to pay it or in a well-known amount, or pursuant to a local custom". This was not, he observed, a tax or duty established by the authorities, but the arbitrariness of the strong, reckoning on weak resistance, rooted in the historical past (p. 13).

Having also analyzed other aspects of this custom, Piip came to the following conclusions, having regard to marine commercial realities:

> [1]. The targeted provision, as payment for services, may occur only if this was agreed in written form in the charter party or freight contract, or other expression of will of the master;
>
> [2]. The amount of the payment is to be established by agreement of the parties;
>
> [3]. Such payment may occur only in the sole instance when the parties have included a condition in a charter party or freight contract concerning the need for such payment in an amount whose determination is provided for by a local custom (pp. 14-15).

Piip touched upon international legal issues in an extensive Report which he gave in November 1909 at Arensburg on the sailing fleet in the Baltic Sea – delivered at the First Congress of Russian Mariners.[358] Analyzing the physical condition and use of the sailing fleet in comparison with the steamship fleet of Russia, Piip considered that the authorities underestimated the potential of the sailing fleet for the economy of the Russian Empire. He proposed several measures to enhance the effectiveness of the sailing fleet: (a) authorize the duty-free import into Russia of large wooden sailing craft from abroad; (b) simplify customs formalities for foreigners, having established a close link between the customs service and the border guard, and liberalize the passport system; (c) reduce port charges and

[358] Ants Piip, Парусное мореходство Балтийского моря. Доклад. Аренсбург. Ноябрь 1909 [Sailing Navigation of the Baltic Sea. Report. Arensburg, November 1909. (M., 1909). 13 p.

remove survival charges (targeted provision, commission agency, and others); (d) build refuge seaports, allowing vessels from abroad to put into them; (e) regulate coastal law in the Baltic territory in the interests of sailors; (f) improve the judicial procedure for the consideration of maritime disputes either by creating special maritime courts or, when considering maritime disputes in ordinary courts, invite an expert assessor.

Lev Adamirovich Shalland *(also Leon-Rodolf, Lev Adolfovich, Lev Vladimirovich, Adamir, Vladimir, and Leo Challandes) (2 November 1868, b. Municipality of Fontaines,*[359] *Canton of Neuchatel, Switzerland – d. 1(13) December 1919, Rostov-on-Don, Russia). Specialist in international law and State law. Counsellor of State.*

Life and career. Having graduated from the III Petersburg Gymnasium, Shalland enrolled in the Law Faculty of St. Petersburg University in 1887 and completed his program in March 1891 with the degree of candidate of law.[360] He remained at the Chair of International Law to prepare for a postgraduate degree and the professoriate from 1 December 1891[361] until 1 April 1894. As part of his postgraduate studies, Shalland was sent abroad to visit the University of Geneva and Heidelberg University (with recommendations from Professor F. F. Martens); at Heidelberg he received the degree of Dr. phil. on 30 October 1893, awarded by the Faculty of Philosophy. The dissertation was published the following year in the German language at St. Petersburg.[362]

In October 1895 he passed the examinations for the magister of international law[363] and found employment with the Ministry of Finances; in 1900 he transferred to the Ministry of Justice.[364] As from 1 July 1901, Shalland was appointed privat-docent at the Chair of International Law of his University, where he offered

[359] Some sources record, incorrectly, that Shalland was born in St. Petersburg.

[360] ЦГИА СПб., fond 14, opis 3, file 26203; also see Starodubtsev, note 4 above, pp. 27, 107, 146.

[361] ЦГИА СПб., fond 14, opis 1, file 9257.

[362] See Leo Challandes, *Das Prinzip der Minoritätenvertretung und die Proportionalwahl* (Spb., Buchdr. V. Trenke & Füsnot, 1894; reprint Norderstedt, Hansebooks, 2017). 48 p.

[363] ЦГИА СПб., fond 14, opis 3, file 14296, l. 58-6; file 14397, l. 2.

[364] ЦГИА СПб., fond 14, opis 3, file 14490.

a special elective course "Private International Law".[365] He submitted his magister dissertation for defense in 1903. The topic was "The Legal Nature of Territorial Supremacy"; the defense took place on 2 November 1903.[366]

The official opponents were Professors M. A. von Taube and I. A. Ivanovskii. Taube in his report gave scathing comments on individual parts of the dissertation, but on the whole rated it as "good, conscientious, deeply thought out, and original – both in respect of the basic idea and the entire structure, a work undoubtedly deserving the learned degree of magister of international law for which the author supplicates".[367]

After his successful defense, Shalland was appointed on 30 January 1904 to the Chair of State Law at the Iurev (Dorpat) University[368] and moved away from the field of international law. From 1904 to 1911 he was professor *extraordinarius*; from 1911 to 1914, acting professor *ordinarius*; from 1914 to 1918, professor *ordinarius* at the Chair of State Law; from 1908 to 1912, Dean of the Law Faculty; and from 1915 to 1918, Pro-Rector of Iurev University. On 24 November 1913 Shalland submitted to St. Petersburg University and successfully defended a doctoral dissertation on "The Immunity of People's Representatives", which ensured his elevation to professor *ordinarius*.[369]

As an expert on State law, Shalland was appointed by the Provisional Government to a Special Meeting attached to the Legal Meeting in order to prepare the draft Basic Laws (Constitution) of the Russian Republic; Shalland drafted §14 "International Relations and Treaties". The commission met from 11 to 24 October 1917; that is, to the eve of the October Revolution that brought the Bolsheviks to power.

In September 1917 Shalland had petitioned the Ministry of Public Enlightenment in Petrograd to evacuate Iurev (Tartu) University to Voronezh in light of the imminent threat of a German invasion. The Soviet authorities decided in spring 1918 to honor that request, evacuating all those who wished by special train to Voronezh. Shalland in Voronezh became one of the founders of the University, Pro-

365 Отчет о состоянии и деятельности Императорского С.-Петербургского университета за 1901 год [Report on the State and Activity of Imperial St. Petersburg University for 1901] (Spb., 1902), p. 21.

366 See L. A. Shalland, Юридическая природа территориального верховенства. Историко-догматическое исследование [Legal Nature of Territorial Supremacy: Historico-Dogmatic Study] (Spb., 1903). Only one volume was published. On the defense, see ЦГИА СПб., fond 14, opis 3, file 14364, l. 8. Butler Ш30.

367 For the text of the review, see Loginova, note 303 above, Annex 14, p. 184.

368 Отчет о состоянии и деятельности Императорского С.-Петербургского университета за 1904 год [Report on the State and Activity of Imperial St. Petersburg University for 1904] (Spb., 1905), pp. 31-32.

369 The defense was reported in Право [Law], no. 6 (1914), pp. 465-471. The dissertation was published in two volumes: Shalland, Иммунитет народных представителей. Юридическое исследование [Immunity of People's Representatives. Legal Study] (Iurev, 1911-1913).

fessor of Law and State, the first dean of the Voronezh Law Faculty, and a member of the Board of that University.

Shalland died in Rostov-on-Don on 13 December 1919 at about 18:00 hours from a heart attack brought on by emaciation and illness; at the time he was visiting colleagues at the Don University en route from the Caucasus, where he had spent two months, to Voronezh, but hoping to find safer employment at the University.[370] He was buried in the Pokrov Cemetery, but that cemetery was closed before the Second World War and destroyed in the 1960s to construct apartment buildings. His personal library became part of the Library of Voronezh University.

International legal views. Before he moved away from the field of international law when he took up his appointment at Iurev (Tartu) University, Shalland made noteworthy contributions to public and private international law. The first was his magister dissertation on the legal nature of territorial supremacy. He noted in the Introduction:

> One would hardly find in the field of public law another question which has been so little explored or scantily illuminated by scholarly critique than the doctrine on the essence of territorial supremacy … territory in textbooks is usually treated in passing … the monographic literature is more than poor and does not encompass the issue in its entirety. Things are even worse in the doctrine of international law. Inquiries of principle are completely lacking. Territory is assimilated to a thing, and accordingly in the domain of inter-State relations civil-law constructions are carried over as a whole (p. 3).

The purpose of the dissertation, Shalland said, was to "elucidate the legal nature of territorial relations from the standpoint of public law" (p. 3). In the doctrinal literature of those times, the concept "State" included only two elements: power and population. As for the third element – territory – the issue was controversial. The merit of Shalland was that he substantiated the status of territory as an integral element of the State and put forward the conception of the formal equality of all three elements of the State. The absence of any one of them, Shalland asserted, deprived a political union of a material element and transformed it into something of another order than a State. No State could exist without space. Therefore, recognition of territory as a significant element of a State was a logical and essential consequence of the contemporary understanding thereof. But territory is not, he said, something that a State possesses or owns, but rather the spatial limit of its exercise of rule. A State has no rights to territory, and there are only rights within the territory. Therefore, the State is no longer identified with the owner of an estate – its power is construed as *imperium*.

In Shalland's view, municipal mechanisms ensured the stability of the regime of territory and limit possible arbitrariness of the government in disposing of territories. Shalland performed a service, it has been suggested,[371] by designating the

[370] See the note by N. A. Alubaeva, in Донской временник. Год 2019-ый [Don Chronicle 2019] (available online).

[371] S. N. Baburin, Территория государства: правовые и геополитические проблемы [Territory

types of such limitations in various States which might be defined as elements of internal law:

[1]. the boundaries of a State may be changed only on the basis of a law;

[2]. the constitution proclaims territory to be inalienable and indivisible;

[3]. the constitution enumerates all lands and regions which are part of State territory;

[4]. the treaties concerning a change of the territory of States must be ratified;

[5]. the government must be empowered by a law to alienate part of the territory (pp. 286-287).

Shalland considered in detail the history of the views and practice concerning territorial supremacy, the types, structure, and content of the legal supremacy of power, the legal nature of the acquisition and exercise of territorial supremacy, and the principal types of territorial changes (conquest, increment, assignment, gift, pledge, lease, cession, occupation, and others). He likewise examined issues of whether a State is required to receive foreigners and has the right to deport foreigners. He concluded that no civilized power believed that it had the right to refuse to admit all foreigners or to arbitrarily expel them. Any refusal to admit groups of foreigners must have a legal basis. Only individuals who represented a danger to the State were subject to deportation. Mass expulsions, especially arbitrary ones, were unspeakable.

This monograph addressed other issues of territory. When considering the problems of "pledge" and "lease", Shalland pointed out that "pledge" as a form of private-law transfer of territory to secure the performance of some obligation had receded into the past. Another private-law form of transfer of territory to another State had appeared at the end of the nineteenth century – the "use" (or lease). Shalland also discussed the legal nature of the coastal (or territorial) sea and coastal maritime navigation (cabotage).

Shalland undertook a study of the extradition by a State of its own citizens; he came to the view that one should reject the position of not extraditing them. He delivered two reports on this issue to the Petersburg Law Society in 1896 and 1899. He favored extradition, except with respect to States which were "half-civilized, barbaric, or wild" and States "whose territories were not the site of the preparation or commission of criminal actions".[372]

of a State: Legal and Geopolitical Problems] (M., 1997), p. 123.

372 Shalland, «Принципы невыдачи собственных подданных» [Principles of Non-Extradition of Own Subjects], Журнал юридического общества [Journal of the Law Society], no. 10 (1896), pp. 86-128. Butler Ш28; Shalland, «О выдаче собственных подданных» [On the Extradition of Own Subjects], Журнал Министерства юстиции [Journal of the Ministry of Justice], no. 4 (1899), pp. 245-247. Butler Ш20.

Still cited today is Shalland's article devoted to theoretical issues of international law.[373] He followed the position of strict étatisme, considering States to be the sole possible subject of international law and regarding international law in the narrow sense only as inter-State law. He emphasized their independence and being subordinate to no one. His approach on the whole was a progressive one for its time:

> One has long since been aware that only States are the subjects of international law. As an international legal relation came into existence, there are two poles thereof – the subject of law and the subject of a duty – which must be States; and therefore States are in a position of equality, being subordinate to no one. As this condition disappears, the relation loses its character and is transformed into an internal legal relation (p. 41).

Although he excluded the interdependence of international public and international private law, Shalland did not deny the possibility of a State entering into property relations in international turnover. Summing up his analysis of international-legal property relations of States which were, in Shalland's opinion, solely of a civilist character, he concluded that all international legal relations have a public character.

As a privat-docent of St. Petersburg University, Shalland was actively involved in investigating issues of private international law; indeed, the majority of his articles were devoted to that branch of law. Many addressed general questions: modern trends in the science of private international law; Russian judicial practice in cases involving foreigners, the application of foreign law by Russian courts, the status of foreign joint-stock societies in Russia; international aspects of family law, law of inheritance, inheritance duties to be recovered from foreigners in Russia, among others.

Shalland considered the character and nature of private international law only from the standpoint of conflicts of law; the last, in his view, was of a private-law nature and fall within the system of municipal law. Accordingly, of all the sources of law applicable for private international law, Shalland recognized only the legislation of States. In exceptional instances he accepted judicial practice as a source of private international law and the views of competent specialists. But even these last two sources, he believed, were recommendatory in nature.

Shalland reviewed Russian and foreign works on public and private international law frequently.

373 Shalland, «Международно-правовое отношение (К вопросу о конструкции международного права)» [International-Legal Relation: On the Question of the Construction of International Law], Вестник права [Herald of Law], no. 8 (1900), pp. 35-66. Butler Ш17.

§7.2.2. *Members of Chair of International Law Who Were Graduates of Other Russian Universities*

Mikhail Ivanovich Dogel *(11 September 1865, b. Heidelberg, Germany – 25 August 1936, d. Paris, France). International lawyer, professor, official of Ministry of Foreign Affairs, privy State counsellor.*

Life and career. Dogel graduated in 1888 from the Faculty of Medicine and Mathematics of Kazan University with the title of true student of the medical and mathematical sciences. He was then employed by the Kazan Governate Board, where he worked until September 1890. After an examination in the State Legal Testing Commission attached to Kazan University, Dogel transferred to the Ministry of Justice and was sent to the Chancellery of the Fifth Department of the Ruling Senate. In Autumn 1892 he was sent abroad at his own expense to visit foreign universities and libraries. Upon returning and passing the magister examinations, he was appointed privat-docent at the Chair of International Law of Kazan University. In 1894 he published a book in Kazan,[374] which he submitted to St. Petersburg University in satisfaction of the requirements for a magister dissertation. He defended successfully on 26 February 1895[375] and was awarded the degree of magister of international law.[376]

The Ministry of Public Enlightenment thereupon transferred Dogel as privat-docent to the Chair of International Law at Kharkov University. This appointment proved to be short-lived; in November 1896 he was transferred with the same rank and title to the Chair of International Law at Kazan University to replace P. E. Kazanskii. He defended a doctoral dissertation at Kharkov devoted to the law of military occupation[377] and was then promoted to be professor and head of the Chair of International Law at Kazan University. In 1905 he moved to St. Petersburg. From 1 May 1911 until 24 April 1913 he was privat-docent at the Chair of International Law in St. Petersburg University,[378] where he lectured on "The History of the Development of International Relations and Law".[379]

[374] M. I. Dogel, «Юридическое положение личности во время сухопутной войны. Комбатанты» [Legal Status of the Individual During Land Warfare: Combatants] (Kazan, 1894).

[375] ЦГИА СПб., fond 14, opis 2, file 925. Also see K. O. Savchuk, «Догель Михайло Іванович» [Dogel, Mikhailo Ivanovych], in Denysov, note 4 above, I, p. 837; Starodubtsev, note 4 above, pp. 15, 18, 40-43, 53-55, 103, 117, 118, 247.

[376] The defense was reported in the Журнал Юридического общества при Императорском Санкт-Петербургском университете [Journal of the Law Society attached to the Imperial St. Petersburg University], kn. 4 (1895), pp. 59-63.

[377] Dogel, О военном занятии (*Occupatio bellica*) [On Military Occupation (*Occupatio bellica*)] (Kazan, 1899).

[378] ЦГИА СПб., fond 14, opis 1, file 10511.

[379] Dogel lectured on Tuesdays, from 12:00 to 13:00, using as the basis of his presentations: F. Laurent, *Histoire du droit des gens et de l'humanité*; Taube, Принципы войны и мира в Средние века [Principles of War and Peace in the Middle Ages], Holzendorff, F. F. Martens, and a number of other monographs. ЦГИА СПб., fond 14, opis 1, file 10511; also see Обозрение преподавания

From 1911 to 1917 he was a member of the Chief Administration for Affairs of the Press. Simultaneously, from 1914 to 1917 he was professor *ordinarius* at the Chair of Police Law of Iurev University.

For some reason all electronic and printed sources which contain Dogel's biographical data omit the fact that he worked in the Ministry of Foreign Affairs. In May 1916 Dogel was appointed to be head of the Legal Unit of the Ministry,[380] succeeding Boris Nolde. The lack of reference to this appointment may be that Dogel did not hold an established appointment in the Ministry and maintained his positions in Iurev and at the Chief Administration for Affairs of the Press.

During the Russian Civil War, Dogel emigrated and lived first in Constantinople, where he was elected Deputy Chairman of the Board of the Russian Committee in Turkey. Thereafter he moved on to Paris. He lectured as a professor at the Russian Law Faculty of the University of Paris (1925-1926); in 1925 he offered a course on "The Development of the Science of International Law in Russian Literature"; in 1926, "Private International Law in Connection with Russian Civil Law". He often spoke to or lectured in Russian émigré organizations.

Dogel died at Paris in 1936 and is buried at the Cimetière Thiais.

International legal views. Dogel was among the early Russian international lawyers, following F. F. Martens, to select as his area of concentration international legal aspects of the law of war, particularly the legal status of disabled persons. Both his dissertations were devoted to these issues: the magister dissertation on the legal status of the individual during war on land and his doctoral dissertation on military occupation. These works combined important conclusions: (1) the purpose of international law with respect to war is not to abolish war, but to subject war to the laws of war; (2) persons who are no longer in a position to continue their participation in a war and the peaceful population should be placed under the protection of international law.

Dogel's magister dissertation addressed the legal status of disabled persons during war – the rights of military servicemen taking part in combat operations, and the rights of peaceful inhabitants. At the outset of his magister dissertation, Dogel pointed to the topicality of his chosen subject:

> The question of the legal status of human beings during war is one of the most interesting in all of international law, and its resolution is vital for the possible humanizing of war itself; only by defining the rights and duties of belligerent States precisely and clearly with respect to the human individual can one hope to mitigate the horrors of war and to subject the manifestations thereof to certain legal norms (p. 1).

на юридическом факультете Императорского С.-Петербургского университета на осеннее полугодие 1912 и весеннее полугодие 1913 года [Survey of Teaching at the Law Faculty of the Imperial St. Petersburg University in the Autumn Semester of 1912 and Spring Semester of 1913] (Spb., 1913), pp. 19-20.

380 See Mikhailovskii, note 270 above, I, p. 67.

At the end of his preface, Dogel expressed the hope that his work on the status of the individual during war (using the example of active combatants) would serve "in Russian literature as an addition to the monograph by Professor Martens 'On Private Ownership During War'" (p. ii). In his introductory remarks when defending his dissertation, Dogel articulated his views on war. He believed that "war is a calamity for States and for their subjects; but it is not an evil originating in the evil of human will". But he followed Niccolò di Bernardo dei Machiavelli (1469-1527) in seeing war as a given: "War is an inevitable step in the life of nations and States which live and die away while undertaking certain missions".[381]

Dogel's dissertation raised a number of topical and complex issues of the law of war . This was evident, for example, when he addressed the controversial issue of who were to be regarded as "legal combatants" and should "participants of partisan detachments in a mass uprising" be deemed to be legal combatants. One merit of the Dogel dissertation was that he formulated a definition of legal combatant before the 1899 and 1907 Hague conventions; in his view:

> a person taking an active part in military actions in the interests and in the name of his State, wearing a well-known distinguishing mark permanent and visible at a long distance, belonging to some militarily organized detachment under the leadership of a responsible commander, and complying with the laws and customs of war (p. 225).

With respect to partisans, Dogel recognized their legality, considering partisan detachments to be organs of social self-government for the defense of the State. In his view, partisan detachments as self-defense organs of the State were formed at the initiative of society itself or individual members thereof. Although not governmental, they were nonetheless State because they pursued a purpose that was a State purpose and acted in the name of and to the benefit of the State (p. 199).

Dogel also demonstrated that prisoners of war were not criminals and therefore not subject to trial and punishment. They had the right to respect of the individual and to release from captivity.

Professors F. F. Martens and N. M. Korkunov were the official opponents at Dogel's dissertation defense; the unofficial opponent was Professor Nikolai Dmitrievich Sergeevskii (1849-1908). They noted both the merits and a series of shortcomings and omissions of the dissertation author (ambiguity, unsystematic account of certain scientific positions, especially when defining the concept of war, the presence of a uniform when determining the status of a combatant, the universality of an uprising on captured territory, the requirement that the population declare to the enemy in good time their intention to resist, punishment for espionage, and others).[382]

Martens said in his report on the dissertation: "... despite major shortcomings in Dogel's work, it all the same is a contribution to the Russian literature on international law. The author displayed a close familiarity with the literature of the

[381] See note 374 above, pp. 59-63.

[382] Ibid., pp. 59-63.

topic he chose and in good faith tried to cast the light of truth and Christian love" on the protection of the individual in the course of a war.[383]

Dogel's doctoral dissertation, defended at Kharkov University, was the first in Russia to consider the regime of military occupation. Dogel's views on the legal limitations on the means and methods of waging war continue to find their place in contemporary writings.[384]

Evald Karlovich Simson *(also Ewald-Wilhelm) (28 February 1869, b. Tartu, Lifliand Governate (now Estonia) – 1918; d. Vyborg, Finland (now Leningrad Region)).[385] Jurist, diplomat, founder and editor of international-legal journal.*

Life and career. Evald Simson graduated in 1891 from the Law Faculty of Dorpat University. At his request, he became a candidate for a judicial post attached to the St. Petersburg District Court and was sent for training in the V Civil Division. On 25 January 1892 his status was redesignated as junior candidate for a post in the judicial department attached to a district court, but on 23 November 1892 he resigned.

In that same year he submitted a dissertation to the Law Faculty of Dorpat University on the non-extradition of own subjects. The reviews by the examiners were highly negative, including that by Grabar,[386] and the Faculty rejected the dissertation. On 22 January 1893 Simson requested the Rector of St. Petersburg University to allow him to defend a dissertation on the same subject, attaching to his request a certificate that he had passed the magister examinations at Dorpat University and six examples of the dissertation.[387] The following day the Rector wrote to the Dean of the Law Faculty, assigning him to organize consideration of the work and attaching the examination certificate and the copies of the dissertation.[388] There is no information in the archives about what happened next.

383 ЦГИА СПб., fond 14, opis 3, file 14298, l. 2; cited in Loginova, note 303 above, p. 105.

384 See, for example, M. A. Mishkuro, «Понятие «незаконный комбатант» и его правовое положение в международном гуманитарном праве» [Concept of "Illegal Combatant" and the Legal Status Thereof in International Humanitarian Law], Отечественная юриспруденция [Fatherland Jurisprudence], no. 3 (2016), p. 20.

385 According to the annual reference work Весь Петербург [All Petersburg], Simson resided in St. Petersburg from 1896 to 1899 at ul. Stremiannoi, no. 8. In 1900 he raised questions about the amenities of his place of residence. ЦГИА СПб., fond 513, opis 83, file 113. He disappeared from sight after that, and no further information has been located about him from 1900 onwards until 1914, when he sought a document from the Law Faculty.

386 Grabar, note 46 above, p. 392. Also see Starodubtsev, note 4 above, pp. 14-15; W. E. Butler, "Ewald-Wilhelm Simson: Estonian/Russian International Lawyer", *Jus Gentium: Journal of International Legal History*, VIII (2023), pp. 145-158.

387 ЦГИА СПб., fond 14, opis 1, file 9350, l. 1.

388 ЦГИА СПб., fond 14, opis 1, file 9350, l. 2.

On 10 September 1894 Simson wrote to the Rector of St. Petersburg University, asking to be allowed to publicly defend a dissertation on another topic – on capture according to the principles of international law.[389] The dissertation had been published as a monograph.[390] The public defense, held on Sunday, 11 December 1894, was successful and the degree magister of international law was conferred.[391] Having completed his magister degree, Simson was appointed as a lecturer. On 18 January 1895 he wrote to the Dean of the Law Faculty requesting that he be allowed to lecture in the capacity of a privat-docent and offer a course on the introduction to international law.[392] In February 1895 the Administrator of the St. Petersburg Educational District accepted the recommendation of the University and authorized him to begin lecturing from the following semester.[393] Simson delivered his first lecture on 7 September 1895. He had been appointed privat-docent in the Chair of International Law from 1 July 1895.

From 1896 Simson worked in the University and the Ministry of Foreign Affairs[394] in the Second Department; he remained with the Ministry until 1916. At the University, Simson offered an elective course on the "Sources and Literature of International Law and the History of International Relations" and from 1896 to 1899, the basic introduction to "International Law". As from 1 July 1899 Simson resigned from St. Petersburg University.[395]

In July 1914 Simson requested the Rector of the University to issue a certificate to him concerning his sojourn at the University for inclusion on a formulary list at the Ministry of Foreign Affairs; Simson specified his position – clerk of the Second Department, Ministry of Foreign Affairs, and, as from 14 April 1913, privy State counsellor.[396] By Ruling of the Department of Heraldry of the Ruling Senate, on 5 June 1914 Simson, together with his daughter Irina, was deemed to be of the ancestral nobility – duly confirmed by the Administrator of the Ministry of Justice on 10 August 1915. Simson lived in St. Petersburg until at least 1917.

International legal views. Many of Simson's views on international law were original and stand out among his Russian contemporaries. In his first, and unsuccessful, magister dissertation on the non-extradition of own subjects, Simson discussed several complex legal issues which attracted a significant audience among

[389] ЦГИА СПб., fond 14, opis 1, file 9350, l. 3.

[390] Simson, О завладении по началам международного права [On Capture according to the Principles of International Law] (Spb., 1894). Butler C76.

[391] ЦГИА СПб., fond 14, opis 1, file 9350, l. 6.

[392] ЦГИА СПб., fond 14, opis 3, file 14299, l. 3, cited in Loginova, note 303 above, p. 67.

[393] ЦГИА СПб., fond 14, opis 1, file 9350, l. 11.

[394] For correspondence among the Ministry, the Administrator of the Educational District, and the Rector of the University on this, see ЦГИА СПб., fond 14, opis 1 , file 9950, l. 15-16.

[395] ЦГИА СПб., fond 14, opis 1, file 9350, l. 7.

[396] ЦГИА СПб., fond 14, opis 1, file 9350 l. 25.

colleagues. Even though there was no dissertation defense, the book has been widely cited.[397]

Simson attempted a new foundation for the extradition by a State of own subjects at the request of another State. The work was divided into two parts: the first contained a detailed survey of the historical and contemporary development of extradition; the second considered the theories of those who supported or opposed non-extradition. Working from the premise that the violation of legal norms of a State was the basis for the punishment and extradition of a criminal, Simson concluded that the offender, whether a foreigner or indigenous, should be extradited to the State whose legal interests were violated. In Simson's view: "Extradition in the legal sense is an act of judicial assistance and consists of the voluntary transfer of a person accused of a crime by that State on whose territory this person is situated to another State, which is the victim of the crime of this person and requests the transfer thereof".

Simson's principal argument in favor of extradition of an own citizen is that the State punishing its own citizen who committed a crime abroad and violated the interests of another State cannot fully and precisely guarantee the protection of the legal interests of the other State, and therefore is obliged to extradite him to the State for punishment.

Simson's second and successful magister dissertation on capture under international law received considerable media attention. His basic positions were as follows: the State, just as any organism, lives and develops; therefore, it is natural that a State aspires to expand the territorial space occupied by it. In Simson's time that was occurring in Africa, which was being divided into spheres of influence and European possessions. The time had come for the adoption of legal norms regulating such acquisitions. The aim of his study, Simson said, was to demonstrate that all means of acquiring State territory should be reduced to occupation or capture. Whereas in private law capture entailed acquiring the right of ownership, then in international law the result of capture is public supreme dominion over the State territory. Therefore, only States may be the subject of capture. The occupation of territory is performed by agencies of the State on its behalf; that is, only on the basis of a *mandatum speciale*.

Occupation, Simson suggested, imposed certain obligations on the State which took possession of some territory, including to respect the rights of the native population and other inhabitants of the occupied territory. The occupying State is obliged to respect and protect the right of private ownership of natives to land. It may convert to its own ownership only that part of the lands of the occupied territory which belong to no one.

The first official opponent of the dissertation, F. F. Martens, singled out what he considered to be an erroneous thesis that the occupied lands are *res nullius*. He proved through historical examples that this was not the case. The same applied to conquest. The other opponents, Professor Sergei Aleksandrovich Bershchadskii

[397] Simson, О невыдаче собственных подданных: Международно-правовое исследование [On Non-Extradition of Own Subjects: International Legal Study] (Spb., 1892). Butler C77.

(1850-1896) and Docent David Davidovich Grimm (1864-1941) also had critical observations.

Simson's views on the system of international law were original and controversial. His book on the subject generated lively discussion.[398] In this work he declared himself to be a "nationalist" in international law. Grabar published a severely critical review, having determined that much was borrowed from the works of others.[399] Shalland was no less scathing and wrote with irony that Simson had set himself the task of seeking a "new substantiation of international law", having already occupied himself with that subject for more than fourteen years.[400]

Simson analyzed foreign and Russian doctrinal systems of international law, including those of Professors F. F. Martens and N. M. Korkunov at St. Petersburg University. The best system, in his view, was that of Professor Karl Kaltenborn von Stachau (1817-1866), of Königsberg University. Simson proposed his own system: Introduction, General Part, and Special Part. The General Part addressed the subject, objects, organs, and means of defending the interests of the State; he placed individual branches of international law in the Special Part: private law, criminal law, means of transport, trade law, and law of the sea. His singling out individual branches into an autonomous section of the system was, for that period, a progressive step forward.

Simson denied the possibility of international communion and general international law between States. He asserted that "international law is not law which operates between nations", that "any law has force and operates only within a State, but between States; that is, there where the supreme power of no State extends, is, so to say, a space without law". In his view, international communion likewise was an "empty concept", that is, without legal substance the therefore should be removed from scientific terminology and is not a subject of international law.

Simson believed that only the international law of an individual State exists: "international law signifies part of the law of the State, precisely as the expression 'private law', 'criminal law', and so on". The civil law of any State, said Simson, contains a Special Part – "Private International Law", which consists of conflicts norms of national private law. The principal task of private international law is the elimination of possible conflicts between the provisions of national and of foreign law. But Simson, working from his perception of international law as part of national law, included private international law within the general international law of a State. He reduced all international law to external State law: "… so-called international law is national, just as any law in general. We must nationalize international law in order to receive the aggregate of truly binding legal norms" (p. 61).

398 Simson, Система международного права [System of International Law] (Spb., 1900). Only volume one appeared. Butler C79.

399 Grabar, Неудачная попытка национализации международного права [Unsuccessful Attempt to Nationalize International Law] (Iurev, 1901). Butler Г335; originally published in Ученые записки Юрьевского университета [Learned Papers of the Iurev University], no. 5 (1901), pp. 1-23. Butler Г336.

400 Shalland, review of Simson in Право [Law], no. 16 (1900), cols. 844-888.

On the basis of the above premises, Simson offered his own definition of international law, which for him was external State law: "The international law of a particular State is the aggregate of those legal norms which have force for the particular State, the organs and subjects thereof, and in general for all persons under its power, and which contain a foreign element or an element relating to something situated abroad" (p. 60).

Simson believed that insofar as, in his view, international law does not exist, then the codification of international law was "inconceivable and impossible". As indicated above, Simson's view concerning his system of international law were sharply criticized in prerevolutionary doctrinal writings. Grabar wrote in his review: "Simson takes under advisement only the will of one State, whereas any international legal norm requires recognition on the part of two States at least. Otherwise, we have to do not with international law, but with State law …".[401]

Nonetheless, the system proposed by Simson was and remains interesting:

System of International Law

Proposed by E. K. Simson

Introductory Part:

1. Basic Concepts
2. Doctrine of Sources of International Law
3. History of the Development of International Law
4. History of the Development of the Science of International Law

General Part:

1. Subjects of International Law
2. Objects of International Law
3. Organs Defending the Interests of the State
4. On Means of Defense of Interests of the State in International Relations. Neutrality

Special Part:

1. Private International Law
2. International Criminal Law
3. Law on Means of International Transport
4. International Trade Law and Law of the Sea

[401] Grabar, note 399 above, p. 12.

This system was a clear departure from the dominant classical division of international law into the Law of War and the Law of Peace.[402]

Journal of International and State Law. Without doubt the most significant of his achievements, Simson was the founder and editor of a specialized periodical publication in Russia: the Журнал международного и государственного права [Journal of International and State Law]. Far superior in concept and execution when compared to its predecessor published by the Russian Society of International Law in 1880 and not emulated in Russia until a century later, this journal was short-lived, but substantial. Six numbered issues appeared in 1897, one volume comprising three issues. By its own numeration, therefore, the journal comprised two volumes in one year.[403]

In his introductory manifesto or "program" for the journal, Simson commented that the "primitive state of publishing … in Russia" made it difficult for young scholars to publish their works and that foreign international lawyers were rarely published in the general Russian legal media. Simson attracted nearly ninety eminent international and public lawyers from all over the world to serve on the editorial board. Among the Russian members were V. N. Aleksandrenko (Warsaw); A. S. Alekseev (Moscow), V. P. Danevskii (Kharkov), V. E. Grabar (Iurev), I. A. Ivanovskii (Moscow), and A. F. Koni (Moscow). From the United Kingdom (G. Burnet (Edinburgh) and from the United States, I. B. Cassody (Madison, Wisconsin) and Charles B. Eliot (Minneapolis) – all of whom contributed articles. Continental Europe provided the balance, including such well-known figures as G. Jellinek (Heidelberg), H. Triepel (Leipzig), F. Zorn (Königsberg), Th. Funck-Brentano (Paris), and P. Fiore (Naples).

Simson struck a careful and well-conceived balance among readership interests: State practice in the form of government documents; substantive articles well chosen to represent public and private international law, State law, theory and practice, Russian and foreign contributors, and comparative public law. He enlisted Professor Kamarovskii (Moscow) to prepare the Chronicle of recent events. Italian judicial practice was examined in detail. Some treaties and other documents were reproduced, but not in all issues. Books reviews were undertaken by Russian and foreign reviewers, accompanied by a conspectus of the leading European international law journals. The contents were as follows:

I. Government Regulations Relating to Ministry of Foreign Affairs

Распоряжения Правительства по ведомству Министерства иностранных дел

[402] See N. N. Kirilovskaia, Система международного права в отечественной международно-правовой доктрине [System of International Law in Fatherland International-Legal Doctrine] (M., 2008), pp. 97-105.

[403] See W. E. Butler, "The Development of International Legal Periodicals in Russia", *Review of Socialist Law*, IX (1983), pp. 367-376; Butler, note 386 above.

I, no. 1 pp. 13-17; no. 2, p. 137-150; no. 3, opp. 281-295.

II, no. 4, pp. 1-8, no. 5, pp. 113-119, no. 6, p. 227-238.

II. Articles

Aleksandrenko, V. N. «Назначение русских дипломатических агентов в XVIII в.» [Appointment of Russian Diplomatic Agents in the XVIII Century], I, no. 1, pp. 51-63; no. 2, pp. 162-172.

Barazetti, Z. «Принципальные точки зрения для разрешения столкновений законов местных и иностранных» [Principal Points of View for the Settlement of Local and Foreign Conflicts of Laws], II, no. 6, pp. 280-290.

Burnet, G. «Частное международное право в Великобритании» [Private International Law in Great Britain], II, no. 5, pp. 169-179.

Cassody, I. B. «Двойственная система правления в Северо-Американских Соединенных Штатах» [Dual System of Government in the North American United States], II, no. 4, pp. 73-76.

Corsi, A. «О необходимости положительной санкции в публичном международном праве» [On the Necessity of Positive Sanctions in Public International Law], II, no. 5, pp. 156-168; no. 6, pp. 273-279.

Eliot, C. B. «Судебный контроль над законодательноой властью в Северо-Американских Соединенных Штатах» [Judicial Control over Legislative Power in the North American United States], I, no. 1 p. 80-86; no. 2, pp. 197-210; no. 3, pp. 318-331.

Fiore, P. «О третейском суде и о его практической приложимости для уничтожения войны» [On the Arbitration Court and its Practical Application for the Elimination of War], II, no. 4, pp. 32-45.

Funck-Brentano, Th. «Международный третейский суд и социальные законы» [International Arbitration Court and Social Laws], I, no. 1, pp. 41-50; no. 2, pp. 151-161.

Heilborn, P. «Международные союзы для охраны промышленной собственности» [International Unions for the Protection of Industrial Property], II, no. 5, pp. 120-134; no. 6, pp. 239-250.Ivanovskii, I. A. «К вопросу о природе государства» [On the Question of the Nature of the State], I, no. 1, pp. 64-79; no. 2, pp. 181-196.

Kamarovskii, L. A. «Новейшие договоры об Африке» [Most Recent Treaties on Africa], I, no. 1, pp. 18-40.

Korostovets, I. «Португальцы в Мозамбике» [Portuguese in Mozambique (Delimitation with Great Britain)], I, no. 2, pp. 211-226; no. 3, pp. 347-362.

Laurent de la Barre, J. de «Занзибарский инцидент (требование о выдаче Сайда-Каледа)» [The Zanzibar Incident (Request for Extradition of Saida-Kaleda)], I, no. 1, pp. 87-95.

Ricci, R. «Право «вето» и предстоящий конклав» [Right of "Veto" and the Forthcoming Conclave], I, no. 3, pp. 307-317; II, no. 4, pp. 22-31.

Sabler, Iu. «О двойном подданстве» [On Dual Subject-ship], II, no. 4, pp. 46-65; no. 5, pp. 135-155; no. 6, pp. 251-272.

Simson, E. K. «Наша программа» [Our Program], I, no. 1, pp. 1-12.

Triepel, H. «О догматической обработке международного права» [On the Dogmatic Processing of International Law], I, no. 3, pp. 296-306; II, no. 4, pp. 9-21.

Ullmann, E. «Основания идеи международного права» [Basis for the Idea of International Law], I, no. 2, p. 173-180.

Zorn, F. «Германская империя» [German Empire], I, no. 3, pp. 332-346; III, no. 4, pp. 66-72.

III. International Chronicle (listed chronologically)

Kamarovskii, L. A. «Заграничное путешествие их Величеств – Решение Критского вопроса – Седьмой общий съезд друзей мира – Современная партия мира – Мир Италии с Абиссинией» [Foreign Trip of Their Majesties – Resolution of Crete Question – Seventh General Congress of Friends of Peace – Contemporary Party of Peace – Peace of Italy with Abyssinia], I, no. 1, pp. 96-109.

___. «1896 г. в международном отношении» [1896 in International Relations], I, no. 2, pp. 240-249.

___. «XVII съезд Института международного права – VII сессия международно-парламентской конференции – Критский вопрос» [XVII Congress of Institute of International Law – VII Session of Inter-Parliamentary Conference – Crete Question], I, no. 3, pp. 368-369.

___. «Англо-Американский третейский договор – Третейский суд между Великобританиею и Венецуелой – Санитарная конференция в Венеции – Треверс Твисс (некролог) – Греко-турецкая война» [Anglo-American Arbitration Agreement – Arbitration Court Between Great Britain and Venezuela – Sanitary Conference in Venice – Trevers Twiss (Obituary) – Graeco-Turkish War], II, no. 4, pp. 77-91.

___. «Предварительный мирный договор между Грециею и Турциею – Еще о греко-турецкой войне» [Preliminary Peace Treaty between Greece and Turkey – Once More on the Graeco-Turkish War], II, no. 5, pp. 180-189.

___. «XVIII Съезд Института международного права в Копенгагене –Торговая конвенция России с Болгарией [XVIII Congress of the Institute of International Law in Copenhagen – Trade Convention of Russia with Bulgaria], II, no. 6, pp. 291-299.

IV. International Treaties and Acts

«Декларация между Россией и Японией, 27 февраля-11 марта 1897 г.» [Declaration between Russia and Japan, 27 February-11 March 1897], I, no. 3, p. 363-364.

«Франция-Великобритания: Конвенция, видоизменящая ст. 7 и 9 трактата о выдаче 14 августа 1896 г.» [France-Great Britain Convention Changing Articles 7 and 9 of the Treat on Extradition of 14 August 1896], I, no. 1, p. 110-111.

«Меморандум, заключенный между Россией и Японией 2-14 мая 1896 г.» [Memorandum, concluded between Russia and Japan, 2-14 May 1896], I, no. 2, pp. 229-231.

«Международный союз для защиты литературной и художественной собственности 1896 г.» [International Union for the Protection of Literary and Artistic Property of 1896], I, no. 1, pp. 111-115.

«О дополнении ст. 3 тарифа консульских пошлин» [On an Addition to Article 3 of the Tariff of Consular Duties], I, no. 2, p. 238.

«Об изменении узаконении о порядке вызова наследников после умерших иностранцев-азияцев» [On Change of the Legislation of the Procedure for the Calling of Heirs After Foreign Asians Have Died], I, no. 2, pp. 238-239.

«Протокол между Россией и Японией 28 мая-9 июня 1896 г.» [Protocol between Russia and Japan, 28 May-9 June 1896], I, no. 2, pp. 227-229.

«Распоряжение о включении Франции в список государств, в которых русские подданные освобождены от представлении обеспечения издержек и убытков ответчика» [Regulation on Inclusion of France on List of States in Which Russian Subjects are Exemption from Submission of Security for Costs and Losses of Defendant], I, no. 2, pp. 237-238.

«Третейское решение тайного советника Ф. Ф. Мартенса по делу "Costa Rica Packet"» [Arbitral Award of Privy Councillor F. F. Martens in "Costa Rica Packet" Case], I, no. 3, pp. 365-367.

«Заключительный протокол русско-германской конференции 9 февраля 1897 г.» [Final Protocol of Russo-German Conference of 9 February 1897], I, no. 2, pp. 231-237.

V. Judicial Practice

Fusinato, G. «Обзор итальянской судебной практики по вопросам международного права» [Survey of Italian Judicial Practice on Questions of International Law], I, no. 2, pp. 250-263; no. 3, pp. 390-402; no. 5, pp. 190-207; no. 6, pp. 300-311.

VI. Bibliography

A. *Journals*

«Периодическая издания» [Periodical Publications], I, no. 1, pp. 133-135; no. 2, pp. 276-278; no. 3, pp. 422-423; II, no. 4, pp. 110-111; no. 5, pp. 225-226; no. 6, p. 322.

Pic, P. «Обзор статей по международному праву, помещенных во французских журналах за 1895 г.» [Survey of Articles on International Law Placed in French Journals for 1895], I, no. 2, pp. 264-271; no. 3, p. 403-414; II, no. 4, pp. 92-105; no. 5, pp. 208-214; no. 6, pp. 312-318.

B. *Book Reviews*

Chicherin, B. N. Курс государственной науки [Course of State Science] (M., 1894-98). 3 pts.: I, no. 1, pp. 116-128 (V. Rennenkampf).

Esmein, A. *Eléments de droit constitutionnel* (Paris, Larouse, 1896). Xi, 270 p.: II, no. 4, pp. 106-109 (X. S. Combothécrea).

Fedozzi, P. *Gli enti colletivi nel diritto internazionale privato, con speciale riguardo al diritto di succssione* (Padova, Fratelli Drucker, 1897). xi, 270 p.: II, no. 6, pp. 319-321 (X. S. Combothécrea).

LeFur, L. E. *État fédéral et confederation d'états* (Paris, Imp. Marchal et Billard, 1896). 839 p.: I, no. 3, pp. 417-421 (L. A. Shalland).

Nagao, Ariga. *La guerre sino-japanoise et le droit international* (Paris, Pedone, 1896). Xii, 310 p.: II, no. 5, pp. 215-224 (L. A. Shalland).

Rivier, A. P. O. *Principes du droit des gens* (Paris, Rousseau, 1896). 2 vols.: I, no. 2, pp. 272-275 (X. S. Combothécrea).

Waurin, L. *Une vue d'ensemble de la question sociale* (Paris, 1896): I, no. 1, pp. 129-132 (X. S. Combothécrea).

Zhigarev, S. A. Русская политика в восточном вопросе, ее история в XVI-XIX веках [Russian Policy in the Eastern Question and History Thereof in the XVI-XIX Centuries] (M., Univ. tip., 1896). 2 vols: I, no. 3, pp. 415-417 (L. A. Kamarovskii).

The archives of the Journal apparently have not survived. It is believed that Simson covered the costs of the journal himself, less whatever revenues may have been received. No copies of the journal are known outside Russia.

Chapter 8
Other Graduates

§8.1. *Graduates Who Prepared for Professoriate but Became Legal Scholars Elsewhere*

The Chair of International Law at St. Petersburg University, just as similar chairs elsewhere in the city, was at the apogee of its development and attracted younger scholars who dreamed of an academic or academic/governmental career. Several promising law graduates remained at the Chair to prepare for the professoriate but then pursued their interests at other institutions of higher education in Russia or abroad.

For them, and for the discipline of international law generally, the second decade of the twentieth century was catastrophic – the First World War, the 1917 Revolutions, the Russian Civil War in rapid succession. Promising careers were interrupted and/or destroyed. Some succeeded in fleeing the Revolutions and found something or nothing relevant abroad. Some were able to complete their magister or doctoral dissertations and were appointed to academic positions in foreign universities; or they emigrated and found positions in institutions organized by the sizable Russian émigré community (B. S. Mirkine-Getsevich, G. I. Mikhailovskii, and M. A. Tsimmerman). Others could not cope with the burdens of the magister program and were removed from it – A. Poltov, L. Rostvorskii, G. S. Sarkisov, N. Stremoukhov, G. Parfenov. The fate of Aleksandrenko was unusual.

Vasilii Nikiforovich Aleksandrenko *(30 January 1861, b. Nezhyn, Chernyhiv Province, Ukraine – 18 July 1909, d. Warsaw). Legal scholar, historian of State and law and of the history and theory of international and State law.*

Life and career. Graduating in 1880 from the Nezhyn Gymnasium, Chernyhiv Province, in Ukraine, he enrolled in 1881 at the Law Faculty of St. Petersburg University.[1] His talents for scholarly research were in evidence during his student years and noticed by the Professor of International Law, F. F. Martens, and the Professor of State Law, A. D. Gradovskii. On their recommendation, Aleksandrenko worked in the libraries of Austria, England, and Germany. In London he found himself attracted by English history. His graduation dissertation he devoted to the "Political System of the Anglo-Saxons". After graduating in 1885, Martens and Gradovskii took the initiative to invite Aleksandrenko to remain at the Chair of State Law to prepare for the professoriate.[2]

Having passed his magister examinations in 1887, Aleksandrenko was sent to England, where he worked in the Public Record Office and other local archives, The British Museum, and other libraries. He collected materials on the history

[1] ЦГИА СПб., fond 14, opis 3, file 21567.

[2] Ibid., file 8695.

of diplomatic relations between Russia and England. Returning to Russia from London in 1888, on the recommendation of Martens[3] he was appointed on 20 November 1888 as acting docent of the Imperial Warsaw University at the Chair of International Law, succeeding Professor Antoni Białecki (1836-1912).

The materials collected in England provided the basis for his magister dissertation on "The English Privy Council and the History Thereof",[4] which he successfully defended in 1891 at Moscow University. He was immediately elevated to the rank of professor *extraordinarius* at Warsaw University from early 1892 at the Chair of International Law. This was followed in 1899 by his masterpiece – a doctoral dissertation on the history of Anglo-Russian diplomatic relations, likewise defended at Moscow University.[5] After the defense, he was appointed professor *ordinarius* at Warsaw University – a position he held for the rest of his life.

He was well appreciated by his colleagues. Grabar wrote of him: "having given his due to State law, he switched to international law on moving to the chair of that subject, but his cast of mind and scholarly tastes were those of a historian, and his best works were devoted to the diplomatic history of Russia".[6]

Views on international law. Aleksandrenko left a rich legacy of legal and historical scholarship. His interests lay primarily in diplomatic and consular law and in diplomatic history, using Anglo-Russian diplomatic relations as his primary examples. But he also published an extensive collection of original sources relating to international law.[7]

Grabar considered that the best and most significant of his works was his doctoral dissertation on Russian diplomatic agents in London. It combined his attraction to English history, his love for working with original sources, and an excellent legal analysis of the organization of the diplomatic service. His study was widely conceived: Russian diplomacy was discussed against the general background of ambassadorial law of the eighteenth century.

As Grabar noted, this study is significantly broader than its title.[8] Volume one of the dissertation is devoted to an extensive survey of the diplomatic relations of Russia with England in the eighteenth century, a description of the diplomatic

[3] See V. A. Tomsinov, "Aleksandrenko, Vasilii Nikiforovich", in W. E. Butler and V. A. Tomsinov (eds.), *Russian Legal Biography* (2007), I, pp. 17-20; G. S. Starodubtsev, Международно-правовая наука российской эмиграции [International-Legal Science of Russian Emigration] (M., 2000), p. 17.

[4] V. N. Aleksandrenko, Английский тайный совет и его история [The English Privy Council and History Thereof] (Spb., 1888-1890). 2 vols. Butler A24.

[5] See Aleksandrenko, Русские дипломатические агенты в Лондоне в XVIII веке [Russian Diplomatic Agents in London in the XVIII Century] (Warsaw, 1897). 2 vols. Butler A66.

[6] V. E. Grabar, *The History of International Law in Russia 1647-1917: A Bio-Biographical Study*, transl. W. E. Butler (Oxford, 1990), p. 427.

[7] Aleksandrenko, Собрание важнейших трактатов и конвенций, заключенных Россией с иностранными державами (1774-1906) [Collection of Major Treaties and Conventions Concluded by Russia with Foreign Powers (1774-1906)] (Warsaw, 1906). Butler A69.

[8] Grabar, note 6 above, p. 518.

service, persons, and institutions subordinate to the diplomatic service (chapters I-III). There follows a description of the diplomatic service of that period and of the sources of ambassadorial law (chapter IV); the development of diplomatic representation abroad in general (chapter V); the appointment of diplomatic agents, documents, audiences, and visits (chapters VI-VIII); national laws of the diplomatic service (chapter IX); international rights and privileges of diplomatic agents (chapter X); their functions in peacetime and war (chapter XI and XII); the procedure for diplomatic relations and correspondence (chapter XIII); the cultural and political influence of England on Russian diplomatic agents (chapter XIV); the chancellery, embassy church, and families of diplomatic agents (chapters XV-XVII); termination of a mission (chapter XVIII); and the College of Foreign Affairs and persons administering the College (chapters XIX-XX).

Aleksandrenko analyzed the difficulties which the early Russian diplomatic agents encountered in England: for the first time they were part of the European diplomatic corps, but their status was legally vulnerable because under Peter the Great the rank of Russia had not been determined in the community of European powers and the Imperial title of the Russian Tsar had not been recognized.

A conflict of national interests and State ambitions ultimately led to a rupture of diplomatic relations in 1720 between Russia and England. Peter the Great decided in 1724 to renew them, but under the following conditions: the King of England would send his Minister to Russia with ambassadorial status and with evidence of his wish to return to the former friendship of the Russian monarch and the credentials of the envoy would contain recognition in writing of the Imperial title as Emperor of All the Russias.

Aleksandrenko drew attention to the fact that Catherine the Great's Declaration on Armed Neutrality, intended to support the American colonies in their war for independence from England, generated dissatisfaction in London and led to the complication of relations between the two courts.[9]

When examining the history of the diplomatic service, Aleksandrenko sketched a full picture of the institution of permanent embassies. There is interesting information about the procedure for the appointment of Russian diplomatic agents in foreign countries, the acts which they issued when sending someone to the diplomatic assignment, the legal and domestic aspects of their sojourn in England attached to the Royal court, diplomatic visits and receptions, and the resolution of diplomatic and important inter-State issues, the rights and privileges of ambassadors, their functions in peacetime and in wartime, the conditions of and procedure for diplomatic correspondence, the distinctive features of diplomatic ceremonial and protocol, among others.

Aleksandrenko devoted several works to diplomatic law. In an extensive review article on Odier and Verzamer,[10] Aleksandrenko noted that the authors had

[9] See I. de Madariaga, *Britain, Russia, and the Armed Neutrality of 1780: Sir James Harris's Mission to St. Petersburg during the American Revolution* (London, 1962).

[10] See the review of F. G. Odier, *Des privileges et immunités des agents diplomatiques en pays de chrétiènte* (Paris, 1890) and Em. Verzamer, *Des franchises diplomatique et spécialement de l'exterri-*

a poor command of the history of the creation of States and the development of their international relations. As a result, they overlooked important facts and legal aspects of the development of ambassadorial law, especially the practice of appointing special embassies during the Middle Ages (unusual in their organization); these practices later influenced the emergence of permanent embassies.

Departing from diplomatic law momentarily, Aleksandrenko analyzed in detail the codification of the laws and customs of law during the 1899 Hague Peace Conference.[11] He prefaced his discourse with a detailed account of the codification of international law as a whole. Curiously, he wrote that, in his opinion, the "first impetus, the first notion, of the possibility of codifying the principles of international law, if not as a whole than at least in individual parts, was inspired by the issuance of the Declaration of Armed Neutrality of 28 February 1790" (p. 83). He was firmly convinced that the adoption of this Declaration by Russia, extensively supported by other States, had a serious impact on the American War for Independence.[12]

Aleksandrenko demonstrated how difficult, in general, the possibility of the codification of international law was. Attempts in the last century by politicians and scholars to undertake such codification had been expressed in various original draft codes. Aleksandrenko summarized some of those better-known: Jeremy Bentham, Abbot Gregoire, Parodo, Domin-Petrushevich, Bluntschli, Field). Great assistance in the cause of codification had been given, he wrote, by the Institute of International Law at Ghent in 1878 (pp. 83-90). But all efforts were without result.

Many jurists did not consider codification to be possible, said Aleksandrenko, or even opposed it. Among these were Bergbohm, Bulmerincq, Holzendorff, Oppenheim, and von Savigny. Their arguments came down to the following:

[1]. Codification weakens the natural, living link with life, that link which exists in customary law. A Code easily might slow down the further development of law;

[2]. Successful codification is possible in an era which is an improvement over the preceding era and when there are jurists having a sense of history and gift for synthesis. The success of codification depends on the degree of the perfection of legal technique, which is possible only if the science of law is highly developed;

[3]. The codification of international law is more complex and difficult than civil law. The interests of the opposing parties in international law concern the

torialité: Étude de droit international et de législation comparée (Brussels, 1891), in Юридический вестник [Legal Herald], IX, no. 2 (September 1891), pp. 163-179.

11 Aleksandrenko, «Кодификация законов и обычаев войны и Гаагские конференции» [Codification of the Laws and Customs of War and the Hague Conferences], Вестник права [Herald of Law], no. 6 (1901), pp. 82-97.

12 On the American side, the 1780 Declaration transformed American perceptions of Russia. Catherine the Great was no longer the "sovereign in petticoats", but the "august sovereign". American patriots no longer viewed her as a threat to American independence. See David M. Griffiths, *No Collusion! Catherine the Great and American Independence*, ed. George Munro (2020), pp. 299-300.

aims of States, and not merely individuals. Therefore the task to reconcile them is far from easy. The elaboration of international law leaves much to be desired, for the civil law has been studied for centuries;

[4]. The existing models of codification are inadequate; gaps exist, contradictions, good intentions of the author rather than the systematic exposition of the law in force;

[5]. Finally, the practical importance of codification, even if such were realized, is undermined by (a) the lack of international courts, and (b) the fact that such a code might not be adopted by individual powers, even those who participated in drawing it up (pp. 86-87).

Aleksandrenko disagreed with the arguments set out above by the opponents of codification. No doubt, he said, there is much in these arguments that is profound and true, but their impact is undermined by the fact that such arguments might be put forward against any codification. It does not follow from the fact that agreement between States is difficult to achieve in international relations that partial codification also is impossible as between certain branches of international law. Well aware of the difficulties, the Institute of International Law assumed the task of promoting the progressive codification of international law (p. 87).

Having considered the individual attempts of scholars and politicians to codify international law, Aleksandrenko concluded that the sole true path to resolving this issue was collective codification – proposals jointly agreed by governments to codify individual branches of international law. Successful undertakings to codify international law were, in his view, the 1864 Geneva Convention, the 1868 Brussels Declaration, and the various Acts adopted at the 1899 Hague Conference.

Georgii Nikolaevich Mikhailovskii *(also Garin-Mikhailovich) (1890, b. Ust-Katav, Urals Province (now Cheliabinsk Region) – 1946, d. correctional labor camp Vorkuta (or Donbass).*

Life and career. The son of Nikolai Georgievich Garin-Mikhailovsky (1852-1906), a noted writer and railway location engineer, Georgii Nikolaevich recorded his birthplace as being in Ust-Katav in 1890, which is also reflected in the Protocol of his interrogation following his arrest in 1945: "born 1890, native of Ust-Katav Station … Russian, stateless, from the nobility, professor of international law, married, no convictions, lived in the city of Bratislav (Slovakia), interpreter of the Ministry of Foreign Affairs of Slovakia".[13]

[13] Отечественные архивы [Fatherland Archives], no. 3 (1997), pp. 59-78. Some sources name Cheliabinsk as his place of birth. His son, Nikolai, also named Cheliabinsk and in Slovakia became a well-known biologist. See N. G. Mikhailovskii, «Мои воспоминания о Русской гимназии в г. Моравска Тржебова [My Recollections of the Russian Gymnasium in Moravská Třebová], Вместе

He graduated with distinction from the Tenishev School (sometimes mistakenly indicated at the Petersburg Gymnasium in the literature) and in 1907 enrolled in two faculties at St. Petersburg University: the Faculty of Law and the Faculty of History and Philology.[14] The Ministry of Public Enlightenment introduced a general prohibition against studying simultaneously in two faculties, so that in 1911 he graduated only from the Law Faculty, with distinction. He remained at the Chair of International Law to complete his magister and prepare for the professoriate. He was initially given an appointment of one year to 1 February 1912,[15] and then renewed for three years (1 February 1912 to 1 January 1915).[16] The renewal involved the possibility of undertaking some lecturing. When petitioning the Law Faculty to allow Mikhailovskii to pursue postgraduate studies, Professor Pilenko noted that Mikhailovskii had taken an active role in seminars and delivered several reports; one on the State system of Turkey had been published in a journal.

In 1912 Mikhailovskii was sent abroad to collect materials for his magister dissertation on the law of the sea and perfect his English language skills. He spent time in London, Paris, Vienna, and then returned to France. In Paris he studied in the consular-diplomatic division of the École Libre des Sciences Politiques until the First World War broke out.

Another report, prepared under the guidance of and, indeed, at the instruction of Professor Taube, dealt with the legally binding nature of international treaties. This was later published by the journal of the Ministry of Foreign Affairs;[17] Mikhailovskii had used materials from the Bibliothéque Nationale in Paris to good effect, and apparently completed the project while in France and sent the manuscript back to St. Petersburg to Taube for publication.

Mikhailovskii returned to Russia when War commenced and, from 12 September 1914, took up service in the Ministry of Foreign Affairs. When his tenure as a postgraduate student at the University expired in 1915 at the Chair of International Law, Mikhailovskii left the University – although according to archival sources he remained at the Chair of International Law until 1918. The archives of the University contain documents that show on 12 December 1918, by decision of a commission of the Council of the I Petrograd University formed to consider petitions of the faculties on the assignment of stipends from 1 January 1919 to 1

[Together], no. 3-4 (2000). Also see Starodubtsev, note 3 above, pp. 40, 42, 68, 71-80, 82-84, 142, 154-163.

14 ЦГИА СПб., fond 14, opis 3, file 48666.

15 ЦГИА СПб., fond 14, opis 1, file 10616. Also see Отчет о состоянии и деятельности Императорского С.-Петербургского университета за 1913 год [Report on the State and Activity of Imperial St. Petersburg University for 1913] (Spb., 1914), p. 71.

16 Отчет о состоянии и деятельности Императорского С.-Петербургского университета за 1914 год [Report on the State and Activity of Imperial St. Petersburg University for 1914] (Spb., 1915), p. 119.

17 G. N. Mikhailovskii, «Юридическая обязательность международных договоров» [Legally Binding Nature of International Treaties], Известия Министерства иностранных дел [News of the Ministry of Foreign Affairs], kn. 5 (1913), pp. 277-311.

January 1920 for individuals remaining to study for the professoriate, the stipend for Mikhailovskii was extended for this period.[18]

Mikhailovskii was a talented individual who advanced rapidly in the Ministry of Foreign Affairs during wartime. Bright, adept in several languages, knowledgeable in the field of international law, well-connected (Nikolai Valerievich Charykov (1855-1930), a well-known diplomat and Deputy Minister of Foreign Affairs was his uncle), within little more than a year he rose to senior positions, including an appointment as secretary of the newly-formed jurisconsult division, headed by Professor Boris Nolde. Mikhailovskii soon became deputy to the head of the division and, from March 1917 under the Provisional Government, head of the international legal section of the Legal Department of the Ministry. He also served as a member of the High Prize Court attached to the Ministry.

As a senior official of the Ministry of Foreign Affairs, Mikhailovskii took part in the preparation of many treaties and personally participated in resolving major foreign policy issues of both Imperial and Provisional governments. He was a member of various interdepartmental commissions, prepared materials for the Council of Ministers and other Russian State institutions, and often expressly for the Minister of Foreign Affairs. His career encompassed both the Imperial and post-Imperial periods; he will have met and collaborated with officials from both eras, including those from foreign missions in St. Petersburg.

Mikhailovskii was hostile to the Bolsheviks. When Leon Trotsky (1879-1940) became the People's Commissar for Foreign Affairs in 1917, Mikhailovskii organized efforts within the Ministry to sabotage the various initiatives in foreign affairs. He left the Ministry but lived in Petrograd until 1918. For some months he worked in the psycho-neurological institute. In October 1918 he left for Crimea, where there was a family estate in Sevastopol, and then moved to Kyiv. From the end of 1918 until May 1919 he taught in the university at Ekaterinoslav (Dnepropetrovsk; since 2016, Dnipr, Ukraine). During the Civil War, he served in the foreign policy departments of the White Guard Government in the south of Russia, headed first by General Anton Ivanovich Denikin (1872-1947) and then Petr Nikolaevich Vrangel (also Wrangel) (1878-1928).

In December 1919 Mikhailovskii was a member of a delegation of the Vrangel Government which traveled to the United States in order to organize assistance from the United States and other western countries to the White movement, but the trip for various reasons never happened.[19]

Emigration. Mikhailovskii left Russia sometime in February 1920. In 1945 he was arrested in Bratislava, Slovakia, by the Soviet counter-intelligence service "Smersh" and died the following year in one of the correctional-labor institutions of the former Soviet Union, probably Donbass or Vorkuta.

[18] ЦГА СПб., fond 7240, opis 14. Mikhailovskii appears on several lists as actually being at the University and receiving a stipend to prepare for the professoriate.

[19] Mikhailovskii recalls the events in considerable detail in his memoirs. See Mikhailovskii, Записки. Из истории российского внешнеполитического ведомства, 1914-1920 [Notes. From the History of the Foreign Policy Department. 1914-1920] (M., 1993).

His memoirs were published in the Russian Federation in 1993, in two volumes. The text was based on a manuscript discovered in the Archive of Foreign Policy of the Ministry of Foreign Affairs. Mikhailovskii wrote his memoirs while he lived in Slovakia; the text was seized when he was arrested there on 21 April 1945. It floated around between archives in Prague and Moscow. Initially it was kept in the Russian Foreign Historical Archive (РЗИА) in Prague, and when that Archive was sent to Moscow, the manuscript first reposed in the Central Archive of the October Revolution and then was transferred to the Archive of Foreign Policy. Grabar mentioned only his surname in connection with his article on treaties; following decades of oblivion, the publication of his memoirs restored him to the pages of history.

International legal views. Having regard to all the tribulations of his life, Mikhailovskii gravitated after the Revolutions in Russia towards journalism and writing. Nonetheless, his two articles published in the journal of the Ministry of Foreign Affairs are of interest. The first addressed the binding nature of treaties, and the second surveyed English prize practice in the context of situations that arose during the First World War.

The article on treaties drew upon materials he gathered while in Paris at the Bibliothèque Nationale. He began with the sweeping statement: "The problem of the binding nature of international treaties might in justice be called the fundamental problem of contemporary international law".[20] In his view, "contemporary international law might be called primarily treaty law". He was persuaded that the "right of existence" of international law itself depended upon the proper resolution of the problem of treaties being legally binding. The force of an international treaty rested on the same force as a law of a State – being the expressed will of the State: "To prove the legally binding nature of treaties means, in our opinion, to show that they also are precisely as binding from the legal point of view as norms of positive law in force within a State" (p. 303).

He devoted great attention to the principle of *rebus sic stantibus*. Having analyzed a broad range of writers and State practice, including a principal proponent in the person of F. F. Martens, Mikhailovskii concluded: "… the *clausula rebus sic stantibus*, as a rule of positive international law, does not exist" (p. 310). If States were permitted to invoke this reason for not complying with a treaty, Mikhailovskii said that abuses would result and references to vital State interests, to arbitrariness, and to a disturbance of normal international communion: "*Pacta sunt servanda* and the *clausula rebus sic stantibus* cannot exist simultaneously" (p. 310). He reasoned that just as a law cannot be changed or repealed except by a new law, an international treaty cannot be changed or repealed other than by a new treaty.

Mikhail Arturovich Tsimmerman *(also Zimmermann) (21 November 1887, b. Kutaisi – 28 May 1935, d. Brno, Czechoslovakia). Talented international lawyer of the interwar generation, well-known in Europe.*

[20] Mikhailovskii, note 17 above, p. 277.

Life and career. Tsimmerman graduated in 1904 from the Imperial Nikolaev Tsarskoe selo Gymnasium and the following year enrolled,[21] and in 1909 graduated, with a first class degree from the Law Faculty of St. Petersburg University. The topic of his graduation dissertation was "Historical Survey of Neutrality in Marine Warfare".[22] During his student days, Tsimmerman was arrested for bringing illegal social-democratic literature into Russia.[23]

In 1909 he enrolled in the Nikolaev Cavalry School (discharged on 22 October 1910 into the reserve with the rank of cornet, and in May 1911 took the officer examination in the school).[24]

As from 1 March 1912 Tsimmerman remained at the Chair of International Law for one year until 1 March 1913 to prepare for the professoriate under the supervision of Professor Taube.[25] On 20 November 1912 he was sent abroad to study international law until 1 September 1913, without a stipend.[26] His work was sufficiently satisfactory that Professor Pilenko recommended to the Faculty that Tsimmerman's sojourn abroad be extended to 1 January 1916 with a stipend of 2,000 rubles per year from an appropriation of the Ministry of Public Enlightenment. That recommendation was accepted.[27] Tsimmerman worked in libraries, attended lectures, and visited tutorials at universities in Paris and Berlin.

When the First World War began, Tsimmerman was called up to active duty as a cavalry officer with the rank of lieutenant. He was wounded at the front in Eastern Prussia and captured by German forces. In German captivity for more than four years (from 22 October 1914 to 8 November 1918), he thrice tried to escape, was recaptured, tried by a court, served punishment, and was confined in a one-window prison at Ingolstadt in Bavaria and then Königstein, in Saxony, where he continued his research. Evidence of this is an article received by the editors of a journal from prisoner of war Tsimmerman in Germany and published under his

[21] ЦГИА СПб., fond 14, opis 3, file 42157.

[22] ЦГИА СПб., fond 14, opis 8, file 1695 (26 November 1909).

[23] ГАРФ, fond 124, file 264, l. 1.

[24] Sergei Gagen, «Русский правовед. Труды Михаила Циммермана актуальны до сих пор» [Russian Jurist: Works of Mikhail Tsimmerman Are Topical to This Day], Пражский экспресс [Prague Express], 15 February 2015; Starodubtsev, note 3 above, pp. 16, 40, 42, 43, 68, 71-78, 80-87, 104, 105, 112, 113, 134, 136, 137, 143, 159, 175-178, 206, 214-216, 250.

[25] ЦГИА СПб., fond 14, opis 1, file 10658, l. 1.

[26] ЦГИА СПб., fond 14, opis 1, file 10658, l. 2-8. Also see Отчет о состоянии и деятельности Императорского С.-Петербургского университета за 1912 год [Report on the State and Activity of Imperial St. Petersburg University for 1912] (Spb., 1913), p. 40.

[27] ЦГИА СПб., fond 14, opis 1, file 10658, l. 10-13; Отчет о состоянии и деятельности Императорского С.-Петербургского университета за 1914 год [Report on the State and Activity of Imperial St. Petersburg University for 1914] (Spb., 1915), p. 120; Отчет о состоянии и деятельности Императорского С.-Петербургского университета за 1915 год [Report on the State and Activity of Imperial St. Petersburg University for 1915] (Spb., 1916), p. 55.

initials.[28] He gave lectures to fellow imprisoned officers and studied foreign languages, including Latin.

After returning to Russia on 20 December 1918, Tsimmerman did not support the Bolsheviks after the October 1917 Revolution and became involved in the Russian Civil War on the side of the White forces. From 1918 to 1920 he was an officer in the Volunteer Army in the south of Russia, and in 1921, together with the remnants of that Army, evacuated to Constantinople. From Turkey he moved on to Czechoslovakia via Yugoslavia. In Prague, having passed the examinations for privat-docent, Tsimmerman became a lecturer at the Russian Law Faculty, affiliated the Charles University. From 1926, having defended the sole magister dissertation written in the Russia Abroad (on interference and recognition in international law), he was appointed a professor at the Chair of International Law of the Faculty.[29]

He eventually made his way to Slovakia, where he died at the age of 47 in the city of Brno.

International legal views (prerevolutionary period). During the years here considered, Tsimmerman was a frequent contributor to the journal of the Ministry of Foreign Affairs – a number of articles and twenty-eight reviews and notes on works by foreign authors. His article on the need to consider at a Third Hague Peace Conference (postponed because of the First World War and never to be held) the protection of private property of subjects of belligerent States.[30] In Tsimmerman's view, the codification of the laws and customs of war was the greatest merit of the First and Second Hague Conferences, but he noted what were material shortcomings of Convention (IV) Respecting the Laws and Customs of War on Land. Most especially this concerned Article 23(g) of the Annex, which imposed the following limitation on belligerents: "(g) To destroy or seize the enemy's property, unless such destruction or seizure be imperatively demanded by the necessities of war". This seemingly unimportant paragraph, wrote Tsimmerman, adopted unanimously at the Conference, had become the subject of polemics and generated in the literature "contrary interpretations" when the "true meaning and significance" of this Article were discussed (p. 89). The problem was that subjects of the belligerents suffered from the legal ambiguity of the Article. Having analyzed the doctrine and practice relating to this problem and the existing customary-law norms for resolving it, Tsimmerman concluded that "only the codification of these norms in a Convention signed by all States-members of the international community can put an end to the chaos in which all questions are found concerning trade and legal relations of subjects of enemy States" (p. 112).

[28] See M. A. Ts[immerman], «Война и право» [War and Law], Известия Министерства иностранных дел [News of the Ministry of Foreign Affairs], kn. 1 (1916), pp. 75-83.

[29] Tsimmerman, Вмешательство и признание в международном праве [Interference and Recognition in International Law] (Prague, 1926). 248 p. See with reference to his sojourn in Czechoslovakia, A. D. Shcherbakov (comp.), Русский юридический факультет в Праге (к 95-летию со дня основания). Сборник документов [Russian Law Faculty in Prague (On the 95th Anniversary from the Day of Founding Thereof): Collection of Documents)] (M., 2017).

[30] Tsimmerman, «Одна из очередных задач Третьей Мирной Конференции» [One of the Next Tasks of the Third Peace Conference], Известия Министерства иностранных дел [News of the Ministry of Foreign Affairs], kn. 6 (1913), pp. 89-112.

Of considerable interest is Tsimmerman's analysis of the incident in 1912 involving the detention by Italian warships of the French postal vessel *Carthage* off the coasts of Sardinia. The vessel, en route to Tunis and Malta, was accused of carrying military contraband. The dispute was referred to the Permanent Court of Arbitration at The Hague in the context of the London Declaration of 26 February 1909 Concerning the Laws of Naval War.[31] He assessed the award positively, taking the view that the Italian authorities had no right to capture the vessel and subject the *Carthage* to sequestration temporarily; therefore, Italy was obliged to pay to the French Republic the sum of 160,000 French francs. This award, Tsimmerman said, "fully corresponded to contemporary legal consciousness" and was of "great value as one of those acts which might strengthen confidence in the impartiality and justice of a court of States" (p. 223).

Tsimmerman's article on "War and Law", which he wrote while a prisoner of war in Germany and sent for publication in Moscow by the journal of the Ministry of Foreign Affairs, is worthy of more than passing note. He considered the causes of war and the role of international law in the limitation thereof from a historical and legal philosophical position. With understandable bitterness, he wrote that

> International law too easily is becoming a toy in the hands of the powerful. In peacetime the functioning of international law is completely normal, but in wartime the restraining principles are weak and, regrettably, make chronic a violation of norms more sacred, defending the weak and defenseless, the wounded and sick.[32]

Tsimmerman put the question: "Can one deny the existence of international law on the basis of violations?" And he came to the conclusion: "The existence of law is not disputed, however, on both sides; and the dispute concerning violations of norms testifies to the recognition of the legally binding force of international positive law". He continued: "Centuries pass, recollections gradually fade of the arduous years of the war of 1914-1915, but never to be forgotten is the meaning of the struggle of nations for their common rights against the aggressor. Law in international life is a synonym of freedom and the denial of one nation being subject to another. War, being violence, may find its cleansing only in the fact that its purpose is the triumph of law (p. 83).

An experienced book reviewer, Tsimmerman had the range and skills to follow foreign international legal literature closely. In his review of Robert Jacomet on the laws of land warfare,[33] he considered the author to have exaggerated when he asserted that international law had achieved significant mitigation in warfare. The reality was, in his perception, that matters were less than good: "... the internationalists usually ignore a number of technical military norms which are contrary to those declarations created at international conferences". Tsimmerman concurred

[31] Tsimmerman, «Решение третейского суда в Гааге 6 (нов. ст.) мая 1913 года и Лондонская декларация 1909 года» [Award of the Arbitration Court in The Hague of 6 (new style) May 1913 and the London Declaration of 1909], Известия Министерства иностранных дел [News of the Ministry of Foreign Affairs], kn. 4 (1913), pp. 219-223.

[32] Tsimmerman, note 28 above, p. 80.

[33] Robert Jacomet (1881-1962), *Les lois de la guerre continentale* (2d ed.; Paris, 1913).

with Jacomet that the serious task was to reconcile military practice agreed in field regulations with existing international norms. But, said Tsimmerman, it would be more useful to show that abyss which separates war as a *de facto* state from war as a legal relation. “This task awaits serious and impartial illumination”.

Tsimmerman cited as an example of the “abyss”, on one hand, the legal norms on the inviolability of private property and, on the other, military practice – when a military commander must decide a military task of destroying a home, structure, fence, trees, or sequester and requisition needed materials, and the like. He did not accept the cruelties of war with respect to the civilian population. It should be recognized as a basic principle of modern warfare that the struggle is being conducted between belligerents, between armed forces, and therefore the peaceful population should enjoy immunity. Hence the legal senselessness of hostages (p. 205). In his view, the internationalists themselves could not effectively resolve these issues because they were unfamiliar with the distinctive aspects of waging warfare. These problems should be resolved by holding international meetings of military specialists, as was done at the 1868 international military conference in St. Petersburg.

Tsimmerman wrote a number of articles on various aspects of the law of war in addition to the piece he prepared while a prisoner of war. He was among the first to address the international-legal dimensions of air warfare,[34] analyzing the extent to which and how this issue was addressed at the 1899 and 1907 Hague Peace Conferences. He offered a number of proposals based on this analysis. In his view, a number of limitations should be introduced in order to humanize air warfare and regulate the use of aircraft:

> [1]. Military operations of belligerent aircraft might occur above the territory of the belligerents or the high seas. No hostile acts may be committed above the territory or the territorial waters of neutrals;
>
> [2]. The crew of aircraft must be part of the armed forces and should openly wear military dress. It was probably not advisable to fix large distinguishing marks on aircraft, for this would only make reconnaissance more difficult;
>
> [3]. Aircraft may shell only forts, fortifications, and the places where forces were located. The shelling and casting of explosives in places where non-combatants were located should be prohibited – cities and villages outside forts should not be shelled without warning;
>
> [4]. Neutral aircraft may be prohibited absolutely from flying over the territory of belligerents;
>
> [5]. Aircraft of belligerents which penetrate neutral territory are subject to sequestration on the part of the neutral State until the military actions end. The pilots may be detained or released on their word of honor (pp. 160-161).

[34] M. A. Tsimmerman, «Вопрос о воздушной войне в международном праве» [Question Concerning Air Warfare in International Law], Известия Министерства иностранных дел [News of the Ministry of Foreign Affairs], kn. 5 (1915), pp. 149-162.

Tsimmerman passed into history as one of the most original and productive international lawyers in the Russia Abroad.[35]

§8.2. *Graduates Who Did Not Complete Magister Degree but Continued International-Legal Research*

Among the protégés of Professors Martens, Taube, and Pilenko were promising students who remained at the Chair of International Law to prepare for the professoriate but for various reasons never completed the magister dissertation. They became legal practitioners but to some extent continued to publish in the field of international law.

Viktor Porfirevich Golubev *(10 January 1884, b. St. Petersburg – d. no earlier than 1935; date and place of death unknown). Specialist in the law of the sea, especially the law of prize.*

There is little information in reference sources and doctrinal writings about Golubev. Grabar knew little about him: "V. P. Golubev served in the St. Petersburg Port Administration. He published more than two dozen articles, most of them on the law of prize".[36] This information, however, is not entirely accurate either with respect to Golubev's research or professional activities. He is now known to have published at least 56 works on various aspects of international law: 39 between 1914 and 1917, and a further nineteen from about 1920 to 1930. Archival sources have provided more insight into his career.

Life and career. Born at St. Petersburg on 10 January 1884,[37] Golubev completed the Tenth Petersburg Gymnasium[38] in 1902 and then enrolled in the Law Faculty of St. Petersburg University. He graduated in 1907 with a first class degree.[39] With the consent of the Rector of St. Petersburg University, he studied in parallel at the Archaeological Institute.[40] On 10 November 1908 the Law Faculty chose Golubev to remain at the Chair of International Law for one year to prepare for the professoriate.

[35] See *Práce ruské, ukrajincké a bêloruské emigrace vydané v Československu 1918-1945: bibliografie s biografickými údaji o autorech* [Works of Russian, Ukrainian, and Belorussian Emigration Published in Czechoslovakia in 1918-1945: Bibliography with Biographical Information on the Authors] (Prague, 1996). Tsimmerman published nine books in the Czech and Slovak languages in Prague, Brno, and Bratislav on international law, primarily relating to the history and the General Part of international law. Many were multilithed or mimeographed with small print runs.

[36] Grabar, note 6 above, p. 449.

[37] In at least one archival source, his year of birth is mistakenly given as 1874.

[38] ЦГИА СПб., fond 14, opis 3, file 39790, l. 4.

[39] РГИА СПб., fond 1405, opis 544, file 3106.

[40] ЦГИА СПб., fond 14, opis 3, file 39790, l. 22.

Simultaneously, he took a position in State service as a college secretary in the Ministry of Justice, assigned to the Zemstvo Section.[41] Archival data associated with that appointment disclose that Golubev was descended from the nobility, Russian Orthodox in faith, had taken no part in military actions, never been convicted of an offense or taken leave, and was unmarried.

Pursuant to an Order of the St. Petersburg Chamber of Justice dated 21 May 1909, Golubev was designated a junior candidate for office in a judicial department attached to the said Chamber, and by an Order of 19 November 1909 was placed at the disposal of the Chairman of the St. Petersburg District Court for training as an investigator.[42] Promotion came two years later when, on 5 December 1911, Golubev was elevated from college secretary to titular counsellor.[43]

Following a lengthy correspondence during 1912 between the Department of General Affairs of the Ministry of Public Enlightenment, Second Department of the Ministry of Justice, and Second Department for Affairs of the Ober-Procurator of the Ruling Senate, by Order of the Ministry of Public Enlightenment of 30 January 1913 Golubev left his position to become an aide VIII class of the Head of the Archive of the Ministry of Public Enlightenment.[44]

Meanwhile, at the University, Golubev prepared for the magister examinations. In November 1909 he submitted a progress report which the Head of the Chair, Taube, considered to be satisfactory. The progress report set out in detail everything he had done and all the literature that he had analyzed.[45] On 21 March 1911 Golubev undertook the magister examination in international law. The following questions were put to him: (1) practice of perpetual peace to the nineteenth century; (2) merchant vessels on the high seas; (3) international motor vehicle and aeronautics law.[46] His answers were deemed to be satisfactory.

On 31 March 1911 Taube assigned Golubev to prepare a written report on "Russo-Swedish Relations in the Eighteenth Century". Golubev submitted a six-page report, likewise accepted as satisfactory.[47]

On 20 February 1912 he took the second set of magister examinations, this time on State law, and was required to address the following questions: (1) North

[41] ЦГИА СПб., fond 14, opis 3, file 39790; РГИА СПб., fond 1404, opis 544, file 3106, l. 24ob.

[42] Ibid., l. 60obverse; l. 27obverse.

[43] Ibid., l. 12.

[44] Ibid., l. 13-22.

[45] ЦГИА СПб., fond 14, opis 3, file 14425; also see E. N. Trubetskaia, История развития кафедры международного права Санкт-Петербургского (Петроградского) университета в 1903-1917 гг. [History of the Development of the Chair of International Law of St. Petersburg (Petrograd) University in 1903-1917] (Spb., 2004), pp. 143-144.

[46] ЦГИА СПб., fond 14, opis 3, file 14460, l. 5.

[47] Ibid., l. 6-806. Golubev later used the report as the basis of an article. See Golubev, «Россия и Швеция в их международных отношениях» [Russia and Sweden in Their International Relations], Вестник права [Herald of Law], no. 3 (1916), pp. 70-71.

American United States; (2) Pufendorf; (3) Local Government. He was unable to answer all the questions of the examiners, however, and received an "unsatisfactory".[48] In May 1912 he was removed from the group of magister postgraduates who remained at the University.[49] From 1913 to 1917 he was employed at the Ministry of Public Enlightenment.

From Spring 1918 Golubev surfaces as employed at the Committee for Hunger in Petrograd; according to some archival data, on 5 October 1918 he was elected as an aide to the Secretary of the Council of Perm University, but there is no confirmation that he took up the appointment. In that year he was mobilized into the Red Army, and after demobilization worked for thirteen years in the merchant seaport of Leningrad. According to the archives of St. Petersburg State University, Golubev worked in 1929 at the Faculty of Soviet Law of Leningrad State University as a senior assistant in the Chair of Economic Law, where he gave tutorials in the course on trade and industrial law.[50] On 20 March 1935 he was arrested and exiled from Leningrad for five years to the northern regions of Kazakhstan (Atbasar, Karaganda Region).[51] Thereafter he disappeared from sight and no further information has been located.

International legal views. Golubev published more than fifty articles on international law, the great majority on the law of prize. Of particular interest were his studies of the territorial sea, the definition thereof, the calculation of the boundaries, regime, and jurisdictional questions.[52]

Having considered historical examples of asserting a breadth of the coastal territorial marine expanse at a maximum (for example, the 100-mile coastal sea in the North Pacific Ocean introduced by Edict of Emperor Alexander I of Russia, repealed, to be sure, in 1824) and at a minimum – 3 miles, and the conflicts arising between States in this regard, Golubev associated himself with the position of the Institute of International Law expressed during 1912 in Resolution 27 (Paris). In that Resolution, the Institute proposed the functional principle of determining the breadth of the territorial sea, depending on the exercise of coastal State functions (neutrality, fishing, customs, quarantine, cabotage, and others) (pp. 35-39).

As regards the various theoretical and practical approaches to the controversial issue of from what line to calculate the breadth of the territorial sea: from the line of lowest ebb tide or the high tide line, Golubev agreed that the line of lowest ebb tide had significant practical advantages; the approach came to be increasingly confirmed in treaty practice and national legislation. The Institute of International Law had endorsed that position in 1894 (pp. 41-44).

48 ЦГИА СПб., fond 14, opis 3, file 14460, l. 14.

49 ЦГИА СПб., fond 14, opis 3, file 14471, l. 30.

50 ОА СПбГУ., fond 1, file 734.

51 ГАРФ, fond P-8409, opis 1, file 1313, pp. 10-17.

52 See Golubev, «Современное определение территориального моря» [Contemporary Definition of the Territorial Sea], Юридический вестник [Legal Herald], kn. 7-8(3-4) (1914), pp. 35-48.

The jurisdiction of States in the territorial sea Golubev discussed by using concrete examples. He analyzed the contradictory practice of States during peace and war. He concluded that the jurisdiction of the coastal State in its territorial waters did not extend to a foreign vessel, except for situations when events on board the vessel threaten the public quiet of the coastal State.

With the outbreak of the First World War, the issue of territorial jurisdiction at sea was exacerbated by the differing views of the law of prize and whether foreign ships and/or cargoes could be captured within the territorial sea. Golubev observed that "persons interested in the ships and cargoes captured by our cruisers attempt to determine these limits to their advantage" (p. 47). Noting the generally-recognized position was that private property at sea was inviolable, Golubev pointed to the equivocal approach in practice. He identified what he considered to be dangerous contradictions in Russian legislation on the law of prize. According to the Instruction of the Procedure for the Stopping, Inspection, and Detention, and also the Allocation and Issuance of Detained Vessels and Cargoes (Article 1), which was an Annex to the 1915 Statute on Maritime Prizes (Article 26), such actions should be undertaken by a "vessel of the Imperial Navy". However, Articles 43, 46, and 48 of this Statute on Maritime Prizes provided that the detention of enemy vessels and cargoes might be performed by merchant ships of the State. Foreign yacht-clubs, motorboats, and the like were even confiscated by instruction of the Head of the City of Petrograd. In Golubev's view, if German shipowners and cargo owners brought suits in Russian prize courts, this may create complex issues for Russia (p. 48).

Closely linked with his views on prize law was Golubev's article on the right of belligerents to capture foreign merchant ships.[53] Having confirmed that the inviolability of private property in naval warfare generates insuperable difficulties, Golubev dwelt on the debates of this issue at the 1907 Hague Peace Conference. He drew attention to the different factual consequences and the public perception thereof involved in the capture of private property during wartime on land or at sea. States more readily agreed to recognize the inviolability of such property during war on land because this property remained on the occupied territory and the occupying State had the possibility by various means to use it. War at sea was another matter.

Maritime shipping was increasing; the capture of foreign private vessels and cargoes not only caused significant losses to their owners, but was capable of undermining the economy of the State of their nationality. Submarines and mines were being improved: private ships and cargoes were being sunk at sea together with their passengers and crews. These considerations exerted influenced governmental circles and public opinion to bring an end to war.

Having analyzed the legal rules governing the capture of foreign commercial vessels, Golubev concluded that in order to prevent such captures it was essential to exclude from this law the mercenary motives of centuries past – profit:

53 See Golubev, «Право захвата воюющими коммерческих судов противника во время морской войны» [Right of Capture by Belligerent Commercial Vessels of Enemy During Naval Warfare], Юридический вестник [Legal Herald], kn. VII-VIII (III-IV) (1914), pp. 306-310. Golubev published several articles on this or similar topics.

> In other words, the abolition of long-established prize remuneration is required, distributed among the members of the crew of the capturing vessel commensurate with the rank and role thereof in taking the prize, and not only with respect to enemy prizes, but also neutral, and in other instances the decision to capture a merchant vessel should not be influenced by considerations of advantage.[54]

Golubev approvingly evaluated the repeal in Russia on 2 August 1914 of Section II, Articles 35-42, of the 1896 Statute on Maritime Prizes relating to prize remuneration for naval vessels which captured prizes, both enemy vessels and neutral ships (p. 308).

The author remains a comparatively unknown figure in the history of international law whose contributions are underappreciated.

Mikhail Davidovich Nemirovskii *(18?-19?). Graduate of St. Petersburg Law Faculty; magister postgraduate, Chair of International Law.*

Life and career. Biographical data on Nemirovskii was not previously available. Grabar mentioned his name and three of his articles.[55] Archival materials now enable some details to be added. Nemirovskii enrolled in the Law Faculty of St. Petersburg University in 1895.[56] Information about his presence in the University is to be found in the numerous protocols of Law Faculty meetings held in St. Petersburg archives.[57] Upon graduating from the Law Faculty, he remained at the Chair of International Law from 3 February 1898 to prepare for the professoriate.[58]

In a letter to the Rector of the University of 9 March 1902, Nemirovskii requested permission to take the magister examination on international law, duly administered on 1-2 April 1902 at a session of the Law Faculty. The following questions were put to him: (1) Relations between Russia and Prussia in the Reign of Emperor Alexander I; (2) Right of Inheritance according to the Principles of Private International Law; (3) Principles of Examination of International Conflicts. His answers were deemed to be satisfactory.[59]

On 9 December 1902 Nemirovskii successfully passed the magister examination in State law.

[54] Ibid., p. 305.

[55] Grabar, note 6 above, p. 460.

[56] ЦГИА СПб., fond 14, opis 3, file 32379.

[57] The protocols are partly produced in T. S. Loginova, История становления и развития кафедры международного права Санкт-Петербургского университета в 1819-1903 г.г. [History of the Origin and Development of the Chair of International Law of St. Petersburg University in 1819-1903] (Spb., 2004), p. 130.

[58] ЦГИА СПб., fond 14, opis 3, file 14344, l. 74.

[59] ЦГИА СПб., fond 14, opis 3, file 14356, l. 68-69.

Nemirovskii applied to the Dean of the Law Faculty on 12 October 1906 to deliver a trial lecture "On the Right of Neutral Maritime Trade during War".[60]

Other archival sources indicate that in 1909 Nemirovskii, according to materials of the St. Petersburg Commercial Court, was entered on the List of sworn *striapchii*.[61] During the mid-1920s, Nemirovskii worked in the Soviet banking system (Leningrad (city) United Society of Mutual Credit for Medium and Small Industry "Vzaimbank" of the People's Commissariat of Finances of the USSR).[62]

International legal views. Grabar was aware of three articles by Nemirovskii. In fact, there are several more. His principal legacy is in the field of international arbitration, writing in an era when the use of force in international relations was common to resolve international disputes. He published his first article on the topic when preparing his magister.[63]

Nemirovskii began by exploring the concept of an international arbitration court. The ruling of such a court, he believed, must differ from similar institutions of civil and international law. He offered the following definition of an international arbitration court: "a legal instrument for the settlement of disagreements between States on the principles of international law by means of judges selected by the common consent of those in dispute (pp. 88-89). Drawing attention to the fact that doctrinal writings often confused two institutions of international law – international arbitration court and international mediation – and analyzing the differences between them, Nemirovskii said that the principal merit of the arbitration court was its legal character. The entire proceeding was based on norms of law. An international arbitration court – in the absence of a permanent international court – was the "sole legal means of defending rights in the field of international relations" (p. 88).

Nemirovskii identified what, in his view, were the essential prerequisites for the consideration of a dispute by an international arbitration court:

(1) only subjects of international law might be parties in the court; insurgents or provinces in revolt within some State might not be a party to a proceeding so long as their autonomy was not recognized by the other powers;

[60] ЦГИА СПб., fond 14, opis 3, file 14388, l. 488.

[61] ЦГИА СПб., fond 243, opis 1, file 2163. On the origins of the *striapchii* in Russia, see W. E. Butler, *The Russian Legal Practitioner* (2011), pp. 32-33. The sworn *striapchii* was introduced by legislation on 14 May 1832 in the commercial courts first established in St. Petersburg and Moscow. Duly registered, sworn *striapchii* enjoyed a monopoly on the right of audience in commercial courts in disputes between private individuals. The list of persons who might engage in commercial court practice included those who submitted evidence of their rank and behavior.

[62] ЦГА СПб., fond РР-1978, opis 6, file 772.

[63] M. Nemirovskii, «О третейском международном суде» [On the International Arbitration Court], Журнал юридического общества при Императорском Санкт-Петербургском университете [Journal of the Law Society attached to the Imperial St. Petersburg University], no. 4 (1898), pp. 83-143; no. 5 (1898), pp. 108-145.

(2) consent of States to submit their dispute for resolution by an arbitration court and the selection of well-known individuals as judges must be clearly expressed; the preliminary conclusion of a treaty – "*compromis*" – between the States in dispute was essential;

(3) the dispute must have a legal character;

(4) the award of the arbitral judges is legally binding on the States which chose them (p. 89).

Nemirovskii divided international disputes into two categories: legal and political. He understood legal disputes to be those which might be settled by legal means in a judicial proceeding. Political disputes, on the contrary, could not be settled by legal means; in order to resolve them, the parties would resort to violence, to war. In the instance of a legal dispute, he said, the norms of international law would need to be so clear that no doubt existed as to the grounds on which the dispute was being decided (p. 90). In the times during which he lived, Nemirovskii considered that disputes affecting the vital interests of States might be resolved only with the assistance of either war or by diplomatic means – negotiations, good offices, mediation. He supported the desirability of diplomatic means for the settlement of international disputes and disagreements.

As for legal disputes, Nemirovskii considered international arbitration to be the most acceptable. Usually an international arbitration court was formed on the basis of a *compromis* agreed between the parties. Nemirovskii understood a *compromis* to be an "international agreement by means of which the parties subject the dispute between them to the award of arbitral judges". The *compromis* must, he said, be carefully prepared and precisely designate the subject-matter of the dispute, the means of forming the arbitration court and the names of the judges, the rules and procedures which the arbitrators should follow, the means of executing the arbitral award, and other essential points (p. 109).

Nemirovskii dwelt on the status of the international arbitration court, the subject-matter of the arbitration, the parties to the dispute, the procedure for agreeing the *compromis* and for forming the tribunal, the requirements for the arbitrators, the grounds and procedure for an arbitrator to recuse himself, the functions of the respective participants in the arbitration, the grounds and conditions for the arbitral consideration of a case to be terminated without terminating the legal relation in dispute, the procedure for rendering and executing the award of the arbitration court, instances of a null award, and the procedure, if any, for appeal.

In his conclusion, Nemirovskii made a number of recommendations: the most acceptable way of forming an international arbitration court was to have neutral judges chosen by the parties in dispute. In the *compromis* provision should be made, if possible, for the creation of courts of cassation to which the parties to an arbitration could appeal the awards of initial arbitral tribunals. Moreover, he added, it would be desirable in international treaties to make the arbitration of a dispute "less occasional".

Nemirovskii hoped that over time an international custom would emerge to the effect that plaintiff and defendant States would exchange "memoires" setting out their positions in a dispute. He expressed the conviction that the development of international arbitration would proceed along the "progressive path" which it had followed down to his time (pp. 143-145).

On 19 October 1907 Nemirovskii spoke at a session of the General Meeting of the Law Society attached to St. Petersburg University on the topic "On the Execution of Foreign Judicial Decisions". The theses of the Report were published in the Law Society journal.[64]

Nemirovskii's report was significant in many respects. First, as was noted at the session of the Law Society to which he reported, this was the first time someone had reported to the Society on an international legal issue. Second, the positions taken by Nemirovskii himself on complex issues of private international law were of considerable interest. Nemirovskii formulated seven basic conclusions; the discussion was so lively that the Society decided to continue the discussion at its meeting on 2 November. At the two sessions combined, seven Society members gave their own detailed analysis of the Nemirovskii report. These collectively generated their own Report, duly published in the Society organ.[65]

Nemirovskii worked in the field of comparative international law. In his article on foreign court decisions, he noted that "the question of the force of the decision of a foreign civil court" encounters two diametrically opposed positions in legal literature. The representatives of the first approach considered a judicial decision to be solely an expression of the supreme power of the State of the court and therefore regarded the execution of such a decision on the territory of a foreign State to be inadmissible because this would be a violation of its sovereignty. One possible exception might be the enforcement of a foreign court decision for reasons of the general benefit and international comity.

The other view held that recognition of the legal force of a foreign court decision was possible, "proceeding from the civil law nature of such a decision" – which is distinct from its public-law operation. Under this approach, the enforcement of a foreign court decision is seen as the application of a private-law norm to a concrete situation to be addressed by a special law for such situations. The enforcement of foreign judicial decisions as an institution of public law is based on this premise: "the rule has been established by the legislative and judicial practice of all States that foreign decisions may not be enforced other than by direction of the local judicial power" (pp. 103-105). On the basis of all the materials duly considered, Nemirovskii formed several recommendations and conclusions that should be taken into account when reworking the Statute on Civil Procedure:

[64] Nemirovskii, «Об исполнении иностранных судебных решений: Тезисы доклада на заседании Общего собрания С.-Петербургского юридического общества» [On the Execution of Foreign Judicial Decisions: Theses of the Report at the Session of the General Meeting of the St. Petersburg Law Society, 19 October 1907], Журнал юридического общества [Journal of the Law Society], no. 5 (1908), pp. 275-276.

[65] See «Протокол заседания Общего собрания Юридического общества, 19 октября 1907 г.» [Protocol of the Session of the General Meeting of the Law Society, 19 October 1907], Журнал юридического общества [Journal of the Law Society], no. 5 (1908), pp. 277-286; «Протокол заседания Общего собрания Юридического общества, 2 ноября 1907 г.» [Protocol of the Session of the General Meeting of the Law Society, 2 November 1907], Журнал юридического общества [Journal of the Law Society], no. 5 (1908), pp. 287-293.

(1) the legal force of the civil decisions of foreign courts must be recognized equally with the decisions of own courts without any special decrees of local courts;

(2) the decision of a foreign court is not subject to recognition if it was adopted with regard to a case not within the jurisdiction of the courts according to the legislation of the particular foreign State;

(3) in order to eliminate possible doubts among persons applying the law, it is desirable that civil procedure legislation expressly set out the rules of international jurisdiction to be recognized by the State concerned. Such rules, Nemirovskii emphasized, must correspond to the requirements of private international law;

(4) the decision of a foreign court also is not subject to recognition if it contains provisions violating the "local social and State order";

(5) the enforcement of foreign decisions also should not be permitted if the party against which reference is made to the decision of a foreign court was not summoned to this court for consideration of the case, as a result of which he could not personally appear to defend his rights or send his representative;

(6) the decision of a foreign court cannot be deemed to have legal force if it did not have such in the State where it was rendered. Thus, the force of a foreign decision is recognized only insofar as it has such according to the foreign laws and to the same extent. Therefore, Nemirovskii was convinced that if a foreign law recognizes lesser force for the decisions of its own courts, then a local court, for example, a Russian court, may not give greater force to a foreign judicial decision than would the law of the foreign jurisdiction. Likewise, if a foreign law recognizes that judicial decisions have greater force than a local, for example, Russian law, the local law must be applied because foreign decisions can never have greater force in a State than the decisions of its own courts (pp. 141-142);

(7) it is necessary to strengthen the position by legislation that if some State does not recognize the operation of foreign laws and decisions of foreign courts on its territory, the other State may as a retaliatory measure grant the right to its own government by way of retorsion to suspend the provisions of its law with respect to the first State concerning the recognition of foreign judicial decisions;

(8) decisions of foreign courts may not be enforced without a special decree or ruling of the local court; that is, unless the foreign judicial decision satisfies all the conditions for recognition of the legal force thereof and also unless the decision is enforceable in the State in which it was rendered (p. 144).

If the system for the recognition and enforcement of foreign judicial decisions were based on the recommendations and considerations set out above, Nemirovskii believed that this would promote the international protection of private rights and interests of States and their subjects (p. 146). He was among the first in Russia to analyze the legal regulation and judicial practice relating to the recognition and enforcement of foreign court decisions.

Georgii Stepanovich Sarkisov *(13 July 1877,*[66] *b. Tiflis – d. no earlier than 1930). International lawyer; leading figure in the Russian pacifist movement; noted film producer.*

Life and career. Sarkisov graduated from the Tiflis Third Gymnasium and enrolled at the Law Faculty of St. Petersburg University in 1902; he finished the University with a first-class degree, having received a "very satisfactory" in all courses. While at University he received in 1901 a gold medal for an essay on the "Codification of the Laws and Customs of War on Land". From 1 September 1902 he was on active military service in the post of Conductor II Class in the Chief Engineer Administration of the Russian Empire.[67]

Sarkisov filed a request on 25 October 1902 in the name of the Rector of the University to remain at the University to study international law.[68] At a session of the Law Faculty on 4 November 1902 he was chosen to remain at the Chair of International Law to prepare for the magister and the professoriate, without stipend, for one year. This period was repeatedly extended with the support of and upon the petition of his supervisor, F. F. Martens,[69] and following his retirement, Taube. He was sent to France for two years (1 November 1903-1 November 1905) for advanced study. The Archives contain his annual reports to the Faculty setting out the results of his visit. In a report from Paris Sarkisov recounted that in addition to visiting the Bibliothéque Nationale and the library of the University of Paris, he had attended lectures at the University, the École libre des sciences politiques, and the College de France; second, attended tutorials; third, studied general courses and monographs on international law; fourth, read books, pamphlets, and periodicals relating to his topic; and fifth, studied the English language.[70]

The extent of supervision and control by the University over young scholars is evident in the fact that Sarkisov's report was considered by the Dean of the Law Faculty, sent to the Rector, then on to the Administrator of the Petersburg Educational District, who submitted this report of a magister postgraduate (with a professoriate stipend) to a Session of the Principal Section of the Academic Committee of the Ministry of Public Enlightenment on 5 January 1905.[71] Sarkisov was extended in the magister program until 1 November 1905.[72]

[66] ЦГИА СПб., fond 14, opis 1, file 9726.

[67] Ibid., l. 5.

[68] Ibid., l. 1-2.

[69] The letter of Sarkisov to Martens is found in ЦГИА СПб., fond 14, opis 3, file 14369.

[70] ЦГИА СПб., fond 14, opis 1, file 9726, ll. 21-29.

[71] ЦГИА СПб., fond 14, opis 1, file 9726, l. 20.

[72] ЦГИА СПб., fond 14, opis 1, file 9726, l. 488.

On 10 November 1907 Sarkisov was given the magister examination in international law at a session of the Law Faculty. The following questions were put to him: (1) Idea of International Organization in Historical Development; (2) Evolution of the Schools of Private International Law; (3) International Arbitration Court.[73] His answers were deemed to be unsatisfactory, and he was dismissed from the University.[74] No further records of Sarkisov's relationship with the Chair of International Law or the University have been located.

He did become involved in the Russian and international pacifist movement; he was among the founders and a member of the Board of the St. Petersburg Peace Society and a member of the editorial collegium of the organ of the Society, Вестник мира: Орган международного права и культуры [Herald of Peace: Organ of International Law and Culture]. He also supported the Committee of the Philanthropic Society "Assistance to Children of Workers of St. Petersburg".

He worked as a jurisconsult at the Ministry of Trade and Industry and achieved a reputation as a film producer. From 1916 he was a stockholder and member of the Board of the Joint-Stock Society "Biokhrom" (later AO "Biofilm") – the first society in Russia engaged in making color cinematic products. Sarkisov left an enormous archive containing materials of his school and University days, visit to Paris, various published and unpublished scholarly works and publicist materials, some of interest and others not, his membership in the Peace Society and other social organizations, correspondence with well-known political and social figures, relatives, and other items of a personal nature.[75]

International legal views. It is no easy task to trace the views of Sarkisov on international law. He did not publish in the large and well-known legal media. Most of his articles on international politics or on legal topics appeared in the journal of the St. Petersburg Peace Society or in St. Petersburg newspapers. His personal archive contains many completed but unpublished items or advanced manuscript drafts. However, his published material provides a general impression of this out of the ordinary jurist and his international legal views.

In an article[76] commemorating the fourth anniversary of the First Hague Peace Conference, held on 6 May 1899, to discuss the ways of bringing peace to the globe, Sarkisov asserted as a convinced pacifist that the Conference should be considered not so much from the results achieved as for the noble idea which the organizers and participants advanced. This was the idea of international peace and amity, which he said must "deeply penetrate into the consciousness of nations" and displace the militant spirit and national intolerance in which nations had been nurtured for many centuries.

[73] ЦГИА СПб., fond 14, opis 3, file 14404, l. 1.

[74] РГИА СПб., fond 1049, opis 1, file 435.

[75] РГИА СПб., fond 1049.

[76] G. Sarkisov, «Славная годовщина (Гаагская конференция)» [Glorious Anniversary (Hague Conference)], Санкт-Петербургские ведомости [St. Petersburg Gazette], 6 May 1903.

Sarkisov analyzed the three basic questions of the Hague Conference: reduction of armaments; prevention of wars with the assistance of pacific means for the settlement of international disputes; and mitigation of the means of waging wars by the establishment of laws of war. As regards disarmament, Sarkisov saw this possibly happening in the long term. But, he believed, the time might be approaching. For him a promising first successful step was the international arbitration court formed on the basis of the Hague Peace Conference. One of the first cases was the dispute between the United States and Mexico relating to the payment by Mexico of the debt of certain church officials (F. F. Martens served as one of the arbitrators). Sarkisov wrote approvingly likewise of the arbitration between England, France, and Italy, on one side, and Venezuela, on the other. Symbolic and significant, in light of these arbitrations, was the decision of the American magnate, Andrew Carnegie, to donate a large sum to build the Peace Palace in The Hague. Sarkisov thought the moment was opportune to conclude special treaties between States recognizing the compulsory jurisdiction of the international arbitration court. In his view, if the majority of parties to the Hague Convention concluded similar bilateral treaties among themselves, the limitation of armaments would be next; it would become possible to reduce the size of forces and to improve the standard of living by diverting the enormous sums spent on weapons.

Sarkisov transitioned from a pacifist evaluation of the Hague conventions to an article published in 1909 analogous in content.[77] Again optimistic, he assessed the results of the 1907 Second Hague Peace Conference positively. In the decade that had elapsed since the First Peace Conference, the world, he suggested, had become a safer place. Countries believed in the possibility of negotiating to create the legal foundations for peaceful relations. The 1907 Second Hague Peace Conference brought 45 countries together, and in four months had achieved much en route to a universal peace:

> The results of this work in the form of two dozen universal international treaties having as their subject-matter, on one hand, the codification of international customs operating during war and, on the other, a number of measures to prevent wars: a law of peace was created in the form of the convention on arbitration, mediation, and commissions of enquiry, and international adjudication in the person of the Hague permanent tribunal.

Sarkisov placed great hopes on the peace societies being formed everywhere. He noted that in Russia the "cause of the Hague conferences attracted great attention so that society … inspired governments to achieve greater successes en route to strengthening law and peace in international relations".

In an article on Russian society and peace,[78] Sarkisov set out the basic purpose of the pacifist movement: "to accelerate the establishment of international peace by means of the organization of an international legal structure". Sarkisov defined the three basic orientations of the pacifist movement:

[77] Sarkisov, «Славная годовщина» [Glorious Anniversary], Вечер [Evening], 6 May 1909.

[78] Sarkisov, Русское общество и мир [Russian Society and Peace], place of publication not indicated, but available in an offprint in the Sarkisov personal archive. РГИА СПб., fond 1049, opis 1, file 370, l. 43-44obverse.

(1) work relating to the creation of the necessary scientific and practical foundation for the legal organization of the international community, strengthening in the popular consciousness the need for and possibility of establishing universal peace through the propaganda of peace and destruction of old prejudices;

(2) work to promote the mutual rapprochement of nations and joint and several activity through achieving common cultural and economic interests: "internationalism is the best and most reliable ally of pacifism";

(3) in the direct impact of the establishment of an international legal order through, especially, the support for and stimulation of governments. Pacifists must "aim their efforts towards the strengthening, expansion, and rapid development of the cause of the Hague conferences: the practice of the arbitration court; the codification of international law; and the reduction of armaments are their most cherished ideals".

Sarkisov believed that the Interparliamentary Union had great promise in the cause of universal peace.[79] He assessed positively other international regional organizations such as the Union of American Republics. In an article on Pan-Americanism based on a Report that Sarkisov delivered on 5 December 1913 to the St. Petersburg Peace Society, he touched upon international legal aspects of the creation, organization, and activities of that Union.[80]

The Sarkisov personal archive contains an unpublished obituary of F. F. Martens.[81]

Sarkisov thus left a larger legacy to the field of international law than had previously been known, especially as a leading Russian international lawyer in the pacifist movement.

[79] Sarkisov, «Междупарламетнский союз и Гаагская конференция мира» [Interparliamentary Union and the Hague Peace Conference], Современная неделя [Contemporary Week], no. 7 (1909).

[80] Sarkisov, «Панамериканизм» [Pan-Americanism], Вестник мира [Herald of Peace], no. 7 (January 1914), pp. 11-12.

[81] РГИА СПб., fond 1049, opis 1, file 370, l. 40-42obverse. The manuscript is dated 10-11 June 1909.

Chapter 9
Honorary and Other Doctorates in International Law

From time to time, but exceptionally, legal scholars from other institutions were given or earned doctoral degrees for outstanding research in the field of international law.

Antoni Władyslaw Emilian Białecki *(Anton (Antonii) Kazimirovich) (11 June 1836, b. Warsaw – 15 November 1912, d. Jordanowice, near Pruszków, Warsaw Governate). Russian and Polish legal historian, specialist in international and State law).*

Life and career. Antoni Białecki was born on an estate near Warsaw.[1] His father, Casimir Białecki, was a well-known figure in the Great Poznan Principality, hence in the Russian language Antoni's patronymic was "Kazimirovich". After graduation from the prestigious St. Anna Gymnasium in Krakow, Białecki enrolled at the Law Faculty of the Jagellonian University. Initially attracted by journalism, he wrote political and literary articles for local newspapers.[2] He was forced by illness to interrupt his studies in 1856 and returned to his village to recuperate by engaging in agricultural work. From 1858 to 1860 he lived in St. Petersburg, seeking manuscripts in archives of the noted religious and socio-political eminence, Jan Długosz (1415-1480), a Polish historian and diplomat and author of a monumental history of Poland in twelve volumes. The results of his archival research he recounted in an impressive volume published at St. Petersburg.[3] Some of his articles appeared in a Russian liberal journal Русское слово [Russian Word].

Białecki moved to Heidelberg, Germany, where he continued his legal studies at the Law Faculty of the local University. In 1862 he defended a dissertation at Heidelberg University on the essence and materials of international law and was awarded the degree of Dr. Phil. That same year he was appointed a lecturer in the Chair of Social and Administrative Sciences at the Chief Warsaw School (the pre-

[1] For biographical notes, see K. P. Krakovskii, Нить времени (Биографии преподавателей юридического факультета Варшавского-Донского-Ростовского университета) [Thread of Time (Biographies of Lecturers of Law Faculty of Warsaw-Don-Rostov University) (Rostov-on-Don, 2003), pp. 57-58; V. M. Syrykh, Правовая наука и юридическая идеология России. Энциклопедический словарь биографий [Legal Science and Legal Ideology of Russia. Encyclopedic Dictionary of Biographies] (Moscow, 2006), I, p. 107; Adam Bosiacki, "Antoni Białecki", in G. Bałtryszajtys (ed.), *Profesorowie Wydziału Prawa i Administracji Uniwersytetu Warszawskiego. 1808-2008* (Warsaw, 2008); Adam Moraczewski, "Białecki Antoni Władyslaw Emiljan", in *Polski Słownik Biograficzny* (Krakow, 1936), II, p. 5; V. S. Ivanenko, "Antoni Białecki: Warsaw International Lawyer", *Jus Gentium: Journal of International Legal History*, VI (2021), pp. 165-170.

[2] Throughout his life he contributed to newspapers, among them: *Tygodnikiem Ilustrowanym, Gazetą Lwowską, Teką Wilenską, Biblioteką Warszawską*, and the Lviv *Dziennikiem Literackim.*

[3] Jan Długosz, *Rękopisma Długosza w Peterburgskich Bibliotekach* (Spb., 1860). [x], 126 p.

decessor from 1862 to 1869 of Warsaw University), where he taught the theory of State law, international law, the history of political sciences, and political ethics. From 1866 to 1869 he was appointed professor *ordinarius* in this Chair. In parallel, until 1876 he offered instruction on political economy in the Leopold Kronenberger Trade School.

Białecki maintained more than a casual interest in agricultural pursuits. An active gardener, from 1874 to 1879 he served as Chairman of the Board, and from 1879 until 1912 as the Chairman of the Society of Agricultural Settlements and Artisan Work. In 1907 he was a founder member of the Warsaw Scientific Society.[4]

As a jurist, he played a major role in drafting the Law on the Transformation of the Warsaw Chief School into the Imperial Warsaw University. When the University opened on 12 October 1869, he held the Chair of International Law as *professor ordinarius*, a position he held until his retirement. Grabar for reasons unknown gave no attention to Białecki as the predecessor of V. A. Aleksandrenko in the Chair, mentioning only that Białecki addressed issues of sources of international law.[5]

It should be noted that when Warsaw University was founded, the condition was imposed that, first, Polish professors in the University were given two years to study the Russian language, after which they were expected to lecture in Russian; second, it was expected that each Polish professor would within three years defend a doctoral dissertation at any of the Russian universities irrespective of whether they already had a doctorate from a western European university. In 1872 Białecki submitted to St. Petersburg University a dissertation on the "Significance of International Law and Materials Thereof"; the Learned Council of the University conferred the degree of Doctor of International Law for this dissertation – duly published by decision of the Council of the Imperial Warsaw University.[6] The topic of the dissertation was virtually the same as that dissertation the author had defended at Heidelberg University, but archival data suggests there was also a public defense in Warsaw.

Having divided his work into two parts, Białecki gave considerable attention to the works of legal scholars who had written on international law. In his preface he observed that State systems were comparatively unstable, constantly changing: "when unleashed political passions strongly rocked social principles – thinkers always, imbued with noble feelings of love for their fellow man, raised their voice in defense of the public order and suggested a system of international legal principles" (pp. i-ii). In Białecki's view, the materials produced by publicists were in a chaotic state and desperately needed ordering and systematization. His predecessor international lawyers had been aware of this, but not succeeded in devising a system for the materials. He concluded: "The question of a rational systematic we

[4] Among his scholarly works in this field were Białecki, *O uprawie kwiatów* (Warsaw, 1856); Białecki, *O ogrodach chłopskich* (Warsaw, 1879).

[5] V. E. Grabar, *The History of International Law in Russia 1647-1917: A Bio-Biographical Study*, transl. W. E. Butler (Oxford, 1990), p. 480.

[6] A. Białecki, О значении международного права и его материалов [On the Significance of International Law and Materials Thereof] (Warsaw, 1872). [РГБ]. Butler Б285.

consider to be most important and the working out thereof the most essential" (p. iv).

A proper and rational system of international law depends upon investigating three issues: (1) the essence and significance of international law; (2) the content and character of the materials thereof; and (3) the influence of guiding ideas on all international law. Only, he said, after a fundamental study of these three questions, after seeking the close organic link between them – can one create a complete and stable system of the science" (p. iv). His work was addressed to the first two of these issues. He regarded the study of concepts concerning the essence, extent, and legal force of international law as the point of departure not merely for building the system thereof, but for all further research and opinions.

In his sole mention of Białecki, Grabar described him as being one of the "representatives of natural law".[7] This is a controversial view and not one confirmed by Białecki's works. Białecki would be more accurately described as belonging to the embryonic sociological school of international law. In his view, international law was part of several sciences, one of which was the social sciences: "the main subject-matter to which all the content thereof relates is the aggregate of social phenomena of human life". But international law was, he believed, part of the State sciences because "social phenomena, the investigation with which it is concerned, arise and develop solely under the influence of State institutions". Only State interests "may belong to the domain of international law …". Not all, however, but only those "in which the idea of law and justice require their own ensuring". Such interests also comprise primarily the subject-matter of international legal norms. It follows that international law comprises "part of legal knowledge because it is concerned principally with the selection and determination of the legal aspect of State relations" (pp. 3-4). Summarizing these preliminary observations, Białecki said:

> From this tripartite relation of international law to social, State, and the legal sciences, it follows that the general essence thereof must be imbued with three ideas: the idea of society, the State, and law. These three ideas impart the basic character to the entire doctrine on international law. The concept thereof is inseparable from the concept of society, the State, and law (p. 4).

Perhaps Grabar considered that Białecki should be categorized as a proponent of natural law because he believed international law to emanate, just as any social phenomenon, from social laws, from the natural aspirations of people and nations with respect to social life, to the coming together of one another, to a social union which comprises the "highest natural law of the world" (pp. 6, 13).

The concept, essence, conditions of origin, development, tasks, volume, subjects, subject-matter, and binding force of international law were considered in Part One of his treatise. Having considered aspects of the concept, Białecki concluded that "according to the contemporary concept of international law, it represents both the aggregate of legal rules determining the external correlation of autonomous States for the purpose of realizing the free combining of peoples" (p.

[7] Grabar, note 5 above, p. 480.

19). Reflective of the legal regulation of international relations at that time, Białecki acknowledged the binding nature of individual categories of international rules, the list of which constantly expanded (for example, the emergence in the second half of the nineteenth century of the principles of defending private ownership and the inviolability of the field health service during war) (p. 141).

In Part Two, entitled "External Expression of International Law", Białecki analyzed the general character of sources of international law and the concrete typed thereof: international customs and treaties, decisions of congresses, legislation of States and judicial precedents, and the opinions of international legal scholars. Commenting on the importance of international customs in the history of the international community, Białecki wrote: these being the "most abundant materials of international law", they occupy in history a

> pre-eminent place and strongly assist the strengthening of the most important principles of international law. The majority of the institutions of international law arose by means of gradual customary formation and were recognized as binding before they were formally sanction by State authorities and found their place in the provisions of treaties (pp. 157-158).

But emphasizing the growing role of treaties in the regulation of relations between nations and States, Białecki gave attention to the definition of this form of international legal cooperation:

> We call the clear statement of consent of two or more States with respect to a known general question an international treaty, as a consequence of which these States recognize their mutual duty to subject their actions to rules or conditions determined in a ... treaty act, that is, a treaty ... A treaty is the concrete expression of general principles of international law elaborated by a civilization of a particular epoch (pp. 185-186).

Białecki was the first in Polish legal science to consider the conclusion of treaties from the standpoint of public international law.[8] He suggested that each of the aforesaid sources of international law contains a basic element influencing international law:

> In international customs – instinctive activity of a nation; in treaties – the will of States consciously expressed; in domestic laws and judicial decisions – the concrete conditions of local being; in the views of publicists – the unrestrained legal consciousness of the human spirit free from any external conditions (p. 255).

No single source of international law is decisive for the international legal system, said Białecki. Each has its own importance and each has its own worthiness and shortcomings. None of these sources contains all the principles of international law, and therefore all are closely linked to one another (p. 256).

[8] Syrykh, note 1 above (2006), I, p. 107.

Białecki published other works in addition to his dissertation[9] and translated Robert von Mohl (1799-1875), *Encyclopädie der Staatswissenschaft* (Tübingen, H. Laupp, 1859) into the Polish language.[10]

Vladimir Emmanuilovich Grabar *(sometimes Hrabar) (10/22 January 1865, b. Vienna Austria – 26 November 1956, d. Moscow, Russia). Historian of international law, academician, professor of international law, dean, librarian, legal adviser.*

Life and career. Grabar was born in Vienna, Austria, at a time when Eastern European movements were finding a firm footing.[11] He was descended from grandparents and parents deeply involved in the movement to incorporate the Carpatho-Rusyn people within a single Russian civilization. The events of 1848 required the Grabar family to move about Europe, eventually settling at Egorevsk, Ukraine. Having a remarkable gift for languages, Grabar enrolled at the Galangan College in Kyiv; upon graduation he enrolled at the Law Faculty of Moscow University, also attending lectures in the Faculty of History and Philology. In his final years at University, an inclination towards international law emerged. In 1885 he submitted a second-year paper to the Law Faculty on the "Right to the Throne and the Order of Succession". For the diploma essay topic set by the faculty in 1888 he presented a thesis (193 pages) about navigation on international rivers, which was awarded a University gold medal. The medal automatically exempted him for submitting a

[9] See Białecki, *O uniwersytetach* (Warsaw, 1865); Białecki, *Przebieg sporu o niewolnictwo i znaczenie zasady strón Zjednoczonych* (Warsaw, 1866); Białecki, *Zadanie Prawa Międzynarodowego i obowiązki strón wojujących* (Warsaw, 1874); Białecki, *Prawidlowość stosunków międzynarodowych* (Warsaw, 1874); Białecki, *O konwencji genewskiej* (Warsaw, 1878); and Białecki, *Prawo w życiu ludzkiem* (Warsaw, 1906); among others.

[10] R. von Mohl, *Encyklopedia umiejętności politycznych,* transl. Antoni Białecki (Warsaw, 1864-1865). 2 vols.

[11] This account is based on Butler, "V. E. Grabar: Profile of a Russian International Legal Historian", in Grabar, note 5 above, pp. xxv-li; Butler, "On the History of International Law in England and Russia" and a biographical sketch, "V. E. Grabar (1865-1956)", both published in Butler, *Russia and the Law of Nations in Historical Perspective: Collected Essays* (2009), pp. 194-206, 493-505, and the materials cited therein. K. O. Savchuk, «Грабар Володимир Еммануiлович» [Grabar, Volodymyr Emmanuilovych], in V. N. Denysov, et al. (eds.), Енциклопедія міжнародного права [Encyclopedia of International Law] (Kyiv, 2014-2019), I, pp. 645-648; G. S. Starodubtsev, Международно-правовая наука российской эмиграции [International-Legal Science of Russian Emigration] (M., 2000), pp. 9, 14, 16, 17, 20-22, 27, 40, 41, 138, 141, 146, 154, 169, 206-208, 255.

candidate thesis, but he did so anyway on the "Status of Aliens among the Ancient Hebrews".

He spent a year in Paris to follow lectures in the universities, including those delivered by Louis Renault (1843-1918) on international law. Without a stipend, he earned his keep by translating and acting as literary correspondent for the newspaper Русские ведомости [Russian Gazette]. Upon returning to Russia, he began work on his magister dissertation, supporting himself with various jobs. In 1893 he was invited with the rank of privat-docent to the Chair of International Law at Iurev (now Tartu) University to replace the recently retired C. M. Bergbohm. Appointed as from 1 July 1893, he arrived in September and remained in Tartu until 1918.

On 10 September 1893 he requested permission to deliver his trial lectures on "War and International Law", outlining the gradual development of rules of law on warfare and criticizing German legal scholars who believed that war was an inherent feature of the human condition. His second lecture was on "The Study of International Law in Russia up to the Mid-Nineteenth Century". On 7 August 1894 Grabar surrendered his Hungarian nationality and formally became a subject of the Russian Empire.

Grabar was awarded his magister degree on 24 March 1901 for a thesis on Roman law in the history of international legal doctrine: elements of the law of nations in works by legists of the twelfth to fourteenth centuries. Academic promotion followed; on 19 July 1901 he was appointed professor *extraordinarius*, and on 30 December 1906, professor *ordinarius*. Twice he was elected Dean of the Faculty of Laws, served as Director of the University Library for five years, and was twice elected chairman of the professorial disciplinary court at the University.

His deep commitment to the history of international law brought him on several occasions to western Europe, where he worked in the archives and libraries with medieval manuscripts.

At the outbreak of the First World War, Grabar was officially offered the Chair of International Law at the Petrograd Higher Women's Courses. This would have brought him to the capital, but the offer apparently was not taken up because Grabar had accepted an offer from Boris Nolde to become a legal adviser to the Russian High Command. The Minister of Public Enlightenment who released Grabar from his academic duties to serve as legal adviser was another international lawyer, Baron von Taube.

Grabar lasted in the position of legal adviser for less than a year, from 2 August 1914 to 7 May 1915. The objectivity of his opinions on the laws of war – he pointed out instances of breaches by Russian forces as well as by the enemy – antagonized a Russian general and led to Grabar's withdrawal for "reasons of health" under the protection of the Ministry of Foreign Affairs. As a jurist of an empirical positivist and historical orientation, Grabar had a devastating way of succinctly setting out relevant data and reaching his conclusions.

The Provisional Government in Russia appointed Grabar as the Administrator of the Riga Education District as from 18 March 1917. His efforts to reorganize the education district brought him into conflict in October 1917 with the Estland Provincial Land Administration. On 9 November 1917 the Executive Committee of the Iurev Soviet of Soldiers' and Workers' Deputies requested the Riga Education District to vacate its premises and turn over its records to the Soviet authorities, relieving Grabar of his post on 11 December 1917. Grabar refused to surrender the records, pointing out that only the central authorities could remove him. The request to turn over the records was made by V. Kakk, Commissar for the Liquidation of Affairs of the Riga Education District. Apparently armed force was used on 19-20 December 1917. On 17 January 1918 the Executive Committee asked Grabar to turn over the records of the Riga Education District once again; in order to avoid scenes of 19-20 December 1917, Grabar said he had no right to do so, but would offer no resistance and confined himself to a protest. Grabar challenged the authority of the Executive Committee to dismiss him and appealed to the People's Commissar for the Enlightenment, Anatolii Vasil'evich Lunacharskii (1875-1933), who, concurring that the local soviet lacked the competence to dismiss Grabar, promptly exercised his own authority and dismissed Grabar on 3 January 1918. The documents are confusing because Lunacharskii on 3 January 1918 had dismissed Grabar from office as of 1 January 1918 and made general provision for disposition of the personnel and assets of the Riga Educational District.

Among the enduring mysteries of the life and career of Grabar was whether he ever completed his doctoral dissertation, whether the dissertation perished, "vanished", and/or was successfully defended, and whether he held a higher doctorate, an honorary higher doctorate, or both. The background, insofar as the facts are known, is as follows.

Grabar's true passion resided in the history of international law in the Middle Ages and before. He never accepted Hugo Grotius (1583-1645) as the "founder" or as the "father" of international law. Giving his due to the Spanish "school", Grabar believed the doctrine or science of international law came into being much earlier. To Grabar, Hugo Grotius was merely one in a long line of important publicists originating in pre-mediaeval times.

For his doctoral dissertation, Grabar turned to Britain, examining the writings of early and long-forgotten jurists in England and Scotland. He visited London, Oxford, and Cambridge on several occasions from the 1890s to the First World War in order to consult archives and correspond with like-minded colleagues, as the notebooks and scraps of paper containing thousands of bibliographical references – now to be found in his personal archive at Tartu University – confirm.

When precisely Grabar formed the intention to write about English contributions to the development of the law of nations cannot be determined precisely. The proposed, perhaps actual, Table of Contents of the dissertation is preserved in the Grabar Archive at Tartu University.[12] Certain portions, perhaps chapters, Grabar published just as the *ancien régime* in Russia was supplanted;[13] others appeared

[12] Translated and published in Butler, note 11 above (2009), pp. 202-203, from Grabar Archive, Tartu University, F.38, s. 150.

[13] Grabar, «Понятие естественного и международного права в английской литературе XII-XIV вв.» [Concept of Natural and International Law in English Literature of the Twelfth to Fourteenth Centuries], Юридический вестник [Legal Herald], kn. 2-4 (1917), pp. 5-30.

from time to time during the Soviet era in Ukraine[14] or in Russia.[15] Only one of these works is now known outside Russia and Ukraine. Their subject-matter remains largely untouched in the United Kingdom.

These works, together with many others treating early international legal doctrine, chiefly in France, Germany, and, to a lesser extent, Italy, constitute a fraction of Grabar's contributions to the history of international law. The documentation deposited at the Tartu University Archive by Maria Evgenevna Grabar-Passek (1893-1975) confirms that Grabar labored for more than seven decades transcribing and ordering extracts from obscure manuscript sources in many languages with a view to preparing a universal history of international law.

The information is conflicting as to the fate of Grabar's dissertation. There are at least three versions as to what transpired. According to the first, the Germans invaded Tartu in spring 1918. During the sacking of the city, Grabar reported that his newly printed book, *De legatorum jure: Tractatum Catalogus Completus ab anno MDCXXV usque ad annum MDCC* (Dorpat, 1918), had been burned by the German forces and his completed doctoral dissertation entitled "The Science of International Law in England Before the Reformation" had perished.[16] Apparently, the manuscript had made an impression, however, and according to various sources the Council of Petrograd University had conferred the doctor of international law *honoris causa* on Grabar, apparently on 27 May/10 June 1918.[17]

[14] Grabar, Питання державного и міжнародного права в Комментариях Джона Мера до Сентенции Петра Ломбарда (До літературної історії міжнародного права середіх віків) [Questions of State and International Law in the Commentaries of John Mair on the Sentences of Peter of Lombardy (On a Literary History of International Law of the Middle Ages], Записки соціально-економічного відділу [Annals of the Socio-Economic Section], V-VI (1927), pp. 292-327 (French summary, pp. 313-318). The work also is known as a separate offprint in monograph format (Kyiv, 1927). A useful abridged version appeared in the Russian language thanks to two Kharkov scholars. See V. S. Semenov and O. Ia. Trahniuk, «Вопросы государственного и международного права в комментариях Джона Мэра к Сентенциями Петра Ломбардского» [Questions of State and International Law in the Commentary of John Mair on the Sentences of Peter Lombard], Московский журнал международного права [Moscow Journal of International Law], no. 4(32) (1998), pp. 187-195. Since then a substantial summary has been published at Kiev in *International Law*, no. 1-2 (2013), pp. 265-295. Also see W. E. Butler, "Volodymyr Hrabar, Peter Lombard, John Mair, and the History of International Law", ibid., pp. 296-304.

[15] See Grabar, «Репрессалии в Англии при Эдуарде II» [Reprisals in England Under Edward II], Ученые записки Института истории Российской ассоциации научно-исследовательских институтов общественных наук [Learned Papers of the Institute of History of the Russian Association of Scientific-Research Institutes of Social Sciences], III (1929), pp. 213-235; Grabar, «Международно-правовые воззрения Джона Виклифа» [International Legal Views of John Wycliffe], Вопросы истории [Questions of History], no. 8-9 (1946), pp. 75-90.

[16] The authority for this is Vsevolod Nikolaevich Durdenevskii (1889-1963), in his preface to Grabar, Материалы к истории литературы международного права в России (1647-1917) [Materials on the History of the Literature of International Law in Russia (1647-1917)] (M., 1958), p. 7: "The manuscript of the doctoral dissertation of Grabar, "Science of International Law in England Before the Reformation", perished in the fire".

[17] See Butler, note 5 above (1990), p. xliii. Also see Butler, "On the Fate of the Grabar Doctoral Dissertation and Degree", *Jus Gentium: Journal of International Legal History*, IV (2019), pp. 593-606.

The second version originated in the diary of Boris Vladimirovich Nikolskii (1870-1919) covering the years 1896 to 1918. Nikolskii was a jurist, poet, and literary critic. Most of his publications relate to his literary interests, but as a jurist he was a specialist in Roman law. In 1915 he published a study of gifts between spouses under Roman law. A monarchist active in Russian politics, he was executed by the Petrograd Extraordinary Commission in 1919. In his diary he recounts meeting Grabar on 23 January 1918:

> Today met at Tarle's.[18] Grabar came with his wife. It turns out that the manuscript of his work of two decades has vanished. For his governorship, he has paid this price. I experienced no Schadenfreude, and mentally I thank God that I can sincerely feel sorry for him, a person completely unknown to me. The fact is that a completely finished manuscript, twenty years of work, 25 to 30 printed quires, two completed articles, and many other manuscript materials, as well as money, he kept in a cupboard in the district. One manuscript he needed. He went to the district – and learned that there was neither a trace of the money or the manuscripts. When precisely in the last two months all this vanished no one knows, and he himself cannot imagine. An agonizing situation.[19]

According to the third version, an official history of Tartu University published in Estonian, Russian, and English language versions, in the section written by A. Kisik, claimed that Grabar actually had defended his dissertation at Voronezh University in 1918.[20]

[18] The reference is to Evgenii [Grigorii] Viktorovich Tarle (1874-1955), historian and, from 1927, member of the USSR Academy of Sciences. From 1913 to 1918, Tarle was a professor at the University of Tartu, where he would have known Grabar.

[19] See B. V. Nikolskii, Дневник. 1896-1918 [Diary. 1896-1918], ed. D. N. Shilov and Iu. A. Kuzmin (Spb., 2015), II, p. 329. Shilov and Kuzmin suggest that the missing manuscript may have been Grabar's work on the history of the literature of international law in Russia. This is most certainly not the case, but rather Grabar's dissertation on the law of nations in England and Scotland during medieval times. Other contemporary sources report the loss of the dissertation; Grabar did not receive the assignment to produce the work on Russian doctrinal writings from the Russian Academy of Sciences until 1914; although he may have started on that project earlier, there is so far no evidence that he did; and he did ultimately complete his Russian project, but not his English project. The two months that had elapsed since Grabar last visited his cupboard coincide more or less that the period when Grabar refused to turn over records to the Iurev Executive Committee. As other diary entries make clear, Nikolskii had known Grabar for many years and intensely disliked him.

[20] "The manuscript was ready of the doctoral dissertation of V. E. Grabar on the topic "The Science of International Law in England Before the Reformation" which he defended at Voronezh in 1918". See A. Kisik, in Karl Siilivask (ed.), История Тартуского университета, 1632-1982 [History of Tartu University] (2d ed.; Tallinn, 1983), p. 145. Also see Siilivask (ed.), *History of Tartu University, 1632-1982*, transl. Ants Aaver (Tallinn, 1985). This is not confirmed by sources at Voronezh State University, who note the conflicting information. See E. V. Sazonnikova, «Навстречу 100-летию юридического факультета Воронежского государственного университета в 2018 г.» [On the 100th Anniversary of the Law Faculty of Voronezh State University in 2018], Вестник Воронежского государственного университета: серия: право [Herald of Voronezh State University. Series: Law], no. 4 (2016), p. 24.

And so the mystery thickens: the dissertation "perished"; the dissertation was stolen or "vanished"; the dissertation survived and was defended at Voronezh.

Grabar and his wife had decided to evacuate with the rest of Tartu University to safety in Voronezh by special train arranged by the Soviet authorities in July 1918, where they formed the nucleus of the newly-established Voronezh State University.

Access to archival documents enables certain events to be confirmed as set out above. Whether Grabar defended a dissertation in Voronezh remains inconclusive, although no evidence has surfaced which would confirm that such a dissertation defense did occur and the dissertation itself, if defended at Voronezh, has not been found.

In St. Petersburg, however, there are materials of considerable interest. On 26 April 1918 the Chancellery of the University received a copy of a letter from the Dean and the Secretary of the Faculty of Law addressed to the Rector of Petrograd University which read as follows:

> I have the honor to submit that the Faculty of Law at a session of 30/17 April of this year by a closed ballot unanimously decreed to petition the Council of the University concerning the conferral on Professor *ordinarius* of Iurev University, V. E. Grabar, the learned degree of doctor of international law without the submission of a dissertation.
>
> The submission concerning this of acting *extraordinarius*, *ordinarius* professor, Baron B. E. Nolde is appended.

The document carries on the left margin the following notation: "Reported to the Council of the University, 10 June 1918. Decreed: to confer the degree of doctor of international law *honoris causa* by a majority of 31 votes against 6".

On 27 April 1939 Grabar wrote to the Director of Leningrad State University to request an instruction to issue him an extract from the Protocol of the session of the Council of Petrograd University of 10 June (27 May) 1918 concerning the "awarding to me of the learned degree of doctor of international law. I need this for submission to the Historical Institute of the USSR Academy of Sciences". The request was signed "Personal Pensioner, Professor Vladimir Grabar"; he added postage stamps for the reply to his home address at Zubovskii bulvar, 15, kv. 15, in Moscow. The Archive of Leningrad University issued the requested information officially as follows:

Archival Reference

According to archival materials of Leningrad State University, this means that professor ordinarius of Iurev University, V. E. Grabar, at a session of the Council of Petrograd State University of 10 June 1918 by a majority of votes was awarded the learned degree of doctor of international law without the submission of a dissertation.

Head of Archive of Leningrad State University: T. Kotin

Archivist: V. Dobrogaev

As is evident from the text of the materials, the Law Faculty requested the awarding of the degree of doctor of international law without the submission of a dissertation; the Council of the University awarded the said degree *honoris causa*. The degree would have been awarded pursuant to a further submission by Baron Boris Nolde of an 8-page detailed list of Grabar's scholarly achievements to the Council of the University.

It happens that sometimes only the text of the Faculty request is read without having regard to the confirmation of what the Council of the University actually awarded. In any event, it is beyond doubt that Grabar was awarded the degree of doctor of international law *honoris causa* without the formality of a defense of published works or a dissertation, which would further explain the absence of a dissertation in Petrograd (St. Petersburg).

The precise form of Grabar's doctoral dissertation is unknown. At a minimum, it was a manuscript written out in hand and existed in but one copy. In those times it could have been typewritten, although the combination of Cyrillic and Latin text would have been a challenge and required either two typewriters or one language typewritten and the other interpolated by hand. One chapter or article based on the dissertation was in press at the time of the October 1917 Revolution and appeared.[21] Upon his election as academician by the Ukrainian Academy of Sciences, he published an appropriate article addressing the Commentaries of John Mair (c. 1467-1550) on Peter of Lombardy (c. 1100-1160) in the Ukrainian language with a French-language summary.[22] His seminal bibliography on medieval ambassadorial law appeared after the Revolution but was in press during the stormy events of 1917/18.[23]

Grabar's friends who arranged the honorary doctorate hoped this degree would acknowledge his excellent dissertation, completed but no longer extant, and ease Grabar's election to the Chair of International Law at Moscow University. Any prospect of the Moscow appointment ended with the reforms in higher education being instituted by the Bolsheviks. From 1918 to 1919 Grabar served as professor at Voronezh University, but illness forced him to return to the Grabar home in Adler, on the Black Sea. On 25 May 1921 Voronezh University authorized his return to teaching and sent the necessary documents, but the post was not taken up.

[21] Grabar, «Понятие естественного права и международного права в английской литературе XII-XVI вв.» [Concept of Natural and International Law in English Literature of the Twelfth to Sixteenth Centuries], Юридический вестник [Legal Herald], kn. 2-4 (1917), pp. 5-30. See W. E. Butler, *Russia and the International Legal System: A Bibliography of Writings by Russian Jurists on Public and Private International Law to 1917 with References to Publications in Emigration* (London, 2006), p. 50, item Г348.

[22] Grabar, note 14 above. See Butler Г345 and Г346. This item appears in the serial publication cited and as a separate offprint, 36 p. For background, see W. E. Butler, note 14 above, pp. 581-593. Also see Semenov and Tragniuk, note 14 above, pp. 178-185.

[23] Grabar, *De legatum jure: Tractatum Catalogus Completus ab anno MDCXXV usque ad annum MDCC* (Dorpat, 1918). The Mattisen printing house burned during the German occupation of Tartu in spring 1918; a substantial portion of the print run of his book perished as a result.

Although Grabar's extensive notes survive in his personal archive at Tartu University, so far as is known, he did not attempt to reconstruct the dissertation or prepare a similar work along analogous lines. His interest in this, primarily pre-Grotian, era of the law of nations did not wane completely. He did make efforts in what must have been difficult and risky times to attract interest abroad in his research, with presumably minimal opportunities in the Soviet Union at the time, but for certain more auspicious periods. Fragments of this interest can be documented; whether they are the "tip of the iceberg" or the entire iceberg remains uncertain. No later than 1923 Grabar was aware that the Carnegie Foundation in New York and Washington DC was well along in producing seminal volumes devoted to the classics of international law. A project initiated by James Brown Scott (1866-1943), the plan was to undertake new translations of the leading publicists accompanied by a facsimile edition of the best version of each author selected. Grabar apparently wrote to Scott in late 1922 or early 1923 expressing his interest in becoming part of the project. Whether that letter actually arrived is uncertain; neither the Grabar archive or the Carnegie Foundation archive contains any indication of such a letter.

In any event, Scott was traveling when the Grabar proposal arrived. George Finch (1884-1957), Secretary of the Carnegie Endowment and eventual biographer of Scott,[24] replied to Grabar on 2 August 1923, noting receipt of the proposal and that Scott would reply upon return.[25] Grabar took advantage of the reply to respond to Finch on 19 September 1923 and make further proposals, as follows:

> … I should suggest to complete the Series of Ancient Authors by Alberico Gentili, who deserves attention more than any other author of the past … His two other works, *De Legationibus* and *Advocatio Hispanica*, are still waiting for an editor.
>
> As to *De Legationibus*, I had opportunity already to prove the necessity of its edition. In my book, *De Legatis et Legationibus tractatus varii*, which appeared in 1905, in explaining the lack of any quotation out of the work of Gentili, I said in the preface: "Quod idem si non fecai, cum ex quellaro opera illo Albertei summa, crius solus abide; nullal alia ex causa id factum existienes, quam quod maxime necessarium esse videbatur, ut Alberici opus saparatium et indigenous edeatur". This has been supported by Prof. Holland in a letter addressed to me.
>
> The *Advocatio Hispanica*, considering cases brought before the Admiralty Court, is a very valuable monument of the XVI century prize law, as interpreted by the civilians of that age – a book of greatest interest for the development of international law.[26]

24 G. Finch, *Adventures in Internationalism: A Biography of James Brown Scott*, ed. W. E. Butler (2012).

25 Scott replied on 7 November 1923 that one edition of Gentili already had been published and another was in press. The Scott Reply is held in the Grabar Archive at the Russian State Library, Ф376, kart. 13, ed. 22.

26 The Letter was received by the Carnegie Endowment on 5 November 1923 and reposes in the Archives of the Endowment held at Columbia University, File C-17. The Letter in the hand of Grabar was written in English and addressed to George Finch, Assistant Secretary of the Carnegie Endow-

On 17 March 1924 Igor Grabar (1871-1960), Vladimir's younger brother, trained in the law but a noted artist, art restorer, cultural historian, sometime diplomat, and eventually Academician of the USSR Academy of Sciences, wrote to Scott in the English language from New York, where he was participating in a Soviet artistic initiative, indicating Vladimir's interest in the project and confirming that a letter had been sent earlier. This Letter further indicated that Vladimir Grabar was considering emigration from the Soviet Union, a prospect that Scott was asked to keep confidential; this intimation may have been made to increase Grabar's attractiveness to the Carnegie Endowment insofar as he could be closer to the central headquarters of the project and available for consultations. Igor's letter, typewritten, enclosed a hand-written letter from Vladimir dated 12 December 1923 in response to James Brown Scott's reply reporting that the Gentili works already were spoken for. On this occasion Grabar made further proposals:

> … I regret I came too late with my proposals as to the edition of the works of Alberico Gentili, but I was very glad to hear they were already included in the list of "Classics of International Law", as I am of the opinion he deserves no less attention than the so-called father (rather stepfather) of International Law.
>
> I come now to you with new proposals I would think necessary to include in the list of the "Classics"
>
> 1. The treatise of Bartolus, *de repressalis*. So far as our knowledge extends, it is the first treatise on international law that ever appeared. It was written in the year 1354, some years before the treatise of Giovanni de Ligano, already published in the series of "Classics".
>
> 2. Zouch, *Solutio Questionis veteris et nouve, sive de Legati delinquentis Indice competante* (first published in 1657). To the edition of this treatise might be joined anonimous treatise, to which Zouch's work is referring: "*Questio vetus et nave: Au legatuus ... salvo Iure gentium capere, retinere et punier liceat?*" (two editions of the same year 1606, one of Paris, the other of Strassbourg). An extrait of Pierre Ayrault (Petrus Aerodius) to whom belongs the real authorship of the conception of "Extraterritoriality" could be also joined to the edition.
>
> Separately to be edited later on the same question the work of Jean Villier de Hotmann, the son of Francais de Hotman.
>
> 3. On war – three different treatises of Spanish authors: Francesco Arias de Valdera, Juan Lopez (Joh. Lupus) and Alvarez Guerrero (can be edited later).
>
> A treatise of Henricus v. Goreuus *Tractatus de bello rusto* (1460).
>
> 4. I have some special proposals concerning maritime international law (Sovereignty of the Seas), which I shall communicate later on. They concern the edition of several English writers on the question of the Sovereignty of the Seas (one of which preserved in ms., not yet edited) . The

ment for International Peace, in Washington DC.

> treatise of Grotius, *De mare liberum*, no doubt should be edited too, but not in connexion with the above-mentioned English authors.
>
> As to me, I am mostly interested in 1) Bartolus, 2) writers on war, specially those of Spanish origin, 3) English authors on the Sovereignty of the Seas. Bartolus and the writers on war could be prepared, I think, in one year; the next year I could begin with the English authors, if you trust to me their edition. I should combine it with a bibliography of the pre-Grotian authors.[27]

On this occasion, Scott replied to Igor Grabar in New York City directly in a letter dated the following day, 20 March 1924, rejecting Vladimir's proposals for financial reasons. He did not divulge future titles for the series. In fact, at this time the "Classics of International Law" series was experiencing financial difficulties because of problems with the translation of Hugo Grotius, *On the Law of War and Peace*. Scott hoped to publish Grotius the following year, to commemorate the 300th anniversary of the first edition of the Grotian treatise. That aspiration was not to transpire, and in fact the Grotius appeared in 1928, published with a false date of 1925. The delays with Grotius held up all other volumes in the series and engaged extra unanticipated costs for the Endowment.[28]

Grabar was a member of the American Society of International Law and somehow managed to pay dues for a number of years. On 18 September 1932 the *American Journal of International Law* received an article from Grabar entitled "Extradition in England Before the Time of Grotius", which was then distributed to the Board of Editors for consideration. The article was not published in the end, being deemed to be "too historical".[29]

Turning away from England to the continent, Grabar published several articles in French[30] journals. These were bibliographical in character, demonstrating his mastery of the original sources, and unlikely to generate political repercussions at home. Throughout these years, at least since 1914, Grabar pursued Russian literature on international law, eventually materializing in his encyclopedic work on the subject.[31] This work appeared posthumously, in 1958, published by "Nauka", the publishing house of the USSR Academy of Sciences.

27 Ibid. The Letter was received at the Carnegie Endowment on 19 March 1924.

28 For full details of this episode, see Butler, *Grotius on War and Peace in English Translation* (2021), pp. 77-131.

29 For Grabar's correspondence and documents, see the Grabar Archive at the Russian State Library, Ф367, kart. 12, ed. 40.

30 Grabar, "Esquisse d'une histoire litteraire du droit international du Moyen Age, du IV au XII siècles", *Revue de droit international privé et de droit pénal international*, XVIII (1936), pp. 7-39, 373-439 ; Grabar, "La doctrine de droit international chez Saint Augustine", *Archives de philosophie de droit et de sociologie juridique*, II (1932), pp. 428-446; Grabar, "Le rôle de Grotius dans le développement scientifique du droit international", *Revue de droit international privé et de droit pénal international*, VI (1925), pp. 537-555.

31 Grabar, note 5 above.

The future Soviet judge in the International Court of Justice, Sergei Borisovich Krylov (1888-1958), wrote to Grabar on 22 May 1941, referring in passing to the fact that the Grabar "work on the history of the science" had gone to press.[32] In fact this was the "initial (broad) version" containing material up to the end of the eighteenth century. Because of the War, the publishing house was unable to complete typesetting and in 1945 returned the materials to Grabar. The part devoted to the first quarter of the nineteenth century, of second half, Grabar had completed by July 1946 when Grabar was attached to the Institute of State and Law of the USSR Academy of Sciences. Conferences on publication of the work were held with the senior staff and technical editors of the Institute at this time.[33]

This would suggest that for various reasons the Grabar work was held up in process, which included wartime exigencies, and possibly political issues, or other complications. Whatever the reason(s), the Grabar volume joined a number of others devoted to matters of pre-revolutionary history that were revived c. 1940 as part of a new emphasis upon patriotism and nationalism, some of which were expeditiously treated, others delayed, and some never published. It may well be that the Grabar fell into the second category.[34]

It transpired that Fedor Ivanovich Kozhevnikov (1903-1998), Русское государство и международное право [Russian State and International Law (1947), appeared a decade before Grabar. The Grabar manuscript was completed by the mid-1940s, subject to occasional emendations as Grabar awaited publication. The two were close friends, although Kozhevnikov was not even close to being the scholar that Grabar was. Kozhevnikov had access to the Grabar manuscript. Any "borrowing" as between the two books would have most certainly been Kozhevnikov adapting from Grabar. It may even be that the Kozhevnikov volume came to fruition because of delays with the Grabar publication, although this is purely speculative.[35]

Grabar retired in 1929 and was awarded a personal pension of 200 rubles per month. For the next quarter century he devoted himself to research on international law in the Middle Ages and to completing his study on the history of international law in Russia. His eightieth and especially his ninetieth birthdays were marked by resolutions of congratulations sent by every Soviet legal institution of consequence; these are preserved in Grabar's personal archive. Grabar died on 26 November 1956 in his ninety-second year.

[32] Letter from S. B. Krylov to V. E. Grabar, 22 May 1941. Russian State Library, Ф376, kart. 5, ed. 38.

[33] See the Memorandum held at Tartu University, F.38, s. 158.

[34] M. P. Lepekhin, *N. V. Zdobnov and His* ***History of Russian Bibliography***, ed & transl. W. E. Butler [Idyllwild, California], 2014) – a detailed account of publishing practices and conundrums during the period concerned.

[35] See W. E. Butler, review of L. Mälksoo, *Russian Approaches to International Law* (2015), in *The American Journal of International Law*, CX (2016), pp. 402-406.

Baron **Aleksandr Nikolaevich Shtiglits** *(7 October 1852 – no earlier than 1917). International lawyer, publicist, public figure.*

Life and career. Shtiglits descended from a noteworthy Russian noble family dynasty.[36] He attended secondary school at the First St. Petersburg Gymnasium, graduating in 1872.[37] That year he enrolled at the Law Faculty of St. Petersburg University.[38] At the end of 1879, Shtiglits passed the examination for the degree of magister of international law at Kharkov University. He submitted in 1881 a magister dissertation "On Military Contraband".[39] The Council of the Kharkov University considered the dissertation to be unsatisfactory on the basis of a review by Professor Vsevolod Pievich Danevskii at that University.[40] In 1882 Shtiglits submitted a magister dissertation to St. Petersburg University, defended with success, on the extradition of criminals.[41] He was awarded the magister of international law and on all future publications indicated this degree. In the early twentieth century Shtiglits was active in the Russian nationalist and Slavophile movements, a committed monarchist. From 1899 to 1918 he served as a member of the Trusteeship Council of the Prince P. G. Oldenburgskii Child Orphan's Home.

International legal views. Grabar judged Shtiglits harshly: "He devoted much time to investigating questions of international law, to which he continued to apply the old epithets 'European' or 'Christian'. His works have disappeared without trace in the history of the Russian science".[42] Modern legal scholars, however, find the contribution of Shtiglits to the science of international law to be useful.

Shtiglits addressed a number of issues in his writings on international law. His works on military contraband began with a general account of warfare, written in 1880 when war had not been outlawed and was considered to be a natural phenomenon. Shtiglits considered war, nonetheless, to interfere in the natural course of a civil society and to violate the "laws of intellectual, moral, and economic development". History, he believed, gives evidence of a "gradual transition from a state of lawlessness, violence, and arbitrariness to a state of lawfulness, legality, advis-

36 Some sources give the year of death as 1914. The reference book Весь Петербург на 1917 год. Адресная справочная книга [All Petersburg for 1917. Address Reference Book] (Pg., 1916), p. 776, however, listed Shtiglits at Nab. Moika, 32. The book was not published for the years 1918 to 1921. The surname Shtiglits was not included in the 1922 edition.

37 ЦГИА СПб., fond 14, opis 1, file 36182.

38 ЦГИА СПб., fond 14, opis 3, file 17642. His father, N. B. Shtiglits, a privy counsellor and Russian ambassador in Italy, filed the application for admission in the name of the Rector. There is no evidence of his graduation from St. Petersburg University.

39 A. N. Shtiglits, Исследование о военной контрабанде [Study on Military Contraband] (Spb., 1880). 228 p. Butler Ш82; Shtiglits, Исследование о военной контрабанде [Study on Military Contraband] (Spb., 1881). 249 p. Butler Ш83.

40 Grabar, note 5 above, pp. 392-393.

41 Shtiglits, Исследование о выдаче преступников [Study on the Extradition of Criminals] (Spb., 1882). Butler Ш84. Also see Shtiglits, *Études sur l'extradition*, transl. L. de Mikor (Paris, 1883). Butler Ш81.

42 Grabar, note 5 above, p. 393.

ability, and love of mankind" (p. 1). Modern warfare can no longer be regarded as lawless because military customs have formed and treaties have been concluded which impose certain duties on belligerents (p. xiii).

The rules regulating military contraband are examples of such international legal obligations – the carriage of military goods by ships of neutral countries and a violation of their neutral status by one of the belligerents. Shtiglits proved that States who wishes to maintain their neutral status must observe complete impartiality and not render any assistance to one belligerent to the detriment of the interests of the other. Each belligerent, he said, has the right to exercise certain control over trade links of neutral States with the other party to the conflict. All goods discovered in a vessel which are directed or capable of strengthening the military might of a belligerent constitute military contraband. The other goods having no military significance to be delivered by neutral States to a belligerent are inviolate and should be allowed to pass without obstruction. He further demonstrated that the carriage of military detachments by the warships of neutral States is a special type of contraband which must result in the arrest of all the individuals being transported and confiscation of the vessel.

As regards extradition, Shtiglits pointed to the increased incidences of an individual committing a crime in one country and fleeing to another to avoid apprehension or prosecution, or the serving of punishment. The flight of culprits in these situations is harmful, Shtiglits argued, to the State where the crime was committed and to all of human society. States over time, said Shtiglits, have become aware of the need to extradite criminals (p. ii). In the past jurists were inclined to treat extradition as a political, and not a legal, issue. Even Professor Martens, Shtiglits pointed out, considered the extradition of criminals to be an act of international comity (p. 28).

States were revising their attitudes and positions; they were concluding bilateral treaties laying down the procedures and circumstances of extradition. These were desirable developments in the interests of the international community.

Shtiglits produced a three-volume treatise on the principles of political equilibrium, legitimacy, and nationality,[43] of which there was a French translation.[44]

Vladimir Antonovich Ulianitskii *(30 January (11 February) 1854 – 1920). Specialist in the history and theory of international law.*

Life and career. Born at Moscow into a noble family, Ulianitskii graduated from the Third Moscow Gymnasium and enrolled in the Law Faculty of Moscow University.[45] Upon completing the course in 1874 with a gold medal for a grad-

[43] Shtiglits, Исследование о началах политического равновесия, легитимизма и национальности [Study on Principles of Political Equilibrium, Legitimacy, and Nationality] (Spb., 1889-1892). 3 vols. in 4. Butler Ш85.

[44] Shtiglits, *De l'équilibre politique, du légitimisme et du principe des nationalités* (Paris, 1893-1897). 3 vols. Butler Ш80.

[45] For biographical data, see Grabar, note 5 above, pp. 429-430; Профессора Томского

uation thesis on the land tax, he remained at the Faculty from 1 November 1875 to 1 November 1877 to prepare for the professoriate at the Chair of State Law. But, having been enticed by international law, on 17 November 1877 he passed the magister examination on international law. From 1878 he worked at the Moscow Chief Archive of the Ministry of Foreign Affairs.

Drawing upon access to archival materials, Ulianitskii published a monograph which he submitted to St. Petersburg University as a dissertation for the degree of magister of international law and successfully defended in 1883.[46] In 1885 the Imperial Russian Academy of Sciences awarded the Uvarov Prize for this work.

Having become a magister and with the approval of the Ministry of Foreign Affairs, Ulianitskii was appointed privat-docent at the Chair of International Law of Moscow University and began to lecture on the theory of international law and on diplomatic history, together with Professor L. A. Kamarovskii (1846-1912). He later published a course of lectures together with Kamarovskii.[47] Two further treatises followed from his relationship to the Moscow Archive. The first explored Russian relations with Central Asia and India,[48] and the second, relations between

университета. Биографический словарь [Professors of Tomsk University. Biographical Dictionary] (Tomsk, 1996), I, pp. 262-264; V. F. Volovich (ed.), Юридическое образование в Томском государственном университете: Очерк истории (1898-1998 гг.) [Legal Education in Tomsk State University: Survey of History (1898-1998)] (Tomsk, 1998), pp. 32-33; V. L. Tolstykh, «В. А. Уляницкий и его работа «Международное право» [V. A. Ulianitskii and his Work "International Law"], in Ulianitskii, Международное право [International Law] (M., reprint ed.; 2010), pp. 7-17; K. O. Savchuk, «Уляницький Володимир Антонович» [Ulianitskii, Volodymyr Antonovich], in Denysov, note 11 above, p. 876; Starodubtsev, note 11 above, p. 200.

46 V. A. Ulianitskii, Дарданеллы, Босфор и Черное море в XVIII веке. Очерки дипломатической истории Восточного вопроса [Dardanelles, Bosphorus, and the Black Sea in the Eighteenth Century. Survey of the Diplomatic History of the Eastern Question] (M., 1883). Sources often mistakenly indicate that the dissertation was defended at Moscow University. See G. G. Krichevskii, Магистерские и докторские диссертации, защишенные на юридических факультетах университетов Российской империи (1755-1918). Библиографический указатель [Magister and Doctoral Dissertations Defended at Law Faculties of Universities of the Russian Empire (1755-1918): Bibliographical Index] (Stavropol, 1998), p. 29. On the defense, see ЦГИА СПб., fond 14, opis 1, file 8407.

47 L. A. Kamarovskii and V. A. Ulianitskii, Международное право. По лекциям Л. А. Камаровского и В. А. Улянинцкого [International Law. According to the Lectures of L. A. Kamarovskii and V. A. Ulianitskii (M., 1908). Butler K251.

48 Ulianitskii, Сношения России с Среднею Азиею и Индиею в XVI-XVII вв.: По документам Московского главного архива Министерства иностранных дел [Relations of Russia with Central Asia and India in the XVI-XVII Centuries: According to Documents of the Moscow Chief Archive

Russia, Poland, Moldavia, Wallachia, and Turkey.[49] In 1899 Ulianitskii left the Archive to take up an appointment as privat-docent at the Chair of International Law of Kharkov University.

On 5 February 1900 Ulianitskii defended a doctoral dissertation at Moscow University on consular law and was appointed professor *ordinarius* of Kharkov University.[50] His stay in Ukraine was brief, however, and on 1 July 1901 he was transferred to the Chair of International Law at Tomsk University by the Ministry of Public Enlightenment. While in Tomsk, Ulianitskii published the last fundamental treatise on international law of the pre-revolutionary period.[51]

On 8 May 1909 Ulianitskii retired and on 28 May 1910 the title of Distinguished Professor of Tomsk University was conferred for 25 years of service to the teaching profession. At his request, Ulianitskii was appointed privat-docent at Kazan University on 23 July 2011 by the Ministry of Public Enlightenment, and there he spent the remainder of his life.

International legal views. When Ulianitskii submitted his treatise on the Black Sea straits to St. Petersburg University in 1883 as a magister dissertation, he was well-known as an international lawyer. Most of his publications were in the field of international legal history, reflecting his work and access to materials in the Moscow Chief Archive at the Ministry of Foreign Affairs. He explained the reasons for choosing his magister topic as follows: "The recent war of Russia against Turkey, its results, and the arguments inspired by it concerning the historical mission of Russia in the East persuaded me to investigate the history of Russian diplomacy with regard to the Eastern Question" (p. 13). The principal task of his treatise was to investigate the "freedom of Russian trade and navigation in the Black Sea" (p. 14). His work began with a sweeping summary from ancient times to the conquest of Constantinople by the Turks in 1453. Thereafter, he divided matters into two periods. The first extended from 1453 to the Russo-Turkish wars under Peter the Great. The second period originated from the end of the seventeenth century to the 1774 Treaty of Kuchuk-Kainardzhi. The Black Sea during all these centuries had been a center of maritime trade and been used by the Black Sea and Mediterranean peoples and nations. But when the Ottoman Porte captured and controlled both side of the Straits, trade from the mid-fifteenth century depended entire on them (p. 20).

Ulianitskii undertook to demonstrate the legitimacy of Russian aspirations to secure its southern Russo-Tatar borders, the economic development of its southern regions, and its longer-term strategic interests by achieving freedom of navigation

of the Ministry of Foreign Affairs] (M., 1889).

[49] Ulianitskii, Материалы для истории взаимных отношений России, Польши, Молдавии, Валахии и Турци и в XIV-XVI вв. [Materials for the History of Mutual Relations of Russia, Poland, Moldavia, Wallachia, and Turkey in the XIV-XVI Centuries] (M., 1887).

[50] Ulianitskii, Русские консульства за границею в XVIII веке [Russian Consulates Abroad in the XVIII Century] (M., 1899). 2 vols.

[51] Ulianitskii, Международное право [International Law] (Tomsk, 1911; reprint ed.; M., 2010).

and trade on the Black Sea and free passage for Russian-flag vessels through the Straits.

In Part One Ulianitskii analyzed the treaty and diplomatic relations of Turkey with other countries, especially in Europe with Mediterranean Venice and Genoa. Turkey has concluded treaties in writing with them on trade and merchant shipping. Trade relations were complicated when the Popes of Rome declared the Porte to be the enemy of the Christian world because of the conquest of Constantinople.

The second period Ulianitskii based on documents discovered in the archives, some of which he published for the first time in his treatise. He addressed the Russian positions when the 1700 Constantinople Peace Treaty, 1739 Belgrade Peace Treaty, and 1774 Treaty of Kuchuk-Kainardzhi were negotiated against the background of regional Black Sea and Straits developments. In his review of Ulianitskii, Martens expressed admiring praise of the "wealth of new materials and facts relating to the history of the past century".[52]

[52] F. F. Martens, reviewing Ulianitskii in Отчет о двадцать восьмом присуждении наград графа Уварова [Report on the Twenty-Eighth Conferral of the Count Uvarov Award] (M., 1886), p. 7.

Chapter 10

Practitioner Graduates Who Continued International-Legal Research

A significant number of graduates from St. Petersburg institutions of higher education pursued careers as civil servants but found themselves in positions where a knowledge of international law was useful or directly involved in the performance of their duties. Some produced contributions to international legal doctrine of quality and importance. Among them were the following jurists.

Liudvig Liudvigovich Gervagen *(5 March 1860, b. village of Azel, Valsk District, Lifland (now Latvia) – d. no earlier than 1928). Civilist.*

Life and career. Gervagen enrolled in the Law Faculty of St. Petersburg University in 1879[1] and graduated in 1883 with the degree of candidate of laws. He remained at the Chair of Civil Law in the Faculty to prepare for the professoriate. In 1890 he was permitted to sit the magister examinations[2] and found employment in the Fourth Department of the Ruling Senate. For ten years he served as justice of the peace and administrator of a prison in Švenčionys, Lithuania, and as deputy chairman in district courts in Krasnoiarsk, Chita, and Łomża (Kingdom of Poland). During the First World War, he worked as a jurisconsult of the Ministry of Justice. In 1917 he was appointed a privy State counsellor and made an honorary citizen by descent. In that same year he joined the Religious-Philosophical Society.

During the Soviet era, Gervagen worked from 1919 to 1920 as the Head of the Archive of the Council of National Economy of the Northern District.[3] During the 1920s, he was employed as the secretary of a people's court. From 1928 he was elected to membership of a church executive organ of the Russian Evangelical Lutheran St. Mikhail Congregation. Thereafter his fate is unknown but is believed by some sources to have perished in the repressions during the 1930s.

International legal views. Gervagen's principal works dealt with civil law.[4] Of special interest in the field of international law were his views on the nature of international legal obligations. During the First World War, Gervagen published a

[1] ЦГИА СПб., fond 14, opis 3, file 20585.

[2] ЦГИА СПб., fond 14, opis 3, file 9126.

[3] ЦГА, fond P-1578, opis 1, file 1244.

[4] L. L. Gervagen, Развитие учения о юридическом лице [Development of the Doctrine on the Juridical Person] (Spb., 1888); Gervagen, «Теория общественных союзов» [Theory of Social Unions], Юридический вестник [Legal Herald], VIII, no. 7-8 (1891), pp. 362-396; Gervagen, Обязанности как основание права [Duties as the Basis of Right] (Spb., 1908); Институт собственности как основание системы гражданских прав, и учение о юридическом лице [Institution of Ownership as Basis of System of Civil Rights and Doctrine on the Juridical Person] (Pb., 1917).

brief monograph on whether international agreements have the property of law[5] – a piece that drew attention from the legal community at the time.[6] The occasion for this work was the outbreak of the First World War, when Germany and Austria-Hungary attacked their neighbors with "complete neglect of their international legal obligations and according to the rule 'the end justifies the means', adhering to the view that external force is higher than international obligations" (p. 58).

Gervagen also responded to the debate extending over many centuries of whether general legal categories extended to international legal norms and obligations. If, he wrote, law is understood as the "aggregate of instructions" issued by State authorities, "it must be acknowledged that international agreements, not being based on a power supreme in any State, do not have the character of law". But if one distinguishes municipal legislative law emanating from the power of a State and international "treaty" law emanating from international agreements, "then international agreements as specific concepts of treaty agreements must be added to the domain of law" (p. iv).

Gervagen addressed the skepticism widely shared at the time and even now relating to the actuality of international agreements in view of their frequent violation:

> The fact that violations of international agreements are often observed in life, even if entire States and nations are such violators, cannot serve as evidence that international agreements lack the character of law because rather often law based on State power is violation, and this circumstance has never served as grounds for denying the property of law for a law based on State power (pp. iv, 32).

Passing on to the international legal duties of States, Gervagen understood by these a situation in which the parties to an international treaty must act or refrain from acting in such a way, so that the performance or fail to perform their promise or their duty arising from an international treaty may entail disadvantageous consequences for them (p. 36). One such unfavorable consequence might be military measures taken against them by the victim State. War, in other words, might be waged to resist a violation of international law (p. 40).

Gervagen devoted a chapter to the law of war (Chapter 2, pp. 40-57). Depending on what purposes the belligerents pursue for waging war, a war may be moral or immoral, aggressive or defensive (p. 41). The second chapter is overwhelmingly humanitarian in tone. In spirit, every military serviceman must lay down a moral principle which should assist him in determining:

(a) war is waged only with the enemy forces, and not with the peaceful population so long as that population does not take part in the war;

[5] Gervagen, Имеют ли международные соглашения свойство права? [Do International Agreements Have the Property of Law?] (Pg., 1915).

[6] Reviewed by S. A. Krichevskii, in Право [Law], no. 6 (1915), cols. 401-402.

(b) it is appropriate to leave inviolate both the life of the peaceful population of the enemy side and the honor of their women and private property of the population;

(c) property of the enemy country should not be destroyed and its population eradicated, for destruction and eradication is immoral;

(d) after a battle it is appropriate to help the wounded or captured enemy and not desecrate them because the enemy also is a person who performed his duty.

The essential moral principles that belligerents should follow were demonstrated by drawing upon an idealized example of the Russian warrior:

> We (as a general rule from which there may be exceptions strictly punished by the military command) do not finish off wounded and prisoners, do not offend the peaceful population so long as it does not resort to weapons; pay for property taken from them essential for military purposes; do not plunder private property; and do not destroy churches, cities, and settlements (p. 48).

If war cannot be avoided, it must be waged according to international rules, wrote Gervagen: "Waging war without complying with the conditions established by a treaty is not only a violation of law, but also is for the greater part an immoral action". A violation of established international norms would be: (a) failure to respect the Red Cross; (b) means of waging war not permitted by international treaties; (c) finishing off wounded and prisoners; (d) deceitful use of enemy or neutral flag or uniform; (e) capture of private property without the fault of the owner; (f) destruction of churches; (g) eradication of the peaceful population; and others (p. 49). If military servicemen are guilty of using unpermitted means of waging war, said Gervagen, they must be prosecuted by their superiors for these violations according to domestic law; if this does not happen, then the government itself must be liable for the failure to convict the guilty (p. 50).

Here Gervagen led his reader to the idea of the need to create a mechanism of international responsibility for a violation of international norms for waging warfare:

> An international court should be established by international treaties and empowered by international treaties to consider cases after the end of the War with regard to the accusation of the State, although it triumphed, of a violation of duties adopted by international treaties relating to the means of waging the war.

Possible forms of punishment for violations of international law, suggested Gervagen, might be the declaration of a warning to the guilty State or the infliction of unpleasantness. The last might consist of the suspension of international economic treaties concluded with States around the world; that is, deprive the guilty State of some sort of economic benefit (pp. 51-52). To some extent Gervagen anticipated the reactions of the international community to the outcome of the First and Second World Wars and the creation of the international military tribunals in Germany and Japan.

Sergei Mikhailovich Goriainov *(4(16) December 1849 – 25 October/7 November or 31 December 1918). Diplomatic historian and international lawyer.*

Life and career. Goriainov enrolled at the Law Faculty of St. Petersburg University in 1867 and graduated in 1871.[7] Upon graduation, he accepted a position in Pavlovsk – a suburb of St. Petersburg – as a justice of the peace; from 1873 as an uezd Marshal of the Nobility; and from 1872 at the chairman of the Pavlovsk uezd zemstvo administration. In 1878 he became a member of the Petersburg District Court. He transferred to the Ministry of Foreign Affairs in 1891, being appointed Consul in Chernovytsa (then Austria-Hungary; now Ukraine). By 1896 he was Consul General in Vienna, and a year later Vice Director of the Department of International Relations of the Ministry of Foreign Affairs (external and internal correspondence on matters of Western Europe and America). In 1898 he was made a privy State counsellor. From 1902 to 1915 Goriainov served as the Director of the Petersburg and Chief Archives of the Ministry of Foreign Affairs. In 1916 to 1917, he was appointed a Senator. He held membership in the Historical Society attached to the St. Petersburg University and in the Russian Historical Society.

International legal views. Central to the scholarly interests of Goriainov were diplomatic history and the international legal regulation of international relations. His two major works were devoted to consuls[8] and to the legal status of the Turkish Straits from the late eighteenth century to the 1878 Congress of Berlin.[9]

With regard to consuls, Goriainov undertook to systematize international and domestic legal norms regulating consuls. Conceived of as a manual, the volume was structured in immense detail into five basic parts, subdivided into sections, chapters, and sub-sections:

(1) consular institutions, rights and privileges "recognized for consuls by virtue of international treaties and on the basis of international custom;

(2) duties of consuls when dealing with administrative, registration, trade, customs, marine, financial, medical, and other issues which arose in relations with subjects of their own and foreign States;

(3) duties of consuls when resolving various court cases;

(4) duties of consuls when certifying various documents.

Goriainov used treaties to which Russia was a party, legislative acts of Russia, Finland, and other countries, explanations and instructions of governmental departments, rulings of Russian and foreign courts, and extensive consular practice.

[7] ЦГИА СПб., fond 14, opis 5, file 3530.

[8] S. M. Goriainov, Руководство для консулов [Manual for Consuls] (Spb., 1903).

[9] Goriainov, Босфор и Дарданеллы: Исследование вопроса о проливах по дипломатической переписке, хранящейся в Государственном и С.-Петербургском главном архивах [Bosphorus and Dardanelles: Study of the Question of the Straits through Diplomatic Correspondence Kept in the State and St. Petersburg Chief Archives] (Spb., 1907).

The manual was well reviewed by colleagues.[10] Ulianitskii gave an extensive review analyzing the merits and shortcomings, but considered the volume to be a significant contribution to the science and practice of consular law and the first study of its kind for the period covered.

In his study of the Turkish Straits, Goriainov turned to a substantial theoretical work of diplomatic and international legal history based on materials in the archives of which he had become the Director. Consisting of fifteen chapters, the author in chronological order documents the various aspects of the political and legal struggle of Russia vis-à-vis the Ottoman Porte and the powers of Western Europe over the ownership of and rights of passage through the Straits. He emphasized that the struggle for control over the Straits had been preceded by competition for ownership or control of the Black Sea itself. Turkey initially regarded the Black Sea as its internal waters and had categorically taken the position that no other States might have their warships in that Sea (p. 1). From the Turkish point of view, this included Russian warships and, insofar as they represented unwelcome competition, Russian merchant ships. These Turkish objectives were achieved in the 1739 Peace Treaty of Belgrade, where it was provided that Russia would have no naval fleet on the Sea of Azov or the Black Sea and that any trade would be conducted through vessels belonging to Turkish subjects. Only after the victory of Russia in conflicts between 1768 and 1774 did the Peace Treaty of Kuchuk-Kainardzhi fundamentally change the situation. Russia received the right to have its own fleet on the Black Sea and the right of free passage from the Black to the Mediterranean Sea and return (p. 2). Goriainov advocated closing the Straits to warships of all countries, including Russia, who had been weakened by the Japanese victory in the Russo-Japanese War of 1904-1905.

This volume too was welcomed by reviewers[11] and enjoyed a French translation.[12]

Iakov Abramovich Kantorovich (Iankel Abramov)[13] *(1 January 1859, b. Minsk – 15 October 1925, d. Leningrad). Civilist, publicist, journalist, publisher.*

[10] See V. A. Ulianitskii, in Отчет о 46-м присуждении премий гр. Уварова [Report on the 46th Conferral of the Count Uvarov Prizes] (Spb., 1906), pp. 43-46; and L. A. Shalland, Журнал Министерства юстиции [Journal of the Ministry of Justice], no. 3 (March 1903), pp. 371-373.

[11] See reviews by Nolde, Известия Санкт-Петербургского политехнического института [News of the St. Petersburg Polytechnic Institute], VII (1907), pp. 254-260; Aleksandrenko, Журнал Министерства юстиции [Journal of the Ministry of Justice], no. 4 (1907), pp. 336-338; and Grabar, Отчет о пятидесятом присуждении наград графа Уварова [Report on the Fiftieth Conferral of the Count Uvarov Awards] (Spb., 1910), pp. 145-168.

[12] Goriainov [Goriainow], *Le Bosphore et les Dardanelles: étude historique sur la question des détroits, d'après la correspondance diplomatique deposée aux Archives centrales de Saint-Petersbourg et celles de l'Empire*, preface G. Hanotaux (Paris, 1910); reviewed by B. E. Nolde, in Русская мысль [Russian Thought], no. 4 (1911), pp. 1-21. Butler Г203.

[13] In 1888, Kantorovich officially changed his forename from Iankel to Iakov. See ЦГИА СПб., fond 19, opis 80, file 15. Also see the entry in G. G. Branover (ed.), Российская еврейская энциклопедия [Russian Jewish Encyclopedia] (M., 1994), p. 546.

Life and career. After completing the Vilna Gymnasium in 1879 (Vilna; today Vilnius, Lithuania), Kantorovich enrolled at the Law Faculty of St. Petersburg University.[14] From 1886 to 1905 he worked as an assistant sworn advokat in a district of the St. Petersburg Chamber of Justice, and from 1905 to 1917 as a sworn advokat of the same Chamber and a sworn striapchii attached to the St. Petersburg Commercial Court.[15]

Using his own resources, he founded, edited, and published Судебное обозрение [Judicial Survey] (1902 to 1905); Вестник сенатской практики [Herald of Senate Practice] (1903 to 1905); and the Вестник законодательства [Herald of Legislation] (1903 to 1905) and was involved in the publication of other journals and dictionaries. After 1917, he worked on the journal Право и жизнь [Law and Life].

International legal views. A productive legal scholar, Kantorovich wrote primarily on aspects of the law of obligations, family, inheritance, intellectual property, civil procedure, and criminal procedure – often with an innovative or original twist (for example, the right to truth, transactions concluded by telephone, the right to one's own image).[16] He was especially interested in author's right. His work on literary property enjoyed three editions during the 1890s.[17] After the adoption in 1911 of the Russian Law on Author's Right, he published a detailed article-by-article commentary.[18]

During the first decade of the twentieth century, Kantorovich became interested in international law, particularly the protection of author's rights in literary, musical, and photographic works. His early publications in this area analyzed Russian cooperation with France and Germany. With respect to France, Kantorovich noted

[14] ЦГИА СПб., fond 14, opis 3, file 22498.

[15] ЦГИА СПб., fond 243, opis 1, file 1779.

[16] Among others: Ia. A. Kantorovich, Женщина в праве [The Woman in Law] (Spb., 1895); Kantorovich, Законы о женщинах [Laws on Women] (Spb., 1899); Kantorovich, Законы о детях [Laws on Children] (Spb., 1899); Kantorovich, Законы о браке и разводе [Laws on Marriage and Divorce] (Spb., 1899); Kantorovich, Законы о безумных и сумашедших [Laws on the Mentally Retarded and Insane] (Spb., 1899); Kantorovich, Средневековые процессы о ведьмах [Medieval Trials on Witches] (Spb., 1896); Kantorovich, Процессы против животных в средние века [Trials Against Animals in the Middle Ages] (Spb., 1897).

[17] Kantorovich, Литературная собственность [Literary Property] (Spb., 1895).

[18] Kantorovich, Авторское право на литературные, музыкальные, художественные в фотографические произведения: Новый закон 15 марта 1911 г., с историческим очерком и с разъяснениями, извлеченными из мотивов Редакционной комиссии по составлению Проекта Гражданского уложения, объяснительной записки к проекту Министерства юстиции и дебатов в Государственной Думе и Государственном Совете [Author's Right to Literary, Musical, Artistic, and Photographic Works: New Law of 15 March 1911 with a Historical Survey and Explanations Extracted from Reasons of the Editorial Commission for the Composition of the Draft Civil Code, Explanatory Memoranda to the Draft of the Ministry of Justice, and Debates in the State Duma and State Council] (Spb., 1911).

that the problems of defending and protecting author's rights had transcended State frontiers and become an issue for the international community. Solely domestic regulation of author's rights had become insufficient. Everywhere situations occurred when various scientific and artistic works were published in one country, translated into the language of another, or reprinted in the same language but in another country, distributed in large editions, with no royalties paid to the author.[19]

Kantorovich believed there were two means available to protect author's rights on the international scale: (1) protection of the rights of foreign authors on grounds identical with the rights of fatherland authors by a law in force in the particular country by which, with or without reciprocity, the rights of foreigners are equated to the rights of citizens; (2) international protection of intellectual property by special or separate agreements with individual States or a general agreement of several States who have formed a single Union (Berne Convention).[20] France was an example of the first approach, having in 1852 accorded to foreigners the identical protections as to French subjects, as was the United States, which granted by an 1891 law the same rights to foreigners as to American citizens, but on the basis of reciprocity. Other countries preferred the second approach; they concluded the 1886 Berne Convention for the Protection of Literary and Artistic Works and formed the Berne Union.

Russia actively promoted original and translated works by foreign authors in its book markets. The Berne Convention was not attractive to a country which aspired to preserve the principle of freedom of translation and the publication of foreign authors. Kantorovich analyzed the pros and cons of the two opposed positions, compared the Berne Convention with applicable Russian legislation, and concluded that the time was not ready for Russia to accede to the Convention. The 1911 Law was a welcome replacement of archaic legislation and introduced self-limitations which represented a gradual transition to acceptance of the international system of protecting intellectual property. The bilateral conventions with France and Germany were seen as steps in this direction.

Although Kantorovich welcomed the Russo-French convention, he believed that the Convention was more beneficial to France than to Russia. The works of Russian authors were not in demand in France and few were translated. French authors, on the other hand, were popular in Russia. The 1911 Law in Russia equalized the rights of all authors, but gave foreign authors certain preferences in litigation and in other respects. Russian authors did not enjoy such rights in France.

The First World Was inspired Kantorovich to turn to the implications of war for the performance of contractual obligations.[21] War changed the legal status of

[19] Kantorovich, Конвенция между Россией и Францией для защиты литературных и художественных произведений [Convention between Russia and France for the Defense of Literary and Artistic Works] (Spb., 1912), p. 3; also see Kantorovich, Русско-Французская конвенция об охране авторских прав [Russo-French Convention on the Protection of Author's Rights], Право [Law], no. 16 (1912), cols. 909-916.

[20] Kantorovich, note 17 above, p. 3.

[21] Kantorovich, «Война и исполнение обязательств» [War and the Performance of Obligations], Журнал Министерства юстиции [Journal of the Ministry of Justice], no. 2-3 (1917), pp. 102-154;

subjects of the belligerents caused by the occupation of foreign territory by enemy forces or the phenomenon of "refugees". Various types of contracts were affected under which, objectively speaking, a party to a contract could not perform his obligations – insurance contract, for example.

Kantorovich believed that war constituted an example of insuperable force; war began from the date of a formal declaration and terminated only after the ratification and publication of a peace treaty. But even after these formalities were completed, war might continue by reason of the continuing occupation of territory, disruption of transport, or other circumstances which make it impossible for a contracting party to perform its obligations. A court considering a contractual dispute should take these matters into consideration.

The obituary of Kantorovich by Professor Liublinskii (*q.v.*) evaluated his contributions as follows:

> Ia. A. Kantorovich did not produce works which were a major contribution to theoretical jurisprudence, but the merit of bringing law closer to the general public will remain long after him. He knew how to select practically necessary and lively topics and to set them out in accessible form. Many issues were advanced by him for the first time in Russian literature.[22]

Vladimir Dmitrievich Nabokov *(8(20) July 1869, b. Tsarskoe selo, St. Petersburg – 28 March 1922, d. Berlin). Jurist, professor, political figure, publicist, and journalist, one of leaders of Constitutional-Democratic Party of Russia (Kadet Party), member of I State Duma, appointed Senator by the Provisional Government, father of Russo/American writer, Vladimir Vladimirovich Nabokov (1899-1977).*

Life and career. Born of a noble family,[23] Nabokov graduated in 1897 with the gold medal from the III St. Petersburg Gymnasium and enrolled at the Law Faculty of St. Petersburg University.[24] In March 1890 he was arrested for a short time for taking part in student disturbances. After graduating in 1891, he was sent abroad, to Halle University in Germany, to continue his education. At the initiative of Professor Ivan Iakovlevich Foinitskii (1847-1913), he was selected in 1892 to remain at the Chair of Criminal Law to prepare for the professoriate. He simultaneously

no. 4 (1917), pp.126-182; no. 5-6 (1917), pp. 115-153. Also published separately: Kantorovich, Война и исполнение обязательств [War and the Performance of Obligations] (Spb., 1917). 149 p.

22 P. I. Liublinskii, «Канторович: некролог» [Kantorovich: Obituary], Право и жизнь [Law and Life], no. 9 (1925), p. 113.

23 His father, Dmitrii Nikolaevich Nabokov (1826-1904), was a State official, Senator, and Minister of Justice under Emperor Alexander II. On Nabokov, see A. A. Matyshev, Энциклопедия репрессированных авторов. 1917-1987. Биобиблиография советской трагедии [Encyclopedia of Repressed Authors. 1917-1987. Bio-Bibliography of a Soviet Tragedy] (Spb., 2023), X, pp. 7-26; G. S. Starodubtsev, Международно-правовая наука российской эмиграции [International-Legal Science of Russian Emigration] (M., 2000), p. 90.

24 ЦГИА СПб., fond 14, opis 3, file 26159.

took a position in the State Chancellery attached to the State Council, remaining there until 1899.

In 1895 he received the court title of gentleman of the bedchamber (камер-юнкер) of His Majesty's court. From 1897 to 1904 he was Professor of Criminal Law at the Imperial School of Jurisprudence[25] and wrote a number of works on criminal law. He began to acquire a reputation as a legal scholar: he was elected Chairman of the Russian Group of the International Union of Penal Law and secretary of the Criminal Section of the St. Petersburg Law Society.

Nabokov became active in Russian political life at the turn of the twentieth century. In 1902 he was elected a deputy of the St. Petersburg City Duma. He was among the founders and subsequently one of the leaders in October 1905 of the Kadet Party and served as the publisher and editor of the Party organ (from 1906 to 1908) – the journal Вестник Партии Народной Свободы [Herald of the Party of People's Freedom] and co-editor of the newspaper Речь [Speech]. In 1903 he published an article in the newspaper Право [Law] under the title "Kishinev Blood Bath" criticizing the Jewish pogrom in Kishinev; for this his court title "gentleman of the bedchamber" was taken away, and he lost his position at the Imperial School of Jurisprudence. He was, however, elected to the I State Duma and became one of the leaders of the Kadet Duma faction. His oratorical skills were in evidence in the political world; he quickly acquired a reputation as the leading Kadet public speaker in the Duma. During the short-lived I Duma, he spoke from the podium no less than 28 times. In those years Nabokov was among the editorial personnel of two leading law media: Вестник права [Herald of Law] and the newspaper Право [Law]. But his activities were not confined to Russia. In 1905 he was among the permanent staff of an illegal émigré journal first published in Stuttgart, Germany, and then moved to Paris – Освобождение [Liberation].

Because he signed the so-called Vyborg Appeal in 1906 – an appeal of a group of deputies of the I State Duma dissolved by the Tsar entitled "To the People from the People's Representatives – which encouraged the people to engage in civil disobedience, he was deprived of parliamentary inviolability and was imprisoned for three months from May to July 1908.

During the First World War he served first as an Ensign in the Home Guard from July 1914 to September 1915, and was then transferred to be a clerk in the Asian Section of the Chief Staff in Petrograd. On 16 March 1917 he was a co-drafter (with Boris Nolde and V. V. Shulgin) of the Act in which Grand Prince Mikhail Aleksandrovich Romanov, younger brother of Tsar Nicholas II, refused to take the

[25] ЦГИА СПб., fond 355, opis 1, file 3963. Also see E. A. Annenkova, Императорское училище правоведения [Imperial School of Jurisprudence] (Spb., 2006), pp. 86-88.

throne vacated by the abdication of the Tsar. The Act transferred all power to the future Constituent Assembly and brought an end to the centuries of Romanov rule in the Russian Empire.

Following the February 1917 Revolution, Nabokov found himself in the narrow group of the new political leadership. He was considered to be a serious contender for the post of Minister of Justice, but it went to Alexander F. Kerensky; Nabokov was offered and accepted the position of Administrator of the Provisional Government; in that capacity he coordinated the work of the agencies of power and the preparation of the major legislative acts. In October 1917 he became a member of the "Pre-Parliament" (Provisional Soviet of the Russian Republic): a member of the Council of Elders, Deputy Chairman of the Pre-Parliament, and Chairman of the Commission for Foreign Affairs.[26]

Nabokov did not support the 1917 October Revolution. In November he was elected a deputy of the Constituent Assembly from the Kadet Party. On 23 November he was arrested as a member of the All-Russian Commission for Elections to the Constituent Assembly. After five days in confinement, he was released, but then arrested again under the Dekret of Soviet Power naming the Kadet Party as the "Party of enemies of the people". This forced him to leave for the Crimea, where his family was already situated.

From November 1918 Nabokov held the post of Minister of Justice of the Crimean Territorial Government, but with the assault by the Red Army on Crimea and the fall of the Crimean Government, he emigrated with his family on 15 April 1919.

Emigration. After some time in London and Paris, in August 1920 Nabokov moved to Berlin. There he published a memoir, several books, and many journal and newspaper articles.

Nabokov was killed on 28 March 1922 in Berlin while trying to prevent the assassination of Pavel Nikolaevich Miliukov (1859-1943) by émigré monarchists. Miliukov was then the leader of the Kadet Party. Nabokov was buried at Tegel Cemetery, near Berlin.

International legal views. Nabokov made no contributions to the theory of international law. Most of his publications were in the field of criminal law. But having been elected Chairman of the Russian Section (or Group) of the International Union of Penal Law and secretary of the Criminal Section of the St. Petersburg Law Society, Nabokov was noteworthy in Russian international legal circles for his fundamental analytical publications on the activities of the International Union of Penal Law and its Russian Group and of international penitentiary congresses.

Nabokov's erudition, command of the disciplinary literature, and knowledge of the principal approaches at the time of the Russian and major European schools

[26] On Nabokov's memoir of these years, see V. D. Medlin and S. L. Parsons (eds.), *V. D. Nabokov and the Russian Provisional Government, 1917* (New Haven, 1976), pp. 33-177. Also see G. L. Arosev, «Владимир Набоков, отец Владимира Набокова» ["Vladimir Nabokov, Father of Vladimir Nabokov"] (M., 2021).

of thought on penal matters were well demonstrated in his extensive publications. His first work of international legal interest was an article on the Petersburg Congress of the International Union of Penal Law, held on 4-7 September 1902 for the first time in Russia, at St. Petersburg University.[27] Nabokov took part, giving a report in the name of the Russian Group of the Union. In those years the International Union of Penal Law, formed back in 1889, was an authoritative international organization composed of legal scholars and practitioners from around the world and determined to promote the development of international cooperation against crime through the discussion of scientific positions, legislative approaches, and the elaboration of agreed reform measures and the unification of domestic criminal legislation of States. Nabokov described the purposes and tasks of the Union as follows:

> The purposes of any similar scientific assembly come down in essence to the following: to popularize the ideas developed by specialists, establish and support a link between society and the individual parts thereof – people of science, serve the cause of communion and mutual exchange of thoughts between representatives of various scientific orientations.[28]

The Congress in St. Petersburg discussed a number of important problems of criminal law and procedure, but two were considered to be vital: first, the role and significance which the criminal law of various countries attached to the mental element of the crime in comparison with its material consequences; second, the need to reform the preliminary investigation and binding over for trial in order to ensure personal freedom and ascertain the truth. In his article Nabokov gave a detailed description of the various positions taken in the basic reports and gave his own critique of each and his vision of the optimal way to find an appropriate solution.

Nabokov's article on the history of the Russian Group of the International Union of Criminal Law contained basically his speech at the opening Congress of the Russian Group in St. Petersburg on 4 January 1909. He cast light on all the complex reversals of fortune in the search for organizational and doctrinal approaches and the foundations for the Group in the context of performing their obligations as a part of the International Union. The congresses of the Group were valuable in that they "theoretically and practically establish the basic guiding points of view"[29] on difficult issues of criminal law policies, which are then presented as an agreed unified scientific-legal position of the Group to congresses of

[27] An official Ministry publication described the event as follows: "On 4 September 1902, at 14:00 hours, in the magnificently decorated hall of the Imperial St. Petersburg University the Ninth Congress was opened of the International Union of Penal Law – the first in St. Petersburg". E. Ginzberg, «IX съезд Международного союза криминалистов» [IX Congress of the International Union of Penal Law in St. Petersburg], Журнал Министерства народного просвещения [Journal of the Ministry of Public Enlightenment], no. 1 (January 1903), pp. 177-194.

[28] Nabokov, «Петербургский конгресс Международного союза криминалистов, его значение и результаты» [Petersburg Congress of International Union of Penal Law, the Significance and Results Thereof], Право [Law], no. 38 (1902), col. 1667.

[29] Nabokov, «К истории Русской группы Союза Криминалистов» [On the History of the Russian Group of the Union of Penal Law], Право [Law], no. 1 (1909), col. 4.

the International Union of Penal Law and to legislative and executive agencies of the Russian Empire.

Nabokov also addressed the preparation, organization, and agenda of the VIII International Penal and Penitentiary Congress held in Washington D. C. in September 1910.[30] The Congress was to discuss the state of penitentiary policy in various countries with reference to the execution of punishment and the treatment of convicts with a view to making recommendations for improvement.[31] The organizer of his Congress, just as all preceding and subsequent congresses, was, unlike the congresses of the International Union of Penal Law, an inter-governmental agency – the International Penal and Penitentiary Commission. In the view of Nabokov, the principal shortcoming in the organization of this Congress was that for the first time it has assembled across the ocean, thereby seriously reducing the participation of Europeans because of the complications of traveling so far. The dates also were complicated for university colleagues, who began the academic year in September. Therefore, Nabokov wrote with some bitterness, the participants were "primarily officials sent by the prison administrations and practitioners" (col. 2215). On the other hand, he approved of the program, which transcended the confines of prison science. In Washington D. C. four basic orientations were discussed: (1) criminal legislation; (2) penitentiary issues; (3) preventive measures; and (4) children and minors. In addition, Congress participants were asked to complete two questionnaires: (1) What significance does the death penalty have in the punishment system of various countries?; (2) How necessary is it to build and organize contemporary prisons and other places of confinement? (col. 2217).

The Congress also considered, Nabokov observed, issues of a purely international-legal character. The section on criminal legislation, in addition to such general questions as the indeterminate sentence, criminal societies, and complicity as a circumstance increasing guilt, there was discussion of the significance and enforcement of criminal judgments of foreign courts, especially with regard to recidivism, limitations of rights, and others. The discussion of the last matter, Nabokov said, "was the result of greater recognition of the need for a certain international solidarity in the struggle against crime" (col. 2219).

In 1913 Nabokov's substantial article appeared on the XII Congress of the International Union of Penal Law, held in Copenhagen from 27-31 August of that year. There were two basic questions on the agenda: (1) measures against generally dangerous crimes; (2) the teaching of the sciences of criminal law. Nabokov was

[30] Nabokov, «К открытию Международного тюремного конгресса в г. Вашингтоне» [On the Opening of the International Penal and Penitentiary Congress in Washington D. C.], Право [Law], no. 38 (1910), cols. 2215-2225. The inspiration for establishing this international forum is credited to Count Vladimir Aleksandrovich Sollugub (1813-1882), Chairman of the Commission for the Reorganization of Prisons in Russia, who wrote to foreign colleagues and suggested that such a forum be created. See N. K. Teeters, "The International Penal and Penitentiary Congress (1910) and the Indeterminate Sentence", *Journal of Criminal Law and Criminology*, XXXIX (1948-1949), p. 618.

[31] See the Программа вопросов, поставленных на разрешение Восьмого Международного тюремного конгресса, имеющего собраться в Вашингтоне с 19-го по 25 сентября 1910 г. (старого стиля) [Program of Questions Put for Solution of the Eighth International Penal and Penitentiary Congress to Assemble in Washington D. C. from 19 to 25 September 1910 (Old Style)] (Spb., 1910), p. 3.

a rapporteur for the first question and not unnaturally devoted most of his space to that issue with some critiques of other reports to the Congress.

But he also dwelt on the proposals made during the Congress for a new approach to teaching criminal law in the light of contemporary requirements of theoreticians and legal practitioners. The Basic Report on this second question was given by Joseph Heimberger (1865-1933), who summarized the responses of States to a questionnaire which he circulated with the following questions: (1) are university students familiarized with the auxiliary sciences of criminal law and are they tested on them; (2) is instruction organized for prison personnel and for candidates for positions in the prison administration; (3) is information communicated to prison personnel about dangerous criminals (recidivists, alcoholics, mentally deficient, indigent, and vagrants). Nabokov reacted positively to the proposal made in the Report to introduce in universities and post-graduate educational institutions the teaching of the following courses: criminal anthropology, criminal psychology, criminal psychiatry, criminalistics, criminal statistics, forensic medicine, and prison science. All individuals applying repressive criminal measures should be knowledgeable about these sciences: police, procuracy, investigators, judges, and agencies executing punishment.

It follows from the foregoing that Nabokov did not make his own contribution to any aspect of international law. His merit lay in the field of jurisprudence; although not an international lawyer, he explained and popularized ideas and proposals advanced by participants in sessions of the said international organizations. The achievements of Nabokov to the law and the legal profession, nonetheless, are significant:

> I think that after all has been said, there is no point asking 'What did Nabokov do?' Vladimir Dmitrievch was a brilliant figure. His temperament and leadership inclinations contributed greatly to the rapid advancement of legal norms in the short interval of prerevolutionary Russia … One regrets only that the lifespan of those norms, like the lift of V. D. Nabokov himself, the 'knight of law', turned out to be so short, like most knights '*sans peur et sans reproche*'.[32]

Dmitrii Petrovich Nikolskii *(25(18) October 1855, b. Perm*[33] *– 10 August 1907, d. St. Petersburg). International lawyer, publicist, engaged with public and private international law.*

[32] P. Krasheninnikov, *The 12 Apostles of Russian Law: Lawyers Who Changed Law, State and Society*, transl. Christopher Culver (2019), p. 69. See also Nolde's address at a memorial service for Nabokov held by the Law Society in Paris on 24 May 1922, translated in Medlin and Parsons, note 26 above, pp. 13-31.

[33] The assertion often encountered that Nikolskii was born at Novgorod in 1857 is mistaken. See, for example, M. D. Elzon, in Сотрудники Российской национальной библиотеки – деятели науки и культуры. Биографический словарь [Personnel of the Russian National Library – Figures of Science and Culture. Biographical Dictionary] (1995), I, p. 372. For his birth certificate issued by the Perm Theological Consistory, see ЦГИА СПб., fond 14, opis 3, file 18590, l. 3. Also see Starodubtsev, note 23 above, pp. 14, 17.

Life and career. Comparatively little is known about Nikolskii. Grabar said he was "unable to obtain more precise biographical information about him".[34] The son of an archpriest, Nikolskii received his secondary schooling at the Perm Theological Seminary[35] and in August 1875 applied to be enrolled in the natural sciences division of the Faculty of Medicine and Mathematics at St. Petersburg University, but was admitted to the Law Faculty.[36] A year later, in September 1876, Nikolskii petitioned the Head of the St. Petersburg Academy of Medicine and Surgery to be admitted to that Academy. The Head of the Academy sought a reference from the Rector of the University and received a positive recommendation, but for whatever reason, Nikolskii remained in the Law Faculty on one basis or another.

In 1883 Nikolskii graduated from the Law Faculty of St. Petersburg University with the degree of candidate of laws, having specialized in international law under the supervision of F. F. Martens. According to archival materials, Nikolskii was sent abroad in 1884-1885 to pursue his legal studies.[37] Upon his return, he worked briefly in the Asian Department of the Ministry of Foreign Affairs. From 1 January 1896 he was transferred to the Historical Division of the Imperial Public Library in the post of an assistant librarian and remained there until 1907.[38]

From February 1907 he was the head of the foreign policy section of the newspaper Россия [Russia], an official governmental publication. He also published articles in other legal and philanthropic journals.

International legal views. Nikolskii was interested in many aspects of international law. Best known was his first and substantial work on extradition, recommended for publication by decision of the Law Faculty and issued a year after graduation from University.[39] The work was dedicated to his teacher, F. F. Martens.

Rich factual material and careful analysis made the book one of the best on the topic in Russian international legal doctrine. Nikolskii worked from two basic categories: territorial supremacy, "which by its essence does not tolerate being

[34] V. E. Grabar, *The History of International Law in Russia 1647-1917: A Bio-Biographical Study*, transl. W. E. Butler (Oxford, 1990), p. 393.

[35] Some sources record that Nikolskii received his general education at the Novgorod Gymnasium. See Elzon, note 33 above, p. 372. The correct data is found in ЦГИА СПб., fond 14, opis 3, file 18590, l. 1.

[36] After two weeks at University, on 2 September 1875, Nikolskii petitioned the Rector to be transferred to the Faculty of Medicine and Mathematics, but the Council of the University left him in the Law Faculty. Ibid., l. 6-8. On 11 October 1875 Nikolskii again petitioned for transfer from the Law Faculty, pointing out that in August illness prevented him from taking the mathematics examination and therefore had been enrolled in the Law Faculty. On 24 October an examination was arranged for him in the field of "lower mathematics", the result of which was "satisfactory". On 14 December 1875 Nikolskii requested financial assistance as a student of the Division of Medicine and Mathematics.

[37] ЦГИА СПб., fond 14, opis 3, file 14199.

[38] Elzon, note 33 above, p. 372.

[39] D. Nikolskii, О выдаче преступников по началам международного права [On the Extradition of Criminals according to Principles of International Law] (Spb., 1884). Butler H63.

subject to foreign laws", and territoriality, according to which "any criminal law operates within the limits of that State which issued it", and "any person within the Russian State, whether Russian subjects or foreigners, is absolutely subject to our criminal laws" (p. 1). But he concluded that a new basic principle was important – the principle of international communion: "The development of contemporary international relations has laid down another guiding principle mitigating the narrow requirements of nationality – the principle of international communion" (p. 2). The objective necessity, he said, of the international communion of nations is the admissibility of an exception from the principle of territoriality: the principle of exterritoriality. The extradition of criminals is connected with this exception.

Nikolskii offered the following definition of extradition: "The aggregate of legal actions by means of which one State extradites to another a person accused of the commission of a crime within the limits of the last State which has the right of trial and punishment is called extradition". Four elements are necessary when deciding to extradite: an accused person, a requesting State (plaintiff), defendant State (State of refuge), and a legal relation between them. The said legal relation between the States is expressed in the form of a mutual agreement which "may be either tacit, implied, determined according to the principle of reciprocity, or written – concluded in the form of a treaty or convention on extradition" (p. 29). The procedure for extradition reflected the state of treaty law obligations of States of that period. In Nikolskii's view, an extradition treaty as an agreement of the will of two States assumes the following: the consent of the defendant State to extradition, which must be certain and free; the legal capacity of the State to conclude a treaty; and a legal reason for the obligation. On this basis, Nikolskii concluded that an extradition treaty acquires legal force only after consent of the State to extradition (p. 30).

Nikolskii's general international legal views may be judged from two of his works: a course of international law,[40] and a lengthy review of Kamarovskii's survey of the contemporary literature of international law.[41]

Concise, but substantive and in many respects original, Nikolskii's course was published in a series called the "Family University" of S. F. Komarskii. Nikolskii suggested that international law had been in existence for all time, but he denied the equality of States, considering this to be a "fiction":

> The equality of States may be recognized only in theory, whereas in fact it does not exist. States are not equal in their rights or in their power. Understandably, treaties concluded between unequal States are virtually never treaties an expression of absolute equality. While making this reservation, one may ascertain the basic rule of international law: all States, despite their relative inequality, are mutually bound to respect one another's independence, comply with the inviolability of boundaries, maintain correct

[40] Nikolskii, Международное право (популярные лекции для самообразования) [International Law: Popular Lectures for Self-Education] (Spb., 1903). Butler H62.

[41] Nikolskii, «Рец. на книгу Камаровский Л. А. Обзор современной литературы по международному праву. М., 1887. 354 с.» [Review of L. A. Kamarovskii, Survey of Contemporary Literature on International Law. M., 1887. 354 p.], Журнал Министерства народного просвещения [Journal of Ministry of Public Enlightenment], no. 1 (1885), pp. 247-259.

relations with one another, and render mutual protection to one another's subjects (p. 9).

As we see, in noting the actual inequality of States, Nikolskii recognized their inter-connection and, indirectly, equality as a legal principle.

The lawfulness and admissibility of interference in the internal affairs of States is closely linked with sovereignty and equality of States. Nikolskii categorically opposed legal recognition of the admissibility of such interference: "interference is a fact, but does not comprise a right"; attempts "to determine when it is legal have no basis whatsoever" (p. 22). Nikolskii also expressed his attitude towards private international law. He understood private international broadly as the "aggregate of rights which States grant to foreigners" (p. 51).

In his review of the Kamarovskii volume, Nikolskii did not agree that the denial of the principle of equality of States "leads to enslavement of the weak by the strong". He said that "taking the unvarnished view is more fruitful than establishing a fiction contrary to international existence and the laws on which it rests" (pp. 247-249).

Nikolskii took a position rather progressive in his day on a number of issues of war and peace, on humanitarian law. In his review of Kamarovskii, he was a firm proponent of disarmament:

> All European States at the initiative of the Great Powers should take part in the discussion of this question; after preliminary conferences a congress should be convened at which by common consent a period is established for disarmament: the decree of the Congress should be guaranteed by the general protection of all States who gave their consent (pp. 247-259).

As for military questions, Nikolskii expressed his views on a controversial issue of the time – the right of a people to engage in partisan warfare against an invader. Using the examples of the 1812 War of Russia against Napoleon and of the Spanish partisans against the French invaders between 1808 and 1813, Nikolskii observed: a "feeling of morality says to us that these people's wars were truly sacred exploits of nations". He was of the view that "every citizen has the right to defend his fatherland: that a people's war is not a crime, but the sacred duty of the people to their fatherland" (pp. 254-256).

Nikolskii displayed an interest of private international law, testimony to which was his detailed analysis of the outcome of the First and Second Hague Peace Conferences on private international law.[42] In this article he formulated his position with regard to this branch of jurisprudence:

> Private international law has significant similarities … with the civil law of individual States because, just as civil law, it is concerned with the in-

42 Nikolskii, «Первая и Вторая международные конференции в Гааге по вопросам частного международного права» [First and Second International Conferences at The Hague on Questions of Private International Law], Журнал Юридического общества при Императорском С.-Петербургском университете [Journal of the Law Society attached to the Imperial S.-Petersburg University], no. 1 (1895), pp. 1-28; no. 2 (1895), pp. 47-68.

> terests of private individuals. It differs sharply from public international law, which permits the resolution of international conflicts and disputes by means of war; that is, by means of violence. In private international law all disputes of private individuals are settled only by a judicial procedure.
>
> Thus, every State has its own civil laws which frequently diverge from the laws of other States in very material features, whereas private international law never differs in firmness and certainty of the principles underlying it. Throughout the entire history of this law there has been a struggle between two basic principles – the personal or national and the territorial or feudal. The task of the science of private international law is that each of these principles be introduced in the respective role … (p. 1).

His analysis of the proposals put forward by delegates, the discussion thereof, and the decisions adopted by the conferences are of interest. Commissions were formed by the conference participants as follows: at the First Conference – (1) on marriage; (2) on the form of acts; (3) on inheritance by operation of law and by will; (4) on the competence of courts and other issues of court proceedings. At the Second Conference – (1) on marriage; (2) on inheritance; (3) on civil proceedings; (4) on trusteeship; (5) on trade insolvency. Indeed, the vice-president of the two conferences and the chairman of both commissions on inheritance was the representative from Russia, F. F. Martens.

Nikolskii noted that the conferences were not expected to adopt legally binding decisions. The participant States will look at their decisions:

> Only as the basis for a change of their domestic laws or the conclusion of new international conventions. But the decisions of the conference were important because they give the possibility in practice to verify what might be expected from joint actions of governments in the domain of private international law (p. 5).

Nikolskii was convinced that the conferences were a great success. Their success, in his view, was to be explained by excellent advance preparation on the part of international lawyers and by the Institute of International Law. He suggested that "it should not be forgotten that questions of private international law lend themselves more to being prepared at conferences than questions of public international law". In Nikolskii's opinion:

> … both conferences made a great step forward by recognition of the principles long since proclaimed in science but previously alien to codes. The conferences significantly facilitated the application in a particular State of foreign laws and thereby worked against that tendency which dominated in the field of public international law. We understand the principle of judicial territorial power. Now the general rule dominates that a foreigner, with few exceptions, is subject to trial in local courts, judged according to local laws. Such a court obviously is far from the highest justice. The task of international law is to try to eliminate this injustice. But such a purpose will be achieved only when in the domain of civil relations of the law of the national situs is supreme over all others. The Hague conferences rendered a great service to all nations in that in moved to the forefront the law

of the national situs. It remains only to wish that the work thereof continues in the same direction and with the same success (pp. 67-68).

Of enduring interest are Nikolskii's commentaries on the decisions and resolutions of the Institute of International Law, many of which reflected the doctrinal positions of his teacher – F. F. Martens.[43]

Andrei Nikolaevich Sobolev *(13 May 1889, b. Moscow[44] – 9 September 1968, d. Moscow).[45] Graduate of St. Petersburg University Law Faculty, author of several works on the law of the sea.*

Life and career. The usual reference sources contain no information about Sobolev. The information herein is based on archival materials and that provided by his relatives.

Sobolev descended from the Russian aristocracy. Having completed in 1907 his Gymnasium education (two years at the Moscow Fifth Gymnasium and six years at the St. Petersburg Sixth Gymnasium), on 16 August 1907 he applied for admission to the Faculty of History and Philology of St. Petersburg University but was enrolled on 19 August in the Law Faculty. On 3 November 1914 he was awarded a certificate confirming that he had completed the full course in the Law Faculty of the University.[46]

According to the Address Book of St. Petersburg for 1917, Sobolev's place of employment was listed at the Library of the Alexander Military Law Academy.[47] During the 1950-60s, Sobolev worked as the head of a Planning Section at the All-Union Scientific-Research Institute for the Construction and Operation of Pipelines.

International legal views. Sobolev gave evidence of an interest in international law during his legal studies. The Chair of International Law arranged a competition for the best essays submitted by students on a topic chosen annually by the Chair and awarded medals to the winners. In 1912 the chosen topic was: "The

[43] Nikolskii, «XVI сессия Института международного права (1895 года)» [XVI Session of the Institute of International Law (1895)], Журнал Юридического общества при Императорском С.-Петербургском университете [Journal of the Law Society attached to the Imperial St. Petersburg University], no. 9 (1896), pp. 63-74; Nikolskii, «XVII сессия Института международного права (1896 года)» [XVII Session of the Institute of International Law (1896)], ibid., no. 3 (1898), pp. 72-87.

[44] Birth certificate issued by the Moscow Theological Consistory. ЦГИА СПб., fond 14, opis 3, file 49627, l. 15.

[45] Year and place of death determined by internet correspondence with Sobolev's relatives.

[46] ЦГИА СПб., fond 14, opis 3, file 49626, l. 1 and 8.

[47] Адресная книга Петрограда. 1917 год [Address Book of Petrograd. 1917] (Pg., 1917), p. 638. His name did not appear in subsequent address books for Petrograd.

1909 London Declaration on Naval Warfare". Four essays were submitted; each was reviewed in the annual report of the University.[48]

The winning essay by Sobolev was entitled: "Le droit ne nait pas des règlements, mais les règlements doivent naitre du droits". By decision of the Law Faculty on 25 November 1913 he was awarded the gold medal. The reviews were highly positive:

> It was not the most extensive, but undoubtedly the content was the best [and created] the impression that the author had a full command of the material at his disposal ... All the conclusions are exceedingly calm, well argued, connected with the large literature known to the author, and testify to the author's skill in orienting himself in very complex legal controversies. If one adds that the entire work is written in a beautiful language, and that the author, judging from the references, has a command of three languages (English, French, and German), one cannot fail to conclude that the work undoubtedly deserves the awarding of the gold medal.

After graduation from the University, Sobolev continued to write about the law of the sea. Much of his attention was devoted to the law of prize, which although considerably written about, in his view raised serious issues for the entire system of the law of the sea. Between 1914 and 1915 he published in six issues of the leading naval journal an extensive article on naval warfare, which in 1915 was published in book form. The work was well regarded by Grabar.[49]

Sobolev pointed out that the outbreak of War had aggravated problems of the law of prize, especially with regard to neutral States. The law of prize was a complex of norms regulating the capture and confiscation of enemy private property during naval warfare; at the turn of the century prize law had been sharply criticized as a survival of the feudal past. In anticipation of war there were even attempts on the part of several States to abolish the law of prize. Only Italy, however, introduced the principle of the inviolability of private property in its legislation during war at sea, and even then only on the basis of reciprocity. But, as Sobolev noted, because other States did not emulate Italy, the right to capture enemy private property at sea was retained.

Using rules of international and municipal law, the materials of international conferences, including the discussion at the founding of the International Prize Chamber and the drafting of the 1909 London Declaration on Naval War, and State practice unfolding in the course of World War One, Sobolev analyzed the following:

(1) the influence of the law of prize on the economic life of States;

[48] Отчет о состоянии и деятельности Императорского С.-Петербургского Университета за 1912 год [Report on the State and Activity of Imperial St. Petersburg University for 1912] (Spb. 1913), p. 251.

[49] Sobolev, Очерки призового права [Essays on the Law of Prize] (Pg., 1915). Butler C113. Grabar called the book a "well-compiled survey of the development of prize law from the fourteenth century to 1914". Grabar, note 34 above, p. 450.

(2) the establishment of indicia under which a ship is an enemy vessel or used as such;

(3) the consequences of a vessel changing the flag State;

(4) the situation of a single (uninterrupted, continuing) voyage;

(5) convoys;

(6) destruction of prizes and remuneration for losses;

(7) consequences of assimilation of a clearly neutral ship to an enemy vessel which arises in instances when the vessel: (1) attempts to run a blockade; (2) carries military contraband; (3) renders other services to an enemy; (4) resists inspection.

As for cargoes, these are not subject to confiscation, Sobolev indicated, unless they constitute military contraband, except when enemy cargo is on an enemy ship (p. 2).

In a concise but impressively profound little book on the law of war at sea and maritime neutrality, Sobolev, observing that the law of naval warfare is less regulated than war on land and there is relatively little legislation and relevant doctrinal writing, undertook to fill this gap in legal doctrine.[50] He began his work by attempting an assessment of the extent to which the law of war was regulated:

> The contemporary law of war is far from perfected. It suffers, it seems, to a significant degree theoretically and was created to a great extent without reflections on the real situation in which one acts during war. The soft chairs of diplomats offer too great a contrast with the trenches of fighters and are completely lacking at sea, and this is not reflected in works of the compilers of conventions, despite the close involvement of practitioners and technical delegates.

Having considered State practice during the First World War with its numerous violations of international legal norms, Sobolev came to a grim conclusion: "it seems now that a violation of law is not an exception, but the execution of international laws". Nonetheless, he remained optimistic. He was convinced that the crimes committed during the war were so cruel and obvious that this "provides assurance that the breaking of the concepts will after the war be based, in any event, on respect for law" (p. 51).

Prince **Viacheslav Viacheslavovich Tenishev** *(11 October 1878, b. St. Petersburg – 7 June 1959, d. Montauban, Department of Tarn et Garonne, France). Political and social figure, deputy of III State Duma.*

Life and career. Descended from an aristocratic family, Viacheslav was the son of Viacheslav Nikolaevich Tenishev (1843 or 1844-1903), a noted ethnog-

[50] Sobolev, О праве войны на море и морском нейтралитете [On the Law of War at Sea and Maritime Neutrality] (Pg., 1915). Butler C109.

rapher, archaeologist, sociologist, industrialist, merchant, sworn advokat, and founder of the Tenishev Real School in St. Petersburg. Viacheslav studied from 1892 to 1897 at the Ia. Gurevich Private Gymnasium in St. Petersburg and graduated with the gold medal.[51] From 1897 to 1901 he studied law at the St. Petersburg University.[52] Upon graduating, he continued his studies in Germany, where he attended lectures at the universities of Berlin and Heidelberg. Upon returning home to Russia, he settled at his estate in the Briansk Governate. Just as his father, he was interested in ethnography, and in 1907 published a book on justice in the Russian peasant milieu.[53]

He was elected in 1904 as the Briansk uezd marshal of the nobility and as a deputy to the Briansk uezd zemstvo, as well as an honorary justice of the peace of the Briansk uezd. At the age of 28 he became a member of the III State Duma from the Orlov Governate. There he joined the "Union of 17 October" and served as secretary of the Fourth Section of the Duma. He became rapporteur of the commissions for judicial reform and for questions, together with serving on others as a member. He spoke in support of the unity and indivisibility of Russia, a bicameral State Duma, and the granting of political freedoms within the framework of the Manifesto of 17 October 1905. He was appointed Counsellor of State.

During the First World War, he headed the Briansk Committee of the Red Cross Society and was a plenipotentiary of the Red Cross at the Briansk District Evacuation Point for Wounded Military Personnel. Together with the Briansk zemstvo, he organized six field hospitals.

Emigration. After the October 1917 Revolution, he emigrated first to Bulgaria, then to France, and lived in Paris. There he worked as the manager of an accounts division in a large bank.

He was active in émigré affairs. During the 1920s he acted as Deputy Chairman of the Union of Russian Nobles in Paris, and later as Honorary Chairman. For many years he was a member of the Board of the Society for the Protection of Russian Cultural Antiquities, and in 1956 was elected a founding member. He lec-

[51] ЦГИА СПб., fond 171, opis 2, file 3249.

[52] ЦГИА СПб., fond 14, opis 3, file 34316.

[53] V. V. Tenishev, Правосудие в русском крестьянском быту [Justice in the Russian Peasant Milieu] (Briansk, 1907; reprinted, 2011).

tured on Imperial Russia during the 1950s and wrote from time to time in Русская мысль [Russian Thought].

He passed away in Montauban, Department of Tarn-et-Garonne, in 1959 and is buried in the local cemetery.

International legal views. Tenishev's contributions to the literature of international law are comparatively modest. His most significant work was devoted to international arbitration, which he published shortly before the First World War.[54] This was a work informed by a pacifist spirit, with faith in the real possibility of averting military confrontation and the achievement of peace on earth. He wrote that two simple truths needed to be demonstrated: (1) the unnecessariness and immorality of the burdens of war; and (2) the need to strengthen and ensure a universal and stable international peace (p. ii).

Tenishev began by examining war as a historical phenomenon, examining its causes and suggesting a classification of these. He considered the classification to have importance: "This attempt was made by the author completely autonomously because not one of the well-known works on perpetual peace or an international arbitration court contains such classifications" (p. iii).

Tenishev identified the historical reasons for war as follows:

(1) the settling of peoples apart throughout the earth and ensuing struggle for access to the best natural wealth. This group settling over time led to the consolidation of territory for individual nations and the founding thereon of their States and cultures;

(2) the intensification of State organization and culture led to a struggle with small public-law formations – with the owners of petty feudal lords and to their violent destruction, to the cessation of private wars between them, and to the destruction of their independence;

(3) the aspiration of central authorities of many States to expand their power by means of military conquests of the territory of other States;

(4) the colonizing conquests, when the quality of State organization and culture of some countries outstrips the same factors in other countries, the nomadic population of which is not in a position to autonomously exploit their natural wealth. From the nineteenth century onwards one observes the continuous historical process of political colonization, with the assistance of wars, of the barbaric peoples of a number of countries (for example, Turkey, Persia, China) if a stable constitutional system has not been established (pp. 2-5).

[54] Tenishev, Вечный мир и международный третейский суд [Perpetual Peace and International Arbitration Court] (Spb., 1909). Butler T54. Also see N. Iu. Nikolaev, «Забытый пацифист» – В. В. Тенишев о войне, третейском суде и вечном мире» ["Forgotten Pacifist" – V. V. Tenishev on War, Arbitration Court, and Perpetual Peace], История государства и права [History of State and Law], no. 22 (2016), pp. 43-47.

In addition to these historical processes which lead to wars, Tenishev singled out wars between nations at approximately the same level of cultural development. The reasons for the majority of such wars were ideological. The general cause, he said, of ideological wars is the false conviction dominant everywhere that one can achieve results by force of arms in an ideological war. The ideas were evaluated not by their merit, which lies solely in their truth, but in the physical force which the progenitors of these ideas possessed (pp. 5-6).

The first type of wars of an ideological nature, Tenishev suggested, were religious wars (crusades) and the Reformation in its various types. The second type was ideological wars for the spreading of political ideas (the French Revolution and partially the Napoleonic wars). The third type was national wars which initially arose as a protest of peoples of many countries against the Napoleonic invasion, and then the Balkan peoples against Ottoman dominance in order to protect their national and cultural identity (pp. 6-9).

Another category of wars, separate from the foregoing, is dynastic wars and wars begun solely in the interests of governments or individual classes of the population. The reasons for these wars Tenishev relegated to the search by capitalist classes for markets to sell the goods they produced. But, in his view, State power was so structured that such wars breaking out because of being advantageous to one government or the interests of the industrial classes he regarded as unlikely (pp. 10-11). On the basis of this analysis, Tenishev concluded:

> It is completely evident that war is not inevitable in any human society, the desire to go to war is not an innate feature of the human character; on the contrary, war exists only so long as nations deem it to be admissible from a moral standpoint. Consequently, when the conviction develops and matures that wars are incompatible with the moral law and the dignity of civilized States – and this … is merely a question of time – then wars with necessity must disappear.

In the view of Tenishev, the greater part of the historical processes which caused wars no longer existed. The majority of disputes, especially those settled with the assistance only of arms, were now readily resolved peacefully. This happened because nations and governments had developed a sense of law and because of the emergence of an international arbitration court. The process underway of the democratization of governments leads to a destruction of all wars not having significance for the nation (p. 11).

.The process of human settlement, said Tenishev, has been completed; armed hostilities for ideologies are impossible, the conquest of countries with an identical culture makes no sense: "Thus, it is incontestable that wars are completely ceasing, and in the near future, by virtue of historical necessity" (p. 12). Wars being a social calamity, Tenishev concluded: "war is senseless, inhumane, and immoral, and all that is connected with war disturbs the human conscience; this position cannot continue; it must be brought to an end" (p. 22).

En route to a universal world, mankind already has overcome many barriers and traveled along a significant path, developed an entire system of international political and legal means for limiting war, settling international conflicts, and establishing peace. These were considered by Tenishev to include mediation, commissions of enquiry, and international arbitration (pp. 22-25). His analysis of the practice with regard to these means led Tenishev to conclude that international arbitration was the most effective of them all.

Therefore, he devoted the largest part of his book (Chapters 3 to 12) to international arbitration. He considered a broad range of issues: from the history of the origin and development of international arbitration to the nineteenth century, its place and role in ensuring a universal peace in the early twentieth century, together with an analysis of the distinctive legal features of its structure, conditions, and procedures. In Tenishev's view, the stability of peace was facilitated significantly by the conclusion of treaties concerning a permanent court of arbitration at the turn of the twentieth century. This process had accelerated, he believed, by reason of the normative-.legal consolidation of the institution of international arbitration at the 1899 First Hague Peace Conference, where it was considered to be the best means for the settlement of legal disputes, especially concerning the interpretation and application of international conventions (pp. 60-62).

Tenishev directly linked the problem of disarmament with the successful strengthening of mediation and arbitration: "One can never believe in the very possibility of disarmament so long as peaceful means for the settlement of international conflicts are not put on a firm basis" (p. 66). Absolutely vital, in Tenishev's view, for the success of arbitration was a precise organization of the structure of the court and the proceedings. To this issue he devoted two chapters (9-10), having considered there both the organizational structure of the court and especially the basic foundations of the proceedings (*compromis*, general conditions and procedures, adoption of an award) (pp. 73-97).

Three major factors, in his view, should facilitate the success of international adjudication:

(1) the establishment in States of a democratic system that would objectively promote the establishment of peace – representative democratic rule in a State dependent on the people and not conducting a militant foreign policy;

(2) the process of the demilitarization of States and disarmament – it is necessary to conclude a general international treaty in which a certain minimum armed forces are established for each State-party and periods for compliance. The failure to comply with the treaty must be considered by an arbitration court;

(3) the codification of international law – it should ensure the normative foundation for normal relations between countries in different spheres of their cooperation.

Tenishev optimistically asserted: the time is not far away when the idea of the inadmissibility of war will become a generally-recognized truth:

A great idea cannot fail to triumph over the traditional inertia of a certain group of persons. All great truths which became the positive heritage of people mankind comprehended slowly, sometimes with grave difficulties. Mankind supposedly did battle with them. Such was the case with two of the greatest ideas which have now received universal recognition: (1) that one person should not own another person as a slave; and (2) that a State should not be governed without the participation of representatives of the people. Not long ago these truths were considered to be unattainable ideals. That is why when they now say that the destruction of war is a fruitless utopia, they should not be believed. The universal peace is required by religion reason, and direct practical necessity; this is one of the greatest moral truths, and mankind is doing battle with it (p. vi) …

The public movement has strengthened in recent decades in favor of peace, a whole series of conventions on the pacific means for the settlement of international disputes, on law during war, and finally, the proclamation from the heights of the Throne of one of the mighty military powers on the need to reduce armaments – all these are true symbols of approaching a new era in the history of mankind (p. 2).

Vasilii Vasilevich Vodovozov *(22 December 1864, b. St. Petersburg – 7 October 1933, d. Zbraslav, Czechoslovakia). Noted Russian publicist, jurist, economist, specialized in electoral, socio-economic, and political topics.*

Life and career. A graduate of the Larin Gymnasium, Vodovozov enrolled at St. Petersburg University in 1883, first in the Faculty of History and Philology and, in 1885, in the Law Faculty.[55] During his University years, he was a member of the Scientific-Literary Society and involved in student organizations engaging in opposition activities. He worked in the newspaper Неделя [Week], where he headed the foreign section and printed some of his own articles.

He was arrested in 1887 for helping to translate a book by Alfons Thun (1854-1886) on the history of revolutionary movements in Russia.[56] He also was accused of involvement in the "Terrorist Faction of People's Will", a dissident movement at the time. Following three months' imprisonment, he was exiled for five years to Arkhangelsk

[55] ОА СПбГУ, fund 1, opis 3, file 573; ЦГИА СПб., fond 14, opis 3, file 23081.

[56] A. Thun, История революционных движений в России [History of Revolutionary Movements in Russia] (1886). He was not listed among the translators, but not all were listed. Vera Zasulich (1851-1919) was the lead translator. See Richard Pipes, *The Trial of Vera Z.* (2010); Jay Bergman, *Vera Zasulich: A Biography* (1983).

Region and then transferred to the Samara Governate. He was given leave in 1890 to take the State examinations at the Law Faculty, after which he returned to complete his sentence at his place of exile. That same year he published an article on the International Penitentiary Congress held in St. Petersburg. From 1893 to 1894 he edited the foreign section of the newspaper Русская жизнь [Russian Life]. During the 1890s, he published articles on socio-political topics and in March 1894 was again banished from St. Petersburg. From 1896 he lived in Kyiv.

He traveled to Bulgaria and other countries of the Balkans, where political crises were in progress. This led to several articles that appeared in major journals: Русское богатство [Russian Wealth] and Вестник Европы [Herald of Europe]. He moved on to Austria and published correspondence for which he was arrested, banished, and deprived for life of the right to enter the country. Arrested again in 1900 in the anti-governmental "Ibsenovskii Case", he was under investigation for two years but released for the lack of evidence. In 1901 he entered Austria under a different surname.

Vodovozov returned to St. Petersburg in 1904 and taught State law, electoral law, and history in various higher educational institutions. From 1904 to 1905 he took part in the "Union of Liberation" and attended its constitutive Congress. He became an editor of Новая газета [New Newspaper] and published several articles on electoral law. In 1906 the Petersburg Chamber of Justice prosecuted Vodovozov for nine "literary crimes" committed in his capacity of editor.[57] That same year he spoke to a Duma political organization of a Narodnik orientation called "Labor Group" and remained active in that anti-Tsarist group until 1917.[58]

Vodovozov served as editor in several opposition newspapers, for which he was sentenced to a year in prison and directed to cease political activities. He continued his scholarly interests, however, and published articles on electoral law. He contributed a significant portion of the legal articles to the Энциклопедический словарь Брокгауза и Ефрона [Encyclopedic Dictionary of Brockhaus and Efron] and the Новый экциклопедический словарь [New Encyclopedic Dictionary].

Vodovozov supported the February 1917 Revolution and welcomed the abdication of the Tsar. He was critical, however, of the unwillingness of the Provisional Government to publish the secret treaties concluded by Imperial Russian with western European powers. In June 1917 the People's Socialist Labor Party was formed, with Vodovozov a prominent member. When the Bolsheviks took power in the October 1917 Revolution, Vodovozov remained in opposition. He was employed from 1917 in the Petrograd Historical Revolutionary Archive and, from 1918, also taught at the III Petrograd University and at the Institute of Journalism.

In 1919 he commenced work as a professor at the Chair of State Law in the Division of Politics and Law of the Faculty of Social Sciences of the University.

57 See Сборник программ политических партий в России [Collection of Programs of Political Parties in Russia] (Spb., 1906).

58 For the polemic between V. I. Lenin and Vodovozov, see V. I. Lenin, «Трудовики и рабочая демократия» [Laborers and Workers' Democracy], in Lenin, Полное собрание сочинений [Complete Collected Works] (5th ed.) XXII, pp. 267-274.

He requested permission to make a visit abroad in 1920, which was refused by the Division on 8 and 29 March 1920 on the grounds that he failed to specify the place and purpose of the trip.[59] He did, however, succeed in visiting Berlin in 1922 on behalf of the People's Commissariat of Enlightenment, and later in 1924 he visited Prague. At his request, the visit was repeatedly prolonged by the People's Commissariat.[60] He did, in fact, never return to Soviet Russia; the Petrograd University relieved him from his post as of 1 October 1924.[61]

Emigration. Having decided to stay in Berlin, Vodovozov returned to his literary and political activities. After removing to Czechoslovakia, he joined the Union of Russian Writers and Journalists in that country and in due course was elected an Honorary Member. His life ended tragically. At the age of 68, in extreme poverty, deaf and blind, he threw himself under a train in Zbraslav.

International legal views. Vodovozov's views on international legal issues are scattered throughout his numerous books and articles devoted to various topics. Most relevant articles appeared in encyclopedias. Summarizing his interests on international law and relations, they reduce to five basic orientations: foreign policy, international law and relations, war and peace, international conferences, and treaties.

With respect to foreign policy, Vodovozov was interested in the Balkans and published several books and articles on this topic. He was critical of the foreign policy and international legal positions of the Tsarist and Provisional governments of Russia on issues connected with the wars and the postwar division of the territories of the Balkan countries, with the exception of the peace treaties and the violations thereof. He favored the active use by Russia of peaceful means for setting the international disputes of the Balkan States; in his view Russia should act as a just arbitrator having regard to the interests of all the States involved in the Balkan conflicts.[62]

In one of his last works in Russia, published in summer 1917, Vodovozov analyzed the causes and consequences for Russia of World War One. The Great Powers, in his view, conspired behind the backs of nations about the division of territories and countries. He demonstrated this by using the example of the expansionist policies of the Tsarist Russian Government:

> The previous Russian Government of former Emperor Nicholas II said that Russia absolutely must conquer German and Austrian Poland and, moreover, the Turkish city of Constantinople, together with the lands along the coast of the two maritime straits: Bosphorus and Dardanelles (Constantinople stands on one of them). He openly stated this wish in the

[59] See Protocols of Sessions of the Politics and Legal Division of the Faculty of Social Sciences, 8 March and 29 March 1920. ЦГА СПб., fond 1, opis 3, file 573.

[60] ОА СПбГУ., fond 1, opis 3, file 573, l. 7-21.

[61] Ibid., l. 24.

[62] See, for example, V. V. Vodovozov, «Бухарестский мир» [Bucharest Peace], Современник [Contemporary], no. 10-11 (1915); Vodovozov, «На Балканах» [In the Balkans], Современник [Contemporary], no. 7-8 (1913).

> State Duma on 27 January and 19 July 1915. Then we knew that our allies: England, France, Italy, already had given their consent to the accession of these lands to Russia after the end of the War (of course, if the war ended with our victory).[63]

Vodovozov categorically opposed the predatory purposes of the War of 1914-1917 which its principal initiators pursued and the participant Great Powers, including Russia. Therefore, Vodovozov emphasized the purpose declared by the Provisional Government which came to replace Tsarism:

> … the most rapid achievement of a general peace not having as its task either the domination of other nations, or taking away their national dignity, or the capture by force of the territory of another … [and we welcome the slogan advanced by the Provisional Government] 'Peace without annexations and contributions on the principles of the self-determination of peoples' (p. 5).

Taking into account, however, that German forces were on the territory of Russia and the authorities of Germany were seizing part of the territory of Russia, including Poland, and aspired to capture and take possession of Serbia against the will of the population, the Provisional Government of Russia should continue the war. Vodovozov expressed the firm conviction: "In order to achieve a peace without annexations and contributions, we must force them to renounce annexations and contributions, and for this we must achieve a victory over them" (p. 15).

Vodovozov thus left his trace in history as a convinced opponent of war and a proponent of peaceful forms of cooperation between nations and States.

[63] Vodovozov, Что такое мир без аннексий и контрибуций [What is a Peace Without Annexations and Contributions] (Pg., 1917), pp. 4-5.

Chapter 11
Contributions to International Law of Colleagues in Other Chairs of Law Faculty

Within the Law Faculty of St. Petersburg University legal scholars associated with other Chairs made their own contributions to international legal doctrine, either directly or contextually. Chief among them were the following.

§11.1. *Chair of Encyclopedia and History of Philosophy of Law*

Aleksandr Semenovich Iashchenko *(24 February 1877, b. Stavropol – 10 June 1934, d. Berlin). Legal scholar, philosopher, publicist, bibliographer, publisher, and a leading exponent of world federalism.*

Life and career. Iashchenko graduated with distinction in 1895 from the Stavropol Classical Men's Gymnasium and immediately enrolled at Moscow University, initially in the Faculty of Mathematics. A year later he transferred to the Law Faculty. Upon graduating in 1900, he remained at the University attached to the Chair of International Law to prepare for the professoriate.

In early 1902 Iashchenko was involved in a criminal proceeding relating to the activities of the Moscow Student Executive Committee, was found guilty, and was exiled to Siberia by judgment of a court. When the term of exile was completed, he passed the magister examinations and from 1905 as a privat-docent began to lecture at Moscow University on international law. That same year he was sent for two years to Paris to work on his magister dissertation. Upon returning, he resumed lecturing at Moscow University.

In December 1908 Iashchenko successfully defended his magister dissertation entitled "International Federalism. Ideas of the Legal Organization of Mankind in Political Doctrines to the End of the Seventeenth Century".[1] He accepted an offer

[1] A. S. Iashchenko, Международный федерализм: Идея юридической организации человечества в политических учениях до конца XVIII века [International Federalism: The Idea of Legal Organization of Mankind in Political Doctrines up to the End of the Eighteenth Century] (M., 1908). Butler Я24.

from 1911 to become privat-docent,[2] and from 10 January 1913, professor *extraordinarius*, at St. Petersburg University in the Chair of Encyclopedia and History of the Philosophy of Law, and from 4 June 1914, professor *ordinarius*. In 1912 he published a monograph on federalism.[3] He also gave tutorials and undertook research on aspects of international law. On 1 February 1913 Iashchenko defended his doctoral dissertation on the theory of federalism at Moscow University.[4] He compiled an extensive bibliography on philosophy and religion, part of which was published by Iurev University.[5]

On 25 May 1917 Iashchenko left Petrograd University to accept a position as professor at Perm University. He worked there until 1919 at the Chair of International Law. In spring 1919 Perm University authorized him to go abroad for research purposes. He found himself a member of a Soviet delegation as an expert on international law in Berlin – whether these were two separate visits or combined into one is unclear. Iashchenko, however, declined to return to Russia and became one of the early Soviet "non-returnees".

Emigration. Iashchenko took up residence first in Berlin and rapidly became one of the central figures in the Russian émigré movement. In 1921 he founded and became the editor of the best Russian journal devoted to bibliography and bibliophilia, Русская книга [Russian Book], renamed in 1922 Новая русская книга [New Russian Book]. Through that publication and related activities, he sought to preserve the unity of Russian culture above and beyond ideological barriers. To that end he cooperated with both émigré and Soviet organizations and literary figures.

In 1924 Iashchenko moved to then Kovno (now Kaunas, the capital of Lithuania during the interwar period) and occupied the Chair of International Law at the Lithuanian University, founded in 1922 and renamed in 1930 the Vytautas Magnus University. Iashchenko gave courses on public and private international law and on international economic law. He put aside his literary, artistic, and bibliographical work; in the early 1930s he returned to Berlin.

Iashchenko died in Berlin on 10 June 1934 and was buried in a local cemetery.

[2] ЦГИА Спб., fond 14, opis 1, file 10486.

[3] Iashchenko, Теория федерализма. Опыт синтетической теории права и государства [Theory of Federalism. Attempt at Synthetic Theory of Law and State] (Iurev, 1912). Butler Я29. On Iashchenko, see G. S. Starodubtsev, Международно-правовая наука российской эмиграции [International-Legal Science of Russian Emigration] (M., 2000), pp. 17, 27, 40, 42, 45-48. 86, 104, 146, 178-182; Yoshiro Ikeda, "Toward an Empire of Republics: Transformation of Russia in the Age of Total War, Revolution, and Nationalism", in Tomohiko Uyama (ed.), *Comparing Modern Empires: Imperial Rule and Decolonization in the Changing World Order* (Tokyo, 2018), pp. 119-146.

[4] Iashchenko, note 3 above. The defense was reported in Право [Law], no. 7 (1913), cols. 434-436. Sometimes the place of defense is incorrectly given as St. Petersburg rather than Moscow.

[5] See Iashchenko (comp.), «Русская библиография по истории древней философии» [Russian Bibliography on the History of Ancient Philosophy], Ученые записки Императорского Юрьевского университета [Learned Notes of the Imperial Iurev University (1915).

International legal views. When Iashchenko joined St. Petersburg University, he was a mature scholar and well-known in international circles for original ideas and positions expressed in his works on international federalism and the theory of federalism published respectively in 1908 and 1912. Together these works addressed the theory and philosophy of law, State law, comparative jurisprudence, and international law. Iashchenko was considered to be a specialist in all three areas: legal philosophy, State law, and international law. In the field of international law he concentrated on the organization of international communion and what he deemed to be the social tasks of international law.

His views on international law – which he understood more widely than most as the "law of mankind" or the law of an international union – were primarily set out in his two monographs and a work on the social tasks of international law.[6] Iashchenko based his theory of the "law of mankind" on two basic doctrinal postulates: denial of the principle of State sovereignty and the idea of the creation of a unified international supreme power above States.

In his view, the entire history of mankind represented an attempt to form a universal State. He described the human condition contemporary to him as "disorganized confederalism" under which international communion is structured on the principles of multiple authority. He predicted a transition to social unions larger than the State and political associations of a higher order; other completely different norms of a qualitatively-different law would operate – what he called "cosmopolitan law".

Iashchenko believed that the international law of his time was unsystemic, obsolete, and even anarchical. But, he believed, it had a promising future as a potentially effective means of uniting all mankind. The chief obstacle to be overcome, in his view, was the division of mankind into independent sovereign States. He suggested in his work on the social tasks of international law that

> international law might stand at the level of the new challenges of life, should choose not the idea of free treaty combinations of sovereign subjects of law, but the idea of the supremacy of the interests of a single international community; that is, a civilized mankind (p. 115).

In his view, the international law of his day was merely at an early stage of development; further development would lead to its being transformed into a "cosmopolitan law" erected above States and individuals, to the formation of a supranational organization and the elimination of State sovereignty. Such a new international (world) law would gradually "organize itself; that is, create the embryos of international agencies". The future world social evolution would be towards a renunciation of State sovereignty, a transition from a "state of amorphous community towards a federative community". Relations within that union would be regulated by a new "law of mankind" – the law of the universal organization thereof.

Iashchenko believed that civilized mankind confronted the "problem of creating a unified law and unified political organization" of a supranational character

[6] Iashchenko, Социальные задачи международного права [Social Tasks of International Law] (Spb., 1911).

standing above various social unions, corporations, and individuals. He added to his cosmopolitan scheme reflections on the solidarity of class interests on an international scale, the "harmonious reconciliation of the interests of different classes", the establishment of a "cooperation of labor and capital" and considered the task of international law to be to defend mankind against the egoism of individual States and individual classes (pp. 118-122).

In his later work on the theory of federalism based on his synthetic theory of law, the State, and the social organization of society, Iashchenko moved away from his earlier notion of the universal organization of mankind and the cosmopolitan theory of law and built a new theory which primarily developed the idea of State sovereignty. He suggested that a "scholar could not close himself off within the framework of a single conception of the origin of State and law and the evolution thereof, having regard to the multi-factored and multi-variant character of this process".[7]

Russian doctrinal writings gave Iashchenko's ideas of world federation, world government, and world "cosmopolitan law" a mixed reception. During the Soviet era, most views were hostile. Levin characterized Iashchenko's conception as "utopian and reactionary".[8] For some contemporary Russian international lawyers the ideas of Iashchenko have resonance in a era of globalization.[9] Others remain critical. When evaluating the ideas and suggestions for a "world federation", "world government", "world cosmopolitan law", and "unified legal order", Marchenko dismissed them as "myths" which do and will exist only in a virtual world.[10]

The discussion of Iashchenko's legacy, however, is far from over.[11]

Petr Davydovich Kalmykov *(27 October 1808, b. Moscow Governate – 18 March 1860, d. St. Petersburg). Specialist in legal theory and State law.*

Life and career. After completing the Third St. Petersburg Gymnasium, Kalmykov enrolled in 1827 at the Faculty of History and Philology of St. Petersburg University. He was among six students who by Imperial behest were chosen to

[7] For details, see A. E. Kravchenko, Синтетическая теория права и государства [Synthetic Theory of Law and State of A. S. Iashchenko] (Belgorod, 2015) (abstract diss. kandidat iurid. nauk).

[8] D. B. Levin, Наука международного права России в конце XIX и начале XX в. [Science of International Law of Russia at the End of the XIX and early XX Centuries] (M., 1982), p. 39. Levin was a graduate of Leningrad University.

[9] For example, L. S. Iavich, «О философии права на XXI век» [On the Philosophy of Law in the XXI Century], Правоведение [Jurisprudence], no. 4 (2000), p. 11.

[10] M. N. Marchenko, Государство и право в условиях глобализации [State and Law in Conditions of Globalization] (M., 2009), pp. 55-60.

[11] Among recent contributions to the dialogue, see V. F. Kalina, «А. С. Ященко как первый российский теоретик федерализма» [A. S. Iashchenko as the First Russian Theoretician of Federalism], Вестник РГГУ [Herald of the Russian State Humanities University], no. 8(70) (2011), pp. 225-231; A. I. Dultsev, «Политико-правовое учение о федерализме в трудах А. С. Ященко» [Politico-Legal Doctrine on Federalism in the Works of A. S. Iashchenko], Право и закон [Jus and Lex], no. 4 (2013), pp. 40-42.

spend three years at the Professorial Institute attached to Dorpat University, then two years abroad to prepare for a professorial appointment at a Russian university. He took up residence at Dorpat in July 1828, where after two years it was decided that he was ready for independent studies; on 24 November 1830 he went abroad and, having accepted the suggestion of M. M. Speranskii, he attended the lectures of Friedrich Carl von Savigny and Georg Hegel. Upon returning to Russia, on 29 June 1834 he was appointed to the Second Department of His Majesty's Chancellery.

On 7 August 1835 Kalmykov was appointed a lecturer at the Chair of the Encyclopedia of Lexprudence and Russian State Laws at St. Petersburg University. A month or so later, on 4 September 1835, he was awarded a doctorate of laws without the submission of a dissertation, having passed the doctoral examinations and defended theses from the "science of lexprudence". The rank of professor *ordinarius* was conferred on 27 March 1837.

At the University, Kalmykov lectured on "Encyclopedia of Lexprudence" and "Russian State Laws" for the remainder of his life. From 1838 to 1860 he also lectured on criminal law at the Imperial School of Jurisprudence and from 1851 to 1860 on the history of Russian law at the Alexander Lycée. For nearly a decade, from 1840 to 1849, he served as the Director of the First St. Petersburg Gymnasium. In 1855 he was the Dean of the St. Petersburg Law Faculty.

In the summer of 1857 he traveled to Germany, Belgium, and France to investigate law faculties in connection with the drafting in Russia of a new University Statute. He did not live to see the result, however, and is buried in the Smolensk Orthodox Cemetery.

International legal views. The sole, but significant and important, contribution of Kalmykov to international legal doctrine was contained in a public lecture delivered on 8 February 1851 on literary property. In Russia its appearance was the first scientific defense of the concept of author's right as a category of jurisprudence.[12] He observed: "The question of literary ownership has not yet been discussed by a single one of our writers" (p. 141). Kalmykov did not confine himself to setting out the right of authors, but also addressed the history of relations between writers,

[12] P. D. Kalmykov, «О литературной собственности вообще и в особенности об истории прав сочинителей в России» [On Literary Ownership in General and in Particular on the History of the Rights of Writers in Russia], Журнал Министерства народного просвещения [Journal of the Ministry of Public Enlightenment], no. 10 (1851), section II, pp. 1-42; no. 11 (1851), section II, pp. 99-156. Separately published in the same year. 93 p.

copyists, and society, describing in detail the fate of the early printers and publishers, the development of printing, the problems of book preservation. In passing he touched upon the intellectual property rights of authors to art. His propositions had and still have significance for international law.

The creative work of an author, he said, is the outcome of his or her mind and fantasy. The fruit of the labors of a scholar, literary figure, or poet should, "beyond any doubt", be in the exclusive ownership of those who produced them. Literary ownership or property, Kalmykov believed, consisted of: (1) the ownership of the author of a work in the original or manuscript and the right to remuneration for his labor; (2) the right of personal obligation between the writer and the publisher under a contract concerning first publication and sale of the original multiplied in a determined number of examples; (3) the right to further multiplication and sale.

The basic problem, in his view, was how to precisely determine the concept and significance of literary ownership or property and to protect it against possible violations – counterfeiting or unlawful reprinting and multiplication. The privilege to exclusively reprint a work within an agreed period should be legislatively consolidated for authors and publishers.

Kalmykov addressed the purely international legal dimension of the issue, observing: "In systems and manuals of the law of nations or inter-State law the question of the mutual protection of literary and artistic ownership usually is ignored or passed over lightly. In his *Traité du droit international privé ou du conflit des lois de différentes nations en matière de droit privé* (Paris, 1843), Foelix devotes several lines rather concisely to this important subject" (p. 140). Kalmykov himself declared: "I confine myself to the domestic organism of the State and leave without attention that significance which the question of the rights of writers has now in the law of nations or inter-State law, the more so that to date only a few States have made the effort to ensure the rights of foreign writers within their own boundaries, and likewise the right of indigenous writers in foreign States" (p. 137).

Despite this disclaimer, Kalmykov gave several examples of international legal regulation of the protection of author's rights: (1) the decree of the German Diet to ensure the literary property of German writers within the German Union, the provisions of which were adopted by Austria and Prussia for areas within their boundaries that were not part of the Union; (2) the 1840 Austrian-Sardinian Convention which recognized literary property and prohibited the counterfeiting of scholarly, literary, and artistic works, to which other Italian principalities and a Swiss canton acceded; (3) the literary property conventions concluded between France and The Netherlands (1840), France and Sardinia (1843); and Great Britain and Prussia (1846). He also commented on the "difficult inter-State question" arising out of Belgian open literary piracy of French publications (pp. 137-138). He assessed positively the few examples from Russian practice concerning "inter-State relations of Russian music writers and artists with foreign music writers, artists, and publishers of musical and artistic works" (p. 139).

Kalmykov's 1851 public address was to be the introduction to a substantial study that Kalmykov never completed.

Petr Efimovich Mikhailov *(30 June 1883, b. St. Petersburg – 19?, date and place unknown). Privat-docent, Law Faculty of St. Petersburg University, specialist in the philosophy of law and history of Russian law.*

Life and career. There is little biographical data on Mikhailov. He is merely mentioned by Grabar with no biographical data.[13] The archives provide some help. Petr Efimovich Mikhailov studied at the Imperial St. Petersburg Theater School and performed as an artist in St. Petersburg theaters. In 1905 he requested permission from the Ministry of Public Enlightenment to sit the test for maturity at the First St. Petersburg Gymnasium, received such authorization, and performed satisfactorily. The certificate, dated 25 August 1905, was necessary for Mikhailov to apply for a university place.[14] That same month Mikhailov applied to the Law Faculty, was admitted, and graduated in 1910.[15] On 26 January 1911 Mikhailov applied to the University for a certificate of loyalty in order to apply to the Ministry of Public Enlightenment to remain at the Chair of International Law to train for the professoriate.[16]

At a session of the Law Faculty on 24 January 1911 Mikhailov was chosen to remain at the Chair of Encyclopedia of Law to prepare for the professoriate. The usual period of one year was given and renewed several times thereafter.[17] Whether Mikhailov actually wrote a magister dissertation is unknown; however, his name does not appear among the individuals who defended dissertations during the first half of the twentieth century.

International legal views. Bibliographical sources, however, indicate that Mikhailov published more than twenty scientific articles, bibliographical surveys, and book reviews, mostly devoted to the history, theory, and sociology of law. He touched upon international legal issues in three of his pieces: on the idea of

[13] V. E. Grabar, *The History of International Law in Russia 1647-1917: A Bio-Biographical Study*, transl. W. E. Butler (Oxford, 1990), p. 394. Also see S. A. Vengerov, where he is mentioned as an author of works on the philosophy of law and the history of Russian law.

[14] ЦГИА СПб., fond 14, opis 3, file 44609, l. 3.

[15] ЦГИА СПб., fond 14, opis 3, file 44609, l. 11.

[16] ЦГИА СПб., fond 14, opis 3, file 44609, l. 22.

[17] ЦГИА СПб., fond 14, opis 3, file 10513; also see Отчет о состоянии и деятельности Императорского С.-Петербургского университета за 1912 год [Report on the State and Activity of Imperial St. Petersburg University for 1915] (Spb., 1913), p. 141.

inter-power law;[18] an armed peace;[19] and a review of Baikov on inter-power law.[20] Two of these works – the article and the review – share a common theme: they express Mikhailov's views on a new idea which emerged in this period of an inter-power law which existed side by side with international law. The originators of this idea were both associated with the Chair of International Law at St. Petersburg University – Docent A. L. Baikov and Professor M. A. Taube. Turning first to von Taube's conception, Mikhailov determined that this conception proceeded along an "unexplored path" (col. 1577).

Mikhailov took the position that Taube's idea should be welcomed as a bold attempt to stir up the "monotonous and boring traditional literature on international law" (col. 1579). On the other hand, Mikhailov believed, this idea should not be accepted for several weighty reasons:

> first, the term introduced by Taube generates objections – inter-power law – because, in his view, there is no legal place for "power" as such: "international law is a powerless law", it does not recognize any powers;
>
> second, the construction suffers from logical and methodological defects, a critique of which Mikhailov developed in detail (col. 1579).

Mikhailov drew attention to the international legal constructions of Baikov and their methodological defects: with regard to Baikov's understanding of "inter-power law", according to which "international" law is subordinate to "inter-power" as a species is subordinate to a genus (p. 377) and that "inter-power law" regulates the "mutual relations of a State with the Roman Catholic Church" (p. 380) – it should be noted that this suffers from methodological ambiguity", analogous to that of Taube (col. 2649).

Of interest are Mikhailov's thoughts on the subjects and subject-matter of international law. He believed that the science of international law mistakenly used the construction "subjects of law" as a foundational analytical category.

Mikhailov set out his political, moral, and international legal views on war and peace in an article on the "armed peace" – a response to the appearance of Miliukov's book on an armed peace and the limitation of armaments.[21] Noting the arms race throughout the world accompanied by the immeasurable growth of the military budgets to the prejudice of social needs that created the illusion of ensuring peace, Mikhailov gave an original critique of this policy:

[18] Mikhailov, «Новая идея «междувластного права» [New Idea of "Inter-Power Law"], Право [Law], no. 27 (1909), cols. 1576-1583.

[19] Mikhailov, «Вооруженный мир» [Armed Peace], Вестник права [Herald of Peace], no. 4 (1913), cols. 13-22.

[20] Mikhailov, «Библиография: А. Л. Байков, Междувластные и властные отношения в теории права. Ярославль, 1912» [Bibliography: A. L. Baikov, Inter-Power and Power Relations in the Theory of Law. Iaroslavl, 1912], Право [Law], no. 48 (1912), cols. 2645-2649.

[21] P. N. Miliukov, Вооруженный мир и ограничение вооружений [Armed Peace and the Limitation of Armaments] (Spb., 1911).

An armed peace is an insurance premium which States are at pains to pay to save themselves in the event of war. They ignore urgent social reforms only to pay a progressing premium for military insurance. From the 'Great Powers' to small States – all try to be prompt payers and at the same time all are exhausted from the burden of these unbearable premiums (col. 15).

The "armed peace" is a breathing space and preparation for the next war. Nations, he said, must reject this. Everywhere a broad movement is developing: "war – to war". In his view, the "peace societies", arbitration courts, and, finally, the Hague Conferences of governments comprised three successive steps in the development of the movement in favor of peace (cols. 20-21).

Mikhailov was a convinced pacifist; he had faith in the progressive development of mankind from a savage and militant past to the establishment of perpetual peace. For him the idea and implementation of an "armed peace" were merely a transitional stage (col. 22).

Lev Iosifovich Petrazhitskii *(also Leon Petrażycki) (13 April 1867, b. Kollontaevo, Sennensk uezd, Vitebsk Governate – 15 May 1931, d. Warsaw, Poland). Russo-Polish legal scholar in the fields of the philosophy and sociology of law, a founder of the psychological theory of law.*

Life and career. Petrazhitskii studied for two years at Kyiv University, initially in the medical faculty, then in the Law Faculty. He graduated in 1890 and remained at the University to prepare for the professoriate. For three years he pursued advanced postgraduate training at Berlin University, where he published a two-volume treatise (in German) that established his reputation in legal circles.[22] In 1896 he defended a magister dissertation at Kyiv University "On the Distribution of Revenues In the Event of the Transfer of the Right of Use under Roman Law".

He was appointed privat-docent at the Chair of the Encyclopedia and Philosophy of Law at St. Petersburg University in 1897. The next year he defended a dissertation for the doctorate of Roman law: "Rights of a Good-Faith Possessor to Revenues from the Point of View of Dogma and Policy of Roman Law".[23] He was then appointed professor *ordinarius* in the Chair of the Encyclopedia and Philosophy of Law, replacing N. M. Korkunov. From 27 April 1906 to 8 September 1915, he held the

[22] L. Petrazhitskii, *Die Lehre von Einkommen. Vom Standpunkt des gemeinin Civilrechts unter Berücksichtigung des Entwurfs eines bürgerlichen Gesetzbuches für das Deutsche Reich* (Berlin, 1893-1895). 2 vols.

[23] ЦГИА СПб., fond 14, opis 3, file 14640; also see Starodubtsev, note 3 above, pp. 107, 218, 261.

non-established post of professor *ordinarius*, and thereafter, established professor *ordinarius* in that Chair. During the academic year 1905-1906 he served as Dean of the Law Faculty. Simultaneously he held appointments at the Higher Women's Courses and at the School of Jurisprudence.[24]

He became involved in political activity, was among the founders of the Kadet Party, and served as a deputy in the I State Duma. After Emperor Nicholas II dissolved the Duma, Petrazhitskii signed the 1906 "Vyborg Appeal", as a result of which he was sentenced to three months imprisonment and deprived of political rights.

He was elected to the Polish Academy of Sciences in 1912. Following the February 1917 Revolution, he was appointed with effect from 1 May 1917 as a Senator in the I Department of the Ruling Senate. He continued his position at what was now the I Petrograd University in the same Chair.[25]

Emigration. In 1921 Petrazhitskii emigrated to Warsaw, took Polish citizenship, and became the Head of a Chair of Sociology specially created for him at Warsaw University. Petrazhitskii regretted the excesses of Polish nationalism and Russophobia that afflicted the Poland of his day. He died on 15 May 1931, deeply depressed by all accounts, either from an apopleptic fit in his study at home or by suicide – the accounts differ. He was buried in Warsaw at the Catholic cemetery in Powązki. His later manuscripts perished in 1944 during the Second World War.

International legal views. Among the most eminent of Russo-Polish legal scholars, he was an individual of many talents and not easy to pigeonhole. His legal doctrines were set out most fully in his theory of law and State.[26] This was in the view of most his greatest work; it continues to inspire discussion and controversy.[27]

Less well-known is that Petrazhitskii contributed to the science of international law. He was seriously interested in public and, especially, private international law and the works of his colleagues who were international lawyers. He acted as an opponent at the defense of Mandelstam's dissertation on the Hague conferences on the codification of private international law.

Drawing upon his background in law and medicine, Petrazhitskii believed that emotions played a special role in human social life; these he divided into ethical-moral emotions and legal emotions. He introduced the concept of intuitive law, juxtaposing it to positive law. Law, he suggested, is rooted in the psyche and emotions of man. Emotions are the main stimulant of the psyche and, simultaneously,

[24] ЦГИА СПб., fond 355, opis 1, file 3997.

[25] ОА СПбГУ, fond 1, opis 1, file 141, l. 15.

[26] Petrazhitskii, Теория права и государства в связи с теорией нравственности [Theory of Law and State in Connection with the Theory of Morality] (reprint ed.; Spb., 2007). 2 vols.

[27] And inspire dissertations. See E. V. Timoshina, Теория и социология права Л. И. Петражицкого в контексте классического и постклассическлого правопонимания [Theory and Sociology of Law of L. I. Petrazhitskii in the Context of Classical and Post-Classical Law Comprehension] (Spb. 2013) (diss. doctor iurid. nauk).

a source of law. Under the impact of emotions, man is inclined to ascribe various rights and duties to external authority, himself, and other people, relying on their inner convictions for how to act in a particular situation. In order to understand the essence of law, Petrazhitskii said, one must draw upon the science of psychology.

As a counterbalance to the étatist and positivist notions of law, Petrazhitskii's view of law as emotion that exists solely within the psyche of the individual was not included in notions of the objective existence of law, or in the traditional understanding thereof only as positive law; that is, a complex of legal norms, principles, and institutions created or recognized by States and operating both within the municipal and inter-State spheres. Within this context, Petrazhitskii's opinions on the correlation between the science of international law and the theory of law are of importance. Having analyzed the various legal theories of his time, he found them all lacking. In his words, they are "jumping about" or "lame"; they do not reflect the true state of affairs, the true objects of reality.

The dominant positivist theory of law, he said, likewise is inadequate. It derives law from the will of the State or from State coercion, thereby creating a problem: although international law from this point of view does not fall under the positivist definition of law, many positivists take into account the realities and deem international law created by the wills of States to be a variety of law.

The concept of international law, suggested Petrazhitskii, may be built only on a scientific concept of law: "for example, the concept of international law = the concept of law + a specific distinction between international law and other types of law; so long as there is no scientific concept of law, there is not and cannot be a scientific concept of international law".[28]

Nonetheless, Petrazhitskii's critique of the positivist and other theories of law for being "crippled" did not escape the same appellation: he did not devote proper attention to international law. Issues of international law he touched upon on incidentally. One reason perhaps is that Petrazhitskii did not consider international law to be a sufficiently mature branch of law or legal system:

> It is regrettable, for example, that contemporary international law (that is, from the standpoint of our theory of law, the imperatively-attributable convictions of people relating to what is its relation to themselves and to their members: ambassadors, combatants, peaceful citizens, and so on during war and peace …) is not yet close to the position: *homo homini lupus* and is still far away from the evangelical principle: *homo homini frater*, but this still very barbaric law contains thousands of such slowly and gradually crystallized stable imperatively-attributable combinations, with regard to which one may say: part of the path from *populus populo lupus* to *populus populo frater* already has been traversed, let us go onward.[29]

[28] Petrazhitskii, Введение в изучение права и нравственности. Эмоциональная психология [Introduction to the Study of Law and Morality. Emotional Psychology] (Spb., 1905), pp. 22-23.

[29] Petrazhitskii, О мотивах человеческих поступков, в особенности об этических мотивах и их разновидностях [On the Motives of Human Behavior, Particularly Ethical Motives and Varieties Thereof] (Spb., 1904), p. 44.

In this value judgment, Petrazhitskii not only demonstrated the weak aspects of international law, but laid out the path towards achieving this high ideal – man is a brother to man and all nations are brothers – being the direction which international law should pursue. The spiritual foundation of the scientific approach taken by "psychologist" Petrazhitskii echoes the "positivist" F. F. Martens, who linked the origin and development of international law not so much with "facts" as with "ideas":

> Facts by their nature are transitional and changeable; they often are the result of arbitrariness or accident. On the contrary, ideas which penetrate into a certain historical era which underlie all facts, augment them, make analysis possible are found in an enormous mass of special conditions and circumstances in which the life of an individual nation develops, just as all nations in aggregate which participate in the European political system. In this respect, ideas play the role of those engines, or levers, of law operating in international relations in various eras and periods of its existence, as do principles in the sense of Montesquieu with regard to the forms and orders of State life.[30]

Petrazhitskii predicted that the development of the science and practice of international law in the future, especially of permanent international courts, would play a great role in the future. He also was the progenitor of the idea of a special new science – the policy of law as an applied discipline called upon to combine the knowledge of law with a social ideal (that is, to provide a scientific resolution of a problem) and to facilitate the development of the principles of a desired, rational law and legislation and, in this sense, generate former natural law doctrines whose basic provisions would extend to international law.[31]

The views of Petrazhitskii on private international law are great interest.[32] He wrote but a single article on private international law, and that concerned, using his expression, the "so-called private international law". He wrote the article in response to a book by A. A. Pilenko on the systematics of private international law. The article addressed what he considered to be the most difficult and topical problems of private international law that "unexpectedly for the author had grown greatly" and gone beyond the framework of a single article.[33]

[30] F. F. Martens, Современное международное право цивилизованных народов [Contemporary International Law of Civilized Nations] (Spb., 1904; reprint ed.: M., 2008), I, p. 25.

[31] O. O. Merezhko, Наука политики международного права: истоки и перспективы [Science of the Policy of International Law: Sources and Prospects] (Kyiv, 2009).

[32] See I. V. Getman-Pavlova, «Проблемы международного частного права в психологической теории Л. И. Петражитского» [Problems of Private International Law in Petrazhitskii's Psychological Theory of Law], Международное публичное и частное право [International Public and Private Law], no. 5 (2009), pp. 5-11; Getman-Pavlova, «Наука международного частного права: проблемы международной вежливости, публичного порядка и отсылки в психологической теории Л. И. Петражитского» [Science of International Law: Problems of International Comity, Public Policy, and Renvoi in Petrazhitskii's Psychological Theory], Международное публичное и частное право [International Public and Private Law], no. 6 (2009), pp. 16-23.

[33] Petrazhitskii, «О старой школе и новых течениях в науке права: по поводу книги проф. А. Пиленко: «Очерки по систематике частного международного права», 1911» [On the Old School

Petrazhitskii investigated private international law from the standpoint of his psychological approach to law. In his view, the term "private international law", just as other terminological constructions such as "conflict of laws", "internal conflicts law", or "international conflicts law" were wrong, and therefore he himself constantly prefaced their use by the expression "so-called". First to be resolved, said Petrazhitskii, was the question of whether private international law really existed. If it exists, then where, in what sphere, and in the form of what law: (a) in the form of a unified international law binding on States; (b) in the form of many internal systems of law in individual States; (c) both a system subject to international law and a multiplicity of systems of respective internal laws exist.

He believed that private international law is the rules on the application of foreign civil laws in a State. The term "international" within the concept "private international law" he understood not in the sense of the transboundary character of the relations regulated, but of an integral aggregate of international unified (treaty and customary) norms on the conflicts of the laws of States. In his view the first cause and basis of private international law is the difference in the various national laws and the existence of gaps in the law of States. The existence among various nations of "different civil laws' was not accidental; it represents something historically inevitable, reasonable, and deserving of approval.

Petrazhitskii applied his theory of the policy of law to private international law. In concluding that there was no system of positive conflicts law, he believed that the dogmatic of private international law must develop by taking into account the policy of private international law, and the need to develop the policy of conflicts law. Proceeding from the reasonable requirements of the policy of law, the principal politico-legal purpose of conflicts norms of private international law was to exclude (1) infringements on the rights of foreigners acquired under the laws of a foreign State; (2) exempting foreigners from duties imposed by foreign legislation that lead to a violation of the rights of other persons in whose interests these duties were established.[34]

The parallel existence of "different civil laws" inevitably generating conflicts of law was objectively necessary, he believed. Therefore, one cannot speak about international or municipal unification of legal concepts. A law of conflicts understood as international law might exist only if a single world State existed. Therefore, the full unification of international conflicts norms cannot be serious because the policy of law must take into account whether this can be implemented – and that, as a rule, is impossible.

He considered that private international law cannot be construed as international law, and therefore does not fall within the system thereof. Criticizing the "internationalist" Pilenko, he demonstrated that the application of foreign laws

and New Trends in the Science of Law: re: the Book of Prof. A. Pilenko, «Очерки по систематике частного международного права» [Essays on the Systematics of Private International Law], 1911», Право [Law], no. 47 (1911), cols. 2609-2619; no. 48, cols. 2694-2710; no. 49, cols. 2767-2776; no. 50, cols. 2851-2865; no. 51, cols. 2906-2918; no. 52, no. 2974-3000. Butler П84.

34 See the Preface by E. V. Timoshina to Petrazhitskii's article, note 31 above, in Правоведение [Jurisprudence], no. 2 (2015), p. 153.

never means the court of one State being subject to the legislative directions of other States. Such subordination would be a material violation of the sovereignty and internal autonomy of States and would lead to chaos. Municipal judges, unlike members of an international tribunal, must adjudicate according to their national legislative acts.

Petrazhitskii criticized several basic concepts of private international law. One was the category of "public policy". He acknowledged that certain laws consolidate the most essential conditions of the existence of society. But what these conditions are is an open question giving great latitude for "reasonable discretion", the reply to which may vary. If one were to imagine that all judges, being "independent, honorable, and idealistic" people are "angels on earth", they nonetheless need guidance in order to take public policy into account on the basis of reasonable discretion. Legal stability and certainty are necessary in order to avoid flagrant and cruel arbitrariness. Sometimes, however, judges are guided by that which they like and what seem to them important national laws, and therefore they relegate them to public policy. And the personal and property rights and the fates of people in this broad realm of law depend on their decisions.

Legal scholars were at one with judges on this matter. Here Petrazhitskii could not resist sarcasm: "ink sticks to the paper in the offices of internationalist scholars, and not human tears, but this ink dries into dots as though they had been mixed with tears" (cols. 2864-2865). Petrazhitskii formulated his own vision of private international law:

(1) private international law is part of the national legal system, part of civil law; therefore it is best designated with the term "conflicts of law";

(2) positive private international law as an integral aggregate of international legal norms does not exist in reality;

(3) the principal function of a conflicts norm is to delimit the territorially different material norms;

(4) the principal source of conflicts law is national legislation. The best means of optimizing positive conflicts law is a separate law containing significant provisions of private international law.

Petrazhitskii thus formulated in the early twentieth century three basic, "eternal", and contradictory problems still topical: the place and role of private international law in the legal systems of States and the international community as a whole. He attempted to present his own original conception, which did not, however, find broad support among his contemporaries. Measured in contemporary terms, "the psychological theory of law makes it possible for us to look anew at many problematic questions of the theory and practice of contemporary international law".[35] Against the background of the "post-modernist chaos" in the science

[35] O. O. Merezhko, «Типология норм международного права в свете психологической теории права» [Typology of Norms of International Law in the Light of the Psychological Theory of Law], in Актуальні проблеми держави і права [Topical Problems of State and Law], no. 62 (2011), p. 281.

of international law, one must return, it is suggested, to the concept of law developed by Petrazhitskii build a science of international law on the foundation of the psychological school of law.

Following the approach of Petrazhitskii, Merezhko defined international law as the "intuitively-attributed convictions of people relating to what are the mutual rights and duties of States, and also other subjects of the international community".[36] Based on Petrazhitskii's doctrine, Merezhko developed the following typology of international law:

(1) intuitive international law;

(2) positive international law;

(3) official international law (within such law he distinguished between internal and external official international law);

(4) unofficial international law.[37]

The same typology, in Merezhko's view, is applicable to private international law. Based on Petrazhitskii's psychological theory, Merezhko gives the following description of private international law:

> Among the fundamental principles of private law characteristic of virtually all national systems of private law and therefore simultaneously principles of private international law are such principles as justice, good faith, and reasonableness. It is not difficult to note that each of these principles has psychological content. In light of the psychological theory of law these principles are an expression of intuitive law, one may even say intuitive private law, because they conceal intuitive legal notions, for example, judges considering a concrete case in the field of private law. For example, in the field of private international law the principle of reasonableness appears in the concept "reasonable period".[38]

Although it was not his primary interest, Petrazhitskii made his own contribution to public and private international law. More than most of his colleagues, his work is finding a new audience among successor colleagues.

[36] Merezhko, Психологическая теория международного права (публичного и частного) [Psychological Theory of International Law (Public and Private)] (Odessa, 2012), p. 22, reviewed in Право [Law], no. 2 (2013), pp. 183-186 (I. V. German-Pavlova); also see Merezhko, "Petrażycki's Psychological Theory of Private International Law", *Jus Gentium: Journal of International Legal History*, IV (2019), pp. 117-144.

[37] Merezhko, «Методологические основы психологической теории международного права» [Methodological Foundations of the Psychological Theory of International Law], Русский юридический журнал [Russian Legal Journal], no. 1 (2012), pp. 48-61.

[38] Merezhko, note 33 above, p. 226.

Petr Alekseevich Pokrovskii *(22 August 1885, b. Samara – 19 October 1916, d. Petrograd). Specialized in the philosophy of law and State law. Docent at the Chair of the Encyclopedia and History of the Philosophy of Law.*

Life and career. Pokrovskii graduated from the Law Faculty of Kharkov University and remained to pursue postgraduate studies at the Chair of State Law. He was successful in obtaining the degree of magister of State Law. For several years he also worked in Kharkov at the newspaper Южный край [Southern Territory] and the St. Petersburg journal Русское богатство [Russian Wealth]. In 1913 Pokrovskii removed to St. Petersburg.

From 1 January 1914 he took up the position of privat-docent at the Chair of the Encyclopedia and History of the Philosophy of Law at St. Petersburg University.[39] There he lectured in the following courses: "Political Doctrines in England in the Eighteenth and Nineteenth Centuries" (1914-1915) and "Evolution of the Idea of Individualism in the Political Doctrine of the Eighteenth and Nineteenth Centuries" (1915-1916).

In parallel with his position at the University, Pokrovskiii joined from 16 May 1916 the Ministry of Foreign Affairs, where he was given the post of librarian of the II Department and as secretary of the Ministry journal Известия Министерства иностранных дел [News of the Ministry of Foreign Affairs]. From 1914 he became a lecturer at the Law Faculty of the Psychoneurological Institute, where he taught general constitutional law.

Pokrovskii died suddenly on 19 October 1916 in Petrograd.

International legal views. Pokrovskii left one specialized study on international law – an article on subjects of international law,[40] together with several book reviews. Of these, the article is of greatest importance, for there he became, in the words of Grabar, "the most resolute opponent of the predominant view of international legal personality".[41] Pokrovskii declared that the question of subjects of international law is a "question of cardinal importance for the entire discipline of international law. One way or another the reply to this question depends on a particular understanding of the said discipline" (p. 177).

Pokrovskii reproached international lawyers because they traditionally treated the problem of subjects of international law "virtually always without any link not only with the concept of law in general, but also with a narrower concept of a subject of rights" (p. 177).

In the view of Aleksandr Nikolaevich Makarov (1888-1973), the Pokrovskii article "brilliantly manifested the scientific credo" of its author on the correlation

[39] ЦГИА СПб., fond 355, opis 1, file 10802.

[40] P. A. Pokrovskii, «К вопросу о субъектах международного права» [On the Question of Subjects of International Law], Известия Министерства иностранных дел [News of the Ministry of Foreign Affairs], kn. 6 (1912), pp. 177-210. Butler П132.

[41] Grabar, note 13 above, p. 485.

of law and State. Pokrovskii was convinced that "no State makes law, law makes the State" (p. 191). An objective legal order reigns in the State, there is no unified, intangible State power in a State, there is merely the "legal powers of individual bearers of power unified by their origin from one legal order".[42]

Pokrovskii opposed the dominant view that only States are subjects of international law:

> But how is such an assertion compatible with the numerous data of positive law according to which individual persons participating in international relations are governed and bound by norms of international law? What will be, from the legal point of view, the status of individual persons and societies participating in international turnover if all the rights and, respectively, legal duties are consolidated only for States?

Pokrovskii noted that representatives of the dominant doctrine could not deny the undoubted fact that "not only States participate in international legal turnover as certain integral entities, but also individual societies and individual persons, and that international legal turnover defends the lawful interests of societies and individual persons". Pokrovskii cited as an example the Geneva Convention for the Amelioration of the Condition of the Wounded in Armies in the Field, which, he recalled, "defends the interests not of States as integral entities but of individual persons having the misfortune to be sick or wounded during war, and also persons and institutions (albeit only partially) intended to assist the sick and wounded' (p. 179).

In his view, even though in international treaties the obligations are placed on the State as a whole, the practical realization of these international obligations lies on the government, concrete departments or ministries, and individuals. Pokrovskii's position was unusual in that he deemed to be subjects of international law all those in whose interests international legal norms are created: States, organs of the State, societies, and private persons (the sick and wounded according to the Geneva Convention, subjects under trade treaties, and so on).

Pokrovskii's review of the Zhilin monograph on the union (unie) and other complex States[43] reflected his approach. The review was sharp in tone, evidence that Pokrovskii had a thorough command of the theoretical and practical materials of a constitutional and international legal nature. The reviewer pointed out the many inaccuracies and mistaken assertions in the book. For example, he drew attention to one place (p. 162) where Zhilin said that a "unie" was a union of two States but in another place (p. 285) the exact opposite – a union of several States

[42] A. N. Makarov, «Памяти П. А. Покровского» [Memories of P. A. Pokrovskii], Известия Министерства иностранных дел [News of the Ministry of Foreign Affairs], kn. 5-6 (1916), p. 293.

[43] Pokrovskii, review of A. A. Zhilin, «Теория союзного государства. Разбор главнейших направлений в учении о союзном государстве и опыт построения его юридической конструкции» [Theory of the Unie State. Analysis of the Principal Orientations in the Doctrine of the Unie State and Experience with Building the Legal Construction Thereof. Kyiv, 1912. 354 p.], Известия Министерства иностранных дел [News of the Ministry of Foreign Affairs], kn. 1 (1913), pp. 173-180. Butler Ж10.

was possible (p. 178). His overall judgment was severe: "Theory in the exposition of Prof. Zhilin loses any aroma of life. The last is not felt therein" (p. 174).

Pokrovskii reviewed Iashchenko on the theory of federalism. His assessment was positive. In a lengthy review (12 pages), he analyzed the best features of the book and pointed to lost opportunities and controversial moments[44]

Pokrovskii passed away in his 32nd year, cutting short what promised to be an impressive career in international law. Many of his positions relating to subjects of international law were prophetic, notably his expansive view of who or what should be deemed to be subjects of international law.

Mikhail Andreevich Reisner *(7 March 1868, b. Vileika, Vilna Governate (now – Molodechenskaia Region, Belarus) – 3 August 1928, d. Moscow). Russian and Soviet legal theorist, constitutional scholar.*

Life and career. Reisner graduated from the Sixth Gymnasium with the gold medal and enrolled at the Law Faculty of Warsaw University, where he graduated in 1892. From 1892 to 1896 he lectured on the legal sciences in the Novo-Alexandria Institute of Agriculture and Forestry (suburb of Novo-Alexandria, Lublin Province, Poland). After passing the magister examinations in 1896 at St. Vladimir University in Kyiv, he was sent abroad for two years to Heidelberg University in preparation for the professoriate. Upon returning, he took a position from 1 September 1898 as professor *extraordinarius* in the Chair of Political Economy and Statistics in Tomsk University; and from 1 July 1899 at the Chair of State Law. He served as secretary of the Law Faculty from 20 October 1898 to 1 November 1900. He delivered lectures on political economy, Russian State law, and the encyclopedia of law and history of the philosophy of law.

On 1 April 1903 he was dismissed with deprivation of the right to teach in Russia. The accusation was abuse of the right to speak, thereby deflecting students from serious scientific work and inspiring in them disrespect and hostility to the legal order in Russia. Persecutions forced him to emigrate. From 1903 to 1906 he worked abroad, including at the École des hautes études en sciences sociales in Paris, and engaged in Party work for the Russian Social Democratic Workers Party (Bolshevik) in Europe and in Russia. He returned to Russia at the end of 1905 and founded a social-democratic group in Narva.

[44] Pokrovskii, review of A. S. Iashchenko, Теория федерализма: опыт синтетической теории права и государства [Theory of Federalism: Attempt at Synthetic Theory of Law and State]. Iurev, 1912. x, 841 p.], Известия Министерства иностранных дел [News of the Ministry of Foreign Affairs], kn. 4 (1913), pp. 224-235. Butler Я29.

From 1906 to 1918 Reisner was privat-docent at St. Petersburg University, initially at the Chair of State Law and then at the Chair of Encyclopedia and History of the Philosophy of Law. He taught in various years the following courses: State Law of Foreign Powers; State and Church in Their Mutual Relations; History of Political Doctrines in Antiquity and the Middle Ages; and "History of Political Doctrines".[45]

From 1907 he was a professor at the Higher N. P. Raev Historical-Literary and Legal Women's Courses. In addition, he held the post of secretary at the Law Faculty of the Psychoneurological Institute.

After the February 1917 Revolution, Reisner was reconfirmed in the post of professor *ordinarius* at Tomsk University. However, on 7 August 1918 by order of the Provisional Siberian Government he was dismissed because he had failed to appear at his place of work. His failure to do so was no doubt partly attributable to serving as Deputy People's Commissar of Justice after the October Revolution. During 1919-1920 he participated in the Russian Civil War first as the head of a political section and then of a political administration. He also was employed at the People's Commissariat of the Enlightenment, where he took part in the reform of higher education.

He was involved in a number of post-October 1917 legal positions and developments. As Deputy People's Commissar of Justice, he headed the Legislative Proposals Commission of the Peoples Commissariat of Justice, was one of the authors of the Dekret of the Council of People's Commissars on the separation of church and State, and took part in drafting the 1918 Constitution of the RSFSR.

Not long after the Bolsheviks seized power, the fate of Imperial Russian legislation was addressed: should positive Imperial Russian law be retained in force, at least in part, or should there be a complete break with the old legal order by repealing that legislation and replacing it with something else. Anecdotal evidence suggests that Lenin, himself a trained jurist, hesitated about so drastic a measure as complete abrogation. Consulting his People's Commissar of Justice, whose deputy was Reisner, a protégé of Petrazhitskii and devotee of the latter's theory of intuitive law, Lenin was persuaded to support Dekret No. 1, "On the Court", terminating the operation of laws of the Russian Empire contrary to the ideas and principles of the Revolution and to substitute in their place a "revolutionary legal consciousness".

Reisner had reinterpreted Petrazhitskii's theory of intuitive law from a Marxist perspective long before the 1917 Russian revolutions.[46] When asked by Lunacharskii, as People's Commissar of Justice, for his advice, the anecdote was related as follows:

> [Reisner] … used Petrazycki's theory of intuitive law to 'persuade his superior, the Commissar of Justice, that it was possible to abrogate *uno actu* the legislation of the Tsarist regime and of the Provisional Government, since

[45] ЦГИА СПб., fond 14, opis 1, file 10014.

[46] M. A. Reisner, Теория Петражицкого: Марксизм и социальная идеология [Theory of Petrazhitskii: Marxism and Social Ideology] (1908), transl. by H. W. Babb in John N. Hazard (intro.), *Soviet Legal Philosophy* (1951).

a substitute already existed in the form of the intuitive law of the working class. Reisner's advice was embodied in the decree On Courts (7 December 1917), according to which the new courts had to render decisions on the basis of the enactments of the 'Workers' and Peasants' Government' and of the revolutionary consciousness of judges which was supposed to coincide with the ideas on justice held by working men. Since, at that time, the enactments of the new government were scarce and unsystematic, the other source, revolutionary legal consciousness had to prevail.[47]

Reisner later deflected criticism made of Lunacharskii and Pēteris Stučka (1865-1932) for drawing upon Petrazhitskii's theory of intuitive law:

> The guilt attributed to Lunacharskii I must to an important degree take upon myself inasmuch as I was the person whose lot it was, in conversation with him, (a) to attest the necessity of organizing revolutionary justice (which Lunacharskii put forward), and (b) to point out the fact that … revolutionary law is already existent and in being, notwithstanding the absence as yet of any legislation confirming it … this was the intuitive law of our revolutionary masses … which … as the class law of the insurgents … comprises completely the entirety of the appropriate legal consciousness … Everyone knows that the turn of the revolutionary masses to intuitive law vindicated itself magnificently.[48]

And so it happened that Reisner refashioned and implemented Petrazhitskii's intuitive law in the service of the Revolution.

Reisner was among the founders in 1918-1919 of the Socialist (Communist) Academy as a center of Marxist socio-political science. Other matters beckoned, however. On 9 February 1919 the Council of Petrograd University confirmed the decision of the Law Faculty to consider Reisner to have left by reason of his failure to return from a trip elsewhere. When the Civil War ended, Reisner returned to academic work and accepted lecturing positions at the Military Academy of the Red Army and the Moscow Psychoneurological Institute. From 1925 to 1928, he was employed at Moscow University, successively holding the positions of professor in the legal-political division; chair of general history and theory of law at the faculty of social sciences; chair of State law of the USSR and State law of bourgeois countries in the faculty of Soviet law.

Reisner died at Moscow on 3 August 1928 of a heart attack.

International legal views. Three works by Reisner dealt with international legal matters. The first concerned perpetual peace.[49] Noting that the unattainable

[47] A. Walicki, *Legal Philosophies of Russian Liberalism* (1987), pp. 287-288. For details, see I. A. Il'in, *On the Essence of Legal Consciousness*, ed., intro., and transl. William E. Butler, Philip T. Grier, and Paul Robinson (2d rev. ed.; 2023), pp. 116-119. Also see Starodubtsev, note 3 above, pp. 14, 17, 18, 20.

[48] Reisner, in Hazard, note 46 above, pp. 86-87.

[49] M. A. Reisner, «Вечный мир» [Perpetual Peace], Энциклопедический словарь Гранат [Encyclopedic Dictionary Granat] (1911), XII, cols. 190-197.

ideal of perpetual peace had ancient origins (col. 190), he undertook a historical excursus and dwelt in detail on the ideas of establishing a lengthy peace, commencing from the ancient world (Babylon, Greece, Jews, Rome), the proposals in the Middle Ages for perpetual peace, and then onto the Renaissance. He drew attention to the fact that in the Renaissance drafts appeared (for example, King Henry IV of France, Abbot St. Pierre) which upheld the idea of the cessation of wars and establishment of perpetual peace by creating a union of States on the basis of a treaty. Reisner dwelt on the treatise of Immanuel Kant (1724-1804) in which draft treaty articles were proposed directed towards the international legal consolidation of the legal foundations and forms of an inter-State peaceful union (cols. 190-194). A union of States created with a view to a perpetual peace, he noted, with common legislative, judicial, and executive organs was becoming for some scholars an "ideal of the science of international law" (col. 194).

Reisner was skeptical about perpetual peace being achieved "now"; the positions of proponents of war among the authoritative State agencies and great industrialists who sought to resolve their economic, political, and territorial problems through wars were strong. More realistic, he thought, were "partial disarmament or suspension of the further growth of armies and navies" (col. 196). He likewise was skeptical about the Hague peace conferences, various pacifist organizations, and peace societies. More significant in the peace movement, Reisner believed, were international organizations, conferences, congresses, and unions which united people's representatives and members of various European parliaments (col. 196).

In another encyclopedia entry devoted to Hugo Grotius (1583-1645), Reisner set out the basic benchmarks in the life of Grotius and expressed a number of interesting thoughts on Grotius' views. Noting that Grotius was an apologist for natural law, Reisner observed that Grotius did not reject war. He demanded certain limitations of military practices, namely the inviolability of the clergy, wives, children, the confinement of killing only to the belligerent parties, and so on.[50]

His next work on war and democracy appeared after the 1917 February Revolution. Reisner condemned the war with Germany and its allies as being conducted in the interests of the Tsar and his "stooges", and described with rapture the overthrow of Tsarism and the lower strata of society acquiring democratic freedoms. As a result of the Revolution, Reisner wrote, one no longer hears high-flown appeals to "eradicate" or to "wipe off the face of the earth" the "vile Teutonic barbarians".[51]

When describing the First World War (to him, the Great European War) as a war of the great European power for a division of spheres of influence, the seizure of disputed territories, and new raw materials and markets for the sale of goods, Reisner viewed it as a commercial "capitalist enterprise":

> The contemporary war is a capitalist enterprise in the full sense of the word. The times are long past when war was a confrontation of the most bravest. Now not only people do battle, but also machines, technical apparatus, chemical, and other appliances. War is waged now not at the front,

[50] Reisner, Гроций Гуго [Hugo Grotius], Энциклопедический словарь Гранат [Encyclopedic Dictionary Granat] (1911), XVII, cols. 178-181.

[51] Reisner, Война и демократия [War and Democracy] (Spb., 1917), p. 12.

> but at the rear, and he triumphs who has the better factories plants, railways, and communications, who has the better technical knowledge and organized labor (p. 14).

Reisner passionately condemned cruel means of waging war which plant capitalist monopolies in nations thanks to the increase of their profits. With surprise he wrote:; "As reality shows, the most cultured and civilized countries of Europe appeared to the world as models of moral decline and social rudeness, which no one might have anticipated" (p. 19).

Having analyzed the appeals for and drafts of schemes for perpetual peace from Hammurabi (c. 1810-1750 BC) – the sixth king of the First Babylonian Dynasty of the Amorite tribe – onwards, Reisner welcomed the Fourteen Points of Woodrow Wilson (1856-1924) and the appeal of the Soviet of Workers' and Soldiers' Deputies of Russia to the working people of the belligerents to end the three-year war on a just basis. Riding the wave of socialist ideas in 1917, Reisner wrote: "If the wealthy and strong cannot create a union of all European countries, then let the proletariat create their own common and unified State, a labor democracy of the United States of Europe. Then perpetual peace will come to the Earth" (p. 32).

Voldemar Evgrafovich (Vladimir Eduardovich) Valdenberg *(23 December 1871, b. Moscow – 1940, d. Leningrad). Historian, legal philosopher.*

Life and career. Educated at the Sixth Gymnasium of St. Petersburg, Valdenberg enrolled in St. Petersburg University in 1890 and graduated in 1894 from the Law Faculty. He remained at the Chair of the Encyclopedia and History of the Philosophy of Law from 1 October 1894 to 1 April 1897 to prepare for the professoriate. From 1895 he taught in secondary schools and lectured at the Private Courses for Commercial Knowledge, subsequently becoming the Director.

On 28 May 1900 he defended a magister dissertation on "Lex and Jus in the Philosophy of Hobbes". From 1901 to 1907 he served as privat-docent at the Chair of the Encyclopedia and History of the Philosophy of Law, offering a course on the "History of the Philosophy of Law". In parallel he offered courses at the Imperial School of Jurisprudence (head of the Chair of the Encyclopedia of Law from 1906 to 1909), Petrovskii Commercial School, and several other educational institutions. He returned to Petrograd University from 1918 to 1924 as privat-docent and from 1919 as professor at the Faculty of Social Sciences offering lectures on the "History of State Ideas in Russia from the Sixteenth to Seventeenth Centuries". Simultaneously he served as the Head of the Archive of Petrograd University.

He moved into librarianship, acting from 1924 as the Head of the Library of the Politico-Legal Division of the Faculty of Social Sciences. From 1924 to 1928 and again from 1934 to 1936 he worked at the Library of the Academy of Sciences (learned secretary, senior librarian, Head of the Journals Division). Twice, in 1929 and 1930, he refused offers to appear on the ballot for election as Corresponding Member of the USSR Academy of Sciences. During the 1930s, he lectured at the Technological Institute and worked at the Geological Committee. From 1937 to 1939 he held a position at the Archive of the Institute of Russian Literature (Pushkin House).

International legal views. A number of Valdenberg's published works touched upon issues of international law. In one of his earliest pieces Valdenberg addressed the ideas of Nicolo Machiavelli (1469-1527) and the reactions to Machiavelli's writings by René Descartes (1596-1650) and Baruch Spinoza (1632-1677). Analyzing the Machiavellian proposition that the "end justifies the means" and the law may be neglected in so doing, Valdenberg addressed the implications for international law:

> It is understandable that in the field of international relations where there is no law Machiavelli should deem permissible all possible actions. All criminal thoughts, diplomatic cunning, intrigues, and plots of one government against another lose their immorality and criminal character if the representative of a State has the power to bring his idea to completion; in war, of course, all is permitted. International law is in essence treaty law; but if compliance with a treaty is deemed to be not binding, then it is clear that relations between States may rest only on force.[52]

The immorality of many of Machiavelli's views, in Valdenberg's perception, reflected the historical experience of preceding times and the times contemporary to Machiavelli himself.

Another work by Valdenberg had implications for private international law – his frequently reprinted textbook on trade law and procedure.[53] At the time Valdenberg wrote his textbook, trade law was in the early stages of forming its conceptual foundations. Valdenberg offered his own definition: "By trade law in the broad sense may be understood the aggregate of legal norms regulating trade and trade activity in general … Trade law in the narrow sense comprises norms which regulate the private relations of persons with regard to trade transactions by those concluding them" (p. 5).

When considering the question of trade legal capacity and dispositive legal capacity, Valdenberg noted that "contracts and obligations peculiar to trade" also appertain to foreigners. However, Russian consuls arriving in foreign countries were deprived of this right. The portions of his textbook relating to trade, stock

[52] V. E. Valdenberg, «Основания макиавеллизма» [Grounds of Machiavellianism], Вопросы философии и психологии [Questions of Philosophy and Psychology], no. 2(37) (1897), pp. 231-232.

[53] Valdenberg, Краткий учебник торгового права и судопроизводства [Concise Textbook of Trade Law and Procedure] (Spb., 1900; 6th ed.; Pg., 1915).

exchange, and banking transactions, the law on bills of exchange, trade proceedings inn courts, arbitration, among others are of undoubted relevance for private international law.

§11.2. *Chair of History of Russian Law*

Viacheslav Mikhailovich Gribovskii *(29 July 1867, b. Suwalki, Kingdom of Poland – d. 21 February 1924, Riga). Authority on Byzantine and Russian law, State law, and State institutions of the eighteenth to nineteenth centuries.*

Life and career. Having graduated in 1887 from the Ninth Gymnasium in Petersburg, Gribovskii enrolled at the Law Faculty of St. Petersburg University, initially in the Oriental Faculty (Arabic-Turkish-Persian Division), but at the end of the first semester transferred to the Law Faculty.[54] Upon graduation from the University, from 1 December 1891 he remained at the Chair of State Law to prepare for the professoriate.[55] He traveled abroad for one year from August 1895 as part of his postgraduate training.

In parallel with his postgraduate studies, Gribovskii was employed between 1891 and 1898 as an official of the State Commission for the Repayment of Debts, from 1894 a candidate attached to the Kronshtadt Naval Court, and from 1896 an ober-auditor and, from 1897, a clerk at the Chief Naval Vessel Administration. Upon returning from his visit abroad, from 1 July 1896 he was appointed privat-docent in the Chair of History of Russian Law at St. Petersburg University, where he offered a course on "State Institutions of Byzantium". On 29 April 1897 by order of the Naval Department he was appointed chief flag-officer of the Command Squadron of the Baltic Sea for the campaign of 1897. That same year he defended a magister dissertation at St. Petersburg University on "People and Power in the Byzantine State: Attempt of a Historical-Dogmatic Study",[56] and on 16 January 1902, a doctoral dissertation: "The High Court and Supervision in Russia in the First Half of the Reign of Empress Catherine the Second".[57]

[54] ЦГИА СПб., fond 14, opis 3, file 26081; also see Starodubtsev, note 3 above, p. 28.

[55] ЦГИА СПб., fond 14, opis 1, file 9259.

[56] V. M. Gribovskii, Народ и власть в Византийском государстве: Опыт историко-догматического исследования [People and Power in the Byzantine State: Attempt of a Historical-Dogmatic Study] (Spb., 1897).

[57] Gribovskii, Высший суд и надзор в России в первую половину царствования Императрицы Екатерины Второй: Историко-юридическое исследование [The High Court and Supervision in

From 1905 he taught the history of Russian law at the Petersburg Archaeological Institute. He served as head of a division of the Chancellery of the Ministry of Railways from 1903, and from 1908, as an official of the Chief Administration for Local Economy of the Ministry of Internal Affairs. For two years, from 1909 to 1911, Gribovskii was a professor at the Novorossiisk University in Odessa at the Chair of Police Law, and then the Chair of Encyclopedia of Law and History of the Philosophy of Law. He returned to St. Petersburg University in 1911; by appointment of the Ministry of Public Enlightenment (without a vote in the Council of the Faculty) be became a professor in the Chair of the History of Russian Law in the Law Faculty – an appointment which generated mass protests by the University students.

Following the October 1917 Revolution, Gribovskii moved to Tomsk in November 1917. There he became a professor initially in the Chair of the History of Russian Law of Tomsk University and, from 22 January 1919, Dean of the Law Faculty. He also taught international law.

Emigration. Gribovskii emigrated to Riga, Latvia, in 1920. There he was appointed a professor of the Latvian University, Director of the Slavic Gymnasium in Riga, and lectured on military psychology in officer courses.

He died on 21 February 1924, and is buried at the Pokrova kapi (built in 1773) in Riga, Latvia.

International legal views. Among Gribovskii's scholarly publications are several articles devoted to international law. The first was a review of a treatise by M. I. Dogel on the legal status of the individual, especially combatants, during war.[58] On the whole, Gribovskii thought well of the Dogel book. But he disagreed with Dogel, who considered the emergence of customs of war not to be the result of the aspiration of nations to regulate various manifestations of war, but rather as a consequence of innate feelings of humanity which have never abandoned mankind. Gribovskii regarded that approach to be a "concession to idealism" and suggested that the customs of war were formed over the centuries as the nations mature culturally (pp. 24-25).

Gribovskii also disagreed with Dogel's definition of combatants. In Dogel's view, combatants were "persons who voluntarily or by order of their government assumed the role of representatives of the State in the event they wage war". Dogel therefore denied the need for the prior authorization of the government for the right of combatants to engage in military actions. Gribovskii did not accept this approach in his review: "Thus, the author recognizes the right for any arbitrarily formed detachment with clearly distinguishable marks and lead by a responsible individual to be a legal combatant acting at the discretion of his own risk and con-

Russia in the First Half of the Reign of Empress Catherine the Great: Historico-Legal Study] (Spb., 1901).

[58] Gribovskii, рец. на кн. М. Догель, Юридическое положение личности во время сухопутной войны. Комбатанты. Казань, 1894 [review of M. Dogel, Legal Status of the Individual During War on Land. Combatants. Kazan, 1894], Журнал Юридического общества при Императорского Санкт-Петербургского университета [Journal of the Law Society attached to the Imperial St. Petersburg University], kn. 2 (1895), pp. 20-28.

science". Dogel's argument that otherwise in the event of a change of monarch or government the combatants must each time request authorization to engage in military actions Gribovskii considered to be unfounded. In such situations, Gribovskii said, the principle of legal succession operates (pp. 26-27).

Gribovskii reviewed the third edition of the F. F. Martens treatise on contemporary international law.[59] He boldly declared his intention: "In fatherland literature so far there does not exist a full detailed analysis of this work" (p. 26). Gribovskii first suggested that the world success of the treatise may be attributed to Martens being a humanist; the book is imbued with a faith in the progressive development of human society. Martens himself, said Gribovskii,

> ... firmly believes in the bright future of mankind; he teaches that the entire course of European history is an unstoppable movement forward from the darkness of ignorance, rudeness, narrow egoism to a world of peaceful struggle for reasonably understood personal interests, to friendly partnership in the achievement of common purposes of cultural development (p. 27).

Gribovskii defended Martens against another review by a colleague in the St. Petersburg University, one which engaged in "unforgivable attacks". The occasion for the "attacks" was the position Martens took with respect to the subjects of international law. Korkunov had reproached Martens by saying it was incomprehensible how private individuals could be subjects of international law. Martens avoided this by using, said Korkunov, "terms which he fabricated": he recognized only States as subjects of international law, rulers as subjects of law in international relations, and, finally, private individuals as subjects of law in the domain of international communion. But Martens did not elucidate the technical differences between the terms he invented and therefore, Korkunov believed, the distinctions he drew did violence to the Russian language (p. 28).

Gribovskii called Korkunov's allegations a "strange spectacle", his conclusions being based on a fleeting acquaintance with the treatise, "hasty", because Martens nowhere called private individuals subjects of international law. Martens wrote that "States, always being the sole subjects of international law, nonetheless in certain instances allow together with themselves the existence in international relations of private individuals, persons, corporations, and so on".

In defense of Martens' position concerning the legal personality of private individuals, Gribovskii made the following arguments:

> First, individuals or corporations are subjects of well-known rights on fatherland territory, and as such they must enjoy defense not only in the motherland, but beyond the limits thereof. Are the said private individuals in a position to defend their right by their own efforts in a foreign country or with respect to it? Of course not ... The fact is that a State fights for a right outside its territory, respect for the individual, freedom of industrial

[59] Gribovskii, review of F. F. Martens, Современное международное право цивилизованных народов [Contemporary International Law of Civilized Nations. 2 vols. Spb., 1895], Журнал Юридического общества при Императорском Санкт-Петербургском университете [Journal of the Law Society attached to the Imperial St. Petersburg University], kn. 9 (1896), pp. 26-36.

> turnover, and so on that belongs to it, but to take advantage of the conclusions of the established position it voluntarily gives advantage to another. Of course, the State also gives this right to those who were active in the struggle, that is, are constituent parts thereof, individuals, social unions, estates, and others (pp. 29-30).

In every society, Gribovskii believed, there are positive interests which force States to acquire rights to the benefit of their subjects. Hence postal, telegraph, and monetary unions are born, and the right of free profession of faith, communication by rail, and others are established.

Finally, the last argument advanced by Gribovskii in support of Martens: he used States as the Roman *familia* and the head thereof in Roman law:

> The entire composition of the Roman family: wife, children, and slaves did not have legal capacity themselves; in their legal relations they were always represented by the father; but did he use personally all the rights to things of which he had ownership? Of course, no. *Pater familias* was merely a legal subject; behind him stood a whole series of factual subjects … who had personal requirements and interests (pp. 30-31).

The State as the head of a large family must be concerned for the well-being of its members.

Another issue in this period was the legal status of Finland within the Russian Empire. Gribovskii reacted to these controversies in a review of Messarosh.[60] Messarosh took a hard line with respect to the Russian administration of Finland and favored the suppression of any manifestations of separatism:

(1) Finland is not a State, voluntarily joined to Russia on the basis of a treaty, but a territory conquered by force of Russian arms and in the ownership and State possession of the Russian Empire on the basis of the Fridrikshamn Peace Treaty as a result of the war between Russia and Sweden;

(2) The emperors of Russia never recognized the constitutional laws of Sweden limiting their autocratic power on the territory of Finland;

(3) All institutions of Finland perceived by Finns as attributes of "statehood" have been given by the Russian emperors;

(4) In connection with the spread and strengthening of Finnish separatism, the complete reorganization of the administration of the territory is need and the replacement of distinctive Finnish features of administration by Russian procedures, including the transfer of Finnish schools under Russian administration.

[60] Gribovskii, review of P. I. Messarosh, «Финляндия – государство или русская окранна. Значение особых учреждений финляндской окраины Российской Империи. СПб., 1897» [Finland – State or Russian Region? Significance of Special Institutions of Finnish Region of Russian Empire. Spb., 1897], Журнал Юридического общества при Императорского Санкт-Петербургского университета [Journal of the Law Society attached to the Imperial St. Petersburg University], kn. 1 (1898), pp. 27-31.

Gribovskii concurred that Finland is not an autonomous State in a personal unie with Russia, but a privileged Russian province. He noted that Finland previously had been a province of Sweden with certain rights and after the successful war between Russia and Sweden had passed to Russia with the same rights. But Gribovskii categorically disagreed with accusations made by Messarosh of the entire nation having criminal intentions and actions and with his proposal to carry out severe measures against Finland and the Finnish people. He was persuaded that the authorities of Russia and Finland would find optimal legal means of settling their problems.

In an article honoring the fiftieth birthday of F. F. Martens, his contemporary and colleague, Gribovskii related many biographical facts that deserve further research.[61]

§11.3. *Chair of State Law*

Prince **Zurab Davidovich Avalishvili (Avalov)**. *(28 December 1875 (1874?, 1876?), b. Tbilisi – 21 May 1944, d. Schwarzenfeld, Bavaria, Germany). Specialist in State law, historian, diplomat, journalist, one of founders of National-Democratic Party of Georgia (1917), and an organizer of Tbilisi University.*

Life and career. After graduating in 1893 with the gold medal from the Tbilisi Gymnasium, Avalishvili enrolled at the Law Faculty of St. Petersburg University, completing the degree in 1898 with the gold medal of the Faculty. He chose to remain to prepare for the professoriate, from 1 November 1898 at the Chair of Civil Law, and from 1 December 1899 to 1 January 1904 at the Chair of State Law.[62]

When preparing his magister dissertation, Avalishvili published a scholarly work on the accession of Georgia to Russia.[63] While pursuing his studies at the University, Avalishvili began to use a shortened version of his surname: Avalov; it appears on his books and articles. From 1901 to 1903 he was sent abroad

[61] Gribovskii, «Юбилей профессора Ф. Ф. Мартенса» [Jubilee of Professor F. F. Martens], Журнал Юридического общества при Императорском Санкт-Петербургском университете [Journal of the Law Society attached to the Imperial St. Petersburg University], kn. 2 (1896), pp. 41-45.

[62] ЦГИА СПб., fond 14, opis 2, file 1414.

[63] Z. Avalov, Присоединение Грузии к России [Accession of Georgia to Russia] (Spb., 1901; 2d ed.; 1906; reprint ed., New York, 1981; Spb., 2009).

by the University for postgraduate studies and attended lectures at the Sorbonne, in Paris.

On 24 May 1906 Avalishvili defended his magister dissertation on the topic "Decentralization and Self-Government in France: Parliamentary Assemblies from the Reform of Bonaparte to Our Days. A Political Study".[64] He was thereupon appointed privat-docent at the Chair of State Law of St. Petersburg University and assisted Professor Korkunov with the sixth edition of the treatise on Russian State law, his contributions duly noted on the book.[65] According to the official University report, in 1908 Avalishvili failed to attend classes without a justifiable excuse.[66]

In 1909 Avalishvili was invited to St. Petersburg Polytechnic Institute as a professor and Head of the Chair of Administrative Law. He returned to St. Petersburg University for two semesters from 1 July 1912 as privat-docent at the Chair of Administrative Law, where he gave a course on the "State Law of Austria". From 1912 to 1917 he served as a legal advisor to the Ministry of Finances of Russia. In St. Petersburg he was elected to the Board of the Law Society attached to St. Petersburg University.

By Edict of the Provisional Government of 5 May 1917 he was appointed to the Ruling Senate with effect from 1 May 1917.[67]

Emigration. On 28 March 1918 Avalishvili left Russia for Georgia and immediately become involved in Georgian domestic politics. A leader of the National-Democratic Party of Georgia, he also played a major part in founding the Tbilisi University, opened in February 1918. He lectured there from 1918 to 1921.

Upon arrival in Georgia, he became the chief advisor on foreign policy to the Government of Georgia and helped chart the overall foreign policy orientation of the country. He represented Georgia at the Paris Peace Conference in 1919 as a member of the official Georgian delegation. In 1921 he helped draft the Constitution of the Georgian Democratic Republic. However, the political situation became such that he moved on to Paris that same year, and from 1940, to Germany.

While in Paris, Avalishvili published in the Russian language a volume of articles and memoirs.[68] In Munich, Germany, he founded the "Headquarters of the

64 Avalov, Децентрализация и самоуправление во Франции: департаментские собрания от реформы Бонапарта до наших дней: политическое исследование [Decentralization and Self-Government in France: Parliamentary Assemblies from the Reform of Bonaparte to Our Days. A Political Study] (Spb., 1905).

65 N. M. Korkunov, Русское государственное право [Russian State Law], ed. Z. D. Avalov, et al. (6th ed.; 1908).

66 Отчет о состоянии и деятельности Императорского С.-Петербургского университета за 1908 год [Report on the State and Activity of Imperial St. Petersburg University for 1908] (Spb., 1909), p. 73.

67 See N. A. Murzanov, Словарь русских сенаторов 1711-1917 гг. Материалы для биографий [Dictionary of Russian Senators 1711-1917. Materials for Biographies] (Spb., 2011), p. 19. He is entered under the surname "Avalov" in the Senate directory.

68 Z. D. Avalishvili, Независимость Грузии в международной политике 1918-1921 гг. [Inde-

Georgian Union" whose purpose was to liberate Georgia from "Soviet imperial dominance". During 1942 he took part in the formation of the "Anti-Bolshevik League" and the "Union of Georgian Traditionalists".

Avalishvili died at Schwarzfeld, in Bavaria, Germany, on 21 May 1944. In 1993 his remains were repatriated to Georgia and placed in the Didube Pantheon in Tbilisi.

International legal views. Avalishvili set out his international legal views in the two aforementioned works. In the preface to his study on the accession of Georgia to Russia, he observed: "The accession of Georgia to Russia was a political event of first importance ... Russia had no economic interests in Georgia and could not involve it in types of 'rectification of boundaries', but Georgia needed the assistance of Russia and ... sought a more local unification" (pp. iii-iv). He stressed that the "idea of accession belongs to Georgia, to its Tsars".

When considering the history of the relations of the Russian State with the Georgian tsars, Avalishvili analyzed the treaties and other legal documents regulating these relations: the 1724 Russo-Turkish treaty, the 1783 Georgian-Russian treaty, diplomatic notes, powers to conduct inter-State negotiations between Georgia and Russia, the 1801 Manifesto on the accession of Georgia to Russia, and others. On the whole, Avalishvili considered the legal aspects of Georgian accession to be positive. He drew up a draft Act on the Independence of Georgia which, following minor amendments, was adopted on 26 May 1918 at an extraordinary Congress of the National Council of Georgia. A Georgian patriot, he upheld the right of the Georgian nation to sovereignty.

In 1920 he sent a special Note to the Supreme Council of the Entente substantiating the case for including native Georgian lands within the western environs of Georgia. These lands, he argued, rightly belonged to Georgia and not to Turkey. The issue was resolved in favor of Georgia.

His second book, published in Paris, contained an account of his participation in the legal preparation of the Georgian Declaration of Independence and the diplomatic negotiations between Georgia and Russia, Turkey, Germany, Ukraine,[69] and other States.

pendence of Georgia in International Politics 1918-1921] (Paris, 1924; reprint ed.; New York, 1982).

69 See on Georgian consular relations in these years T. Korotkyi and A. Khevtsurian, "Island of Hope in the Vortex of Revolution: The Georgian Consul General in Odessa: 1918-1919", *Jus Gentium: Journal of International Legal History*, IV (2019), pp. 95-115.

Vladimir Matveevich Gessen *(also Wolf Munishevich). (13 April 1868, b. Odessa – 1(14) January 1920, d. Ivanovo-Voznesensk). Specialist in State law and international law, noted political figure. Senator. State counsellor. Talented publicist and poet.*[70]

Life and career. Sources vary with respect to details of Gessen's life. This account relies principally upon archival sources.[71] Gessen graduated from the Nikolaev Gymnasium in Odessa and, in 1891, from the Law Faculty of Novorossiisk University with a first-class degree. He then spent three years abroad. In Germany he attended lectures and prepared for the magister examinations; in the Austro-Hungarian Empire he worked at the Russian consulate in Budapest. Upon returning to Odessa, he was appointed privat-docent at Novorossiisk University.

In 1896 he removed to St. Petersburg. After passing the magister examination in State law, he was appointed privat-docent in State law at St. Petersburg University, where he offered a course on the "General Doctrine on the State".[72] In parallel, he became in 1899 a non-established lecturer at the Alexander Military Law Academy; in 1901 – a lecturer at the Alexander Lycée; in 1902 – docent at the Chair of State Law of the Polytechnic Institute.

The Ministry of Justice hired Gessen in the position of junior clerk of the Second Department, where he served from 1899 to 1902. He represented the Ministry of Justice as a member of the Russian delegation at the First Peace Conference in The Hague in 1899 and published an article on the occasion.[73]

From 1902 to 1912 he was privat-docent at the Chair of Police Law at the University.

[70] See V. M. Gessen, Желтые листья: стихотворения [Yellow Leaves: Verses] (Spb., 1911). César Antonovich Cui (1835-1918) and Vladimir Edouardovich Den (1867-1933) wrote several works for choir and romances based on Gessen's poems.

[71] ЦГИА СПб., fond 14, opis 2, file 1064. Also see Starodubtsev, note 3 above, pp. 13, 16, 17, 25, 41, 93-94; A. S. Okatova, Учение В. М. Гессена о государстве [V. M. Gessen's Doctrine on the State] (Tambov, 2009) (diss. kand. iurid. nauk).

[72] ЦГИА СПб., fond 14, opis 2, file 1064.

[73] Gessen, О значении Гаагской конференции [On the Significance of the Hague Conference], Журнал Министерства юстиции [Journal of the Ministry of Justice], no. 3(2) (1900), pp. 55-109. For the quality of his work at The Hague during the Conference, Gessen was awarded the Order of Orange-Nassau by the Queen of The Netherlands, a foreign decoration the Emperor of Russia was pleased to allow Gessen to accept. ЦГА СПб., fond 2998, opis 1, file 509, l. 2ob.

One of the founders and co-editor of the authoritative legal newspaper of a liberal bent, Право [Law], he contributed many articles and served as co-editor of the journal Вестник права [Herald of Law], being no less active on that law review. On matters of law and legal policy, he became one of Russia's most influential publicists.

Gessen was involved in the protests against the slaughter of the participants in the demonstration of 4 March 1901 at Petersburg; on 28 April 1906 he was tried for publishing an issue of Право [Law] containing anti-governmental materials. He published in 1906 a volume devoted to autonomy, federation, and the nationality question.[74]

The year 1910 was auspicious for Gessen. On 15 February and 22 March respectively he was appointed professor *extraordinarius* by the Alexander Lycée and the Polytechnic Institute. On 13 December 1910 Gessen defended his magister dissertation and was awarded the degree of magister of State law. The official opponents were Professors I. A. Ivanovskii and M. A. Taube.[75] He ceased his lecturing at St. Petersburg University on 1 July 1912. From then on, his principal place of work was the St. Petersburg Polytechnic Institute as professor and in various years short-term appointments also as professor at the Alexander Military Law Academy, the Alexander Lycée, and the Higher Women's (Bestuzhev) Courses.

On 9 December 1916 Gessen defended his doctoral dissertation at Moscow University on the "Fundamental Principles of Constitutional Law", with success.

Gessen was engaged in Russian political life. Elected in 1908 as a deputy of the II State Duma, where he chaired two committees, he was a member of the Central Committee of the Kadet Party. In his capacity as a Duma deputy, he was involved in drafting several legislative acts relating to basic civil freedoms, especially the inviolability of the individual, repeal of the death penalty, and others. The February 1917 Revolution brought more responsibilities. The Provisional Government appointed Gessen a Senator of the First Department of the Ruling Senate on 3 May, with effect from 1 May 1917, allowing him to retain his position as professor at the Polytechnic Institute and Alexander Lycée. He served as a member of the Special Meeting to draft the Statutes on elections to the Constitutive Assembly, and in October 1917 was elected to the Provisional Council (Pre-Parliament) of the Russian Republic.

The Soviet authorities persecuted Gessen as a member of the Kadet Party; he was dismissed from all the higher educational institutions of Petrograd. In 1918 he was forced to leave Petrograd for the South of Russia. He lived in Rostov-on-Don,

[74] Gessen, Автономия, федерация и национальный вопрос [Autonomy, Federation, and the Nationality Question] (Spb., 1906). Butler Г43 [MH-L]. Also see Yoshiro Ikeda, "Toward an Empire of Republics: Transformation of Russia in the Age of Total War, Revolution, and Nationalism", in Tomohiko Uyama (ed.), *Comparing Modern Empires: Imperial Rule and Decolonization in the Changing World Order* (Tokyo, 2018), pp. 119-146.

[75] See Gessen, Подданство, его установление и прекращение [Subjecthood, Establishment and Termination Thereof] (Spb., 1909). Butler Г59. The defense was reported in Право [Law], no. 51 (1909), cols. 2879-2882.

and then returned to Petrograd. During 1919 he worked as a professor at the Chair of State Law at the I Petrograd University.[76]

According to the Plan for lecturing in the 1919-1920 academic year confirmed on 13 October 1919 at a session of the Politico-Legal Section of the Faculty of Social Sciences of the University, Gessen was to lecture on the following subjects: "Fundamental Principles of the State System of Contemporary Capitalist States" and the "Public Law of Citizens".[77] The following day the Politico-Legal Section adopted a decree to recommend to the Faculty of Social Sciences to confer on Gessen the title of professor on the basis of his magister degree.[78]

At the invitation of the Rectorate of the newly-formed Ivanovo-Voznesensk Polytechnic Institute – created in 1918 on the base of the evacuated Riga Polytechnic Institute, Gessen moved to that locality, having accepted the post of professor in the socio-economic faculty to teach a course on State law. At the Institute of Public Education in Ivanovo-Voznesensk, he also taught a course on "State Law' and a new subject – the "History of Public Education in Russia".

His life ended tragically. Sent by the Rector of the Institute to Nizhnii Novgorod to prepare an inventory of the property of the Riga Polytechnic Institute stored in railway cars, Gessen fell ill with spotted fever (typhus); upon his return to Ivanovo-Voznesensk he died on 14 January 1920 at the age of 52 from heart complications. He was buried within a fenced enclosure of the Exaltation of the Cross Church in Ivanovo-Voznesensk; by decision in 1932 of the Ivanovo Regional Executive Committee that church and its graveyard were demolished. At present, the site is Revolution Square with a monument to the revolutionary events from 1905 to 1907.

International legal views. Although Gessen was primarily a professor of State law, he did render services to the field of international law. His first contribution to legal scholarship was an article on peace, written in a pacifist vein.[79] Four years later he was inspired to write again on the same topic.[80] In both pieces Gessen condemned war and the concomitant enormous losses and destruction; exploring in detail the history of the idea of perpetual peace and contemporary ways of achieving this.

Gessen believed that the idea of peace was stronger than military aspirations; with each year the peace movement gathered more adherents. An example was the proliferation of peace societies throughout the world: "If all members of peace societies scattered throughout the world were to assemble together, they would comprise a mighty 'army of peace' exceeding the numbers of their many awesome and

[76] ОА СПбГУ., fond 1, opis 1, file 141, l. 14.

[77] ЦГА СПб., fond 7240, opis 14, file 85.

[78] ЦГА СПб., fond 7240, opis 14, file 85, l. 32.

[79] Gessen, «О мире» [On Peace], Вестник Российского общества Красного Креста [Herald of the Russian Red Cross Society] (1895).

[80] Gessen, «О вечном мире» [On Perpetual Peace], Журнал Министерства юстиции [Journal of the Ministry of Justice], no. 4 (1899), p. 145-189. Also published as a small monograph, 47 p.

mighty 'armies of war'" (p. 17). A large role, in his view, was being played by the Institute of International Law, founded at Ghent in 1873, which by "promoting the development and codification of international law … thereby renders an invaluable service to the cause of peace" (p. 17).

Gessen had faith in the reason of mankind and in the progress towards peace. Much had been done, he said, in the nineteenth century to create the international legal foundations of peace:

> By its nature international law is hostile to war: *la force prime le droit*. With the development of international law, the number of international cases increases to be settled by legal means; by virtue of the law of the solidarity of social phenomena the time must come when the resolution of even a few cases by means of war proves to be impossible. War suffocates in an atmosphere of law (pp. 34-35).

He had great hopes for the forthcoming 1899 First Hague Peace Conference, called upon, in his view, to lay the legal grounds for a stable peace. He came to an optimistic conclusion:

> An obstinate and arduous struggle has lasted for centuries between law and force. Slowly and gradually pushing force aside, law is capturing ever more and broader spheres of human life. The idea of rights is not a national idea, but a universal idea. In its forward movement, it does not stop, cannot stop, at the boundaries of a State. Already now we are commencing a gradual transition towards international communion from a natural to a legal state; with the completion of this transition the era of war ends and the era of peace begins (pp. 46-47).

Gessen returned to the topic of war and peace in 1915.[81] The causes of the First World War, he believed, should be placed on German militarism. He considered the political and legal aspects of the actions of the belligerent States. Writing in the second year of the War, Gessen was confident that the combined civilized nations would triumph: "War for peace, war for law – the password and slogan of the contemporary Great War … To affirm on a stable foundation of the rule of law is the most important purpose of the contemporary war" (pp. 504-505).

He touched upon aspects of the law of war in an article on war and diplomacy[82] and another on specific unlawful actions of one of the belligerents.[83]

His magister dissertation on what in modern parlance is the law of citizenship but in Imperial Russia was the law governing subjects of the Crown addressed the interface between State law and international law. Grabar regarded it as "one of the

81 Gessen, «Война и право» [War and Law], Вопросы мировой войны: Сборник статей [Questions of World War: Collection of Articles] (Pg., 1915), pp. 484-506.

82 Gessen, «Война и дипломатия» [War and Diplomacy], Право [Law], no. 25 (1915), cols. 1753-1762; no. 26, cols. 1801-1813; no. 27, cols. 1849-1859.

83 Gessen, «Германская армия и право войны» [The German Army and the Law of War], Речь [Speech], nos. 210, 216, 219, 227 (1914).

best works in world literature on the question of citizenship".[84] Gessen constantly turned to issues affecting both municipal and inter-State legal aspects. He considered citizenship to be an institution not only of State law, but also of international law. Gessen distinguished between the concepts of "subject-hood" and "citizenship" from the standpoint of international and of State law. In an absolute monarchy only subjects may be under the authority of the ruler, whereas in constitutional States the relations between the individual and the State authorities are of a dual nature: a citizen being a subject of public rights and duties is under the authority of the State, but insofar as he belongs to a particular State and is subject to norms of law created by that State, he also remains a subject. Gessen emphasized the international legal character of subject-hood:

> The international legal nature of subject-hood determined the character of its regulation; such regulation may not be a matter of the free discretion of an individual State; by its very essence it assumes the existence of a certain complex of international legal norms ensuring a well-known co-ordination of the normative definitions of individual legislation (p. 142).

Gessen explored the differences in the concept and status of subjects and foreigners. He concluded that the doctrine on State law was not in a position to offer a concept of the correlation between being a subject and the concept of being a foreigner. Such a qualification was, he believed, within the realm of international law. The doctrine of State law should receive the international legal concept of subject-hood readymade from international law.

Section V of the book considered the "international principle" in which Gessen explores such complex issues having an international legal dimension as "dual subject-ness" and "statelessness", compulsory uprooting, legal capacity of foreigners as a condition of their naturalization, freedom of expatriation, compulsory deprivation of subject-hood, termination and change of subject-hood, among others (pp. 394-442).

Ivanovskii had a high opinion of Gessen's monograph.[85] Gessen, in his view, unlike the majority of foreign authors in whose works an analysis of positive law dominates, gave attention to theoretical issues in substantiation of the legal nature of citizenship.[86]

In a significant work on the law of prize,[87] Gessen offered an interesting definition:

[84] Grabar, note 13 above, p. 504.

[85] I. A. Ivanovskii, «Новая теория подданства» [New Theory of Subject-Hood], Вестник Европы [Herald of Europe], no. 3 (1910), pp. 354-372.

[86] Also see Eric Lohr, "The Ideal Citizen and the Real Subject in Late Imperial Russia", *Kritika*, V, no. 2 (2006), pp. 173-174; Lohr, *Nationalizing the Russian Empire: The Campaign against Enemy Aliens During World War I* (2003), pp. 168-169, 206-207; Lohr, *Russian Citizenship: From Empire to Soviet Union* (2012).

[87] Gessen, «Очерк призового права» [Survey of Prize Law], Право [Law], no. 35 (1914), cols. 2473-2482; no. 38, cols. 2634-2636.

> By the law of prize is understood the aggregate of norms regulating the right of capture and confiscation of private, enemy, or neutral property belonging to a State during naval warfare – ships and their cargoes on the high seas or in the territorial waters of the belligerent powers (p. 2473).

He analyzed in depth the positive treaty and customary norms and doctrinal problems with respect to the concept of the law of prize, the subjects and objects thereof, the operation of prize law in time and space, the boundaries of the territorial and high seas, and the types of prizes (absolute and conditional war booty), detention and confiscation of prize, and others. One of the most controversial issues of the law of prize was determining the nationality of war booty. Gessen took the view that the basic question of the law of prize is to what extent the law of maritime booty extends to instances: (a) when a ship of enemy nationality carries neutral cargoes; and (b) when cargo belonging to enemy subjects is carried on neutral vessels" (col. 2477). Gessen believed that States holding opposite positions on this question could not reach a compromise, and because "the 1909 Convention on the Law of Naval Warfare did not touch this issue at all of who is the owner of the captured cargo" and left this issue open, "the enemy or neutral character of the cargo is determined by the legislation of the State capturing the prize" (col. 2636).

Gessen's publications demonstrate the wide range of his scholarly interests in the field of international law: relations of dependent and independent States;[88] the legal status of foreigners;[89] the influence of naturalization on the family of a foreigner,[90] among others.

Mikhail (Moisei) Borisovich Gorenberg *(1865, b. Poltava Governate – 27 November 1918, d. Petrograd). Specialized in Russian and foreign constitutional law.*

Life and career. Gorenberg graduated in 1882 from the Gymnasium in the City of Poltava, Ukraine and from the Law Faculty of St. Petersburg University in 1886. He remained at the University to prepare for the professoriate at the Chair of State Law and was sent abroad for two years to European universities. Upon his return he was accepted by the University as privat-docent at the Chair of State Law without the defense of a magister dissertation. He served as privat-docent from 1899 to 1917 at the Chair of State Law of the University (in 1905-1906 at the Chair of Finnish Law), where he offered courses on "General State Law"; "State Law of Foreign Powers"; "State Law of Contemporary Federations"; "Finnish Law"; "State Law of England"; and others.

88 Gessen, «Вассальное государство» [Vassal State], in Словарь юридических и государственных наук [Dictionary of Legal and State Sciences] (Spb., 1901), I, cols. 1490-1493.

89 Gessen, «Иностранцы» [Foreigners], in Новый энциклопедический словарь [New Encyclopedic Dictionary] (1914), XIX, cols. 489-492.

90 Gessen, «О влиянии натурализации на семью иностранца» [On the Influence of Naturalization on the Family of a Foreigner], Журнал Министерства юстиции [Journal of the Ministry of Justice], no. 7(2) (1896), pp. 35-58.

From 1894 to 1895 and 1899 to 1917 he acted as a sworn advokat in the St. Petersburg Judicial Chamber district.

International legal views. Although he concentrated solely in his academic life on State law, Gorenberg touched upon issues relating to international law. This was especially true of his principal work on the unie State.[91] Even though Gorenberg stated in the title of his book that he was to examine the ideas of modern German publicists, he in fact undertook a comprehensive comparative analysis of the entire literature on this type of State.

The German nation was chosen to be examined because in Gorenberg's view it demonstrated the vast complexity and distinctive features of forming legal paths, foundations, and forms of combining sovereign States into a new unified single State formation:

> There had to be an infinite number of attempts to unify, the beginnings of which are lost in the depths of German history; there had to be the disappointment of 1848, subsequent reaction, and new plans for reform; finally, the great events of 1866 and 1870, which ended with the formation of the North German Union and the German Empire so that the rest of the country looked with a feeling of contentment on results so costly to achieve and so that the human mind would turn from developing plans for the future to an investigation of the present (p. 17).

Gorenberg was one of the earliest Russian scholars to examine so intensively the legal structure of a State based on federative principles. Of interest to international law is that aspect of Gorenberg's work which explores the prerequisites and circumstances that lead to sovereign States as subjects of international law voluntarily agreeing to limit their own sovereign rights and enter into a union of States while giving up an appreciable extent of their sovereignty. Gorenberg explored a vast range of views, approaches, and theories of German scholars on the nature and essence of sovereignty, the nature of sovereign States, treaty and coercive forms of creating federations, the mutual relations between federal or central authorities and institutions and those of the constituent units, among others. Comparisons were explored with the United States of America and Switzerland.

Gorenberg observed that a unie State is a voluntary combination of sovereign States who have transferred part of their sovereignty to a single union which creates a new State that enters into political and legal relations as a single entity and individual juridical person, being a subject of international law in foreign relations. Historically, he noted, such unie States do not necessarily last forever, but become unitary States, or a confederation.

The relations between the central authorities and the units of "complex" State were addressed by Gorenberg in his article on the conflict that arose between, on one hand, the State Duma and Imperial Government of the Russian Empire and,

[91] M. V. Gorenberg, Теория союзного государства в трудах современных публицистов Германии [Theory of Unie State in Works of Contemporary Publicists of Germany] (Spb., 1891).

on the other, the authorities of the Grand Duchy of Finland.[92] Gorenberg analyzed the normative legal foundation of Finland being part of the Russian Empire and the special character of relations between officials and agencies of the two countries. He demonstrated that although the Grand Duchy was an integral part of the Empire, Russian laws had no preferential force over Finnish laws and, with few exceptions, did not operate on Finnish territory. Rather, they exist and operate in parallel. These observations had implications which were taken into account when adjusting the status of the minister-state secretary.

Aleksandr Dmitrievich Gradovskii *(13(25) December 1841, b. khutor Volchii Valuiskogo uezd, Voronezh Governate (now Volokonovskii District, Belgorod Region) – 6(18) November 1889, d. St. Petersburg). Noted Russian legal scholar and publicist, "creator of the science of Russian State law", major figure in Russian legal doctrine in the nineteenth century.*

Life and career. After graduating from the Second Gymnasium of Kharkov, Gradovskii enrolled at the Law Faculty of Kharkov University and graduated in 1862 with the degree of candidate of laws. He found employment in the Chancellery of governors – from 1863 at Kharkov, and from 1864 at Voronezh. By 1865 he had removed to St. Petersburg, where he undertook to prepare for a lecturing career by himself. He took the magister examinations in 1866 at St. Petersburg University[93] and defended his magister dissertation on State law[94] on the topic "Higher Administration of Russia of the Eighteenth Century and the Procurators-General";[95] his official opponents were Professors Semen Vikentevich Pakhman (1825-1910) and Ivan Efimovich Andreevskii (1831-1891).

Academic appointments ensued. On 10 October 1866 he became privat-docent,[96] and in January 1867 was unanimously elected an established docent and at

[92] Gorenberg, «Запрос о действиях финляндского министра статс-секретаря» [Question on the Actions of the Finnish Minister State Secretary], Право [Law], no. 8 (1908), pp. 417-425.

[93] ЦГИА СПб., fond 14, opis 1, file 6342.

[94] ЦГИА СПб., fond 14, opis 3, file 14131.

[95] A. D. Gradovskii, Высшая администрация России XVIII ст. и генерал-прокуроры [Higher Administration of Russia of the Eighteenth Century and Procurators-General] (Spb., 1866).

[96] ЦГИА СПб., fond 14, opis 1, file 6397.

the age of 25 held the Chair of State Law at St. Petersburg University. He immediately began to lecture on State law. At the same time, he was appointed professor *extraordinarius* at the Alexander Lycée and at the Higher Women's (Bestuzhev) Courses. Shortly after defending his doctoral dissertation in 1868,[97] he was elected professor *extraordinarius* and, a year later, professor *ordinarius*, at St. Petersburg University.[98]

Gradovskii retired from the University on 29 August 1889.[99] On 19 September 1889 the Council of the University elected him an Honorary Member of the University. He was best known in the fields of State law and administrative law, and his career flourished during an era of unprecedented academic freedom in Russia – the 1860-1880s. The bibliography of his works is testimony to a talented and multi-faceted scholar;[100] his collected works were published in nine volumes.[101] Most important was his first treatise in three volumes,[102] followed by a significant contribution to comparative legal studies.[103]

Gradovskii died on 6 November 1889 and was buried at the Lazarev Cemetery in the Alexander Nevsky Monastery; in 1936 his ashes were transferred to the Literary Bridge of the Volkovo Russian Orthodox Cemetery of St. Petersburg. His contributions were so substantial to the development of Russian State and law that he is called by many the "father" of the science of the State.

International legal views. It is not widely known that Gradovskii had an interest in international relations and international law. He published several substantive studies of relevance in his large legacy of publicist articles and topical sketches. Among the matters of discussion in his day were proposals for a "world State", or a "world monarchy" to be managed or governed by a universal world

[97] Gradovskii, История местного управления в России [History of Local Administration in Russia] (Spb., 1868). vol. 1 only.

[98] ЦГИА СПб., fond 14, opis 1, file 6516.

[99] ЦГИА СПб., fond 14, opis 3, file 14271; fond 139, opis 1, file 7664.

[100] «Библиографический указатель трудов А. Д. Градовского» [Bibliographic Index of Works of A. D. Gradovskii], Журнал Министерства юстиции [Journal of the Ministry of Justice], no. 3 (1897), p. 391-409.

[101] Gradovskii, Собрание сочинений [Collected Works], ed. A. A. Shakhmatov, et al. (Spb., 1899-1904). 9 vols.

[102] Gradovskii, Начала русского государственного права [Principles of Russian State Law] (Spb., 1875-1883). 3 vols. Korkunov praised this work as the "first, truly scientific" account of Russian State law; it surpassed all preceding literature. All future textbooks on the subject, he said, would rely on Gradovskii. See Korkunov's article on Gradovskii in Биографический словарь профессоров и преподавателей Императорского Санкт-Петербургского университета за истекшую третью четверть века его существования. 1869-1894 [Biographical Dictionary of Professors and Lecturers of the Imperial St. Petersburg University for the Past Third Quarter its Existence, 1869-1894] (Spb., 1896), p. 211.

[103] Gradovskii, Государственное право важнейших европейских держав. Историческая часть. Лекции, читанные в 1885 году [State Law of Major European Powers. Historical Part. Lectures Delivered in 1885], ed. N. M. Korkunov (Spb., 1895).

authority. The aim was to overcome the existing inter-State and inter-nationality rivalries and wars and to create an interaction of individuals, nations, and peoples without conflicts.

In 1872 Gradovskii produced two works, one on contemporary views on the State and nationality, and the other on the State and nationality, together with analogous pieces in a volume of collected articles.[104] In these articles Gradovskii concluded that the time had come to review notions of the State through the prism of national principles. Of international legal interest was Gradovskii's reaction to the "world State", "national question", and "national-progressive State".

He criticized the ideas and proposals for a "world State" or a "world monarchy" in the context of the national question, which he had studied in depth and which during the second half of the nineteenth century was in the center of public attention and had attracted the interest of legal science. The Greek struggle for independence, the unification of Italy, the unexpectedly rapid amalgamation of the Prussian *lände* into a unified Germany required, in his view, theoretical reflections on the role of the national factor in the fates of individual nations and States and of the world community as a whole.

Gradovskii believed that the principles of "national statehood" and the idea of a "world State" were incompatible. He criticized the view of J. C. Bluntschli, who had denied the significance of national States and regarded the idea of a "world State" as the ideal of human progress. The various schemes for creating a "world State" might be realized only by acts of violence, which in Gradovskii's view would represent an infringement on the freedom and uniqueness of individuals and nationalities and therefore was unacceptable (p. iii).

He understood that for multinational Russia the correlation between the power of the State and the interests of the numerous nationalities within the Empire was an awkward and challenging issue. This inspired him to study the nationality question in the context of contradictory world processes and the study of ideas competing in Russian society of "conservatives", "liberals", westernizers, and Slavophiles. The ideas of "sovereignty" and of the "national" or "multinational" State, "world State", "world government", "universal citizenship", and the like were at the center of the discussion.

Gradovskii devoted considerable attention to the national question, defended the principle the "diversity of national peculiarities", acknowledged the "political autonomy of peoples", and recognized their right to national statehood. He proceeded from the fact national differences in the world are a reality dictated by objective reasons. Therefore, the "diversity of national peculiarities is a fundamental condition of the correct course of world civilization". Such diversity enriches mankind with invaluable experience. But no nation has the right to absolute sway over other nationalities; not one of them possesses a monopoly on truth. Therefore, one need not suppress and soften national distinctions and peculiarities but, on the contrary, one should create conditions for the normal existence and development

104 Gradovskii, Национальный вопрос в истории и литературе (Сборник статей) [The National Question in History and Literature (Collection of Articles)] (Spb., 1873).

of nations. Gradovskii opposed an aggressive foreign policy of States seeking to subject other nations to themselves.

He took the view that political autonomy was an important condition for the development of a nation and people. Given the constant wars and territorial conquests in Europe, Gradovskii attached significance to European powers acquiring freer political forms, the creation of autonomous States, and the affirmation of the principles of equality and development. He recognized the lawfulness of the struggle of peoples for national self-affirmation and welcomed the formation of national States in Greece, Italy, and Germany. On this ideological foundation, Gradovskii supported the theory of the "national-progressive State", underlying which was the principle of internal unity and solidarity uniting governmental and social elements of political nationality, the individual, society, and the State. In his opinion, among the main purposes of any State is an independent foreign policy directed towards the defense of its interests and increase of own prosperity.

Gradovskii was among those early Russian jurists who had begun to support human rights. "Respect for the human individual" is the highest criterion for evaluating the dignity of the State. Therefore, the existing shortcomings of political and social life show, using Gradovskii's words, the following "simple truth": no social and political institutions may develop, or take root, if the human individual is not ensured his elementary rights.

Ignatii Aleksandrovich Ivanovskii *(16 December 1868, b. village of Germanovka, Kyiv Governate (now Obukhovsk District, Kyiv Region) – 1933, d. Leningrad). Specialist in State and international law, Dean of the Law Faculty, St. Petersburg State (Petrograd) University.*

Life and career. Ivanovskii graduated from the Second Kyiv Gymnasium and in 1877 matriculated at the St. Vladimir Kyiv University, completing his degree in 1881. He remained at the University attached to the Chair of International Law to prepare for the professoriate. On 5 November 1882 he was appointed a lecturer at the Chair of International Law of the Imperial Novorossiisk University in Odessa. After defending a dissertation *pro venia legendi* in 1884 on the 1864 Geneva Convention,[105] he was elected privat-docent at the Chair of International Law by the

[105] I. A. Ivanovskii, Женевская конвенция 10-22 августа 1864 г.: Положительный международный закон об участии больных и раненых воинов во время войны [Geneva Convention of 10-22 August 1864: Positive International Law on Participation of Sick and Wounded Fighters During War] (Kyiv, 1884). Butler И16.

Council of Novorossiisk University. He also held a lectureship in the field of political economy at the nearby Odessa Commercial School.

In 1889 Ivanovskii defended a dissertation at Kyiv University for the degree of magister of international law on the topic “Mutual Assistance of States in the Performance of Investigations in Criminal Cases”[106] and was elected professor *extraordinarius* in the same Faculty.[107]

He transferred in 1896 to St. Petersburg University and from 1 July took the post of professor *extraordinarius* at the Chair of State Law.[108] There he taught courses on Russian and foreign State law and lectured as well at the Imperial Alexander Lycée and the Alexander Military Law Academy.[109] With the consent of the University, he acted as the inspector of classes at the Lycée. He was elected to the Institut de droit international in 1896.

From 1899 to 1901 he acted as a tutor on the science of the State to Grand Duke Mikhail Aleksandrovich Romanov (1878-1918), the Heir to the Throne. As of 1 January 1900 Ivanovski became a privy State counsellor, and on 9 November 1900 by ruling of the Governing Senate (together with his wife and three children), he was elevated to the ancestral nobility of the Russian Empire.[110] From the year 1900 he was a member of the Learned Council of the Ministry of Public Enlightenment.

Ivanovskii apparently had no doctorate ambitions; he was content with his magister degree and greatly enjoyed lecturing. He was said to have been “one of the outstanding university lecturers”.[111] Moreover, he supervised several magister students in the fields of State and international law, among them A. L. Sakketti. Ivanovskii was an active member of the Law Society attached to St. Petersburg University and the Russian Group of the International Union of Penal Law.[112] In 1912 he retired from his established post in the University, having completed thirty

[106] I. A. Ivanovskii, Взаимное содействие государств в производстве следствий по делам уголовным [Mutual Assistance of States in Performing Investigations in Criminal Cases] (Odessa, 1889).

[107] L. Iu. Kudinova, «Ивановский Игнатий Александрович» [Ivanovskii, Ignatii Aleksandrovich], Профессора Одесского (Новороссийского) университета: биографический словарь [Professors of Odessa (Novorossiisk) University: Biographical Dictionary] (2d ed.; Odessa, 2005), II, pp. 482-483; K. O. Savchuk, «Івановський Ігнатій Олександрович » [Ivanovskii, Ignatiy Oleksandrovich], in V. N. Denysov and Iu. S. Shemshuchenko (eds.), Енциклопедія міжнародного права [Encyclopedia of International Law] (2014-2019), II (2017), pp. 504-505; Starodubtsev, note 3 above, p. 16.

[108] ЦГИА СПб., fond 14, opis 1, file 9432.

[109] ЦГИА СПб., fond 14, opis 1, file 3645.

[110] ЦГИА СПб., fond 1343, opis 35, file 9969.

[111] See his entry in K. K. Arsenev (ed.), Новый энциклопедический словарь [New Encyclopedic Dictionary], (Spb.-Pg., 1914), XVIII, p. 937.

[112] Русская группа международного союза криминалистов [Russian Group of the International Union of Penal Law] (Spb., 1911), p. 11.

years of service, but remained at the Chair of State Law in a non-established position.[113] In 1908 the title of Distinguished Professor of St. Petersburg University was conferred, and in 1913 the State title of privy counsellor.[114]

In 1905 he played a role in drafting materials of the governmental Commission for preparing the draft law on the founding of the State Duma. He served as Dean of the Law Faculty of Petrograd University, from 15 September 1904 for a term of four years; from 1917 to 1919 he worked[115] as a professor at the Chair of State Law from 1917 to 1919 at the First Petrograd University and from 1918 to 1919 simultaneously as Dean of the Faculty.[116]

According to the "Teaching Plan" for the 1919/20 academic year confirmed at a session of the Politico-Legal Section of the Faculty of Social Sciences on 13 October 1919, Ivanovskii planned to deliver lectures on the "General Doctrine of the State" and "International Law (Introduction and Doctrine on the Structure of an International Union).[117] The Politico-Legal Section of the Faculty of Social Sciences did, however, on 20 October 1919 decree to submit a proposal to the said Faculty on conferring the rank and title of professor, given that Ivanovskii had a magister degree.[118] From May 1923, given his age, Ivanovskii became a supernumerary professor of Petrograd University. He retired from the University in 1924 because the courses he taught were eliminated, but he continued to lecture at the Petrograd Polytechnic University until 1929. He died at Leningrad in 1933 and is buried in Smolensk Russian Orthodox Cemetery.

International legal views. Ivanovskii's early training was in the field of international law. His early works on the 1864 Geneva convention and on international assistance in criminal investigations were discussed above. He set out his views on the nature and substance of international law in his lectures,[119] defining international law as the "aggregate of legal norms determining the mutual relations of powers as autonomous political entities" (p. 6).

His positions initially echoed those of the St. Petersburg School of International Law; that is, of F. F. Martens and his followers. For example, when considering the essence of international law, Ivanovskii perceived it in the harmonious combination of two basic principles: subjective – the idea of the autonomy of separate States; and objective – the idea of the international community as given.

113 ЦГИА СПб., fond 139.

114 See S. V. Volkov, Высшее чиновничество Российской империи. Кратаий словарь [High Officials of the Russian Empire. Concise Dictionary] (Moscow, 2016).

115 ЦГА СПб., fond 7240, opis 14, file 85, l. 1-21. Ivanovskii flatly refused to be a candidate for the post of Chairman of the Politico-Legal Section of the Faculty of Social Sciences. Ibid., l. 21-22.

116 ОА СПбГУ., fond 1, opis 1, file 141, l. 14ob.

117 ЦГА СПб., fond 7240, opis 14, file 85, l. 29ob-30.

118 ЦГА СПб., fond 7240, opis 14, file 85, l. 32.

119 I. A. Ivanovskii, Определение, основные начала, задача и значение международного права. Вступительная лекция [Definition, Basic Principles, Task, and Significance of International Law. Inaugural Lecture] (Odessa, 1884). 14 p. Butler И28.

Even though fate took Ivanovskii to the Chair of State Law at St. Petersburg University, he never lost his interest in international law. During his Petersburg period, Ivanovskii's first contribution to legal scholarship dealt with the application in Russia of foreign judicial decisions in criminal cases.[120] He noted that, unlike the great majority of European jurisdictions, Russian legislation contained no provisions regulating the grounds and procedure for the recognition and enforcement in Russia of foreign criminal judgments. As an example, he cited a decision of the Ruling Senate of Russia of 28 April 1892 in a specific case (the initiation in Vilnius by a Russian investigator of a criminal case against a Russian subject for participation in a forgery in Switzerland of Russian credit securities; this individual had served a three-year term in a Swiss prison). Supporting the decision of the Ruling Senate not to prosecute the individual twice for the commission of the crime on the principle of *non bis in idem*, Ivanovskii disagreed with the "silence of Russian laws" on the issue:

> The Ruling Senate finds that, despite the absence in our law of a categorical provision on the significance of foreign judicial judgments in criminal cases, when there is such a judgment and the guilty person has served the imposed punishment abroad, a new prosecution in Russia for the same act should not occur. From this standpoint, one cannot agree, and the considerations cited by the Senate in support thereof cannot be accepted, for they are inaccurate, contain completely untrue conclusions from incontestable principles, and, finally, give an incorrect interpretation of both laws and international treaties (p. 19).

Ivanovskii published three works and several book reviews which demonstrated the breadth of his knowledge and erudition. His review of V. M. Gessen's monograph on subjecthood, defended by Gessen as a magister dissertation on State law,[121] Ivanovskii considered to be an excellent work: "the question of citizenship is one of the most important in the sciences of State and international law. It has enormous practical and theoretical significance" (p. 354). Gessen's distinctions between "subjects", "citizens", and "foreigners" Ivanovskii considered to be controversial but well argued.

Of interest were his comments on Pilenko's monograph on the systematics of private international law:[122]

> Private international law … is a branch of jurisprudence to a great extent conditioned by the specific nature of both the sphere of regulation of private international law and the functioning thereof: when resolving individual issues from the domain of private international law it is necessary to

[120] Ivanovskii, «О значении в России иностранных судебных приговоров по уголовным делам» [On the Significance in Russia of Foreign Judicial Judgments in Criminal Cases], Право [Law], no. 1 (1898), pp. 16-19; no. 2 (1898), pp. 9-16.

[121] Ivanovskii, «Новая теория подданства» [New Theory of Citizenship], Вестник Европы [Herald of Europe], no. 3 (1910), pp. 354-372.

[122] Ivanovskii, review of A. A. Pilenko, Очерки по систематике частного международного права. Критический этюд [Essays on the Systematics of Private International Law], Журнал Министерства юстиции [Journal of the Ministry of Justice], no. 9 (1911), pp. 282-310.

> reckon with the principle of the independence and autonomy of individual States, members of an international union, on one hand, and with the idea of international communion, with the need to promote the development and legal protection of international civil turnover, on the other (p. 85).

When he prepared the review, Ivanovskii had formulated his own understanding of private international law. Earlier, criticizing Danevskii for a definition of private international law that Ivanovskii considered to be unacceptable,[123] Ivanovskii offered the following definition:

> … private international law is the aggregate of legal norms determining the law of which State and which power should be applied to a particular private law relation which arose in the sphere of international turnover or … is the aggregate of legal norms determining the competence of legislation and agencies of power of individual States with respect to private law relations which arose on the basis of international turnover.[124]

Therefore, when undertaking the review of Pilenko, Ivanovskii was already "armed". Pilenko had structured his study basically on a successive analysis of the principal categories and concepts of the conflicts of law, among them *comitas gentium*, *ordre public*, and *renvoi*. He wrote in his preface that these important concepts and categories of private international law "are set out by the authors without a system, because no concepts are embedded in them". Criticizing Pilenko's attraction to theory, Ivanovskii noted that possibly the "entire dialectic will prove to be merely a game with legal concepts unrealizable in practice". Ivanovskii added that Pilenko's study did not provide a new autonomous systematic or even indicate the path to finding one (pp. 308-309). But all credit to Pilenko, he said, for giving a rather full picture of the state of theory and practice on the issues which the book treated and some fresh thoughts (p. 114).

Grabar wrote of Ivanovskii that his works were distinguished by a punctilious conscientiousness and written from the point of view of a consistent positivist-dogmatist: "his lectures always rich in content and full of scholarly enthusiasm, deeply impressed his listeners; a significant number of contemporary specialists in State law who have made their mark in the literature and the chair were his pupils".[125]

[123] Danevskii defined private international law as a "system of legal norms under the protection of international law applicable to civil-law relations between subjects arising in the sphere of international turnover". See V. P. Danevskii, Пособие к изучению истории и системы международного права [Manual for the Study of the History and System of International Law] (Kharkov, 1892), II, p. 17. Butler Д20.

[124] See Ivanovskii, «Новый курс международного права» [New Course of International Law. Review of Danevskii, note 123 above, in Юридическая летопись [Legal Chronicle], II (1892), p. 292.

[125] Grabar, note 13 above, p. 424.

Baron **Sergei Aleksandrovich Korf** *(also Korff) (19 February 1876, b. St. Petersburg – 8 March 1924, d. Washington D.C., United States). Scholar of State and international law; professor at Russian, Finnish, and American universities.*[126]

Life and career. Educated by home tutoring in early life, at the age of 13 he enrolled at the Imperial School of Jurisprudence, where he graduated with the gold medal in 1898.[127] He was a pupil of F. F. Martens, who taught the course on international law at the Imperial School of Jurisprudence. By special authorization of the Ministry of Public Enlightenment, in 1899 he took the State examinations at the Law Faculty in St. Petersburg University. From 1 February 1900 to 1 January 1903 he was a magister postgraduate at the Chair of State Law of St. Petersburg University and remained there to write his magister dissertation and prepare for the professoriate with a Demidov stipend.[128] As part of his degree program he was sent to Heidelberg University, where he attended the lectures of Georg Jellinek. Upon his return to Russia, he accepted a position at the Ministry of Finances, where he held various positions between 1899 and 1906.[129] From 1899 to 1901 he traveled abroad to Paris, Berlin, and London, and in 1902, on the eve of the Russo-Japanese War, to Manchuria, China, Japan, and the United States.

[126] On Korf, see Starodubtsev, note 3 above, pp. 29, 40, 122, 128-129; K. S. Belskii, «Профессор С. А. Корф – видный русский государствовед, административист и юрист-международник (К 130-летию со дня рождения)» [Professor S. A. Korf – Eminent Russian Specialist on State Law, Administrator, and International Lawyer (On the 130th Anniversary of His Birth)], Государство и право [State and Law], no. 3 (2007), pp. 76-82; W. E. Butler and V. S. Ivanenko, «Барон С. А. Корф: тернистый жизненный путь и творческий вклад ученого-государствоведа в науку международного права (к 100-летию со дня смерти)» [Baron S. A. Korf: Thorny Life Path and Creative Contribution of Constitutional Scholar to the Science of International Law (On the 100th Anniversary of His Death)], Вестник Санкт-Петербургского Университета [Herald of St. Petersburg University], no. 1 (2024).

[127] ЦГИА СПб., fond 355, opis 1, file 1596.

[128] ЦГИА СПб., fond 14, opis 1, file 9465.

[129] For details, see A. V. Pavlov, Научно-педагогическая и политическая деятельность С. А. Корфа (1876-1924) в России и эмиграции [Scientific-Pedagogical and Political Activity of S. A. Korf (1876-1924) in Russia and in Emigration] (Spb., 2006) (diss. kand. iurid. nauk); E. V. Petrov, С. А. Корф (1876-1924): правовед, дипломат, общественный деятель [S. A. Korf (1876-1924): Jurist, Diplomat, Public Figure] (Spb., 2018).

Korf represented the interests of Russia at the VII International Conference of the Red Cross in 1902 held at St. Petersburg, being assistant to the secretary of the Conference; he was a member of the Russian delegation to the 1899 and 1907 Hague Peace Conferences, and organized the work of the Russian Section at the 1904 World's Fair in St. Louis, Missouri. Upon returning from his visits abroad, Korf renewed his postgraduate studies for the magister degree of St. Petersburg University.

On 22 October 1906 he defended a magister dissertation in the field of State law on the nobility and the estate administration thereof.[130] The Russian Revolution of 1905 forced Korf to leave St. Petersburg for Helsinki.[131] In Finland he progressed from being the curator of a Slavic collection at Helsinki University and professor of State law to Governor-General of the country.

From 1905 until 1918 Korf served as a supernumerary lecturer and, from March 1907, as professor of Russian State Law and the History of Russian Law at the Imperial Alexander University in Helsingfors. By instruction of Emperor Nicholas II he was given a special award for lecturing in the amount of 8,000 marks per year.[132] While in Finland, Korf between 1905 and 1907 was a member of an anti-governmental "Committee for Giving Assistance to Needy Russian Political Emigrants" in Finland and signed an Appeal published in the newspapers "To Free Citizens in Free Countries" seeking donations for "freedom fighters" expelled from Russia. His actions generated a severe reaction in Russian governmental circles and in many respects predetermined his future fate: he was disgraced and deprived of his honorary court position of gentleman of the bedchamber.

Apprehensive, not without reason, of academic disgrace after the events following the "Appeal", Korf was forced to seek an appropriate place to defend his doctoral dissertation. He chose Tartu University, where on 5 December 1910 he successfully defended (for four hours) the first volume of a treatise on administrative justice in Russia,[133] becoming one of the leading Russian authorities in this field. From 1 July 1908 to 3 May 1910 he served as privat-docent at the Chair of State Law of St. Petersburg University.

He took an active role in numerous European and international associations, being elected a member of the Association of Comparative Jurisprudence in Berlin in 1911; in 1912 he was elected Executive Secretary of the IX International Con-

[130] Korf, Дворянство и его сословное управление за столетие 1762-1855 годов [The Nobility and Estate Administration Thereof in the Century from 1762 to 1855] (Spb., 1906). The official opponents were Professors I. A. Ivanovskii and V. N. Latkin.

[131] In June 1905 Korf married Aletta Louise van Reypen, a United States citizen and daughter of William K. van Reypen, a Rear Admiral and President of the American Red Cross. Korf had made the acquaintance of the Rear Admiral at an international Red Cross conference in May 1902 at St. Petersburg This marriage played a fateful role in Korf's future after the Russian revolutions in 1917.

[132] See Pavlov, note 129 above, p. 7. The appointment itself and unusual salary raised questions. Korf did not yet have his research degree and, although multilingual, did not speak Finnish – a requirement at the time. See Petrov, note 129 above, pp. 113-114.

[133] Korf, Административная юстиция в России [Administrative Justice in Russia] (Spb. 1910). 2 vols.

ference of the Red Cross in Washington D.C.,[134] and in 1913 he took part in the World Congress of Historical Sciences at London University. In that same year he began to lecture at the Academy of Trade in St. Petersburg.

From 24 April 1915 he was professor at the Petrograd Higher Women's Courses, and in 1916, Professor of International Law at the Petrograd Institute of Higher Commercial Knowledge.

After the February 1917 Revolution, Korf was appointed by the Provisional Government to be the assistant Governor-General and, from October 1917, the acting Governor-General of the Grand Duchy of Finland. He participated in October 1917 in the work of the Special Commission for the Legal Meeting to Draw Up the Draft Basic State Laws" of Russia. Not being sympathetic to the October Revolution and the Soviet Government, on 8 November 1917 – the second day following the Revolution – he officially resigned as Governor-General of Finland.

Emigration. Apprehensive of arrest by the Soviet authorities, during the first half of 1918 he traveled from Finland to Sweden, then in December 1919 to England and France, where he played an active role in the formation of anti-Bolshevik organizations. In Paris he became the Chairman of the "National and Democratic Bloc of Russian Political Organizations Abroad". By August 1919, he was in the United States, where in January 1920 he initiated the formation and headed new anati-Bolshevist structures: a Committee for the rebirth of Russia and the Russian Information Bureau. As the Soviet authorities consolidated their power, Korf recognized the futility of his political efforts and decided to devote himself to scholarly research. In January 1921 he was invited by Georgetown University to lecture on the history of the Slavic world at the recently founded Walsh School of Foreign Service. From May 1921 he was attached to the Department of Political Science at Georgetown, where he offered courses on the History of Russia, Comparative Analysis of State Government; Diplomatic History of Contemporary Europe, and Diplomatic Procedure and Customs. While maintaining his position at Georgetown and lecturing at The Johns Hopkins University, from the end of 1923 he served as a Professor of History at Columbia University. Brown University awarded him an honorary doctorate.

He was a productive scholar. In 1920 he prepared a syllabus for a course on Russian history.[135] A work on Russian foreign relations followed in 1922.[136] A year later he published the N. W. Harris Lectures.[137] He was involved in the early activities that led to the formation of the Hague Academy of International Law and delivered lectures on the history of international law.[138] He joined or was elected

[134] For his Report on the Conference, see Korf, "The Ninth International Red Cross Conference", *American Journal of International Law*, VI (1912), pp. 858-864.

[135] S. A. Korf, *The History of Russia from Earliest Times: A Preliminary Syllabus* (New York, Institute of International Education, 1920). 14 p.

[136] Korf, *Russia's Foreign Relations during the Last Half Century* (New York, 1922).

[137] Korf, *Autocracy and the Russian Revolution* (London, 1923).

[138] Korf, "Introduction à l'histoire du droit international", *Recueil des cours*, I (1925), pp. 1-23; Korf, "An Introduction to the History of International Law", *American Journal of International Law*,

to a number of American learned societies, including the American Society of International Law.

Korf died of a heart attack on 8 March 1924 while at work in the School of Foreign Service at Georgetown University.

International legal views. Korf is best known as a significant Russian legal historian and specialist in State law. Russian federalism was a particular interest from the outset. His international legal views are to be found principally in his works on federalism and in publications specially devoted to international law. In 1908 Korf published a monograph on federalism in which, having regard to the causes of the Russian Revolution of 1905 to 1907, he concluded: "The centuries-old conflicts of the peoples populating Russia may be settled peacefully only pursuant to the great principle of national self-determination, and best of all be satisfied by principles of federalism.[139]

The book addressed the following: colonial federalism; the formation and essence of American federalism; ideas of European federalism; and especially consideration of its future correlation between international communion and the union of States in their self-government; and the purpose and legal construction of federations. Of particular relevance to international law is the section on the "international union of States" in which Korf formulated his position regarding the unification of all States and the organization of an international legal union. In his view, the the development of mankind was proceeding in the direction of unification, in the course of time, of nations and States into an international union combining different States with different degrees of unity standing above individual States (p. 75).

Korf distinguished two organizational forms of such a union: inter-State organizations and supranational organizations. Positive examples, Korf said, already existed. Inter-State unions are created to unify State interests in individual spheres of administration; for example, by creating general courts of free cities (the States of Thuringen, two Mecklenburgs, Lubeck) or a customs union (for example, the customs Union of the German States between 1867 and 1871). International supranational unions are the river commissions on the Rhine (1815) and Danube (1856), the International Telegraph Union (1865), the Universal Postal Union (1874), the International Commission for Weights and Measures (1875), among others (pp. 77-79). Although these organizations "do not have their own executive and judicial organs, nonetheless they bear the ineffaceable imprint of supranational agencies to which the Contracting Powers assign administrative domain" (p. 77). Such a combination of States is fully justified and acceptable because "States combine by means of a treaty without losing own sovereignty; in other words, while retaining all their supreme power and limiting themselves voluntarily only in certain strictly defined domains by treaty" (p. 89). Korf was persuaded: "The further the

XVIII (1924), pp. 246-252.

139 Korf, Федерализм [Federalism] (2d ed.; Pg., 1917), p. 3. Also see Yoshiro Ikeda, "Toward an Empire of Republics: Transformation of Russia in the Age of Total War, Revolution, and Nationalism", in Tomohiko Uyama (ed.), *Comparing Modern Empires: Imperial Rule and Decolonization in the Changing World Order* (Tokyo, 2018), pp. 119-146.

international communion developed, which in our time already is not in a state to do without this kind of united organizations, the more clearly shines the benefit of the existence of these supranational agencies" (p. 78). In the complex period of the dissolution of the former Soviet Union and the search for models of State construction in post-Soviet space, federalist ideas were unexpectedly in fashion. Korf's publications on federalism became part of the dialogue.[140]

Korf's career coincided with major political and territorial changes in Russia and elsewhere – the collapse or dissolution of empires, the formation of new States, new territorial claims and conflicts. Korf concluded that ethnographic principles should underlie these processes: disputed territory should pass to that State whose inhabitants were ethnically, historically, and culturally cohesive: "in the event of honorable relations with one another, neighbors have a magnificent opportunity to precisely determine their own ethnic composition".[141]

Korf left a number of original studies devoted to issues of international law. One result of his visit to Manchuria and China was an article on mixed courts in Manchuria and Shanghai;[142] he was among the first Russian legal scholars to investigate legal aspects of mixed courts in remote territories important to the Russian Empire.

Korf addressed the principle of the equality of States in international law.[143] He concluded that revisions were necessary: even though the principle of equality had been unceremoniously violated by the Great Powers, who were not inclined to see small States as their partners, the principle, however weak, guaranteed a certain autonomy for small States in their relations with the Great Powers. Korf believed that the time had come to "found an international organization, for the historical development of international communion indicates to us clearly that the external form of an organization may be built only on an aristocratic principle". But the small States would agree to such an "aristocratic international organization" under certain conditions. By such conditions Korf understood, first, "reconciliation of the contradiction of the hegemony of the Great Powers with the defense of the rights and autonomy of the small powers"; and second, the management of such an international organization may be assigned to a small State. Only under these conditions may small States renounce the principle of equality and possibly "substitute the political hegemony of the Great Powers with the legal principle of inequality" (pp. 146-147).

140 See Korf, «Возможна ли в России Федерация?» [Is a Federation Possible in Russia?], Современные записки [Contemporary Notes], no. 3 (Paris, 1921), pp. 173-190; reprinted in Новое время [New Times], no. 33 (1991), pp. 40-42.

141 Korf, ibid. (1921), p. 131.

142 Korf, «Железнодорожный смешанный суд в Маньчжурии» [Railway Mixed Court in Manchuria], Право [Law], no. 35 (1903), cols. 2021-2028; no. 36, cols. 2056-2064; Korf, «Смешанный суд в Шанхае» [Mixed Court in Shanghai], Журнал Министерства юстиции [Journal of the Ministry of Justice], no. 10(2) (1903), pp. 93-116.

143 Korf, «Принцып равенства государств в современном международном праве» [The Principle of Equality of States in Contemporary International Law], Известия Министерства иностранных дел [News of the Ministry of Foreign Affairs], kn. 1 (1914), pp. 136-147.

In later years Korf published works on the international legal status of States,[144] colonies,[145] war,[146] aircraft,[147] and others. He supported, for example, the prohibition of the use of aircraft in war and insisted on the complete prohibition of air warfare:

> … it would be disgraceful for people in the twentieth century to introduce the of a new and barbaric means of eradicating the enemy by dropping projectiles from aircraft … we believe in the insistent necessity and duty of cultured mankind to prevent with all its power the introduction of new means of elimination, and the use of aircraft to drop projectiles undoubtedly belongs to these.[148]

He advanced the doubtful thesis of using aircraft for intelligence purposes (pp. 60, 71). Tsimmerman published a critique of Korf's views on air warfare, which he considered to be erroneous and, in practice, unrealistic, especially confining the use of aircraft in war to reconnaissance missions. Tsimmerman observed that an adversary would defend itself from an aircraft by opening fire from the ground, and the pilot would have no choice but to drop projectiles on the adversary in the interests of self-defense.[149]

As the First World War unfolded, Korf condemned the perfidy of the Great Powers, for they had initiated it. Reflecting liberal views pervasive in Russian society[150] and disillusioned by the collapse of the international legal order, Korf substantiated the need for reform on the basis of new international legal principles. In an article on international law in the contemporary war, Korf considered the war to be the outcome of the aspiration of a number of powers to confirm their almightiness as a State, most aggressively demonstrated in the international relations and practices of Germany. In Korf's view, the ideal of international law is the creation of:

144 Ibid.

145 Korf, «Колониальные конференции» [Colonial Conferences], Юридические записки [Legal Notes], no. 4 (1911), pp. 626-689.

146 Korf, «Международное право в современной войне» [International Law in Contemporary War], M. K. Tugan-Baranovskii (ed.), Вопросы мировой войны. Сборник статей [Questions of World War: Collection of Articles] (Spb., 1915), pp. 507-531; Korf, «Английский взгляд на защиту частной собственности на море во время войны» [English View of the Defense of Private Property at Sea During War], Право [Law], no. 26 (1917), cols. 1845-1849.

147 Korf, «Аэропланы в современной войне» [Airplanes in the Contemporary War], Вестник мира [Herald of Peace], no. 1 (1912), pp. 14-15; Korf, «Воздухоплавание» [Air Navigation in International Law], Русская мысль [Russian Thought], no. 12 (1913), pp. 51-72.

148 Korf, note 147 above (1913), pp. 56-57.

149 M. A. Tsimmerman, «Вопрос о воздушной войне в международном праве» [Question of Air Warfare in International Law], Известия Министерства иностранных дел [News of the Ministry of Foreign Affairs], no. 5 (1914), p. 162.

150 See V. V. Shelokhaev and K. A. Solovev, «Российские либералы о Первой мировой войне» [Russian Liberals on the First World War], Новейшая история России [Modern History of Russia], no. 3 (2014), pp. 184-196.

> an international legal order which does not depend on the will of individual participants of communion, which would ensure the growth of international relations in the domain of law in parallel with the colossal development of social and economic relations of cultured nations and would guarantee the new international legal order against external and internal violations, and not only in quiet peacetime, but also in stormy – war.[151]

He emphasized that international law pursues humanitarian purposes relating to the improvement of international relations, aspiring to eliminate violence and other flagrant and mass displays of force (pp. 508-509). Korf believed that war will end with the triumph of reason and peace and considered the tasks of any congress convened to conclude a peace would include the restoration of international law. He made a number of proposals to limit armaments and restrain militarism (pp. 530-531).

Korf was disturbed about enhancing the effectiveness of the institutionalized mechanisms of international law. His views continue to have resonance with respect to modern international organizations.[152] He set out basic principles for the institutionalization of the international community – what he called the principle of aristocracy on condition of guarantees given by the governments of the Great Powers that would defend the rights and interests of small States. Korf linked the creation of such a reliable foundation of international relations with the domestic law of States. The Great Powers, he said, must initially be bound by domestic law, and for this municipal constitutional guarantees were essential.

Many of his ideas and proposals were embodied in the documents of the 1919 Versailles Peace Conference and League of Nations.

Nikolai Mikhailovich Korkunov *(14 April 1853, b. St. Petersburg – 27 November (10 December) 1904, d. Station Udelnaia, St. Petersburg). Specialist in State law, made contributions to the science of international law.*

Life and career. After graduating from the First St. Petersburg Gymnasium, Korkunov matriculated at the Law Faculty of St. Petersburg University in 1870[153] and graduated in 1874 with the degree of candidate of laws and the gold medal for an essay on State law. He remained at the University to prepare for the professoriate. In spring 1876 he passed the magister examinations,[154] but commenced his career as a lecturer in law at the Imperial Alexander Lycée, where he taught the

151 Korf, note 146 above (1915), p. 508.

152 M. A. Pshenichnov, «К вопросу об историко-правовом генезисе гармонизации российского законодательства» [On the Question of the Historical Legal Genesis of the Harmonization of Russian Legislation], Вестник Нижегородской академии МВД России [Herald of the Nizhnii Novgorod Academy of the Ministry of Internal Affairs of Russia], no. 1 (2010), p. 51.

153 ЦГИА СПб., fond 14, opis 3, file 16571; Starodubtsev, note 3 above, pp. 16, 20.

154 ЦГИА СПб., fond 14, opis 1, file 7581.

Encyclopedia of Law.[155] He lectured at that institution for twenty years. In 1878 he was invited to the St. Petersburg University while retaining his position at the Lycée; at the University he was initially appointed a lecturer, from 1884 a privat-docent, and gave the course on Encyclopedia of Law.[156]

In all he held three lecturing positions simultaneously: from 1879 at the University and the Alexander Lycée, and on international law at the Military Law Academy, where he worked until 1896. Comparatively late in his career, in 1893 – long after having achieved an international reputation for his scholarship – Korkunov submitted a magister dissertation to the Iurev University: volume one of his treatise on Russian State Law. The originality of this work was sufficient, by way of exception, to be accepted as a dissertation even though it was a textbook. Following a successful defense Korkunov was awarded the degree of magister of State and international law – Iurev University combining under its Statute the two fields together in a single degree. A year later, at St. Petersburg University, Korkunov defended a doctoral dissertation on the topic "Edict and Law" These two dissertations opened the door to elevation: from 1894 he became professor *extraordinarius* at the Chair of State Law; from 1894 to 1896, secretary of the Law Faculty; from 1896, professor *ordinarius* at the Chair of Encyclopedia and History of the Philosophy of Law. He was involved in editing the biographical dictionary of professors and lecturers at the University for the preceding quarter century.[157]

In State service Korkunov was an aide to the State secretary of the State Council and served on the governmental Commission for the codification of the basic laws of Finland. Talented in many callings as so many of his colleagues, he wrote poetry and shared interests in art and culture.[158]

In the late 1890s Korkunov became gravely ill and resigned in 1898 from all academic posts. He passed away on 27 November (10 December) 1904 at the age of 52 in the Emperor Alexander III Charitable Home near the Udelnaia Railway

[155] ЦГИА СПб., fond 14, opis 1. file 3704.

[156] ЦГИА СПб., fond 14, opis 1, file 7883.

[157] See Биографический словарь профессоров и преподавателей Императорского С.-Петербургского университета за истекшую третью четверть века его существования 1869-1894 [Biographical Dictionary of Professors and Lecturers of Imperial St. Petersburg University for the Past Three Quarters of a Century of its Existence] (Spb., 1896). 2 vols.

[158] Korkunov, Стихи [Verses] (Spb., 1899).

Station; he was buried at the Smolensk Cemetery, but details of the gravesite have been lost.[159]

International legal views. Korkunov's career in the world of legal scholarship began with publications on international law. In 1877 he published his first two articles, both on legal issues that contended with the realities of State practice and international legal doctrine. The first was devoted to privateers, which operated under letters of marque issued by belligerent States to private shipowners allowing them to attack and capture enemy vessels.[160] Korkunov went beyond the narrow topic implied by the title and made certain theoretical generalizations:

> In the field of international law, there is no other sanction for the force of treaties than the reciprocity arising from their advantages and disadvantages. If it is so advantageous for a State to derogate from the performance of treaties previously concluded that these advantages exceed the harm which may occur from retorsion by the other contracting party, there is nothing in force or in law to compel a State to perform such a treaty.[161]

The second addressed the treaty-law guarantees of neutrality, especially important for small States: treaty neutrality is of special significance with respect to small States whose territory is adjacent to a powerful neighbor.[162] He analyzed the factual and legal status of neutrality and the rights and duties of neutral and belligerent States and their subjects.

Korkunov did not lecture on international law at the University; however, he did teach the course at the Alexander Lycée and the Military Law Academy, together with the course on the State law of foreign powers. His lectures on international law were transcribed by the students, edited, repeatedly published in student editions, and acquired a considerable audience.[163] Grabar considered Korkunov's course to be among the best: "It was the most original of the manuals extant, not

159 For a biography of Korkunov, see A. I. Ekimov, Коркунов [Korkunov] (M., 1988). On Korkunov's contributions to legal theory, see O. V. Shapoval, Учение Н. М. Коркунов о праве [Doctrine of N. M. Korkunov on Law] (Krasnodar, 2005) (abstract diss. kand. iurid. nauk); L. S. Zolotareva, Психологическое правопонимание: историко-сравнительный анализ учений Л. И. Петражицкого и Н. М. Коркунова [Psychological Law-Comprehension: Comparative Historical Analysis of the Doctrines of L. I. Petrazhitskii and N. M. Korkunov] (Saratov, 2008) (abstract diss. kand. iurid. nauk); V. P. Horbatenko and K. O. Savchuk, «Коркунов Микола Михайлович», in V. N. Denysov note 107 above, II (2017), pp. 799-801.

160 Korkunov, «О каперах» [On Privateers], Журнал гражданского и уголовного права [Journal of Civil and Criminal Law], no. 1 (1877), pp. 108-156.

161 Ibid., p. 155.

162 Korkunov, «Юридическое положение нейтральных» [Legal Status of Neutrals], Журнал гражданского и уголовного права [Journal of Civil and Criminal Law], no. 4 (1877), p. 108.

163 See Korkunov, Лекции по международному праву, читанные в I-м классе Императорского Александровского лицея 1883/4 года [Lectures on International Law Delivered to the I Class of the Imperial Alexander Lycée in 1883/4] (Spb., 1885) 260 p.; Korkunov, Международное право. Лекции, читанные в Военно-юридической академии [International Law. Lectures Delivered at the Military Law Academy] (Spb., 1886). 334 p.

only Russian but also foreign".[164] Another specialist has said that Korkunov's work "bears the clear imprint of his individuality".[165] According to Grabar, Korkunov rendered "greater service to international law than many of the internationalists *pur sang*",[166] although many of his views were received with diffidence by international lawyers.

His theoretical legacy was fundamental and became classical for the general theory of law and the branches of that science. Korkunov took the view, for example, that the essence of law is embodied in real social relations; it establishes the rights and duties of subjects of these relations and thereby creates "orders of social relations". Any attempt to scientifically define the law by its content leads to the establishment of definitions indicating not what any existing law (whatever its ontological status) is in reality, but what it should be in someone's subjective view. Instead, the definitions of law merely contemplate the ideal of its future development, which in form are arbitrary and in content ideological.[167] Korkunov was convinced that law was created in order to achieve common purposes; law "merely determines the framework for the realization of diverse interests which comprise the content of social life".[168] The principal purpose of law is to demarcate the social interests and ensure their joint existence. The significance of law is that it makes subjects aware of the proper order of social relations (p. 227).

Thus, Korkunov, seeking to ascertain the legal nature and purpose of international law, offered an original definition of international law: the doctrine concerning a complicated form of the protection of social relations through the joint activity of several State powers". Korkunov thereby robbed international law of its basic content – the political relations between States.[169]

Korkunov was convinced that the jurist is obliged to research only the real phenomena of legal reality, to study law as it was lived, law in movement, and not fabricate it by structuring some unreal legal constructions. He criticized the science of international law: the existing constructions of international law are a blind imitation of obsolete constructions of private law formed during an era when natural law was dominant. International law should be cleansed of its ancient scholastic dust.[170]

He criticized the doctrine on the basic rights of States when he analyzed the essence of international law. The target was the still powerful school of natural law.

164 Grabar, note 13 above, p. 465.

165 A. V. Poliakov, «Государственно-правовое учение Н. М. Коркунова» [State-Law Doctrine of N. M. Korkunov], Kodeks info., no. 5 (2002), p. 117.

166 Grabar, note 13 above, p. 440.

167 Poliakov, note 165 above.

168 Korkunov, Лекции по общей теории права [Lectures on the General Theory of Law] (reprint ed.; Spb., 2003), p. 36.

169 Grabar, note 13 above, p. 478.

170 Korkunov, «Международное право и его система» [International Law and the System Thereof], Юридическая летопись [Legal Chronicle], no. 10 (1891), pp. 232, 251.

In his view, the "remnants of long obsolete theories somehow reign in other legal sciences". Therefore, he put the question: "why not liberate international law from the scholastic rubbish which encumbers it?"[171]

As for the State in international relations, Korkunov affirmed the right of a State to self-preservation and the concomitant duty to respect the inviolability of other States, the right of a State to independence and the concomitant duty of non-interference in the internal affairs of other States, the right of a State to equality and other basic rights – all these were questions, he said, of fact and not law, and therefore do not lend themselves to legal regulation and cannot be regarded as legally mediated. And, he added, many factors in international life are beyond legal substantiation: "A particular State exists, of course, not because the right to existence is recognized, but because it exists" (p. 256).

One cannot, for example, regulate legally the interference or non-interference in the affairs of States. From an analysis of international facts Korkunov drew the concept of admissible interference in the internal affairs of States. In his view, "to refrain from interference in the affairs of other States would mean to remain a non-participating witness to the most terrible violence ..." (pp. 256-257). Therefore, he acknowledged a definition of the lawfulness of war for the purposes of compelling another State to perform obligations placed on it by treaties or by customary norms of international law (p. 255). On the other hand, he opposed attempts to legally regulate the resolution of political disputes between States, interference, war, and neutrality. These were, he stressed, facts to which norms of law were not or should not be applicable.

His radical views on international law generated objections on the part of those adherents of the dominant orientation, as did his original approach to State law. Korkunov reduced international law to international administrative, criminal, and civil law. He addressed such fundamental issues of international law as the correlation between principles of international legal capacity and sovereignty, international communion, and the international protection of rights. In an article on international criminal law[172] he raised basic issues. His views were affected by the level of cooperation between States on criminal matters, and there was no thought of creating a supranational international criminal court. In his opinion the State itself was capable of effectively combatting crimes having an international character: "only the State as a participant of international communion should ... protect by its punitive power all the rights which have received international recognition".

171 Korkunov, «Лекции по международному праву профессора Н. М. Коркунова, читанные в Военно-юридической академии в 1883-1884 гг.» [Lectures on International Law of Professor N. M. Korkunov delivered at the Military Law Academy in 1883-1884], in Золотой фонд российской науки международного права [Golden Fund of the Russian Science of International Law (M., 2007),

172 Korkunov, «Опыт конструкции международного уголовного права» [Attempt at Construction of International Criminal Law], Журнал гражданского и уголовного права [Journal of Civil and Criminal Law], no. 1 (1889), pp. 106-142. Butler K132.

He criticized the system of international law as unsatisfactory because many issues of international law do not relate to the law of peace or to the law of war.[173] Therefore, he offered his own system of international law, dividing it into two parts and four basic sections: General Part (international protection of rights) and Special Part (right of foreigners, right of international communion, right of war).[174] Korkunov included in the Special Part the so-called private international law, the basis of which was the law of foreigners. He considered private international law to be a natural addition to civil and criminal law within the national legal systems of States.

Korkunov could not fail to consider such issues as the effectiveness of international law and guarantees of States to ensure compliance with its norms and principles. He acknowledged that the protection and defense of rights in relations between States differed from the system within a State. International law operates in difficult and particular circumstances and many political, military, economic, and cultural factors are relevant. This led Korkunov to conclude: "The international protection of law is less reliable precisely because it depends upon a large number of factors" (p. 49).

Maksim Maksimovich Kovalevskii *(27 August 1851, b. Dvurechnyi Kut, Kharkov Governate – 23 March 1916, d. Petrograd). Jurist, historian, ethnographer, sociologist, comparative lawyer; associate member (from 1899), academician (from 1914) of the Imperial St. Petersburg Academy of Sciences; member of foreign academies of sciences and institutes. First professional sociologist in Russia.*

Life and career. After graduating from the Third Kharkov Gymnasium in 1868, Kovalevskii enrolled at the Law Faculty of Kharkov University, where he completed his course of study in 1872 with the degree of candidate of laws and remained at the Chair of State Law of European Powers to prepare for the professoriate. From 1872 to 1876 he continued his studies abroad in preparation for the magister examination on State law and international law, first in Berlin and then in Paris. In France he attended lectures at the College de France, École libre des sciences politiques, and the École des chartres; in London he undertook research at The British Museum and the Public Record Office.

In 1876 he joined Moscow University. After passing his magister examinations and defending, in 1877, a magister dissertation on the "History of Police Administration (Security Police) and Police Court in English Counties from Ancient

[173] Korkunov, note 163 above, p. 13.

[174] Ibid., p. 48.

Times to the Death of Edward III",[175] he was appointed to the Chair of State Law and Comparative History of Law. This was followed in 1880 by the defense of a doctoral dissertation, "The Social Structure of England at the End of the Middle Ages", whereupon he was appointed professor *ordinarius*.

In his lectures Kovalevskii made the case for reforms in Russia on the basis of the priority of human values and the freedom of the individual. Following the entry into force of the 1886 University Statute, he was dismissed in 1887 from Moscow University by instruction of the Minister of Public Enlightenment "for a negative attitude towards the State system of Russia". For eighteen years Kovalevskii lived in forced emigration, principally in France (where he owned a villa at Bouleaux, not far from Nice); he had a command of English, French, German, Italian, and a number of other European languages, was involved in scientific, pedagogical, and social activity, lectured at universities in Europe and the United States, and was in touch with leading figures throughout the world, including Karl Marx and Friedrich Engels. He published widely on legal history and sociology; in 1895 he was elected vice-chairman (and in 1907, chairman) of the International Sociological Institute in Paris, where he became one of the organizers of the École russe des hautes études de sociales de Paris.

The revolutionary events of 1905 to 1906 in Russia enabled Kovalevskii to return. On this occasion he chose to live in St. Petersburg. In 1905 he was appointed to the Chair of Political Economy at the St. Petersburg Polytechnic Institute, and from the end of 1905, professor of State Law at the Institute.[176] From 1906 to 1916 Kovalevskii was professor *ordinarius* of State Law at St. Petersburg University.[177] There he lectured on general constitutional law, the constitutional law of foreign powers, and the history of State institutions. From 1907 to 1914 he was chairman of the Professorial Disciplinary Court of the University, and from 1914, Chairman of the Law Society attached to the University.

In parallel with his work at the University, Kovalevskii was among the founders in 1907 of the Psychoneurological Institute, where he created and headed the first Chair of Sociology in Russia. From 1910 he was Dean of the Law Faculty. He succeeded in St. Petersburg in forming his own school of sociology; his works in this field are considered to be the highest achievement of Russian sociological thought in the early twentieth century.

From 1910 to 1911 he headed the Higher Courses of P. F. Lesgaft and, in parallel, continued to work at the Polytechnic Institute and the Higher Women's (Bestuzhev) Courses.

[175] M. M. Kovalevskii, История полицейской администрации (полиции безопасности) и полицейского суда в английских графствах с древнейших времен до смерти Эдуарда III: К вопросу о возникновении местного самоуправления в Англии [History of Police Administration (Security Police) and Police Court in English Counties from Ancient Times to the Death of Edward III: On the Question of the Origin of Local Self-Government in England] (Prague, 1877).

[176] ЦГИА СПб., fond 478, opis 23, file 139.

[177] ЦГИА СПб., fond 14, opis 1, file 10024.

Upon his return to his homeland, Kovalevskii became politically active at once as a founder of a Party of democratic reforms which demanded cardinal changes in the socio-economic and political system of Russia. Later he joined the Progressive Party, founded in 1912, and a member of its Central Committee. He was elected in 1906 to the I State Duma from the Kharkov Governate, and in 1907 became a member of the State Council (the upper chamber of the Russian parliament) from the Academy of Sciences and universities of Russia, where he worked on the Commission of Legislative Proposals. In July 1906 he headed the first delegation of the State Duma to the XIV Congress of the Inter-Parliamentary Union in London, becoming in due course a member of the Executive Council of the Union.

During 1906 to 1907, Kovalevskii published the journal Страна [Country], and from 1909 until his death was the publisher, editor, and a leading publicist of the influential liberal journal Вестник Европы [Herald of Europe]. In December 1909 he became the head of the newly-created St. Petersburg Peace Society – which existed until 1915 as a division of the international pacifist society "Peace", with its own publication, the Вестник мира [Herald of Peace], issued monthly from 1912 to 1914. In 1912 he was elected vice-president of the XIX Universal Peace Congress in Geneva, and in that same year nominated for the Nobel Prize by the Russian Inter-Parliamentary Group for Assistance in Spreading Peace and Humanism.

He held leadership positions in other scientific, philanthropic, and pacifist organizations, among them the Russian Peace Society, the Society for Slavic Scientific Unity, the English Society of Friends of Russian Freedom, and the American Society of Friends of Russian Freedom. The United Kingdom selected Kovalevskii as an arbitrator in a dispute with the United States.[178]

The outbreak of the First World War found Kovalevskii at a Carlsbad resort. As a well-known subject of the Russian Empire, he was interned by the Austro-Hungarians, but thanks to a well-orchestrated international protest and the petition of influential friends he was released after seven months. He returned to Russia via Romania in February 1915 and immediately took up his active scientific and socio-political life.

The years of exhausting labor had undermined his health. He died on 23 March 1916, age 65, and was buried at the Nikolsk Cemetery at the Alexander Nevsky Monastery. The first sociological society in Russia, initiated by him, but formed only after his death was re-constituted in the Russian Federation in 1993 under the name "Kovalevskii Sociological Society".

International legal views (Petersburg-Petrograd Period). A productive scholar, Kovalevskii left a bibliography of 677 publications which is probably not complete. Issues of international relations and international law figure among them. Most often Kovalevskii addressed international legal issues in his studies of historical, sociological, and political distinctive features of the development of society, State, law, and relations between peoples and States or peace and war, and the

[178] Отчет о состоянии и деятельности Императорского Петроградского университета за весеннее полугодие 1916 г. [Report on the State and Activity of Imperial Petrograd University for the Spring Semester of 1916] (Spb., 1916), pp. 28-34.

future of mankind.[179] Several dealt expressly with international law, two of which date from his pre-Petersburg period[180] and one from his time in St. Petersburg.[181]

Kovalevskii approached issues of international relations and international law from humanist and pacifist positions based on his theories of sociological factors and doctrines concerning a peace-making environment, solidarity, and progress. Relying on his doctrine, Kovalevskii maintained that any group in the world of fauna or the human world "is primarily a peace-making environment from which elements of struggle have been eliminated and their place taken by solidarity or the creation of a commonality of interests and mutual dependence".[182] Mankind, experiencing further social development, progress and a deepening solidarity, has moved from alliances of nomadic hordes, through kinship organizations and unseparated families to tribal federations which over time formed "one political whole – the State", and States, in turn, formed a more complex social structure – a universal community of States. Regulators of social relations such as morality, religion, and law emerged in parallel on the basis of these principles of peace-making and solidarity.

Under the impact of inter-tribal and international religions, military conquests, and international trade, the sphere of solidary encompassed all peoples and States. In an article on progress Kovalevskii demonstrated this socio-political progress of "peace-making and solidarity" by using the example of European nations and States: thanks to general Christian values, they formed a political union which, although amorphous, took the form of the Holy Roman Empire. The next step in the development of solidarity was connected, in Kovalevskii's perception, with the decline of the feudal system and Christian (Catholic) unity. During this period, the principle of solidarity manifested itself "in the creation of political bodies from the scattered principalities and city republics, a united commonality of language and nationality, economic interests, and a readiness for a common political life".[183]

In the course of historical progress with the decline of the Holy Roman Empire, "concern for the maintenance of international amity and peace fell on allianc-

179 M. M. Kovalevskii, «Мир» [Peace], Запросы жизни [Queries of Life], no. 11 (1911), pp. 4-5; Kovalevskii, «Освободительное движение на Балканах» [Liberation Movement in the Balkans], Вестник Европы [Herald of Europe], kn. 11 (1912), pp. 321-330; Kovalevskii, «Судьба Балкан» [Fate of the Balkans], Вестник Европы [Herald of Europe], kn. 1 (1913), pp. 197-223; Kovalevskii, «Вторая Балканская война» [Second Balkan War], Вестник мира [Herald of Peace], no. 5 (1913), pp. 3-8.

180 Kovalevskii, «Взгляд на истории русской дипломатии в Швеции (на основании данных Королевского архива в Стокгольме)» [View on the History of Russian Diplomacy in Sweden (on the Basis of Data of the Royal Archive in Stockholm), Юридический вестник [Legal Herald], no. 5 (1887), pp. 16-58; Kovalevskii, «Кодификация международного права» [Codification of International Law], Юридическая газета [Legal Newspaper], no. 60 (1898), pp. 1-2.

181 Kovalevskii, «Порто-Франко во Владивостоке» [Porto-Franco in Vladivostok], Вестник Европы [Herald of Europe], no. 1 (1909), pp. 423-437.

182 Kovalevskii, Социология [Sociology] (Spb., 1910), I, p. 63.

183 Kovalevskii, «Прогресс» [Progress], Вестник Европы [Herald of Europe], no. 2 (1912), pp. 259-260.

es of the Great Powers". The first was formed on the basis of the 1815 Congress of Vienna, the Holy Alliance, which thereafter was replaced by two military and political alliances confronting one another – the Triple Alliance (German, Austria, and Italy) and the Entente (Russia, England, and France). Kovalevskii noted positive and negative aspects in the new system of military and political alliances in the cause of maintaining peace: "The new system of counterbalances has served to secure peace, but by straining all the financial resources of the State to create unprecedented armies and navies" (pp. 254-255).

Issues of war and peace were closely linked with Kovalevskii's ideas of peace-making, solidarity, and progress. As a convinced pacifist, he condemned war and believed that any controversial issues between States might be resolved by peaceful means on the basis of solidarity and peace-making.[184] The conflicts between States and civil wars within States Kovalevskii believed to be a temporary and annoying obstacle to the objective aspiration of European nations for peace and unification. Testimony to this was the wide dissemination of pacifist ideas, the activities of inter-parliamentary groups and peace societies, and the successful work of the 1899 and 1907 Hague peace conferences, which consolidated the system of arbitration, limitation of the cruelty of wars by introducing more precise restraints for waging them. Kovalevskii, however, was convinced that the "political evolution of nations and States is evident not merely of the amelioration of the terrors of war, but the more frequent replacement thereof by an agreement of the interested parties with the direct or indirect participation of all, some, or one member of an international union" (p. 256).

But, in his view, armed conflicts and wars can be avoided. Human reason and political consciousness provide an accurate understanding that the "benefits of peace" may be sacrificed only in exceptional instances and "in the interests of preserving one's autonomy and territorial integrity and composition" (p. 256). The just armed struggle of the Balkan nations against Turkish domination was, said Kovalevskii, such an instance.[185] He also considered the First World War to be such an instance, appealing for solidarity and the combined efforts of States for just armed resistance against the German "enlightened barbarians". Kovalevskii criticized Germany, the homeland of Immanuel Kant and Johann Wolfgang von Goethe (1749-1832), a country which dreamed of freedom and perpetual peace, but transformed itself into a hotbed of reaction, militarism, and war. The reason for this, said Kovalevskii, was the nature of German statehood created in 1871 by Prussia through the unification by "iron and blood" of the many German principalities.[186] Kovalevskii appealed to States to unite against Germany and its allies with a noble view in mind – the "erection in the world of an order based on recognition of the principle of the equality of States and the right of peoples to self-determination of their political fates".[187]

[184] Kovalevskii, Ученый, государственный и общественный деятель и гражданин. Сборник статей [Scholar, State and Public Figure, and Citizen: Collection of Articles] (Pg,, 1917), p. 39.

[185] Kovalevskii, note 179 above (1912).

[186] Kovalevskii, «Германцы против англичан» [Germans against the English], Вестник Европы [Herald of Europe], no. 5 (1915), p. 284.

[187] Kovalevskii, «Иностранное обозрение» [Foreign Survey], Вестник Европы [Herald of Eu-

Kovalevskii was optimistic about the progress of mankind. He saw the further development of "peace-making, solidarity, and progress" in the formation of national and federal unions, and this would lead to their unification into a single international union that ultimately would become "the completion of the entire process of the development and ultimate strengthening of the idea of the human species" (pp. 350-351).

The international union posited by Kovalevskii was not a world State with a supranational government, but a union of "autonomous political entities entering into permanent unions or federations with one another and inspired to preserve peace by economic calculations and concern for the possible development of their production through an expansion of exchanges – and this was conceivable only under free markets" (pp. 257-258).

Free trade Kovalevskii considered to be a major condition for the maintenance of such peace. If conflicts between States often are caused by the struggle for new markets, then for such struggle to cease there must be "open doors to any foreign good". But as the national economy transitions from being closed and self-sufficient, States become interested in the possibility of free exchange and are equally hostile to open or covert war which represents an artificial moving off from markets for their goods. He came to the view on the basis of these considerations that "the fate of the world is closely intertwined with the fates of trade".[188]

Kovalevskii believed that the international union contemporary to him rested upon the "existence of autonomous States which combined each into a single political whole on the basis of the historical past and community of interests to a greater degree than a single language or faith". Kovalevskii perceived these States as being based on the principles of self-determination of a people, self-determination of the individual, parliamentary democracy, and recognition of human rights. He regarded such States as having an aspiration to place all inhabitants on an equal footing, to be concerned for their education free of charge, to actually ensure to every citizen who has fallen into need the right to work, to expand the range of persons who take part in political elections, the possibility for people's representatives to have an impact on legislative activity by means of their personal participation and through any kind of associations or unions (p. 258).

Being a sociologist, Kovalevskii stressed in his conclusion that his scheme merely "established some of the upper columns, indicates a general trend"; only the general contours of the evolution of the State and an international union are sketched. "I am drawing", he said, "a future in the form of stable harmony not only of private individuals and individual groups within a single national and State whole, but also in permanent amity and mutual assistance in a world economy of autonomous States and the union thereof" (p. 260).

During his Petersburg-Petrograd period, Kovalevskii published several articles inspired by specific events having international legal implications. Three discussed above dealt with Balkan matters and the wars of 1912 and 1913. In his view

rope], no. 10 (1915), pp. 350-351.

188 Kovalevskii, note 183 above, p. 257.

the Balkan wars were a just liberation struggle of the southern Slavic countries and Greece for political independence in the name of human rights and freedoms, equality of nations, and the establishment of prolonged peace in Europe.

Kovalevskii touched upon other issues of international law in various works, including the limitation of poisonous weapons, ensuring the freedom of the straits, compliance with the rules of naval warfare, and the defense of ethnic minorities against persecution and destruction.

Kovalevskii's views on international law were developed from a sociological perspective, so it is hardly surprising that his relevant works are interspersed with materials of a sociological or political science nature. Against this background, of interest is his article on porto-franco (free port), a calque in Russian from the Italian – an internal port or on the coast to which the State grants the right in international trade by sea to duty-free exports and imports. The institution of porto-franco was introduced in Russia on 16 April 1817 by Edict of Alexander I initially for Odessa (from 1819 to 1859), and then gradually to Kamchatka (from 1828), Batumi (from 1878 to 1885), Vladivostok, and other ports of the Maritime Province (1862 to 1901, 1904 to 1909). In his article on the subject,[189] he used official materials from the State Duma, accessible to him as a member of legislative committees which discussed this issue. With respect to the Far East, he argued that porto franco should be used to encourage the import of foreign goods to the mouth of the Amur River; numerous petitions from foreign merchants supported such a change. He thoughtfully analyzed the history of the question, noting that the situation was complicated by the 1905 Treaty of Portsmouth ending the Russo-Japanese War, that the port of Dalnyi (with Port Arthur Fortress) had passed to Japan who had declared it to be a free port, and all this weakened the competitiveness of Vladivostok as a port. He made the case for Russia taking legislative measures to create favorable conditions for foreign merchants in their international trade with the Far East.

Nikolai Ivanovich Lazarevskii *(24 November 1868, b. Warsaw – 26 August 1921, d. suburb of Petrograd). Specialist in State and administrative law of Russia and western Europe, active in the State Duma; publicist, Pro-Rector of Petrograd University.*

Life and career. After graduating in 1887 from the First St. Petersburg Gymnasium, Lazarevskii matriculated at the Law Faculty of St. Petersburg University.[190] He was awarded the gold medal for an essay on "The State Doctrine of Spinoza in Connection with his General Philosophical System". In 1891 he graduated from the Law Faculty and from 1 November 1892 to 1 May 1895 he remained to prepare for the professoriate at the Chair of State and Police Law.[191] During these years he

189 Kovalevskii, note 181 above, pp. 423-427.

190 ЦГИА СПб., fond 14, opis 3, file 26224. Also see A. A. Matyshev, Энциклопедия репрессированных авторов. 1917-1987. Биобиблиография советской трагедии [Encyclopedia of Repressed Authors. 1917-1987. Bio-Bibliography of the Soviet Tragedy] (Spb., 2020), VII, pp. 32-34.

191 ЦГИА СПб., fond 14, opis 1, file 9316.

was sent abroad for postgraduate studies and visited universities in Strasbourg, Heidelberg, and Toulouse.

After returning to Russia in 1896, he delivered two trial lectures to the Law Faculty of the University and was granted the right to lecture with the rank and title of privat-docent. But on 24 May 1896 he was appointed as junior assistant clerk in the Zemstvo Division of the Ministry of Internal Affairs, and from 1897, an official for special assignments in the Ministry of Finances, being first assigned to the jurisconsult unit.

In 1898, together with V. M. Gessen and other noted legal scholars, he founded the liberal newspaper Право [Law] and served for many years as a co-founder and executive editor. He was as from 1 January 1905 appointed privat-docent at the Chair of State and Police Law in St. Petersburg University. On 20 May 1906 he defended a magister dissertation, "Responsibility for Losses Caused by Officials"; his official opponents were Professors I. A. Ivanovskii and L. I. Petrazhitskii. He was awarded the magister of State Law. From 1905 to 1913 he lectured on "Russian Administrative Law" (1905-1906); "State System of France" (1906-1907); "Russian State Law (tutorials) (1908-1909); and Russian State Law" (1911-1913).

From 1906 to 1916 he was appointed professor at the Higher Women's (Bestuzhev) Courses, where he lectured on "Russian State Law" and "Western European State Law" and offered a special course of lectures on self-government, decentralization, and autonomy. Simultaneously, he served from 1914 as a jurisconsult at the Ministry of Finances.

After the February 1917 Revolution, he was involved in reforms of the State: by Edict of the Provisional Government of 8 May 1917 he was appointed a member of the Ruling Senate; acting Deputy Minister of Finances of the Provisional Government; Chairman of the Legal Meeting – a special agency to prepare drafts of major legislative acts; and from 11 to 24 October 1917, Chairman of the Special Commission for preparing draft Basic Laws (Constitution) of the Russian Republic attached to the Legal Meeting for the convocation of the All-Russian Constitutive Assembly.

On 8 March 1918 Lazarevskii was elected docent at the Chair of Administrative Law of St. Petersburg University. After the reorganization of 1918-1919, the Law Faculty of the University he continued to work within the Faculty of Social Sciences of the University, and Lazarevskii continued in his post as Professor at the Chair of Administrative Law of the now renamed I Petrograd University.[192] According to the lecturing Plan for the 1919/20 academic year confirmed by the Politico-Legal Division of the Faculty of Social Sciences on 13 October 1919, Lazarevskii was to lecture on the "Theory of Law (from the Dogmatic-Legal Point of View)" and tutorials on legal theory.[193] On 20 October 1919, the Division decreed to recommend that the Faculty of Social Sciences confer the title of professor on Lazarevskii because he held the degree of magister. From 1918 Lazarevskii was an assistant pro-rector of Petrograd University.

Lazarevskii was arrested on 13 December 1919 at his flat, sent to Moscow, and confined in the Butyrka Prison; he was later released. In 1921 he acted as the Pro-Rector of Petrograd University and professor of the Institute of National Economy and the Institute of Economic Research. He offered a special course on "Russian Electoral Law in its Past and Present". He was arrested again in the well-known "Petrograd Fighting Organization" case (V. N. Tagantsev). By Decree of the Presidium of the Petrograd Gubernia Extraordinary Commission of 24 August 1921 Lazarevskii was sentenced to death by shooting; the date of the actual execution varies, from 26 August 1921 or 29 August 1921. In May 1992 Lazarevskii was rehabilitated by decision of the Chief Military Procuracy.

International legal views. Lazarevskii touched upon matters of public international law in several works, most especially his article on treaties.[194] This was the first occasion in Russian international doctrine that the role of the State Duma in the conclusion of international treaties was discussed. Lazarevskii observed that in connection with the forthcoming accession of the Russian Empire to the 1901 International Sugar Convention "for the first time since the introduction of popular representation in Russia the question arises of its participation in the conclusion and introduction into operation of an international treaty" (col. 3207). However, he said, not a single Article of any legislative act makes provision for the participation of the Duma or of the State Council in the matter of concluding international treaties. Such participation is consolidated solely for the Emperor, who is "the supreme leader of all foreign relations of the Russian State with foreign powers" and, *inter alia,* concludes treaties with foreign States. Lazarevskii pointed out that the constitutional provision of Russia repeated western constitutions of the first quarter of the nineteenth century, and therefore "Russia in the twentieth century is prolonging the same evolution which Western Europe underwent in the nineteenth century, little by little granting to popular representation its share of participation in the cause of bringing a treaty into execution when this affects law in force" (col. 3213).

Referring to Article 86 of the Basic Laws of the Russian Empire that "no law may ensue without the approval of the State Council and State Duma and take

[192] ОА ЦГА СПбГУ., fond 1, opis 1, file 141.

[193] ЦГА СПбГУ., fond 7240, opis 14, file 85.

[194] N. I. Lazarevskii, «Международные договоры и народное представительство» [International Treaties and Popular Representation], Право [Law], no. 50 (1907), cols. 3207-3217. Also see W. E. Butler, "On the Ratification of Treaties in Prerevolutionary Russia", *Jus Gentium: Journal of International Legal History*, VII (2022), pp. 7-23.

force without confirmation of the Sovereign Emperor" and Article 94, according to which a "law may not be repealed other than by force of a new law", Lazarevskii came to the following conclusion:

> From these two Articles it follows beyond doubt that the Sovereign, having the right to conclude any treaties alone by his power, may not impart binding force to these treaties because this would be contrary to the literal meaning of Article 86. However, from the undoubted meaning of Article 94 it arises that although the provisions of a treaty in which there are provisions which are contrary to laws in force, these last all the same must be deemed to have retained their full force so long as new laws do not establish that which is in the agreement of the Sovereign in the treaty concluded by him; thus, so that the provisions of a treaty replace and repeal laws in force it is necessary that the treaty, insofar as it affects legislation in force, be in the form of a law; that is, it is necessary that this part of the treaty be approved by the State Council and the State Duma.

Here Lazarevskii addressed the conflict arising between the International Sugar Convention and Russian legislation. According to Article 3 of the Convention, Russia was obliged for six years not to export sugar with a refund of excise in a quantity exceeding one million tons. Russia, however, had a law in force which provided that if native sugar were exported abroad the exporter has the right to a refund of excises, with no indication of the quantities of sugar involved. In Lazarevskii's view, the only way to eliminate this conflict would be to change the Russian law, which could only be accomplished by the popular representative agency – the Duma.

Lazarevskii concluded: "… in those instances when international treaties concluded by the Sovereign affect legislation in force, the participation of popular representation in the matter of executing these treaties is legally insurmountable" (col. 3217).

In 1915 Lazarevskii published a book on the causes of the First World War analyzing the diplomatic, military, strategic, technical, and moral aspects of the war.[195] He recalled that the two Hague Peace conferences were held at the initiative of Russia to agree the creation of an international arbitration court in order to eliminate disputes and prevent wars, but regrettably the treaty norms on the limitation of armaments and ameliorating the cruelties of war were not fully achieved (p. 56). But those norms intended to humanize war and adopted at these Conferences were being flagrantly violated by Germany. Lazarevskii was upset by the cruelty of the German forces. A manual for officers prepared by the German General Staff warns German military personnel against "exaggerated humanitarian views" with regard to the methods and means of waging war; as for prisoners of war, in order to prevent escapes the most "merciless application of all means at the disposition of the escort" was recommended. One may continue to fire at an enemy who has surrendered and raised a white flag if this is necessary in order to "occupy certain points", and so on (p. 52).

[195] Lazarevskii, Причины и задачи войны 1914-1915 гг. [Causes and Tasks of the War 1914-1915] (Pg., 1915). 64 p.

He completed his work with the observation: "We and our Allies uphold the highest principles of law and truth to the benefit of the entire world" (pp. 59-60).

Aleksandr Nikolaevich Makarov *(also Makarow) (4 August 1888, b. Tsarskoe selo, St. Petersburg – 13 May 1973, d. Heidelberg, Germany). Specialist on State law and private international law.*

Life and career. Makarov graduated in 1906 with the gold medal from the Karl Mai School in St. Petersburg and matriculated at the Law Faculty of St. Petersburg University.[196] He completed his degree with a first class result in 1910 and was invited to remain at the Chair of State Law to prepare for the professoriate from 1 January 1912 initially[197] and then 1 January 1914 with a University stipend.[198]

In 1913 he passed the magister examinations.[199] After receiving his magister of State Law, he was from 1 July 1914 appointed privat-docent at the Chair of State Law. During the academic year 1915-1916 he offered a course on "Central Administration in Russia from the Early Nineteenth Century" and gave tutorials on Russian State law. Simultaneously, he worked at the Imperial Public Library from 1 December 1914 as a volunteer in the Legal Section of the Library, and from February 1915, he was hired by the Ministry of Public Enlightenment and then sent to work in the Public Library. From 16 January 1916 he became an assistant registrar of the Library, but was dismissed that year to take up a position in the Ministry of Foreign Affairs as Librarian in that Ministry, with the rank of college secretary. In 1917 became the secretary of the editorial board of the journal of the Ministry of Foreign Affairs – Известия Министерства иностранных дел [News of the Ministry of Foreign Affairs].

[196] ЦГИА СПб., fond 14, opis 3, file 46093; Starodubtsev, note 55 above, p. 227.

[197] ЦГИА СПб., fond 14, opis 1, file 10433; Отчет о состоянии и деятельности Императорского С.-Петербургского университета за 1912 год [Report on the State and Activity of Imperial St. Petersburg University for 1915] (Spb., 1913), p. 39.

[198] Отчет о состоянии и деятельности Императорского С.-Петербургского университета за 1913 год [Report on the State and Activity of Imperial St. Petersburg University for 1913] (Spb., 1914), p. 70. According to the Report for 1914, Makarov was without a stipend from 1 September 1910 to 1 July 1914. See Отчет о состоянии и деятельности Императорского Петроградского университета за 1914 год [Report on the State and Activity of Imperial St. Petersburg University for 1914] (Spb., 1915), p. 122.

[199] ЦГИА СПб., fond 14, opis 3, file 14509.

From 11 to 24 October 1917 he participated in the work of the Special Commission attached to the Legal Meeting to prepare the Basic Laws (Constitution) of the Russian Republic; together with others he worked on §6 (on parliament) and §16 (on the procedure for review and guarantee). After the 1917 October Revolution, Makarov remained to work at Petrograd University as a professor. In 1923 he was dismissed from the University. But from 1921 until the end of his sojourn in the Soviet Union he was a professor at the Petrograd Engels Institute of National Economy.[200]

Makarov left in 1925 for a year's visit to Berlin in order to do work and research on private international law; at his request, the visit was extended for a further year. He did not return to the Soviet Union. Although he spent the remainder of his life in Germany, he never took German citizenship and remained an apatride.

He died in Heidelberg on 13 May 1973 and is buried in a local cemetery.

International legal views. In his early years Makarov had an interest in both public and private international law. In 1915 he published a substantial study of dual citizenship, or to use the language of empires – dual "subject-hood". He analyzed the issues that arose from the enactment in Germany of a 1913 law legalizing the possibility of dual citizenship. In Makarov's view, this German legislation pursued the political interests of rising German nationalism, being directed towards preserving Germanic subject-hood for Germanic peoples living outside Germany. The legislation would allow the "use of the privileges" granted to Germanic peoples "for personal interests of those" acquiring German citizenship and for "the political interests of Germany". He believed that being affiliated with two States simultaneously was, in principle, unacceptable.[201] Makarov rejected the legislative possibility of permitting statelessness, which in his opinion was, "from the international legal standpoint, an unmitigated evil" (no. 38, col. 2388). The inadmissibility of dual citizenship had long been a stable axiom of international legal doctrine (cols. 2395-2396).

Analyzing the legislation of France, England, and Russia on citizenship, Makarov concluded it was necessary to resist the implementation of the German legislation. The task, as he understood it, was twofold: first, to render harmless the naturalizations of German subjects which had occurred under the 1913 law; and second, to establish a procedure under which these naturalizations would become legally impossible in the future (col. 2349).

Having determined that the Russian legislation on subject-hood was utterly unsuitable for coping with the German law (col. 2442) and having analyzed the proposals put forward by the Ministry of Internal Affairs of Russia in the form of a draft law for admission to and withdrawal from Russian subject-ship, Makarov expressed the hope that Russian legislation would "prove to a sufficient degree to be adapted to eliminating those highly undesirable consequences for us which arise from the consistent application of the new German law on subject-hood". For the

200 ЦГА СПб., fond 2998, opis 1, file 554.

201 A. N. Makarov, «Германский закон о подданстве 1913 г. и двойное подданство» [German Law of 1913 on Subject-Hood and Dual Subject-Hood], Право [Law], no. 37 (1915), col. 2314.

moment, he said, one must struggle against those instances of dual subject-hood which occurred before the war by reason of applying the 1913 German law and exclude from Russian subject-hood those "dual subjects" (col. 2446).

Makarov addressed the legal nature and distinctive features of unions of States in a book review of Korf's work on the autonomous colonies of Great Britain.[202] This was an issue always at the interface between international law and municipal law. Makarov criticized Korf, who had asserted that the British Empire, being a federation, has features of a union State (pp. 338-339). But Korf maintained that a union State exists so long as parts thereof are not sovereign. Makarov categorically disagreed, pointing out that England itself as part of the British Empire was a wholly sovereign State. Moreover, using the example of the United States of America, Switzerland, and Germany, Makarov demonstrated that

> integral parts of an integral Union participate in creating the legal will of this whole, whereas the autonomous colonies of Great Britain do not participate in the creation of Imperial legislation; it is created by English legislative bodies and already prepared, in force, is passed on to the colonies to be applied (p. 341).

Aleksandr Sergeevich Muliukin *(2 September 1873 – after 1944). Historian of Russian law and specialist in State law.*

Life and career. Of the nobility. In 1893[203] he enrolled in the Law Faculty of St. Petersburg University and graduated in 1897. His student graduation diploma was awarded a silver medal. After University graduation, he took a position in the Ministry of Justice and was sent to the Chancellery of the Fourth Department of the Ruling Senate. From 1899 he served as a clerk in the Department of Public Enlightenment and eventually achieved the rank of court counsellor.

In parallel, from 1897 he remained at the Chair of State Law to prepare for the professoriate. On 18 October 1909 he defended a magister dissertation at St. Petersburg University[204] on the "Arrival of Foreigners in the Muscovy State. From the History of Russian Law of the XVI-XVII Centuries".[205] From 1 January to March 1910 Muliukin acted as privat-docent at the Chair of State Law in St. Petersburg University, assigned to offer a course on the history of Russian law. At the end of March 1910, however, Muliukin was transferred to the position of acting professor *extraordinarius* at the Chair of the History of Russian Law in Novorossiisk University (Odessa), where he worked until 1920. He also served as secretary

[202] S. A. Korf, Автономные колонии Великобритании [Autonomous Colonies of Great Britain] (Spb., 1914), reviewed by A. N. Makarov in Журнал Министерства юстиции [Journal of the Ministry of Justice], no. 4 (1915), pp. 336-342.

[203] ЦГИА СПб., fond 14, opis 3, file 29744. Also see Matyshev, note 190 above, X, pp. 504-505.

[204] Grabar erroneously believed the defense was at Novorossiisk University. See Grabar, note 13 above, p. 426.

[205] A. S. Muliukin, Приезд иностранцев в Московское государство. Из истории русского права XVI-XVII вв. [Arrival of Foreigners in the Muscovy State. From the History of Russian Law of the XVI-XVII Centuries] (Spb., 1909).

of the Law Faculty. In Odessa he offered additionally courses on the history of Russian State law and court procedure.

During the summer months from 1912 to 1915, Muliukin traveled abroad for research purposes. In 1916 he defended a doctoral dissertation at Kharkov University on the history of the legal status of foreign merchants in Muscovy.[206] From 1915 he was professor *ordinarius* at the Chair of Police Law and lectured on administrative, police, and canon law. When the Novorossiisk University was reorganized in 1920, Muliukin moved over to the Odessa Humanities-Social Institute, and from 1921 to 1922, to the Odessa Institute of National Economy. In the course of a "purge" of the Institute, he was arrested on the night of 17/18 August 1922 and dismissed for sabotage of Soviet power together with other professors. In October 1922 he left Ukraine for Varna, Bulgaria, and then settled in Sofia. He had a private law practice in emigration. His fate thereafter is unknown.

International legal views. The legal status of foreigners in medieval Rus and Muscovy was a principal area of Muliukin's research and is directly relevant to the field of international law. In his monograph and articles based on chapters thereof, Muliukin explored the legal regulation within medieval Rus of the admittance, reception, sojourn, and commercial activities of foreigners over five centuries, principally merchants. He wrote that medieval Rus was open to all foreigners, that Slavic hospitality reflected an enduring interest in the cultures and material wealth of foreigners.[207] Medieval Rus evolved from rules of customary law regulating foreigners (right of free arrival and departure, frequent initiative of good will, communion, exchange of goods) to treaties of the fourteenth to fifteenth centuries which made provision for conditions and the procedures for admittance and sojourn of foreigners on the territory of Muscovy as a major prerogative of State power.

Russian legal regulation in the sixteenth and seventeenth centuries reflected the centralization processes of the Muscovite State and expanded diplomatic, commercial, and other links with neighbors on all sides. For the purposes of legal regulation, foreigners were classified into groups: merchants, servitors, clergy, scholars, teachers, engineers, craftsmen, doctors, midwives, pharmacists, travelers, individuals of free professions, and accompanying personnel (suites, servants, protection, relatives, and the like). Foreigners arrived voluntarily at their own initiative, or by invitation, or on urgent matters or to enter the service of the Russian sovereign. Muliukin concentrated on foreign traders, the international and domestic legal conditions and procedures for admittance, movement, sojourn, and other activities in Muscovy, including the registration of their nationality, profession of faith, and trade interests. Treaties entered into by Muscovy consolidated special privileges and preferences for the foreign merchants of favored States:

> The provisions of treaties on trade, and especially on the free arrival of merchants of a particular nationality in Russia, excluded the law of mer-

[206] Muliukin, Очерки по истории юридического положения иностранных купцов в Московском государстве [Essays with Regard to the History of the Legal Status of Foreign Merchants in the Muscovite State] (Odessa, 1912). Butler M256. [РГБ].

[207] Muliukin, «Приезд иностранцев в древнюю Русь» [Arrival of Foreigners of Mediaeval Rus], Журнал Министерства юстиции [Journal of the Ministry of Justice], no. 9 (1907), p. 123.

chants from the unilateral will of the territorial authority and placed it under the control of international communion. The legal consciousness of that time clearly took account of the formal force of international treaties in comparison with domestic legislation ...[208]

Muliukin thus demonstrated that often foreign merchants, and sometimes foreigners of other professions, were in Russia under conditions more favorable than those enjoyed by Russian subjects.

Aleksandr Liverievich Sakketti *(13(26) August 1881, b. St. Petersburg – 15 February 1966, d. Moscow). Specialist in the theory and history of law, State law, and international law.*

Life and career. After completing his secondary education at the First St. Petersburg Classical Gymnasium in 1901, he matriculated and, in 1908, graduated from the Law Faculty of St. Petersburg University with a first-class degree.[209] At the suggestion of M. M. Kovalevskii, in autumn 1908 Sakketti remained at the Faculty of State Law to prepare for the professoriate[210] for one year until 1 December 1909, without stipend;[211] he was sent abroad to attend lectures on the philosophy of law and State law at German universities. From December 1908 until August 1911 Sakketti was registered at the Ministry of Justice of Russia as a candidate for judicial office and assigned to the Chancellery of the First Department of the Ruling Senate.

Up returning from abroad, he passed the magister examinations in State law and international law during 1912 and 1913. In 1914 he was appointed privat-docent at the Chair of the General Theory and Encyclopedia of Law of Petrograd University. During the War years, from 1914 to 1918, Sakketti devoted himself to instruction at the University, giving lessons on the philosophy of law and offering a course on the "Political Doctrines of the Renaissance". He published several articles, pamphlets, and courses on the theory of law (mimeographed versions),

208 Muliukin, Приезд иностранцев в Московское государство: Из истории русского права XVI и XVII веков [Arrival of Foreigners in the Muscovite State: From the History of Russian Law of the Sixteenth and Seventeenth Centuries] (Spb., 1909), p. 171.

209 ЦГИА СПб., fond 14, opis 3, file 38693.

210 ЦГИА СПб., fond 14, opis 1, file 10219.

211 Отчет о состоянии и деятельности Императорского С.-Петербургского университета за 1913 год [Report on the State and Activity of Imperial St. Petersburg University for 1908] (Spb., 1909), p. 71.

and worked on his dissertation. Later observers commented that "already in these works he showed himself to be a mature scholar".[212]

The closure in 1919 by decision of the People's Commissariat of the Enlightenment of all law faculties of universities and their transformation into legal divisions of Faculties of Social Sciences led to mass curtailment of instructional plans and lecturing personnel, including at Petrograd University. Sakketti moved first to Kostroma, and then to Moscow, where he continued to engage in lecturing and research. He died on 15 February 1966 in Moscow.

International legal views. In the Russian-speaking world of international law the surname "Sakketti" is commonly linked with the treatise by Hugo Grotius on the law of war and peace. Sakketti displayed his lexical talents and remarkable classical erudition, having devoted decades of labor to producing a meaningful translation – a challenge confronting Russian scholars since Peter the Great first commissioned a translation back in 1712.[213] Sakketti began his translation of Grotius early in his career; his first attempt to publish Grotius in 1902 was frustrated by the Russian censor, apparently for theological reasons rather than objections to the Grotian natural law approach.[214] Sakketti persisted, polishing his text over the years; in 1948 Book 1 of the Grotian treatise was issued with a preface by Andrei Ivanovich Denisov (1906-1984).[215] The entire work, translated from the Latin text published at Amsterdam in 1646 and containing Grotius' last corrections, appeared in 1956 under the general editorship of the former judge on the International Court of Justice, Sergei Borisovich Krylov (1888-1958).[216]

Sakketti produced other works on various aspects of international law. On 19 February 1915 he reported to the Petrograd Philosophical Society on "The State and Nationality", later published as an article.[217] The Report considered from an international legal perspective the relations of the authorities and nationalities in

212 G. V. Savenko, «Александр Ливериевич Саккетти» [Aleksandr Liverievich Sakketti], Правоведение [Jurisprudence], no. 5 (2002), p. 233; Starodubtsev, note 3 above, pp. 20, 41.

213 See W. E. Butler, "Grotius' Influence in Russia", in Hedley Bull, B. Kingsbury, and Adam Roberts (eds.), *Hugo Grotius and International Relations* (1990), pp. 257-266; revised in Butler, "The Influence of Hugo Grotius in Russia", in Butler, *Russia and the Law of Nations in Historical Perspective: Collected Essays* (2009), pp. 185-193.

214 H. Grotius, О праве войны и мира [On the Law of War and Peace] (Spb., [1902]). 50 p. Butler Г413. Grotius was for many years on the Vatican Index of prohibited books; this may have influenced the Russian censor. See Robin Vose, *The Index of Prohibited Books: Four Centuries of Struggle Over Word and Image for the Greater Glory of God* (London, 2023).

215 Grotius, О праве войны и мира [On the Law of War and Peace] (M., 1948), pp. i-xv.

216 Grotius, О праве войны и мира [On the Law of War and Peace] (M., 1956; reprint ed.; 1994). Sakketti produced an introduction for this work: Sakketti, «Гуго Гроций и его трактат «О праве войны и мира» [Hugo Grotius and his Treatise "On the Law of War and Peace"], in ibid., pp. 6-9. Also see Sakketti, «Гроций как ученый-гуманист, юрист и историк» [Grotius as Humanist Scholar, Jurist, and Historian], Советский ежегодник международного права 1959 [Soviet Yearbook of International Law 1959] (M., 1960), pp. 261-270.

217 Sakketti, «Государство и народность» [The State and Nationality], Юридический вестник [Legal Herald], no. 12(4) (1915), pp. 5-16; also separate offprint, M., 1915.

a multi-national State, the conflicts between which often were internationalized and complicate international relations. He asked how relations between the authorities and nationalities should be structured, what principles should operate to govern these relations and what was a reasonable nationality policy, and what precisely was the danger of nationalism and social upheavals arising. In his view, nationalism might manifest itself in two forms: either the predominant nationality subordinates the government to its exclusive aims and prejudices the interests of other nationalities, or the State in the person of the government is penetrated by the exclusive interests of one of the nationalities. In the first instance there is the domination of one nationality and the oppression of the others; in the second, the State and the nationality are simultaneously corrupted. The State overlooks its universal foundations and tasks, principles of freedom and equality, throws an organic substance over the people's life and the development of the people. But, Sakketti acknowledged, complete non-interference on the basic of nationality is as pernicious as is national oppression.

The world is multi-faceted and multi-national. The unity of mankind on the basis of nationality, in Sakketti's view, is possible only in the form of suppressing other nationalities in the interests of a single dominant one, or in the form of absorption by one nationality or merger of several into one. International law has the ability and capacity to embody freedom and equality of nationalities. But what should be the organization of world inter-State relations?

There are no obstacles in the essence of the State, said Sakketti, to the realization of unified world domination. A confederation, that is, a permanent union of sovereign States on the basis of a treaty, a union constitution, successfully combines State universalism with national particularism. In his various schemes for perpetual peace, Immanuel Kant acknowledged the union structure as the completion of unity ("political cosmos") on condition of the rational structure of the State (implementing principles of freedom and equality within and ensuring such without; that is, a union of equal, independent States).[218] Of course, said Sakketti, within the bowels of this organization an irrational principle will continue to fester – the life of nations which at any moment may burst its banks, overcome all barriers, and destroy the symmetrical harmony of the social cosmos.

In his article on the territoriality of a State, Sakketti reminded his readers that "the determination of the legal nature of State territory is among … the most controversial questions of the theory of public law and the proper structuring of the legal concept of State territory has generated material and profound disagreements …".[219]

Having analyzed several western-European theories relating to concepts of territory and finding them to be in some respects paradoxical, he wrote:

> Territory from the international viewpoint is an object of a unique right to a thing; States as subjects of international communion have divided

[218] See Savenko, note 212 above, p. 234.

[219] Sakketti, «Основные учения о территориальности государства» [Basic Doctrines on the Territoriality of a State], Известия Министерства иностранных дел [News of the Ministry of Foreign Affairs], kn. 1 (1915), p. 204.

> and legally consolidated among themselves certain parts of earthly space. Norms consolidating for them rights to territory are undoubtedly of an international nature. From the standpoint of State law, territory is a legal fact which conditions the arising (and, respectively, termination)of certain relations of subordination ... On the basis of such a qualification, a certain geographical space becomes the basis for subordinating persons located thereon to a certain power. Therein lies the unique function of State territory, which distinguishes territory from things in private turnover (pp. 218-219).

Having put the question of whether territory is an essential and material indicator of a State, Sakketti offered his own answer: the location of a State on a certain territory generates certain relations which are part of a State, and territoriality is not an essential indicator. Nonetheless, Sakketti believed that territoriality was usually a condition for delimiting spheres of domination between States and in reality always is present (pp. 218-223). He concluded: "territoriality of States, that is, the delimitation of their spatial limits, in fact always exists for reasons of practical advisability and is based on norms of objective positive law" (p. 224).

§11.4. *Chair of Police Law*

Vladimir Fedorovich Deriuzhinskii *(17 March 1861, b. Smolensk – 19 December 1920, d. Buyuk-Dere, near Constantinople, Turkey). Professor of police law, publicist.*

Life and career. Upon graduating from the Smolensk Gymnasium, Deriuzhinskii enrolled in 1878 at the Law Faculty of Moscow University. He remained to train for the professoriate after completing University at the Chair of Police Law and was sent abroad to study at the University of Paris and Heidelberg University in 1884-1885. Upon returning from Europe, he successfully defended at Kharkov University in 1886 a magister dissertation on the "Habeas Corpus Act and its Suspension under English Law: Survey of the Basic Guarantees of Personal Freedom in England and the Temporary Limitation Thereof".[220]

[220] The magister defense was reported in the Журнал Юридического общества при Императорском Санкт-Петербургском университете [Journal of the Law Society attached to the Imperial St. Petersburg University], no. 8 (October 1896), pp. 42-49.

He was then appointed privat-docent at the Chair of Police Law of Moscow University in that same year, becoming Professor *extraordinarius* from 1891 of Police Law at Iurev University. In 1895 he removed to St. Petersburg, becoming a lecturer at the Alexander Lycée[221] and editor of the Journal of the Ministry of Justice and, from 1897, editor of the journal Трудовая помощь [Labor Assistance]. From 1902 to 1916 Deriuzhinskii was professor at St. Petersburg University in the Chair of Police Law, where he offered a general course on police law.[222] He became a consultant attached to the Ministry of Justice in 1915 and was active in a number of social organizations.

Following the February 1917 Revolution, the Provisional Government appointed him Senator and a member of the Special Commission for drawing up a draft of the Basic Laws.

When the Bolsheviks came to power in October 1917, Derzhiuinskii continued to work at the University until 1919. After the reorganization of the Law Faculty in 1918-1919, he lectured in the Politico-Legal Division of the Faculty of Social Sciences of the University as a professor at the Chair of Administrative Law.[223] He resigned with effect from 1 November 1919 from the University because of "domestic circumstances" and the need to leave Petrograd for an extended period.[224]

He traveled to Crimea and lectured during the 1919-1920 academic year at Tauride University in Simferopol. When the White movement was defeated in the Russian Civil War, he moved to Turkey. On 21 December 1920 Deriuzhinskii died of a heart attack (according to other sources, from typhus) in a Russian refugee camp on the Bosphorus, near Constantinople.

International legal views. As a specialist in criminal law, Deriuzhinskii took part in organizing international efforts to curb trafficking in women. An international movement to combat this phenomenon commenced in the early twentieth century. Russian jurists were involved in the search for legal mechanisms to counteract this practice. Several legal scholars at the Chair of Criminal Law in St. Petersburg University took part, including Deriuzhinskii.

Deriuzhinskii was at the very origin of the said international movement. In June 1889 he was sent by the Russian Government to London in order to attend the First International Congress to Repress the White Slave Trade. The representatives of ten European countries and the United States took part. The Congress decided to form national organs in each country to combat trafficking in women. In Russia, the Russian Society for the Defense of Women was formed in 1900. Deriuzhinskii served as a member of its Board from 1900 until 1918. He was the empowered representative of Russia in subsequent international congresses and conferences devoted to this question.

[221] ЦГИА СПб., fond 14, opis 1, file 3602.

[222] ЦГИА СПб., fond 14, opis 1, file 9688; fond 14, opis 1, file 16115

[223] ОА СПбГУ., fond 1, opis 1, file 141.

[224] ЦГА СПб., fond 7240, opis 14, file 85. The session of the Politico-Legal Division was held 3 November 1919.

He published two articles on the subject. In the first, he shared impressions of attending the International Conference to Repress the White Slave Trade, held at Paris from 15 to 25 July 1902 with the participation of fifteen European and one South American States. Deriuzhinskii took part in the work of the Conference as a representative of the Ministry of Justice from the Ober-Procurator section and editor of the Journal of the Ministry of Justice. His article surveyed the white slave trade, pandering, and prostitution. He set out the results of the 1899 London Conference on the same subject convened at the initiative of non-State organizations; the London Conference had drafted measures to counteract the white slave traffic and proposed they be discussed by the general public and governments so that legal decisions might be taken.[225]

When preparing for the 1902 Paris Conference, many proposals of the London Conference were taken, reflecting the serious intentions of the organizers to use governmental and non-governmental resources to combat this social evil. According to the Program of the Paris Conference, possible domestic criminal law measures and agreed international legal measures were discussed; the Russian delegation played a significant role in the discussion. These included an international convention on the white slave trade and an administrative agreement to adopt provisional measures until the Convention entered into force. The discussion at the Conference concentrated on the following:

(1) the determination of the jurisdiction of prosecutions;

(2) the determination of the grounds and procedure for the extradition of perpetrators and others complicit;

(3) the expeditious execution of instructions to arrest suspects and assignments to investigate criminal actions;

(4) the supervision over the departure and arrival of persons suspected of committing the criminal acts and of their victims; reports to the governments of those countries to which these victims belonged; and their deportation to their homeland;

(5) the respective instructions on measures to combat the white slave trade to diplomatic and consular agents of various States.

Deriuzhinskii understood that the aforesaid conventions and agreements must be realized, *inter alia*, by making adjustments to the criminal legislation of the States which ratified them.[226]

[225] V. F. Deriuzhinskii, «Международная борьба с торговлею женщинами» [International Struggle with Trafficking in Women], Журнал Министерства юстиции [Journal of the Ministry of Justice], no. 7-8 (1902), pp. 174-186.

[226] An administrative agreement was signed and ratified in 1904, and entered into force in 1905. The International Convention for the Suppression of the White Slave Traffic, signed at the Second Conference on 4 May 1910, entered into force in 1920.

His second article on this subject was published twelve years later.[227] It took into account that internationally agreed legislative and practical measures had been taken by States to reduce the white slave trade as a result of the Conferences at London and Paris. Deriuzhinskii noted: "These two acts laid the foundation for the international struggle against the white slave trade for the purposes of depravity and created a firm legal basis for the work of the National Committees to realize the tasks of this struggle in individual countries", including in Russia (p. 202).

This article analyzed the Fifth International Congress on the white slave trade held at London from 17-21 June 1913; Deriuzhinskii officially represented the Ministry of Finances. He said that this Congress adopted a number of resolutions on material aspects of this complex issue. (p. 202). One major issue was the trade in and use of children for depraved purposes. As a result of the discussion in which the Russian delegation took an active role, the Congress adopted legislative and practical measures to prevent trade in children and child prostitution. These concerned the suppression of various concealed forms of such trade, for example:

(1) the use of international theatrical agencies to conceal trade in children who were to be used for performances in theaters, circuses, concerts, music halls, and other forms of amusement where children are used for depraved actions;

(2) the hiring of youth in various drinking institutions (inns, taverns, bars, cafes, and the like) in which children are used for depraved actions;

(3) the use for the purpose of enticing minors for depravity of *poste restante*, indicating the addressees by numbers or initials.

A Report of the Russian delegation was delivered on the legislative measures combatting trade in children and child prostitution, after the discussion of which the Congress adopted several recommendations addressed to the governments of States. Thus, in his official capacity as the Russian representative to international congresses devoted to suppressing the trafficking in women made his own contribution to the development of international law.

Konstantin Iakovlevich Zagorskii *(3 March 1859, b. Kyiv – 9 November 1934, d. Moscow). Authority on the law of railways. Served in the central administrative departments of the Imperial Russian and Soviet railway system.*

Life and career. After graduating from the First Kyiv Gymnasium, Zagorskii enrolled at the Kyiv University, where he remained for one year. In 1877 he transferred to the Law Faculty of St. Petersburg University, graduating in 1882 with the degree of candidate of laws.[228] He remained to prepare for the professoriate at the Chair of Political Economy and Statistics within the Law Faculty.

[227] Deriuzhinskii, «Пятый международный конгресс по борьбе с торгом женщинами» [Fifth International Congress for Suppression of the White Slave Trade], Журнал Министерства юстиции [Journal of the Ministry of Justice], no. 1 (1914), pp. 200-210.

[228] ЦГИА СПб., fond 14, opis 3, file 19452 (1877).

His magister dissertation, “Theory of Railway Tariffs. Tasks of Management, Principles of Structuring and Application, and Forms and Types of Tariffs”, he defended at the University in 1902 and became a magister of political economy and statistics.

From 1904 to 1907 as a privat-docent at the Chair of Police Law of St. Petersburg University he lectured on the “General Part of Administrative Law” and also taught at the Polytechnic Institute.

A noted specialist on railway policy and tariffs, from 1889 to 1890 he served in the Department of Trade and Manufactures of the Ministry of Finances and, from 1891, in the Department of Railway Affairs. From 1899 he was the representative of the Ministry of Finances on the Tariff Committee and on the Commission of New Railways, and later a member of the Council for Tariffs and representative of the Special Meeting on Railway Affairs. In 1916 he became Head of International Transport Affairs of Russian Railways.

From 1913 to 1917 he was a counsellor of the Petersburg City Duma.

After the October Revolution, he remained in his position as head of international transport affairs of the People’s Commissariat of Railways, and during the 1920-30s as a member and deputy head of the tariff committee of the People’s Commissariat and a consultant to other executive Soviet agencies. In 1918 he participated as a railway expert in the Soviet delegation to conduct peace negotiations with Ukraine, and in 1921 with Poland. A new tariff system for the RSFSR was developed under his guidance in 1922.

From 1919 he continued to engage in teaching. He lectured at the Karl Marx Institute of National Economy, the First Moscow State University, the Institute of Transport Engineers, and others and became a full member of the Institute of Economics of the Russian Association of Scientific Research Social Sciences Institutes. On the publishing front, he collaborated with the Вестник финансов [Herald of Finances], Торгово-промышленная газета [Trade and Industry Newspaper], Русское экономическое обозрение [Russian Economic Survey], Народное хозяйство [National Economy], Русский экономист [Russian Economist], and certain other publications.

International legal views. In several of his writings on railways Zagorskii touched upon international legal matters. In railway development he attributed importance to such domestic factors as ensuring the timely and efficient movement of freight and passengers and to effective administrative structures, but also to such external factors as security and safety, consolidation of military power, development of international railway links and carriages, and the attraction of foreign investment capital.[229]

[229] K. Ia. Zagorskii, «Железнодорожные тарифы в России и Германии в связи с экономической политикой этих стран» [Railway Tariffs in Russia and Germany in Connection with the Economic Policy of These Countries], in Ministry of Finances, Материалы к пересмотру русско-германского торгового договора [Materials for a Revision of the Russo-German Trade Treaty] (Spb., 1914), pp. 1-2.

The expansion of international rail traffic seriously aggravated the issues of payment for the carriage of goods and services provided. Each partner-country of Russia fixed its own prices, and the rivalry and competition created additional problems. The situation was complicated by the railways being in private ownership by various competing companies which sought to attract custom by lower tariffs. Imbalances were created between domestic and international tariffs for carriage. Zagorskii counseled that the solution lay in State involvement in regulating tariffs.

Another issue of concern to Zagorskii was the use of trade customs and exchange rules for the grain trade.[230] One of the "dark aspects" of the grain trade in Russia, he said, was the inadequacy of certain customs and rules regulating grain turnover and relating to the conclusion and performance of transactions and the disputes accordingly arising between the parties. In western Europe and the United States, he observed, such trade customs and rules were published and administered by special boards, exchanges, or dispute settlement procedures. Grain, he observed, was a major Russian export and deserved similar treatment. His article was based on published collections of such rules issued by the major European and American grain markets. He especially drew attention to trade rules and customs which by reason of their origin could not be equated to legislation or to customary law.

§11.5. *Chair of Finnish Law*

Eduard Nikolaevich Berendts *(also Eduard Khristof Nikolaevich) (21 December 1860, b. St. Petersburg – 4 August 1930, d. Tallin, Estonia). Specialist in State, administrative (police), and financial law, first Professor of Finnish Law at St. Petersburg University.*[231]

Life and career. Berendts was schooled in St. Petersburg, first at the Gymnasium of the Chief German School (1871-1873), and then at the Chief School attached to the St. Peter Evangelical Church, in which great attention was devoted foreign languages, including Scandinavian. From 1880 Berendts was a student of

[230] Zagorskii, Торговые обычаи и биржевые правила как один из элементов организации хлебной торговли. Доклад Отделению Вольного экономического общества 18 апреля 1892 г. [Trade Customs and Exchange Rules as One Element of Organizing the Grain Trade. Report to the Division of the Free Economic Society of 18 April 1892] (Spb., 1893).

[231] On Berendts generally, see K. S. Belskii, «Доктор финансового права, ученый-административист и сенатор Российской империи (К 150-летию со дня рождения Э. Н. Берендтса» [Doctor of Financial Law, Scholar-Administrative Lawyer, and Senator of the Russian Empire (On the 150th Anniversary from the Birth of E. N. Berendts)], Государство и право [State and Law], no. 12 (2010), pp. 60-69; P. S. Zinovatnyi, «Служить правде»: Э. Н. Берендтс (1860-1930). Краткий очерк жизни и творчества» ["Serve the Truth": E. N. Berendts (1860-1930). Concise Survey of Life and Creation], in E. N. Berendts, Русское финансовое право [Russian Financial Law] (M., 2014), pp. 308-340; S. A. Egorov, «Берендтс Эдуард Николаевич» [Berendts, Eduard Nikolaevich], in V. M. Syrykh (ed.), Правовая наука и юридическая идеология России. Энциклопедический словарь биографий [Legal Science and the Legal Ideology of Russia: Encyclopedic Dictionary of Biographies] (M., 2009), I, pp. 67-69.

the Division of Administrative Sciences of the Law Faculty of St. Petersburg University.[232] He graduated in 1884 with the degree of candidate of laws.

Berendts took up employment in the Ministry of State Properties, initially in the Department of the State Treasury and, from 1887, in the Department of Cultivation and Agricultural Industry. He submitted documents in 1887 to St. Petersburg University to be admitted to the program for the magister of financial law.[233] After the defense in 1891 of a magister dissertation on the "State Economy of Sweden",[234] Berendts was appointed acting professor *extraordinarius* at the Chair of State and Administrative Law of the Demidov Law Lycée in Iaroslavl, where he lectured on administrative law.[235]

Berendts continued his work on the State economy of Sweden and in 1894 defended volume two of his treatise as a doctoral dissertation; he thereupon became professor *ordinarius* at the Demidov Law Lycée. From 1894 to 1900 he served as Chairman of the Iaroslavl Academic Archive Commission and the Временник Демидовского юридического лицея [Chronicle of the Demidov Law Lycée]. Berendts was appointed in 1900 assistant to the State secretary of the State Council and an official for special assignments attached to the Minister-State Secretary for the affairs of the Grand Duchy of Finland.

On 28 May 1901 the Chair of Finnish Law was created at the Law Faculty of St. Petersburg University and the post introduced of supernumerary professor *ordinarius*, which was held from 4 June 1901 to 1904 by Berendts. He gave courses on "Finnish Administrative Law" and the "Fundamental Principles of Finnish Civil Law".

He was the first elected Director for the academic year 1904-1905 of the Demidov Law Lycée.

Following the publication of the Manifesto by Emperor Nicholas II on 17 October 1905 "On the Improvement of State Order", Berendts temporarily left State service and engaged in socio-political activity as a member of the Central Commit-

232 ЦГИА СПб., fond 14, opis 3, file 21059.

233 ЦГИА СПб., fond 14, opis 1, file 8806.

234 E. N. Berendts, Государственное хозяйство Швеции [State Economy of Sweden] (Spb., 1890-1894). 2 vols.

235 See his inaugural lecture, in Berendts, Вступительная лекция, читанная и. д. экстраординарного профессора государственного и административного права [Inaugural Lecture Delivered by the Acting Professor Extraordinarius of State and Administrative Law] (Iaroslavl, 1891).

tee of the right-liberal political party “Union of 17 October”, commonly known as the Octobrist Party; he headed the Iaroslavl division of the Party. During 1906, he edited the newspaper Северянин [Northerner] in Iaroslavl.

From 1907 he became Professor of Financial Law, History of Russian Law, and Finnish Law at the Imperial School of Jurisprudence in St. Petersburg, and simultaneously lectured in lexprudence at the Nikolaev Cavalry School of Officers and Junkers. He re-entered State service in 1908. From 15 February 1908 he was appointed a member of the Council of the Chief Administration for Affairs of the Press in Russia.[236] He was appointed likewise a member of the Academy Committee of the Ministry of Public Enlightenment. From April 1914 he became a member of the Ruling Senate of the Russian Empire and, from June of the same year, a Senator of the First Department of the Senate to review decisions of governate institutions, where he worked until October 1917. While serving as Senator, he was the editor and co-author of volumes three and four of the jubilee edition of the History of the Ruling Senate; he personally wrote the sections on the “Draft Reforms of the Senate in the Reign of Emperors Alexander I and Nicholas I” and “Draft Reforms of the Senate during the Second Half of the Nineteenth Century”.[237]

He wrote articles for leading Russian general and legal journals. Being a supporter of a strong monarchy, he was opposed to both the February and the October 1917 revolutions. With the shutting down of the Ruling Senate and the School of Jurisprudence, Berendts found himself unemployed. He emigrated to Estonia in 1918 and acquired Estonian citizenship. From 1 August 1919 he became a consultant on statistics at the Ministry of Internal Affairs in Estonia and from 1 October 1919 to 1930, a professor at the Chair of Financial Law in the Law Faculty of Tartu University.

Berendts died in Tallinn on 4 August 1930 and was buried at the Kopli Cemetery, founded in 1774 and completely destroyed in 1945 by the Soviet occupation authorities; the area is now a public park.

International legal views. Although primarily a specialist in the fields of administrative and financial law, Berendts made his mark on the science of international law. The first of his scholarly publications in this domain was devoted to the Berlin Conference on the workers’ question.[238] The article analyzed the discussions and outcome of a special Berlin diplomatic conference on the international protection of labor held on 15-16 March 1890 convened at the initiative of Germany to consider the international regulation of “factory legislation”. The Conference suggested several measures for the protection of labor that remained, as Berendts observed, merely wishes.

[236] РГИА, fond 776, opis 23, file 18.

[237] ЦГИА СПб., fond 355, opis 1, file 5470. Also see РГИА СПб., fond 1405, opis 528, file 17; opis 544, file 1060.

[238] E. N. Berendts, «Берлинская международная конференция по рабочему вопросу» [Berlin International Conference on the Workers’ Question], Юридическая хроника [Legal Chronicle], no. 11 (1890), p. 425-431.

But on matters of Finnish law, Berendts remained the greatest specialist on the Finnish question and related issues of Finnish law. The so-called Finnish question was one of the legal status of Finland, which arose after the accession of the territory of Finland to the Russian Empire as a consequence of the Russo-Swedish War of 1808-1809. There were strong international legal elements in the legal status of Finland: sovereign rights (its legislative body – the Sejm, which had the right of legislative initiative); in the sphere of trade, Finland had its own customs legislation with Russia and the countries of western Europe; its State revenues did not flow to the general treasury of the Russian Empire; Finland had its own financial system, monetary system, bank, and post office. Therefore, the problem of determining the legal status of Finland was in that period one of the most topical theoretical and political issues in Russia. The basis thereof was differences in the approaches of politicians, officials, and scholars to understanding the legal status of Finland. Some proceeded from the theory of the union (unie) – the theory of a special State within the Russian Empire; others, from the theory of conquest (the incorporation of a province within the Empire). The Grand Duchy of Finland was considered also as a sovereign State and as part of a real unie with the Russian Empire, and as a vassal State, a protectorate of Russia.[239]

As a legal scholar, Berendts analyzed the theory widely shared in Finland of a special legal status of the Finnish State. This theory was based on 1809 Treaty of Fredrikshamn which ended the Russo-Swedish War, in the course of which Finland was conquered by Russian forces. According to the Treaty, Sweden renounced its eastern province of "Finland" to the benefit of Russia. His analysis of the specific historical facts led Berendts to the following conclusions:

> (1) I do not recognize Finland as a State – not as a non-sovereign State having State autonomy under the Russian power nor as a State standing with Russia in a real or other personal unie, nor as a State which is a protectorate of Russia, nor as a vassal State. I do not recognize Finland as a State because I consider a State to be only that territorial-public union which autonomously may decide its own fate during peace and during war and, consequently, is a subject of international law. A State may be large or small. This is immaterial. Most important is that a union have the right of self-determination and was an autonomous member of the international community. Whether this autonomy is based on an own right given by no one, or is given by another State which creates a new State with an autonomous existence is all the same. Of decisive significance is the right of political self-determination irrespective of the source and factors which created it. Finland is not a subject of international law; it has no right of political determination; consequently, it is not a State;
>
> (2) Finland is an integral part of Russia incorporated by virtue of Article 4 of the 1809 Fredrikshamn Treaty. It is a region (territory, province) subject to an indivisible, unified Russian supreme power. Russia assumed no in-

239 See S. A. Nikiforova, «Проблемы совершенствования государственно-правовой системы России в теоретическом наследии Э. Н. Берендтса» [Problems of Improvement of the State-Legal System of Russia in the Theoretical Legacy of E. N. Berendts], Вестник Санкт-Петербургского университета МВД России [Herald of St. Petersburg University of the Ministry of Internal Affairs of Russia], no. 4 (2015), pp. 68-70.

ternational legal obligations with respect to preserving any special Finnish statehood;

(3) Finland enjoys an autonomy given to it not on the basis of a treaty concluded between Emperor Alexander I and the population of the part of the Kingdom of Sweden conquered by him, but by virtue of the free decision of the Russian monarch which, having the force and power of a conqueror, might at his discretion determine the procedure for the administration and legislation in the newly-conquered territory. He gave autonomy to Finland not by prescription of positive law, but according to considerations of justice and political advisability.[240]

Berendts concluded that Finland is a special autonomous State-legal system within the Russian State. He believed that the Grand Duchy of Finland was an incorporated province of the Russian State. Nonetheless, he emphasized the importance of taking into account national traditions in all spheres of public life and administration and made the case for a bilateral compromise – the foundations of a constructive interaction between the Russian Imperial State and the parts thereof.[241]

In the early twentieth century the Finnish Question became a burning topic with international legal resonance. In 1910, seventy-three professors from German, Austrian, Swiss, and Dutch universities published an Appeal "In Defense of Finland" which demonstrated the need to preserve the legal order in Finland, based on international law, the inviolability of which was threatened by various decisions of the Government of the Russian Empire – the occasion for the Appeal was the decision of the Russian authorities to credit revenues from Finland to the general treasury for military needs, the participation of Finnish authorities in national legislation, and changes in the procedure for the submission of the Emperor's Report on Finnish affairs affecting the interests of the Empire. The Appeal was based on three principal propositions:

(1) the Grand Duchy of Finland was acquired by Russia from Finland with the consent of the population thereof;

(2) the Emperor of Russia, Alexander I, promised to give autonomous existence to Finland with the rights of accession to Russia but as an autonomous State;

(3) inasmuch as the 1809 Fredrikshamn peace treaty, signed according to the outcome of the Russo-Swedish War of 1808-1809 and in accordance with which Finland became part of the Russian Empire with the rights of an autonomous principality, contains a reference to the promise of Alexander

[240] Berendts, «К вопросу о юридической силу старых шведских основных законов в Финляндии» [On the Question of the Legal Force of Old Swedish Basic Laws in Finland], Журнал Министерства юстиции [Journal of the Ministry of Justice], no. 2 (1915), pp. 17-18.

[241] Berendts, К вопросу о правовом положении Финляндии [On the Question of the Legal Status of Finland] (Spb., 1910), p. 18.

I to grant to Finland the status of a special State, this promise acquired the character of an international legal obligation of Russia.

The published Appeal, moreover, asserted: "the existing disagreement between the Russian government and the Finnish people also affects the common interests of the nations of Europe and even all cultured States". These actions of the government of the Russian Empire, in the view of the European professors, "must generate in each cultured and rule-of-law State the most sorrowful attention and amazement".

Berendts reacted to this Appeal and set out his arguments against the European scholars in a lengthy Report presented on 31 January 1910 to the General Assembly of the St. Petersburg Club of Public Figures. Having analyzed the legal status of Finland from the standpoint of international law and Russian law, he formed the following conclusions concerning the unfounded claims against Russia:

(1) *With regard to the assertion that Russia acquired the territory of Finland with the consent of its population.* In the early eighteenth century and the period of possession by Napoleon, when force dominated and not law, norms of international law did not exist providing for any agreement between the conqueror-State and the population of a conquered territory concerning the future State-legal position of this territory;

(2) *With regard to confirmation of the special status of Finland as a State.* Finland as an autonomous formation within Russia possesses a number of indicia of statehood which testify to the extensive autonomy, but not sovereignty, thereof;

(3) *With regard to the reference of Austro-German scholars to the status of the Friderikshām Peace Treaty as containing international legal obligations of Russia.* There are no provisions in the said treaty enabling such a conclusion to be drawn.

The Club of Public Figures, having heard the Berendts Report on the Appeal of the European professors, adopted a decision to fully support the following conclusions expressed in the Report:

(1) the 1809 Fredrikshamn peace treaty did not contain an international legal obligation to grant the status of a "special State" to Finland;

(2) the rights of Finland are not a question of international law, but of the internal law of the Russian Empire.

The general meeting of the Club resolved to print the Berendts Report for general information at its own expense.

§11.6. *Chair of Civil Law and Procedure*

Vasilii Ivanovich Adamovich *(19 December 1856, b. St. Petersburg – after 1917, date and place unknown). Specialist in civil, trade, and Roman law; privat-docent, Chair of Civil Law and Chair of Civil Procedure and Trade Law.*

Life and career. Adamovich graduated in 1877 from the Karl Mai Gymnasium and enrolled at the Law Faculty of St. Petersburg University.[242] His graduation thesis, defended in 1881, earned him the gold medal of the University. From 1881 to 1884 he remained at the University to prepare for the professoriate. He was appointed privat-docent at the Chair of Civil Law and Procedure, where he served from 1884 to 1888, and then privat-docent at the Chair of Trade Law and Procedure from 1888 to 1904 at the University.[243] Among the courses he taught were: "Trade Law (Doctrine on Trade Transactions and Merchant Shipping Law)", "Trade Law and Trade Procedure", and "Trade Law with the Inclusion of Maritime, Bill of Exchange, and Trade Procedure". From 1885 to 1914 he also was employed at the Chancellery of the State Council.

In 1899 he defended a magister dissertation on the counterclaim.[244] He applied in 1903 for a competitive appointment as professor *extraordinarius* at the Chair of Roman Law in the Imperial Novorossiisk University at Odessa and was elected; he served as professor *ordinarius* in that Chair from 1907 to 1910. He returned to St. Petersburg in 1910 and taught for the next four years at the School of Jurisprudence. Simultaneously, from 1910 to 1914 he was an official for special assignments, V Class, of the Ministry of Public Enlightenment. Between 1914 and 1917 he was a member of the Council of the Chief Administration for Affairs of the Press of the Ministry of Internal Affairs. He retired in April 1917 and his whereabouts thereafter are unknown. He gave his personal library to the University, numbering 1,625 volumes.

[242] ЦГИА СПб., fond 14, opis 3, file 19303. Also see Shilokhvost, Русские цивилисты: середина XVIII – начало XX в. Краткий биографический словарь [Russian Civilists: Mid-XVIII – Early XX Century: Concise Biographical Dictionary] (M., 2005), pp. 10-11.

[243] ЦГИА СПб., fond 14, opis 1, file 8468.

[244] V. I. Adamovich, Встречный иск (К учению о зачете) [Counter Suit (On the Doctrine of Set-off)] (Spb., 1899). 290 p.

International legal views. Adamovich published his views on issues of international law in his works on trade law[245] and in a critique of German justifications of the First World War. He touched upon public international law and international conflicts law. Most attention was accorded to trade law, which he considered to be the "branch of legal science concerned with trade activity".[246]

In his discussion of the sources of trade law he enumerated the classical legislative sources (laws, statutes, edicts, and others), including foreign laws concerning maritime trade. Foreign laws apply, he wrote, "when determining the rights and duties of intermediaries relating to the conclusion of transactions, so-called ship brokers: the last are required to possess sufficient information concerning the statutes and rules of commercial shipping in foreign States". Nonetheless, said Adamovich:

> It is not difficult to be convinced that there is extensive access in Russia to foreign legislation; first, one should not lose sight of the whole number of treaties, declarations, and trade treaties concluded by Russia with various States, especially in recent times; second, one should not lose sight of several Articles of the Statute on Civil Procedure (464, 465, 707-709, 1273-1281) treating the recognition of the force of the treaties and acts concluded abroad with regard to laws existing there; although these articles are contained in a procedural law and have significance for new civil judicial institutions, nonetheless – in the material law sense – they have identical significance for trade in general (p. 12).

In order to provide a court with the possibility to apply a foreign law (one can never impute to a court the duty to know foreign legislation), the acts drawn up according to foreign legislation must be submitted in a case not other than with the certification of the Russian embassy, mission, or consulate that they truly were drawn up according to the laws of that State. In addition, in the event in general of difficulty in applying a foreign law, irrespective of recourse to knowledgeable persons such as, for example, a ship broker on merchant shipping law, a court may request the ministry of foreign affairs to communicate with the respective foreign government to provide an opinion on the question which has arisen.

If trade laws are insufficient, then civil laws and customs applicable in trade are applied. The conditions for the application of a custom, according to Adamovich, are: (1) a custom must have arisen on the basis of trade relations; (2) a custom must be generally-known, become a fully mature norm of a customary legal relation, and pass through all known stages (pp. 13-14). A custom must not be contrary to good morals or morality. The existing sense of legal relations can never be distorted by a custom; for example, the insertion in a clause of the right of a person hiring out a thing to demand the return of the thing at any time despite the money paid. A custom must be applied in courts *ex officio*; that is, without awaiting the initiative of the parties in litigation – unlike a general civil custom. Consequently,

245 Adamovich, Конспект лекций по торговому праву [Conspectus of Lectures on Trade Law] (Spb., 1899); Adamovich, Конспект лекций по торговому праву. 1897-98 акад. год [Conspectus of Lectures on Trade Law. 1897-98 Academic Year] (Spb., 1898).

246 Ibid. (1899), p. 4.

a general civil court acting instead of a commercial court is obliged, when considering a trade case, to apply a custom at its own initiative.

Adamovich played a special role in the "duel of intellectuals" at the beginning of the First World War. A "Manifesto of 93 Scholars: Appeal to the Civilized World" was published in the German press on 4 October 1914, signed by ninety-three representatives of the intelligentsia in Germany – among whom were rectors of German universities, well-known cultural figures, and scholars, such as the eminent international lawyer, Franz von Liszt. The Appeal contained a justification of the war unleashed by Germany, which, the Appeal said, Germany had been forced to begin as a defensive measure against the threat of England, France, and Russia. In addition, the authors of the Appeal justified the actions of German forces in the captured territories, asserting that the forces were not violating the requirements of international law and were complying with the laws and customs of war. Not one German soldier had committed any cruelties or evil deeds and they were not infringing the life and health of peaceful inhabitants or their property on the territories occupied by German forces. Russia was portrayed in the Appeal as a barbaric country, unworthy of being in the family of civilized nations. As a supplement to the Appeal, on 16 October 1914 a "Declaration of Lecturers of Higher Schools of the German Empire" was published and signed by more than three thousand German docents and professors.[247]

Insofar as the military facts indicated the contrary (for example, the world public was aware of the destruction of the Belgian city of Louvain (Leuven) by the Germans, including the destruction of the University and burning of its library), and retaliatory protest appeals emerged in Europe and America – so-called "professorial manifestos". In Russia, Adamovich took on the task of preparing, formulating, and editing the reply of the English-French-Russian community. A book published under his editorship contained materials reflecting the positions of England, Russia, and France and refuted the arguments of the German scholars. The authors stated that there was no violation which the governments and military forces of Germany and Austria-Hungary had not committed in complete disregard of the customs of war and international conventions sealed by the signatures of representatives of the Empire at war with the Allies. Concrete examples were given of the unfounded militant position taken by the representatives of the Austro-German public.[248]

[247] «Минифест 93 ученых. Призыв к цивилизованному миру. Манифест Германских университетов» [Manifest of 93 Scholars. Appeal to the Civilized World. Manifesto of German Universities], Две культуры (К философии нынешней войны) [Two Cultures (On the Philosophy of the Present War)] (Petrograd, 1916), pp 122-133.

[248] V. I. Adamovich (ed.), «Протест представителей русской науки против неправомерного ведения войны Германией и Австро-Венгрией» [Protest of Representatives of Russian Science against the Unlawful Waging of War by Germany and Austria-Hungary], in Оправдывание представителей германской интеллигенции нынешней войны и способа ее ведения Германией и Австро-Венгрией и отповедь представителей интеллигенции во Франции, Англии и России [Justification by Representatives of the German Intelligentsia of the Present War and Means of Waging it by Germany and Austria-Hungary and the Rebuke of Representatives of the Intelligentsia in France, England, and Russia] (Pg., 1915), pp. 36-43.

After the aforesaid publication, the Council of Petrograd University adopted a decision to revoke its 1897 decision to confer the title of "Honorary Member of the University" on one of the German signatories of the Appeal, the international lawyer Franz von Liszt, author of the well-regarded treatise on international law translated and republished several times in the Russian language.[249]

Aleksei Nikolaevich Geine *(13 June 1871, b. St. Petersburg – presumably 1917, d. Petrograd). Civilist, specializing in intellectual property law, family law, and the law of the Kingdom of Poland, poet.*

Life and career. Graduated in 1890 from the Fifth Gymnasium and enrolled in the Law Faculty of St. Petersburg University, completing his studies in 1895. The following year he remained at the Chair of Civil Law to prepare for the professoriate and for this purpose was awarded the P. P. Demidov stipend. He was appointed privat-docent at the Chair of Civil Law of the University as from 1 January 1900. There he offered courses on "Russian Civil Law, Special Part, Law of Obligations"; "Family Law"; "Author's Law"; "Contract of Purchase-Sale"; "Bearer Securities"; and others.

Simultaneously he held various posts from 1895 in the judicial department attached to the Petersburg Judicial Chamber. In June 1899 he was appointed to the First Department of the Ministry of Justice and assigned to the jurisconsult unit.

International legal views. Although he produced no works specially treating international law, Geine addressed international legal aspects of author's right in a 1905 article.[250] He noted that author's right in architecture had only been recognized from the second half of the nineteenth century because such works were not considered to be art. But public opinion had changed and legislation in some European jurisdictions followed.

Geine undertook an extensive analysis of European legislation protecting the rights of architects and compared those enactments with Russian. Legislation generally, he noted with regret, did not contain a General Part as was routinely advocated in doctrinal writings but instead applied concrete literary author's right to architecture – which in his view was inappropriate given the special qualities of

[249] On all the complexities involved in this decision, see E. A. Rostovtsev, «Казус профессора фон Листа (эпизод из университетской истории периода Первой мировой войны)» [Causus of Professor von Liszt (Episode from the University History of the Period of the First World War)] in Уроки истории – уроки историка. Сборник статей к 80-летию Ю. Д. Марголиса (1930-1996) [Lessons of History – Lessons of a Historian (Collection of Articles for the 80th Birthday of Iu. D. Margolis (1930-1996)] (Spb., 2012), pp. 308-315.

[250] A. N. Geine, «Авторское право на произведения зодчества (так называемая архитектурная собственность) (в т. ч. анализ норм международного права о защите авторского права архитекторов-художников)» [Author's Right in Works of Architecture (So-Called Architectural Ownership) (Including Analysis of Norms of International Law on the Protection of Author's Right of Architects-Artists)], Вестник права [Herald of Law], no. 7 (September 1905), pp. 297-349. Also published as Geine, Авторское право на произведения зодчества (так называемая архитектурная собственность) [Author's Right in Works of Architecture (So-Called Architectural Ownership)] (Spb., 1905).

architectural creation. He then turned to the regulation of these matters by international law.

He welcomed the decision of the First International Literary Congress held at Paris in 1878 to encourage the protection of architecture just as was done for painting. Two years later the position was legally consolidated by the Convention on Author's Right concluded on 16 June 1880 between France and Spain because both parties understood when exchanging instruments of ratification that architectural works were included. Geine was understandably disappointed when the 1886 Berne Convention on the Protection of Literary Property extended protection only to architectural plans and drawings (Russia acceded to the Berne Convention on 13 March 1995).

Geine was silent in his writings about the reasons for the Russian refusal to ratify the 1886 Berne Convention or to take part in later literary conferences.

Aleksandr Grigorevich Goikhbarg *(also Avraam Moshovich-Gertsevich, Abramko Gertsev)*[251] *(8(21) March 1883, b. small town of Derzahnia, Letichevskii uezd, Podolsk Governate, Ukraine – 1 January 1962, d. Moscow). Civilist, private international law specialist.*

Life and career. Information varies as to precisely where Goikhbarg was born; some sources indicate the small town of Derazhnia, others mention Galuzintsa. In either case, the place was within the Pale of Settlement in Letichevskii uezd, Podolsk Governate, in Ukraine, to the family of a former Moldovian subject attached to a local petty bourgeois society.[252]

After graduating in 1902 with the gold medal from the Second Zhitomir Gymnasium, he matriculated at the Law Faculty of Kyiv St. Vladimir University, but was expelled after three semesters in 1904. From 1906 to 1909 he was a student at the Law Faculty of St. Petersburg University.[253] From 1 March 1910 he remained at the University Chair of Civil Law to prepare for the professoriate;[254] this period was extended to 1 March 1914. In December 1912 and October 1913 he passed his magister examinations, and in 1914 defended a magister dissertation "On Pledge". From 1914 to 1917 he was privat-docent at the Chair of Civil Law of the Univer-

[251] Certificate on Appearance for Performance of Military Duty, 18 December 1906. ЦГИА СПб., fond 14, opis 1, file 10345.

[252] ГАРФ, fond 533, opis 1, file 1284, l. 2. See the biography of Goikhbarg by O. Iu. Shilokhvost, Александр Гойхбарг: Горькая судьба Красного Трибониана. Биография создателя первого советского Гражданского кодекса [Aleksandr Goikhbarg: Bitter Fate of the Red Tribonian: Biography of the Creator of the First Soviet Civil Code] (M., 2020), p. 14. Also see «Гойхбарг Александр Григорьевич» [Goikhbarg, Aleksandr Grigorevich], in G. G. Branover (ed.), Российская Еврейская энциклопедия [Russian Jewish Encyclopedia] (2d ed.; M., 1994), I, p. 331; Shilokhvost, note 242 above, pp. 44-45.

[253] ЦГИА СПб., fond 14, opis 16, file 27.

[254] ЦГИА СПб., fond 14, opis 1, file 10345.

sity, where he led tutorials on civil law, the law of obligations, and insurance law. In the spring semester of 1917 he lectured on bankruptcy law and procedure.[255]

During the periods from 1910 to 1911 and from 1914 to 1916 he lectured on civil law and procedure and on family law at the Higher (Bestuzhev) Women's Courses. From 1915 he lectured on "Bankruptcy Law" at the Petrograd Institute of Higher Commercial Knowledge.[256] Political activities engaged much of his time; he frequently changed his party orientation; however, from 1904 to 1917 he was a member of the Russian Social Democratic Workers' Party (Menshevik). Nonetheless, throughout 1905 he was the co-editor of the first legal Bolshevik newspaper, Новая жизнь [New Life]. When the Bolshevist newspaper was closed down, he began to place his articles in the Вестник гражданского права [Herald of Civil Law], published by Maksim Moiseevich Vinaver (1863-1926), an anti-Bolshevik leader.

Following the October 1917 Revolution, Goikhbarg left the Party of the Menshevik socialists and joined the Bolsheviks. For a few years, until 1924, he became an eminent Party and State figure, regarded as the "father" of the first Soviet civil code and an author of works on private international law.

International legal views. Goikhbarg is known to legal history primarily as a specialist in civil law – the general theory of civilistics, contract of insurance, land law, economic law, and family law. Less known is that Goikhbarg wrote about private international law in the Imperial and Soviet eras. His first article concerned war and the rights of private individuals and juridical persons, especially the legal status of foreign subjects on the territories of belligerent powers.[257] In his second article Goikhbarg analyzed legal aspects of possible payments by subjects of enemy powers. This especially concerned prisoners of war, who had to act through their attorneys. Among the questions addressed were: did legal means exist in connection with the war for unilateral delay of payments or non-payments? Were remittances abroad by foreign subjects used or not used to strengthen the might of their respective countries? To both these questions Goikhbarg gave a negative response.[258]

At the height of the First World War, Goikhbarg published a book that proved to be of practical use on land ownership and land use by foreign subjects. The work

[255] Обозрение преподавания наук на Юридическом факультете Императорского Петроградского Университета в осеннем полугодии 1916 года и в весеннем полугодии 1917 года [Survey of Teaching of Sciences at the Law Faculty of the Imperial Petrograd University in the Autumn Semester of 1916 and Spring Semester of 1917] (Pg., 1916), pp. 6, 10.

[256] ЦГИА СПб., fond 14, opis 1, file 10345, l. 55.

[257] A. G. Goikhbarg, «Являются ли иностранцы субъектами права по общим законам или только в силу конвенций» [Are Foreigners Subjects of Law under General Laws or Only by Virtue of Conventions], Вестник права [Herald of Law], no. 37 (1914), cols. 1088-1092.

[258] Goikhbarg, «К вопросу о способах задержания платежей подданным враждебных держав» [On the Question of Means of Delaying Payments to Subjects of Enemy Powers], Вестник права и нотариата [Herald of Law and the Notariat], no. 35 (1914), cols. 1037-1041.

appeared in two volumes with slightly varying titles.[259] In volume one Goikhbarg undertook a commentary on three laws of 2 February 1915 devoted to aspects of land possession and land use in Russia by Austrian, German, Hungarian, or Turkish subjects (that is, subjects of the powers fighting against Russia), and also of German, Austrian, and Hungarian émigrés who had become Russian subjects. Goikhbarg pointed out that although these laws were adopted in the heat of war, they were not "wartime laws"; they were intended for general application: first, these laws were retroactive; second, these laws were intended for peacetime. Goikhbarg identified flagrant contradictions permitted by the draftsmen (for example, the first two articles of the Law of 2 February contained norms contradictory to one another: Article 21 established an absolute prohibition against the acquisition of immoveable property by any means, and Article 2 permitted such acquisition by way of inheritance).

According to the 1915 laws analyzed by Goikhbarg, subjects of powers fighting against Russia (except subjects of Bulgaria) were all prohibited from acquiring throughout Russia the right of ownership and other rights to a thing in immoveable property, and also the right of possession and use of immoveable property separate from the right of ownership (for example, the right of lease and rental, except for the rental of apartments, houses, and other premises). They were also prohibited from managing the said property as attorneys or as managers. These limitations extended not only to natural persons, but also to any type of society or partnership. In addition, limitations were imposed on certain categories of "suspicious Russian subjects". Thus, any type of society of colonists – émigrés of German origin – could not acquire any rights to immoveable property on the territory of the Russian Empire. Individual Russian subjects from among Austrian, Hungarian, and German émigrés also were so limited, but only outside urban settlements. However, these limitations did not extend to acquisition by right of inheritance.

In his second volume Goikhbarg produced a commentary on the Law of 13 December 1915 which made certain changes in legislation enacted earlier in that year and took into account the implementation of the Law of 2 February 1915. The December changes expanded the range of persons falling under the limitations; clarified the localities where the legislation applied; and expanded the legal relations to which the operation of the legislation extended. Added to the range of subjects from Germany, Austria-Hungary, and Turkey were descendants through the male line who were subjects or held citizenship of other foreign States if they became subjects of these foreign States after 1 January 1880.

Goikhbarg argued that the application of the December Law might be unfavorable. For example, that Law might generate protests on the part of neutrals or even powers friendly to Russia. Retaliatory limitations on the part of other powers might be introduced by invoking the principle of reciprocity. And the Law might be a barrier to attracting foreign investors, especially American, in the natural re-

[259] Goikhbarg, Землевладение и землепользование подданных враждебных держав и немецких выходцев [Land Possession and Land Use by Subjects of Enemy Powers and German Emigrants] (Pg., 1915). 2 vols. Volume two contained a Composite Text of the laws of 2 February and 13 December 1915.

sources of Russia. Other complexities might affect Russian subjects of foreign origin.

Goikhbarg followed other aspects of private international law: change of the legal status of trade enterprises of foreign States; remuneration for war losses; and others.

Adolf Khristianovich Golmsten *(25 November 1848, b. Oranienbaum, St . Petersburg Province – 6 July 1920, d. Station Lykoshino, Novgorod Governate). Specialist in civil law and procedure.*[260]

Life and career. After graduating from the Second Petersburg Gymnasium, Golmsten enrolled at the Law Faculty of St. Petersburg University, which he completed in 1873 with the degree of candidate of laws. He then was sent abroad, where for two years he pursued studies in civil law and procedure at universities in Berlin, Munich, and Heidelberg. From 1877 he worked in the Legislative Division of the Ministry of Justice, and from 1882, served as a member of the Commission for Preparing the Draft Russian Civil Code. During the period from 1884 to 1886, he acted as a senior aide of the jurisconsult of the Ministry of War.

In 1886 he passed the magister examinations and defended a magister dissertation on the "Principle of Identity in Civil Procedure" at the Kyiv St. Vladimir University. From 1889 he became privat-docent,[261] from 1895 – professor *extraordinarius*, and from 1908 – professor *ordinarius*[262] at St. Petersburg University in the Chair of Civil Procedure and Trade Law. At various times he was a lecturer at the Chair of Civil Procedure of the School of Jurisprudence; Chair of Civil Law at the Alexander Lycée; Chair of Civil Law and Chair of Civil Procedure at the Military Law Academy; and Chair of General Lexprudence at the Mining Institute. However, a doctoral dissertation submitted for discussion by the Law Faculty on 4 March 1891 on the topic "Historical Survey of Russian Bankruptcy Procedure" was deemed to be "unsatisfactory". In 1914 the degree of Doctor of Civil Law was conferred on Golmsten by recommendation of the Council of Kazan University

[260] Shilokhvost, note 242 above, pp. 46-47.

[261] ЦГИА СПб., fond 14, opis 1, file 9009.

[262] ЦГИА СПб., fond 139, opis 1, file 8392.

for the aggregate of his scholarly publications, a decision duly confirmed by the Ministry of Public Enlightenment.

During the academic year 1898-1899 he was the secretary of the Law Faculty, and on 18 September 1899 appointed the Rector of St. Petersburg University for four years. On 13 October 1908 the title of "Distinguished Professor" was conferred in honor of his serving for thirty years in the University.[263] From January to October 1912 he was the Dean of the Law Faculty.

He was appointed a member of the Commission for the Review of Legal Provisions with regard to the Judiciary attached to the Ministry of Justice in 1894. From 1882 to 1886 and again from 1888 to 1891 he was the editor of the civil law section of the Журнал гражданского и уголовного права [Journal of Civil and Criminal Law]. His publishing record was impressive in his chosen field: five editions of a Учебник гражданского судопроизводства [Textbook of Civil Procedure]; four editions of revising, augmenting, and editing D. I. Meier, Русское гражданское право [Russian Civil Law]; a monograph on Исторический очерк конкурсного процесса [Historical Survey of Bankruptcy Procedure], a course on trade law Курс торгового права [Course of Trade Law]; two volumes of legal studies Юридические исследования [Legal Studies], and more than one hundred articles in legal journals.

When the Law Faculty of St. Petersburg University was reorganized in 1918-1919, Golmsten continued to lecture in the Politico-Legal Division of the Faculty of Social Sciences of the University as a professor at the Chair of Civil Law and Procedure.[264] The instructional plan for the 1919/20 academic year, confirmed on 13 October 1919, included Golmsten teaching a lecture course on the "Science on the Civil Court" and giving tutorials on civil law.[265] A week later the Politico-Legal Division recommended that the title of professor be conferred on Golmsten.[266] The archives, however, indicate that even after the establishment of Soviet power Golmsten remained a Distinguished Professor at the Chair of Civil Law and Procedure.

Golmsten retired in 1919, having spent his entire academic career at St. Petersburg (Petrograd) University. He died on 6 July 1920.

International legal views. Two of Golmsten's numerous publications are directly concerned with international law. The first was a succinct but detailed piece on the draft trade treaty between Russia and Germany.[267] Golmsten noted that although the treaty concerned chiefly issues of trade and navigation, it touched upon

[263] ЦГИА СПб., fond 139, opis 1, file 16074.

[264] ОА СПбГУ, fond l, opis 1, file 141, l. 14.

[265] ЦГА СПб., fond 7240, opis 14, file 85, l. 30.

[266] ЦГА СПб., fond 7240, opis 14, file 85, l. 32.

[267] A. Golmsten, «Заметки по поводу проекта торгового договора между Россией и Германией» [Notes with Regard to the Draft Trade Treaty between Russia and Germany], Журнал Юридического общества при Императорском Санкт-Петербургском университете [Journal of the Law Society attached to the Imperial St.-Petersburg University], no. 3 (1894), pp. 1-4.

other important domains of legal life, especially the right to acquire immoveables and the right to sue. He demonstrated that those who prepared the draft treaty, accidentally or deliberately, included seriously flawed provisions. For example, according to the Statute on Civil Procedure, foreigners who were not in Russian service and did not possess immoveable property in Russia, experienced limitations in that they were obliged, at the demand of their defendants, to submit security for costs in a case and those losses which the defendant might sustain.

At the time, Golmsten noted, the duty when filing suit to provide security extended to all foreigners without distinction of nationality. The text of the draft treaty with Germany, however, was so drawn up that upon its entry into force German subjects would be exempted from this duty; the French, English, Italians, and other foreigners must bear the entire burden of these limitations. Of course, Golmsten observed, thanks to this exemption Russian subjects would not be obliged to provide security when filing suit in German courts. But if one takes into account the significant numerical superiority of Germans in Russia versus Russians in Germany, the disproportion is unjust. The Germans in Russia will have significantly greater privileges over other foreigners than Russians in Germany (p. 2).

The draft treaty further provided that the subjects of the Contracting Parties shall be "granted the right to have recourse, being guided by the laws of the country, to judicial institutions both in order to bring suits and to defend their rights, and in this respect they shall enjoy all the rights and privileges given to local subjects" (p. 2). Thus, the Germans in Russia and the Russians in Germany are equated in rights with local subjects in respect of the right to bring suit. However, in Golmsten's view, this would create problems for other foreigners. It would be desirable, he suggested, to make a special reservation that such a right is recognized with respect to the right of subjects of the Contracting Parties to acquire immoveables; according to the special clause, this right would be recognized insofar as this is permitted to foreigners of any other nationality" (p. 3).

The second work by Golmsten on international law was a lengthy review of Ovchinnikov on the law of prize.[268] Golmsten stated at the outset that his book review had been prepared on the basis of a Report in his capacity as an official opponent in the defense by Ovchinnikov of a dissertation submitted to the Military Law Academy. Affirming the topicality of Ovchinnikov's thesis, Golmsten quoted the view of J. C. Bluntschli – that prize law was a "blank spot in international law" (p. 13). He dwelt on the methodological foundations of the study, considering them in many places to be mistaken, analyzed the historical part of the study with an abundance of examples of the operation of prize law, and devoted attention to the philosophical (that is, the doctrinal) aspect of the work.

He was critical of Ovchinnikov's account of the legal grounds for the right of a State to authorize the taking of prizes (vessels and cargoes) in the ownership of private individuals. Ovchinnikov had reviewed the various opinions on this question and suggested that the law of prize derived from the purpose of war – to weaken

[268] Golmsten, review of I. A. Ovchinnikov, Призовое право [Prize Law] (Spb., 1897), vol. 1, in Журнал Юридического общества при Императорском Санкт-Петербургском университете [Journal of the Law Society attached to the Imperial St.-Petersburg University], no. 3 (1894), pp. 12-33.

the enemy. Golmsten reproached Ovchinnikov for this view, based on the use of doubtful methodological methods:

> The principal methodological requirement here is the equal reproduction of the opinions which agree with the view of the author and which disagree with him; one must devote an identical place to one and the other, concealing nothing from either side. If this requirement is not satisfied, then one receives an incorrect impression of the state of the question (pp. 18-19).

In other words, Golmsten said that Ovchinnikov gave more attention to those with whom he agreed in comparison with those with whom he disagreed. Golmsten then turned to the dogmatic aspect of the work under review – the concrete legal phenomena and legal relations determined by particular legal norms. The principal requirement of the dogmatic method, Golmsten believed, was that the dogmatic researcher must rely on legal norms – legislative, international customary rules, or treaty provisions. His review was a veritable conspectus of the law of prize itself: subjects, object, means of capture, procedure for acquiring rights to a prize, variants of judicial decisions in contested situations, ways of determining the nationality of ships and the role of the flag, including the presence or absence of a patent for the flag, legal aspects of the sale of an enemy ship to subjects of a neutral State, normal conditions for purchase-sale, and the grounds for a sold vessel to fly a particular flag.

Vladimir Mikhailovich Gordon *(25 October (6 November) 1871, b. Lokhvitsa (now Poltava Region) – 3 January 1926, d. Kharkov).*[269] *Civilist, specializing in civil and trade law and civil procedure. Academician, All-Ukrainian Academy of Sciences.*

Life and career. After graduating in 1890 from the Kishinev Gymnasium, he enrolled in that year with an Imperial stipend and completed in 1894 the Law Faculty of St. Petersburg University. In 1896 he remained to prepare for the professoriate with a P. P. Demidov stipend and simultaneously assigned to the III Department of the Ruling Senate. From 1897 to 1899 he traveled to universities and libraries in Berlin, Leipzig, Munich, Vienna, Switzerland, and Paris. He was appointed privat-docent from 1 July 1899. His magister dissertation on "Ground for Suit Comprising a Change of Suit Demands" led to his appointment as professor *extraordinarius* in 1903 at the Demidov Juridical Lycée, He defended his dissertation

[269] I. P. Safronova, in Iu. S. Shemshuchenko (ed.), Юридична енциклопедія [Legal Encyclopedia] (Kyiv, 1998), I, p. 617.

for the doctor of civil law in 1906 on the topic "Suits on Recognition" and became professor *ordinarius* at Kharkov University He taught at various institutions, including the Demidov Lycée in Iaroslavl for five years from 1901 to 1906 and universities in Kharkov and Crimea.

From March to November 1917 he was again at Petrograd University, where he taught a course "Trade Law and Trade Court Procedure" and simultaneously served as a Senator in the IV (Cassation) Department of the Ruling Senate. From the end of 1917 throughout 1918 he lectured at the Chair of Trade Law of the Moscow Commercial Institute and the Moscow Higher Women's Courses. At a session of the Council of the Law Faculty of Petrograd University on 13 January 1919 it was decided to consider him to have left the University as not having returned from a business trip.

From 1920 to 1922 he was a professor at the Tauride University in Simferopol. In 1920 he also returned to Kharkov University where he was Head of the Chair of Civil and Trade Law and from 1921 to 1922 a jurisconsult at the People's Commissariat of Justice of the Crimean Autonomous Soviet Socialist Republic. From 1922 he was professor of trade law and Dean of the Law Faculty at the Institute of National Economy in Kharkov and from 1923 head of the Chair of Problems of Contemporary Law. For some years he also served as the Head of the Legal Department of the People's Commissariat of Internal Trade of the Ukrainian SSR. He was elected on 9 March 1925 to the All-Ukrainian Academy of Sciences, where he was Head of the Chair of Civil Law.

International legal views. Gordon did not produce works devoted solely to international law. In a study of the world unification of the law on bills of exchange, however, he expressed views of international legal interest. On the eve of the First World War, he believed such a unification process was underway: "Both a natural inclination for community life, an *appetitus societat*, and practical necessity will lead mankind towards unification".[270] And he believed this process was underway. Differences in speech drew mankind towards the formation of a single language. And the diversity of legal norms "causes concern about the elimination of conflicts, towards the creation of an international and inter-State law". He was persuaded that mankind "wishes to completely destroy difference in law, create a single law" so that in the future all would live under one law. The unification of the law of bills of exchange was one step forward on this path.

He saw the idea of a single, universal, world bill of exchange law emerging in the eighteenth century, and he viewed the unification of Germany after 1870 as evidence that such a unified law could be achieved. Extension of the German bill of exchange statute to other countries would even be a positive step. He nonetheless recognized the serious arguments against such unification, not least that the diversity of national legislation on the subject was rooted in their respective legal systems and traditions, languages and customs. He was optimistic that sundry international conferences devoted to such unification had made progress and might

[270] V. M. Gordon, «Мировое объединение вексельного права» [World Unification of Bill of Exchange Law], Журнал Министерства юстиции [Journal of Ministry of Justice], no. 2 (1912), p. 154 (also available as separate offprint.

ultimately achieve a result and welcomed Russian participation in such efforts. He did not live to see the Convention on the issue.

Avgust Isaakovich Kaminka *(9 September 1865, b. Kherson – autumn 1941, d. Riga, Latvia). Civilist, public and political figure, publicist, publisher.*

Life and career. After graduating from the First St. Petersburg Gymnasium in 1882, he enrolled in 1884[271] and in 1888 graduated with the degree of candidate from the Law Faculty of St. Petersburg University. He remained at the Chair of Civil Law to prepare for the professoriate and was sent to attend lectures and work in libraries at the universities of Berlin and Heidelberg.

Upon returning to Russia in 1902, he passed the magister examinations and successfully defended a magister dissertation on joint-stock companies.[272] Kaminka devised a definition of the joint-stock company which became the foundation of the contemporary definition in Russia. His supervisor was Nikolai Lvovich Diuvernua (1836-1906).[273] From 1 July 1894 Kaminka was appointed privat-docent at the Chair of Civil and Trade Law and Procedure of St. Petersburg University.[274] In 1912 he resigned from the University as privat-docent, but he returned for the academic year 1918/19 as professor at the Chair of Civil Law and lectured on the "History of Trade Law"; "Bill of Exchange Law", and "Questions of the Codification of Civil Law".

Kaminka held additional positions in parallel with his University appointment. From 1909 he served as a professor of the Higher Women's (Bestuzhev) Courses and at the St. Petersburg Institute of Commercial Knowledge (from 1910),[275] where he lectured on trade law.

[271] ЦГИА СПб., fond 14, opis 3, file 24036.

[272] A. I. Kaminka, Акционерные компании: Юридическое исследование [Joint-Stock Companies: Legal Study] (Spb., 1902).

[273] Diuvernua translated and edited the classical work on the reception of Roman law by the Dutch legal scholar, W. Modderman (1838-1882), *Die Reception des römischen Rechts* (Jena, 1875). See Modderman, Рецепция римского права [Reception of Roman Law] (Spb., 1888).

[274] ЦГИА СПб., fond 14, opis 2, file 894.

[275] ЦГА СПб., fond 2998, opis 1, file 537.

Kaminka was a practicing lawyer from 1895 to 1917 as a sworn advokat of the St. Petersburg District Chamber of Justice and a sworn *striapchii* attached to the St. Petersburg Commercial Court.[276]

In 1898, together with young colleagues, Kaminka founded a weekly newspaper of a liberal orientation, Право [Law], and became a co-editor. He published widely in other legal journals of the period. When the 1905 Revolution occurred, he became an organizer and leader of the Constitutional Democratic Party (Kadets), being elected to its Central Committee.

After the October 1917 Revolution, he initially remained at the University and continued to lecture. University records indicate that he was elected as professor *ordinarius* by the Council of the First Petrograd University for the 1918/19 academic year and appointed as acting professor *ordinarius* (supernumerary) from 17 October 1918 at the Chair of Trade Law and Procedure.[277] He did not support the Bolshevik Revolution, however; he attempted to resist. With P. N. Miliukov in Kyiv he entered into negotiations with the ambassador of Germany in Ukraine about the Germans rendering assistance against the Bolsheviks.

In January 1919 he was arrested in Petrograd, transported to Moscow, and placed in Butyrka Prison. Thanks to the efforts of his influential pupil, graduate of St. Petersburg University, and former colleague on his newspaper, A. G. Goikhbarg, he was released. In February 1919 he emigrated (his second attempt) to Finland; he lived in Berlin from 1920, became there a co-founder of the publishing house Слово [Word], and one of the founders and leaders of the widely-distributed émigré newspaper Руль [Rudder] (1920-1931); he initiated the formation and was chairman of the Russian Academic Group in Berlin; and he was among the founders of the "Union of the Russian Sworn Advokatura", also in Berlin. He joined the Organizational Committee of the Russian Scientific Institute in Berlin, formed on 17 February 1923, and lectured there on Russian trade law.

As the political situation changed in Germany and the Nazi Party came to power, Kaminka moved to Riga, Latvia, where the Russian Law Society operated from spring 1929 and regularly published the journal Закон и суд [Law and Court].[278] Kaminka became the head of the editorial committee and regularly contributed articles on State law, joint-stock company legislation, and private international law.

276 See Shilokhvost, note 242 above (2005), p. 79.

277 ЦГА СПб., fond 7240, opis 14, file 26 ; fond 2998, opis 1, file 557; ОА СПбГУ, fond 1, opis 1, file 141.

278 Закон и суд: Вестник русского юридического общества [Law and Court: Herald of the Russian Law Society] (Riga, 1929-1938); reprinted as (Riga, Latvijas Juristu biedriba. Senatora Augusta Lebera fonds, 2000). 10 vols. in 8. Copies of the original journal are rare and not well-known, one of apparently two Russian-language journals in emigration devoted entirely and exclusively to law. There are important articles on public international law and Imperial Russian law. The Latvian Government closed the journal in 1938 by refusing to re-register the organization sponsoring its publication. In a Letter from the Latvian Ministry of Justice dated 18 July 1938 it was said that the publication did not "correspond to the spirit and aims of recent legislation of our State inasmuch as it still lives too much in the practice and theory of the jurisprudence of former Russia". Reviewed in *Sudebnik*, V (2000), pp. 829-831 (W. E. Butler).

On 1 July 1941 German forces entered Riga. Mass extermination of the Jews commenced, and Kaminka is believed to have perished in the Riga ghetto during autumn 1941.

International legal views. Kaminka made his reputation primarily in the field of civil and trade law. Several publications, however, are concerned with private international law. Of importance is a series of articles on war and private law published in Право [Law].[279] Kaminka devoted each installment to a particular topic. In his view, many legal norms, principles, and institutions of a public and private character were subjected to unforeseen trials and required rethinking and adjustments.

An analysis of the operation of legal norms during war is rather useful, given the importance of legal life that continues even on the fields of battle:

> Legal status during war represents two peculiarities. First, an awareness of the significance and important of law is blunted; second, laws are applied, albeit specially intended for war but drafted during peacetime, when people do not really imagine war. And when it begins and horrors develop inevitably one after another, these laws either cease to operate with that force they were calculated to do or they prove in general to be completely unsuitable to these new conditions.

Despite the fact, Kaminka noted, that many centuries of experience have shown that contracts with the subjects of belligerent States should be recognized during war, nonetheless "a distinctive feature of war is that general principles of law lose significance, and a situation ensues under which many questions ultimately are resolved by force" (cols. 2617-2618). Among the controversial issues of jurisprudence, he said, is the borderline between public and private law ... That border separating these two domains is distinguished by a significant indefiniteness and changeability in time. The central part of private and public law is characterized by unique features that are impossible to combine" (cols. 2841-2842). The "noise of weapons and the clatter of horse's hoofs" may deaden the voice of private law, but cannot and must not force it to be silent. War, he observed, is waged by States, and not by individual citizens. Therefore, during war citizens do not lose the rights belonging to them because the tasks advanced by the interests of war do not cause this. The conclusion is unavoidable that the civil rights of subjects of belligerent States during war should be fully recognized in a belligerent State (cols. 2617-2618).

The sacred nature of private rights even during war is beyond doubt. But what of the rights of the belligerent parties themselves? What if governmental budgetary revenues invested in foreign banks and securities during a war prove to be residents of the opposing party? States wage war between themselves and, consequently, there are no grounds to mutually recognize State ownership. Thus, a private-law transaction in which the Russian Government entered into with banks

[279] A. Kaminka, «Война и частное право» [War and Private Law], Право [Law], no. 34 (1914), cols. 2433-2437; no. 38, cols. 2617-2624, 2681-2688; no. 42, cols. 2841-2848; no. 44, cols. 2976-2983; no. 48, cols. 3266-3274; (1915), no. 10, cols. 704-711.

abroad may be complicated, in the event of war, by public-law elements (no. 42, cols. 2844-2845).

Kaminka believed that priority should be given to norms of private law; the interests of world monetary circulation and inter-State financial relations counseled this approach. Just as a careless debtor ultimately loses credit, so too a State which encroaches upon the ownership of another, albeit in a state of war, cannot count upon a postwar restoration of its solvency and reputation as a debtor in good faith. The expropriation of the gold reserve of a belligerent country will ultimately lead to a reduction in the balance of payments of the expropriating country.

Kronid Ivanovich Malyshev *(25 September 1841, b. Sukhoborskoe, Cheliabinsk uezd, Orenburg Governate – 3 January 1907, d. St. Petersburg. Russian jurist who founded the civilist conception of private international law – the doctrine on the domestic conflicts of law.*

Life and career. Contemporaries regarded Malyshev as the "luminary of Russian civilistics",[280] the progenitor of the conflicts of law component of private international law. He received his primary education at the Cheliabinsk Theological School and Ufa Seminary, and higher education initially at the Kazan Theological Academy, from which at the age of 23 in 1864 after finishing the third year he transferred[281] to the Law Faculty of St. Petersburg University.[282] Experiencing serious financial difficulties and supporting himself with incidental earnings, Malyshev was able to graduate from the Faculty in 1868 and remained at the Chair of Civil Law and Procedure to prepare for the professoriate.[283]

280 Iu. V. Tai, Светило русской цивилистики [Luminary of Russian Civilistics], in K. I. Malyshev, Избранные труды по конкурсному процессу и иным институтам торгового права [Selected Works on a Bankruptcy Proceeding and Other Institutions of Trade Law] (reprint ed.; M., 2007), pp. 7-44.

281 Seeking to enroll at the Law Faculty of St. Petersburg University but lacking resources to pay for travel, Malyshev mostly walked from Kazan to St. Petersburg or caught rides on strings of carts. On Malyshev, see V. S. Ivanenko, "Kronid Malyshev and the Renaissance of Private International Law", *Jus Gentium: Journal of International Legal History*, III (2018), pp. 539-551.

282 ЦГИА СПб., fond 14, opis 5, file 2792.

283 ЦГИА СПб., fond 14, opis 1, file 6821.

On 10 April 1871 Malyshev defended a dissertation for the degree of magister of civil law.[284] Having become a Docent at the Chair of Civil Law, he was sent abroad for two years, where he studied the peculiarities of civil and trade practice and law, the legal foundations of the activity of stock exchanges, banks, enterprises, customs houses, joint-stock societies, and the like in Western Europe and North America. While abroad, Malyshev visited about 2,000 trade institutions, gathering material concerning the organization and activity. Upon returning to Petersburg, he from 11 September 1873 lectured at the University on civil procedure and then on civil law.[285] On 20 September 1875 Malyshev introduced at his own initiative a course of lectures on "Trade Law", a new course not yet part of the syllabus of law faculties in Russian universities. Malyshev resigned from the University in 1882 to take a civil service position and devoted himself to lawmaking and codification. From 1882 to 1893 he was a senior official in the Codification Section of the State Council, and when that section was abolished, held from 1893 to 1895 the office of Secretary of State of the division for the Digest of Laws of the State Chancellery. From 1894 to 1906 he served as an active member of the Committee and Editorial Commission for preparing a draft Civil Code of Russia, and simultaneously from 1895 as a member of the Consultation Committee attached to the Ministry of Justice. He died on 3 January 1907 and is buried at the Nikolskii Cemetery in the Alexander Nevsky Monastery.[286]

International legal views. It should be noted that Malyshev has entered the history of Russian doctrine as the greatest civilist of the second half of the nineteenth and early twentieth centuries in Russia; one of the progenitors of the Russian school of civil law and procedure as evidenced by his erudite scholarly works and lawmaking activity. While in his lectures, scientific publications, and practical activity he attached important significance to theory, especially its critical component, Malyshev favored a close link between legal science and legal practice; he drew attention to the usefulness and necessity of studying concrete legal relations, the distinctive features of transactions and obligations, and the procedure for handling cases in various institutions, without which, in his view, legal theory is dormant.

One of his auditors and subsequently a noted specialist in the field of civil law, Professor Igor Matveevich Tiutriumov (1855-1943), recalled: Malyshev's lectures were distinguished by being "always picturesque and the clarity of thoughts expressed, astonishing concision and precision of definitions, always enthusiastically

[284] K. I. Malyshev, Исторический очерк конкурсного права [Historical Survey of the Bankruptcy Process] (Spb., 1871). Professor S. V. Pakhman (1825-1910) called the dissertation a "model for future works of our civilists". Cited in M. Kantor, «Кронид Малышев (1841-1907)» [Kronid Malyshev (1841-1907)], Вестник гражданского права [Herald of Civil Law], no. 8 (1916), p. 5.

[285] ЦГИА СПб., fond 11, opis 1, file 782 (1874).

[286] Malyshev bequeathed his personal library (10,000 volumes) and author's rights to Tomsk University ("the most eastern Russian university at which a law faculty will exist"). On his gravestone this inscription is engraved from a grateful University: "Imperial Tomsk University to Professor Kronid Ivanovich Malyshev". See E. A. Maleev, «История одного памятника» [History of One Monument], Правоведение [Jurisprudence], no. 6 (1987), p. 89.

visited by attendees, surprised by the enormous erudition of the professor, and carried away from the lectures great interest in the courses he taught".[287]

Another specialist on the life and works of Malyshev, G. M. Kolonozhnikov, noting the "enormous" services of Malyshev in the field of the science of civil law and practice, wrote: "In his day the name of this scholar enjoyed the greatest popularity and authority in the learned and judicial worlds".[288] In legal doctrine Malyshev usually is linked with the birth of the Russian science of private international law: Malyshev is "the founder of the civilist conception of the understanding of private international law"[289] who "substantiated" this conception,[290] developed the doctrine of "so-called inter-regional conflicts",[291] thereby making an "exceedingly large contribution to the Russian science of international law".[292] The view has been expressed that Malyshev advanced a "dual conflicts theory – the existence of autonomous intra-conflicts and international private law".[293]

This view is not completely accurate. Although Malyshev was a pioneer in analyzing many aspects of private international law, the foregoing statement requires clarification.

Malyshev's contributions to legal scholarship began in the 1870s. Russia was experiencing positive socio-economic and legal development: serfdom had been abolished, the economy had begun to grow, trade links had been strengthened among regions within Russia, and foreign trade had grown significantly. But complex problems had been discovered that affected the operation in the Russian Empire of general civil legislation and local laws, principally on conquered territories of the Empire: the provisions of the French Code Civil (in force in parts of the

287 I. M. Tiutriumov, «Памяти Кронида Ивановича Малышева» [In Memory of Kronid Ivanovich Malyshev], Журнал Министерства юстиции [Journal of the Ministry of Justice], no. 1 (1907), p. 208.

288 G. M. Kolonozhnikov, Кронид Иванович Малышев: Биография и характеристика. С портретом и списком трудов [Kronid Ivanovich Malyshev: Biography and Characteristics. With a Portrait and List of Works] (Tomsk, 1917), p. 1.

289 G. K. Dmitrieva (ed.), Международное частное право [Private International Law] (3d ed.; Moscow, 2015), p. 43.

290 V. A. Kanashevskii, Международное частное право [International Private Law] (Moscow, 2009), p. 39.

291 M. M. Boguslavskii, Международное частное право [International Private Law] (Moscow, 2009), p. 39.

292 S. N. Lebedev and E. V. Kabatova (eds.), Международное частное право. В 2-х томах [International Private Law. In Two Volumes] (M., 2011), I, p. 47.

293 Iu. A. Komnatnaia, «Эволюция отечественной доктрины международного частного (коллизионного) права в дореволюционный период: Михайл Игнатьевич Мыш» [Evolution of Russian Doctrine of International Private (Conflicts) Law in the Pre-Revolutionary Period: Mikhail Ignat'evich Mysh], in E. N. Kamyshanchenko and Iu. L. Rastopchina (eds.), Современные проблемы социально-экономического развития России [Contemporary Problems of the Socio-Economic Development of Russia] (Belgorod, 2012), p. 364.

Kingdom of Poland which had acceded to Russia),[294] Swedish laws (in Finland), civil codes of the Baltic "Ostsee" provinces based on the legal acts of Polish and Swedish kings, Roman law, and local city statutes; Byzantine sources (in Bessarabia), the Lithuanian Statute in the Chernigov and Poltava provinces, among others. All this when entering into civil law relations and trade links led to conflicts of both "inter-regional laws" and conflicts of "nomadic" or "different nationality" laws. This was especially evident in court disputes.

Russian legal science could not fail to react to this anomalous situation in the legal space of the Russian Empire. Malyshev could not stand aside.

Malyshev was a leading scholar in the fields of civil law and procedure, noteworthy for his scholarly approach and conscientiousness. But for all of his scholarly reticence and diligence, he did not study international law; he does not have a single work devoted to international law. Consequently, Malyshev did not directly research private-law relations in the international, or inter-State, sphere. He mentioned them only in volume one of his course on general civil law of Russia when analyzing the relationship of Russian civil law "to other branches of public law".[295] In this volume under a separate point "Relation to International Law" (very concise – in all, several lines), Malyshev, while adhering to a civilist conception of international private-law relations, identified their content through the prism of international civil relations. Private law relations he considered within the State with the participation of foreigners and within the international community of States. Having analyzed the correlation of civil and international law, he at the juncture thereof identified international private-law links. Malyshev wrote that the science of civil law:

> investigates private law relations in all forms of civil existence, beginning with the family and kin and ending with the State and an international union. In international existence one should distinguish public relations – between States – and private relations – between individual subjects of civil turnover; on this basis the theory of international law is divided into droit international public and privé. The last is nothing other than part of civil law; that is, the theory of civil relations in international existence. It developed comparatively recently, together with the complication of private international relations … (I, p. 12)

Taking into account the expanding and complicated international ties, Malyshev planned to investigate the "theory of civil relations in international existence (or according to another expression of his, the theory of "inter-State conflicts law"). To this problem he intended to devote the last volume of his contemplated three-volume course of civil law. In that volume Malyshev planned to discuss the "international relations of Russian civil law" because he considered that the material for such a theory "assumes the knowledge of all individual institutions of civil

[294] M. Gałędek and A. Klimaszewska, "A Controversial Transplant? Debate over the Adaptation of the Napoleonic Code on the Polish Territories in the Early 19th Century", *Journal of Civil Law Studies*, XI, no. 2 (2018), p. 270.

[295] K. Malyshev, Курс общего гражданского права России [Course of General Civil Law of Russia] (Spb., 1878), I, pp. 11-12.

law and has, in addition, significance for the theory of procedure" (I, p. 12). But he was not fated to complete this.[296]

But without polishing his notion of "inter-State conflicts law", Malyshev successfully undertook a study of so-called "inter-regional conflicts", having formed a distinctive theory of "inter-regional conflicts law" (I, pp. 135-137) (which was at that time in Russia auspicious).

Malyshev discovered the problem of multiplicity, or in his expression, "laws of various localities" in the extremities of the Russian Empire when delivering his course on "Trade Law". Malyshev was the first in the history of St. Petersburg University to at his own initiative deliver this course in 1875.[297] He was among the first in Russia to publish scholarly works on this branch of law. Regrettably, the course of lectures on "Trade Law" was not published, but Malyshev did publish a substantial inaugural lecture for this course.[298] Malyshev contended that underlying the formation of the science of trade law should be: (1) materials of history and comparative jurisprudence, including norms of foreign law; "trade links various nations with one another; trade disputes arise often between subjects of different States and are resolved not only according to local, but also foreign, laws"; (2) the study of customary trade law, which is possible "only by means of familiarity with real life, with the business methods and customs of trade", including the forms of trade in foreign States; (3) judicial practice; for "judicial decisions often reflect business methods and customs of the trading world" (pp. 61-64).

In this inaugural lecture Malyshev drew attention to the diversity of norms regulating trade law relations in various localities of Russia:

> Trade legislation of our country differs in various territories of Russia: in some places we have the French Code de Commerce in force, in others Swedish laws, Lubeck Law, and various local sources, and in yet others the Russian Digest of Laws. In principle each of the territories upholds its own legal orders (p. 68).

This in practice led to legal conflicts between "native" laws. Malyshev considered it important to summarize the diverse legal practices. It does not follow, he wrote, to suppose "that this task is easy; some diverse sources –Russian, French, Swedish, Romano-Germanic – indicate that this may be resolved only through

296 See Tiutriumov, note 287 above, p. 212.

297 However, as Professor O. Iu. Skvortsov noted, the delivery of this course proved to be not for long and not successful: "There were both objective reasons (lack of compulsory courses of trade law in the universities of Russia) and subjective: Malyshev significantly was deflected by work on the courses of civil law and civil procedure". See O. Iu. Skvortsov, «Очерк жизни и творчества К. И. Малышева» [Survey of Life and Creativity of K. I. Malyshev], KODEKS-info, no. 7-8 (2002), p. 112.

298 See Malyshev, «Об ученой разработке торгового права в России (Вступительная лекция по торговому праву в С.-Петербургском университетом 20 сентября 1875 г.» [On the Instructional Development of Trade Law in Russia (Inaugural Lecture on Trade Law in St. Petersburg University, 20 September 1875)], Журнал гражданского и уголовного права [Journal of Civil and Criminal Law], no. 6 (1875), pp. 44-65.

comparative-historical research, that the world outlook should be broad and the conclusions precise and correct" (p. 59). Consequently, Malyshev in his course on "Trade Law" addressed the conflict of "laws of different places", the scientific resolution of which he undertook in a fundamental work – the first volume of his course on the civil law of Russia.[299] The topicality and need to investigate the "indigenous", "regional", "laws of different places", the identification of legal conflicts between them, and development of an individual branch of law was significant for an Empire composed of heterogeneous and contradictory internal legal orders.

Malyshev explained the urgency of the problem. In his view, individual localities in Russia (especially the "western belt of the Empire": Bessarabia, Kingdom of Poland, Finland, Baltic, and others) "from the standpoint of civil law still might be called special States ... [more] than either Prussia or Bavaria in the German Empire" (I, p. 168). On these territories legislative acts of various legal systems operated: the Digest of Laws of the Russian Empire, Code Civil of Napoleon, own laws in Poland, the Baltic, Bessarabia, Finland, and other remote localities.

In practice all this led, in the words of Malyshev, to "laws of different places", by which he understood "laws operating in various localities of the same country or in different States" (p. 169), which already testified to the international legal character of conflicts situations arising. The problem was that of delimiting the spheres of operation of laws in various localities of the Russian Empire.

In Malyshev's view, the resolution of particular conflicts problems "should be sought solely in Russian legislation". The legislative regulation of similar situations laid the basis for forming "municipal conflicts law". In order to resolve conflicts with the participation of foreign subjects he stipulated the need to apply not only Russian law, but also the comparative jurisprudence and international agreements. Malyshev believed: "in order to usefully compare one should take into account here other historical-comparative materials of science, such as principles of Roman law formed in the Middle Ages in the West – the theory of the so-called *statuta personalia, realia and mixta*, the legislation of Western States in the event of the conflicts of laws of different places and the most recent western theories" (I, pp. 139-140).

In recognizing international treaties as a source of conflicts law, Malyshev acknowledged the international legal component of conflicts situations with the participation of foreigners. Nonetheless, he insisted on the national civilist nature of private international law, categorically denying not only its affiliation to the international system of law, but in general its autonomous character.

In his treatise, Malyshev considered the judicial procedural aspects of legal norms in conflicts situations. In analyzing the application of foreign law by Russian courts, Malyshev concluded that the duties of the court to apply foreign law not only emanated from international comity, but were based on the legislation of the country of the court considering the case in dispute. Malyshev did not avoid the correlation of different laws in the course of a court proceeding: the *lex fori*, the *lex loci*, place of residence or origin, motherland, and nationality or subjectship

[299] Malyshev, note 295 above, I, p. v.

of the person (*lex domicilii, originis, patriae, civitatis*), law of the location of the thing (*lex rei sitae*), and law of the performance of an act or action (*lex loci actus, contractus, solutionis, delicti commissi*) (I, p. 138-139, 144):

> … with regard to various questions concerning the fate of law, the laws of all the said localities should be applied in a court and not one has predominance over the others. One cannot say that the application of the laws of one locality was a general rule and the application of laws of other localities was an exception. To be sure, the court applies usually the laws of its area (*lex fori*), but then only when there are no grounds for the application of outsider laws (*domicilii, rei sitae*, and so on) (I, p. 145).

The application of "outsider laws" may arise "only with regard to those cases in which some element of the case (or person, property, or action) transcends the limits of the local domain of law" (I, p. 148). But, said Malyshev, the issue remains controversial as to what laws a court needs to "discuss" when determining the legal consequences of the civil status of a person, having in view the need to ensure the interests of trade relations, credit, and the security of civil turnover:

> Especially with respect to international private existence it is understandable that the State, in accepting foreigners and protecting their person and civil rights equally with their own subjects, is not obliged to acknowledge all the same diverse personal and property privileges and limitations to which they are subject and their status in each of their fatherlands and cannot place duties on their subjects when concluding transactions with foreigners to cope with their *statuta personalia*.

This also concerned Russia:

> In our fatherland foreigners form a special estate and are subject to the operation of Russian laws: if a transaction concluded by them in Russia satisfies the conditions of legal capacity and dispositive legal capacity under Russian legislation, it will be fully valid, although limitations lie on them according to the laws of their fatherland. On the other hand, each person having general civil legal capacity and dispositive legal capacity according to the laws of his foreign fatherland is deemed among us to be a person with full legal capacity and the transactions concluded by them in Russia are binding.

In sum, Malyshev concluded: "The volume of legal capacity and dispositive legal capacity of a person should be discussed according to the laws of his place of residence or other formal grounds under which his status is confirmed" (I, pp. 154-155).

The value of the research undertaken by Malyshev on the conflicts aspects of laws of different places was enhanced by a special annex, published in 1880, to his course on the general civil law of Russia. In this annex, in addition to general Russian civil laws, he systematized (on the basis of primary sources) the Baltic Ostsee laws, laws of the Kingdom of Poland, Finnish and Swedish laws, Bessarabian sources – the Six Book Armenopulo and collection of laws of Donich – Jewish and Muslim laws, and materials of customary laws of eastern foreigners and native Russian population, and judicial practice.

Nolde favorably assessed the contribution of Malyshev to the science of private international law:

> It would be no exaggeration to say that no one in the history of Russian jurisprudence could earlier or later be compared with Malyshev in his knowledge of positive Russian and foreign law and his literary Russian and foreign erudition. This is genuine scholarship, not taken on hire, because Malyshev most often is the first along those paths of scholarship which he noted: behind him there are no predecessors, and he collected everything himself. The astonishing diligence made Malyshev courageous, and he was not stopped by tasks which, without exaggeration, one must call gigantic … One may boldly say that Malyshev created the dogma of the Russian domestic conflicts law.[300]

As the first study in the Soviet Union on private international law by Makarov noted, Malyshev made an "enormous step forward in the autonomous development of a Russian science of conflicts … Malyshev mastered … not only the classics of the science of conflicts in the West, but in general the entire literature which … had emerged in the light of his study; not confining himself to a doctrinal approach to conflicts problems, Malyshev gave a model dogmatic evaluation of the Russian internal; that is, inter-regional, law of conflicts".[301]

Lazar Adolfovich Lunts (1892-1979), believed that the most important "stage in the development of the Russian science of private international law was the works of K. I. Malyshev, distinguished by a great perfection in the form of exposition and comprehension of the vast material of Russian and foreign law".[302]

The contributions of Malyshev are acknowledged by contemporary specialists. Abdullin noted the high theoretical level of the discussion of inter-regional conflicts in Russia. Malyshev pointed to the civilist nature of private international law, relegating this to the internal law of a State.[303] He investigated conflicts chiefly between laws of Russia of different places. Even though he did not complete the section of the course devoted to the international law of conflicts, "nonetheless", as was justly noted, "the contribution of K. I. Malyshev to the science of interna-

[300] B. E. Nolde, «М. И. Брун (1860-1916) и наука международного частного права в России» [M. I. Brun (1860-1916) and the Science of Private International Law in Russia], Вестник гражданского права [Herald of Civil Law], no. 3-5 (1917), p. 17.

[301] A. N. Makarov, Основные начала международного частного права [Basic Principles of Private International Law] (M., 1924), p. 38.

[302] L. A. Lunts, Курс международного частного права [Course of International Private Law] (3d ed.; M., 1973), I, p. 148.

[303] A. I. Abdullin, Очерки истории науки международного частного права в России (проблема понимания природы международного частного права в трудах отечественных правоведов XIX – начала XX в.) [Survey of the History of the Science of Private International Law in Russia (Problem of Understanding the Nature of Private International Law in the Works of Russian Jurists of the XIX and Early XX Centuries)] (Kazan, 2004), p. 24.

tional private law in Russia is enormous. That which he has done is enough for us to recall his name with gratitude".[304]

Thus, the times were appropriate for Malyshev to lay the foundations for one of two basic concepts of private international law – the municipal (national-law) civilist conception, which in the twenty-first century is accepted by the majority of scholars.[305] Malyshev developed his conception solely within the framework of civil law and for municipal-law purposes. First, this reflected the complexities generated by domestic regional conflicts of laws in the Russian Empire. Second, this reflected the low standard of international legal regulation of private law relations. The first multilateral unification treaties began to emerge at the turn of the twentieth century. Third, the higher normative and scientific quality of the civil law, whose sources emanated from Roman law, were relevant. The legal argumentation of Malyshev was used to develop a civilist conception of private international law.

Sergei Pavlovich Nikonov *(2 August 1867, b. Elabuga (other sources specify Urzhum), Viatka Governate – d. no earlier than 1928, probably in Vladivostok). Specialist in the fields of trade law and procedure.*

С. П. Никоновъ

Life and career. Nikonov graduated in 1886 from the Kazan Third Gymnasium with the gold medal and in 1890 from the Law Faculty of Kazan University with a first class degree and a gold medal for an essay on "Suretyship as Security for Obligations". He remained at the University in the Chair of Civil Law to prepare for the professoriate. In 1891 he was sent to Germany to participate in a legal seminar at Berlin University. There he spent two and a half years studying Roman law. He was appointed privat-docent from 1895, and from 1901 professor *extraordinarius* at the Chair of Civil Law of Demidov Law Lycée in Iaroslavl.

On 22 April 1901 he defended a magister dissertation at St. Petersburg University on "Sequestration in Civil Law" and was awarded the degree of magister of civil law. With effect from 1 March 1903 he became professor *extraordinarius* at the Chair of the History of Roman Law in the Law Faculty of Kharkov University. There he lectured on the history of Roman law and gave tutorials on civil law and procedure. At Kyiv St. Vladimir University in May 1909 he defended a dissertation, successfully, on "*Actio spolii*" for the degree of

[304] G. K. Dmitrieva (ed.), Международное частное право [International Private Law] (3d ed.; M., 2015), p. 45.

[305] See Iu. A. Komnatnaia, Эволюция отечественной доктрины о коллизионном праве в середине XIX – начале XX века [Evolution of Russian Doctrine on the Conflicts of Law in the Mid-Nineteenth and Early Twentieth Centuries] (Stavropol, 2011), pp. 21-22 (abstract diss. kand. iurid. nauk).

doctor of civil law.[306] On the basis of this achievement, Nikonov was elevated on 26 July 1909 to professor *ordinarius* at the Chair of Civil Law and Civil Procedure of Novorossiisk University in Odessa.

Nikonov was appointed professor *ordinarius* of St. Petersburg University on 15 July 1912 at the Chair of Trade Law and Procedure by instruction of the Minister of Public Enlightenment – without a vote in the Council of the Law Faculty.[307] He offered a course on "Trade Law". On 7 April 1917 the University dismissed him from his teaching position. From 1917 to 1920 he served as professor *ordinarius* at the Chair of Trade Law in the Law Faculty of Tomsk University, where he delivered a course on trade law.

In December 1919 he undertook a trip to the Far East in order to examine trade relations between Siberia and foreign States. Throughout the 1920s he was professor at the Far Eastern University, where he offered courses on civil law, economics, trade, and industry and, in 1920-1921, was Dean of the Faculty of Social Sciences. He lived in Vladivostok until 1928, after which his fate is unknown.

International legal views. In the few works in which Nikonov addressed private international law he displayed a good knowledge of the theoretical and practical aspects. In 1913 he published an article on the participation of Russia in treaties regulating the protection of industrial property. He commented on the unbridled unfair competition and commercial piracy, including the counterfeiting of foreign trademarks and factory marks, industrial designs, and utility models and their arbitrary use by foreign inventors.[308] To reduce the incidence of these phenomena, States enter into treaties with one another; these cumulatively are creating an international system for the protection of industrial property. By 1913 Russia had concluded such treaties with seven States. Nikonov noted that the treaties were highly diverse; there was no uniformity as to the subjects and objects of the legal relations being protected.

For example, there was no unity with respect to the types of industrial property subject to international protection. The treaties ranged from "complete and real protection of the manufacturing industry of subjects of the Contracting Parties" to a detailed enumeration of the objects to be protected: "rights of ownership in inventions, patents on inventions (including patents to improvements), trademarks (including factory seals), models, and drawings", and so on. Nor was there uniformity with respect to the use of rights granted: either subjects of the Contracting Parties may use all these rights *a priori*, or prior application is required. Nikonov noted many ambiguities and contradictions in this sphere, and these, in practice he said, lead to confusion and complications. The importance was noted of the signature in Paris on 20 March 1883 of the Convention for the Protection of Industrial Property, to which there were originally thirteen parties and by 1913 had grown to twenty-two.

306 S. P. Nikonov, *Actio Spolii* (Kharkov, 1908). 302 p.

307 ЦГИА СПб., fond 11, opis1, file 10644 ; also see Starodubtsev, note 3 above, p. 185.

308 Nikonov, «Россия и международная охрана промышленной собственности» [Russia and the International Protection of Industrial Property], Юридическая известия [Legal News], no. 12-13 (1913), p. 308.

Nikonov analyzed the 1883 Convention, with the changes and additions made at Madrid in 1891; Brussels in 1897 and 1900; and Washington D.C. in 1911), and the relevant rules in Russian legislation and judicial practice, including criminal prosecutions. He concluded that the "rules in the 1883 Convention" are fully consistent with Russian legislation and urged Russia to become a Party to that Convention in the 1911 version agreed in Washington D.C. (p. 351).

His second article addressed the law of the sea – the legal status, right of ownership, and right of use of various coastal sea waters of the Russian Empire.[309] These matters, he believed, were insufficiently treated in doctrinal writings. The principal issue, Nikonov said, is whether the coast is *res communes omnium* and precluded from being in private ownership, or is encumbered by common interests in navigation and fishing; or the possessors of maritime parcels have the full right of ownership – and no rights of general participation in their use have been established in a law. The problems were aggravated because that the Russian legal system had so-called "laws of different places": the Digest of Laws of the Russian Empire, the Napoleon Code Civil, laws in Poland, the Baltic, Bessarabia, Finland, and other border localities; this led to conflicts of legislative norms and law enforcement practice.

In Nikonov's view, in light of the draft Russian Civil Code being discussed, a State creating cities and settlements along the coast using treasury land might allocate coastal marine parcels for the common needs of fishing; but it would be inadvisable to "infringe upon the existing full ownership of private persons, slowing down the settling of the seacoasts" (p. 58).

Although Nikonov purported to consider only the municipal legal aspects of this issue, it did have implications for international law. He considered, for example, the issue of border control over persons and goods crossing the maritime boundary and coasts (p. 49).

Mikhail Iakovlevich Pergament *(28 July 1866, b. Feodosia, Tauride Governate, Crimea – 21 February 1932, d. Leningrad). Noted civilist and international lawyer.*

Life and career. After graduating from the Richelieu Gymnasium in Odessa, Pergament enrolled at the Law Faculty of Novorossiisk University, graduating in 1890 with the gold medal awarded for a work on the "Legal Nature of the Real Unie".[310] He remained at the Faculty to prepare for the professoriate and was sent abroad to study Roman law at the universities in Heidelberg and Berlin. He passed the magister examinations in 1896 and was appointed privat-docent at Novorossi-

[309] Nikonov, «О пользовании морским берегом в России» [On Use of the Maritime Coast in Russia], Журнал Министерства юстиции [Journal of the Ministry of Justice], no. 4 (1912), pp. 26-58.

[310] M. Ia. Pergament, Юридическая природа реальной унии [Legal Nature of the Real Unie] (Odessa, 1893). Butler П34. Also see Starodubtsev, note 3 above, pp. 217, 225, 230-233, 236, 237, 261-263.

isk University, where he lectured on Roman law. In 1899 he defended a magister dissertation at St. Petersburg University.[311]

He was transferred to the post of professor *extraordinarius* at the Chair of Russian Civil Law and Procedure at Iurev University in 1903. He moved on in 1906 to St. Petersburg University as professor *extraordinarius*, and from 1907 to 1911 acted as Head of the Legal Cabinet. During this same period, he was a member of the Professorial Disciplinary Court of the University. From 1906 to 1917 he was professor and Dean of the Law Faculty of the St. Petersburg Higher Women's (Bestuzhev) Courses.

Along with several other professors at St. Petersburg University, he resigned in 1911 as a protest against the dismissal of professors at Moscow University by the Minister of Public Enlightenment, Lev Aristidovich Kasso (1865-1914). From 1912 he was professor and pro-rector of the Institute of Higher Commercial Knowledge, known from 1917 as the Commercial Institute, and later renamed the F. Engels Institute of National Economy. After the February 1917 Revolution, he returned to Petrograd University as professor *ordinarius*, from 20 March 1917, at the Chair of Civil Law, and from 17 June 1917 simultaneously as the Head of the Legal Cabinet.

By Edict of the Provisional Government, he was appointed from 1 May 1917 as a Senator of the IV Department of the Ruling Senate. In summer 1917 Pergament was elected professor at the Petrograd Commercial Institute while retaining his University appointment.

When the Bolsheviks came to power in October 1917, Pergament became actively involved in several institutions of higher education, research centers, and other organizations in Petrograd/Leningrad. He traveled abroad – generating serious disagreements as to whether he emigrated, which is not the case – and took part in the international activities of Soviet Russia.

International legal views. Pergament was an individual of broad interests and many talents who made a serious contribution to international law – mostly in the Soviet era. Only one work prior to 1917 dealt directly with aspects of international law: an article on war and insuperable force.[312]

The outbreak of war, Pergament noted, was often accompanied by references either to "insuperable force" or to "*force majeure*" – concepts which overlap but

[311] ЦГИА СПб., fond 14, opis 2, file 1357. See Pergament, Договорная неустойка и интерес в римском и современном гражданском праве [Contractual Penalty and Interest in Roman and Contemporary Civil Law] (Odessa, 1899). 349 p.

[312] M. Ia. Pergament, «Война и «неопреодолимая сила» [War and Insuperable Force], Право [Law], no. 36 (1914), cols. 2521-2533.

are not synonyms – as grounds for the termination of contracts, relieving parties of obligations they assumed. One can find neither in legal doctrine nor in judicial practice, he said, uniformity or consistency in what constitutes insuperable force. In Russia the question became more salient because the Council of the Congresses of Representatives of Industry and Trade had raised the possibility of deeming war to be *force majeure* and therefore giving the right to dissolve trade contracts (col. 2533).

The international dimension of the issue Pergament discussed through examples: A. sold timber in a neighboring neutral country. But with the declaration of war, a governmental prohibition followed on the export of grain and bread. Does A. have the right to not deliver the timber sold to the purchaser, having in view the prohibition introduced on trade? Pergament concluded that the answer was obviously: no. The subject-matter of the contract was timber, not bread. There A. should bear responsibility for the failure to perform the contract because there was no causal link between the failure to deliver the timber and the prohibition on the export of bread.

Another example: B. purchased a good within the country, intending to export that good to other countries. But with the declaration of war the export of goods was prohibited. Is B. obliged to accept the purchased good which he planned to export? Pergament gave a positive reply: the obligation remained in force, the seller has the right to demand strict performance, and the foreign contracting parties, to receive the good. Justifying that reply, Pergament emphasized the "motives" for the transaction: if the motives of the transaction had been specified in the purchase-sale contract – the export by the purchaser of the good to other countries, then one might refer to the "*force majeure*" of war as insuperable force and not accept the good.

Pergament analyzed problems – known to have arisen in practice – of performing obligations in wartime relating to the acquisition of raw materials for subsequent processing, or the failure by French and Belgian firms to pay contracting parties in Russia within the agreed periods – these firms referring to a moratorium introduced in their countries on financial payments. In maritime trade similar problems arose: many countries referring to the *force majeure* of war as insuperable force and terminating contracts of carriage by sea.

Pergament took the view that international trade should not suffer during wars because trade is "nothing other than an uninterrupted chain in which an individual contract is merely a link in an endlessly long series of links"; during wartime confrontations and actions, these are often interrupted (col. 2531).

On behalf of the Law Faculty of St. Petersburg University, Pergament together with privat-docent Baron Aleksandr Emilevich Nolde (1873-1919) reissued in 1910 a concise survey of foreign information on the Digest of laws of the western governates, originally published back in 1837; only fifty copies were printed in 1837 and the book had become impossible to find. The book was immensely useful in comparative legal research, especially codification work and private international law, for it contained the texts of Ukrainian, Belorussian, Polish, and Baltic materials indispensable when analyzing conflicts of law situations.[313]

Vladimir Valentinovich Rozenberg *(1 July 1879, b. Peterhof, St. Petersburg Governate – d. 1940?). Specialist in civil, financial, trade, stock exchange, and intellectual property law.*

Life and career. After graduating from the Fifth Gymnasium in St. Petersburg in 1897, Rozenberg completed legal studies and graduated from the Law Faculty of St. Petersburg University in 1901 with a first class degree. He then joined the Chancellery of the Civil Cassation Department of the Ruling Senate and remained there until 17 April 1902. From 17 January 1905 he took up service in the Chancellery of the Ministry of Finances.

In 1902 he chose also to remain at the Chair of Roman Law of St. Petersburg University to prepare for the professoriate with a Demidov Stipend for two years, extended for a further year in 1904. After passing the magister examinations in 1905, he was appointed privat-docent at the Chair of Russian Civil and Trade Law and Procedure of the University, a position he held from 1 July 1905 to 1 January 1907 and again from 1 January 1914 to 1919. During his first lecturing appointment he offered the course on "The Stock Exchange and Exchange Operations"; from 1914 he taught a comprehensive course on intellectual property. At the same time, he was a professor at the Higher Commercial Courses.

The Council of the Law Faculty on 13 January 1919 considered that he had left the University, a decision duly confirmed on 9 February 1919. In November 1920 he evacuated from the Crimea to Yugoslavia. He was elected to membership of the Russian Scientific Institute in Belgrade. His fate thereafter is unknown.

International legal views. Rozenberg devoted several articles to issues of international law, one of which remains of special interest. During the First World War he drew attention to what he called a "burning issue" of legal relations arising in connection with the sojourn of enemy subjects on the territory of belligerents. In his comparatively concise but dense article he addressed a broad range of questions – from the concept of private military law and the legal status of foreigners in peacetime to various forms of limiting rights in wartime. On one hand, he observed, the "colossal successes" in the international legal community should not be materially affected during wartime merely because of differences in nationality or citizenship. But he was obliged to acknowledge that the War begun in 1914 had destroyed normal international communion and by its unexpected cruelty was more than combat between two or several armies; it was a war between peoples. All means and methods harmful to the rival would be used to the death.[314]

313 M. Ia. Pergament and A. E. Nolde (eds.), Обозрение исторических сведений о составлении свода местных законов западных губерний [Survey of Historical Information on Composing the Digest of Local Laws of Western Governates] (St. Petersburg, 1910). 63 p. Nolde had defended a magister dissertation on this subject in 1906 at St. Petersburg University.

314 V. V. Rozenberg, «Современные правоотношения к неприятельским подданным» [Contemporary Legal Relations with Enemy Subjects], Вестник финансов, промышленности и торговли [Herald of Finances, Industry and Trade], № 26 (1915), с. 598-603; № 27 (1915), с. 5-9;

During the early days of the War, there were three categories of enemy subjects within the Russian Empire: (1) prisoners of war, including individuals who potentially might be combatants of other States; (2) persons evicted from their residence in certain localities; (3) individuals who remained in their places of initial sojourn. But the status of these persons was not determined by the Statute on prisoners of war or any other enactments but for those which prohibited prisoners of war from bearing arms, having horses, or carrying military papers. Rozenberg noted that the legal status of these persons was being formed gradually by administrative agencies and essentially amounted to local supervision over enemy subjects sent to their respective areas. The legislator repealed the operation of any privileges and advantages granted to enemy subjects on the basis of reciprocity or treaty and established various limitations on foreign natural and juridical persons with respect to land ownership or possession, industry, trade, banks, patents, access to courts, and others.

Early on in the War certain aspects of the issue were addressed by special treaties. Rozenberg drew attention to the Russo-German treaty in late 1914 pursuant to which the two parties on the basis of reciprocity granted to their subjects free departure from the enemy country to their homeland with the right to remove personal property except for gold coins and bank deposits.

Most attention was given to the legal status of juridical persons formed outside Russia but with a presence on Russian territory; their status was governed by treaties, for example, with Austria-Hungary and Germany. Rather than close down the operations of such juridical persons, as did England and France, Russia placed their operations under local control. He noted, moreover, that England and France had begun to deny the validity of transactions concluded with enemy subjects. Russia, however, pursued a legal policy of compliance with the rights of enemy subjects as private individuals. The sole limitations introduced by wartime legislation related to prohibiting the enrichment of enemy subjects in Russia by stipulated means.

№ 28 (1915), c. 49-54; № 32 (1915), c. 227-236; also a separate booklet: Rozenberg, Современные правоотношения к неприятельским подданным: С приложением узаконений по этому предмету [Contemporary Legal Relations with Enemy Subjects: With an Annex of Legislation on this Topic] (Pg., 1915). 55 c. Also see by Rozenberg, «Вашингтонская конвенция» [Washington Convention], Вестник Центрального банка [Herald of the Central Bank], № 10 (1913), c. 5-7; № 12 (1913), c. 7-9.

§11.7. *Chair of Criminal Law and Procedure*

Ivan Iakovlevich Foinitskii *(29 August 1847, b. Gomel uezd, Migolev Governate – 19 September 1913, d. St. Petersburg). Criminologist, professor of criminal law at St. Petersburg University, State and public figure.*

Life and career. Foinitskii was born into a serf family beholden to Count Ivan Fedorovich Paskevich-Erevanskii (1782-1856), Serene Prince of Warsaw. The Countess Paskevich paid attention to a capable peasant youth and with her assistance he received a Gymnasium education. He was first schooled in Chernyhiv, and then at the Mogilev Gymnasium, where he graduated in 1864 with the gold medal. In 1868 he completed the course of study at the Law Faculty of St. Petersburg University with the gold medal for an essay "On Measures for the Suppression of Means of an Accused Evading Investigation and Trial".[315] He remained at the Faculty to prepare for the professoriate and immediately began to lecture, from 1868 to 1871, on criminal law at the Auditor School (later transformed into the Military Law Academy).

Having passed his magister examinations,[316] in 1871 Foinitskii defended his magister dissertation: "Swindling under Russian Law". He was promptly elected by the Council of the University as an established docent in criminal law[317] and sent abroad for further postgraduate studies. His travels took him throughout Europe; he attended lectures in Germany, Switzerland, Austria, France, Italy, and England, where he visited many places for the confinement of convicts.

He offered two courses at the University in 1873: the course on criminal law for students in the administrative division, and a special course on prison science for all students of the Law Faculty. Following the example of most of his colleagues, he held more than one appointment; in his case he lectured on criminal procedure at the School of Jurisprudence and the course on encyclopedia of law at the Alexander Lycée.[318] From 1876 he was deputy ober-procurator of the Criminal Cassational Department of the Ruling Senate, and in 1900 he was appointed a Senator of that Department. He also was a deputy in the St. Petersburg City Duma from 1904 to 1909.

[315] ЦГИА СПб, fond 14, opis 5, file 2873.

[316] ЦГИА СПб, fond 14, opis 3, file 14147.

[317] ЦГИА СПб, fond 139, opis 1, file 6578.

[318] ЦГИА СПб, fond 11, opis 1, file 4055.

In 1881 Foinitskii defended a doctoral dissertation and was confirmed as professor *extraordinarius* (from 1882, *ordinarius*) at the Chair of Criminal Law and Procedure of the University.[319] He was appointed Distinguished Professor *ordinarius* from May 1896. During the academic year 1902-1903 he served as Chairman of the Professorial Disciplinary Court of the University. At Foinitskii's initiative, a Cabinet and Museum of Criminal Law attached to the University were founded. He bequeathed his impressive personal library to them.

Foinitskii was involved in the formation of the Law Society attached to the University, prepared the draft Charter of the Society, repeatedly was chosen to be secretary of the Council, member of the Council, vice-chairman, and chairman of the Criminal Division. He attended from 1872 several international congresses: among them the International Penitentiary congresses at London (1872), Rome (1885) and Paris (1895). In 1890 Foinitskii was one of the principal organizers of the St. Petersburg international penitentiary congress. He became in 1889 a member of the International Union of Penal and Penitentiary Law and took part in its congresses in Brussels, Berne, Linz, Paris, and Christiana (Oslo).

Foinitskii initiated the formation of the Russian Group of the International Union of Penal and Penitentiary Law and served as chairman until January 1905. He founded the St. Petersburg Society of Protection in 1905.

He is regarded as an initiator of the system of special courts in Russia for youths and the opening of the first such court in St. Petersburg. His ideas were influential in the development of the Leningrad School of Criminal Law and continue to be significant in the post-Soviet era. However, in 1912 he was dismissed by the Minister of Public Enlightenment from the University by reason of his resistance to the proposed revisions of the 1864 judicial reform.

Foinitskii died suddenly on 19 September 1913 from a heart attack in St. Petersburg and is buried at the Voskresensk Cemetery of the Novodevichy Monastery.

International legal views. The international legal dimensions of Foinitskii are similar to those of his colleague, A. A. Zhizhilenko; that is, they relate mostly to involvement in the congresses of the International Union of Penal and Penitentiary Law and the international penitentiary congresses, which commenced in 1846. On the basis of that participation, Foinitskii formed a positive view of the International Union – an association dedicated to addressing problems of criminal law in a freer and more academic climate, convening without long intervals between meetings, considering itself to have a broad remit to discuss problems, and deliberating without officiousness.[320] The hope and expectation of Foinitskii was that general approaches to combatting criminality would be agreed and even coordinated at the international level; to this end he was the founder of the Russian Group of this Union and served as Chairman. The Russian Group contributed to improving and advancing the theory and practice of criminal law in their country. In the late

[319] I. Ia. Foinitskii, Ссылка на Западе в ее историчкском развития и современном состоянии [Exile in the West in its Historical Development and Contemporary State] (Spb., 1881). 351 p.

[320] Foinitskii, «Международный союз уголовного права» [International Union of Criminal Law], Юридический вестник [Legal Herald], VI, no. 1 (1890), p. 4.

years of Foinitskiii's life many colleagues separated themselves from their founder because of the sad history in January 1905 of the closure of the Kyiv congress of the Group.[321]

Foinitskii's international legal views are to be found in his Reports on participation in the international congresses. He set out in his Report on the Linz Congress (1895) the historical background of the International Union and his involvement in that Congress. Four questions preoccupied the delegates: (a) reform of university education in preparing practitioners of criminal law; (b) the influence of new ideas on the doctrines of complicity and attempt; (c) sexual homicide; and (d) the reduction of the length of proceedings concerning recidivism.[322]

The most controversial issue was the proposal by an Austrian criminal law specialist to create special Chairs of criminalistics in all universities (p. 112). On this question the Bureau of the Union requested Foinitskii to express his views, he having submitted an abstract to the Congress on this question. Foinitskii said that "all the information necessary for a judicial investigator" is so extensive that an entire lifetime is insufficient to acquire such and it could not be provided by a university course. Therefore the clinic for the criminal lawyer is prison, and not the Cabinet of Criminalistics – the last is an art, not a science which perhaps 1/20 of the students will acquire in university courses, so making such courses compulsory is not useful for 19/20 of the students concerned (p. 113).

In his Report on the Rome Congress, Foinitskii observed that congresses initiated by legal scholars had become more pragmatic. Primary attention had shifted from legal scholars devoting themselves to prison studies (professors of criminal law, directors of penitentiaries, pastors, medical personnel, and so on) to governments, which issue invitations, distribute necessary expenses among themselves, and send their own delegates. Whereas private individuals take part in the congresses, the executive organ of the International Union consisted entirely of governmental representatives.[323] There were delegates from fifteen European and two North American countries in the Rome Congress (1885).

According to the agenda of the Rome Congress, the first section discussed: (a) the compatibility of a fixed deprivation of certain civil and political rights with the requirements of the penitentiary system; (b) the limits of the power of a court when determining the amount of punishment; (c) the possible substitution of other forms of punishment for imprisonment; (d) the legal responsibility of trustees and educations for criminal acts committed by children; (e) the power which should be granted to a criminal court with regard to sending minors to educational or correctional institutions, but in case of acquittal for the "lack of reason" and in the event of their being sentenced to deprivation of freedom.

[321] Foinitskii, «Некролог» [Obituary], Отчет о состоянии и деятельности Императорского С.-Петербургского университута за 1913 год [Report on the State and Activity of the Imperial St. Petersburg University for 1913] (Spb., 1914), p. 33.

[322] Foinitskii, «Линцский съезд Международного союза уголовного права» [Linz Congress of International Union of Criminal Law], Журнал Министерства юстиции [Journal of the Ministry of Justice], no. 1 (1896), p. 109-136.

[323] Foinitskii, Пенитенциарный конгресс в Риме [Pententiary Congress in Rome] (n.p., n.p.), p. 4.

The second section discussed the internal regime of places of confinement: prison systems, prison architecture, prison administration, and activities in prisons.

Section three considered a wide range of issues: the international exchange by States of convicts (and the possibility of special provisions being included in extradition treaties for the exchange of convicts sentenced for certain general criminal acts), the establishment of refuges for persons freed from places of confinement, the best means for the proper exchange between States of data concerning records of conviction; the pursuits of convicts on holidays; the visiting of convicts by members of philanthropic societies, and so on.

In an article on the war and the court, Foinitskii, disclaiming any special competence in the field of international law, nonetheless formulated a number of theoretical positions of considerable interest. When analyzing the work of a French jurist, he suggested that "law is, above all, a formal concept; it exists where a court exists".[324] He believed in the gradual humanization of social relations: "international relations are managed by laws of the moralization of struggle conditioned by a gradual replacement of war by a court, the order of force by an order of law" (pp. 81-82).

When Foinitskii was forced to leave the University by the Minister of Public Enlightenent, Kasso, because he resisted changes in the 1864 judicial reforms, the University students prepared an address to Foinitskii in which they said: "Professor Foinitskii is not leaving the Chair, but the Chair is leaving Professor Foinitskii".[325]

Sergei Konstantinovich Gogel *(21 May 1860, b. Granovo, Gaisinsk uezd, Podolsk Governate – 6 April 1933, d. Berlin). Specialist in criminal law and policy.*

Life and career. After completing his secondary education at the Nikolaev Tsarsko selo Gymnasium, Gogel enrolled at the Law Faculty of St. Petersburg University, where he graduated in 1885.[326] He remained at the Chair of State Law to prepare for the professoriate and was sent to Vienna, Austria, for further studies. For personal reasons, however, Gogel cut short his foreign trip and returned to Russia, where he quickly found employment as an assistant procurator in the St. Petersburg District Court. He moved on to the Ministry of Justice and took part in drafting laws on the extradition of

[324] Foinitskii, «Война и суд» [War and Court], Журнал гражданского и уголовного права [Journal of Civil and Criminal Law, no. 4 (1873), p. 81.

[325] V. V. Vodovozov, «Иван Яковлевич Фойницкий» [Ivan Iakovlevich Foinitskii], Современник [Contemporary], no. 10 (1913).

[326] ЦГИА СПб., fond 14, opis 3, file 19968; also see Starodubtsev, note 3 above, pp. 58, 61, 68-69, 117.

criminals, pardon, and rehabilitation. He joined the editorial board of the Журнал Министерства юстиции [Journal of the Ministry of Justice].

In 1906 he was appointed privat-docent at the Chair of Criminal Law of St. Petersburg University, where he lectured in the course "Court of Jurors" (1906-1907) and "Criminal Policy" (1907-1911). He published a text on criminal policy and criminal sociology,[327] and in 1910 defended a magister dissertation at Kharkov University on the "Role of Society in the Cause of Struggle against Criminality".[328] He resigned from St. Petersburg University on 31 October 1911 and became a professor and Rector of the Psychoneurological Institute.

He was elected in 1916 Vice President of the M. M. Kovalevskii Sociological Society and was a member of the Russian Group of the International Union of Penal Law.

After the February 1917 Revolution, Gogel was a member of the Commission for the revision of judicial statutes attached to the Provisional Government and a Senator of the I Department of the Ruling Senate.

Following the October 1917 Revolution, he found employment at the Academy of Sciences and the Public Library. By 1919 Gogel was lecturing in Kyiv. The following year until 1921 he was a lecturer and Director of the Legal University in Sevastopol, and with it evacuated in November 1920 to Constantinople. He moved on to Prague, where from 1922 he was a professor at the Russian Law Faculty, and then a lecturer at the Russian Scientific Institute in Berlin. He was a member of the Committee of Congresses of Russian Jurists Abroad and active in seeking recognition for Russian émigrés as political refugees. He was a member of the Committee for the Protection of Russian Emigrants.

Gogel died at Berlin on 17 March 1933 and is buried at the Russian Orthodox Cemetery in Tegel, near Berlin.

International legal views. Several of Gogel's works on criminal law and policy address matters of international law. His article on trafficking in women took into account the results of the 1895 International Penal and Penitentiary Congress held in Paris and the forthcoming 1899 International Congress on the White Slave Trade in London; it was intended to illuminate the legal aspects of this issue.[329] He singled out two groups of actions to prevent this criminal act.

The first group was actions undertaken by criminal elements to entice women by fraud into houses of depravity. Giving examples of such enticement, he observed that international procuring was tempting for criminals: "… it is easier to

[327] S. K. Gogel, Курс уголовной политики в связи с уголовной социологией [Course of Criminal Policy in Connection with Criminal Sociology] (Spb., 1910). 505 p.

[328] Gogel, Роль общества в деле борьбы с преступностью [Role of Society in the Cause of the Struggle against Criminality] (Spb., 1906).

[329] S. K. Gogel, «Юридическая сторона вопроса о торговле белыми женщинами в целях разврата» [Legal Aspect of Question on Trade in White Women for Depraved Purposes], Вестник права [Herald of Law], no. 5 (1899), p. 108.

persuade naïve women" to improve their fate in a far away, remote country than at home, where any deceitful promises might easily be verified (p. 114).

The second group consisted of actions undertaken to keep women in houses of ill repute for their enslavement and quiet exploitation. This is slavery, and the criminal law and administrative measures must be deployed to combat it. Gogel believed that "if there were no slavery, there could not be a sale into slavery".

In his view, national and international legal measures were needed to counteract the trafficking in and the enslavement of women. Those States where prostitution had been legalized needed to adopt legislative and administrative measures regulating the legal relations in public houses between the masters and the prostitutes, the conditions and procedures for prostitutes becoming resident in these houses, the right to leave freely when they wished, and strict punishment to be applied for violently preventing women from leaving. Provisions should be made in legislation for the international type of procuring in the form of enticing women abroad by way of lies, violence, and threats. Control by State agencies should be strengthened over the operations of public houses, police powers should be delineated to prevent arbitrariness, extortion, and failure to punish the owners of public houses and the prostitutes themselves, and health supervision should be introduced or strengthened by local authorities. Gogel was optimistic that all these measures, properly introduced, would reduce international procuring.

Gogel delivered Reports at sessions of the Russian Group of the International Union of Penal and Penitentiary Law in 1900. The first was devoted to the protectorship in Russia.[330] He drew upon propositions advanced at the 1846 international congress, taking the view that a protectorship over convicts released from prison could only be introduced if additional prison reforms were made. He associated himself with remarks made by the delegates of the United States at the London Conference that no measures to reform criminals would work unless individuals were given proper support by society and the opportunity to earn a decent wage (p. 328). Analyzing similar foreign institutions, Gogel recommended measures to be introduced in Russia and prepared a draft Statute of a Chief Society for the Protectorship and for local societies (pp. 353-358).

Gogel's second report to the Congress addressed the issue of children who had been arrested and were serving terms of punishment.[331] Society, said Gogel, was unaware that innocent children were in prisons because their parents were criminals. If this were well-known, they would prohibit the confinement of innocent children in a climate of social evil and moral depravity so typical of prison conditions (pp. 334-335). The way out was to develop an extensive system of child accommodation under the patronage of philanthropic societies.

[330] Gogel, «О развитии и правильнопостановке патроната в России» [On the Development and Proper Placement of the Protectorship in Russia], Журнал Министерства юстиции [Journal of the Ministry of Justice], no. 8 (1900), pp. 328-358.

[331] Gogel, «Об удалении невинних детей из тюрем» [On the Removal of Innocent Children from Prison], Журнал Министерства юстиции [Journal of the Ministry of Justice], no. 9-10 (1900), pp. 261-344.

Pavel Isaakovich (Isaevich) Liublinskii *(10 September 1882, b. Grodno, Russian Empire – 28 December 1938, d. Leningrad). Noted criminologist, public and political figure.*

Life and career. Liublinskii graduated from the Fifth Petersburg Gymnasium and in 1900 enrolled at St. Petersburg University, graduating from the Law Faculty in 1904 with a first class degree.[332] He remained at the Faculty from 1 September 1904 until 1 September 1905 to prepare for the professoriate at the Chair of Criminal Law and Criminal Procedure.[333] This period was extended several time until March 1908, but without stipend.[334]

In 1904 Liublinskii was arrested for the possession of revolutionary literature and cooperation with leftist factions of the State Duma. He was sent abroad in 1907 for postgraduate research, in particular to study the English judicial system. That same year he passed the examination for the degree of magister of criminal law[335] and defended his magister dissertation.[336] In 1907 he became the Keeper of the Cabinet of Criminal Law of the St. Petersburg University Law Faculty. His successful magister dissertation led at once to his being confirmed as privat-docent at the Chair of Criminal Law and Criminal Procedure at the University.[337] He simultaneously lectured from 1909 to 1916 on criminal court organization and procedure at the St. Petersburg Higher Women's (Bestuzhev) Courses.

[332] ЦГИА СПб., fond 14, opis 3, file 37462.

[333] ЦГИА СПб., fond 14, opis 3, file 14369. He was awarded a Demidov stipend of 600 rubles per year.

[334] Отчет состоянии и деятельности Императорского С.-Петербургского университета за 1908 год [Report on the State and Activity of Imperial St. Petersburg University for 1908] (Spb., 1909), p. 70.

[335] ЦГИА СПб., fond 14, opis 3, file 14403.

[336] P. I. Liublinskii, Свобода личности в уголовном процессе: Меры, обеспечивоющие неуклонение обвиняемого от правосудия [Freedom of the Individual in Criminal Procedure: Measures Ensuring the Accused Does Not Evade Justice] (Spb., 1906). 701, viii p. On the dissertation defense, see Liublinskii, «Этическое начало и свобода личности в уголовном процессе: Речь перед диспутом» [Ethical Principle and Freedom of the Individual in Criminal Procedure: Address Preceding the Defense], Право [Law], no. 50 (1907), cols. 3217-3223; also see «Диспут П. И. Люблинского в Санкт-Петербургском университете» [Defense of P. I. Liublinskii in St. Petersburg University], no. 7 (1908), cols. 401-410.

[337] Note 334 above, p. 61.

He served as editor of the Журнал уголовного права и процесса [Journal of Criminal Law and Procedure], the organ of the Russian Group of the International Union of Penal and Penitentiary Law (also serving as secretary of the Group), and published widely in other leading legal journals of the time. During the First World War, he delivered public lectures on the "Legal Status of Our Prisoners of War".[338]

After the February 1917 Revolution, on 28 April 1917 he was appointed by Edict of the Provisional Government to an office in the Ruling Senate. When the Bolsheviks came to power in October 1917, Liublinskii remained in Russia. He lectured on criminal law and procedure at the Petrograd (Leningrad) University, the Bestuzhev Courses, the Psychoneurological Institute, and later, at the legal institutes and A. I. Gertsen Leningrad Pedagogical Institute, which had detached themselves from the Faculty of Soviet Law of Leningrad State University.

A productive legal scholar, Liublinskii published about fifty monographs and more than 310 articles, notes, and reviews on criminal law, criminal procedure, criminalistics, international law, and other legal issues.[339] He had a command of the Latin, English, Greek, Italian, Spanish, German, and French languages. For his services to legal scholarship the degree of doctor of juridical sciences was conferred on Liublinskii in 1938 without the defense of a dissertation; that is, on the basis of his published works. In 1930 he was elected to membership in the American Academy of Social and Political Sciences.

Liublinskii died in an accident in December 1938, the precise date being either 20 or 28 December; printed obituaries give the date as 20 December,[340] whereas archival records give the date of 28 December.[341] An important Russian bibliophile, Liublinskii's library of 10,000 volumes, of which 1,500 were early printed books, was acquired by the Leningrad State University in 1945 by decree of the Council of People's Commissars of the RSFSR.

International legal views. Of Liublinskii's oeuvre of more than 350 titles, approximately twenty relate to international law. Many were inspired by his participation in the International Union of Penal and Penitentiary Law (founded in 1888) and the international penitentiary congresses, held from time to time beginning in 1846. Liublinskii took part of the congresses between 1905 and 1917. Often he spoke at meetings of the Russian Group of the International Union. In 1910, for example, he was sent officially to the conference and congress held in Brussels and Washington D.C. While in the United States, he defended the reports of the

[338] Отчет состоянии и деятельности Императорского Петроградского университета за весеннее полугодие 1916 г. [Report on the State and Activity of Imperial Petrograd University for the Spring Semester of 1916] (Spb., 1916), p. 137.

[339] See the «Библиография печатных трудов П. И. Люблинского» [Bibliography of Printed Works of P. I. Liublinskii], Ученые записки Ленинградского юридического института [Learned Papers of Leningrad Juridical Institute], no. 1 (1939), pp. 112-127.

[340] N. N. Polianskii, «Некролог (П. И. Люблинский)» [Obituary (P. I. Liublinskii)], Социалистическая законность [Socialist Legality], no. 1 (1939); M. Shargorodskii, «Некролог (П. И. Люблинский)» [Obituary (P. I. Liublinskii)], Ученые записки Ленинградского юридического института [Learned Papers of Leningrad Juridical Institute], no. 1 (1939), pp. 110-112.

[341] ОА СПбГУ, fond 1, opis 1, file 797, l. 3.

Russian Group of the International Union, which criticized the Tsarist policies of repression for political crimes. Reports in Washington D.C. from the Russian participants included: "Courts for Minors in Russia", "On Measures to Improve Conditional Release", and "The Death Penalty and Public Opinion".

In 1917 Liublinskii published a substantial article on international criminal law during war.[342] He noted that the First World War had drawn attention to gaps in the legal regulation of matters that required doctrinal consideration and normative legal resolution. Among these, Liublinskii enumerated: (a) responsibility of prisoners of war for crimes committed before being taken prisoner; (b) responsibility of interned enemy subjects; (c) responsibility of allied forces for acts committed on the territory of allies and against an allied State. He analyzed the problems of bringing prisoners of war to responsibility for crimes committed before they were taken prisoner and concluded that governments should exercise restraint in view of the impossibility to fully and impartially conduct an investigation and of possible reprisals on the part of the State of which the prisoner of war is a subject.

But after the War comes to an end, if sufficient information is gathered, it would be possible to bring the guilty to responsibility on the basis either of a general international agreement or of a bilateral agreement between the interested States. If the respective acts were not covered by an amnesty, then the interested State, he suggested, might insist on one of two alternatives: either trying the individual in its own courts, or extraditing the individuals to the State of which they are subjects on condition they would be tried there (p. 224).

As for the responsibility of interned enemy subjects, Liublinskii was persuaded that although they often were equated to prisoners of war, including in Russia, they should be subject to general civil jurisdiction and any exceptions for individuals found to be in areas in which a "military situation" may have been declared (pp. 228-229).

The responsibility of allied forces for acts committed on the territory of allies and against the allied States raised issues of the extent to which the principle of exterritoriality was engaged. Liublinskii concluded that if the subjects of any third power are in the army present on another's territory, they are subject to trial for military crimes by that army in which they happen to be (p. 230).

His Reports on the congresses of the International Union of Penal and Penitentiary Law were of doctrinal and practical importance. These took the form of scholarly articles regularly appearing in Russian journals and newspapers. He published these materials in 1915 in a separate book.[343] Reassessing the positive and negative

[342] P. I. Liublinskii, «Вопросы международного уголовного права в связи в настоящей войной» [Questions of International Criminal Law in Connection with the Present War], Известия Министерства иностранных дел [News of the Ministry of Foreign Affairs], no. 1-2 (1917), pp. 216-238.

[343] Liublinskii, Международные съезды по вопросам уголовного права за десять лет (1905-1915) [International Congresses on Questions of Criminal Law for Ten Years (1905-1915)] (Pg., 1915 ; reissued M., 2012 ; 2d ed.; 2014). 379 p. In the Preface to the 2014 reprint, V. S. Ovchinskii and A. V. Fedorov wrote: "almost a century later, its reissue is of interest for scholars and practitioners living and working in the early twenty-first century and the continuing traditions of the said

contributions of each congress in the decade under consideration, he believed the congresses had been useful to academic lawyers and legal practitioners. Among other constructive contributions, in his view the congresses ultimately resulted in legislators hearing the informed voices of academic specialists.

On the negative side, Liublinskii mentioned the seemingly incidental selection of Congress participants, the difficulty of discussing scientific issues in general meetings, the chaotic nature of the discussion, the occasional nature of meetings and lack of permanent cooperation among participants from various countries. He was skeptical about the need for three different associations of criminal law specialists (pp. 362-365). The time had come for more stable forms of scientific cooperation than a congress – the congresses had performed their role successfully. He suggested the creation of a free international scientific institution – an international institute of criminal law (p. 367). The outlines of such an institute were drafted, as were the twelve primary tasks such an organization should perform (pp. 367-370).

In his collected articles and in general Liublinskii believed in the progress of the science of law and legal practice. This approach had been evident in his magister dissertation and present throughout his professional life.

Nikolai Dmitrievich Sergeevskii *(7 October 1849, b. rural village of Bolchino Porkhovsk uezd, Pskov Governate – 25 September 1908, d. St. Petersburg). Noted criminologist, Professor of Criminal Law, St. Petersburg University, public figure.*

Life and career. Having graduated in 1868 with the gold medal from the Pskov Governate Gymnasium, Sergeevskii enrolled in the Law Faculty of St. Petersburg University. Completing his legal studies in 1872, he remained at the Chair of Criminal Law to prepare for the professoriate.

In 1874 he accepted an invitation to serve as acting docent at the Demidov Juridical Lycée in Iaroslavl, where he remained until 1882. During the years 1875 and 1876, Sergeevskii passed his magister examinations and then spent the next two years abroad at universities in Austria and Germany. His dissertation for the magister of criminal law he defended in 1880 at St. Petersburg University "On the Significance of the Causal Link in Criminal Law", his official opponents being Professors N. S. Tagantsev and I. Ia. Foinitskii.

He served from 1882 to 1894 as adjunct-professor at the Alexander Military Law Academy and simultaneously lectured on criminal law from 1882 to 1895 at

congresses in contemporary scientific-practical forums" (p. vii).

the Alexander Lycée, serving as a member of the Council from 1884 to 1901. From 1906 he taught at the School of Jurisprudence.

At St. Petersburg University he was elected docent at the Chair of Criminal Law but did not take up the post. From 1 November 1882 he was selected as professor *extraordinarius* there. He did serve as Dean of the Law Faculty from 1887 to 1888. His doctoral dissertation "Punishment in Russian Law of the XVII Century" he defended in 1888, the official opponents being Professors I. Ia. Foinitskii and V. Sergeevich. He resigned from the University in 1901.

From 1890 to 1892 he was the publisher and editor of Юридическая летопись [Legal Chronicle] and from 1894 to 1895, editor of the Журнал Министерства юстиции [Journal of the Ministry of Justice]. He was designated a Distinguished Professor in 1903.

From 1893 he served as an aide to a State-secretary and from 1897 as State-secretary of the State Council and section head of the Digest of Laws of the State Chancellery, where he undertook the systematization of financial laws. As from May 1906 he was a member of the State Council of the Russian Empire.

He died on 25 September 1908 and is buried in the Smolnyi Russian Orthodox Cemetery; the site of the grave has been lost.

International legal views. Several works by Sergeevskii address issues of international law. He explored the status of criminal legislation of the Grand Duchy of Finland in correlation with similar legislation of the Russian Empire, which led him to consider the legal status of the Grand Duchy itself and larger questions of conflicts of law between the two entities. Noting the separatist trends between the Russian Empire and the Grand Duchy, the aim of his study was to explain "the public law status of Finland within the Russian State".[344]

Sergeevskii drew attention to the fact that Finland before becoming part of Russia in 1808 pursuant to an 1809 Russo-Swedish peace treaty was an integral part of the Kingdom of Sweden and did not enjoy "State solitariness" or even provincial autonomy. Upon becoming part of the Russian Empire, Sergeevskii observed, Finland was granted rights in "State law, political, economic, financial, tax, and other spheres" to a greater extent than any other formation in the world. Nonetheless, Finland was dissatisfied with its status within the Russian Empire by reason of three Russian legislative acts: the Manifesto on the procedure for adopting general laws in Russia; the Manifesto on introducing the Russian language throughout the Empire, and the statute on military service in Finland.

Sergeevskii is generally classified in Russian historiography as a monarchist, being of the view that the Western European parliamentary-constitutional model was not appropriate for Russia. He concluded that Finland must be an inseparable part of the Russian Empire and bound by legislative provisions just as other parts of the Empire which were essential to the existence of the Empire. From the standpoint of international law and of Russian legislation Finland was and must remain

344 N. D. Sergeevskii, К вопросу о финляндской автономии и основных законах [On the Question of Finnish Autonomy and Basic Laws] (Spb., 1902), p. 1.

an integral part of a unified Russian State to which all laws of the Russian Empire extended.

Pitirim Aleksandrovich Sorokin *(2 February (21 January) 1889, b. Turya, Iarenskii uezd, Vologda Governate (now Kniazhpogostskii District, Republic Komi) – 10 February 1968, d. Winchester, Massachusetts, United States). Russo-American jurist, sociologist, and culturologist. One of the founders of the Russian sociological school of criminal law and criminology.*

Life and career. Son of a Russian itinerant craftsman and Komi mother, Sorokin did not have formal primary or secondary schooling and, from the age of eleven, left an alcoholic and abusive father to make his own way in the world. He gravitated towards revolutionary ideas. At the age of seventeen, he joined the Socialist Revolutionary (SR) Party. He was arrested in 1906 and imprisoned for two years in Kineshme; there he devoted himself to self-education with a penchant for reading materials with a socio-philosophical and revolutionary bent. In spring 1909 he passed the external examination for a certificate of maturity at a Gymnasium in Velikii Ustiug (Vologda Governate) and enrolled that autumn in the private Psychoneurological Institute.[345] Not long before his enrollment the sole Chair of Sociology had been created at that Institute, and Sorokin became secretary to M. M. Kovalevskii.

In 1910, unable to pay tuition fees, he was dismissed from the Psychoneurological Institute, whereupon he matriculated at the Law Faculty of St. Petersburg University,[346] received an Imperial stipend, and became a pupil of L. I. Petrazhitskii. Even in his student years he was active in the world of legal scholarship – expeditions, popular pamphlets, reviews, essays, surveys of foreign philosophical and sociological literature. He undertook some part-time lecturing at the Psychoneurological Institute.

Sorokin was arrested again in 1913, on this occasion for a pamphlet he wrote in commemoration of the 300th anniversary of the House of Romanov; thanks to the intervention of Professor Kovalevskii, he was released. During the winter of 1912-1913, at the age of 24, Sorokin published his first scholarly monograph during the year of his University graduation – a survey of criminological theories.[347]

[345] ЦГИА СПб., fond 115, opis 2, file 8799.

[346] ЦГИА СПб., fond 14, opis 3, file 56272.

[347] P. A. Sorokin, Преступление и кара, подвиг и награда: Социологический этюд об основных формах общественного поведения и морали [Crime and Chastisement, Exploit and Reward: So-

Sorokin graduated in 1914 with a first class diploma and remained at the Chair of Criminal Law and Procedure with a stipend from the Ministry of Public Education to prepare for the professoriate under the supervision of A. A. Zhizhilenko. The initial period granted was from 15 September 1914 to 15 September 1915 and renewed periodically until 1 January 1917.[348] Sorokin also worked as an assistant to Professor Kovalevskii at the Chair of Sociology in the Psychoneurological Institute. During this period, Sorokin served as editor of the SR newspaper Народная мысль [People's Thought] and, from 1917, Дело народа [Matter of the People].

During 1916 he passed the magister examinations;[349] on 17 February 1917 he was successfully examined for the degree of magister of criminal law. On 17 April and 1 May 1917 he delivered two trial lectures on criminal law. He was thereupon appointed privat-docent at the Chair of Criminal Law and Procedure of St. Petersburg University. He prepared his magister dissertation; the defense was assigned for March 1917, but he was consumed by revolutionary events and the defense was postponed. He continued to be politically involved. After the February 1917 Revolution he became a secretary for science and advisor of the Chairman of the Provisional Government, Aleksandr Fedorovich Kerensky (1881-1970).[350]

The October 1917 Revolution found Sorokin on the other side, in support of the SR opposition to the Bolsheviks. He was elected in November 1917 to the Constituent Assembly from the Vologda Governate on the SR list. Together with many rightist SRs, he was arrested on 2 January 1918 and accused of being involved in the attempted assassination of V. I. Lenin. He spent two months in the Peter and Paul Fortress, being released thanks to politically influential university classmates and friends from the leftist SRs. He moved to Moscow, participated in the "Union for the Renaissance of Russia" movement, and prepared for an armed uprising against the Soviet authorities in the Vologda Governate. In summer 1918 he was rearrested and sentenced to death.

While in prison he wrote a repentant letter to the local newspaper in Velikii Ustiug which was reprinted in the central newspaper Правда [Truth].[351] He acknowledged the collapse of the SR policies and declared that he was withdrawing from the SR Party and from political life in general. Reacting favorably to the letter, Lenin in reply wrote a gracious article[352] and, after publication, revoked the

ciological Study on the Principal Forms of Social Behavior and Morality] (Spb., 1914; reprinted: Spb., 1999; M., 2006).

348 ЦГИА СПб., fond 14, opis 1, file 10917.

349 ЦГИА СПб., fond 14, opis 3, file 14605.

350 A. F. Kerensky, *Russia and History's Turning Point* (New York, 1965); Kerensky, *The Catastrophe: Kerensky's Own Story of the Russian Revolution* (New York, 1927; reprint ed.; 1971).

351 «Отречение Питирима Сорокина» [Renunciation of Pitirim Sorokin], Правда [Pravda], 20 November 1918.

352 Lenin, «Ценные признания Питирима Сорокина» [Valuable Acknowledgements of Pitirim Sorokin], Полное собрание сочинений [Complete Collected Works], (5th ed.), XXXVII, pp. 188-197.

death penalty; Sorokin was released from prison at the end of 1918 and returned to Petrograd University.

Following the reorganization of the Law Faculty of the University in 1918/1919, Sorokin continued to work in the politico-legal division of the Faculty of Social Sciences of the University, but now at the Chair of Political Economy and Statistics[353] and, from 31 January 1920, in the post of professor.[354] On 13 October 1919 the Politico-Legal Division of the Faculty of Social Sciences confirmed the instructional plan for the 1919/20 academic year; Sorokin was listed as giving the principal lecture course "The System of Sociology".[355] During 1920, the academic title of professor was conferred on Sorokin for the aggregate of his scholarly publications; he created and headed the Chair and Division of sociology in the socio-pedagogical division of the Faculty of Social Sciences.

During these years, Sorokin worked as well at the Psychoneurological Institute, renamed the Socio-Bibliological (from 1919, Sociological) Institute (and from 1921, as Head of the Chair of Sociology), and Agricultural Institute, Institute of the National Economy, and occasionally lectured at other institutions of higher education. The apogee of his publications during his Russian period was a two-volume treatise on the system of sociology.[356] On 22 April 1922 Sorokin defended the theses of his treatise at the Council of the Historical Institute attached to St. Petersburg University. The official opponents were professors Nikolai Ivanovich Kareev (1850-1931), Konstantin Mikhailovich Takhtarev (1871-1925), and Ivan Ivanovich Lapshin (1870-1952). The Institute unanimously awarded Sorokin the degree of doctor of sociology.[357]

By Decree of the Collegium of the State Political Administration of 26 September 1922, Sorokin was exiled from Russia.

Emigration. Sorokin lived first in Berlin, then by invitation of the President of Czechoslovakia, Thomas Masaryk (1850-1937), he moved to Prague University, and in 1923, to the United States. His first position was as a professor of sociology in the University of Minnesota (1924-1930); he became a citizen of the United States in 1930. That same year he accepted a position at Harvard University, where he headed the first sociology department in that country. In 1937 he was elected President of the International Institute of Sociology. During the 1950s, he founded the Center for the Study of Creative Altruism at Harvard University and became the Director.

Honors from his colleagues came in the form of being elected President of the American Sociological Association, the International Society for the Comparative Study of Civilizations, and the International Congress of Sociology; and honorary

353 ОА СПбГУ, fond 1, opis 1, file 141.

354 ЦГА СПб, fond 7240, opis 14, file 134.

355 ЦГА СПб, fond 7240, opis 14, file 85.

356 Sorokin, Система социологии [System of Sociology] (Pg., 1920). 2 vols.

357 Санкт-Петербургский университет [St. Petersburg University], no. 8 (1998), p. 28.

memberships in the American Academy of Arts and Sciences and the academies of Romania, Belgium, and Czechoslovakia.

International legal views. Widely known throughout the world as a leading sociologist, Sorokin wrote on international law or on matters directly affecting international law. These works have been overlooked, one may suppose, because he published them in the pre-revolutionary period, he was strongly and outspokenly anti-Soviet, and when he emigrated, they were simply forgotten. And his contributions to sociology, pioneering in their day, overshadowed his contributions to international law.

Being a sociologist, he approached international law from a sociological point of view. While a University student and shortly afterwards, he published two short items on his specialty at the time – criminal law.[358] He turned in 1917/18 to books of an international legal orientation. At this stage of his life, Sorokin was sympathetic to socialist ideals and schemes for building a just international world. In his view, a State unites people belonging to different classes. The alliance of classes transcends State boundaries: the proletariat of Russia, England, France, and other countries belong to a single class and constitute a unified whole. The internationalist alliance of the proletariat of different countries is an expression of this "whole", embodied in the phrase "Proletarians of All Countries, Unite"; the aspiration is to create a world proletarian State on new international principles. Nevertheless, Sorokin believed that the fall of the States contemporary to him and the worldwide unification of mankind would be completed not by replacing State organization with class organization and not by substituting class egoism for the existing State egoism, but rather in the form of a supra-class and supra-national unification of all people; each individual would be equal with others, without distinction of citizenship, class, sex, religion, kinship, and so on. Only such a world society, in his view, might be an ideal of the future.[359]

The horrors of the First World War persuaded many political scientists and legal scholars to seek a way of building a stable "peace for the world"; Sorokin was of this inclination. In two virtually identical books published in 1917, Sorokin evaluated two basic schemes for building the future peace being widely discussed in scientific and political circles. The first scheme was based on the principle of retaining the principles of the State (on one hand, to keep existing States, but undertake a territorial regrouping by strengthening the "reliable, honorable, and peaceful" States by adding territory to them and, on the other hand, weakening (by "deducting" territory, reducing military strength, etc.) the bloodthirsty and militant States aspiring to place force above law). The ultimate aim of this scheme was to re-draw the territories of States and equalize their status and strength in accordance with geographical and military-economic criteria.

[358] Sorokin, Преступность и ее причины [Criminality and the Reasons Therefor] (Riga, 1913). 46 p.; Sorokin, «Третья» школа и спор «классиклов» с «социологами» в уголовном праве [The "Third" School and Dispute of the "Classics" with the "Sociologists" in Criminal Law] (M., 1915). 20 p.

[359] See M. A. Mentiukova, Государственно-правовые воззрения Питирима Александровича Сорокина [State-Law Views of Pitirim Aleksandrovich Sorokin] (Spb., 2010), p. 14 (abstract diss. kand. iurid. nauk).

The second scheme was based on the principle of national priority (in essence, each nation forms a State; national States are separated out in multi-national States, and the nations residing on the territories of two or more States should form their own national State or accede to an existing national State).[360]

Sorokin addressed the weak aspects and contradictions of both theories and demonstrated that neither scheme guaranteed peace; they were utopian and unsuited to establishing the creation of peace on earth (p. 8). Rejecting both schemes, Sorokin offered his own. What was needed, he said, was a supranational union – the members of which would be existing States combined into a single supranational State (p. 17). He acknowledged that his scheme was infinitely more difficult to realize than the other proposals, but "if mankind wants a stable peace", it needs to undertake this scheme. There was, he believed, no other way (p. 18).

His scheme might be significantly advanced in the near future if several avenues were pursued, among them:

(1) the formation of an inter-State court to settle disputes between States, the enforcement of which would depend upon all States except the offending or violating State;

(2) the adoption by an international congress of two basic legal norms: (a) the prohibition to use war to resolve inter-State disputes and conflicts; (b) the obligation of States when any conflict arises between them to refer the dispute for resolution by an international court and accept the decisions of the court. Sorokin was persuaded that his scheme was realistic: "the adoption thereof would signify replacement of the principle of force by law" (pp. 20, 24). He was a proponent of a "world federation of States" which on the basis of a carefully developed international law would act as an arbitrator in conflicts between States.

In the field of international relations and international law Sorokin elaborated his so-called "theory of fluctuations". In his perception, "revolutions and wars were nothing other than the logical and factual consequence of a disintegration of the permanent system of relations". If the political and legal system was stable, war should precede a lengthy period of the forming, development, and improvement of peace. Thus, war cannot be constant or permanent.

Sorokin offered an analysis that contrasted the duration of wars, the size of the population of States, the size of their armies, the intensity of combat operations, and other factors as the basis for comparing the wars of Antiquity, Middle Ages, and Renaissance. On this basis of this historical material, he concluded that when contrasting the First World War with the wars of the Middle Ages – which lasted for centuries but ended in certain battles – and with the wars of Ancient Greece from the sixth to the second centuries accompanied by an occasional dash of scientific and philosophical innovation, they were not to the benefit or interests of modern society. Consequently, he said, the "simple number of years of war and peace is an inadequate indicator of the dynamics of war and peace", but this is

[360] Sorokin, Основы будущего мира [Fundamental Principles of the Future Peace] (Pg., 1917), pp. 4-7.

what researchers rely upon then they insist that wars predominated in ancient international relations and then deny the existence of international law in Antiquity.

He admired the Roman achievements. It was astonishing that the Romans maintained peace within such a vast empire: for Sorokin, the "Pax Romana was a magnificently organized peaceful coexistence". Thus, the theory of fluctuations reflected the distinctive features of the alternating periods of peace and war in ancient history.[361]

Sorokin published more than forty books and about 1,000 articles, many republished, translated, or reprinted throughout Europe, Asia, Latin America, and Africa.

Nikolai Stepanovich Tagantsev *(19 February (3 March) 1843, b. Penza – 22 March 1923, d. Petrograd).*[362] *Pre-eminent specialist in criminal law, senator, privy counsellor, member of State Council of Russian Empire, honorary member of Russian Academy of Sciences.*

Life and career. Tagantsev graduated from the Penza Male Gymnasium with the silver medal and enrolled in the Law Faculty of St. Petersburg University in 1859, finishing in 1863 with the degree of candidate of law. He was selected to remain to train for the professoriate at the Chair of Criminal Law and Procedure and sent to Germany for two years, where he worked on a magister dissertation under the supervision of Karl Joseph Anton Mittermaier (1787-1867). The dissertation, devoted to recidivism, was successfully defended and on 8 December 1867 Tagantsev was appointed privat-docent at the Chair of Criminal Law and Procedure in St. Petersburg University, advancing from 15 October 1868 to an established docentship, and from 1869 to professor *extraordinarius*.

In parallel, Tagantsev was appointed professor *extraordinarius* at the Imperial School of Jurisprudence and from 1892 to 1907, a Distinguished Professor; from 1867 to 1872 professor *extraordinarius* at the Alexander Lycée; from 1871 to 1873 a professor at the Military Law Academy; and from 1878 to 1882, at the Higher Women's Courses.

[361] See O. V. Butkevych, У истоков международного права [At the Sources of International Law] (Spb., 2008), pp. 25-26.

[362] Murzanov, note 190 above, p. 418. Murzanov gives the date of death as 21 March 1923, at 10:40 hours.

He defended a doctoral dissertation on crimes against life under Russian criminal law and received the doctor of criminal law as from 5 February 1870. He was appointed professor *ordinarius* at St. Petersburg University, and from 1871 to 1878 was secretary of the Law Faculty and for many years a member of the University court. From 1873 to 1878 he served as the editor of the Журнал гражданского и уголовного права [Journal of Civil and Criminal Law]. In 1877 he became a co-founder and from 1878 to 1883 a Deputy Chairman of the Criminal Division of the Law Society attached to St. Petersburg University.

In 1877 he taught criminal law in the Winter Palace to the son of Emperor Alexander II, the Grand Prince Sergei Aleksandrovich. About that time he became a member of a Commission appointed by the State Council to consider prison reform. He acted as defense counsel in the "Case Concerning Propaganda in the Empire" – a political trial instituted against revolutionary narodniks.

In 1882 he resigned his teaching positions at the University and the Lycée to devote himself to assisting in the codification of Russian criminal law. He had completed his three-volume Course of Russian Criminal Law, rich in comparative and international materials (1874-1880). In 1881 he was appointed a consultant to the Ministry of Justice and a member of the Committee to draft a new Statute on Punishments and in 1903 appointed to the Commission to draft a new Criminal Code. He became in 1890 the Chairman of the Commission to draft preliminary proposals for the revision of Finnish criminal legislation and thereafter a member of committees to prepare new legislation on court organization and criminal procedure. He personally drafted much of the reform criminal legislation. On 23 December 1887 he was appointed a Senator in the Department of Cassation of the Ruling Senate, becoming privy counsellor as from 1 January 1903. On 17 April 1905 he was appointed a member of the State Council, and on 3 May 1917 became a Senator of the First Department of the Senate.

He was a member of the Permanent Court of International Arbitration at The Hague in 1909 and 1915.

In December 1917, Tagantsev was elected an Honorary Member of the Russian Academy of Sciences. By Decree of the Law Faculty of St. Petersburg University adopted 25 November 1918 Tagantsev was invited to become a lecturer in the Faculty, but the invitation was not taken up.

Upon his death on 22 March 1923, Tagantsev was buried at the Mitrofanevskoe Cemetery; the cemetery was later destroyed and the gravesite not preserved.

International legal views. Tagantsev left an enormous literary legacy, several items of which are of interest to international law.

In 1878 Tagantsev was among the initiators of transformations in the system of punishments in Russia and in that capacity took part in the Second International Penitentiary Congress held at Stockholm. His article on the Congress also appeared as a separate book.[363] He favored such congresses for the opportunity

[363] N. S. Tagantsev, Стокгольмский тюремный конгресс [Stockholm Penal Congress], Журнал гражданского и уголовного права [Journal of Civil and Criminal Law], no. 2 (1880), pp. 28-90. The

to exchange views with other specialists on prison systems and possibly develop common or similar norms for organizing penitentiaries. His substantial report summarized in detail the reports and oral remarks made with emphasis on controversial issues. With regard to the international aspects of the Congress, he noted the need for mutual assistance of States in the prevention and detection of crimes, the establishment of greater unity in the provisions of extradition treaties, the creation of better methods to facilitate treaty implementation, and the formation of stabler links between law enforcement agencies.

The Stockholm Congress discussed a project to create a permanent international penitentiary commission to be composed of official representatives of States. Such a commission would have three tasks: (1) to collect factual material concerning crimes committed by persons released from prison; (2) to generalize progressive experience in prison administration and make recommendations to governments of States; and (3) to arrange for regular future congresses. Participation in the Congress strengthened the position of Tagantsev in his capacity as a member of the Ministry of Justice commission charged with recommending urgent reforms in the Russian prison system.

At the turn of the nineteenth and twentieth centuries, Tagantsev became involved in clarifying the legal status of the Grand Duchy of Finland and its relations with the Russian Empire. During the 1880s separatist trends intensified in Finland, expressed in attempts to configure the legal status of Finland as a "State within a State", its relations within the Russian Empire as an inter-State unie, and the Grand Duchy as an autonomous subject of international law. These attempts were in evidence when the Finnish parliament confirmed a draft Criminal Code of Finland to replace the Swedish Code of 1734. The draft adopted by Finnish parliament on 7 December 1889 was confirmed by Emperor Alexander III and published in April 1890. The evidence in that document of separatist tendencies generated a negative reaction in Russian academic and governmental circles. The Code was supposed to enter into force on 20 December 1890, but at the last moment the entry into force was suspended – a development in which Tagantsev was directly involved.

Tagantsev became an outspoken opponent of the Code and actually spearheaded a considerable public opposition movement. In 1890 he was appointed by the Emperor to head a special commission to draw up preliminary proposals for the revision of Finnish criminal legislation. He set out his views in an article also released in book form.[364]

In Tagantsev's view, the problems with the 1889 Finnish Criminal Code were three: (1) provisions affecting the international relations of the Russian Empire with foreign States and not consistent with laws of the Empire; (2) provisions

book appeared under the same title. 63 p.

[364] Tagantsev, «Высочайший манифест 1/13 декабря 1890 г. и Финляндское уголовное уложение» [His Majesty's Manifesto of 1/13 December 1890 and the Finnish Criminal Code], Юридическая летопись [Legal Chronicle], I (1891), pp. 97-146; separate booklet. Spb., 1910. 44 p. Also see Tagantsev, Великое княжество Финляндия: Выдержка из лекций по русскому уголовному праву (Т. 1, 2-е изд. 1902 г., с. 245 -252) [Grand Duchy of Finland: Extract from Lectures on Russian Criminal Law (2d ed.; Vol. 1 (1902), pp. 245-252)]. (СПб., 1910). 17 p.

separating the interests of Finland from those of Russia and equating the last with regard to the prosecution of certain crimes on Finnish territory against foreign powers; and (3) provisions effectively repealing legislation considered to be binding throughout all of Russia, including Finland.

As for the international-legal status of Finland – a notion that Tagantsev believed was being pushed by the Swedish component of Finnish society – Tagantsev was firmly of the view that Finland was an integral part of the Russian Empire, possessed autonomy in managing Finnish affairs, and had its own special legislation for this purpose, but this did not make Finland a State within a State. In international relations Finland was part of Russia; diplomatic relations were solely with Russia; diplomatic representatives of foreign States were accredited only to the Russian court; only Russia might declare war and conclude peace; treaties were concluded only between Russia and foreign powers. All provisions of the Finnish Criminal Code affecting these matters were superfluous, Tagantsev argued.

Tagantsev resisted categorically those provisions addressed to crimes against the State. The external security of Finland should be protected by the same measures as protected Russia. Any infringement against Finland by a foreign State was also an infringement against Russia, and *vice versa*. Finland, he said, cannot have allies and enemies separately from Russia, or its own armed forces, fortifications, and so on. Any provisions treating treason must be identical in both jurisdictions.

Aleksandr Grigorevich Timofeev *(22 December 1867, b. St. Petersburg – d. after 1917). Specialist in criminal law, consul abroad.*

Life and career. Having graduated in 1886 from the Fifth St. Petersburg Gymnasium, Timofeev studied law at St. Petersburg University, finishing in 1890. As a student he received a gold medal for a written essay on correctional institutions for young offenders.

He served from 1894 as privat-docent at the Chair of Criminal Law of the University and simultaneously lectured at a commercial school. In 1897 Timofeev published a history of corporal punishments in Russian law, followed by a second expanded version in 1904. He submitted the second edition to Novorossiisk University in Odessa as a magister dissertation. The defense was held in 1905, generated sharp discussion, lasted for ten hours, and ended in scandal. The occasion turned into political and the police were summoned. The Council of Novorossiisk University refused to confirm the magister degree. Timofeev urged the Ministry of Public Enlightenment to appeal to the Ruling Senate. Three years later, in autumn 1908, the Council of the University confirmed the magister of criminal law for Timofeev.

In St. Petersburg University Timofeev also offered courses on "Criminal Law", "Criminology", "Criminal Law Policy", "Crimes Against the State", "History of Judicial Rhetoric", and "The 1864 Judicial Statutes". He worked at the University until 1915.

At the St. Petersburg Commercial School, Timofeev lectured on consular law. During the First World War he accepted an assignment as supernumerary consular agent in Kandahar, Afghanistan, from 1915 to 1917.

International legal views. Several of Timofeev's works engaged his views on international law, rather unusual for a specialist on criminal law. For reasons unclear, the St. Petersburg Commercial School persuaded him to offer lectures on consular law as a "supplemental course". These appeared as a concise lithographed manuscript text intended for non-lawyers but nonetheless of the standard expected by this discipline at the time.[365]

Timofeev had a strongly positive view of the role of the consul in defending the commercial and diplomatic interests of the sending State. In his view, the development of a country's foreign trade depended upon the consul, as well as the acquisition of new markets and the acquisition of desirable imports. He considered in detail the procedures for opening consulates, the appointment of consuls, their citizenship, rights, and privileges, the distinctive features of consulates and consuls in the Orient, administrative, judicial, and notarial functions, and relations with local officials and natives of the receiving country. He considered consuls in the Christian and non-Christian worlds and their respective roles in peacetime and wartime. Much attention was devoted to the implementation of trade treaties and conventions (pp. 148-217) applicable to the carriage of goods by sea or river, post and telegraph, fishing, and the like. Attention was given to intellectual property.

Timofeev also touched upon a concern of his day relating to the correlation of central Empire power and authority and that of nationality-based and other entities within the Empire. His article was widely cited then and since. The central authorities preferred centralized territorial administration throughout the country and opposed granting extensive rights to entities at the middle and local levels, what were known as autonomies. In the world of legal scholarship, especially in liberal circles, there was sentiment for some form of federation within the Empire, whether based on nationality principles or simply efficient management principles.

Timofeev identified as the most important feature of an entity within a federation as opposed to an entity within a unitary State: the inviolability of the rights of a subject of the federation against interference by the central authorities.[366] An autonomy exercises the rights of another and is therefore controlled by the central authority. But he did not see compelling reasons to change the existing correlation between the Empire and the various forms of local government.

[365] Консульское право и международные торговые трактаты России: Лекции, читанные в Дополнительном Практическом классе / Санкт-Петербургское коммерческое училище [Consular Law and International Trade Treaties of Russia: Lectures Delivered in the Additional Practical Class /St. Petersburg Commercial School] (Spb., 1898). 98 c.

[366] Timofeev, Самоуправление и автономия. Очерк [Self-Government and Autonomy. Essay] (Spb., 1906), pp. 11-12.

Aleksandr Aleksandrovich Zhizhilenko *(16 December 1873, b. Borovichi, Novgorod Governate – 11 August 1931, d. Leningrad). Specialist in criminal law and one of founders of Russian criminology.*

Life and career. After graduating in 1891 from a Gymnasium in Kalice, Poland, Zhizhilenko enrolled in the Law Faculty of St. Petersburg University.[367] Completing his degree in 1895, he remained to prepare for the professoriate at the Chair of Criminal Law for one year with a Demidov stipend.[368] He was sent abroad immediately to Germany and spent about two years studying with Franz von Liszt, who specialized both in criminal law and in international law. Upon returning home, Zhizhilenko began to lecture on criminal law at the Alexander Lycée.

By petition of the Law Faculty of St. Petersburg University and by decision of the Administrator of the Petersburg Education District, Zhizhilenko was appointed in February 1898 the Keeper of the Cabinet of Criminal Law; from autumn 1898 he was granted the rank and title of privat-docent as an assistant to give tutorials on criminal law. Following the successful defense on 19 November 1900[369] of a magister dissertation on the "Forgery of Documents. Historico-Dogmatic Study",[370] by decision of the Council of the University of 18 December 1900 the degree of Magister of Criminal Law was conferred. On 1 June 1901 Zhizhilenko was appointed professor *extraordinarius* at the Chair of Criminal Law and Procedure of the St. Petersburg Law Faculty. The Administrator of the Education District on 12 November 1901 confirmed Zhizhilenko in the post of secretary of the Law Faculty for a term of four years, repeatedly reconfirmed until August 1913.

The Ministry of Public Enlightenment on 11 October 1905 authorized Zhizhilenko to deliver courses on criminal procedure and the doctrine of punishments. In addition to the University, Zhizhilenko taught criminal law at the Higher Women's (Bestuzhev) Courses and at the Institute of Higher Commercial Knowledge.

In 1915 Zhizhilenko defended his doctoral dissertation at Kharkov University on "Punishment. The Concept Thereof and Distinction from Other Means of Law

367 ЦГИА СПб., fond 14, opis 3, file 28474.

368 ЦГИА СПб., fond 14, opis 3, file 14399. The period at the Faculty was extended several times.

369 The defense was reported in Право [Law], no. 51 (1900), cols. 2468-2472.

370 See A. A. Zhizhilenko, Подлог документов. Историко-догматическое исследование [Forgery of Documents: Historico-Dogmatic Study] (Spb., 1900). 746 p.

Enforcement",[371] whereupon he was elected professor *ordinarius* of the Chair at St. Petersburg University.

Zhizhilenko served as Vice Chairman and Chairman of the Criminal Division of the Law Society attached to St. Petersburg University. He was active in the Russian Group of the International Union of Penal and Penitentiary Law and a member of the Committee of the Literary Fund. Two important legal publications enjoyed his support as a member of the editorial board – the Журнал уголовного права и процесса [Journal of Criminal Law and Procedure] and the newspaper Право [Law].

During the Revolutions of 1917 and Civil War, Zhizhilenko remained in Russia. The Provisional Government on 7 March 1917 appointed him Head of the Chief Prison Administration of Russia while remaining a University professor. By Order of the Ministry of Public Enlightenment of 20 February 1917, he was confirmed as from 1 January 1917 as professor *ordinarius* at the Chair of Criminal Law of the University. As Head of the Prison Administration, he spoke out in favor of humanization of the procedures and departmental institutions for the execution of punishments, respect for the personal dignity of convicts, initiated training courses for prison personnel, and opposed capital punishment.

After the October 1917 Revolution, Zhizhilenko continued as a professor at the University and other institutions of higher education in Petrograd/Leningrad. The rank and title of professor was again conferred in 1919 on the basis of his magister degree.[372] About 1930 Zhizhilenko was subjected to public criticism in the Soviet press as one who bore the imprint of bourgeois ideology. He died on 11 August 1931 and is buried at the Smolensk Cemetery in Leningrad; his grave has been preserved.

International legal views. Zhizhilenko's views on international law emerged in two connections and international forums: the International Union of Penal and Penitentiary Law, formed in 1888, and international penitentiary congresses, which date back to 1846. Of the congresses, there were twelve in all, the last held at Washington D.C. in 1910; they were revived in 1925 during the interwar period. Representatives of Russia took part in those, both officials and legal practitioners, medical doctors, architects, clergy, and others.[373] These were forums for scholars and legal practitioners from various countries to discuss general positions and prepare proposals for their governments, especially their legislative bodies, to approximate or unify material and procedural norms relating to criminal law, procedure, and penology. Zhizhilenko wrote more than ten articles and reports on these matters.

[371] Zhizhilenko, Наказание: Его понятие и отличие от других правоохранительных средств [Punishment: Concept Thereof and Distinction from Other Means of Law Enforcement] (Pg., 1914). 676 p. This work was awarded the M. P. Akhmatov Prize by the Russian Academy of Sciences.

[372] ЦГА СПб., fond 7240, opis 14, file 85, l. 32.

[373] See R. I. Ivaniakov and E. A. Kruglova, «Деятельность международных пенитенциарных конгрессов и съездов в XIX – начале XX века» [Activity of International Penitentiary Congresses and Assemblies in the XIX and early XX Centuries], in Уголовно-исполнительная система: право, экономика, управление [Penal System: Law, Economy, Administration], no. 1 (2015), pp. 18-22.

In an article on the Brussels penal congress,[374] Zhizhilenko noted that the emergence of international congresses convened to develop positions an exchange of information was among the major achievements of the nineteenth century. Among these the International Congresses on Penal and Penitentiary Law occupied a special place because the international struggle against crime was so important. Even though decisions of the Congresses were not binding, governments took them into account. He believed the Congresses had done much to approximate the positions of States and improve criminal legislation (p. 127).

At the Brussels Congress of 1900, some 173 reports were presented, of which thirteen were from the Russian delegation and ten of these were submitted to the penitentiary commission formed by the Law Society of St. Petersburg University. Among the issues discussed at the Congress with active Russian participation: (1) providing remuneration to the victim of a crime by the criminal; (2) the international legal aspects of the extradition of criminals, especially the extradition of one's own subjects. A joint Report submitted by Professor I. A. Ivanovskii and Magister of International Law, L. A. Shalland, refuted arguments made by opponents of the extradition of own subjects: "... extradition of own subjects not only does not infringe on the dignity of the country extraditing them", they said, but failure to do so would reflect unfavorably on the impartiality of foreign judges in matters concerning foreigners. Non-extradition should occur when the circumstances of the case show that the *forum deprehensionis* gives more advantages than the *forum detecti commisi*, or if the infringement is directed against Russia and co-citizens of the accused (p. 142).

After sharp debates, the Congress decided that extradition of own subjects would be a desirable means of ensuring the proper administration of justice when it occurs between countries whose criminal legislation rests on analogous grounds and there is mutual trust in the courts. Zhizhilenko criticized this approach as being "insufficiently certain" because in practice it might make matters more difficult. For example, how does one in practice determine that one State refuses extradition to another on the basis that its courts are untrustworthy, and what is understood by the formulation that criminal legislation rests on analogous grounds, and so on. Zhizhilenko considered the proper approach to be that the Congress should decide, on one hand, the conditions of the extradition of own subjects and, on the other, define those instances when their extradition for one reason or another may not occur (p. 143).

He then turned to a related issue: what principles should guide the determination of the jurisdiction of courts of another country where crimes were committed either abroad or with the participation of own subjects or foreigners abroad. The Congress adopted a decision under which every State may punish, under its own laws, crimes and offenses committed outside its territory by its own subjects or by foreigners as the principal culprits or co-culprits. The prosecution of the guilty should not be affected by the sojourn of the culprits on the territory of the victim State. Punishment of its subjects is possible also when the incriminating acts are

[374] Zhizhilenko, «Международный пенитенциарный конгресс в Брюсселе 1900 года» [International Penitentiary Congress in Brussels in 1900], Вестник права [Herald of Law], no. 2 (1901), pp. 126-159.

punishable in that country on whose territory the crime was committed. Prosecution, however, of the guilty may occur only in the event of the guilty being situated on national territory.

Attention was devoted at the Congress to identifying measures for improving the penitentiary institutions of States (the organization of medical and health services, the participation of medical doctors in determining the conditions for confining convicts, experience with reformatories (United States), the basis for solitary confinement, combatting recidivism, including among minors), and to crime prevention (should emigration be included among the measures for the prevention of crimes by minors, or deportation to a colonial possession, among others).

§11.8. *Chair of Political Economy and Statistics*

The Chair of Political Economy and Statistics before the 1917 October Revolution was part of the Law Faculty of St. Petersburg University.

Iosif Mikhailovich (Moiseevich) Kulisher *(1 August 1878, b. Kyiv – 17 November 1933, d. Leningrad). Russian and Soviet economist and jurist, publicist, historian, public and political figure.*

Life and career. Iosif Kulisher graduated with the gold medal from the German Gymnasium attached to the St. Anna Evangelical Lutheran Church in St. Petersburg and in 1896 enrolled at the Law Faculty of St. Petersburg University. Even in his student years he began to undertake economic research. His essay "On Revenue from Capital" was awarded a gold medal. During and after his law studies he published several articles in German journals on economics.

After graduation in 1900, the Law Faculty invited Kulisher to remain at the Chair of Political Economy and Statistics to prepare for the professoriate, but this proposal was not confirmed by the Administrator of the Educational District. Kulisher went abroad to Berlin, Halle, Vienna, and Leipzig to attend lectures and use libraries. Upon his return, Kulisher passed the magister examinations in political economy, statistics, and financial law. In 1905 he was appointed privat-docent at the Chair of Political Economy in the Law Faculty and delivered a course on the history of economic existence.

From 1905 he became a college secretary in the trade section of the Ministry of Finances, elevated in 1907 to be an official on special assignment, while remaining a privat-docent at the University. In 1908 Kulisher defended his magister dissertation "Survey from the History of the Forms of Industry in Western Europe from the XIII to the XVIII Centuries". To his workload he added in 1910 the position of docent of the Higher Commercial Schools, and from 1916, professor. He was elected professor in 1915 at the Psychoneurological Institute.

His articles appeared in Русское богатство [Russian Wealth], Русская мысль [Russian Thought], Русское экономическое обозрение [Russian Economic Survey], *Jahrbücher für Nationalökonomie und Statistik*, among others. His expertise caused him to be invited to take part in drafting Russian legislation on the income, trade, and other taxes submitted to the State Duma.

From 1921 to 1924 he was Director of the Economic Scientific Research Institute attached to Petrograd University and, from 1930 to 1932 taught at the Leningrad Financial-Economic Institute.

International legal views. Kulisher is noteworthy as an economist for the legal approach he took in his studies. This was evident in his early history of customs policies: a comparative analysis of rich factual materials gathered from legal systems throughout the world. He concluded that rulers over the centuries arbitrarily established customs duties and charges which were nothing other than outright robbery. The imposition at the boundary of various road, bridge, port, transit, convoy, market, and other charges in order to obtain travel or passage documents supposedly in the interests of financing repairs or construction or providing services were actually spent for other purposes. In fact, he argued, all these imposts were essentially payment for entry to another monarch's territory. Matters began to change in the eighteenth century when arbitrarily determined charges were replaced by those legislatively created in order to pursue protectionist objectives. Kulisher also gave attention to export duties and import prohibitions.[375]

During the First World War, Kulisher decided to investigate the export policy and practice of European States and determine the reasons, means, and consequences for the sharp increase in Germany's foreign trade, that country having moved to the forefront of European powers in this respect.[376] In his view export was no longer merely a supplement to domestic production. England had thrived on export markets, but was an exception among European States. Now the situation had changed, and all European countries needed and competed for export markets, especially Germany. Having analyzed German export policies, Kulisher concluded that German leaders and entrepreneurs understood that foreign trade and export at the turn of the centuries had become the major structural element in the economic development of Germany. This led Kulisher to undertake a major treatise on international trade policy.[377]

375 I. M. Kulisher, Очерки по истории таможенной политики [Essays on the History of Customs Policy] (Spb., 1903), pp. 1-8.

376 Kulisher, «Германский экспорт и борьба с ним» [German Export and the Struggle Against It], Вестник финансов [Herald of Finances], nos. 5, 7, 14 (1915); issued as separate offprint (1915). [2], 61 p.

377 Kulisher, Основные вопросы международной торговой политики [Basic Questions of International Trade Policy] (Pg., 1918-1919). 2 vols.

In his final work of the pre-Soviet era, Kulisher analyzed world trade and categorically opposed certain theories prevalent in the West that world trade would recede and domestic production again would be the predominant source of economic growth for each country. On the contrary, he believed world trade would be restored after the War, but more likely not based on the earlier customs union. New arrangements would arise. For Russia this meant the expanded export of Russian goods and greater inclusion in international trade turnover. He made specific policy recommendations to the Provisional Russian Government to this end.[378]

Semen Osipovich (Iosifovich) Zagorskii *(1882 – 17 March 1930, d. Geneva, Switzerland). Specialist in law and economics, journalist, public figure.*

Life and career. The son of a military doctor, he graduated from the Law Faculty of St. Petersburg University. During his student years he was active in Marxist circles and experienced arrests. After graduation, he remained at the Chair of Political Economy and Statistics to prepare for the professoriate. From 1 January 1916 he was appointed privat-docent at the Chair of Statistics of the Law Faculty of St. Petersburg University, where he offered a course on "Syndicalism and Trusts". He also lectured at the Petersburg Polytechnic Institute, Higher (P. F. Lesgaft) Commercial Courses of Pobedinskii, and at a private university attached to the Psychoneurological Institute. He combined lecturing with acting as a department head at the Ministry of Labor of the Provisional Government.

Following the October 1917 Revolution, he removed to Odessa and there collaborated on the editorial boards of several local periodical publications. In 1919 he moved on to France, where he worked in the Russian Economic Bureau. In March 1922 he took a position in Geneva, Switzerland, as head of the Russian Section of the International Labour Organisation. From 1923 he lectured at the Law Faculty of the Russian Division of the University of Paris, offering a course "International Economic Policy of Russia at the End of the XIX and Early XX Centuries".

He was among the organizers in 1926 of the Franco-Russian Institute of Social and Political Sciences, became a member of the Council of professors of the Institute, and taught a course on the "Economic System of Soviet Russia".

International legal views. Although Zagorskii wrote on economic and social issues, some touched upon matters of international legal interest. In 1917 he produced a substantial study of the economic and political reasons for the First World War, discussing in detail the 1916 international economic conference in Paris.[379] Eight States took part in the Conference, including Russia, England, France, and Italy. Despite their differences, these powers sought to resist a new postwar threat on the part of Germany and its allies. The Conference decisions contemplated a

[378] Kulisher, Будуще нашей внешней торговли [Future of Our Foreign Trade] (Pg., 1917).

[379] S. O. Zagorskii, Война после мира (По поводу Парижской экономической конференции союзников) [War After Peace (On the Occasion of the Paris Economic Conference of Allies)] (Spb., 1917). 393 p. On Zagorskii, see Starodubtsev, note 3 above, p. 122.

system of measures intended after the War not to allow the rebirth of Germany, to create an economic and customs union, and to isolate those countries through a protectionist policy and the introduction of trade sanctions. The ultimate purpose of the Conference was to affirm in Europe the dominance of a French-English-Russian bloc with a view to forming a unified customs union. Underlying all the decisions of the Conference, observed Zagorskii, was the intention to carry on the war against Germany in the sphere of the economy.

In an article written in advance of his monograph Zagorskii examined the other side of the equation – how a victorious Germany might organize the European world.[380] He considered the foreign policy, economic, and international legal ideas of the German ruling elites and German legal scholars and their embodiment in German policies during the second half of the nineteenth and early twentieth centuries with regard to creating a powerful customs or even economic union in Central Europe. Zagorskii called this scheme an attempt to unify the Central European States by trade treaties.

Such treaties were concluded initially between Germany, Austria-Hungary, and Italy, then between Germany and Belgium and Switzerland, followed by the accession of Romania and Serbia. Leading these arrangements was Germany, who regarded these measures as preliminary steps towards the unification of Central Europe and the construction of a United States of Europe. In his perception these German policies were also directed against the protectionism of Russia, who averted these intentions by acceding to the trade treaties in 1894.

Zagorskii also noted aspirations in Germany to create in Europe a large State on federative principles. Supporters of this approach pointed to the examples of the United States of America, the United Kingdom, and the Russian Empire. They also observed that the Baltic, Central, and Northern European countries had no direct access to warm Mediterranean ports, and the Mediterranean countries had no direct access to the Baltic coasts and ports. Even United Germany had but one river; the other European rivers were partly in the hands of others. Zagorskii quoted Franz Liszt, the international lawyer, when endorsing the advantages of a European federative State or organization.

[380] Zagorskii, «Происхождение идей объединения Европы под гегемонией Германии. Историческая справка» [Origin of the Idea of an Association of Europe under the Hegemony of Germany], Вестник Европы [Herald of Europe], № 2 (1915), pp. 130-150.

Chapter 12
St. Petersburg Law Graduates Making Incidental Contributions to International Legal Scholarship

The individuals herein had usually a tangential and fleeting relationship with the field of international law. They pursued other career paths but will have contributed in at least one publication, sometimes more, to the development of international law.

Ottokar Karlovich von Aderkas *(1859, b. Peydehof, Livonian Governate – 1921, d. Arensburg, Estonia). Russian public figure, privy counsellor.*

Life and career. Graduated from the Law Faculty of St. Petersburg University in 1881 and from that year became secretary of His Imperial Majesty's Chancellery for the institutions of Empress Maria Fedorovna. From 1895 he served as Director for the management of children's orphanages. He published several reports on international congresses dealing with the affairs of children and charity.[1]

Dmitrii Ivanovich Azarevich *(1 October 1848, b. Mogilev Governate – 1920). Specialized in the history of Roman and Byzantine law.*

Life and career. Graduated from the Law Faculty of St. Petersburg University in 1870, Azarevich was invited to remain at the Chair of Roman Law to prepare for the professoriate. He later held positions as professor at the Demidov Juridical Lycée in Iaroslavl, the Novorossiisk University in Odessa, and Warsaw University. He left three works of interest to the world of international law.[2]

[1] O. K. Aderkas, Краткий отчет о Пятом Международном конгрессе по делам слепых в Амстердаме [Concise Report on Fifth International Congress in Amsterdam for Affairs of the Blind] (Spb., 1885); Aderkas, Четвертый Международный конгресс по вопросам общественного и частного призрения в Милане [Fourth International Congress for Public and Private Charity in Milan] (Spb., 1906); Aderkas, Международные конгрессы по общественному и частному призрению в Копенгагене и по семейному воспитанию в Брюсселе [International Congresses for Public and Private Charity in Copenhagen and Family Nurturing in Brussels] (Spb., 1911); Aderkas, Международный конгресс по вопросам народного образования в Милане [International Congress for Public Education in Milan] (Spb., 1907); Aderkas, Международный конгресс по вопросам охраны детей и борьбы с детской смертностью в Брюсселе [International Congress for Protection of Children and Infant Mortality in Brussels] (Spb., 1907); Aderkas, Отчет о Международном конгрессе по вопросам воспитания и охраны детей в Льеже [Report on International Congress for Nurturing and Protection of Children in Liege] (Spb., 1906); Aderkas, Отчет о Международном конгрессе по общественному призрению и благотворительности в Париже [Report on International Congress on Public Charity and Philanthropy] (Spb., 1900); Aderkas, Отчет о Шестом Международном конгрессе для улучшения быта слепых, состоявшемся в городе Кельне на Рейне, в июле 1888 года [Report on Sixth International Congress for Improvement of Existence of Blind, Held in Cologne on Rhein] (Spb., 1889).

[2] D. I. Azarevich, Античный мир и христианство [The Ancient world and Christianity] (Iaroslavl,

Aleksandr Pavlovich Bashilov *(10 November 1849, b. St. Petersburg – d. ?). Specialist on trade law.*

Life and career. Having graduated in 1871 from the Law Faculty of St. Petersburg University, Bashilov served on the staff of the Ruling Senate and as a jurisconsult to the Stock Exchange Committee. He was active in preparing draft legislation in the fields of trade and industry and took part in international congresses on trade law at Antwerp in 1885 and Brussels in 1888. From 1883 he taught trade law at the School of Jurisprudence. His treatise on trade law addressed both the international character of trade law and conflicts of law arising out of trade relations.[3]

Samuil Iosifovich Dobrin *(1885-1959). Civilist, trade law, Soviet affairs.*

Life and career. Graduated from St. Petersburg Law Faculty in 1909 and became an assistant to a sworn advokat, Maksim Moiseevich Vinaver (1863-1926). Froom 1925 he served with the Trade Representation of the USSR in London and decided to remain, becoming a British citizen on 21 November 1933. He wrote extensively on Soviet legal affairs, including issues of public and private international law.[4]

Konrad Konradovich Dynovskii *(5 December 1863 – no earlier than 23 June 1930, d. Warsaw). Civilist.*

Life and career. Graduated from the Law Faculty of St. Vladimir University in Kyiv in 1886. From 1905 to 1912 served as privat-docent at the Chair of Civil Law and Procedure at the Law Faculty of St. Petersburg University, and also in the Department of Cassation of the Ruling Senate as Deputy Ober-Procurator, jurisconsult in the Ministry of Finances, and member of the consultation office attached to the said Ministry. He achieved a reputation by reason of two cases following the Russo-Japanese War: the first concerning armour which did not arrive in France, and the second in Berlin concerning the return of the ship *Angalt* to Russia, illegally seized by German subjects while the shop was en route to Port Arthur and carried military cargo. In connection with this second case he edited and wrote

1880); Azarevich, Очерки по торговому праву [Essays on Trade Law] (Warsaw, 1897), reprinted as Azarevich, Очерки по торговому праву. История торговли и торгового права. Права и обязанности торговца [Essays on Trade Law. History of Trade and Trade Law. Rights and Duties of Trader (2d ed.; Moscow, 2016).

[3] A. P. Bashilov, Русское торговое право [Russian Trade Law] (Spb., 1887).

[4] S. I. Dobrin, Вопросы министра юстиции Правительствующему сенату о праве неприятельских подданных на судебную защиту [Questions of the Minister of Justice to the Ruling Senate on the Right of Enemy Subjects to Judicial Defense], Право [Law], no. 6 (8 February 1915), cols. 345-355' Dobrin, Гражданско-правовое положение в России подданных воюющих с нею держав [Civil Law Status in Russia of Subjects of Belligerent Powers], Вестник Гражданского права [Herald of Civil Law], no. 6 (October 1914), pp. 60-98, published as separate pamphlet under same title in 1914. Also see Dobrin, "The English Doctrine of the Renvoi and the Soviet Law of Succession", British Yearbook of International Law, XV (1934), pp. 36-45; Dobrin, "Law Relating to Anglo-Soviet Trade", Law Times, CLXXXVII (1939), pp. 33, 51; Dobrin, "State-Owned Ships and Contraband of War", Law Times, CLXXXIX (1939), pp. 299, 316.

the introduction to a volume of documents and commentary published at Berlin on State immunity with respect to the enforcement of foreign judicial decisions.[5]

Boris Isaakovich Elkin *(1887, b. Kyiv, Ukraine – d. 1972, London, England).[6] Legal practitioner in the field of civil and trade law, journalist, legal publisher, and public figure.*

Life and career. Graduated from the Law Faculty in 1910, he was a publisher and legal practitioner; sworn advokat in St. Petersburg. In 1913 he became the editor of the weekly newspaper Право [Law]. Close politically to P. N. Miliukov (and his executor after Miliukov's death in 1943 and editor of the last (posthumous) volume of Miliukov's memoirs), Elkin was a member of the Kadet Party. Not sympathetic to the October 1917 Revolution, he emigrated in 1919 to Germany, where he founded and was the chief editor of the publishing house «Слово», considered one of the best Russian émigré publishing houses during the 1920s. There he was a member of the Board of the Russian Sworn Advokatura in Germany. He served as Chairman of the Union of Russian Publishers and Booksellers in Berlin. In 1933 he moved to Paris, and in 1940 to the United Kingdom, where he was called to the Bar.

He published from time to time in England – articles on Russian politics and intellectual life leading up to the during the 1917 revolutions[7] and later an important article on Freemasonry in Russia.[8]

Ivan Egorovich (Johann August) Engelman *(25 June (7 July) 1832, b. Mitau, Courland – d . 4 September 1912, Iurev).[9] Legal historian, civilist.*

Life and career. Graduated from the Mitau Gymnasium in 1850 and enrolled at the Law Faculty of St. Petersburg University in 1851, completing the course of study in 1855 with the degree of candidate of sciences. He received the gold medal of the University for a diploma dissertation on the civil laws contained in the Pskov

[5] K. K. Dynovskii, *Unzulässigkeit einer Zwandvollstreckung Gegen ausländische Staaten* (Berlin, 1910).

[6] See Branover, Российская еврейская энциклопедия [Russian Jewish Encyclopedia) (M., 1997), III, p. 456.

[7] See, for example, B. E. Elkin, "The Russian Intelligentsia on the Eve of the Revolution", *Daedalus*, LXXXXIX (1960), pp. 472-486.

[8] B. I. Elkin, «По вопросу об источниках частного международного права» [On Sources of Private International Law], Закон и суд [Law and Court], I. no. 5 (1929), cols. 187-188; Elkin, "Attempts to Revive Freemasonry in Russia", Slavonic and East European Review, XLIV (1966), pp. 454-472.

[9] On Engelman, see the biographical sketch by V. S. Em and V. V. Voronoi, in the reprint edition of Engelman, О давности по русскому гражданскому праву [On Limitations under Russian Civil Law] (reprint ed.: M., Statut, 2003), pp. 7-22; Shilokhvost, Русские цивилисты: середина XVIII – начало XX в. Краткий биографический словарь [Russian Civilists: Mid-XVIII – Early XX Century: Concise Biographical Dictionary] (M., 2005), pp. 164-165.

Sudnaia Gramota, published that same year at the expense of the University.[10] He accepted a position in the Ministry of Public Enlightenment and simultaneously pursued his magister of civil law degree, duly awarded in 1859 for a work on the acquisition under Russian law of the right of ownership in land.[11] In December 1860 Engelman was unanimously elected acting professor *extraordinarius* and from 1861 to 1867 was professor *ordinarius* at the Chair of Russian Law and from 1889 to 1900, professor ordinarius at the Chair of Civil Law, Dorpat University. From 1887-1882 and from 1891 to 1894 he was elected Dean of the Faculty. His talents were recognized by other universities; the School of Jurisprudence and the Alexander Lycée offered his positions as early as 1860, but these he declined in favor of the position in Dorpat (Iurev, now Tartu). He retired in 1900.

Originating in a German-language family, Engelman published his doctoral dissertation in that language,[12] followed by a Russian-language version.[13] Several ppublications touched upon issues of private international law.[14] He held various editorial positions in the specialist legal media: from 1867 to 1892 he was editor of *Dorpater Zeitschrift für Rechtswissenschaft* and from 1893 to 1896, *Dorpater juristische Studien*. He published biographies of leading Russian public figures and statesmen from time to time in *Baltische Monatschrift*. In recognition of his contributions to legal scholarship, he was appointed Distinguished Professor or an honorary member of the St. Vladimir University in Kyiv and the Iurev University. The Emperor of Russia awarded him the Order of St. Stanislav, first degree; Order of St. Vladimir, third degree; Order of St. Anna, second degree; among others.

[10] I. E. Engelman, Систематическое изложение гражданских законов, содержащихся в Псковской судной грамоте [Systematic Account of Civil Law Contained in the Pskov Sudnaia Gramota] (Spb., 1855). 182 p.

[11] Engelman, О приобретении права собственности на землю по русскому праву [On the Acquisition of the Right of Ownership in Land under Russian Law] (Спб., Тип. Н. Тиблена и Ко., 1859). xxxii, 187 p.

[12] Engelman, *Die Verjährung nach russischen Privatrecht: historisch-dogmatische Abhandlung* (Dorpat, 1867). Vi, 243 p.

[13] Engelman, О давности по русскому гражданскому праву [On Limitations under Russian Civil Law] (2d ed.; Спб., 1868; 3d ed.; Spb., Senatskaia tip., 1901; reprint ed.: M., Statut, 2003). The German language version was regarded as the first edition and the Russian language version as the second.

[14] Engelman, "De l'execution des jugements en Russie", Journal du droit international privé, no. 3-4 (1884) ; Engelman, «Об исполнении иностранных судебных решений в России» [On the Execution of Foreign Judicial Decisions in Russia], Журнал гражданского и уголовного права [Journal of Civil and Criminal Law], № 1 (1884), стр. 75-121, offprint published separately as Engelman, Об исполнении иностранных судебных решений в России [On the Execution of Foreign Judicial Decisions in Russia] (Spb., 1884); Engelman, «Отвод по необеспечению исцом-иностранцем издержек по делу и убытков ответчика» [Challenge for Impecuniousness of Foreign Plaintiff for Costs in Case and Losses of Defendant], Журнал Министерства юстиции [Journal of the Ministry of Justice], № 10, ч. 2 (декабрь 1896), pp 143-164; Engelman, "Russland", in F. Leske and W. Löwenfeld (eds.), Die Rechtsverfolgung im internationalen Verkehr (Berlin, 1896-1901), II, pp. 553-754.

Aleksandr Fedorovich Fedorov *(5 June 1885, b. St. Petersburg – 17 March 1935, d. Berlin). Specialist in civil, trade, and maritime law, composer, and editor.*

Life and career. A graduate of the Law Faculty of St. Petersburg University in 1879, Fedorov became Professor *ordinarius* at the Chair of Trade Law, Novorossiisk University. He published major works on trade law and maritime law.[15]

Dmitrii Aleksandrovich Filosofov *(30 January 1861, b. St. Petersburg – 6 December 1907, d. St. Petersburg). Senior State official.*

Life and career. Graduated jointly from the faculties of physics and mathematics and of law, St. Petersburg University in 1886. Appointed to the State Chancellery in 1887. From 1905 to 1906 served as the State Controller of the Russian Empire; Minister of Trade and Industry from 1906 to 1907 and member of the State Council from 1906. Co-authored several short pieces on customs duties, maintenance of diplomatic personnel, and railways.[16]

Ozer Abramovich Finkelshtein *(21 September 1863, b. Kovno – d. 28 September 1932, Kaunas). Legal practitioner and public figure in Lithuania.*

Life and career. Graduated from the St. Petersburg University Law Faculty in 1888. Published on aspects of private international law in the form of submissions to the State Council through the Ministry of Finances.[17]

[15] A. F. Fedorov, К вопросу об авторском праве на произведения литературные, художественные и музыкальные [On Question of Author's Right to Literary, Artistic, and Musical Works] (Odessa, 1896); Fedorov, К вопросу о предполагаемом возобновлении конвенции с Францией о литературной и художественной собственности [On Question of Proposed Renewal of Convention with France on Literary and Artistic Property] (Odessa, 1891); Fedorov, Морское право [Maritime Law] (Odessa, 1913); Fedorov, Торговое право [Trade Law] (Odessa, 1911).

[16] D. A. Filosofov, Об обложении таможенной пошлиной некоторых иностранных товаров, привозимых в Приамурский край: представление Членам Государственного Совета [On Levying Customs Duty on Certain Foreign Goods Imported into Amur Territory: Submission to Members of the State Council] (Spb., 1900); Filosofov, О дополнении Устава промышленного и Устава таможенного постановлениями, касающимися изготовления и привоза из-за границы огнестрельного оружия образцов, употребляемых в войсках: представление Членам Государственного Совета [On an Addition to the Industrial Statute and Customs Statute of Provisions Concerning the Manufacture and Bringing in from Abroad of Samples of Firearms Used in Forces: Submission to Members of the State Council] (Spb., 1900); Filosofov, Об увеличении содержания Российско-Императорского посла в Вашингтоне: представление Членам Государственного Совета [On Increasing Maintenance for the Russian-Imperial Ambassador in Washington: Submission to Members of the State Council] (Spb., 1899); Filosofov, Об утверждении Дополнительной конвенции от 16 июня 1898 г. к Международной конвенции от 14 октября 1890 г. о перевозке грузов по железным дорогам: представление Членам Государственного Совета [On Confirmation of the Supplementary Convention of 16 June 1898 to the International Convention of 14 October 1890 on the Carriage of Goods by Railway: Submission to Members of the State Council] (Spb., 1899).

[17] O. A. Finkelshtein, «Ликвидация неприятельских предприятий» [Liquidation of Enemy Enterprises], Право [Law], № 17 (1917), cols. 959-971.

David Samsonovich Fleksor *(1871, b. Soroki, Bessarabian Governate -1936, Rybinsk, Iaroslavl Region). Specialist on water law and the law of land tenure.*

Life and career. Graduating in 1893 from the Law Faculty of St. Petersburg University, he achieved a reputation in natural resource law and worked in the Ministry of Land Cultivation and State Property. His early interests were in family law and conflicts of law, producing articles on the subject[18]

Pavel Ivanovich Georgievskii *(18 January 1857, b. myza Tsarskaia Slavianka, Tsarskoe selo uezd, St. Petersburg Governate – 25 March 1938, d. Prague, Czechoslovakia).*

Life and career. Graduated f rom the Law Faculty of St. Petersburg University in 1879 and remained to prepare for the professoriate at the Chair of Political Economy and Statistics. In 1885 he was appointed privat-docent at the said Chair and defended a magister dissertation on the "International Grain Trade".[19] His doctoral dissertation followed in 1887 on "Financial Relations of the State and Private Railway Societies". In due course he became Professor *ordinarius* at the said Chair. In 1911 he became Director of the Central Statistical Committee of the Ministry of Internal Affairs and was appointed a Senator in 1916.

Georgii Konstantinovich Gins (Guins) *(15(28) April 1887, Novogeorgievsk, Warsaw Governate, Poland – d. 23 September 1971, Redwood City, California).*[20] *Civilist and important legal theoriest.*

Life and career. Born into the family of a Russian military officer stationed at the time in Poland and a mother of Greek descent from Kishinev, then part of Bessarabia and now Moldova. He graduated from a Gymnasium in Kishinev with the gold medal, enrolled at the Law Faculty in Petersburg University, and graduated in 1909. He remained to train for the professoriate, completed his magister degree, and was appointed privat-docent at the University in 1916 in the Chair of Civil Law. In parallel he worked at the Ministry of Agriculture, which sent him

18 Branover (ed.), note 6 above, III, p. 227, See D. S. Fleksor, «О праве иностранцев на усыновление детей по закону 12 марта 1891 г.» [On the Right of Foreigners to Adopt Children under the Law of 12 March 1891], Судебная газета [Judicial Newspaper], № 15 (1895); Fleksor, «Усыновление русскоподанного иностранцем» [Adoption of a Russian Subject by a Foreigner], Юридическая газета [Legal Newspaper], № 30 (1894).

19 P. I. Georgievskii, Международная хлебная торговля [International Grain Trade] (Spb., 1885). Apparently intended as a multi-volume work, only the first appeared, devoted to England, France, and Germany.

20 See his obituary in *The Russian Review*, XXXI (1972), pp. 104-106 (Dimitri von Mohrenschildt). Also see G. S. Starodubtsev, Международно-правовая наука российской эмиграции [International-Legal Science of Russian Emigration] (M., 2000), pp. 27, 40, 54, 186, 191-192, 197-200, 203, 205, 206, 218-226, 228-230, 234, 237, 239, 241-245, 254-255, 261.

to Turkestan to investigate the legal principles associated with the distribution of irrigation waters.[21]

Following the February 1917 Revolution, Guins was appointed chief jurisconsult at the Ministry of Food Supply. Following the October Revolution, he left with his family for Omsk. There he taught Civil Law at the Polytechnic Institute and acted as executive secretary of the Siberian provisional government at Omsk. Later he held several significant posts in the cabinet of Admiral Aleksandr Vasilevich Kolchak (1874-1920), experiences later related in his political memoir.[22] When the Omsk regime fell in 1920, Guins emigrated first to Harbin, Manchuria, where he taught at the University in exile founded there, worked as an administrator on the Chinese Eastern Railway, and served in a variety of other positions.[23] The Second World War and hostilities in Manchuria saw him emigrate to the United States in 1941. He settled first in the San Francisco area and then accepted a position at the University of California Berkeley, where he held appointments in the Slavic Department and then the Department of Political Science. He retired in 1954 from the University and joined the United States Information Agency in Washington D.C. in an editorial position on the Voice of America.

On the basis of publications in Harbin he became a leading figure in the solidarist movement. In the United States he published two books[24] and numerous articles on legal, sociological, and cultural subjects.

Aleksandr Aleksandrovich Girs (Giers) *(14 May 1850, b. St. Petersburg – 5 November 1923, Maribor, Slovenia). Russian diplomat.*

Life and career. Graduated from the Law Faculty in 1872 and joined the Ministry of Foreign Affairs from 1872 to 1915. He served as Russian Consul in a number of countries, producing materials of historical interest and consular memoirs.[25]

[21] At this time he published two works on colonialism. G. K. Guins, «Переселение и колонизация» [Resettlement and Colonization], Земельная политика в колониях [Land Policy in Colonies] (Spb., 1913); Guins, «Колонии и колонизация» [Colonies and Colonization], Новый энциклопедический словарь Ф. А. Брокгауза и И. А. Эфрона, XXII (1915), pp. 221-235.

[22] G. K. Guins, Сибирь, союзники и Колчак [Siberia, The Allies, and Kolchak] (Peking, 1921). 2 vols.

[23] See V. Ponomareva, "Legal Space in Harbin: The Russia Abroad", *Journal of Comparative Law*, VIII (2013), pp. 247-263.

[24] Guins, *Soviet Law and Soviet Society* (The Hague, 1954); Guins, *Communism on the Decline* (New York, 1956).

[25] A. A. Girs, Австро-Венгрия, Балканы и Турция. Задачи войны и мира [Austria-Hungary, Balkans, and Turkey. Tasks of War and Peace] (Tg., 1917); Girs, Россия и Ближный Восток. Материалы по истории наших отношений с Турцией [Russia and the Near East. Materials on the History of Our Relations with Turkey] (Spb., 1906); Girs, «Из прошлого российского консульства в Яссах» [From the Former Russian Consulate in Jassy], Русская старина [Russian Antiquity], LXXXIX, no. 2 (1897), pp. 315-325; Girs, «Молдавия и Валахия перед Турецкой войной 1787 г. (Из прошлого российского консульства в Яссах)» [Moldavia and Walachia Before the 1787 Turkish War], Русская старина [Russian Antiquity], XCVI, no. 12 (1898), pp. 633-655. Also mentioned in Starodubtsev, note 20 above, p. 76.

Aleksandr Solomonovich Goldenweiser *(14 February 1855, b. Kanev, Kyiv Governate – 24 May 1915, d. Kyiv). Civilist, advokat, publicist, bibliophile.*

Life and career. Graduated from the Law Faculty of St. Petersburg University in 1876 and became a noted sworn advokat, serving for many years as the Chairman of the Kyiv Commission of Sworn Advokats. He published short pieces on international aspects of juvenile affairs.[26]

Samuil (Shmuel) Iakovlevich Ianovskii *(1876, b. St. Petersburg – 1944, d. Tel Aviv, Israel). Legal practitioner, wrote on emigration law.*

Life and career. Graduated from the Law Faculty of St. Petersburg University in 1899. Organizer of student Zionist group at the University. In 1903 he published an Index of literature on Zionism. Assistant to a sworn advokat from 1905. From 1910 he was a member of the Central Committee of the Zionist Movement in Russia. Active during the Russian Civil War in Zionist activities in Odessa and the Crimea. Emigrated to France from 1920 to 1926; resident from 1927 in what is modern Israel.[27]

Leonid Nikolaevich Iasnopolskii *(1 February 1873, b. Kyiv – 23 May 1957, d. Kyiv). Specialist in trade law, political economy, and budgetary law, public figure.*

Life and career. Graduated from the Law Faculty of St. Petersburg University in 1895. Deputy of the State Duma, First Convocation; specialist in the field of

[26] A. S. Goldenweiser, Вопросы малолетних на Международном пенитенциарном конгрессе в Вашингтоне [Questions of Youth at the International Penitentiary Congress in Washington] (Kyiv, 1911); Goldenweiser, О Международном пенитенциарном конгрессе [On the International Penitentiary Congress] (Kyiv, 1911); Goldenweiser, Современная система наказаний и ее будущность по трудам Парижского пенитенциарного конгресса [Contemporary System of Punishments and Future Thereof According to Works of the Paris Penitentiary Congress] (Kyiv, 1896).

[27] Branover, note 6 above, III, p. 502. See S. Ia. Ianovskii, «Право въезда в чужую страну» [Right of Exit to Another Country], Журнал Министерства юстиции [Journal of the Ministry of Justice], № 10, ч. 2 (1909), pp. 107-134; Ianovskii, «Русское законодательство и эмиграция» [Russian Legislation and Emigration], Журнал Министерства юстиции [Journal of the Ministry of Justice], № 9 (апрель 1909), pp. 87-114; Ianovskii, «Эмиграция с точки зрения права: По поводу законопроекта об эмиграции, разрабатываемого особым совещанием при Министерстве Торговли и Промышленности» [Emigration from Standpoint of Law: On Occasion of Draft Law on Emigration Worked Out by Special Meeting attached to the Ministry of Trade and Industry], Журнал Министерства юстиции [Journal of the Ministry of Justice], № 3, ч. 2 (1908), pp. 31-66; Ianovskii and A. I. Kastelianskii (eds.), Справочная книга по вопросам эмиграции [Reference Book on Questions of Emigration] (Spb., 1913).

political economy and budgetary law.[28] He edited a two-volume encyclopedia on banking[29] and brief works on the Russo-German trade treaty.[30]

Petr Davydovich Kalmykov *(1808-1860). Published on intellectual property law.*

Life and career. Professor at the Chair of Encyclopedia of Lexprudence and Russian State Laws at St. Petersburg University from 1835 to 1860.[31]

Robert Khristianovich Kalveit *(18?-after 1916). Legal practitioner.*

Life and career. Graduated from the Law Faculty of St. Petersburg University in 1898. In the early twentieth century he worked in the St. Petersburg justice of the peace system. During the First World War, he published on the carriage of goods by rail during wartime.[32]

Nikolai Platonovich Karabchevskii *(29 November 1851, b. Kherson Governate – 22 November 1925, d. Rome, Italy). Advokat.*

Life and career. Graduated from the St. Petersburg Law Faculty in 1874 and became one of the leading Russian advokats of his generation. He was among the founders of the influential Russian newspaper Право [Law] and served as editor. In 1904 he founded the philanthropic fund for young advokats and a year later was among the co-founders of the Russian Union of Advokats. From 1913 he served as Chairman of the Petersburg Council of Sworn Advokats. During the First World War he acted as the Chairman of a Commission for the Investigation of German Cruelties. He went abroad in 1917 to Scandinavia in order to collect information on the status of Russian prisoners of war and remained an emigrant, taking up res-

[28] L. N. Iasnopolskii, Очерки русского бюджентого права [Essays on Russian Budget Law] (M., 1912).

[29] Iasnopolskii (ed.), Банковская энциклопедия [Banking Encyclopedia] (Kyiv, 1914-1919). 2 vols.

[30] Iasnopolskii, Значение русско-германского торгового договора [Significance of the Russo-German Trade Treaty] (Kyiv, 1913); Iasnopolskii, Позиция России по отношению к новому русско-германскому торговому договору [Position of Russia With Regard to the New Russo-German Trade Treaty] (Kyiv, 1914).

[31] P. D. Kalmykov, О литературной собственности вообще и в особенности об истории прав сочинителей в России: Рассуждение ординарного профессора Императорского Санкт-Петербургского университета, читанные на Публичном акте Университета 8 февраля 1851 года [On Literary Property in General and Especially the History of the Rights of Compilers in Russia: Discourse of Professor Ordinarius of Imperial St. Petersburg University Delivered at a Public Act of the University, 8 February 1851] (Spb., 1851).

[32] R. Kh. Kalveit, «Бернская конвенция о перевозке грузов по железным дорогам и война» [Berne Convention on Carriage of Goods by Railway and War], Право [Law], № 27 (1916), cols. 1557-1573. Butler K72.

idence in Italy. In the field of international law he published on maritime matters and prisoners of war.[33]

Aleksandr Fedorovich Kerensky *(4 May 1881, b. Simbirsk – 11 June 1970, d. New York City). Advokat, State official.*

Life and career. Graduated from the Law Faculty of St. Petersburg University in 1904. He served in the State Duma prior to the February 1917 Revolution. Successively thereafter the Minister of Justice, Minister of War and the Navy, and Chairman of the Provisional Government of the Russian Republic between March and November 1917. After the Revolution, emigrated to Paris, then the United States in 1939 and remained there. Active in Masonic circles, he is buried in Putney Vale Cemetery, London, England. He is known to have published one pamphlet in the field of international law.[34]

Mark Osipovich Kosven *(11(23) January 1885, b. Brest-Litovsk – 18 June 1967, d. Moscow). Legal historian, ethnographer.*

Life and career. Graduated in 1904 from the Petersburg Gymnasium and completed a two-year course at the University of Paris in 1906. At St. Petersburg University he completed the course at the Law Faculty in 1909, where he attended the lectures of M. M. Kovalevskii. During the First World War, Kosven worked for the Russian Red Cross Society. On the basis of materials gathered there, he published his first work on prisoners of war.[35] In 1917, he served as Secretary of the International Congress for Affairs of Prisoners of War, held at Copenhagen, Denmark. After the 1917 Revolutions, he remained in the military-sanitary section of the Red Army. From 1921 to 1924 he was involved in Soviet economic work. Thereafter he devoted himself to ethnography and history, producing classic works on the early societies in the Caucasus, Central Asia, and Siberia.

Aleksandr Mikhailovich (Moiseevich) Kulisher *(1890, b. St. Petersburg – 1942, d. Drancy, France).*

Life and career. Graduated from the Law Faculty of St. Petersburg University in 1911. Appointed privat-docent at the Chair of State Law of St. Petersburg University for 1918-1919. Emigrated to Berlin and Paris in 1917, where he was active

33 N. P. Karabchevskii, К делу о потоплении парохода «Владимир» итальянским пароходом «Колумбия» (Odessa, 1894), reprinted in Karabchevskii, «Дело о крушении парохода «Владимир» [Case Concerning the Wreck of the Steamship "Vladimir"], in Karabchevskii, Около правосудия. Статьи, речи, очерки [About Justice. Articles, Speeches, Essays] (Tula, 2001), pp. 159-186; Karabchevskii, Мирные пленники. В курортном плену: Впечатления и наблюдения [Peaceful Prisoners. In Resort Captivity: Impressions and Observations] (Pg., 1915).

34 A. F. Kerensky, Об армии и войне [On the Army and War] (Pg., 1917).

35 M. O. Kosven, Военнопленные. Очерк по международному и воинскому праву [Prisoners of War. Essay on International Law and Military Law] (Pg., 1915); Kosven, «Задержание санитарного персонала неприятелем» [Detention of Sanitary Personnel by Enemy], Вестник Красного Креста [Herald of the Red Cross], № 7 (1915), pp. 2987-2997.

on the newspaper Последние новости [Recent News]. Extensively involved in the Zionist movement, he was interned by the German occupying forces in France and died there in a concentration camp.[36] While in Russia he published extensively on home rule and Irish affairs.

Evgenii Mikhailovich (Moiseevich) Kulisher *(4 September 1881, b. Kyiv – 2 April 1956, d. Washington D.C.). Specialist in criminal law.*

Life and career. Graduated from the Law Faculty of St. Petersburg University in 1906 and undertook, but apparently did not complete, magister studies there. He became an assistant to a sworn advokat attached to the St. Petersburg Judicial Chamber and an advisor to the St. Petersburg okrug court, also serving in private practice. He was a member of the Russian Committee of the Union of Criminalists and from 1917 to 1918, privat-docent at the Chair of Criminal Law and Procedure of St. Petersburg University.[37] In 1921 he emigrated to Germany, Denmark, France, and the United States and from 1942 served as an expert on migration issues with the International Labour Organisation. In the United States he worked with various governmental agencies and the Library of Congress.

Georgii (Gavriel) Adolfovich Landau *(1877, b. St. Petersburg – 15 November 1941, d. Surmogsk Concentration Camp, Usol Camp, Molotov Region). Philosopher, publicist, and public figure.*

Life and career. Graduated from the Law Faculty of St. Petersburg University in 1902.[38] Published extensively in Jewish and Russian publications. One of found-

[36] Branover, note 6 above, II, p. 103; Starodubtsev, note 20 above, pp. 88-89, 146. See A. M. Kulisher, Государственное единство Англии и гомруль [State Unity of England and Home Rule] (M., 1914); Kulisher, «Ирландский гомрул и английский федерализм» [Irish Home Rule and English Federalism], Юридический вестник [Legal Herald], кн. IX(I) (1915), pp. 45-87; Kulisher, Автономия Ирландии [Autonomy of Ireland] (M., 1915); Kulisher, «Автономия Ирландии» [Autonomy of Ireland], Юридический Вестник [Legal Herald], кн. VI (II) (1914); кн. IX (I) (1915).

[37] See E. M. Kulisher, «Вопрос об «опасных преступниках» на брюссельском конгрессе» [Question of "Dangerous Crimes" at the Brussels Congress], Право, no. 5 (1911), cols. 264-276; Kulisher, «Юбилей Союза криминалистов» [Jubilee of the Union of Criminalists], Право [Law], no. 4 (1914), cols. 264-269; Kulisher, «Брюссельский съезд международного союза криминалистов и вопрос об общеопасных преступниках» [Brussels Congress of the International Union of Criminalists and the Question of Generally Dangerous Crimes], Труды Юридического общества при Императорском Санкт-Петербургском университете [Proceedings of the Law Society attached to the Imperial St. Petersburg University], IV (1912), pp. 32-56; Kulisher, review of: N. Hermann Kriegsmann (1882-1914). Einführung in die Gefangnisskunde, Журнал уголовного права и процесса, издаваемый при Русской Группе Международного союза криминалистов [Journal of Criminal Law and Procedure, Published attached to the Russian Group of the International Union of Criminalists], no. 3 (1913), pp. 170-172.

[38] Branover, note 6 above, II, p. 120. He left two articles relating to international law. G. A. Landau, Идея этнической государственности [Idea of Ethnic Statehood], Северные записки [Northern Notes], (April 1915). pp. 187-205; Сумерки Европы [Twilight of Europe], Северные записки [Northern Notes] (December 1914), pp. 28-54, expanded into a book: Landau, Сумерки Европы [The Twilight of Europe] (Berlin, 1923).

ers of the Jewish Democratic Group (1904) and the Union to Achieve Full Equality of Jewish People in Russia (1905), he joined the Kadet Party in 1905. A leading figure in Zionist circles, he emigrated to Germany after 1919 and from 1921 to 1931 was deputy editor of the Kadet newspaper there. In 1933 he emigrated to Latvia, settled in Riga, and worked on the newspaper Сегодня [Today]. Arrested by Soviet security authorities in 1941, he died in a correctional-labor camp.

Vasilii Nikolaevich Latkin *(10 December 1858, b. Krasnoiarsk – 1927). Legal historian.*

Life and career. Graduated from the Law Faculty of St. Petersburg University in 1882. Appointed privat-docent from 1886 to 1889 and professor *extraordinarius* from 1889 to 1891 at the Chair of Russian Law, serving as professor *ordinarius* from 1891 to 1911 and Distinguished Professor *ordinarius* from 1911 to 1913 and 1916 to 1917 in the Chair of the History of Russian Law. He produced one book review relating to international law.[39]

Maksim Iakovlevich (Max, Matayahu, Matthasia Zusmanovich) Lazerson *(1 February 1887, b. Mitau, Courland Governate – 29 November (or 1 December) 1951, d. New York). Jurist, sociologist, historian, and journalist.*

Life and career. Often confused with his brother Maurice (Moisei, Morits) Iakovlevich Lazerson (1880-1961),[40] Max Lazerson graduated from the Law Faculty of St. Petersburg University in 1910 and was appointed privat-docent at the Chair of State Law from 1917 to 1918. He published several items relating to international law before the Russian revolutions[41] and extensively later on diplomatic

[39] See Latkin's review of Muliukin on the arrival of foreigners in Muscovy in the Журнал Министерства юстиции [Journal of the Ministry of Justice], no. 9 (November 1909), pp. 417-421.

[40] Edward Kasinec, "The Confiscation of Art, Icons and Valuables in Revolution: The Witness of Maurice Lazerson ("M. J. Larsons")", in Princeton Yurii-Leving (ed.), *A Blue Brick: Festschrift for John E. Bowlt on the Occasion of His 80th Birthday* (2023). Maurice Lazerson worked for the Soviet Government during the 1920s and published memoirs of that period under the pseudonym M. J. Larsons, *An Expert in the Service of the Soviet*, transl. Angelo S. Rappoport (London, 1929). It first appeared in German as Larsons, *Als Expert im Sowietdienst* (Berlin, 1929) and later in Russian as Larsons, На Советской службе. Записки спеца [In Soviet Service. Notes of a Specialist] (Paris, 1930). Maurice likewise was trained as a jurist, obtaining his law degree at the University of Dorpat/Tartu, then led by Professor V. E. Grabar.

[41] Max Lazerson, Автономия и федерация [Autonomy and Federation] (Pg., 1917); Lazerson, Война и международная политика [War and International Politics] (Pg., 1917); Lazerson, «Государство без территории» [State Without Territory], Русская мысль [Russian Thought], no. 2 (1915), pp. 89-92; Lazerson, К международной постановке еврейского вопроса (С прил. документов) [On International Raising of the Jewish Question] (Pg., 1917); Lazerson, Национальность и государственный строй: юридико-политические очерки [Nationality and the State System: Legal-Political Study] (Pg., 1918). Also see Lazerson, Общая теория права [General Theory of Law] (Riga, 1930). He is mentioned in Starodubtsev, note 20 above, pp. 40, 46, 149.

history and international relations.[42] Before coming to New York just before the Second World War, he spent some years in Riga, where several books appeared.

Nikolai Antonovich Lenskii *(14 December 1886, b. Minsk – 11 November 1937, d. Camp Sandarmokh, Medvezh'egorsk District, Karelia). Specialist in administrative and agricultural law.*

Life and career. Graduated from the eight-year Tenishev School in St. Petersburg and studied the Latin language independently to a standard satisfactory for admission to the Law Faculty of St. Petersburg University, where he graduated in 1911 and remained to prepare for the professoriate at the Chair of Police Law. He passed the magister examinations and served from 1911 to 1916 as privat-docent at the said Chair. From 1914 he also served as an official on special assignment attached to the Resettlement Administration of the Ministry of Agriculture. In October 1917 he was a member of the Special Commission attached to the Legal Meeting for Drafting the Basic Laws (Constitution) of the Russian Federation. His fate during and after the 1917 revolutions is unknown. From 1921 he was professor and from 1924 to 1929 Rector of the Kuban Agricultural Institute, founded at Krasnodar in 1922. One source claims that he was a professor at Leningrad State University from 1927 to 1928.[43] In 1930 he was arrested in the Labor Peasant Party case and in 1931 sentenced to the death penalty for "wrecking" and "counter-revolutionary group activity", commuted to ten years deprivation of freedom in a concentration camp. Released ahead of time, in 1937 he was Director of a Technical School of the White Sea-Baltic Canal. Arrested in October 1937, he was convicted of "counter-revolutionary agitation" on 23 October 1937 and executed.

International legal views. Lenskii was the author of a perceptive pamphlet on the Chinese-Japanese conflict and two relevant book reviews.[44]

Isaak El'evich (Il'ich) Levin *(12 July 1887, b. Kyiv – 25 April 1945, d. United States). Russian economist specializing in foreign investment.*

[42] Lazerson, *Russia and the Western World: The Place of the Soviet Union in the Comity of Nations* (New York, 1945); James T. Shotwell and Lazerson, *Poland and Russia, 1919-1945* (New York, 1945); Lazerson, *The American Impact on Russia, Diplomatic and Ideological, 1784-1917* (New York, 1950); and others.

[43] Source cited in A. A. Matyshev, Энциклопедия репрессированных авторов [Encyclopedia of Repressed Authors 1917-1937 (Spb., 2020), VII, p. 283.

[44] N. A. Lenskii, Дальневосточный конфликт и задачи внешней политики [Far Eastern Conflict and the Tasks of Foreign Policy] (Petrograd, 1915); Lenskii, review of: N. A. Gromov, Цензура и шпионство по законам военного времени [Censorship and Espionage According to the Laws of Wartime] Изд. Б. А. Суворина. Pg., 1914. [VIII] 146 p. in: Право [Law], no. 40 (1914), cols. 2763-2764; Lenskii, review of: N. V. Iastrebov, Галиция накануне великой войны 1914 года. С картой Галиции и Буковины с Угорской Русью [Galicia on Eve of the Great War of 1914. With Map of Galicia and Bukovina with Hungarian Rus] Pg., 1915, in: Право [Law], no. 3 (1915), cols. 172-173.

Life and career. An economist by training, he graduated in 1909 from the St. Petersburg Polytechnic Institute and received his doctorate of political economy in 1912 at the University of Freiburg in Germany. His magister of political economy he received at Moscow University in 1915. From 1915 to 1918 he was privat-docent at the Chair of Political Economy and from 1918 to 1919 at the Chair of State Law of Petrograd University. He published two brief pieces on foreign investment in Russia, contributions to private international law.[45]

Petr Ivanovich Liashchenko *(22 October 1876, b. Saratov – 24 July 1955, d. Moscow). Russian and Soviet economist.*

Life and career. After graduating in 1894 from the First Classical Saratov Gymnasium, he enrolled in the Physics and Mathematics Faculty, graduating in 1899, and the Law Faculty, graduating in 1900, at St. Petersburg University. He spent the years 1900 to 1901 in further studies at Leipzig University and was appointed privat-docent from 1903 to 1913 in the Chair of Political Economy in the Law Faculty. From 1914 to 1917 he moved to Tomsk University as Dean of the Law Faculty, and became Rector of the Don Institute of National Economy (Rostov on Don) from 1918 to 1922. He then moved to government service from 1922 to 1926 in the People's Commissariat of Agriculture. From 1926 he was a professor in the Institute of Red Professoriate and Moscow University; from 1935 at the Communist Academy and Institute of the Economy as a Senior Scientific Associate, and in the same capacity from 1942 at the Institute of History of the USSR Academy of Sciences and at the Institute of Economics at the Academy of Sciences of the Ukrainian SSR. He was elected an associate member of the USSR Academy of Sciences and in 1949 awarded the Stalin Prize for his *History of the National Economy of Russia, to the 1917 Revolution* (1949).[46]

Iurii (Georgii) Sergeevich Lukianov *(9 August 1887-after 1918). State official and author of works on neutrality.*

Life and career. Graduated from the Law Faculty of St. Petersburg University in 1910, he was employed from 1911 in the Chancellery of the State Duma. His graduation dissertation was published as an article in the Journal of the Ministry of Justice; the full text remains in the archive.[47]

45 I. E. Levin, Германские капиталы в России [German Capital in Russia] (2d ed.; Pg., 1918); Levin, Новые тенденции в экономических кризисах [New Trends in Economic Crises] (Pg., 1916).

46 His principal work of international legal interest was P. I. Liashchenko, Зерное хозяйство и хлеботорговые отношения России и Германии в связи с таможенным обложением [The Wheat Economy and Grain Trade Relations of Russia and Germany in Connection with Customs Levy] (Pg., 1915). The work was produced as part of materials for a revision of the Russo-German trade treaty.

47 Iu. S. Lukianov, «Очерк развития понятия о нейтралитете до XIX столетия» [Essay on the Development of the Concept of Neutrality Up to the XIX Century], Журнал Министерства юстиции [Journal of the Ministry of Justice], № 7 (September 1913), pp. 93-126; № 8 (October 1913), pp. 121-146; Lukianov, Историческое развитие понятия нейтралитета до XIX столетия (Диссертация студента) [Historical Development of the Concept of Neutrality Up to the XIX Century (Student Dissertation)], ЦГИА СПб., fund 14, opis 8, file 967.

Mikhail Mikhailovich Mikhailov *(24 September 1827 – 4 November 1891, d. Iaroslavl). Civilist.*

Life and career. Graduated from the Law Faculty of St. Petersburg University in 1846, serving as an adjunct from 1851 to 1867 and professor *extraordinarius* from 1867 to 1869, and then professor *ordinarius* from 1869 to 1876 at the Chair of Civil Law of the said University. He lectured on civil law and trade law and, at the Konstantinov Military School, on military law, including the laws of war.[48]

Vladimir Alekseevich Miliutin *(4 December 1826, b. St. Petersburg – 5 August 1855, d. Ems, Germany). Specialist in State law.*

Life and career. A graduate of the Law Faculty of St. Petersburg University in 1847, he served with the Department of Agriculture of the Ministry of State Property from 1848. From 1850 to 1853 pursued magister studies and acted as an adjunct professor at the Chair of Russian State Law. In 1853 he was appointed a professor at the Chair of Law of Public Decorum and Amenities and simultaneously in 1852 to 1853 served as Professor of Police Law at the Alexander Lycée. He was an active member from 1849 to 1852 in the Russian Geographical Society, serving as secretary from 1853 to 1855 and editor of the Вестник Русского географического общества [Herald of the Russian Geographical Society]. He published a survey of the diplomatic relations between ancient Russia and the Roman Empire.[49]

Iakov Abramovich Natanson *(18? – after 1914).* Graduated from the Law Faculty of St. Petersburg University in 1910 and wrote on aspects of private international law.[50]

Aleksandr Mikhailovich Naumov *(1 November 1835, b. St. Petersburg – 14 December 1879). Publicist, journalist, active member of Free Economic Society.*

Life and career. A graduate of the Law Faculty of St. Petersburg University in the 1850s, he defended a magister dissertation at Moscow University on 4 February 1856 devoted to navigation on the Scheldt. The official opponents were Vasi-

[48] M. M. Mikhailov, Торговое право. Лекции, читанные в 1857-1860 [Trade Law. Lectures Delivered in 1857-1860] (Spb., 1860); Mikhailov, Военно-уголовное право: Курс военно-уголовных законов и военного судопроизводства, читанный в Константиновском военном училище в 1869-1870 гг. [Military Criminal Law: Course on Military Criminal Laws and Military Proceeding Delivered at the Konstantinov Military School in 1869-1870] (Spb., 1871).

[49] V. A. Miliutin, «Обзор дипломатических сношений Древней России с Римской империей», Современник, no. 7 (1851), pp. 1-28; no. 8 (1851), pp. 29-62.

[50] Ia. A. Natanson, «Война и право германских и австрийских подданных на судебную защиту в русских судах» [War and the Right of German and Austrian Subjects to Judicial Defense in Russian Courts], Право [Law], no. 39 (1914), cols. 2695-2707.

lii Nikolaevich Leshkov (1810-1881) and Mikhail Nikolaevich Kapustin (1828-1899). The book was well received.[51]

Pavel Ivanovich Nebolsin *(18 August 1817, b. Nizhnii-Novgorod Governate – 18 August 1893, d. Vilnius). Historian, ethnographer, economist.*

Life and career. Graduated from the Law Faculty of St. Petersburg University in 1838, he was employed by the Criminal Law Department of the Ruling Senate from 1838 to 1846. In 1848 he was elected to the Imperial Russian Geographical Society. From 1850 to 1852 he was assigned by the Society to travel to the Caspian Sea area and the Bukhara Orde to investigate trade and industrial relations of Russia with Central Asia, which led to his book on the subject.[52]

Leopold Nikolaevich Nisselovich *(30 August 1856, b. Bausk, Courland Governate – 1914, d. Geneva, Switzerland). Legal practitioner, financial law, public figure.*

Life and career. Graduated from the Law Faculty of St. Petersburg University inn 1880, serving in the Ministry of Finances from 1880 to 1882. From 1882 to 1907 he was a sworn advokat of the Petersburg Judicial Chamber. Elected to the III State Duma, he served as a deputy from 1907 to 1912. He published on private international law aspects of stock exchanges.[53]

Baron **Aleksandr Emilevich Nolde** *(20 August 1873, b. Ekaterinoslav, now Dnipropetrovsk, Ukraine – 5 November 1919, d. Terioki, now Zelenogorsk, Leningrad Region). Civilist.*

Life and career. Graduated from the Law Faculty of St. Petersburg University in 1896 and remained to prepare for the professoriate at the Chair of Roman Law and completed a magister degree. From 1900 appointed privat-docent at the Chair of Civil Law and simultaneously employed at the Ministry of Public Enlightenment. In 1912 served as a professor at the Alexander Lycée, St. Petersburg Higher Women's Courses, and librarian at the Public Library. From 24 March 1914 he became an assistant to the State-Secretary of the State Council for the Division of the

[51] V. E. Grabar, *The History of International Law in Russia 1647-1917: A Bio-Biographical Study*, transl. W. E. Butler (Oxford, 1990), p. 373. A. M. Naumov, Судоходство по Шельде. Опыт приложения начал международного права к судоходству по рекам: Историко-юридическое исследование [Navigation Along the Scheldt. Attempt to Apply Principles of International Law to Navigation on Rivers] (M., 1856). The defense was reported in Московские ведомости [Moscow Gazettes], no. 16 (7 February 1856), p. 131, cols. 1-2.

[52] P. I. Nebolsin, Очерки торговли России со странами Средней Азии, Хивой, Бухарой и Кокандом [Essays on Trade of Russia with the Countries of Central Asia, Khiva, Bukhara, and Kokand] (Spb., 1855).

[53] L. N. Nisselovich, О биржах, биржевых установлениях и мерах ограничения биржевой игры: Обозрение важнейших законодательств сравнительно с русским правом [On Stock Exchanges, Stock Exchange Statutes, and Measures of Limitation of Stock Exchange Gambling] (Spb., 1879).

Digest of Laws. Became a Senator by Edict of the Provisional Government of 16 June 1917. He was killed when attempting illegally to cross the Finnish-Russian border. He left two publications on private international law.[54]

Baron **Adolf Maksimovich (also Genrikhovich) Nolken** *(30 July 1860, b. Livonian Governate – 1919, d. Petrograd). Legal practitioner, Senator.*

Life and career. Graduated in 1882 with the degree of candidate of laws from the St. Petersburg University and began employment on 25 July 1882 in a Department of the Ministry of Justice. From 22 September 1910 served as a Senator in the Civil Cassation Department of the Ruling Senate until 1917. Author of works on bills of exchange and relevant treaties.[55]

Georgii Fedorovich Parfenov *(1878 – April 1942, d. Leningrad). Wrote on the law of war.*

Life and career. Graduated from the Law Faculty of St. Petersburg University in 1900 and worked at the Ministry of Justice, initially in the Second Section of the First Criminal Department and in 1916 as acting Vice Director of the First Department. He perished during the blockade of Leningrad during the Second World War. He published two pieces on the law of war.[56]

Nikolai Nikolaevich Pokrovskii *(27 January 1865, b. St. Petersburg – 12 December 1930, d. Kaunas, Lithuania). Diplomat, politician.*

[54] N. A. Murzanov, Словарь русских сенаторов 1711-1917 гг. Материалы для биографий [Dictionary of Russian Senators 1711-1917. Materials for Biographies] (Spb., 2011), p. 312. See A. E. Nolde, «Заметки: может ли быть передаваем по надписям вексель, о взыскании по которому состоялось решение иностранного суда» [Note: Can We Transfer an Endorsed Bill of Exchange, Concerning Execution Under Which the Decision of a Foreign Court Has Occurred], Вестник гражданского права [Herald of Civil Law], no. 4 (1913), pp. 156-159; Nolde, «Об ограниченной ответственности судохозяев по уставу торговому» [On Limited Responsibility of Shipowners under Trade Statute], Журнал Министерства юстиции [Journal of the Ministry of Justice], no. 7 (September 1908), pp. 1-37; no. 8 (October 1908), pp. 85-110.

[55] Murzanov, note 54 above, p. 312. See A. M. Nolken, Всеподданнейшии доклад сенатора, тайного советника, барона Адольфа Нолькена о заключении им. 10/23 июля 1912 года в городе Гааге, Международной конвенции об объединении законоположении о векселях [General Report of Senator, Privy Counsellor, Baron Adolf Nolken on Opinion of 10/23 July 1912 in the City of The Hague of International Convention on Unification of Law on Bills of Exchange] (Spb., 1912); Nolken, «Гаагская международная конференция 10/23 июля 1912 года об объединении законоположений о векселях» [Hague International Conference of 10/23 July 1912 on Unification of Law on Bills of Exchange], Журнал Министерства юстиции [Journal of the Ministry of Justice], no. 2, ч. 2 (1913), pp. 181-221; no. 3, ч. 2 (1913), pp. 263-309; no. 4, ч. 2 (1913), pp. 234-264; Nolken, Объединенное законодательство о векселях (Гаагская конвенция 10/23 июля 1912 г.) в применении к России [Uniform Legislation on Bills of Exchange (Hague Convention of 10/23 July 1912) in Application to Russia] (Spb., 1913).

[56] G. F. Parfenov, «Война» [War], in A. F. Volkov and Iu. D. Filippov (eds.), Словарь государственных и юридических наук [Dictionary of State and Legal Sciences] (Spb., 1901), cols. 2234-2237; Parfenov, «Вооруженный мир» [Armed Peace], ibid., cols. 297-229.

Life and career. Attending the law faculties of both Moscow and St. Petersburg universities, Pokrovskii graduated from the Law Faculty of St. Petersburg University in 1888 and joined the Ministry of Finances. He became Deputy Chairman in 1903 (Chairman in 1904) of the Department of Taxation in the said Ministry. Appointed Deputy Minister of Finances in 1906, from 1914 to 1916 he served on the State Council. Throughout most of 1916 he was a State Inspector. On 30 November 1916 he became the last Minister of Foreign Affairs of the Russian Empire and in that position opposed a peace treaty with Germany. He strongly favored arrangements to attract American financial capital to Russia and proposed to create a special commission dedicated to this aim. After February 1917 he acted as Chairman of the Russo-American Committee on Assistance to the Economic Rapprochement between Russia and the United States. From August 1917 he was Deputy Chairman of the Chief Administration of the Russian Red Cross Committee. He emigrated to Lithuania after the October 1917 Revolution, accepting a position at the Vytautas Magnus University. He left two articles of international legal interest; his memoirs were eventually published.[57]

Vladimir Aleksandrovich Posse *(10 May 1864, b. Novgorod Governate – 21 October 1940, d. Leningrad). Jurist, publisher.*

Life and career. Posse studied both at the Faculty of History and Philology (expelled in 1887) and the Law Faculty of St. Petersburg University, graduating from the Law Faculty in 1888. In early 1899 Posse became editor of the journal Жизнь [Life], published until 1901 when it was suppressed by the Russian authorities. Posse moved to Ireland and then London, where he tried to secure financial support to revive the journal, succeeding in issuing six issues in 1902 together with other publications. He sometimes used the pseudonym "F. S. Rosin". Posse returned to Russia in 1905 and published a journal Жизнь для всех [Life for All] from 1908 to 1918. In spring 1917 he founded a movement which favored a peace with Germany. Under the Soviet Government he worked briefly with the People's Commissariat of Agriculture. His autobiography appeared in 1933.[58]

Isaak Moiseevich Rabinovich *(20 March 1859 – 25 November 1929, d. Berlin). Legal practitioner, specialist in the law of railways.*

57 N. N. Pokrovskii, «Об итогах экономической конференции» [On the Results of the Economic Conference], Коммерсант [Kommersant], 6 July 1916; Pokrovskii, Доклад об условиях развития нашего экспорта [Report on the Conditions of the Development of Our Export] (Spb., 1915). For his memoirs, see Pokrovskii, Последний в Мариинском дворце: воспоминания Министра иностранных дел [Last in the Mariyinsky Palace: Recollections of the Minister of Foreign Affairs] (M., 2015).

58 V. A. Posse, Из истории франко-русского союза [From the History of the Franco-Russian Alliance] (Geneva, 1902); Posse, Национальная автономия и всемирная федерация (Сборник). I. Политические слова, понятия и вещи. II. Национальная автономия и всемирная федерация. III. Формы правления и демократия [National Autonomy and World Federation (Collection). I. Political Words, Concepts and Things. II. National Autonomy and World Federation. III. Forms of Government and Democracy] (Spb., 1906). For his autobiography, see Posse, Пережитое и продуманное. Молодость. 1864-1894 [Meditations About the Past. Youth. 1864-1894] (Leningrad, 1933).

Life and career. Graduated from the Law Faculty of St. Petersburg University in 1882. A legal practitioner, he became a sworn advokat in St. Petersburg. Through his publications he is regarded as one of the pioneers in Russian railway law.[59] After the 1917 revolutions, he emigrated to Germany in 1920, where he published a reference manual and posthumously an article on private international law.[60]

Nikolai Mikhailovich Reinke *(27 October 1849, b. St. Petersburg – 11 March 1927, d. Warsaw, Poland). Senator, ober-procurator.*

Life and career. Graduated from the Law Faculty of St. Petersburg University in 1872 with the degree of candidate of laws. From 24 July 1872 served in the Chancellery of the Fourth Department of the Ruling Senate. Was appointed Privy Counsellor from 1 January 1910 and became a member of the Ruling Senate from 1 January 1911. He published important works on Russo-Polish conflict of laws.[61]

Iurii Vladimirovich Sabler (from 1915: Desiatovskii) *(1876-1918). Diplomat.*

Life and career. Graduated from the Law Faculty of St. Petersburg University in 1901 and served in the Ministry of Foreign Affairs, including as First Secretary of the Russian diplomatic mission in Bulgaria. From 1915 he became the acting Head of the Mission in Bulgaria and a member of the consular department of the Ministry of Foreign Affairs. Killed in 1918 during the Kronshtadt Uprising. He published on State sovereignty and dual citizenship.[62]

[59] I. M. Rabinovich, «Международная конвенция о перевозке грузов по железным дорогам: Русский и французский текст с приложениями и с разъяснениями по протоколам бернских конвенций 1878, 1881, 1886 и 1890 годов» [International Convention on Carriage of Goods by Rail: Russian and French Text with Annexes and Explanations Under Protocols of Berne Conventions of 1878, 1881, 1886, and 1890], Журнал гражданского и уголовного права [Journal of Civil and Criminal Law], nos. 1-2 (1893), Прил. № 3, pp. 1-40; no. 3 (1893), Прил. № 1, pp. 41-88; no. 4 (1893), Прил. № 2, pp. 89-136; no. 5 (1893), Прил., pp. 137-168; no. 6 (1893), Прил., pp. 169-181; issued in monograph format as an offprint: (Spb., 1893). Also see Starodubtsev, note 20 above, p. 101.

[60] Rabinovich, Русские в Германии: Юридический справочник [Russians in Germany: Legal Manual] (Berlin, 1921); Rabinovich, «Применение советского права в Германии» [Application of Soviet Law in Germany], Закон и суд [Law and Court], no. 10 (1930), cols. 347-350; nos. 11/12 (1930), cols. 383-388.

[61] Murzanov, note 54 above, p. 365. N. M. Reinke, Каким гражданским законам подведомы русские уроженцы, пребывающие в Царстве Польском? [To What Civil Laws are Russian Natives Subject Who Arrive in the Kingdom of Poland?] (Warsaw, 1884; 2d rev. ed.; Warsaw, 1892); Reinke, «Очерк русско-польского междуобластного частного права» [Survey of Russo-Polish Inter-Regional Private Law], Журнал Министерства юстиции [Journal of the Ministry of Justice], no. 9 (November 1908), pp. 19-88; no. 10 (December 1908), pp. 1-56; Reinke, Очерк русско-польского междуобластного частного права [Survey of Russo-Polish Inter-Regional Private Law] (Spb., 1909).

[62] Iu. V. Sabler, «К учению о суверенитете в государстве» [On the Doctrine of Sovereignty in the State], Журнал Юридического общества при Санкт-Петербургском университете [Journal

Dmitrii Iakovlevich Samokvasov *(27 May 1843, b. Stakhorshina, Chernohiv Governate – 18 August 1911, d. Moscow). Legal historian.*

Life and career. Graduated from the Law Faculty of St. Petersburg University in 1868, Samokvasov wrote on early Rus diplomatic and treaty relations.[63] He was a professor at Warsaw University and Distinguished Professor of Moscow University.

Boris Evgenevich Shatskii *(7 November 1889-1941, d. Santiago, Chile). Specialized in State law.*

Life and career. Graduated from Law Faculty of St. Petersburg University in 1911, received magister degree and was appointed privat-docent at the Chair of State Law. Following the 1917 February Revolution in Russia, Shatskii became Director of the Russian Information Bureau of the Provisional Government. In autumn 1917 he was a member of the Special Commission attached to the Legal Meeting to Draft the Basic Laws (Constitution) of the Russian Republic. He emigrated to Germany and France, then in 1934 to Chile, where he held an academic appointment at the Universidad de Concepción. He published on recognition and international affairs.[64]

of the Law Society attached to St. Petersburg University], no. 7 (July 1896), pp. 50-82; Sabler, «О двойном подданстве» [On Dual Subjectship], Журнал государственного и международного права [Journal of State and International Law], II, no. 4 (1897), pp. 46-64; no. 5, pp. 135-155; no. 6, pp. 251-272.

[63] D. Ia. Samokvasov, Главнейшие моменты в государственном развитии древней Руси и происхождение Московского государства [Major Moments in the State Development of Medieval Rus and Origin of the Muscovy State] (Warsaw, 1886); Samokvasov, «Речь на торжественном акте Императорского Варшавского университета 30 августа 1886 года: Свидетельства современных источников о военных и договорных отношениях славяноруссов к грекам до Владимира Святославича Равноапостольного» [Address at the Solemn Occasion of Imperial Warsaw University on 30 August 1886: Evidence of Contemporary Sources on Military and Treaty Relations of the Slavic Rus with the Greeks Before Vladimir Sviatoslavich the Great], Варшавские университетские известия [Warsaw University News], no. 6 (1886), pp. 1-48; Samokvasov, Свидетельства современных источников о военных и договорных отношениях славяноруссов к грекам до Владимира Святославича Равноапостольного (Речь на торжественном акте Императорского Варшавского университета 30 августа 1886 года) Evidence of Contemporary Sources on Military and Treaty Relations of the Slavic Rus with the Greeks Before Vladimir Sviatoslavich the Great (Address at the Solemn Occasion of Imperial Warsaw University on 30 August 1886)] (Warsaw, 1886).

[64] Starodubtsev, note 20 above, pp. 54-55, 58, 61, 89-90, 92, 100, 103, 117-118, 122. See B. E. Shatskii, Государственно-правовое положение Бельгии (в связи с её оккупацией Германией) [State-Law Status of Belgium (in Connection with its Occupation by Germany)], Право [Law], no. 45 (1914), cols. 3055-3059; «Вопрос о признании Советской России в Соединенных Штатах» [Question Concerning Recognition of Soviet Russia in the United States], Право и хозяйство [Law and Economy], no. 2 (1925), pp. 4-6; Shatskii, «Защита русских интересов в Америке» [Defense of Russian Interests in America], Закон и суд [Law and Court], no. 4 (1929), cols. 127-130; Shatskii, «Иностранная политика Американских Соединенных Штатов и задачи пацифизма в Америке» [Foreign Policy of American United States and Tasks of Pacifism in America], Известия Министерства иностранных дел [News of the Ministry of Foreign Affairs], no. 4 (1914), pp. 104-132; Shatskii, Иностранная политика Американских Соединенных Штатов и задачи пацифизма

Iakov Mikhailovich Sheftel *(11 (12//24) May 1882, b. Zhitomir, Volhynia Governate – 7 May 1973, Paris, France).*

Life and career. Graduated from the Law Faculty of St. Petersburg University in 1904 and worked as a sworn advokat in the Petrograd Judicial District. Emigrated in 1917, lived in London in 1921 and the moved to Paris. Became a French avocat and established his own law office in Paris (6, rue Sainte-Beuve, 16e). Sheftel was active in the Russian Parliamentary Committee, where he gave reports in 1921; he lectured between 1928 and 1932 at the Russian Commercial Institute in Paris and in the Franco-Russian Institute; he also served as Chairman of the Association of Former Students of St. Petersburg University. He was a member of the Association of Russian Advokats in France, being elected to the internal audit committee of the Association and serving a term as Chairman of the Association. During the 1930s, he was a member of the Committee of the Red Cross. In 1939 he was chosen as a member of the Jubilee Committee honoring Professor Valerian Konstantinovich Agafonov (1863-1955). An active Mason, he was a co-founder of the Free Russia Lodge (1931) and a member of the Northern Star (1928-1955) Lodge. He published on naval and prize law during the First World War and on private international law later.[65]

Karl Vasilevich von Shneider *(25 January 1837, b. St. Petersburg – 29 December 1914, d. St. Petersburg). Senator, privy counsellor, civilist.*

Life and career. Graduated in 1859 as candidate of law from the Law Faculty of St. Petersburg University in 1859 and accepted employment on 24 December 1857 in the Ministry of Justice. Made a privy counsellor on 15 May 1883 and a

в Америке (Доложено в Общем собрании Санкт-Петербургского отдела Общества Мира, 5 декабря 1913 года) [Foreign Policy of American United States and Tasks of Pacifism in America (Reported at the General Meeting of the St. Petersburg Section of the Peace Society, 5 December 1913)] (Spb., 1914).

[65] Starodubtsev, note 20 above, p. 103. See Ia. M. Sheftel, (comp.). Право морской войны: Положение о морских призах (изд. 1914 г.) с разъяснениями по решениям Высшаго Призового Суда, дополнетельными инструкциями и правилами и с приложением применяемых в настоящее время в России постановлений международных конвенций, касающихся права морской войны [Law of Naval Warfare (1914 ed.) with Explanations Regarding Decisions of Supreme Prize Court, Additional Instructions and Rules and Annex of Provisions of International Conventions Concerning Law of Naval Warfare Applied at Present in Russia] (Petrograd, 1915); Sheftel, «Русское призовое право» [Russian Law of Prize], Право [Law], no. 11 (1915), cols. 793-801; no. 12 (1915), cols. 868-881; Sheftel, Русское призовое право [Russian Law of Prize] (Petrograd, 1915); Sheftel, К вопросу о пределах ответственности страховщиков при морском страховании военного риска [On the Question of the Limits of Liability of Insurers under Military Risk Marine Insurance] ([Petrograd, 1915]); Sheftel, «К вопросу о юридическом статусе русской эмиграции во Франции» [On Question of Legal Status of Russian Emigration in France], Право и хозяйство [Law and Economy], no. 3 (1925), pp. 7-11; Sheftel, «Правовое положение заграничнаго имущества русских акционерных предприятий «национализированных» советскими декретами» [Legal Status of Foreign Property of Russian Joint-Stock Enterprises "Nationalized" by Soviet Dekrets], Закон и суд [Law and Court], no. 13 (1930), cols. 419-423; no, 14/15 (1930), cols. 453-458; no. 16 (1930), cols. 499-504; no. 17 (1931), cols. 533-538; no. 18/19 (1931), cols. 595-602; no, 20 (1931), cols. 645-652.

member of the Ruling Senate from 15 January 1892. On behalf of the Russian Government he took part at The Hague in an international conference concerning the unification of bills of exchange, producing an article on the subject.[66]

Genrikh Borisovich Sliozberg *(1863, b. Mir, Minsk Governate – 1937, d. Paris, France). Specialized in criminal law and procedure.*

Life and career. Sliozberg graduated from Law Faculty of St. Petersburg University in 1886 and remained to prepare for the professoriate. He was sent to German universities and returned to defend his magister dissertation in 1889 on criminal law. Practiced law, from 1893 as an assistant sworn advokat and from 1904 as a sworn advokat. He was active in the Law Society attached to St. Petersburg University and from 1899 to 1902 edited the Society's journal, Вестник права [Herald of Law].[67] He was prominent in Jewish affairs in Russia and assisted a United States congressional committee investigating the reasons for Jewish emigration from Russia. On numerous occasions he defended the interests of victims of pogroms in suits against the local administration. Persecuted by the Soviet authorities, he emigrated to France in 1920, where he headed the community of émigré Russian Jews in Paris. He published his memoirs in 1934 in three volumes.[68]

Konstantin Nikolaevich Sokolov *(7 August 1882, b. St. Petersburg – 20 March 1927, d. Sofia, Bulgaria). Specialist in State law, journalist.*

Life and career. Graduate of the Law Faculty of St. Petersburg in 1904, then appointed privat-docent at the Chair of State Law of the University, a position held from 1909 to 1917. There he produced a substantial study of Parliamentarianism.[69] He offered courses on "Legal Theory of the Parliamentary System" and the "State

66 K. V. von Shneider, «Международная конференция в Гааге для подготовления единообразных норм вексельного права» [International Conference at The Hague to Prepare Uniform Norms of Bill of Exchange Law], Журнал Министерства юстиции [Journal of the Ministry of Justice], no. 1 (1911), pp. 1-19.

67 G. B. Sliozberg, «Финляндский проект уголовного уложения» [Finnish Draft Criminal Code], Журнал гражданского и уголовного права [Journal of Civil and Criminal Law], no. 8 (October 1887), pp. 124-130; Sliozberg, «Защита на предварительном следствии (Доклад конгрессу Международного Союза криминалистов в С.-Петербурге в сентября 1902 г.) [Defense at the Preliminary Investigation (Report to the Congress of the International Union of Penal Law in St. Petersburg in September 1902)], Вестник права [Herald of Law], no. 6 (1902), pp. 111-125; Sliozberg, «Санкт-Петербургский конгресс Международного союза криминалистов» [St. Petersburg Congress of the International Union of Penal Law], Вестник права [Herald of Law], nos. 7-8 (1902), pp. 127-147; Sliozberg, Законы о евреях и практика их применения [Laws on Jews and the Application Thereof] (Spb., 1907); Sliozberg, Сборник действующих законов о евреях (по Своду законов по продолжению 1906 г.) [Collection of Laws in Force on Jews: According to the Digest of Laws, as of 1906] (Spb., 1909).

68 Sliozberg, Дела минувших дней: записки русского еврея [Matters of Time Past: Notes of a Russian Jew] (Paris, [Imp. Pascal], 1933-1934. 3 vols; reprinted: M., Секачев, 2017). 2 vols.

69 K. N. Sokolov, Парламентаризм: опыт правовой теории парламентарного строя [Parliamentarianism: Attempt at Legal Theory of Parliamentary System] (Spb., 1912).

Law of France". As a journalist, he was head of the foreign section of the newspaper Речь [Speech]. In autumn 1917 he was a member of the Special Commission attached to the Legal Meeting to Draft Basic Laws (Constitution) of the Russian Republic. Active in the White movement against the Bolshevik authorities,[70] he emigrated to Bulgaria in 1919, becoming a professor at the Sofia University. There he produced a text on the General Part of State Law (1923). He wrote a substantial article on Belgian neutrality.[71]

Petr Berngardovich Struve *(26 January 1870, b. Perm – 22 February 1944, d. Paris, France). Jurist, economist, historian, philosopher, sociologist, editor.*

Life and career. Initially enrolling in the natural sciences at St. Petersburg University in 1889, he transferred to the Law Faculty in 1890 and graduated in 1894. Struve became a major economist, publicist, historian, sociologist, and philosopher. He found employment in September 1893 at the Library of the Ministry of Finances, but was dismissed the following year because he had been arrested. He became a prominent representative of the "Legal Marxist" grouping and traveled to France and England on several occasions in the late 1890s and early 1900s. In 1906 he was appointed a lecturer, from 1908 privat-docent, and from 1914 professor *extraordinarius* at the Chair of Political Economy of the Petersburg Polytechnic Institute. He defended his magister dissertation (1913) and doctoral dissertation (1917) in the field of political economy. From 1916 to 1918 he was privat-docent at St. Petersburg University at the Chair of Russian History. From 1915 to 1917 he acted as Chairman of the Interdepartmental Committee for the Limitation of Trade and Supply of the Enemy attached to the Ministry of Trade and Industry. During 1917 he became the Director of the Economic Department of the Ministry of Foreign Affairs of the Russian Republic. He was a co-founder of the Kadet Party in 1905 and edited a number of journals, including Русская мысль [Russian Thought]. In May 1917 he was elected to the Russian Academy of Sciences. When the October 1917 Revolution brought the Bolsheviks to power, Struve fled to the south of Russia, returned to Moscow for some months in 1918, emigrated first to Finland, then to Paris and London, where he represented the Government of General Wrangel, back to southern Russia, and in November 1920 to Bulgaria, and ultimately to Paris, where he remained. With respect to international law, he wrote interesting works on international trade policy.[72]

[70] He wrote memoirs of his experiences with General Anton Denikin (1872-1947): Sokolov, Правление Генерала Деникина (из воспоминаний) [Government of General Denikin (From Recollections)] (Sofia, Российское-болгарское изд-во, 1921). The publishing house was founded by P. B. Struve, who had been part of the Denikin movement. There was a Chinese translation of the book in 2007.

[71] Sokolov, «Нейтралитет независимой Бельгии» [Neutrality of Independent Belgium], Русская мысль [Russian Thought], no. 1, ч. 2 (1915), pp. 139-164.

[72] P. B. Struve, «Великая Россия: из размышлений о проблеме русского могущества» [Great Russia: From Reflections on the Problem of Russian Might], Patriotica (Spb., 1911), pp. 73-96; Struve, К критике так называемой теории международной торговли [On a Critique of the So-Called Theory of International Trade] (Pg., 1918); Struve, «Современное международное положение под историческим углом зрения» [Contemporary International Situation from the Historical Angle],

Vadim Vladimirovich Telesnin *(1889-not after 1937). Early specialist in aviation law.*

Life and career. Graduated from the Law Faculty in 1911, he worked in the fields of railway and water transport with an abiding interest in the emerging promise of aviation law.[73] Executed in 1937 for alleged counter-revolutionary crimes.

Fedor Gustavovich (Thorner, Th. von) Terner *(12 October 1828, b. St. Petersburg – 20 August 1906, d. St. Petersburg).*

Life and career. Graduated from the Law Faculty in 1850 with the degree of candidate of law. Appointed from 11 January 1851 to the Special Chancellery of the Ministry of Foreign Affairs, he became privy counsellor on 12 December 1875 and a member of the Ruling Senate from 14 September 1892, and joined the State Council on 1 January 1896. On 1 January 1898 he became an actual privy counsellor. In 1881 he attended as an official Russian representative an international monetary conference in Paris and published his Report and impressions.[74]

Igor Matveevich Tiutriumov *(23 May 1855, b. village of Volchevo, Novgorod Governate – 29 March 1943, d. Narva-Jöesuu, Estonia). Civilist, but active in criminal law matters.*

Life and career. Graduated from the Law Faculty of St. Petersburg University in 1878 with the degree of candidate of law. From 31 May 1878 to 1 January 1883 he remained at the University to prepare for the professoriate at the Chair of Civil Law A noted civilist, he was appointed privat-docent and professor at the Chair of Civil Law of the University. In 1906 he was appointed Ober-Procurator of the Second Department of the Ruling Senate, made a privy counsellor from 1 January 1914, and from 10 March 1916 became a member of the Ruling Senate. He served as a member of the State Council from 16 January 1915, elected from the Novgorod Governate Zemstvo Assembly.[75] In 1919 he emigrated to Estonia, where he became a professor at Tartu University.

Patriotica (Spb., 1911), pp. 128-140; Struve, Торговая политика России [Trade Policy of Russia] (Spb., 1913); Struve, «Унижение России (Аннексия Австрией Боснии и Герцеговины)» [Humiliation of Russia (Annexation by Austria of Bosnia and Herzogovina)], *Patriotica* (Spb., 1911), pp. 197-199.

73 V. V. Telesnin, Идея мира и воздухоплавание [Idea of Peace and Air Navigation], Вестник мира [Herald of Peace], no. 3 (March 1913), cols. 41-48; Telesnin, Идея мира и воздухоплавание [Idea of Peace and Air Navigation], Общество мира в Москве [Peace Society in Moscow] (1911-1913), pp. 27-36; Telesnin, Что такое международное право [What is International Law] (M., 1914; 2d ed.; 1917).

74 F. G. Terner, Доклад г-ну управляющему Министерства финансов представителя русского правительства на Международной монетной конференции в Париже [Report to the Administrator of the Ministry of Finances by the Representative of the Russian Government at the International Monetary Congress in Paris] (Spb., 1881); Terner, "Die Ergebnisse der internationalen Münzkonferenz inn Paris mit spezieller Beziehung auf Russland", *Russische Revue*, X, no. 9 (1881), pp. 253-277.

75 Murzanov, note 54 above, pp. 444-445. I. M. Tiutriumov, «О деятельности комитета Русской

Moisei Lvovich Trivus *(1865, b. Berdiansk, Tauride Governate – 1955). Specialist on trade law, conflict of laws, writer, publicist.*

Life and career. Graduated from the Law Faculty of St. Petersburg University in 1887. Active in Jewish affairs and organizations, with extensive publications in the Russian language in the Russian Jewish press.[76]

Petr Pavlovich Tsitovich *(7 October 1843, b. Chernihiv Governate – 19 October 1913, d. St. Petersburg). Civilist.*

Life and career. Graduated from the Law Faculty of Kharkov University in 1866, he remained at the Law Faculty to prepare for the professoriate at the Chair of Civil Law. He was awarded the magister of civil law in 1870 for a dissertation on "Basic Moments in the History of the Russian Law of Inheritance" and the doctorate of civil law for his dissertation "Money in the Field of Civil Law". From 1873 he worked at the Novorossiisk University in Odessa and from 1884 at the St. Vladimir Kyiv University. In 1900 he became professor *ordinarius* at the Chair of Trade Law of the St. Petersburg University. His lectures on trade law, maritime law, and the law on bills of exchange delivered in 1900 and 1901 were published in four volumes.[77]

Vladimir Mikhailovich Ustinov *(31 January 1870, b. St. Petersburg – 11 February 1941, d. Leningrad). Specialized in State law.*

Life and career. Graduated from the Law Faculty of St. Petersburg University in 1893 and served as privat-docent from 1900 to 1901 at the Chair of State Law.

группы Международного союза криминалистов» [On the Activity of the Committee of the Russian Group of the International Penal Union], Право [Law], no. 34 (1904), pp. 1676-1681; Tiutriumov, «Письмо в редакцию» [в дополнение к письму, напечатанному в № 34 "Права" и касающемуся деятельности комитета Русской группы международного союза криминалистов]» [Letter to the Editor (in Addition to the Letter Printed in No. 34 of "Law" and Concerning the Activity of the Committee of the Russian Group of the International Penal Union], Право [Law], [№ 1-52] (1904), p. 3021; Tiutriumov, (comp.). «Русская группа Международного Союза криминалистов: протоколы заседаний 26 ноября, 21 декабря 1899 года, 8 января 1900 года» [Russian Group of the International Penal Union: Protocols of the Sessions of 26 November and 21 December 1899, and 8 January 1900], Журнал Министерства юстиции [Journal of the Ministry of Justice], [№ 1 (January) - № 2 (February)] (1900), pp. 292-347; Tritriumov, «О подсудности местным национальным судам исков предъявляемых к правительствам иностранных государств» [On Jurisdiction to Local National Courts of Suits Against Governments of Foreign States], Закон и суд [Law and Court], no. 2(62) (1936), cols. 3147-3152; № 3(63) (1936), cols. 3185-3191.

[76] Branover, note 6 above, III, p. 162. M. L. Trivus, «К вопросу об обязательности для Прибалтийских губерний общерусских торговых законов: по поводу статей г. Фон-Резона (*О торговом праве Прибалтийских губерний*)» [On the Question of General Russian Trade Laws Being Binding for the Baltic Governates: on the Article of von Rezon (On Trade Law of the Baltic Governates)], Журнал гражданского и уголовного права [Journal of Civil and Criminal Law], XXI, no. 9-10 (1891), pp. 55-66.

[77] P. P. Tsitovich, Очерки по теории торгового права [Essays on the Theory of Trade Law] (Spb., 1901-1902). 4 vols.

From 1901 he was privat-docent at the Faculty of Law of Kharkov University, and from 1906, at Moscow University. In 1907 he collaborated with Mikhail Nikolaevich Gernet (1874-1953) and Ivan Borisovich Novitskii (1880-1958) to produce the first edition of a standard introduction to Russian State, civil, and criminal law,[78] adding Ivan Aleksandrovich Il'in (1883-1954) to the fourth and last edition.[79] Ustinov was executive editor of the newspaper Утро России [Morning of Russia]. In 1919 he was sentenced to death in connection with the Tactical Center Case, replaced by deprivation of freedom for five years. He lectured in the Faculty of Social Sciences at Moscow University from 1921 to 1922.[80]

Dmitrii Efimovich Vasilevskii *(1781, b. Kaluga Governate – 1844). Legal philosopher.*

Life and career. Vasilevskii graduated from the Division of Philosophical and Legal Sciences at the Petersburg Pedagogical Institute in 1809. From 1809 to 1816 he was a lecturer at the Chair of Logic and Psychology of the Institute. In 1817 he became a magister at the Chair of Philosophy of Moscow University. From 1820 to 1823 he was at the Law Faculty of Göttingen University for advanced studies and later defended a dissertation for the degree of doctor of philosophy. He was among the early Russian legal scholars, serving as professor *extraordinarius* and *ordinarius* at Moscow University, to lecture on international law. He left a brief work on the art of negotiation.[81]

Vladimir Ivanovich Veshniakov *(16 November 1830, b. St. Petersburg – 6 February 1906, d. St. Petersburg). State official, Senator, Academician.*

Life and career. Graduated from the Law Faculty of St. Petersburg University in 1852, he worked for many years in various assignments within the Ministry of State Property (1852-1893), including as Head of the Department of Agriculture and the Agricultural Industry and as Deputy Minister. Appointed to the Ruling

[78] V. M. Ustinov, M. N. Gernet, and I. B. Novitskii, Основные понятия русского государственного, гражданского и уголовного права: Общедоступные очерки [Basic Concepts of Russian State, Civil, and Criminal Law: Generally Accessible Essays] (1907; 3d ed.; 1910).

[79] The Il'in contribution has been separately published in his collected works. See I. A. Il'in, «Общее учение о праве и государство» [General Doctrine on Law and State], in Il'in, Собрание сочинений в десяти томах [Collection of Works in Ten Volumes] (M., 1994), IV, pp. 47-147.

[80] On international law, see Ustinov, «Идея национального государства» [Idea of the National State], Труды Юридического Общества при Императорском Харьковском Университете [Proceedings of the Law Society attached to the Imperial Kharkov University], I (1904), pp. 20-43; Ustinov, Идея национального государства [Idea of the National State] (Kharkov, 1903; 2d ed.; 1906); Ustinov, «Организация помощи русским военнопленным» [Organization of Assistance to Russian Prisoners of War], Юридический вестник [Legal Herald], no. 12(4) (1915), pp. 145-152; Ustinov, Организация помощи русским военнопленным [Organization of Assistance to Russian Prisoners of War] (Kharkov, 1915).

[81] D. E. Vasilevskii, О том, что нужно негоциатору для приобретения искусства вести переговоры и совещаться о делах государственных [What Does a Negotiator Need to Acquire to Art of Conducting Negotiations and Advising on State Affairs] (M. 1824).

Senate in 1883, he became a member of the State Council in 1893. Member of the Russian Archaeological Society from 1877; elected an Honorary Member of the Russian Academy of Sciences in 1896. He published on international aspects of intellectual property and on statistics.[82]

Aleksandr Fedorovich Volkov *(1867-1927). Specialist in trade law and commercial arbitration.*

Graduating from the Law Faculty in 1893, he was awarded the degree of doctor juris at Heidelberg University in 1895. Appointed privat-docent in 1900 at the Chair of Trade Law with the rank of privat-docent at St. Petersburg University. He published works on the international grain trade[83] and commercial arbitration.[84]

Grigorii Samuilovich Voltke *(1864, b. Odessa – d. no earlier than 1916). Civilist, publicist, journalist.*

Life and career. Graduated in 1889 from the Law Faculty of St. Petersburg University. Sworn advokat in the St. Petersburg Judicial Chamber. As a publicist he also used two pseudonyms: L. Vladimirov and G. Samoilovich. Produced a book on the laws governing inhabitants of frontier borderlands and a review of P. E. Kazanskii on administrative unies of States.[85]

Konstantin Konstantinovich Zlobin *(10 March 1814, b. Volsk, Saratov Governate – 31 August 1877, d. Samara. Orientalist, archivist.*

[82] V. I. Veshniakov, Международный статистический конгресс в Гааге [International Statistical Congress at The Hague] (Spb., 1869); Veshniakov, Об уничтожении привилегий на изобретения [On the Elimination of Privileges to Inventions] (Spb., 1870); Veshniakov, О причинах возвышения Московского княжества. С ист. карт. и родословной табл. русских князей [On the Reasons for Ennoblement of the Muscovite Princedom. With Historical Maps and Genealogical Table of Russian Princes] (2d ed.; Spb., 1909).

[83] A. F. Volkov, Биржевое право: Биржевой суд и правила биржевой торговли хлебными товарами. Т. 1. (Материалы Калашниковской хлебной биржи г. С.-Петербурга в связи с практикой западно-европейских бирж) [Exchange Law: Exchange Court and Rules for Exchange Trade in Grain Goods. Vol. 1 (Materials of the Kalashnikov Grain Exchange of St. Petersburg in Connection with the Practice of Western European Exchanges] (Spb., 1905); Volkov, Курс международной хлебной торговли [Course of International Grain Trade] (Spb., 1910).

[84] Volkov, Торговые третейские суды (Историко-догматическое исследование) [Trade Arbitration Courts (Historico-Dogmatic Study)] (Spb., 1913); reprinted in serial form: Третейский суд [Arbitration Court], № 2/3, № 4-6 (1999); № 1, 2, 4 (2000); № 1, 2, 3-4, 5-6 (2001); № 1-6 (2007); № 1-6 (2008); № 1, 2, 4 (2009).

[85] G. S. Voltke, Законы о пограничных жителях и пограничных сношениях. Их история, современное значение и желательные изменения [Laws on Frontier Inhabitants and Frontier Relations. Their History, Contemporary Significance, and Desirable Changes] (Spb., 1903); Voltke, review of P. E. Kazanskii, Всеобщие административные союзов государств (Odessa, 1897), 3 vols. in Журнал юридического общества при Санкт-Петербургском университете [Journal of Law Society attached to St. Petersburg University], no. 3 (March 1898), pp. 26-36.

Life and career. Graduated from the Law Faculty of St. Petersburg University in 1834. Served in the Ministry of Foreign Affairs from 1836 as an interpreter. Became a Head of Division from 1843 and Vice Director of the Asian Department from 1856. In 1864 he became the Director of two archives: the St. Petersburg archive and the State Archive of the Russian Empire. In his archival post he published an important volume on Russo-Swedish relations.[86]

86 K. K. Zlobin, «Дипломатические сношения между Россией и Швецией в первые годы царствования императора Александра Первого до присоединения Финляндии в России» [Diplomatic Relations between Russia and Sweden in the Early Years of the Reign of Emperor Alexander I Until the Accession of Finland to Russia], Сборник Императорского Русского исторического общества [Collection of the Imperial Russian Historical Society], II (1868), pp. 1-95. Also published as offprint as separate volume.

Chapter 13
Scholars from Other Faculties Who Contributed to International Law

During the period here considered, scholars or graduates in other faculties of St. Petersburg University made significant contributions to international legal doctrine. The Faculty of History and Philology and the Faculty of Oriental Languages were especially noteworthy in this respect. International law was an integral part of the curriculum for students of oriental languages. Professor F. F. Martens was among those offering lecture courses to language students. Those language graduates who later accepted positions in the Ministry of Foreign Affairs had sufficient background in international law to be useful in diplomatic and consular positions. Three such individuals are discussed in detail, followed by briefer notices on a number of others.

Nikolai Viacheslavovich Bogoiavlenskii (Nicholas Bogoyavlensky) *(19 February 1867 – 20 June 1945). Russian consul, writer.*

Life and career. Little is known of Bogoiavlenskii. Some sources indicate that after completing studies at the Vologda Seminary he enrolled at the Lazarev Institute of Oriental Languages in Moscow and then took up service in the Ministry of Foreign Affairs. The list of graduates from the Lazarev Institute, however, does not contain the name Bogoiavlenskii. It has now been established that he studied Chinese, Mongolian, and Manchurian in the Faculty of Oriental Languages at St. Petersburg University[1] and was awarded a medal for an essay.[2]

From 1892, Bogoiavlenskii served as the Russian Consul in Chuguchak (Sinkiang-Uighur District of China).[3] He was stationed at Kharbin during the Russo-Japanese War, where the quality of his work earned the praise of the Minister of Foreign Affairs, Count V. N. Lamzdorf. In 1908 he was appointed to the newly-established post in the diplomatic section: Plenipotentiary Representative of the Ministry of Foreign Affairs attached to the Governor-General of the Amur Territory in Khabarovsk, and remained there until autumn 1912.[4] From September 1913[5]

[1] ЦГИА СПб., fond 14, opis 3, file 26598.

[2] ЦГИА СПб., fond 14, opis 3, file 15665.

[3] N. V. Bogoiavlenskii, «Юрисдикция русских консулов в Западном Китае и судебная деятельность Чугучакского консульства» [Jurisdiction of Western Consuls in Western China and Judicial Activity of the Chuguchak Consulate], Журнал Министерства юстиции [Journal of the Ministry of Justice], no. 3 (1898), pp. 28-70; Bogoiavlenskii, Западный Застенный Китай: Его прошлое, настоящее состояние и положение в нем русских подданных [Western Walled China: Past Thereof, Present State, and Status Therein of Russian Subjects] (Spb., 1906). [iv], 418 p.

[4] T. Ia. Ikonnikova, «Оформление отношений с консульском корпусом в Приамурском генерал-губернаторстве (1908-1912 гг.)» [Formalization of Relations with the Consular Corps in the Amur General-Governate (1908-1912)], Россия и АТР [Russia and the Asian-Pacific Region], no. 1 (2012), pp. 26-34.

[5] President Woodrow Wilson "recognized" the appointment of Bogoiavlenskii as Consul of Russia

to 16 November 1933,[6] Bogoiavlenskii served as Russian Consul General in the United States, based in Nome, Alaska, and Seattle, Washington.[7] He remained in the United States after his retirement from consular duties[8] and became a citizen of the United States. He is buried at the Washelli Cemetery in Seattle, Washington.

International legal views. Bogoiavlenskii drew upon his experience as an international legal practitioner in the Russian and Soviet consular service to produce contributions to legal scholarship. His first article on the subject addressed specific issues that he encountered when performing consular functions.[9] In his view, consular activity in China and other Asian countries differed significantly from what Russian consuls did in European and other western countries – a reality that generated surprise and misunderstanding: "Under the name of consular jurisdiction in the East is understood the granting to consuls of civilized nations in the Orient the right to judge and punish subjects of one's own State residing in the district of the consulate" (p. 29). He pointed out that consular jurisdiction began to be established by European Powers initially in Muslim countries, and then eastward to China and Japan. Over time, European countries adopted detailed legislation on judicial activity of consults in international treaties with the countries concerned. Regrettably, said Bogoiavlenskii, Russia had lagged behind, and Russian legislation on this matter was brief and left much to be desired. He quoted Martens, who had noted the shortcomings of Russian legislation and wrote that little was known how Russian consular courts in China and Japan were structured and operated.[10] Bogoiavlenskii set out to rectify this situation.

He noted that Russian legislation and Sino-Russian treaties did not lay down a procedure for the settlement of many issues that arose. He addressed, giving examples, the conditions and procedure for consular courts in China to operate when settling civil and criminal cases involving Russian subjects or performing

on 22 November 1913. The official document was auctioned in 2019.

6 His status as Russian Consul was terminated and exequatur revoked "in view of the recognition of the Union of Soviet Socialist Republics by the Government of the United States". The telegram of notification was published in the *American Journal of International Law*, XXVIII (1934), pp. 14-15.

7 His reports sent in 1914 on his reception in Seattle, the 11,000 Russian émigrés in the western United States, and the potential for improved trade relations between Seattle and Vladivostok are reproduced in A. N. Iakovlev (ed.), Россия и США: дипломатические отношения 1900-1917 [Russia and the United States: Diplomatic Relations 1900-1917 (M., 1999).

8 A letter from the Counsellor of the Plenipotentiary Representation in the United States, Boris Evseevich Skvirskii (1887-1941), to the People's Commissar of Foreign Affairs, Maksim Litvinov (1876-1951), dated 19 July 1934 reported that, according to the Department of State, in a letter of 12 June 1934, Bogoiavlenskii had ceased his consular activity, closed the office, and left Seattle. See A. N. Iakovlev (ed.), Советско-американские отношения 1934-1939 [Soviet-American Relations 1934-1939] (M., 2003), Doc. No. 98, p. 185.

9 Bogoiavlenskii, «Юрисдикция русских консулов в Западном Китае и судебная деятельность Чугучакского консульства» [Jurisdiction of Russian Consuls in Western China and Judicial Activity of the Chuguchak Consulate], Журнал Министерства юстиции [Journal of the Ministry of Justice], no. 3 (1898), pp. 28-70.

10 F. F. Martens, Современное международное право цивилизованных народов [Contemporary International Law of Civilized Nations] (Spb., 1883), II, p. 96.

investigative actions on behalf of Russian courts with respect to Russian subjects living or hiding in his consular district.

He made suggestions for improving the legislative and administrative regulation of consular jurisdiction in the Orient and the training of consular personnel. Given that judicial matters fall within consular duties in the East, he urged that Russian consults have sufficient legal training. This meant expanding the legal component when training orientalists in Russia, especially in the fields of civil and criminal law (pp. 68-69). Much of the material in this article was reiterated in his treatise eight years later (1906). His perceptive observations were reinforced by the open publication of some of his consular reports at the time.[11]

Georgii Vasilevich Forsten (Torsten) *(30 May 1857, b. Fredrikshamn (now Hamina), Grand Duchy of Finland – 2 July 1910, d. Parish of Yoros, Grand Duchy of Finland). Specialist on international relations of Scandinavian countries.*

Life and career. After graduating from the Sixth St. Petersburg Gymnasium, Forsten enrolled in the Faculty of History and Philology of St. Petersburg University, graduating in 1881 and remaining to prepare for the professoriate. He defended his magister dissertation in 1885 on "The Struggle for Dominance in the Baltic Sea in the Fifteenth and Sixteenth Centuries".[12] Sent abroad for two years to undertake research, Forsten visited Germany, Italy, France, Belgium, Denmark, and Sweden to attend lectures and seminars and work in the archives of Berlin, Dresden, Munich, Venice, Florence, Rome, Paris, Brussels, Copenhagen, and Stockholm. The outcome of his studies was an early article on the history of international relations based on archival and library resources.[13]

Upon returning from abroad, Forsten taught and pursued research at the Chair of Universal History in the Faculty of History and Philology of St. Petersburg Uni-

[11] See Bogoiavlenskii on Russian trade with the region in Сборник консульских донесений [Collection of Consular Reports], VI (1899), pp. 461-475.

[12] G. V. Forsten, Борьба из-за господства на Балтийском море в XV и XVI столетиях [The Struggle for Dominance in the Baltic Sea in the XV and XVI Centuries] (Spb., 1884).

[13] Forsten, «Архивные занятия в Париже, Брюсселе, Копенгагене и Стокгольме по истории Скандинавских стран и Московского государства в XVI и XVII столетиях» [Archival Engagements in Paris, Brussels, Copenhagen, and Stockholm Relating to the History of Scandinavian Countries and the Muscovite State in the XVI and XVII Centuries], Журнал Министерства народного просвещения [Journal of Ministry of Public Enlightenment], no. 6 (1887), pp. 50-74.

versity, from 1887 as privat-docent, from 1896 as professor *extraordinarius*, and from 1899 to 1910, as professor *ordinarius*. He taught in addition from 1891 at the Higher Women's (Bestuzhev) Courses; in 1893 the Chair at the Institute of History and Philology attached to the Ministry of Public Enlightenment; and in 1896 at the Nikolaev Academy of the General Staff. In 1894 he defended at St. Petersburg University a two-volume doctoral dissertation which continued the topic of his magister. The doctoral dissertation too was based on foreign archives.[14]

International legal views. Forsten concentrated his scholarly research on the diplomatic relations of Russia, Sweden, Livonia, Poland, Prussia, and Denmark, his central concern being the Baltic Sea. His interest in these matters, he said, was dictated by several considerations. First, commencing in the sixteenth and seventeenth centuries new large Baltic powers pursued competing interests, including Muscovy and the Russian Empire; second, the relations of the Baltic States, including Russia, had received little attention in Russian studies. Prior to the mid-seventeenth century commercial and political hegemony appertained to the Hanseatic League, which combined more than 130 Baltic cities, about a hundred of which were seaports, that granted to League members and specific traders certain commercial privileges. Forsten believed that the discovery of the Americas and new sea routes to colonial countries inflicted a decisive blow on the Hanseatic League, whose decline in turn generated new States elevated to the stature of a European power, namely Denmark, Russia, Sweden, and Poland, who one after another sought to secure the wealthy legacy of the League and competed among themselves to do so. This in turn raised issues of the territorial possession of the Baltic coasts.

Archival research underlay his magister and doctoral dissertations, and he continued to visit archives abroad after publishing his doctorate. He published several monographs and numerous articles of relevance to international law. In their efforts to dominate the Baltic, States used the full arsenal of their capabilities: political, military, diplomatic, trade, and international legal. Forsten explored the open and concealed efforts in negotiations to conclude numerous treaties, the complexities of complying with these, and the sundry violations. He commented on one consistent factor in these: "All the coalitions which we encountered … were concluded against Russia: fear of Russia is the cement which binds States to one another".[15]

Nikolai Ivanovich Veselovskii *(24 November 1848, b. Moscow – 12 April 2010, d. Petrograd). Professor at the Chair of the History of the Orient; specialist in the history and archeology of the South of Russia and Central Asia; corresponding member, Russian Academy of Sciences.*

Life and career. After completing studies at the Gymnasium in Vologda, Veselovskii enrolled in 1869 in the Faculty of History and Philology of St. Petersburg University (Arab-Turkic Division), graduating in 1873. He remained at the

[14] Forsten, Балтийский вопрос в XVI и XVII столетиях (1544-1648) [The Baltic Question in the XVI and XVII Centuries (1544-1648)] (Spb., 1893-1894). Volume one was devoted to the struggle for Livonia, and volume two to the struggle of Sweden against Poland and the House of Habsburg.

[15] Forsten, ibid., I, p. 717.

University to prepare for the professoriate. Having passed the magister examinations, he published his first serious research study and defended it successfully in 1877 as a magister dissertation.[16] From 1878 to 1882 he was privat-docent at the Chair of the History of the Orient; from 1884 to 1890, professor *extraordinarius*; from 1890, professor *ordinarius*; and from 1903, Distinguished Professor.

As an historian, Veselovskii pursued many aspects of Russian history and the relations of Russia with the inhabitants of Central Asia, publishing several monographs and articles on this subject.[17] In 1916-1917 he published a four-volume concise List of professors at the history and philological, oriental languages, physics and mathematics, and law faculties of St. Petersburg University from 1819 onwards.

As an archeologist, Veselovskii conducted research in Central Asia, the South of Russia, and Crimea, locating hundreds of kurgans and ruins of ancient urban settlements during expeditions and excavations. The treasures and items found enriched the museums of Russia; many are presently in the State Hermitage at St. Petersburg. Veselovskii's gifts as an archeologist were recognized by election to membership in the Russian Archeological Society (1881); the Imperial Archeological Commission (1885); the Moscow Archeological Society (1887); head of the Orientall Division of the Russian Archeological Society (1908); and Chairman of the Archeology and Archeography Section of the Society of Military History (1908).

International legal views. Several of Veselovskii's works are relevant to the field of international law. These concern the distinctive features of the relations between medieval Rus and the peoples of Central Asia, including ambassadorial protocol and ceremony.

In Veselovskii's view, the Grand and appanage princes of Rus had long maintained relations with the Golden Horde and Mongolia. From times immemorial in the East diplomatic links had been established that differed from European practices. This was especially evident with respect to envoys and ambassadorial ceremonial. Veselovskii acknowledged that the Russians had borrowed ambassadorial

[16] N. I. Veselovskii, Очерк историко-географических сведений о Хивинском ханстве от древнейших времен до настоящего [Survey of Historico-Geographical Information on the Khiva Khanate from Ancient Times to the Present] (Spb., 1877). ЦГИА СПб., fond 14, opis 3, file 15622.

[17] Among these, Veselovskii, Памятники дипломатических сношений Московской Руси с Персией [Monuments of Diplomatic Relations of Muscovite Rus with Persia] (Spb., 1890-1898). 3 vols.

ceremonial from Eastern neighbors. Therefore, ambassadorial ceremonial during the Muscovite period of Russian history was primarily Asian in character and insofar as it differed, did so for religious reasons.

Thus, in Rus ambassadors did not pass between two flames prior to an audience with the Tsar, as was compulsory in some khanates in order to supposedly destroy any possible evil intent on the part of ambassadors. This was considered to be a pagan practice in Rus and therefore incompatible with Christianity. Similarly, in Russia the practices of kowtowing, or the ambassador kneeling to kiss the feet of an oriental ruler, were rejected. In the Russian view, one only kowtowed to God, and as for the second, in the Russian view the human body below the waist was unclean and, consequently, an ambassador who kissed someone's feet debased himself.[18]

Ambassadorial ceremonial in all its details was directed towards an external public expression of honor with respect to three subjects: the sovereign who sent the envoy; the sovereign receiving the envoy; and the envoy himself. These three orientations of honor were concentrated on the person of the envoy. What reception was extended to an arriving envoy also elevated the honor of the sending State. An envoy had the right to being received attentively and to special respect. This was reflected in the premise provided him, the provisions supplied, horses, escort, and gifts for the envoy himself and his suite.

But in many countries of the Orient another view was embedded of receiving envoys: humiliation of the arriving envoy so as to raise the significance of the receiving sovereign in the eyes of the people. Traditionally, envoys were received in the Orient as spies, treated with suspicion, and subjected to constant observation. But the majority of diplomatic customs Russian princes borrowed from the Golden Horde and over time adapted them to their circumstances until the reign of Peter the Great. Only during the reign of Tsar Peter were the diplomatic links of Russia reoriented towards the countries of Europe and the practices of European diplomatic ceremonial introduced.

§13.1 *Other Scholars and Graduates*

Vasilii Vladimirovich Bartold *(25 November 1869, b. St. Petersburg – 19 November 1939, d. Leningrad). Noted Russian and Soviet orientalist, historian, and philologist. Academician, Russian and USSR Academy of Sciences.* Graduated from the Faculty of Oriental Languages, St. Petersburg University, in 1891; privat-docent and professor in the said Faculty from 1891 to 1919. Relevant works on the Islamic world and China.[19]

18 Veselovskii, «Татарское влияние на посольский церемониал в Московский период русской истории» [Tatar Influence on Ambassadorial Ceremonial in the Muscovy Period of Russian History], in Отчет о состоянии и деятельности Императорского С.-Петербургского университета [Report on the State and Activity of the Imperial St. Petersburg University for 1910] (Spb., 1911), pp. 1-19.

19 V. V. Bartold, История изучения Востока в Европе и России: Лекции, читанные в Импера-

Vasilii Vasilevich Bauer *(13 December 1833, b. St. Petersburg – 18 November 1884, d. St. Petersburg). Historian of antiquity and the Middle Ages.* Bauer graduated from the Faculty of History and Philology of St. Petersburg University in 1855. From 1863 to 1880 he was privat-docent and then professor at the said Faculty and from 1880 to 1882, Dean of the Faculty. His works of international legal interest addressed Russian relations with the Holy Roman Empire.[20]

Mikhail Nikolaevich Berezhkov *(30 October 1850, b. Mosttsa, Vladimir Governate – April 1932, Ukraine).* Historian. Graduating in 1875 from the Faculty of History and Philology of St. Petersburg University, Berezhkov defended his magister dissertation on Russian history in 1879. From 1886 to 1904 he was Professor of Russian History at the A. A. Bezborodko Institute of History and Philology in Nezhyn, Ukraine. Berezhkov published on trade relations with the Hanseatic League, prisoners of war in Crimea, and ambassadorial law.[21]

Pavel Vladimirovich Bezobrazov *(14 February 1859, b. St. Petersburg – 13 September 1918, d. Petrograd).* Specialist in Byzantium and the Middle Ages, publicist, translator. Bezobrazov graduated in 1883 from the Faculty of History and Philology of St. Petersburg University. From 1888 to 1895 he was privat-docent at the Chair of Universal History of Moscow University. In 1890 he defended his magister dissertation at St. Petersburg University and from 1913 to 1916 was privat-docent at the Chair of Universal History

торском С.-Петербургском университете [History of the Study of the East in Europe and Russia. Lectures Delivered at the Imperial St. Petersburg University] (Spb., 1911); Bartold, Мусульманский мир [The Muslim World] (Pg., 1922); Bartold, Образование империи Чингис-хана [Formation of the Empire of Genghis-Khan], Записки Восточного отделения императорского Русского археологического общества [Notes of the Oriental Division of the Imperial Archeological Society], X (1896), pp. 105-119.

[20] V. V. Bauer, Конспект лекций по истории германо-романского мира XVI и XVII столетий [Conspectus of Lectures on the History of the Germano-Roman World of the XVI and XVII Centuries] (Spb., 1885); Bauer, «Сношения России с императорами Священной Римской Империи в конце XV и начале XVI столетий» [Relations of Russia with Emperors of the Holy Roman Empire at the End of the XV and Early XVI Centuries], Журнал Министерства народного просвещения [Journal of the Ministry of Public Enlightenment], no. 3 (March 1870), pp. 75-93.

[21] M. N. Berezhkov, «О торговле русских с Ригой в XIII и XIV веках» [On Trade of Russians with Riga in the XIII and XIV Centuries], Журнал Министерства народного просвещения [Journal of the Ministry of Public Enlightenment], no. 2 (February 1877), pp. 330-357; Berezhkov, О торговле Руси с Ганзой до конца XV века [On Trade of Rus with the Hanseatic League Before the End of the XV Century] (Spb., 1879; reprinted M., 2016); Berezhkov, Русские пленники и невольники в Крыму [Russian Prisoners of War and Slaves in Crimea] (Odessa, 1888); Berezhkov, Древнейшая книга Крымских посольських дел: 1474-1505 гг. [Most Ancient Book of Crimean Ambassadorial Affairs: 1474-1505] (Simferopol, 1894).

of St. Petersburg University. He published articles on Russian relations with England, France, and Turkey.[22]

Vasilii Alekseevich Bilbasov *(1838, b. Poltava – 1904, d. Pavlovsk). Historian and publicist.* Having graduated in 1861 from the Faculty of History and Philology of St. Petersburg University, he defended his magister dissertation there in 1863 and his doctoral dissertation in 1867. From 1866 he was privat-docent at the Chair of Universal History. He published on the accession of Courland, Anglo-Russian relations, and Count Andrei Ivanovich Osterman (1686-1747).[23]

Vladimir Feofilovich Botsianovskii *(15 June 1869, b. Skoromokha, Zhytomir uezd, Volnyhia Governate – 16 July 1943, d. Moscow). Literary historian and critic.* A graduate of the Faculty of History and Philology of St. Petersburg University in 1892, Botsianovskii produced works on the Russian Red Cross Society and on German atrocities in the First World War.[24]

Fedor Aleksandrovich (Friedrich-Agafon-Marie) Braun *(20 July 1862, b. St. Petersburg – 14 July 1942, d. Leipzig, Germany).* Historian and philologist, Corresponding Member, USSR Academy of Sciences. Braun graduated from the Faculty of History and Philology of St. Petersburg University in 1885. From 1900 to 1920 he served as Professor at the Chair

[22] P. V. Bezobrazov, «О сношениях России с Францией» [On Relations of Russia with France], Русское обозрение [Russian Survey], no. 1 (1891), pp. 205-236; no. 2 (1891), pp. 587-624; no. 3 (1891), pp. 306-337; no. 4 (1891), pp. 604-638; no. 5 (1891), pp. 279-313; no. 6 (1891), pp. 609-660; no. 8 (1891), pp. 548-593; no. 9 (1891), pp. 5-54; no. 10 (1891), pp. 498-547; no. 11 (1891), pp. 173-241; no. 12 (1891), pp. 204-266; Bezobrazov, О сношениях России с Францией [On Relations of Russia with France] (M., 1892); Bezobrazov, «Раздел Турции» [Partition of Turkey], Сообщение Императорского Православного палестинского общества [Report of the Imperial Orthodox Palestine Society], XXVII (1916), pp. 204-266; Bezobrazov, Раздел Турции [Partition of Turkey] (Pg., 1917); Bezobrazov, «Россия и Англия» [Russia and England], Русское обозрение [Russian Survey], no. 9 (1892), pp. 279-301; no. 10 (1892), pp. 774-803; no. 11 (1892), pp. 302-345; no. 12 (1892), pp. 759-790.

[23] V. A. Bilbasov, «Присоединение Курляндии» [Accession of Courland], Русская старина [Russian Antiquity], no. 1 (1895), pp. 1-55; Bilbasov, «Россия и Англия в XVIII веке» [Russia and England in the XVIII Century], Русская старина [Russian Antiquity], no. 10 (1893), pp. 1-37; Bilbasov, Review of A. A. Kochubinskii, Граф Андрей Иванович Остерман и раздел Турции: Из истории Восточного вопроса. Война пяти лет (1735-1739). Одесса, 1899. 526 p. [Count Andrei Ivanovich Osterman and the Partition of Turkey: From the History of the Eastern Question. War of Five Years (1735-1739). Odessa, 1899. 526 p.], in: Журнал Министерства народного просвещения [Journal of the Ministry of Public Enlightenment], no. 6 (1900), pp. 331-347.

[24] V. F. Botsianovskii, Исторический очерк деятельности Российского общества Красного Креста [Historical Survey of Activity of the Russian Red Cross Society] (Spb., 1896); Botsianovskii, «Немецкие зверства и международное право» [German Atrocities and International Law], Вестник Красного Креста [Herald of the Red Cross Society], no. 4 (1915), pp. 1240-1251.

of the History of Western European Cultures and Dean of his Faculty. From 1921 he removed to Germany and worked at Leipzig University. He published on Gothic-Slavic Relations with particular attention to Goths on the Wisla up to the fifth century.[25]

Vadim Apollonovich Butenko *(12 July 1877, b. Gori, Tiflis Governate – 14 September 1931, Camp Mai-Guba, Karelia).* Specialist in nineteenth-century French history. Graduated in 1900 from the Faculty of History and Philology of St. Petersburg University and from 1907 to 1917 was privat-docent at the Chair of Universal History in the said Faculty. Relevant publications addressed the Congress of Vienna, Holy Alliance, and Hundred Years War.[26]

Nikolai Dmitrievich Chechulin *(15 November 1863, b. Cherepovets, Novgorod Governate – 14 February 1927, d. Borisoglebsk, Cherepovets Governate).* Historian, collector, member of the Russian Historical Society; Corresponding Member, Russian Academy of Sciences. Chechulin graduated in 1885 from the Faculty of History and Philology of St. Petersburg University. From 1891 to 1913 he was privat-docent at the Chair of Russian History of the said University. He left two works of interest to international law.[27]

Olga Antonovna Dobnash-Rozhdestvenskaia *(31 May 1874, b. Kharkov – 30 August 1939, d. Bolshie Izory, Leningrad Region).* First female in

[25] F. A. Braun, Разыскания в области гото-славянских отношений [Searches in the Field of Gothic-Slavic Relations] (Spb., 1899).

[26] V. A. Butenko, «Борьба европейских держав за Бельгию» [Struggle of the European Powers for Belgium], in M. I. Tugan-Baranovskii (ed.), Вопросы мировой войны [Questions of the World War] (Pg., 1915), pp. 48-60; Butenko, «Венский конгресс» [Congress of Vienna], in Отечественная война и русское общество [Fatherland War and Russian Society] (1912), VII, pp. 1-20; Butenko, «Нейтралитет Бельгии» [Neutrality of Belgium], in E. D. Grimm, M. M. Kovalevskii, and B. V. Formakovskii (eds.), Россия и ее союзники в борьбе за цивилизацию [Russia and its Allies in the Struggle for Civilization] (1916), I(3), pp. 117-202; Butenko, «Священный союз и международная политика эпохи реставрации» [The Holy Alliance and International Policy of the Restoration Epoch], Книга для чтения по истории нового времени [Book for Reading the History of the New Time] (M., 1913), IV(4.1), pp. 105-127; Butenko, «Соединенные Штаты и мировая политика» [United States and World Politics], Биржевые ведомости [Stock Exchange Gazette] (22 March 1917), p. 3; Butenko, «Столетняя война» [Hundred Years War], Энциклопедический словарь Гранат [Encyclopedic Dictionary Granat] (7th ed.; M., 1926), XLV(IV), pp. 640-645; Butenko, Review of A. Debidour, *Histoire diplomatique de l'Europe depuis la congrès de Berlin jusqu'á nos jours* (Paris, Alcan, 1916), in Исторические известия [Historical News], no. 1 (1917), pp. 136-139.

[27] N. D. Chechulin, Внешняя политика России в начале царствования Екатерины II [Foreign Policy of Russia At the Beginning of the Reign of Catherine II] (Spb., 1896); Chechulin, Политика России в Польше перед первым разделом [Policy of Russia in Poland Before the First Partition] (M., 2016); Chechulin, Заметки о внешней политике России в начале царствования Екатерины II [Notes on the Foreign Policy of Russia at the Beginning of the Reign of Catherine II] (Spb. 1895).

Russia to successfully defend a magister dissertation in the field of universal history, medievalist, paleographer, doctorate from the University of Paris, and Corresponding Member, USSR Academy of Sciences. She graduated in 1899 from the Faculty of History and Philology of the Higher (Bestuzhev) Women's Courses and from 1915 to 1919 was privat-docent and then professor at the Chair of Universal History of St. Petersburg University. She wrote on the Crusades and French history.[28]

Vasilii Vasilevich Grigorev *(15 March 1816, b. St. Petersburg – 19 December 1881, d. Pavlovsk, suburb of St. Petersburg).* Professor at the Chair of the Orient, public official, numismatist. Grigorev graduated in 1834 from the Division of Oriental Languages of the Faculty of History and Philology of St. Petersburg University. He published several works on relations with Central Asia and other nomadic peoples.[29]

Ervin Davidovich Grimm *(8 January 1871, b. St. Petersburg – 18 February 1940, d. Leningrad).* Historian, last Rector of the Imperial St. Petersburg University. Grimm graduated in 1891 from the Faculty of History and Philology of St. Petersburg University. From 1894 to 1896 he was privat-docent at the Chair of Universal History of the said Faculty and again from 1894 to 1896 and from 1899 to 1918 successively privat-docent and professor at the same Chair as well as Dean of the said Faculty and Pro-Rector and Rector of St. Petersburg University. He wrote on alliance policy during the First World War.[30]

[28] O. A. Dobnash-Rozhdestvenskaia, Что такое Франция в прошлом и настоящем и за что она воюет [What is France in Past and Present and For What Do They Fight] (Pg., 1917); Dobnash-Rozhdestvenskaia, Эпоха крестовых походов (Запад в крестоносном движении) [Epoch of the Crusades (The West in the Crusade Movement)] (Pg., 1918).

[29] V. V. Grigorev, О древних походах руссов на Восток [On Medieval Campaigns of the Rus to the East] (Spb., 1835); Grigorev, Об отношении России к Востоку [On the Relations of Russia to the East] (Odessa, 1840); Grigorev, «Об отношениях между кочевыми народами и оседлыми государствами» [On the Relations between Nomadic Peoples and Settled States], Журнал Министерства народного просвещения [Journal of the Ministry of Public Enlightenment], no. 3 (1875), pp. 1-27; Grigorev, Русская политика в отношении к Средней Азии [Russian Policy with Respect to Central Asia] (Spb., 1874); Grigorev, Разбор сочинения П. И. Небольсина, Очерки торговли России со Среднею Азиею [Analysis of the Work by P. I. Nebolsin, Survey of Trade of Russia with Central Asia] (1856).

[30] E. D. Grimm, «Борьба народов» [Struggle of Peoples], in M. N. Tugan-Baranovskii (ed.), Вопросы мировой войны: Сборник статей [Questions of the World War: Collection of Articles] (1915), pp. 2-20; Grimm, «Происхождение современной группировки держав» [Origin of the Contemporary Grouping of Powers], in E. D. Grimm, M. M. Kovalevskii, and B. V. Formakovskii (eds.), Россия и ее союзники в борьбе за цивилизацию [Russia and its Allies in the Struggle for Civilization] (M., 1916), I(1), pp. 11-50.

Dmitrii Grigorevich Ianchevetskii *(1873 – 28 August 1938, d. Iaroslavl).* Orientalist, journalist, editor. Ianchevetskii graduated in 1895 from the Faculty of Oriental Languages of St. Petersburg University. During the Russo-Japanese War, First World War, and civil conflict in Russia, Ianchevetskii worked as a journalist and editor-in-chief of several newspapers. As the Vienna correspondent of Новое время [New Times], Ianchevetskii was accused on 21 August 1915 of espionage by the Austrian authorities and sentenced to death by hanging, duly replaced by life imprisonment at the request of Emperor Nicholas II and the intercession of the King of Spain. He was released in 1916. Of interest to international law was his article on Russian policies in the Far East.[31]

Nikolai Vladimirovich Iastrebov *(10 June 1869, b. Vetluga, Kostroma Governate – 25 May 1923, d. Prague, Czechoslovakia).* Historian and Slavic philologist. Iastrebov graduated in 1895 from the Faculty of Oriental Languages of St. Petersburg University. From 1902 to 1919 he was docent and professor at the Chair of Slavic Philology of the said University. After the 1917 revolutions, he emigrated to Czechoslovakia. Of interest to international law, he wrote on Galicia.[32]

Nikolai Ivanovich Kareev *(6 December 1850, b. Moscow – 18 February 1931, d. Leningrad).* Historian and sociologist, Corresponding Member, Russian Academy of Sciences; Honorary Member, USSR Academy of Sciences. Kareev graduated in 1873 from the Faculty of History and Philology of Moscow University and served from 1885 to 1923 as privat-docent and professor at the Chair of Universal History of St. Petersburg University. He published books and articles of international-legal interest on territorial issues.[33]

Nikolai Ivanovich Kostomarov *(16 May 1817, b. Voronezh Governate – 19 April 1885, St. Petersburg).* Historian, Corresponding Member, Russian Academy of Sciences. Author of a well-regarded multi-volume history of Russia in accounts of the lives of its principal personalities. Kostomarov graduated in 1837 from the Faculty of History and Philology of Kharkov University. From 1859 to 1862 he was a professor at the Chair of Russian

[31] D. G. Ianchevetskii, Гроза с Востока: Задачи России, задачи Японии на Дальнем Востоке [Threat from the East: Tasks of Russia, Tasks of Japan in the Far East] (Revel, 1907; 2d ed.; 1908).

[32] N. V. Iastrebov, Галиция накануне Великой войны 1914 года [Galicia on the Eve of the 1914 Great War] (Pg., 1915).

[33] N. K. Kareev, Европа до и после войны в территориальном отношении [Europe Before and After the War Territorially] (Pg., 1922); Kareev, «Польский вопрос в историческом освещении» [The Polish Question Historically], in M. I. Baranovskii (ed.), Вопросы мировой войны: Сборник статей [Questions of the World War: Collection of Articles] (Pg., 1915), pp. 61-85; Kareev, Южные славяне и Италия на Адриатике [Southern Slavs and Italy on the Adriatic] (Pg., 1917).

History of St. Petersburg University. Primarily a medievalist, he published works on government and trade of international-legal interest.[34]

Mikhail Semenovich Kutorga *(18 September 1809, Mogilev – 7 June 1886, d. Borka estate, Mogilev Governate).* Specialist in ancient Greek history, Corresponding Member, Russian Academy of Sciences. Kutorga graduated in 1833 from the Professorial Institute organized at Dorpat University. From 1834 to 1869 he served as a junior scientific associate and professor at the Chair of Universal History and from 1844 to 1859 at the Chair of the History of the Orient, at St. Petersburg University. Of interest to international law is his treatise on the Persian wars.[35]

Vladimir Ivanovich Lamanskii *(2 July 1833, b. St. Petersburg – 2 December 1914, d. Petrograd).* Historian and Slavist, Academician, Russian Academy of Sciences. Lamanskii graduated in 1843 from the Faculty of History and Philology of St. Petersburg University. From 1863 to 1899 he was privat-docent, docent, and professor at the Chair of Slavic Philology at the said University and Dean of the Faculty from 1883 to 1885. Of interest to international law remain his works on territorial issues.[36]

Ivan Ivanovich Lappo *(28 August 1869, b. Tsarskoe selo – 23 December 1944, Dresden, Germany).* Historian. Lappo graduated in 1892 from the Faculty of History and Philology of St. Petersburg University and from that year he began to teach history in various gymnasia of the City. In 1901 he defended a magister dissertation on the Polish-Lithuanian Commonwealth.[37] This earned him an appointment as privat-docent at the

[34] N. I. Kostomarov, Мысли о федеративном начале в Древней Руси [Thoughts on the Federative Principle in Medieval Rus] (Spb., 1861); Kostomarov, Очерк торговли Московского государства в XVI и XVII столетиях [Survey of Trade of the Muscovite State in the XVI and XVII Centuries] (Spb., 1862); Kostomarov, Севернорусские народоправства во времена удельно-вечевого уклада [Northern Russian People's Rule During the Appanage-Veche Formation] (Spb., 1863). 2 vols.

[35] M. S. Kutorga, Персидские войны: Критическое исследование событий этой эпохи древней греческой истории [Persian Wars: Critical Study of Events of this Epoch of Ancient Greek History] (Spb., 1858).

[36] V. I. Lamanskii, Три мира Азийско-Европейского материка [Three Worlds of the Asian-European Mainland] (Spb., 1892); Lamanskii, Review of A. A. Kochubinskii, Граф Андрей Иванович Остерман и раздел Турции [Count Andrei Ivanovich Osterman and the Partition of Turkey. Odessa, 1899] (Spb., 1901).

[37] I. I. Lappo, Великое княжество Литовское за время от заключения Люблинской Унии до смерти Стефана Батория: 1569-1586 [Grand Principality of Lithuania from the Conclusion of the Lublin Unie to the Death of Stefan Batory: 1569-1586] (Spb., 1901). Vol. 1 only published. Also see Lappo, Великое княжество Литовское во второй половине XVI столетия [Grand Principality of Lithuania in the Second Half of the XVI Century] (Iurev, 1911). Lappo continued to publish on this topic in emigration, as well as studies of the Lithuanian Statute.

Chair of Russian History at St. Petersburg University. From 1905 to 1918 he served as Professor of Russian History at Iurev University, and from 1919 to 1921 at Voronezh University as part of the evacuation eastward of Iurev University. He emigrated in 1921 to Czechoslovakia, where until 1933 he was privat-docent at the Russian Law School in Prague. In 1933 he removed to Lithuania as a professor at the Vytautas the Great University in Kaunas, becoming a privat-docent at Vilnius University in 1941 and junior assistant at the Institute of Law and the Economy in 1942. His magister dissertation remained his principal service to international law.

Nikolai Iakolevich Marr *(25 December 1864, b. Kutaisi – 20 December 1934, d. Leningrad).* Specialist in the Orient and Caucasus, philologist, historian, ethnographer, archeologist, Academician, Russian Academy of Sciences; Academician and Vice President, USSR Academy of Sciences. Marr graduated in 1888 from the Faculty of Oriental Languages of St. Petersburg University. From 1891 to 1919 he was privat-docent and professor at the Chair of Armenian and Georgian Languages at the said University and Dean of the Faculty from 1911 to 1919. He wrote two works of relevance to international law.[38]

Pavel Pavlovich Mitrofanov *(3 December 1873 – 4 March 1917, d. Petrograd).* Historian of Austria, publicist. Mitrofanov graduated in 1896 from the Faculty of History and Philology of St. Petersburg University. He was employed by various educational institutions in St. Petersburg, and from November 1904 was privat-docent at the Chair of Universal History at St. Petersburg University. He published on Austrian foreign policy and on Russo-German relations.[39]

Vitold Vladislavovich Novodvorskii *(14 June 1861, b. Igumen uezd, Minsk Governate – 25 November 1923, d. Vilnius, Poland).* Historian specializing on Polish-Russian relations. Novodvorskii graduated in 1885 from the Faculty of History and Philology of St. Petersburg University. From 1900 to 1906 he was privat-docent at the Chair of Universal History of the said University. He emigrated to Poland in 1918. His study of the Muscovy-Polish struggle for Livonia is of interest to the field of international law.[40]

[38] N. Ia. Marr, Антиох Стратиг. Пленение Иерусалима персами в 614 г.: Грузинский текст [Antiochus Stratigus. Captivity of Jerusalem by the Persians in the Year 614: Georgian Text] (Spb., 1909); Marr, Батум, Ардаган, Карс – исторический узел межнациональных отношений Кавказа [Batumi, Ardagan, Kars – Historicall Juncture of Inter-Nationality Relations of the Caucasus] (Pg., 1922).

[39] P. P. Mitrofanov, Леопольд II Австрийский [Leopold II of Austria] (Pg., 1916). Vol. 1(1) only; Mitrofanov, "Offener Brief über das Verhältnis von Russland und Deutschland", in H. Delbrück (ed.), *Preussische Jahrbücher*, CXLVI (1914), pp. 385-398.

[40] V. V. Novodvorskii, Борьба за Ливонию между Москвой и Речью Посполитою (1570-1582).

Sergei Fedorovich Platonov *(28 June 1860, b. Chernyhiv – 10 January 1933, d. Samara).* Historian. Corresponding Member, Russian Academy of Sciences; Academician, USSR Academy of Sciences. Platonov graduated in 1882 from the Faculty of History and Philology of St. Petersburg University and from 1888 to 1918 served as privat-docent and professor at the Chair of Russian History in the said University. His contributions relevant to international law are devoted principally to the eighteenth century.[41]

Mikhail Aleksandrovich Polievktov *(5 April 1872, b. Kaluga Governate – 21 December 1942, d. Georgia).* Historian and specialist in Caucasian studies. Polievktov graduated in 1894 from the Faculty of History and Philology of St. Petersburg University and from 1903 to 1918 was privat-docent at the Chair of Russian History of the said University. Four of his works prior to 1918 are of interest to international law.[42]

Aleksandr Evgenevich Presniakov *(3 May 1870, b. Odessa – 30 September 1929, d. Leningrad). Historian.* Corresponding Member, Russian Academy of Sciences from 1920. Presniakov graduated in 1893 from the Faculty of History and Philology of St. Petersburg University. From 1907 to 1918 he was privat-docent at the Chair of Russian History of the said University. His study of inter-appanage princely relations is of relevance to international law.[43]

Историко-критическое исследование [Struggle for Livonia between Moscow and Rzeczpospolita (1570-1582). Critical Historical Study] (Spb., 1904).

41 S. F. Platonov, Великий Новгород до его подчинения Москве в 1478 и после подчинения до Ништадского мира 1721 г. [Great Novgorod Before its Subordination to Moscow in 1478 and After Subordination to the Peace of Nystad of 1721 (Novgorod, 1916); Platonov, Review of N. D. Chechulin, Внешняя политика России в начале царствования Екатерины II (1762-1774). СПб. 1896 [Foreign Policy of Russia at the Beginning of the Reign of Catherine II (1762-1774) (Spb., 1896], in Журнал Министерства народного просвещения [Journal of the Ministry of Public Enlightenment], no. 1 (1897), pp. 170-175; no. 2 (1897), pp. 163-177.

42 M. A. Polievktov, Балтийский вопрос в русской политике после Ништадтского мира (1721-1725) [The Baltic Question in Russian Policy After the Peace of Nystad (1721-1725)] (Spb., 1907); Polievktov, «Герцог де Лирия и его проект учреждения испанского консульства в России» [Duke of Liria and His Project of Establishing a Spanish Consulate in Russia], Сборник статей, посвященных С. Ф. Платонову [Collected Articles Dedicated to S. F. Platonov] (Spb., 1911), pp. 375-414; Polievktov, «Гольштинский вопрос и политика России на Балтийском море в первую половину XVIII столетия» [Holstein Question and Policy of Russia on the Baltic Sea in the First Half of the XVIII Century], Русская старина [Russian Antiquity], no. 1 (1907), pp. 199-219; no. 3 (1907), pp. 643-667; no. 6 (1907), pp. 482-503; no. 11 (1907), pp. 413-425; Polievktov, Проект союза России с Сардинским королевством в царствование императора Павла I [Project of an Alliance of Russia with the Kingdom of Sardinia in the Reign of Emperor Paul I] (Spb., 1902).

43 A. E. Presniakov, Образование Великорусского государства. Очерки по истории XIII-XV столетий [Formation of the Great Russian State. Survey of History from the XIII to XV Centuries] (Pg., 1918).

Mikhail Ivanovich Rostovtsev (Rostovtzeff) *(29 October 1870, b. Zhytomyr – 20 October 1952, d. New Haven, Connecticut).* Historian of ancient Greece and Rome. Academician, Russian Academy of Sciences; sometime President, American Historical Association; honorary doctorates of many universities. Having begun his university studies at Kyiv, Rostovtsev graduated in 1892 from the Faculty of History and Philology of St. Petersburg University. From 1899 to 1918, privat-docent and professor, Chair of Classical Philology, of the said University. In 1918 he emigrated, first to Sweden, then to England, and in 1920 to the United States, where he accepted a chair at the University of Wisconsin-Madison before moving on to Yale University in 1925, where he taught until his retirement in 1944.[44] Two of his works are of interest to international law.[45]

Sergei Mikhailovich Seredonin *(30 August 1860, b. St. Petersburg – 26 July 1914, d. Krasnnoe, Iaroslavl Region).* Historian. Seredonini graduated in 1883 from the Faculty of History and Philology of St. Petersburg University and from 1892 to 1914 was employed as privat-docent at the Chair of Russian History of the said University. Of relevance to international law was a Report delivered on 12 March 1912 to the Russian Historical Society on the political reasons for the War of 1812 against Napoleon.[46]

Evgenii Frantsevich Shmurlo *(29 December 1853 – 7 April 1934).* Historian. Corresponding Member, Russian Academy of Sciences. Initially enrolled in 1874 at the Law Faculty of St. Petersburg University, but transferred to the Faculty of History and Philology, from which he graduated in 1879. From 1889 to 1891 he was employed as privat-docent at the Chair of Russian History in the said University, but from 1891 to 1903 served as professor at the Chair of Russian History in Iurev University. From 1903 he served as a correspondent of the Russian Academy of Sciences in Rome attached to the Vatican Archive, being elected to as Corresponding Member of the Russian Academy of Sciences in 1911. He emigrated to Italy in 1918 and on to Czechoslovakia in 1924. Of interest to international law were his collected documents and descriptions of Italian archives on Russo-Italian diplomatic relations.[47]

[44] On Rostovtsev, see G. W. Bowersock, “Rostovtzeff in Madison”, *American Scholar*, LV (1986), pp. 391-400; Arnaldo Momigliano, “M. I. Rostovtzeff”, *The Cambridge Journal*, VII (1954), pp. 334-346; M. A. Wes, *Michael Rosatoovtzeff, Historian in Exile: Russian Roots in an American Context* (Stuttgart, 1990); G. S. Starodubtsev, Международно-правовая наука российской эмиграции [International Legal Science of Russian Emigration] (M., 2000), pp. 27-28.

[45] M. I. Rostovtsev, Национальное и мировое государство [National and World State] (M., 1915); Rostovtsev, Рождение Римской империи [The Birth of the Roman Empire] (Pg., 1918).

[46] S. M. Seredonin, Политические причины войны 1812-го года [Political Reasons for the War of 1812] (Spb., 1912).

[47] E. F. Shmurlo, Восток и Запад в русской истории [East and West in Russian History] (Iu-

Ivan Petrovich Shulgin *(15 November 1784, b. Kostroma Governate – 12 May 1869, d. St. Petersburg).* Historian. Academician, Russian Academy of Sciences. Shulgin graduated in 1814 from the Chief Pedagogical Institute in St. Petersburg. From 1833 to 1843 he served as professor at the Chair of Universal History, Dean of the Faculty of History and Philology, and Rector of St. Petersburg University. His work on the history of the European political system is relevant to international law.[48]

Evgenii Viktorovich (Grigorii Vigdorovich) Tarle *(8 November 1874, b. Kyiv – 5 January 1955, d. Moscow).* Historian. Academician, USSR Academy of Sciences. Tarle graduated in 1896 from the Faculty of History and Philology of St. Vladimir Kyiv University. Fromm 1903 to 1913 he was privat-docent and from 1918 to 1930 professor at the Chair of Universal History of St. Petersburg University. He prepared an anthology of articles and documents useful for international lawyers.[49]

Aleksandr Antonovich Tsagareli *(9 December 1844 – 12 November 1929, d. Tiflis, Georgia).* Historian and philologist. Tsagareli studied from 1868 to 1870 at the Faculty of History and Philology of St. Petersburg University and then spent two years in German universities pursuing language studies. He graduated from St. Petersburg University in 1872. From 1872 to 1916 he was privat-docent, docent, and professor at the Chair of Armenian and Georgian Languages of the said University. His works on Russian relations with the Caucasus are of interest to international law.[50]

Nikolai Gerasimovich Ustrialov *(16 May 1805, b. Bogoroditskoe, Orlov Governate – 20 June 1870, d. Tsarskoe selo).* Historian. Academician, Russian Academy of Sciences. Ustrialov graduated in 1824 from the Faculty of History and Philology of St. Petersburg University and served from 1830

rev, 1895); Shmurlo, Россия и Италия: Сборник исторических материалов и исследований, касающихся сношений России с Италией [Russia and Italy: Collection of Historical Materials and Studies Concerning the Relations of Russia with Italy] (Spb., 1907-1915). 3 vols. in 6.

48 I. P. Shulgin, История политической системы европейских государств (в течение трех последних столетий) [History of the Political System of European States (During the Three Last Centuries)] (Spb., 183?). 483 p. (lithographic reproduction of handwritten text).

49 E. V. Tarle, Запад и Россия. Статьи и документы из истории XVIII – XX вв. [The West and Russia. Articles and Documents from the History of the XVIII to XX Centuries] (Pg., 1918).

50 A. A. Tsagareli, Сношения России с Кавказом в XVI-XVIII столетиях [Relations of Russia with the Caucasus in the XVI-XVIII Centuries] (Spb., 1891); Tsagareli, Переписка грузинских царей и владетельных князей с государями российскими в XVIII столетии [Correspondence of the Georgian Tsars and Sovereign Princes with Russian Sovereigns in the XVIII Century] (Spb., 1890); Tsagareli, Грамоты и другие исторические документы XVIII столетии, относящиеся к Грузии [Instruments and Other Historical Documents of the XVIII Century Relating to Georgia] (Spb., 1891-1898). 2 vols. in 3.

to 1844 as lecturer, junior scientific associate, and professor at the Chair of Russian History and Dean of the Faculty of the said University. His work on the Grand Principality of Lithuania is of international legal interest.[51]

Vasilii Grigorevich Vasilevskii *(2 February 1838, b. Ilinskoe, Iaroslavl Governate – 25 May 1899, d. Florence, Italy).* Specialist in Byzantine studies. Academician, Russian Academy of Sciences. Vasilevskii graduated in 1860 from the Faculty of History and Philology of St. Petersburg University. He served as privat-docent and professor from 1870 to his death in 1899 at the Chair of Universal History of the said University. Author of works on relations between Byzantium and Pechengs, trade of medieval Kyiv, and Baltic affairs.[52]

Georgii Vladimirovich Vernadskii (George Vernadsky) *(20 August 1887, b. St. Petersburg – 12 June 1973, d. New Haven, Connecticut).* Leading American historian of Russia, early proponent of Eurasianism. Vernadsky studied history at Moscow University, graduating in 1910, moving to St. Petersburg University where he was privat-docent from 1913 to 1917 at the Chair of Russian History. His magister dissertation was devoted to the consequences of Freemasonry for the Russian Enlightenment. Not a supporter of Bolshevism, he lectured for a year after the 1917 October Revolution at the University of Perm, then moved on to Kyiv and Simferopol. In 1920 he left Russia for Istanbul, then to Athens, and in 1921 on to Prague, where he taught for four years at the Russian School of Law. In 1927 he was appointed Research Associate in History at Yale University, elevated in 1946 to a full professorship, which he held until his retirement in 1955. Diplomatic history was a special interest, and he published several works of international-legal interest.[53]

[51] N. G. Ustrialov, Исследование вопроса, какое место в русской истории должно занимать Великое княжество Литовское? [Study of the Question of What Place in Russian History Should the Grand Principality of Lithuania Occupy?] (Spb., 1839).

[52] V. G. Vasilevskii, «Византия и печенеги (1048-1094)» [Byzantium and the Pechengs (1048-1094)], Журнал Министерства народного просвещения [Journal of the Ministry of Public Enlightenment], Part 164 (II) (1872), pp. 116-165, 243-332; reprinted in Vasilevskii, Труды [Works] (Spb., 1908), I,, pp. 1-175; Vasilevskii, Древняя торговля Киева с Регенбургом [Ancient Trade of Kyiv with Regenburg] (Spb., 1888); Vasilevskii, Review of Балтийский вопрос в XVI и XVII столетиях (1544-1648) [The Baltic Question in the XVI and XVII Centuries (1544-1648)]. Spb., 1893-1894. 2 vols.; Акты и письма к истории Балтийского вопроса в XVI и XVII столетиях [Acts and Letters on the History of the Baltic Question in the XVI and XVII Centuries] Spb., 1896. 2 vols.] (Spb., 1896).

[53] G. V. Vernadskii, Против Солнца. Распространение Русского государства к Востоку [Against the Sun. Extension of the Russian State to the East] (M., 1914); Vernadsky, *Political and Diplomatic History of Russia* (1936); Vernadsky, *Medieval Russian Laws* (New York, 1947).

Egor Egorovich Zamyslovskii *(18 June 1841, b. Grodno (now Belarus) – 21 May 1896, d. St. Petersburg).* Specialist in Russian medieval history, Corresponding Member of the Russian Academy of Sciences. Zamyslovskii graduated in 1862 from the Faculty of History and Philology of St. Petersburg University. From 1871 to 1890 he was privat-docent and professor at the Chair of Russian History of the said University. He touched upon international legal issues in his many works on Russian foreign relations under Ivan the Terrible and Feodor Alekseevich.[54]

Aleksandr Ivanovich Zaozerskii *(21 March 1874, b. Apukhtino, Tver Governate – 1 October 1941, d. Leontevskoe, Iaroslavl Region).* Historian specializing on the period of Muscovy. Zaozerskii graduated in 1910 from the Faculty of History and Philology of St. Petersburg University. From 1915 to 1923 he was privat-docent and then professor at the Chair of Russian History of the said University. He produced several works on the diplomacy of Muscovy.[55]

Valentin Alekseevich Zhukovskii *(6 May 1858, b. Voronezh – 17 January 1918, d. Petrograd).* Orientalist specializing in Persian language and literature, ethnography, and history, Corresponding Member of the Russian Academy of Sciences. Zhukovskii graduated in 1880 from the Faculty of Oriental Languages of St. Petersburg University. From 1886 to 1918 he was privat-docent and professor at the Chair of Persian Language of St. Petersburg University and from 1902 to 1911, Dean of the Faculty. Among his diverse interests were the Russian consul in Persia and the Panama Canal.[56]

[54] E. E. Zamyslovskii, «О сношениях с Западом при Иоанне Грозном» [On Relations with the West Under Ivan the Terrible], Русский вестник [Russian Herald], no. 4 (1889); Zamyslovskii, «О сношениях России с Англией в царствование Ивана Грозного» [On Relations of Russia with England in the Reign of Ivan the Terrible], Древняя и Новая Россия [Ancient and New Russia], no. 6 (1876), pp. 160-173; Zamyslovskii, «Сношения России с Польшей в царствование Феодора Алексеевича» [On Relations of Russia with Poland in the Reign of Feodor Alekseevich], Журнал Министерства народного просвещения [Journal of the Ministry of Public Enlightenment], no. 1 (1888), pp. 1-23; no. 2 (1888); no. 3 (1888), pp. 161-197; Zamyslovskii, Сношения России с Польшей в царствование Феодора Алексеевича [Relations of Russia with Poland in the Reign of Fedor Alekseevich] (Spb., 1888); Zamyslovskii, Сношения России с Швецией и Данией в царствование Федора Алексеевича [Relations of Russia with Sweden and Denmark in the Reign of Fedor Alekseevich] (Spb., 1889).

[55] A. I. Zaozerskii, «К характеристике Московской дипломатии XVII века» [On the Characteristics of Muscovite Diplomacy of the XVII Century], Сборник статей, посвященных С. Ф. Платонову [Collected Articles Dedicated to S. F. Platonov] (Spb., 1911), pp. 335-355; Zaozerskii, К характеристике Московской дипломатии XVII века [On the Characteristics of Muscovite Diplomacy of the XVII Century] (Spb., 1911); Zaozerskii, «Ордин-Нащокин Афанасий Лаврентьевич» [Ordin-Nashchokin, Afanasii Lavrentevich], Новый энциклопедический словарь [New Encyclopedic Dictionary], XXIX, cols. 630-634.

[56] V. A. Zhukovskii, Русский императорский консул Ф. А. Бакулнт в изучении бабизма [Russian Imperial Consul F. A. Bakulin in the Study of Babism] (Pg., 1917); Zhukovskii, Панамский канал, его история и сооружение [The Panama Canal, its History and Construction] (Pg., 1917).

Chapter 14

Russian Group of International Union of Penal Law

attached to St. Petersburg Law Society

Reference has been made above to individual Russian jurists active in forming the Russian Group of the International Union of Penal Law. The Group is of sufficient moment to deserve separate discussion as an integral part of the St. Petersburg School of Law. The Group was attached to St. Petersburg University, having been founded by University personnel in 1897. Foinitskii took the initiative to establish the Group. Russian participation in the International Union was one of the early and major instances of sustained Russian involvement in what today would be called "international legal space". Both legal scholars and legal practitioners were involved. Russia made its own contributions to this domain of legal science, notwithstanding a negative image abroad for repressive penological practices associated with political offenses, and in turn was influenced by deliberations and discussions within the International Union.

The International Union was founded in 1888 by criminal law specialists from the academic world and governmental agencies in Europe and North America, including Russia. The founders hoped to encourage the "approximation, harmonization, and unification" of criminal legislation and prepare agreed international legal principles and norms in this sphere. The creation of the International Union had been preceded more than four decades earlier by the initiation from time to time of international penitentiary congresses. They were heavily attended by governmental officials, which many believed was a disincentive to the free exchange of views, the agreeing of conceptual positions, and the adoption of concrete decisions on the matters being discussed. The solution was a separate permanent organization of criminal law specialists.[1]

The International Union appealed to all States to cooperate in the cause of improving international criminal law, to undertake measures to study and suppress international crimes by conducting international police measures agreed by States. The organization was not merely to improve methods of prosecuting criminals, but also to study the causes of national and international crimes.

The International Union's principal form of activity was periodically convened congresses or conferences, initially every year and, from 1897, once every two or three years. In all before the First World War twelve congresses were held: Brussels (1889); Berne (1890); Christiana (1891); Paris (1893); Antwerp (1894); Linz (1895); Lisbon (1897); Budapest (1899); St. Petersburg (1902); Hamburg (1905); Brussels (1910); and Copenhagen (1913).[2] The agenda of the congresses included

[1] I. Ia. Foinitskii, «Международный союз уголовного права» [International Union of Criminal Law], Юридический вестник [Legal Herald], VI(1), no. 9 (September 1890), p. 4.

[2] Liublinskii, Международные съезды по вопросам уголовного права за десять лет (1905-1915) [International Congresses on Questions of Criminal Law for Ten Years (1905-1915)] (Pg., 1915).

general issues of criminal law and criminal policy of States and topical specific issues: complicity, rehabilitation, responsibility and punishment of minors, conditional conviction, execution of punishments, short-term confinement and measures to replace it; recidivism, protection over persons released from confinement, education on criminal law, the training of practitioners, among others.

National groups which operated independently but within the framework of the International Union were organized in a number of countries. Their aim was to promote the development of new orientations in the science of criminal law, prepare Congress materials in advance for regular sessions, assist in putting forward draft decisions and recommendations for consideration of the congresses and, once a Congress had adopted a decision or recommendation, to seek its implementation in their respective country. They also prepared legislative initiatives for consideration in their own country.

Russian criminal law specialists, having taken part in the International Union from its inception, decided to create their own Russian Group in 1897.[3] The Russian Group was attached to the Law Society, which had existed since 23 February 1877.[4] The Charter of the Russian Group was confirmed by the Minister of Public Enlightenment on 5 June 1897.[5] Article 1 of the Charter provided that "The Russian Group of the International Union of Penal and Penitentiary Law shall be founded … for the scientific working out, dissemination, and application of the provisions of criminal law corresponding to the tasks of the Union and conditions of Russian life".

These aims were clarified in Article 3 of the Charter:

> The Russian Group shall collect materials with regard to questions to be discussed by the Union, disseminate scientifically worked out provisions of criminal law by means of the press, public lectures, conversations, and so on, prepare Russian reports for congresses of the International Union, and resolve questions to be transferred by the Union for discussion of groups or initiated by the group itself for submission to the Council.

The leadership of the Russian Group was entrusted to a Committee consisting of a Chairman and three members (secretary, treasurer, and librarian) elected for a term of two years (Article 4, Charter). Meetings of the Russian Group were to be convened by the Committee no less than once a year. Questions were discussed at

[3] The Protocol of the session of the Committee of the Russian Group of the International Union of Penal and Penitentiary Law, held 25 November 1897, was published in the Журнал Министерства юстиции [Journal of the Ministry of Justice], no. 10 (1897), p. 362.

[4] There is a substantial literature on the Law Society attached to St. Petersburg University. See «К двадцатипятилетию деятельности Юридического общества при Императорском Санкт-Петербургском университете» [On the Twenty-Fifth Anniversary of Activity of the Law Society attached to the Imperial St. Petersburg University], Журнал Министерства юстиции [Journal of the Ministry of Justice], no. 2 (1902), pp. 247-259.

[5] The Charter, sometimes called the Statute, was published in the Журнал Юридического общества при Императорском Санкт-Петербургском университете [Journal of the Law Society attached to the Imperial St. Petersburg University], no. 7 (1897), p. 1-2.

meeting submitted by the Union or initiated by the Group itself (Article 5, Charter). The initiator of the Russian Group, Professor I. Ia. Foinitskii, was elected the first Chairman and also Chairman of the Central Committee of the International Union of Penal and Penitentiary Law. According to the List of members of the Russian Group, at the time of its creation two members of the Group represented St. Petersburg University: Professor I. Ia. Foinitskii and I. A. Ivanovskii.[6]

By 1902 membership of the Russian Group had increased to 253 members, of whom sixteen were from St. Petersburg University.[7] When the Russian Group wound up, on 1 January 1914, it had 330 members, of whom 155 were from the St. Petersburg Law Society.

The first session of the Russian Group on 25 November 1897 determined the questions to be addressed in priority: conditional conviction and conditional early release.[8] Having agreed its position on these issues, the Russian Group should have submitted it to the International Union of Penal and Penitentiary Law. The issue, however, generated a sharply divided discussion within the Group. Conditional conviction was considered at the First Congress of the Russian Group held at St. Petersburg in 1899. The Congress discussed the essence and forms of conditional conviction, world practice, the conditions and procedures for its application, the organization of a probation period, the consequences of application – all of which generated sharp controversy, including among those from St. Petersburg University.

Zhizhilenko, for example, said that the purpose of a conditional conviction is to remove the "incidental criminal" who has committed an offense for the first time from the deleterious influence of prison and place him in reliable hands so that he returns to an honorable life.[9] On the other hand, N. D. Sergeevskii pointed out that the actual conditional conviction comes down to granting the possibility for a certain interval of time to commit one criminal act without punishment.[10] By a majority vote the Congress of the Russian Group approved the institution of conditional conviction and considered it desirable to implement the introduction thereof as soon as possible.[11]

[6] Международный союз криминалистов. Русская группа [International Union of Penal and Penitentiary Law. Russian Group] (Spb., 1897), pp. 5-6.

[7] Международный союз криминалистов. Список членов Русской группы Международного союза криминалистов [International Union of Penal and Penitentiary Law. List of Members of the Russian Group of the International Union of Penal and Penitentiary Law] (Spb., 1902). 15 p.

[8] Note 3 above, p. 362.

[9] A. A. Zhizhilenko, «Программа вопросов по содержанию института условного осуждения (Составлена для Русской группы Международного союза криминалистов» [Program of Questions Relating to the Content of the Institution of Criminal Conviction (Drawn Up for the Russian Group of the International Union of Penal and Penitentiary Law)], Журнал Министерства юстиции [Journal of the Ministry of Justice], no. 5 (1898), p. 360.

[10] See the Protocols of the Sessions of the Committee Журнал Министерства юстиции [Journal of the Ministry of Justice], no. 2 (1899), p. 65 (Annex).

[11] Ibid., p. 82. Also see S. M. Kostina, «Роль Русской группы Международного союза

Thereafter, the congresses of the Russian Group considered topical issues of criminal law and practice, international cooperation in combatting crime, prepared, confirmed, and submitted to congresses of the International Union proposals and draft decisions on various problems of criminal law, determined the principal orientations for the improvement of criminal and criminal procedure legislation and of judicial practice, chose the problems and topics for undertaking scientific research, and heard reports concerning the results.

The role of the Russian Group in developing criminal policy within Russia and in influencing the positions of the International Union was considered to be significant. The Russian Group sought to reform Russian legislation on criminal law, criminal procedure, and penal policy by adapting the best ideas approved by the International Union, having regard to foreign experience where relevant and instructive.[12]

Representatives of the Russian Group devoted considerable attention to coordinating the efforts of States in developing measures to combat international organized crime. Liublinskii constantly emphasized that crime was becoming increasingly international. He noted that a special class of traveling individuals with criminal intent were active in a number of countries. The efforts of States against these individuals, he believed, were mostly unsuccessful because of complicated international police relations and the lack of a uniform search organization, disagreements over the rules for extradition, definitions of individual crimes, rules relating to complicity, jurisdiction, and so on.[13] And the Congresses periodically contemplated certain measures to enhance the effectiveness of this struggle. A resolution of the Hamburg Congress in 1905 acknowledged the need to take agreed international measures against crime. It was recommended to establish central agencies in all States within the police departments of large cities. These central agencies were intended to collect all information about international crimes and criminals and to exchange the information with other States with a view to taking measures for the prevention of crimes and punishment of criminals. Many of these proposals were later implemented within the League of Nations, United Nations, and Interpol.

Members of the Russian Group attended international penal congresses held in London (1872), Stockholm (1878), Rome (1885), St. Petersburg (1890), Paris (1895), Budapest (1905), and Washington D. C. (1910).

криминалистов в истории становления института условного осуждения в дореволюционной России» [Role of the Russian Group of the International Union of Penal and Penitentiary Law in the History of the Development of the Institution of Conditional Conviction in Prerevolutionary Russia], Право: история, теория, практика [Law: History, Theory, Practice] (Spb., 2011), pp. 33-37.

[12] V. S. Miridonova, «Научно-исследовательская деятельность Санкт-Петербургского юридического общества» [Scientific-Research Activity of the St. Petersburg Law Society], Вестник Нижегородского университета им. Н. И. Лобачевского. Серия: Право [Herald of the N. I. Lobachevskii Nizhnii-Novgorod University: Series Law], no. 1 (2002), p. 63.

[13] Liublinskii, «О деятельности Международного союза криминалистов в период 1902-1908 гг.» [On the Activity of the International Penal and Penitentiary Union in 19021908], Право [Law] no. 10 (1909), cols. 630-642.

The First World War, the Revolutions of 1917, and the Russian Civil War put an end to international cooperation in criminal law. The activities of the Russian Group ceased, and research in the world of criminal policy diminished drastically. The International Union experienced a similar fate for similar but different reasons and was not reconstituted until the mid-1920s.

ELSEWHERE IN ST. PETERSBURG

Chapter 15

Individuals Elsewhere in St. Petersburg Contributing to International Law

§15.1. *Imperial Alexander Lycée*

The Imperial Alexander (originally, Tsarskoe selo) Lycée was founded in 1810, opening on 19(31) October 1811, as the elite Russian institution of higher education for the privileged classes. Originally, the Lycée was placed within the jurisdiction of the Ministry of Public Enlightenment, but in 1822 was made subordinate to the military.

On 6 September 1843 the Lycée moved from Tsarskoe selo, a suburb of St. Petersburg, to the center of the City, taking over the premise of the Alexander Orphan's Home. By order of Emperor Nicholas I, the Lycée was renamed in honor of its founder and became the Imperial Alexander Lycée.

The Lycée was a closed educational institution in the sense that it admitted only children of the Russian ancestral nobility. Admission took place every three years; children aged ten to fourteen were eligible for consideration on the basis of exemplary morality and sound health. At the outset, the number of pupils admitted was dependent on an appropriation from the State Treasury. At the end of the nineteenth century admission was extended to pupils able to pay their own way. In 1902, for example, of 220 pupils admitted, fifty were supported by the Treasury and 170 paid tuition. Those supported by the Treasury fell into three groups: (1) graduates of senior preparatory classes by petition of their parents; (2) pupils who distinguished themselves at classical gymnasia in St. Petersburg and were recommended by pedagogical councils; and (3) children of generals and civil servants not lower than a privy State counselor.

The course of study was initially six years (two three-year courses; in 1836, four courses for eighteen months each). In 1877 the Lycée was transformed into a six-class program.

Unlike comparable European institutions which readied graduates for entry into universities, the Alexander Lycée provided training equivalent to that of a university. Between 1817 and 1916, the Lycée graduated 1,919 individuals (72 cycles of admission). Depending on the quality of their results, Lycée graduates took positions in State service at levels from the fourteenth to the ninth category or enlisted in the military on the same conditions as graduates from the Corps of Pages – the most prestigious military academy in Imperial Russia.

The instructional syllabus of the Lycée was oriented towards the humanities and the law. Following much reconsideration and revision, the instructional program included the same subjects as the University Law Faculty. Knowledge of international law the pupils received from Professor A. P. Kunitsyn, and then from professors also employed by St. Petersburg University – I. I. Ivanovskii, N. M.

Korkunov, F. F. Martens, A. A. Pilenko, and I. A. Ivanovsksii – the first two of which published their lectures at the Lycée.[1]

From 1912 to 1914 the professor *extraordinarius* (by joint appointment) of international law was Boris E. Nolde, also teaching at the Polytechnic Institute, and a graduate of the St. Petersburg University Chair of International Law.

One of those who taught international law at the Alexander Lycée was a graduate of that institution.

Vladimir Pavlovich Bezobrazov *(15 January 1828, b. Vladimir – 10 September 1889, d. Noskovo, Dmitrovskii uezd, Moscow Governate).*

Bezobrazov was born in Vladimir on 3(15) January 1828 and died from gangrene of the foot following an unsuccessful operation on 10 September 1889, the father of three sons and three daughters. He married on 5 September 1852 the daughter of a Privy Counsellor, Elizaveta Dmitrievna Maslova (1836-1881).

Well-known as an economist, publicist, editor, senator, professor of political economy and financial law at the Imperial Alexander Lycee, and member of the Academy of Sciences,[2] he entered State service in 1847 at the State Chancellery;

[1] See I. I. Ivanovskii, Курс международного права и дипломации, преподаваемый в Императорском Александровском лицее [Course of International Law and Diplomacy Taught at the Imperial Alexander Lycée] (lithographed manuscript; Spb., 1860); Ivanovskii, Международное право. Лекции, читанные в Императорском Александровском лицее. 1876-1877 гг. [International Law. Lectures Delivered at the Imperial Alexander Lycée. 1876-1877 (lithographed manuscript; Spb., 1877); N. M. Korkunov, Право войны: Лекции, чит. проф. Коркуновым в 1883-1884 г. в I кл. Алекс. лицея [Law of War: Lectures Delivered by Professor Korkunov in 1883-1884 to the First Class of the Alexander Lycée] (Spb., [1884]); Korkunov, Лекции по международному праву, читанные проф. Коркуновым в 1-м классе Алекс. лицея 1884/5 года [Lectures on International Law Delivered by Professor Korkunov to the First Class of the Alexander Lycée 1884/5] ([Spb., 1885]).

[2] See the obituary of Bezobrazov by F. de Martens, "M. Vladimir de Besobrasof", *Annuaire de l'Institut de droit international*, XII (1892-1894), pp. 332-335; V. M. Koretsky, "Vladimir P. Besobrasof (1828-1889)", *Institut de Droit International, Livre du Centenaire 1893-1973* (1973), pp. 32-44; Koretsky, «Академик В. П. Безобразов в институте международного права» [Academician V. P. Bezobrazov in the Institute of International Law", Советский ежегодник международного права 1972 [Soviet Yearbook of International Law 1972] (1974), reprinted in V. N. Denysov (ed.), В. М. Корецкий: Избранные труды [V. M. Koretsky: Selected Works] (1989), II, pp. 337-344; N. A. Murzanov, Словарь русских сенаторов 1711-1917 гг. Материалы для биографий [Dictionary of Russian Senators 1711-1917. Materials for Biographies] (2011), p. 45; G. I. Starodubtsev, Международно-правовая наука российской эмиграции [International-Legal Science of Russian Emigration] (M., 2000), p. 16; V. S. Ivanenko, Санкт-Петербургская школа международного права [St. Petersburg School of International Law] (3d rev. ed.; 2023), pp. 575-576; V. N. Denysov, «Безобразов Володимир Павлович» [Bezobrazov, Volodymyr Pavlovich], in V. N. Denysov and Iu. S. Shemshuchenko (eds.), Енциклопедія міжнародного права [Encyclopedia of International Law] (2014-2019), I, pp. 225-228; W. E. Butler, "Vladimir Pavlovich Bezobrazov: Co-Founder of the Institute of International Law", *Jus Gentium: Journal of International Legal History*, VIII (2023), pp. 297-301. Koretsky's tribute to Bezobrazov, given his early and long-term interest in international economic law, places special emphasis on the Bezobrazov contributions to political economy and law.

from 1849 worked in the Department of Various Duties and Charges of the Ministry of Finances; transferred in 1854 to the Ministry of State Properties, where he was a section head and in 1857 became editor of the Журнал Министерства государственныйх имуществ [Journal of the Ministry of State Properties].[3] From 1860 he became an official on special assignment of the Ministry of Finances, where he traveled throughout the country extensively to collect information on landowner relations with land banks, financial turnover, and other statistical data on industry, trade, and factory production; he also was sent abroad to investigate models of financial management in banking. During the 1850-60s, he was an acknowledged supporter of abolishing serfdom.

He was elected to the Russian Academy of Sciences in 1867, and in 1869 became Professor of Political Economy and Financial Law at the Alexander Lycée, where he taught until December 1878. Well connected to the Palace, in 1870 he taught political economy and State finances to Grand Princes Aleksei Aleksandrovich and Nikolai Konstantinovich, and in 1876 to Sergei Aleksandrovich and Konstantin Konstantinovich. He was appointed a Privy Counsellor on 1 December 1874 and from 1 January 1885 was a member of the Ruling Senate in the Department of Heraldry.

From 1873 to 1880 he acted as the publisher of an important encyclopedic work, the Сборник государственных знаний [Collection of State Knowledge]. The eight volumes included articles by leading Russian international lawyers, among them F. F. Martens, I. E. Andreevskii, M. I. Gorchakov, A. D. Gradovskii, and the editor himself.[4]

He published widely on economic, financial, political, and social topics, including international relations more than international law. Koretsky observed that: "The interest of Bezobrazov in problems of foreign policy, the role of Russia in Europe and the Orient, and issues of foreign trade led him, an economist, to problems of international law. This was a natural path".[5]

Nonetheless, by background and experience Bezobrazov was an unexpected and unlikely Russian jurist to be invited by Europeans to act as a co-founder of the Institut de droit international. Why and how he should have been chosen for this task remains something of a mystery, but he was invited by foreign colleagues in August 1873 in his professorial capacity to take part on behalf of Russian colleagues in discussions to found an international academic body for research on international law. He had published only one brief article in the field of international

[3] In the same year he began to serve as editor of the Вестник императорского русского географического общества [Herald of the Imperial Russian Geographic Society] and in an editorial capacity for nearly two decades on Русский вестник [Russian Herald].

[4] Bezobrazov, «Брюссельская конференция для установления правил и обычаев войны» [Brussels Conference to Establish the Rules and Customs of War], Сборник государственных знаний [Collection of State Knowledge], II, pp. 1-40, which also appeared as a separate pamphlet (Spb., 1875), 42 p. See in general W. E. Butler, *Russia and the International Legal System: A Bibliography of Writings by Russian Jurists on Public and Private International Law to 1917 with References to Publications in Emigration* (2006).

[5] Koretsky, note 2 above, p. 191 (Russian text).

law[6] and was at work on or had just completed a study of war and revolution.[7] He was not regarded in his time or later as an international lawyer, although he was a significant public figure, knowledgeable about international affairs generally and Russian foreign policy, considered to hold progressive views, and well disposed to the emerging discipline of international law.[8]

No doubt the election soon after the Institut de droit international was founded of F. F. Martens (1845-1909) and L. A. Kamarovskii (1846-1912) as members facilitated Bezobrazov in the performance of his international legal representation in that body. He produced one article for a Russian audience on his activities in the Institute, in which he expressed his understanding of the discipline:

> International law is primarily an applied science, and its major issues are not purely theoretical, but questions of the application of general principles of justice to the practical relations of legislation and policy, and therefore by its very procedure as practical questions and very complex ones, they permit discussion, and even need such, among specialists.[9]

§15.2. *Imperial School of Jurisprudence*

The Imperial School of Jurisprudence, founded in 1835 by Prince Petr Georgievich Oldenburgskii (1812-1881) from his own resources, was designed especially to produce graduates for careers in State service. Related to the Emperor Nicholas I, Prince Oldenburgskii submitted his plans for the School directly to the Emperor and received a favorable response both the monarch and Mikhail Mikhailovich Speranskii (1777-1839), whose counsel the Emperor solicited for the project. In his capacity as a member of the Ruling Senate, Oldenburgskii was sensitive to the fundamental changes underway in Russian society and the need for qualified, legally-trained personnel to assist the Government in pursuing appropriate policies.

The School was founded by Edict of the Emperor of 9 May 1835 and placed within the system of the Ministry of Justice. Oldenburgskii acquired and renovated

[6] V. P. Bezobrazov, «Бернский международный конгресс» [Bern International Congress], Современная летопись [Contemporary Chronicle], no. 34 (September, 1865), pp. 1-4.

[7] Bezobrazov, «Война и революция. Очерки нашего времени» [War and Revolution: Outlines of Our Day], Русский вестник [Russian Herald], no. 9 (1872), pp. 157-202; no. 2 (1873), pp. 504-581; no. 4 (1873), p. 429-481; id, Война и революция. Очерки нашего времени (Moscow, 1873). 224 p. Despite its title, this work is more on international politics and economics than law.

[8] See A. A. Dorskaia, «Институт международного права: опыт неофициального научного сообщества» [Institute of International Law: Experience of an Unofficial Scientific Society], Известия Российского государственного педагогического университета им. А. Н. Герцена [News of the Herzen Russian State Pedagogical University], no. 134 (2010), pp. 190-191.

[9] Bezobrazov, Международный институт международного права в Генте [International Institute of International Law in Ghent] (Spb., 1874), p. 3. Also see Bezobrazov, «Институт международного права с 1873 г. по 1876 г.» [Institute of International Law from 1873 to 1876], Журнал Министерства просвещения [Journal of the Ministry of Enlightenment], no. 10 (1876), pp. 170-192.

a premise in central St. Petersburg, duly dedicated on 5 December of the same year with the Emperor and senior officials in attendance of the occasion. 54 students were admitted to the entering class from 292 applicants.

In every sense of the word this was an institution for the elite. Students were no younger than twelve years or older than seventeen. The maximum entering class was one hundred persons. Only children of the ancestral Russian nobility might apply, a requirement gradually but slowly liberalized to extend to other social strata. The full course of study required six years, later extended to seven, and the syllabus was oriented towards a career in State service. Tuition was charged for some, but a limited number of stipends were available. All students boarded in the School, and all classes were held in the same building.

International law was part of the curriculum. Professors F. F. Martens taught that subject from 1871 to 1909, succeeded after his death by M. A. von Taube, from 1909 to 1917.[10]

Graduates were required to spend up to six years within the Ministry of Justice system; those who graduated with distinction were awarded State service ranks of IX or X class. Usually they were assigned to the Chancellery of the Ministry or to the Ruling Senate, and the rest, to the staff of courts in the various governates. During the eight or so decades of its existence, the School graduates more than two thousand jurists, many of whom attained senior public office or appointments in diplomatic service. Professor A. L. Baikov was among the graduates.

The School was liquidated by decision of the Soviet authorities on 18 June 1918.

Among graduates who made a significant contribution to international law was:

Sergei Nikolaevich Tregubov *(24 October 1866, b. St. Petersburg – 29 July 1945, d. Birkenwerder (near Berlin), Germany). Procurator, professor, specialist in criminalistics, military lawyer, senator.*

Life and career. In 1888 Tregubov graduated with the silver medal from the Imperial School of Jurisprudence and accepted a position with the Ministry of Justice. The following year he became a Deputy Procurator in Ferghana, followed by similar postings in Tashkent, Vitebsk, and St. Petersburg. From 1899 he was a Procurator of the Tashkent, then Penza, and from 1902, St. Petersburg district courts. In 1910 he became a senior jurisconsult at the Ministry of Justice and a member of the consultation office attached to the Ministry. From 1915 he was elevated to the Director of the First Department of the Ministry of Justice and during

[10] I. V. Olimpieva, «Профессорско-преподавательский состав Императорского училища правоведения на службе российской юстиции» [Professorial-Lecturer Composition of the Imperial School of Jurisprudence in the Service of Russian Justice], Известия Юго-Западного государственного университета. Серия «История и право» [News of the South-Western State University. Series History and Law], no. 3 (2016), pp. 31-39.

1916 to 1917 acted as a consultant of questions of military justice for the High Command of the Russian Army.

Tregubov was the first in Russia to offer a course on criminalistics as a Professor of Criminal Law at the Alexander Academy of Military Law and at the Imperial School of Jurisprudence. He published several articles on the subject.

In 1916 he joined the First Department of the Ruling Senate and became an auditing senator the following year. He did not support the October 1917 Revolution and joined the White movement. From 1919 he was a member of the Senate of the Armed Forces of the South of Russia – the combined armed formations of the White movement. In 1920 Tregubov emigrated to Serbia and became a professor at Belgrade University. In Belgrade he acted as an advisor to the Ministry of Internal Affairs and served as a member or executive of several émigré organizations of jurists. With respect to international law he compiled and edited an important collection of extradition treaties and an article on espionage.[11]

§15.3. *Alexander Academy of Military Law*

This Academy was one of the oldest institutions of higher education in the Russian Empire with a military profile. Its origins trace back to 26 April 1866, when it was created to train officers and attached to a School for Auditors in St. Petersburg, duly transformed on 30 March 1867 into an Academy of Military Law by behest of Emperor Alexander II. The initial purpose of the Academy, formed during the far-reaching judicial reforms in Russia, was to improve the system of education in military law and train military officer lawyers. The Academy was renamed in 1908 the Alexander Academy in honor of Emperor Alexander III.

In its time the Academy was believed to be the first educational institution in the world dedicated to training officers for careers in military law. The Academy accepted officers no higher than captain from all kinds of forces who had served as an officer for at least four years and were recommended by their respective command.

Completion of the course of study required three years. Officers were selected on the basis of competitive examinations. Intake of students was limited to 45 officers from land forces and no more than five naval officers, together with a small number of supernumerary officers chosen by the Academy with subsequent confirmation by the Minister of War. Beginning in 1880, the Academy trained officers

[11] S. N. Tregubov (comp.), Сборник заключенных Россией действующих конвенций о выдаче преступников и непосредственных сношениях русских пограничных судебных учреждений с иностранными судебными местами. Особое приложение к Настольной книге криминалиста-практика [Collection of Conventions in Force Concluded by Russia on Extradition of Criminals and on Direct Relations of Russian Frontier Judicial Institutions with Foreign Courts: Special Annex to Manual of Criminalist-Practitioner] (Spb., 1908); Tregubov, «Шпионство и соприкасающиеся с ним преступные деяния по закону 5 июля 1912 года» [Espionage and Similar Criminal Acts Under the Law of 5 July 1912], Журнал Министерства юстиции [Journal of the Ministry of Justice], no. 2 (1913), pp. 37-58.

from the Bulgarian and Serbian armies. In all, the Academy graduated about 1,000 military jurists.[12]

The instruction in the Academy was undertaken principally by professors from the Law Faculty of St. Petersburg University. International law was among the eleven subjects taught. The instructor was M. V. Piunovskii, a graduate of the said University Law Faculty, who intended to publish his course of lectures but succeeded in issuing only those dealing with the law of war.

From 1879 to 1896 the Chair of International Law at the Academy was held by N. M. Korkunov, also a Professor at St. Petersburg University (see above) where he lectured on State law. At the Academy, Korkunov also lectured on the comparative State law of foreign countries. His students at the Academy took his lectures on international law down verbatim and published them in lithographed format.[13] In their final form his lectures on international law were transcribed and published by Lieutenant Shidlovskii and became quite well-known, being republished in 2009.[14]

The Soviet authorities closed the Academy of Military Law in December 1917.

Mikhail Vasilevich Piunovskii *(18?-dates unknown). International lawyer, specialist on the law of war.*

Life and career. There is little information on Piunovskii. He enrolled at the Law Faculty of St. Petersburg University in 1865[15] and graduated in 1870,[16] having produced a graduation dissertation on the "Problem of Cognition according to Kant, Fichte, and Hegel and the Closely Related Problem of Morality and Law".

According to Grabar, in 1879 Captain M. V. Piunovskii passed the examination for the magister degree of international law at the Law Faculty of Kharkov University.[17] But the standard reference work on Russian dissertations does not mention

[12] Iu. V. Riazantseva, «Создание, становление и деятельность первой высшей военно-юридической школы в России. К 150-летию Александровской военно-юридической академии» [Creation, Development, and Activity of the First Higher School of Military Law in Russia. On the 150th Anniversary of the Alexander Academy of Military Law], Вестник военного права [Herald of Military Law], no. 1 (2016), pp. 125-132.

[13] N. M. Korkunov, Лекции по международному праву, читанные в Военно-юридической академии в 1883/4 [Lectures on International Law Delivered at the Academy of Military Law in 1883/4 (lithographed manuscript; Spb., 1884); Korkunov, Право войны. Лекции, читанные в Военно-юридической академии в 1881-82 академ. году [Law of War. Lectures delivered at the Academy of Military Law in the 1881-82 Academic Year] (lithographed manuscript; Spb., 1882).

[14] Korkunov, Международное право: Лекции, читанные в Военно-юридической академии [International Law: Lectures Delivered at the Academy of Military Law] (Spb., 1886; reprinted: M., 2009).

[15] ЦГИА СПб., fond 14, opis 5, file 3060.

[16] ЦГИА СПб., fond 14, opis 12, fille 34.

[17] V. E. Grabar, *The History of International Law in Russia 1647-1917: A Bio-Biographical Study*, transl. W. E. Butler (Oxford, 1990), p. 410.

the defense of a magister dissertation by Piunovskii.[18] Nonetheless, it is documented that in 1876-1877 Piunovskii lectured on international law at the Academy of Military Law; the section of his course of lectures on the law of war was published in installments in a leading Russian newspaper between 28 November 1876 and 19 April 1877.[19] Piunovskii's reputation as an international lawyer, however, rests on a collection of materials on the laws and customs of war.[20]

International legal views. Piunovskii's manual on the law of war, published by the Russian Army during the War against Turkey in 1877-1878, took the form of questions and answers, using the 1874 Brussels Declaration concerning the Laws and Customs of War. There were 109 questions with precise responses. The answers to the questions suggest an author with humanitarian values whose views were influenced by F. F. Martens, his teacher at the St. Petersburg University. Piunovskii defined war as an open struggle of two or several armies of two or more hostile States and as a "means by which a dispute is resolved between two or several States" (p. 5). War might commence, in Piunovskii's view, only when a State: (a) violates the law of another State or insults the honor and dignity of its sovereign, government, or the entire nation;; (b) arbitrarily seizes the lands of another State, harms its trade or otherwise violations its material or moral interests; (c) fails to perform obligations assumed and, notwithstanding peaceful demands to perform them, continues with hostile intent and actions to avoid performing its obligations; (d) rejects satisfaction offered by another State (p. 5).

If war cannot be prevented, it must be waged in compliance with the established laws and rules formed over the centuries or consolidated in conventions: "Observance thereof not only makes war itself honorable and in good faith, but delivers to the belligerents important and material advantages" (p. 6). The laws and rules of war concerned these matters addressed in his manual:

(a) the conduct of belligerents relative to the sick, wounded, and killed in all battles, as well as the persons and institutions connected with their fate;

(b) the means by which one may harm the enemy and from whose us one must refrain;

(c) the status of prisoners of war;

(d) the means of intercourse between the belligerent armies;

[18] See G. G. Krichevskii, Магистерские и докторские диссертации, защищенные на юридических факультетах университетов Российской империи (1755-1918). Библиографический указатель [Magister and Doctoral Dissertations Defended at Law Faculties of Universities of the Russian Empire (1755-1918): Bibliographical Index] (Stavropol, 1998).

[19] See M. Piunovskii, «Лекции по международному праву» [Lectures on International Law], Русский инвалид [Russian Invalid], no. 264 (28 November 1876), pp. 2-3 to no. 84 (19 April 1877), pp. 2-3 (titles vary). Butler П121.

[20] Piunovskii, «Законы и правила войны по международному праву» [Laws and Rules of Warfare under International Law], Военный сборник [Military Collection], № 6, отд. 1 (1877) приложение, с. 1-43. Butler П119. Also published separately. Butler П120 [ИНИОН]

(e) the definitions of whose who must be considered combatants and those who are not (combatants and non-combatants), and those who have the right to take advantage of the protection of laws of war and those who may not;

(f) the status of enemy property during war;

(g) the means by which compliance with the laws of war may be ensured (pp. 6-7).

Addressing the question of whether the laws and rules of war must be executed without exception or whether the failure to comply with them is permitted, Piunovskii responded as follows. Non-compliance with the laws and rules of war is possible in two instances: (a) when extreme necessity requires this; or (b) when the opposite party provides occasion for this. In all other instances deviation from the laws and rules of war is not justified. But in some cases even extreme necessity or any other reason would not justify failure to comply with the laws of war – to engage in inhumane and cruel behavior, such as torture or tormenting the enemy, or murdering an armed or unarmed enemy (pp. 6-7).

In his other responses to the questions he raised, Piunovskii set out the provisions of laws and rules for the behavior of belligerents in various situations, demonstrating on the whole a humane approach to legal relations which in the second half of the twentieth century came to be called "international humanitarian law". The same approach was evident in this lecture. Controversial in his time was the right of the general population to resist an approaching enemy or an enemy already occupying territory. Piunovskii said there was no unity of views on this question either in theory or in practice. Many authorities drew no distinction between an uprising against an invading enemy and an "insurrection" against one's own government. In his view, the population had the right, proceeding from sacred patriotic feelings, to rise up against an "occupier", in which case the occupier must not engage in unjustified cruelty and must comply with the laws and rules of war.

§15.4. *Imperial Nikolaev Marine Academy*

The Marine Academy is not merely the oldest military educational institution in Russia, but one of the earliest secular such institutions in the country.[21] The history of the Marine Academy commences with the Marine Guard Academy founded by Peter the Great in 1715 in St. Petersburg on the basis of a navigation school. This was followed in 1827 by the creation of a senior officer class attached to the Marine Cadet Corps, transformed in 1862 into the Academy Course of Marine Sciences within which the international law of the sea was part of the program of instruction. Finally, in 1877 this became the Nikolaev Marine Academy, which in 1910 became an autonomous military instructional and research educational institution.

21 L. A. Ivanashchenko, «Военно-морская академия и развитие международного морского права в России» [The Naval Academy and Development of the International Law of the Sea in Russia], Московский журнал международного права [Moscow Journal of International Law], no. 4 (1994), pp. 117-118.

Instruction was suspended from the outset of the First World War until 1916. Students admitted in November 1916 graduated in 1918. During the Soviet period, the Academy was repeatedly reorganized and continues to function in the Russian Federation as the N. G. Kuznetsov Naval Academy – a naval instructional and research center.

International law formed part of the Academy syllabus from the earliest years. The new Statute on the Nikolaev Marine Academy adopted in 1896 provided for a separate course on the "International Law of the Sea". The first lecturer in the Marine Academy was I. A. Ovchinnikov, who collaborated closely with the Law Society attached to St. Petersburg University and with the Chair of International Law of that University. He was succeeded in 1917 by M. Ia. Rapoport.

Ivan Aleksandrovich Ovchinnikov *(11 November 1865 – 11 December 1917, d. near Sochi). Lt. General, specialist on the law of the sea, professor.*

Life and career. Data on the life and career of Ovchinnikov is scarce and often inconsistent. Russian naval archives have been helpful, as have a few secondary sources.[22] In 1880 he enrolled in the Marine Cadet Corps in St. Petersburg,[23] enlisting in naval service in 1883, graduating from the Corps in 1886,[24] and assigned to sea duty as a midshipman. In 1887 Ovchinnikov undertook a foreign voyage as watch officer on board the frigate *Dmitrii Donskoi* to the coasts of Korea and Japan.

Ovchinnikov graduated in 1892 from the Academy of Military Law.[25] From 1894 to 1895 he attended lectures at the Law Faculty of the University of Lausanne, Switzerland, where the instruction was in the French and German languages. He was appointed a lecturer from 1896 on the international law of the sea at the Nikolaev Marine Academy and at the Marine Cadet Corps, and a year later at the Academy of Military Law. In 1897, having achieved the rank of Lieutenant, Ovchinnikov defended a dissertation at the Academy of Military Law on the law of prize. The official opponents were A. Kh. Golmsten,[26] Professor of Civil Procedure at St. Petersburg University, and M. I. Sveshnikov, privat-docent of State law at the said University. Thereafter, Ovchinnikov advanced successfully in naval service and educational employment.

[22] G. S. Starodubtsev, «Иван Александрович Овчинников (К 130-летию со дня рождения)» [Ivan Aleksandrovich Ovchinnikov (On the 130th Anniversary of His Birth)], Московский журнал международного права [Moscow Journal of International Law], no. 4 (1995), pp. 129-136

[23] РГАВМФ, f. 432, opis 5, file 6576.

[24] РГАВМФ, f. 406, opis 9 (available online).

[25] According to a number of publications, including the Guide to naval archives, Ovchinnikov graduated in 1892. But his name does not appear in the Lists of Academy graduates for the 1880s and 1890s.

[26] Golmsten's review was published in the Журнал Юридического общества при Императорском Санкт-Петербургском университете [Journal of the Law Society attached to the Imperial St. Petersburg University], no. 4 (1897), pp. 12-33.

In 1903 Ovchinnikov became a Lt. Colonel; in 1904 an officer of field rank for special assignments attached to the Head of Chief Naval Headquarters; in 1907, a Colonel; in 1911, a Major General; and in 1915, Lt. General of the Fleet. Ovchinnikov taught the law of the sea until 1917 at the Academy of Military Law and the Nikolaev Marine Academy, from 1910 with the rank of professor *ordinarius*.

During the First World War, Lt. General Ovchinnikov was the head of the Central Information Bureau on Prisoners of War attached to the Russian Red Cross Society.

Ovchinnikov was a member of the Russian delegations to the 1899 Hague Peace Conference, Second Hague Peace Conference in 1907, and international conferences in Brussels (1905) and London (1909).

Ovchinnikov died tragically near Sochi on the Black Sea on 11 December 1917 when he and his wife and her parents were killed by thieves ransacking their dacha.

Grabar wrote that Ovchinnikov "was the most eminent of the Russian specialists on the international law of the sea, especially as regards the law of war".[27]

§15.5. *Others Associated with St. Petersburg*

Some individuals were part of the St. Petersburg School of International Law without a known association with the University or other educational institutions in the city. Among these was a figure known, until recently, solely as the author of a brief monograph on international law: N. S. de Galet.

Nikolai Spiridonovich de Galet *(?-1864, d. St. Petersburg). Author of monograph on international law.*[28]

Life and career. Little is known of this individual. He is presumed to be a foreigner, probably French or Spanish in origin, with a russified forename and patronymic which did not appear on his book and were unknown to his colleagues. In 1860 he published a monograph simply entitled "International Law" in Russian.[29] It received a harsh reception from D. I. Kachenovskii, who characterized the

[27] Grabar, note 17 above, p. 441.

[28] See S. V. Bakhin, "N. S. de Galet: Forgotten Name in the History of Private International Law", *Jus Gentium: Journal of International Legal History*, VI (2021), pp. 133-144. Bakhin suggested that "de Galet" may be a version of "La Gaulette", an island discovered in the early sixteenth century by the Portuguese and later belonging to the Dutch, French, and British and now part of the Republic Mauritius. De Galet was buried on 1 January 1865 at the Smolensk Orthodox Cemetery in St. Petersburg. See Grand Prince Nikolai Mikhailovich, Петербургский некрополь [Petersburg Necropolis] (Spb., 1912), I, p. 528. In the English-speaking world we give Joseph Story credit for inventing the expression "private international law", leaving the interesting issue of whether De Galet took the term from Wheaton or was familiar with Story.

[29] N. S. de Galet, Международное право [International Law] (Spb., Tip. Eduarda Pratsa, 1860). 139 p. Butler Д38.

volume as produced by "… a foreigner who had a poor command of the Russian language, expounded his views aphoristically and almost incomprehensibly".[30] Grabar called the review a "damaging but deserved critique" of a work "which contained many flagrant errors and which was a 'watered down compilation' from Wheaton, whose views he distorted".[31]

Most of the monograph is devoted to public international law, especially the law of the sea (blockade, right to fly a flag, inspection of cargo on the high seas, exterritoriality of warships, jurisdiction over crimes committed on a merchant ship, and others). Chapter Five, devoted to "civil and criminal law", does touch upon certain conflicts of law issues. For all of his faults, de Galet seems to be the first to use the expression "private international law" in the Russian language – certainly earlier than other individuals previously given credit for this. The relevant passage is as follows:

> In all instances of a court proceeding, a [foreign subject] is subject to that law to which he is subject in the views of jurists, or to complex laws to which his case belongs. This law is called *private international law*. As a consequence of this law, no State has the right to ownership even of its own subject if he is outside this State, for otherwise this would be interference to the prejudice of international law …[32]

De Galet was thus of the opinion that private international law and international civil procedure were subject to public international law.

Stepanov is rightly regarded primarily as an international lawyer based in Ukraine, for he spent most of his career at Kharkov University. A career in St. Petersburg was within his contemplation, however, and he took employment in that city from 1830 to 1831 before returning to Kharkov. For our purposes, that is time enough to include him in the present volume.

Tikhon Fedorovich Stepanov *(1795, b. Voronezh – 1847, d. Kharkov). Specialized in political economy and the law of nations; author of first Russian textbook on international law.*

Life and career. Born at Voronezh, Russia,[33] Stepanov completed studies at the Voronezh Theological Seminar in 1814 and then enrolled at Kharkov University in

[30] Журнал Министерства юстиции [Journal of the Ministry of Justice], XVI, no. 4 (1863), pt. 2, pp. 207-228.

[31] Grabar, note 17 above, p. 468.

[32] Galet, note 29 above, pp. 48-49.

[33] This biographical sketch draws upon Grabar, note 17 above; V. S. Semenov and N. N. Ulianova, «Первый русский курс международного права» [First Russian Course of International Law], Советский ежегодник международного права 1960 [Soviet Yearbook of International Law 1960] (Moscow, 1961), pp. 243-254; Denysov and Savchuk, note 3 above; V. Levitskii, «Степанов» [Stepanov], in D. I. Bagalei (ed.), Юридический факультет Харьковского университета за первые 100 лет его существования (1805-1905) [Law Faculty of Kharkov University for the First Hundred Years of its Existence (1805-1905)] (reprint ed.; Kharkov, 2007), pp. 277-279; F. K., «Степанов

the Faculty of Morals and Politics. During his early years at University, he attended lectures on politics and language, and during his third year, on Roman law and medicine. He graduated in 1819 with the degree of candidate "with distinction", only to see the degree retracted, together with several other students, as a result of a denunciation by a trustee of the University. He resat the examinations in 1821 and received the degree of candidate of legal sciences.

In 1823 he found employment as an instructor in universal history and geography at the Kharkov Institute of Noble Maidens and various part-time appointments in local boarding schools, including the De Roberti boys boarding school. He defended a dissertation on political equilibrium for which the degree of magister of political history and statistics was conferred in 1824 by Kharkov University. At about this time the Rector of Kharkov University offered Stepanov appointment to the Chair of Russian Law; the offer was rejected partly because Stepanov was not interested in this subject and partly because he intended to pursue a civil service career. From July 1830 to 1831 he moved to St. Petersburg to take up a civil service position in the State Commission for the Repayment of Debts.

During his years in Kharkov and St. Petersburg, Stepanov did not produce works of scholarship in the disciplines of economics, political economy, or law; however, he did devote himself energetically to a large number of journal and newspaper articles on philosophical topics and matters of political economy during the 1820-1830s.[34] Those published between 1830 and 1832 he deployed to advantage to seek appointment to a University position.

In 1832 he returned to Kharkov University in the position of professor *extraordinarius* in the Chair of Political Economy and once more a lecturer at the Institute of Noble Maidens, elevated to professor *ordinarius* in 1836. He served as a Syndic of Kharkov University from 1833 to 1834.[35] He was elected Dean of the Faculty of Morals and Politics in 1835 and in 1837 became Pro-Rector of Kharkov University. In 1839 he was assigned to supervise the instructional component in the Pedagogical Institute formed within the Kharkov University with the rank and title of Director.

Тихон Федорович» [Stepanov, Tikhon Fedorovich], Русский биографический словарь [Russian Biographical Dictionary] (reprint ed.; Moscow, 1999), vol. Smelovskii – Suvorina, pp. 398-399; K. O. Savchuk, «Степанов Тихон Федорович» [Stepanov, Tikhon Fedorovich], in Denysov, note 2 above, III, pp. 779-780.

34 These all seem to be devoted to political economy. An extensive list is given by F. K., note 242 above, p. 399. Reference is made to an unpublished manuscript attributed to the period 1824 to 1826 "On Philosophical and Political-Diplomatic Principles", whose whereabouts is unknown.

35 Under the 1804 Statute on universities in the Russian Empire, a Syndic was an administrative position filled by a member of the professorial staff to assist with judicial matters within the University, including the preparation of decisions by a University court in accordance with University statutes and State laws. A Syndic served on the Board of the University with the right of a consultative vote and might be delegated to represent the University in administrative or judicial proceedings connected with the University.

The University Statute of 1835 enhanced the status of international law or the law of nations ("all-people's law", or "people's law")[36] in the University curriculum. Stepanov was assigned to lecture on this subject as from 1837. This doubtless became the occasion for writing his treatise on the subject.

Stepanov taught at Kharkov until 1845, when ill-health forced him to retire. He died in 1847 not long after completing his treatise on international law. He left an autobiography completed in 1845 or 1846 (the sources differ on the date). Levitskii had access to this material, which otherwise remains unpublished.[37]

Stepanov's intellectual legacy in the field of international law will not be fully appreciated until the publication of the complete text of his two-volume treatise. Grabar had a high opinion of Stepanov on the basis of what was known about his approach to the law of nations. Stepanov was, Grabar wrote, an "… original thinker" who equal was "difficult to find … among foreign international lawyers". Among Russian international lawyers, Grabar believed that Stepanov occupied "… a place second only to V. A. Nezavitovskii".[38] F. K., on the other hand, commenting principally on the basis of Stepanov's contributions to political economy rather than public international law, described Stepanov as more an "… eclectic and gifted publicist than an independent and profound scholar", although acknowledging that Stepanov was rightly considered to be the best specialist on political economy, an outstanding and talented lecturer who had a significant influence upon his audience, a man deeply sincere, eloquent, and honorable, and of enormous impact in his discipline.[39] His former student, M. De Poulet, described Stepanov as a talented and eloquent lecturer who treated critically the realities of the time, "opposing them in a most courageous and passionate way".[40]

Until the publication of the translation of an excerpt from Stepanov's treatise, what little we have known about his approach to the law of nations was based upon the inaugural lecture which he delivered upon his appointment to the Chair of Political Economy in 1832. This lecture addressed the essence, importance, and purpose of the political sciences and was plainly drawn upon by Stepanov when composing the first chapter of his treatise some years later.[41] Many passages in the texts are near identical; the views which he expressed in 1833[42] had not been significantly revised.

36 The term "international law" was not introduced until the 1863 University Statute.

37 Levitskii, note 33 above, p. 277.

38 Grabar, note 17 above, p. 303.

39 F. K., note 33 above, p. 399.

40 M. De Poulet, «Харьковский университет и Д. И. Каченовский: Культурный очерк и воспоминания из 40-х годов» [Kharkov University and D. I. Kachenovskii: Cultural Essay and Memoir from the 1840s], Вестник Европы [Herald of Europe], no. 1 (January 1874), pp. 75-115; no. 2 (February 1874), pp. 565-588.

41 T. F. Stepanov, Речь о сущности, важности и назначении политических наук [Address on the Essence, Importance, and Purpose of the Political Sciences] (Kharkov, 1833). 64 p.

42 The address was delivered at a solemn meeting of Kharkov University on 30 August 1833. The printed text of the address a decade later had become a veritable *cours* on political economy "unique

It should be noted that Stepanov anticipated Nezabitovskii in treating as subjects of "all-people's law" not only peoples, but people; that is individuals or natural persons (whom he calls "inseparables" throughout his text). He actually used the expression human rights in connection with their being tantamount to subjects of all-people's law. In general, Stepanov used the views of Georg Friedrich Martens (1756-1821) as a foil for his remarks, herein often referred to as the "writer" or the "publicist".

Something of Stepanov's views on diplomacy can be gleaned from his 1833 lecture, where he wrote: "Diplomacy is concerned with the laws of physical and moral life of nations in their mutual relations; it should demonstrate the rules which nations are obliged to follow in their constant interactions".[43] As Grabar observed,[44] Stepanov used the word "diplomacy" in two senses:

> By diplomacy I understand the conditional law of nations in general. The authorities usually treat Europe only and consider it in this respect the positive law of the nations of Europe.
>
> … I call diplomacy conditional law if we separate it from the natural law of nations. In this event politics and political economy will also constitute conditional sciences, and natural law will embrace that unconditional science which expounds the purely unconditional principles and rules which serve as the basis for uncovering the life of societies and nations.[45]

The two-volume treatise on public international law completed by Stepanov in 1847 was never published. Although the Russian censor had approved the manuscript for publication, it is presumed that Stepanov's untimely death precluded its appearance. For decades the manuscript was believed to have been lost or to have been destroyed during the Second World War and so recorded by Grabar.[46] In 1960 the manuscript was reported to have been discovered and identified in the Archive of Kharkov University in Ukraine.[47] At present the manuscript is held by the Central State Historical Archive of Ukraine in the City of Kyiv, fond 2055, delo 5.[48]

in Russian literature". See Levitskii, note 33 above.

43 Stepanov, note 41 above, pp. 41-42.

44 Grabar, note 17 above, p. 301.

45 Stepanov, note 41 above, p. 42.

46 See Grabar, note 17 above, p. 303.

47 Semenov and Uliainova, note 33 above, pp. 243-254.

48 V. N. Denysov and K. O. Savchuk, «Степанов Тихон Федорович» [Stepanov Tikhon Fedorovich], in Iu. S. Shemshuchenko (ed.), Антологія української юридичної думки [Anthology of Ukrainian Legal Thought] (Kyiv, 2004), VIII, p. 38. Denysov and Savchuk transcribed the first chapter of the manuscript, composed in the Russian language, for the aforementioned Anthology. That Chapter is available in English in a translation by W. E. Butler. See T. F. Stepanov, "All People's Law in Aggregate with Diplomacy", *Jus Gentium: Journal of International Legal History*, VIII (2017), pp. 39-72.

ANNEX

Personnel and Graduates of St. Petersburg Educational Institutions Serving in the Ministry of Foreign Affairs

(Preliminary List)

Introduction

The present Annex is both a preliminary list and something of an experiment. St. Petersburg offers some unusual advantages as a metropolis. Among great cities of the world, its origins are comparatively recent and certain (1702). A decade later, St. Petersburg became the capital of one of the largest States on the planet and maintained that status until the end of the Romanov Dynasty in 1917 – a comfortable periodization.

The city was founded as the nucleus of a "bootstrap" operation: to provide a "window on the West"; to continue processes of transformation, modernization, and reform on a new scale with intensified energies; to assert a rightful place for Russia in Europe as a Great Power; to educate and train the rising generations of Russians in the sciences and humanities, including the science of law, in order to create a domestic supply of civil servants who might fully assume the competent administration of the realm. The Russian State assumed the primary role for initiating or creating, financing, and structuring the measures necessary to achieve these ends. Foreigners were invited or recruited to jump-start the process on a significant scale.

The law of nations was an integral component of the process from the outset. The Petrine State conducted foreign relations with a new assertiveness and direction. Books were written or translated, treaties negotiated and published. The exercise was overwhelmingly State conceived, directed, and supported to satisfy State requirements; the Church and private entrepreneurship or philanthropy played throughout a marginal role. The College of Foreign Affairs, later the Ministry of Foreign Affairs, and to a lesser extent, the military and commercial ministries, appointed or hired graduates of Petersburg institutions of higher education who had studied the law of nations, or international law, as an obligatory part of their training.

These individuals, to adapt the terminology of V. E. Grabar, became the "legists" of Russia – increasingly Russians rather than foreigners and proficient in foreign languages – who as diplomats and consular officials had status, privileges, and immunities under international law. They were all practitioners of international law, responsible for the performance of Russian treaty obligations and customary international law. Their instructions from the MID encapsulated their country's perception of their legal role in the international community; their reports to the Ministry represent State practice and their understanding of their respective positions and duties. St. Petersburg institutions of higher education in particular encouraged, in ways that provincial universities could not, the symbiosis between teaching and practice. Joint appointments between the University and the MID were routine and not the exception. For University graduates of quality in law there was no need to choose between an academic and a government career; most chose both, to the benefit and advantage of the State and the individual.

The List below contains 367 individuals with minimal overlap in respect of the main body of this work.[1] It emphasizes the relationship with the MID and contains little information about other accomplishments of the individuals concerned. In some cases the information is fragmentary, and doubtless other individuals remain unknown to us. But most names are unknown to historians of international law, and undeservedly so. The archival sources based on the State practice generated by these "legists" is a key to understanding the role of international law in the policy process, the extent to which international law guided, or not, the formulation, conceptualization, and implementation of foreign policy.[2]

§1. *Ministers and Deputy Ministers*

1. **Artsimovich, Vladimir Antonovich** (12 December 1857 – after 1918). Graduated in 1880 from the Law Faculty of St. Petersburg University, joined the Ministry of Foreign Affairs (MID) from 1881: supernumerary official in Department of Foreign Relations; from 1882, clerk, 8th class; Vice Consul in Torna, Austria-Hungary; from 1891, Consul in San Francisco, California; from 1900, Consul General in Berlin; from 1910, Department of Personnel and Economic Affairs MID; from 1914, Senior Advisor, MID; from 1914-1918, Deputy Minister of Foreign Affairs; from 1916-1917, Senator; after 1917, in emigration.

2. **Petriaev, Aleksandr Mikhailovich** (27 October 1875 – 9 November 1933, d. Belgrade). Graduated in 1897 from the Law Faculty and Faculty of Oriental Languages – a polyglot who knew fourteen languages, he joined the MID from 1897: from 1897, I Asian Department; from 1902, dragoman and secretary, Consulate General in Constantinople; from 1906, Consul General in Constantinople; from 1910, Consul General in Bitola, Macedonia, Ottoman Empire; from 1913, envoy inn Albania; from 1916, advisor to II Political Section of MID. In 1917, Deputy Minister of Foreign Affairs, Provisional Government. Emigrated to Yugoslavia.

3. **Pokrovskii, Nikolai Nikolaevich** (27 January 1865, b. St. Petersburg – 12 December 1930, Kaunas, Lithuania). Privy counsellor. Graduated in 1888 from the St. Petersburg University Law Faculty, Pokrovskii was from November 1916 to March 1917 the last Minister of Foreign Affairs of the Russian Empire. From August 1917, Deputy Chairman and then acting Chairman, Chief Administration, Russian Red Cross Committee.

[1] This List has drawn upon archival sources and benefited from Iu. V. Ivanov and E. Iu. Ivanova, Последние дипломаты Российской империи 1900-1917 [Last Diplomats of the Russian Empire 1900-1917 (M., 2021) and Russian Wikipedia lists of graduates from the respective institutions.

[2] Consider, for example, the records of the Council of Ministers of the Russian Empire as evidence of international legal issues arising before that body, the role of international lawyers in advising that body, and the decisions taken. See W. E. Butler, "Russian and Soviet State Practice and the Law of the Sea: New Perspectives", in R. A. Kolodkin and S. M. Punzhin (eds.), *International Law of the Sea: Essays in Memory of Anatoly L. Kolodkin* (M., 2014), pp. 18-39.

4. **Shtiurmer, Boris Vladimirovich** (15 July 1848, b. Baikovo estate, Tver Governate – 20 August 1917, d. Petrograd). Full privy counselor. Graduated in 1872 from the Law Faculty of St. Petersburg University. Chairman, Council of Ministers, Russian Empire. Joined MID from 7 June 1916 as Minister of Foreign Affairs while resigning as Chairman of Council of Ministers. Dismissed 10 November 1916; arrested 28 February 1917 and confined in Peter and Paul Fortress; died in prison hospital.

§2. *Members of Faculty of Law of St. Petersburg University*

5. **Baikov, Aleksandr Lvovich** (30 April 1874, b. St. Petersburg – 31 December 1943, Paris, France). International lawyer and legal philosopher. From 1897 to 1901, awarded professorial stipend; magister of law. Privat-docent at Faculty of Law of St. Petersburg University from 1901 to 1908. From 1896 to 1909, served as interpreter and official of central apparatus, MID; Director, II Department; participated in preparing draft treaties. Emigrated to France.

6. **Dogel, Mikhail Ivanovich** (11 September 1865, b. Heidelberg, Germany – 25 August 1936, d. Paris, France). International lawyer, diplomatic historian. From 1912 to 1918 privat-docent, Chair of International Law, St. Petersburg University. Head, Jurisconsult Section, MID in 1916-1917. Full privy counselor from 1913. Emigrated to France.

7. **Gorovtsev, Aleksandr Mikhailovich** (21 January 1878 – 27 October 1933, Paris, France). International lawyer, diplomat, publisher. Privat-docent, Chair of International Law, St. Petersburg University, from 1912 to 1918. Sent by MID to China, served in Kharbin, Chifu, and other cities. Emigrated to France.

8. **Makarov, Aleksandr Nikolaevich** (4 August 1888, b. Tsarskoe selo – 13 May 1973, d. Heidelberg, Germany). Specialist in private international law. Privat-docent and professor, Chair of State Law, St. Petersburg University. Worked at MID in 1916 to 1917. Emigrated to Germany.

9. **Mandelstam, Andrei Nikolaevich** (6 March 1869, b. Mogilev – 27 January 1949, d. Paris, France). Docent and professor, Chair of International Law, St. Petersburg University. Worked at MID from 1893 to 1917, represented Russia at international conferences; Director, Legal Department, MID of the Provisional Government. Full privy counselor from 1915. Emigrated to France.

10. **Martens, Fedor Fedorovich** (10 August 1845, b. Pernov, Livonian Governate – 7 June 1909, d. Valk Station, Livonian Governate). International lawyer, diplomat, legal consultant, and international arbitrator. From 1871 to 1903, docent, professor, and Head, Chair of International Law, St. Petersburg University. Joined MID from 1869 to 1909 as ambassador on special assignment; member, Council of MID; represented Russia at many international conferences. Full State counselor from 1881; privy counselor from 1891.

11. **Müller, Gerhard Friedrich** (29 October 1705, b. Herford, Westphalia – 11 October 1783, Moscow). Historiographer, State official. First Rector, St. Peters-

burg University. Full State counselor. Head, Archive of the College of Foreign Affairs of Russia from 1766 to 1783.

12. **Nolde, Boris Emmanuilovich** (14 December 1876, b. St. Petersburg – 28 May 1848, d. Lausanne, Switzerland). International lawyer, diplomat, historian. Professor and Head, Chair of International Law, St. Petersburg University from 1917 to 1919. Joined the MID from 1899 as clerk; from 1902, clerk of 8th class, 1st Department; from 1907 to 1914, aide to the State secretary and jurisconsult of MID; from 1914, Head of Jurisconsult Unit; in 1917, Director, 2d (consular) Department. Initiator and editor-in-chief, Известия Министерства иностранных дел [News of the Ministry of Foreign Affairs] from 1912 to 1917.

13. **Pokrovskii, Petr Alekseevich** (22 August 1885, b. Samara – 19 October 1916, d. Petrograd). Specialized in the philosophy of law and State law. Privat-docent, Chair of the Encyclopedia and History of the Philosophy of Law from 1914 to 1916. Joined the MID in 1916 as Librarian of the 2d (consular) Department.

14. **Simson, Ewald Karlovich** (28 February 1869, b. Tartu, Livonian Governate – 22 June 1918, d. Vyborg, Finland). International lawyer, diplomat. Privat-docent from 1895 to 1899, Chair of International Law, St. Petersburg University. Joined MID from 1895; from 1915 to 1916, Clerk in the 2d (Asian) Department.

15. **Strube de Piermont, Friedrich Heinrich** (1 January 1704, b. Germany – 1 August 1790, d. near St. Petersburg). Academician. Taught the law of nations at the St. Petersburg Academy University. Assisted the College of Foreign Affairs from 1757 to 1775.

16. **Taube, Mikhail Aleksandrovich von** (15 May 1869, b. Pavlovsk – 29 November 1961, d. Paris, France). International lawyer, diplomat, international arbitrator. Joined MID from 1892 as Cler, in 2d (newspaper) Expedition; from 1900 to 1904, Head, 1st Section; from 1905, Vice Director, 2d Department; from 1907, Legal Advisor of MID; from 1909, member, Council of MID. Legal and diplomatic representative of Russia at many international conferences. Emigrated to Finland, Sweden, Germany, and France.

17. **Timofeev, Aleksandr Georgievich** (2 December 1867, b. St. Petersburg – after 1917). From 1895 to 1915, privat-docent, Law Faculty of St. Petersburg University. Joined MID in 1915; Consul in Kandahar, Afghanistan, from 1915 to 1917.

§3. *Graduates of the Faculty of Law of St. Petersburg University*

18. **Argutinskii-Dolgorukov, Prince Vladimir Nikolaevich** (24 March 1874, b. Tiflis, Georgia – 9 December 1941, d. Paris, France). Art historian, collector, merchant. Chairman, Commission for the Study and Description of St. Petersburg. Graduated in 1896 from the Law Faculty of St. Petersburg University and the Cambridge University in England. Joined MID from 1898 in the 2d Department; from 1899 to 1912, secretary of Russian Embassy in Paris, where he facilitated the organization in Paris of the "Russian Seasons" of Sergei Diaghilev. Emigrated after 1917 to Paris.

19. **Bezobrazov, Nikolai Aleksandrovich** (17 October 1816, b. St. Petersburg –15 October 1867, d. Tsarskoe selo). Jurist, writer. From 1852, full State counsellor. Joined MID in 1839, serving from 1839 to 1841 at the Russian Mission in Naples, Italy, and from 1841 to 1843 at the Asian Department in St. Petersburg.

20. **Bok, Nikolai Ivanovich** (18 October 1880, b. St. Petersburg – 27 February 1962, d. New York). Jurist, diplomat, Catholic cleric, University lecturer. Graduated in 1903 from the Law Faculty of St. Petersburg University. Joined MID from 1903 as Clerk, 2d (consular) Department; from 1912 to 1915, secretary of the Russian Mission at The Vatican; from 1916 to 1917, acting *chargé d'affaires* at the Vatican. After 1917, Chairman, Committee for Assistance to Russian Refugees in Italy. Emigrated to Italy, Japan, and United States.

21. **Botkin, Petr Sergeevich** (21 August 1865, b. St. Petersburg – 9 July 1933, d. Veuve, Switzerland). Full privy counsellor, jurist, diplomat. Graduated in 1887 from the St. Petersburg University Law Faculty. Joined MID from 1887 to 1890 as Clerk, Asian Department; from 1890 to 1895 as second secretary of the Russian Embassy in Washington D. C., including as Head of the Mission; from 1896 to 1899 as secretary of the Mission in Sofia, Bulgaria; from 1899 to 1901 in Lisbon, Portugal; from 1901 to 1906 in Brussels, Belgium; and in 1906 at London. From 1907 to 1912, he was Resident-Minister and Consul General in Morocco, and from 1912 to 1917, envoy in Portugal. He played an active role in the work of the Commission to reorganize the MID and was a Russian delegate to international congresses and conferences. According to von Taube, Botkin was a possible candidate to become the Minister of Foreign Affairs in 1914. Emigrated to France and Switzerland.

22. **Buksgevden, Baron Karl Karlovich** (2 March 1856, b. Dorpat – 4 August 1935, d. Brussels, Belgium). Graduated in 1878 from the Law Faculty of St. Petersburg University. Joined MID from 1882 in the Personnel and Economic Affairs Department; from 1891 as acting Head; from 1892 as Vice Director; and from 1897 as Director of the said Department. From 1910 to 1917 he was Envoy Extraordinary and Minister Plenipotentiary to Denmark. He emigrated to Belgium.

23. **Gambs, Prince Ernest Ernestovich** (1882 – after 1928). Graduate of the Law Faculty of St. Petersburg University. Joined MID from 1906 in the 2d Department; from 1911 to 1912, acting Consul in Cardiff and Newport, Wales; from 1915 to 1917, Vice Consul at the Consulate General in London. Also served in The Netherlands. Emigrated to the United Kingdom.

24. **Girs (Giers), Aleksandr Aleksandrovich** (4 May 1850, b. St. Petersburg – 5 November 1923, d. Maribor, Slovenia). Studied from 1868 to 1872 at the Law Faculty of St. Petersburg University. Joined MID from 1884 as secretary and dragoman, Consulate in Salonika; consul from 1884 to 1886 in Jerusalem; from 1887 to 1889 in Trieste; from 1889 to 1899 in Jassy Romania; Consul General from 1899 to 1901 in Cannes; from 1901 to 1902 in Bender, Persia; from 1902 to 1905 in Salonika; from 1906, Head, Newspaper Expedition of MID. From 1910 to 1912, advisor of MID and representative of MID on the Special Meeting for Revision of the Rules for the Administration of Maritime Commercial Ports. Emigrated to Yugoslavia.

25. **Girs (Giers), Mikhail Nikolaevich** (22 April 1856 – 27 November 1932, Paris, France). After completing the Marine Cadet Corps from 1875 to 1877, Girs studied at the Law Faculty of St. Petersburg University. Joined MID in 1878. From 1879 he was Vice Consul at Zara, Yugoslavia; from 1880, first secretary of the Mission in Serbia, acting as *chargé d'affaires* from 1882 to 1883; from 1883, second secretary of the Embassy in the Ottoman Empire; from 1884 to 1887, first secretary of the Mission in Persia; from 1888, official for special assignments, 5th class, attached to MID; from 1889, advisor to MID and envoy extraordinary and minister plenipotentiary from 1895 to 1898, in Brazil and Argentina; from 1898 to 1901 in China; from 1901 to 1902, in Bavaria; from 1903 to 1912, in Romania; ambassador extraordinary and plenipotentiary from 1912 to 1914, Ottoman Empire; and from 1914 to 1917, where he was doyen of the diplomatic corps in Rome. Emigrated to France.

26. **Goriainov, Sergei Mikhailovich** (4 December 1849, b. Odessa – 5 November 1918, d. Russia). Graduated from the Law Faculty of St. Petersburg University. Privy counsellor. Joined MID from 1891 as Consul in Czernowitz, Austria-Hungary; from 1896, Consul General in Vienna; from 1907, Director, Department of Internal Relations; from 1902 to 1915, Director, St. Petersburg and Main Archive of MID.

27. **Iazdovskii, Aleksandr Stepanovich** (1879-1937). Attended Law Faculty of St. Petersburg University. Joined MID from 1904 to 1911 as secretary of the Vice Consulate and from 1913 to 1917 as Head of the Consulate in Antwerp, Belgium.

28. **Iazykov, Petr Aleksandrovich** (1882 – not before 1917). Attended Law Faculty of St. Petersburg University. Joined MID from 1908 to 1914, serving in the central apparatus and the Russian Embassy in Germany. From 1914 to 1917, administrator of the Committee of Grand Princess Elizaveta Fedorovna for Philanthropic Assistance to Families of Persons Called Up for War.

29. **Ignatev, Aleksei Nikolaevich** (28 July 1874, b. Constantinople – 17 January 1948, d. France). Graduated in 1897 from the Law Faculty of St. Petersburg University. Joined MID from 1897 as attaché of the Russian embassy in Turkey; from 1901, attaché of the embassy in Italy. From 1909 to 1911, Vice Governor of Podolsk and Governor from 1911 to 1915; from 1915 to 1917, Governor of Kyiv. In 1917, representative of Red Cross in Romania. Emigrated to France.

30. **Ivanov, Nikolai Alekseevich** (1884 – 1941). Graduated 1908 from the Law Faculty and Faculty of Oriental Languages, St. Petersburg University. Joined MID from 1910 as Sinologist, serving in consular posts in Peking, Kharbin, Kuldzhu, and Hankow. From 1915 to 1916, secretary and dragoman, Consulate in Hankow, then Vice Consul and Consular Judge at the Consulate General in Shanghai. After 1919 emigrated to China.

31. **Kandaurov, Leontii Dmitrievich** (1880, b. Warsaw – 1936, d. Nyon-sur-Seine, France). Graduated in 1903 from the Law Faculty of St. Petersburg University. Joined MID in 1904; from 1906 to 1912, served in the 2d Department; from 1912 to 1913, Vice Consul in Sarajevo; from 1913 to 1917, Vice Consul (Consul from 1917) in the Consulate General in Paris. Emigrated to France.

32. **Kantemir, Antiokh Dmitrievich** (10 September 1708, b. Constantinople – 31 March 1744, Paris, France). Graduated in 1727 from the Petersburg Academy University. Joined the College of Foreign Affairs from 1731 as Resident in the United Kingdom; negotiated recognition by the British Government of the Imperial title for Russian sovereigns and the appointment of a British representative in Russia. During the dispute over the Polish succession, Kantemir negotiated an Anglo-Russian alliance against France. In 1734 was actively involved in the trade treaty negotiations between England and Russia. In 1737 negotiated renewal of Franco-Russian friendly relations. From 1738, envoy, then ambassador extraordinary in France.

33. **Karasev, Konstantin Alekseevich** (dates unknown). Graduated from St. Petersburg University. Joined MID from 1894 as secretary in Department of Internal Relations; from 1897, secretary of Consulate in Lviv, Austria-Hungary; from 1898, Vice Consul in Stockholm; from 1898 to 1911, Consul in Memel, Germany; from 1911 to 1914, Consul in Lubeck, Germany. In 1917, diplomatic official attached to Headquarters of Supreme Command of Russian Army.

34. **Kazanskii, Mikhail Vasilevich** (1887-1915). Graduated in 1908 from the Alexander Lycée and in 1909 sat the examinations for the Law Faculty of St. Petersburg University. Joined MID from 1912 as secretary of the Consulate in Prague; from 1913 as Vice Consul in Lviv (then Poland); from 1914 secretary again of the Consulate in Prague; and after the declaration of war in 1914, as Vice Consul in Bergen, Norway. In 1915 he died in Poland in combat on the front.

35. **Lashkarev (Loshkarev), Sergei Sergeevich** (29 December 1816 – 1 July 1869, d. St. Petersburg). Graduated in 1838 from the Law Faculty of St. Petersburg University. Full State counsellor. Served in MID from 1838 to 1839.

36. **Lashkevich, Georgii Nikolaevich** (30 June 1886, b. St. Petersburg – 22 August 1938, d. Kommunarka, Moscow Region). Graduated in 1908 from the Law Faculty of St. Petersburg University. Joined MID as Clerk, 8th class, in the 2d Department. During the Soviet period, he served in the People's Commissariat for Foreign Affairs in the Economic and Legal Section; as plenipotentiary representative in France; the Service for Affairs of the League of Nations attached to the General Secretariat of the said Commissariat. Executed for counter-revolutionary crimes.

37. **Maslov, Nikolai Nikolaevich** (dates unknown). Graduated from the Law Faculty of St. Petersburg University. Student file dates from 1890. Joined MID as Clerk, 6th class, and Head, Accounts Unit, 1st Department; from 1916 to 1917, senior secretary of the jurisconsult unit of MID.

38. **Metsler, Karl Eduardovich** (1886 – 1940, d. Shanghai, China). Graduated in 1907 from the Law Faculty of St. Petersburg University and the Institute of Oriental Languages attached to the MID. Joined MID from 1911: from 1912, student at the Embassy of Russia in Peking; from 1912, secretary of Russian Mission in Seoul, then the Consulate in Kabdo; from 1915, in Sharasum, Korea; from 1916, secretary and dragoman in Canton; from 1917, Vice Consul, Consulate General of Russia in Shanghai. After 1917, emigrated to Shanghai, China.

39. **Mikhailovskii (Garin-Mikhailovskii), Georgii Nikolaevich** (1890, b. Ust-Katav, Urals Governate – 1946, d. Correctional Labor Camp, Vorkuta (or Donbass). International lawyer, diplomat, writer. Joined MID in 1914 as secretary; from 1915, aide to Head, Jurisconsult Unit; from 1917, Head, International Legal Section, Legal Department. Emigrated to Czechoslovakia.

40. **Muravev, Nikolai Valerianovich** (28 September 1850, b. Kostroma – 14 December 1908, d. Rome). Graduated in 1870 from the Law Faculty of St. Petersburg University. From 1894 to 1905, Minister of Justice and Procurator General. Full State counsellor. Joined MID from 1905 to 1908 as Ambassador Extraordinary and Plenipotentiary to Italy.

41. **Muromtsev, Mikhail Ivanovich** (1854 – after 1917). Graduated in 1873 from the Law Faculty of St. Petersburg University. Served in administrative and instructional posts at MID. From 1902 to 1914, Vice Director, Department of Personnel and Economic Affairs; from 1916, member of MID Council. Lectured on international law in the Instructional Division of Oriental Languages attached to MID. Dismissed in November 1917 without right to pension for insubordination to the Council of People's Commissars.

42. **Nabokov, Konstantin Dmitrievich** (1872, b. Rostov-on-Don – 18 March 1927, d. London, England). Graduated in 1894 from the Law Faculty of St. Petersburg University. Joined MID from 1894 as Secretary of the Chancellery; in 1905 was a member of the Russian delegation to the conference in Portsmouth, New Hampshire, to conclude the Russo-Japanese peace treaty. From 1906, secretary of Mission in Belgium; from 1910, first secretary of Embassy in Washington D.C.; from 1912, Consul General in Calcutta, India; from 1916, Counselor to Embassy in London; from 1917, temporarily managed the embassy while remaining in post as Counselor with conferral on him personally of rank of Envoy Extraordinary and Minister Plenipotentiary in England. From 1918 to 1920, diplomatic representative of Kolchak Government in London. Emigrated to Norway.

43. **Nekliudov, Mikhail Sergeevich** (1873 – no earlier than 1917). Graduated from the Law Faculty of St. Petersburg University; student file dated 1891. Joined MID from 1909 to 1910 as Clerk, 1st Department; from 1917, assigned to Vice Consulate in Hakodate, Japan. Emigrated to Japan, where he committed suicide.

44. **Nelidov, Aleksandr Ivanovich** (11 June 1835, b. Dubrovka, Smolensk Governate – 5 September 1910, d. Paris, France). Graduated in 1855 from the Law Faculty and the Faculty of Oriental Languages of St. Petersburg University. Joined MID from 1855 in the Asian Department; from 1856 to 1861, junior secretary of the Mission in Greece; from 1861 to 1864, junior secretary and 1864 to 1869, senior secretary, Mission in Bulgaria; from 1869 to 1874, senior secretary, Mission in Austria; from 1874 to 1877, Counselor, Embassy in Turkey, repeatedly administering the Embassy in the ambassador's absence during the Russo-Turkish War of 1877-1878; Director, Diplomatic Chancellery, Commander-in-Chief, Army in Balkans; participated in negotiations with Turkey to conclude armistice and peace as plenipotentiary with N. P. Ignatev he signed the Peace of San Stefano; in 1878 participated in the Congress of Berlin; from 1879, envoy to Saxony and Duchy of Saxen-Altenburg; from 1882, administrator of the Embassy; from 1883, ambassador to Turkey. In 1885 and 1886, participated in Constantinople Conference of

Ambassadors on the Bulgarian question. From 1897, Ambassador Extraordinary and Plenipotentiary in Italy; in 1898 he participated in the international conference in Rome on combatting anarchism and terrorism. From 1903 to 1910, Ambassador Extraordinary and Plenipotentiary to France; in 1907, Chairman, Second Hague Peace Conference.

45. **Nikolskii, Boris Vladimirovich** (3 October 1870, b. St. Petersburg – 11 June 1919, d. Petrograd). Legal historian. Graduated in 1893 from the Law Faculty of St. Petersburg University. Joined MID from 1896; from 1902, assigned to 1st Department. Professor at Iurev University from 1913 to 1918. His doctoral dissertation was twice rejected for defense (1903 and 1914). A leader of the monarchist organization "Union of the Russian People", sometimes known as the "Black Hundred", he was arrested in 1919 and executed for "affiliation with counter-revolutionary activity" and rehabilitated in 2002.

46. **Nikolskii, Dmitrii Petrovich** (25 October 1855, b. Perm – 10 August 1907, d. St. Petersburg). International lawyer and publicist. Graduated in 1883 from the Law Faculty of St. Petersburg University. Joined MID from 1883 to 1895; then worked in the St. Petersburg Public Library and served as head of the foreign policy section in the newspaper Россия [Russia].

47. **Osten-Saken, Baron Fedor Romanovich** (1832, b. St. Petersburg – 19 March 1916, d. Petrograd). Graduated in 1853 from the Law Faculty of St. Petersburg University. Joined MID from 1853 as official; from 1856 as head of Desk; from 1857, as official on special assignments, 8th class; from 1859, senior head of Desk; from 1860, head of Section; from 1865, as official on special assignments, 6th class; from 1853, Clerk, 5th class, Asian Department; from 1871, Vice Director, and 1875 to 1897, Director, Department of Internal Relations; from 1897 to 1908, member, MID Council. Privy counsellor.

48. **Persiani, Ivan Aleksandrovich** (17 February 1872, b. St. Petersburg – 8 February 1930, d. Belgrade). Graduated in 1894 from the Law Faculty of St. Petersburg University. Joined MID from 1894 in Central Asian Section; from 1916, Counselor of Embassy in Italy and from 1917, *chargé d'affaires* of Embassy. Emigrated to Italy, then Yugoslavia.

49. **Petrashevskii (Butashevich-Petrashevskii), Mikhail Vasilevich** (13 November 1821, b. St. Petersburg – 7 December 1866, d. Minusinsk, Enisei Governate). Graduated in 1841 from the Law Faculty of St. Petersburg University. Joined MID in 1839 as interpreter. Arrested in 1849, sentenced to execution by firing squad, replaced by hard labor in perpetuity.

50. **Planson (Planson-Rostkov), Georgii Antonovich** (6 April 1859, b. Kharkov – after 1937, d. supposedly in France). Graduated in 1883 from the Faculty of Oriental Languages and in 1887 from the Law Faculty of St. Petersburg University. Joined MID from 1888 as Clerk of 1st (Asian) Department; from 1902, official in Diplomatic Unit attached to Chief Head, Kwangtung Region; from November 1902, *chargé d'affaires* in China; from 1903 to 1905, Head, Diplomatic Chancellery attached to Governor in Far East, Admiral E. N. Alekseev; member of Russian delegation in Portsmouth, New Hampshire to negotiate peace treaty with Japan in 1905; from 1905 to 1908 and 1910, Consul General in Korea; from 1908, Vice

Director of 1st (Asian) Department of MID; from 1910 to 1916, *chargé d'affaires* and Consul General with personal rank of Resident Minister in Siam; from 1916 to 1917, Envoy Extraordinary and Minister Plenipotentiary attached to Switzerland. After 1917, emigrated to Switzerland and France.

51. **Ragozin, Konstantin Lvovich** (1887, b. Kazan – 19?). Graduated from the Law Faculty of St. Petersburg University. Joined MID as official in 2d Department; conducted legal affairs for Russian natural and juridical persons abroad. From 1912 to 1914, Vice Consul in Varna, Bulgaria.

52. **Sabler (from 1915, Desiatovskii), Iurii Vladimirovich** (1876-1918). Graduated in 1901 from the Law Faculty of St. Petersburg University. Joined MID from 1902 as interpreter in the 2d Department; from 1913 to 1915, first secretary and in 1915, acting Head of Mission in Bulgaria; from 1915, 2d (consular) Department of MID; from March to May 1917, first secretary, Russian Embassy in Washington D.C.

53. **Savinskii, Aleksandr Aleksandrovich** (1868, b. Kovno, Lithuania – 1934, d. Paris, France). Graduated in 1891 from the Law Faculty of St. Petersburg University. Joined MID from 1891; from 1892, Department of Personnel and Economic Affairs; from 1895, supernumerary official; from 1900, 1st secretary of MID Chancellery; from 1901 to 1903, Vice Director, Chancellery; in 1904, official on special assignment attached to MID; from 1905 to 1910, Director, MID Chancellery; from 1911, envoy to Sweden; from 1913 to 1915, envoy to Bulgaria. Emigrated to France.

54. **Sobolev, Andrei Nikolaevich** (13 May 1889, b. Moscow – 9 September 1968, d. Moscow). Graduated in 1914 from the Law Faculty of St. Petersburg University. Joined MID in 1917 as secretary-assessor of Minister of Foreign Affairs of the Provisional Government, P. N. Miliukov.

55. **Struve, Petr Berngardovich** (26 January 1870, b. Perm – 26 February 1944, d. Paris, France). Graduated in 1894 from the Law Faculty of St. Petersburg University. Joined MID in 1917 as Director, Economic Department, Provisional Government.

56. **Tal, Pavel Iakovlevich von** (1857 – after 1916). Graduated in 1861 from St. Petersburg University. Joined MID, serving from 1880 to 1884 as consul in Memel, Germany; from 1885 to 1891, in Königsberg; from 1891 to 1895, in Chicago, Illinois; from 1895 as Consul in Lubeck, becoming Consul General from 1901 to 1906; from 1907 to 1914, Consul General in Bremen, Germany.

57. **Terner, Fedor Gustavovich** (12 October 1828, b. St. Petersburg – 7 August 1906, d. St. Petersburg). Graduated in 1850 from the Law Faculty of St. Petersburg University. Joined MID from 1851 as interpreter; from the 1850s to 1870s, worked in Ministry of Finances on international legal issues; from 1864, Vice Director, Department of Foreign Trade; in 1867, Russian delegate to international statistical congress at Florence, Italy; represented Russia in 1869 at opening of Suez Canal; representative at 1875 Russian/Austro-Hungarian conference to conclude trade and customs agreements; in 1881 represented Russia at Paris conference on correlation between gold and silver; from 1881 to 1882, plenipotentiary of Russia on Turkish reparations for Russo-Turkish War of 1877-1878.

58. **Tolstoi, Count Dmitrii Ivanovich** (30 May 1860, b. St. Petersburg – 5 March 1941, d. Nice, France). Graduated in 1883 from the Law Faculty of St. Petersburg University. Joined MID from 1884 to 1900 as official in Department of Internal Relations; then secretary, Chancellery of MID, then official on special assignments. Emigrated from 1920 to various European countries, finally settling in France.

59. **Tolstoi, Count Sergei Petrovich** (1875 – 1937). Graduated in 1898 from the Law Faculty of St. Petersburg University. Joined MID, serving as secretary of the Embassy in Italy, Mission in Greece, Embassy in France; from 1913, secretary, MID Chancellery. Emigrated to France, from 1932, in United States.

60. **Ubri, Pavel Petrovich** (4 November 1818 – 6 February 1896, d. Naples, Italy). Graduated in 1838 from the Law Faculty of St. Petersburg University. Joined MID from 1839 as college secretary, Russian Mission in Frankfurt-on-Main; from 1840, third secretary; from 1842, second secretary, Chancellery of Vice-Chancellor K. V. Nesselrode; from June 1842, senior secretary, Russian Mission in Lisbon; from 1846, junior secretary of Embassy in Vienna. Served as "right hand" of Chancellor A. M. Gorchakov at 1853 Vienna conference. From 1856, Counselor, Russian Mission in Berlin; from 1858, Counselor, Embassy in Paris; from 1862, Envoy Extraordinary and Minister Plenipotentiary in Prussia, Mecklenburg-Schwerin, and Mecklenburg-Strelitz; from 1871, Ambassador Extraordinary and Plenipotentiary in Germany. In 1878, third plenipotentiary of Russia at Berlin Congress. From 1879 to 1881, Ambassador Extraordinary and Plenipotentiary in Vienna; from 1882 to 1895, member of State Council and full privy counsellor.

61. **Vasilevskii, Prince Nikolai Sergeevich** (1883-1927). Graduated in 1908 from the Law Faculty of St. Petersburg University. Joined MID as 2d secretary of the Chancellery.

62. **Volkonskii, Prince Aleksandr Mikhailovich** (1866-1934). Military diplomat, from 1930, Catholic cleric. Graduated from the Law Faculty of St. Petersburg University and a two-year course at the Nikolaev General Staff Academy. In 1895, member of the Embassy Extraordinary to Persia. He was sent in 1897 to Peking, thereafter preparing a Memorandum "On the Need to Strengthen Our Strategic Position in the Far East" and arguing the inevitability of a military conflict with Japan and the unreadiness of Russia for war. From February to April 1908 and again from 1915 to 1917, military agent of Russia in Italy. Emigrated to Italy.

63. **Voznesenskii-Vladimirov, Arsenii Nikolaevich** (1881-1937). Graduated in 1899 from the Law Faculty and the Faculty of Oriental Languages of St. Petersburg University. Joined MID as a jurist, Sinologist, and Japanologist: Vice Consul in Shanghai from 1913 to 1915; first Plenipotentiary Representative of Soviet Russia to China, but did not take up the post because of Chinese refusal at the end of 1917 and early 1918 to recognize this position and issue an entry visa.

64. **Vulf, Nikolai Pavlovich** (1877 – after 1927). Graduated in 1899 from the Law Faculty and Faculty of Oriental Languages of St. Petersburg University. Joined MID from 1899 as a student trainee at the Russian Mission in Peking; in 1904, secretary of the diplomatic chancellery attached to the Imperial Governor in the Far East; in 1908 as secretary of the Consulate General in Jassy, and a similar position

at Barcelona (1910) and Marseilles (1915); and secretary (1915) and Vice Consul (1916) in Florence. He returned to the Soviet Union in 1926.

65. **Zhukovskii, Vladimir Grigorevich** (31 March 1871, b. Samara – July 1922, d. Novo-Nikolaevsk, Russia). Graduated in 1897 from the Law Faculty of St. Petersburg University. Joined MID from 1897 to 1899 as Clerk, 2d Department; from 1899 to 1902, secretary of the Consulate, Galac, Romania; from 1902 to 1903, secretary, Consulate General in Jerusalem; from 1903 to 1907, Vice Consul in Adrianople; from 1907 to 1910, Consul in Königsberg; from 1910 to 1917, Consul in Prague; from February 1917, in the MID apparatus.

66. **Zlobin, Konstantin Konstantinovich** (10 March 1815, b. Volsk, Saratov Governate – 31 Augus 1877, d. Samara). Graduated in 1834 from the Law Faculty of St. Petersburg University. Joined MID from 1836 as interpreter in the Department of Internal Relations; from 1843, Head of the Division; from 1856, Head, Asian Department; from 1861, Head, St. Petersburg Chief Archive of MID; from 1864, Director of two archives, St. Petersburg and State Archive of Russian Empire. From 1845 to 1847, on behalf of MID undertook diplomatic visits to Constantinople, Athens, Vienna, and London.

§4. *Lecturers and Graduates of the Faculty of Oriental Languages*

67. **Adamov, Aleksandr Alekseevich** (1870-1938). Graduated in 1891 from the Faculty of Oriental Languages of St. Petersburg University (Arabic, Persian, Turkish-Tatar Division). From 1892 to 1894 Adamov studied in the Instructional Division of Oriental Languages attached to the Asian Department of MID. Joined MID from 1894 as Consul in Tevriz and Kerman, Persia; first Russian consul in Basra, and Consul in Baghdad; from 1914, Consul in Erezum, Turkey, then in Belgrade.

68. **Adlerberg, Nikolai Nikolaevich** (1848-1951). Student file dated 1867 from the Faculty of Oriental Languages of St. Petersburg University. Joined MID from 1894 attached to Mission in Bavaria. Reportedly declined invitation from Lev Trotsky and G. V. Chicherin to join People's Commissariat of Foreign Affairs. Arrested in 1929 and exiled to Siberia. Year of death not verified.

69. **Akhsharumov, Dmitrii Dmitrievich** (1834-1910). Graduated in 1846 from the Faculty of Oriental Languages of St. Petersburg University. Joined MID in the central apparatus until 1849.

70. **Antipov, Vasilii Konstantinovich** (1879-1948). Student file dated 1899 of the Faculty of Oriental Languages of St. Petersburg University. Joined MID in 1906 as dragoman (1906) and secretary (1907) of Russian Consulate in Reshteh, Persia; from 1910, secretary of Consulate General in Jerusalem; from 1915 to 1917, Vice Consul, Kazvina, Persia. Emigrated to Turkey.

71. **Avtonomov, Aleksandr Aleksandrovich** (1884-1938). Historian, philologist, keeper of weapons division in Hermitage Museum. Student file dated 1903 of the Faculty of Oriental Languages of St. Petersburg University. Joined MID from 1908 as Clerk; from 1916 as secretary in the IV (Far Eastern) Political Section.

72. **Balabin, Viktor Petrovich** (1811-1864). Graduated from the Noble Boarding School attached to St. Petersburg University. Joined MID from 1832; from 1835 interpreter in Department of Internal Affairs, then secretary of Russian Mission in Paris. From 1852 to 1853, senior secretary, Mission in Constantinople; from 1856 to 1858, Counselor of Embassy in Paris; from 1858 to 1860, in Austria on special assignment; from 1860 to 1864, envoy, then ambassador, to Austria.

73. **Baranovskii, Aleksandr Rafailovich** (1874-1944). Graduated in 1896 from the Faculty of Oriental Languages of St. Petersburg University. Joined MID from 1897; from 1902, secretary and dragoman, Consulate in Isfahan; from 1903, second dragoman, Mission in Teheran; from 1914 to 1917, Consul in Bucharest. Emigrated to Romania and France.

74. **Batiushkov, Georgii Dmitrievich** (1866-1923). Student file dated 1885 of the Faculty of Oriental Languages of St. Petersburg University. Joined MID from 1890, freely speaking seventeen foreign languages; Consul, then Consul General, in Beirut, Ottoman Empire. Director, 1st (Asian) Department of MID.

75. **Belchenko, Andrei Terentevich** (1873-1958). Graduated in 1897 from the Faculty of Oriental Languages of St. Petersburg University. Joined MID from 1898 as Sinologist; from 1901, as secretary-dragoman of Russian Consulate in Hankow; from 1902 to 1904, as second dragoman, Mission in Peking; from 1904, Consul in Hankow; from 1906, acting Consul in Newchwang; from 1910 to 1913, Consul in Fuzhou; from 1913 to 1914, Consul General in Canton; from 1914 to 1917, Consul General in Hankow. Emigrated to China and then the United States.

76. **Beliaev, Aleksei Konstantinovich** (1870-1960). Student file dated 1888 of the Faculty of Oriental Languages of St. Petersburg University. Joined MID from 1894, serving from 1895 as secretary, Consulate in Skopje, Ottoman Empire; from 1897, secretary and dragoman, Consulate General in Erezum; from 1899, Vice Consul in Prizrena; from 1906, Consul General in Smyrna; from 1910, Consul General in Salonika; from 1913 to 1916, political agent in Bukhara. In 1917, envoy in Persia. Emigrated to Yugoslavia and France.

77. **Beliaev, Dmitrii Dmitrievich** (1882-1960s). Student file dated 1900 of the Faculty of Oriental Languages of St. Petersburg University. Joined MID from 1904; from 1906, administrator, Consulate in Kermanshah, Persia; from 1908 to 1909, administrator, Consulate in Jeddah, Turkey; from 1910, secretary, Consulate General in Tavriz, Persia; from 1912, secretary, Consulate General in Erezum; from 1913, secretary, Consulate General in Bender-Bushir, Persia; from 1915 to 1916, first dragoman, Mission in Persia. Emigrated to Turkey and Belgium.

78. **Ber, Nikolai Alekseevich** (1879-1940). Student file dated 1897 of the Faculty of Oriental Languages of St. Petersburg University. Joined MID from 1902. From 1912 to 1917, first secretary of Embassy in Belgium; from 1917 to 1921, first secretary of Embassy in Sweden. Emigrated to England.

79. **Berens, Eduard Liudvigovich** (1875 – after 1940). Student file dated 1897 of the Faculty of Oriental Languages of St. Petersburg University. Joined MID to serve in consular posts in China as student-apprentice at Mission in Peking; in 1908, secretary of Consulate in Chuguchak; from 1909, secretary-dragoman, Ulia-

sutae, Mongolia; from 1912 to 1915, secretary of Consulate General in Kashgar. In August 1915 assigned to Press Section of MID.

80. **Bludov, Count Andrei Dmitrievich** (1817-1886). Graduated in 1842 from the Faculty of Oriental Languages of St. Petersburg University. Joined MID, from 1848 as secretary of Embassy in Vienna; from 1855, senior secretary of Mission in Hanover; from 1856, in London; from 1861, Envoy Extraordinary and Minister Plenipotentiary to Greece; from 1865, in Salonika; from 1869 to 1886, in Belgium.

81. **Bobrovnikov, Ivan Aleksandrovich** (187? – after 1917). Graduated in 1901 from the Faculty of Oriental Languages of St. Petersburg University (Chinese-Manchurian Section). Joined MID from 1905, serving in consular posts in China: from 1905 to 1906, secretary of Consulate in Turfan; from 1907 to 1909, secretary, Consulate General in Kashgar; from 1910 to 1914, secretary of Consulate in Newchwang; from 1915 to 1916, secretary of Consulate in Kharbin.

82. **Bogoiavlenskii, Nikolai Viacheslavovich** (1867-1945). Graduated in 1892 from the Faculty of Oriental Languages of St. Petersburg University (Chinese-Manchurian-Mongolian Section). Joined MID from 1892 as Consul in Chuguchak (capital of Sinkiang); during Russo-Japanese War, 1904 to 1905, diplomatic representative in Kharbin; from 1908 to 1912, official in diplomatic unit as plenipotentiary representative of MID attached to Governor-General of Amur Territory in Khabarovsk; from September 1913 to 1917, Consul General in Seattle, Washington, and Nome, Alaska; thereafter, informally until diplomatic relations were established in 1933 between the United States and the Soviet Union. Emigrated to United States.

83. **Bogoiavlenskii, Pavel Georgievich** (1870-1911). Graduated in 1894 from the Faculty of Oriental Languages of St. Petersburg University. Joined MID from 1897; from 1900, dragoman of Political Agent in Bukhara; from 1901, secretary, Consulate General in Meshed, Persia; from 1904, second secretary of Mission in Teheran; from 1908 to 1911, Consul in Isfahan, Persia.

84. **Bogoiavlenskii, Sergei Georgievich** (1878-1944). Student file dated 1898 of the Faculty of Oriental Languages of St. Petersburg University. Joined MID from 1898 in central apparatus; from 1910 to 1914, Vice Consul, Plovdiv, Bulgaria, attached to the Mission in Sofia.

85. **Brandt, Georgii Vilgelmovich (Vasilevich)** (1854 – after 1920). Graduate of the Faculty of Oriental Languages of St. Petersburg University. Joined MID from 1882 to 1884 as attendee at Instructional Division of Asian Department; from 1884, student at Russian Embassy in Constantinople; from 1899, Vice Consul in Burgas, Eastern Rumelia; from 1914 to 1915, Consul in Trapezund, Turkey; from 1916 to 1918, Consul in Rio de Janeiro, Brazil.

86. **Bratsev (Bratsov), Vladimir Aleksandrovich** (c. 1878 – 1942). Student file dated 1896 of the Faculty of Oriental Languages of St. Petersburg University. Joined MID from 1901 as Sinologist; secretary of Consulate General in Kharbin; from 1913, administrator of Consulate General in Hankow; in 1914, Consul in Jilin; from 1915 to 1917, secretary and Vice Consul in Shanghai. Emigrated to China.

87. **Bravin, Nikolai Zakharovich (Zakharievich)** (1881-1921). Student file dated 1856 of the Faculty of Oriental Languages of St. Petersburg University. Joined MID from 1905 in central apparatus; from 1907 to 1909, acting Vice Consul in Seystan, Persia; from 1909 to 1911 served in consulates in Bombay and Calcutta; from 1911 to 1913, served consulate in Addis-Abebe; in 1914, Consul in Kazvina, Persia; from 1915 to 1916, Consul in Seystan and Hoe, Persia.

88. **Brodianskii, Lev Grigorevich** (1878-1942). Student file dated 1895 of the Faculty of Oriental Languages of St. Petersburg University. Joined MID from 1900 to 1901 as student at Mission in Peking; from 1903 to 1904, secretary and dragoman at Consulate in Hankow; from 1906 to 1909, secretary and dragoman at Consulate in Shanghai; from 1910, Vice Consul in Chemulpo, Korea; from 1911, in Seoul; from 1913 to 1917, Consul General in Kulja, China.

89. **Brunner, Nikolai Fedorovich** (1859-1936). Student file dated 1879 of the Faculty of Oriental Languages of St. Petersburg University. Joined MID from 1851 in central apparatus; from 1894, Vice Consul in Stockholm; from 1898 to 1899, Consul in Newcastle-on-Tyne, England; from 1899 to 1902, Vice Consul in Leipzig; from 1916, Consul General in Genoa. Emigrated to Sweden.

90. **Brunnert, Ippolit Semenovich** (1881-1948). Student file dated 1901 of the Faculty of Oriental Languages of St. Petersburg University. Joined MID and from 1907 to 1917 was a student and then dragoman at the Russian Mission in Peking. Emigrated to China, where he became a professor at Peking University.

91. **Bubnov, Petr Nikolaevich** (1882-1933). Student file dated 1901 of the Faculty of Oriental Languages of St. Petersburg University. Joined MID from 1901 as secretary of the Russian Embassy in France; secretary of Consulate in Bitola, Turkey. Emigrated to France.

92. **Budberg, Andrei Andreevich von** (1836-1916). Student file dated 1856 of the Faculty of Oriental Languages of St. Petersburg University. Joined MID from 1862 in central apparatus; from 1865, official on special assignment attached to Governor of Kingdom of Poland; from 1874, secretary of Embassy in Germany; from 1897 to 1903, Resident Minister in Saxe-Weimar and Saxe-Altenburg; from 1903 to 1906, envoy in Württemburg.

93. **Budberg, Andrei Fedorovich von** (1817-1881). Graduated from St. Petersburg University. Joined MID from 1841 in Department of Foreign Relations; from 1842, third secretary of Chancellery of Vice-Chancellor; from 1845, junior, and from 1846, senior secretary; from 1848, *chargé d'affaires* of Mission in Frankfurt-on-Main; from 1849, acting *chargé d'affaires*, and from January 1850, Counselor of Mission in Berlin; from 1851, Envoy Extraordinary and Minister Plenipotentiary to Prussia and simultaneously Grand Duchies of Mecklenburg-Schwerin and Mecklenburg-Strelitz; from 1852 to 1855, simultaneously Head of Mission in Hanover; from 1856 to 1858, Ambassador Extraordinary and Plenipotentiary to Austria-Hungary; from 1858 to 1862, Envoy Extraordinary and Minister Plenipotentiary to France; from 1868, member of State Council while remaining in MID; full privy counsellor from 1867.

94. **Budberg, Baron Fedor Andreevich** (1851-1916). Student file dated 1871 of the Faculty of Oriental Languages of St. Petersburg University. Joined MID from

1873; from 1879, aide to secretary of Embassy in Constantinople; from 1882, acting second secretary of Embassy in London; from 1883, second secretary and from 1893, first secretary of Embassy in Vienna; from 1896 to 1897, Counselor of Embassy in Berlin; from 1898, Counselor of Embassy in Vienna; from 1904, Envoy Extraordinary and Minister Plenipotentiary in Sweden; from 1909 to 1916, Envoy Extraordinary and Plenipotentiary to Spain.

95. **Bukeveden, Nikolai Aleksandrovich** (1868-1921 or 1925). Graduated from St. Petersburg University. Joined MID: from 1902, first secretary of Embassy in Japan; from 1905, member, Russian delegation to Peace Conference in Portsmouth, New Hampshire after Russo-Japanese War of 1904-1905; from 1906, first secretary of Embassy in Turkey; from 1910 to 1913, acting *chargé d'affaires* of Russia in the United States; from 1914 to 1916, Director, Diplomatic Chancellery attached to Headquarters of Supreme Commander-in-Chief in the Far East; from 1916 to 1917, Envoy Extraordidnary and Minister Plenipotentiary in China, occupying the post until 1920, when the Chinese authorities closed the Russian diplomatic representation. Emigrated to China, then to France.

96. **Chakhotin, Stepan Ivanovich** (1857 – 1919). Graduated 1880 from the Faculty of Oriental Languages of St. Petersburg University. Joined MID from 1883 as Consul in Constantinople; from 1895 to 1915, Consul in Nisha, Serbia.

97. **Chirkin, Sergei Vissarionovich** (1875 – 1943). Graduated 1900 from the Faculty of Oriental Languages of St. Petersburg University. Joined MID from 1902 as student in Instructional Division. Served from 1902 in 1st Department ("Persian Desk"); from 1903, student at Mission in Teheran; from 1904 to 1906, secretary and dragoman, Consulate in Isfahan, Persia; from 1906, secretary, and from 1907, administrator of Consulate in Bombay, India; from 1911 to 1914, secretary of Consulate General, Seoul, Korea; from 1915, diplomatic representative of MID attached to Turkestan Governor-General; from 1917, administrative residency in Bukhara, Bukharan Emirate. Emigrated to Korea.

98. **Den (Dan), Vasilii Egorovich von** (1884 – 1954). Student file dated 1902 from the Faculty of Oriental Languages of St. Petersburg University. Joined MID during First World War as Vice Consul in Paris and, ca. 1920, secretary of Embassy. Emigrated to France.

99. **Desnitskii, Ivan Ivanovich** (1882 – 1922). Student file dated 1902 from the Faculty of Oriental Languages of St. Petersburg University; had command of fourteen languages. Joined MID from 1908; from 1912, second secretary of Mission in Peking. Emigrated to China.

100. **Diachenko, Nikolai Nikolaevich** (18? – 19?). Student file dated 1893 from the Faculty of Oriental Languages of St. Petersburg University. Joined MID from 1897; from 1902, secretary of Consulate in Rushchuka, Bulgaria; from 1903, secretary and dragoman, Consulate General in Salonika, Greece; from 1905, Vice Consul in Sofia; from 1906, secretary of Diplomatic Agency in Bulgaria; from 1908 to 1910, secretary of Mission, and from 1909 to 1910, *chargé d'affaires* in Montenegro.

101. **Diakov, Aleksei Alekseevich** (1876 – 1940). Graduated 1902 from the Faculty of Oriental Languages of St. Petersburg University. Joined MID from 1902

as Sinologist; from 1903, student-trainee, at Mission in Peking; from 1904, dragoman at Consulate in Urga; in 1905, dragoman and from 1906 to 1912, secretary of Consulate in Kulja; from 1912 to 1917, Consul in Tufan, but actually in Ürümchi.

102. **Dmitrevskii, Pavel Andreevich** (1851 – 1899). Graduated 1875 from the Faculty of Oriental Languages of St. Petersburg University, with specialization in Chinese-Manchurian-Mongolian. Joined MID from 1876; from 1882 to 1883, acting Consul, and from 1884 to 1892, Consul, in Hankow; from 1893 to 1896, Consul in Tiantsin, temporarily from 1892 to 1893 administering Mission in Seoul, Korea; from 1896 to 1899, Consul General in Shanghai.

103. **Dolbezhev, Boris Vasilevich** (1881 – 1910). Graduated 1903 from the Faculty of Oriental Languages of St. Petersburg University, specializing in Mongolian, Chinese, and Manchurian. Joined MID as Sinologist; from 1905, dragoman at Consulate in Urga; from 1908, secretary of Consulate in Chuguchak, then in Ürümchi.

104, **Dolbezhev, Vladimir Vasilevich** (1877 – 1958). Graduated 1897 from the Faculty of Oriental Languages of St. Petersburg University, specializing in Mongolian, Chinese, and Manchurian. Joined MID from 1898 in consular service in China and Mongolia; from 1898 to 1900, as dragoman of the Consulate General, and from 1902 to 1904, administrator, of the Consulate in Urga; from 1905 to 1906, Consul in Tufan; from 1906 to 1909, Consul in Uliasutae; in 1909, secretary of Consulate in Ürümchi; from 1910 to 1916, Consul in Chuguchak. Emigrated to China and the United States.

105. **Eltekov, Nikolai Kuzmich** (1876 – 1936). Student file dated 1894 from the Faculty of Oriental Languages of St. Petersburg University. Joined MID from 1901 as diplomatic official of Chancellery of Governor for Far East; from 1904 to 1905, secretary of Commander-in-Chief at Port Arthur; from 1906 to 1910, acting secretary of Russian Mission in Siam, and as *chargé d'affaires* from 1909 to 1910; from 1910 to 1916, diplomatic official on special assignment to Irkutsk Governor-General. Emigrated to China.

106. **Essen, Otton Antonovich (Otto Peter)** (1843 – 1909). Student file dated 1861 from the Faculty of Oriental Languages of St. Petersburg University. Joined MID from 1901 to 1909 as Consul General in Breslau, Germany.

107. **Fedorov, Vladimir Mikhailovich** (18? – 19?). Student file dated 1899 from the Faculty of Oriental Languages of St. Petersburg University. Joined MID from 1913 to 1915 as dragoman, Consulate in Kashgar.

108. **Fitingof-Shel, Baron Aleksandr Borisovich** (1855-1926). Student file dated 1873 from the Faculty of Oriental Languages of St. Petersburg University. Joined MID from 1898 to 1902 as Consul in Le Havre and Rouen; Consul General in Baghdad; envoy to Greece. From 1913, Consul General in Florence; from 1916, at MID in St. Petersburg.

109. **Flit, Vasilii Iakovlevich van der** (1887 – 1948). Student file dated 1896 from the Faculty of Oriental Languages of St. Petersburg University. Joined MID from 1891; from 1893, at Embassy in Berlin; from 1895, aide to secretary and from 1902, second secretary, of Embassy; from 1906, first secretary of Mission in Den-

mark, administering Mission in 1906 in absence of envoy; from 1908, first secretary of Embassy in Berlin; from 1911, Resident Minister in Hesse and Saxe-Coburg-Gotha; from 1914, Director of 1st Department. Emigrated to Denmark.

110. **Gadzhemukov, Vasilii Nikolaevich** (1880 – 1956). Graduated in 1904 from the Faculty of Oriental Languages of St. Petersburg University. Joined MID from 1904; from 1906, stationed in Embassy in Constantinople; from 1908, held various consular positions in Ottoman Empire: Jerusalem, Jaffa, Skopje, Mitrowize, Beirut, Constantinople. Fromo 1914, Vice Consul in Dedeagach, Bulgaria; from May 1917, Consul and head of Dersiman area, Turkish province of Tunjeli. Emigrated to Constantinople, and in 1922, to Marseilles, France.

111. **Gagarin, Prince Sergei Andreevich** (1887 – 1941). Student file dated 1905 of the Faculty of Oriental Languages of St. Petersburg University. Joined MID from 1914 as secretary of the 2d Political (Near Eastern) Section; secretary of Embassy in Constantinople. Emigrated to United States.

112. **Gagelstrom, Viktor Vladimirovich** (1883 – no earlier than 1917). Student file dated 1901 of the Faculty of Oriental Languages of St. Petersburg University. Joined MID from 1906 as student at the Mission in Peking; from 1910 to 1912, dragoman at the Consulate General in Kashgar; from 1913 to 1915, secretary and dragoman of the Consulate in Canton; from 1915 to 1917, secretary and dragoman at the Consulate in Shanghai; in 1917, Vice Consul of the Consulate General in Kharbin. Emigrated to China and New Zealand.

113. **Geltske, Karl Andreevich** (1826 – 1910). Graduated 1848 from the Faculty of Oriental Languages of St. Petersburg University. Joined MID from 1848 in Chancellery; from 1852, third secretary; from 1853, second secretary; from 1857, first secretary; in 1865, secretary of Mission and simultaneously Consul General in Hamburg; from 1874, *chargé d'affaires* and from 1876, Resident Minister in Hamburg, Lubeck, and Bremen; from 1880, Envoy Extraordinary and Minister Plenipotentiary in Darmstadt; from 1882 to 1897, Resident Minister in Saxe-Weimar; from 1897 to 1908, special envoy of Russia in Italy and Egypt.

114. **Girs (Giers), Mikhail Mikhailovich** (1877 – 1932). Graduated 1900 from the Faculty of Oriental Languages of St. Petersburg University. Joined MID from 1902 in the Asian Department; from 1903 to 1913, various consular assignments in Persia, including Teheran. From 1913 to 1914 Political Agent in Bukhara; from 1915 to 1916, MID official for frontier relations attached to Governor of Caucasus in Tiflis; from 1916 to 1917, senior secretary of 3d (Central Asian) Division of MID. After 1917 remained in Soviet Russia; executed in 1930 as part of so-called "Academy of Sciences" case.

115. **Glinka, Dmitrii Grigorevich** (1808 – 1883). Graduated in 1824 from Noble Boarding School attached to St. Petersburg University. Joined MID: from 1825 as Clerk; from 1831, second secretary of Russian Mission in Copenhagen; from 1837, senior secretary of Mission in Stockholm, acting as *chargé d'affaires* from 1841 to 1844; from 1846, Counselor in Berlin; from 1850, *chargé d'affaires* attached to Court of Hesse-Darmstadt, Hesse-Kassel, and Nassau. From 1856, Envoy Extraordinary and Minister Plenipotentiary in Rio de Janeiro; and from 1871 to 1883, in Lisbon, Portugal.

116. **Golenishchev-Kutuzov, Vladimir Viktorovich** (1879 – 1934). Graduated 1906 from the Faculty of Oriental Languages of St. Petersburg University. Joined MID from 1906 as secretary of Consulate in Bitola, Serbia; from 1907, service in diplomatic representations in Turkey, Balkans, and India. From 1915 to 1916, secretary of Consulate in Maku, Persia. Emigrated to Tunis and France.

117. **Golstunskii, Konstantin Fedorovich** (1831-1899). Orientalist, professor. Head, Chair of Mongolian and Kalmyk Languages, St. Petersburg University. Simultaneously worked in MID from 1865 to 1899 as a translator, VII class, of the Asian Department.

118. **Golubinov, Sergei Petrovich** (1879 – 1951). Graduated 1901 from the Faculty of Oriental Languages of St. Petersburg University. Joined MID from 1901; from 1904, dragoman of Political Agent in Bukhara and secretary of Consulate General; from 1908, in Tevriz; from 1910, in Teheran; from 1911, Vice Consul in Urmi, Persia; from 1913, Consul in Rio de Janeiro; from 1915 to 1920, Consul in Isfahan. Emigrated to France and Germany.

119. **Grave, Vladimir Vladimirovich** (1880 – 1930). Graduated 1901 from Alexander Lycée. Joined MID from 1901 and was assigned in 1902 to the 1st Department; served on several commissions for the revision of the Sino-Russian boundary; from 1910, dragoman; from 1911, aide to Director, 1st (Far Eastern) Department; from 1912 to 1920, first secretary of Mission in Peking. Active in the White movement, he migrated to China and joined the Russian-Asian Bank in Peking.

120. **Grevenits, Baron Georgii Aleksandrovich** (1857 – 1939). Student file dated 1875 from the Faculty of Oriental Languages of St. Petersburg University. Joined MID from 1890 as third secretary, from 1891 as second secretary, from 1894 as secretary, and 1898 to 1899 as Counselor, of the Chancellery; from 1900 as first secretary and from 1902 as Counselor, of Embassy in London; from 1904 to 1908, Resident Minister in Saxe-Weimar, and from 1916, at the MID in St. Petersburg. Emigrated to Finland, Germany, and Italy.

121. **Grigorev, Nikolai Nikolaevich** (1881 – 1933). Student file dated 1899 from the Faculty of Oriental Languages of St. Petersburg University. Joined MID from 1905 as Persian specialist; initially as secretary and dragoman at Consulate in Isfahan; from 1909, dragoman of Consulate General at Bushir; from 1909 to 1913, secretary, dragoman, and administrator, Consulate General in Meshed; from 1915, consul in Astrabad; from 1917, administrator of Consulate in Jilin. Emigrated to France.

122. **Grosse, Viktor Fedorovich (Karl Georg Theodor)** (1869-1931). Graduated 1892 from the Faculty of Oriental Languages of St. Petersburg University, Chinese-Manchurian-Mongolian category. Joined MID Joined MID from 1892, basically in consular service in China. First as Clerk in Asian Department; from 1893, as student in Peking; from 1896, as secretary of Consulate in Tiantsin; from 1899, as Consul in Chifu; from 1892, as Consul in Newchwang (during Russo-Japanese War, as Commendant in Yingkou); as Consul General from 1906 in Yokohama, from 1910 to 1920, in Shanghai. Emigrated to China.

123. **Grushetskii, Aleksandr Nikolaevich** (1862 – 1910). Graduated 1886 from the Faculty of Oriental Languages of St. Petersburg University with Chinese-Manchurian specialization. Joined MID from 1886 as student at Mission in Peking; from 1889, governate secretary in Asian Department; from 1892, secretary of Consulate in Korea; from 1893 to 1897, secretary of Consulate in Lviv, Austria-Hungary; from 1900, official in Diplomatic Unit attached to Amur Governate General; from 1903, similar post attached to Far Eastern Governor; from 1907 to 1910, Consul General in Mukden, China.

124. **Iakimov, Nikolai Petrovich** (18? – 19?). Student file dated 1893 from the Faculty of Oriental Languages of St. Petersburg University. Joined MID as student at Embassy in Turkey; from 1914, Consul in Adrianople, Turkey; from 1915 to 1916, military attaché in Romania.

125. **Iakovlev, Nikolai Nikolaevich** (18? – 19?). Student file dated 1905 from the Faculty of Oriental Languages of St. Petersburg University. Joined MID as official in central apparatus; from 1915 to 1916, dragoman, Consulate General in Meshed, Persia.

126. **Iakushev, Boris Sergeevich** (18? – 19?). Student file dated 1907 from the Faculty of Oriental Languages of St. Petersburg University. Joined MID from 1915 to 1916 as secretary of Vice Consulate in Belgrade; from 1920, secretary of Mission in Greece.

127. **Ignatev, Vladimir Ivanovich** (1853 – 1902). Student file dated 1870 from the Faculty of Oriental Languages of St. Petersburg University. Joined MID from 1876; from 1880, student at Russian Mission in Persia; from 1885, dragoman and secretary at Consulate in Astrabad; then Clerk in Asian Department; from 1891 to 1893, diplomatic official attached to Head of Trans-Caspian Region; from 1895, Political Agent in Bukhara.

128. **Iudin, Nikolai Petrovich** (18? – 1917). Student file dated 1889 from the Faculty of Oriental Languages of St. Petersburg University. Joined MID as official in Asian Department; from 1914 to 1916, senior secretary, Far Eastern Division of MID.

129. **Iurenev, Aleksandr Nikolaevich** (1843 – after 1908). Student file dated 1863 from the Faculty of Oriental Languages of St. Petersburg University. Joined MID from 1901 to 1902 as diplomatic agent in Odessa; from 1903, at MID in St. Petersburg.

130. **Iuzefovich, Trofim Pavlovich** (1840 – 1883). Student file dated 1860 from the Faculty of Oriental Languages of St. Petersburg University. Joined MID from 1873 as Consul in Tulcha, Turkey; from 1876 to 1877, Consul General in Salonika. During Russo-Turkish War of 1877-1878, worked in Provisional Russian Administration of Bulgaria; in 1877, appointed Governor of liberated Tulcha; then became official of Russian Chancellery of Russian Commission in Bulgaria; and after termination of its operations, head of section of foreign links in Bulgaria.

131. **Ivanov, Ivan Aleksandrovich** (1835-1908). Graduated 1858 from St. Petersburg University and the Instructional Division of Oriental Languages attached to MID. Joined MID from 1860 as student trainee at Mission in Constantinople, and

then secretary and dragoman at several consulates; from 1868, Consul in Adrianople; from 1877 to 1878, during Russo-Turkish War was stationed at Chancellery of Head of Civil Affairs attached to Commander-in-Chief of Army; from 1894 to 1905, Head of Instructional Division of Oriental Languages attached to 1st (Asian) Department of MID.

132. **Kalmykov, Andrei Dmitrievich** (1870-1941). Student file dated 1891 of the Faculty of Oriental Languages of St. Petersburg University, fluent in fourteen languages but specializing in Armenian, Persian, Turkish, and Tatar. Joined MID from 1891 in Asian Department; from 1895, at Consulate General in Tevriz, Persia; from 1896, second secretary at Mission in Teheran; from 1897, Consul in Astrabad; from 1898 to 1900, secretary of Mission and *chargé d'affaires* in Bangkok, Siam; from 1900 to 1906, Commissar for frontier questions in Ashkhabad; from 1906 to 1910, Political Secretary for frontier questions attached to Governor General of Trans-Caspian Region (Tashkent); from 1911, Consul General in Skopje, Northern Macedonia, Ottoman Empire; from 1912, in Smyrna, Turkey. Emigrated to United States.

133. **Khadzhi-Lazarro (Khadzhi-Lazarri), Ivan Nikolaevich** (1880 – 1960s). Student file dated 1904 of the Faculty of Oriental Languages of St. Petersburg University. Joined MID from 1914, secretary of Consulate General in Erzerum, Turkey; Consul in Galac, Romania; Consul in Athens, and Consul General in Piraeus, Greece. Emigrated to Greece.

134. **Kholodkovskii, Vladimir Nikolaevich** (18? – 1958). Student file dated 1908 of the Faculty of Oriental Languages of St. Petersburg University. Joined MID as secretary, 2d Political Section. Emigrated to United States.

135. **Kolesov, Nikolai Fedorovich** (18 – 19?). Student file dated 1885 of the Faculty of Oriental Languages of St. Petersburg University. Joined MID from 1890 as Sinologist; from 1891, student trainee at Mission; from 1897, second dragoman and, from 1903, first dragoman, and from 1906, Consul General in Peking. Emigrated to China.

136. **Kolokolov, Sergei Aleksandrovich** (1868 – 1921). Graduated 1892 of the Faculty of Oriental Languages of St. Petersburg University, specializing in Chinese, Manchurian, and Mongolian. Joined MID from 1895 on consular service in China as dragoman of Consulate in Kulja; from 1896 to 1901, as secretary of Consulate in Kashgar; from 1901 as official in diplomatic unit attached to Head of Kwantung Region in Port Arthur; from 1902, secretary and dragoman, and from 1904, Consul General in Kashgar; from 1909, in Fuzhou; from 1910, Consul in Mukden. Emigrated to China.

137. **Koloshin, Ivan Petrovich** (1827 – 1891). Graduated from the Faculty of Oriental Languages of St. Petersburg University. Joined MID from 1848; from 1853, junior secretary of Mission in Belgium; from 1856, senior secretary of Mission; from 1871, *chargé d'affaires* of Russia in Spain; from 1876, Envoy Extraordinary and Minister Plenipotentiary in Baden; from 1882, member of MID Council.

138. **Kormazov (Karmazov), Aleksei D.** (18? – ?). Student file dated 1861 of the Faculty of Oriental Languages of St. Petersburg University. Joined MID from

1865 as Sinologist; from 1866 to 1869, secretary of Consulate in Ugra; from 1871 to 1873, secretary of Consulate in Tiantsin.

139. **Korostovets, Vladimir Konstantinovich** (1888 – 1953). Student file dated 1906 of the Faculty of Oriental Languages of St. Petersburg University. Joined MID from 1912 to 1917 as "private" secretary of three ministers of foreign affairs. Emigrated to Poland, Germany, and England.

140. **Kotsebue-Pilar von Pilhau, Dmitrii Fedorovich** (1872 – 1939). Student file dated 1894 of the Faculty of Oriental Languages of St. Petersburg University. Joined MID from 1902, serving at Embassy in Italy; from 1908, secretary at Mission in Hesse-Darmstadt; from 1915, in Christiana, Norway; from 1917, *chargé d'affaires* in Oslo. Emigrated to Estonia.

141. **Kozakov (Kazakov), Grigorii Aleksandrovich** (1869 – 1919). Student file dated 1887 of the Faculty of Oriental Languages of St. Petersburg University. Joined MID from 1893; from 1894 to 1895, student, and from 1897, acting dragoman at Mission in Japan; from 1899, secretary of Consulate General in Bombay; from 1901, Vice Consul, Masampo, Korea; from 1904, first secretary of Mission in China; first secretary, newly-opened Embassy in Tokyo after Russo-Japanese War; from 1910, official on special assignment attached to MID; from 1914, Head of 4th Political (Far Eastern) Section of MID. Emigrated to Finland and Sweden.

142. **Kratirov, Nikolai Nikolaevich** (1880 – 1952). Student file dated 1898 of the Faculty of Oriental Languages of St. Petersburg University. Joined MID as Clerk, 2d Department; Consul in Rome. Emigrated to France.

143. **Kristi, Khristofor Petrovich** (19? – 1937). Student file dated 1892 of the Faculty of Oriental Languages of St. Petersburg University. Joined MID from 1902 as secretary and dragoman, Consulate in Newchwang and Consul in Tiantsin; from 1907, Consul in Liverpool, England; from 1915 to 1917, Consul in Oslo. Emigrated to Norway.

144. **Krotkov, Nikolai Nikolaevich** (1869 – 1919). Graduated 1894 from the Faculty of Oriental Languages of St. Petersburg University, specializing in Manchurian and Chinese. Joined MID from 1894 as Sinologist; from 1894 as dragoman at Consulate in Kulja and Inspector of Consular School of Interpreters and Translators; secretary of Consulate in Jilin, Tsitsikar, and Kulja; Consul in Ürümchi until 1912; from 1914 to 1915, official on special assignment attached to Minister and agent of Ministry of Trade and Industry in Bulgaria.

145. **Kudashev, Nikolai Aleksandrovich** (1868 – 1925). Graduated from the Faculty of Oriental Languages of St. Petersburg University. Joined MID from 1893 as aide to secretary; from 1898, second secretary of Embassy in Turkey; from 1901, first secretary of Embassy in Japan; member, Russian delegation to Portsmouth, New Hampshire, peace conference to end Russo-Japanese War; from 1905, aide to first secretary of Embassy in Turkey; from 1906, first secretary of Embassy in United States; from 1908, second secretary of Embassy in Turkey; from 1910, Counselor of Embassy in United States; from 1913, Counselor of Embassy in Austria-Hungary. From 1914 to 1915, Director, Diplomatic Chancellery, Headquarters of Supreme Commander-in-Chief, coordinating activities of Headquarters and MID. From 1916, envoy in China. Emigrated to China and France.

146. **Kukhnov, Aleksandr Ivanovich** (18? – 1931). Graduated 1900 from the Faculty of Oriental Languages of St. Petersburg University. Joined MID from 1896 as executive of central apparatus; before 1917, Consul General in Bordeaux, France. Emigrated to France.

147. **Kurenkov, Mikhail Pavlovich** (18? – 19?). Graduated 1900 from the Faculty of Oriental Languages of St. Petersburg University. Joined MID as official in Diplomatic Unit attached to Amur Governate-General; Head, Commercial Section, Board of Chinese Far Eastern Railway. Emigrated to China.

148. **Kuzminskii, Mikhail Nikolaevich** (18? – 19?). Graduated 1901 from the Faculty of Oriental Languages of St. Petersburg University. Joined MID from 1902 to 1904 as a Sinologist and student trainee at the Mission in Peking; from 1905 and 1907-1910, secretary and dragoman of the Consulate in Ugra; from 1906, secretary and dragoman, Consulate in Uliasutae; from 1911, secretary of the Consulate General in Kharbin; from 1912 to 1913, Consul in Kobdo; from 1913 to 1917, Consul in Sharasum. Emigrated after 1917.

149. **Landezen, Artur-Karl Iulevich** (1874 – 1935). Graduated 1898 from the Faculty of Oriental Languages of St. Petersburg University. Joined MID from 1902 as Sinologist and dragoman at Mission in Peking and secretary of Consulate; from 1903, secretary of Consulate in Jilin and from 1911 to 1914, in Kharbin; from 1915 to 1920, Vice Consul in Kobe. Emigrated to United States.

150. **Lavdovskii, Vladimir Nikolaevich** (18? – 19?). Graduated 1902 from the Faculty of Oriental Languages of St. Petersburg University. Joined MID from 1907 to 1910 as dragoman of Russian Consulate in Kulja; Consul in Kiakhta.

151. **Lavrov, Mikhail Ivanovich** (18? – 19?). Graduated 1886 from the Faculty of Oriental Languages of St. Petersburg University. Joined MID as Sinologist: from 1902 to 1906, secretary of Consulate General in Kashgar; from 1907, Vice Consul, Consulate General in Kharbin; from 1910, Vice Consul, and from 1912 to 1916, Consul in Kvachen. Emigrated to China.

152. **Likhachev, Sergei Aleksandrovich** (1886 – 19?). Student file dated 1905 of the Faculty of Oriental Languages of St. Petersburg University. Joined MID from 1905 as secretary of Mission and, from 1906, as *chargé d'affaires* in Ethiopia; from 1909, at the Embassy in Italy; from 1912 to 1914, secretary of Mission and *chargé d'affaires* in Morocco; from 1915 to 1918, Consul General in Montreal.

153. **Liuba, Vladimir Fedorovich** (1861 – 1928). Student file dated 1881 of the Faculty of Oriental Languages of St. Petersburg University, specializing in Chinese, Mongolian, and Manchurian. Joined MID from 1886 as Sinologist and interpreter attached to Governor-General of Steppe Territory; from 1890, dragoman, and from 1895 to 1899, secretary of Mission in Ugra; from 1899 to 1902, first representative of MID in Manchuria, with rights of Consul in Jilin; from 1904 to 1906, Consul in Ugra; Consul General from 1907 to 1909 in Kharbin and from 1909 to 1911, in Uliasutae, and from 1911 to 1913, in Ugra; from 1913 to 1916, in Kobdo, temporarily administering the Consulate; in 1916, at Sharasum; from 1917 to 1919, Consul in Kulja under Provisional Government and White regimes. Emigrated to China.

154. **Liutsh, Iakov (Rudolf-Alexander) Iakovlevich** (1854 – 1919). Graduated 1878 from the Faculty of Oriental Languages of St. Petersburg University. Joined MID from 1878 as official in Chancellery of Turkestan Governor-General; from 1883 to 1894, secretary of Consulate in Kashgar; from 1894, official in Diplomatic Unit attached to Amur Governor-General and, from 1899, Turkestan Governor-General; from 1902 to 1910, Political Agent in Bukhara; from 1911 to 1921, Consul General in Seoul, Korea.

155. **Lukashevich, Nikolai Nikolaevich** (18? – 19?). Graduated 1914 of the Faculty of Oriental Languages of St. Petersburg University. Joined MID from 1915 to 1918 as student trainee Sinologist at Mission in Peking.

156. **Maksimov, Viktor Aleksandrovich** (18? – 18?). Appointed lecturer and privat-docent in Faculty of Oriental Languages from 1866 to 1867. Graduated 1867 from the Faculty of Oriental Languages of St. Petersburg University. Joined MID from 1866 and served at Mission in Turkey; from 1873 to 1877, Consul in Bitola, Serbia; from 1884 to 1887, as Consul in Trabzone, Turkey; and from 1890, Consul in Jerusalem.

157. **Malinin, Evgenii Dmitrievich** (1888 – 1923). Graduated 1911 of the Faculty of Oriental Languages of St. Petersburg University. Joined MID from 1911 in 1st Department of MID; from 1912, student trainee at Embassy in Japan; from 1915, secretary of Consulate at Dalnii, China; Vice Consul, Kobe, Japan. Emigrated to Japan.

158. **Margaritov, Ivan Nikolaevich** (1885 – 1977). Student file dated 1904 of the Faculty of Oriental Languages of St. Petersburg University. Served MID as commercial attaché in Italy; from 1914, as military attaché in Rome. Emigrated to Italy.

159. **Martinovich, Nikolai Nikolaevich** (1883 – 1954). Graduated 1907 from the Faculty of Oriental Languages of St. Petersburg University, specializing in Arabic, Persian, Turkish, and Tatar. Joined MID from 1907 as Vice Consul in Alexandria, Athens, Salonika, Istanbul, and Kandia, Crete. Emigrated to Czechoslovakia and United States.

160. **Melnikov, Aleksandr Aleksandrovich** (1827 – 1913). Graduated 1849 from the Faculty of Oriental Languages of St. Petersburg University, specializing in Arabic, Persian, Turkish, and Tatar, and from the Instructional Division of Oriental Languages attached to MID in 1851. Joined MID from 1851 as student trainee; from 1857, as junior secretary attached to Mission in Persia; from 1860, Asian Department of MID; interpreter VII class, then senior Head of Desk; from 1864, interpreter VI class; from 1865, Head of 1st Division; from 1868, Clerk VI class; from 1871, Clerk, V class; in 1873, elevated to full State counsellor; from 1875, Vice Director of Asian Department; from 1883 to 1886, Envoy Extraordinary and Minister Plenipotentiary in Persia.

161. **Meshcherskii, Prince Dmitrii Viktorovich** (1875 – 1933). Student file dated 1896 of the Faculty of Oriental Languages of St. Petersburg University. Joined MID from 1901 as Sinologist and dragoman at Consulate in Kulja; from 1905, secretary of Consulate in Tiantsin; from 1907 to 1909, Vice Consul in Kwanchentse; from 1911, Consul in Jilin; from 1915 to 1917, Consul General in Kashgar. Emigrated to Poland.

162. **Miller, Aleksandr (Friedrich) Iakovlevich** (1868 – 1940). Student file dated 1880 of the Faculty of Oriental Languages of St. Petersburg University. Joined MID from 1893 as student trainee in Mission at Teheran; from 1894 to 1899, dragoman of Political Agent in Bukhara; from 1899 to 1905, Vice Consul in Seystan, Persia; from 1906, first dragoman at Mission in Teheran; from 1907, Consul in Liverpool, England; from 1908, Consul in Astrabad; from 1910, Consul General in Tevriz; from 1913 to 1915, Diplomatic Agent, and from 1915 to 1916, Consul General in Ugra; from 1916 to 1917, Resident, and then Political Agent in Bukhara. Emigrated to France.

163. **Mukhin, Nikolai Iakimovich** (18? – 1873). Graduated 1832 from the Faculty of Oriental Languages of St. Petersburg University and Instructional Division of Oriental Languages of MID. Joined MID from 1841 as third dragoman of Mission in Constantinople and from 1844, as second dragoman; from 1847, secretary of Mission in Persia; from 1850 to 1853, Consul General in Adrianople; from 1853 to 1856, Consul General in Serbia; from 1856 to 1859, Consul General in Syria and Palestine (with Residence in Beirut); served in central apparatus of MID; from 1862 to 1873, Consul General in Palermo, Italy.

164. **Muliukin, Nikolai Sergeevich** (1876 – ca. 1960s). Student file dated 1897 of the Faculty of Oriental Languages of St. Petersburg University. Joined MID from 1903 and served in Diplomatic Chancellery of Governor in Port Arthur, Far East; from 1906, secretary and dragoman of Vice Consulate in Chifu, China; from 1907, acting secretary of Consulate in Tiantsin; from 1912 to 1914, secretary of Consulate General in Shanghai; from 1915, Vice Consul of Consulate General in Chifu. Emigrated to China.

165. **Murkos, Georgii (Iurii) Abramovich** (1846 – 1911). Student file dated 1866 of the Faculty of Oriental Languages of St. Petersburg University. Joined MID from 1901 to 1906, at Moscow Main Archive of MID.

166. **Nekrasov, Vladimir Ivanovich** (1873 –1923). Graduated 1898 from the Faculty of Oriental Languages of St. Petersburg University. Joined MID from 1898; from 1901 as dragoman, then secretary, of Consulate General in Tevriz, Persia. From 1901, secretary, Consulate General in Bombay, then Vice Consul in Seystan; from 1910 to 1913, Consul in Reshteh; in 1913, Consul in Isfahan; in 1917 appointed by Provisional Government as Head, 3d Political Section, MID, responsible for Persian and Central Asian affairs. Emigrated to Turkey.

167. **Nikitin, Vladimir Konstantinovich** (1877 – 19?). Student file dated 1897 of the Faculty of Oriental Languages of St. Petersburg University. Joined MID from 1901 as Sinologist and student trainee at Mission in Peking; from 1902, secretary of Consulate General in Shanghai; from 1904, dragoman of Consulate in Newchwang; from 1910, Vice Consul in Kharbin; from 1911 to 1917, Vice Consul in Aigun.

168. **Nikolai, Baron Nikolai Pavlovich** (1818 – 1869). Graduated from the Alexander Lycée and St. Petersburg University. Joined MID from 1839; from 1841, junior secretary of Mission in The Hague; from 1845, junior secretary of Embassy in United Kingdom; from 1850, official on special assignment, VI class, attached to State Chancellery; from 1854, Counselor of Mission in Berlin; from

1855, Counselor, Embassy in United Kingdom; Envoy Extraordinary and Minister Plenipotentiary in Switzerland; from 1860 to 1867, in Denmark.

169. **Nikolskii, Nikolai Petrovich** (1868 – 1966). Student file dated 1888 of the Faculty of Oriental Languages of St. Petersburg University. Joined MID from 1896 as Persian specialist; from 1897, secretary and dragoman, Consulate in Reshteh and Astrabad; from 1898, dragoman at Mission in Teheran; from 1903, Consul in Kermanshah; from 1914, Consul General in Meshed. Emigrated to France and United Kingdom.

170. **Nikonov, Mikhail Nikolaevich** (1832 – 1902). Graduated from the Faculty of Oriental Languages of St. Petersburg University. Joined MID from 1855 as junior and from 1866 as senior Desk Head; from 1868, Clerk, VII class, and from 1873, V class, in Department of Economic Affairs and Accounts; in 1874, member from MID in special commission attached to Ministry of War for questions of military duty; in 1875, member of provisional MID commission for the recovery of customs duties and related reports; from 1884, Director, Department of Personnel and Economic Affairs.

171. **Obnorskii, Nikolai Aleksandrovich** (18? – 19?). Student file dated 1891 of the Faculty of Oriental Languages of St. Petersburg University. Joined MID from 1900 as Clerk, 1st (Asian) Department; from 1905, second secretary of Russian Mission in Serbia; from 1910, Embassy in United States; from 1911, secretary of Mission in Montenegro; from 1915 to 1916, *chargé d'affaires* in Montenegro; from 1916, first secretary of Mission in Serbia.

172. **Okunev, Grigorii Nikolaevich** (1823 – 1883). Graduated 1844 from St. Petersburg University. Joined MID from 1846 as Clerk, Department of Internal Relations; from 1847, Clerk of Chancellery of MID; from 1849, junior secretary and from March 1856, senior secretary of Embassy in Rome; from September 1856, senior secretary of Embassy in France; from 1870, *chargé d'affaires* of Russia in France; from 1875, Envoy Extraordinary and Minister Plenipotentiary in France.

173. **Orlov, Arkadii Aleksandrovich** (1870 – 1940). Student file dated 1890 of the Faculty of Oriental Languages of St. Petersburg University. Joined MID from 1896; from 1897, first dragoman, Consulate General in Constantinople; from 1898 to 1902, secretary of Extraordinary Mission in Abyssinia; from 1903, Vice Consul in Skutari, Turkey (now Albania); then Consul in Mitrowice, Turkey (now Kosovo); from 1906, Consul in Uskube, Turkey (now Skopje, Northern Macedonia); from 1911, Consul General in Baghdad; from 1913 in Tevriz; from 1916, Ugra; simultaneously from 1917, in Kobdo. Emigrated to China.

174. **Ostrovskii, Dmitrii Nikolaevich** (28 March 1856 – 30 March 1938, d. Paris, France). Student file dated 1875 of St. Petersburg University. Joined MID from 1878; served from 1889 to 1893 as Consul, Hammerfest, Norway; from 1893 to 1895, in Klaipeda; from 1895 to 1897, in Newcastle-on-Tyne; from 1898 to 1899, Leipzig; from 1899 to 1914, Consul General in Danzig.

175. **Panafidii, (Panafidin), Petr Grigorevich** (1848 – after 1916). Graduated 1874 from the Faculty of Oriental Languages of St. Petersburg University. Joined MID from 1874; from 1875, student trainee at Mission in Teheran; from 1878, secretary and dragoman, Consulate in Astrabad; from 1883, secretary of Consulate

General in Tevriz; from 1888 to 1893, Consul in Baghdad; from 1897, Consul General in Isfahan, then in Meshed; from 1903 to 1919, in Constantinople. From 1913 to 1916, served in central apparatus of MID.

176. **Perovskii (from 1907, Petrovo-Solovovo), Count Mikhail Mikhailovich** (1870 – 1954). Student file dated 1888 of the Faculty of Oriental Languages of St. Petersburg University. Joined MID as first secretary and as official for special assignments of MID. Emigrated to France.

177. **Petrashevskii, Ignatii Baltazarovich** (1796 – 1869). Graduated 1831 from St. Petersburg University with studies at the Institute of Oriental Languages of MID, specializing in Turkish, Persian, and Arabic. Interpreter and Lecturer at St. Petersburg and Berlin universities. Joined MID from 1833 to 1840 as dragoman and secretary of Mission in Constantinople. Subsequently served as Consul in Turkish cities of Smyrna, Salonika, Alexandria, and Jaffa.

178. **Piper, Leonid Adolfovich** (18? – 19?). Graduated 1883 from the Faculty of Oriental Languages of St. Petersburg University. Joined MID and served in the central apparatus; from 1902, secretary and dragoman, Consulate General in Salonika.

179. **Pisarev, Vissarion Modestovich** (1877 – 1917). Graduated 1900 from the Faculty of Oriental Languages of St. Petersburg University. Joined MID and served in Constantinople; from 1915 to 1916, Vice Consul in Prizren, Serbia.

180. **Pletner, Orest Viktorovich** (1892 – 1970). Student file dated 1911 of the Faculty of Oriental Languages of St. Petersburg University, specializing in Japanese. Joined MID from September 1917 as dragoman and attaché in Mission at Tokyo. Emigrated to Vietnam and Japan.

181. **Pokotilov, Dmitrii Dmitrievich** (1865 – 1908). Student file dated 1883 of the Faculty of Oriental Languages of St. Petersburg University. Joined MID from 1887 as Sinologist; from 1893, in service of Ministry of Finances as Head of Division for Korea and Japan; from 1894 to 1904, Director, Peking Division of Russo-Chinese Bank; from 1897, representative of Ministry of Finances in China; from 1905, Ambassador Extraordinary and Plenipotentiary in China; in 1905, member of Russian delegation to Portsmouth, New Hampshire peace conference; from 1905 to 1908, envoy to China.

182. **Polianskii, Zinovii Mikhailovich** (1871 – 1919). Student file dated 1889 of the Faculty of Oriental Languages of St. Petersburg University, specializing in Chinese, Mongolian, and Manchurian. Joined MID from 1893 in Asian Department; from 1895, student trainee at Embassy in Tokyo; from 1901, Vice Consul in Seoul, Korea; from 1903, Vice Consul in Chemulpo, Korea; and from 1905, in Shanghai; from 1906, Consul in Nagasaki, Japan; from 1909, interpreter, VI class, Asian Department; from 1910 to 1914, Consul in Königsberg.

183. **Polikarpov, Sergei Ivanovich** (18? – 19?). Student file dated 1905 of the Faculty of Oriental Languages of St. Petersburg University. Joined MID as Sinologist and served in Embassy in Peking; from 1914 to 1916, secretary of Vice Consulate in Khailar, China.

184. **Popov, Georgii Konstantinovich** (1879 – 1929). Student file dated 1899 of the Faculty of Oriental Languages of St. Petersburg University. Joined MID from 1903 as Sinologist; from 1909, dragoman of Consulate in Kharbin; from 1912, secretary of Consulate in Ugra; from 1914, Consul in Vana; from 1915 to 1920, Vice Consul and administrator of consulate, and Consul General in Kharbin. Emigrated to China.

185. **Popov, Mikhail Mikhailovich** (18? – 19?). Student file dated 1884 of St. Petersburg University; from 1901 to 1903, graduate of Lazarev Institute of Oriental Languages, specializing in Chinese. Joined MID from 1903 to 1904 as secretary of consulate in Baghdad; from 1904 to 1905, administrator of Consulate in Basra; from 1905 to 1906, and in 1913, secretary and dragoman of Consulate in Urga; from 1907 to 1912, secretary and from 1913 to 1916, Vice Consul, Consulate General in Kharbin. Emigrated to China.

186. **Popov, Pavel Stepanovich** (1842 – 1913). Graduated 1870 from the Faculty of Oriental Languages of St. Petersburg University, specializing in Chinese. Joined MID from 1870 as student trainee at Mission in Peking; from 1873, second dragoman, and from 1877, first dragoman of Mission; from 1886 to 1902, Consul General in Peking. From 1902, Head, Chair of Chinese Language, Faculty of Oriental Languages of St. Petersburg University. Author of important dictionaries of Chinese language.

187. **Poppe, Nikolai Gotfridovich** (1870 – 1913). Student file dated 1889 of the Faculty of Oriental Languages of St. Petersburg University. Joined MID from 1895; from 1899 to 1901, secretary of Consulate in Tiantsin; from 1901 to 1902, secretary of Consulate in Shanghai; from 1907 to 1909, Consul General in Tiantsin; from 1909 to 1913, Consul General in Kharbin.

188. **Pustoshkin, Konstantin Pavlovich** (1859 – 1922). Student file dated 1878 of the Faculty of Oriental Languages of St. Petersburg University. Joined MID from 1885 as Consul in Naples, Italy; from 1887 in Amsterdam; from 1890, in Brodach, Austria; from 1903 to 1909, Consul General in Lviv (Lemberg); and from 1913 to 1918, Naples. Emigrated to Italy.

189. **Ramming, Martin-Gothard-Theodor Nikolaevich** (1889 – 1988). Student file dated 1908 of the Faculty of Oriental Languages of St. Petersburg University. Joined MID from 1912 to 1923 as student trainee, then dragoman, at the Mission in Japan. Emigrated to Germany.

190. **Razdolskii, Kazimir Stanislavovich** (18? – 19?). Student file dated 1897 of the Faculty of Oriental Languages of St. Petersburg University. Joined MID from 1911 as secretary of Consulate in Kobdo, China; from 1917, at Russian Residenceship in Bukhara.

191. **Razumovskii, Sergei Pavlovich** (1875 – 1947). Student file dated 1896 of the Faculty of Oriental Languages of St. Petersburg University. Joined MID from 1914, as Vice Consul in Jaffa, Ottoman Empire; then attaché at Diplomatic Agency in Egypt; until 1917, Consul in Cairo.

192. **Renne, Baron Arved-Adolf-Edgar Frantsevich** (18? – 19?). Student file dated 1908 of the Faculty of Oriental Languages of St. Petersburg University.

Joined MID from as secretary and dragoman, Consulate in Aigun, Manchuria; from 1915 to 1921, attaché in Tokyo. Emigrated to Japan.

193. **Rospopov, Nikolai Aleksandrovich** (c. 1865 – 1940s). Student file dated 1884 of the Faculty of Oriental Languages of St. Petersburg University. Joined MID from 1890 to 1895 as student trainee in Tokyo; from 1896, Vice Consul in Seoul; from 1899, Consul in Chempulpo, Korea; from 1905 to 1906, financial agent of Consulate in Shanghai; from 1907, Consul General in Dairen; from 1910, Consul in Nagasaki; from 1915, Consul General in Singapore. Emigrated to France.

194. **Rozdolskii, Kazimir (Valerian) Stanislavovich** (18? – 19?). Student file dated 1900 of the Faculty of Oriental Languages of St. Petersburg University. Joined MID from as official of central apparatus; from 1914 to 1916, secretary, Consulate General in Kashgar, China.

195. **Rozhdestvenskii, Petr Sergeevich** (1870 – 1915). Graduated 1892 of the Faculty of Oriental Languages of St. Petersburg University. Joined MID from 1892 as student trainee in Peking; from 1896, administrator of Consulate General in Hankow; from 1898 to 1902, served at Embassy in Washington D.C.; in 1905 participated in Portsmouth, New Hampshire, peace negotiations to end Russo-Japanese War; from 1905, second secretary, Mission in Peking; from 1908 to 1909, first secretary of Mission in Bucharest; from 1909 to 1915, Consul, then Consul General, at San Francisco, California.

196. **Rudanovskii, Petr Konstantinovich** (c. 1870 – 1904). Graduated 1892 from the Faculty of Oriental Languages of St. Petersburg University. Joined MID from 1902 as second secretary, Embassy in Turkey; from 1903 to 1906, Consul in Singapore.

197. **Sabanin, Andrei Vladimirovich** (1887 – 1938). Student file dated 1904 of the Faculty of Oriental Languages of St. Petersburg University; studied at the said University from 1904 to 1905, and then from 1906 to 1908 at Alexander Lycée. Joined MID from 1908; from 1910, Clerk in 2d Department; in 1917, senior clerk, MID; from 1920 to 1937, Head, Economic and Legal (from 1931, Legal) Section of NKID of RSFSR and then USSR.

198. **Sekretarev, Petr Petrovich** (1852 – 1922). Graduated 1898 from the Faculty of Oriental Languages of St. Petersburg University. Joined MID from 1898 as Vice Consul in Haifa, Palestine; from 1902, secretary and dragoman in Consulate at Trapezund, Turkey; Vice Consul in Cairo. From 1916 to 1917, acting diplomatic official attached to Governor-General of Turkestan.

199. **Serafimov, Boris Savvich** (1882 – not before 1940s). Graduated 1907 from the Faculty of Oriental Languages of St. Petersburg University, specializing in Arabic, Persian, Turkish, and Tatar languages. Joined MID from 1909 in 1st (Asian) Department; from 1911, acting secretary and dragoman of Consulate in Aleppo, Syria; from 1914, third dragoman of Mission in Constantinople; in 1917, stationed at Mission in Berne, Switzerland. Emigrated to Bulgaria.

200. **Sergeev, Vasilii Sergeevich** (1857 – 1910). Student file dated 1875 of the Faculty of Oriental Languages of St. Petersburg University. Joined MID from 1881 as Clerk in Asian Department; from 1888, first secretary of Mission in Serbia and,

from 1893, in Sweden; from 1900, Counselor in MID; from 1906 to 1909, Envoy Extraordinary and Minister Plenipotentiary in Serbia; from 1910, in Sweden.

201. **Shapshal, Sergei Markovich (Mordukhaevich, Mordkhaevich)** (1873 – 1961). Student file dated 1894 of the Faculty of Oriental Languages of St. Petersburg University, specializing in Arabic, Persian, Turkish, and Tatar. Joined MID from 1901 to 1908 as interpreter and performing diplomatic work in Persia, also serving as personal secretary and dragoman of Shah of Persia; from 1908 to 1917, in central apparatus of MID as interpreter in Political Section and lecturer in Turkish language at Instructional Division of Oriental Languages attached to MID.

202. **Shcheglov, Andrei Nikolaevich** (1857 – after 1920). Student file dated 1875 of the Faculty of Oriental Languages of St. Petersburg University. Joined MID from 1880; from 1885, secretary and dragoman of Diplomatic Agency and Consulate General in Cairo; from 1890, secretary of Mission in Japan; from 1895, official on special assignment for frontier relations attached to Commander-in-Chief of the Civil Unit in the Caucasus; from 1896, first secretary of Mission in Persia; from 1898, first secretary of Embassy in Turkey; from 1902 to 1905, Resident Minister in Montenegro; from 1906 to 1907, envoy to Bulgaria. Emigrated from 1920.

203. **Shchekin, Mikhail Sergeevich** (1871 – 1920). Student file dated 1889 of the Faculty of Oriental Languages of St. Petersburg University. Joined MID from 1908 as Consul in Trieste; from 1910, first secretary of Mission in Peking; from 1912, Counselor of Mission in Tokyo. Emigrated to Japan.

204. **Shcherbatskii, Aleksandr Ippolitovich** (1874 – 1952). Student file dated 1898 of the Faculty of Oriental Languages of St. Petersburg University. Joined MID from 1898 as aide to secretary and, from 1902, second secretary of Embassy in Turkey; from 1910, first secretary of Embassy in Japan; from 1914 to 1915, Counselor to Embassy in Washington D.C.; from 1916, envoy to Brazil and jointly Uruguay, Paraguay, and Chile. Emigrated to Germany, France, and United States.

205. **Shebunin, Aleksei Fedorovich** (1867 – 1937). Student file dated 1885 of the Faculty of Oriental Languages of St. Petersburg University. Joined MID from 1889 as secretary; from 1902, Vice Consul, Consulate General in Cairo; from 1914, Consul General in Constantinople. Emigrated to France.

206. **Shilling, Baron Gustav Gustavovich (Gustav-Tobias) von** (1859 – 1912). Student file dated 1878 of the Faculty of Oriental Languages of St. Petersburg University. Joined MID in central apparatus; secretary of Embassy in Italy; official on special assignments, VI class.

207. **Shirkov, Vasilii Ivanovich** (18? – 19?). Student file dated 1889 of the Faculty of Oriental Languages of St. Petersburg University. Joined MID as a Turkologist from 1902, as secretary and dragoman, Consulate General in Erzerum; from 1907, Consul in Bitlis.

208. **Shrut, Aleksandr Vasilevich** (1881 – 1970). Student file dated 1901 of the Faculty of Oriental Languages of St. Petersburg University. Joined MID from 1905 as official in the Department of Personnel and Economic Affairs. Emigrated to Czechoslovakia.

209. **Shtaveman, Petr Fedorovich** (18? – 19?). Graduated 1905 from the Faculty of Oriental Languages of St. Petersburg University. Joined MID as official in the Political Section.

210. **Shtein, Evgenii Fedorovich** (1869 – 1961). Graduated 1892 from the Faculty of Oriental Languages of St. Petersburg University, specializing in Chinese, Manchurian, and Mongolian. Joined MID from 1892 as Clerk, Asian Department; from 1893, student trainee at Mission in China; from 1895, secretary and dragoman, and then Counselor, *chargé d'affaires*, and temporary administrator of Mission in Korea; from 1904, by decision of MID, member of Prize Court in Vladivostok regarding Japanese vessels detained or seized during Russo-Japanese War; from December 1905, secretary of Mission in Montenegro; from 1908, secretary of Mission in Brazil; and from 1910, simultaneously *chargé d'affaires*; from 1916 to 1917, first Envoy Extraordinary and Minister Plenipotentiary of Russia in Argentina, until 1923.

211. **Shuiskii, Nikolai Alekseevich** (1852 – 1909). Graduated 1876 from the Faculty of Oriental Languages of St. Petersburg University. Joined MID from 1882 and served in consulates in China, Korea, and Japan. From 1898, Consul in Tiantsin; from 1902 to 1909, Consul General in Fuzhou, China.

212. **Shulga, Nikolai Andreevich** (1883 – after 1917). Student file dated 1901 of the Faculty of Oriental Languages of St. Petersburg University. Joined MID from 1909 at Political Agency in Bukhara; from 1911, dragoman of Political Agency in Bukhara; from 1914, first dragoman and, from 1916, acting first secretary of Political Agency in Bukhara; from 21 May 1916, temporarily administered Political Agency in Bukhara; from 1917, secretary of 3d Political (Central Asian) Section of MID.

213. **Simonolevich, Konstantin Iosifovich** (18? – 19?). Student file dated 1903 of the Faculty of Oriental Languages of St. Petersburg University. Joined MID as official; from 1915 to 1916, secretary of Consulate in Tsitsikar, China.

214. **Skorodumov, Vasilii Aleksandrovich** (1880 – 1932). Student file dated 1898 of the Faculty of Oriental Languages of St. Petersburg University. Joined MID from 1903; from 1906 to 1907, attaché at Mission in China; from 1908 to 1914, dragoman of Embassy in Japan; in 1914, acting Consul in Kobe and, in 1915, at Nagasaki; from 1915 to 1916, Vice Consul in Pusan and Mozanpo. Emigrated to Japan.

215. **Skriabin, Nikolai Aleksandrovich** (1849 – 1914). Student file dated 1872 of the Faculty of Oriental Languages of St. Petersburg University. Joined MID from 1878 at Embassy in Turkey; from 1879 to 1881, secretary and dragoman of Consulate General in Salonika; from 1899 to 1900, at Adrianople; from 1901 to 1904, Consul General in Jannina, Turkey; from 1904 to 1909, in Erzerum; from 1911 to 1914, in Lausanne, Switzerland; from 1914, at central apparatus of MID.

216. **Smirnov, Aleksei Aleksandrovich** (1857 – 1924). Graduated 1891 from the Faculty of Oriental Languages of St. Petersburg University, specializing in Arabic, Persian, Turkish, and Tatar languages. Joined MID from 1881 in Asian Department; from 1885, aide to secretary of Embassy in Turkey; from 1891, second secretary of Embassy in Turkey; from 1897, first secretary of Embassy in Athens;

from 1905 to 1911, Consul General and diplomatic agent in Egypt; from 1911 to 1923, Envoy Extraordinary and Minister Plenipotentiary in Egypt; doyen of diplomatic corps in Cairo. Emigrated to Egypt.

217. **Smirnov, Nikolai Aleksandrovich** (1861 – 1930). Student file dated 1885 of the Faculty of Oriental Languages of St. Petersburg University. Joined MID from 1902 as secretary of Mission in Dresden; from 1914, Consul General in Trieste. Emigrated to Germany.

218. **Smogorzhevskii, Sigizmund Bronislavovich** (1884 – 1931). Student file dated 1903 of the Faculty of Oriental Languages of St. Petersburg University. Joined MID from 1912 as Vice Consul in Algiers; from 1918 to 1919, attached to Russian Embassy in Paris. Emigrated to Poland.

219. **Sokolov, Afinogen Afanasevich** (18? – 19?). Graduated 1908 from the Faculty of Oriental Languages of St. Petersburg University. Joined MID as Sinologist from 1913 to 1915, dragoman of Consulate in Kulja; from 1915 to 1916, Consulate General in Kharbin.

220. **Sokov, Sergei Vasilevich** (18? – 19?). Graduated 1886 from the Faculty of Oriental Languages of St. Petersburg University. Joined MID from 1894 to 1909 as dragoman of Russian Consulate in Kulja; from 1909 to 1914, Consul General in Kashgar; from 1914, Consul General in Kulja.

221. **Somov, Aleksandr Sergeevich** (12 August 1859 to 1928). Student file dated 1879 of the Faculty of Oriental Languages of St. Petersburg University. Joined MID from 1888 to 1892, second secretary of Mission in Serbia; from 1892 to 1895, in Romania; from 1895, first secretary of Mission in United States; from 1897, first secretary of Mission in Japan; from 1897 to 1903, in Romania, where he administered the Mission; from 1903 to 1908, in Persia. From 1908, Consul General in Korea; from 1911 to 1913, Political Agent in Bukhara.

222. **Stal von Golshtein, Baron Aleksandr Avgustovich** (1877 – 1937). Orientalist, Egyptologist, Sinologist, and privat-docent, Chair of Sanskrit Language in Faculty of Oriental Languages, St. Petersburg University. Joined MID from 1904 as attaché in 1st Department; from 1905, secretary of Consulate in Bombay.

223. **Stefanovich, Grigorii Feofilovich** (18? – 19?). Student file dated 1913 of the Faculty of Oriental Languages of St. Petersburg University. Joined MID from 1915 to 1916, dragoman, Consulate General in Kashgar. Worked in Soviet institutions after 1917.

224. **Stolitsa, Sergei Nikolaevich** (18? – 19?). Student file dated 1891 of the Faculty of Oriental Languages of St. Petersburg University. Joined MID as official of central apparatus; from 1902, third dragoman at Embassy in Turkey, and from 1914, second dragoman.

225. **Stolypin, Nikolai Arkadevich** (1814 – 1884). Graduated 1834 from St. Petersburg University. Joined MID from 1835 as official of central apparatus; from late 1840s to early 1850s, senior secretary, missions in Baden and Frankfurt-on-Main. From 1854 to 1865, *chargé d'affaires* in Baden. From 1865 to 1871, envoy in Württemberg; from 1871 to 1884, in The Netherlands.

226. **Strebulaev, Nikolai Ivanovich** (18? – 19?). Student file dated 1878 of the Faculty of Oriental Languages of St. Petersburg University. Joined MID as Turkologist from 1902, secretary of Consulate in Harput, Armenia; from 1913 to 1916, Consul in Skopje, Serbia.

227. **Struve, Nikolai Berngardovich** (18? – 19?). Student file dated 1882 of the Faculty of Oriental Languages of St. Petersburg University. Joined MID from 1897 as Vice Consul in Frankfurt-on-Main; from 1900 to 1911, first Consul of Russia in Montreal, Canada; from 1911 to 1912, Consul in Lisbon.

228. **Subbotin, Nikolai Nikolaevich** (18? – 19?). Student file dated 1906 of the Faculty of Oriental Languages of St. Petersburg University. Joined MID from 1913 to 1914, secretary of Consulate General in Berlin.

229. **Tideman, Petr Genrikhovich** (1872 – 1941). Student file dated 1890 of the Faculty of Oriental Languages of St. Petersburg University. Joined MID as Sinologist from 1895 as student trainee at Mission in Peking; from 1899, dragoman attached to Diplomatic Unit of Chief Head of Kwantung Region; from 1902, Vice Consul in Chifu; from 1904, official VI class in Mukden; from 1906, aide in Diplomatic Unit attached to Amur Governor-General; from 1908, Consul General in Hong Kong; from 1911, in Newchwang (Yingkou); from 1915 to 1917, in Tiantsin. Emigrated to China and Canada.

230. **Timchenko-Ostroverkhov, Andrei Nikolaevich** (18? – 19?). Student file dated 1882 of the Faculty of Oriental Languages of St. Petersburg University. Joined MID from 1894 as Sinologist; from 1894 to 1899, Consul in Chifu; from 1899 to 1902, Consul in Newchwang; from 1903 to 1904, Consul in Hankow; from 1915 to 1917, Consul General in Canton.

231. **Tolmachev, Nikolai Sergeevich** (18? – 19?). Student file dated 1903 of the Faculty of Oriental Languages of St. Petersburg University. Joined MID from 1912 as dragoman of Consulate in Kulja.

232. **Trautshold, Vilgelm Vilgelmovich (Vasilii Vasilevich)** (1877 –1937). Student file dated 1895 of the Faculty of Oriental Languages of St. Petersburg University. Joined MID from 1901 to 1904, at Embassy in Japan, during Russo-Japanese War being assigned to Chief Headquarters of Russian Forces. From 1905 to 1906, secretary of Mission in Bangkok, Siam; from 1906 to 1912, Vice Consul in Hakodate, Japan; from 1912 to 1913, Vice Consul in Dalian, China; from 1913, Consul General in Kharbin. Emigrated to France.

233. **Trotskii, Aleksandr Sergeevich** (1879 – 1940). Student file dated 1900 of the Faculty of Oriental Languages of St. Petersburg University. Joined MID as student trainee at Embassy in Peking; administrator of Vice Consulate in Hakodate, Japan; from 1912 to 1917, Vice Consul in Chongjin, Korea. Emigrated to China.

234. **Tseidler, Ludwig Ferdinandovich** (1863 – 1916). Graduated from the Faculty of Oriental Languages of St. Petersburg University, specializing in Arabic, Turkish, and Persian languages. Joined MID as official in Asian Department; from 1902, Consul in Reshteh, Persia; from 1904, Consul in Leipzig; from 1912, Consul in Stettin. In 1915, temporary administrator of Consulate in Oslo, Norway.

235. **Tukhodka, Sergei Vladimirovich** (1874 – 1954). Graduated 1892 from the Faculty of Oriental Languages of St. Petersburg University, specializing in Turkish and Albanian languages. Joined MID from 1898 to 1902 as secretary of Consulate (temporary administrator from 1901 to 1902) in Jeddah, Saudi Arabia; from 1902 in Prizren, Serbia; from 1907, Consul in Kosovo Mitrowice, and simultaneously as Commissar of the Great Powers on Crete; from 1910, secretary of Consulate in Damascus and Consul in Basra, Iraq. From 1912, Consul General in Skopje; from 1914, in Baghdad. From 1 March to 18 October 1914, first dragoman of Embassy in Constantinople, until First World War began; in February 1917, MID official attached to Headquarters of Commander of Black Sea fleet; from 1917, Consul in Varna, Bulgaria. From 1920, emigrated to Constantinople and Paris. Served as representative of League of Nations Nansen Committee in Constantinople.

236. **Tuzhilin, Aleksandr Vasilevich** (18? – 19?). Graduated 1904 from the Faculty of Oriental Languages of St. Petersburg University. Joined MID as Sinologist from 1911 as secretary and dragoman of Consulate in Tsitsikar; from 1914, secretary and dragoman of Consulate in Jilin; from 1916 to 1917, secretary and dragoman of Consulate in Newchwang. Emigrated to China.

237. **Umniakov, Ivan Ivanovich** (1890 – 1976). Student file dated 1902 of the Faculty of Oriental Languages of St. Petersburg University. Joined MID as auditor in Instructional Division of Oriental Languages; from 1916 to 1918, worked in Russian Political Agency of MID in Bukhara.

238. **Ungern-Shternberg, Baron Rolf Rudolfovich** (1880 – 1943). Student file dated 1897 of the Faculty of Oriental Languages of St. Petersburg University. Joined MID from 1909 as aide to secretary and, from 1911, as second secretary of Embassy in Constantinople; from 1913, second secretary of Embassy in Paris; from 1917, first secretary of Mission and *chargé d'affaires* in Portugal. Although one of the few Russian embassies abroad to recognize the Soviet authorities, the Baron did not return to Russia and emigrated to Portugal, Germany, China, and Japan.

239. **Usatyi, Pavel Kirillovich** (18? – 1927). Student file dated 1899 of the Faculty of Oriental Languages of St. Petersburg University. Joined MID from 1904 as student trainee in Peking; from 1907, dragoman of Consulate General in Kharbin; from 1914, Vice Consul in Khailar, Inner Mongolia; from 1917, Vice Consul in Tsitsikar. Emigrated to China.

240. **Uspenskii, Konstantin Viktorovich** (1881 – 1940). Student file dated 1900 of the Faculty of Oriental Languages of St. Petersburg University. Joined MID as Sinologist from 1910 as dragoman of Consulate in Kulja; from 1913 to 1916, secretary of Consulate General in Tiantsin. Emigrated to China.

241. **Uspenskii, Viktor Matveevich** (1845 – after 1901). Student file dated 1866 of the Faculty of Oriental Languages of St. Petersburg University. Joined MID as Sinologist from 1872 as student trainee at Mission in Peking; from 1874, secretary of Consulate General in Tiantsin; from 1879, secretary of Consulate in Ugra; from 1885, Consul in Kulja; from 1887 to 1901, Consul General in Turfan.

242. **Vakhovich, Aleksandr Stepanovich (Augustin Stefanovich)** (1858-1904). Student file dated 1878 of the Faculty of Oriental Languages of St. Petersburg Uni-

versity. Joined MID from 1882 to 1904, acting from 1891 as dragoman of Mission in Peking; from 1901 to 1902, Vice Consul in Fuzhou; from 1902 to 1904, Consul in Hankow, China.

243. **Valter, Aleksandr Aleksandrovich** (1879-1940). Student file dated 1897 of the Faculty of Oriental Languages of St. Petersburg University. Joined MID from 1901 as Sinologist, initially as student at Mission in Peking; from 1901 to 1902, dragoman and administrator of Consulate in Kulja; from 1904, secretary of Consulate in Chuguchak and, in 1906, Ugra; from 1907 to 1909, secretary-dragoman and administrator, Consulate in Newchwang and, from 1909 to 1911, Kashgar; from 1911 to 1917, Consul in Uliasutae, Mongolia. Emigrated to China.

244. **Vasilev (from 1912, Vasilev-Vasilkov), Aleksandr Konstantinovich** (18? – 19?). Graduated 1892 from the Faculty of Oriental Languages of St. Petersburg University. Joined MID from 1897 in the 2d Department; from 1910 to 1911, Consul in Paris; from 1912 to 1917, Consul General in Algiers and Tunis.

245. **Veber, Karl Ivanovich von (Friedrich Theodor)** (1841-1910). Student file dated 1861 of the Faculty of Oriental Languages of St. Petersburg University. Joined MID from 1865 at Mission in Peking; from 1871 to 1873, secretary and Vice Consul, Hakodate, Japan; from 1874 to 1875, Vice Consul in Yokohama; from 1876 to 1884, Consul in Tiantsin, China; from 1883 to 1884, envoy to China; in 1884 concluded Treaty between Russia and Korea on trade; from 1884, first Russian official representative in Korea as acting *chargé d'affaires*, from 1895, *chargé d'affaires*; and from 1888 to 1897, Consul General.

246. **Verkhovtsev, Mikhail Sergeevich** (18? – 1941). Student file dated 1891 of the Faculty of Oriental Languages of St. Petersburg University. Joined MID as secretary of Consulate in Lviv, Poland; later Consul in Bordeaux, France. Emigrated to France.

247. **Vestman, Vladimir Ilich** (2 September 1812, b. St. Petersburg – 15 May 1875, d. Weisbaden, Germany). Graduated in 1829 from Noble Boarding School attached to St. Petersburg University. Joined MID from 1829 in various administrative positions; from 1845, Vice Director, and from 1846 to 1865, Director of MID Chancellery; from 1866 to 1875, Deputy Minister of Foreign Affairs.

248. **Vilm, Artur Karlovich** (1867 – 1934). Student file dated 1886 of the Faculty of Oriental Languages of St. Petersburg University. Joined MID from 1890 as Clerk in Asian Department; from 1892, student; from 1897, dragoman at Russian Mission in Tokyo; from 1904, diplomatic official attached to Headquarters of Commander-in-Chief off 1st Manchurian Army; from 1911, Consul and from 1912, Consul General, in Yokohoma. Emigrated to Japan.

249. **Volkov, Antonii Moritsevich (Volf (or Vulfson), Anthony Moritz)** (1866 – 19?). Student file dated 1884 of the Faculty of Oriental Languages of St. Petersburg University. Joined MID from 1890; from 1904 to 1908, Consul in Astrabad, Persia; from 1908 to 1914, Consul in Liverpool, England; from 1914 to 1916, Consul in Chicago, Illinois, with personal rank of Consul General. Emigrated to United States.

250. **Zabello, Georgii Parmenovich** (1864 – 1946). Student file dated 1882 from the Faculty of Oriental Languages of St. Petersburg University. Joined MID from 1902 in Consulate at Rome. Last Consul General of Russian Empire at Rome. From 1904 to 1917, representative of Russia at the International Agrarian Institute. Emigrated to Italy.

251. **Zherebtsov, Dmitrii Mikhailovich** (1859 – 1932). Student file dated 1880 from the Faculty of Oriental Languages of St. Petersburg University. Joined MID as official, IV class, on special assignment.

252. **Zhukovskii, Sergei Valentinovich** (1883 – after 1945). Student file dated 1901 from the Faculty of Oriental Languages of St. Petersburg University, specializing in Arabic, Persian, Turkish, and Tatar. Joined MID from 1906 as Clerk of Asian Department attached to Khan of Khiva and in 1913 to Emir of Bukhara during their sojourns in St. Petersburg; from 1915 to 1916, acting secretary, Instructional Division of Oriental Languages attached to MID; from 1916, official of MID for frontier relations in Ashkhabad attached to Head of Trans-Caspian Region. Emigrated to Persia, France, and Austria. Returned to Soviet Union after Second World War.

253. **Zhukovskii, Valentin Alekseevich** (1858 – 1918). Student file dated 1876 from the Faculty of Oriental Languages of St. Petersburg University, specializing in Arabic, Persian, Turkish, and Tatar. Corresponding member, Russian Academy of Sciences; professor of St. Petersburg University. Joined MID from 1905 as Head, Instructional Division of Oriental Languages attached to 1st (Asian) Department.

254. **Zinovev, Aleksandr Dmitrievich** (1854 – 1931). Student file dated 1873 from the Faculty of Oriental Languages of St. Petersburg University. Joined MID from 1871 as Diplomatic Agent in Romania; from 1876, envoy and Minister Plenipotentiary in Persia; from 1883, Director, Asian Department of MID; from 1901, envoy to Sweden; from 1897, ambassador to Turkey. Emigrated to Italy.

§5. *Graduates of the Faculty of History and Philology*

255. **Bek, Aleksandr Khristianovich** (1810 – 1878). Graduated from the Faculty of History and Philology of St. Petersburg University. Joined MID from 1842 as senior secretary of Mission in The Hague; from 1854 to 1856, Director of Department of Economic Affairs and Accounts; from 1868 to 1876, member of MID Council; from 1878, Director of St. Petersburg and from 1879 to 1890, of Main Archive of MID.

256. **Brosse, Lavrentii Marievich** (1839 – 1906). Graduated 1860 from the Faculty of History and Philology of St. Petersburg University. Joined MID from 1862; from 1868, as dragoman and interpreter and, from 1885, Clerk of the Asian Department; from 1889, Consul General in Barcelona; from 1889 to 1898, Consul in Bordeaux; from 1902 to 1906, Consul General in Barcelona.

257. **Chicherin, Georgii (Iurii) Vasilevich** (1872 – 1936). Graduated 1895 from the Faculty of History and Philology of St. Petersburg University. Joined MID from 1896 to work in the Archive. After October 1917, served as Deputy People's

Commissar of Foreign Affairs to Lev D. Trotsky and from May 1918 to 1930, as People's Commissar of Foreign Affairs of the RSFSR and USSR.

258. **Izvolskii, Petr Petrovich** (1863 – 1928). Graduated 1885 from the Faculty of History and Philology of St. Petersburg University. Joined MID from 1886 to 1887 as official of Department of Internal Relations.

259. **Kratirov, Aleksei Nikolaevich** (1882 – 1958). Graduated c. 1906 from the Faculty of History and Philology of St. Petersburg University. Joined MID as Clerk in 2d Department; from 1912 to 1916, Vice Consul in Hammerfest; attache at Embassy in Italy. Emigrated to Italy, then to France.

260. **Onu, Aleksandr Mikhailovich** (1865 – 1935). Graduated 1889 from the Faculty of History and Philology of St. Petersburg University. Joined MID from July 1917 as Consul General in London, England. Emigrated to England.

261. **Pavlov-Silvanskii, Nikolai Pavlovich** (1869 – 1908). Graduated 1892 from the Faculty of History and Philology of St. Petersburg University. Joined MID as Clerk, VII class; senior Clerk; from 1902, aide to Director, of Main and St. Petersburg archives of MID. From 1907, Professor at Higher Women's Courses specializing in medieval Russian History.

262. **Petkovich, Konstantin Dmitrievich** (1826/27 – 1897). Graduated from the Faculty of History and Philology of St. Petersburg University. Joined MID from outset of Crimean War; from 1853 served in Diplomatic Chancellery of Commander-in-Chief of Russian forces in the Balkans; from 1856, secretary of Consulate General and, from 1859, Consul, and from 1861, Consul General at Ragusa (Dubrovnik); from 1869 to 1896, Consul General at Beirut.

263. **Polivanov, Evgenii Dmitrievich** (1891 – 1938). Graduated 1912 from the Faculty of History and Philology and the Faculty of Oriental Languages of St. Petersburg University. Joined MID from 1917. After February 1917 Revolution, Head of Press Section of MID of Provisional Government; after October 1917 Revolution to early 1918, Head of Eastern Section of People's Commissariat of Foreign Affairs and acting People's Commissar for Foreign Affairs of Lev D. Trotsky; prepared first draft of Brest Peace Treaty. On behalf of Council of People's Commissars in 1917 to 1918 organized the translation and publication of secret treaties of Imperial and Provisional governments.

264. **Ukhtomskii, Baron Esper Esperovich** (1861 – 1921). Student file dated 1880 of the Faculty of History and Philology of St. Petersburg University. Joined MID from 1884 in Department of Spiritual Affairs of Foreign Professions of Faith; from 1886 to 1890, sent to China and Mongolia to study Buddhism and collect articles of Eastern art which were transferred to The Hermitage and other museums. From 1897, head of delegation sent to China to expand Sino-Russian cooperation, including the Chinese-Russian Railway. From 1896 to 1917, editor and publisher of Санкт-Петербургские ведомости [St. Petersburg Gazette].

265. **Vizel, Bernard Franz Oskar Oskarovich** (20 August 1864, b. St. Petersburg – 27 September 1918, Geneva, Switzerland). Graduated 1888 from the Faculty of History and Philology of St. Petersburg University. Joined MID from 1896 to 1901, Vice Consul in Hamburg; from 1901 to 1911, Consul in Hammerfest, Nor-

way; from 1911 to 1912, Consul General in Wroclaw, Poland; from 1912 to 1916, Geneva, Switzerland; from 1917, in Naples. Emigrated to Italy.

§6. *Graduates of the Faculty of Physics and Mathematics*

266. **Ermolov, Nikolai Sergeevich** (1853 – 1924). Military attaché, Lt. General. Graduated 1874 from the Faculty of Physics and Mathematics of St. Petersburg University. In 1876, passed examinations for Mikhailov Artillery School. Participated in Russo-Turkish War of 1877-1888. In 1883, graduated from the Nikolaev Academy of the General Staff. From 1891 to 1905 and 1907 to 1916, served as military agent (attaché) of Russia in United Kingdom. During Spanish-American War of 1898, served as military observer attached to Headquarters of United States Army in Cuba.

267. **Lodyzhenskii, Nikolai Nikolaevich** (1842 – 1916). Began University studies at Moscow University and transferred to the capitol, graduating 1869 from the Faculty of Physics and Mathematics of St. Petersburg University. Joined MID from 1869, during the 1870s to 1880s serving in consular posts in Austria-Hungary (Chernowitz, Belgrade, Sarajevo) and during the 1880s, in Bulgaria and Romania. Representative of Russia on International Danube Commission. From 1891 to 1894, Consul in Königsberg; from 1895 to 1902, Consul General in Galac, Romania; from 1902 to 1906, in New York.

268. **Lopukhin, Vladimir Borisovich** (1871 – 1942). Student file dated 1890 of the Faculty of Physics and Mathematics of St. Petersburg University. Joined MID from 1898 to 1902 as Clerk in Department of Foreign Relations; from 1910, Clerk in Department of Personnel and Economic Affairs (transformed in June 1914 into the 1st Department; from 1914, acting Vice Director, and from 1916, Vice Director, and from 19 January 1917, Director, 1st Department. Sole senior official of MID who did not emigrate.

269. **Panaev, Aleksandr Ippolitovich** (1856 – after 1923). Student file dated 1877 of the Faculty of Physics and Mathematics of St. Petersburg University. Joined MID from 1891 in Department of Personnel and Economic Affairs and official on special assignments attached to MID. Emigrated to Germany from 1923.

270. **Peshchurov, Dmitrii Alekseevich** (1833 – 1913). Diplomat, Sinologist, and professor. Graduated 1853 from the Faculty of Physics and Mathematics of St. Petersburg University. Joined Ministry of Internal Affairs from 1856 in Russian Orthodox Mission in Peking. Joined MID from 1861 as Consular Agent in Tiantsin; from 1867, interpreter, then dragoman, of Asian Department; from 1902, dragoman V class in Asian Department. Simultaneously, from 1867, lecturer; from 1870, privat-docent; from 1890, Professor of Chinese Language in Faculty of Oriental Languages, St. Petersburg University and author of Russian-Chinese dictionary (1891).

271. **Struve, Kirill Vasilevich** (1835 – 1907). Graduated 1856 from the Faculty of Physics and Mathematics of St. Petersburg University. From 1858 served as astronomer in military-diplomatic mission in the Khanates of Bukhara and Khiva. Joined MID from 1860 in Asian Department; from 1862, led Commission for the establishment of new Western Chinese boundary. From 1865 to 1866, ambassa-

dor to Bukhara; from 1866 to 1868, diplomatic official attached to Orenburg and, from 1868 to 1873, attached to Turkestan Governors-General. From 1873 to 1874, *chargé d'affaires* and Consul General and, from 1874 to 1876, Resident Minister, and from 1876 to 1882, envoy to Japan. From 1882 to 1892, Envoy Extraordinary and Minister Plenipotentiary to the United States. From 1892 to 1905, envoy to The Netherlands. In 1884, Head of Russian delegation to International Meridian Conference in Washington D.C. at which the Greenwich Meridian was recognized officially. Retired in 1903.

§7. *Graduates of Alexander Lycée*

272. **Abaza, Aleksandr Nikolaevich** (4 August 1872, b. Tiflis – 6 November 1925, d. Alexandria, Egypt). Graduated 1895. Joined MID from 1895, IX class, and held various consular posts. From July 1910, Consul General in Melbourne, Australia; first official representative of Russia to visit New Zealand, Tonga, Samoa, Fiji, and the New Hebrides.

273. **Arsenev, Boris Konstantinovich** (17 December 1875, b. St. Petersburg – 7 November 1925, d. Paris, France). Graduated 1896. Joined MID from 1895, IX class, and held various consular posts. From 1910 to 1912, Consul General in Bombay, and then in Calcutta.

274. **Bakh, Genrikh Genrikhovich** (1881 – after 1961). Graduated 1902. Joined MID from 1907, IX class, and held diplomatic and consular posts in Bulgaria, United States, and Persia. From 1916, first secretary of the Mission in The Netherlands; from September 1917, *chargé d'affaires.*

275. **Bartolomei, Mikhail Fedorovich** (3 March 1836 – 18 October 1896, d. Berlin, Germany). Graduated 1854. Joined MID from 1858, IX class, and held diplomatic posts. From 1880 to 1852, Envoy Extraordinary and Minister Plenipotentiary consecutively in Greece, United States, and Japan.

276. **Baumgarten, Apollon Aleksandrovich von** (18? – 1914). Graduated 1875. Joined MID from 1875, XII class, and served from 1894 to 1912, as Consul General at Frankfurt-on-Main, Germany.

277. **Bazili, Nikolai Aleksandrovich** (1883 – 1963). Graduated 1903. Joined MID from 1903, IX class, and held administrative and diplomatic posts. From 1916 to 1917, Director, Diplomatic Chancellery attached to the Headquarters of the Supreme Commander-in-Chief.

278. **Beger, Aleksandr Fedorovich** (2 September 1823 – 8 April 1895, St. Petersburg). Graduated 1842. Joined MID from 1842, IX class, and held diplomatic and consular posts. From 1861, Consul General in Beirut; from 1869 to 1876, Envoy Extraordinary and Minister Plenipotentiary in Persia.

279. **Belostotskii, Vladimir Vasilevich** (January 1852, b. St. Petersburg – 24 May 1895, d. St. Petersburg). Graduated 1874. Joined MID from 1874, XII class, and held diplomatic and consular posts, including Vice Consul in Frankfurt-on-Main.

280. **Berg, Aleksandr Fedorovich** (24 January 1803, b. Dorpat – 2 March 1884, d. London, England). Graduated 1821. Joined MID from 1824, X class, and held diplomatic and consular posts, including from 1858 to 1860, in Naples, Italy, and from 1861, in London, England.

281. **Biutsov, Evgenii Karlovich** (1837 – 17 October 1904, d. Baden, Austria). Graduated 1856. Joined MID from 1858, IX class, and served from 1871 as Consul in Yokahama, Japan. From 1873 to 1883, Envoy Extraordinary and Minister Plenipotentiary to China; from 1884 to 1889, in Greece; from 1889 to 1897, in Persia; and from 1897 to 1904, in Sweden and Norway.

282. **Biutsov, Konstantin Evgenevich** (1873 – 8 June 1932). Graduated 1894. Joined MID, IX class, and served as State-secretary of Near Eastern Section. Emigrated to France.

283. **Bulakh, Aleksandr Iurevich** (4 April 1875 – 24 September 1918, d. Petrograd). Graduated 1895. Joined MID from 1901, IX class, and held diplomatic and consular posts, including from 1905 to 1910, Vice Consul in Colombo, Ceylon.

284. **Burnashev, Aleksandr Nikolaevich** (1870 – 1921). Graduated 1893. Joined MID, XII class, serving from 1916 as Consul in Hull, England.

285. **Charykov, Nikolai Valerievich** (8 January 1855, b. Viatka – 12 September 1930, Istanbul, Turkey). Graduated 1875. Joined MID from 1875, IX class, and held various senior diplomatic posts. From 1907, Deputy Minister of Foreign Affairs; Chairman, Commission for Reforming the Personnel Establishments of MID Central Institutions. Appointed Senator in 1909. Died in emigration.

286. **Chevati, Konstantin Stepanovich** (c. 1811 – 28 June 1862, d. Livorno, Tuscany). Graduated 1829. Joined MID from 1829, IX class, and held diplomatic and consular posts in Poland, Germany, and Austria-Hungary. From 1852 to 1862, Consul General in Livorno, Italy.

287. **Danzas, Boris Antonovich** (1 September 1838 – 13 January 1893, d. Berlin, Germany). Graduated 1859. Joined MID, IX class; secretary of Embassy in Washington D.C., then Counselor, Embassy in Dresden, Saxony; official on special assignments attached to Minister.

288. **Engelgardt, Aleksandr Sergeevich** (13 June 1833 – 18 July 1889). Graduated 1851. Joined MID, IX class, serving as Vice Director, Asian Department; member of MID Council.

289. **Fren, Rudolf (Andreas Rudolf) Khristianovich** (12 January 1812, b. Kazan – 19 August 1872, d. Ancona, Italy). Graduated 1828 from Tsarskoe selo Noble Boarding House. Joined MID from 1830, XII class; attended Instructional Division of Oriental Languages attached to MID; from 1833 held diplomatic and consular posts in Turkey, Egypt, Crete, and Persia; from 1859, Consul in Ancona, Italy.

290. **Gamm, Aleksandr Fedorovich** (25 December 1861 – 3 June 1946). Graduated 1883. Joined MID from 1883, IX class; from 1898, Consul in Berlin; from 1902, in Stettin; from 1923, Consul General in Berlin and Head, consular unit in Germany.

291. **Ganzen, Fedor Karlovich** (1862 – 29 April 1909, d. Genoa, Italy). Graduated 1881. Joined MID from 1881, IX class; from 1907 to 1909, Consul General in Genoa, Italy.

292. **Girs (Giers), Nikolai Karlovich** (21 May 1820, b. Radivilov, Volhynia Governate – 26 January 1895, d. St. Petersburg). Graduated 1838. Joined MID from 1838, X class; held various diplomatic posts. From 2 December 1875, Deputy Minister of Foreign Affairs and simultaneously administrator of Asian Department with rights of Director; participated in four meetings with Emperors of Russia, Austria-Hungary, and Germany between 1882 and 1895 as Minister of Foreign Affairs between those years.

293. **Glinka, Nikolai Dmitrievich** (1838 – 1884). Graduated 1857. Joined MID, IX class; from 1881 to 1885, Consul General in Frankfurt-on-Main, Germany.

294. **Gorchakov, Prince Aleksandr Mikhailovich** (4 June 1798 – 27 February 1883). Graduated 1817, classmate of Alexander Pushkin. Joined MID from 1817, IX class, and held various diplomatic assignments; from 1856 to 1882, Minister of Foreign Affairs. Succeeded in securing European recognition of Russian renunciation of 1856 Treaty of Paris denying Russian naval egress from the Black Sea. Secured European neutrality in Russo-Turkish War of 1877-1878.

295. **Goriainov, Mikhail Sergeevich** (9 November 1878 – 19?). Graduated 1901. Joined MID from 1902, IX class; from 1912, Vice Consul in Stockholm, Sweden; Vice Director, 2d Department; from 1916, official on special assignments.

296. **Guk, Vladimir (Valter) Ivanovich von** (18? – 19?). Graduated 1892. Joined MID from 1895, IX class; from 1895, secretary of Consulate, Newcastle-on-Tyne, England; from 1898, Vice Consul in Stockholm, Sweden; from 1900 to 1904, Vice Consul in Naples, Italy; in 1905, Vice Consul in Hamburg, Germany; in 1906, Vice Consul in Oslo, Norway; in 1907, Consul General in Lisbon, Portugal; in 1909, Consul General in Cadiz, Spain; from 1908 to 1914, Consul in Antwerp, Belgium; from 1914 to 1916, Consul in Brussels, Belgium, including April to June 1916 as *chargé d'affaires*; from May 1917, first secretary of Embassy in Washington D.C.

297. **Igelstrom (Igelstrem), Gustav Viktorovich** (18? – 19?). Graduated 1874. Joined MID, XII class, serving as Consul General, Sarajevo, Bosnia and Herzogovina.

298. **Iurev, Vladimir Vladimirovich** (18? – 19?). Graduated 1903. Joined MID, IX class; from 1906, Vice Consul in Bari and Naples, Italy.

299. **Izvolskii, Aleksandr Petrovich** (18 March 1856, Moscow – 16 August 1919, d. Barritz, France). Graduated 1875. Joined MID from 1875, IX class, in various diplomatic posts; from 1906 to 1910, Minister of Foreign Affairs. Died in emigration.

300. **Karchevskii, Petr Vikentevich** (14 February 1837 – 16 December 1905, d. Marseilles, France). Graduated 1856. Joined MID from 1860, IX class; from 1866, Consul in Jassy, Romania; from 1878, Consul General in New York; from 1880, Consul General in Copenhagen; from 1886 to 1904, Consul General in Marseilles.

301. **Kartsov, Andrei Nikolaevich** (1835 – 24 September 1907). Graduated 1856. Joined MID from 1856, IX class; from 1862, Consul in Jerusalem; from 1866, Consul General in Corfu; from 1875 to 1877, diplomatic agent and Consul General in Serbia; from 1879, Consul General in Naples, Italy; from 1880 to 1906, Consul General in Paris, France.

302. **Kartsov, Iurii Sergeevich** (11 November 1857 – 7 August 1931). Graduated 1877. Joined MID from 1877, X class; from 1879 to 1886, diplomatic service in Near East and southern Europe: Vice Consul in Mosul; Consul in Palestine; diplomatic agent in Serbia. From 1893 to 1895, Consul in Newcastle-on-Tyne, England.

303. **Kassini, Artur Pavlovich** (1835 – 1919, d. Paris, France). Graduated 1854. Joined MID from 1854, IX class; from 1884, *chargé d'affaires*, and from 1888, Resident Minister attached to Free Hanseatic Cities in Hamburg; from 1891 to 1896, Envoy Extraordinary and Minister Plenipotentiary in China; from 1897, Minister, and from 1898, Ambassador Extraordinary and Plenipotentiary to United States; from 1905 to 1909, the same to Spain.

304. **Kister, Baron Anatolii Ottonovich** (18? – 19?). Graduated 1885. Joined MID, IX class; from 1902, Consul in Hong Kong and Singapore; Consul General in Stockholm.

305. **Korostovets, Ivan Iakovlevich** (25 August 1862 – 1 January 1933, d. Paris, France). Graduated 1884. Joined MID from 1884, XII class; from 1899, Vice Director, 1st Department; from 1900, administrator, Consulate in Tiantsin; from 1902, Consul General in Bushera, Persia; from 1910, Head of Mission in Mongolia; from 1908 to 1912, Envoy Extraordinary and Minister Plenipotentiary in China; from 1913 to 1915, same in Persia; from 1915 to 1917, member MID Council.

306. **Kotsebue, Vasilii (Vilgelm Avgustovich) Evstafevich** (7 March 1813, b. Revel – 24 October 1887, d. Revel). Graduated 1832. Joined MID, IX class; from 1865, *chargé d'affaires* in Saxony; from 1865 to 1869, Baden, Germany; from 1869 to 1878, Envoy Extraordinary and Minister Plenipotentiary in Saxony; from 1878 to 1879, same in Switzerland.

307. **Kozakevich, Pavel Mikhailovich** (1859 – 1 August 1931, d. Turin, Italy). Graduated 1881. Joined MID, XII class; from 1897 to 1899, Vice Consul in Catania, Italy; from 1900 to 1909, Consul in San Francisco, California; Consul General in Genoa.

308. **Krupenskii, Vasilii Nikolaevich** (22 August 1869, Riga – 5 April 1945, Cannes, France). Graduated 1889. Joined MID from 1889, IX class, serving in embassies at Turkey, China, United States, and Austria-Hungary; from 1911 to 1916, Envoy Extraordinary and Minister Plenipotentiary in China; from 1916, same in Japan, remaining in this post under Provisional Government.

309. **Laksman, Aleksandr Alfonsovich (Afanasevich)** (18? – 1891). Graduated 1835. Joined MID, XIV class; Consul General in Lisbon, Portugal.

310. **Lobanov-Rostovskii, Prince Aleksei Borisovich** (18 December 1824, b. Voronezh Governate – 18 August 1896, d. Shepetovka, Volhynia Governate). Graduated 1844. Joined MID from 1844, IX class; held various diplomatic posts. Chief

Plenipotentiary of Russia at 1878 Congress of Berlin; from 1895 to 1896, administered MID, then Minister of Foreign Affairs.

311. **Lomonosov, Sergei Grigorevich** (1799 – 13 October 1857, d. San-Danello Estate, Florence, Italy). Graduated 1817. Joined MID, IX class; from 1841, *chargé d'affaires* in Denmark; from 1841 to 1848, Envoy Extraordinary and Minister Plenipotentiary in Brazil; from 1848 to 1853, same in Portugal; from 1853 to 1857, same in The Netherlands.

312. **Loris-Melikov, Iosif Grigorevich** (15 September 1872 – August 1948, d. Paris, France). Graduated 1894. Joined MID from 1894, IX class, held administrative and diplomatic posts. From 1916, *chargé d'affaires* and Consul General with personal rank of Envoy Extraordinary and Minister Plenipotentiary in Siam; in 1917, same post.

313. **Loviagin, Aleksandr Aleksandrovich** (18? – 19?). Graduated 1912. Joined MID, IX class, as Vice Consul in Stockholm, Sweden. Emigrated to Germany.

314. **Loviagin, Aleksandr Evgrafovich** (1861 – 19?). Graduated 1886. Joined MID from 1889, X class; from 1895, Vice Consul in Amsterdam; from 1898, Vice Consul in Torun, Poland; from 1909, Consul in Memel, Germany; from 1909 to 1917, Consul General in Oslo, Norway.

315. **Lysakovskii, Aleksandr Iosifovich** (12 August 1879 – 18 March 1941). Graduated 1899. Joined MID, IX class, holding various administrative and diplomatic posts. From 1916, administrator of MID Press Section; from 5 July 1917, Resident Minister, Vatican, with personal rank of Envoy Extraordinary and Minister Plenipotentiary.

316. **Makeev, Aleksandr Nikolaevich** (1873 – 19?). Graduated 1892. Joined MID, XII class, serving as Vice Consul in Catania, Italy; administrator, Consulate in Amsterdam; Consul, Lausanne, Switzerland.

317. **Matiunin, Nikolai Gavrilovich** (2 February 1849, b. Vitebsk – 18 May 1907, d. St. Petersburg). Graduated 1869. Joined MID from 1897, XII class; from 1897 to 1898, *chargé d'affaires* in Korea; from 1898 to 1899, Consul General in Melbourne, Australia.

318. **Muravev, Valerian Nikolaevich** (28 February 1885, b. Moscow – 1930 or 1932). Graduated 1905. Joined MID from 1905, IX class; from 1907, secretary, Second Hague Peace Conference. From 1914 to 1917, Vice Director, Diplomatic Chancellery attached to Headquarters of Supreme Command. From September to October 1917, Head of Cabinet of Minister of Foreign Affairs.

319. **Neratov, Anatolii Anatolievich** (2 October 1863, b. St. Petersburg – 10 April 1938, d. France). Graduated 1883. Joined MID, IX class; from 1910 to 1917, Deputy Minister of Foreign Affairs under five different ministers; from November to December 1916, temporarily administer MID. During Civil War, acting Minister of Foreign Affairs of Government of General A. N. Denikin, then representative of White Movement in Turkey. Died in emigration.

320. **Perovskii, Petr Nikolaevich** (1818 – 13 August 1865, d. Genoa, Italy). Graduated 1835. Joined MID from 1841, XII class, serving in Asian Department. From 1852, Head, 1st Division of Asian Department; from 1863 to 1865, Consul General at Genoa, Italy.

321. **Persiani, Aleksandr Ivanovich** (23 November 1842, b. Athens – 19 September 1895, d. St. Petersburg). Graduated 1862. Joined MID from 1862, X class; from 1877, diplomatic agent and Consul General; from 1878, Resident Minister; from 1889, Envoy Extraordinary and Minister Plenipotentiary in Serbia.

322. **Poklevskii-Kozell, Stanislav Alfonsovich** (1868, b. Talitsk, Perm Governate – 1 May 1937 or 1939, d. Bucharest, Romania). Graduated 1886. Joined MID from 1886, IX class, held administrative posts in MID and diplomatic posts in Tokyo and London. From 1909 to 1913, Envoy Extraordinary and Minister Plenipotentiary in Persia, and from 1913 to 1916, the same in Romania.

323. **Protopopov, Evgenii Sergeevich, Prince Ukhtomskii** (12 July 1875, b. Riga – 5 January 1945, d. Berlin, Germany). Graduated 1897. Joined MID, X class, serving from 1913 to 1914, Vice Consul in Vienna; Consul General in Nice.

324. **Rashet, Aleksandr Emmanuilovich** (1805 – 1860). Graduated 1824. Joined MID, XII class, serving as Consul in Brodach, Austria-Hungary.

325. **Rikhter, Aleksandr (Christof Friedrich) Borisovich** (18 June 1809 – 16 April 1859). Graduated 1826. Joined MID from 1826, IX class, serving in administrative and diplomatic posts; from 1856 to 1859, Envoy Extraordinary and Minister Plenipotentiary in Belgium.

326. **Rostovskii, Aleksandr Arkadievich** (18 October 1860, b. Kherson – 26 July 1903, Bitola, Macedonia). Graduated 1883. Joined MID from 1883, IX class, holding administrative and diplomatic posts in Bulgaria, Palestine, Greece, Lebanon; from 1893, Vice Consul in Brindisi, Italy; from 1895 to 1899, Vice Consul in Bitola, Macedonia; from 1899 to 1903, Consul in Skopje.

327. **Saburov, Petr Aleksandrovich** (22 March 1835 – 18 March 1918, d. Petrograd). Graduated 1854. Joined MID from 1856, IX class, serving in administrative and diplomatic posts in Bavaria and England. From 1869, *chargé d'affaires* in Karlsruhe, Germany; from 1870, Envoy Extraordinary and Minister Plenipotentiary in Greece; from 1879 to 1884, Ambassador Extraordinary and Plenipotentiary in Germany and simultaneously Envoy to Mecklenburg-Schwerin and Mecklenburg-Strelitz.

328. **Sazonov, Sergei Dmitrievich** (27 July 1860, b. Riazan Governate – 25 December 1937, d. Nice, France). Graduated 1883. Joined MID from 1883, IX class; held various diplomatic posts. From 1909, Deputy Minister; from 1910 to 1916, Minister of Foreign Affairs. During Civil War, acted as Minister of Foreign Affairs in Government of A. V. Kolchak. Died in emigration.

329. **Sementovskii-Kurilo, Dmitrii Konstantinovich** (16 September 1854, b. St. Petersburg – 13 January 1911, d. Sofia, Bulgaria). Graduated 1880. Joined MID from 1880, IX class; from 1900 to 1906, Vice Director, and from 1906 to 1907,

Director, Asian Department of MID. From 1907 to 1911, Envoy Extraordinary and Minister Plenipotentiary in Bulgaria.

330. **Serzhputovskii, Anton Adamovich** (c. 1832 – 14 December 1901, d. Naples, Italy). Graduated 1851. Joined MID from 1859, XII class; from 1869 to 1875, Consul in Reshteh, Persia. Consul General in Naples.

331. **Shilling, Baron Ernest Ottonovich von** (1882 – not before 1937). Graduated 1897. Joined MID, X class, serving as Consul in Chicago; from 1912 to 1914, Consul General in Breslau, Germany; from 1914 to 1923, Consul General in Copenhagen.

332. **Shishkin, Nikolai Pavlovich** (11 August 1830, b. Iaroslavl – 11 November 1902, d. Gatchina, Petersburg Governate). Enrolled in 1841; left at wish of parents in 1845. Joined MID from 1853, holding various diplomatic posts. From 1891 to 1897, Deputy Minister of Foreign Affairs. In 1895 after death of Minister Giers and in 1896 after death of Lobanov-Rostovskii, temporarily administered the MID. From January 1897, member of State Council.

333. **Shneider, Vasilii Karlovich** (1872 – 11 February 1903). Graduated 1894. Joined MID, X class; from 1902 to 1903, Vice Consul, Colombo, Ceylon.

334. **Shtofregen, Aleksandr Kondrat'evich** (18? – 7 February 1844). Graduated 1832. Joined MID, XII class; administered Consulate General in Amsterdam, Netherlands.

335. **Sivers, Count Lev Egorovich** (18? –5 June 1875, d. Amsterdam, Netherlands). Graduated 1836. Joined MID, X class; served as Consul General in Amsterdam.

336. **Solovev, Iurii Iakovlevich** (1871 – 1934). Graduated 1893. Joined MID from 1893, IX class, serving in administrative and diplomatic posts in China, Greece, Montenegro, and Romania. From 1909 to 1911, first secretary of Mission in Stuttgart, Württemberg; from 1911 to 1912, *chargé d'affaires* in Wurttemberg; from 1912 to 1917, Counselor of Embassy in Madrid, repeatedly assuming direction of the Embassy. One of two Russian diplomats who agreed to cooperate with the Soviet authorities; from 1922 to 1927, worked in People's Commissariat of Foreign Affairs of RSFSR and USSR.

337. **Stuart, Baron Dmitrii Fedorovich** (18 May 1838 – 1 April 1902, d. St. Petersburg). Graduated 1859. Joined MID from 1859, IX class, serving in administrative and consular posts. From 1876 to 1878, Consul General in Bucharest; from 1878 to 1879, Resident Minister in Romania; from 1879 to 1902, Director, State and St. Petersburg Main Archives of MID.

338. **Tatishchev, Boris Alekseevich** (23 July 1876 – 22 November 1949). Graduated 1896. Joined MID from 1898, IX class, serving in administrative and consular posts in Germany, Greece, and France. From 1902, official on special assignments attached to MID. From 1916 to 1917, Director, 1st Political Section and Head, Chancellery of MID. In 1920, Deputy Minister of Foreign Affairs in Government of General P. N. Vrangel.

339. **Taube, Baron Konstantin Ferdinandovich** (18? – 19?). Graduated 1877. Joined MID, IX class; Head, statistical committee of MID.

340. **Tillo, Georgii Eduardovich** (1870 – 1934). Graduated 196. Joined MID, IX class, serving as Vice Consul, San Remo, Italy.

341. **Tolstoi, Count Aleksandr Aleksandrovich** (1869 – 1939). Graduated 1891. Joined MID, X class; from 1912, first secretary of MID Chancellery; from 1916, official on special assignments attached to MID; member, MID Council.

342. **Tsur-Milen, German Kasparovich von** (18? – 19?). Graduated 1896. Joined MID, IX class, serving as Consul, Mannheim, Germany; from 1913, Consul in Finnmarken, Sweden; from 1915 to 1916, Consul in Hammerfest, Norway.

343. **Vadbolskii, Prince Aleksandr Alekseevich** (12 January 1838 – not before 1913). Graduated 1859. Joined MID, IX class, and served as Vice Consul in Fiume, Italy.

344. **Veiner, Arkadii Petrovich** (1875 – 1965). Graduated 1894. Joined MID, IX class, from 1894 and held administrative and consular posts, including from 1897 as Vice Consul in New York, Chicago, and San Francisco; from 1914 to 1916, Vice Consul of the 2d Department; from 1916 to 1917, member of MID Council.

345. **Vestman, Aleksandr Vladimirovich** (1 December 1846 – 17 April 1923). Graduated 1868. Joined MID from 1869, IX class, and held administrative and diplomatic posts, including from 1891 to 1900, Resident Minister in the Free Hanseatic Cities (Hamburg); from 1900 to 1902, envoy to Berne, Switzerland; from 1902 to 1912, envoy in Munich, Bavaria.

346. **Vrangel, Baron Aleksandr Egorovich** (23 February 1833 – 12 September 1915). Graduated 1853. Joined MID from 1857, IX class, and held administrative and diplomatic posts, including from 1879 to 1897, Consul General in Danzig; from 1897, Resident Minister, and from 1898 to 1906, envoy to Saxony and Braunschweig.

347. **Zhadovskii, Valerii Vsevolodovich** (26 June 1836, b. St. Petersburg – 14 April 1916, d. Rome, Italy). Graduated 1857. Joined MID from 1857, X class, serving from 1897 to 1899, Envoy Extraordinary and Minister Plenipotentiary to Serbia; from 1899 to 1902, in Portugal; and from 1902 to 1906, in Switzerland.

§8. *Graduates of Imperial School of Jurisprudence*

348. **Baikov, Aleksandr Lvovich** (30 April 1874, St. Petersburg – 31 December 1943, Paris, France). Graduated 1895. Joined MID from 1896, IX class, serving in Department of Internal Relations; Director, 2d Department.

349. **Brosse, Fedor (Theodore) Lavrentevich** (29 November 1873, b. St. Petersburg – 10 September 1953, d. Stockholm, Sweden). Graduated 1897. Joined MID from 1897, XII class; held various posts in central apparatus of MID and consulates. Vice Consul in Hamburg, Lubeck, Hammerfest. From 1913 to 1914, Consul in Mannheim; in 1917, Consul General in Stockholm, Sweden.

350. **Butkevich, Evgenii Adolfovich** (1874 – 1949). Graduated 1896. Joined MID from 1899, X class; held various posts in central apparatus, embassies, and consulates in Turkey and Macedonia. From 1911 to 1916, Consul in Newcastle-on-Tyne, England.

351. **Dubiagskii, Nikolai Ivanovich** (18? – 14 October 1942, d. Sofia, Bulgaria). Graduated 1907. Joined MID, IX class; from 1915 to 1916, Vice Consul in Kaval, Greece; from 1916, served at Embassy in Rome.

352. **Gornostaev, Lev Nikolaevich** (1881 – 2 January 1940, d. Geneva, Switzerland). Graduated 1902, having studied at Law Faculty of St. Petersburg University for one year(1899). Joined MID from 1904, IX class; official in 2d Department of MID. From 1912, Vice Consul in Bari, Italy; from 1915 to 1916, Vice Consul of Consulate General in Genoa; from 1921 to 1923, Vice Consul in Geneva, Switzerland. Emigrated to Switzerland.

353. **Islavin, Lev Vladimirovich** (5 April 1866, b. St. Petersburg – 28 June 1934, Austria). Graduated 1889. Joined MID, X class; from 1897, Vice Consul in Vienna; from 1901 to 1902, Consul in Rome; from 1904, Consul General in Nice; from 1907 to 1914, Consul General in Vienna; from 1915 to 1919, envoy in personal capacity in Montenegro.

354. **Kolchanovskii, Nikolai Petrovich** (1892 – 1940). Graduated 1914. Joined MID, IX class; from 1917, official of 2d Department. After October 1917, deputy head, Economic-Legal Division, People's Commissariat of Foreign Affairs of RSFSR.

355. **Korf, Baron Oskar Aleksandrovich** (1883 – 1 August 1958). Graduated 1904. Joined MID from 1905, IX class; from 1912 to 1915, Vice Consul in New York.

356. **Lavrov, Boris Adrianovich** (18? – 1958). Graduated 1906. Joined MID, IX class; from 1914, Vice Consul, Frankfurt-on-Main, Germany.

357. **Muravev-Apostol-Korobin, Vladimir Vladimirovich** (9 December 1864 – 14 October 1937, d. Bursinel, Switzerland). Graduated 1887. Joined MID, XII class; from 1903 to 1904, *chargé d'affaires*, in Serbia; from 1908 to 1910, Consul General in Budapest.

358. **Ogarev, Mikhail Nikolaevich** (26 December 1844 – 3 January 1900). Graduated 1866. Joined MID, XII class; from 1877, Consul in Rostock and Weimar, Germany.

359. **Palen, Petr Konstantinovich (Peter Karl Johann) von** (11 November 1859, b. St. Petersburg – 7 December 1912, d. Gross Aux, Courland). Graduated 1880. Joined MID, IX class; from 1908 to 1912, Envoy Extraordinary and Minister Plenipotentiary to The Netherlands.

360. **Peterson, Ivan Karlovich** (25 August 1859 – 17 June 1940). Graduated 1881. Joined MID from 1881, XII class; from Consul General in Amsterdam; from 1902, Consul in Jassy, Romania; from 1915 to 1916, Consul General in Rotterdam.

361. **Polovtsev, Aleksandr Aleksandrovich** (1867 – 12 February 1944, d. Paris, France). Graduated 1888. Joined MID from 1896, X class; from 1906 to 1907, Consul General in Bombay, India; during First World War, participated in Russian delegation at international inter-Allied conferences. From 1916 to March 1917, Deputy Minister of Foreign Affairs.

362. **Rikhter, Vladimir Konstantinovich** (1881 – 14 October 1940, d. Paris, France). Graduated 1904. Joined MID, IX class; from 1915, Vice Consul, Sulina, Romania; from 1916, Kustendja, Romania.

363. **Rozen, Baron Roman Romanovich** (12 February 1 847, Revel, Courland Governate – 31 December 1922, New York). Graduated 1868. Joined MID from 1872, X class; from 1872 to 1875, Vice Consul, Yokohama, Japan; from 1877 to 1879, secretary of Embassy, and from 1879 to 1883, *chargé d'affaires* in Japan. From 1884 to 1890, Consul General in New York. From 1890 to 1895, Envoy Extraordinary and Minister Plenipotentiary in Mexico; from 1895 to 1897, in Serbia; from 1897 to 1899, in Japan; from 1899 to 1901, in Bavaria; from 1901 to 1902, in Greece; from 1903 to 1904, in Japan; from 1905 to 1911, in United States. Served as Second Plenipotentiary of Russia during negotiations at Portsmouth, New Hampshire, to settle Russo-Japanese War in 1905.

364. **Rudanovskii, Vasilii Konstantinovich** (1868 – 1932). Graduated 1888. Joined MID, XII class; interpreter VII class of 2d Department of MID; from 1907 to 1917, Consul on Malta.

365. **Rutskii, Petr Albinovich** (1880 – 1953). Graduated 1904. Joined MID from 1905, IX class; from 1905, official of 2d Department; from 1911, secretary of Consulate in Antwerp, Belgium; from 1912, Consul in Valpariso, Chile; from 1913, secretary of Consulate General in New York; in 1914, acting Consul in Montreal, Canada; from 1915 to 1917, Consul General in New York.

366. **Shlippenbakh, Baron Albert Albertovich** (1846 – 1920). Graduated 1868. Joined MID, X class; from 1895, Consul in New York; from 1908, Consul General in Chicago.

367. **Stakhovich, Mikhail Aleksandrovich** (8 January 1861, b. Palna Estate, Orlov Governate – 23 September 1923, Aix en Provence, France). Graduated 1882. Joined MID, XII class; from March to September 1917, Governor-General of Finland; from September 1917, Ambassador Extraordinary and Plenipotentiary in Spain.

INDEX OF NAMES

www.ingramcontent.com/pod-product-compliance
Lightning Source LLC
LaVergne TN
LVHW081943200926
848484LV00009B/2501

* 9 7 8 1 6 1 6 1 9 6 8 7 5 *